Critical acclaim for Tag Gallagher's
John Ford: The Man and His Films

"An almost flawless blend of criticism and biography . . . a fascinating work. The thoroughness of [the] research is evident on every page. . . . While Mr. Gallagher concentrates on film analysis, his book is also brimming with entertaining asides. . . . An impressive achievement."
—**Gil Johnson**, *New York Times Book Review*

"Tag Gallagher has performed a monumental task of scholarship in reconstructing the mind and psyche of movie director John Ford. . . . Taking the book as straight biography of my friend of 40-odd years, I found it fascinating and informative, filling many gaps in my own knowledge."
—**Philip Dunne**, *Los Angeles Times*

"[This is] a major labor of love, a tremendously useful book on the teaching level, and a solid and enjoyable read on a personal level. . . . One of the major film books of recent years." —**William K. Everson**, *Films in Review*

"Tag Gallagher is as immersed in Fordiana as anyone on the planet. . . . [This book] will deservedly become the central data bank in its territory."
—**Geoffrey O'Brien**, *The Village Voice*

"Rich in fascinating anecdotes and character traits. . . . Like a lawyer building his case, [Gallagher's] accumulation of data regarding Ford's thematic and stylistic features, the reminiscences of associates, to what Ford contributed to his scripts all fashion a provocative view of Ford's intentions and achievements." —*Variety*

"Gallagher has deftly interwoven detailed interpretations of Ford's major works with knowledgeable analysis of the man. . . . This is [the] definitive [Ford biography] and possibly one of the best of its kind. Highly recommended." —*Library Journal*

"Will be the prime source for future research on the film director many consider to be America's finest." —*Choice*

"An admirer of Ford's achieveme[nt] Gallagher for his new biography documents his life and catalogs Ford's [films]."

D1492906

[grate]ful to Tag [b]oth richly [both richl]y on all of [B]oston Globe

Roberto Rossellini on the set for *La lotta dell'uomo per la sua sopravvivenza*.

The Adventures of
ROBERTO
ROSSELLINI

Tag Gallagher

DA CAPO PRESS • NEW YORK

Library of Congress Cataloging-in-Publication Data

Gallagher, Tag.
  The adventures of Roberto Rossellini / Tag Gallagher.
    p.   cm.
  Filmography: p.
  Includes bibliographical references and index.
  ISBN 0-306-80873-0
  1. Rossellini, Roberto, 1906– . 2. Motion picture producers and directors—Italy—Bi-
ography. I. Title.
PN1998.3.R67G36 1998
791.43'0233'092—dc21
[B]   98-29342
                                                                                              CIP

Photo and text credits can be found in the Acknowledgments on pages 776–777

Published by Da Capo Press, Inc.
A Subsidiary of Plenum Publishing Corporation
233 Spring Street, New York, N.Y. 10013

Manufactured in the United States of America

He could have been a minister, a cardinal, a banker . . .
—Sergio Amidei

And so my brother Roberto set off on a great adventure . . .
—Renzo Rossellini

This book is for Phoebe Ann Erb

Contents

Preface

In 1974, while visiting a friend in Los Gatos, California with scarcely a dime in my pocket, I learned that Pacific Film Archives was showing Rossellini's *The Age of the Medici* over three nights in Berkeley. I walked to the interstate and hitched a ride. My driver was a Chicano in a beat-up car. He showed me an iron rod he kept under the seat for unruly passengers and negotiated the jammed highway by going seventy in the service lane. As he dropped me off, he mentioned he was checking into a psychiatric hospital.

The first segment of *The Medici* ended at midnight. My bed was fifty miles away with no way to get to it. I tried sleeping across the street in a University of California dormitory lounge, but a guard threw me out. I found a bush, and it started to rain.

All the next day it poured. I sat in a small museum, saw the second part of *The Medici* that night, got drenched afterward, and for two dollars found space with some other strays on the floor of an apartment, where flood lights and rock music blared through what was left of the night until we were kicked out at seven. The rain had stopped. I waited fourteen hours and saw the third part of *The Medici*.

I cannot imagine a better context for a Rossellini movie: confusion, chaos, out-on-a-limb, obsessed. And the movie: order, but something more: providence, amazing grace. Never have house lights coming on jarred me so precipitously out of one world and into the next. It was devastating.

Why?

Eventually I would learn that Rossellini's real life, outside the "new reality" he created in his pictures, was perpetually in turmoil, and not unwittingly. Yet the man himself had a calm about him, a confidence, charm, and fascination that everyone who knew him remarked on and that ought to be present on every page of this book—but is not—because it explains why so many people wanted to love, serve, and be acknowledged by him. Sooner or later, inevitably, they would feel betrayed. The house lights would come on. Long before then Rossellini would have gone on to new conquests, refusing to look back, "going to meet the future," as he would say. Part of him never left you; you did not stop loving him.

Why did Rossellini devastate people?

I met him once, for a two-hour interview. He bought me a beer and told me it was easy to borrow all the money I needed for anything. "People don't try," he explained. I understood what people meant about him.

"These are my *things*," his sister Marcella Mariani and wife Marcella De Marchis both told me when I asked them questions, as though in the very act of speaking they would be giving away parts of their selves. I wanted to reply that he was "my thing" too. My experience was of a different order, however. The Rossellini I knew was an artistic consciousness, nearly as unknown to them as the supple human being was to me. Yet for both of us, what we knew was mystery.

Neo-realism was an effort, born in pain and confusion during the war and Resistance, to take stock of what Italians had been through, to sift through a mystery, to make sense. It was premised on the heady assumption that our lives need not be ruled by fortune or evil, that, if we are willing to be intelligent, we are capable of imposing our fantasies on History, changing the concept of the universe, and creating a "new reality."

This had been the message of *Open City, Paisà,* and the other neo-realist films. It was also the message of the Italian Renaissance depicted in *The Age of the Medici.* In spite of the confusion, private and public, of the decades between these films—the 1940s, '50s, and '60s—Rossellini stayed loyal to the Resistance commitment to create a new culture. This was the great adventure toward the future, the "new."

Gerald Mast told me when I began this book fifteen years ago that biography is fiction. I did not believe him then; I do now. Everything here is based either on my own experience of the movies or of what people have told me in interviews. Written sources are no more reliable, often less so. Rossellini's own statements are the most unreliable of all, even, or particularly, in the simplest things: indeed, defending him often entails attacking his words. Official documents were rarely obtainable and these are notoriously unreliable in a country that until recently has made a fine art of fictionalizing accounts. The best I could do was to follow Benedetto Croce's advice, try to inject myself into the hearts and minds of the real people who have become my "characters," and hope that they will at least agree that we saw the same movie.

Note: Throughout the book, **bold** *footnote numbers designate editorial comment. Other footnotes are purely bibliographic. Unless specified otherwise, all translations have been made by the author.*

1

Fantasy

At ten minutes before one on Wednesday afternoon, May 8, 1906, Roberto Gastone Zeffiro Rossellini began a life of adventure, conveniently, in one of Rome's wealthier families. The Rossellinis, besides being debonair, gay, and fashionable, were bohemian, quixotic, outré, and always prodigal. It was entirely to one person that their fortune was due: the oddly-named Zeffiro ("zephyr") who, having no children of his own, had taken his nephew into his house and business, married him to his mistress's stunningly beautiful niece, and assumed the title of *nonno* ("grandfather") to their children. Appropriately, his name had been passed down to the first-born.

Zeffiro Rossellini had risen from poverty. Born in 1848 of peasant stock and orphaned while young, he raised his brothers Luigi and Ferdinando while working as a bricklayer near Pisa in his native Tuscany. Around 1870 he moved south to Rome. The city was small then, with barely 200,000 inhabitants, and it stank of misery, with people living ten-to-a-room in certain districts. But a Piedmontese army, blowing a hole through the old Roman walls at Porta Pia, had just put an end to the Popes' thousand-year rule and announced the first unification of Italy since the ancient empire. Since the Romans were unenthusiastic, regarding the Piedmontese as foreign occupiers and "Italy" as some new-fangled concoction of the devil, the new government, to win their sympathy, began spending vast sums on spectacular buildings. Forty thousand officials had to be housed in the new capital, a rail line was built to link Rome with the prosperous north, and masses of immigrants poured in from the impoverished south.

Zeffiro became a contractor, gentrified his name from Rosellini to Rossellini, and rode the crest of the boom. In the next decades Rome's population would triple, land speculation would skyrocket, and new construction would bury the old baroque city beneath a new modern one. Zeffiro built railroads in Puglia and houses and office buildings in Rome. He was the first to stretch the city beyond the Aurelian walls into the Parioli countryside, where most middle-class Romans live today. He was tall, im-

1

posing, and elegant, with a florid Umbertine mustache and terrifying authority.

But to his "grandchildren" he was sweet and indulgent. Each morning they would troupe into his bedroom, kiss him, and get a fond smack on the cheek in return. They were awed by him. Nonno had even been a *garibaldino*. True, he had been dragged back home only a few days after running off to join Giuseppe Garibaldi's campaign of 1866. Yet he had worn, however briefly, the famous red shirt that the followers of the man who "made" Italy wore, and this shirt, for him, as later for Roberto, meant glory and freedom—Garibaldi's *republican* freedom. The "junk," as Zeffiro called the royal arms of the House of Savoy, was glaringly absent from the center of the tri-color flag *he* flew during World War I—letting it wave boldly from his carriage as he rode around Rome, and attracting not a few stares. He had gotten to know Garibaldi during the impecunious soldier's last years and would send him woolen socks, underwear, and money. Befriending the sons as well, he became Menotti Garibaldi's executor. Garibaldi memorabilia formed a shrine in his studio—letters, pictures, a sword, the famous boot shot through at the battle of Aspromonte, and most sacred of all, in its small round frame, a piece of the hero's beard. All through their childhood this relic held Roberto and his brother Renzo in thrall: one day, if they behaved, said Zeffiro, the beard would be theirs. Liberty was Zeffiro's religion and would be the leitmotif of Roberto's films.

Zeffiro had built himself a large residence at Via Nerva, 1, in Piazza Sallustio, where Roberto was born, followed by Renzo (February 2, 1908) and sister Marcella (September 9, 1909). The *palazzo* marked the city's farthest limits at the time. Elegant Via Veneto lay a few blocks to the east, but a dirt cycling course could be glimpsed to the west and, beyond that, toward Porta Pia, vineyards and artichoke fields. "There were empty lots and gardens all around us, and wide sections of the Aurelian wall," Roberto recalled. "On the Pincio there were still goat herds, vineyards, cows, and dairies. The old quarters with their orange and rust-colored houses hadn't been torn down yet."[1] The characteristic sound was not today's constant revving of engines but the occasional rhythmic clatter of horse hooves and carriage wheels along pebbled streets. Rome was renowned for its quiet.

"Our home," recalled Roberto, "was full of happiness. And imagination. Unrestrained fantasy. My parents didn't try to restrain this fantasy. They encouraged it. Fantasy in everything, games of the wildest imagination. We weren't a traditional family. We didn't try to hold on to anything, not even our wealth. We spent immediately."[2]

Rome was a puritanically modest society. The nouveaux riches Rossellinis were regarded as eccentric. They enjoyed showing off their wealth, flinging their money around in a city of impoverished people. They displayed themselves in a rotogravure where their darling children, who had won a beauty contest, were gamboling naked on a bed. They assumed the mores of a noble house. Breakfast, dinner, supper, they kept an open table; people of all sorts—from Roman princes to impoverished painters—were free to drop by and eat even when the family was away. Roberto's father Beppino (né Angiolo Giuseppe) often came home with a dozen unanticipated guests. Elettra, Roberto's mother, never knew who anyone was. "Sometimes I just couldn't stand it," she said, "and I'd run back home to my mother."[3] For the children it was great fun and wonderful training for the future. "The house was always full of intellectuals and artists," said Roberto. "I never saw a businessman there. So I grew up in a rather special atmosphere."[4]

"Roberto had personality and agility," Renzo recalled. "As first-born he also enjoyed unconfessed but instinctive protection from our parents, especially from mama. He was brown-haired, with eyes as sharp as pins, all nervous, restless, aggressive, and volatile. I was just the opposite: blond, quiet, submissive, easily contented. For friend and plaything Roberto had me; for companion and despot I had him. My attachment to him was morbid. It was as though I took my first steps only to run after [him]."[5]

The boys had a battlefield in their playroom, with mountains, bridges, tunnels, shrubbery, and a railway all around, inaugurated in 1911 when Italy went to war against Turkey. Roberto had a wondrous sword; Renzo, twenty months younger, just a toothpick, and he had to be a Turk. Worse, Roberto would fire lead balls at him from a great big cannon, and Renzo had to fight back with a popgun and cork bullets.

Roberto got what he wanted, always. For one period, he refused to go out without wearing a leash, because he had decided he was a dog. Elettra was helpless; the rest of the family followed in the wake of maternal submission. Once he had a tantrum returning from a party; he went rigid, threw himself on the street, tore his brand new clothes to shreds; and everyone stared helplessly. (Renzo tried the same thing, but Donato the butler just picked him up and carried him home.) On another occasion Roberto's desire for a stupendous rocking horse in the window of the corner toy store required a two-month campaign, and perhaps for this reason within hours of receiving it, he had torn off its ears and crinoline tail, and had turned its belly into a soup kettle.

Roberto Rossellini would owe his success to tenaciousness and charm. He would chart the course of human history in terms of our innate impulse for freedom.

"My mother was a housewife," said Roberto, "very near-sighted, very timid, and very funny. It was impossible not to get along with her."[6] Elettra was tender but nervous, passing quickly from laughter to tears to laughter. When provoked, she'd administer little slaps, then smother them in kisses. She was still slapping Roberto long after he reached adulthood.

"I was strongly attached to both my parents, but in different ways. Toward my mother I felt tenderness, toward my father, deepest admiration. He was an exceptional man."[7]

He was the only one to interfere with Roberto's tyranny. For example, Roberto, to get to sleep at the hunting lodge at Ladispoli, had established that each night the carriage would be brought out and harnessed; Aunt

Fortù would mount up front beside the coachman and blow her hunting horn (*ta-too, ta-too, ta-too*), and off they would gallop into the night, whereupon little Roberto, in his mother's arms in back, would blissfully drift off to sleep. And all went well until the evening Beppino arrived unexpectedly, nearly rammed the horn down Fortù's throat and, hoisting and spanking the startled Roberto, hauled him off to bed.

Yet, ritual morning kisses and special occasions aside, Roberto's father was seldom around. He had his business, a social life, and lady friends. Elettra, who had borne Roberto at seventeen, was eight years her husband's junior, virtually confined to the house by the semi-cloistered mores of the day, and utterly incapable of coping with her children. "We were all too much for her," said Marcella.[8] Roberto agreed: "I still remember the prayer she used to have us children recite with her in chorus. She'd say, 'Those mothers, those wives, who have suffered so many torments, Jesus, you who love them, help them in your mercy.'"[9]

Their daily care was relegated to Donato, the dozen servants, and a succession of governesses. Only at Sunday supper did the children eat with their parents, until they were ten or eleven. The father so admired was thus somewhat distant, and the mother so tender was slightly withheld.

The result, in a child as demanding and undisciplined as Roberto, was insecurity and guilt. At seven he was still wetting his bed ("I perspired," he would explain). At six, he agreed to wear an angel costume he loathed in a church procession, on condition that he not be seen in it by his mother, but when he spotted her hiding behind a column, he ran sobbing to clutch her, then erupted in fury. He tore off his wings, kicked everyone within reach, shrieked and shouted, and had to be dragged outside. But he wasn't punished. Elettra blamed herself for breaking her word.

Even when he was thirteen: "I have a vivid memory of the traumatic reaction I had the day my mother, a very gentle person, came home with her [lovely, long] hair bobbed."[10] He cried for hours. Gentle Elettra had been caught up by the suffragette movement. She had a healthy, ironic wit, would eventually find a life outside the family cloister, and would leave her husband in 1926.

The children, unaware of any unquenched needs, would recall their childhoods in heavenly terms. They themselves would become parents conspicuous for spasmodic eruptions into, but general absence from, their children's lives.

The governesses represented a tapestry of languages. The first governess, Léontine Niaudeaux, was French and for this reason French, not Italian, was the first language the children learned and the language that was spoken in the family. "Allez, mes enfants," Léontine would say. Although she used the elevator herself, she insisted that the children walk. (In contrast to everyone else in Rome the eccentric Rossellinis lived on the top floors of their huge *palazzo* and rented out the lower ones.)

Then came Margaretha, a German. Beppino admired German culture and literature; but the language was quickly forgotten when the First

World War began. "Mademoiselle," a Frenchwoman, came next; then an English governess, pale and terribly thin after her six-month escape from Russia's revolution; then soon after another English girl, Mabel, who so quickly succumbed to Roberto's charms that she learned Italian, but no one learned English. Among themselves, the children had their "secret" language.

The butler Donato, an ex-soldier from Tuscany, personified professional pride and total dedication, according to Renzo. No Rossellini would ever expect anything less. Donato was paid 25 lire a month (four dollars in 1918) and never took an hour off. In white tie he served the elegant evening meal, then sat upright and impeccable in the hallway until Beppino or Zeffiro came home—often at two or three in the morning. Otherwise he devoted his time to the children. He took the boys to Villa Borghese where he taught them to ride bicycle and race hard; he gave them their baths, brought them home from school, told them stories, defended them against their parents' (often justified) anger, and, above all, taught them not to take life's difficulties too heavily to heart—though here, again, the judgment is Renzo's: others would say the Rossellinis took life's difficulties with inveterate hysteria.

Donato's good humor left him prey to the boys' exuberance, but he never lost patience—except once. That occasion was the Royal Derby, the year's social highlight, which was all the more special in that the cloistered ladies of those days had few opportunities to sport themselves. Elettra decided to go by car—a show-offy display indeed. Cars were expensive: a good auto worker might earn 1,500 lire a year but a car cost 15,000 to buy and 10,000 a year to maintain. Only 7,000 cars were to be found in all of Italy. Of course the Rossellinis were among the first to have one in Rome, which had been Beppino's idea. Elettra preferred the carriage with its coachman and lackey, but for Derby Day it occurred to her that dignity might be maintained by placing Donato in the coachman's livery beside the uniformed chauffeur. The coachman was a small man, alas, and Donato, after squeezing into the livery, scarcely dared move lest he burst out of it. Roberto and Renzo teased him mercilessly at the track, pulling his tails and knocking off his top hat and kicking it around like a ball, and Donato, running after the hat, split open his pants. Still he clung to the dignity of his profession and, home at last, opened the door for Elettra with customary reserve. The boys merrily snatched apart his tails to show the burst pants and Donato, mortified to tears, ripped off the top hat, the white cotton gloves, and the liveried tail coat, and bashed them to the ground with blasphemy. The boys went into hysterics. Elettra, proper, refined, yet nearsightedly oblivious to all that had transpired, demanded, "Donato! Explain your vulgar behavior!"

Even getting the car started was an adventure. Its chain transmission so wore out Fernando the chauffeur that a muscle-bound mason had to traipse over every morning from Beppino's workyard to give the "Fides" its morning crank-up. For the 25-mile drive to Ladispoli milk cans full of gasoline had to be loaded onto the rear—none would be found en route—and a good supply of spare tires as well. Astride this mountain perched Donato, a rifle slung on his shoulder. Elettra, her maid, Renzo, and Marcella sat on the back seats, Roberto up front. "Faster! Faster!" he'd shout every time they encountered a horse and gig. "Slowly, Fernando, go slowly!" Elettra would admonish from the back. Rare was the trip without a flat tire or two or three; replacing them was a dirty, exhausting job, for wheels could not be removed as today: tire and tube had to be manipulated directly on the chassis, after which the air pump, leaking everywhere when it worked at all, required four or five hands to operate. The Fides would boil over on steep hills, and everyone except Elettra would get out and walk behind. They wore raincoat-like coveralls, so dusty were the roads, and rubber goggles that left black residue on their faces for days afterward. Tasty snacks, when tires were being changed or the radiator cooling, made the long waits more endurable. Donato, with his gun, stood guard by the roadside for, in Elettra's opinion, it was at such moments that the brigands were most likely to attack.

In reality no brigands existed. But Elettra—timid in any case and inspired in this instance by a Bartolomeo Pinelli print, *The Brigands of the Roman Countryside*, that hung at home—had convinced herself and her children that attack was imminent. She had heard a noise one night at Ladispoli when everyone was asleep. Tiptoeing to the window, she fired a hunting gun into the air and screamed, "Donato! Donato! To arms! The brigands are here!" Dogs, hens, and ducks awoke for miles around. A candle was found, guns were distributed to young and old, and an armed vigil was maintained till dawn.

This small house near the beach of Ladispoli, to which Zeffiro's bizarre mistress Fortù had been exiled by universal decree, was the least of the family properties. A little south of Anzio was Circeo, an entire peninsula complete with a papal title, "Baron of San Felice Circeo," which Zeffiro had contemptuously bestowed on his dog. Then there were blocks of land in central Rome, including a palazzo on Via Boncompagni where Elettra had lived before her marriage, and various three- or four-storied villas. The one at Ardenza, a fashionable sea resort, had a sober elegance. Another just south of Rome between Frascati and Grottaferrata so enchanted the children with its three acres of gardens, lake, and cane forest that Renzo named it *The Garden of Klingsor* and Roberto forty years later would try to lure Marcella to India by telling her it was "another Grottaferrata." Zeffiro liked to wheel and deal. He would build a new villa with great enthusiasm, then quickly get bored, sell it, and start another. In design, however, each was as unremarkable as the next.

The children were aware of their advantages. From the top floor at Piazza Sallustio they looked down on the little paint store where their actual grandfather, Beppino's father Luigi, made a modest living selling paint to Zeffiro, his brother and only customer. Luigi lived a few blocks away, across Via XX Settembre, in a sad, dark, fifth-floor apartment with no elevator, no radiators, and a tin bathtub that had to be filled by hand. It was a typical middle-class home of the time, but it contrasted badly with Zeffiro's lordly splendor and modern conveniences. Luigi was a true bohemian; he asked little of life and enjoyed himself to the hilt. With easel, paints, and brushes, he would wander out into the countryside and lose himself staring at dawns, noons, and evenings. He painted for the love of it, in the bright, contrasty style of the *macchiaioli*, always landscapes with colorful birds in them, because Luigi was a passionate hunter and carried a gun along with his easel. Between shots, he would sketch canvases that for the most part he left unfinished. Optimistic, expansive, and pleasure-loving, he was also a diabetic. But dieting was impossible for someone who spent his day's happiest hours at table eating highly spiced country fare like *spaghetti alla amatriciana* with authentic pecorino, lamb or chicken *cacciatore*, and saddle of pork with raw broccoletti fried in oil, garlic, and red pepper. These were prepared by Natalina, a feisty peasant who ruled the house. She had served the family for 48 years (for five lire a month, which she never received) and called everyone *tu* rather than the formal *Lei* (driving Roberto's mother up the wall). Luigi's wife, Giuseppina Benedetti, Roberto's grandmother, was an invalid who suffered through a succession of operations over many years and quarreled endlessly with Natalina in between. Roberto and Renzo, accustomed as they were to the refined service and precise etiquette on which their mother insisted, were embarrassed by Luigi's shabby surroundings and Natalina's way of putting the food on the table in big dishes and leaving everyone free to help themselves. They begrudged the second-class seats Luigi bought them at movies and the single mandarin punch they were given to share between them at the Caffè dell'Indipendenza afterward, where Luigi stopped to swap hunting yarns with other old men. But they cherished their grandfather's good humor, his long, wonderful bedtime stories (an inspiration for the stories Roberto would tell), and his zest at table. As he drank, he sang "Viva il vino spumeggiante" ("Hooray for sparkling wine") from *Cavalleria rusticana*, or a ditty that went:

> Our fathers drank!
> Our mothers drank!
> We're their children!
> Let's drink too!

Then, over pears and cheese, Natalina would come sit and listen, and Luigi would begin to recite Dante, at length, with wide-ranging tone and emotion, and eventually crying rivers of tears and drawing his listeners into his grief too, until there was nary a sound in all the room except sobbing.

The play between fantasy and reality that so characterized the Rossellinis and that would haunt Roberto's films was typical of Italy as a whole.

In the Italy of his youth, poverty was of stupendous proportions. Hundreds of thousands lived in caves or mud huts. Few of the women and children who constituted the bulk of the industrial work force and even fewer of the agricultural workers earned a living wage. Thousands died each year of malaria; many regions lacked drinkable water. Half the population was illiterate—eighty percent in parts of the south. Most people could not even hope for a job unless they left Italy. So eight million did, between 1871 and 1914—100,000 a year in 1876, 500,000 in 1901, 872,000 (or one in forty) in 1913. Italy was providing no opportunity for her people.

Such facts were ignored. Segments of Italian society were as modern and prosperous as any on earth. Well-off citizens like the Rossellinis gave less thought to poverty than well-off Californians do to Alabama blacks today. Modern Italians were looking to the future. The new Italy was rising up around them. Why think about things that were shameful and humiliating? Haunted by centuries of foreign contempt, manipulation, and occupation, they sought to forge a national identity and to claim, in international affairs, the parity with England and France they believed they deserved. To achieve these ends, they recognized only dimly the need for internal development. Self-assertion and conquest abroad seemed more immediately important. "Italy must not only be respected," declared King Vittorio Emanuele II, "she must make herself feared." Prime Minister Cavour's final word on Garibaldi took a similar stance: "Garibaldi has rendered to Italy the greatest service that a man could render her: he has given the Italians confidence in themselves: he has proved to Europe that Italians can fight and die on the battlefield to reconquer a fatherland."[11]

Italian foreign policy followed a consistent course from unification through Mussolini; it was a reaction to the humiliating impression that Italy owed its unity to gifts from Garibaldi and Napoleon III. Thus in 1866, when Austria offered to cede Venice, Italy went to war anyhow, to conquer it. In 1911, when Turkey accepted an Italian ultimatum to cede Libya, Italy went to war anyhow, to conquer it. In 1915, when Austria offered to cede Trent, Trieste, and Fiume to keep Italy out of the First World War, Italy went to war anyhow, to conquer them. To assert herself as a great power was everything. Twenty years later Mussolini, too, would be unable to resist the call to glory.

How many died to "prove" something to Europe? The glory was façade. Italy was no great power. She lacked natural resources, industrial production, capital, and an educated or disciplined citizenry. In Ethiopia in 1896 her army was massacred. In Libya her troops huddled in a few coastal citadels. In World War I more than 650,000 Italians were killed, half a million were mutilated, another million wounded, and 148 billion lire was spent—twice the total of all government expenditures since 1861.

After so pointless a waste, glory would seem more important than ever and failure to achieve it would be blamed on foreign powers. Self-delusion was the kernel of Italian politics, in reaction to centuries of foreign occupation, papal repression, stultifying provincialism, military ineptitude, and economic powerlessness against the world-wide aggrandizement of England, France, and America. Hold on to your idea, it was believed, and you can achieve anything. Had not the Risorgimento—that "revolution of the disinherited, of the starry eyed"[12]—shown this was true? Tiny bands of ex-officers, doctors, lawyers, writers, and students had pushed and pulled Italy into unity, against the desires not only of the Church and the land-owning aristocracy, but of most of the populace as well. And these same starry-eyed leaders had been ruling ever since by virtual martial law, implementing liberal ideas with violent methods and seeing themselves as the historical agents for releasing the subconscious desires of the Italian nation. They were still ruling now. Mussolini would be their heir.

In Germany it was the military establishment that had created the nation. In Italy it was the poets. Germany had been forged of steel, Italy of dreams. War would give their dreams substance, Italy's poet statesmen believed, and would bind and invigorate national character. Gabriele D'Annunzio, the era's dominant literary figure, evoked the Roman Empire and preached that Nietzschean-like supermen were above morality. "Man the prow and sail toward the world!" he shouted. Marinetti's 1909 *Futurist Manifesto* equally extolled conquest and power, preaching how poetry and violence spring from an identical impulse, how war is the world's sole purifier. Democracy, justice, the sacredness of life—these were degenerate idiocies concocted by and for the weakest and least worthy elements of society.

(In America, the argument for entry into World War I was almost identical. War would "forge a national soul"; give birth to "a new religion of vital patriotism—that is, of consecration to the State"; imbue citizens with "a strong sense of international duty." War, above all, would bring about a "change in the whole attitude of the people." It would create a New America, one in which citizens would ask not what their country could do for them but what they could do for their country.[13])

Philosophically Italy's leaders had started out as liberals and still called themselves that, although they no longer were. In theory they were slowly pushing Italian society toward a vision in which restriction of any sort was minimal, competition and "harmonious discord" were encouraged, and each individual might fulfill his idiosyncratic potential. This was the ideology that Roberto Rossellini grew up in, and that he would endeavor to propagate through his films by combining art with ideological agenda in the age-long Italian fashion. But during all the decades preceding World War I, the masses had been unfriendly and reactionary, a drag against progress. The Church was hostile and forbade Catholics to vote. Labor opposed *any* bourgeois government and refused all cooperation. Parliament was hopelessly factionalized and debated interminably without ever agreeing to anything. Thus the "liberals" ineluctably succumbed to the conclusion that liberty would have to be imposed through dictatorial methods, iconoclasm, and war—the techniques validated by the Risorgimento.

In so polarized a society, government was possible only though *trasformismo*, a policy whereby opposition leaders were given seats in the ruling coalition and successive ministries were brought to power by slight shifts to the right or the left: it perpetuated a ruling class, accommodated moderate change, and avoided extremes (and it is still the rule in Italy today). But as the elite joined the power clique, they sacrificed their followers and principles to tactical expediency, left a residue of cynicism, and confused any clear conflict between alternative policies. Given the intransigent, permanently discordant nature of Italy's rival ideologies, politics, and class interests, such tactical expediency was a necessity and confusion of conflict was a step toward cooperation. But *trasformismo* instituted corruption and ineffectualness (also still the rule today), and created a parliament that was happiest when a strong leader came along to monopolize responsibility. Even wholehearted republicans like Garibaldi favored dictatorship out of frustration. Thus successive ministers—Cavour, Depretis, Crispi, and Giolitti—promulgated laws by decree and then had them confirmed retroactively by parliament (also still the practice in Italy today).

At all times Italy's elite overwhelmingly deplored the ways by which policy was implemented. But few disagreed with the broad outlines of that policy and almost no one opposed the assumptions that underlay it. Thus Fascism, when it came, seemed, like Woodrow Wilson's quashing of free speech during the World War, a necessary expediency at a time of crisis. The Italy Mussolini would inherit was already functioning: a police state that was authoritarian and corrupt; a government that survived by manipulating defects and weaknesses; a population that was prosaic and pedestrian; a ruling class inspired by the highest ideals.

When the First World War broke out, Italy stayed out, in accord with the desires of most of parliament and almost all of the public. Strident voices, however, demanded intervention. Sympathies sided with France and against Germany and Austria, despite Italy's nominal partnership with the latter in the Triple Alliance. In the Rossellini home, Beppino's pro-neutrality caused violent clashes with the ultra patriotic Zeffiro. Ten long months passed, with mounting slaughter in northern Europe and mounting pressure for intervention in Italy. Beppino was overheard whistling Wagner on a trolley and escaped a beating only by claiming (falsely) that he had been whistling German music in scorn. Finally Italy was thrust into the war by executive decree. Prime Minister Salandra and Foreign Minister Sonnino, succumbing to territorial bribes dangled by the Entente, deceived the cabinet, signed a treaty with England, and had the king issue a war decree. They mobilized violent street demonstrations, brought D'Annunzio back from France to excite war fervor, and, when parliament at last was allowed to convene, arranged for mobs to storm its buildings. Giolitti, the nation's leading politician, had opposed the war. Now the king threatened to abdicate and Giolitti caved in. National honor was at stake and effective opposition impossible.

Italians flocked to the colors. "A great élan of patriotic zeal [shook] the entire city," Roberto recalled. "We were fighting against the Austrian-Hungarian Empire, we were going to free the irredentist provinces. Not a day passed without parades, speeches, and demonstrations, even in the school

I went to. How could anyone resist such a wave?"[14] Beppino was mobilized as an industrialist to construct air camps at Montecelio and Furbara. On occasional weekends he was able to visit his family.

Roberto and Renzo, nine and seven, were all for war. At school the beadle would announce the end of class by crying, *"Finis!* Death to Giolitti!" and the children would march home chanting mournfully, "Down with the Austrian flag! Death to Franz Josef! Long live Oberdan!" (Oberdan, from Austrian-occupied Trieste, had tried to assassinate the Austrian emperor Franz Josef in 1870.) At home they set up their playroom battlefield. On Thursdays and Sundays they went off to a meadow near Via Brescia for military training with the "Young Explorers." When gawking street boys attacked with stones, the uniformed Explorers retaliated with broccoli-stick bayonets salvaged from the dumpings of a nearby market. Roberto's pugnacious grandmother lived across the meadow and would yell threats and curses helplessly from her balcony. (This was Elettra's mother, Amalia del Monte, a Roman from Anagni. She had separated from Giuseppe Bellan, a wealthy grain merchant whose French ancestors had established themselves in Rovigo, near Venice, during the Napoleonic wars. It was so that she would avoid her parents' quarrels that Elettra had originally been sent to Rome.)

Zeffiro's other nephew, Eugenio (his brother Ferdinando's son), was 25, six-foot-three, a grenadier captain stationed in Tripoli, and frustrated. Feisty old Zeffiro had wanted this new war, but now he refused to listen to Eugenio's requests for help in obtaining a transfer to the Alpine front, where the fighting was. The war entered its second year, however, and the need for soldiers grew, so Eugenio got his transfer all the same. At dinner at Grottaferrata that May, Beppino was telling a story about Mascagni, when the doorbell rang, "signorino Eugenio" was announced, and the table fell silent and still. Beppino went to the door and returned. "Eugenio's leaving," he said softly. "He's here to kiss us goodbye." Eugenio walked in, smiling. Everyone else was close to tears. Beppino poured some wine and handed him a glass. "Let us drink," he said, "to your health, to your glory, to our country's victory." Elettra started to cry.

The children were still awake past midnight when their father got back from the station. "Go to bed," he said. "Eugenio's glad to be going. He's happy and confident. Italy needs soldiers like him."

On Mount Cencio every foot of advance or retreat cost mountains of corpses and Eugenio lasted less than 48 hours. "I can still hear the howl of pain that erupted from nonno Zeffiro," wrote Renzo, who was eight at the time. "That a grandfather of that mettle could cry like that tells us something of the tragedy we passed through. I remember that elegant, austere, Umbertine monument of a man lying prostrate, while my mother laid cold compresses to his forehead."[15]

The casualties mounted by the tens of thousands. Rome's gas lamps were painted blue. Only women, children, and old men were to be seen. The beadle at school, with four sons at the front, grew meek and quiet.

Fear and heartbreak replaced enthusiasm. Bread tickets became sacred documents, symbols of the nation's united effort. Then in 1917 Germany locked Lenin in a train and shipped him to Russia. They hoped he would undermine the government and he did. The Russian front collapsed, and fifteen German and Austrian divisions were shifted to Caporetto in Italy, where in October an offensive devastated the Italian army. One quarter of a million men were captured in twelve days; twice as many more were killed, wounded, or missing. The 700,000 who survived retreated precipitously one hundred miles to the river Piave. The German army was twenty miles from Venice. But the nation rallied as one, and the worst military disaster in modern Italian history was followed by its most heroic resistance.

Renzo recalls how he and Roberto helped make socks and scarves to send up to the front, and *ingegnosi*—strips of rolled-up newspaper covered with wax, which burnt slowly and could be used to warm soldiers' mess kits. Then one evening Donato came home late, wearing a uniform several sizes too small. The children burst into tears. Even at 41, overweight, and one-eyed, Donato was in better shape than most conscripts from the South. Yet instead of being sent into battle or even out of Rome, he was assigned to valet a general in a nearby ministry! Well! It was one thing to lose one's best servant, the children's best friend, to Italy in her direst hour. It was quite another to lose him to a gentleman. Beppino befriended the general and an arrangement was worked out. For the next year, Donato's days were divided in two.

In the summer of 1918 the army withstood a new Austrian push on the Piave, then counter-attacked and, exactly a year after Caporetto, won the decisive battle of Vittorio Veneto. The war was over. Rome's Via Veneto was renamed Via Vittorio Veneto. Italy had a victory at last.

The Rossellinis moved twice during the war. They left Piazza Sallustio in 1916 for a temporary apartment adjoining the Hotel Carleton (which Zeffiro then owned) on Via Collina, just around the corner. Marcella woke up one morning there and saw the house walls across the street severing apart; it was the Avezzano earthquake. The new home was ready in 1917, constructed by the Rossellinis of course: a huge building at Via Ludovisi 16, just off Via Veneto. The entire block, including the Hotel Regina (across Via Veneto from the present American embassy), was theirs. Once again they lived on the upper floors.

Beppino spent the postwar years in Venice. In partnership with a Swiss company run by brothers named Sleiter, he reconstructed the bridge over the Piave at Priula, rebuilt areas of Conegliano, Spresiano, and Nervesa devastated by the war, and in Padua built the model "Garden City" quarter. He fell madly in love with Venice. Each day, though exhausted at work, he would wander for hours in the city's narrow streets, and during his weekend visits to Rome would try to share his discoveries with his children. "The men of action of that time," wrote Renzo, "combined the religion of work with an intense spirituality, a renascent humanism that expressed itself in passionate love of art. . . . The first time I went to Venice, I was shaking with excitement, so great was the spell my father had cast over me. But . . . when I woke . . . and saw the lagoon appear through the train window, the sight was more wonderful than any I've imagined before or since; I felt a sense of stupor, of magic, of enchantment."[16]

To be near Beppino, the family passed part of the summer at a villa on the Venice Lido. Elettra bore her last child there in 1922, Micaela, nicknamed Micci (*Mee*-chee). Renzo also lived for a time with his father in Venice proper, where he became deeply involved with music; at sixteen he published the first of his many operas for Ricordi.

Marcella studied art in Rome. She went each day to a studio on Via Margutta, accompanied by her governess, as custom demanded. (A young woman would no more go out without her governess than without her hat.) But musicians outnumbered artists at Via Ludovisi, for music was Beppino's primary passion, as well as Renzo's. The composer Mascagni was a family friend, Molinari, Respighi, Alfano, and Zandonai came also; and Marcella first heard herself addressed as *signorina* by Puccini himself. On Sundays, Renzo and Marcella, and occasionally Roberto, attended matinees at the opera. The new operas they usually knew even before their premieres, having played them at home on the piano.

Roberto staged plays at home: mime dramas accompanied by piano or dramas of the French revolution. He adored fancy dress, and would take so long fussing over the wigs and costumes of his cousins Luisa and Renzo Avanzo (drafted for the occasion) that just as they were ready, it would be time to go home. The red velvet curtains in the hallway formed a sort of proscenium. Once Donato walked through them into a duel between Roberto and his brother, and Renzo's bamboo sword tipped over Donato's tray and hit him in his one good eye. It looked as though he would lose his sight entirely. Roberto took the blame and resolved to say 5,000 "Hail Marys" every night for a miracle. Donato's eye was saved, but not due to Roberto. He kept falling asleep before completing his daily quota and soon became hundreds of thousands of "Hail Marys" behind.

To opera, theater, music, and art, Roberto preferred the movies. He went every day, often twice a day. He had a free pass to the Corso Cinema, which his father had built in 1918. It was the first large, modern movie house in Rome, the first with a roof that could be slid open on hot summer nights. Called the Étoile today, it was then the center of Rome's movie world. Douglas Fairbanks and stars from all over the world would come to see it when visiting Rome. Roberto met many of them. "So I saw it born, the cinema, I saw Griffith born," he said, when he was 66.[17]

Sometimes, using his pass, he'd take his whole class to the movies. Roberto and Renzo had transferred in the fall of 1917 to the Collegio Nazareno, a school for privileged boys run by the Scolopi fathers. Several of their schoolmates went on to distinguished careers: Giorgio Amendola a Communist Party leader, Guglielmo Ceroni a top reporter for *Il Messaggero*,

Marcello Pagliero an actor and filmmaker, Giovanni Mosca a brilliant journalist, Sergio Fenoaltea an ambassador, and another a cardinal. Roberto, having flunked the year before at the Tasso School, was the oldest in his class by age but the furthest behind academically, and he scorned to wear the school's Etonesque uniform. He took Italian, Latin, and Greek (both written and oral), history and geography, French, mathematics, and natural history. His grades were never better than the lowest possible for passing, and even these were obtained through charm rather than scholarship. A classmate, Franco Riganti, recalls him as lazy, perpetually dreaming, and distracted, but as more intelligent than most and fascinating even to his peers.[18] In Roberto's opinion school was utter damnation. "Those years were absolutely wild, horrible, and cruel. It was *so* boring! I learned to sleep with my eyes opened and fixed on my schoolmaster."[19] Paradoxically, though, he esteemed his teachers—Alberto M. Ghisalberti in history, Pietro Paolo Trompeo in Italian, and the famous Dante scholar Luigi Pietrobono, who, defying Croce, championed the poetic role of allegory in the *Divine Comedy*.

Boredom inspired Roberto to miss school as often as possible. Ill health resulted in absences of long duration. He seemed prone to every possible disease. He caught malaria at Ladispoli, a mild form of cholera at Ardenza, got appendicitis at Bocca d'Arno in 1918, and that fall missed an entire trimester at Nazareno. The following winter, 1919–1920, at the end of a three-year influenza epidemic that claimed half a million lives in Italy—27 million worldwide—Roberto's lungs became infected. For three months the thirteen-year-old hung between life and death. Part of one lung was removed in an operation and Elettra, only 31 and at the peak of her beauty, vowed to the madonna to wear black all the rest of her life if her son were spared.

He was and she did. She looked stunning in black and permitted herself mauve as well. Roberto spent a year convalescing, missing two-thirds of the 1919–1920 school year and all of 1920–1921. Then he damaged his kidneys.

This occurred at Cortina d'Ampezzo in the Dolomites, where the Rossellinis had been spending their Augusts since 1919. A popular resort today, it was an unknown region then, and Beppino took his family exploring in a chauffeur-driven touring car. The children were thrilled to see real snow for the first time. They saw shrapnel, too, and a skeleton uncovered by melting snow. In these Nibelungen valleys two armies had struggled for more than two years without advance or retreat. Now the dead of both sides kept company in numerous small cemeteries, where white Italian crosses stood beside grey Austrian ones. Here and there some crosses had messages written on them like "Mama, I'm here."

In August 1921, Beppino and his children decided to climb a glacier that churned down a ravine between the first and second "Monk's Hat." Having driven to the tree line along a stream bed, they started hiking up a rocky stretch of ground toward the ice. The glacier had seemed close by, but it took several hours to reach it. Once there, however, enthusiasm sprouted wings and they leapt up along the ice flow.

High up the glacier, Renzo, suddenly faint, stumbled, and started to fall. Although he caught his balance, he had startled ten-year-old Marcella, so that she fell almost straight down, sliding like a bullet 350 yards along the ice. Beppino tried to grab her, but she struck him in the chest, turning her feet-first and knocking down her father. He tumbled down too, along with a family friend, Sandro Ferraguti, whom the speeding Marcella also struck. She halted, finally, on rocky ground at the glacier's base and lay there bruised and bleeding, her clothes in shreds. Her first thought was to see if her watch was still running. It was. Ferraguti landed half conscious in a snow bank. Beppino came to rest gracefully and unhurt beside his daughter.

Meanwhile, up on the glacier, thirteen-year-old Renzo looked down and, only now aware of the terrifying height, began to tremble. Roberto, ever resourceful, started using his hands, walking stick, and heels to carve out a niche for himself, and Renzo tried to imitate him. He put his foot on a soft spot, however, and felt himself falling, but was grabbed just in time by the remaining member of the party, a banker from Padua, who held onto him tightly. And like that they stayed the next four hours: Roberto in his niche, Renzo fastened to the banker, Marcella and Ferraguti down below. Only Beppino was able to move. Shouting instructions to wait, he went off for help toward a mountain refuge he suspected was not too far away. They could hear his strong voice echoing through the valleys as he disappeared, "Help! Help!" Then for an eternity there was silence.

Back at the car, the chauffeur had woken from a nap, started to worry, and went looking for the family. He found Marcella at the base of the glacier, bleeding and turning blue from the cold, and carried her in his arms to the car, where he revived her by vigorous massage with gasoline. Roberto, Renzo, and the banker, however, waited amid growing desperation until two guides arrived from the refuge.

It was late when they got back to Cortina, where Elettra was waiting. Marcella was cut badly, all had frozen fingers and sunburnt faces. "Let's sing," said Beppino, "and hide our misery."

Roberto was back in school that fall, but with weakened kidneys and persistent pleurisy.

In adulthood, physical effects from his adolescent illnesses did not linger; in fact, he was almost never sick at all. But mentally, sickness was a catalyst whereby character traits already present were amplified.

Sickness encouraged his love of indulgence. It was nice to miss school, to stroll in the mountains where doctors sent him for his lungs, and to have nothing he *had* to do. "I remember those days as extraordinarily happy. Taken care of by everyone, babied by everyone, I got along just fine. It was a very fertile period for me from every point of view. It gave my life a new orientation."[20] But such indulgence made the spoiled boy a spoiled man, one who flew into blind rages when frustrated, one who was sporadically disabled by overpowering headaches (which, it seems, were psychosomatic in origin, although never treated as such). Yet if Rossellini had not had so absolute, so infantile a need to get his way, could he have succeeded in making the films he did?

Sickness encouraged insecurity. He became a lifelong hypochondriac; his bedside was lined with dozens of little bottles of medicine, all of which travelled with him in a special little suitcase wherever he went; and every year he had a blood transfusion. His hypochondria had a positive side, though. It contributed to his generosity—which was extraordinary in any case, singularly so in one so self-indulgent—toward anyone ill or grieving. It was natural for him to spend the night with a school friend who had lost his parents, or to buy Marcella another dog when Ior, her little Pekinese, died, and to stay up all night with her telling her stories: Ior would surely be reincarnated, he explained, and come back as a man, and one day she might marry him. Roberto had a strong, open energy and people instinctively turned to him in a crisis.

Sickness encouraged consciousness of death. Death would be a dominant motif in his films: heroes would die and stare at death in virtually every one, and his famous "neo-realism" would evoke sensation of the precious precariousness of each fleeting moment. Off screen Roberto's nervousness was amplified. Boredom became intolerable. Life had to be challenged, attacked every instant, with reckless speed in a Ferrari, with profligate spending, with unrestrained sexuality, with artistic ambitions as monumental as they were impractical. Thus he accomplished monuments. Obstacles erected by others were rarely as awesome as the fear of the void that impelled him forward. The mere threat of dulled consciousness terrified him: he rarely drank, not even wine; dentists, he claimed, had to give him extra doses of Novocain to overcome his automatic rejection of numbness of any kind.

Roberto's manic search for security required constant refreshment. His addiction to bed became legendary. Convalescence encouraged his penchant for lying in bed two or three days at a stretch, reading Dumas, Verne, Salgari, Stendhal, Balzac, Dostoyevsky, and Tolstoy. Home meant family and servants who would do his bidding, and baby and mother him. "And so my brother Roberto set off on a great adventure," wrote Renzo in early childhood, inside the cover of *The Great Explorers*, their favorite book. "He took along everything he might need. And when he got to the doorman, he cried and came back home."[21]

Youth

At war's end, twelve-year-old Roberto, sheltered in his privileged world,
was only dimly aware of the violence and chaos shaping his future.

War had not united the nation the way it was supposed to. The working classes were furious. They hadn't wanted the war. To get them to fight
it the government had announced it was a "war for the proletariat" and
had promised free land and higher wages.[1] But all they got—the million
and a half wounded, and the millions of other veterans—was unemployment.

The nationalists felt humiliated. The Allies, after rewarding themselves,
had reneged on their territorial pledges to Italy—whereupon D'Annunzio
had recruited a private army and occupied Fiume.

The middle classes were terrified. As prices soared and the lira shrank
to seventeen percent of its prewar value, their savings and rental income,
along with the war bonds they'd patriotically purchased, became tickets to
the poor house. They had been the bulwark of progressive civilization.
Now their sons—200,000 ex-officers—sought work in vain, and bread and
coal were severely rationed, while political power was passing into the
hands of those who wanted to destroy everything they'd struggled for.

Bolshevik revolutions had just occurred in Russia, Germany, and Hungary, whetting the thirst for justice of laborers who had been brutally savaged for centuries. As the Socialist chief Pietro Nenni said, "All the extraordinary and clamorous events at the end of 1918 and the beginning of 1919
fired the imagination, and inspired the hope that the old world was about
to collapse and that humanity was on the threshold of a new era and a new
social order."[2]

"I remember," said Roberto, "how on the First of May the workers
would come out in their Sunday clothes, a red flower in the button hole,
and go eat outside the city walls."[3] Their leaders were romantic figures
from the last century, with flamboyant whiskers, drooping black neckties,
and wide-brimmed hats. But their parades, demonstrations, and violent
language inspired panic. Having won control of Milan, Bologna, and two-
thirds of the rural North, they were transferring contracts to their friends,

denouncing the king to his face in parliament, and demanding forced expropriation of capital and a Soviet republic. Red flags flew from churches; Monday replaced Sunday as rest day; children were named not after saints but Ateo, Spartaco, Lenin, Ribellione. Seventeen hundred strikes were called in 1919, nineteen hundred the following year. Looting and window-smashing became daily events. In one year, 145 people were killed, 444 wounded. Finally the Socialists occupied factories all over the country, tore down the owners' names, put up pictures of Lenin, and for a month tried to run the companies themselves.

The government was helpless. After a nation-crippling, two-month strike by railway and postal workers, it not only capitulated, it paid out back wages for the entire strike period.

Theoretically, the government wasn't supposed to do anything. The liberalism Roberto Rossellini grew up in was supposed to be beyond politics and ethics; or rather, it incorporated them within a complete idea of the world and reality. In liberalism, wrote Benedetto Croce, "is reflected all the philosophy and religion of modern times, centered in the idea of dialectics, that is, of development. By means of the variety and conflict of the spiritual forces, dialectics continuously enriches and ennobles life and imprints upon it its only and complete meaning."[4] In other words, liberalism, rather than allowing select authorities to prescribe the course and curtail conflict, was based on trust in each individual and favored competition and cooperation "in harmonious discord." Under no circumstances, said Croce, "should we take from man his human faculty of erring and of sinning, without which not even good can be done.... [T]he liberal concept is not meant for the timid, the indolent and the pacifistic."[5]

"Trust the individual" became one of Roberto's pet phrases. But in 1920 there was outrage at the government's refusal to impose order. Few trusted dialectics to surmount the ideological chasms that were destroying the nation.

It seemed, rather, that liberalism was the cause of the collapse. The Liberals had destroyed their own elitist rule by widening the franchise and instituting proportional representation. A majority of seats in parliament had been won by the new mass parties, the anti-clerical Socialists, and the Vatican-run, anti-Marxist *Popolari*, who hated each other as much as they did the industry-backed, anti-clerical Liberals. No working majority was possible. The nation was drifting into endemic civil war.

Then toward the end of 1920, amid chaos and despair, disciplined bands of war veterans began to inspire hope and promise order. They vowed to maintain the social hierarchy and repress subversion, to call the deputies to their duty and rejuvenate the nation. The war *had* been worth fighting, they insisted, and they pledged to fulfill its revolutionary hopes. Thus they won support from the middle classes and the government, and newspapers portrayed them favorably. They called themselves Fascists.

History has condemned them. Countless books, in hindsight after World War II, have told us they were gangsters. And they were. But they rose to power amid tremendous enthusiasm, and Italians were loyal to them for twenty years.

The Fascists were violent. They yanked red flags off streetcars, poured quarts of castor oil into Bolsheviks, sacked and burnt Socialist newspaper offices, and drove out Socialist farm unions that, in a time of falling prices, were extorting small farmers into hiring more laborers than they needed. And people applauded. Somebody at last was doing something. The destruction, the fires, the beatings and maimings, even the murders were overlooked. Town halls were invaded, socialist councils were forced to resign, and administration of cities all over the north—Ferrara, Rovigo, Bologna, Cremona, Ancona, Terni—was forcibly commandeered. The Socialists, in protest, attempted a half-hearted national strike, whereupon the Fascists grabbed hold of Milan and ran the streetcars themselves, and scored a public relations victory. The Liberal experiment looked dead. The king, the military, and Pius XI refused to oppose the Fascists. The Fascists were saving Italy from Communism; they were the people who could make things work.

When Benito Mussolini, the Fascist leader, called for a "March on Rome" if order was not restored, he was invited to form a government. In effect, the Liberals gave up and called in a Strong Man.

On October 30, 1922, Mussolini arrived by train from Milan, took a taxi to the Quirinal palace, and presented himself to the king in a black shirt, unpressed trousers, scruffy shoes, and a growth of beard. "I've come straight from the battlefield," he said.

The city was a boiling cauldron, Roberto recalled. Bombs were exploding. Civil war was brewing. That evening the street in front of his house, Via Lodovisi, was taken over by black-shirted *squadristi* carrying hand guns, rifles, and bludgeons. Some policemen took refuge in the Rossellini gateway and were preparing for combat on the stairs. Giant searchlights were shooting their beams into the night. Roberto led Renzo and Marcella down to a ground-floor room where they nailed their faces to the window. Mussolini was about to appear on the balcony of the Hotel Savoia, directly across the street, and they didn't want to miss his slightest movement. "I was sixteen and excited by the smell of gunpowder."[6]

It was then that his father came home, pulled open the door, and shouted, loud enough to be heard across the street, "Remember, kids. Black's good for hiding dirt."

A few words called everything into question. All Italy was hailing Benito Mussolini. America and England and the whole world, almost, would join the cheering. Parliament, by a three-to-one vote, was about to give him full powers for a year to carry out whatever reforms he thought necessary. His would be the first government in Italian history to be supported by monarchy, army, Church, industry, and middle class, and he was socialist at heart. The Pope would proclaim him "a man sent us by Providence." There was every reason for Roberto, Renzo, and Marcella to feel a surge of enthusiasm as Mussolini stepped out onto his balcony. It was to prevent a Bolshevik blood bath that young people from all over Italy had "marched" on Rome; only Communists and a few Socialists had offered opposition. Giuseppe Rossellini's cynicism—or rather, his adoration of liberty, his conviction that Mussolini would be "a dictator, the ruin of us all"[7]—was a remarkable stand on principle, courageously at odds with his time and class. It was a lesson Roberto would never forget. Ideology—islands of ideology, each claiming transcendence—had destroyed liberal democracy; he would make it his life's work to destroy ideology.

These decisions came later. In the fall of 1921, Roberto was back at the Nazareno. He had kept up his studies with private tutors and, despite 23 days of absence, completed middle school (*ginnasio*) in 1922. But the following year, in the middle of his second trimester of high school (*liceo*), he dropped out of Nazareno entirely. The only thing he was learning at school, he realized, was how to fake it. It was a skill he understood already; he knew that his professors, like many people, desired a façade and nothing more. "Fortunately," as he put it, the Spanish flu intervened when he was thirteen and he spent the next eighteen months in bed with purulent pleurisy. Finally his lungs were cut open. "I was emptied of two kilos of puss—and all the twisted truths, useless facts, and dubious methods that, despite myself, I had accumulated at school. I was cured." Now with a tutor he studied math and physics for pure enjoyment, and would have gone on to the University, except that the University required a high school diploma, which would have meant learning Latin and Greek all over again. "I couldn't make myself do it."[8]

He was sixteen and had become an heir. Bedridden Zeffiro had died in 1924 and bequeathed his fortune to Roberto and Renzo. (Women were generally excluded from succession. Zeffiro had sighed with relief when Elettra's fourth child had proved to be female: he would not have to remake his will.) How much this fortune amounted to, we do not know. Besides real estate and investments, there were eight million lire in cash. No one worried about preserving this legacy. In Rome's decadent upper-class, wealth was to be spent ostentatiously, saving was ignoble. The whole family feasted with hearty appetite, and Roberto gobbled quickest and ate the most.

"I did every stupid thing it's possible to do in that situation between seventeen and twenty. I failed to get my [high school] diploma, I chased girls, I was constantly crazy in love, I competed on motorcycles and automobiles in Fiats, Salmsons, and Amilcars, taking every risk, animated by a rage to live that never subsided day or night. And my father watched me with love."[9]

Roberto had piano lessons, too. But compared to Renzo and Marcella, scarcely anything indicated a career in the arts for Roberto. His obsessions were mechanical and sexual. He had a laboratory on the top floor on Via Ludovisi and, with Marcella as his gofer, he busied himself with experiments in solar energy and inventions for racing cars. First came a modified compressor that juiced up a broken down Fiat 509, then a new-fangled spark plug and a fuel-conserving motor, both of which he sold to Bugatti. For friend and counselor he had Baratelli, a passionately serious engineer who wore an elastic band around his forehead, claiming it helped him think—so Roberto wore one too. When Baratelli needed to illustrate a point, he was wont to halt the car wherever it was and, oblivious to traffic whizzing by left and right, get out and draw diagrams on the middle of the road.

Roberto got his first car at fifteen, a fire-red Chiribiri. He had been driving since he was nine, taught by his aunt, the baronessa (Maria) Antonietta Avanzo, whom he adored. In complete contrast to her sister, the gentle, feminine Elettra, Antonietta was fiery-eyed, assertive, and a race driver. One of the first women to race in the Indianapolis 500 (in a bright red Ferrari and a matching bright red jump suit), she had lived in Paris and Australia, was friends with Agnelli and Ferrari, and had been nicknamed Nerissa by D'Annunzio because of her jade-black eyes and hair. When, some decades later, her son (also named Renzo) demanded a halt to her racing, contending it ill-suited a middle-aged woman, she took up big game hunting in Africa instead.

Roberto soon got a Bugatti, started racing at eighteen, and kept at it through the 1950s. He was fearless. Tires might blow at 150 mph (as one did), or the car might bang into Via Veneto's Porta Pinciana (as one did), but his hands stayed steady, cool, and calm. Not so Renzo. Fraternal subservience and Roberto's enthusiasm overcame the terror of riding as mechanic, but Renzo claimed his life-long heart palpitations began then. Sometimes, in desperation, he would turn off the motor or try to press the brake pedal, and huge fights would break out. It didn't matter. Not once in all his life did Roberto finish in the money. He was usually last, with a million good reasons why. Nor was he a winner at selling cars, custommade ones, in the late twenties—a fiasco that ended with Roberto paying off large debts incurred, it is said, by his partner.[10]

But he was a winner with girls. He claimed his first victory at fourteen (a year before his first car), and thereafter his sister never knew which of her friends were really her own, for everyone she knew was in love with Roberto. It was less his body that attracted them—although he was good looking then, five foot eight with brown eyes—than his charisma and enthusiasm. He found all women irresistible. Certainly there is no rumor of his ever resisting. "I started going to the bordello quite young and would spend whole days there in search of a kind of glory by fucking one after another each of the seven girls who rented their bodies there."[11] Devotion to the flame of the moment was all consuming. When a Yugoslavian rejected him in his early teens, he resolved on suicide, took three aspirin, and went to bed. Disaster struck again, some years later, when he fell under the spell of Titi Michelle, whose father had been physician to the exiled king of Serbia. She was pretty, elegant, and very coquettish, but she went home to Savoy in France, leaving Roberto pining behind. Determined to follow, he secured his doctor's unwitting cooperation to contrive a need for mountain air to refresh his tubercular lungs. His goal was Bardonecchia, a ski resort in the Piedmontese Alps near the French border. Since he didn't have a passport, he sneaked past the border guards and walked through the train tunnel connecting Italy to France. Marcella, whom his parents had insisted he take along, was left back at the hotel, where Crown Prince Umberto was also staying. She was happy as always to oblige Roberto even though, lacking an escort, she could not leave her room the three days he was gone, even to dine. Valuing conspiracy in discretion above curiosity, she did not think to inquire how he had fared with Titi when he returned or ever afterward. Others say he was rebuffed, but he was too proud of his border escapade to mourn.[12]

This was in 1927, when Roberto was 21. We know almost nothing about his adventures during his teens and twenties, nor did his family know much at the time. "I left home fifty times when I was seventeen, eighteen, nineteen, twenty," for weeks and months at a throw, he later recalled.[13] He was "wild," but elegant and full of practical jokes, hung out in cafes and socialized with playboys like himself. Whoring was popular, drugs were in, women were sport. For contrast he went often to Naples, where he found pleasure in wandering without money and sleeping on park benches. He would have agreed with Croce's favorite aphorism, that Naples was not at all spiritually integrated with the rest of Italy, especially not with the restrained culture Roberto knew in Rome. Particularly in the Amalfi region he found a personal source of truth in its harmony of the spiritual and earthy. Later, he would make six movies there.

One friend's impoverished grandfather lived in slum housing near the Naples station. Although dressed in tatters, he was always impeccably groomed and spent his days on his balcony fishing for rats in the garbage-strewn courtyard below. They were as big as cats. He would strangle them, wait for a neighbor to open a window, then throw one in.

How different Roberto's experiences were from those of others his age!

"When I was twenty," said the novelist Vitaliano Brancati, "I was a Fascist down to my hair roots. Fascism for me was a wondrous credo. I experienced the joy of a herded animal: the joy of being in accord with millions of people—of feeling what they felt. An optimism of a third order invested me. I felt like a giant of the group even in my solitude. . . . I experienced deeply in 1927 what it is like for a twenty-year-old, inclined to meditation, fantasy and sloth, to admire a man of action and violence: to believe that a new delightful morality was about to be born."[14]

For many who were young, Fascism was adventurous, idealistic, magical, full of imagination and energy. It hailed the brave new world that was worth a fight to create, a world of justice, of plenty, a world where capital and labor would cooperate harmoniously, where class strife, corruption, and debauched lifestyles like Roberto's would be swept away along with the traditional Establishment.

Fascism was also attractive to militarists, gangsters, and Futurists who worshipped strength and violence. Often it had the effect of terrorizing opponents into silence. But until 1935 Fascism had a progressive side as well, a dynamic liberalism, and ought not to be confused with Nazism or the reactionary regimes we call "fascist" today. Such regimes try to demobilize their masses, to reduce them to passive participation, and to return to traditional, pre-revolutionary models. Fascism, in contrast, wanted to mobilize the masses, to transform society in new, untried directions, and to create a new type of man. It was authoritarian, but revolutionary.

For the Nazis the man of the future already existed, but he was being suffocated by modernism (i.e., the last two centuries) and the great task was to restore the old, immutable, pre-Napoleonic values like race.[15] Fascism wanted just the opposite—a new phase of civilization, engaged masses, not passive ones. It sponsored unions, after-work activities, sports, debates, and cultural activities to attach people to the revolutionizing process. Especially through education, it was believed (following the illuminists, Rousseau, and Jefferson), the new type of citizen could be created. Renzo De Felice writes: "Reading the books written by Fascists, looking at Fascist publicity, what's striking is the vital optimism: the joy, the youthfulness, the life, the enthusiasm, the [concept of] struggle as a struggle for life. It's a perspective which—even though in Fascist terms—is one of progress. In Nazism even the idea of progress did not exist."[16]

The Fascist state, declared Giovanni Gentile, the regime's philosopher, is "a spiritual creation . . . an ethical state . . . an idealist state."[17] Unlike socialists, communists, and positivists, Fascists denied that spirit was subservient to matter, that anything was historically inevitable or evolutionarily predetermined. They vaunted the primacy of the will, the total freedom of the individual to carve out his own destiny. When the Marxist Turati told parliament that "Democracy [i.e., socialism] will win, because it must win, because it is history; yes, for this simple reason," Mussolini replied, "History does not have fixed rails like a railway." And Turati retorted, "I know . . . the will for you is everything, and ignores the causes which determine and moderate it. The trouble is that reality is not in agreement . . . with you, and economics is not literature or romance."[18]

But Fascism was romance. When critics charged it lacked ideology and was merely a means to power, Mussolini agreed. Fascism regarded itself as the first realistic political movement free both from moral and intellectual preconceptions. Practice would precede and form values instead of the other way round. "I declare to you," Mussolini told the nation, "that the twentieth century shall be the century of Italian power, it shall be the century during which for the third time Italy shall be the guide of human civilization. Outside our principles there is salvation neither for individuals nor above all for peoples. Ten years from now Europe will be Fascist."[19]

Mussolini shut down newspapers, abolished parties, jailed his critics (particularly on the extreme left), unleashed goon squads, repressed religious liberties, and ten thousand Italians emigrated to escape him. But he also suppressed the mafia, demoted the Fascist Party to an athletic and leisure-time organization, repressed class warfare by subjecting unions to state planning, reconciled the Vatican, and restored religion to the schools. The regime generally left people alone. There were no more broken windows, a shopkeeper knew his store would still be there the next morning, the trams were running, women could walk the streets unmolested, and children were safe going to school. There was some price security for the farmer, the renter, the wage earner. The state's finances were in order; inflation was checked; unemployment, the bureaucracy, and the deficit were all being reduced; and an impressive public works program was under way. Few countries could boast comparable achievements. Italy was a tyranny, but in the twenties and thirties few countries, no matter how democratic in name, permitted their citizens more actual freedom.

People were arrested for thinking or speaking. Crime, corruption, unemployment, and anything unflattering was censored out of the media. Privilege ruled. Yet the Germans were constantly agog at the amount of dissent Mussolini tolerated. In America at the time, by comparison, censorship of racist lynchings, war crimes, corruption, and exploitation of labor was routine; "free speech" often existed more in theory than practice. "I know no country in which, speaking generally, there is less independence of mind and true freedom of discussion than in America," wrote de Tocqueville.[20] Americans during the war had been sentenced to ten years in prison for writing letters to the newspaper saying the government favored profiteers, or for making a movie, *The Spirit of '76*, that cast British troops in an unfavorable light during the Revolution.[21] In most of the world, free speech was synonymous with anarchy and disruption. In America, again by comparison, over a forty-year period thousands were jailed, deported, or fired for thinking, speaking, listening to, or possessing dissident writing; socialist legislators were denied their elected seats; labor struggles were routinely blamed on foreign communist agitators; and goon squads regularly suppressed peaceful demonstrations with violence and murder, even gassing babies. Mussolini's prisons were relatively empty, violent crime was rare, and city dwellers had no need to barricade themselves behind security guards. By 1932, 22,173 political prisoners had been released, and most of the remaining 373 were confined to islands or small towns rather than to prisons. Mussolini's victims were chiefly militant Communists. Still today, many Italians credit him for saving Italy from "going Communist." During the Depression, Italy's forward-looking social legislation spared it the traumas of massive unemployment, homelessness, organized crime, class warfare, racism, lynchings, and massacres that were encouraging not a few Americans to hope that Roosevelt would suspend the Constitution and assume near-dictatorial powers.[22] Almost every book published since World War II condemns Fascism out of hand on the grounds that it was anti-democratic. But where was the "Democracy" to which Fascism is compared? Was it in the United States where two million wandered homeless, where other millions languished in jails, where non-whites had few freedoms and could even be lynched with impunity, where the press seldom printed the truth?

World War I had turned European civilization upside down more thoroughly than any event in history. A generation of youth had been wiped out, everyday morality had been destroyed, class relations were in turmoil, and virtually every nation in Europe was experiencing problems similar to Italy's. Fascism's response, as De Felice points out, "was the attempt of the middle class, of the petite bourgeoisie . . . to impose itself as a class, as a new force. In this sense the Fascist movement was an attempt to propose new, 'modern' and 'more adequate' solutions, [such as] a modern sort of inter-class corporatism."[23] Thus, compared to Russia, Germany, France, Spain, and most of the non-European world, Italy under Mussolini was the envy of the world. Sovereigns and politicians and poets, too, from all over— George V, Churchill, Thomas Edison, Gandhi, J. P. Morgan , T. S. Eliot, Ezra Pound, George Bernard Shaw, W. B. Yeats—hastened to applaud Mussolini's accomplishments.

And so did the Italian people. In a freely-conducted plebiscite in 1929, in which ninety percent of the electorate participated, 8,519,559 voted approval, and only 135,761 expressed dissent. "Despite the misgivings of certain intellectuals, students, and workers," states Tannenbaum, "most of them, along with almost everyone else, viewed the Fascist regime as 'normal' and did what it required more often out of conformity than fear."[24]

But not Roberto. He was terribly out of step, a high-rolling flower child, addicted to liberty, to license even, as to a drug. Like his libertine family, he despised the lower-middle-class virtues that Fascism was institutionalizing. For him Fascism was the antithesis of Risorgimento liberalism, although masquerading as its fulfillment. In later years Roberto recalled the era in ho-hum tones. Fascism gained power dramatically, he contended, but soon afterward even the fanatics regarded it as a bad joke. He contrasted public feeling after the Second World War—a sense of victory in defeat—with the sense of defeat in victory that followed the First World War, infecting Fascism as well. One Mussolini hymn was titled "Me ne frego" ("I don't give a damn").

The Fascist creations were the militia, community organizations, corporate structures, and tens of thousands of little jobs—which weren't to be discounted in a country full of unemployed and hungry citizens. The Fascists weren't revolutionaries, they behaved like normal people living normal lives, nothing like the black masses of National Socialism. Often at the whorehouse, Roberto would be made to hide in his room so that Balbo or some other Fascist bigwig wouldn't be seen. It was hard to be intimidated by people like that.

Roberto lived within Fascism from age 16 to 38. During that period, when virtually no one travelled anywhere, Italian culture was all he knew. Yet, by dropping out of school, avoiding military service because of his bad lung, and being rich, he was largely unaffected by Fascism—aside from having to rush with his whore. "[I] lived the bohemian life, traveling about . . . and being in love all the time."[25] His companions were like himself: irresponsible, unemployed, and privileged, living in the gilded margins of the real world. They paid no attention to politics. Their youthful revolt was not against Fascism but conformity of any sort. Confronted by middle-class sobriety, they delighted in flaunting cynicism and insulting convention. One friend, who by birth belonged to the Pope's Noble Guards, would take his post at the Vatican drugged out of his mind on cocaine, in full uniform, and would perpetrate so many jokes that they had to dismiss him.

Roberto, also on cocaine, got into an encounter with a militia captain in a Naples theater and slapped him—for reasons he could not remember later. They were both about 22. The insulted captain challenged him to a duel. Roberto and his friends could not keep from laughing. Early the next morning they went to the Solfatore of Pozzuoli, an area of tiny volcanic craters that give off sulphur fumes (where Roberto would later film a scene in *Voyage in Italy*). They tore off their right sleeves and faced off with swords. After simultaneously scratching each other, they stopped. For the rest of his life Roberto enjoyed displaying his scar.

Slapping a uniformed officer in a public place was a scandalous—and jailable—offense, however, and the cocaine added to the mess. Giuseppe Rossellini had to defend his son from the police, which wasn't easy. Roberto was impossible. When he was home, he was always late, always forgetting appointments, and his money lenders were always pacing to and fro outside on the sidewalk. Paternal fury had no effect. Roberto's excuses were so extraordinary and detailed—on one occasion he claimed he had met the Queen of England and fixed her car—that even though no one believed him, his sins were forgotten.

"My father was a man of exceptional dimension: courageous, intelligent, cultivated, of a liberalism and generosity of mind I've encountered in few others," said Roberto. "This didn't prevent me from revolting against him when the moment came. I couldn't stand his telling me what to do. The moment he'd begin a reprimand, I'd leave the house slamming the door, going somewhere else to live, making debts my father paid."[26] Roberto's brother Renzo, who sulked over Roberto's conduct all his life, would go looking for him. His parents would box his ears.

Roberto was following his forebears' examples, in any case. None of them counted money, restrained a whimsy, or honored a marriage. His mother's parents had separated, his aunt was separated, nonno Zeffiro had lived openly with his mistress Fortù. (Zeffiro had had a wife but none of the children saw her—ever.) Beppino's philandering ("When my father died, three wives were crying under his bed," Roberto would later say) reached such a point that in 1926 Elettra left him and, taking her youngest child, went north to Comerio, on Lake Varese, where her eventual second husband lived.

Roberto spent money on cars, flowers, women, and clothes, frivolously. One friend, Eugenio Silenzi, recalls him buying a pair of sunglasses for a thousand lire—more than most white-collar workers could hope to earn in a month.[27] He took twenty or thirty people to supper every night. A lot of money he gave away casually. Rarely was he home before three in the morning. "I tended to prodigality, to excess," he understated in 1973, although he had not changed a whit. "I've always been thoughtless. I can't calculate the risks, I live on enthusiasm. I'm always making plans for the future. My policy is always to burn my bridges behind me. It's a grave defect."[28] Even in debt he didn't change; he would borrow more money and give that away, too. This was the D'Annunzian side of Roberto, the one who lived in a fabulous dream world full of refined gentlemen and marvelous women spending their lives amid licentiousness, subtle conversations, and perilous love affairs.

Liliana Castagnola, a third-rate vaudevillian from Naples, was one such woman. Eight years Roberto's senior and with intense black eyes, hair short like a boy's, and a sensual mouth, she was a *femme fatale* on whom many a fortune and, legend has it, even a life was squandered. Roberto, with faithful Renzo beside him, raced his car while Liliana watched from the stands and, each time he passed, threw her a kiss with one hand while steering with the other, then with two hands while steering with none—a ploy that moved Renzo to speak to him afterward. They spent all day in bed making love, said Roberto, until hunger forced them out to a restaurant, and then they had to rush back to bed before they had time to eat.[29]

The romance's end is mysterious. Liliana was found dead on March 3, 1930. By some accounts, she killed herself for the actor Totò with an overdose of sleeping pills. By other accounts, harder drugs were involved. By Roberto's account, she killed herself for him, by burning coal so that carbon gas asphyxiated her.[30] He was boasting: it is likely she who jilted him. But around this time, due perhaps to the scandal around Castagnola, but more probably to cocaine and the slapping incident with the militia captain, Roberto's father, as much to keep the police at bay as from bewilderment at his son's behavior, consigned him to a mental sanitarium (a *casa di cura per alienati*) near Naples.

It was a harrowing experience that left terrible memories. Roberto emerged after a month or two and got into a taxi. It is not clear whether he escaped or was free to leave. In any case, the friend he went to see was not at home and he had no money to pay for the taxi. He had himself driven across town in search of another friend who wasn't in either. A third and a fourth were also out. Roberto suggested they go to Rome.

There was no gas, the cab driver was broke, and Rome was 140 miles away. But credit was available: the driver's little boy was deposited at the gas station as security, and on they went to Rome.

Once home, Roberto told the butler to pay the cab fare. The butler went down, came back up, and told Beppino he didn't have enough money. Beppino asked, "How much is it?"

"Twelve hundred lire!" Enough to support a family for two months.

Beppino paid, and nearly cracked his son's skull. It was the only time in his life that he was violent with Roberto.

"I still have the scar," Roberto would brag to friends.[31]

"My father gave me the will to lead an adventurous life or, if you prefer, a courageous life. Despite this, I opposed my father. I felt that what he wanted for me wasn't enough. And I think he was pleased that I rebelled, because for him that was a sign of courage. My stubbornness appeared as a sign of vitality to him.[32] He used to tell me that you have to be daring, always. The important thing is always to be moving forward."[33]

Giuseppe Rossellini, for his part, had assumed his duties in the family firm quite against his own bohemian inclinations. He was proud of the house with the tall, tall tower engineered by the Sleiters that he had built atop Monte Mario for the baritone Titta Ruffo (Via del Sassoferrato 11), and the one—the first on Via Po—that he had built for Pietro Mascagni. But he was far more Luigi's son than Zeffiro's nephew, and he was not good at business.

He had wanted to be a singer and had sung the tenor roles in *La Bohème* at Rieti and *L'Amico Fritz* at Prato. The cult of Mascagni, the creator of *Cavalleria rusticana*, was a virtual religion in the household; its morning ritual featured Beppino singing "*Tu ch'odi lo mio grido*" while shaving. Entire nights were passed conversing with his idol. Once Mascagni phoned at 5 A.M. desperate for a nightingale. Beppino woke up a pet store owner and arrived breathless with a nightingale and a box of worms. But it wouldn't even peep. They tried everything, they even brought over Marinetti, whom all Italy was whistling at in scorn, but to no avail.

Art and ideas invigorated Beppino, business depressed him; he dreamed of vast projects, spent wildly, made bad deals, acquired a slightly shady reputation, and eventually ran his company into the ground. Yet, writes Renzo, "he was the sort of man to merit the esteem and friendship of many famous people. My brother and I owe to our father the teaching that has gotten us through so many difficulties in life: that without iron faith and intangible ideals you are lost and will end up with nothing."[34]

Zeffiro had been self taught and was proud of it. But Beppino resolved late in life to remedy his lack of formal education. Rising before dawn, he would read the classics and write. By 6:30 he was at his workyard. At 1:00 he came home, exhausted, for dinner. In the afternoons he went to his office at 54 Via Margutta. After supper he went back to his studies. Fortunately he needed little sleep. He had a fine book collection, wrote poetry, occasional newspaper pieces, and, after ten years of constant refining, published a novel, *Sic Vos Non Vobis* (Rome: Edizioni Sapientia, 1928).

"It was my father who gave me my zest to understand," said Roberto.[35] Every Sunday a band of friends would gather at Beppino's house: musicians, painters, novelists, they were all crazy for knowledge and beauty. Among them was Odoardo Gori, a poet and philosopher whose refinement left a lasting impression on Roberto. And the famous writer Massimo Bontempelli, who with Malaparte had founded a magazine, *Novecento* ("Twentieth Century") which, in an age when Italians tended to feel culturally inferior to the French, gave evidence of Italian culture also in a French edition, *Cahiers d'Italie et d'Europe.*

The *cenacolo*, or coterie, met for more than ten years. They'd come for dinner and stay into the evening, thirty of them, declaiming verses, playing scores on the piano, showing paintings and watercolors. Among them was Renzo's impoverished music teacher, Giacinto Sallustio, who adored Croce and whose "concerts" at the Radium Cinema, where he played the great masters and totally ignored the silent films he was supposed to be accompanying, attracted a clientele all their own.

They all argued madly about literature, politics, sports, women, life, death, and anything. No subject was taboo, no opinion forbidden. Often fights would break out in thundering Roman voices. The neighbors across the street would run to their windows to discover what was going on when the shouting got wild. Then Sallustio would stomp out, announcing he was going off to read a few pages of Croce to restore his sanity.

"But the arguments themselves were superb," said Roberto. "And I, when I was thirteen or fourteen, was admitted into this circle where I had the right to say no matter what to try to rival intelligence with the old men. This type of duel gives you passion for intelligence your entire life, thirst for knowledge, a need to understand."[36]

The group included Alfredo Panzini, a Socialist; Mario Montesi, a city councilor who wrote classical tragedies in verse and whose Catholicism clashed with Beppino's liberalism; Giuseppe Adami, a noted writer; Titta Ruffo, the baritone; Willy Ferrero, a conductor; Mascagni, Zandonai, and Alfano, composers; Marcello Piacentini, an architect; and Angelo Bencini, a public works contractor (building tunnels in Sicily with Beppino) and bibliophile whose father had been a *garibaldino*. Gori, an ex-priest teaching Italian at the Nazareno, had a passion for defending the Italian language against the incursions of foreign words. They were middle-class, but generally left-leaning. Beppino, with Socialist friends, was no ordinary industrialist. "Each of them reflected on his own hopes, once golden, now deluded [under Mussolini]. The first world war hadn't been over long and literature was trying to recompose itself, to find a face. Bontempelli was working hard in the twenties."[37]

Bontempelli was one of the most important writers of the era. He thought the new realities of the twentieth century required a new literature. His solution was to return to the myth-making techniques of primitive peoples. "The true role of narrative art," he said, "is this: to relate dreams as if they were reality, and reality as if it were a dream." His "Twentieth Century" magazine, at the center of the cosmopolitan Stracittà movement, promoted the most advanced art of the 1920s and had an editorial board that included Pierre McOrlan, Georg Kaiser, Ramon Gomez de la Serna, James Joyce, and Ilya Ehrenburg. Later, with Anton Giulio Bragaglia and Alessandro Blasetti, Bontempelli started *Cinematografo*, one of the first magazines to deal culturally with film. His futuristic proclamation, that "the new century demands only one quality of its poets: that of knowing how to be candid, of knowing how to marvel, of feeling that the universe and all of life are a continuous and inexhaustible miracle,"[38] might have been Roberto's own artistic credo. In the sixties and seventies we shall find him loudly denouncing "modern" art and cinema as wallowing in fear and alienation; we shall see him advocating Bontempelli's notion of art as celebration of progress and innovation.

Croce - *l'aria d'Italia*

This notion was also a Crocean notion, as almost all of Roberto's notions would be. Benedetto Croce (1866–1952) was an Hegelian philosopher, historian, and literary critic. But the description is misleading. He was the "air of Italy." For half a century his thought, in turbulence with Catholicism, defined Italian mindsets. Roberto soaked him up like a sponge, as he would existentialism, phenomenology, Marxism, and whatever else was in the air. The sponge could no more have avoided Croce than it could have avoided Christ. Croce was the bright, new, *secular* liberalism, the *cenacolo*, and represented Roberto's father's values. Christ was the transcendent, the sacred, grace and the incarnation, and represented Roberto's mother's values. Both were everywhere—and their conflicts resound in Roberto's films as in his personality. His "neo-realism" was quintessentially Crocean: a reliving of the past (a *ricorso*) in order to create a new human reality today. In his two most personal works, *Voyage in Italy* and *Viva l'Italia*, two of Croce's family have roles. Formal study of Croce would come only late in life, when he would follow Croce's criticisms in his movie depiction of Descartes. In the intervening years, whenever Roberto would leap excitedly on a "new" idea, it would usually be a Crocean idea—a *ricorso* of his youth.[39]

Roberto's life-long polemic against "theories" and "intellectuals" stems from Croce, who, like him, scorned academia, never bothered to get a degree, and opposed the thinkers fashionable outside of Italy—Freud, Darwin, Comte, Marx—who dealt in theory, claimed we can only know abstractions, and insisted we are slaves to psychic, genetic, or material forces. To the contrary, for Croce and Roberto *real* experience was just that: not something we are taught at school through abstractions, but something we know and feel directly. Theories, concepts, opinions, all threaten to corrupt our ability to experience reality directly for ourselves. For Roberto, fond of cocaine and shunning theory, the act of grasping the world directly was an obsession—as sexual as intellectual—in his life, conversation, friendships, and methods of filmmaking. Like Croce, Roberto's whole life was a polemic that we need not be slaves, we *are* capable of controlling our destiny and, in Roberto's words, can "revise the whole conception of the universe."[40]

We can do so because there is no objective reality, only the human reality humans create, which changes constantly. Revolution is perpetual. Each age has its own peculiar philosophy, attitudes, institutions, aesthetic tastes, and so on. For Croce, history is not "what happened," it is a story with emotion and meaning for today. ("History" and "story" are a single concept in Italian and French—*storia, histoire*.) Not only history, but every concept changes constantly. "There is no such thing as the true (logical) sense of a word. The true sense of the word is that which is conferred upon it on each occasion by the person forming a concept." (Philosophy's job is to figure out what, for example, Socrates meant by "wisdom.") Genuine speech is "poetry," individual intuition—as opposed to "prose," when we ape theory rather than think for ourselves. Thus poetry can contain no "signs," because a sign stands for something else, whereas poetry stands for itself. "Born as poetry, language was afterwards twisted to serve as a sign."[41]

History, similarly, does not stand as a sign of reality; history *is* human reality *today*, an art rather than a science, a myth. Documents, statistics, and judgment are not to be slighted, but what is crucial is intuition—the way we know our friends. "Do you wish to understand the true history of a neolithic Ligurian or Sicilian? Try, if you can, to become a neolithic Ligurian or Sicilian in your mind.... Do you wish to understand the true history of a blade of grass? Try to become a blade of grass."[42] As we "rerun" the past and integrate it into our sense of the present, art and imagination will bring us closer to reality, and the heroic virtues of the past will be renewed in us.

It was from Giambattista Vico (1668–1744), the only other Italian philosopher of note since the Renaissance, that Croce adapted his notion of *ricorso*, as well as the notion of history as the expression of human will and deeds, and therefore a more certain source of knowledge about humanity than the natural sciences or psychology can be. Vico, like Croce, opposed the notion that human nature is constant, contending that, since we are historical entities, our human nature changes over time. Vico saw art, poetry, philosophy, religion, myth, economics, and politics as interrelated keys to a culture.[43] Bontempelli, with his interest in myth-making, was following Vico and Croce, as Rossellini would do in his movies.

For Croce, as for Rossellini, history was the story of liberty emerging. Human nature, ever changing, was the only transcendental. There were no absolutes, no "normal," no "sanity," no "reality." The basic political axiom was that individuals must be trusted and free. Liberty was the mantra of Roberto's life, its impulse always the decisive moment in his movies. "There were no rules for him," his own daughter marveled.[44] Had such not been the case, how could he have persevered from failure to failure? "We no longer believe," Croce wrote, "like the Greeks, in happiness of life on earth; we no longer believe, like the Christians, in happiness in an otherworldly life; we no longer believe, like the optimistic philosophers of the last century, in a happy future for the human race.... We no longer believe in anything of that, and what we have alone retained is the consciousness of ourselves, and the need to make that consciousness ever clearer and more evident, a need for whose satisfaction we turn to science and to art."[45]

Rossellini would speak of this severe moral commitment and constant study as the "moral attitude" (one of his favorite phrases) at the basis of "new-reality" film—a need for each of us to make our individual consciousness ever clearer and create a "harmonious discord." The world's hope needs each of us courageous enough to be maximally ourself—even, Roberto would insist, at the risk of looking ridiculous. "I must admit, I'm always for the 'crazy' people."[46]

Beppino's last building project involved construction of the Barberini Cinema and the opening up of Via Barberini and Via Bissolati.[47] It was a particularly tormented job, entailing extensive demolition of older buildings, and he was simultaneously forgoing sleep to pursue his studies. He caught a cold that turned into pneumonia and in three days he was dead, on March 6, 1931. He was fifty. The children were waiting in an adjoining room in the middle of the night when Dr. Nicola Sforza, one of the tenants, came and hugged them. "Now," he said, "you're on your own."

They were indeed. Within a few months they discovered they were virtually broke. In Rome today people still say that Giuseppe Rossellini's death was a suicide brought on by his firm's collapse.

Where had all the money gone? No one knew. Postwar inflation had taken its toll. Expenses had spiraled upward, while income from property—rented out on long leases before the war—had fallen disastrously. And Beppino had been a bad businessman. But most of the money had simply been squandered.

Renzo and Marcella went to live with their mother in Comerio. The building on Via Ludovisi was sold. Roberto stayed in Rome to salvage what he could.

A few hours after Giuseppe Rossellini's death, some police had come to question him, as they had six months earlier. The family concluded that the police had intended to arrest him and send him into internal exile. Roberto, in the words of a *New York Times* reporter, claimed in 1949 that his father's loss of money "resulted from political complications, and to say now that his father was 'anti-Fascist' would sound 'unconvincing.' He said that his father was 'big enough and so well known' that he was able to maintain his prosperous business without having to submit to the Mussolini clique. But the Fascist officials moved in on Joseph Rossellini's death; were, in fact, 'coming to arrest my father on the very day he died and we were maneuvered in an extremely complicated way out of our rightful inheritance.'"[48]

Beppino, we know, was a left-leaning Liberal. He admired authors like Anatole France, an anti-bourgeois, communist crusader for social justice, and moderate Socialists like Prampolini, Turati, Bissolati, and Enrico Ferri. Some of the regime's victims had been his friends; Matteotti, for instance, was Titta Ruffo's brother-in-law. Beppino disliked Mussolini and had not kept his opinions to himself, supposedly, when the Duce had shown up for the Barberini dedication.

But he was not under investigation by the police.[49] The family legend that he was slated for internal exile derives entirely from a rumor reported to Antonietta Avanzo by one of her friends.[50] At the time of Beppino's death, the regime was releasing political prisoners, not collecting more of them from the ranks of harmless industrialists who had not only profited from the regime but were serving it. Rossellini's patron and protector was Marcello Piacentini, the regime's favorite architect;[51] it was due to Piacentini that he had received highly visible government contracts like that for Piazza Barberini—a showplace for the regime. Bontempelli and others in the *cenacolo* were closely associated with the regime. There is little basis, either, for the allegation that the family inheritance was lost as a result of political conspiracy. Roberto himself never repeated this charge, nor have any of his family or friends reiterated it; his sister Marcella denied it: all concur that the fortune was lost through inflation, Beppino's incompetence, and wild spending.

Roberto's similarities with his father were striking. Both were dreamers. Both spent recklessly, dressed dapperly, loved promiscuously, smoked incessantly, made a religion of liberty, and had the manners of grand seigneurs. Roberto too undertook to educate himself late in life—and spent ten years rewriting the same book.

Many of these qualities, it has been said, along with chameleon-like abilities in social situations, were typical of wealthy Romans of that era. But Beppino's sudden death, coming as it did amid Roberto's defiance and dissipations, left an exceptional void in his son. True, Roberto had seen his father infrequently until 1924, when Beppino's affairs in Venice had finished, and by then Roberto was rarely at home himself. But by 1926, with Elettra hundreds of miles away, Beppino was the only parent on the scene and in any case the sole point of stability or discipline Roberto's life had ever had, or ever would have. "He was dominated by his father," his sister said.[52] His father was someone he admired and depended on, before whom he was shy and intimidated, and to whom he never got close. He spoke rarely of him in later life, even to his intimates, except to note how often he had failed him and how terrible it was to have one's father die that way. "You live with such remorse," he told his daughter Ingrid.[53]

Yet if guilt was a constant element in Rossellini's life, it was an oddly irrational guilt. He liked confessing and being forgiven, but he did not as a result change or confront responsibilities more maturely. As we shall see, he spent his life searching for father figures, shying away from his own ever-increasing patriarchal roles, while paradoxically encouraging revolt against any sort of authority. Till his dying day he carried with him a small photo of his father. He regarded it as a sort of life force and would study it questioningly whenever he had a problem. The photo would smile, he contended, when his father approved of his decisions.

Roberto treated his own son as his father had treated him. Even after Roberto's death, he would appear in his son's dreams, raising his hand, and commanding, "Stop!"

Passing Time

While Renzo languished melancholically in Comerio, teaching music in nearby Varese for 300 lire a month, Roberto continued his madcap existence in Rome. He had little contact with his family during the next four or five years. They were 300 miles from Rome, he was something of a black sheep in their eyes, and his handling of the estate produced ill feeling. He himself took less than a year to eat up his part of the inheritance. But there does not seem to have been a part for anyone else. He seldom discussed this period in later years.

Roberto was able to depend on friends such as Marcello Pagliero, Adolfo Sansoni, and Marcellino Caracciolo. They had a loose sort of gang that shared everything, sometimes lived together, and, undecided about what to do with their lives, passed their days in snobbistic pleasures of the *dolce vita* sort. Pagliero was later to star in *Roma città aperta*. Sansoni, from Bologna, was a Fascist consul and, married to a Wülf, one of the richer people in Europe; eventually he became a film producer. "Sansoni was a great friend of Roberto's," recalls Franco Riganti, "inasmuch as all his life he lent Roberto money on the heaviest terms."[1] Caracciolo came from a thousand-year-old Neapolitan family full of princes and archdukes, bore the title Duke of Laurino, lived at the Excelsior Hotel, and drove race cars. He was rich enough, but had narrowly missed inheriting a truly immense fortune by refusing one evening to play "train" with a senile uncle with whom he had been playing train for years, chanting "choo-choo" with the butler and all the chairs. Marcellino had sent his brother Lucio instead, whereupon the uncle had changed his will and died, and Lucio, who until that night had never had to play train or do anything, became Duke of Acquara. Marcellino eventually married an English woman from South Africa whose father owned a diamond mine. They divorced but stayed friends, and when she remarried he went to England for the ceremony— but was barred from entering when he told immigration he'd come to witness his wife's marriage. (Both Caracciolo dukes would later appear in *Voy-*

age in Italy. In *Viva l'Italia* Lucio's son plays a wounded soldier, a daughter plays a nurse, and another daughter the Queen of Naples. Marcellino Caracciolo served as an assistant director on many Rossellini pictures. Roberto's son Renzo married a Caracciolo.)

Amaldo de Los Vargas, a Socialist deputy from Volterra, became a sort of father and tutor to Roberto after Beppino's death. "What he gave me was the taste for not believing in universal and eternal ideas, and when I rediscovered this attitude in Marx, it was absolutely clear."[2] (Not believing in universal ideas was, of course, a Crocean attitude. Rossellini claimed that "Marxist" belief in dialectical materialism was a betrayal of Marx's own ideas.)

Roberto was extremely tied to Los Vargas and attracted to his quick intelligence, love of paradoxes, and insolence. Once, as he was about to board a train, Los Vargas was jerked aside by a nervous Fascist who shouted, "I have seven deaths on my conscience, and you're going to be the eighth," to which Los Vargas replied, "Bravo, buffone!" and went calmly to his compartment. Roberto credited Los Vargas in helping him turn his youthful revolt toward something concrete—toward movies.

Rome was Italy's Hollywood and, thanks to the movie theater his father had built, Roberto had always partied in the circles of Rome's film people. "When I was young and foolish,[3] I spent disproportionately long hours in the stalls."[4]

Charlie Chaplin was his favorite—because of Chaplin's great humanity, he claimed, but in fact what actually attracted Rossellini to Chaplin was the tramp's *revolt*. The tramp is persistently horrible, destructive, and mean, particularly in his early films. Fereydoun Hoveyda once said as much to Roberto: "It's this *inhumanity* that, unconsciously, attracts you."

"Not true," Roberto had parried.

Yet what do Chaplin's films resemble if not another Rossellini love, the Neapolitan *commedia dell'arte*. The tramp is malicious and violent, irreverent and subversive, always debunking things like heroism, glorious war, love, and sanctity, always rejecting accepted authority. Like most Rossellini films, Hoveyda observes.[5]

Roberto would rail against authority in any form. Yet he may have been the only person in Italy who never drove through a red light. Similarly, he admired the Roman ability to be "infernal" and "diabolic," but needed to bow before father figures, confess his sins, and be forgiven. Deliberately in his films he would contrast characters' unfettered emotions with their orderly dress and appearance, believing that order, virtue, and civilization are so many veneers to which obeisance must from time to time be made, but that unfettered human instinct is the reality.

All of which he could find in Chaplin.

He also loved Griffith and Stroheim and, above all, Murnau. "Murnau's influence is far back," he said in 1959, "but that was the invisible spring that started things going."[6] In the Murnau of *Sunrise* and *Tabu* there is a *poetic* realism—an intense way of showing the world around a character—that is far closer, stylistically and temperamentally, to Rossellini, than the social realism of Griffith and Stroheim. Thus equally important is King Vidor, who married the two realisms. *Hallelujah* and *The Crowd*, Roberto said, "made an unforgettable impression.[7] In *The Crowd*, do you remember, when they marry without their families' knowing, and he shaves to look nice and clean to meet the family, and then the in-laws arrive unexpectedly, and he goes out and has forgotten to wipe off a bit of soap still on his earlobe, you know? Things like that really struck me and perhaps put me on the road toward truth, toward reality."[8]

King Vidor is the primary model, cinematically, for the "neo-realism" shared by filmmakers otherwise as diverse as Rossellini, De Sica, and Visconti. Reviews of *The Crowd* printed in 1928 could have been reprinted in 1948 as reviews of the Italian films with only name changes. For example, Gilbert Seldes wrote on *The Crowd*: "Negatively the picture is extremely important because it breaks completely with the stereotype of the feature film. There is virtually no plot; there is no exploitation of sex in the love interest; there is no physical climax, no fight, no scheduled thrill. The characters, all commonplace people, act singularly unlike moving picture characters and singularly like human beings; there is no villain, no villainy, no success."[9]

Reality could also be sought in Rome's night life. Caffè Rosati in Piazza del Popolo and Caffè l'Arago in Via del Corso were after-theater haunts for vaudeville and cinema people and fertile grounds for womanizing. Roberto would stay up talking with Aldo Vergano, Ferdinando Poggioli, Ivo Perilli, and Leo Longanesi until he fell asleep with his head against the wall. It was "by chance—or rather by love" that he drifted into filmmaking, he told François Truffaut, who explained: "He was in love with a girl who had been noticed by some producers and hired to make a movie. Purely out of jealousy, Roberto went with her to the studio and, since it was a low-budget production, and they saw him doing nothing, and since he had a car, they sent him every day to pick up the male star, Jean-Pierre Aumont, at his home." Roberto, Aumont recalled, "looked like a decadent Roman emperor."[10]

The girl was Assia Noris and the picture was not the one with Aumont (her second), but her first one, *Tre uomini in frack* or *Trois hommes en habit* (Mario Bonnard, 1932).[11] Its producer, Peppino Amato, as well as two of the "Three men in tails"—Eduardo and Peppino De Filippo, Neapolitan vaudeville brothers so poor they had had to borrow their tail coats from a waiter—were denizens of Roberto's cafés. Roberto liked teaming up with the De Filippos to play elaborate practical jokes on Amato.

Amato had been a shoeshine-boy, actor, and filmmaking pioneer in Naples. He had emigrated to the United States, failed as a film producer there, and turned to the local mafia for help. After selling carpets for a while, he managed to set himself up as a film importer and return to Italy. Genial, semi-literate, a Latin lover, and a wild gambler, he quickly became Italy's most adventurous and perhaps most colorful producer—and a wonderful victim. One of Roberto's more elaborate gags, in the forties, involved convincing him that Greta Garbo wanted to return to the screen under his aegis. After three months of (fabricated) international correspondence, Amato made his way, shaking with nervousness to an Excelsior apartment where De Filippo waited in dress and wig. Just as Amato went to knock on the door, he stopped and, fearing Garbo or fearing a trick, walked away without opening it.

Assia Noris was to become one of the most famous divas of European cinema. A Russian exile, she had come with her mother from Cannes to visit some Russians living in Italy. They had gone to a show at the Teatro Argentina in Rome but, not understanding a word of Italian, were spending the second act over tea in the lobby when Amato—"a character out of Gogol," recalls Noris—"approached mama and said he was looking for a girl like me for Peppino and Eduardo De Filippo's first film, *Tre uomini in frack.* He said I'd play a young American who asks her daddy to buy her Tito Schipa, so she'd have him with her always, with his beautiful voice and his songs, and so save money on records. . . . I shot the film and went back to school in Cannes to tell my friends about my adventure."[12]

Noris describes herself as a school girl never out of her watchful mother's eye. But she was a twenty-year-old radiant blonde, already separated from her first husband. She and Roberto were a familiar sight among Rome's night people for the better part of a year—four years, according to some.[13]

"When I knew Rossellini," Noris relates, "he was a young playboy, very handsome, very skinny, very brilliant. Our parents were in agreement, so we got married in a Russian church, and I felt very happy, even though frightened, young as I was. But our private marriage never happened, I don't know why. My father came to get me in a hotel in San Remo, and after 48 hours the marriage was annulled. . . . [This] would have been considered a scandalous episode, but Fascist censorship forbade its publication."[14]

The wedding, which took place in Nice, was actually a farce in which an actor friend posed as a Russian priest. Afterwards Roberto took Assia to Varese and to general surprise—for he'd had no contact with his family for a year or so—presented her to his mother as his wife. Real or unreal, the marriage soon ended. Roberto liked to say that it was he who left her, after her father found them in bed while he was holding her down and twisting her ankle. By other accounts it was she who left him.

The morning after arriving in Varese, she came downstairs in a riding habit and inquired where the horse was. "The horse? What horse?" Elettra replied. "We only have an old donkey to carry sacks from market."

Assia went back upstairs, changed her clothes, and left.[15] "What I like about a man," she declared, "are his arms, his tenderness; I like to feel small and protected. Instead, though, I always make the wrong choice, because they all want me to play the mama."[16]

To replace Roberto, she turned to the director Mario Camerini, whom she hoped would make her a big star. And he did—by accentuating her exoticness with a Russian accent, though she had never spoken that language, and by encouraging the rumor that she was really a princess.

Roberto was insanely jealous for a time, the gossips say. He spied on the lovers and lurked behind doors with a toy pistol in hand. But the manic phase did not last long. His name was soon linked with Ingriduccia, Laura Nucci, and hosts of others.

Even at seventy, Roberto would devote more time and energy to making women than to making films—which in his circles was considered merely good taste. He worked because he was broke. In 1932 friends found him a job at Caesar Film as a dubbing assistant. The Italian cinema in those days was fighting a pitiful losing battle even in its own movie houses, where in 1930 a mere twelve Italian pictures were in distribution against 290 American ones. To save the industry, the government enacted a law in 1933 making it obligatory to dub foreign films into Italian and adding an import tax which was kicked back to Italian film producers as a subsidy. Like all such laws, then as now, the subsidy system was controversial because a "quality" clause might favor films deemed politically or morally pleasing.

At Caesar Film, Roberto helped prepare Italian versions of American productions, and French versions of Italian productions like Noris's. His job was purely technical, so he enjoyed it at first and had fun inventing sound effects and editing film. Although the work got boring, he still needed money so he continued to slog on fitfully during the next few years, also working at I.C.I. (Industrie Cinematografiche Italiane). But the tedium was so repugnant to Roberto that, in later years, he would refuse to have anything to do with the sound editing of his films—often with ruinous results.

An easier source of occasional income was, as he put it, "in a sort of black market cinema. Three scenarists exercised a quasi-monopoly in Italy at the time, getting 200,000 lire for each of their bagatelles. One of them [Caesare Vico Lodovici], whom I knew well and who was very fond of me, suggested I write stories for him at three thousand a piece. I learned later that he never even read them. [But] since I was regarded as an original, as someone perhaps not completely idiotic, but a bit eccentric, this friend gave me the chance to work. He'd give me a thousand lire in advance. And with a thousand lire I could get by for, I don't know, twenty days, a month. A thousand lire was real money then. When I was close to the end of the thousand lire, I'd do the first half of the script, because then I could get the second thousand lire, and then, finally, when I was really desperate, I'd do the second half. And all of this would take me two days work.[17] I'd go to

Via Principe Amedeo, where the only typists were, and spend a few hours there dictating."[18]

Ghostwriting was common in the Italian film industry; everyone did it and still does. Roberto concluded there was nothing sacred about a script; scriptwriting was just an easy way to make money. "It was so mechanical that the experience really disenchanted me completely."[19]

There is, then, every reason to take Rossellini at his word that he only took up filmmaking reluctantly, quite late in life, "because until then I had a better profession, that of the family son, and I liked it more."[20] He was, said Eugenio Silenzi, "brilliant—self-taught rather than studied—a marvelous conversationalist, and a font of culture."[21] But it was obvious he had no purpose in life. When Sergio Amidei, a socially committed idealist, arrived in Rome in 1936 and met, that very first day, Roberto with Aldo Vergano and Fernando Poggioli at a restaurant on Via Zucchelli, his attraction to Roberto was ardent and immediate but his assessment was scathing. He thought Roberto a big waster, dissolute and brilliant, a big spender, a do-nothing far more interested in actresses than cinema. Indeed, it was Roberto's ability to waste everything—money, women, time—that, coupled with his ambiguous and cunning gentleness, made him appealing to women, Amidei concluded. Little had changed in the four years since he was with Assia Noris, when Roberto's friends had joked, "He's courted the cinema so much that he's gotten stuck there. They've made him go to work!"[22]

Roberto's reputation as a brilliant conversationalist never disguised his lack of academic discipline and formal education. He had trouble adding numbers in his head and never mastered sure command of the Italian language. He spoke an Italian remarkable (among a people who adore long, complicated rambling) for its clear short sentences and simple vocabulary. He read omnivorously but superficially; any sort of deep, comparative analysis was beyond his patience. He grasped people and things wholly, but uncritically. He prided himself for his receptivity and openness—justly—but even his closest friends judged him lacking in principles, religion, or ideals consciously his own. With Catholics, it was agreed, he was Catholic, with Communists Communist, with Buddhists Buddhist—and never insincerely or inconsistently.[23] Always he was charming, winning, inspiring, because, denying self-definition (but not self-purpose), he had a unique ability to feel others, to become others, and to appear to them as the channel through which their deepest aspirations would be fulfilled. "Roberto dreamed his way through life," said Franco Riganti.[24] And he took people along.

Enrico Fulchignoni, one of Roberto's most constant friends, saw his character as twofold: part product of a superficial society, part dominated by "doubt, rage, and the search for—and stubborn affirmation of—human dignity.

"Roberto [in the thirties] had a reputation as a wit and an adventurer, a man from a good family, full of charm and courteous arguments. He was proud of having grown up with the grace of those well-born and well-raised. A physical laziness at a time when it was in good tone—at the dawn of Fascism—to exhibit as much athletic talent as possible was one of the first manifestations of his snobbery. And, one thing leading to another, this snobbery, evolving in the midst of Rome's bourgeoisie, pushed the adolescent toward a career of pugnacious anticonformity that was to be one of his life's regal characteristics. What usually distinguishes the bourgeoisie, someone once wrote, is its quest for immobility: nothing should change, nothing should move, children should not have ambitions too high or too risky."

Yet Roberto was impassioned by cars and speed. In some ways he typified his generation—young enough to have missed World War I but old enough to suffer from disenchantment—insatiable youths who needed racing or a war to calm them down. "He was always busy, full of projects, a bluffer and a spendthrift, bold with women, curt and crafty with creditors. The fairy godmothers who bestow talents had, with no contradiction, given him a fickle heart, a refined mind with a taste for the exquisite, and, at the same time, an irresistible vocation for turbulence. So much so that even then he had already plunged into an incessant and infinite series of worries, fights, debts, and deceits in order to provide himself with the superfluities his prejudices convinced him were necessities."

He could have gone on this way, Fulchignoni argued, neither happy nor unhappy, a part of the sick culture that adored D'Annunzio, because D'Annunzio's verse, novels, and plays represented a middle class "such as the Italians would have liked to have been. And they were the opposite." D'Annunzio glorified risk and decadence in ways that appealed to bored, snobbish imaginations thirsting for power, heroism, war, and blood; it was a theatrical pastiche, false and literary. People modeled themselves after D'Annunzio's characters, speaking, writing, living, and dressing like them.

"Rossellini could have been satisfied with this ersatz, like so many others," concluded Fulchignoni. "And so it is all the more surprising that he revolted against all conformity."[25]

While Roberto pursued his explorations, others in his family were settling down. Marcella had married Mario Mariani, an architect who worked at the Vatican, in 1932. And on April 26, 1934, Renzo had married a young pianist, Lina Pugni, 23 days after meeting and conducting her in Beethoven's *Emperor Concerto* in Varese.

Roberto had shown up sometime later, Lina recalls, with Assia Noris, and, on learning that Lina came from a wealthy family, he had promptly hit her for a loan. Renzo and his mother had been horrified. "Never, *never* lend money to Roberto!" they had warned—too late. Forty-three years later, when he died, he still had repaid none of it.[26]

Renzo's son Romano Franco (called Franco) was born November 7, 1935, in Rome, where he and Lina had taken an apartment at 4 Via Jacopo Paulo. Renzo was writing criticism of music (and film, occasionally) for *Il*

Messagero, and in 1937 began composing for films, with a score for Camerini's *Il signor Max.*

Roberto's mother got married, too, to a second ex-opera singer. Taurino Parvis was born in Cairo, but half Spanish, and a baritone; he had been in San Francisco with Caruso during the famous earthquake. Now he was a lawyer operating dubbing studios in Rome and Barcelona. In 1939 he brought Elettra and her youngest child Micci to Spain, where Parvis's mother lived. Micci married and had children there. After the war Elettra spent twenty years commuting back and forth between Barcelona and Rome.

Roberto, by 1936, had sunk to his life's low point. Like most Italians, he always dressed well but his shoes had holes in them. He commuted to Rome from Ladispoli, where he was able to live for free with his mad aunt Fortù in the "hunting lodge"—actually a small cottage—that was given to her before Zeffiro's death and was all that remained of the Rossellini millions.

Fortunata Bellan had come to Rome from Venice many years before as Zeffiro's mistress, and she had brought Elettra and Antonietta, her brother's children, along with her. But her outrageous behavior—gambling in particular—had resulted in her banishment by unanimous family verdict to Ladispoli where, free to indulge her fancies, she dwelt quite happily. At 75 she had not mellowed and was still reputed the "best shot" in town. Wrote Renzo: "Forgetting her long-gone youth that had been so gay and wonderful, the luxury and vast world she had known and appreciated, she accepted exile and 'confinement' good-humoredly and with a Dionysian enjoyment of nature. Regardless of the weather or season, Zia Fortù—as we called that dear woman—would rise at dawn, take her rifle, hang a hunting pouch and basket on her shoulder, and go out into the fields. . . . Even in old age, near and over eighty, Zia Fortù shot her rifle with only one arm; with the other she would flash a little mirror or wave, the two classic ways of attracting skylarks. Once her bag was full, she started gathering that exquisite and tender chicory, bitter-rich, that is found only in the Roman countryside. Back home, every day of the year, no matter the weather, she would put on a flaming red bathing suit and take a dip in the sea."[27] Her hunting dog, Cirillino, went swimming with her. To catch frogs, she would tie a long string to a cane, with a squashed snail on the end of the string, which she would then drag through the water while whistling; without the whistling, which aroused the frogs' hunger, the trick would not work.

Fortù ate eight times a day, and at least as often changed her elaborate costumes, completely, even her wigs, to which her hats were attached—she was bald. She had an 1890s fixed-wheel bicycle on which she would ride, in light blue pajamas, to Velletri's Etruscan tombs and back—about twenty miles—and on which she would occasionally even hunt and shoot. She wore boots, gambled, and cussed like a man, and spent her evenings in the local trattoria drinking with the hunters. She kept her hunting horn by her bedside to summon her servants. And she kept a pet pig that roamed freely around the house, and on which, as her private protest against Mussolini, she had painted an Italian flag.

An exceedingly kind woman, she must have been a wonderful aunt. And Ladispoli must just as certainly have been a wonderful place to have been a child, and thus, too, a good place for Roberto to retreat to later. The town had not grown much since the 1920s when there were but ten houses, a broken-down church, a small hotel for hunters, some wooden beach stalls, and the trattoria, where the fare was eel, lamb, and boar. Even so, Fortù's cottage was rather isolated, the last one at the end of town. Across from it, on the beach, was the *Torre Flavia*, an old, ruined tower on whose stones could be found masses of seaweed, shells, bones from various sea creatures, and, farther down where the water lapped, fabulously colored rocks. In back of the house a path led across a little stone bridge to the reserve. The bridge crossed a nameless stream, referred to as "the ditch," from which one could fish by net and catch, besides tiny fishes and eels, five-pound mullets in the rainy season. Beyond the ditch stretched the reserve, the *Campo del Mare*, a vast, swampy plane dotted with reflection pools, without sign of humanity for as far as one could see, but home to Fortù's quails, rabbits, foxes, ducks, and, especially, frogs. Altogether, the voices of these creatures made a sonorous concert.

"We met by chance toward the end of May, on the beach at Ladispoli," recalled Marcella De Marchis. "We were both fishing for shrimp on the old Odeschalchi castle. Roberto weighed 195 pounds [and was five foot eight]. He had on a sailor's jacket, a pair of fishing trousers all in pieces like the ones boys wear today, with ten lire in his pocket, and in the course of half an hour managed to expound at least a hundred of his marvelous projects. It was during the Fascist era, then, with all its emphasis on muscles and athletic prowess, and, well, Roberto was nothing like that. But for a nineteen-year-old girl, romantic and adventurous as I, who'd played pirate till just recently, such an encounter couldn't help but be magical."[28]

She thrust out her arm in a vigorous handshake. It was like being yanked by a rope, Roberto thought. He showed her how to present her hand delicately so that he could kiss it politely. She adored this.[29]

"And after that half-hour Roberto seemed in my eyes to be trim, his hair (which was always sparse) looked abundant, and I was ready to swear on even the most fantastic of his projects as though on the Gospels. What got me were his dreams: to live on an island, fishing and hunting. I spent hours listening to him. We'd fish for shrimp and octopus, then cook them on rocks in the sand.

"Fifteen days after we met, while we were in water up to our chests, Roberto, between shrimps, asked me to marry him. Naturally I accepted immediately. But my mother went into shock. In the state he was in then, there was no way Roberto could represent, in my parents' eyes, the 'proper' sort of match for a traditionally raised, middle-class young girl. To support us, he had only his dreams and a room in his Zia Fortù's cottage. But I was determined despite everything and everyone, and Roberto, in case they refused, was even planning to abduct me and shut me up in a convent until I'd be old enough to marry without their consent."

Marcella, or Marcellina, as she immediately became to avoid confusion with Roberto's sister Marcella, was well aware of Roberto's past history, his many affairs, his squandered inheritance. His whole family had an aura that scandalized her parents. Tongues wagged that it was a hopeless mismatch, that Roberto, ten years older, lusted for her lithe body and glittering jewels—her father Raimondo De Marchis, owned two jewelry stores in Rome—and that a dissolute, upper-class bohemian like Roberto could not possibly find intellectual compatibility with an unsophisticated university student ten years his junior.

None of this mattered to Marcella. Roberto was the first person in her life to kiss her on the lips. She was his first virgin, he told her.

Her parents thought otherwise. She was locked in her room, escaped at five in the morning, and phoned Roberto from Piazza San Silvestro. He told her to go stay with her married sister Vevi, who sided with him. He came there himself a few hours later, along with her father. They put her in one room while they discussed matters in another. Then Roberto left.

"My mother dragged me off to Chianciano and locked me in a hotel, and my parents stayed absolutely incommunicado, even refusing to accept telegrams. But Roberto made huge scenes with my older sister and her husband, an important person in aviation, and, having finally won them over, sent my brother-in-law to talk to my mother."

Marcella was coming from the beach one morning with her mother when a friend gave her a secret message. Roberto was in town and she could see him that night. The friend introduced her to Montesano, who invited Marcella and her mother to a dance that night. There, among the plants, she spotted Roberto as he lit a cigarette. Vevi's husband arrived, her mother ordered champagne, and unenthusiastically toasted her engagement. A few days later, Roberto took Marcella to visit his father's grave.

"Our wedding was another big shock, because Roberto, who had adored his father, didn't want any ceremonies. One of my sisters had just been married in April in a huge to-do. And then when I said that I didn't want to wear white—not because of anything to do with virginity but because of Roberto's feelings [of respect for the death of his father four years before]—it was another big scandal. We were married in a little church at Palo, just south of Ladispoli, on September 26, [1936]. The witnesses were Cesare Vico Lodovici and General Assanti, a family friend of the Rossellinis. On the marriage record, as Roberto's profession, the priest wrote, 'registratore cinematografico'"—"film recording machine," a mistake for *regista*, director.[30] Roberto insisted that Marcella not wear high heels because they made her too tall. He was so embarrassed at being a newlywed that he would not permit a single photograph and wore his oldest suit.

Nor did he want to seem to be on a honeymoon, so he invited Vevi and Nino Barbieri, Renzo and Lina Rossellini, and a third couple to come along with Marcella and him for two days at the Park Hotel in Frascati, just south of Rome. In their room were white roses, which Roberto asked the maids to remove. He put a portrait of his father on the bureau.

"From Frascati we went straight back to Ladispoli, where Zia Fortù had put bunches of wildflowers all over the house for us. She greeted us in a wonderful, thirty-year-old evening gown sparkling with sequins and rhinestones, with very high-heeled, pointed shoes that made her suffer terribly, and with, on a leash, her favorite goose, for whom she had made for the occasion a new, little cotton-checkered suit. (Sometimes, Zia Fortù even went to Rome with her dressed-up goose.) The first night was hilarious. The cottage was half dilapidated, the oldest in Ladispoli, and the rain poured down mercilessly through the holes in the ceiling. Roberto and I spent the night with the umbrella opened over the bed."[31]

Their married life was secluded. They saw friends in Ladispoli but, avoiding middle-class society, rarely partied in Rome. The lifestyles even of Roberto's sister Marcella or cousin Renzo Avanzo seemed foreign.

A minor problem was Fortù's penchant for poker in the afternoon. Normally she won, but occasionally she lost. Typical was the day Roberto and Marcellina came home to find every mattress in the house gone and hear Fortù's forthright explanation. "Dear Babies," she said, "I lost at cards and I cannot live owing money, so I sold the most sellable thing I found in the house: the mattresses."[32]

Finally Working

"Immediately after our wedding, Roberto got really serious about finding work. Till then he'd always lived capriciously, from hand to mouth, but now everything changed. Projects that he'd often talked about but had been too lazy to work out began taking form. He'd always hated sitting down and writing after he'd sold a subject by talking it up. Eventually he'd find himself forced to put it down on paper anyhow, and since he always waited till the last minute, he'd end up staying up all night writing. So to create the illusion of working at night (since ideas came less easily by day), he used to close the shutters and light the lamp and go on like that, without feeling either sleepy or hungry."[1]

What were the projects? We have no idea. In 1936 he worked on *La fossa degli angeli*'s script without credit and assisted its director, Carlo Ludovico Bragaglia. Lodovici continued to pay him for scripts. But his ideas, excitedly conceived in conversation, came out dull and tawdry on paper. Writing was never to be his métier. The harder he tried, the more stilted his expression became. Roberto needed to concretize his thoughts at the exact moment that they first came to him.

He started a film—who knows where he got the money? Then, the following spring 1937, he ran into Franco Riganti in Piazza Fiume. He hadn't seen him since the Nazareno days, when Franco had courted Roberto's cousin at Via Ludovisi.

Roberto looked bad-off now, Franco thought. He listened compassionately as Roberto showed him the hole in his shoe and told him that Marcellina was about to have their first baby, and that he was desperate for work. Riganti had been working for the producer Alfredo Guarini (Isa Miranda's husband) and was starting a big film of his own. When Roberto exaggerated his experience, claiming he'd worked with Jean Renoir in France, Riganti understood he was trying to sell himself. He knew Roberto.

He followed him to Via del Tritone where, in a carriage stall inside a courtyard, Roberto showed him what he'd shot for *Prélude à l'après-midi d'un faune,* a short in which he planned to combine Debussy's music with Mallarmé's poem. Nijinsky had made a scandalous ballet out of the combination in 1912. A mermaid emerges from the sea, dances with a faun, and leaves behind a veil for the faun's masturbatory fantasies. Roberto had had help from an old retired cameraman, but was doing everything himself now, shooting a bit every few weeks, any time he got money for film. He had discovered he could make sea sounds by rubbing a newspaper against the wall, and was proud of it. But his set consisted of a sorry-looking fake tree and a tank of water, in which a girl was trying to look mermaidishly naked in a chain-mail-like top and tights. It was a painfully bad film, Franco thought; even the photography was ugly. Yet he was genuinely happy to see Roberto after so many years. Like many another friend in many another year to come, he wanted very much to help him.[2]

Riganti's new film, *Luciano Serra pilota* ("Luciano Serra, pilot"), was going to tell the story of a World War I ace who, unable to adjust to peacetime, leaves his wife and little boy and takes up commercial flying in South America. When he comes home, he learns his son is an army flyer in Ethiopia. To reach him, he enlists as a foot soldier. But Ethiopian rebels attack his train, and a plane that tries to help is forced down when its pilot is hurt. Serra runs across the field of battle and, though fatally wounded, flies the plane to safety, only realizing afterward that the pilot is his son.

The picture was nominally under the supervision of the Duce's son, 21-year-old Vittorio Mussolini, who had co-authored the story with Fulvio Palmieri, one of his teachers at the Tasso school. Because of Mussolini's involvement, and because the movie deals with Italy's invasion of Ethiopia, *Luciano Serra* has always been regarded with suspicion—which has spilled over to Roberto because of his eventual involvement with it. Even its star, Amedeo Nazzari, claims "it looks completely like one of the regime's propaganda films. It attempted to affirm that aviation was an important armament, neglected, and thus to be encouraged."[3]

Perhaps so. But the actual inspiration for *Luciano Serra* lay closer to home, in Vittorio Mussolini's and Franco Riganti's passion for flying. The Fascist regime, apart from newsreels, did not make propaganda movies. It had indeed occupied itself with film production. It set up an overseeing directorate under Luigi Freddi in 1934, created financing mechanisms at the Banca Nazionale del Lavoro in 1935, fostered film clubs through the Gioventù Universitaria Fascista (GUF), initiated the Venice Film Festival, opened the Centro Sperimentale di Cinematografia (one of the world's best film schools) in 1935, sponsored three film journals that same year (*Cinema, Bianco e Nero, Lo Schermo*), blessed the privately financed Cinecittà (a giant film studio) in 1937, rebated taxes on imported films to the domestic industry, and monopolized the importation of films in 1938. But none of these efforts was designed to control film content or generate propaganda. The goal was to rescue a national cultural industry in dire straits. Support was given to private and local initiatives. Most of the measures continue to this day and have been imitated by every nation that has sought to preserve native filmmaking in the face of American competition. The postwar glories of Italian film could not have occurred without the nurturing policies of the Fascist regime.

Scripts were reviewed and there was a bias in favor of movies that would both entertain and imbue "healthy moral principles." But the bias was not enforced. Censorship under Fascism was less severe than under Christian Democracy in the 1950s, and under neither regime were restraints comparable to the repression in America. Neither the regime nor the Church could be criticized; murder, suicide, adultery, seduction, theft, and corruption were all discouraged, as was serious discussion of political, social, religious, or sexual problems. Evidence of hunger, unemployment, prostitution, or poverty was rare, and in general no civil servants, police, or priests were portrayed. But all such restrictions were gotten round with a little invention—or even indulged in flagrantly. The more formidable restriction was that most of what the regime was discouraging was in fact also bad box office in conservative Italy and appealed chiefly to the intelligentsia—as postwar moviemakers eventually discovered to their own discouragement. Similar production codes existed in the U.S. and were enforced rigorously (by a combination of Hollywood's own production code and local governments) in support of banks, corporations, racism, and even lynching.[4] Italy was far more open. "Fundamentally," wrote Cesare Pavese, "humanistic intelligence—the fine arts and letters—did not suffer under Fascism; they managed to follow their own bent, cynically accepting the game as it was."[5]

"My father," wrote Vittorio Mussolini, who besides producing films was editor of *Cinema,* the most important of the film magazines, "followed my film activity sympathetically and often gave me valuable and sensible advice. Among other things, not to make propaganda films. 'In Italy,' he said, 'only two really Fascist films have been made: Blasetti's *Vecchia guardia (Old Guard)* and Forzano's *Camicia nera (Black Shirt).* Their lackluster success tells you how poorly the people support official propaganda. I don't think even the Russians enjoy watching some Stakhanovistian hero up on the screen turning out tons of iron ingots while not pausing even to kiss his fiancée.'

"After dinner, he would usually go downstairs to the first-floor living room where projection equipment had been installed. . . . My father rarely watched an entire film. . . . He was tired and often fell asleep. When the subject interested him, he'd look at some parts of it every evening. He sought diversion. Sad, heavy movies bored him. [He did not like gangster or mystery films.] He preferred light comedies or slapstick like Mack Sennett with big chases and pies in the face. Among foreign actors he preferred types like Wallace Beery or the Barrymore brothers; among Italians, Musco, Nazzari, De Sica. Actresses: Greta Garbo, Alida Valli, and Lilia Silvi. Generally he watched films in a strange position . . . due to his stomach pains. He leaned his back against the back of a chair, folded his legs up against his stomach, pushed out his stomach, and put a hand behind his waist or head."[6]

Father Mussolini, incidentally, had a stern sense of money. Unlike other world leaders, he never amassed an estate nor even collected his salary, and left his family poor when he died. On one occasion Vittorio and Riganti had an opportunity to make a profit of several million dollars overnight by purchasing prints, with borrowed money, of Disney's *Snow White* and selling them to Germany, with which Disney refused to deal. Vittorio needed his father's permission. He approached him while he was shaving—always the best time—and explained the deal.

"No," said his father.

"But . . . why not?"

"Too much money too easily."

And that was that.[7]

Vittorio Mussolini was a fanatic for Hollywood movies. He liked their "freshness, boldness, strength, and rowdy but healthy exuberance." As a producer, he tried to foster "a cinema of the open air, following the American model as an example of an art that was healthy and alive rather than [as communists would claim] 'decadent, degenerate, and bourgeois.'"[8] Russian movies were enjoying great prestige at the Centro Sperimentale just then. But Vittorio had doubts; they reflected an unfree society, he felt, whereas King Vidor's films, for example, seemed to him the very models for a cinema with social conscience. Fascism had a strong and democratic left wing.

Luciano Serra pilota was an attempt to imitate Hollywood, as Vittorio Mussolini said. "The airplanes correspond to the 7th cavalry, the Ethiopians to the Indians. Errol Flynn could be substituted for Amedeo Nazzari without changing anything. *Luciano Serra pilota* was not at all a Fascist propaganda film . . . any more than *The Lives of a Bengal Lancer* is an English propaganda film. It was only an exaltation of the sacrifices made by Italians."[9]

In contrast to *The Lives of a Bengal Lancer* (Hathaway, 1935) or *Gunga Din* (Stevens, 1939) which celebrate and whitewash British imperialism, or *Sergeant York* (Hawks, 1941) which sanctifies war, *Luciano Serra pilota* ignores any such issues in Ethiopia. Its silence is culpable: Ethiopia became Italy's Vietnam. But in contrast to the Hollywood pictures, *Luciano Serra* lacks innocent flag-waving and sincerely patriotic rhetoric. What postwar critics objected to was its love of Italians flying, which had militarist implications. To love Italy, they said, was to be Fascist; even kissing your baby becomes a Fascist sermon.

Listen, for example, to Mino Argentieri's judgment of *Luciano Serra:* "The confusion, the perplexity of the character who is transformed from a negative to a positive being is really the confusion and perplexity of the country, which Fascism [allegedly] banished, salvaging all the national energies—including those that had deviated or gone astray—for a destiny of greatness achieved by a heroic act in which the objective and subjective are reunited." And, citing Argentieri, American historian Edward R. Tannenbaum adds that *Luciano Serra*, rather than presenting a superman hero with which Italians could not identify, used "a much more insidious and effective technique of propaganda [that] encourage[d] them to identify themselves with an ordinary and even confused man who finally does the right thing."[10]

Tannenbaum implies that "the right thing" Luciano Serra finally does is a patriotic gesture, thus Fascist. In actuality, neither his going to Ethiopia nor his attempt to help the downed flyer has any connection with the national effort, let alone with the Fascist Party. In order for Tannenbaum and Argentieri to ferret out the movie's "insidious" propaganda, they have to invent implications based on associations the movie itself does not make. We should not be surprised: such critical methods were once the standard fashion by which all cinema produced during the Fascist era was judged, condemned, and secreted from view. The same methods, in the early seventies, were used to show that depiction of a Christmas dinner was insidious propaganda for bourgeois patriarchal Christian capitalism. No wonder, then, that Roberto tried all his life to distance himself from his early movies. To many people, their simple existence was an indictment.

How do we assay Rossellini's moral responsibility in the Fascist period? How do we assay another filmmaker's moral responsibility in the Vietnam period? Do we condemn Rossellini for participating in a film like *Luciano Serra pilota*, in which the sins of Italy's imperialism in Ethiopia are never mentioned? Do we condemn Gary Cooper for whitewashing British imperialism in *Lives of a Bengal Lancer* or Cary Grant in *Gunga Din*? How many films should be damned for *not* underlining the sins of aggression? The difference is that the American pictures glorify it.[11]

Few Italians, moreover, saw Italy's politics in the negative light we do today. Theirs was a poor country, with a huge surplus population and little arable land. Ethiopia offered the same solution as New England had to the Pilgrims. Didn't England, France, the United States, even Belgium and Portugal have immense colonial empires (half the world, in fact)—which, rather than actually *settling*, they just ruthlessly exploited? If these empires opposed Italy's benign plans to develop parts of Africa, Italians argued, wasn't it obviously because they had designs of their own against territories, such as Ethiopia, in which Italy had long-standing treaty rights? Italian colonies in Somaliland and Eritrea, moreover, had long been victims of terrorist border raids from Ethiopia. Ethiopia was seen as a primitive and chaotic area, greatly in need of Italy's assistance. Colonialism, a dirty word today, was then a radical, progressive idea. Wasn't it Europe's *duty* to bring civilization to the world?

These were the arguments advanced at the time. They masked mass murder and an invasion planned three years earlier and were no different than other arguments of other governments all over the world, and they were generally believed.

Military operations had begun in October 1935. Some Italians had been enthusiastic, some lukewarm, hardly anyone contrary. Then the League of Nations—England and France, in effect, the arch imperialists—voted sanctions and waves of nationalism swept through Italian hearts. At the tomb of the unknown soldier, the king and queen threw their wedding rings into a cauldron to be melted down to finance the war effort, while simultaneously, all over Italy, other husbands and wives did the same. Bishops contributed their episcopal crosses. Restaurants served "Sanction Soup." (Americans retaliated with the "Gibson," an oliveless martini.)

Internationally Ethiopia was the turning point for Fascism. The world turned from admiration to condemnation. Still today Ethiopia is cited as evidence that Fascism was evil. Less cited are the Philippines, where 600,000 Filipinos died on Luzon alone during the American conquest, where U.S. Marines on Samar were ordered to kill everyone older than ten.[12] Or Namibia or Kenya, where the Germans and English stole all the land, killed off half the native inhabitants, and reduced the remaining people to slave laborers who needed police permits to travel in their own country. Or British Bengal in 1943, where the British stood guard over abundant stocks of food while three million people starved to death, simply because they could not afford prices that had quadrupled from wartime inflation. By ascribing evil to "Fascism," we proclaim our virtue, which is one of the advantages of theory over intuition.

The Italians murdered tens of thousands, and built roads, schools, and hospitals they could not afford to build at home. "It is doubtful whether any other European power . . . ever poured such resources of men and money into any colonial possession as did Italy during its short tenancy," comments the *Encyclopædia Britannica.*[13] Rather than exploiting her colonies, Italy exploited herself on their behalf. Or one could say it is what Fascism did.

At home Mussolini's defiance of the Great Powers raised his prestige to its highest pitch. Soon third-graders were copying a dictation exercise that went: "One year has passed since November 18, 1935: we have shown the world that we are the strong ones, the just ones, the best ones. The fifty-two sanctionist nations denied us bread, iron, gold, coal, and cloth; we found it all anyway: bread from the fields of Italy. Iron from the houses of Italy. Gold from the women of Italy. White coal from the waters of Italy. Black coal from the mines and forests of Italy. They wanted to humiliate us, but our victory and sacrifice has raised us above them."[14]

Luciano Serra pilota began filming (pro-formally if not actually) on April 21, 1937, to inaugurate Cinecittà. Vittorio's father showed up for the ceremonies. He had read the picture's plot summary while shaving; now he watched as Serra was filmed telling his wife why he has to leave home. A title had not been decided on; the Duce made the winning suggestion.

Riganti introduced Roberto to *Luciano Serra's* director, Goffredo Alessandrini. Though only two years older than Roberto, Alessandrini had been directing since 1931 and was one of Italy's top filmmakers. He was a Fascist and cultured. Born in Egypt and educated in England, he spoke English, French, and Arabic. Roberto was all smiles, ingratiating himself instantly.

Alessandrini already had an assistant but, knowing of Roberto's baby, he accepted him anyway, and Roberto began drawing a weekly salary.

A day or so later Alessandrini's wife, Anna Magnani, came by and remarked how "the new face" kept following her husband around "like a faithful dog." He wanted to become a director, someone told her, and she replied that he didn't seem particularly able, that at best he might end up making cheap little "B" pictures.[15]

Roberto and Alessandrini were quickly united by a "big sympathy," as Riganti put it. And since there was nothing for Roberto to do as an assistant, he was assigned instead to the script, which needed injections of life and constant rewriting as production progressed.

Vittorio Mussolini played almost no role in *Luciano Serra*'s production, and Rossellini met him only much later. Vittorio got married during the picture and made a pilgrimage to America. He was received at the White House by Franklin D. Roosevelt and in Hollywood by Norma Shearer, Tyrone Power, Shirley Temple, Bette Davis, and Ida Lupino, with whom he made a little documentary. His plan was to entice American filmmakers to Italy where, using blocked funds, they would make movies in double edition and improve the national product by their influence. A deal was struck with Hal Roach, which collapsed immediately when Father Mussolini promulgated his anti-Jewish laws.[16] At the same time a furor erupted, more in Italy than the U.S., over lines in Vittorio's recent book, *Voli sulle ambe*, exhorting Italian boys on the beauties of war, "the most beautiful and complete of all sports," and how it had been "sad but diverting" to watch from the air Ethiopian tribesmen "bursting out like a rose after I had landed a bomb in the middle of them."[17]

The twenty-year-old author had swallowed Fascist rhetoric virginally and unquestioningly. Otherwise, even anti-Fascists regarded him as well-intentioned and kind-hearted. "A good person, on a human level," said the Communist Giuseppe De Santis.[18] "Vittorio wasn't a bad guy," said Gianni Puccini, another Communist; "quite the contrary: he was just lazy and weak, and more ingenuous than stupid. . . . He was more a movie fan than a gerarch. . . . He didn't have the stuff of a tyrant; he was apathetic, tolerant, and sad. None of us [committed anti-Fascists] were ever able to hate him."[19]

"Vittorio and Bruno Mussolini," said Marcella De Marchis, "were both very fine fellows, embarrassed by their parentage. . . . People never talked to them about politics, though they could make jokes about the regime then. Vittorio always behaved decently."[20] One day at the Villa Glori racetrack, during the period when the Duce's posters were altered into Latin— *Duce* became *Dux*—Riganti asked Vittorio if he'd heard the latest: how Storace, the unpopular party secretary who was always aping his master, wanted to change his name to Storax? Vittorio found this quite funny, whereas his brother Bruno, standing behind them, nearly summoned the police.[21]

Luciano Serra's interiors were shot in Rome. Then the troupe went north to Udine and Arona, where the "South American" scenes were filmed. On the train back to Rome, Roberto decided to have a serious talk with Riganti. They were close friends now; Roberto's son, Marco Romano, had been born July 3 at Marcella's parents' house, and Riganti was the baby's godfather.

"Franco," said Roberto, eventually, "I have something extremely important to tell you. It's about the film. But I can't lose my salary, and I will if I tell you this. So I want your promise that I'll stay. Otherwise, I won't tell you."

"Well, what it is?"

"No. You have to promise first."

"Oh, come on, Roberto. Just tell me what it is!"

"No. I'm afraid if I tell you the truth, you'll get mad and have me fired."

"Okay. I promise. Now, what is it?"

What it was was that in Roberto's estimation Alessandrini was doing everything wrong. Roberto detailed his criticisms and said he wanted freedom to develop the script without regard to Alessandrini—although the film would be completely ruined anyway, unless Riganti took steps immediately, by firing Alessandrini and replacing him with Roberto.

This was Roberto's first real job and he wasn't intimidated by false modesty. He was so frustrated with the way someone else was doing something that, for the first time in his life, he felt compelled to get involved himself, to take on responsibility himself. The feeling that cinema was something *he* could do and that someone else would mess up was and remained a motivation for stealing time from his *dolce vita* as a playboy.

Roberto did not get Alessandrini's job; he remained behind in Rome when the troupe went to Africa. But his complaints were taken seriously. Memos were written and recriminations exchanged, and by the time the troupe got to Agordat in Ethiopia, Riganti was barely on speaking terms with Alessandrini and the company was divided into rival factions. They were quartered at an airfield and for the battle scenes had at their disposition battalions of Italian and Ascari (Eritrean) soldiers, a search plane, a squadron of fighter planes, a train, and fifty trucks. It was October, boiling by day, freezing by night, and the altitude of the high plateau made everyone light-headed. Now it seemed to Riganti that Roberto was right, that Alessandrini was wasting time and working at a snail's pace. In a letter to Rome, he lambasted his director and asked that Roberto be sent down to take charge of a second unit.

So Roberto was to have his chance after all. He travelled via Bengazi, Cairo, and Khartoum, and arrived on a rainy day. Alessandrini received him frigidly and protested vehemently to Riganti. Roberto, finally intimidated, came crying to Riganti and, to avoid confronting Alessandrini, in Riganti's words, "he promptly came down with every ailment known to mankind, his liver, his kidneys, his head."[22] His asthma constricted his breathing, he nearly collapsed walking up a hill, he never stopped complaining. One day he felt well enough to go hunting but shot down an owl—an omen of bad luck. Alessandrini shot next, and missed Riganti's head by six inches.

The idea had been for Roberto to work during the battle with Aldo Tonti, the still-photographer, and a hand-held Avia. Roberto rarely got out of bed. After eight days he left for Rome.

Tonti shot alone. He was with the troupe only to take publicity stills, but his work was judged superior to that of the two senior cameramen. In a few years he would be rated one of the world's premier cinematographers. In the 1950s he was one of Roberto's closest collaborators.

Riganti did not leave Africa until mid-January. He narrowly survived a bizarre accident when his tiny plane struck a wire, flipped over, and landed upside down. Then he was laid up in Rome for two months with appendicitis and a contagious disease. Eventually Roberto's stories got back to him second-hand, stories of Roberto's erotic adventures in Egyptian harems and hair-raising exploits in darkest Africa—stories that everyone swallowed whole.

There was still a lot to be done on *Luciano Serra*. Nazzari, the star, had not gone to Ethiopia, so now shots of him taken in Rome had to be inserted into the Ethiopian footage—a tricky business that was splendidly accomplished. Giorgio Simonelli had taken over for Alessandrini, who had gone on to another film, and Roberto was devising dialogue that would enable the three sets of footage to go together.

Roberto, however, did not feel like going to Rome these days. He had gone on to other things. The censors, he lied, had suppressed his (unfinished) *L'après-midi d'un faune* because of "a few frames judged obscene."[23] Now he was doing a "documentary" about fish called *Fantasia sottomarina*, at home in Ladispoli, and Riganti, therefore, had to go to Roberto. Getting Roberto's attention was not always easy, even so. Roberto's habit was to sleep late and then spend hours in the bathroom with the telephone and a hoard of books. He had a theory that man was most inspired when defecating, and he liked to converse from across the bathroom door. It was from a mutual friend, Carlo Bugiani, that Riganti learned the trick; if he wanted to talk to Roberto, this was the moment to get him.

In this fashion Roberto worked on *Luciano Serra pilota* through August 1938. By coincidence, Vittorio Mussolini had asked Renzo Rossellini to do the music after admiring his scores for other films. The picture was finished just in time for the Venice Film Festival, where it won first prize, sharing the prestigious Mussolini Cup with Riefenstahl's *Olympia*. Michelangelo Antonioni, writing in Padua's *Corriere Padano*, declared it "undoubtedly the first great Italian film. [It] will find a place among the most respected works of our time. And for that we have to be grateful to Vittorio Mussolini."[24]

For Franco Riganti, *Luciano Serra*'s financial success—until 1943 it had the highest grosses of any Italian film ever made—meant that he was able, with Vittorio Mussolini as titular head, to get financing from Fiat, Gaggia, Cini, and other large firms to buy Europa Film from Alfredo Sansoni and set up a company, ACI (L'Anonima Cinematografica Italiana), that would produce and distribute films and exhibit them in its own chain of theaters. With assistance from minister Dino Grandi, who hoped economic ties would help keep Italy out of the coming war, Riganti worked out co-production agreements with British companies, secured backing from Lord Hardwick (an Isotta-Fraschini representative), and signed Leslie Howard to a contract.

And Roberto Rossellini? Somehow the legend grew that it had really been *Roberto* who had shot those wonderful battle scenes in Africa, not to mention much of the rest of the film in Rome.

Fantasia sottomarina ("Undersea fantasy") tells the tale of two fish in love, threatened by an octopus and saved by an eel. Though only ten minutes long, it took months to make and did not obtain a release for nearly two years.

In 1929 Roberto had met and befriended three Japanese biologists exploring undersea life in the Bay of Naples. He had gone along on their dives, developed a life-long passion for the world he discovered there, and wanted to put it on film. So, lacking the equipment to film underwater, he set up a three-by-nine foot aquarium at Ladispoli on Zia Fortù's roof and filmed the fish he had caught fishing—then fried and ate them.

Rodolfo Lombardi was Roberto's photographer. Soon there were three aquariums. "Every morning," recounts Marcellina, "Roberto would go to Civitavecchia to get live saraghetti [the fish starring in his film], but it was the middle of August and right after the first shots the saraghetti would invariably die and Roberto, to make them seem alive, devised an original scheme: he filled the saraghettis' stomachs with lead pellets to keep them horizontal, tied two strands of my hair to the fins of the dead fish to hold them up invisibly, and with a thin little stick manipulated them like puppets."[25]

According to Roberto, the drolly humorous picture was a surprise to many people who had never seen live fish close-up—although many documentaries of the period were fish-oriented. *Fantasia sottomarina* was bought by Incom, a short-film company, and played for a week in Rome in April 1940. Its story and humor depend on an accompanying narration; the pictures alone convey almost nothing.

Riganti, meanwhile, as soon as he had set up ACI, had put Roberto on a regular salary of 1,500 lire a month in ACI's story and script department.[26] Working there too were the well-known comedy writer Luigi Chiarelli, Raffaele Saitto, Umberto Bianchini, and, a bit later, Marcello Pagliero and Federico Fellini. "There was a great deal of envy in film circles for all those who were working in my company," recalls Riganti.[27] In Roberto's case, the job was a sinecure, a gift from Riganti. Roberto was too lazy and distracted ever to write anything, Riganti knew, and in two years he never did; nor did he work on any specific pictures. Yet he participated in story conferences and, says Riganti, his ideas were always among the most fruitful. From time to time, when he needed money, he would find Riganti and make up a movie idea off the top of his head. Once it was *La linea della critica* ("The critic's line"), a marvelous story drawn from Faulkner's *Pylon*. Another time, in August 1939, Roberto came to visit Riganti in the hospital, told a horse story called *Pesce d'Aprile* ("April Fool's Day") and got 2,000 lire. It was not just charity. Riganti had enormous respect for Roberto's talent. "His aspirations were always so elevated that their actualization would always be inferior to his dreams. He had the heart of a caliph." Roberto would later claim that "people used to think of me as a crazy guy full of ideas whom they ought to be afraid of."[28]

This "wasn't true, not true at all," according to Riganti. "People weren't afraid of him. They didn't think he was crazy—just full of ideas." And sometimes, during meetings, they were slightly awed at Roberto's way of uttering phrases—like, "This denouncer of ACI wears the masque of Flaubertian infamy"—which no one could make head or tail of but which left everyone impressed just the same.

Vittorio Mussolini recalls Roberto as "typically Roman" but exceptionally "*simpatico*." Vittorio was shy and avoided society. But he partied with Roberto, went to racetracks, drove cars, and took out girls. He was struck by Roberto's peculiar way of softly chatting in a woman's ear. And how he always needed money. "He'd get 20,000 lire for three pages, then be quiet for three days, and then be back again."[29]

Outside of work Franco and Roberto were closer than ever. They would frolic naked on ACI's terrace overlooking Piazza di Popolo and make love in foursome. They frequented a whorehouse on Via degli Avignonesi where they would pass a girl between them. Roberto always kissed the madam's hand and always took two girls for himself. On weekends Riganti would bring his wife and son out to Ladispoli. They even shared the same car; Roberto would drive it into Rome in the morning, Riganti would use it during the day, Roberto would drive home in it at night. The car was a rented one, until Roberto proved it was more economical to buy a Ballila, in Roberto's name with Franco's money.

Shortly before setting up ACI, Riganti had found financing through Excelsior Film, a firm he had begun in the name of his sister Elisabetta, for Roberto to make a second fish film, *Il ruscello di Ripasottile* ("The brook of Ripa Sottile"). It too was shot at Ladispoli, in a little brook behind Fortù's house (the "ditch"?), probably during 1940, again in collaboration with Rodolfo Lombardi. The story was written by Elisabetta Riganti and, as in most of Rossellini's later movies, is melodramatic. Trout eggs hatch, all the brook's creatures rejoice, and the news spreads from the fish to the birds to the turtles, the ducks, the rabbits, and so on. But the vicious pike hear too and start swimming toward the newborns. Alarm spreads and all the creatures join forces. The birds try to peck the pikes and a terrific battle rages (we see fish with swollen eyes), until, in the nick of time, the birds wake a fisherman and he, with one sweep of his net, eliminates the pike. Unlike *Fantasia sottomarina, Il ruscello* involved substantial expense, elaborate equipment, a great many workers—and a thousand little tricks. Roberto found a street performer at Piazza Vittorio whose dozen trained birds (with their wings clipped) could pick up slips of paper that told people's fortunes, pull carriages, and walk in file. Intricate special effects, like the pike swimming upstream, were shot at Rome's Istituto Ittogenico, using long glass tubes with rolling scenery behind them.[30] No copy of *Il ruscello* is known to have survived, yet one has the impression that Roberto was still a putterer, attracted to filmmaking essentially for its technical challenges.

In light of the volumes of rhetoric Rossellini's later movies would spawn about "realism," "neo-realism," "reality," and "things in themselves," it is well to recall that movies like *Il ruscello di Ripasottile* were, in their day, routinely called *documentaries*, because of their focus on the natural world. Yet, as contemporary British documentaries by Jennings, Watts, and Wright illustrate, their interest is less in showing *things* than in conveying subjective impressions, inventions, and fantasies. Said Roberto, affectionately, "The fantasies of my youth are there, my discovery of life, of a buzzing hornet, of fish passing over a stretch of water."[31] Thus, early on, we note that "realism" in the context of Rossellini means not the reality of the perceived object; it means the reality of the perceiving subject's relationship to his object.

Once *Il ruscello* was finished, Roberto had the idea of trying to sell it to Scalera Films, which had purchased Caesar Film and become the dominant Italian studio. Roberto had known the Scalera brothers, Michele and Salvatore, since the time of his engagement with Marcellina through friendship with the family of Emanuele Limongelli, whose daughter Anita had married Michele Scalera's son (and would become Renzo Rossellini's second wife in the 1950s). Through the Limongellis, Roberto had befriended Massimo Ferrara Santamaria, a lawyer whose aunt was Michele Scalera's wife and who, with the Scaleras occupied with building railroads in Libya, was running the film company as its managing director. As in the case of Riganti, Ferrara was delighted to help Roberto any way he could.

Roberto showed him the documentary, then titled *Anche i pesci parlano* ("Fish speak too"), Ferrara recalls, and it needed editing.[32] Riganti was expecting Roberto to make a deal for ACI, but Roberto made a deal selling himself along with the movie. He phoned Marcellina excitedly to tell her he would be making 5,000 lire a month. This was an exaggeration; Ferrara's salary was only 2,000.[33]

Scalera had obtained backing for a series of animal shorts and needed someone to make them. Roberto plunged in enthusiastically. He arrived at Ladispoli with animals of all sorts distributed among pockets and cages and started sixteen documentaries, no less, all at once. A slew of titles were annouced: *La foresta silenziosa* ("The quiet forest"), *Primavera* ("Spring"), *Re Travicello*, and *La merca*; and perhaps *Il brutto idraulico* ("The ugly plumber").[34] Fellini recalls finding Roberto at Scalera kneeling under small reflectors. "Inside a small enclosure made of nets and rope were a turtle, two mice, and three or four roaches. He was shooting a documentary about insects [*La vispa Teresa*], doing one frame a day, very complex and laborious, with great patience."[35]

"He kept shooting for months," Fellini adds, probably with his customary exaggeration. For, in fact, Roberto's enthusiasm flagged quickly.

Scalera announced two seven-minute animal pictures in October 1940. *La vispa Teresa* ("Lively Theresa") is based on a well-known song. I have been unable to see the surviving print, which was only discovered in 1997. Gianni Rondolino describes it as charming and amusing, like a home movie. A girl, about ten, tries to catch a butterfly but all the other insects intervene to save it—the same story of collective protection by the weak against the strong as in *Fantasia sottomarina*, *Il ruscello*, and *Il tacchino prepotente*.

Il tacchino prepotente ("The bullying turkey"), whose working title had been *La perfida Albione*, was a satire in which "Perfidious Albion," a big turkey representing England, goes around pecking at the hens, representing the nations of Europe, until defied by a rooster representing Italy. "Rossellini detested it," said Ferrara, "[though his] genius was such that he could achieve extraordinary effects out of nothing. He used to tell me, 'It's the only time that, through my weakness, I made a work of propaganda.'"[36] A print of *Il tacchino* was also discovered in 1997, but I have not seen it.

La vispa Teresa was rejected and, although Ferrara said that "*La perfida Albione*" was distributed by Scalera, there were no press notices of it, and no one outside of Scalera is known to have seen it. In the surviving print of *Il tacchino prepotente*, moreover, there are no specific allusions to England or Italy, only a comic protest against a bully that might as well be Mussolini; and in place of the Scalera logo is that of Fincine, a company which did not exist before 1947. Was the movie re-edited to confront the new postwar realities?[37]

"Scalera," said Riganti, "was very irritated with Rossellini for the bad quality of the shorts he had made and considered him in default of his contract."[38]

"5,000 lire a month was richness itself," said Roberto. "But I was so eager to do nothing of what was expected of me that I ended up getting fired."[39]

Roberto stayed on ACI's payroll, even during his brief richness. *Il ruscello* was released after almost a year, in May 1941, and was greeted as an advance on the "exquisite" *Fantasia sottomarina*. "Both the director and cameraman demonstrate perfect mastery of technique . . . with the result that the film is suffused with uncommon poetic grace," said *Rivista del Cinematografo*.[40]

The War Trilogy

La nave bianca, Un pilota ritorna, L'uomo dalla croce

"How distant our fate was then!" Vittorio Mussolini sighed. "Only a madman could have foreseen that the same people—who on the night of May 9, 1936 were cheering deliriously in every square in Italy as they heard my father emotionally announce the return of the Empire to Rome's seven sacred hills—would some of them participate and almost all of them assist, silently, at the tragic butchery in Piazzale Loreto"—where in 1945 the Duce's corpse was displayed hanging upside down for public mutilation.[1]

What happened to destroy Fascism's dreams? How did it sink to mass infamy? Was it never, as most books now claim, anything but a farce manipulated by Mussolini for no other end than his own thirst for power?

Croce had condemned Fascism early on "as blind instinct and irrationalism, as shouting and gesticulation that would lead to totalitarianism."[2] In Roberto's opinion, Fascism got bad only after twelve years in power, when it was tired and tried to compete with Nazi Germany by becoming "solemn" and constructing a mystique of dogma and ritual. Fascism had been a political movement, but it tried to become a chivalrous order, whose hierarchies could be distinguished by their age: those who had joined before the March on Rome, those who had joined during the March, and those who had joined after it.[3] Mussolini slogans that once had been exciting now sounded flatulent: "If I advance, follow me. If I retreat, kill me. If they kill me, revenge me."

Fascism had been an exasperation of the militant liberalism that had propelled Italy since 1860, an assertion of will in response to frustration following World War I. It was revolutionary and youthful, but middle-class and conservative. Generations would have had to pass before society could have been radically transformed and true Fascist institutions could have arisen. Meanwhile Mussolini was far from absolute dictator. In regions like Emilia he was able to set up social security, health, and pension programs for farmers and workers that their ancestors had never dreamed of; in other regions he was powerless to prevent property owners from exploiting and terrorizing peasants. The Depression put dreams on hold; fictions took their place, and military glory. The war effort in Ethiopia imposed dogma in place of the free debates that, formerly, Mussolini had insisted youths indulge in. Teachers were put into uniforms; the lesson in schools, universities, and scouting groups was "to serve in silence and to obey with humility."[4]

The result was the antithesis of Fascism's progressive side. Mussolini became god. "Everything is in the state; nothing human or spiritual exists outside the state," said the state.[5] Simone Weil met a "pleasant, cordial, and very naive" Fascist student in Rome in 1937 and remarked, "I would prefer hardship and starvation in a salt mine to living with the narrow and limited horizon of these young people. I should feel the mine less suffocating than that atmosphere—the nationalistic obsession, the adoration of power in its most brutal form, namely the collectivity . . . the camouflaged deification of death."[6]

The pleasant student was the exception. Most people subscribed to the Party cynically or with no thought at all, just to hold their jobs. Then as now they loathed the mediocre bureaucrats, the sycophancy and corruption of daily life. But they trusted Mussolini. "The Italian nation," proclaimed Gentile, "marches . . . without hesitation, without question, its eyes fixed on the heroic man of exceptional talents. . . . Mussolini goes forward with confidence, in a halo of myth, almost chosen by God, indefatigable and infallible, the instrument employed by Providence for the creation of a new civilization."[7]

"It was all artificial," Roberto said. "It was so artificial that when Mussolini was dedicating Pomezia, the Town of Apples, built on the newly drained Pontine Marshes, he was given a huge American apple, which the people pretended had been grown in Pomezia. He bit into the apple, shouted, 'What comes from the earth must go back to the earth!' and threw it into the crowd and hit an old lady in the eye. The poor woman lost her sight; she could not find a doctor willing to treat her for an injury inflicted by the Duce.[8]

"The years of Fascism were twenty years of total darkness. I know because I lived through it. It was like being kept in a state of ignorance. . . . We were tormented, wounded, confused—we didn't know what was happening. The motto of Fascism was 'To believe is to fight': to believe in what existed and nothing else. There was not the least trace of dialectics. . . . It was living death."[9]

Italians imagined they were prosperous, powerful, and modern. In reality their growth rate was among Europe's lowest; the average person spent half his income just on food; poverty abounded. But the newspapers kept silent and few people travelled. Mussolini's famous dictum—"Illusion is perhaps the only reality"—was rueful. He knew institutions are maintained through illusion. How else can we win tomorrow's battles?

"Truth," moreover, was available. The Vatican's *L'Osservatore Romano* was uncensored and sold everywhere. Radio broadcasts from abroad, often in Italian, were easily received. People did not listen. Like Americans during the Vietnam War, people felt their nation's critics sounded alien and hostile, thus false. They cheered Mussolini because foreigners had been ridiculing them for centuries, and he founded an Empire, protected his neighbors, and arbitrated world affairs. Posterity has condemned his maneuvers as bloody and self-interested—and posterity is correct. But Mussolini was a minor devil compared to the power mongers of England, Spain, France, Germany, Russia, Belgium, and America. The flaw in Italian policy long antedated Fascism—an idealism that contradicted self-interest and, often, reality as well. A nation founded by dreams thought dreams were enough.

The worst dream was Ethiopia. Officially the war had ended eight months before Riganti and Alessandrini went there to scout locations in 1937. Everyone they talked to assured them *Luciano Serra* could be filmed in perfect safety. Four days later everyone they had talked to was massacred. Four years later people were still being massacred. Although rarely mentioned in the news, Ethiopia had become Italy's Vietnam—an effort almost as large by a nation inestimably poorer. 650,000 soldiers, two million tons of equipment, and vast sums of money were involved, year after year. Renzo Avanzo was there, leading a band of rangers and knowing he would be dismembered piece by piece if caught. Tales drifted back of gross mismanagement, systematic exterminations of educated Ethiopians, ten-for-one reprisals, and massacres of tens of thousands.

At home, prices inflated and social programs were cut back. But in Ethiopia construction of roads, schools, and hospitals went on unabated. Simultaneously Mussolini sent 60,000 soldiers (and a portable movie projector) to Franco in Spain. Spain was becoming a Soviet satellite and Italy had to save liberty, religion, and Western civilization.

It turned into another bad dream. "Instead of . . . a war of starving peasants against land owners and their clerical accomplices," Simone Weil discovered, "[it] had become a war between Russia, Germany and Italy. . . . I never saw anyone express even privately repulsion, distaste or even disapproval at the useless bloodshed. . . . I met, to the contrary, peaceful French people, whom until then I hadn't despised, who wouldn't have gotten the idea of going off themselves to kill, but who were bathing in this blood-drenched atmosphere with visible pleasure. . . . An abyss separated the armed people from the disarmed population, an abyss totally similar to the one that separates the poor from the rich."[10]

Mussolini retorted by summoning his people to greatness. Listening to foreign broadcasts was banned and the *squadristi* were revived to hunt down transgressors; Jews were banned and driven off the streets; women were banned from professions and told to stay home; handshakes were banned and replaced with the Fascist salute; *Lei* (the word everyone used for "you") was banned and replaced with the more egalitarian *voi*; the old way of marching was banned and replaced by the German goose-step; even Saturdays were banned and replaced by "Fascist Saturdays," when every male was expected to be in a stadium or on a parade ground. "Giovinezza" was played at the slightest pretext at sports and movies, and woe to anyone who declined to stand up and join in! "War alone," the Duce proclaimed, "brings up to their highest tension all human energies and imposes the stamp of nobility upon the peoples who have the courage to make it."

In Ladispoli in 1939, Roberto, Marcellina, Zia Fortù, and the whole town watched a ceremony commemorating the March on Rome. It was held in the large, unpaved public square, in the middle of which the regime had constructed a pedestrian obstacle, a monumental baroque concrete urinal.

Mussolini had just made a speech in Rome perched on a tank. In Ladispoli the orator stood on a tractor and bellowed how the Duce, if he had been in Hitler's place, wouldn't have been content with invading just Austria and the Sudetenland. For the finale, there was to be a procession of Ladispoli's seven original squadristi (from *before* the March). A platform had been improvised in front of the urinal to seat those who were courting rank in the Fascist hierarchy. There were so many of them that the platform collapsed.

The squadristi, so as not to be seen prematurely, hid in the urinal. From time to time their heads would bob up like jack-in-the-boxes to check what was happening. Finally they marched out brandishing kitchen knives and singing manly Fascist hymns. They stank of urine and excrement, according to Roberto, and clouds of millions of flies were buzzing around their heads.

Nonetheless, Italy might have stayed Fascist into the 1950s, had Mussolini not joined the Germans and their war.

Why did he? Because his ambitions for conquest, in combination with English and French irresolution, left little alternative.

England and France, after giving the private impression that they would countenance Italy's invasion of Ethiopia, publicly denounced it; while the Allies squabbled, Hitler militarized the Ruhr unopposed (a bitter defeat for Italian foreign policy) and refused to cut off fuel shipments to Italy. England and France, while privately supporting Italy's intervention in the Spanish Civil War, publicly denounced it; while the Allies squabbled, Hitler annexed Austria (which had been under Italian protection) and sent a few thousand troops to Franco. England and France, having cast Italy as an enemy, offered no resistance as Germany took over Czechoslovakia, seduced Russia, and conquered Poland and then France itself. The war was over. Hitler had no opponents left—certainly not in an Italy exhausted by Ethiopia and Spain. Clearly Italy would be next, unless it accepted the *faits accomplis* and Germany's friendship.

Hitler was terrifying but not yet identified with extermination, slave labor, and unending war. He was a heinous dictator in a world full of dictators, and intelligent, having engineered prosperity amid worldwide depression and having undone much of the injustice of the Treaty of Versailles through brilliant diplomacy and rapid "surgical" strikes. American corporations such as Exxon and Texaco saw no reason not to go on sending him vital military supplies even after his invasions of Poland and France.[11] Points in favor of Italian alliance with Germany—besides lack of alternative—were Hitler's sincere admiration for Mussolini and Mussolini's desire to conquer Albania, Greece, and Tunisia. Moreover, if Germany was hated by Italians, England and France, who monopolized most of the world's riches, were not loved. "They tell us what we may buy and what we may sell," Gandhi complained.

Still for nine months after Germany invaded Poland, Mussolini did nothing. "The Duce's reactions are varied," wrote Foreign Minister Galeazzo Ciano. "At first he agrees with me [that the Germans will drive us to destruction]. Then he says that honor compels him to march with the Germans. Finally he states that he wants his part of the booty. . . . Then, too, he fears . . . that a denunciation of the [alliance] . . . might induce Hitler to abandon the Polish question in order to square accounts with Italy. . . . The Duce is really out of his wits."[12]

"All those [German] troops, all that formidable machinery, are getting closer," Mussolini explained to his wife. "Soon they will be at our frontier, and if they wish, the Germans won't even need to cross France. We have a common border. Within hours they can storm Italy. But there's something else we can be sure of—whether we go into the war or not, the Germans will occupy Europe. If we're not there with them, they'll be able to dictate their conditions to tomorrow's Europe, and that'll mean the end of Latin civilization. . . . Not only in the acquisitive interest of Italy, but also to prevent her suffering the same fate as Poland, Holland, and so many other countries, I must fight."[13]

"Sometimes," said Vittorio Mussolini, "if you don't go to the war, the war comes to you."[14]

In effect, the Duce tried to declare war in order not to fight it. This he did in June 1940, after the French had signaled surrender and the war appeared over. Italians were ashamed and horrified. Roberto, who had been against intervention in Spain, hoped Italy would lose. Marcella swore to kill herself and her children if Hitler won. Even Ciano told the king he would "consider a German victory the greatest disaster for our country."[15] Even the king, Mussolini groaned, "at heart still hopes for a British victory."[16]

Italians hoped the war would be brief and that Mussolini would miraculously pull them through. People who were ashamed went loyally off to war to fight for a cause they hoped would fail. Posterity has ridiculed them. They failed in France, fled in Greece, surrendered in Africa, got lost in Russia. Their Navy's inability to supply Rommel lost North Africa. Their Army's inability to hold Greece, by delaying Hitler's invasion of Russia, lost the entire war.[17]

The truth was they had nothing to fight with; Ethiopia and Spain had totally exhausted their resources. "Clowns, tragic clowns ... have brought our country to the ... necessity of ... invoking outside intervention to be protected and defended!"[18] Ciano moaned, and cited the case of an eighteen-year-old sent the day he was mobilized to the Greek front, without knowing what a gun was.[19] He could have added that the officers were not much better prepared; that the troops sent against France and Russia carried 1891 rifles, wore cardboard shoes, and froze in summer uniforms in the Alps and the steppes; that the tanks in Africa could not stop even an ordinary bullet; that the navy lacked radar, armor, or air support. He did note that in Germany Italian workers were disciplined with bites from attack dogs, while in Libya "the Germans took all our trucks in order to withdraw more rapidly, leaving our divisions in the middle of the desert, where masses of men are literally dying of hunger and thirst."[20]

Gradually, it is said, the truth became obvious that Italians had been duped by twenty years of platitudes, that they were victims of an enormous deception. But what was this "deception"? That Italy was a great power? It had not been invented by Fascism but by Salandra and Sonnino when they brought Italy into World War I; by D'Annunzio and Marinetti; by Depretis, Crispi, and Giolitti when they pursued grandeur and conquest in Africa; by Vittorio Emanuele II and the poets who dreamed up the Risorgimento. Mussolini's insistence on sending Italian troops to fight Bolshevism alongside the German army, when even Hitler preferred their staying home, was simply a continuation of the policy of Cavour, who, by sending troops to the Crimea in 1855, had launched Italy onto the stage of European politics. Did reality contradict idealism? Well, then, the solution was just to wish all the harder!

In later years, after the war, great clamor would proclaim that the new Italian cinema ("neo-realism") could at last show the "truths" smothered by the deceiving rhetoric of Fascism. It would do no such thing. By then Fascism and Mussolini were merely convenient bogeymen. And the Allies who had gone to war to preserve Poland's independence had declared victory, forty million lives later, with Poland (and half a dozen other formerly independent countries) in the power of a dictator who had himself begun the war by conquering Poland.

*

Rossellini's first three features deal in turn with the Italian Navy, Air Force, and Army, and were made during World War II in collaboration with celebrities of the regime. Therefore he has been accused of manufacturing propaganda, having Fascist sympathies, and being an opportunist.

Are the accusations justified?

Memories of the Fascist years are so clouded by recrimination or loyalty, by desires to present the past in its most damning or flattering light, that the context for a verdict—an understanding of what daily life under

Fascism was like—is likely to elude us. Moreover, at the time of the first of these films Rossellini was 35 and had been living under Mussolini's rule for nineteen years—all his adult life; his notions of Fascism, then, were certainly quite different from ours today. As we quoted Croce earlier: "Do you wish to understand the true history of a neolithic Ligurian or Sicilian?" "Try, if you can, to become a neolithic Ligurian or Sicilian in your mind. . . . Do you wish to understand the true history of a blade of grass? Try to become a blade of grass."[21]

Long before 1940 Fascism had become an object of mockery and scorn for Roberto, with his disgust for ready-made opinions, mass ideologies, and middle-class myopia. In Ladispoli, accompanied by Fortù's flag-painted pig, he would stand outside the house and lampoon the Fascist salute to annoy the gerarch who lived next door. In Rome his café companions, some of whom had participated in the March on Rome and then been shunted aside, enjoyed the privilege of moaning and groaning and making fun of the gerarchs. His director friend Aldo Vergano had even attempted to assassinate Mussolini in 1925. With family and relatives, too, Roberto would joke about the regime, whereupon visiting friends, government functionaries would hold their hands over their ears and cry in horror: "Stop! Stop! We're not supposed to hear this!"

Yet how far did Roberto's attitude go beyond mere cynicism? To what degree was he conscious of Fascism's deception or the nature of the war? To what degree was he collaborating or resisting in the autumn of 1940 when he began *La nave bianca* ("The white ship"), a documentary about a hospital ship intended to show how well the Navy took care of its sailors?

All Italy, after all, was Fascist. Everyone had been part of it for twenty years. And rather than being, as in Germany, a fierce and efficient tyranny suddenly in control of every fiber of the nation, Fascism was an old habit, a lazy delusion, an indulgence by a people sheltered from the currents of intellectual Europe. Fascists were as ordinary as Reaganites. Roberto's upbringing, the *cenacolo*, set him somewhat apart, but not enough to prevent his outlook from being provincial, introverted, and aesthetic. To travel from Rome to Naples was to visit the world's end. No framework—no organized opposition—existed within which to evaluate political events. Roberto's dislike of Fascism was not due to reasoned conviction or political awareness. No one who knew him thought him the least interested in politics. "I was anti-Fascist out of fidelity to my father," he admitted, "because, you know, the moment you're inside a mechanism, you don't understand things very well; we were incredibly ignorant.[22] By simple fidelity to my father, to my grandfather, I held apart from Fascism, whose wing could have pricked me like others. The Fascist machine, with its songs, its flags, its simplifying passwords, was a grand mechanism to bite the young. I had extreme adroitness in escaping it, resisting all the pressures exercised then."[23]

It was a casual resistance. He enjoyed the parades occasionally, he admitted, and cheered when Mussolini revived the Roman Empire—it all seemed harmless enough—and he even looked on the Duce, for a while, as a kind of father figure.[24] He was friends with Mussolini's sons, "terribly affected" by Bruno Mussolini's death in 1941,[25] and frequented the salon of Mussolini's daughter, Edda, who was married to Galeazzo Ciano, the Foreign Minister, who together with Mussolini had forged the German alliance.

Such friendships became compromising later, after Fascism's fall. During the regime's twenty years they were unremarkable. Rome was a small world, as intimate as a college campus, particularly its cultural world where, by virtue of a sort of *a tempore* absolution, clerics and vaudeville players, professors and industrialists, politicians and musicians, aristocrats and women mingled freely. It was unlikely that Roberto—or anyone moving in this world—would not have had friends in every camp, Catholic, Fascist, Communist, and Liberal. He had grown up with them, had attended the same schools, and now encountered them at the same theaters, cafés, bordellos, receptions, and every day on the street. The camps mingled. Vittorio Mussolini was a familiar figure in the movie world and saw nothing bizarre in having Communist friends, and neither did they, although he was also living a quite different existence as an air force captain and they as infiltrators. Ciano, happier as *bon vivant* than minister, socialized widely; he would stop by the *Messaggero* newspaper offices, where Renzo Rossellini knew him, and groan, "Mussolini's mad! He's dragging us into a catastrophe!" Ciano lived in the same building as Franco Riganti.

Roberto, in any case, had no moral qualms about making films with backing from Fascists—or from anyone. Later he would be backed by Communists, then by Americans, then by Christian Democrats, then by Schlumberger, finally by Communists again. At one point in the 1960s he would negotiate simultaneously to make films with Mao Tse Tung, the Shah of Iran, Allende, the Vatican, and the Rockefeller Foundation. It wasn't where you got the money that counted, he preached, but what you did with it.

In 1941 he was thrilled to be making his first real movie. It brought him close to the war, close to the biggest thing happening. Playboy that he was, he found a new world to explore.

La nave bianca, though produced by Scalera, was the project of Navy Commander Francesco De Robertis and the Navy Film Bureau, the Centro Cinematografico del Ministero Marina.

De Robertis was a precursor of neo-realism. In opposition to fictional, star-laden cinema, he shot authentic stories in authentic locations with authentic people playing the roles. He had been an amateur moviemaker, despised by the professionals, when, back in 1937, he had submitted his first scenario, *Il nastro azzurro* ("The Blue Ribbon") to Luigi Freddi, the head of the Direzione Generale per la Cinematografia, the government directorate charged with reviewing scripts, distributing prizes, and regulating international film exchange. "The film, which was never shot, had been entirely worked out in its author's mind," wrote Freddi. "[De Robertis] had put together a shooting script of 800 pages, with each scene shown, framed, drawn in a rectangle and accompanied by a description and precise technical directions!"[26]—a thing unheard of at the time.

Il nastro azzurro was turned down. But De Robertis kept coming back with new proposals. First he directed a documentary short, *Mine in vista*, then in 1939, when public interest was aroused by the combination of a Hollywood submarine-rescue film (Lloyd Bacon's *Submarine D-1*) and an actual submarine disaster (despite rescue attempts, the British submarine *Thetis* had sunk with all its crew), the Navy decided to back De Robertis's film about a successful rescue: *Uomini sul fondo* ("Men undersea": *SOS Submarine*). And Michele Scalera, at the urging of Ivo Perilli and Leo Longanesi, agreed to produce it.[27]

"It was only after months and months of opposition, struggle, skepticism, and every kind of obstacle that the film got under way," said De Robertis. "No one believed real sailors could be substituted for actors. No one believed a Navy officer could, just like that, turn himself into a story writer, scenarist, director, and everything. I'm referring to the Film Bureau, the various production houses, all the movie people involved. . . . It was a real battle. Even after shooting began it didn't end. It went on all through production, in the form of the most amicable and respectful lack of confidence, on and on right up to the first private screening, which was for the film crew, when, finally, I received the first and most expressive sign of faith when Monaco, the chief electrician, shook my hand firmly and said, his voice breaking with emotion, 'Commander. . . ! I was really worried!'"[28]

Uomini sul fondo showed the Navy's efficiency and concern for its men. But there was little to cheer in its bleak tale of trapped men struggling to survive. Amid the bombast of Italian militarism, the commonplace authenticity of De Robertis's images had the effect of demystifying war and deflating optimism. Nonetheless, it scored a substantial commercial success.

De Robertis met Rossellini at Scalera, liked Roberto's fish films, and had him visit La Spezia where *Uomini* was being shot. De Robertis developed a warm affection for Roberto while the film was being edited in January 1941, and talked with him about a movie about a hospital ship. He was four years Roberto's senior.

De Robertis began shooting *La nave bianca*, ran afoul of Michele Scalera, who felt he was spending too much, and simultaneously fell sick. Massimo Ferrara decided, with De Robertis's concurrence, to give their friend Roberto his first chance to direct.[29] "I must admit," added Ferrara, "that I was a bit worried, because De Robertis was a very demanding director. Yet Roberto managed to make the film for me at a much more modest cost. Roberto was intelligent. He had ways all his own of finding solutions. De Robertis's ideas were more grandiose, whereas Roberto's were closer to my own. I had limited means then, the Scalera brothers were in Africa, and I had to get along with what was available. De Robertis thought he had the whole Navy at his disposition. But it was wartime. De Robertis created illusions."[30]

De Robertis had prepared a detailed storyboard and Roberto was obliged to follow it.[31] He began filming in February or March 1941 at Jonio, near Taranto, the Navy's largest base, where a British air raid had sunk three battleships, two cruisers and two fleet auxiliaries the previous November—essentially eliminating the Italian Navy from the war. Among Roberto's troupe from Scalera were people like Carlo Carlini who would still be working with him 35 years later. At Easter, Marcellina came with their son Romano, who was nearly four, and watched Roberto shoot on the hospital ship *Arno*, then found them their first apartment in Rome, Via Ipponio 8, near Porta Metronia. But Roberto was still shooting in July when De Robertis and Bellero intervened at the Navy Ministry's insistence. Over Roberto's objections they added new material (chiefly on the technical aspects of navigation) and back in Rome at the end of July, shot many interior scenes, including the war ship's command deck, on sets constructed at Scalera. Editing began in August. Battle footage—Roberto had shot none— had to be incorporated from material shot independently for LUCE newsreels. (Details are given in the filmography.)

"Then the jealousies began," said Marcella De Marchis.[32] And the huge fights. "Even though he wasn't well, De Robertis had an overbearing character," said Massimo Ferrara. "[He] was analytical, precise. He was the first in Italy to invent what's called the storyboard today. Just the opposite of Roberto."[33]

Controversy has raged over whether *La nave bianca* is a Rossellini film, a De Robertis film, or both. Bellero claims that only a few scenes of ships going in and out of harbor are by Rossellini.[34] And Mario Bava charges that "De Robertis was . . . a real genius, the inventor of neo-realism, not Rossellini who stole everything from him. De Robertis . . . had affection for Rossellini and had him do *La nave bianca*, then redid it all himself and left on Rossellini's credit."[35] (Actually, like all Navy films, *La nave bianca* had no credits—except, oddly, Renzo's, for the music—so Roberto's name was neither left on nor taken off.)

De Robertis, ever the gentleman, limited himself to innuendo. "Roberto Rossellini," he wrote in 1949, "has always figured—in practice and for the public—as the director of *La nave bianca*. Over this paternity is hidden a question so delicate as to impose on me the duty of leaving its clarification to the propriety and professional loyalty of signor Rossellini. . . . *La nave bianca* originated in my mind as a simple documentary short showing, through a wounded sailor, the Navy's medical care during war. It was only late in production that the idea came up, and was forced on us, of lengthening it into a 'film spectacular.' Accordingly, I, not without asking my conscience for forgiveness, expanded the short by inserting into it an extremely banal love story between the sailor and a Red Cross nurse."[36]

Roberto used *La nave bianca* to advance his career in 1941 and forever after spoke of it as his. But simultaneously he distanced himself from it by denouncing the mutilations. He too had set out to do a ten-minute short on safety methods, he said, but had had the film taken away from him to be redubbed, recut, and have scenes added to it by others, so that the entire thing had been transformed. The whole of the naval battle was his, he maintained, but "half" the film was not. All the love story of the sailor and his female penpal, he said, was De Robertis's "responsibility."[37] "After I finished the film, it made everyone so angry [because of its anti-heroic depiction] that we had to make some compromises. . . . The romance was put in to tone things down."[38] They wanted to "correct" his film, to sweeten and sentimentalize it. There were troubles with the censors, fights over the love story, and meddlings by the producers.

But if only a modest movie about safety was intended, why had Roberto spent months shooting 15,000 meters of film and emphasizing themes of fear? If De Robertis "redid it all," why does Rossellini's assistant claim the tack-tack montage is Rossellini's?[39] If Rossellini was not "responsible" for the love story, why did he proudly lay claim to the scene where the sailor tries to steal a flower for the girl?[40] Was this something he shot because he was told to? Or does the reference to "the love story" mean only its second half, when the girl shows up to nurse the wounded sailor?

In any case, in 1941 Roberto was complaining loudly to anyone who would listen that the movie was his, that Fascist officials had disliked it, that his name had been taken off to punish him, and that it was being released anonymously.[41]

Despite the quarrels, De Robertis, an exceptionally generous soul, appeared as godfather at the baptism of Roberto's second child, Renzo Paolo, born August 24 and dubbed "Renzino"—"I never saw him after that," said Marcellina[42]—and the two still seemed friends when *La nave bianca* debuted the last night of the Venice Film Festival, September 14, 1941.

On that occasion—perhaps because of Roberto's complaints—no one questioned his authorship. "We Italians have a director who with his first work can already boast a notable success. We are speaking of Roberto Rossellini," Massimo Mida reported.[43]

La nave bianca astounded people; it was awarded a special jury prize ("The Fascist Party Cup") and greeted as a revelation.[44] *Cinema* bestowed its rarely awarded four stars. "Rossellini's work is not a simple visual exposition of the facts," its reviewer wrote. "It is a real *cinematic* narrative enriched by elements completely new for its genre, by unexpected possibilities, by a dramatic tension deriving not from without—from a scene staged and constructed—but from the emotions themselves, from emotions determined by real facts, real details, authentic characters, guided, chosen, and presented by the excellent director."[45]

It was a subtlety, perhaps a contradiction, to proclaim, as most did, that Rossellini filmed facts and was nonetheless a poet. And the subtlety would degenerate through decades of repetition by countless critics eager to emphasize the directness of Rossellini's style, in contrast to the supposedly patched-on emotions (the "rhetoric") of commercial cinema. De Robertis himself contributed by remarking that *La nave bianca*'s "style resulted not from an aesthetic choice but from the necessity of the subject."[46] Emphasis on documentary style fueled the theory that (as Perilli put it) De Robertis influenced Rossellini's "tendency to make a film real, quasi documentary, unrhetorical,"[47] or (as Mario Bava put it) that everything worthwhile in Rossellini was imitation of De Robertis.

But what was the issue? Documentary or art?

The reasons why Mida attributed *La nave bianca* to Rossellini rather than to De Robertis were its precision in aesthetic choice, its creative, poetic, human approach to reality and documentary.[48] Fulchignoni noted how at the high point of emotion at the end of the film, looks take the place of dialogue;[49] but the emotion is patched on, created by montage. Under the influence of Eisenstein's *Potemkin* (Russian silent masterpieces were all the rage at the Centro Sperimentale) De Robertis had had Rossellini film looming gun-turrets and sleeping-sailors in strung-hammocks. And Rossellini, following De Robertis's storyboard, had cut the battle footage into tiny snippets with tack-tack montage rhythms, à la Eisenstein. Under the influence of *Uomini sul fondo* and De Robertis's storyboard, he had severely limited the connotation of each shot and manipulated time with elliptical editing. To this extent *La nave bianca* is a De Robertis film executed by Rossellini, both of them imitating Eisenstein. Rossellini's own style, markedly different, can be seen in the frequent long takes and the camera's constant movement as it pans right and left and dollies in and out. His camera is already aggressively curious.

The extent to which *La nave bianca* was De Robertis's or Rossellini's became embarrassing in the postwar period. It was charged that *La nave bianca* was Fascist propaganda: by showing the wounded well-cared-for, it inculcates blind trust in superiors, praises dedication to duty, and encourages the young to come to war.[50]

Such may have been the Navy's or even Scalera's intention—though it seems a dubious recruiting ploy—and indeed *La nave bianca*'s commercial success was hailed by the Ministry of Culture's Committee for Political and War Films, which gave Rossellini its official blessing and instructed critics to support the picture. But of course the movie frustrates propagandistic intentions. The fragile humanness of the sailors is opposed by their ever more brutal environment. Our particular sailor is prevented by duty from seeing the girl penpal who has travelled the length of Italy to meet him; the flower he saved for her is thrown callously into the sea; he is transported into a totally nightmarish battle. Is this a way to encourage the young to come to war?

Mussolini's slogans, written on the walls of the boat, have been cited as proof that the movie is propaganda. But the words "He Who Stops Is Lost" signal the battle's second half—after our sailor has been wounded and while he is being operated on—and seem singularly appropriate to a renewed onslaught of hell and terror: to an existence Rossellini depicts not as brave aggression but as cacophony desperately endured. Likewise, the looming gun barrels that open the movie, punctuate its sequences, and signal the ship's survival quickly lose force as a tribute to majesty and become instead figures of war's dreadful menace, of a machine's dehumanizing power. "Men and Machines Are One," proclaims the second slogan, damningly; for Rossellini juxtaposes *Metropolis*-like scenes of sailors serving machines with our poor boyish sailor constantly overwhelmed, down-beaten, deprived, almost killed by machines. Amid this "nightmare of cruelty" (in Rossellini's words) the transfer of our sailor to the white calm of the hospital ship and his eventual awakening in front of the almost haloed presence of the pretty nurse (who is also, by appropriate coincidence, the girl he was longing to see) comes as a relief nothing short of a miracle. To state, as Baldelli does, that such an experience is an inducement to enlist or an assurance that one's loved ones are being well cared-for is absurd. *La nave bianca*'s vision of war is utterly antithetical to Fascism—and nothing like it would have been permitted in an American war documentary.

"Do you have any idea of what a warship is like?" Roberto once asked his interviewers. "It's terrifying. There are these little guys who know nothing at all, poor country folk dragged off to work machines they don't understand. The only thing they know is that when the light's red they're supposed to press a button, and when it's green they're supposed to pull a switch; that's all. They're imprisoned in this life, no: sealed up, literally sealed up, so that if a torpedo hits they'll drown but other sections won't. Even the ventilation is cut off so that gas won't get in. Sealed up, deafened by a vague, incomprehensible noise, knowing nothing, they have to watch a red light and a green light. From time to time a loudspeaker says something about the Fatherland and then everything becomes silent again.[51] There is no heroism, because the men are like so many sardines in a can.[52] No heroism, apparently, and yet it's staggeringly heroic."[53]

Once *La nave bianca* is experienced in this context (as a horror film) everything changes. For example: the way, just before battle and just after mass, the men cry, "Viva il Re! Saluto il Duce!" On the surface, this smacks of flag waving. In context, we cut to it so suddenly, and cut away from it so abruptly, that its documentary quality is enhanced; it seems a stolen glimpse of history, a poignant absurdity, an heroic folly—as though Riefenstahl's loving portraits of nubile Aryan youths saluting Hitler at Nuremberg had been juxtaposed with the carrion they became. How often hideous evil results from beautiful, noble emotions!

Amédée Ayfre, citing Rossellini's description of life on a warship, asked: "Is this not, in a few lines, the most striking description ever given of the *huis-clos* of the human prison? Without doubt one can always cry out, weep, shout, trying to establish communication, but the 'human voice' has its limits and on the other end of the line no one ever answers."[54] Tragedy in Rossellini, as Brunello Rondi has pointed out, is always the result of some artificial system imposing a repressive schematicness (like Fascism) on the natural, free-flowing development of instinctual people.[55] Thus we need not go so far as Mida and declare that "Rossellini interpreted a need for truth fermenting in our people under Fascism."[56] The battleship's cannon are aimed at *us*.

La nave bianca's opposition to Fascist ideals can be found on many levels:

- Fascism regarded human will rather than history as determining events. But in *La nave bianca* Rossellini shows Mussolini's machines (specifically Mussolini's, since they bear his words) brutalizing human wills.

- Fascism regarded war as ultimate fulfillment. But in *La nave bianca* war is a horror movie and machines with Mussolini's words on them brutalize the supposed heroes.

- War requires an individual to integrate himself into the group. But in *La nave bianca* the group ethic is split. One sense of group (machine-like militarism) is opposed to another sense (friends and loved ones). Unlike Riefenstahl's *Triumph of the Will*, where an assortment of youths announcing themselves with different regional accents indicates their unity under the Führer, the differing regional languages of *La nave bianca*'s assorted youths are an anti-Fascist protest—dialects were forbidden in movies as contrary to Mussolini's effort to impose a single version of Italian upon the whole nation. The boys' camaraderie exists in an entirely different moral sphere from their military duties: we never see them *working* together. The moment Rossellini liked best was when "the flower hooked by the sailor is about to fall."[57] For him, human progress depended on individuality. "As in *Uomini sul fondo*," says *La nave bianca*'s opening legend, "all the characters in this story are seen in their own environment and their own real life, and are followed through the *spontaneous truthfulness* of the expressions and *natural humanity* of those feelings that constitute the *ideological world of each person*." [emphases added]

- In contrast to Fascist rhetoric, which subjugated facts to political needs, *La nave bianca*'s realistic presentation of the war machine was subversive. The essence of neo-realism, Rossellini later said, was its moral attitude: to be as honest as possible.

"The Italian cinema," Roberto declared, "was Fascist from head to foot then. It paraded in black shirt, with flags rattling in the wind and a martial hymn in the mouth. I employed all my talents to make films without falling prisoner of that system. True, I had to make extraordinary contortions. At the end, I had become as strong, supple, and ungraspable as an eel. Because of my growing reputation, special lines were cast specially for me, bait was thrown my way, attempts were made to lock me into rules of chain mail. Wasted effort. I managed to escape to fry my fish elsewhere. The only thing left for the defeated fishermen was to grab violently away from me the film I had made outside the rules, to try to fix it. . . .

"With some variations, the same thing happened with . . . *Un pilota ritorna* and *L'uomo dalla croce*. I tried to film the truth but it was just the truth that was unsupportable."[58]

*

Roberto's next project was about a bomber pilot and Italy's invasion of Greece. *Un pilota ritorna* ("A pilot returns") was made with the participation of the Air Force, produced by Franco Riganti's ACI-Europa, and based on a story idea by ACI's chairman, Vittorio Mussolini (under the anagramatic pseudonym Tito Silvio Mursino). The Duce's son had been a bomber pilot in Greece and Albania. He had toured the Russian front with his father and Hitler in August 1941—and had watched Hitler sit petrified when the Duce took over the controls of their plane. Vittorio had then been put in charge (though not by his father) of the Air Force's film operations. He mounted cameras on planes and filmed footage for intelligence and newsreels. "We also shot some documentaries and prepared a series of feature films whose purpose was to publicize our air corps's heroism."[59]

There were three such features. Besides *Un pilota ritorna* ACI produced another Tito Silvio Mursino story, *I tre aquilotti* ("The three eagles," 1942), directed by Mario Mattoli, to whose script Roberto may have contributed. The third picture, *Gente dell'aria* (Pratelli, 1943), was produced by ENIC from a story by Bruno Mussolini, Vittorio's brother, also a pilot, who had died in an air accident in 1941.

A full-length treatment for *Un pilota ritorna* by Rosario Leone had been deposited at the Ufficio della Proprietà Intellettuale (the copyright office) in June 1941. Roberto was announced as director toward the end of July, but was uncertain of his appointment until *La nave bianca*'s success in mid-September.[60] Then he wanted to start shooting right away, even though dialogue still had to be written and he intended to throw away most of Leone's treatment. Bursting with enthusiasm, he claimed he'd do the whole film in "thirty days, sixty at most," on location near Viterbo, where he had found an old church that he planned to convert into a shooting stage.

"This began my fight with Rossellini," Riganti says. "To begin shooting a film that was all exteriors at the beginning of the winter season looked like madness to me." Besides, he knew Roberto. Production would drag on well into winter; the weather would multiply the difficulties and expenses of shooting on location. They should wait until spring. "But Rossellini, with the help of the lawyer Antonio Tenni-Bazza, managed to prevail over me by getting Vittorio's authorization."[61]

Shooting began October 20, 1941. Roberto used real combatants, real bullets, even real English and Greek prisoners of war. He himself, his publicists said, clocked 200 hours flying time, got his eye badly swollen while filming stretched out beyond the machine-gun turret, and once almost fell out when he tried to open an Alcione cockpit 10,000 feet up. Three soldiers were killed when 200 smoke bombs, sent to Viterbo by truck for the battle scenes, were sequestered by the Air Force, and an airman, not knowing what he was doing, pulled one of the bombs' heads, causing it to explode and igniting the others. It was scant consolation that an official inquest placed the blame on the Air Force rather than the film company.

One reason for the increased costs of filming on location was Roberto's need for inordinate quantities of lighting equipment, every piece of which would have to be on hand every day, holidays included, whereas in a studio, rental would have been charged only for what was used each day. Accordingly Riganti, who was convinced that Roberto would be shooting for months, had proposed buying the equipment rather than renting it and, finding himself again overruled thanks to Roberto's optimism, had done so anyhow, disguising the purchase in weekly rental invoices. And he was right. Six months later Roberto was still shooting. But Riganti hadn't been able to buy the actors, all of whom had to be paid pro rata for three months after their contracts expired December 31, 1941. Costs thus "exceeded any reasonable expectation" and, financially, *Un pilota ritorna* was "a real disaster," mitigated only by what could be recouped from the purchased equipment.[62]

Shooting had been protracted by Roberto's capriciousness. Unable to work when not in the mood, he would lie in bed for days in Viterbo's Albergo del Angelo. At other times, he would film skillfully for thirty hours straight. Was he still using cocaine? "The set wasn't stressful, but very calm, very relaxed," recalled Massimo Girotti, the star. "Roberto never made me feel the weight of the dialogue. Somehow, almost without noticing it, I would begin my lines."[63] Roberto was popular with his crew, too; film workers were already among Italy's highest-paid, and Roberto's methods earned them weeks of overtime. But his irregularities made him the despair of his producers throughout his career. During *Un pilota ritorna* there was the added problem that the company was shooting on a military base and expected to conduct itself punctiliously. Instead, Roberto would saunter in at ten, eleven, or twelve, unperturbed that everyone had been waiting for him since 7:30. Once Mario Gabbrielli was sent to uproot him from his bed. Roberto punched him in the nose and landed him in the hospital. Confronted with Riganti's attempts to control expenses, Roberto countered with seduction. He convinced Riganti's friends that Riganti was the enemy; among the converts was Aldo Moggi, Vittorio Mussolini's pilot, whom Riganti had brought into the film business to supervise flying sequences. It was a devastating lesson for him. "I realized Roberto would walk over my body, destroy me, anything, to get his own way." Since he wanted to stay friends with Roberto, he resolved never to work with him again.[64] Such would be the pattern of nearly all of Roberto's friendships.

Vittorio Mussolini was on active service with the Air Force and had almost nothing to do with *Un pilota ritorna*. But he too had difficulties with his friend Roberto. Always cautious and prudent, Mussolini had insisted on a thoroughly prepared shooting script before production began, whereas Roberto, even had he been capable of finalizing his every move beforehand, had no intention of restricting himself, let alone putting together a shooting script, and therefore had set on a course of deception. "He'd use me as an accomplice," said Marcellina. "'Ask Marcella,' he'd say; 'I was working all night, wasn't I, Marcella? You tell them!' And then he said the script was ready but that he'd left it at Ladispoli. In fact, we had spent the night playing cards with friends and then gone hunting with them at dawn."[65] Roberto worked at the script all during production itself, often just before shooting. When the movie debuted, a proper scenario still did not exist.

A dozen hands had contributed to the initial scenario, among them Massimo Mida (Puccini), his brother Gianni Puccini, Michelangelo Antonioni, Lianna Ferri, and Margherita Maglione, who served also as Roberto's assistants. "Rossellini had moved to Rome only shortly before this time," Antonioni recalls. "He lived in an almost empty house; there was a large bed in one room, a table and a few chairs in another, the rest was empty. Roberto was nearly always in bed. We worked there, on the bed."[66] Antonioni favored a colder, more formal, detached and traditional style than the new, direct, emotional style desired by Rossellini, Leone, Mida, and Vittorio Mussolini.[67]

The Puccini brothers worked at *Cinema*, a magazine edited by the Duce's son, staffed with many Communists, and less reticent in its opinions than was *American Film* in the 1980s. Communists were often tolerated in influential positions, as "left-wing Fascists." Umberto Barbaro, for example, a teacher and second-in-command at the Centro Sperimentale, was unmolested, once Centro president Luigi Chiarini assumed responsibility for him, and was able to publish translations of Communist theorists like Eisenstein, Pudovkin, Kuleshov, and Balazs years before the rest of the world; it was only when the Christian Democrats came to power that Barbaro was forced out. Marcella De Marchis has claimed Vittorio Mussolini "knew very well what sort of people he had around him at *Cinema*."[68] Mussolini himself has said he would have fired them, had he known,[69] and one of them agrees—Massimo Mida, who adds that Mussolini was involved in the wars and rarely in the office.[70] Vittorio has said he was surprised and furious when Gianni and Dario Puccini (Mida's brothers) were arrested and he learned they were Communists.[71] For years they had been calling him a "traitor," he complained, for liking American movies more than Italian ones. "They were more 'Fascist' than I was. They always thought the pictures I liked weren't 'Fascist' enough."[72]

Mussolini did not wonder about whether his associates joined the Fascist Party or not. Concerning Roberto, "I wasn't curious. I didn't care about his politics. I had twenty directors without [membership] cards. Mastrocinque and Mattoli were known anti-Fascists." He didn't regard Roberto as anti-Fascist, or as anything else, either.[73]

Mussolini's insouciance even extended to hiring a columnist notorious for his lampoons of the Duce in a French Communist newspaper, *Ce Soir*— in this case to work for the second production company with which Vittorio was involved, ERA Film, headed by Angelo Rizzoli, *Cinema*'s publisher. "Overcoming the opposition of the Minister of Popular Culture, to direct the film *Tosca* I succeeded in signing the famous director Jean Renoir, who, because of his anti-Fascist background, was the least suitable person at that moment," Mussolini wrote. France was at war with Germany; Renoir had Communist associates and his *Grand illusion* had had limited screening in

Italy because it glorified pacifism. "But I thought and still think it is preferable to gain the friendship of intelligent adversaries than the opportunistic sympathy of foolish friends. The French director came to Rome and found himself comfortable, so much so that he was thinking, after *Tosca*, of shooting a film on the Pontine Marshes and the colonies in the reclaimed zones. Unfortunately the war's course surprised us. Renoir directed only *Tosca*'s first scene, at Palazzo Farnese at night,[74] then, due to my intervention with my father, he was able to leave Italy without any problems a few hours before the outbreak of hostilities [when Italy attacked France]. He sent me a friendly letter promising we would make some other film together after the war. Perhaps I am being immodest, but evidently we belonged to that world of gentlemen whose types tend to get lost in the quagmire of intolerance."[75]

In fact, Renoir's departure for Italy coincided with a break from his Communist supporters. He "didn't say goodbye," wrote Aragon. He was "going to Mussolini," jeered others. Two years earlier, during Renoir's period of solidarity with the Popular Front, Renoir had declined to come to Venice to receive a reward for *La Grand illusion*. Now, after *La Règle du jeu*'s disastrous reception and his mobilization into the Army as a Lieutenant, he was happy to respond to his government's request to propitiate Mussolini by going to Rome to direct *Tosca* and to lecture at the Centro Sperimentale—all the more so in that it was a means of avoiding his creditors (*La Règle* had cost five million francs, a colossal sum). The alliance with the Communists had been one of mutual convenience. Renoir, like Rossellini, did not believe in the possibility of justice on earth, and had refused to inscribe in any political group. But the Party had wanted his prestige. And he had needed the Party's immense support in cultural circles; had seen it as the strongest opposition to Nazi Germany; and had been captivated by the buoyant hopes and enthusiasm of his many Communist friends, among them Marguerite Renoir, his occasional mate and editor. But in 1939 he had broken with Marguerite and her friends and had begun a life-long romance with Dido Freire. Simultaneously, the Party's support for Stalin's non-aggression pact with Hitler had left him permanently disenchanted with politics—and with friends whose idealism he had formerly admired.[76]

And of course he fell in love with Rome. In January 1940 he took a luxurious apartment near San Stefano Rotondo on whose walls Dido painted Amazon scenes. There he stayed until June, when, with Italy about to enter the war, he found himself an enemy alien, was assaulted in a restaurant, and was forced to flee. When he returned to Europe from America after the war, he didn't return to Paris, he came back to Rome.

Renoir's first tour guide in Rome had been his assistant, Luchino Visconti. The movie community's welcome contributed to his love affair with the city. In France he was being denounced by all factions and for every reason: his greatest film had been excoriated by the critics, then banned by the government; his creditors were pursuing his purse; and his first wife was ready to skin him alive. In Italy his cult could scarcely have been more estimable. Not only were his movies cited by everyone as high art, models for the Italian cinema to come and the epitome of social engagement, but they had gained the added piquancy of having to be viewed semi-clandestinely. Rossellini too was an admirer, especially of *La Grande illusion*, which impressed him immensely. "In *Un pilota ritorna* his influence is clear."[77] Roberto may have been introduced to Renoir at this time, when he was still a year away from *La nave bianca*, but if so, Renoir did not recall it when the two became friends after the war.[78]

For most Italians the years 1939–43 were uneasy times. For the clandestine Communists at *Cinema*, Mida recalls, they were "full of fear," despite Vittorio Mussolini's support. Talking to others was always "problematic." Someone like Roberto, who seemed to be searching for his own personality, was not the sort Mida could fully trust. Wanting the war to be lost, Mida regarded his own participation in a movie like *Un pilota ritorna* as "a compromise. *L'uomo dalla croce* was another compromise. But we didn't consider it serious, something to be sorry for later. We tried to mitigate the propaganda and to be sympathetic. Rossellini wanted even the enemies to be people and not caricatures. He understood things but he didn't want to be compromised like us, yet at the same time he wanted to be inside things and to make films at any cost. Visconti didn't have money problems [making *Ossessione*], and the rest of us were still young. Rossellini couldn't afford to wait for better times."[79]

"We thought we were making a patriotic film, but not propaganda," said Massimo Girotti.[80]

"[Vittorio Mussolini] used to call me 'the citizen who protests'!" Marcella De Marchis said; "Neither I nor Roberto ever enrolled in the Fascist party."[81] Yet Roberto had made enemies, former friends like Scalera among them. They resented his winning a choice assignment like *Un pilota ritorna*. They complained loudly that it was an outrage—not to say suspicious—for this Rossellini to be working for the Duce's son, to be making a film for the Air Force in the middle of the war, and not even to belong to the Fascist Party. Thus, according to Riganti, Roberto, saying he feared gossip might force his removal from the picture, asked Riganti to arrange for him to see Vittorio Mussolini in order to procure a Party card. "The ritual of cinema was fantastically complicated then," Roberto explained later. "If you didn't have a tiara on your head, a pastoral staff in your hand, a ring and a cross, you didn't get to make films."[82] But Riganti pointed out that joining the Party would not squelch the accusations; it would merely look opportunistic. What was needed was a pre-dated card that would make it appear that Roberto had been a loyal Fascist for many years. Such cards were not too difficult to obtain, for salaries in Mussolini's Italy were affected by status or longevity within the Party, and as a result falsification was endemic. According to Riganti, he asked a militia member named Sisti Evangelista to get such a card for Roberto in exchange for a production job on the film, and Roberto later told Riganti that the card designated him as a "founder of the Fascist party at Ladispoli." Concludes Riganti: "That way, at least, everyone had to believe it."[83]

Roberto's accepting a card for a year no more suggested loyalty to the Party than having a driver's license. It was common to joke that PNF (Partito Nazionale Fascista) really stood for *per necessità familiare* (for family necessity). Pius XI quipped that membership was "a bread card." But within the Rossellini family the card had become a question of high honor. Because Renzo had refused to have a card, his appointment to a professorship—and a secure income—at the University of Rome had been blocked, and he had been eking out an uncertain livelihood writing film music and criticism. When at last a job did materialize at the Conservatory of Pesaro, it turned out to be due to his composer friend Zandonai, who had subscribed Renzo in the Party without his knowledge. Renzo had been outraged and shamed—and grateful when the job and membership finally expired after a year.[84]

After the war, Roberto made a point of declaring publicly and frequently that he had never had a card. His sister and wife regarded his word as sacred on this matter and have insisted, despite Riganti's account, that Roberto never had a card. The question is thus Roberto's word to Riganti versus Roberto's word to his family. Party records cannot be checked, because they no longer exist. Riganti himself never saw the card, and Roberto's quip about "founder of the Party at Ladispoli" may have been just a joke, concedes Riganti, like Zia Fortù painting an Italian flag on her pig. In either interpretation, Roberto would have regarded it as farce, as one of the "extraordinary contortions" by which he asserted his independence of the regime.[85]

It must be said that Renzo's stand on principle was extraordinary—and a nightmarishly daunting example for an older brother, and all the more so because there was almost no one else in Italy, however much they detested the regime, who took the card seriously enough to deem it worth a fight.

Roberto's real "secret" was that he had become ambitious. It was a quality he took pains to conceal. Like his decadent companions, he cultivated pleasure in behaving like a dilettante, in emulating the legendary Roman father who on his death bed had counseled: "My sons, you must all try to have an occupation in life. Life without an occupation is contemptible and meaningless. But always remember this: you must never allow your occupation to degenerate into work."[86]

Roberto, seeking redemption in his father's eyes, would eventually transform dilettantism into a sort of liberation humanism. He was mastering the art of intrigue and the "*volto sciolto e pensiero stretto*" (open countenance and concealed thoughts) counseled by Lord Chesterfield. The flatulent revolt of his youth was ripening in middle age into the courtly skills defined ages earlier by Baldassare Castiglione: "To behave with decorum, to win the favor of one's superiors and the friendship of one's equals, to defend one's honor and make oneself respected without being hated, to inspire admiration but not envy, to maintain a certain splendor, to know the arts of living, to converse with wit and facility, to be in one's proper place in war, in a salon, in a lady's boudoir, and in a council chamber, to live in the world and at the same time to have a private and withdrawn life."[87]

Un pilota ritorna's reputation long suffered—along with Rossellini's—from the unofficial ban against showing "Fascist" films that more or less prevailed from the end of the war into the 1980s; from the tendency of a succession of voices (Visconti, Jean Gili, and others) to condemn the picture as "Fascist propaganda" without seeing it; and from the reluctance of Rossellini (and his family) to discuss this period of his life. In 1949 Rossellini told *The New York Times* that he had only been "technical director" on the two pictures.[88] In 1974, pressed by Savio, he took refuge in evasions and outright lies. "It's antipathetic to speak about them," he responded, referring to *Pilota* and *L'uomo dalla croce*, "because it has become so much a way of proclaiming oneself a victim of political pressure, which is boring. I can say this, that certainly all the dialogues of *Pilota ritorna* were changed. All."[89]

As long as the film remained unseen and the facts were unknown—that Roberto had been wildly enthusiastic about doing it and that his dialogues had not been changed—his explanation seemed reasonable enough. Yet his defensive posturing was counterproductive, because it seemed to affirm that he had opportunistically collaborated in a shameful project. And the posturing was wrongheaded, because *Un pilota ritorna* requires no apologies.

It does start out like propaganda. Our pilot flies a bombing run from Italy to Greece, with Rossellini emphasizing the personableness of the flyers, the mechanics of their work, and the joy of returning home; nothing even hints at what happens to those beneath their bombs. But then our pilot is shot down in a dogfight with the British and finds himself caught up in something bigger than his patriotism. Along with other prisoners, hostages, and refugees, he experiences war as a victim while the British army retreats before the Germans. Now Rossellini emphasizes suffering: the plight of the civilians, a dying father, a sick child, a soldier having his leg amputated, the terror and screaming of people caught in a bombardment. "I have never," proclaimed Jean Rouch, "in the whole history of the cinema seen a film more decisively against war than this one that Rossellini managed to make in Fascist Italy at war. A film, moreover, in which English, Italians, Greeks, Yugoslavs are all on the same level, and never like actual enemies, and in which, instead, the sole god of war is a German pilot in a Stukas [strafing them all indiscriminately]. . . . It's a truly moral portrait of war."[90]

How could such a film have been allowed? It never would have been permitted in America during World War II. Not only is war shorn of all its glory and reduced to individual cases of misery, but Italy's ally is depicted as a mechanical assassin, while her enemies come through as gentlemen.[91] A commanding officer answers his subordinates' Fascist salutes with a little jerk of his hand, like something out of Chaplin's *Great Dictator*. In direct contradiction to official propaganda, the ground crew remarks that the bombs they load are always defective and always have to be replaced. The hero is caught in a bombardment by his own planes. Even the film's dedication—"with fraternal heart to the pilots who have not returned from the skies of Greece"—manages to sound pessimistic and like a protest; indeed, the thrice-repeated evocation of coming home as war's ultimate joy cannot help but imply that home ought never to have been left in the first place. "I'm sure," said Riganti, "that in Roberto's mind the frequent repetition of 'coming home' would be interpreted as a message of peace (coming home not to fight again but to bring the war to an end)."[92] As in *La nave bianca*, the woman (Michela Belmonte, Maria Denis's sister) is no Valkyrie but an archetype of compassion surrounded with a halo of magic, and the hero (Massimo Girotti, boyishly resembling Richard Greene) is no Siegfried but a passive, morose sort, who wakes from depression only under Belmonte's spell, and whose sole heroic act consists in stealing a British plane so that he can go home.

That final sequence, inspired by the impressionistic train ride in Renoir's 1938 *La Bête humaine*, is one of the more ambitious in Rossellini's career. After the black, cacophonous, rocket-streaked night comes the exhilaration of dawn and the open sky and an accelerating montage twixt pilot and ground—the rapid passage of ports, fields, cities, and train tracks, punctuated with vaunting thrusts upward by the camera. Sighting his English plane, the Italians try to shoot it down, but Girotti lands with only a hand wound and in progressively closer shots is surrounded by his comrades.

But an anti-war film had not been Vittorio Mussolini's intention; he supported the war and his father to the bitter end. In his story, the hero is a good Fascist with seventy missions to his credit, who defends the war, who escapes at the end not by plane but by foot, and who reaches not Italy but the German lines in Greece, and shouts "Viva Hitler!" In Rossellini's movie, almost nothing of Mussolini's story survives,[93] and Mussolini does not believe that any of Rossellini's dialogues were altered.[94] Franco Riganti denies absolutely that the dialogues were altered. "It was Rossellini's character never to allow liberty or independence to anyone. Given his character, it was inconceivable, for him, that anyone would receive credit, praise or success from a work that depended on him."[95]

The invasion of Greece in October 1940 had been a disaster; only Hitler's intervention had prevented the Italians from being thrown into the Mediterranean. None of this can be divined from *Un pilota ritorna*. It was promoted as "a page of heroism in the blazing atmosphere of the air war," and ministers and gerarchs flocked to its premiere, April 8, 1942, at Rome's Supercinema. Its reception with the public was tepid; amid successive defeats, goon-squad beatings and castor oil, and severe rationing, there was little enthusiasm for war movies. "It told neither the truth nor lies," Riganti said. "It was hard to tell exactly whose side the director was on: he didn't seem to want to offend either Italians or Germans or the English or anyone else."[96] Vittorio Mussolini found it disappointing, quite aside from ideological values.[97]

But the critics, whether because they did or did not get the point, praised *Un pilota ritorna* highly and at Venice in September gave it the National Cinematic Prize for the best political and war film; the glass cup on its marble base was so heavy Riganti had to leave it behind: he couldn't lift it. *Un pilota ritorna* was "a film without rhetoric," said *Corriere della Sera*, which liked the humanity with which the enemy was depicted.[98] But Giuseppe De Santis, in Vittorio Mussolini's *Cinema*, gave it only two stars ("mediocre") and, though also praising "the noteworthy assumption of an objectivity shorn of rhetoric and party spirit," found fault with nearly everything else. It had tried to imitate *La Grand illusion* but utterly lacked Renoir's poetic gift for creating feeling cinematically. The drama was weak, the characters simplistic, the documentary side unpoetic, the sound, lighting, and editing sloppy. And if it were trying to be a propaganda, it failed at that, too, for "to propagandize means to reawaken faith and wisdom in souls that have become numb ... to create a general awareness ... by which every man will feel himself indissolubly linked in a relationship of rights and duties with others."[99]

De Santis is partly correct. Rossellini's first solo feature does imply more deep feeling than it achieves. It is a lightweight action movie, the work of a brilliant technician rather than an artist. The months he spent at ACI personally doing all the editing[100] are immediately apparent. *Pilota* is a montage film, constructed in tidy sequences, with Hollywood-like pacing and story sense, like other ACI products and subsequent Rossellini movies. And crowds are manipulated with an inspired sense of choreographic composition. It is already evident that Rossellini is a great portrayer of war. But these masterful battle scenes, with glimpses of the British columns fording a river, gain their power more from painterly instinct and love for pageantry than from any devotion to newsreel-like photography. Here vast vistas and long takes anticipate *Viva l'Italia*.

But there is too much chorus and not enough individuality. The principal actors are handled perfunctorily, as in a documentary. Rossellini is as yet incapable of building empathy between them. When he tries to break into a Renoiresque fullness of character, the result is a banal, sentimental love scene. *Pilota* resembles *La Grand illusion* in that it is about prisoners of war, but it only hints at the solidarity that transcends war. Yet there are existential touches: space seems imprisoning despite a fluid camera, and languid 360-degree pans search every horizon, meditating on time and space and who we are, before returning to their starting point no more the wiser.

"Roberto and I," said Marcella De Marchis, "separated definitely in 1942, when Renzo was one. As soon as he became successful, women began besieging him like mosquitos. They were everywhere, in the closet, under the bed. He could be charming when he wanted to, there's no doubt.[101]

"Things had gone along without a cloud until [that] May . . . when Roberto had his first extramarital affair." Marcella was still nursing Renzino. "From the perspective of years later, I think that had I been less young and less impulsive, that is, had I been able to accept this first incident as an inevitable and surmountable fact, perhaps things would have gone differently. We were then still at Ladispoli where Roberto was shooting a film. . . . The female lead . . . was a German dancer from Totò's company, a girl 24 years old, with big green eyes and a rather tragic family past. Roberto, who has always been inclined to protect the weak and oppressed, let himself be transported from an initial affection into a quite different feeling, one which a wife tolerates with difficulty. Incapable of pretending, it did not occur to him to hide this relationship from me, and things reached such a point that I was obliged to request, out of respect for myself, a legal separation. Roberto accepted unwillingly, but showed no intention of wanting to break off his relationship with the German dancer.[102]

"I tried to save anything I could—the great love, the children. But I always told him, 'The important thing is that you be free.' Of course, I said it while crying, but I was convinced of it even if inside I felt deathly despair. He adored me then, and from then on. And he respected me. I left with the two children for Cortina [on July 26], to get away, and Roberto gave me no peace (twenty phone calls a night, telegrams, letters, everything). But I didn't want to know what he was doing."[103]

The dancer's name was Roswitha Schmidt. She was scarcely his first infidelity. She was 23 and had come to Italy with a dance troupe from Berlin that was touring in a variety show, *Volumineide*, in which Magnani and Totò were featured. An agent had spotted her at Rome's Teatro Argentina in February or March and pointed her out to Roberto. She had had a son, Viktor, in 1937 by a man who didn't love her, who was being raised by her aunt in Vienna. Roswitha was timid, not in the least self-assertive, and in no way ambitious to become an actress. ("She has an interesting face and is not lacking in energy," De Santis later wrote, "but she's too immobile in her expressions."[104]) But Roberto gave her a screen test and then bought out her contract with the dance company virtually without consulting her. She was to be paid 15,000 lire for three months and then rejoin the dance troupe. In any event, the film's production was prolonged through most of the year, by which time the troupe was long gone.

Roberto brought Roswitha home frequently. Marcellina was there, of course, and at Ladispoli there was Zia Fortù, whose kind blue eyes beamed on Roswitha charmingly. When Marcellina left for Cortina the lovers took an apartment at 6 Via Parco Pepoli, at first in the basement, later, after Aldo Vergano moved to Milan, in Vergano's apartment on one of the upper floors.

Roberto had had no desire to leave Marcellina. She was devoting her life unreservedly to him and was (he claimed) the best of women sexually. But he wanted other women, too. Lots of them. He was like a caliph, said his friends, who counseled Marcellina not to run away. But Roswitha turned out to be one of the longest loves of Roberto's life. After his attempts failed to reconcile Marcellina to the new arrangement—he brought both women to Venice that September—he had every intention of marrying Roswitha once he was free to do so. Yet still he carried on countless side affairs (actress Laura Nucci among them) of which Roswitha, all trusting, knew nothing until years later.

Marcellina went from Cortina to Hungary, where she obtained an annulment, on Roberto's claim that he had been under the influence of drugs at the time of their marriage. The Italian courts refused to recognize the Hungarian annulment, however, and further litigation was frustrated by the collapse of the Italian state. Roswitha's marriage remained a hope for the future. In the meantime, the fact that Roberto was known to have a German companion helped his career during the war,[105] just as his collaboration with Amidei would help him after the war.

L'uomo dalla croce ("The man of the cross") began production in July 1942. Roberto again refused a soundstage and had all the sets constructed on location, near Ladispoli. Halfway through, everything burned down. Roberto went crazy, cursed wildly at everyone, and calmed down just as suddenly; half an hour later, affable, witty, and full of charm, he took the whole crew for drinks. "Films are demanding creatures," he said during a break for the Venice Festival. "You think you can get away from them for a few days, and instead they follow you; you're forced to think about a new shot, a dialogue line that needs to be changed, a scene not yet clear. Only when the film's completely done and running in the movie houses can you free yourself from its tyranny."[106]

L'uomo dalla croce is based on the life of Father Reginaldo Giuliani, a chaplain on the Russian front. Caught between Russian and Italian artillery while tending a wounded soldier, he takes shelter in an isba along with a Russian commissar and his girlfriend and twenty or so women and children. He cares for the wounded through the night, delivers and baptizes a baby, and converts the girl after a Russian kills the commissar. The Italians retake the village at dawn, but the chaplain is shot by a dying Russian soldier and, fatally wounded, crawls over to murmur the "Our Father" in his ear.

Asvero Gravelli wrote the story and script and supervised the production. He was a well-known Fascist news commentator with a nightly radio show and was the editor of two Fascist journals, *Gioventù Fascista* ("Fascist Youth") and *Antieuropa*. His film—"Dedicated," as an end title announces, "to the heroic chaplains fallen among the Godless in barbaric lands"—supposes that a crusade against atheistic Communism is a noble project for Church and Army.

This was a common idea at the time—to liberate the Russian people from Stalin. Its advocates did not know about the twenty million people the Germans were slaughtering in the Soviet Union. "But what could one know?" said Roberto. "The things one heard were so vague. Now if you're ignorant about something, it's important to make an effort and try to get out of that ignorance. But then there weren't any ways of learning anything.[107] What we thought we understood about Soviet realities was only so much parroting. Under those conditions, there was no way the picture could not have turned out lame-brained and foolishly ambitious."[108]

Even Italy's foreign minister knew next to nothing. A report from a friend late that May left Ciano skeptical: "The brutality of the German, which has now reached the proportions of a continuing crime, stands out from his words so vividly and so movingly as to make one skeptical of its truthfulness. Massacres of entire populations, raping, killing of children— all this is a matter of daily occurrence."[109] If even Ciano was bewildered, what could Rossellini know?

Marcella De Marchis claims Roberto made *L'uomo dalla croce* because "he needed money to eat."[110]

In fact, there were other movies Rossellini could have made instead. *Un pilota ritorna* had been a personal success, despite losing money. ACI had announced in October 1941 that he would direct *Rapsodia ungherese*, a film about the composer Liszt. In March 1942, Riganti had hoped, and ACI had announced, that he would do Salgari's *Predoni del Sahara*.[111] Then Scalera had announced a children's adventure film, *L'espresso del Guatemale*, in April and *L'attendente* in September.

But Roberto, whether because he had alienated both ACI and Scalera or because he wished to pursue his trilogy of war films, chose to work for Continentalcine instead, a company which almost immediately was absorbed by Cines in order to avoid bankruptcy. Riganti theorized that Roberto was "jumping to the party in power."[112] It looked at the moment like the Axis would win the war. The Japanese were in Singapore; the Germans were advancing into the Caucausus; Mussolini had gone to Tripoli in preparation for a triumphal entry into Alexandria.

In any case, *L'uomo dalla croce* only sketchily acknowledges the intentions of Gravelli's script. Like *Un pilota ritorna* it is anti-imperialist, depicting Italians as obsessed with machinery and mechanical maneuvers, their enemy as dependent on animals and nature. Unlike *Pilota*, it does not try to transfer responsibility to the Germans, who are never mentioned, though Russia was full of them and the Italians were just along for the ride. Merely showing Italians fraternizing with Russians undermined German objectives: any German caught doing so would have been shot on the spot.[113] Rather than Gravelli's holy crusade, it is themes of love and tolerance that dominate the picture: the theme (from *La Grand illusion* and *Un pilota ritorna*) of a brotherhood of suffering transcending enmity; the theme of a chaplain mediating between Italians and Russians, as in *Roma città aperta*, where another priest will unite Communists and Christians;[114] and the theme, most crucially, of hope. *L'uomo*, Rossellini said, "poses the same problem [as *La nave bianca*]: men with hope, men without hope. It's rather naïve, but such was the problem."[115] The problem, amplified by the war, would soon send torrents of hope and despair coursing through *Roma città aperta, Paisà, Deutschland im Jahre Null, Una voce umana, Stromboli, Francesco giullare di Dio, Europe '51,* and even *Desiderio.* But in *L'uomo dalla croce* the problem is abstract and dim, for Rossellini is not yet a moviemaker with real people. His priest is an outline, his other characters bare figures in the chorus.

Many of Rossellini's admirers and most of his friends thought *L'uomo* one of the worst ("ugliest") films they'd ever seen.

The Communist De Santis, in contrast, was unbothered. He praised Rossellini, among recent filmmakers, as "the most devoid of polemic sense, the furthest from having an ax to grind." He thought Rossellini's idea of "recreating an objective reality without useless decoration and fancy frills" was an "exceptionally combative and polemical" ideal, in light of the degree to which Italian cinema had abandoned realism and put D'Annunzio-like romance in its place. Yet, said De Santis, Rossellini's ideal was unfulfilled, because his successful scenes (the spectacular, documentary-like battles) were constantly undercut by his intimate scenes, which were inflated with voids and the cheapest sort of worn-out melodrama. It almost seemed as though "two different heads had presided over the film's production," one that loved the authentic, the other that wallowed in "rhetoric."[116]

De Santis was working for Rossellini at that moment. Otherwise, *L'uomo dalla croce* got lukewarm reviews and few patrons. By the time it opened (mysteriously, not until June 1943, although its immanent release had been announced back in October when it was in editing), events had passed it by.

It no longer looked as though the Axis would prevail. By November 1942, Rommel had been beaten at El Alamein, and the Americans had landed in Algeria. Italians in Russia were defending the Don with one man every twenty feet, one machine gun every mile, with ammunition so low that a shot could not be fired without regimental authorization, with almost no food and only thin clothing against forty-below temperatures. Flanked on December 16, they started a 300-mile death march in icy wind. Their German allies seized their vehicles and threw their wounded out onto the snow to take their places in peasant huts. As many Italians died from the cold and the Germans as from Russian bullets. Their tales came wending home long before the survivors.

Hitler had declared war on the U.S. in December 1941, after Pearl Harbor, and the Duce had toddled along, ablaze with Fascist honor. Ciano had reflected in his diary, "The Minister from Cuba came to declare war. He was very emotional and was disappointed that I did not share his emotion. But, after having had the good fortune, or is [it] the misfortune, to declare war on France, on Great Britain, on Russia, and on the United States, could the good man really think that I would turn pale on learning that Sergeant Batista was mobilizing against us the forces of Cuba on land and sea and in the air? Ecuador, too, has declared war, but I had my secretary receive the Minister."[117]

A year later, public feelings had hardened, although *L'uomo dalla croce*'s release was still six months away. At *Il Messaggero*, where Renzo worked, his colleagues would spit at the large glass-covered photo of Mussolini in the entrance hall, then wipe the glass clean with a handkerchief—to avoid being put in prison. And at night, when wardens patrolling the curfew would spot a violation and shout "*Luce! Luce!*" ("Light!"), they would be answered by contemptuous hoots, "Prrrt!" and would call back, "We said 'luce,' not 'Duce'!"

Renzo Rossellini published an open letter to his brother in *Cinema*, in January 1943. "You have just finished your third movie, my brother Roberto, and I have just scored it: we've rediscovered each other through work and are happily collaborating again. . . . Our tastes and life styles, so different in the banal terms of daily life, are perfectly . . . sympathetic in inmost feeling. . . . We are spiritually close again when once we thought ourselves launched along opposite roads in life. . . . While I was losing myself in a sea of notes and melancholy, you were starting your long path of fatiguing experiences in the disorganized and troubled search for an ideal wherein you might appease your restless and discontented soul. These were the years of separation. Years which little by little brought me a certain, even premature, fortune, we might say, and which for you were not only adverse but cruel. Among the many things I have to reproach myself for, two appear unpardonable to me: having taken your lack of discipline for materialism, and your contradictions for absentmindedness. Alone by myself, and enchanted with music like Gazzano's poet that wants to dream at any cost, I almost did not see you, I almost did not hear you. Two years ago, seeing your first sequences in *La nave bianca*, I miraculously rediscovered you; and with my heart full with emotion as never before, I wanted to express all my joy to you, all my fraternal trembling. The long silent parts of your film that were left solely to my discretion were the invitation to our meeting. And you remember how in a few days, [scoring *La nave bianca*], I filled page after page with notes that were never unworthy, because they all vibrated with fraternal love. The poetry of your narrative, the attention of your eye for the big little passions of little people, of simple hearts, were the tenderness of our infancy, were our ideals from always. . . . [And then came] *Un pilota ritorna*, a film which is certainly unmistakably yours, with those long silences, with that grandiose rhythm made almost out of nothing, full of astonished stares."[118]

According to Roberto, he was under a cloud at the moment his brother's letter appeared, but the facts are difficult to ascertain. In 1949 he told *The New York Times*, "My name was taken off [*L'uomo dalla croce*], too, [and then the authorities] suspended my license (work permit) for ten months in 1942–43."[119] A year later he told Vernon Jarrat the ban was not political but due to his squirming out of a contract with Scalera.[120] A few years later he told Brusasca that Scalera had done the squirming: "Scalera Film informed me that war was one of the cases of *force majeure* that might entail suspension of my contract with them; they thus reserved the right to interrupt my salary without further notice. An independent producer offered me work, I notified Scalera and signed the contract. I had two children and it was clear that hard and dangerous times were at hand. The members of the [producers'] consortium decided that no one would distribute film that bore my name and only they had nationwide distribution networks. I was consigned to hunger and for a very long year did not manage to work."[121] In 1974 he told Savio, "I can't recall what motivated it. Ad personam, probably. Motives were always a bit cloudy. Hard times were coming and I had a terror of not being able to work."[122] To Toscan du Plantier in 1976 he claimed that the motives were political, that Italian producers collectively blacklisted him for eleven months for indiscipline, insolence, and a penchant for causing them problems; and that he had appealed to Vittorio Mussolini, who headed the consortium of producers, citing in his defense an anti-strike law the Duce had promulgated, and claiming he was being prevented from working—at which Vittorio had laughed merrily.[123]

In actuality, Rossellini's name appeared on *L'uomo dalla croce*, and only a few months passed between his finishing that picture and starting his next one. The "authorities" could not have "suspended" his license or work permit, for no such permit existed in 1942/43. Only ironically could Scalera have cited war as an excuse to suspend his contract, for they had not given him the contract until after Italy had entered the war. As for the producers' consortium, they issued no bans.

This consortium was ANCILS (an acronym for ACI, Nationalfilm, Cines, ICI, Lux, Scalera). It was founded and chaired by Riganti toward the end of 1942. "Its principal activity," he said, "was to control production costs and regulate distribution. I don't remember the consortium ever taking disciplinary steps against Rossellini. I personally would have had to issue and distribute the ruling against him; and I do not remember ever having done so either against Rossellini (whom I always defended and helped) or against anyone else with the exception of a Venetian exhibitor and the Leoni brothers, film distributors. I do believe that Michele Scalera, after his great love for Roberto [and] seeing himself betrayed by Roberto's certainly unorthodox behavior, may have tried to get revenge. But I and Vittorio Mussolini always protected Roberto even if he made no bones about caring for nothing except his own interests. It's natural that years later, when he had become the great director everyone was singing hosannas about, he would have tried to make himself sound like a victim of Fascism, a line that was very useful for him, politically. It's impossible to keep up with the inexhaustible imagination of Roberto Rossellini who obviously always tried to recount the facts of the past distorted to yield the maximum benefit. Among all the many liars I've known in life Rossellini occupies a place on the highest level in that he had the great merit of *living his lies*, that is, telling them and remembering them and thus running no risk of giving himself the lie by forgetting. Which takes away nothing from the fact that Roberto Rossellini was one of the greatest talents, and not just of Italian film, as his life and achievements prove."[124]

Rossellini's first features—aside from topicality, documentary flare, and an *au courant* cynicism toward Mussolini's vastly unpopular war alliance— were mechanical films by a youth playing with cinema and imitating Eisenstein, Renoir, and Hollywood. They were certainly not yet movies by an artist.

World War II Comes Home

"The Rossellini of those years [was] an incredible character," recalled Giuseppe De Santis, "[especially in] his great ability to find money, always, anyway, and everywhere. . . . For example, he had become friends with a bank teller to whom he'd give movie tickets as though he'd gotten them for free, whereas he had actually bought them the normal way. And in exchange for such an act on the part of a director, the teller used to lend him all the money he needed, which he'd pay back when he could. (He was incredibly generous with me, he helped me like a father.)

"We were scripting *Desiderio* and one night were coming back from Diego Calcagno's. It was May 1, 1943, we were coming down the Aventine hill in a taxi on our way to our respective homes when a police patrol stopped us and asked for our papers. I didn't have my Fascist Party card. To be clear, I'd forgotten it, I'd left it in a drawer, because at that time the PCI (Italian Communist Party) had told us to work within the mechanisms of Fascism, to camouflage ourselves inside these organisms. . . . Anyhow, I didn't have the card and I could have run into trouble. Then intervened Rossellini who enjoyed great prestige with Vittorio Mussolini and the Fascist Federation and everything was smoothed over, since he freed me from any suspicion. . . .

"There wasn't a true and a sham Roberto. Roberto is all one, true from some points of view, false from others, a joker from still others. . . . He belonged to that great family of Cagliostros, like the Fellinis, like the great Mississippi gamblers, people who have great natural abilities plus the ability of getting themselves involved in things and always making out in them. . . . Yet it should be emphasized that Rossellini did it always with an enormous respect for other people and always with a great sense of generosity. I can't say as much for other, similar characters, but for Roberto I can. The number of people he's helped are infinite, including me when I was young."[1]

"I think," said Carlo Lizzani, "that the long chats in the *Cinema* office, the solidarity with Rossellini during the work on [*Desiderio*] . . . , when Giuseppe De Santis became [his] assistant, gave Rossellini a decisive push toward the choices he made. I don't mean that the same total understanding was created between our group and Rossellini as between us and Visconti, Zavattini, or De Sica. But comparisons exaggerate when they ignore that an understanding did exist. We began to feel Rossellini was one of us and to support him as soon as we saw certain scenes in *Un pilota ritorna* that were dry and incisive."[2]

Roberto had entered the film world sideways at the top, through family connections and boyhood friends. He had never been on more than the outer fringes of the leftist litterati at *Cinema* or the *Centro Sperimentale* where, besides filmmakers, writers, and painters like Purificato and Guttuso also gathered. Nonetheless they hoped to "bring him over," as when Mida, amid praise for *La nave bianca*, admonished that Rossellini would need to "persist with the humble world and simple characters" if he wanted to achieve "real success."[3]

These youths saw themselves as the cinema of the future. And they tried to formulate what that cinema should be. The "style to be created" would achieve a new artistic truth and sweep away centuries of rhetoric. *Cinema*'s agenda—which was also Fascism's and the inevitable result of the Liberals' widening of the franchise after the war—was to involve the popular classes and thereby transform Italy's mandarin culture. Most Italians were utterly uninvolved in the nation's life, culturally or politically; book readers were rare even among the middle classes. "It is difficult for an Italian writer to establish an intelligent relationship with his audience," remarked Moravia. "The reading public in all older societies used to be made up of the courtly section of the community. In Italy, it was not replaced by any other reading public, either bourgeois or popular.... The lack of a social climate, in which culture is a social fact, comes from the failure of our middle classes to establish a democracy in our country; a failure not only moral, but political, economic, and consequently, cultural as well."[4]

But the movies were one cultural medium that was speaking to all the people. Mightn't it be the means to the new society? No, said Mussolini, except for newsreels. Yes, said *Cinema*. "Follow the people!" was their slogan, but they wanted to lead. They were students and teachers, products of sophisticated literary educations, property owners rather than workers; many of them were Communists but their class values were represented in the regime. Fascism had a strong left wing, probably a majority, in favor of a socialist Fascism, shorn of militarism and repression and oriented toward the working classes.[5]

The Communist Party and America, along with certain writers and films, were their rallying points—because they represented (except for the Church) the sole energetic alternatives to the fascist Fascists. A new generation of writers—Cesare Pavese, Elio Vittorini, Vasco Pratolini (eventually dubbed "neo-realists")—were looking to America as a paradigm of democracy and progress and were striving to imitate Dos Passos, Hemingway, Steinbeck, Saroyan, Caldwell, and Faulkner, whose works were appearing in translation and were being taught at the Centro Sperimentale. The

Americans' unblinking concentration on the unflattering realities of everyday life, their populist revolutionary fervor, their direct, unrhetorical prose, looked poles apart from Fascism. The same was true of many Hollywood movies, King Vidor's in particular, and while Vittorio Mussolini was arguing that Italian movies should be more like American movies, his colleagues at *Cinema* were looking for inspiration from Giovanni Verga, a nineteenth-century novelist whose naturalism resembled the American writers. Instead of describing victorious armies, Verga wrote about the downtrodden people of the South, about adultery, hunger, and injustice, about men who became bandits out of despair, and he used language that mirrored his characters' own regional dialects and thought patterns. Verga wanted to remove the writer's personality in favor of "scientific" analysis of the bio-social determinants in which the characters struggled. (Thus the lamentable myth that "realism" is truth without an author.)

Nothing quite like Verga existed in Italian cinema, nothing so rigorously attentive to the lowest classes and corruption, unless one referred back to Martoglio's melodramatic 1914 *Sperduti in buio* (as De Santis often did). But in French cinema, in Carné and Duvivier and especially the friend-of-the-fellow-travelers Renoir (*Toni*, *La Chienne*, and *La Bête humaine*), there was a realism that seemed to presage the "style to be created": an attention to environment and how it influenced people, a refusal to make facile moral judgments, a loosely-knit narrative, and characters who did not appear to be acting. French films also had an additional attraction: "For a certain period American films were the ones one saw in public," Lizzani says, "whereas French films were seen in private, almost in secret. They had to be seen at Cineguf [the Fascist student movie club] or the Centro Sperimentale, because the great period of French realism was detested by the regime.... I remember that [Renoir's] *La Grande illusion* was a film we talked about trying to imagine what it was like."[6]

Roberto followed these events, saw the French films, read the American novels, listened to the discussions. It was an exciting time to be dreaming up a future cinema, a time of "the talks, the secret debates, the sort of cultural guerrilla warfare in which we believed with all our hearts ... in the years of *fronde* ... when we were young," as Carlo Lizzani puts it.[7] Alberto Lattuada showed Renoir's *La Marseillaise* at a Milan film club shortly before Italy declared war on France; some students applauded the French anthem, others hooted them down singing "Giovinezza," and the tumult reached such a point that Lattuada had to spend the night hiding in the prop room out of fear for his life. "Our enemies were precisely those who denied cinema the possibility of being art," Lizzani said.[8]

The chance came to put dreams into action when De Santis met Luchino Visconti. Visconti was a cultured Milanese aristocrat and heir to a castor oil and perfume firm (which had benefited greatly from Mussolini's exclusion of French products). But he had gone to France, shed his title, converted from Fascism to Communism, and worked under the fabled Renoir, designing costumes for *Day in the Country* and *Tosca*. He wanted to film Verga's *L'amante di Gramigna*, a story about Sicilian brigands, and was wealthy enough to finance it all by himself. He hired De Santis, Mario Alicata, Gianni Puccini, Pietro Ingrao, and Michelangelo Antonioni to collaborate on the script. They were all writing for *Cinema* and, Antonioni excepted, members of the PCI (Alicata was also the editor of *L'Unità*, the underground Party newspaper). But the Minister of Culture vetoed Verga. "No more bandits!" he scrawled on the script's cover, though there hadn't been any bandit movies yet. And Visconti decided to follow an old Renoir suggestion and adapt a minor American novel by James M. Cain, *The Postman Always Rings Twice*. (It had been filmed in 1939 in France by Pierre Chenal as *Le Dernier tournant*, and would be filmed subsequently in America in 1946 by Tay Garnett with John Garfield, and yet again in 1981 by Bob Rafelson with Jack Nicholson).

Visconti called his version *Ossessione* ("Obsession"). Its tale of an innkeeper's wife who seduces a drifter into murdering her husband displayed life's squalid side. It was set in smoky rooms, ugly suburbs, and the hostile, sad landscapes of the Po valley. A whore represented virtue and a homosexual liberty. Greed, malice, and selfishness, the film suggested, are natural factors in life.

Ossessione has gone down in history as an act of resistance against Fascist censorship and the Pollyanna values of the time, a legend its reception helped to create. Vittorio Mussolini slammed a door at the first screening (May 16, 1943) declaring "That's not Italy"; a minister labeled it degenerate; crowds railed against it in Bologna; a bishop was asked to bless a theater sullied by it in Salsomaggiore; and it was shown in only a few cities.

But the legend is specious. *Ossessione* was not anti-Fascist; it was hyper-Christian, seeing goodness where others saw filth and asserting cosmic morality. The Duce refused to suppress it (he never suppressed movies); the Rome premiere had been sponsored by ACI, Vittorio Mussolini's own company, and organized by Franco Riganti, for the explicit purpose of "removing any bureaucratic or censorship problems"[9]; and the film would have been produced by ACI, too, except that Visconti had demanded total control over even the budget ("It would have been suicide," said Riganti[10]). That *Ossessione* fared badly at the box office had little to do with Fascism, which fell from power shortly after *Ossessione* opened in Bologna and Genoa, little to do with the Germans, who allowed its Milan release in May 1944, and much to do with wartime audiences, who wanted escapist entertainment rather than depressing aestheticism. Two paeans to Fascism, *Vecchia guardia* and *Camicia nera*, had received equally poor distribution in the mid-thirties, for similar reasons. Vittorio Mussolini's opposition was aesthetic, not censorious, and was part of the debate at *Cinema*. He admired Renoir and supported Visconti, but he argued against European brooding and for Yankee practicality and optimism. He argued that French naturalist movies, of the sort *Ossessione* imitated, were jaded and flaccid, thus dangerous as models—in contrast to Hollywood, which, like Fascism, was youthful and fresh.[11] But young Vittorio's preferences were in no way a government directive. Not only was Vittorio at odds with staff at *Cinema* and the movies they preferred, but in *Bianco e Nero* Luigi Chiarini was free to rebut that French cinema represented life as it is, that politicians can try to change the way things are, but that art's duty is to present problems, not to solve them. Seeing that issue of *Bianco e Nero* on the Duce's table made the Minister of Culture tremble. But Mussolini said, "It's good for this magazine to pull my son's ears when he says stupid things. Ah, I really enjoyed this magazine." Concludes Chiarini: "A great, great deal of the dictatorship was due to people's cravenness; those who wanted to be independent, could be."[12]

Ossessione was less innovative than part of a trend.[13] *Cinema* was disgusted with escapist conventions and had been thirsting for movies that would capture the taste of actual life—the perennial refrain of critics everywhere. Yet veristic melodramas like *Ossessione* had been fashionable for half a century. Particularly in 1942–43, movies were dealing with working people, local customs, and social problems—such as Mattoli's *L'ultima carrozzella*, Blasetti's *4 passi fra le nuvole*, Bonnard's *Campo de' Fiori*, or De Sica's *I bambini ci guardano*, which chronicled the anguish of a small boy watching his parents' marriage break up, a supposedly taboo subject. War-time movies, rather than affirming middle-class values, were portraying their disintegration and searching for higher ideals—the opposite of what was occurring in America, where pictures like *Sergeant York* depicted killing the enemy as a wholesome Christian tradition.[14]

But, in keeping with its legend, *Ossessione*—partly for its populism, partly for its outrageousness, partly for its legend, partly because it did deal with certain "realities," and partly because its editor Mario Serandrei used the term "neo-realism" in a note to Visconti comparing it to French movies, but mostly because of the clique promoting it—has been said to have begun the "neo-realist movement." And the fact that the "Communist" Visconti was making *Ossessione* during the very months (starting June 1942) that the "Fascist" Rossellini was making *L'uomo dalla croce* (starting July 1942) has been taken as illustrative of the gulf of virtue separating the two filmmakers.

The comparison is invidious. Visconti was his own producer and financier, responsible only to himself, and rich enough not to be concerned if his film didn't earn back its cost. No other Italian filmmaker enjoyed such freedom, or even came close to the sort of dominance Capra, Ford, Sternberg, Hawks, or Lubitsch exercised in Hollywood. Rossellini did not have Visconti's option of setting up his own film company—although he would eventually do so. In 1942 he had to work within other people's structures. Oddly, it was the propaganda film that offered some degree of control and freedom. Its semi-documentary style was novel; it didn't require the lighting, acting, and story construction that audiences demanded (and still demand) in fiction films. And because it didn't require these things, it didn't require studio production, where they were best achieved, which meant that there were fewer bosses around watching what one was doing.

The cry for "realism" in cinema has usually been accompanied by a cry for freedom from industry structures, and not just in the war years or Italy. "We should make films as simply and straightforwardly as possible," wrote Leo Longanesi back in 1933, "films without artifice, shot without scripts, as much as possible filming real things. What our films lack is reality. We should go out onto the highways, carry the camera into the streets, into courtyards, into barracks, into garages. . . . It will be enough just to go out onto the street, to stop somewhere and observe what happens for half an hour, with attention and without preconceived ideas of style."[15] And John Ford was dreaming the same dream three years later in Hollywood: "Eventually . . . we'll go out to a Maine fishing port or to an Iowa hill and employ ordinary American citizens we find living and working there, and we'll plan a little story, and we'll photograph the scene and the people. That's all pictures should do anyway, and it'll be enough."[16]

This cry for simplicity and realism was only vaguely answered by what Visconti was doing. It was *Ossessione*'s "overall restraint and pictorial elegance," deriving from French naturalist cinema, that impressed Sarazani in 1945, when *Ossessione* finally opened commercially in Rome.[17] But *Ossessione* was not the style "to be created." "What sort of mental confusion makes people attach Visconti to a movement [neo-realism] that *Ossessione* preceded by two years?" asked Henri Langlois. "Visconti's art and Visconti himself belong to an entirely different discipline . . . : Italian classicism. . . . To separate [Visconti] the filmmaker from the [Visconti] who staged Chekhov, Pirandello, and Goldoni in the theater is to give up any possibility of understanding the originality of Visconti's art. . . . People tend to confuse neo-realism with the scenery of Italian life and to imagine that any film whose action is set there belongs to the same school."[18] *Ossessione* was "a typical manifestation of the culture opposed to Fascism" (within Fascism), cautions Mario Alicata, and ought not to be linked unthinkingly with neo-realism; before neo-realism would be born, whole chapters of Italy's history—the war, the Resistance, the liberation—still had to be experienced, which would create a new culture.[19]

Ossessione was a product of Italy's mandarin culture. So too was *I bambini ci guardano*, although its style is not so different from *Shoeshine* or *Bicycle Thieves*. But that difference, and not the older style, was what Casiraghi and Viazzi were referring to in 1942 when they wrote that "within a few years people [might] speak of an Italian school and, especially abroad, of a certain flavor; of an immediacy of execution; of a style and, perhaps, of a manner typically and purely Italian."[20] They were thinking not of *Ossessione* nor of anything related to American novelists, Verga, Renoir, the art history books, or socio-political agenda within which *Cinema* had been theorizing and Visconti filming; they were referring to a semi-documentary, De Robertis's *Uomini sul fondo*.

The "style to be created" never got created. *Ossessione* was a culmination of a tradition of painterly naturalism and melodrama, not the initiation of a new, iconoclastic realism. De Robertis and Rossellini, on the other hand, since they could not be integrated into the structures of *Cinema*'s version of art history, did seem to represent something different. They had an advantage. Free from the overtones of past culture, lacking the literary filters through which a Visconti viewed reality, unattached from any political movement, their mixture of reportage and novel could confront the present with a new eye. This is why *Cinema* had endorsed, rather than opposed, *L'uomo dalla croce*.

Desiderio

Ossessione's encouragement to air dirty linen and, even more, De Santis's influence on Rossellini, gave *Desiderio* its initial impetus. Rossellini was also connected to Visconti though marriage (Roberto's cousin Renzo Avanzo to Visconti's sister Uberta) and friendship (Roberto's sister Marcella with Uberta). But the two men loathed each other. Roberto could not abide Visconti's homosexuality and affectations of Marxism, and even took the position that a Milanese was not really an Italian. ("Lombardy and Piedmont are two regions that, for those born like me on this side of the line, are not part of the 'real' Italy. To us their inhabitants are, in some mysterious but undeniable way, like foreigners."[21]) For his part, Visconti was outraged when Giuseppe De Santis "defected" to Rossellini—"[He] wouldn't speak to me for some time and did everything to hinder the collaboration," said De Santis[22]—and Visconti later berated *Desiderio* as a "faithful copy" of *Ossessione*.[23]

This last charge is untrue, for De Santis was to leave the picture unexpectedly, and Rossellini, as usual, would throw away his script, alter the ending, and reshape the whole into the most seminal of his early pictures.

Desiderio ("Desire") had as its original title *Scalo merci* ("Freight yard"). Like Renoir's *La Bête humaine*, its setting was to be the railroad yards. But after the first day of shooting, July 19, 1943, a rewrite became unavoidable, for that morning the U.S. Army dropped 700 tons of bombs on the location, Rome's San Lorenzo Station. It was "a bad day to start a movie," said Roberto.[24] "We were shooting at the Titanus [studio]," said De Santis, "and Rossellini, Girotti, Elli Parvo, and I took refuge in a grotto."[25]

The planes flew in low in four waves starting at 11 A.M. and continuing for three hours. Anti-aircraft fire failed to shoot down even one plane, and many Romans cheered the bombs as they cringed in terror. Fourteen hundred were killed, six thousand wounded, most of them civilians. Vittorio Emmanuele III came to inspect the damage that afternoon. He found fires still burning and the wounded moaning on the ground: no one had taken charge. The people stared at the king in glacial silence. The bombing of Rome had come as a shock; it belied Roosevelt's personal promise to Pius XII. The Romans had thought themselves immune in their artistic city; now they took fright. The Duce was in Feltre that day, attending spellbound to Hitler's promises of ultimate victory and ignoring his generals' pleas to repudiate the German alliance, and the raid was intended to pressure the

Italians. But Mussolini had already lost his supporters' confidence. Massive Communist-organized strikes for peace had been plaguing industrial production since March, and the Allies, who had landed in Sicily on July 9, were encountering little opposition as they swept across the island. As long as Mussolini had kept the poor in check, guaranteed profits, and won easy victories, he had been supported by industry, Church, the civil service, and the army. But they had all been basically at odds with him and now the time had come to jettison him and try some other *combinazione*. Fascism had never been more than a temporary expediency, anyway: unlike Nazism and Soviet Communism, it had not altered the fundamental structures of society. Thus on July 25, around 10:45 at night, an announcement came over the radio that Mussolini had been dismissed by the king and replaced by Marshall Badoglio. "The war continues," the announcement concluded, but the crowds surging into the streets and tearing down fasces everywhere, paid little attention.

The next day, an undeclared holiday, it was hard to find a Fascist in Italy. Such *trasformismo* was not unprincipled opportunism or even mere necessity; it was simply a refusal to accept someone else's "principles" as binding upon them and their families. In De Santis's words, they "knew no lies."[26]

Most people had little belief in Fascism, in Roberto's opinion. They went along and responded to the regime's incentives. For example, raises were given to those who had children—"which encouraged people to fuck and people liked that a lot."[27]

If it was hard to find Fascists on July 26, it was also because Fascists had gone into hiding. Those who had not were hunted down in the streets. Many festering grudges were settled that day.

For Franco Riganti it was a business day like any other. He bicycled over to Via delle Vite where he was to meet Roberto, and found himself engaged by a passing acquaintance. "Let me shake your hand," the man declared. "There are few people in Italy today of your courage and principle. I am proud to know you."

Riganti held out his hand, puzzled. "Well, thank you. But, eh, might I ask what courage you're referring to?"

"Why, your lapel pin, of course."

Without realizing it, Riganti had grabbed a blazer with the Fascist pin attached. He could have been assaulted at any moment. Once his friend had gone, he quickly removed it.

Roberto arrived with a Christian Democrat pin in his lapel.[28] For Visconti, the transfer of loyalties from monarchism to Fascism to Communism had entailed orgies of conscience-wrestling. Roberto, who never bestowed loyalties to begin with, felt no such pangs; but today was an exception.

To avoid the bombs, however, he did some *trasformismo* on *Desiderio*: the parents his prostitute heroine returns to (in an attempt to recover her virtue in preparation for marriage) would now be a lumbering family in

Tagliacozzo rather than a railroading family in Rome. Tagliacozzo was in the Abruzzi mountains, sixty miles from the bombs, and Roberto had a friend, Zenobbi, who owned a woodmill in nearby Cucuzzo. So, after shooting interiors at Rome's Farnesina studio, he transported his troupe to a hotel in Tagliacozzo. Massimo Girotti, the male lead, was a veteran of both *Un pilota ritorna* and *Ossessione*. Elli Parvo, the female, was having an affair with Roberto, unbeknownst to Roswitha.

De Santis had quit the film for clandestine activities in Rome. A half-dozen parties outlawed by Mussolini were trying to form a shadow government to pressure Badoglio into a quick peace. But Badoglio and the Allies were dragging their negotiations, and the Germans, no fools, were moving divisions into Italy. When an armistice was finally announced on September 8, the Germans rode into Rome by one gate as the king and Badoglio fled south by another. The Army, left without leadership, orders, transport, or fuel, was quickly disarmed, and 700,000 soldiers were sent to German prison camps; only the Navy managed to transfer itself to the Allies. Mussolini was rescued and installed by Hitler in the town of Salò on Lake Garda, near Milan, as head of the neo-Fascist Repubblica Socialista Italiana. He was only a puppet trying to moderate the German occupation; he could have retired to Spain instead.

Naples, meanwhile, had suffered two hundred Allied bombardments. Every morning 300,000 people woke up not knowing where they would find anything to eat. Roberto had an 82-year-old painter friend, Ezechiele Quadrascioni, who camped out in a cave and went right on painting in the dark. Finally the city rose up, threw out the Germans, and handed itself over to the Allies. But the liberators regarded Italians as Nazi-Fascist enemies and the Allies' first act was to disarm the urban partisans. Soon, amid bombs, typhus, and water and food shortages, everything was for sale in the desperate city, including children and even the occupiers themselves: black soldiers in particular were made drunk, sold over and over, and progressively despoiled. The Germans withdrew to the Gustav Line, seventy miles south of Rome. Their idea was to fight a holding action; the Allies' idea was to tie down German troops; neither was trying to conquer. Italy had become a backwater battleground, its people hated by both sides, its fate to endure a long, painful rape. Mussolini's war had brought disaster to his people, but his downfall brought worse.

In Tagliacozzo Roberto tried to go on with his movie. When German patrols came by, Roswitha would smile reassuringly, and Roberto would turn on his charm and mention Vittorio Mussolini—and later brag how he had manipulated them. But his producer, Federigo D'Avack, had run out of money and, to raise more funds, was trying to sell the Germans movies he'd made with Miriam di San Servolo—whose sister and ticket to stardom was Claretta Petacci, the Duce's mistress. (Roberto had doctored the script of one of her D'Avack films, *L'Invasore*, a cape-and-sword adventure which was also stranded for lack of funds.)

D'Avack never showed up. Eventually the Tagliacozzo hotel ran out of patience, took away the mattresses, closed the kitchens, and seized the camera, film, and props. With nothing left to do, the troupe returned to Rome in a freight car. To pay them, Marcellina sold a diamond brooch her father had given her.

Desiderio was not completed until after the war, in the fall of 1945, and then not by Roberto, who had gone onto other things, but by his friend Marcello Pagliero (whose own unfinished 1943 film, *07... tassì*, would be completed by Alberto D'Aversa). Even then its troubles were not over. Two weeks after its release in August 1946, when it had already been demoted to second-run, the Catholic Cinema Center forced its withdrawal and had various sexual references eliminated before permitting its reissue, where-upon it passed unnoticed.[29] Released in New York as *Women* in 1950, it was dismissed as "a disjointed affair told at a pedestrian pace . . . obvious and . . . familiar."[30]

The first, and very much the better, half of the picture is Rossellini's.

> Paola Previtali (Elli Parvo) is a Milan call girl desperately unhappy with her life. A horticulturist offers marriage and a fresh start, but Paola decides first to go home to conceal her profession and recover respect-ability. There, however, in the Abruzzi mountains, her father refuses to speak to her, a former lover blackmails her for sex, and her sister's hus-band (Girotti) lusts after her. When her sister (Roswitha Schmidt), the only person to whom she has been close, tells her to go away, Paola real-izes that she cannot escape her past. Hours before her fiancé arrives, she throws herself from a bridge.

In De Santis's original script, Girotti plots to murder his wife (as in *Os-sessione*); the fiancé dies accidentally; and Paola returns in despair to Milan rather than killing herself. Rossellini's changes diminished *Desiderio*'s resem-blances to Visconti or Renoir and turned it into a peculiarly Rossellinian type of plot. Whether his milieu is a battleship-prison, a concentration camp, a Russian hut, the party life of a Milan call girl, or the middle-class values of her rural family, Rossellini's effect is the same: a society of constriction, perverted values, misery, and enslavement. And whether the central char-acter is a sailor, a flyer, a chaplain, or a whore, the drama is the same: the yearning of the downtrodden for freedom, virtue, happiness, and self-reali-zation. *Desiderio*'s linkage of milieu and character, so typical of Rossellini and so prominent, later, in "neo-realism" did not require *Ossessione*, natu-ralism, or even Jean Renoir as precedent; the linkage is there already in *La nave bianca*, in Stroheim, Murnau, and Vidor even earlier, and innately in Roberto's intense sensitivity to the world and people around him. Still, the desolately stunning scene of *Desiderio*'s Paola walking the barren Abruzzi hills, struggling homeward in hope of salvation yet doomed to friendless solitude, introduces something new, something that will be typical of post-war European thought. Past Rossellini heroes simply tried to preserve down-home idealism amid war's inhumanity; future heroes discover that such idealism has everywhere ceased to exist and must be reconstructed afresh, within themselves, alone. These new heroes do not choose heroism; they merely take the only route available. Not until they feel themselves crushed; not until absolute solitude is forced upon them; not until their world of family, friends, and moral values has turned alien, confining, and suffocating do they become desperate. They thrash about looking for answers or anchorage, but find only miscomprehension and, worse, a void, into which they thrust themselves, because only there can they be true to their new sense of self and find peace in death or transfiguration.

Rossellini's refusal to believe that solutions can be found *through* society (in which he resembles Vidor) was fashionable when "society" meant Fascist, as in *Desiderio*. But it would lead him into difficulties once the war was over and "society" meant what "Fascism" had meant: the beautiful new world everyone was pitching in to build. To the left, who suspected that earthly paradise might be attained by fine-tuning society's material conditions, Rossellini would eventually become irrelevant, even anathema. To Catholics, too, Rossellini's "despair of history"[31] would be troubling. Yet the suicides and flights of insanity that will climax so many Rossellini pictures strike us not as statements of nihilism, but as affirmations of some smoldering fire that burns within and redeems, by its rebellion, even the most corrupted society.

There is much more movement of camera and actors in *Desiderio* than in *La nave bianca* or *Un pilota ritorna*. "One stylistic problem in which we were all very involved was that of movement within the shot," Lizzani recalled. "Every breakdown of action into separate shots seemed like a prison to us, and each of us tried in our own way to pass from one 'cut' to another without cutting, to connect different 'scenes' with the same meaning in the same shot."[32] But even more than motion, it's a sense of vitality and depth of feeling that distinguish Rossellini's sections of *Desiderio* from Pagliero's tepid and more realistic scenes. Indeed, the contrast with Pagliero makes it apparent how subjective and poetic—how much *more* than "real"—is Rossellini's "realism." Reality for him is not the world of objects but the world of feelings which brute reality reflects. And these feelings come through best, not by heavy-handed symbolism (like the hearse Paola meets as she walks homeward—a literary, Viscontian touch, redundant in its implications), but rather by oxymoronic juxtaposition (as when Paola, worn out by moral lassitude, falls asleep in the greenhouse surrounded by plants and filtered luminosity). Rossellini never allows "things to speak for themselves," despite what critics claim. The loveless severity of the home in the Abruzzi, the gay innocence of Anna's wedding, even the desire-laden stares of the characters, are never *just* staged and filmed (as Pagliero does), but rather their emotions are highlighted by Rossellini's lighting, cutting, and choice of the most invasive camera angle possible. Rossellini's defenders have praised his "almost magical ability to catch in the air the profound sense of his time"[33]; but the reality Rossellini grasps is one he himself creates.

Paola is the first full-fleshed character in Rossellini, and it is with *Desiderio* that we first perceive artistic depth in his movies. Perhaps this is so because Rossellini, all of whose characters are oppressed and suffering, is better able to express sympathy for women; his men are almost always more theoretic, less empathetic. Or perhaps it was Pagnol who nudged him beyond documentary. *Marius* (1930), *Angèle* (1934), and *La Femme du boulanger* (1938), Roberto claimed, were "neo-realism before the fact." Before he saw these Pagnol movies, in Italy before the war, he had expected every film—*and life as well*—to follow the D'Annunzian model of a man, a woman, and a rival—all trading words of burning passion. "Pagnol turned me topsy-turvy. His films hit me like a fantastic gust of truth."[34] Roberto experienced Pagnol's characters as warm, sensual creatures who pulsed and perspired, and suddenly realized what he had known all along: that people in real life are like the people in Pagnol. Roberto now experienced the people around him in a new way. He had learned a valuable lesson.

Visual artists, like dime novelists, usually find their techniques of depicting people by imitating the techniques of their predecessors and by imitating life as well. Rare in history is the artist who learns to draw a human hand by starting with a hand, rather than with a picture of a hand. They copy the picture, because the picture already possesses "conventional" realism: everyone agrees that the picture looks like a hand, regardless of whether a hand looks like the picture. Thus, in effect, conventional realism is reality, the reality we live in. If we can draw a hand a different way, and get people to accept it, we can create a new reality to live in. Roberto, late in life, would make a stupendous film (*The Age of the Medici*) recounting the boldest attempt of this sort in human history: the Renaissance invention of perspective—as a means of reshaping our reality.

Occupation

Marcellina had moved back to Rome in 1942 and taken an apartment on Via Lima. Roberto would come Sundays to lie in bed and play with the boys, but Marcellina never again consented to sex.

After Rome was bombed, she took the children to Ladispoli. Zia Fortù was no longer there. She had died, wrote Renzo, "with the years of Methuselah, by falling off her [1890] bicycle, which she was so insanely jealous of. Coming down the hill from Cerveteri with her legs unable to keep up with the frenetic whirl of the pedals, she took a curve at a fantastic velocity and ended up banging her head into a curb stone. Knowing her, I can say she would have laughed heartily at her spectacularly ridiculous accident."[35]

There were no bombs in Ladispoli, but the Germans arrived in September. Marcellina phoned Roberto and followed his advice. She rented the house to a "very civil" German colonel for 12,000 lire a year—the Germans were requisitioning houses in any case—and left with the boys for Tagliacozzo.

She found Roberto's sister Marcella and Visconti's sister Uberta already there. The two friends had come in August and already Germans were everywhere. Luchino Visconti and Renzo Avanzo had been put to work as street cleaners. To escape the Germans, Uberta had hired a man and his car and gone looking with Roberto for a village without Germans. As they drove along a hillside, a squadron of American planes had appeared and began diving toward them. Deaf as a doorknob, their driver had continued placidly on his way. When at last their frantic shouts had made him stop, they had jumped into a ditch.

Uberta found a house in nearby Verrecchie and stayed three months, giving lessons to local children to pay her keep and aiding American and German soldiers trying to escape. Girotti and his wife were in the house as well, along with Marcella and Roberto, and now Marcellina and the children. Roberto had insisted on having the only room with a bathroom—on the balcony outside—and soon regretted it, because the whole house was perpetually going through his room. But he himself had been perpetually coming and going, no one knew why or where, as had been his habit since his teens.

What he concealed from the ladies—as a matter of good manners—was that he was living a second existence not too far away with Roswitha. Roswitha was going by the name Roswitha Rossellini and not until decades later would either Roswitha or Marcellina learn that the other had been in Tagliacozzo. The Roswitha-Roberto home was a flea-infested wooden silo up the mountain from the Zenobbi family, near Avezzano. The Zenobbis also supplied polenta, a mule on which to ride down to Tagliacozzo, and two pet ducks to keep Roswitha company when Roberto went off. Roswitha had "the eyes of a cat but a heart of marzipan," De Angelis recalled, and was "very well known at Tagliacozzo for her love for the young ducklings, whom she fed and nursed as if they were human babies."[36] A German colonel befriended her too, as a fellow German, and from time to time would call on her to interpret. He was unaware that three English soldiers were hiding farther up the mountain in a charcoal hut linked by telephone to the silo. When snow came and the English shivered in their short pants, Roswitha and Roberto found blankets and invited them for a rough sort of dinner. Two were brothers captured in North Africa who had been interned in different camps and had met on the road after escaping. The third had an infected leg. Roberto had gotten some spaghetti from Marcellina which he had cooked with garlic, oil, and peperoncino, and he was just putting it on the table when the door opened and a German patrol appeared. Notices had just been posted that any Italian caught helping an escaped prisoner would be shot on the spot.

The three Englishmen were sitting at the table in their uniforms. A German officer was standing in the snowy doorway with his long, grey-green raincoat, silver pendant, and machine gun. Roberto was standing holding the bowl of spaghetti.

He put down the bowl and threw his arms around the German. He embraced him, squeezed him, and slobbered uncontrollably for mercy.

The German didn't understand Italian. He thought Roberto was an insane homosexual, pushed him off violently, and asked the way to Cappadocia.

Roberto, recovering, pointed the way with his hand, and the officer went back out into the snow without asking to stay and rest. In the dimly lit room, he hadn't seen the Englishmen.

"Two or three times during the war," he commented later, "I had the taste of real fear in my mouth. It has a special taste."[37]

Roberto had been making frequent trips to Rome with a jeep and armed driver lent him by the Germans. Ostensibly he was bringing back movies for them to see; he brought back supplies for the English soldiers as well. He was not, though, the sort to enlist with the partisans; he never had a military man's courage and, in any case, had a family and Roswitha to provide for. One reason Marcellina came to Tagliacozzo with the children in the first place was to try to escape across the mountains to the Allies. And later, at Christmas, Renzo Avanzo and Luchino Visconti would manage to escort some POWs to safety. But the route was too perilous.

After the Germans came, Roberto moved Marcellina to a second mountain hut, with a family so poor the mother counted out the beans before cooking them. Her sons were soldiers who had come home after their units dissolved. In October, Roberto took Marcellina, Renzino, and Romano back to Rome in a truck. He himself stood on the running board all the way, hanging onto a window, scanning the skies. At each sign of a plane, he would make the truck stop and they would run and hide in the bushes.

In Rome, Marcellina stayed with her parents for a few days until Roberto installed her and the boys in a Spanish convent on Via San Sebastianello, just off Piazza di Spagna. A convent was safe from bombing, in theory. Marcellina stayed for nine months, quite comfortably, in a large sunny room with three beds. She could take the boys to the Villa Borghese, which was right behind the convent, or go play bridge at friends' houses. When sirens sounded, the Via del Tritone tunnel, which was a few blocks away, filled with refugees. The convent was filled with women and children, all of whom went to Mass every evening—except for Marcellina, who had been asked not to come because Romano was so irrepressible a pest. Not until after Rome was liberated did she discover that "Anna" was actually Esther and "Maria" actually Rachele. They were all Jews. "One can pray to God anywhere, anytime," they told her, "even in a Christian church. We were guests, we were being saved from deportation."[38]

In Tagliacozzo, Roberto spent his time reading, novels sometimes, history mostly. He carried his father's picture everywhere, Roswitha recalls, and would press it to his forehead, then bow down to earth and up to heaven. They never discussed politics.

The German colonel, however, was determined to save Roswitha. His regiment had been ordered to the north, to Salò; politely and kindly, he offered to take her along, and was puzzled by her reluctance to return to Hitler's full protection. She was in love with Roberto, she protested. The colonel was scandalized. Inconceivable that a good German could be in love with an Italian!

"Love is international," she joked.

"Well, you can leave him and come with us."

"But I'm engaged!"

"You're not married?" More scandal.

"No," she replied, enjoying his discomfort. "You see my fiancé is still married."

The colonel became really upset. "Well, all the same," he decided finally, "I will still afford you this exceptional opportunity to retreat with us. You can even bring your Italian along!"

He departed thinking she had agreed.

She and Roberto went back immediately to Rome, to the Via Parco Pepoli apartment, and fell asleep in the unaccustomed comfort of their own home, satisfied they had eluded the privilege of going to Salò.

But in the middle of the night came a banging on the door that wouldn't stop. Roswitha struggled awake—Roberto was dead to the world—and called out: "Who's there?"

It was a German sergeant. They were to come down immediately, and bring their things. The colonel was waiting, with his regiment.

Roswitha got Roberto together somehow, threw everything into bags, to make it look as though they were leaving for good. Outside the colonel greeted her cordially and escorted them to a truck. The column started through Rome, heading north. It was 5 A.M.

Late that evening they arrived in Gardone, near Salò. The colonel was terribly pleased to have been so helpful. They thanked him profusely, waved as his column drove off, crossed the road, and hitchhiked back to Rome.[39]

The years 1942 and 1943 had been the most prosperous ever for the Italian film industry. One hundred twenty-two films had been produced in 1942, six times as many as in 1935, and the number of admissions, 470 million, had almost doubled. In 1943, despite the fall of Mussolini, invasions by both Allies and Germans, and the outbreak of civil war, 72 films had been made before everything had shut down. So important were movies that one of the first actions of the neo-Fascist state in Salò was to relocate the film industry to the north, in a "Cinevillaggio" near Venice. Luigi Freddi, Mussolini's film czar, had started phoning stars and directors on September 8—the first day of the armistice and German occupation. Many filmworkers dutifully reported and would produce seventeen films in 1944 and four in 1945. Many others refused to go, went into hiding, or fled: among them, Mario Soldati, Dino De Laurentiis, Riccardo Freda, Alida

Valli, and Renato Castellani. There was a general panic, in fact, for with the German occupation Fascists who had vanished July 25 reappeared to settle scores and avenge insults. Blood was flowing.

Pressure was put on leading names by the Minister of Culture. In Vittorio De Sica's case, Goebbels's undersecretary summoned him directly.

"I can't go," he replied. "I'm making a film for the Vatican."

"Ah!" said the undersecretary, bowing his head with respect.

No one knows why the Vatican, just at this time, decided to finance producer Salvo D'Angelo's *La porta del cielo* ("Heaven's gate"), a movie about sick pilgrims travelling by train to Loreto in hope of a miracle. But the Vatican had what no one else had—film stock—and could provide church basements to shoot in, sheltered from the bombings. Its liaison included Monsignor Giovanni Montini, the future Pope Paul VI.

Maria Mercader, the star, insisted that De Sica, her lover, direct the film, and the Vatican made no objection. De Sica had broken with his wife Giuditta Rissone years before, but the irregularity of his situation had continued to perturb him, particularly the specter of his young daughter Emy not finding her parents in bed together. His habit had been to start every night in his wife's bed, slip over to Mercader's once Emy was asleep, and return to his wife before Emy awoke. (Emy, naturally, knew what was going on.)

La porta del cielo began filming that September in St. Paul's Basilica. Work went slowly because no one wanted to finish while the Germans were still in the city, and under the cover of the production the Basilica gradually became a refuge for almost 3,000 people. De Sica tried to maintain the site's dignity, but the priests were soon finding condoms in the confessionals.

Cinema, with Vittorio Mussolini gone, had become a center for revolution. Carlo Lizzani relates how "many meetings were held at my house around the start of September with members of the Party directorate of the [Committee for National Liberation], and you can imagine my emotions in front of these personages, their talks and their plans, which were also military plans to organize the struggle against the Germans. . . . Then came September 8 and even my house became dangerous. The real, actual Resistance began then, and I had my baptism of fire with two other guys one night when we were writing the names of Rosa Luxemburg and Karl Liebknecht [leaders of the 1919 Communist revolt in Berlin] on walls, for the sake of German soldiers who might remember them! Five minutes before midnight we were on our way home when two SS cars blocked our path. My hands were covered with red paint, and I had the presence of mind to raise them and rub them in the face of the German who had his machine gun on me, knocking it aside. Profiting from the confusion, we ran separately down three different side streets and they didn't manage to catch us."[40]

*

When Roberto got back to Rome after his trip to Salò (probably in December), his position was precarious. For one thing, he had been good friends with Freddi before the war and had refused the summons to work for the Fascists in the north. For another, a personal vendetta had been undertaken against him by a Fascist whose name or reasons have not come down to us, but upon whom Roberto later modeled the Tarcisio character in *Era notte a Roma.* "I had to hide from him for months. He was crippled and that gave me some insight into his psychology, which gave rise to the character in the film."[41]

At first Roberto and Roswitha lived in Alberto Consiglio's apartment. Roberto was scared to return to his own home. He had gone to Via Parco Pepoli and had seen the concierge across the street, and the man had signaled him—he only had one hand—to meet him down the block. Roberto had followed him at a distance until they were far enough from the house, and the concierge had warned him, "Whatever you do, don't go home! They're after you, they've come several times for you."[42]

For Roberto and Roswitha, months of wandering began. They changed addresses almost every day—by five o'clock, when the curfew began and they had to be off the street. "The main thing was not to stay in the same house, because if someone saw me it was really very dangerous. There were a lot of police, Fascist police, normal police, German police, volunteer groups."[43]

"Believe me," he told students at Yale thirty years later, "when you have passed through fear, you can have a lot of resentment. It's really difficult to forget fear, to forget you were hunted like an animal, not anymore like a human being."[44]

Food was one reason Roberto had placed his wife and children in the convent. Since convents were supplied by the Vatican, they were the only places one could be sure of eating adequately. Up until Mussolini's fall, despite hard rationing elsewhere, Romans had still been able to eat gloriously in restaurants, but now there was little to be had, even with money—which hardly anyone had—and everyone lost weight. Roberto, wandering from house to house, lost fifty to seventy pounds but from fear more than the scarcity of food. He was using a phony ID card with the name of someone in Florence, and so could not get ration coupons. It was winter and a cold one, too, for the city had little coal or charcoal. To keep people docile and terrorized, the Germans were apt at any moment to descend on some neighborhood street and "rake up" all the men they found—a *rastrellamento.* Some would be released after a night or two, others sent to labor gangs in Germany, others "questioned" by the dreaded Gestapo in Via Tasso. Roberto saw Massimo Mida on Via Nizza one day, embraced him hurriedly, and said he couldn't stay with him. He was too scared, he explained, because Mida's brother Gianni Puccini was in jail and Mida could be arrested at any moment. Mida laughed.[45]

In January the Americans landed at Anzio. The news was all over the city instantly. The Germans had been taken completely by surprise. The road to Rome was clear. Anzio was only 35 miles away. The Americans would arrive at any minute.

But the incredible happened. For days, the Americans sat watching on the beach, while the Germans occupied the high ground above them and boxed them in.

Surely, it was nonetheless expected, the Americans would break loose any day. But what would happen then? Would Rome become another Stalingrad? And what about the Americans? They regarded Italians as enemies. Their bombs were falling on women and children, even once on the Vatican itself, and everyone had heard how their artillery had bombed away at little villages in the South, destroying everything even when the Germans had evacuated them days before. The inhabitants would risk their lives to go tell the American soldiers they were wasting their ammunition, but the Americans wouldn't believe them. They thought it was a trap. They snickered when Italians protested they had been hoping for liberation for years.

As everyone waited, Rome was unnaturally quiet. Cars and buses were few, and even bicycles had been banned as a potential threat.

Bicycles became tricycles, which hadn't been banned, by the addition of a small training wheel. And bartering became the city's life. Roberto would ride around on his "tricycle" with clothes, shoes, clocks, and Marcellina's jewelry. He needed to pay the nuns for keeping Marcellina and the children and to get food for himself and Roswitha. When he ran into a friend, they would swap wares—a necktie for some handkerchiefs—so that each of them could offer a variety of items. When Marcella took advantage of the black market for cigarettes, Roberto lectured her severely.

One night, walking down from Monte Savello, Roberto was stopped by two policemen. There had just been a *rastrellamento* and Roberto was one of the last to be nabbed. He handed over his phony papers and one of the policemen pocketed them, and said, "Come with us."

They started down toward Via del Mare, to a police station 300 yards away, and Roberto began discussing the situation in the tones of an upper-class, cultivated gentleman. "I understand you're obliged to verify my identity. You are doing your job. But, you know, I was just on my way to see my children and give them a thousand lire that I managed to find for them. Since I'm not going to be able to give it to them myself, would you be willing to take it, and get it to them in my place?"

The policeman on his right took the money.

They walked on a few dozen yards. "And for my partner?"

"You can search me," replied Roberto. "It's a miracle I had that!"

They walked on. The police station was only a few feet away. Just as they got there, the policeman said, "Keep walking straight ahead." He was free.[46]

In this way, Roberto and Roswitha passed the months of November, December, January, and February. He was 36. Friends would give them an address where they could sleep. "I'd arrive around five o'clock in homes of people absolutely unknown to me and we'd spend the night together playing cards and become very good friends and swear to be friends the rest of our lives. (I've never seen them again.)."[47]

Often he didn't know in the morning where he'd lie down that night. While waiting to find out, he'd walk around the whole day long, until the curfew at five. Without a ration card, he resorted to picking dandelions near the Baths of Caracalla, where they were plentiful. Once indoors, he'd ask his hosts to let him boil them. But there was never any salt. He developed a skin irritation which he called "famine leprosy."

All the while, there were bombing raids and contradictory rumors about the Americans. "They're coming!" "No, they're not!"

In March, tired of wandering from house to house and sick of boiled dandelions without salt, Roberto and Roswitha decided to risk going home and getting a bath. Water was severely rationed, but each apartment had a tank on the roof. They waited until just before curfew, then sneaked in quickly.

"I'd left a cat there. When she saw me come back, she was all over me. But the neighbors had taken all my water, so I wasn't able to wash, and I threw myself on the bed to sleep. Toward ten, the cat was in heat, and I began to feel the taste of fear in my mouth, fear that the meowing would attract all the Fascists and Germans in Rome to my house. I put her outside and she meowed even more. I looked around for some valerium, and gave her some, but she went on meowing even worse. Something had to be done, so with the help of a toothpick dipped in hot water I fashioned a little tail and with this all the rest of the night I masturbated the poor beast, who continued to moan, on and on, in her strange language of desire and suffering. A night of hell! Curfew lifted at seven and I didn't wait a minute more to slip into the street and flee in utter terror. That was the most terrifying night of my life. Ten years later I learnt by chance that valerium is an aphrodisiac for cats."[48]

The terror reached its apex on March 23, 1944. Partisans exploded a bomb in Via Rasella, near Roberto's favorite whorehouse and favorite restaurant,[49] killing 32 patrolling Germans. In reprisal, 335 Italians were taken the next day to an abandoned quarry, the *Fosse Ardeatine,* and in its caves executed one by one with shots in the back of their heads. The caves were sealed with mines, but a victim's son dug in with his hands and spread the news.

Renewed arrests followed all over Rome. Roberto was out trying to sell an overcoat when he was stopped and made to line up with others. Trembling with fear, he thrust the rolled-up coat into the arms of the German guarding him, and escaped into the entrance of the building behind him. By luck it was a building Zeffiro had owned and he knew it well.

Fellini, typically embroidering this or a similar incident, claimed to have been arrested himself on October 23, 1943, but to have pretended to recognize a Wehrmacht officer and embracing him crying "Fritz! Fritz!"

and then, after the truck had gone, to have apologized to the officer for mistaking him for someone else.[50]

Collective misery promoted solidarity. In the afternoons, the variety theaters were popular. At five, people would gather in a friend's kitchen—the only room likely to have a bit of warmth—and start partying. The Occupation was a season of fear and deprivation, but it was also a period of prodigious community and euphoric dreams.

With little to do but read, listen, barter, and dream, Roberto was in the process of idealizing the sort of films he wanted to make, toward which *Desiderio* had been pointing. In the meantime, he decided to write a novel, purchased some paper, and phoned a writer friend, Raoul Maria De Angelis, who had been at Tagliacozzo, to find out how to go about it. De Angelis did not believe such things could be taught, and he thought Roberto rather flighty in any case. But, seduced by Roberto's ingenuous trust, he was soon discoursing on time, intrigue, characters, feelings, catharsis, and so on, and illustrating these concepts with examples from Flaubert, Tolstoy, and Stendhal. "Rossellini listened with reverent attention," De Angelis remembers, "and then concluded that writing a novel that way was difficult and that he would have to find another formula, would have to invent another technique, one more similar to that of movies and American novels—which he seemed much more familiar with than I would ever have suspected.

"'I need,' he told me in so many words, 'a depth of field that probably only the cinema can provide. I need to see people and things from every side, and to be able to use cuts and ellipses, dissolves and inner monologues. I don't mean like Joyce, but like Dos Passos. To take things out or leave them alone, or to insert something near an action which might be its distant cause. I'd use the camera to follow a character obsessively: contemporary anguish derives precisely from this inability to escape the lens' implacable eye. Do you agree?'

"Indeed, I agreed so much that, sick to death of the impersonal eighteenth-century sort of novel, in which the maximum of bravura was achieved with the maximum of distance, I was already at work on a novel (that later became *Panche gialle*) constructed with as much arbitrariness as I could manage. . . . Only by means of the arbitrary can one infallibly show the hundred different ways in which a single reality is capable of appearing.

"'But don't you also think,' Rossellini added, 'that in letting the character go wherever he wants, there's a risk of seeing him disappear around the first corner? He has to be followed, his movements and lines have to be controlled, he has to be reduced to impotency; otherwise we run into trouble. The camera inserts itself between the character's destiny and the plot's necessity, determining a new fatalness. Have you understood me completely? Why don't you try a novel like this too? With more stories, linked together by memory, time, space, a different "continuum," with four or five dimensions. In cinema it can be done. I shall do it.'

"'You'll do it,' I said, "but with words it's impossible. Not that I won't try. In fact, to tell you the truth, I've already started. In the first chapter . . .'

"He interrupted me. 'This neo-realist current is all very well, but it has one essential defect: it's too much newsreel. Tragedy doesn't mean a black newsreel-look. Comment is needed, an arbiter; the crowd can be used like a chorus, with an individual in the foreground, voices and echoes in the background. The night is not made only of stars, and a city at night doesn't live through neon signs alone. If a character is followed as I say, it becomes a special sort of surveillance: his anguish explodes then. Don't misunderstand me: I'd like to give you some examples.'

"'*Le jour se lève*,' I suggested [Carné's film].

"'It's a good example, but it's not enough for me.' (Perhaps he was thinking [ahead to] the ruined German houses in *Deutschland im Jahre Null*, to scenery commenting more powerfully than could a thousand masques on the common tragedy of man and city.)

"'You need more space?'

"'Not in the sense of bigger and smaller. I need greater depth.'

"'We all do,' I protested.

"'Agreed,' Rossellini consoled me. 'And now go on about your novel.'

"And so it was that I did not teach the director Rossellini to write novels with words. It was he, on the contrary, who gave me an advance look at a few of the tricks of his singular technique, convincing me that cinema and novel are developing together, and will be ever more interrelated."[51]

Evidently, Roberto's attitude toward movies had changed a lot from his purely technical exercises with fish and airplanes. What had brought about this change? What had made him aspire to art?

He had spent the Occupation listening. It was unlike Roberto to be so quiet. Yet sitting with legs crossed and head back, with his fingers twisting a lock of hair behind his ear, he would listen to conversation of a sort he had never experienced before. At Gaston Medin's on Via Gregoriana there was Ivo Perilli, whose film *Ragazzo* had the distinction of being the sole film ever to be refused a censor's visa,[52] and who could remember every book he had read in his entire life, an ability that had made him an invaluable collaborator on more than a hundred movies. (As chief scenarist, however, he was to be avoided at all costs, for he could not resist taking the plots and characters of four or five different books and trying to combine them. He would construct immense narrative puzzles—and then get hopelessly lost in them.)

More important were the long nights spent at Amidei's, where artists, writers, filmmakers, and the Communist Party's leading lights sat conversing. Roberto discovered, said Pajetta, "that a Communist worker who had done seven years of jail was perhaps the most interesting person he had ever encountered: rich with a culture the director had only heard of (and then only vaguely)."[53] This was Celeste Negarville, a Communist military expert Amidei had known in Turin. Negarville had been jailed by the Fascists in 1927 and released in a general amnesty in 1934, then had run the Paris office of the PCI for a year, and in Moscow had served in the presidium of the International of Young Communists. In September 1943, he had come to hide out in Amidei's apartment as the PCI representative to the military command of the Committee for National Liberation. Negarville had a proletarian roughness about him and approached politics with an élan that almost seemed cynical, yet none of this clashed with a taste for culture and art and a vague cosmopolitan air. Rossellini modeled *Roma città aperta*'s partisan hero on him, and used his alias, "Gino," for another partisan in the same film. After the war Negarville became a minister and then returned to Turin as its mayor.

Amidei was not himself a member of the Party. But Negarville's presence attracted others to his home: Renato Guttuso, who became one of Italy's leading artists; Giorgio Amendola, who headed Rome's Communists, had been a movie buff in exile in Paris, and had known Roberto at the Nazareno school; Mario Alicata, the energetic, charismatic editor of *L'Unità*; Pietro Ingrao, the Centro Sperimentale graduate who went on to become president of Parliament; and even Palmiro Togliatti, the legendary head of the PCI, who slept at Amidei's when he returned to Rome toward the end of the war. Italy's Communist leaders were men of deep culture, hypnotic charm, and inspiring compassion. Roberto would sit listening with the same outward detachment he gave Perilli; but he absorbed everything like a sponge. It was Amidei in particular (according to many who knew Roberto) who got him to understand the "humanistic approach"—the social and political role an artist might play.[54]

Sergio Amidei had been born October 30, 1904, in Trieste, then part of the Austrian-Hungarian Empire. As Italians, he and his family had been interned in a concentration camp during World War I and afterward had moved to Turin. Yet Amidei always looked back nostalgically on his middle-European origins, found Southern ways alien, and liked to consider himself an Austrian exiled in Italy. His youth was rather Bohemian. He attended university for a bit, worked in a factory where he formed close friendships with Communist unionists, joined a third-rate theater troupe, and at age twenty drifted into cinema as a jack of all trades: writer, actor, grip, and at one point even director, until, in a typical outburst of his famous and fiery temper, he threw everything he had shot into a furnace. The Turinese film industry was wiped out by Hollywood in the late 1920s (along with virtually the whole of Italian cinema). But talkies were coming in and Amidei packed two silent films in one suitcase, a phonograph and some sound-effects records in another, and, keeping his secrets closely guarded, embarked on a tour of the South, where he presented his "sound movies" in little villages where real talkies had not yet arrived. In 1936, as we saw, he settled in Rome and met Rossellini. By the time the war began, he had established himself as a good adapter of novels and was in demand by top directors. He valued precision and structure in his work and prided himself on being a skilled artisan who could fashion anything on demand. His serious political formation (a rare thing in Italy, where everyone dabbles in politics), his theatrical background, and his Austrian heritage added up to enormous experience and had a significant impact on Rossellini.

Copies of *L'Unità* and all the other democratic papers were kept hidden at Amidei's, awaiting distribution by scores of volunteers—Marcella Mariani Rossellini and Uberta Visconti among them. "[We felt] a bit hunted," Amidei recalled, "but, except for a few incidents, [there was] very little fear, considering that the police almost certainly knew everything and would have arrested us if they had wanted to."[55]

Toward the end of winter, when danger seemed more imminent, the Communists left. Then came the police, who searched Amidei's apartment and confiscated the gold bars Amidei had prudently purchased a few years earlier. Amidei himself fled across the roof—his apartment was on the top floor of 51 Piazza di Spagna—and hid on the roof of the building next-door, the Spanish embassy to the Vatican.

The get-togethers continued in other quarters. Alicata recalls Roberto and Amidei taking part in a series of "very impassioned meetings" that tried to formulate "a sort of declaration by progressive intellectuals, less as part of the anti-Fascist struggle than as a cultural program of the Resistance to be developed at the moment of liberation."[56] The new buzzword was "national-popular cultural," which was what Italy did not have, which was why Italy had succumbed to Fascism, which was now defined as warfare by the industrial class against the working class.[57] The Liberals' experiment of imposing progressive ideas from the top down had failed, partly because Crocean thinking lacked moral absolutes and was thus "involuted" (another buzzword)—in the sense that Liberal response to Fascism had been meditation rather than action.[58]

The new thinking that Roberto heard so earnestly being discussed around the kitchen stove had its source in Antonio Gramsci, a sickly, hunchbacked dwarf who had risen from abject poverty in Sardinia to leadership of the Italian Communist Party and martyrdom in Mussolini's prisons where, despite constant insomnia, headaches, angina, gout, and tuberculosis, he had penned piles of notebooks of social and literary commentary. Combining Croce and Marx, he created the Euro-Communism of the rest of the century. The "hegemony" (rulership) of one class over others was due not solely to economics but to many cultural factors. Revolution is intellectual and emotional rather than materialist. "Every revolution," he wrote, "has been preceded by hard critical thinking, the diffusion of culture, and the spread of ideas among men who are at first unwilling to listen, men concerned only with solving their private economic and political problems."[59]

The way to convert Italians to Communism, Gramsci argued, was to respect Catholicism while forging alliances between the working classes and the intellectuals and artists. Thus would be created a culture both national *and* popular—the only sort of culture capable of abolishing exploitation.

Ideas rule people; change ideas, change hegemony.[60]

Roberto had always felt that movies were important. Now it came home to him that he himself had responsibility in society, and that he could fulfill that responsibility by telling the stories of the people around him. But he preferred existential search to the left's sociology; he was more interested in the "involution" preceding action.

His friends on the left, moreover, saw Roberto neither as one of their own nor as an artist. He was charming, yes, with streaks of brilliance and a dazzling ability to find money and make things happen. No one had seen *Desiderio*, and no one knew what was passing through Roberto's soul that winter. As De Angelis remarks, Rossellini's depth would come as a revelation even to those who liked and respected him.

The Resistance activities in Rome were part of a vaster national movement. Before Mussolini's fall, the left had been organizing workers and students, the Catholics had been working on women and peasants, and the Liberals on the king. As uneasy as they were with each other (for Fascism's attempt to transcend Italy's ancestral divisiveness had ended in exacerbating it), they had been united in their opposition. By the spring of 1943 they had succeeded in sabotaging the war and igniting universal disaffection. Even the Vatican curia, where twenty old cardinals had died, now dreamed of an international Christian Democrat bloc and a purge of pro-Fascist priests.

The Allies, however, were still refusing to recognize the Committee of National Liberation, only begrudgingly employed a few brigades of the regular Italian army, and sometimes behaved as though they wished all the partisans would just go home. A lot of Italians wished the same. Citing the Via Rasella massacre, they argued that the Resistance brought about civilian reprisals without advancing victory.

At Guadalajara in Spain, however, anti-Fascist exiles had defeated 30,000 Fascists, and had been beaming home broadcasts ever since. In the north of Italy 80,000 partisans, many priests among them, were beginning a full-scale war against Mussolini's army of Salò. The time had come for Italians to reclaim their virtue and self-respect by taking the field against Fascism and Nazism. For most of the country the partisans were heroes.

Their numbers swelled from 80,000 in March to 250,000 in April. Yet 153,600 of them were Communists, and some of their leaders had been trained in Russia and seemed more interested in seizing political power than in fighting Nazi-Fascism. During the Ossola Valley battles, it was charged, the Communist Garibaldi Brigades had refrained from supporting the centrist Di Dio partisans who were being decimated.[61] Would these armies not become the basis for a Communist coup d'état?

Visconti fell in with the Resistance as a result of sheltering some partisans who had fought in Spain. At first he participated in a Communist-

Catholic group that trafficked in dynamite, grenades, small arms, and leaflets. Then he enlisted in GAP (Gruppi d'Azione Popolare), an elite band of Communist terrorists who had engineered the Via Rasella action, and was given a gun. On April 15, however, the night before his first GAP action—he was supposed "to kill someone," says his biographer without saying whom[62]—he was arrested by the Italian police, beaten, and kept twelve days without food. Meanwhile, in a twist worthy of Stendhal, Police Lieutenant Koch had found the actress Maria Denis caretaking Visconti's house and had fallen desperately in love with her. She prevailed upon him to have Visconti transferred to a kinder prison, where Uberta Visconti and Marcella Rossellini were able to bring him food—although the Fascist guard wouldn't let them tell him that the explosions he kept hearing were the cannon of the approaching Allies.

By then, Roberto and Roswitha, after living with various friends (Giovanna Scotto and Diego Calcagno among them) had moved into a pension near Babington's Tea House, just across Piazza di Spagna from Amidei's.

Toward the end of May, to keep the Romans from knowing what was going on, the Germans turned off the city's electricity. But their weary, blood-stained, dirty columns retreating northward up Via Flaminia made it "certain, absolutely certain, even probable," as Peppino Amato put it, that an end was near.[63]

Meanwhile Roberto and Roswitha had disappeared from view, and no one knew where they had gone. Later he would say he had gone "to meet the Americans, to meet the future.[64]

"The Americans had landed at Anzio on January 22 and news of it had immediately begun to arrive in Rome. A day or two later it was said people had seen an American jeep in Frattocchie. So I had anxiously gone down the Via Appia, beyond Via Tor Carbone where you can see Frattocchie in the distance, hoping to see the jeeps. But I didn't. So I had returned discouraged to Rome.

"Then I went down again, on June 3."

Roswitha was with him (although Roberto omits this fact as usual), and they were on bicycles.

"Just at the curve [where Via Ardeatina splits off from Via Appia Antica] I saw four soldiers coming, four soldiers in uniforms unknown to me, with helmets I didn't know. Then I saw that on their cartridge belts, which were made of grey cloth, there was a rather big 'U.S.' and I hazarded to call 'Hello' and one of them interpreted for me in shaky Italian, Italian-American Italian.

"Via Appia was interrupted because the Germans had mined it where it crosses the Marana [Creek] and the road [had] been blown up, along with the bridge and the face of the house there. On the front wall of this house, though, was a telephone and I began dialing the numbers of a bunch of friends. Finally one answered who lived in Viale Medaglie d'Oro, and I asked him what was happening where he was, and he, poor fellow, replied, 'Nothing. What do you think's happening?' So I asked, 'But what are the Germans doing?' He said, 'The Germans? Just what they're supposed to be doing: nothing.' 'But aren't they retreating?' 'Why should they be retreating?' 'But, look, I'm here on Via Appia, I'm here with some Americans.' He let out a huge yell and hung up.

"Then I called some women who were there, who had just appeared from that house, and I asked them if they had some wine. And they brought a flask of wine and this Italian American, to be polite and gracious toward these women who were offering him wine, started to say, '*Io, io Caputo*,' because his name was Caputo, and these women, because the Germans had been there up to five minutes before, replied, '*Niente kaput! Tutto evviva!*' with enormous enthusiasm. ['Nothing's kaput! Everything's hooray!']

"I was really scared that the same thing would happen that had happened in January, that they'd stop and turn back. So I tried every way I could to entice them. I invited them to my house. But they were rather diffident. And after they had seen the walls of Rome, they drew back, and with an enormous sadness I watched them vanish down the Via Appia. I followed them from afar just like a straw dog, and I saw that around the curve, near the Quo Vadis chapel, some tanks had come. The soldiers got up on the tanks and they withdrew. And so there I was left alone on Via Appia. I went back home. The next morning I went out at dawn and Rome by then had been occupied by the Americans."[65]

Many in Rome were unaware when they awoke that morning that anything had changed. In St. Paul's Basilica, production of *La porta del cielo*, now in its ninth month, was proceeding as usual, thanks to electricity supplied by the State Railways. Tremendous noises outside attracted the troupe's curiosity. The Americans had begun to enter the city in the middle of the night. Their columns were still pouring in. They would pour in all that day. De Sica's cameramen rushed out of the church, spread themselves throughout the city, and began filming the arriving Americans.

That evening a script girl, Jone Tuzzi, came hurrying down to Piazza di Spagna where crowds had gathered to cheer the Americans. She ran right into Roberto's arms. He was pale, thin as a poplar, and smoking a Camel. "We have to make a movie," he said. "Right now. All we have to do is look around us and we'll find all the stories we need."[66]

Open City

Roberto was not one to keep his enthusiasms to himself. Later, to be sure, when a project started to take form, when it was necessary to make a *combinazione* and engage people in his plans, he could be adroit, secretive, and downright Machiavellian. But initially, when an idea was just taking form, when a new thought, like a new woman, was taking possession of his imagination, he would blabber on almost mindlessly to anyone who would listen. Other people who carried on that way became objects of amusement, but not Roberto. No matter how fanciful or improbable his ideas, he entranced his listeners, not only convincing them that the dream *could* and *would* come true, but, like a coach, engaging them *in* the dream, making them share it, making them believe it was their own, making them *want* it to come true. "Are you with me?" he would ask, plaintively; and, if he didn't, people would wish he had.

So Roberto talked and talked. It was fine to dream of making a film without a plot, without a script, without actors, without a studio or sets—although no one, not Jone Tuzzi, not even Roberto could imagine even vaguely what such a film might be like—and it was fine to dream of making a film without money—as far as Roberto was concerned all he'd need to solve that obstacle would be a pocketful of *gettoni* (tokens) for the telephone. But not even Roberto's magic tongue could overcome one necessity that no movie could do without: raw film stock, of which there was absolutely none to be found.

The first days of liberation were halcyon. The Americans brought white bread, cigarettes, and chocolate bars, luxuries the food-loving Romans had been able to enjoy for many cold, damp months only in their imaginations. To be sure, that white bread, whiter and softer than anyone had ever seen, was a feeble substitute for the mighty feasts they had dreamed of, but it savored of America and richness, and as such played its part in determining Italy's political future. The day after the Americans came, half of Rome flocked to Saint Peter's Square, and the Pope, to his bewilderment, found himself greeted by the enthusiastic waving of hundreds of red flags with hammers and sickles on them. Far from resenting the Church for the aid and comfort she had given Fascism, the crowd was expressing its gratitude to the Pope for saving Rome, and to the clergy for sheltering the persecuted during the Occupation, forging papers, and obtaining food coupons for them.

The next day came news of the Allied landings in Normandy.

Visconti had been released June 3, as a parting gift by Police Lieutenant Koch to his unrequited love as he fled Rome. Maria Denis thought she had saved Visconti's life. Others thought he had been let go, like other prisoners, to mitigate reprisals after the Allies arrived.[1] Visconti thought she had compromised his heroism. He let it be believed she had been a collaborator and Koch's lover and never spoke to her again.

De Sica's cameramen sold their footage of the arriving Americans to those same Americans, netting 300,000 lire. But when they went back to San Paolo and *La porta del cielo*, they found the basilica's door barred by a cardinal and two Palatine guards. The mess inside took three days to clean up. De Sica claimed all his life that the film was the finest he ever made.[2]

The realities of their situation became apparent to the Romans after a few weeks. There were no jobs and few opportunities; the economy was in ruins. The curfew was still in effect. Ration cards were still required. For staples like white flour, olive oil, sugar, or coffee, the black market was the only source—at Tor di Nona, on a half-sunken street near the Tiber—but even there film stock was not to be found. A new currency, the Am-lira, was issued by the American military, and as prices began doubling overnight, it seemed appropriate that the new notes were made of paper that resembled newsprint. People continued to survive by bartering. Roberto was in the market one day with Roswitha's astrakhan coat over his arm when he bumped into Amidei, who was peddling wine to American soldiers. Almost immediately Roberto started talking about the films he wanted to make.

Meanwhile he was carving out a role as a mediator in his new-found identity as a Christian Democrat. Together with Aldo Vergano (representing the Action Party), Alfredo Guarini (the PCI), and Socialists and Communist-Catholics, he organized the Sindicato dei Lavoratori del Cinema (Film Workers Union), a subcommittee of the Committee of National Liberation. Its chief purpose was to intervene just after the liberation of Rome when U.S. Rear Admiral Emery W. Stone expropriated Cinecittà as a refugee camp and tried to suppress the "so-called Italian film industry" on the grounds that it had been "invented by the Fascists."[3]

Along with Diego Fabbri and Amidei, Roberto issued an appeal for an entente between Catholic and Marxist intellectuals and held numerous meetings to develop cultural programs in cooperation, a cause that met with some success during the euphoria of the first period of reconstruction, and in which he loyally persevered to the end of his life when, having made *The Messiah* for the Marxists, he was about to make *Karl Marx* for the Catholics.

For the purges had already begun. Everywhere, in each profession, commissions were set up to bring Fascist criminals and profiteers to a sort of private justice. But in civilized Rome the affair collapsed even before it began. Anyone who had gotten anywhere trembled for his or her position; some went into hiding, others hypocritically posed as anti-Fascists and took to screaming loudly against their private enemies. So much dirt was thrown in every direction that anything resembling truth was hopelessly buried in a vast sandstorm of lies. "The Commission for Purging Directors, Assistant Directors and Screenwriters in Cinema," consisting of Guarini, Barbaro, Camerini, Visconti, Mario Chiari, and Mario Soldati, began meeting in July and, on behalf of "The High Commissioner of Purges," compiled lists of those who had compromised themselves before Mussolini's fall and those who had gone north to Salò. This too was an Italian comedy. No sooner was someone accused than he could cite poverty and a hungry family in his defense. Even those who had made movies featuring black-shirt heroes could claim they had been lampooning Fascism or, at worst, acritically exhibiting its worst aspects, so that people could see the regime's perfidies for themselves. Rossellini, it appears, was not under suspicion and was not called to testify[4]; the commission's president, Guarini, was his colleague on the Sindicato Lavoratori del Cinema and, in any case, Roberto's films and collaborations were not considered reprehensible. Ultimately only three directors, Alessandrini, Gallone, and Genina, were punished—with six-month suspensions—but even these pats on the wrist were not administered, for the three had some of the best box-office records in the Italian cinema and were needed to make films. It was symptomatic of the times that *Pian delle stelle*, the first film to be made in praise of partisans, was directed by Giorgio Ferroni, who only a few months before had been loyally serving Salò, and that Alessandrini himself only narrowly missed directing *Il sole sorge ancora* ("The sun rises again"), a film directly produced by the National Association of Partisans.

In France a blood bath of vengeance baptized the Liberation. In northern Italy, in Florence and Milan, in April–June 1945, there were orgies of death as partisan death squads murdered 12-15,000 people. Franco Zeffirelli, a partisan himself, was mistaken for a Fascist and managed to save himself from summary execution only by making himself appealing to a homosexual Communist leader.

Yet overwhelmingly people wanted peace and work, not ideological vendettas. In contrast to France the purges in Italy were minimal, partly by will of the Communist Party which sensibly refused to divide the country chasing after Fascists. The first concern of its leader, Togliatti, when he became Minister of Justice was to pronounce a total amnesty. Stalin himself had pulled the rug out from under the militant Communists by recognizing Badoglio's government and conceding Italy to Allied dominion. Togliatti even cooperated with the Christian Democrats' bitterly-resented policy of disarming the partisan bands.

Italians also declined to indulge their shame as Germany and France were doing. The last twenty years would simply be buried, ignored. Movies would not mention Fascism and virtually no one would object; the new Italian cinema would make the Germans the scapegoats for everything.

Italians would not feel guilty; they would just forget to remember, and forge ahead. Most of them had not really taken a part in Fascism. Roberto, like everyone, knew people who had dressed like Fascists for years and were stupefied to be treated like Fascists when the purges began. "I'm convinced they were absolutely sincere," he remarked.[5]

Few movies of any sort were made during 1944 and 1945; the Italian cinema virtually ceased to exist. Its prewar prosperity had in great measure been due to Mussolini's policy of limiting, then banning, the importation of American pictures. Hollywood could amortize its pictures in its home market—which already permitted scales of production no other nation could compete with—and then dump them onto foreign markets at prices far below those native producers required in order to survive. Italy's film industry had already been destroyed once by this practice, during the twenties, and now, with Hollywood's exports protected by a secret no-quota clause inserted into the peace treaty imposed upon Italy by the Allies, it was in peril again. Even in 1938, a good year, Italian films had netted less than 14 percent of Italian box office receipts, versus 64 percent earned by American films; whereas by 1941 the embargo had raised the Italian share to 41 percent. But between 1944 and 1949 Hollywood would dump approximately 3,500 films into Italian theaters and snare up to 80 percent of the receipts. England, France, and other nations would also pour in films. Under such conditions it was to be difficult for an Italian film to obtain screen time in its own country. Liberation had brought a new occupation.

Worse, most Italians preferred it that way, at least at first. A few movie theaters managed to reopen, powered by dynamos, since there was still no electricity one could count on, and by stolen gasoline, since none could be bought but much could be stolen from army trucks by the hoards of orphaned boys that competed for the shoeshine trade. But the cinemas showed American movies, not Italian ones. Italian films were *old*. They reeked of Fascism and shame. Two of the biggest stars, Osvaldo Valenti and Luisa Ferida, were now said to have been drug addicts who got their kicks torturing partisans in Salò.[6] Not for thirty years would Italians bear to look again at films from the Fascist era (and Valenti and Ferida be exonerated). Rejection was total, blind, absolute, and uncompromising. American films, even dubbed into execrable Italian-American, represented the future. The former stars of Cinecittà were not to be seen in movie theaters but in the variety houses, where the demands of the new era were quickly adjusted to, and where an Anna Magnani, saucy, disheveled, and erupting with vitality, represented rejuvenation.

And so, by early August, on a blisteringly hot afternoon, Roberto was still talking eagerly about the films he was going to make. And his friends Sergio Amidei and Alberto Consiglio were talking just as eagerly about the films they were going to make. All three were captivating conversationalists, and all the more primed by that special inspiration that overcomes an Italian as he sits down to a meal. As Ugo Pirro dramatizes it, presumably from Amidei himself,[7] they were the only diners remaining in *Il cacciatore*, a small trattoria with paper tablecloths in back of the *Messaggero* building where, in accordance with the traditional affinities of Italians and their restaurants, especially during times of common misery, credit was accorded regular customers, and one ate meat and pasta abundantly, despite the rationing and daily price increases. Amidei had no need for credit. He earned good money but even though he would throw it away on ill-advised investments and romances, he tended to be parsimonious and he knew enough to avoid giving so profligate a borrower as Roberto the impression that he possessed spare cash. Roberto paid rarely, but when he did he tipped lavishly, guaranteeing future credit and loving service, but infuriating Amidei who, with his "Austrian" obsession with provident living, was simultaneously attracted and repelled by Roberto's "Roman" insouciance for the morrow.

Talking of cinema meant talking of events in the war that was still going on, of friends who had died, of things they themselves had experienced, and, in vague terms, of how the new sense of the world such moments had given them might be translated into a new sort of movie. For the first time in Italian history the masses were going to be part of the political arena. A fresh critical angle was needed on reality to reflect the new, popular world and to tear away the veil of lies under which Mussolini's regime had tried to conceal the realities of Italian life. At least, that was the way the Communist-leaning Amidei saw matters. Consiglio, a monarchist, and Roberto, a Christian Democrat of sorts, were less idealistic and dogmatic. They all agreed that what they wanted was not to chronicle huge, shameful events (like the massacre that had followed the incident on Via Rasella, a block away), but something humbler, something to revitalize the spirits of the Italian people, something positive.

As Pirro dramatizes the scene, Amidei dominated the conversation with an imperious, irascible tone and fluent concision. He tended, however, to keep his hand in front of his mouth, in order to conceal his brown, macerated teeth. (A local wit had nicknamed him "Teruel," after a Spanish city Franco's bombings had reduced to rubble, then changed it to "The White Cliffs of Dover" when Amidei bought a set of dentures. Amidei himself never knew about either nickname, says Pirro. He would have erupted like a volcano.)

Amidei was working on a story about the black market at Tor di Nona for director Alessandro Blasetti and producer Peppino Amato. But so far all he had was a beginning.

One night around ten, he recounted to Roberto and Consiglio, a German patrol knocks rudely on a door in Piazza di Spagna. The door doesn't open, but the noise alerts the neighbors, who peek out at the Germans, afraid to show themselves. Upstairs on the top floor, a man is sleeping on his couch, fully dressed. When the Germans shoot the door open downstairs, he knows he's the one they're after and quickly climbs out onto the roof. At the risk of his neck he makes his way across to a neighboring terrace. Meanwhile the

Germans find the man's bed unslept in and, although the landlady tells them he never came home that night, they go out onto the roof and stare around anyway. The moon is shining brightly; the man, crouched frozen in fear behind a plant, covers his white socks with his hands. Calling the landlady, the Germans ask her whom the terrace belongs to. "The Spanish embassy," she replies. So the Germans, not daring to violate Spanish diplomacy, go away. But, being Germans, they ingenuously leave their phone number with the landlady, just in case the man comes home.

"Fantastic!" exclaimed Roberto, as Amidei stroked his mustache in self-satisfaction, "but it doesn't have anything to do with the black market."

Amidei snorted, according to Pirro. "The man is a black marketer."

"At Piazza di Spagna?! A black marketer should live near Via di Panico."

"There's no Spanish embassy on Via di Panico. I like the idea of a black marketer living at Piazza di Spagna."

"It's too arbitrary, it seems false."

"But what difference does it make?" objected Consiglio.

"In fact, it does," interrupted Amidei, irritated. "I was that man. The whole thing really happened. I didn't make any of it up. We can't go putting the Spanish embassy any old place we want."

"And by the same token the black marketer cannot live in Piazza di Spagna," declared Roberto. "Your story didn't happen to a black marketer. And that should tell us something else. . . . "

Roberto paused, for once not languishing in his customary indifference.

"Does the man have to be a black marketer? If you want to make it really true, since you were being hunted by the Germans for political reasons, your man ought to be hunted for the same reasons. And, besides, the Germans didn't go around in the middle of the night looking for black marketers. You know, we could do a film in episodes, a lot of short stories, and this could be one of them."

Roberto hardly took a breath.

Consiglio was right, no one had ever cared if things in films were "really real"—except perhaps Roberto and De Robertis in their war films, and even then, only occasionally. But Amidei was listening—an act for him equivalent to admitting someone else was right, says Pirro.

"People want long stories," Consiglio objected, absolutely correctly, "with a beginning and an end, even if your idea might be easier."

But Consiglio, Pirro tells us, was a journalist, Neapolitan, and charmingly cynical, and ready to write about anything for anyone ready to pay. Movies for him were merely one more of his sidelines, of less personal importance than the fine little book he would one day write about pasta, called *Macaroni, With a Hundred Recipes.*[8]

Roberto and Amidei ignored him, pursuing their common obsession.

"But Amato wants a film on the black market," Amidei pointed out, even though he had already lost interest in it.

"Have you told Blasetti the story yet?" asked Roberto.

"No."

"Or Peppino Amato?"

"Him neither."

"So don't. Think up some other crap. Don't waste this idea. It's not impossible that you will be starting a film in a few days. I have some negotiations under way and this beginning could be used."

Amidei smelled blarney; he didn't have a great deal of respect for Roberto and his flighty ways. He hadn't even bothered to see his films (and when he did, years later, he said they were Fascist and said he wouldn't have worked with Roberto had he known them at the time[9])—and, as one of the most professional and respected scenarists in the industry, he even felt justified in regarding Roberto as a bit of an interloper. But something in the way Roberto talked convinced him that, even if what Roberto was saying wasn't true yet, it might be true presently.

At least, this is the way Pirro, echoing Amidei, claims Amidei felt. Ugo Pirro and Amidei were both screenwriters and took a writer's point of view. Two of Pirro's films won Oscars: *Investigation of a Citizen above Suspicion* (Elio Petri, 1970) and *Garden of the Finzi Continis* (De Sica, 1971).

The reality is that Roberto, with three solid pictures behind him and with unequalable abilities at finding money, was far more capable of bringing an idea to fruition than Amidei. Amidei needed Roberto, if he was ever to turn his dream of a populist cinema into reality; Roberto did not need Amidei. And in fact, Roberto did have some negotiations under way.

They left the restaurant, each paying for himself, "alla romana," and walked lazily with frequent stops. Consiglio, according to Pirro, recalled mention of a priest somewhere in the suburbs, called Don Pietro Pappagallo, who was making phony identity cards for the Resistance.

"A priest who helps underground Communists! That's good. Because it's true. It could be another episode. Write it up," exclaimed Roberto, good-naturedly taking command, like a born director.

Amidei didn't much like the idea. He didn't much like priests, even if they were broadminded, disobedient, and helpful to Communists. "Cockroaches," the Romans called them, with their ageless contempt for the clergy. But Amidei liked the name Pappagallo ("parrot") and he liked the idea of a priest counterfeiting documents in his sacristy. "It would even be funny," he observed. "But we'd need an actor like Fabrizi."

Aldo Fabrizi was a vaudeville star who had made three highly successful movies the year before Mussolini's fall: *Avanti c'è posto, Campo de' fiori,* and *L'ultima carrozzella.* Roberto knew and liked these films. They were comedies, shot on location with a realistic feel to them, and, rather than playing stock roles, Fabrizi's characters had been working-class Romans such as one encountered every day. Nonetheless Amidei was being flippant and Roberto countered sarcastically. "Sure," he said, "we could turn the whole thing into a Roman farce!"

But abruptly he stopped, and stared across Via del Tritone. "Those guys are getting a film together," he declared, and hastily quitting Amidei and Consiglio, sauntered across the intersection to where two men were standing.

The two were Salvo D'Angelo, erstwhile producer of the infamous *Porta del cielo*, and Commandant Carlo Civallero, erstwhile Navy filmmaker who, like many of his colleagues in the Navy film section, had eagerly made the transition into the civilian film industry, albeit retaining his former title. Seeing them together and knowing their reputations, Roberto had immediately leapt to the conclusion that they wouldn't be talking to each other unless about a movie and unless they'd found money. As always with opportunity in view, Roberto didn't hesitate.

"What's the film?" he asked, casually.

"A film. We'll see. Maybe the Countess has something in mind, but if you have some ideas, keep them to yourself."

They were entering the building housing the Florida nightclub, on the corner of Via di Capo le Case, above which the Countess Chiara Politi, an ex-mistress of Egypt's King Faud and with a teenage son by him, had her offices: Nettunia Productions. D'Angelo and Civallero were taken by surprise by Roberto's attaching himself to them, but they figured his charm might be useful—they didn't have the Countess's money yet—and a director might be useful, and, at any rate, neither felt capable of shooing the redoubtable Rossellini away.

"I'm already working up some ideas with Amidei and Consiglio," Roberto exaggerated, indicating the two across Via del Tritone.

"On what?"

"The story of a priest, a film in episodes. Perhaps we'll call it *Storie di ieri* ('Stories of yesterday')." He said it as though he'd hired Amidei and Consiglio to help develop ideas of his own, and, sensing that D'Angelo, Civallero, and the Countess as well would be scared off by anything politically daring, he began with the priest rather than with Amidei's story. But they still looked dubious, so he went on. "These days a film in episodes is the only thing feasible. We'll shoot one episode, close down, and edit it. If there're money problems or production problems we'll work them out and then start shooting again. The script, of course, has to be iron tight. So, you see, the problems are minor, easily solvable one at a time. And besides," he added decisively, "I know where to find film stock."

They were admitted by a butler (secretly the Countess's lover). A poster for *Rossini*, her only other attempt at production (and a fiasco at that) decorated the hallway. "Let's hope she doesn't want to do Verdi," quipped Roberto.

The Countess Politi was in her fifties and visibly charmed by Roberto who, according to Pirro, took charge of the meeting, speaking, as usual, with calm indifference, and letting it be known that it was his old friendship and esteem for D'Angelo and Civallero that had led him to unite his interests with theirs. The two men bristled at this but preferred not to undo the progress Rossellini was making. For in Roberto the Countess sensed a kindred soul. She too was a gamesman and enjoyed making hard-nosed producers think she could finance a film. Her friends in Milan would provide all the money they needed, she told them, confiding that she had information that it was only a matter of a few weeks before Milan and northern Italy would be liberated from the Germans.

Eager for an advance, Roberto, according to Pirro, promised the Countess a story on paper the next day. "I'll take care of it," he told D'Angelo and Civallero, on the way out.

The two were now convinced that without Rossellini they would have gotten nowhere.

Actually the truth was that no one was anywhere. Roberto had merely an extremely hypothetical *combinazione*—various fish dubiously eyeing an as yet undefined bait, without even a hook to hold them if they bit. Amidei certainly wasn't to be trusted too much: at this point Blasetti and Amato represented advantages infinitely more substantial than Roberto. So, even though Amidei's Piazza di Spagna apartment was only a block away, Roberto, according to Pirro, resisted the temptation to go tell him about Politi, and instead, catching a ride on one of the lumbering, wobbly, old trucks that then substituted for buses, he went home to Via Parco Pepoli and lay down in bed. Around 4:30, when it was likely Consiglio had returned to consciousness after a long siesta, he called him, told him they had a chance to get money quickly, and asked him to get the story of Don Pappagallo onto paper immediately.

Consiglio had worked for Roberto on *L'uomo dalla croce.* Accustomed to churning out copy on a moment's notice, he sat down at his typewriter, and without even thinking of what he would write, tapped a title, "La disfatta di Satana" ("The defeat of Satan"). But given Satan, Pirro explains, Consiglio needed a villain, and Kappler, the Gestapo commander who'd been in charge of the Fosse Ardeatine massacre, was the perfect model. So there'd be torture and an execution scene. Except there was a problem: even though no one had heard of him, Don Pappagallo was still alive and in Rome. Then Consiglio remembered another priest, Don Giuseppe Morosini, whose execution by the Nazis was well known. Morosini, a former military chaplain who had joined Rome's partisans, had smuggled plans of the German deployment at Monte Cassino to the Allies, and had then been betrayed to the Gestapo, who found arms and a transmitter for men he was hiding. The Pope had been unable to save him. At his execution, March 4, 1944, he kissed a crucifix, blessed the firing squad, and announced his forgiveness of those who had betrayed him. The volley left him wounded but conscious, and the officer had shot him through the head.

Morosini had been an unrelentingly severe personality, however. Aside from his execution, there was not much about him that was appealing. So Consiglio combined him with Don Pappagallo. When completed, the story approximated the second half of what would become *Roma città aperta.* Manfredi is captured during a *rastrellamento* and ordered deported to Germany. But planes attack the column of prisoners, and Rainer, the German commander, turns out to be an old friend, who frees Manfredi and deserts. Luisa, another of Manfredi's friends, sends them to Don Pappagallo, who frequently helps fugitives. But Luisa denounces them to the Gestapo Colonel Bergmann in exchange for cocaine, and the SS storm into Don Pietro's rectory. Rainer kills himself (like the Austrian deserter in *Roma città aperta*), Manfredi is tortured to death, and Don Pietro is shot.[10]

Before supper, he had finished the story, a simple story without Communists or heroines of a priest shot by the Germans. He then went to Amidei's, where he was to meet Rossellini, and, by prior agreement with Roberto, in order not to offend Amidei, presented the story as an article he'd written that might be a possible subject for their film.

Having read it, Amidei stood up and began pacing nervously about the room, as was his wont when something caught his imagination. "It needs Fabrizi," he declared again.

Roberto fingered a lock of hair. Actors held no fascination for him. The theater with its eternal mannerisms and stilted talk, talk, talk bored him to tears, even the actresses: what need did he have to fantasize about them when he could take them to bed whenever he chose? Left to himself, he might never have considered Fabrizi.

"I had *him* in mind," he joked, indicating Consiglio.

Amidei stopped pacing, and fixed a stare on Consiglio, as though making a screen test, then responded decisively: "No. Better Fabrizi," he said, and Roberto began to suspect Fabrizi was going to be necessary if his *combinazione* was going to come off.

He changed the subject. One of the episodes, he thought, should be about the small boys of Rome who'd taken part in the Resistance. And he recounted other ideas that came to him to the pacing Amidei, ideas that were more like fragmentary images rather than stories with beginnings and ends. What appealed to Roberto was the juxtaposition of heroism with childishness.[11]

"I don't know . . ." Amidei reacted. His mind was elsewhere. He had just remembered the incident of a pregnant woman, Maria Teresa Gullace, who had been killed in front of her husband and children on Viale Giulio Cesare on March 3, 1944. Gullace's husband had been awaiting deportation, she had thrown him a food packet through the barracks window, and a German had casually shot her in the face with a machine-gun. Amidei had seen the story in a copy of *L'Unità* during one of his clandestine sessions with Alicata and Ingrao. It had stuck in his mind because of the stupidity of the headline: "IMMEDIATE REVENGE OF A WOMAN KILLED BY THE GERMANS." "Imagine! A murdered woman who revenges herself immediately afterward! Ha!" Amidei exclaimed.

"But it's perfect for the film!" exclaimed Roberto.

The murdered woman became the model for sora Pina, the character eventually played by Anna Magnani.

*

The above is Pirro's and Amidei's account.

In fact, however, Roberto and Consiglio had been discussing the Don Morosini story with Countess Politi since June, months before.[12] Neither the writer nor the Countess were chance encounters. Amidei did not know this at the time and never learned of it afterward.

Roberto encouraged people to think he worked miracles. His collaborators were pieces of reality to be used in the same way as the pieces of reality before his camera. He saw no need to let them know what their colleagues were doing; indeed, the less they knew, the easier it was to control them. Eventually, as one might expect, Roberto's tactics caught up with him in the form of indignation, resentment, and broken friendships; but by then he was off onto a new project and new collaborators.

It was a lawyer friend Attalante who, according to Roberto, had told him he knew a Countess with lots of money who had just arrived from Milan and wanted to invest.[13] And the Countess, after Roberto had outlined his project, had replied that she had five million lire that she would give him the day he started shooting, but not before. She distrusted film people totally.

Leaving Amidei's, Roberto walked up the Spanish Steps to Via Gregoriana. With the loss during the Occupation of the cafés as places to meet and chat in, Gastone Medin's apartment had taken their place, and the habit continued. It was late, but Roberto loved roaming about during the wee hours and Roswitha, waiting at home, was too obedient to object. "He treated Roswitha like a slave," said Mario Del Papa; "he treated Marcella De Marchis worse."[14]

At Medin's he found Ivo Perilli and Turi Vasile, and toward morning Roberto, in search of more material with which to coax an advance from the Countess, and without mentioning Amidei or Consiglio, asked them if they had any story ideas for Fabrizi, then began to recount his latest discovery. He had discovered he could hold back his orgasms, and thus satisfy his partner, by thinking of something else while physically occupied in coupling. Oblivious to Vasile's blushing, he continued: "For example, tell yourself the story of your next film. Or count sheep, like when you're trying to get to sleep. Or mentally recite a poem."[15]

They met the next day at Nettunia. Roberto read their treatment—written that morning—about a truck driver (Fabrizi) who, after hazarding the war-torn highways and sacrificing himself for his son, enters a Rome he no longer recognizes. "I'll give it to the Countess," Roberto said. "If I get an advance, we split it three ways."[16]

When Amidei failed to show up at *Il cacciatore* at the usual time, Roberto started worrying. If Amidei had got to talking to Blasetti, if the unpredictable Amato had suddenly decided to rush an Occupation film of his own into production, Roberto's project was imperiled.

Amidei arrived at last, squabbling furiously with Maria Michi, who was more than holding her own. Roberto relaxed. They had obviously been fighting all morning.[17]

Michi had been a movie usherette. But one day she and Doretta Sestan had been fired for doing imitations in the balcony, a protest had followed, and Michi had met Eduardo De Filippo. "You're like an orchid in a chamber pot," he had told her, studying her eccentric, street-wise face, and he had given her a few small parts in his plays. But Michi had soon passed to the actor Renato Cialente, resulting in one of the countless triangles that enlivened her life. Without hiding his jealousy, De Filippo had struggled to direct Gorki's *Lower Depths*, while Michi, ignoring him completely, had responded only to Cialente's instructions. Meanwhile, she had entered the circle around Togliatti, Negarville, and Amendola, was running from house to house distributing underground news sheets, and Amidei had fallen in love with her. But the Gorki play, premiering November 28, 1943, had been greeted too enthusiastically—as a covert protest against the Occupation—with the result that the Germans had run down Cialente with a truck as he pedaled his tricycle slowly down the Corso. Michi and Amidei had been walking on the sidewalk alongside him and he had died in their arms. Since Cialente had been his close friend, Amidei had kept his feelings for Michi hidden, but now she had passed to him.

It was not a peaceful union. She was not disposed to play a docile role, and Amidei, habitually sullen, authoritarian, and overbearing in his relations with others, Pirro maintains, was prone to indulge his lovers, to make himself an easy victim of their betrayal, and then to become suicidal. He suffered from solitude, which he would never admit (like the horrible teeth that he was always trying to hide from view), and his need for companionship led him time and again into impossible love affairs: married women, adolescents, lesbians, and tramps, for all of whom he was always trying to get parts in his films.

As Pirro dramatizes it, Consiglio entered the restaurant and joined them. After Michi had subsided, Amidei confessed he had seen Amato that morning, but that Amato hadn't cared for his story. Roberto turned gloomy.

Time passed in general silence, until Amidei put down his fork, carefully wiped his mouth, and stared solemnly at Roberto. "The man the Nazis arrest and torture," he announced, as though delivering an ultimatum, "is a Communist leader and it's Maria who'll betray him. The other man, who's partnered with that Teresa Gullace whom I'll call *sora* [signora] Pina is a printer and prints *L'Unità* clandestinely."

"Maria who?" asked Roberto.

"Her!" growled Amidei, indicating Michi. "She looks like an informer. Doesn't she?!"

Amidei had imposed his girlfriend on the production and she, eager for the role, wisely kept silent. But Communists in a film could pose serious problems, and Consiglio, who was shortly to begin writing for a ferociously anti-Communist, pro-monarchist magazine, couldn't suppress his alarm:

"You mean they're *both* Communists?"

"Yesss, sssir!" hissed Amidei, looking like a general, and went back to eating. Roberto eyed Consiglio: this was not the moment to stir up Amidei; better to humor him. There had never been one Communist hero in an Italian film,[18] let alone two, and leaguing them with a priest-martyr perfectly echoed the image the Party currently wished to project. Even in the halcyon days of 1944 it was a risky move. A decade later it would be worse. An incredible uproar would explode over *Don Camillo*, an innocuous comedy about a priest and a Communist mayor, which both the Christian Democrats and the Communists would damn as a betrayal. And most of Italy's filmmakers would sign a published protest against the politicians.

Consiglio tried another tack, summing up what they had so far:

"The priest dies shot, the Communist dies tortured, the pregnant woman dies machine-gunned. If we don't kill off a little boy, too, we have three dead already. Isn't it a bit much?"

Roberto responded quickly before Amidei could explode. "It's okay for now," he said.

More urgent now was money. That afternoon Roberto met Civallero at Countess Politi's. He gave her Consiglio's story and, carefully leaving out the Communists, recounted the ideas for the three episodes—the priest, the truck driver, the boys: *Storie di ieri, oggi e domani* ("Stories of yesterday, today, and tomorrow"). The Countess was fascinated.

They'd have to move quickly, he emphasized, before anyone else, like Amato, launched a similar project, and for this he'd have to pay something to his collaborators. Reluctantly, she advanced 15,000 lire.[19] Amidei drew up a contract for Consiglio, September 12, 1944.

It wasn't much, but it was a beginning. Thereafter they met nightly, Amidei writing, Consiglio talking, Roberto listening, suggesting, and, above all, telephoning, which he liked best. The script progressed slowly; mostly they talked about other things. From Steinbeck's *The Moon Is Down* they took the idea of a drunken German officer bemoaning German war crimes. From Ferenc Molnar's "I ragazzi della via Pal" (a popular children's book in the 1920s that had been made into a short film by Monicelli in 1935 and had served as the source for Frank Borzage's *No Greater Glory* in 1934), they took the idea of schoolboys playing war. Inevitably, given Amidei's insistence on well-developed intrigues and interrelated characters, the little episodes that Roberto had originally envisioned coalesced into a single long film. The boys joined Don Pietro's parish, one of them became sora Pina's son, and her illicit pregnancy would soon be legitimized in Don Pietro's church. And Maria Michi's character, besides being an informer (a species so loathed that even to show one smacked of forgiveness), became a drug addict and a lesbian to boot. (After the picture opened, Michi experienced her character's shame directly. Blackmarket cigarette vendors refused to sell to "this shameful woman!" and a German-hating Pole tried to kill her with a knife.)

But the problem Amidei could not solve was how to postpone sora Pina's death beyond the end of the movie's first half, a "flaw"—stars simply do not die halfway through a movie—that greatly offended his tradition-bound sense of proper story construction.

Meanwhile, the week after reading their treatment, Roberto gave Perilli and Vasile 2,000 lire a piece. He had gotten 6,000 from the Countess, he said, and they did not know whether to believe him. "Now do the script quickly, and we'll see," he said.

"How much?" asked Perilli.

"As much as I can get." He shrugged his shoulders.

"We'll have a contract?"

"Write it yourself and I'll sign it."

"Why won't the Countess sign it?"

"Okay," said Roberto, reflecting. "As soon as we've set up the company." And he dismissed them.[20]

Besides Fabrizi, Amidei was set on Magnani, whom he'd known in Turin. They both had personalities that suited their roles, were top box-office stars as well, and yet were still new enough to personify the Resistance rather than the Fascist era—as Clara Calamai also was. All three, more importanty, were "bankable." With them it would be possible to raise money to make the movie, without them it would be impossible. But money from whom? The Countess Politi was questionable: she had provided additional small advances, but the bulk of her funds were still in Milan, behind German lines, and might not be sufficient for a feature even if she could get to them; after all, she had originally contracted for a series of shorts. To make matters worse, she had vanished a week earlier.

Perilli and Vasile finished writing their script in three weeks. Roberto threw it on the table without looking at it. "I'll read it."

"And the Countess?" Perilli asked.

"She'll read it too."

"And the contract?"

Roberto played with his hair. "I'll have it drawn up."

"How much?"

"Next week."

Perilli almost shouted. "I said how much?!"

Roberto shrugged. "I hope to get 15,000. Five apiece."[21]

Additional sources for money would have to be found, for which they would need a distribution contract—a guarantee that an established firm was prepared to market the picture to theaters. To get a distributor, they would need bankable stars. But to get the stars to get the distributor to get the money, they would need money.

Roberto and Amidei sat on a doorstep one morning pondering their impasse. Vittorio De Sica came walking up Via Bissolati.

"What are you doing?" he asked.

They shrugged. "Looking for money. We don't have money to go ahead with the film," said Amidei. "And you, what are you up to at the moment?"

De Sica smiled sadly. "I'm looking for money, too. What's your film?"

"You know . . . about Don Morosini, that priest the Germans shot. And yours?"

"Mine? It's about children, but it's still all vague."[22]

De Sica went on his way, leaving Roberto and Amidei curious and jealous. They couldn't believe De Sica had no money. He was as successful as an actor could be, both in film and theater, and his credit as a director (*Teresa Venerdì, Maddalena zero in condotta, Un garibaldino al convento, I bambini ci guardano* [*The Children Are Watching Us*]) was infinitely greater than Rossellini's. But in fact it would take two long years for De Sica to find money and make *Shoeshine*, his film about Rome's war-orphaned children. The penalty of his success as an actor was that he was typecast as a dapper gentleman; few Italians shared his desire to expose their nation's dirty linen, especially in gray depressing art films that no one would go see.

Fabrizi was playing at the Salone Margherita, just off Piazza di Spagna. Roberto and Amidei met him backstage and together they walked next door to the popular Caffè Rampoldi where, to avoid interruptions from friends, they sat in a corner in the back. Cordially but warmly—for neither of them knew Fabrizi well and actors almost never read scripts—Amidei told him about the film. He spoke as though it were a series of personal reminiscences of those times. Fabrizi listened, impassively at first, then, it seemed, with boredom and impatience, and Roberto, sitting there smoking and listening, became more and more convinced they had been foolish. Even if Fabrizi *had* liked *La nave bianca*, he was infamous for his ill-tempered cynicism; he had never played a dramatic role, why on earth would he risk his reputation to do so now? Amidei, experiencing the same misgivings, began to emphasize the funnier scenes. But, telling the film this way, putting it all together for the very first time, he himself, and Roberto, too, began to realize how extraordinary, how novel their story was. Fabrizi, however, leaned forward and lowered his head onto his chest. *He was falling asleep!* Concluding quickly, Amidei suppressed a furious desire to kick him in the ass. The silence was acute.

Finally Fabrizi looked up. His eyes were full of tears. He stood up and thanked them; he wanted to make the film.

"I want a million," he added, as he walked away.

A million lire! Roberto had spent the whole morning on the telephone trying to find ten thousand. But nothing fazed him.

"We'll find it," he mumbled.

"How? Where? When?" exclaimed Amidei. Roberto's eternal confidence dismayed him, even annoyed him at times. For his part, Roberto forbore mentioning that he had found a sheep and cattle farmer who was willing to take a chance; Amidei would not have approved.

"We need someone to convince Fabrizi to take 200,000," he said, instead.

"And who might that be?" asked Amidei, fascinated despite himself.

"His name's Fellini. He's a gag writer for curtain raisers, and spends a lot of time with Fabrizi. He couldn't care less about films." The last part wasn't quite true, but Roberto, Pirro points out, knew that Amidei had grown jealous of his work and would resent new interference.

"And Magnani? How much will she want?" Amidei asked.

"Magnani? As sora Pina?"

"Who else were you thinking of?"

"In fact I haven't thought about it."

"Well, do!"

"Actually," confessed Roberto, trying to hide his embarrassment, "Civallero's been talking to Calamai." Clara Calamai had starred in *Ossessione.*

"And what do you think of that?"

"Sergio, we must make this film, even if we have to sell our underwear. If they want Calamai, let them pay her. But for the other roles, I want new faces, people never seen before. I can't stand overacting! And, anyhow, Calamai's preferable to Amedeo Nazzari." Nazzari had been the star of *Luciano Serra pilota* who had refused to go to Ethiopia.

"So now Nazzari's involved?"

"The Countess suggested him as the Communist. But I said no." This was probably untrue: Roberto didn't want Amidei to insist on Magnani.[23]

He got free of Amidei and walked through the long tunnel to Via Nazionale. Just across the street from the Palazzo delle Esposizioni was The Funny Face Shop, a big store with three windows where American soldiers went to have their faces drawn into whimsical cartoons—holding up the Tower of Pisa, netting a mermaid in the Gulf of Naples, a gladiator spearing a lion in the Coliseum—or to record their voices onto discs to send home, or to buy a woman. Federico Fellini worked here. Tall and skinny, still only 24, he had come to Rome from Rimini five years before. His facility at drawing caricatures had gained him a post at *Marc'Aurelio*, a weekly humor magazine, and, as most of *Marc'Aurelio*'s staff doubled as screenwriters (Steno, Metz, Marcello Marchesi, Cesare Zavattini, Ettore Scola, Bernardino Zapponi), Fellini too entered the movies. He had known Roberto distantly when they both worked for Riganti and had gained Fabrizi's confidence by supplying him with the idea for his first film, *Avanti c'è posto . . .* But never before in his life had he made anywhere near as much money as he was now, drawing caricatures at The Funny Face Shop at three dollars and ten minutes apiece.

This evening the Shop was so jammed with half-drunk GIs grabbing the female clerks and impatiently pressing for service that Roberto, to get to Fellini, had to push his way through the crowd pretending to be a manager trying to deal with their complaints. Fellini, busy drawing the portrait of a Chinese-American soldier, wasn't impressed by Roberto's whispered proposition in his ear that he collaborate on a film about Don Morosini. To Fellini the Italian cinema seemed all but dead now that Hollywood movies were back, and he couldn't see himself propagandizing the Resistance, given his conviction that, with the Nazis already beaten, it was only provoking bloody reprisals. But Roberto, amid smiles at the Americans, pleaded that no one could write so well for Fabrizi, and that Amidei's Italian was hopelessly inadequate for dialogue. "If Fabrizi reads those dialogues, he'll turn down the part, even though he liked the story so much he cried. We need you."

Fellini went on sketching. He suspected ulterior motives somewhere in Roberto's flattery, but he was young, it was good to feel needed, and, besides, he was never able to refuse people flatly—a problem that in the years ahead would lead him into innumerable subterfuges to avoid confrontations, like answering his phone with a woman's voice. He heard himself giving in to Roberto, agreeing to do whatever he asked; but privately he was wondering if he couldn't escape out the back door.

With this conflict raging in his mind, he showed the finished drawing to the soldier and his life nearly came to a violent conclusion that very moment. The Chinese-American took one look at the pastel portrait, screamed "I'm not yellow!," grabbed a razor from his pocket, and lunged for Fellini's face.

Roberto smoothly intervened, handing a pink pastel to Fellini and gently restraining the raging soldier. The MPs arrived quickly—they were stationed just across the street and used to crossing it—and took charge of the Chinese-American. They also closed up The Funny Face Shop for the night.

Fellini let himself be led through the tunnel, now lined with gaudily painted prostitutes trying to attract passing cars. "Excuse me, Roberto," he sighed as they emerged. "Since you're taking me to Fabrizi, tell me exactly what I have to tell him. Is it a question of money?"

Roberto laughed. "He asked for a million. We can give him two hundred thousand."

"Ah!" said Fellini. "Now all is clear."[24]

A week passed. Perilli and Vasile still did not have their contract. Roberto was still evasive. Perhaps the script would be used; the Countess would be back in a few days. Perilli and Vasile lost hope.

Then Countess Politi reappeared. She had gone to Milan, taking mountain trails across the Allied and German lines, and had brought back to Rome a suitcase containing three million lire, or so she said.

Roberto phoned Perilli. The Countess had given him twelve thousand, he said, "four thousand for each of us!"

The contracts were signed September 18, 1944. But where was their money? Roberto was never in when they phoned. Finally Vasile learned that the Countess had brought back three million, not twelve thousand—

and that the money would finance not their story for Fabrizi, but one by Amidei.

Vasile confronted Roberto, who "looked at me as though he were thinking, 'What does this microbe want?' I exploded in rage." Whereupon Roberto, confronted with his own lack of candor, "replied to me with elevated calm that he had commissioned a script, not a film. This wasn't his affair. Impatiently I blurted, 'Well pay us, at least!' And he started screaming like a maniac. He said he would not permit his propriety to be doubted; he said he had never been in debt to anyone; he said we were in debt to him for the benevolence he had shown us. And at this point there came out of him a terrible blasphemy. I went blind. I jumped to my feet and yelled with all my breath: 'Don't *blaspheme*, for heaven's sake!' Suddenly he broke out laughing. He laughed till tears came to his eyes, and his hilarity's contagion infected Ivo Perilli, too. I looked at them bewildered, as though they had just thrown a bucket of dirty water over me. Maybe I was about to cry. Maybe Rossellini realized it. He put his hand on the back of my neck, drew me to him, and said, 'I like you.' And went out of the room. Shortly later he came back waving the big thousand-lire bills. 'The Countess heard everything. And she's paid!' "[25]

On September 28 Roberto signed Ubaldo Arata, one of Italy's most prestigious cameramen. Arata had been making movies since 1911; his credits included Camerini's *Rotaie*, Ophuls's *La signora di tutti*, and *Luciano Serra pilota*. Shooting would have to begin by mid-January, or they would lose Fabrizi. Roberto also signed Vito Annicchiarico, a ten-year-old shoeshine boy working in Largo Tritone across from the Countess's office, whose father was missing in Africa and whose mother was in the hospital, to play Pina's son for 13,200 lire a day.

But was there money? The Countess's money (closer to one million than to three) was a considerable sum in the North, where the neo-Fascist government was maintaining price controls, and a whole movie could be made for three million. Once into liberated territory, however, where inflation raged unchecked, the money shrunk to a quarter of its value and was barely enough to get shooting started. They would still need Fabrizi.

Fabrizi was hanging tough. Day after day, amid constant threats to terminate negotiations completely, he eased his demands not at all, or perhaps ever so slightly. Day after day, while praising Fellini's efforts, Roberto kept Amidei abreast of the tedious progress. Meanwhile Roberto was meeting secretly with Fellini, going over the scenes Amidei had written, and the next day presenting rewrites to Amidei. "I spent all night on these, Sergio," he'd explain, "all by myself." And Amidei, knowing Roberto, and suspecting something was afoot, would take the rewrites wordlessly, and then secretly restore his own version, keeping only the changes he liked. Eventually, when Roberto decided he had prepared the ground sufficiently, he pointed out that Fabrizi would have much more confidence in the film, and therefore be much more eager to sign, if Fellini were taken on as a collaborator. This was incontrovertible. More importantly, Amidei appreciated the idiomatic poetry of the dialogues Fellini had written. He knew he couldn't write that way himself. "I realized back in 1922 when I arrived in Turin that I'd never learn to speak Italian [the way Italians do]."[26] So Amidei not only accepted Fellini but, departing from his usual rigidity, even consented to a few work sessions at Fellini's apartment—in the kitchen, of course, the only room with heat during that bitterly cold winter when not a few in Rome froze to death.[27] When Amidei would fly into rages, Roberto would intervene and, talking to each of his collaborators separately, impress his own ideas into the scenario.

Fellini's and Amidei's contracts are both dated October 21.[28] Fellini would receive 25,000 lire.

Amidei had already graphed the movie's action, laying it out scene by scene, step by step, until the whole narrative arch had been formed. Fellini's contribution, aside from completing the dialogue Amidei had begun, was to add gags for Fabrizi—like the frying pan Don Pietro uses to knock out the paralytic in the apartment building the Germans raid. Nonetheless, the film still didn't interest Fellini. He was involved only out of affection for Roberto.

A Jewish writer, Diena, also participated in these sessions. But at a certain point he announced that a Communist hero was against his conscience and he quit. This in itself was unheard of, but what truly floored Roberto, Amidei, and Fellini was that Diena returned the small advance he had been given. Diena was clearly not cut out for the movies.

The news spread, however, and served to provoke a storm of protest over the next few weeks. First came Angelo Besozzi, who with Civallero had assumed the functions of managing producer, to demand that the Communist be changed into a follower of Marshall Badoglio.

This was more insidious than it sounds. As head of the nominal Italian government, Badoglio represented the principle that the king was still king and that the Italian state continued, despite the cessation of Fascism. Seven other parties existed, however, which Badoglio refused to recognize: the Christian Democrats, the Socialists, the Communists, the Liberals, the Action Party, Labor, and the Republicans. The right wing of these shadow parties, thrown perforce into coalition, hoped to supplant Badoglio but were not opposed to certain principles he represented. They were willing to accept the king (or the king's son) and they lived in dread of the "Wind from the north"—the eruption onto the political scene of the popular masses and partisan bans that would surely occur once all Italy was freed. To them—Besozzi and Civallero—a Badoglian hero meant order, stability, and renewal of traditional values. But to most people, and to the virulent left wing in particular, Vittorio Emanuele was *"il re fellone"* ("the criminal king") and the break with Fascism meant Liberation, a new beginning, a return to the Risorgimento, a total break with the Piedmontese dictatorship of the last 85 years.

To this virulent left, according to Pirro, Rossellini was someone who should be purged, because of his "Fascist" past; his participation in any picture celebrating the Resistance was an offensive mockery. And, according to Pirro, it fell to Amidei, with his impeccable credentials and friendships with the Communist hierarchy, to defend Roberto to his comrades on the one hand, and his Communist hero to Besozzi on the other. And naturally, still according to Pirro, this defense on two fronts was accomplished by Amidei with his customary, implacable ferociousness, with the result that a deep solidarity was forged between himself and Roberto. The Countess, meanwhile, far from being scared off by the fracas, sat back happily relishing each delicious tidbit of the scandal; now more than ever was she committed to the film, and to Roberto—who, some said, had taken her to bed.[29]

According to Roberto's sister Marcella, however, it was out of jealousy and a desire to inflate his responsibility for *Roma città aperta* that Amidei (through Pirro and others) claimed he had protected Roberto and, worse, claimed that Roberto required protection in the first place.[30] No contemporary witness supports the contention that Rossellini was suspect or in need of protection; on the contrary, Mario Del Papa, Franco Riganti, and two Communists, Massimo Mida and Giuseppe De Santis, all deny it.[31] Besides, many of Amidei's Communist friends were Roberto's friends as well; they were Party leaders who had watched Roberto's life during the Occupation and had spent many a long night sharing with him their plans and dreams. Some of them had known Roberto much longer than they had known Amidei, from boyhood even. Naturally there were wild idealists to whom anyone not a card-carrying partisan was objectionable; there were crass opportunists ready to transmute personal jealousies into ideological denunciation; and there were (and are) those eager to melodramatize any sort of squabble. But Roberto, far from being under a cloud for his supposed Fascism, was generally trusted by people on the left as—at worst—a good soul who would profit from their guidance.

To play the two Communists Roberto, never eager to exert himself in talent searches and always eager to avoid dramatic actors and surround himself with friends, resorted to the architect Francesco Grandjacquet, who had had a part in *Desiderio*, and to his school chum, the Bohemian, ever-drinking Marcello Pagliero. Both had credentials in the Resistance, Grandjacquet as a member of the partisan group GAP, Pagliero for having made the Fosse Ardeatine episode of *Giorni di gloria*, the partisan-produced film to which Visconti, De Santis, Serandrei, and Barbaro had also contributed immediately after the liberation. Yet neither Roberto nor Amidei could decide which of them would play the heroic martyr Manfredi and it was Maria Michi who ultimately made the choice. She could see herself as Pagliero's lover, she said, but his soft, unheroic face, perpetually indifferent and half-awake, made her mad, so mad that she could well imagine wanting to betray him. At this, a fight exploded between Michi and Amidei, who lambasted her for being ready to betray someone just because she didn't like his face. Grandjacquet was cast as Pina's lover.[32]

Face was the problem, too, in casting the role of Kappler. Few of Roberto's acquaintances looked German, and none of them would stoop to playing a Gestapo colonel. But one day Amidei, still with visions of Magnani as Pina even though negotiations were going on with Calamai, went to see Anna in her current revue, *Con un palmo di naso*, with Totò, and afterwards drifted backstage. There Magnani, in the midst of a brutal battle with her lover Massimo Serato, dominated even more thoroughly than on stage. So lost was Amidei in his fascination with her acrobatic gesticulations and screaming profanity, that he barely glimpsed a Satanic male dancer standing nearby. But he did recall this person when he met Roberto the next morning, and suggested he might be the Kappler they needed.

But who was he? Amidei phoned Magnani.

"He's an Austrian. A big queer!" she snorted.

"Wonderful! What's his name?"

"Harry Feist." She was in a bad mood.

"Where can we find him? Where's he live?"

"How the hell would I know?!" grunted Magnani, and hung up.

It was evident she was still distraught over Serato and had been waiting desperately for him to call—whereupon she would have destroyed him as thoroughly as a voice could. Nonetheless, Pirro says, Amidei would have called back as many times as he had to in order to curse her out for her rudeness. But Roberto, now that he knew this Harry Feist was a dancer, an Austrian, and a homosexual, was eager to see him: he sounded perfect for Kappler.

They walked to the Galleria Colonna, where vaudeville people tended to gather late in the morning, and bumped into Nando Bruno, a character actor whom they immediately hired to play the sacristan. A few minutes later they spotted Feist, sinuous and unreticently gay. Feist was Jewish, had lived unmolested in Italy since the late twenties, and the prospect of appearing as so despicable a character initially terrified him, but stronger than his fear, says Pirro, was his exhibitionism—the masochist thrill of imagining himself loathed by everybody—and, of course, the uses to which he could put his salary.[33]

Roberto found Giovanna Galletti's face and manners—she was a dramatic actress, after all—perfect for Ingrid, the German lesbian (although her voice would later be dubbed by Roswitha). Amidei's landlady and maid would play themselves. And there was a new title. No one liked *Storie di ieri*, so Amidei, as was his wont, had gone into the library at Piazza di Spagna and, accompanied by Roberto, had thumbed randomly through the card catalogue, until a novel called *Città chiusa* ("Closed City") had caught his interest. "*Città aperta*," he said: *Open City*. And so it became.

It summed up the movie in an ironic twist.

*

Roberto had rented a makeshift studio, 180 by 60 feet, belonging to Liborio Capitani, a single semi-basement shared by two large buildings, the Braschi and Tittoni palazzi, at Via degli Avignonesi 30, a few blocks from the *Cacciatore* restaurant but near the *Gallo d'Oro* trattoria. Totò would film *Il ratto delle sabine* ("The rape of the Sabines") here in September; before that it had housed a dog-race arena. A few doors away, at number 7–8, had been Anton Giulio Bragaglia's Teatro degli Indipendenti, site of legendary "Futurist Evenings" like the night Marinetti improvised long dialogues with volcanoes consisting of nothing but onomatopoetic noises. Roberto had four sets constructed: the sacristy, Marina's room, the Gestapo office, and the salon—all in a row. Although a few props had to be rented, like the piano, almost all the furnishings came from Roberto's or Michi's homes and almost all the costumes were the actors' own clothing.

In the same building, number 30, above the studio, was a bordello run by Tina Trabucchi. Roberto would go there and rest when he was tired. Mussolini had frequented it during the years he had lived on nearby Via Rasella and now, as spoils of war, Allied soldiers were the principal clients. Only whites were permitted in Madama Trabucchi's (a limitation not imposed by the ladies themselves) and other, less legal, whorehouses had sprung up nearby to cater to clients of other colors. The soldiers often wandered around drunk and confused in the darkness, with the result that throughout the shooting of *Roma città aperta* they would come bang on the door of the film studio by mistake. On the first night they found themselves greeted by a priest (Fabrizi) who would raise his eyes to heaven, beg forgiveness, and solemnly direct them to the appropriate door.

Filming would take place at night, because electricity was not reliably available during the day. It wasn't reliably available at night, either, but the chances of brown-outs were fewer, and it was easier to steal electricity from the nearby offices of *Stars and Stripes*, the U.S. Army newspaper. In this they were aided by Pilade Levi (or Pilate de Levi), an Italian Jew who'd emigrated to America and was now heading the Army's psychological war program in Rome. When theft failed, they had batteries and a generator; but the generator needed gasoline, which could only be bought on the black market, which required money, which they usually didn't have. By shooting without sound, without even a scratch track, they cut costs in half.

Regardless, there was still never enough light, because lamp bulbs couldn't be found, and the few they had produced a dim, yellowish glow. The result looked more like a church than a movie set. Arata was screaming threats to quit. "I want light! I can't doooooo this! You can't see *anything, anything, anything!*"[34]

Roberto tried to calm him. The light was perfect for the style he wanted, he explained, because he wanted everything "thrown away"—the lighting, the recitation, the framings—the last thing he wanted was the usual, polished, studio look. To Arata, this sounded like blarney, just what he expected from Rossellini; if he finally capitulated and agreed to go ahead and shoot, it wasn't because Roberto had convinced him that the picture wouldn't embarrass him professionally; it was because he was convinced that no one would ever see it anyway, because it would never get finished. And in truth no one, not even Arata, would be able to see the scenes he shot that night. They had no money to develop the film—and no lab would give them credit. Probably it would all come out too dark; probably not a single frame of anything would be usable.

Shooting, on that first night, January 17–18, 1945, was delayed by compromise until after midnight; Roberto had wanted the 17th because it was Marcella De Marchis's 29th birthday, but Italians considered seventeen an unlucky number. First Fabrizi (who still hadn't signed his contract) crossed himself, then Roberto, then everyone else, even Amidei—although he turned around so no one would see him. Roberto was 38 years old.

They began with scenes of Don Pietro and the Germans, then the torture scenes. Then the landlord appeared on the staircase yelling for his rent. Roberto yelled back.

"Get off my ass!"

"You're the one who's on my ass!" Capitani screamed. "Your countess palmed off a rubber check for 17,000 lire on me!"

(Two days earlier, January 15, Nettunia Productions had had to borrow 25,000 lire from a textile merchant, Aldo Venturini, a Rossellini family friend.)

It was a disaster. But Roberto went on, inventing ridiculous stratagems day by day, living from hope and getting others to share it, and indulging in acrobatics that a dozen times could have landed him in prison.

The crew were dubious and Roberto preoccupied; Amidei was carried away by excitement, by, as he called it, "the joy of saying the truth.... Before we had said the truth very little, now everything we were saying and doing was true, joyfully true, even the lost war, because it wasn't we who had lost it but Fascism. The force of the new Italian cinema was this: the euphoria of the truth."[35]

But a particular sort of truth. For Amidei the truth meant a film that would show the evilness and corruption of the Nazis (Fascism was scarcely alluded to), the goodness and heroism of the Roman people, how much those people had suffered on behalf of right and justice, and how the triumph of the people was inevitable. Every incident and every person thus had some correspondence with actual incidents and people, but thus also melodrama was at the core of Amidei's conflict of good against evil. His characters were stereotyped—the good fatso priest who's always good; the hero who's always heroic; the sadistic Nazi who's always bad; the lesbian drug-addict who sinks to perfidy and causes the hero's tragedy; the innocent mother who suffers and dies; the orphaned child. Evil on one side was as concentrated as good on the other: torturers, sexual "perverts," drug addicts, drunkards, betrayers, and shadowy interiors *versus* mothers, children, freedom fighters, a priest, and sunshine. Pitted against stereotypes of eternal damnation were stereotypes of nationalism, Christianity, solidarity, populism, morality, and existentialism. But revolutionary art is always this way, and revolutionary art was what Amidei intended: a movie that would articulate the experiences and dreams of the masses, a movie that would proclaim the truth of the revolution. The conventions Amidei was manipulating, moreover, were, despite hundreds of years of wear, still vital in theatrical revues and *commedia dell'arte*. Both vaudeville and the *commedia* staged fables using stock characters wearing masks as an outline for improvisation on themes of current interest. In Amidei's film, as directed by Rossellini, the shock of that improvisation would be overpowering: the emotion-charged actuality to which the old conventions were wedded; the off-handedness with which human failings were depicted in an age when "good taste" censored everything; and above all the experience of moral redemption through suffering. So overpowering that few would notice the melodramatic structure.

The shock was an outcome of conflict between Amidei and Rossellini. Roberto's intentions were quite different. In making *Roma città aperta* he was no more a Communist than he was a Fascist when making *L'uomo dalla croce*. He was not politically motivated, he was not interested in revolutionary popularism, he did not want to push people toward some new ideology (Communism) to replace an old ideology (Fascism). Instead he wanted to explore the past, to relive it, to understand it. He wanted to come to terms with the fear he had experienced. "I could have made *Roma città aperta* like propaganda, against everything," he later explained. "I tried not to. I tried to explore and understand, because I had the feeling that we were all responsible for what happened, all of us. Now, how to solve that problem?"[36]

"I posed [to] myself two goals: one, the moral position: to look without mystifying, to try to make a portrait of us, of us then, as honestly as possible.[37] [It was] didactic, precisely because the effort I made . . . was to achieve understanding of events in which I had been immersed, by which I had been shaken. It was the exploration not only of historic facts, but really of attitudes, of behavior that that certain atmosphere, that that certain historical situation had determined.[38] The other goal was to break the industrial structures of those years, to be able to conquer the liberty to experiment without conditions. Once those two goals are achieved, you find the problem of style already resolved automatically. When you give up pretending, manipulating, you already have an image, a language . . . , a style. When, to kill the industrial structures of cinema, you leave the sound stage . . . and shoot on the street . . . like someone who lives and belongs there, you discover as a result that you possess a style. The language, the style of neo-realism are here: it's the result of a moral position, of looking critically at the obvious."[39]

Thus the tension in Amidei's screenplay and *commedia* between actuality and melodrama was brought to life by Roberto's spontaneity.

This Crocean attitude toward history—a desire to make the past spontaneously present, to relive it in present consciousness—was unique with

Rossellini in film. Many films had told history, or used it as a background to explore ideas and characters, or to propagate ideas. But it is hard to think of one that historicized events to relive them, to understand them. Renoir's *La Marseillaise* (1938), for example, is Crocean in that it constantly implies analogies between populist causes during the French Revolution and Popular Front crises in 1938. But the film's style is unceasingly presentational; it seeks to demonstrate a thesis, not to inquire into an event.[40]

Thus Amidei represented traditional principles of dramaturgy yoked to radical political purposes, whereas Roberto represented radical principles of dramaturgy yoked to traditional humanist purposes. They were indeed an odd couple and in the weeks ahead would clash repeatedly over issues deriving from their opposing attitudes. And Amidei would often prevail.

Amidei, for example (according to Pirro), insisted that the torture scenes be detailed. For him it was important to show what the Germans were capable of (and he hadn't yet learned of the concentration camps). Roberto, however, thought such detail excessive and argued that the more that was shown the less horrible it would seem, that things persistently realistic end up looking false, and that these scenes would clash with the off-handed manner of the rest of the film. Amidei was not present when the scenes were shot,[41] but got his way in the end. (The scenes strongly resemble those Renoir shot for *Tosca* in 1940.[42])

Amidei also prevailed over Rossellini in imposing a transcendental vision of history: spring *will* come, truth *will* triumph. *Roma città aperta* is a melodrama demonstrating why good must defeat evil. Roberto would have to wait for his next film, when he would have more control, before he could relive history without a thesis as his guide.

Nonetheless, Amidei continued to believe (with justification) that Roberto wanted to make the picture politically ambiguous; periodically he would demand that his name be taken off.

This argument continued all through the preliminary editing, at which point Amidei insisted that the film, in its rough cut and without sound, be shown not only to his political gurus, Negarville, Amendola, and Alicata, but to two Russian generals as well. (Negarville was now the editor of *L'Unità* and undersecretary of state in Parri's cabinet.) Roberto resisted as best he could, but ultimately capitulated on the understanding that he would not be bound by the Communists' verdicts.

Much to everyone's amazement, the Russians decreed it would be politically mistaken to insist on detailed depiction of torture. The Russians had their own acts of torture to conceal, of course, but at the time, long before Khrushchev's denunciations of Stalin, no one in Italy expected this was the case, and the generals' verdict was accepted as authoritative.[43]

That first night of shooting, these disagreements still lay in the future. Sergio and Roberto left at dawn together. Tipping his hat, Roberto gaily exchanged quips with the prostitutes who, they too, had also finished work.

*

Word began to spread that this *Città aperta* might turn out to be something after all. It would be "the first film worthy of representing the new Italian cinema," the Roman newspaper *Star* predicted on January 20. And since, the gossips said, Magnani was out and Clara Calamai was procrastinating over her contract,[44] other actresses, Assia Noris and Isa Miranda among them, were trying to grab the role of sora Pina. In the past, before the war, a phone call would have sufficed to interest their producers in a movie they liked and, for the price of Pina, Roberto's financial problems would have instantly been resolved. Now things were different. The producers did not have confidence in Rossellini. He had put together a *combinazione* of filmdom's top and most respected talents, but he was the weak link: as a director of actors, as a maker of story movies rather than action films, his record was mediocre at best; as a man of affairs, as a fiduciary investment, he was the bubonic plague. Besides, producers were timid about committing money in these uncertain times, and a movie about Communists and torture sounded triply unsafe: why not a pleasant comedy? After all, people wanted to feel good, not relive those horrible months.

Rossellini for his part would not have allowed his earthy woman-of-the-people to be portrayed by actresses whose stock in trade was their glamour, sophistication, and starry-eyed mystery. Nor did he want to chain himself to a producer of the old style: it was that sort of cinema he was dedicated to escaping ("destroying," he would say). In later years, however, after *Roma città aperta*'s success and after Pina had proved the most memorable role in the entire history of Italian film,[45] Calamai would lament that Rossellini had wanted her but that a previous commitment to Camerini had prevented her from accepting, Miranda would give a similar explanation, and Noris would charge that it hadn't been her fault at all: her mother had forbade her to work with that Rossellini character.[46]

Meanwhile the Countess's money was almost used up. Roberto was spending more time in the little food shop next door, phoning for money and film stock, than in the studio directing. "I sold my bed to begin the film," he declared a year later, "and then it was the turn of a dresser and a glass wardrobe."[47] "Roberto had to sell everything to make *Roma città aperta*. Everything!" wailed Marcella De Marchis. "My fur, my gold bracelet, everything we had, for little pieces of film! We lived on bread and *caciotta* [a soft white cheese]."[48]

Film stock sometimes could be obtained only in short ends left over from other projects, or in rolls manufactured for Leica still cameras. Eventually it appears to have been an American reporter, Donald Downes, who came to the rescue, purloining film from the American news agencies. "What do *they* need it for?" he would shout. "They only tell lies."[49] The stock he stole was Dupont I or II, a high-definition negative; nothing better could be had even in Hollywood.

As long as he kept the film going, Roberto reasoned, he was sure to find a way to complete it. He spent hours on the food shop's pay phone. Someone would be sent to fetch him when they were ready to shoot. Once or twice he told them to go ahead without him. When the scene didn't particularly interest him, he had every confidence that actors and cameramen could act and photograph just as well whether he were there or not.[50]

It was more important to keep the company together, even when there wasn't enough money to pay them. Once he came up with 50,000 lire, wrote out checks totaling 200,000, and sent his assistant Alberto Manni to stand in front of the bank on Via del Tritone. When someone came along whose name appeared in a little red booklet Roberto had given him (cagily calculating who really needed money and who did not), it was Manni's duty to divert them to a café on the other side of the street and gradually persuade them not to cash the check that day.

One time Roberto took a little gold chain off his neck and instructed Manni to sell it for 14,000. Another time he desperately phoned a friend who agreed to lend the day's receipts from his chain of movie theaters if the sum were repaid on Monday; and after going all around Rome to various box offices, Roberto and Manni were able finally to pay the crew—in small change.

Amidei went to see Amato. Amato was the sort who embarked on new adventures daily. He dropped them just as quickly, but one never knew where his whims might lead. It was always worth seeing him.

He held court in a smoking jacket in his room on the first floor of the Excelsior, the same room that during the Occupation had been occupied by the German General Kurt Maeltzer, the commander of the Gestapo on whom *Roma città aperta*'s Kappler was based. Perhaps for this reason, or perhaps for another, says Pirro, Amato decided a film on the Resistance was not such a bad idea, provided that it was apolitical. He always insisted his projects be apolitical, although it was never quite clear what he meant by that, or exactly how a film on the Resistance was to be apolitical. Somehow Amidei avoided arguing and Amato agreed to advance 250,000 lire in exchange for the right to sell the film outside of Italy (a prospect neither Amidei nor Roberto had even considered). But Amato insisted Magnani be cast as Pina.

In fact, Clara Calamai was being impossible. As an established star and, on the basis of *Ossessione*, as *the* star of the new Italian cinema, she felt she had a right to find difficulties. Civallero talked to her gently and showed her Amidei's outline and a few of the finished scenes. A special make-up artist, Alberto De Rossi, was hired just for her on February 19. But she didn't trust Roberto—he was a "documentary" filmmaker, after all—and she didn't have confidence in his descriptions of her scenes; she wanted to see them on paper. The part of sora Pina seemed small—and not without reason, for Amidei, determined to sabotage her, had held back the texts of her best scenes (including the one where, walking with Don Pietro, she wonders if Christ has abandoned them). Calamai, says Pirro, insisted her death be postponed until the end of the movie, when she also wanted a monologue to recite as she died.

Roberto was called to the Excelsior, and they went together, the three of them, to Via dell'Amba Aradam, near San Giovanni, where Magnani lived in an apartment abandoned to her by Alessandrini. Although Anna had had a series of liaisons after Alessandrini had left her, and a child by Serato, she kept this apartment always, never sharing it with any of her lovers.

She greeted them in rage. Serato had been cruel, they had fought, he still had not called, she had been waiting for days. All this she acted out scene by scene, then, bursting into tears, threw herself onto the couch. Amidei and Amato looked on, frozen in amazement. Roberto bent down to comfort her. As always, he could not resist someone in trouble. She lay sobbing and he stroked her hair and wiped her cheeks.

She sat up at last, placed the phone beside her in case Serato should call, and listened as Amidei told her the story of the film. Again she cried, but this time for Pina, and they watched in fascination as she stood up and started walking around the room, already Pina. She insisted at first on being paid one lire more than Fabrizi, who had finally signed for 400,000 (for the moment). But this would only have outraged Fabrizi. She promptly accepted the same salary.

The very next day Amato was already talking to the Countess as though he were about to renege. But he signed and advanced 250,000, of which 40,000 went immediately to secure Magnani.

Now that the film had a legitimate producer and distributor, they could finally see what they had shot.

Together with Amato, they screened the footage two days later. Arata sighed with relief: it wasn't very good—it was clumsy and a bit under exposed—but all of it was usable. Roberto and Amidei smiled faintly; they still didn't know how good it was, but they really liked what they saw.

Amato, however, jumped screaming to his feet. It looked horrible, horrible. It was technically contemptible, he had been lied to, he wanted nothing more to do with the whole affair. "I'll eat this contract, I hate it so much!" he screamed, and, Pirro says, actually tore off a piece and stuffed it into his mouth. And under that contract, which he had dictated himself, he was demanding restitution of the money he had advanced.

"You don't understand anything," Amidei pronounced sententiously and stomped out. Then, once outside, he screamed at Michi all the things he would have screamed at Amato, had not Amato already been screaming himself.

Rossellini, in contrast, sat smoking, his legs crossed and his hand, as usual, fidgeting with a lock of his hair. He was trying his best to look indifferent, for he knew Amato for what he was: a self-made scrapper who'd scratch and tear and lie and weasel for the sake of scoring a petty one-upmanship over a business partner, but who, a moment later, would casually throw away a fortune on the spin of a roulette wheel. Roberto was trying to provoke Amato. And his indifference was already having an effect. For Amato, shifting the drift of his diatribe, was now suggesting that perhaps he'd forget about demanding his money back, if the negative were handed over to him. In other words, he'd finish the picture himself, as he had done once before, with triumphant results, in the case of Blasetti's *Quattro passi fra le nuvole* ("Four steps in the clouds"), and in this way, he'd show Rossellini and Amidei how it *ought* to be done.

Roberto, sensing his only hope lay in raising the stakes, casually announced he was disposed to honor Amato's claim, but in IOUs signed by himself personally.

It was a preposterous proposal, an utter bluff. They both knew Roberto wouldn't be able to pay back the IOUs. But here he was willing to ruin himself (IOUs, or *cambiali*, are legal notes in Italy, and freely sold and resold, until someone decides to collect) by betting everything on a film Amato wasn't willing to bet a single lira on. It was a wager Amato couldn't refuse. He no longer cared whether he collected the money or not. He just wanted the picture to fail and Rossellini to be proved wrong.[51]

Without Roberto's ability to bluff—to put forth a bold front and generate confidence—*Roma città aperta* would never have gotten made. He was, after all, a Roman among Romans: proudest of his bravado when the odds were greatest against him. Nothing inspired him to bold acts more surely than his own fear. As though to dazzle himself with his own virtuosity in the art of life, he suicidally added one ball after another to those he was already juggling—barely. Directing *Roma città aperta* was a full-time job in itself. But at the same time he was searching out film stock, mollifying Amidei, manipulating Fabrizi, nursing Magnani through multiple crises, scurrying for money to keep the picture going, day by day hunting food and provisions for Roswitha on the one hand and Marcellina and their two boys on the other, and meanwhile, between Madama Trabucchi's whores, having an affair with Carla Rovere, an actress in the film. Pirro claims Roberto broke down one night and started to cry.

But that would have been even more extraordinary than Roberto's juggling, and completely out of character.[52]

One evening he, Amidei, and their Countess were introduced to a British intelligence agent, who gravely informed them that their work had propaganda value which merited assistance. He wrote out a check for 150,000 lire, as an advance.

To clear the check, Roberto's banker wanted five days. The banker's niece, more susceptible to charm, cashed it immediately. Within hours the entire sum vanished into creditors' pockets. Five days later, the niece appeared on the studio staircase: the check had been as phony as the agent.[53]

When money was scarce, Fabrizi and Magnani, as the least in need, were the least regularly paid. They continued out of sympathy and trust, although on several occasions production was suspended for a week or more, while they worked jobs that paid immediately.[54]

The daily chaos continued for two-and-a-half months.[55] Roberto added to it by regularly disappearing. Fortunately, some of the crew, like Manni and Carlo Carlini, had worked with the maestro before; and some of the actors, like Pagliero and Grandjacquet, were old friends and would have been surprised only by an absence of chaos. Most people found Rossellini unsupportive. Pirro describes the set as a madhouse. Harry Feist was strutting around offending everyone and being offended. Pagliero simply refused to act or recite; he would only blankly repeat what Roberto said, and even then required vast quantities of wine and whisky to function; and when Roberto disappeared to make phone calls, so would Pagliero, for a drink in the brothel. Fabrizi behaved like a prima donna, insisting on flattery and coaxing, sick with insecurity. Amidei would spat raucously with Michi, then hover like a commissar, vainly trying to enforce observance of every comma and apostrophe in his script. Arata never ceased yelling, moaning, and groaning: there was never enough light, never the proper equipment, never enough film; sometimes there wasn't even a door in a set where a door was supposed to be.

And all the while, the instigator of it soared serene and apparently indifferent. Rossellini's manner as a director could not have been more opposite the chaos and deviousness of his manner as producer. On the set, no difficulty was an obstacle, no problem really important. Amidei's elaborate schemes were reduced casually to the merest essential, and Roberto couldn't have cared less about his hysterics. Protests, yells, curses, and complaints passed over him as though he were on another planet. In fact, he took note of everything and would eventually put it to use, and his casualness was a maneuver calculated to increase everyone's absolute dependence upon him.

Then, when the situation demanded, no one could be more sympathetic than Roberto. More often, actors were merely precious. Thirty years later, when someone asked about the wonderful "emotional quality" of Fabrizi's performance, Roberto was ready.

"You remember," he answered, speaking English, "the scene when Fabrizi realizes Manfredi [Pagliero] is dead and he blesses him? Well, Fabrizi said to me, 'You must do me a favor. I want to cry. I want really to cry.' So I said, 'Okay, cry, then.'

"We spent half a day waiting for him to cry. Then we said, 'How can you cry?' 'Well, you know, I think, for example, of a little white flower.' So he said, 'Be ready! When I snap my fingers, start shooting because I will be crying.'

"And so we wait for hours. Then he says, 'May I have a cognac?' Yes, okay, you can have a cognac.' So finally after twenty cognacs, he gets totally drunk and he thought about that little white flower and starts to cry.

"I called him later into the projection room, and I said, 'You can see what a masterpiece you have made.' It was absolutely disgusting. The tears were coming out of his nose in balloons, from his mouth. Exploding! It was absolutely a disgusting scene!

"He said, 'But I really cried!'

"'I know you really cried. But what does it mean to really cry? It means nothing at all!'

"So we had to do the scene again. And it was very easy. With a few drops of glycerin he was crying. It was nothing at all!

"How can an actor in a studio with the lamps, the electrician around, and everybody tired of waiting—how can he get into the mood? Actors know just two, three, or four tricks, and they always play on those kinds of tricks. But if you want something else, you must invent things and you must make them at ease. To 'feel,' to 'participate' to me means nothing at all."[56]

Rossellini's methods of shooting brought him into constant conflict with Amidei. "Accustomed as I was to conventional methods," Amidei later admitted, "I was continually balling him out for not knowing how to shoot a film. But he was the one who was right."[57] Convention, in prewar Italy as well as in Hollywood, decreed that a scene in a room between two people, for example, would be edited into a dozen or more short takes, so that certain moments could be given suitable dramatic emphasis. But Rossellini, whether through laziness or genius (one was never sure), had even in *Un pilota ritorna* favored a simpler approach: when possible, he liked to film such scenes in one long single take. This approach was in practice much more demanding on the actors who, instead of concentrating on what they would do during the next eight or ten seconds, were now left to themselves for a minute or more. Yet when they made mistakes or moved awkwardly or flubbed a line, Rossellini would often refuse to do the scene over, on the grounds that their awkwardness was "natural." Since no actor wants to appear inept, they often suspected that Rossellini just did not care. In fact, he did not care for the slow, belabored theatricality that was then the fashion in Italian pictures.

Amidei objected that audiences wouldn't understand, that scenes required editing in order for the correct interpretation to come through. Rossellini retorted that he didn't want to interpret, that audiences should be free to interpret for themselves—if they wanted to. Someone else objected that, no, audiences didn't want to interpret, they wanted to be entertained; long takes are dramatically flat and boring, and require work from audiences. Rossellini replied that there was no point in making films if they all had to follow the same formula, that people had been led around by their noses for years by Fascism, and that now it was time to reject all that and find a fresh way to say new things.

As much as possible, he tried to put into practice the sort of "stream of consciousness" cinema he had theorized about during the Occupation. But the simple flowing style he had sometimes managed in previous films (like the long circular pans in *L'uomo dalla croce*) was often impossible now. There wasn't room for such maneuvers in the Avignonesi studio, and often there weren't lengths of film long enough either; at times he was compelled to re-compose scenes to fit the shortened time he could keep the camera running. Nonetheless, "it's enough just to follow the actors," he would say again and again—never adding that he usually set up a scene so that the poor actors, when it came time to move, had very few choices about where to go. Yet he always kept his actor at the center of frame, and it always seemed that the camera would follow the actor's cue, moving just after he did rather than anticipating beforehand which direction he might take. Had the camera moved first, it would imply the character was doing the correct thing, that somehow his actions were preordained, and that God or fate was watching over him. Rossellini's following camera, on the other hand, implied that the character was on his own, that there were no preordained right or wrong choices, and that responsibility ultimately rested in the individual.

A scene, nonetheless, usually had a point. And Rossellini, contrary to every norm at the time, would refuse to underline that point. Amidei, ob-sessed with the messages in his scripts, would want to develop a scene's point and emphasize it in some way, but Rossellini would try to have it occur naturally, as though resulting from the simple course of events, and might even transform a point into a question. At heart, he didn't care about the script or telling a story "well." What interested him was not the plot but its pauses: the contrasts between characters, between characters and their background, insights into people, in other words, that manifest them-selves only on the screen and scarcely at all in the plot.[58] For him, the essence of film drama lay in *expectation*: here was this poor minuscule be-ing trying to go about his life, but all along forces outside of him dominate him, unknown to him, and they strike terribly just when he feels free and secure from worry. In *Roma città aperta* the terrible forces were the Ger-mans, while the Romans dreamed of freedom.

Roberto's casualness and the continual feuding with Amidei almost combined with a silly mistake to shut down the film. Jone Tuzzi discovered that they had filmed the scene where a fur coat (Marcella Rossellini's in real life) is taken back from Michi, but they had forgotten to film the scene where she is given it. Tuzzi remembered typing the scene, but the script had always been a collection of constantly revised pages rather than a sin-gle, bound entity, and now the pages were missing as well.

Everyone searched madly as Amidei launched furiously into Roberto: he hadn't even noticed! He didn't give a damn! In fact he was deliberately trying to sabotage the film's political message! Roberto shouted back, and Michi, deciding it was all a plot to cut her out of the film, began to cry. The crew watched a three-ring circus.

Tuzzi ran home, found the pages, and returned. The battle was still raging. Afraid to admit the truth, she claimed she'd found the scene in Countess Politi's office.[59]

*

Meanwhile, Franco Riganti asked Roberto for a job. Back in 1943 he had been on top of the world with a prospering production company and theater chain. But when it had become apparent that the war was going to be lost, his board of directors—large corporations like Fiat that had grown fat under the Duce—had summoned him and told him to sack Vittorio Mussolini: it was time for a new image. But Riganti had refused to play the executioner; Vittorio Mussolini had been his friend and had helped him; it was a matter of loyalty and honor.

Five minutes later, he had been out on the street and out of a job.

The next two years had been difficult. For a while after the liberation, he had driven a truck, but mostly his family had had to get by on what they could sell from their home.

Riganti had profited from friends in the regime, as had Rossellini and his father, but he had never been one of them. Luigi Freddi, the government film czar, had thrice attempted to have him sent into internal exile, into confinement in some primitive town in the South, objecting that Riganti refused to wear black shirt and published articles that were anti-Fascist. During the Occupation, Riganti had sheltered fugitives in his apartment, among them the partisan Valeriano Olivieri, with his wife and child, the Communist Nino Vicentini, the Senator Alessandro Brizzi, who became Badoglio's minister of agriculture, and two Jewish women. Fortunately the apartment was large; unfortunately a high-ranking German officer had taken over Ciano's apartment on the top floor. Not only were sentries perpetually patrolling the premises, but every other day the German would make a tour of his neighbors' doors, politely asking if they needed anything, then clicking his heels and saluting.

When Riganti heard Roberto was starting a film, he contacted him.

They met in Piazza Navona.

"Caro Franco, what can I do for you?" asked Roberto.

Franco told him his situation.

"Franco, how can I present you with your political past?" Roberto replied. The film was dominated by Communists; if he gave an ex-Fascist a job, he himself would be kicked out.

Franco said he was desperate. He would do anything. Even run errands.

His hands were tied, Roberto said, a bit too suavely, a bit too gaily.

Riganti went away without mentioning the little pile of IOUs Roberto had signed in the days they had been brothers.[60]

Some who knew Rossellini well deny this incident could have happened: Roberto was not the sort to refuse a friend or have his actions curtailed by stupid prejudices. Others estimate him less highly. In Amidei's words, Roberto "always had something he needed to be forgiven for"[61]; his career, like his romances, was punctuated with innumerable charges of "betrayal."

Amidei always contended that Rossellini had been politically questionable in 1945 and had needed his protection to make the transition into the new Italian cinema. Pirro, Roncoroni, and others have concluded that, as a result, Roberto was constrained by his collaborators, in evidence of which is the fully-dialogued script he was obliged to respect, something even the Fascists had been unable to make him do. Marcella Rossellini and others, on the contrary, dismissed notions that Roberto required protection. True, Amidei's contribution was immense; and Roberto was always "susceptible" to his friends and to Amidei in particular. But Roberto was not subservient. He regarded Amidei as a hysteric and provoked him often. Amidei would accuse him of changing "everything" and would demand his name be taken off the film credits. But Amidei, far from being the hovering commissar Pirro portrays, was rarely on the set (Vito Annicchiarico never saw him there); his fighting was a desperate rearguard action, according to Marcella Rossellini, to constrain the meteoric Rossellini and preserve some of his script's radical politics against Roberto's centrism.[62]

Undoubtedly, Roberto was using his Communist friends as he had used De Robertis, Riganti, and the Fascists, as he would use Americans and anyone else, as he had, in his own words, during Fascism—employing extraordinary contortions and all his talents to make films without falling prisoner to the system, evading baits thrown his way, being "strong, supple, and ungraspable as an eel."[63]

In fact, he had made no secret of his Fascist antipathies then, and was making no secret of his Christian-Democrat sympathies now. But even an eel, when he's producing his first independent film with shaky financing and shaky reputation, has to make concessions to hold his *combinazione* together. Rossellini succeeded in emphasizing the Church's role in the Resistance. But, Marcella Rossellini to the contrary, the movie itself is evidence that he did concede to Amidei on the torture scenes, the transcendental view of history, the melodramatic characters, and the tight plotting. And he was afraid to hire Franco Riganti.

It looked likely, in 1945, that the Communists would inherit leadership in Italy. Despite the mildness of the initial purges, the war still was not over, and it must have been far from clear to Roberto whether he himself would make the transition from filmmaker of the regime to filmmaker of the liberation. Riganti had not. Bontempelli and Mascagni, Roberto's family's most eminent friends, had found their postwar careers destroyed by their support of Fascism. How was Roberto's case different than Riganti's? There was reason for fear.

Probably Roberto saw Amidei and the Communist Party as a safe conduct into postwar cinema. Events would prove his judgment correct. Without the Party's support, he could not have made *Roma città aperta*, and without the Party's forceful endorsement, the picture could not have been hailed as so important in Italy and France. The picture's success, and its Christian aspect, would decrease Rossellini's dependence on the Party; indeed, the

Party would feel obliged to back the film despite its Christianity—but also to feel betrayed and ready for retribution when the chance came.

At the beginning of April, after ten weeks of daily catastrophe, one of Roberto's thousands of phone calls finally paid off. Aldo Venturini, who had already lent money because of family ties with the Rossellinis and friendship with Fabrizi (with whom he had served in the cavalry in Sicily), had never had anything to do with show business before and never would again. But Roberto "bewitched him," said Amidei,[64] and he agreed to buy out the Countess and assume responsibility for the movie's completion. Venturini's money had come from purchasing textiles in Prato, which then was still behind the German lines, and selling them on Rome's black market. Roberto induced him to invest on the basis of a distribution agreement with Artisti Associati, an old firm recently taken over by Besozzi and Ferruccio Caramelli, who were pledged to advance four million lire upon receipt of the completed picture. Why did Countess Politi sell her share? We do not know; no one remembers. But Venturini's accounts indicate that, as of April 1, Politi was credited with 1,600,000 lire for her investment in the film, and Roberto 1,211,893.80. Fabrizi's contract was rewritten for a million lire.

Roberto bought a used bicycle and displayed it to the troupe for all to admire. When there were fifteen minutes to spare, he'd hop on and take a ride, following a long circular route that went gently downhill. Once at the bottom, he'd leave the bike, walk back to Via degli Avignonesi by a shorter route, and have Manni retrieve the bicycle.

By April 21, Venturini and his associates had put an additional 1,677,482.35 into the film.[65]

Anna Magnani, meanwhile, was playing at the Teatro Quattro Fontane in a revue called *Soffia so'*. She wasn't to begin shooting until March, as her scenes involved the redressing of a set.

Roberto sent Jone Tuzzi to help her select sora Pina's wardrobe from old clothes in Anna's own closet. Anna was annoyed at his insistence that she appear visibly pregnant. She never felt confident of her appeal and worried excessively that cameramen were being less than kind to her. And now this Rossellini, not content with the tried and true convention that movie stars need only be *said* to be pregnant and needn't *look* pregnant, was insisting she wear belly padding. Nearly three years ago she had lost the greatest chance of her career for the opposite reason, when Visconti, knowing she was pregnant even though she hardly looked it, had taken sadistic pleasure in insisting she have an abortion, and she instead had chosen her son Luca's life over the starring role in *Ossessione*. Clara Calamai had replaced her then, and now Magnani was replacing Calamai in *Città aperta*.

Anna was expected on the set Saturday morning at ten. The hour was mutually inconvenient. Anna was a night owl addicted to after-theater partying. She rarely rose before three in the afternoon. Morning set calls were the bane of her existence. But since her evenings were tied up at the Quattro Fontane, there was no other choice, and Roberto, too, had had to shift to daytime hours.

On Saturday, just after midnight, his phone rang. It was Anna. She was at a hospital. Luca had polio. Could Roberto come?

Luca, now two, had been feverish the last few days and Anna had been going home early. On Friday night, as she took her bows at the theater, a call had come that he was delirious. Influenza was in season and this was not abnormal. Yet she had found her boy's legs so dead and unfeeling, that they seemed almost detached from his body. She had phoned Serato, Luca's father, and together they had rushed the child to a nearby clinic.

It was all her fault, Anna felt. She had been deserted in babyhood by her mother, a teenager who had gone off to Egypt with an Austrian and who had accepted his demand to leave "the mistake" behind in return for marriage and a new life. Anna had grown up with a grandmother and five aunts, dreaming of a city of gold and a mother who'd say, "Now you'll stay with me always." When she was nine, the mother had come back with her second child, Anna's blonde half-sister, and Anna had clung and clung, incapable of saying a word, her face buried in her mother. Her mother had tried to pull her away, to see what she looked like, but Anna had held on, until finally she had relaxed into a calm cry. Three days later the mother had gone back to Egypt, and Anna, who could hardly read, had been put in a convent where she was lonely and miserable. Her one joy had been music. She took refuge in fantasy. Theater and movies became her real life. Hiding the truth, she gave it out she had been born in Egypt.

Wasn't Luca suffering just as she had? Wasn't his father, for all practical purposes, nonexistent? Hadn't his mother shunted him aside, sacrificing him for her career, deserting him for long periods? Wasn't it her fault that now he would be crippled for life?

By the time Roberto arrived at the hospital, she had made the only possible decision. She would give up the film, and not only the film but her entire career, and dedicate the rest of her life to Luca. She told Roberto the moment she saw him.

He made no response. Right then he didn't give a damn about the film. He was utterly destroyed by her tragedy, worse, by the child's tragedy. Not for anything in the world would he attempt to change Anna's mind. He promised, as she asked, not to breathe a word to anyone of what had happened or of her decision: she did not want Luca pitied. Inwardly Roberto promised himself that, whatever happened, the woman to replace her would not be Clara Calamai a second time. He would spare her that humiliation, even if it meant abandoning the film.

At Via degli Avignonesi everyone was expecting Magnani. The car and driver assigned her were about to leave to pick her up. Then Roberto, looking as though he'd spent the night carousing, arrived and announced he had changed his plans for today. Anna would not be coming. The crew assumed there'd been a fight. Later, vague rumors of Luca's illness began to circulate, but Roberto dismissed all queries with an authoritative wave of his hand: there was nothing to worry about, only a touch of influenza.

In reality, the film's situation could scarcely have been worse. What would they do without Magnani? Could they replace her? With whom? Amidei's irrational opposition to Calamai would cause a furor—and someone as vain as Calamai would never accept the part after they'd rejected her in favor of Magnani—and yet there was simply no other candidate at hand. But the next day was Sunday, things might change over the weekend, and so Roberto, where others would have panicked, said nothing, did nothing, and waited.

He spent Sunday as usual, at Marcella De Marchis's, rolling in bed with Romano and Renzino. He kept in contact with Anna through long phone calls to the hospital. He never mentioned the film. But he realized she would need her career, not only to provide for Luca, but because it was as necessary to her as the air she breathed. He squeezed his own boys, to be sure they were still there, still healthy. There had been other cases of polio in Rome recently, and Roberto feared Romano and Renzino would catch the dread disease too, if he were to think too much of his selfish reasons for wanting Anna to return to the film.

On Monday he let Magnani's driver go as scheduled to pick her up at Via dell'Amba Aradam. No one suspected anything, and Roberto was determined to act calm. He waited at the studio door, ready to sneak away if the car came back empty.

It came back with Magnani inside. And this is how Pirro has described (or invented) the scene. She got out holding her little dog, caressing it as though it were a baby but otherwise furious, as though fresh from a fight with Serato. Let them think whatever the hell they wanted as long as they didn't ask questions or try to be nice.

"Where is he?" she growled.

No one was sure. Rossellini never went far; he was here just a minute ago; probably he was in the bar.

Someone was about to go find him, but a menacing glance from Magnani halted him; she went herself.

He was stirring his coffee in the bar, recounts Pirro. He liked it tepid and with lots of sugar.

"Hey! Have a coffee?" said Roberto, as he turned to kiss her on the cheek—his usual way of greeting everyone, men as well as women.

"Let's go!" she replied, impatient to get started.

Roberto swallowed his coffee. But she stopped him as they started out.

"Robbé, I can't. And don't you dare ask me how Luca is. I need money, a lot of money, I have to give him back his legs, I have to buy them. I have to work and I have to make myself well paid. Meanwhile I want the money you owe me the first day of work. Do you have it?"

"Yes."

"Okay, let's hurry up and finish this damn thing. And anybody dares take pity on me, they can go fuck themselves. It's my own private shit!"

"Am I allowed to ask you how he is?"

"No! I told you!"

"How is he?"

"Bad, Robbé! Bad!" She burst into tears.

Roberto pushed her quickly into a doorway; people were passing. She hid her face behind him and he stroked her hair. They looked like two lovers making up after a quarrel.

Magnani's dog barked, unhappy at being on the ground and ignored, and Anna, wiping her eyes, growled affectionately down at her pet.

"And you keep quiet!"

Dogs were easier to love than people. She rambled on incoherently.

"Every time one of my dogs dies, something else bad happens. I lost one two months ago. I love them so much; they're always faithful. I bet you don't like dogs, do you? You get away with everything, a born betrayer! You don't care about anyone, just about children! Well, you can fuck Roswitha around, but not me!"

"You see, it's all my fault!" Roberto put in.

Magnani laughed through her tears.

They went inside the studio. The make-up man approached but she shooed him off. "No," she announced to Roberto. "No make-up. This is the face I have. Take it or leave it."

In fact, with her swollen eyes and difficult bone structure, Magnani needed make-up if she didn't want to look older than she was. But Rossellini loathed starlet's painted faces and he grabbed at the opportunity.

"No, no make-up," he agreed, "it's fine as it is, better in fact . . . truer."

Magnani hadn't looked Roberto in the face since her arrival. But she did now.

"What are you up to? Trying to screw me? You want me to look ugly?"

"You're beautiful the way you are."

"But you know it's better I make-up. You're too clever!"

Rossellini squinted, acting like a director, and stepped back and inspected her calmly.

"No," he said, half to himself, "we'll shoot just as you are."

"All right! So I stay out of the barber's chair. But let's get started. We're wasting time."

"You need to put a dress on."

"Which one?"

"Anyone you like." And he started to explain the scene.

"I know what to do," she barked.

Magnani wanted to fight, says Pirro. Roberto foiled her every attempt. As far as he was concerned she was already sora Pina. Whatever she said or did, that was sora Pina, and he couldn't get angry with one of his own movie characters. And Pina she became the moment the clapboard sounded. She was in Pina's apartment, wearing Pina's worn jacket and checkered scarf, and there wasn't enough food. Suddenly she moved around the set with that complete absence of self-consciousness people have at home alone. The staring film crew simply did not exist, nor did that other Magnani exist, the little girl dreaming of her lost mother, the woman eternally betrayed by her lovers, the mother racked with grief and guilt for a toddler struck down by polio. Perhaps it's a cliché that actors act to escape themselves and become someone else. But anyone who has seen Anna Magnani change instantaneously from a neurotic, withdrawn wall-flower into a soaring, vibrant presence would not doubt it in her case.[66]

"If Serato didn't exist," said Roberto at the end of the day, "we'd have to invent him!"

Magnani didn't understand the joke: Serato provided a public explanation for the hostile attitude she'd displayed all day. So, planting her palms on her hips, thrusting her back up and her chest out, she retorted in a low, sarcastic growl: "What do you mean? Go tend your own stable!"

Roberto was pleased. She was responding as he hoped she would. The ice was broken between them.

"I meant," he said, "that if you go on fighting with Serato every night and coming to work every morning with that same look on you, we'll have a sora Pina no one will ever forget."

She looked like she was about to attack him.

"You're a sly one," she hissed. "But you don't fool me. And don't waste your time trying."

The crew were leaving. Work was over for the day.

"Come on," she said.

"Where?"

"Just come on, that's all."

He followed her, writes Pirro. They walked toward Piazza Venezia, then into the warren of little streets off to the right. It was cold and getting dark. They talked of growing up in Rome, and, near Piazza Campitelli, Anna showed Roberto the house she had lived in. She pointed out the window of her room. It was a pretty and simple room, but she had been all alone there. . . .

Abruptly she stopped. She had almost told him the truth. She'd never done that with Serato, and it scared her. She turned on Roberto:

"Why the devil am I talking to you like this? I know you couldn't care less."

"On the contrary . . ."

"No. You don't care about anything. Go fuck yourself!"

They walked on a ways, then separated.[67]

It was spring when they went onto location near Via Casilina. Out of the studio and onto the streets meant unpredictability, less constraint by Amidei's shooting plan, and more freedom to suit the moment. Now Rossellini directed with a surer hand and livelier inspiration.

Magnani and Fabrizi had the benefit, too, that first day, of one of Fellini's and Amidei's best scenes—the one Amidei had refused to show to Calamai:

> PINA: I've had to sell everything to live, to keep going. And life keeps getting worse. How'll we ever forget all this suffering, all these worries, all this fear? Doesn't Christ see us?
>
> DON PIETRO: A lot of people ask me that, sora Pina. Doesn't Christ see us? But are we sure we didn't deserve this plague? Are we sure we've always lived according to the Lord's laws?

Magnani had come to trust her director. Closeness had been established and would continue throughout the shooting. They enjoyed spending the intervals between shots together, Anna talking of Luca or of Serato's cruelties toward her, Roberto talking of his children. When the day's work was over, they would walk along the Tiber and Anna, when she thought no one was watching, would sing. It was strange how Roberto seemed to calm her and make her feel young, hopeful, and carefree. It was not yet a romance; there was too much fear for that. Besides, they were both involved with others. Anna had Serato, and Roberto, besides Roswitha, had Carla Rovere who, much to everyone's amusement, was so inspired by Roberto's singling her out, that she had assumed the airs of a prima donna and was playing every little scene as Pina's sister as though it were the hysterical climax of some nineteenth-century tragedy.

One night in Trastevere in the middle of a scene, Serato burst upon them like a wintry gale. Magnani halted in mid-breath, paused barely long enough to aim, then hurled herself toward Serato howling at the top of her lungs her most scatological litany of curses and imprecations, biting, scratching, kicking. Serato, suddenly on the defensive, tried to immobilize her by grabbing her by the hair.

Roberto sat watching with interest. Bruno Todini, a massive lawyer who'd joined the crew out of love for the movies, took hold of Serato and dragged him effortlessly away.

Magnani drew breath and straightened her dress. Then, realizing her lover was escaping, she went charging after him. Outside, she saw Todini driving off with Serato on the back of the production truck. Screaming, she gave chase, almost grabbed the tailgate, but tripped and ended up lying in the dust.

Amidei had seen it all. Coming over, he tried to help Magnani to her feet. She practically spat at him, so he left her there and, going inside, found Roberto still sitting as though upon a throne, impassively studying his set-up with the camera's eyepiece.

"Say, Roberto, I just got an idea for the *rastrellamento* scene," he told him. "That business of Anna in the middle of the crowd getting machine-gunned by accident, it's always seemed rather flat to me."

Amidei had written it the way it had actually happened to Teresa Gullace. Sora Pina would see her fiancé in a prison window, walk toward the window, and get killed.

"Wouldn't it be better if we have Anna run desperately after the truck taking her man away, and then, suddenly, a gun burst shoots her down?"

Roberto thought for a second. "Sounds like a good idea. But how come it just came to you now?"

Amidei was lighting a cigarette. "Oh, I was outside and I saw Magnani" he started, then huffed, "What's it to you how the hell I get my ideas?!" and stalked off.[68]

The scene in question was to be shot the following week on Via Raimondo Montecuccoli, off Via Prenestina southeast of the train station, where Pina lived in a workers' tenement. To Rossellini's frustration, his demand for four trucks and eighty extras to play German soldiers had been cut to two trucks and thirty extras by De Martino, Venturini's less-than-confident production manager. And, oddly enough, thirty proper German uniforms had not been found, and belts and buckles borrowed from some Roman garbage men had been substituted for SS insignia—the "N.U." (*Nettezza Urbana - City Sanitation*) of the garbage men's attire fortunately being indistinguishable on the screen. To find real Germans was next to impossible. "All the time I was searching for Germans," Roberto moaned.[69]

A problem arose the night before, when the actor playing the Gestapo sergeant who was to slap Pina got himself arrested. He was an Austrian who had been drafted into the Wehrmacht, had found himself fighting partisans in Italy, and had changed sides to fight with, rather than against, them. A great talker, he fascinated Rossellini. The Germans, he said, were doomed to lose the war, because they didn't know how to dodge bullets; Italians, in contrast, heard bullets coming in time to get out of the way. He was amused at playing a Gestapo agent in an anti-Nazi movie and went around Rome showing off a photo of himself and Harry Feist in their uniforms. One night he showed it to some American MPs who decided he was a Nazi criminal bragging of his perfidious past, so they hauled him off to jail. It fell to Roberto to talk his actor free.[70]

Real trouble came the next day. A crowd had gathered as usual to stand and watch the filming, and when they saw the trucks drive up and the SS dismount and spread out, they didn't like it. They didn't like seeing Germans, even fake Germans, on the streets of Rome again, repeating the same outrages that had been commonplace a few months before. The war was still going on in the North, some of the onlookers had lost sons and husbands recently, and all of them had suffered at the hands of the Germans. The film's few real Germans—POWs on loan—were bad enough, but the spectacle of fellow Romans masquerading as German soldiers for a few lire a day was even worse. Some in the crowd began to cry out to the extras, telling them they ought to be ashamed; others, suspecting the extras were at least Fascist sympathizers, spat and threw stones. "Go make movies somewhere else!" they yelled, threateningly.

The situation was dangerous. A few days before, as Rossellini had been about to film a scene where the Gestapo arrest Don Pietro, Manfredi, and an Austrian defector, a trolley had come passing by and the conductor, not perceiving Arata with a hand-held camera hiding in a doorway, had halted his trolley, jumped out, and tried to intervene. His passengers had joined in, yelling, cursing, and brandishing rifles. Now, this time, with gun-bearing SS troops all over the place, the crowds might really turn violent.[71]

Many in the company grew afraid. Some of the extras began taking off their uniforms. One threw his helmet on the ground. He was a Communist, he declared; and once the people had announced their opposition, he could not even pretend to be a Nazi.

Roberto, as usual at such moments, stayed on the sidelines watching with detached interest. But Amidei bounded eagerly into the middle of the scene and launched into a harangue. "I'm a Communist," he yelled. "I suffered from the Nazis, I was persecuted by them. But I'm the one who wrote this film. So if you want to get mad at someone, it's me you should be after, not these extras. They're people just like you. They're forced to put on enemy clothing to earn a living. But also they want to record forever what you Romans endured."

The cast-off helmet was lying a few feet away. Amidei picked it up and pushed it back onto the extra's head. "It's precisely *because* you're a Communist," he shouted, "that you *should* be playing a bad German in the first film that's anti-Fascist."[72]

The crowd quieted. A few began suggesting ideas. The scene ought to end with the Germans being lynched, they said.

Filming recommenced. The people from the tenement, women and children and babies and old men, were lined up against the wall on the sidewalk outside, held at bay by the Germans. It was time for Magnani's big scene, the moment that would make the new Italian cinema famous all over the world. Roberto, usually afraid to waste a foot of negative, had put two cameras on top of buildings and a third on the street.

"I hadn't rehearsed the death scene," Magnani recalled later. "With Rossellini, great director that he was, we didn't rehearse: we filmed. He knew that once he had prepared the surroundings I would function. During the scene of the *rastrellamento*, when I came out the door onto the street, unexpectedly I saw it all again, I went back to the time when all over Rome the young people were being taken away. Boys! The people against the wall were real people, ordinary people. The Germans were real Germans from a concentration camp. All of a sudden I wasn't me anymore, understand? I was the character. And, yes, Rossellini had prepared the street in a way that was really hallucinatory. The women had actually turned white telling each other how much they resented the Nazis! This made me feel the anxiety I showed on the screen. It was terrible! That was the way Rossellini worked. And at least with me, it worked.[73] A miracle.

He materialized what I felt. All it took was a gesture, a movement of an eye, and I was on my way."[74]

Sora Pina chased after the truck carrying Francesco away, then fell to the ground, tearing skin from her palms and elbows, ripping her stockings, and bloodying her knee. Then she lay still on the street, her skirt pulled shamelessly up above her thigh, her little boy crouched over her crying uncontrollably.

Rossellini went to help Magnani to her feet.

"Can you do another?" he asked. Someone in the crowd had laughed.

"Sure, sure. Don't worry about me, it just means I won't jump around quite as much at the theater. The scene's the important thing," she said, and went to change her stockings. But the little boy, Vito Annicchiarico, had really gotten scared and was in a corner still crying uncontrollably.

Amidei, however, had had another idea. If they strung a line across the street, they could use it to trip Magnani and make her fall even better!

"So she'll break a leg?!" yelled Roberto, and he went off to tell Magnani: "You know what this delinquent thought up? To trip you with a rope!"

But Magnani, instead of getting mad, went over and reassured Amidei. "Don't worry," she said, "I'll do it well. You'll see, you'll be happy."[75]

Roberto surely recalled a similar scene in King Vidor's 1925 *The Big Parade*—one of the most famous scenes in movies—where Renée Adorée chases the truck taking John Gilbert away.

Earlier, when the crowd had been threatening, Fabrizi had hidden inside the doorway and later he had been so worried that someone might try to "save" him from the Germans, that he had hurried nervously through his scenes. The lesson had not gone unnoticed by Rossellini, who appreciated the touch of realism that such things added to Fabrizi's performance. Accordingly, he sought out other, similar opportunities for improvement. In a playground scene with kids playing ball, for example, he told the actor there were still some old mines buried in the ground; Fabrizi was so scared that instead of throwing the ball, he always handed it instead.

Then, the first week of June, came the end of filming, the execution scene, where Fabrizi is shot by a firing squad. None of the firing-squad extras had ever handled rifles before; the rifles themselves were so antiquated, that no one could tell if they were actually loaded, or if the safety catches would work. Then a black cat crossed Fabrizi's path as they started rehearsing. So Rossellini, who never rehearsed, rehearsed this scene four times. It wasn't just that he enjoyed putting people in embarrassing situations. It was also true that Fabrizi's manner invited such treatment. "Fabrizi hated [Vito], the little boy," Amidei said. "Because, great actor that he is, he understood that the boy had an extraordinary face, and so he always tried to turn him to the side, so that he'd be seen less well whenever they had a shot together, so that the boy wouldn't steal the scene from him."[76]

Fabrizi, for his part, never forgave Roberto. "It's *my* film," the actor declared a quarter century later. "I proposed it to the woman who gave the money, I thought up the scene with the bomb and hitting the old man on the head with the frying pan, and the film's end. I chose Rossellini and found the financing. Take the scene where the Germans are after me! 'Rossellini's realism', say the critics! It's the realism of that trolley car, of those terrified people! Rossellini?! Rossellini had nothing to do with it! He didn't understand any of it! He used to curse and throw his hat on the ground. 'How can I be a serious director with forty meters of film?' he'd scream."[77]

Meanwhile, spring had come. The Allies had advanced beyond Florence at last, the Germans were giving up, and Mussolini, along with the faithful Claretta Petacci, was captured and shot by Communist partisans. Two days later, April 30, Hitler took his own life in his Berlin bunker. The war was over.

Mussolini's dead body, in company with Petacci's and those of thirteen other Fascists, was hung upside down like beef carcasses from the girders of a bombed-out filling station in Milan's Piazzale Loreto. "At first," writes historian Richard Collier, "the crowds had been no more than curious—circling the bodies as they sprawled on the pavement as if at a macabre lying-in-state. Someone had placed a scepter in Mussolini's hand and his head lay propped on Claretta's white blouse. Newsmen stood by registering quick clinical impressions. Stan Swinton of *Stars and Stripes* noted Claretta's neat ringlets, a glimpse of baby-blue underwear. Milton Bracker of the *New York Times* watched photographers tilt the Duce's face towards the sun, supporting his jaw with a rifle-butt. Abruptly a jungle savagery set in. A man darted in to aim a savage kick at Mussolini's head—to the *New York Times* man the sound was 'a hideous crunch.' People began to dance and caper round the corpses; to the *Baltimore Sun*'s correspondent, Howard Norton, their mood was 'black, ugly, undisciplined.' One woman fired five shots into Mussolini's prostrate body—one for each of the sons she had lost in the Duce's war. Another ripped off his shirt, fired it and tried to thrust it in his face. Others moved in to commit the supreme indignity on a man once mobbed by hysterical women whenever he took a bath; spreading their skirts, they urinated upon his upturned face. To one partisan commander it was suddenly like 'a savage circus.' His chief, Italo Pietra, set ten men to fire in the air, striving to keep the crowd at bay—but it was hopeless. Hacking, cursing, swaying, the people were trampling the corpses, blind with the hatred of years. Even 300 *carabinieri* couldn't restrain them; hastily they retreated, uniforms rippled to shreds. Next the Fire Brigade struggled to the scene, but even their white hissing jets could not extinguish that hatred."[78]

There is something to be said for a nation that spews vengeance on its leaders and spares its common people. More symptomatic than the desecration of Mussolini was the partisans' execution of Gentile, the aged, eminent, and gentle scholar who had struggled to articulate a philosophy for the regime. It's deadly for ideologues out of season.

It was in July that Rossellini met the man who more than any single individual was to make him and the new Italian cinema famous around the world. Roland Ernest "Rod" Geiger was 29 and a mere pfc after sixteen months in the U.S. Army. But his talents as a painter and his experience creating stage sets at his father's theater school in New York had served him well in the relaxed atmosphere of the American occupation forces in Italy. He had created a German-weapons orientation exhibition covering five acres near Volturno, and then had been asked to decorate an officers club in Rome (on the present Olympic site).

What he wanted to do was to meet film people. His brother-in-law, André R. Heymann, had been importing films like Pagnol's *Harvest* before the war. Now to Geiger, Rome looked like opportunity. Something was happening here. His assets were eighteen dollars, his next month's army pay, and the confidence that he could talk his way into anything. Italians found him charming; even nasty Amidei hymned that Geiger was "*uno piccolo piccolo*, an elf, very beautiful, with the sweetest little face, he was like a little angel."[79] What Geiger lacked in credibility, Italian imagination (and desperate need for capital) would more than compensate for: any American associated with film was automatically bigger-than-life, and Rod, despite his height, was, if not a big man, certainly the sort of man the times required—one who would work miracles.

People were delighted to show him uncompleted movies. Gaspero del Corso, an art dealer related to Visconti, led him to Renato (or Renzo) De Bonis, who was trying to complete *Desiderio*. De Bonis led him to a lab to meet Rossellini and see part of *Città aperta*.

"Fortune led me to Technostampa," said Geiger.[80] Amidei came too, as well as Pagliero, who had been born in London, spoke excellent English, and translated for everyone.

It was hot and humid. Geiger ordered a Martini and Rossellini squeezed in beside him. "You will see only a few rushes," he explained, "and you will excuse me we have not dubbed in the sound."

In fact, Roberto was showing off his masterpiece, a scene he had labored over as never before, of the German soldier machine-gunning Magnani as she runs screaming after the truck taking away her fiancé. Even without sound, Geiger was overwhelmed. "Groping for words, I clasped Rossellini's hand, and in that hand shake he understood my feelings. I had seen a great piece of art. But as I carefully looked into the face of this thin, tired-looking man, I began to understand that I was alone in this belief."

Geiger told Roberto he was eager to help him any way he could.

Fellini, who was not at Technostampa that day, thirty years later invented a different story about how Geiger entered Roberto's life. According to Fellini, Geiger came stumbling drunk out of the whorehouse on Via degli Avignonesi, tripped on an electric cable, and landed on his nose; then, when he realized a film was being shot, claimed he was a producer and shouted, "I'll buy it."

Fellini eventually recanted his story.[81] But not before a generation of film historians had solemnly inscribed it as fact. And it does touch on a poetic truth. Geiger and Roberto were well matched; they were both flying on a wing and a prayer. Roberto would never find a producer whose invincible optimism and wizardry were better suited to his madcap projects.

Friendship came immediately, deep and all-trusting. They were together constantly during the next weeks. Rod watched Roberto edit *Open City*, sat on his roof with Roswitha as the strains of opera wafted across the Roman night from the nearby Baths of Caracalla, and all the while Roberto spun dreams and set up his next picture.

At Fono Roma, where Roberto mixed music and dialogue and edited film, the gunshots that Geiger could now hear killing Magnani made the sequence even realer than real, not only because of added reverberation, but because we never see a gun firing—and never notice that all the Germans have their hands down.[82]

Theorists of the Russian school contend the true creativity in moviemaking occurs during editing. To Roberto, in later years, such labor became insufferable; his cutting became simple and his sound notoriously uneven. But in the forties he loved tinkering with footage, and he tinkered with *Città aperta* most of the summer. There was much to do. Renzo had composed and conducted the music (stealing from his score for *L'uomo dalla croce*) and had paid the musicians out of his own pocket. Meanwhile, since everything had been shot silent, the actors were coming to FonoRoma and recording their dialogue; ambient sound and sound effects were being added; and everything was being synchronized with the pictures. It was painstaking work and, as Roberto later admitted, "Since I'm an extremely negligent technician, I confess there are times when lip movements don't always coincide with the words."[83]

Nonetheless he spent weeks on end obsessively tied to the moviola. In an innovation, for which he has never been acknowledged, he discovered that when a shot's pace seemed slow, its rhythm could be sped up by subtly and painstakingly editing out single frames in the middle of the shot—the jumps would be imperceptible. He worked over Magnani's death scene in this way. "The rhythm's the thing," he insisted throughout his career.[84]

Rhythm was the problem with the execution scene that ends the picture. Don Pietro gets out of a truck, walks over to a chair and is tied to it. "The whole scene was tremendously flat, something was missing. I saw the shots only three months [after we filmed them]. And there was very little material, because . . . I had a repulsion against doing [extra] angles. I wanted to take risks, I like that. [But now] I was worrying about what to do."[85]

The solution, he said in 1971, was "really for me the most illuminating experience in my life. Just at the last moment I thought of giving the scene a certain kind of rhythm. It was very simple, we set up a microphone and with a finger I beat a chair, thump, thump, thump, and that little, nearly imperceptible noise completely changed the rhythm of the scene. So through that I learned that the main thing is to find the right rhythm: the [right] movement of the camera and people." Careful direction of the actors is unnecessary if the initial idea is right. "That scene was flat because the rhythm was not right. So I had to cheat a little and add that rhythm through the sound which underlined a certain tone. I think the scene is quite moving."[86]

All the while Roberto was putting together a *combinazione* for the next film. He told Rod Geiger he would officially be *Città aperta*'s producer, introduced him to Venturini, and immediately began discussing plans. Geiger would buy the Western-Hemisphere rights to *Città aperta*, arrange for its exhibition in America, and help finance new pictures. It would all be done with IOUs, and Roberto would set up the deals.

"Are you with me, Rod?"

At the beginning, in April 1945, when Roberto had met Alfred Hayes at a trattoria,[87] this next film had been only one vague concept among dozens of others that Roberto was excited about that day. Hayes had been a Brecht-like Communist playwright and poet (Paul Robeson had recorded his working-class ballad "I Dreamed I Saw Joe Hill Again"); now he was a sergeant writing for *Stars and Stripes*. It was only on July 28, when Geiger recruited Thomas Mann's son Klaus, a corporal also writing for *Stars and Stripes*, that a definite project began to materialize. The two screened *Città aperta*, had dinner afterward with Rossellini, Amidei, Hayes, and Pagliero (who was completing *Desiderio*); went to the beach the next day with the same group; saw *G.I. Joe*; went to a party at the Arduini's with Fini, Praz, and Moravia; talked again with Rossellini on July 31; and on August 2 went with him to Leoncavallo's opera *Bajazzo*.[88]

The Americans' idea was to trace the Italian campaign via seven sketches of American GIs encountering Italy and discovering Italians. It would be called *Seven from the U.S.* It would counteract the racism Americans had cultivated toward Italians during the war. Like *Città aperta*, it would show that Italians, too, had died for freedom.

Roberto was enthusiastic. It was a perfect vehicle to continue his reliving and historicization of recent events. And after the constraints of *Città aperta*'s convoluted plotting, the sketch format would give him the Dos-Passos-like improvisatory freedom he had been theorizing about during the Occupation. It would be a Rossellini movie, not an Amidei film.

Klaus Mann had lived through the whole Italian campaign. Within a few weeks, he would have a detailed treatment ready. "Rossellini is without any doubt a high-class director," he wrote his mother.[89]

Almost the next day, there was a crisis. *Città aperta*, still without sound, was shown to Artisti Associati, with whom Roberto had the distribution contract promising four million lire, and they hated it. "It's not a film," they declared. "By the terms of our agreement, you were to deliver a film.

We don't consider this a film." It was more newsreel than story, they complained, as they walked out.[90]

A day or two later, Roberto came wailing to Geiger. "My God! Venturini's ruined everything! He's sold the film to Minerva. You've got to do something!"

According to Roberto, Venturini had panicked. Without consulting with him, he had accepted an offer from the Greek Angelo Mosco of Minerva Film to buy him out for thirteen million lire. Venturini had been sobbing, "I risked my life against machine guns to earn this money that is my children's bread. Look what you've done to me! Why didn't you want to make a real film?"

With the Western-Hemisphere rights to *Città aperta* in the hands of Mosco and with Venturini disinterested in further adventures, all Roberto's and Geiger's elaborate plans would collapse. "You've got to do something!" Roberto insisted.

What Geiger had to do, it turned out, was to buy back the American rights from Minerva for five million lire ($25,500). It would all be done with IOUs. Roberto would arrange the deals.

Geiger thought he had a potential source of funds through his commanding officer, First Lieutenant Robert Lawrence, 25, who, Geiger believed, had a rich uncle. Lawrence could also help with the Army and the U.S. embassy and give invaluable advice. He became Geiger's partner.[91]

Meanwhile, for *Seven from the U.S.*, Roberto had found a new source of funds through Renato Campos, a stockbroker who came from one of Rome's best families and had been friends with the Rossellinis for years. Much older than Roberto, he had fought with the Arditi, the elite soldiers of World War I whose daring escapades had provided almost the sole romantic thrills of that drearily tragic war. In 1921 he had joined the Rossellinis on their tours of the Dolomites when, Renzo recalled, they had looked up to him like an Achilles or an Aeneas.[92]

It was Campos's wealthy business partner who came up with most of the money. Mario Conti was involved in olive oil, fishing boats, and scrap metal, always cleverly. He gathered up tons of aluminum sheets the Americans had thrown away, melted them into bricks, and sold them back to the Americans at an excellent profit.

Conti joined Roberto, fifty-fifty, in forming Organizzazioni Film Internationali (OFI) to produce *Seven from the U.S.* in association with Geiger and Lawrence. On August 11, he agreed to lend Geiger the five million lire ($25,500) that Mosco was demanding for *Città aperta*'s western rights. To acquit this loan, Geiger was to repay Conti $28,000.

The only actual money Geiger paid out was $620 to his lawyer, Massimo Ferrara (who, as former boss at Scalera, knew all about Rossellini and IOUs). Geiger's company, Foreign Film Productions (an American company registered in New York, albeit set up in Italy), would handle *Città aperta* and assume a fifty percent interest in *Seven from the U.S.* For *Seven*, they were to supply raw stock, pay Klaus Mann, and pay and maintain the

American actors in Italy. Since the actors were paid at American scale, $250 per week, dollar costs would be comparable to OFI's lira costs for the rest of the production. Geiger and Lawrence established an office at 68 Via Regina Elena and signed Rossellini to a contract at $10,000 per year (which was never paid). Now all they needed was a distributor and money.

A few days later Amidei heard some friends laughing about the idiot who had paid such a sum for *Città aperta*. The friends were right: even $1,000 would have been sensational. No Italian picture since *Cabiria* had made the slightest impression in the United States—and *Cabiria* had been in 1914. All Italy was in shambles. *Città aperta* was horribly expensive by Italian standards, and was rumored to be a disaster and unreleasable. Mosco must have been overjoyed to have collected five million lire on the eleven (not thirteen!) million he had agreed to pay a few days before.

In fact, what Venturini had sold Mosco were originally the rights to Italy only. It was *after* Geiger paid Mosco that Venturini found himself being taken to dinner by Minerva's Milan agent and being "morally obliged to accept seventeen million [total] in *contanti* [IOUs] to cede the rights for the whole world to Minerva."[93]

Venturini, moreover, who had first been delighted to make an unexpected profit from the seven million he had invested, subsequently maintained for the rest of his life that Roberto had tricked him, that he had accepted Minerva's offers only after Roberto had advised him to do so, that Roberto had set up the deal with Minerva in the first place, and that he had paid Roberto a commission of ten percent.[94] Whenever he saw Geiger, he would touch him for good luck and exclaim, "Oh what a mistake I made!"[95] Ironically, he was pursued by tax collectors who couldn't believe he had profited so little, and by bill collectors for Fabrizi's cassock and the 37 pairs of boots lent by the Ministry of War which were never returned (and were used again in *Paisà*).

Had Roberto, after the disaster with Artisti Associati, convinced Minerva to buy *Città aperta* by assuring them that his American would immediately give them five million? Had he taken a commission as well on the money Geiger was paying Minerva?

Roberto later claimed he took no salary, never owned a share in the picture, never made a penny from its huge earnings, and was stuck with the responsibility for its accumulated debts, which he continued to pay off for "years and years." He also claimed that it was he who had borrowed five million from "some friends" to repurchase Minerva's American rights, and that Geiger gave *him* a note for $28,000 "of which I've never seen a penny."[96]

To the contrary, according to Venturini's accounts, Roberto was repaid 1.2 million lire and received 18,500 per week, totaling 150,000 by September.[97] And Roberto, who had not worked since 1943 and had been peddling his clothes on the street during the Occupation, was now maintaining himself and his two households, going nightly to The 57 Club and other hot spots, driving a *topolino* (a little Fiat 500), and, to Geiger, seemed in no need for funds.

It wasn't clear to Geiger how the figure of $25,500 was arrived at. He was under the impression that *Città aperta* had cost $110,000, but probably wouldn't have cared had he known the true cost had been $35,700. It seemed cheap compared to what his brother-in-law had made from *Harvest* and *Baker's Wife*. He had faith in *Città aperta*, *Seven from the U.S.*, and, above all, in Roberto.[98]

No wonder the Italians called Rod Geiger "a little angel"! He was repaying most of *Città aperta*'s cost and, in the process, providing insurance for investors in the new film. The avant-garde would follow in his wake. "He was the fortune of the Italian cinema," Fellini acknowledged.[99]

Città aperta's first screening took place August 28, 1945, under the auspices of the U.S. Information Agency at the Italian underministry for press and spectacle, Via Veneto 108. The audience—only a few dozen—consisted of friends and journalists, chiefly American. Klaus Mann wrote program notes for the occasion and they are worth quoting, for they established the tone of most subsequent praise of the picture.

> The film you are going to see is based on events that have actually [taken] place. While Allied troops were fighting their way to the Italian capital, another Battle of Rome was going on within the 'open city' itself. Those who faced the Nazi-Fascist enemy on the beachhead of Anzio or in the Cassino area were hardly aware, at the time, of that other war which had to be waged in darkness and secrecy.
>
> But later, after the liberation of the capital, some of us came in contact with former members of the Resistance movement and were told the story of Rome's underground struggle.
>
> The film, ROME OPEN CITY, has the accuracy and freshness of such a firsthand account. It's a factual report—enacted by people who have witnessed, or participated in, the real drama.
>
> Anyone who has lived in Rome will find familiar faces among the characters appearing on the screen.... [T]hey are indeed the plain people of Rome: we recognize their features, gestures, voices.
>
> ... ROME OPEN CITY will be welcome to the American public as a significant document and as a promising, candid message from liberated Italy.[100]

The audience loved it. Luchino Visconti declared, "I remember being the first to jump up and applaud after Magnani's famous death scene [at the intermission]. I was really enthusiastic. But we all felt that way. [It] reinforced the 'charge' we all felt in those days, our exaltation at the sight of a flag in the wind."[101]

Roberto was waiting outside, feigning indifference. "I hugged him for all of us," Blasetti recalled. "We were grateful."[102]

The next day Pfc Rod Geiger got his orders to go to Naples and wait for his boat home. The film, he expected, would reach New York ahead of him. Captain Andy Anderson was sending it in the embassy's diplomatic pouch, in order to skirt the importation complication that no trade relations existed between Italy and the United States just after the war. But Bob Lawrence called five days later and presently arrived in an army jeep with Roberto and Fellini and 150 pounds of 35mm film. To accommodate its six thick reels, Geiger had to throw almost everything out of his barracks bag and ask the soldier behind him to help hoist it onto the ship. He had already mailed Mann's treatment for *Seven from the U.S.* to his father in New York.

The transport, an old Liberty ship carrying thirty soldiers, didn't leave Naples until September 9, then broke down near Gibraltar and stopped for repairs. Roberto, not one to wait calmly for the fullness of time, made frantic transatlantic calls—no easy task in those days—to Geiger's father to find out what had happened to his movie. It was "something I found in Italy," Geiger told U.S. Customs, September 20, when he got home.

Città aperta premiered on Monday, September 24, at the Quirino Theatre as part of the "Primo Festival Internazionale della musica, del teatro e del cinematografo"—the first big art show of the new Italy. It was one of only a few Italian entries in a series of seventeen pictures dominated by big international spectacles Italians had missed during the war—*The Thief of Bagdad, Les Enfants du paradis, Henry V, Ivan the Terrible, That Hamilton Woman,* and *Four Feathers.*

In years to come, historians would concur in judging *Roma città aperta* as a landmark in Italian history, not merely in Italian cinema. Here at last was the first wonderful step toward a "national-popular" culture, as Amidei had hoped. It was revolutionary—it was the first time in an Italian movie that common people were shown as the makers of history, not simply its victims.[103] It doesn't matter that the people's heroes are nearly all slaughtered; as the boys start down the Gianicolo hill after Don Pietro's execution, we know what the future will be.

"At last we've seen an Italian film!" the Communist Carlo Lizzani cried out, "a film that talks about our things, the days of oppression and death, a world alive with people and places we've rarely seen appear in our cinema."[104]

It was, Massimo Mida explained, "that true, unrepeatable, renovating work that Italian art had been awaiting for years . . . , a film that destroys a tradition of mediocrity with the violent force of an explosion blasting open a road through a mountain hitherto impassable. . . . After twenty years of Fascism, everyone felt utter disgust for anything smacking of rhetoric. But Roberto Rossellini caught accurately the suffocated, brooding feelings of the population during the German Occupation. . . . Reality acquired a new dimension; the document became history. . . . If today the cinema is considered the most vital art, the art richest in ferment . . . , the credit is largely *Roma città aperta*'s."[105]

Also beyond the borders of Italy it played a role few movies have been privileged to play. Italy was despised, sharing the odium of Nazi Germany plus the contempt accorded incompetency. But, wrote Renzo Rossellini,

"*Roma città aperta* revealed Italy's true face to the world. A face unknown. The defeated country, ravaged length and breadth by invading armies, gone to war without honor, despised and ridiculed, hated and raped, degraded into servility by long years of dictatorship, could expect neither tolerance nor understanding nor even pity. The public opinion of the entire world was against us, and could not be otherwise. It was this film that, starting in America, managed to attract empathy and attention to our land, that through captivating little details managed to make known unknown truths: the courage, the heart, the nobility of the Italian people, their love for liberty, their heroism... and the unity they miraculously achieved in their struggle for liberation. [De Gasperi, Italy's postwar prime minister,] told me one day... how it was specifically this film that had encouraged certain currents of world opinion, so that we found, if not friendship, at least understanding, when we sat down at the Peace Conference table."[106]

"Our ambassador didn't have to wait any more in Washington," De Gasperi told Roberto.[107]

In *The Nation*, James Agee would charge that the movie was "Communist propaganda.... Audiences are being sold a bill of goods."[108] He was terribly wrong. *Roma città aperta* was a marriage of Marxism and Christianity. It fulfilled Amidei's hopes by showing that the solidarity that should have prevented World War I was winning World War II. It fulfilled Rossellini's hopes in affirming, Croce-like, that out of defeat can come victory and that the victory of the spirit is non-ideological.

But no such praise, according to Roberto in later years, was in the hearts or minds of those who attended *Città aperta*'s public premiere at the Festival that September 24. And his account of what occurred and, even more, of what was thought there, eventually became one of the great "legends" of Rossellini's career and of Italian film history. It was a legend created largely by Roberto himself in the early 1950s, at a time when he was justly claiming to be an artist perennially misunderstood and perennially ahead of his time—and unjustly claiming that he had always been persecuted and opposed.

"Some people were there to whistle," he said. "The critical reception ... was frankly and unanimously unfavorable."[109] "I was treated almost like an imbecile because they said I confused newsreels with art."[110] Even the USIA screening had been "a great delusion" for most of those who attended.[111] No one had wanted to show the film. In screening after screening, exhibitors and distributors had universally rejected it as inconsequential and uncommercial (on one such occasion, Roberto bragged, he had opened his fly and peed at them). It had made it into the "little festival" only because, at the last moment, an Italian entry was required. And that audience had watched in glacial silence, granting only perfunctory applause. They were hostile, hoping it would fail, Roberto contended. People from the "old" cinema dreaded the "new"; intellectuals thought the Occupation was being commercially exploited; the left resented him as a reactionary; the old *Cinema* crowd around Visconti, to whom Rossellini was something of an interloper and trespasser, was still dreaming of a far more literary film than the maverick *Città aperta*.[112] Indeed, according to Roberto, he never would have even been able to have made the picture, had not the established powers momentarily lost control. "In 1944, immediately after the war, everything had been destroyed in Italy. In the cinema as elsewhere. Almost all the producers had disappeared.... So we enjoyed immense freedom; the absence of organized industry favored the least routine enterprises. All initiative was good. It was this situation that permitted us to undertake works of an experimental character.... [Later, after *Roma città aperta* had come out,] I proposed to some of my colleagues to found an association modeled on United Artists [where filmmakers were their own producers] so that we could avoid the vexations that would not fail to come along with the reorganization of the Italian cinema by the producers and the businessmen. But no one wanted to be associated with the maker of *Roma città aperta*; obviously he wasn't an artist.[113] I waited a year to get confirmation from the public and Italian critics that *Roma città aperta* was a good, excellent film."[114]

The legend is blarney. It is true that *Roma città aperta* was a challenge to the industry: it abandoned certain traditions of quality, assumed a political stance, portrayed recent events, dealt with controversial issues, and took license in language, drugs, sex, violence, and choice of heroes. But, though independently produced at a time when a once flourishing industry was disorganized, *Roma città aperta* was not made to spite the establishment, nor even despite the establishment, but rather by established filmmakers with established methods of production and financing. It was not shot on the street by improvisation with non-professional actors, as Rossellini's legend would later insist, but mostly in a studio with famous stars and a detailed script. *Roma città aperta*'s revolutionizing innovations were in content rather than technique. It is self-interested to credit, as Rossellini subsequently did, the license that permitted that content to the disorganization of the industry rather than to the revolutionary chaos of the entire nation. Or to claim that a business association failed to materialize for reasons of artistic reputation.

As we have seen, the businessmen had quickly accepted *Città aperta* once it looked profitable, once Geiger entered the affair. And the overflowing, distinguished nature of the Festival audience indicates (as does the allegation of such profuse varieties of enmity) that even before its premiere *Città aperta* was anticipated as a major event. The undersecretaries of war, foreign affairs, and communications were present; all three grades of seats plus standing room were sold out. That the audience reacted "glacially" is contradicted by newspaper reports that they were "profoundly moved"; that they were "moved [and] applauded at length"; that they received the picture "with the liveliest unanimity"; that "Rossellini spoke to people's hearts . . . , it was applauded with enthusiasm."[115] In fact, the popular success was spectacular. It played at the Quirinetta September 27–28 retitled *Roma città aperta*, then on October 8 moved to the Capranica and Imperiale, two of Rome's largest theaters, where three weeks later crowds were still fighting to get in, and it ran an extraordinary 48 days.[116] Fabrizi's and Magnani's names were as big as the title. It became the best grossing Italian picture of the 1945–46 season. It earned 61 million lire and was seen by almost three million Italians in its first four months of exhibition alone—figures that tripled during the next eight months.

A few of the first reviews were derogatory. Roberto carried one of them around with him for the rest of life to show people how he had been misunderstood. Here it is in its entirety:

> The dramatic days of the nine months of the occupation of Rome have furnished the material for this film by Roberto Rossellini, gray and documentary in tone, at times sincere and effective, often shoddy and rough. Anna Magnani, as usual, alternates between flashes of high quality and heavy vulgarity. Aldo Fabrizi, pervaded with reverential timidity in front of a character inspired by Don Morosini, feels trapped and neutralized. There are many good intentions but not a little roughness and incapacity, mixed with characters and possibilities of relief, in the other performances, improvised or debuting on the screen.[117]

The Vatican's *L'Osservatore Romano* had much worse to say, plus constant denunciation of Roberto's "very questionable taste" and Fabrizi's syntheticness. And the paper of the ruling Action Party declared the film a "failed experiment" whose "rhetoric and bad taste, and false representation of people and things . . . fails to recreate the atmosphere, thoughts, anxieties, and life of the period."[118]

But only five of the initial reviews we have found were hostile, five were mixed, and thirteen were very favorable. By late October, when *Roma città aperta* had opened in Milan and other cities, the reviews, spurred by popular success, were all but unanimously laudatory. The picture was "almost a miracle," gasped Indro Montanelli in *Corriere della sera*.[119]

The most perceptive analysis was by Ennio Flaiano, who would become Fellini's constant scenarist. Anticipating the phenomenological line later adopted by French critics, Flaiano said "Rossellini's direction sticks to the essential, avoids detours, and points up the facts with which the film abounds, working them out with a precision and impassivity that reminds us of the spirit at play in the pictures of another Roman, Antonio Donghi. Everything here is said without apparent effort or grand invention. Rossellini uses real houses, real people, real talk: the effect is thus achieved with quotidian means, copying life with the punctiliousness of one who sees only appearances [phenomena]. Rossellini forbids himself, a priori, any lyric inquiry [i.e., poetic elaboration]. For him two and two make four every time, whereas for us it sometimes makes five and even three." If Italian films wished to conquer foreign markets, said Flaiano, they would have to follow *Roma città aperta*'s example and express "our life" with simple concepts rather than with Fascism's manic exhibitionism—a prediction that proved accurate.[120]

Michelangelo Antonioni loved *Roma città aperta* for its "serene analysis of a psychological condition characteristic of Rome under the Occupation."[121] Maurizio Barendson reported it was "the biggest surprise of the Festival..., true and simple, told and interpreted with courageous and precise language.... It moved the audience by its narrative bravura and the reconstruction of [Rome's] ambience."[122] *Il Messaggero* declared that "Rossellini has established himself among the very greatest of the rare cinematic intelligences of the entire world."[123]

Alberto Moravia, Italy's foremost novelist, was also without reservations. The film owed its success to its "clearness," he wrote. "The principle of veristic art [Verga's melodramatic form of naturalism] is clearly and vigorously applied. The characters talk in Romanesco or German; the social settings are presented precisely, just as in Fabrizi's and the De Filippos' comedies and dialect dramas; facts themselves are coordinated and recounted as in a newsreel, without omission of even the crudest details (as in the torture scenes for example), without intrusions of fantasy or rhetoric."[124]

Moravia, however, was unique in accepting the torture scenes. Most reviewers agreed with *Il Tempo*'s Fabrizio Sarazani in condemning their "ruthless verismo" as anti-esthetic and less effective than allusion. There was general agreement too that the second half was weaker than the first. "Wax-museum truth is never art," Sarazani argued; "Rossellini has fallen into Grand Guignol rhetoric."[125]

It was a phrase Roberto quoted the rest of his life to demonstrate the stupidity of his critics. Yet Sarazani was saying that Roberto had been right in opposing Amidei; far from misunderstanding Rossellini's art, the critics were demanding its purification. "At some point [in the second half]," explained Fabio Carpi in *L'Unità*, "literature prevails over cinema, reality is left behind [and] characters are substituted for people."[126]

Indeed, what triggered misgivings was *Roma città aperta*'s overwhelming emotional force. "One cannot deny in this work of Rossellini a profound and vast human significance, a pure and objective verismo, a lively and pungent sense of suffered reality," wrote Vittorio Ragusa; but "the actuality of the events described in this film operate on our soul, and this might somehow weaken the serenity of our judgment."[127]

Granted, "it's not a masterpiece," summed up one critic, conceding that *Roma città aperta* failed in the traditional aesthetic categories, "but maybe it's better than a masterpiece, because it moved us and spoke to our hearts, exciting unrhetorical emotions..., the passions that made us live and cry for an entire year."[128]

"It's flawed," agreed Guerrasio, "but we'd love to have many more such mistakes."[129]

*

It is these *aesthetic* misgivings in the first reviews, rather than the outright pans, that demonstrate the left's initial opposition to the picture, according to a study by Alberto Farassino. It was not the movie the left had wanted, Farassino says. They thought it more newsreel than art, thought the actors just let themselves be photographed, and concluded that it had no real value as truth and that its "language" was not to be imitated.[130] Since the left had the sympathy of most of the country's cultural leaders and represented the strongest hope that a far more just society would be built from Italy's ashes, the left's condescension would have upset Roberto. Also it would have embarrassed his relations with Amidei. Amidei was one of "the left." He had clashed with Roberto constantly during production over issues of politics and literary taste. Continuing clashes during *Paisà*'s scripting were just at this time motivating Roberto to throw Amidei off the new film, in order to make it his own way—which was the way the left was now opposing. Like the critics, Amidei regarded Roberto as "flawed," as unschooled and politically naive, but as able to capture things and emotions with a power that excited the crowds, the masses, the "people"—and that seemed all the more powerful to these anti-intellectual intellectuals for being "raw," "instinctive," and "unrhetorical," in other words, for being unschooled and politically naive. Rossellini posed a dilemma.

Thus on one hand, in the Socialist *Avanti!*, Alberto Vecchietti felt compelled to denounce *Roma*'s lack of schooling. He was furious that the Nazi colonel's predictions that the unity of the Resistance was a delusion and that the right would soon turn against the Communists had not been answered in the film. He cited this failure as an instance not of political incorrectness but of ineptitude—as evidence that *Roma città aperta* alluded to a lot of themes without knowing how to develop any one of them.

On the other hand, in the Communist *L'Unità* Umberto Barbaro, the respected Communist professor at the Centro Sperimentale during the Fascist years, approved *Roma città aperta*'s political correctness (the "objectivity so lacking in rhetoric and implicit political judgment so judicious and fair") in showing hatred, filth, wretchedness, corruption, treachery, squalor, torture, crime, and ghastliness; and applauded Rossellini's ability to manipulate the audience's emotions in the right directions, his skill at juggling "grotesque comedy and heart-rending pathos in a simple plot," his capacity to arouse "immediately in the entire audience the most avid concurrence and, as they remembered that recent tragedy, the deepest emotions." But Barbaro gave *Roma* short shrift at the end of an article lavishing more enthusiastic praise on the non-crowd-pleasing Russian film, *Lenin 1918*.[131]

In other words, once it became apparent that Rossellini's movie was a huge emotional success with the public, the left concluded, according to Farassino, that their best course was to embrace and even to impose the film. It did show the way, it was a film that had finally said the truth, was on the side of truth, and so it had, obligatorily, to please.[132] "Maybe ten years from now people will judge it as only a good piece of work. Yet it resembles certain revolutionary songs that don't excite musicians but make governments fall," wrote Baracco.[133]

Some reviewers went back, saw it again, and radically changed their minds. "Act of Contrition" was the headline on one such second opinion.[134]

Sponsorship by the left was an immeasurable asset for Rossellini at this point in his career. All the pundits were promoting his film, his wisdom, his inestimable value to the new "Risorgimento" (although none of the left would have dared use that word after the Fascists' long exploitation of it).

Ironically, the left's support would rebound in the 1950s, when some who had thought him an ally would conclude they had mistaken their man, would turn on him, call him a "spiritualist," and denounce his betrayal. He had not after all, they would say, been interested in class struggle but rather in "Catholic historicism." He had made the priest, not the Communist, the chief character, and the priest symbolized not the Catholic partisan but the spirit's indomitability. Thus all the deaths, here and in *Paisà*, all the gains in consciousness, appear to amount to mere generalities that offer no lessons to rationalize human conduct. Rossellini (they would charge) avoids the need to investigate the actual, historical Resistance, the need to illuminate the dialectic among the concrete social forces involved in it, the need to examine history's laws and forces. In his ahistorical, spiritualist vision it is not the dialectical forces of history which will make possible humanity's triumph but rather Christian love.[135]

This seems true. *Roma città aperta*'s dialectics are eternal and Manichaean rather than specific and socio-economic. But few movies illuminate dialectical forces of any sort, almost none examine history's "laws," and the movies Italian Marxists eventually would make would notably fail to do either. Flawed as it was, *Roma* had no competition to point to. What would continue to trouble the left was that it was the unqualified Rossellini, with his uncouth melodrama (rather than more suitable craftsmen like Visconti, Zavattini, or De Santis) who, despite his Catholic historicism and in spite of Amidei's guidance, had made the definitive artistic statements of the postwar and had seemed at the time to have caught its vital élan.

To explain this embarrassment, they fell back on the myth of the instinctual artist (a close cousin to Rousseau's noble savage): Rossellini had been so far "out of it" that he had not realized the need to inspect, organize, classify, and place data within a theoretical context. And it was his lack of intellectual grounding and independence from literary tradition, that gave him an advantage! He thrived on confusion and chaos, trusted his raw intuition, and nurtured his receptivity; and evidently it took ingenuousness of that order to express postwar Italy's state of soul, to catch that feeling for the moment that was not in Amidei's script.[136]

Eminent non-Marxists have reached similar conclusions. José-Luis Guarner emphasizes the "absolute spontaneity" with which natural locations are integrated into the film, with which actors identify with their characters, with which characters and locations *become* the film. This is what is so original about *Roma città aperta*: its spontaneity. "In other Italian films, like *Ossessione* or Mario Soldati's little known *Eugenia Grandet* (1946), success is achieved by a conscious effort of reconstruction. In *Roma città aperta* it is simply *discovered*, thanks to humble, careful observation. Everything seems miraculously to have been seen for the very first time, just as it did at the birth of the cinema."[137]

Visconti reconstructs, Rossellini discovers. Perhaps this is true, whatever it means. Anyone can "discover" reality with a camera; amateur photographers do it with every shot, and also feel they're seeing things for the very first time. But the valid distinction between Visconti and Rossellini is between self-consciousness and intense receptivity, as Guarner make clear. It is absurd to suggest that Rossellini was too naive to know what he was doing, that his art is a product of subconscious impulse rather than intentional craftsmanship. The proof of this is that Rossellini has proven nearly impossible to imitate, except for his weakest passages. It is nonsense to proclaim that Rossellini's art is discovering a pre-existent world rather than creating a new one—one that no more exists outside his cinema than Wordsworth's daffodils outside his poetry or Toynbee's theory of history outside his writing. The past no longer has reality. It can be explored only in the imagination. To recreate it is to make art. Art is always "a ritualistic reordering of reality,"[138] even, or especially, when the ritual is a means of coming to terms with overwhelming events.

Spontaneity is Rossellini's deliberate and persistent theme, however, and always suggests revolutionary utopia, whether as the end point of Marxist evolution, Rousseau's savage, or the Christian innocent. In contrast, any "system"—like the police commissioner's map quadrants in *Roma città aperta*—is burdensome, repressive, unnatural. Rossellini's heroes thirst for the spontaneous; they're dreamers groping for a better world without knowing precisely what's wrong with this one, how to achieve a better one, or what the new one would be like. "[This winter] will end," Francesco the Communist tells sora Pina; "it will end, and spring will come back too, and it will be more beautiful than ever, because we'll be free. We have to believe it, we have to want it! See, I know these things, I feel them, but I don't know how to explain them to you. Manfredi'd know how: he's an educated man, he's studied a lot, and travelled. He really knows how to talk. But I think that's the way it is, that we shouldn't be afraid, either now or in the future. Because we're right, our way is right. We're struggling for something which has to come, which cannot not come! Maybe the road will be a bit long and difficult, but we'll get there, and we'll see that it's a better world! And what's more our children will see it!"

Yet Rossellini was criticized for this very speech. By not specifying the real enemies, the specific means to attain the better world, or what was meant by the "right way," it was charged, the speech avoids all controversies in favor of an "equivocal" homily with which no one can disagree. True. *Roma città aperta* "hides" the fact that the Badoglians (like the Christian Democrats) were attempting to undermine the Resistance and the left, just as it "hides" the fact that there was no democratic procedure in the Communist organization. But such criticism ignores the historical moment, the spirit that made the postwar so euphoric. Togliatti himself, on Stalin's orders, had decreed a policy of cooperation by the Communists with the democratic parties. There was to be no anti-clericalism, no attempt to repeal the Church's privileges, above all, no return to the slogan-flinging disruptions that had brought Mussolini to power. Italy was too wrecked for fresh revolutions. *Roma città aperta*'s insistence on the vague but essential unity of the Resistance was absolutely in accord with PCI ideology at the time. Unity and healing were more important than exact analysis. Which is why, after initial protests by a few rebel film critics, the Party rallied to the movie's support.

Nonetheless it is almost true that love is the only "political" solution Rossellini offers—in any of his films. "My personal 'neo-realism,'" he admitted, "is nothing but a moral position that can be put into four words: love of one's neighbor."[139] And Gian Luigi Rondi has shown that *Roma città aperta*, like *Paisà* and *Deutschland im Jahre Null*, is a vision of a world without God, an icy representation of a time and a society that has forgotten the principles of love; contrasted to it are the pity and fellowship of Don Pietro, sora Pina, the schoolboys, and the partisans, who go even into battle with deep feeling rather than hate: a desperate questioning of the *raison d'être* of injustice, absurdity, and cruelty.[140] Thus *Roma città aperta*'s most moving moments are the small acts of charity: Don Pietro telling Manfredi he didn't talk under torture; Francesco caring for Pina's son Marcello after her death; the school friend who puts his arm around Marcello's shoulder as they walk down the hill after Don Pietro's execution.

As inhumanity is contrasted with love, so confusion is contrasted with certainty. One need not go so far as Henri Agel, the French Catholic, and view the story as "essentially a development in time of . . . the atemporal clash of forces of good and evil . . . [in which] the priest assumes the sufferings of his companions, lifting them onto the supernatural plane."[141] For *Roma città aperta*, melodrama though it be, is clearly rooted in a specific time, place, and political goal. Agel observes that Don Pietro is militant only ambivalently, in spite of himself: he is presented as someone whose actions (his curses of Nazi-Fascists first in front of Pina, then in front of the colonel) surpass his thoughts, as if to say that the Church is with those who struggle but also carries its message of peace: Don Pietro's commitment is to charity rather than to the Resistance itself[142]—although here again the movie is being accurate about the Church's role during the Occupation.

Agel has a point: after Manfredi's death, the priest's immediate repudiation of his damnation of the Germans ("My God? What have I said?") does, along with the framing and cutting, mark his curse as prophetic. And also marks the priest as possessed of a moral certainty that places him alone in the film above the temporal struggle. Or almost alone: for, unnoticed by either Agel or the Stalinists, Manfredi is there too, directing his partisans from a hill literally *above* the conflict as they, like avenging angels, sweep over the German convoy. Both of them, priest and Communist, are the stuff of martyrs. We know they will never capitulate, are never tempted to. Just as sora Pina regards Don Pietro as an oracle of The Truth, so too Francesco, in the speech quoted above, regards Manfredi. Neither counsels love so much as constancy (or, much the same thing: resistance). Don Pietro counsels obedience to God's commandments as an answer to the Nazi occupation, while in a parallel scene Manfredi lets Marina know that she damns herself in his eyes for failing to be true to her own better self. Thus both men represent standards of moral purity that are beyond the reach of ordinary mortals. Indeed, it is Marina's spite at Manfredi's moral aloofness that inspires her to betray him. He is no ordinary "man of the people"; he is able to confront Marina with herself but he is too inhuman to be able to improve her. The "supernatural plane" offers no solutions. As Don Pietro says, "It's not difficult to die well. It's difficult to live well"—or to remedy temporal suffering.[143] The movie's siting is poetic: Rome, "the center of Christianity."[144] The presence of St. Peter's cupola, at the movie's beginning[145] as well as at its end looming over everything, like Don Pietro and Manfredi but eternally, marks not the subsumption of temporal woes into spiritual hopes, but the eternal struggle that human values demand. Almost everyone who is good dies in *Roma città aperta* and still it is an optimistic picture, because St. Peter's *plus* the fraternity of the boys foretells the victory of the spirit, of "Rome." What most movingly documents the courage of the Roman people in front of the Fascists and Germans is their humor. Far from being exalted by Rossellini's camera at the moment of their ultimate sacrifice, both Don Pietro and Manfredi—viewed at human levels by non-heroic friends and having ceased to be the point of interest even in their own death scenes—are shorn of their heroic dimensions in order to return them to the people.

In New York Rod Geiger went straight to Joe Burstyn, who had distributed the French films Rod's brother-in-law had imported. A p.r. man for New York's Yiddish theater, serious about films and the avant-garde, Burstyn was small, under five feet and hunchbacked, yet saintly-looking with white hair, and, as Geiger put it, "the soul of Arthur Mayer"—his partner, who in between exploitation of horror flicks consented to exhibit Burstyn's money-losing treasures at his Rialto Theater and ended his days lecturing on cinema aesthetics at Dartmouth College.

Burstyn couldn't decide whether he was moved or disgusted by *Open City*. But he wasn't undecided about its commercial possibilities. "My God! Italian films . . . ! *No one* goes to see them!"

Geiger found some Italian women who fought over this Italian film and Burstyn began to see potential. But he thought the title should be "Nightmare," until two in the morning, when he phoned to say it was a stroke of genius; Open City: Open Girls!

Mayer–Burstyn contracted with Foreign Film Productions to distribute *Open City* and made a verbal commitment for *Seven from the U.S.* The box-office gross was to be split fifty-fifty, after promotional costs; no advance was paid. For the subtitling Geiger imported a dupe negative and engaged Pietro Di Donato, author of a 1939 book *Christ in Concrete* that Roberto had read in translation and that he and Geiger planned to film after *Seven*.

Now Geiger had to find $28,000 for Conti and more money for Foreign Film Productions' fifty-percent share in *Seven from the U.S.*, then budgeted at $75,000. Bob Lawrence's uncle saw the movie and was uninterested. Geiger's uncle was interested, but attached too many strings. A boyhood friend came through: Oswald Landau, whose father owned a Swiss bank, agreed to supply all the money Geiger needed in return for a fifty-percent interest in Foreign Film Productions. As it turned out, most of the new money would come from Foreign Film Productions' profits from *Open City*. Upset by the two uncles and the general treatment of returning GIs, Geiger at this point gave Lawrence, as a fellow soldier, 25 percent of Foreign Film Productions.

While Roberto continued to phone frantically from Rome, next to deal with was the Legion of Decency. Its Italian equivalent, the Centro Cattolico Cinematografico, although counseling that the torture scenes might be too much for children, had enthusiastically recommended *Roma città aperta* for adults, lauding its rich humanism, exaltation of heroic sacrifice, and "dramatic, shifting rhythm that often achieves perfection." But Americans were made of sterner stuff, and here were sadists, lesbians, cocaine addicts, couples living openly in sin, Communists, and, worst of all, a toddler on a potty. "You're a nice boy," Monsignor John T. McClafferty told Geiger. "People don't want to see films like this. Why do you want to show it?"

"It's a true experience of the war, and of people," Geiger replied. He agreed to some cuts, and collected some conscientious reporters, an Italian priest who wept profusely, and a letter from the Vatican (forged for Roberto) claiming that Pope Pius XII had seen *Roma città aperta*, found it inspirational, and urged everyone to see it.

McClafferty watched a second time, pondered whether to condemn the movie for showing a priest engaged in politics, and did—as "morally objectionable to all" due to "deceit sympathetically treated; excessive gruesomeness; suggestive costumes and implications; use of narcotics."[146]

Thus inspired, Mayer–Burstyn advertised the film as "Sexier than Hollywood ever dared to be." One ad showed two girls in rapt embrace; another ("designed to tap the sadist trade," according to Mayer[147]) showed a man being flogged.

Some torture scenes were toned down (as was done also in Italy), but the toddler continued to offend, and the Motion Picture Producers Association withheld its seal until it was removed. "I've been reproached so many times for it," said Roberto, "but that baby on that potty wasn't at all there for sensation but to convey a sense of the obvious, to bring the human being as near as possible to what's in reality. Only that way, afterward, do you see the heroism, the hero. What do you expect from a hero? That he act like a hero, of course. Zorro is Zorro, and that's all there is to it. But if you catch him also in his humblest moments, off his pedestal, then later, when he gets back on the pedestal, you believe in him more."[148]

Open City's American premiere—the title never included the *"Rome"* added in Europe—was held at the World Theater, 153 West 49th Street, on February 25, 1946, as a benefit for the God Parents for Italian War Orphans Committee.

Janet Flanner's write-up in *The New Yorker* three months earlier had already baited interest. Geiger had invited her to the USIA-sponsored screening in Rome in August and she had reported back to America that this was "the first great film on the resistance to come out in Europe, maybe the best film Italy has ever produced."[149]

Now New York agreed. Bosley Crowther in *The New York Times* praised its documentary "wind-blown look of a film shot from actualities, with the camera providentially on the scene," its "candid, overpowering realism," and its passionate "admiration for the people who fight for freedom's cause. It is a quiet exaltation."[150] John Mason Brown in *Saturday Review* agreed with this impression: "Its anguishes do not appear to have been tricked. [It is] as if we had eavesdropped on the actual speech of mortals tested almost beyond mortal endurance.... People act like people, not actors.... [The] characters appear to have been photographed without knowing it."[151]

Life said many Americans thought it was an actual documentary.[152] Reviewers too assumed that most of the actors were non-professionals (and that Magnani was simply a "cafe singer"), and focused on Rossellini's roughness, the "ugly photography and bad sound" (*New York Sun*[153]), which they identified with realism. *The New York Telegram* warned of female bodies shown without the "customary restrictions." *Life* warned of "violence and sexuality produc[ing] a sensation of dangerous and desperate struggle such as Hollywood rarely achieves."[154]

Emotion, most of all, was identified with realism. In a second review, Crowther talked not about "quiet exaltation," but about "a deep, genuine moral tone..., a screen drama of tremendous power in which the techniques of realism—and the attitudes—are shatteringly employed."[155]

James Agee in *The Nation* judged *Open City* "one of the most heartrending pictures in years, as well as one of the best." He liked its freshness, vitality, and immediacy. Even "a casual little scene" between Francesco and Pina contained "an oxygen-sharp, otherwise unattainable atmosphere, almost a smell of freedom." There are "kinds of understanding which most films entirely lack, or reduce to theatricality ... [such as] the sizing-up look and the tone and gesture with which the Gestapo officer opens his interrogation" of Manfredi.[156]

But it was emotion, atmosphere, and "kinds of understanding" that Agee distrusted, as had Umberto Barbaro. Although *Life*, in a seven-page spread, maintained that *Open City* showed that Italians still possessed the nobility that Mussolini had tried to destroy,[157] many critics wryly remarked on what Italians had avoided noticing: that German Nazis rather than Italian Fascists are the enemy, that Mussolini is never mentioned. But it wasn't *Open City*'s soft line on Fascism that disturbed Agee. After a few weeks' reflection, he decided the movie lacked intellectual depth, was Communist propaganda, and could hoodwink us.

In other words, it didn't come down firmly enough on the right side. Ironically, the same problem had bugged Italian Communists.

Agee may have been irked by assessments from the American left. *The Daily Worker* charged that *Open City* pointed up the lukewarm anti-fascism of Hollywood films. *Open City* was "a true film of the people [in which] people play their own roles again, in a drama they lived once before," said *P.M.*[158] "It . . . has the shattering impact of *Potemkin* . . . the awesome strength of the people in concentrated, unwavering struggle for freedom," hailed *New Masses*.[159]

Agee was answered by Dorothy Thompson in *The Boston Globe*, who was haunted by depths Rossellini's critics had avoided. "Does it mean," she asked, "that in this world, as it still is, there is no happy ending for the pure—except to see God? *Open City* is actually a morality play, in which the human race, eternally struggling to become human, are the actors. But, in the words of Schiller's Marquis Posa, one comes away convinced that 'man is greater than you esteem him!' . . . [T]he solidarity between anti-Fascists," whether Communist or Catholic, "arises not out of conformity of ideological aims, but from the imperatives of each personal character. . . .

"Posa's words were addressed to his king, as this film should be addressed to the peace-makers, sternly to remind them that, however frontiers, spheres of influence, and ideological lines may be drawn, humanity, whatever its class, or creed, shares common hopes, faith, vices, and virtues, and an indivisible destiny."[160]

Open City's success, however, was due mostly to word of mouth. It ran at The World for twenty months, until October 1947 (when it was replaced by Zampa's *Vivere in pace*). The little theater had only 299 seats, which meant there was usually a line outside to attract additional interest. U.S. grosses were at times estimated as high as $1.6 million, which may have been twice the truth. But even the true earnings were unprecedented for a subtitled import, and were in no wise due to patronage by Italian-Americans (who, according to Geiger, paid little attention to it).[161] With *Open City*, Geiger and Burstyn opened up the American market to foreign films in general, and to Italian movies in particular. Its success made it possible for other filmmakers to raise money for other raw, investigative, slices of life, in which audience and filmmaker would join in searching for a "new realism" on which to build a better world from the war's ashes.

Italians, particularly on the left, had hailed *Roma città aperta* for its content. To American eyes its revolutionary novelty lay not in content but style—its documentary-like "realism." While Hollywood films had a long history of populism, and while anti-Nazi movies abounded, realism of any sort had been rare of late. Hollywood had been spoiled by the extraordinary prosperity of the war years, when competing forms of recreation were curtailed and more people went to the movies—any movie—than ever before or since—with the result that formulaic, studio-shot, mindless entertainment had become the rule. Thus *Open City's* impact was shattering. Far more than in Italy, it made other movies look insipid.

Geiger helped create the Rossellini myth. "We talked of [making the film] constantly [during the German occupation]," he told a gullible reporter; "a few days after Rome was liberated we took an old loft building where we made our interiors."[162] Yet talk of "realism" was to confuse the actual issue for years to come. Historically it was not novel at all. Documentary and fiction had been mixed in American cinema from its very beginning. American pictures by Griffith, Chaplin, Stroheim, and Vidor were Rossellini's models and inspiration. Even in 1945, as one reviewer pointed out, *Open City* could be compared to *The House on 92nd Street*, in which an actual F.B.I. operation is re-enacted "with realism as the primary motif."[163]

Aesthetically it was moronic to regard *Open City* as though it were some sort of newsreel rather than carefully constructed art. One had to ignore, for example, Rossellini's continuous, melodramatic manipulation of light: how he situates most of the movie in cramped interiors, outer darkness, and deep shadows to suggest the human struggle; how he emphasizes Pina's naturalness by having daylight enter the apartment to warm and highlight her features; how he paints the corrupt Marina with harsh, bright, artificial lighting; how light around the Gestapo is dense and stagnant; how in the jail cell, where hope is gone, one can barely see.[164] One had to ignore the concocted story as well, not to mention "the excellence of the players," although as Bazin noted this was "what naturally first struck the public."[165]

In comparison, documentary style in *The House on 92nd Street* is severe and unyielding. Rossellini's genius was not his realism, but his ability to overwhelm people with emotions *linked* to actuality—which is quite a different thing. As Guido Fink has written, Rossellini starts out with history but "sacrifices any pretense of exact fidelity for a freer immersion into the very heart of what James called 'the infinite tragedy and pity of the past'.... Don Morosini has become Don Pietro, a more universal personage, detached from any anecdotal contingency: his realness, like the rest of the film's realness, is internal rather than circumstantial in nature.... The wounds of the war and occupation [are] still visible on the streets and neighborhoods where Rossellini ... carried his camera, and they appear even on the actors' faces.... [But the fact that these are] among the most convincing images of this period ... is explained less by the intrinsic authenticity of the non-professional actors and the scenery than by the manner—almost the anguish—with which the camera scrutinizes and explores them.... Rossellini's technique remains always the same [throughout his career]: it's just to explore, to scrutinize, to try to understand the events happening under the camera's eye.... [He] tends to limit his direction to a preliminary organization of material already given and known in the abstract (e.g., Don Pietro's execution, or St. Francis's kissing the leper, or Cardinal Mazarin's death): the fact that he already knows, that we ourselves know, thanks to newspapers, anthologies, or history books, what the screen is going to show us, subtracts nothing from the mystery of the gestures, of the faces, of the human actions, the mystery that reveals itself in its limpid and crystalline purity only in front of the camera."[166]

Roma città aperta, then, is somewhat realist in content but expressionist in means. Rossellini was not a "realist." If he filmed "real things," it was in order to establish a moral relationship between people and things, between us and his film. The difference between news and history, as Croce said, is that one is a science, the other an art. Romans had watched in 1945 while nudging each other and whispering, "That happened to me last year." But *Roma città aperta* was not just *set* in recent events, it historicized those events, made them art, turning them into a paean to Italian defeat, showing that "Spring" would come as a result. History for Rossellini, as for Croce, was the story of liberty emerging. Liberty may be squashed for the moment with the torture and death of Manfredi and the execution of Don Pietro, but liberty burns like a fire within people, alive in the quintessentially Resistance alliance of the Italian Church and the Communist Party, alive in the camaraderie of the little-boy-partisans trouping down the Gianicolo toward the dome of St. Peter's. This was a message Italians wanted—to see the light of heroism that shone in the dark tunnel of shame during Fascism, defeat, and occupation. "Rossellini," one Italian critic remarked, "has looked with the eyes of a poet, not of a newsman."[167]

Paisà

It is not the cause for which men took up arms that makes a victory more just or less, it is the order that is established when arms have been laid down.
                                                                                    —Simone Weil

Italy had declared war on Germany in September 1943. But the Allies went on treating her like an enemy and behaving like conquerors, ruling the country, imposing a vindictive treaty, and only begrudgingly permitting Italians to join the fight. As far as most Americans and Britons were concerned, Italians were just as bad as Germans or Japanese; they just merited less respect.

Seven from the U.S. was intended to change this impression. The Americans involved in its planning—Rod Geiger, Klaus Mann, Alfred Hayes, and Bob Lawrence—were experiencing the real Italy firsthand and wanted to tell the folks back home about it. There would be no "sugar coating," said Geiger.[1] *Seven from the U.S.* was to be a film *for* Americans, addressed *to* Americans, and *about* Americans, Americans discovering Italy. It would be a sort of diary of the war, introducing seven Americans as they sailed toward the first Allied landing in Sicily, July 2, 1943, and following the war up the boot of Italy toward the Alps twenty months later; it would depict "not warfare but . . . , as realistically and faithfully as possible, the life of Americans in Italy, of their relationships with Italians," as Klaus Mann put it in a prospectus composed for the U.S. Embassy.[2] The Americans would be "the most representative types." Each would die, and a white military-cemetery cross would conclude each episode to show "that the film intends to be a warm and respectful homage to the memory of those Americans who lost their lives for the liberation of Italy, and that it intends to be a message to their nation."[3]

This American perspective is strongly reflected in Mann's initial outline, which Geiger took with him to New York in August 1945.[4]

But, as Geiger said, "Movies that make Italians known can't be made except by Italians and in Italy, not in Hollywood."[5] And the participation of such fiercely proud Italians as Rossellini and Amidei in so American-directed a project was incongruous. Americans were their liberators and frequently their friends, but Americans were also their conquerors, their occupying army, their dictators, and frequently their despisers; it was difficult not to resent them at times. Besides, what was more vitally important at the moment: to send a fawning message to the Americans thanking them in the guise of a tour of Italy replete with apologies for being Italian? Or to send a message to Italians, a compassionate message to themselves, telling them they had reasons for pride?

Not surprising, then, that in the movie that emerged, *Paisà*, it is the Italians who are the protagonists, whereas the Americans have been reduced to witnesses who seldom understand what is going on, to "strange new Barbarians," in the words of a British critic, "[who] are taken apart gently, like a mechanical toy, to see how they tick. And here they are: indifferent, obtuse, kindly savages."[6] In each episode, the naiveté of the American characters is unmasked, and they are taught pointed lessons in humility—usually at the cost of Italian lives. "Rossellini ingeniously contrives to load the dice against the Allies," concluded a second British critic. "[He has] great skill in selecting incident, and even greater skill in giving his work a political slant the more telling for its subtlety."[7]

Nonetheless, during the initial script conferences (June to September 1945) Roberto—whether because he was still involved with *Roma città aperta*, or because he wanted to attract American money, or, most likely, because at the moment he was working empathetically with Americans—seems to have accepted their slant for the film. At any rate, an American slant dominates the preliminary treatments. The Rome episode is a good example. The first treatment, by Hayes and Mann, is about an American tank driver who, having been befriended by a "nice" girl on the day of Rome's liberation, returns months later and discovers she has become a whore. Everything, including the flashback, happens from the American's perspective, and even after a second whore explains the brutal circumstances that have forced nice girls onto the streets, the soldier jilts his former friend. But in the filmed version everything, including the flashback, happens from the girl's perspective and the soldier never connects her with their past: the "moral revelation" is hers, not his. The shift is thus from an American's disenchanting but instructive encounter (in which the girl is incidental) to an Italian's moral confrontation with herself (in which the soldier is incidental). Similar shifts in perspective occurred in each of *Paisà*'s episodes between script and production.

This shift is key to Rossellini's concept. It is why *Paisà* wears the aura of a national epic. Although the immediate impression of each episode is negative—the heroine dies, the heroes die, the whore goes unredeemed—each incident implies a new Italy reborn from the ashes: a nation of fraternity, tolerance, and commitment; the dream of the Resistance.

Paisà's message is emphatic for Italian viewers, who identify with the Italian characters. It will be diluted for American viewers who identify with the American characters. An American-oriented experience of *Paisà* goes against its grain, and American viewers would do well to experience each episode from within the sensibility of the Italians.

Even in mid-1946, a year after *Paisà*'s conception, the Italian cinema was still, Rodolfo Sonego recalls, very much an "artisanal craft, improvised day by day and without big production and distribution organizations. Money was still being found in rather adventurous ways. There wasn't much money, there wasn't much film. . . . Amidei was the center of the Italian cinema, everyone passed through him, actors, directors, writers. There had been the great revelation of *Roma città aperta*, and a degree of expansion was already under way. . . . A gleam of light had opened up in the world, and we felt, even with a bit of certainty, that our cinema was good, that it could be good. The people all around us were so much alive! It was an extraordinary time, after the war, after twenty years of Fascism. Everything was grist for cinema. Even the little movies, the ones improvised week by week, in which everything was invented as quickly as possible (and which the critics loathed ferociously), even these were always inspired by everyday reality, and so had an inner strength to them. Seen again today, they still have their authenticity; they are inventories of our misfortunes, but also of our ability to rise again, our vitality."[8]

To Rod Geiger in August 1945, Rome felt "like Athens."[9]

Said Roberto, "We had been under the domination of the Germans, under the Fascists, under persecution, and then one beautiful day the others arrived, as enemies. Three days later they realized we weren't enemies, because we were people like them. I remember a phrase that in Rome was on everyone's lips, 'He's poor mama's boy too,' and this realization produced an extraordinary fraternity during the war (which they managed to kill in three years), a wonderful fraternity."[10]

Fraternity is evoked by Rossellini's title, *Paisà*, adopted two months into the shooting. The word was not Italian but a corruption of the Italian-American "paesano" ("countryman" or "buddy") that Allied soldiers used in greeting Italians. "Paisà" was also the name of Rod Geiger's dog, an Irish Setter whom he left in Rome with Mario Conti when he sailed home in September. The dog reminded Roberto of the four GIs he had encountered before Rome's liberation, on the road just outside the walls, who had kept calling him "paisan, paisan."

Roma città aperta had been a triumph for Rossellini as producer, *Paisà* would be his triumph as director. But the fact that Roberto initially planned to hand *Paisà*'s actual direction over to a number of other directors whom he would merely supervise indicates that he still thought of himself as primarily an organizer rather than the creative artist the movie reveals.

He prepared with great care. Once again he divided his writers into competing teams. At first Amidei worked with Hayes, Mann with Pagliero, while Roberto and Geiger injected ideas of their own. Then Hayes left, and Pagliero, when he wasn't drinking, got involved directing his own movie,

Roma città libera. Mann continued alone, or vainly attempted to collaborate with Amidei. For each episode, a succession of detailed treatments was prepared and repeatedly revised; complete dialogues were composed and these too were repeatedly revised.

The whole film, in its scripted form, was essentially Mann's work, although still without Rossellini's Italian slant. Klaus Mann (1906–49) was deeply cultured, adored Italy, had traveled widely before the war, published twenty books, and served in the American army's Psychological Warfare Branch in North Africa, Italy, and Germany. Despite his adopted country's mistreatment of him—the U.S. Army had interned him as a homosexual for nine months before acceding to his stubborn petitions that he be allowed to serve—Mann was fiercely pro-American. He had begun work on the script August 4, a week after his first discussions with Rossellini, and had signed a contract August 14. He conferred constantly with Lawrence but fought constantly with Amidei, and by November 15 was fed up, announced he was quitting, and even offered to forego $1,000 of the $2,500 due under his contract. "I am through. The Italian text of Amidei's new versions . . . makes it quite clear that there is no place or function for me in the present setup. What Rossellini wants me to do is to act as Amidei's translator. I refuse to accept this role. . . . Amidei tries everything to spoil what I have done. . . . Everything might have worked out all right . . . if it had not been for Amidei's perfidy and Rossellini's weakness. . . . [But] Rossellini backs Amidei. [And] Amidei is against me. So I have to go. . . . Amidei wins."[11]

Weeks of talks, fights, and reconciliations followed, with Lawrence as mediator. By November 23, Mann felt "a bit more Italian again," he wrote his mother, but added, "they are quite too vain and treacherous. *Kazelmacher* [bastard-makers]."[12]

Mann wearied Roberto. He worked with devilish efficiency, dialoguing an entire sequence in a single night, and his enthusiasm was pesky. When he didn't have a lover he was morose and lonely. Every two or three nights he would take a "nightwalk" and pick up a male prostitute. In fact, Roberto had gotten what he wanted out of him; he didn't want him around when filming started and used Amidei to get rid of him.

An agreement was signed, December 14, promising screen credit only to Amidei, with the words "In collaboration with Klaus Mann,"[13] and on December 22 Mann left for Zurich, where his parents lived.

Then Roberto got rid of Amidei.

Amidei had wanted a traditional, well-prepared, well-crafted production. He envisioned a progression from south to north, toward civilization, toward the men of the north, the six-and-a-half-foot partisans, who were upholding Italy's dignity in the foothills of the Alps. (He insisted on their height, and their encounter with an American parachutist who would be a full foot shorter and would condescendingly tell them to stop fighting and go home.)

Roberto, in contrast, was even more reluctant to engage in national-populist flag-waving than he had been during *Roma città aperta.* He had paid his tribute to the Party, and the Church too; now he wished to express his own feelings. He determined to go as far as possible away from traditional studio filmmaking. He wanted to shoot spontaneously on the streets, to get out and explore, to show Italians of different regions to each other. He wanted the Dos Passos–like ellipses and silent monologues he had dreamed about during the Occupation. He wanted leaner, less embroidered facts than in *Roma città aperta*. There were personal differences with Amidei as well. Roberto was carrying on a casual affair with Maria Michi (who, it is said, would go back and forth between him, Amidei, and others[14]) and had become openly scornful of Amidei's lecturing manner. And Amidei was alienating everyone else by his unwillingness to suffer contradiction.

Principally, Roberto wanted to be free. Twenty-five years later he told an American audience, "You have no idea—this is really a confession—how much I hate *Open City* and how much I love *Paisan* more. *Open City* is full of old ingredients.... *Paisan* [is] purer ... less seductive.... [Just] the facts are all there. My starting point was a moral position [to show facts honestly in order to understand fully], so I had a feeling that I was cheating a little bit [in *Open City*—for example, by having the boys whistle outside Don Pietro's prison cell], so I tried to purify the thing."[15]

Paisà would be the true debut of Rossellini, moviemaker.

By December, aside from Hayes ("Rome"), none of the writers except Mann had contributed much that would survive in the finished movie.[16] Accordingly Roberto, seeking to "Italianize" Mann's scenario, turned to Fellini, and reworked the outline with him. On December 28 he hired Massimo Mida as well, offsetting the "Catholic" Fellini with a Communist. "I bumped into Roberto on Via Nizza," said Mida. "He'd been looking for me ... and sent me immediately to his place, where Fellini was working on the scenario.... I never met Klaus Mann or Alfred Hayes or even Marcello Pagliero."[17] Fellini and Mida would each receive 12,000 lire a week plus 1,500 for expenses, would travel with the production, do rewrites as conditions suggested, and act as assistant directors.

For Mida, to work with Rossellini meant to break with Visconti, with whom he had made *Ossessione*. "Visconti was cutting, peremptory, even scornful and bitter with me, his accusations mixing anger with disillusion. Was I then not free to accept a director's offer, for an important film that would take a long time, an author who had already done *Roma città aperta* and was not, in substance, that far away from our [Communist] group? Besides, I ... had already collaborated on the script of Rossellini's *Un pilota ritorna* in 1942. Certainly the encounter with Luchino didn't make me hesitate, I began work the next day, with Fellini, on *Paisà*'s treatment.... But certainly it was no accident that after that encounter-collision with Luchino a caesura occurred between us, something irreparable.... Somehow I had left the 'clan,' I would no longer have the privilege of his high protection."[18]

Nor was Rossellini less jealous. "If I had dinner with Visconti," said Rod Geiger, "Roberto would sulk. He was very possessive. I belonged to him. He'd have a hemorrhage if I saw Visconti."[19]

On December 9, Roberto, still living at 20 Via di Parco Pepoli, signed a two-year contract with Geiger and Lawrence at $15,000 per year, after taxes, plus ten percent net profits, with an option for two additional years. No money changed hands then or ever, although for legal purposes a memo was composed stating that Roberto had received $4,000. Geiger, who was still in New York, had secured half of *Paisà's* financing from Landau and a distribution agreement with Burstyn. Since Conti and Campos were supplying the rest of the money in Italy, the film effectively had five producers (including Roberto). Geiger had announced the actors were on their way, so the production crew had been hired and everything was ready, and they all drove out to the airport with flowers the day Harriet White was to arrive. But she wasn't on the plane—and wouldn't arrive for another two months, along with the rest of Geiger's troupe. Geiger claimed the State Department had promised transportation, then had reneged. Conti insisted Geiger and Lawrence pay half the two million lire it had cost to keep the crew sitting around doing nothing.

Geiger had written his father Joseph, the theater coach, in August 1945 to engage Frances Farmer, Myron McCormick, William Gargan, and Canada Lee. He ended up with unknowns. Rossellini took no part in this casting; he didn't even see photos; they were all off-Broadway players: Harriet White, Dotts M. Johnson, Gar Moore, Tony La Pena, Dale Edmonds, and Bill Tubbs. Tubbs, for example, had been appearing in a play, *Flamingo Road*, that had closed before Christmas, meaning that he would be out of work until the following fall; so he accepted Geiger's offer of $200 a week even though he had just gotten married.

They sailed from New York on February 2, on the Swedish ship *Gripsholm*, the first passenger boat to Europe since the war had begun. Also on board was Lucky Luciano. The crime boss was being deported to Italy, where the American government had generously re-established the mafia lords who had been political victims of Fascist tyranny.[20] Lucky played shuffleboard with Tubbs.

The ship arrived and Roberto was waiting at the pier with Annalena Limentani, his translator and girlfriend of the month; she was Jewish and Roberto had helped hide her family during the Occupation. An American MP chased him nastily away.

"You guinea bastard! Get off this pier!" he yelled.

"Si, signor sergente," acknowledged Roberto meekly, bowing Indian fashion.

Such, often, were American-Italian relations. Tubbs was immediately won to Roberto's side. Tubbs was a drinker, he had been drunk the whole voyage to Italy, and that day, eating at Zia Teresa's, he was overcome with compassion when he saw *"burro"* on the menu. "The poor burros!" he cried, refusing to eat a mouthful, deaf to protests that *"burro"* means "butter."[21]

(According to Fellini, in fantasy invented twenty years later, the effervescent Geiger had asked, "'Whom do you want? Gregory Peck? Just let me know, I'll get them all for nothing, they'll do it for me.' Then he went to America and one day sent us a telegram, saying: 'Come to Naples because I'm arriving.' So we went to Naples. We saw a big steamship dock; we saw a little guy appear. It was Geiger getting off with six people, and he said, 'These are the big new American stars. What's Gregory Peck? What's Lana Turner?'—we believed it all because we didn't know anything—'This man here is better than Paul Robeson!'—and he presented a Negro—'This woman is better than Lana Turner!'—and so on."[22])

Shooting of the "Sicily" sequence had already begun on January 15 at Maiori, south of Naples near Amalfi, following Mann's script fairly closely. Rossellini could afford to record sound this time, although the "scratch track" thus obtained would have to be redubbed later. But frequent power failures were still making steady filming impossible. Now Geiger solved the problem by acquiring a German generator that Army inventories had missed. From then on, whenever he and Roberto fought, the generator was the first thing each would grab. The Army, through a friend of Lawrence's, also provided eight soldiers, a tank, three jeeps, some machine guns, and even three German prisoners of war. After the film was finished, the Army had questions for Roberto and Geiger about where so much equipment had come from.

Roberto was on fire, more enthusiastic than ever before (or afterward) at the prospect of shooting a picture.

"**Sicily**" sets the tone of *Paisà*. The American soldiers have landed on what to them seems a primitive, savage land, the land of their enemies, whereas to the Sicilians these newest conquerors are beings from another planet. Two opposite ways of life encounter each other,[23] people in different worlds fail to recognize each other. This "dialectic" will reappear in each of *Paisà*'s six episodes.

The Americans' column, or what we can glimpse of it on this night-blackened film, is ragged and disorderly, but not so disorderly as Rossellini's raw, hasty storytelling. The movie, jumping from one plot line to another, with this plot or that plot intruding abruptly and without explanation, seems almost incomprehensible at times. Only when the Sicilian girl and the American GI, despite mutual mistrust and no common language, find they want to be friends, do things become vivid, in a cave. Then, out of the blue, Joe is shot. We thought the love story was privileged; but, no, another subplot—a bunch of German soldiers wandering around in the night—has imposed itself and destroyed privilege.[24] Heroes, then, are impotent. Or nearly so. For in company with the shooting stars that briefly streaked across this dark world's dome, we spot sparks of an indomitable moral force, a will to resist, though even futilely.[25] The sole close-up of the

Sicilian marks this moment, with the rocky wall behind her as she determines to pick up Joe's rifle and attack the Germans. Yet Rossellini, having reached this point, ends rapidly rather than celebrating her action. The Germans throw the girl off a cliff. Joe's comrades are sure it was "that dirty little Eyetie" who killed him.

"Sicily"'s key elements of plot and theme will be repeated in each of *Paisà's* episodes. There will always be the dialectic of non-communication. Characters will always be *searching*, wandering countrysides or city streets, adventuring often in a maze. Their search will almost always end in a womb-like chamber (often a cave), where they will realize a discovery of truth. Impulse will always trigger this realization; a collision of love and catastrophe, a confrontation with shame, will always trigger the impulse. Truth will always be a moral revelation of human fraternity. But far from confirming the precepts of Party or Church, truth will always fly in the face of accepted, conventional belief; this very personal truth will always, in Roberto's phrase, "revise the whole conception of the universe,"[26] always inaugurate a "new realism," always be scorned by the world, always isolate the hero, and often entail his or her death.

This thematic pattern, a kind of Messiah myth, echoes the moral adventure of Roberto's own life. Indeed, it recurs not just throughout *Paisà* (and *The Messiah*), but in most of Roberto's movies to come.[27] To some degree it was already present in *Desiderio* and even *Un pilota ritorna*.

In contrast, in *Roma città aperta*, impulse produces not moral realization but simply action—both the big heroic actions (Pina running after the truck; the priest's curse; the boys' camaraderie at the end) and the key nefarious actions (the German's shooting Pina; Marina's betrayal of Manfredi). This is because in *Roma* (as in *L'uomo dalla croce*), truth is already known, there is no need for search or revelation, only for hope and resistance. These *wartime* pictures want to demonstrate that human impulse is untrustworthy without proper ideological support. Whereas *Paisà* and all subsequent Rossellini films want to demonstrate that human instinct can be relied upon independently of ideology. In these *postwar* films, evil is always the product of methodical planning and insensitive dedication to ideology (Germans executing partisans in "The Po Delta"; Edmund murdering his father in *Deutschland*; papal police executing Italian patriots in *Vanina Vanini*; Louis XIV constructing totalitarian monarchy; Saul of Tarsus stoning Stephen to death so that people will say he "preserved the purity of the laws"); and redemption always comes when an individual confronts his or her personal shame. The "new" Italy is already born at "Sicily"'s end.

Roma città aperta, in glaring contrast to subsequent Rossellini movies, rejects the possibility of *individual* revelation or redemption. The film permits a German officer to verbalize his shame when drunk, then underlines the shallowness of his honest feelings by showing him, sober, mechanically administering Don Pietro's execution; he is bad by definition. The film permits no suspicion of even a glimmer of moral honesty in Marina, because she, a collaborator and drug addict, is bad also by definition. In any other Rossellini movie it would be precisely this fallen woman whom the plot would be seeking to redeem; here she is irredeemable. Manfredi's efforts to make her confront her shame push her impulsively to betray him; her very nature is evil. Manfredi dies a martyr of righteousness, not of charity. The two ex-lovers destroy each other through a species of intolerance, but this is not a similarity that this wartime film acknowledged. (It is a postwar theme, and Rossellini will take it up in *Fear* and *Vanina Vanini*.)

When she was not being filmed Carmela Sazio (the Sicilian) would watch sullenly from the sidelines and erupt furiously at the slightest provocation from any of the crew. She was fifteen and, more than just her first film, this was her first experience of civilization. Two months before she had been walking toward a fountain with a water jug on her shoulder, looking like a figure out of a nineteenth-century Neapolitan painting, when Roberto, driving around in search of local faces, had noticed her. "She was a little animal," he said, "not understanding anything, moving only by impulsions. It's a common characteristic of thousands of girls in Sicily."[28] Her father was a miserably poor fisherman in Santa Maria La Bruna, "a real, actual stone-age village," according to Massimo Mida, with "filthy little streets submerged in stagnant water. . . . It was enough just to see it to realise how unknown some parts of Italy still are."[29] Maiori, a small seaside town, seemed "a paradise, a metropolis" to Carmela and at first she was dimwitted. To get her to move quickly in a scene, Roberto had to yell and curse at her. Retakes were numerous. Yet little by little she was "weaned" by contact with the troupe. She learned to bathe herself and watched the local girls, timidly at first, then with morbid curiosity. "Instinctively she . . . evaluated our every act, sifted our every feeling through her baby-like mentality. . . . Her fifteen years were not equivalent to even ten of a city child's."[30]

Now, Robert Van Loon, one of the eight GIs lent to Rossellini, was playing Joe, and according to Rossellini's morality of the cinema, if a "real" situation did not exist, a "real" situation had to be created.[31] That is, if in the film Carmela and Robert were to feel the first groping pangs of love despite the cultural abyss separating them, the same thing had to happen in real life. As with Chaplin, love is always the moment of truth for Rossellini, always sincere and ingenuous; but unlike Chaplin, Rossellini's poetry is never studied, and the "acting" in such scenes often seems "bad." Van Loon was a tall, "blond, slouching cowboy with a shrewd, intelligent face," fresh off a southwestern ranch where his father worked as a butcher. And just after his almost-love scene was filmed with Carmela, he took her "under his protection," as Rossellini had planned. "She became calmer, she sweetened," recounted Mida. "They stayed off by themselves, together for hours at a time, naturally without talking. They looked in each other's eyes, held hands, smiled. But I don't think they ever kissed."

Finally came the day of parting. For the troupe it loomed tragically. What were they to do about Carmela? Now that they had introduced her to a whole new world, was she simply to be sent back to her wretched hovel? She had fallen in love with Roberto, too.

"She wrote us a letter, a few days after leaving, all filled with sorrow: the wound had already opened. We were sure, though, that with the passage of time, she would adjust to things. It was significant that she had taken pen in hand and written us a letter. No matter how ungrammatical, it proved Carmela had succeeded in perfectly expressing her state of mind. . . . Deliberately we decided not to respond. That was best, perhaps."[32]

A few years later they learned she had become a prostitute.[33]

The Germans are not depicted kindly: the ones Carmela attacks are throwing dice to see who gets to rape her first. The German actors' names are even omitted from the credits; one was a wanted criminal, unbeknownst to the troupe. They were guarded by an escort supplied by the American army. But the guard, according to Roberto, "didn't care about the film. He would disappear and come back only on Saturday, when we gave them their living expenses. But those three Germans were prisoners of war. And to be a prisoner without a guard, they felt terrible, poor things. So they searched for a guard. And [when] they learned there was a convent of Franciscan monks nearby, they went there and said, 'Please, can we be your prisoners.'[34] At least there they had rules to comply with and they would not be in danger if they spent the night there. And that's how I found the monastery. When I went there to collect the prisoners I met the monks, who were moving in their simplicity."[35]

Accordingly, Roberto, who had planned to shoot a monk story in **Romagna**, decided to do it in Maiori instead, and to dub the monks later into Romagnolo.

But it was Fellini and Geiger who had found the monastery, according to them. The moment "Sicily" had finished shooting, Roberto had run off to Rome or Capri with Roswitha, leaving everyone suspended in Maiori until he chose to return. Fellini and Geiger took a walk on the beach and there was the monastery.[36] Fra Raffaele was standing as immobile as Totò, Fellini thought. "Since I had often been placed in religious pensions when I was little," Fellini said, "I went inside with great interest, and I encountered an atmosphere of infinite grace, almost like a pastel. There were five or six monks, very poor and extremely simple."[37]

"We were invited to dinner. It was just as in the film," said Geiger. There was a reading from the New Testament, and then, although the monks were eating only wine and nuts, a big tray of awful smelling broccoli was brought in just for the visitors. They were embarrassed, and the Father Superior explained it was a prayer: by giving the broccoli to their guests, they hoped eventually to get more food for themselves.[38] Of the war and all that had transpired during the past ten years, the monks had only the vaguest notions.

"I got Rossellini to come eat one evening in this little convent," said Fellini, and, after discussions with him, "I wrote [the treatment for the episode] during a stay I made there."[39]

The story involved three chaplains. Geiger enlisted the Protestant chaplain and a Jewish OSS sergeant from his former company, then went to collect Bill Tubbs in Capri, where his wild drinking had exiled him to the ministrations of a priest. The good man was appalled to learn Tubbs would impersonate the Catholic chaplain. But Tubbs had promised, "Let me know a week in advance, and I'll sober up." And he was as good as his word all ten days of his episode. Whereupon he went straight back to his bottle, got mad at Roberto, whom he ordinarily adored, and took off after him with a forty-five.[40]

In contrast to "Sicily"—where the script had been followed more or less faithfully during the shooting—the entire "Romagna" episode evolved from the situation and characters at hand. Various other stories had been developed: one about a tragic encounter between an American chaplain and a dedicated Fascist teenager; another (by Amidei) in which monks in Mussolini's home town, in response to Allied looting and inedible American canned food and to vindicate Italian culture, serve some American chaplains a wonderful Italian feast, culminating with a roast pig and the speech, "It's not just *that one* [Mussolini pig] who comes from Predappio, but this one too"; and a third story (by Pagliero) about an American chaplain who flees to a monastery but then goes back to the front lines.[41]

For the new story, only a few bits from the second were retained, with an undeveloped idea from the third: the idea, according to Fellini, of "an encounter between some American chaplains and Italian monks, that is, between two types of religion: an active faith such as soldier-priests might have, and that very meditative faith, made only of prayers, which exists in certain medieval convents found in Italy."[42]

Three American chaplains visit the monastery, but the Franciscans are shocked to learn that one of them is Protestant and another Jewish, and even more shocked to learn that the Catholic chaplain has made no efforts to convert them. "I've never asked them anything," he explains, "because I've never thought I could judge them. I know them too well. They're very good friends. Perhaps you, in this peaceful world, in this atmosphere of untroubled meditation, consider me guilty. I don't feel guilty." At dinner, however, the monks persist. They serve the chaplains but fast themselves— as a prayer for "the light of truth" to descend on the two non-Catholics. And now the Catholic chaplain responds: "What you've given me is such a great gift that I feel I'll always be in your debt. I've found here that peace of mind I'd lost in the horrors and the trials of the war, a beautiful, moving lesson of humility, simplicity, and pure faith. *Pax hominibus bonae voluntatis* [Peace to men of good will]."

The episode has provoked puzzlement and bitterness. The eminent aesthetician Rudolf Arnheim wrote in *Bianco e Nero* that American audiences, "confronted at the end with the liberal chaplain's speech exalting the monks' serenity at the very moment they've given proof of the same sort of intolerance that helped cause the war, don't quite understand what it is all about and go away confused and unhappy."[43] Pio Baldelli, contending that "audiences share" the chaplain's initial "indignation" at the suggestion he ought to have been proselytizing his colleagues, also finds the episode incomprehensible. Rossellini is unaware, he charges, of the monks' "intolerance and puerile fanaticism," their "lack of respect and trust"; instead of condemning the monks, Rossellini evades the issue out of laziness or muddled thinking, and retreats "to his mother's womb, to mythic infancy."[44] Brunello Rondi, on the other hand, while agreeing that the friars are "pharisees" alongside the chaplain's refusal to judge his friends, feels that Rossellini is clearly lamenting their intolerance. As the monks enter the chapel, Rondi points out, their prayer—"My soul is sad as death"—echoes, voice-off, over shots of the empty refectory, an empty cell, an empty corridor, "with an effect identical to the one in *Deutschland im Jahre Null* when Hitler's voice on the record resounds through the [empty] corridors of the [half-destroyed] Chancellery . . . : Christ's words are . . . borne 'against' the convent."[45]

All such theories are excessively negative. After all, tolerance must also tolerate intolerance (or else what is there to tolerate?), and the chaplain's emotions are far above the petty and pedantic, self-righteous condemnation Rossellini's critics desire. The guiding idea of the Italian Resistance and the postwar period was not to purge every person or idea one found disagreeable; in the new Italy ideological differences would be transcended through fraternity, even Fascists would be reincorporated. And *Paisà* demonstrates this idea, as we have observed, in each of its episodes, as characters inhabiting mutually uncomprehending universes momentarily bridge gaps dividing them. True, the monks exhibit intolerance. Cut off (as Renzo Rossellini says) from the nihilism and upheaval of faith caused by the war, from the dilemma of a world with—or without—God, they affirm a primitive faith and security lost elsewhere.[46] Their faith is undoubting, thus intolerant. But their intolerance, in contrast to the bracketing brutality of "Florence" and "Po," does not exclude or condemn. It tries to bridge ideological differences through fraternity, to construct a community through prayer. Is the chaplain to condemn this effort?

The question is the key to *Paisà*. Has the war taught us anything?

The chaplain finds a new spiritual light, says Renzo Rossellini,[47] and grows morally. As in each of *Paisà*'s episodes, a character undergoes a war-inspired trauma so overwhelmingly convulsive that, as happened to Paul on the road to Damascus, his entire attitude toward life is totally reconstructed. In "Sicily" a primitive, fifteen-year-old girl is suddenly moved to attack German soldiers; in "Romagna" a chaplain, sensing his own pettiness, is suddenly moved to a higher level of understanding by the monks' simplicity. These moments of grace are never pondered over, never considered; they are always instinctual, always blinding revelations, always triggered by impulse, always motivated by love, always confront shame. Carmela, loving Joe, does not stop to consider she will be killed; the chaplain, loving the monks, does not stop to consider intolerance caused the war. The world, as Croce says, is what we make it; there is no "right" way of seeing, there is no question of conforming to reality; but there is the power of making the world conform to us, of making it a "grace."

Paisà hopes for similar growth in us. Can we accept the monks' effort? Can we understand why the chaplain reacts as he does?

Usually, no. The new world of tolerance has not come about. We expect comical embarrassment or an argument from the chaplain—conventional responses, conventional morality—but instead he resolves the episode "in love and respect,"[48] which we do not understand. The unconventional, morally innovative resolution does not seem to be a resolution. We thought we knew where the story was going, now we don't know where it went. We say Rossellini was confused.

"Romagna" represents a turning point in Rossellini's career: here, as in nearly every movie he would make during the next twelve years, his critics and audiences would fail to understand. And for always the same reason. In most movies, heroes' reactions mirror public consensus; they react to problems as most people would, or would like to. But now Rossellini's heroes react from private revelation or private trauma, and in ways that often defy public consensus. Not only do they see problems differently, they see different problems. The obvious problem in "Romagna"—the monks' intolerance, which seems to be the dramatic conflict—is not at all what interests the chaplain, for he sees with "new spiritual light."

Roberto was attracted by innovative perspectives. "My aspiration, my great dream, is that each person be himself, with all the risks this entails, including the risk of being a fool. If you're authentically yourself, you have such a load of honesty that you must perforce lead to something."[49] The Maiori monks appealed to him for the "fantasy" in which they "really" lived, their "simplicity" which was unfathomably "complex," the unconscious hilarity that rendered their most ordinary actions deeply moving. He did not have to script these qualities into the film.

"Perhaps you remember the scene where one of them goes into the kitchen, lifts the lid off the pot and says, 'Ah, that smells good!' That was Fra Raffaele, who was very old and didn't understand much that went on. I told him to go into the kitchen, bend over to sniff at the pot, and say the line. 'Okay?' I asked, and he said, 'Si, signore.' So he stuck his head so far down into the pot that I had to sit on the floor and pull him back so that he wouldn't burn himself. He was so ingenuous. Fellini . . . had to instruct the monks to come one by one into a cell where I had the camera. When it came to Fra Raffaele he stood back for Fellini, because he didn't want to go through the door before the director's assistant. It came out as a comedy quite naturally."[50]

On the last day of shooting Fra Claudio learned Mida was a Communist and spent the night in tears.

The troupe moved on to **Naples**. Meanwhile Roberto edited what had been shot so far. "One evening," Fellini recalls, "I found Rossellini working in the silence and darkness of a small room at the moviola. He was pale, twisting a lock of his hair, and holding his eyes fixed on the little screen where a first, approximate cut of the monks episode was unrolling. The images were silent, you heard only the buzz of the film rolls. Enchanted, I stayed there watching. What I saw seemed to me to have that lightness, mystery, grace, and simplicity that cinema so rarely manages to attain."[51]

"My personal contribution to Rossellini's work was completely secondary," Fellini has said, "for Rossellini had very precise ideas, he knew exactly what he wanted, and we were like two friends joking and exchanging opinions. Perhaps I often drew his attention to certain situations, or oriented him in some direction, but no more than that."[52]

In later years, piqued at Fellini's success and incensed at Fellini's being given too much credit for *Paisà*, Roberto would claim Fellini was obsequious, forever trailing after him asking, "*Posso? Posso?* [May I? May I?]"[53] This seems untrue. They "were great friends," said Amidei, "two marvelous liars, two fantastic characters, though in slightly different keys."[54] And there were mutual gags. One night at supper, in front of Mida and Vasco Pratolini, Roberto spiced Fellini's omelet with cocaine—with no effect but laughter, alas.[55] Their friendship was delicate, said Fellini, without expectations and with reciprocal mistrust, more "cat and fox" than master and apprentice.[56] Fellini had more perspective, said Geiger, and was more open to ideas; he balanced Roberto, who had grown up in an environment that was "more aesthetic than real. You never knew where Roberto was politically. Probably he was only political to the extent it related to his ability to use people. He loved the Amalfi monks, for example, but it might not have occurred to him to introduce chaplains of three different faiths into the monastery, or to see the political side of the 'Naples' episode." For that he needed Fellini.[57]

Fellini cites *Paisà* as the turning point in his life. Before it, he had undertaken scriptwriting without enthusiasm; movies had not interested him as much as journalism or caricatures. When visiting a set, he had never felt at ease or understood what all the dozens of people were doing; it felt absolutely foreign. Then, "seeing Rossellini at work, I discovered for the first time that it was possible to make films with the same intimate, direct, immediate rapport as a writer writes or a painter paints.[58] I understood . . . there wasn't anything particularly difficult about filming, or so mysterious or technical about all that equipment as to require special initiation—except knowing how to say with simplicity what one had seen. . . . I suddenly glimpsed a whole new world: that look full of love with which he enveloped things and which inspired each one of his shots. . . . The principal lesson I got from Rossellini was a lesson in humility.[59] His humility in front of life . . . , his extraordinary trust in things, in people, in people's faces, in reality. Looking at thing[s] with love, and with that communion that is established from one moment to another between a face and me, an object and me, I understood that the profession of director could fill my life, could be rich enough, passionate enough, exalting enough, to help me to find a sense in existence.[60]

"For me, the *Paisà* trip constituted a discovery of Italy.[61] We were surrounded by a whole new race of people, who seemed to be drawing hope from the very hopelessness of their situation. There were ruins, trees, scenes of disaster and loss, and everywhere a wild spirit of reconstruction. In the midst of which, we did our tour. The troupe of people working on *Paisà* travelled through an Italy they scarcely knew, because for twenty years, we'd been in the grip of a political regime which had literally blindfolded us.[62] But at the same time as this moving discovery of my own country, I realised that the cinema miraculously made a big, double game possible: to recount a story and, while telling it, personally to live another, an adventure, in the company of characters as extraordinary as those of the film being made—often even more fascinating—and which would be evoked in another film, in a spiral of invention and life, observation and creativity, simultaneously spectator and actor, puppeteer and puppet.

"During *Paisà* there wasn't the indescribable confusion of the studio around us. The film was done entirely on location. But the chaos was even greater.[63] Rossellini pursued his film in the middle of the streets, with Allied tanks passing one meter in back of us, with people crying and screaming from the windows, with hundreds of people around us trying to sell us something or steal something from us, in that incandescent stew pot, in that swarming lazaretto that was Naples, and then in Florence and Rome, and the endless swamps of the Po, with every sort of problem, shooting permits revoked at the last minute, schedules canceled, money mysteriously disappearing in the infernal merry-go-round of the improvised producers, who were always more able, infantile, lying, and adventurous. So I think I received a lesson from Rossellini never translated into words, never explicit, never defined into a program; I think I learned one could keep one's balance in the middle of the most unfavorable, the most contrary conditions, and at the same time turn these adversities and contradictions to one's own advantage, and transform them into a feeling, an emotional value, a point of view. This was what Roberto did. He lived the life of the film like a wonderful adventure to be lived and simultaneously to be told. He had a way of abandoning himself to reality, always attentive, limpid, fervent. He placed himself naturally at a point that was impalpable yet impossible to mistake, that was in between the indifference of detachment and the gaucherie of attachment, and that permitted him to capture, to fix reality in all its spaces, to look at things simultaneously from inside and outside, to photograph the air around things, and to reveal that surprising, ungraspable, dodecaphonic, mysterious, magical something that life has."[64]

The press of crowds on Naples's streets almost led to disaster when a jeep ran out of control and knocked down two bystanders. But rather than being angry, the injured turned all their solicitude onto the distraught driver, the actor Dotts Johnson, sported their slight bruises and insisted on buying him drinks. "Okay, paisan," they assured him, "okay." Next day, however, when Roberto held a meeting to compensate those who had been injured, besides the two who had been hurt 41 others showed up claiming "internal injuries." One man, holding up the bandaged arm of his eight-year-old son, asked for 100,000 lire to compensate for the child's inability to use his arm to beg on buses during the next ten days. Amused by it all, and loving Neapolitan bravura, Roberto gave money to all the claimants.[65]

Partly to protect the troupe from the crowds (and from the police), and partly as a lark, Roberto hired a couple of mafiosi. They proved useful one night in extricating Roberto and Geiger from jail—they had been picked up for lack of papers—and were also used as extras. The mafiosi liked the work so much that Roberto couldn't get rid of them; they stuck to him throughout *Paisà*'s shooting. Roberto was well connected in Naples.

Racism was a taboo topic in American films and Geiger's original conception of "Naples," worked out in a series of treatments by Klaus Mann, had dealt with it single-mindedly, using the Italian boy as a mere sounding board. A black MP (named "Lincoln," then "Ariel," finally "Joe") is slain by robbers, whereupon he admits to fourteen-year-old Renato, whom he has promised to take to America, that his tales about how wonderful America is were concealing bitter truths of poverty and discrimination. "You're better off here," he concludes, and dies.

The filmed version is much different. Nine-year-old Pasquale is now the chief object of prejudice, and the story's "revelation" is now not the black's refutation of the American dream but his realization that the Neapolitans are worse off than American blacks. He flees in terror from a shame that the boy has long since confronted and accepted. Thus again a story about an American has become a story about Italy. How dare we judge others? In the new Italy, there will be a new kind of tolerance. The point of the episode now comes in the moments of recognition between the boy and the black.

This revised "Naples" was conceived on location by Fellini and Roberto when they first laid eyes on the cave of Mergellina and its horde of refugees. But it really took form only when Roberto saw the boy and the black together exchanging lines and smiles. Originally the boy was to have been played by Vito Annichiarico, the boy in *Roma città aperta*. But during the shooting of "Sicily" in Maiori another boy had attracted Fellini's attention, Alfonsino Bovino.[66] Roberto was so enchanted with the eleven-year-old that Vito was sent tearfully back to Rome, losing not only his role to Alfonsino but also the cowboy suit Rod Geiger was bringing from America. The black, Dotts Johnson, in contrast, was an actor, not a real soldier. He had worked for Geiger's father, played two or three years in the American

Negro Theater, been Canada Lee's understudy in *Anna Lucasta*, and was touring Canada in *Hasty Heart* when Geiger's father hired him after Lee, for whom "Naples" had originally been scripted, became unavailable. Rossellini's improvisatory style of non-acting was initially quite difficult for Johnson to get used to.[67] For Roberto, emboldened by his successful experiments with "Romagna"'s occasionally unpredictable monks, had decided to rely heavily in "Naples" on the spontaneously improvised gestures and dialogue of its two characters.

Serceau has pointed out how Rossellini, in contrast to De Sica's small-boy films (*The Children Are Watching Us, Shoeshine, Bicycle Thieves*), refuses to identify the spectator's point of view with the boy's, refuses to allow the boy to be merely a symbol of need or the plight of his "class," and instead, more Marxist than the Marxists, emphasizes the distance, the contradictions, between the boy and the soldier. It is far from clear who is victim and who exploiter.[68] The GIs are occupying Naples, but the kids sell the right to despoil them after getting them drunk. In one of the changes from Klaus Mann's version, it is now not the Neapolitan boy who looks up to the black MP as personifying the nobility and advanced civilization of America, it is only the black MP himself who admires his image. And then he gets drunk and admits that image is a fraud. But even as he admits the reality of his past, he still refuses to focus on the reality of his present. To him, this boy is merely a boy of a nation beneath him, a thing. But the boy sees the man as not entirely a thing.

"There's a line that has enormous importance for me," said Rossellini, "when the Negro is falling asleep and the child tells him, 'Watch out if you sleep! I'll steal your shoes.' The Negro does go to sleep and the kid does steal his shoes. That's correct, that's normal, that's the extraordinary *game* where the limits of morality are."[69]

The economic sphere is distinct from a deeper morality.

But the MP still does not get the point. We see him patrolling in his bright new jeep and bright new uniform—the conqueror striding a wasteland of urban destruction which Italian audiences (but not American) were aware had been created by American bombs, not German bombs. He has forgotten that as a black he is a tool and far from being the man in charge. He arrests Pasquale for stealing his boots, asks him where his parents are, and stares at him heartbroken when the boy replies, "Boom! Boom! Understand? The bombs." When the MP sees that the boy is living in a cave with thousands of children made homeless by the bombs, his reaction is yet again to run away from a reality, baffled.

Moments of empathy, of genuine intuition despite incomprehension, are *Paisà's* point, and the point of Rossellini's life and all of his movies. In "Naples," as in all four of *Paisà's* first episodes, that empathy is still incomplete. In Pasquale's line (as in Carmela's close-up) Italian empathy leaps like a flash of miracle all the voids separating people. But the Americans seem incapable of reciprocating—yet. This is why, when finally an American chaplain makes the leap at the end of "Romagna," the chaplain speaks as though possessed by a revelation (like Don Pietro toward the end of *Roma città aperta*). It is why the story concludes as though with a miracle (as in *Stromboli* and *Voyage in Italy*), and why both the chaplain's colleagues and *Paisà*'s audiences are baffled.

Roberto was staying at the Miramar Hotel in Naples that March when the New York reviews of *Open City* arrived. As Geiger read him the clippings—mixing his minimal Italian with Roberto's minimal English—Roberto got paler and paler. "Oh my God!" he said softly and sadly, clasping Geiger's hand, "How can I live up to this responsibility? How are we going to equal this with *Paisà*?"[70]

Burstyn, in fact, had wired Geiger to bring Roberto to America to publicize *Open City*. Roberto's request for a visa, however, was denied by American officials in Rome, possibly for reasons relating to his Fascist connections, more likely due to his police record relating to cocaine and the events that had led to his sanitarium commitment around 1929.[71]

The troupe moved on to **Florence**, another city that had suffered from the war. When the Allied advance had halted at the Gothic Line for the winter of 1944–45, the English, already occupying the southern half of the city, had refused to cross the Arno River. On August 8, the Germans had blown up the Arno bridges and the partisans had been left to fight alone against the Germans and Fascists. For a week Florence had become a battlefield.

Rossellini recreates that August 8th battle. The brief but stunning scenes of violence, the terror of open spaces, moved Brunello Rondi to remark mystically that Rossellini somehow managed to "see things as though stripped of any mediation or attenuation, discovering angles of vision that, in a certain sense, had never before appeared in cinema."[72] Auriol in contrast was moved to remark that Rossellini was an artist creating: the two English officers "are painted as by a novelist, not photographed as by a reporter."[73] Serceau, in agreement, remarks that Rossellini was a pamphleteer, representing "the situation of an Italy in which the élan for liberation and revolution was up against the indifference of the Allies. . . . A few shots suffice for Rossellini to make the spectator feel the real isolation of the partisans. Remember that right bank of the Arno, with its empty streets blocked and criss-crossed by German patrols, those partisans fighting alone on one side of a street against the Fascists, while on the other side of the river two Allied [English] officers, a map of the city on their knees, try like tourists to make out the famous monuments."[74]

Neither "Florence" nor the city itself had figured in previous treatments. In its place had been an entirely different nurse story for Harriet White set in Naples, whereas the black MP episode had been set in Littoria, a Naples suburb. But in Naples Roberto had met Vasco Pratolini, who was then writing *Cronache di poveri amanti* (which Lizzani later filmed), had asked him to edit "Sicily"'s dialogues, and to help work out the new story for Florence.

"When I arrived in Florence," Roberto recalled, speaking in English, "there were formations of partisans who had fought against the Fascists and Germans, and there were also other sorts of partisans who had organized themselves after the Germans left the town. I remember I met the chief of the partisans, and I asked him what he had done during the war. 'I didn't do anything, because it was forbidden by the Germans. We organized things that we would do after the Germans left, the mail, telegraph, things like that.' The partisans who fought were crazy people, and there were practically none of those crazy people in town. The chief was called Lupo [wolf] because everybody had a name that wasn't their real name. And I knew this Lupo had had a love affair with a Peruvian girl, who was a painter.

"More or less I rebuilt the story I got from gossip I heard in the streets. Those were the modifications." The Peruvian girl became an American nurse. Desperate to see Lupo, her lover, again, before being shipped out, she crosses the Arno. A dying partisan tells her Lupo was killed that morning. "I made up the story and in the story everyone talks about Lupo and Lupo is never seen. Years later I was in Peru and met some Italians [who] invited me to stay in their house. One night I start my souvenirs of Florence, and the man starts to cry—because he was Lupo. Now he's totally fascist."[75]

The dialogues were completed with Fellini, on location, while former partisans gathered round and gave their opinions.

This was how Roberto loved to work. And he was surrounded by friends and family. Marcellina came to Florence with Romano and Renzino. Roswitha was there already, having made most of the campaign once Limentani was out of the way. The soldier cousin Renzo Avanzo was among the partisans, and ended up playing the male lead, when the actor originally hired demanded 10,000 lire.[76] The producer Renato Campos (the one the Rossellinis regarded as "an Achilles, a Hector, an Aeneas"[77]) appears as an old soldier watching the battle from a rooftop—actually his own house on Via Lutezia. Cast as his daughter was Fellini's wife, Giulietta Masina, in her first movie (the steps leading to Campos's rooftop are those of Masina's house, on the same street). Fellini himself, on a day when Roberto was sick, made his debut as a director with the shot of the Florentines using rope to pull water flasks across the no-man's land of a street; he had to fight with Otello Martelli to put the camera at ground level, in order to suggest the Florentines' subjectivity. Two days later, he recalls, he was pleased at seeing his first rushes projected, "and I felt Roberto's hand caressing me in the dark, on the back of my neck."[78] Fellini also assisted Massimo Mida, who had already done some shots of Germans marching in the night in "Sicily," in directing a number of rooftop scenes, including that of the museum piazza with motorcycles.[79]

The beginning of the episode—the scenes in a hospital—were filmed on an estate belonging to Count Roncioni located on Via Vecchia Lucchese between Pisa and Lucca, where, according to Roberto, his ancestors had lived as peasants. The old count could find no traces of a "Rosellini" in the family records, but he was happy to lend his villa in exchange for a tidy payment.[80]

And there was Roberto's servant Mandrino, always in trouble. During "Sicily" he had gotten knocked out and stuck in a hole, where he stayed for hours calling for help. During "Naples" his coat had been caught by the MP's jeep, dragging him along the street. During "Florence" Roberto sent him to a distant rooftop with instructions to start smoke spewing forth at a signal from Roberto's handkerchief. When after two takes smoke still did not appear, they went to investigate and found Mandrino unconscious on the terrace, knocked out by his own fumes. "I'm always innocent," Mandrino maintained.[81]

Later Harriet White would marry Gaston Medin, Roberto's friend from Occupation days, and appear in Fellini's *La dolce vita* as Anita Ekberg's secretary.

It was Geiger everyone was mad at. He could be charming. "Boyish enthusiasm gushes continually from his words, his smiling eyes, his cordial gestures, the pores of his skin," remarked one reporter.[82] But much like Roberto, critics exclaimed, he liked to live in high style, flying around Italy with his flame of the moment, making black-market money deals, and charging expenses to the film. There were complaints he was causing delays and not paying bills. The $28,000 loan for *Roma città aperta* had, according to Geiger, been repaid in January, when he and Campos went to the Banco di Roma with a suitcase to collect it in small lira notes, and had then dedicated it to *Paisà*.[83] Geiger had also brought back $10,000 for Conti from American travelers checks Conti had had him cash for him in New York. Lawrence, however, asserts that $22,000 remained unpaid, and that in April, in Florence, Roberto blew up at Geiger and threatened to kick him off the picture.[84] To pay the crew Roberto was borrowing box-office receipts on Friday and paying them back (regularly) on Monday, according to Del Papa.[85] Yet "Conti must have been in awe of Geiger," says Lawrence. "I recall that Geiger had borrowed the equivalent of $10,000 (I believe) from Conti and failed to pay him back. Conti was livid and came to me asking for help. Then shortly thereafter [having seen Geiger] he asked me if Geiger needed more money—unbelievable."[86]

The problem, according to Geiger, was that Landau in New York was upset that the film was going over its twelve-week schedule and had ceased sending money. Shooting should have finished in March, a month ago, but the situation was even worse than *Un pilota ritorna* and Roberto would still be shooting in July. *Paisà* would turn into the most expensive Italian film since the war. It would cost five or six times what *Roma* had, almost $100,000 (fifty to sixty million lire[87]). (In comparison, Zampa's *Vivere in pace* cost sixteen million that same year, De Sica's *Bicycle Thieves* sixty million in

1948, after much inflation.) Meanwhile each American actor had to be fed, housed, and paid until his or her sequence was shot (thus Bill Tubbs finished in a few weeks but Gar Moore lasted six months). Landau, having paid his agreed twelve weeks, had thrown up his hands and Geiger eventually had to borrow money from Conti. Geiger himself was unconcerned; he had rented a villa in Rome, was sometimes with Valentina Cortese, sometimes with Maria Michi, and, having seen *Open City* already repay its absurd price and finance *Paisà*, regarded all the fuss as piddling: *Paisà* was an important film, absurdly cheap by American standards. He flew to New York for a week, straightened things out with Landau, and, incidentally, purchased rights to Pietro di Donato's *Christ in Concrete*, a story of an Italian family struggling through the Depression in New York City, which Roberto had read in Italian and intended to film in New York after *Paisà*. (*The New York Times* reported Rossellini was talking to Walter Wanger and was coming to New York "in a week or so [with] one film in mind: *Christ in Concrete*.[88]) When Geiger got back to Italy, "Florence" was still being shot. He repaid Conti's loan and a week or so later, at the beginning of May, left for California, not to return until August.

Meanwhile, Conti was still scavenging for money; Lawrence, left in Rome to handle the production, was unable to make sense of Geiger's accounts; and Roberto was becoming increasingly erratic. Often he would start at noon and work until midnight; other times he would shoot 24 hours and more without a break. Once, when the crew had been on location and waiting since eight in the morning, he phoned at two to say he was in Venice and would be back in "two or three days."[89] And Tony La Pena was constantly complaining, because Roberto had taken a terrific aversion to him and, after keeping him on salary for four months, would decide not to use him at all—until seven years later in *Voyage in Italy*.

A big fight started in mid-May, when a Metro-Goldwyn-Mayer representative arrived in Rome, denounced Geiger's deal with Burstyn—a fifty-fifty split after advertising expenses—as an outrageous rip-off, contracted for the Italian distribution rights to *Paisà*, and tried to obtain its worldwide rights. Conti was relieved. But Geiger, in New York, was outraged when he heard the news from Lucy Kroll of the Sam Jaffe Agency (to whom he had delegated power to negotiate Rossellini's and Magnani's interests). Metro had purchased *worldwide* rights, he was told, but the U.S. rights, which belonged to Foreign Film Productions, not to Roberto or Conti, had already been pledged to Burstyn—a pledge Geiger now formalized in writing, effectively nullifying Metro's deal. Geiger was convinced that an independent foreign picture would not make money for its producers when distributed by a major like Metro (as the case of *The Search*, a popular Swiss production distributed by Metro, would shortly confirm).

"The Po Delta." In Florence, Renzo Avanzo, always a great storyteller, had caught Roberto's attention with tales of his adventures during the war. While serving with the American OSS behind German lines, he had found himself in the Po marshes with the partisans. The 5th Army, he recalled, needed lots of water in the Po, whereas the Germans wanted it dry. Then General Alexander had made his infamous proclamation, telling the partisans to go home for the winter. But going home wasn't always an option. ("These people aren't fighting for the British Empire. They're fighting for their lives," an OSS officer declares in the film—a line scripted by Geiger). Avanzo had witnessed the fate of partisans the Germans captured, their corpses adrift on rafts with a sign, "PARTIGIANO."[90]

The Po Delta marshes were familiar territory to Renzo and Roberto. Their mothers, Elettra and Antonietta Bellan, had come from Cavarzere, near Rovigo. "[My mother] spoke often of this earthly refuge," Roberto said: "The birds flying over the delta, the lantern in the house hallway, the last embers dying in the ashes . . . I knew that area well. I spent my childhood there and went back all the time for vacation. Then I started to hunt and fish."[91]

The *Paisà* troupe found themselves wandering, as Fellini recalled, "one day from morning to night in the muddy delta of the Po, in search of a cabin known as the 'Pancirli shack' that Rossellini remembered having seen in his childhood, thirty or thirty-five years before. We had a local guy as a guide who had a black band over his eye. People said he had been stealing eels one night, and the landowner, a countess, had fired a whole rosary's worth of lead at him from her window. This squinter, who limped in the bargain, dragged us all day long through mud and water without ever managing to find the cabin. Then at sundown he threw himself at Rossellini's knees and asked him to discharge his rifle into his remaining eye. But we had no rifles, or any other weapons, and Rossellini burst out laughing. He was, however, stubbornly determined to continue the search himself, and he dragged our whole caravan behind him through a landscape out of a Kurosawa film. From time to time our trucks would sink into the bog, and big black birds would come hovering lower and lower. There were moments of revolt; our porters wanted to turn back. Rossellini climbed onto a jeep and made a speech, promising everyone a pint of rum. It was night, we didn't know where we were anymore, or what we were doing in these interminable swamps. Suddenly a little boy rose up out of the reeds, he was three years old at most. 'I'm a Socialist,' he announced, in Venetian dialectic, and led us quickly to the Pancirli shack, which in fact was located nearby, right near where we had started from that morning. We ate eels cut up alive and cooked on brush fire. The night was totally black, like in Xenophon's *Anabasis*."[92]

These marshes near Porto Tolle belonged to Eustachio Avanzo, Roberto's uncle. One of the men, Cicognani, was his overseer, whom Roberto had known from childhood. "The Po Delta" was shot in ten or fifteen days here, with former partisans from the neighborhood playing themselves, reenacting themselves, restaging events that had actually happened to them. Fellini and Vercours set down their dialogue.

The partisans are surrounded by Germans and are out of supplies. Their American advisers arrange an air drop, but the supplies disappear in the water. A family gives them shelter; the Germans retaliate by shelling the family. In the act of rescuing two downed English pilots, the partisans are captured. The Germans bind their hands and shove them into the water. Startled, an American and an English officer rush forward in protest, and are shot dead. (All these events actually occurred.)

Fellini describes Rossellini's way of working as "instinctive, without preconceived ideas, and rarely constricted by theoretic codes or iron conventions, because, in effect, he was trying to find his own style, he was trying to express himself with precision. Just think of that magnificent ending of *Paisà*: the Germans, in the Po marshes, pushing the partisans into the water. Martelli, the cameraman, was tearing his hair out. 'It's impossible to do it! There's no light anymore!' he cried in his dialect. And there was Rossellini (absolutely determined to get back to Rome—God knows why, perhaps some bills were due or he had a date with some woman) cursing and screaming, yet ending up by giving form to an exceptional idea: with only two cameras, without the least detail, he shot the scene in long shot. The sequence gains an extraordinary force thereby: you don't see the partisans fall from the boat, you only hear the sounds of their dropping, one after the other. Rossellini had arrived at this dénouement quite simply because he had to finish and speed off to Rome—or was it the other way around? He had created the indispensable conditions, the state of friction where the spark takes fire and burns, and dissolves the fog bridling the idea, bridling feeling's direct expression, its most faithful and clearest translation—perhaps the only correct one among innumerable possibilities.

"One could say—and some critics haven't missed any chance to say it—that Roberto's fondness for mysterious incidents like this went to extremes, and that he provoked them too regularly and recklessly. Yet [he had the ability] to transform obstacles and hostile situations into emotive facts, into feeling, into point of view."[93]

Amidei was disappointed. *Paisà* was supposed to conclude with *his* story about the band of (six-foot-six) partisans operating in the Val di Susa above Aosta in Piedmont, their soft-spoken intellectual leader called "Guernica," and Johnnie, the Italian-American parachutist who despises all Italians as corrupt and Fascist and all Italian women as virtueless. Crudely Johnnie would try to make love to Anna, but after seeing her and her comrades executed en masse in a Turin square, he would take her red handkerchief, join the partisans, and become the new "Guernica," thus affirming his Italianness and allying himself with the proletariat.[94]

Supposedly this sequence was not shot because Roberto had lingered so long in Florence that there was no longer enough snow to be found in Piedmont. Supposedly he didn't want to work with Tony La Pena, who was to play Johnnie. Supposedly Roberto and his troupe were worn out from their labors since January—his liver was so aching that he wore pressed against it a San Pellegrino bottle filled with hot water. Supposedly

Conti and Landau were reluctant to embark on an ambitious, arduous, and expensive production amid mountains and snow, especially with yet another episode still to be filmed in Rome. But now, whatever the reason, in place of the tall men of the North Amidei had dreamed of, heroically defending the fatherland against the background of the Alps, here were these grubby swamp folk drowning like so many pieces of garbage. Years later Amidei was still moaning about it. "I don't want to judge it as art, but it's discomforting, it's pessimistic. The partisans almost look like chicken thieves."[95]

Roberto had not wanted Amidei's story; he had not wanted that sort of conclusion for *Paisà*. There were two points at issue. One was the question of mythifying the partisans as mighty indomitable heroes, thus giving a non-pessimistic finish to *Paisà*'s saga of Italy's humiliation. The other was the question of linking the partisans to the class struggle that the Communists hoped would emerge triumphant from the war's ashes. True, the Resistance had been liquidated by victory; the Allies' first order of business in the spring of 1945 had been to disarm the partisans and dissolve the workers' councils that had taken over factories in the north—and the coalition government in Rome had cooperated. But the *issues* the Resistance posed were very much alive in May 1946, when Rossellini was filming "The Po Delta," because Italy's first postwar elections were a month away and the Communists were confident a new era was about to begin. Should not six-foot-tall partisans and Alps proclaim triumph?

Rossellini's obsession with shame and defeat seems to go in exactly the opposite direction. "Heroism is presented not as the capacity to act but as the capacity to suffer," observes Warshow.[96] "Eisenstein offered heroes and hosts of heroes, Rossellini proposed people. Eisenstein offered glory, Rossellini proposed meditation and sorrow," writes Valmarana.[97] And Robin Wood illustrates: "In place of Eisenstein's precise, architectural compositions, [there is] a constant fluidity, the camera moving in nearly every shot, characters and objects entering and leaving the continually shifting frame . . . , a sense of total instability. In place of Eisenstein's confident moral assertion [his "body of 'correct' answers offering a position of moral and ideological certitude"], there is a poignant desperation, a sense of a world in which nothing is certain, a world where there is nowhere to go, no dogma to cling to, no creed to rely on."[98] "The war for Rossellini," Valmarana states, "is the chaos that destroys all. Heroes, even *Roma città aperta*'s dubious and defeated ones, have disappeared; now there are just people trying to save their own lives . . . or bury a dead man. The war has . . . no protagonists, only victims. *Paisà*'s concluding title . . . does not consecrate a victory . . . but only says 'This happened in the winter of 1944. By the beginning of spring the war was already over.' And the sun of liberation that is rising that day is not bright or consoling. It indicates the end of a nightmare, but it lights a world of desolation and ruin, of blood and struggle."[99]

Yet Brunello Rondi is wrong to maintain that Rossellini's theme is "the despair of history."[100] The opposite is true. As with Croce, Augustine, Hegel, and Marx, history is the story of liberty emerging. By reliving the past we make it part of us, observe our chains, and declare our freedom. Each episode of *Paisà* confronts a national shame—thieving children, prostitution, intolerance, the taint of Nazism, the ineffectualness of the Resistance—and in each case Rossellini sees not defeat but, as with Christ's death on the cross, the triumph of the free spirit. Characters wander mazes—city streets, hillsides, swamps—and find solutions always unexpectedly, in confronting their shame, and then impulse takes over. Appropriately they confront themselves in "caves" (actual caves in Sicily and Naples, a doorway in Florence, a dark bedroom in Rome, a refectory in Romagna), except in "The Po Delta," where the solution dissolves into primal fecundity—water. Says Agel, "While feeling the partisans' bodies drop into the sea, the certitude is given us that the death of these martyrs composes the substance of a refound freedom. There is not symbolism here nor even analogy, but identification, as in Hugo's great images."[101] "The Po Delta"'s ending generates emotions resembling those of Murnau's *Sunrise*, Jennings's *Diary for Timothy*, and much Rossellini to come (e.g., *Giovanna d'Arco al rogo*): a premonition of freedom in presence of death; of resurrection. "All human history," said Roberto, "consists of passages from slavery to liberty, even though at a given moment slavery may be stronger.[102] I want my cinema to be a message of faith, of hope, of love . . . , an appeal to humanity."[103]

Impulse replaces heroism, the unreflected, primal impulse for fraternity of doomed and deserted people—giving food, saving flyers, persisting. The parallel with the myopic "resistance" of the monks is not casual. As the American chaplain applauded the monks to universal bafflement, now suddenly the American and English officers on the Po, whose comrades scorned and suspected the Italians earlier, throw themselves into a shared death with them—an action as ineffectual as it is symbolic, at last echoing Carmela's suicidal impulse in "Sicily." The movie's title has become a reality: *paisà*.

Impulse expands fraternity out of the cave and into the sea. Sartre and Camus too base truth on intuition, but their *élan vital* remains in a void, whereas in Rossellini, as in Croce, it is always implemented into society. This is eminently Italian: Aeneas's founding of Rome, the Italian city state, the Renaissance, the Risorgimento, the Resistance, all have been mythified as results of impulse triggered by collision of love and catastrophe. Thus we begin to comprehend the paradox of *Paisà*'s aesthetic impression—that so much failure inspires confidence in the future—and how so ostensibly negative a movie was an apt national epic on which to found the postwar Italian state.

"Thank heaven," wrote Valmarana, "Rossellini never believed in the blood of martyrs that renders the earth fecund. Perhaps had his lesson been better heeded . . . , the bad mythology of the Resistance—those myths of fruitful sacrifice, of heroes showing the shining way, of the need to die for the new fatherland—that bad mythology which, not too differently, had been the ideology of Fascism and was hence . . . the easiest to recycle would have had less of a polluting effect on history . . . , and the Resistance would have remained what in reality it was and ought to have remained: the suffering of humble and oppressed people, their redemption after almost thirty years of injustice and violence."[104]

Freddy Buache charged Rossellini with forgetting that the Resistance was a proletariat revolt braked by the bourgeoisie.[105] On the contrary, rebutted Paolo Gobetti, a Communist partisan leader, linkage to class struggle falsifies the Resistance—as in Vergano's *Il sole sorge ancora* (or Bertolucci's *1900*) with its cinematic references to Eisenstein and Pudovkin. "It is only in [*Roma città aperta* and *Paisà*] that the partisans can recognize themselves on the screen."[106]

"There is no strained rhetoric," writes Baldelli, "yet leaving the theater we recognize our people in these chicken thieves, and the whys and wherefores of civic commitment by conscientious Italians."[107]

"The Po Delta" is the great Italian national-populist masterpiece. It arose from the people as few films have done and fulfilled art's prime social function at a moment of unparalleled need.

It is also Rossellini's most extreme experiment in off-the-cuff filmmaking, and not just in the way the picture was conceived and executed. Much more than in "Sicily" there is an impression of "enormous ellipses—or better, gaps,"[108] as Bazin put it. Complex series of actions—e.g., the partisans being given food at a fisherman's cabin, /their hearing the German guns firing, /the crying baby amid the corpses of his family—are reduced to brief fragments already elliptical themselves. Rather than the usual filmic method, in which the actions a filmmaker selects to show have been crafted to mesh effortlessly into a logically developing story, Rossellini's "facts" seem to maintain their autonomy, and to require our active effort to find the story. "The mind has to leap from one event to the other, the way one jumps from stone to stone to cross a river." And sometimes the mind slips, for narrative is an abstraction. "Facts are facts, our imagination makes use of them, but serving our imagination is not their *a priori* function."[109]

In Pontecorvo's *Kapo*, a cadaver stuck on barbed wire is the object of a forward tracking shot by the camera. "The most perfect example of cinematic immorality," Ayfre called it, paraphrasing Rivette. "Death thereby becomes the object of pure curiosity and the means of propaganda. Rossellini . . . too . . . films a cadaver. But his camera stays silently and respectfully immobile, and it is death that, borne by the current, comes slowly closer to the camera lens. How can one not see that this single inversion is enough to change everything? It is no longer a matter of raping a cadaver but the tragic reality of death which comes itself to pose to the living its ineluctable interrogations."[110]

The documentary, newsreel look of the photography, along with the total absence of any character development (the partisans never really individuate themselves), increases the sensation of Rossellini's modesty in front of his material. "The Po Delta," Bazin says, resembles oral rather than written literature, a sketch rather than a painting. Even the roughness of the camera movements contributes to the effect; lacking the "almost god-like character of the Hollywood crane," they make us feel that everything we see is from a human point of view.[111]

Yet Rossellini's "human point of view," while it does not compel us to connect facts, is far from the impassive, objective attitude Bazin and Rivette suggest. His eye is savage, full of passion; its rawness gives the impression of truth: conviction. It is not the *images* that are true. How can an image be false? Rather it is the emotions that lack inhibition. Rossellini's art owes a lot to his long apprenticeship as a spoiled child.

After "The Po Delta" it is puzzling that Rossellini made **"Rome"**—the third episode in the completed *Paisà*. How could he have taken cinema to its outer limits and then retreated so far? "Rome"'s content is postwar—a sympathetic treatment of prostitution—but its style is a regression to the 1930s. It is the only episode in the film that leaves us feeling comfortable with our understanding of the "facts" we have seen and how they are connected. Not only is the story development traditional (the characters' present circumstances are set against their pasts—in flashbacks—whereas elsewhere in *Paisà* there is only present tense); but "Rome" is the sole episode in *Paisà* that seems *dramatized*. Francesca, the object of long close-ups and monologues, dominates the action rather than being part of it, just as Maria Michi, richly acting and reciting the part, dominates the character rather than simply being her. While *Paisà*'s other episodes are situations with an encounter, "Rome" is an encounter with a situation. Moreover, it reiterates and simplifies "Naples": an Italian is introduced exploiting a drunken American, but in "Rome" we realize the Italian is the only victim.

On its own terms "Rome" is a moving vignette. Serceau argues it illustrates Rossellini's advance over *Roma città aperta*, for rather than stigmatizing its prostitute character by having her incarnate political and ideological points of view, as he had done in the earlier film, he is now concerned with how others represent us: once Francesca and Fred have "codified" their rapports, no communication is possible.[112]

It is in context, within *Paisà*, that "Rome" has provoked harsh verdicts. The usually sympathetic Brunello Rondi judged it "a complete, hopeless failure . . . , forced and false. Anyone who knows Sergio Amidei . . . and who then sees *Paisà* can sense the enormous distance, moral and stylistic travelled from Amidei's scenario. . . . Rossellini's 'fiat' (it's impossible to imagine 'The Po Delta' scripted at a work table) is in profound, categorical opposition to Amidei's 'style.' 'Rome'—a 'closed,' sentimental, melodramatic novelette—is representative of Amidei's style, like a sort of traditional sediment that the director was unable to remove."[114]

Even Amidei himself, thirty years later, declared, "Rossellini didn't like it, and, reseen today, I must say that I don't like it anymore either."[115]

The explanation for "Rome" is quite simple. Once Roberto was back home, tired, his enthusiasm waning, eager as always to be engaged with his friends, back again in the same Capitani Studio where *Roma città aperta* had been filmed, he had fallen under Amidei's spell.[116] June was over before he finished. And he still had to go down to Anzio to shoot "Sicily"'s final shot.

National elections were held June 2. To save the monarchy Vittorio Emmanuel III had abdicated at the last moment in favor of his son Umberto II, but he had clung to his throne too long: 54 percent voted to abolish it. The South voted for the king, as did many Catholics. As did Renzo and Marcella Rossellini. The king appeared to them as a principle of order amid the bewildering proliferation of political parties. Roberto voted to throw him out. In Parliament, the Christian Democrats won 207 seats, the Socialists 115, the Communists 104. This gave the left a majority, but it continued to cooperate in dismantling the Resistance.

Roberto was annoyed by Rod Geiger's interference in the Metro deal. He took to referring to him as a crook and nurtured Lawrence's dissension by talking of contracting himself to Lawrence alone. By the time Geiger got back on August 12, Roberto had won over Lawrence to his conviction that Metro would give *Paisà* the same nationwide exhibition in America that a Hollywood picture would receive, in contrast to the single art house in which Burstyn was exhibiting *Open City*.

Geiger thought this was nonsense, accused Lawrence of sabotage, and, to emphasize his point, stole the generator. Roberto was furious. Others producers were paying to use that generator! He stole it back.

Whereupon Geiger, in flagrant perfidy—gave Visconti—of all people!— the Italian stage rights for Lillian Hellman's *The Little Foxes* and, worse, *Christ in Concrete*, which Roberto wanted to film in New York and had been trying to get David Selznick to back.

Roberto was rabid. But there was something he couldn't resist in Geiger. Geiger, with his panache for selling ideas and unreserved creative support, was the best producer he would ever have. And when he heard that the strange American had access to blocked funds (to film the opera *Boris Godunov* with Alessandrini for Boris Morros), he had a pretext for reconciliation. "Why can't we do *Christ* together?" he asked Rod, through Mario Del Papa.

But other events intervened.

Romano

Whether it was Geiger, Riganti, Amidei, or a female lover, Roberto's affairs followed a pattern. He almost melded into the other person. Then, out of their presence, escape mechanisms sprang into action. He would seek new alliances, ridicule old comrades, and exploit their tensions with others—who became convinced *they* were his special friend, *they* alone understood him. Relationships became emotional battlefields. Male friendships survived (when they did survive) with long separations or professional divorce. Female friendships survived by being desexualized. Mistresses became wives, then mothers, then sisters.

Marcellina was the first wife to undergo the transition. She was his "cousin," he boasted. Beginning with the "Rome" episode, she worked on the costumes in almost all of his films. He purchased a comfortable ground-floor apartment for her and their children at 52 Via Carroncini in Parioli. The cottage at Ladispoli, which he had also given her, was a wreck. American machine guns had strafed it in 1944, the furniture, plumbing, and windows were ruined, and Roberto's books and papers had been stolen (along with Garibaldi's beard, some say—others say Roberto sold it).

"I brought furniture and mattresses and pots and linen from Rome," said Marcellina, "without worrying about there being no panes in the windows and the sea breezes blowing freely through. The children were happy to be living like pioneers; it was almost like camping in a ruined world. I was planning to spend the whole summer there with them when Roberto came and suggested I take the children on a fifteen-day trip to Spain where lived my mother-in-law, who hadn't hugged little Romano for years and hadn't even seen Renzino. [Elettra had spent the war in Spain, and her youngest child Micci had married a Spaniard.] I wasn't enthusiastic about the proposal: it was the middle of summer and I was afraid the heat might harm the children, but it would have been impossible to restrain their eagerness. The following morning, although I had put Roberto off while trying to decide, Romano (who was then nine) got up very, very early and went by himself to call his father from the Ladispoli post office to tell him how happy he'd be to take the trip. It would be his first sea voyage. And all it took was that phone call in order for Roberto, without even waiting for my response, to make all the arrangements for our trip: his children's desires were the sole law of his life."[117]

Romano, from all reports, was an extraordinary child. "He had inherited from his father that remarkable charm by which he could fill anyone he met with enthusiasm," said Alberto Manni, Roberto's valet.[118] "He was the very image of Roberto Rossellini," said Franco Riganti, his godfather, "very intelligent and engaging. He had an amazing ability to reason, and to entertain, a real genius. There was an enormous difference in talent with Renzino; Romano had all his father's best qualities."[119] "He was a little devil," said Lina, Renzo's wife, whose son Franco, two years older than Romano, was making the trip as well. "'Don't you worry,' he told me, 'I'm going to take care of Franco!'"[120]

"We left for Barcelona on August 1, 1946. Roberto accompanied us to the station in Rome, supplied us with all we needed for the trip, and till the last moment hugged the children, who were terribly excited over the idea of this long voyage. Until the train had vanished, Roberto stayed on the platform waving goodbye with a handkerchief." He could happily ignore his children for months at a time, but moments such as this affected him deeply.

"Two days later we left Genoa for Spain. Our ship was an old wreck, *Sister*, that limped along. But none of us paid any attention, we were so happy to be aboard. The children spent the first few hours playing pirate." The crossing was stormy, taking two and a half days, and Romano fell ill but recovered. "In Barcelona Romano never stopped admiring the things he saw; everything made him happy and enthusiastic. Twenty-four hours later we went to my mother-in-law's house at Villa Nueva, a large property on the sea thirty miles from Barcelona.

"The children called it 'The Earthly Paradise.' It was the first time they could live with freedom and tranquillity, without fear of warnings or mines. Romano, after a few days of this, said to me: 'Too bad we're leaving in a few days. I'd like to stay here a month at least.' "[121]

Roberto, meanwhile, exhausted with editing *Paisà*, had taken Roswitha to Capri, where they stayed with the novelist Curzio Malaparte. Watching the two men together was a spectacle for Roswitha; they both talked endlessly of their own projects, not paying the slightest attention to what the other was saying.

"We were supposed to leave the seventeenth," Marcellina continues, "but on the thirteenth late in the afternoon Romano was struck by a strong fever that got hourly higher, and the doctors urgently called to his bedside couldn't identify the cause.

"That night we took him to a clinic in Barcelona, where he had an emergency operation for an inflamed appendix. All the latest equipment was used and the operation went very well, but the tardy identification of the illness annulled the effects of the surgery. By ten the next morning my child was dead."[122]

Phone service between most European countries had not yet been restored. Marcellina had telegraphed Renzo in Rome at 6:30 that morning, that Romano's situation was serious and he would be operated on. Lina phoned Manni, who arrived just as a second telegram came announcing the boy's death. Rather than telegraphing Roberto at Capri, it was decided to send Manni to Naples by taxi. "From there," Manni recalled, "I phoned Capri, to a friend of the director, who told me Roberto was boating off the Amalfi coast. What could I do? I told him what had happened and asked him to send me the director as soon as he found him, but without telling him anything.

"In the middle of the night, in fact, Rossellini rushed into my room. He was a bit worried but thought it was something to do with work, and I didn't have the courage to tell him the truth. So I advised him to return immediately with me to Rome so that he could personally solve the problems that had come up. The director had an old 'topolino' [Fiat 500] at Naples and we left right away for Rome. I had now decided his brother would be the one to tell him the truth. Indeed, once in Rome, parked in front of the house, I let the director go up alone. A scream reached me shortly after through the stairwell."[123]

Lina had ushered Roberto into Renzo's studio, then left the room, but listened outside. "Roberto, Romano is dead," Renzo had said, then collapsed onto the couch. Roberto had stood still with no reaction. "It's impossible," he had said, at last.[124]

In Barcelona, Marcellina had been put to sleep with drugs. "Since Spanish custom forbids the mother participating in the funeral, I could not even attend Romano's. As soon as he was placed in Barcelona's cemetery, I went to find him. They'd put him in a niche way up high, nameless. With a ladder I climbed up and on the fresh cement wrote my child's name. The next morning I had to board the boat to return. My fellow passengers, who were the same as those I had come with, were struck at seeing me alone with Renzino, and ours was a very sad voyage." Elettra kept Franco with her in Spain for a while, to ease Marcellina's return trip.

"Two days before Romano had gotten sick, their grandmother had given the children two Australian parakeets which distracted Renzino a bit from thinking of his dead brother during the voyage. We kept them in our cabin, in a cage. Just after we got back to Rome, one of the parakeets, Romano's in fact, flew away, we never knew how.

"Roberto was waiting for us at Genoa, in the same hotel where the children and I had spent the night preceding our departure. He appeared stricken, and hadn't had the courage to come to the port for fear of seeing us disembark without Romano. If for me our child's death had been tragic, for Roberto it was even more so. . . .

"We stayed awake until dawn, beside each other, but without speaking of what had happened. We went back to Rome together and that same evening [August 28, 1946] Roberto left for Spain, to bring the child's corpse back to Italy. He said he would only return with the child, at whatever cost. (International laws are strict on this subject and require a minimum of two years for an affair of this nature.)"[125]

Roberto had not been idle during the days before Marcellina's return. His reaction to Romano's death, according to Manni, was "terrible. He was destroyed by sorrow, behaved like a hunted animal, and gave himself up to his grief with utter passion. He wouldn't have peace, he said, until he had gotten his son's body back. 'We have to get him back right away, we have bring him back to Italy tomorrow,' he kept repeating at every moment with repressed fury. He seemed to have a physical need to touch him, to embrace him. The days that followed were extremely sad, spent going from one ministry or embassy to another, and, what was worse, accomplishing nothing. . . . All the people he knew, all the recommendations they gave him, all his threats and implorings achieved nothing. The necessary authorizations seemed impossible to obtain without following a horribly slow bureaucratic passage. Seeing after several days that nothing could be done in Rome, Rossellini went to Spain and for two weeks went back and forth between Madrid and Barcelona, trying to move or obtain the sympathy of government people in every department. Meanwhile he arranged for Romano's corpse to receive the injections needed to conserve it, and had a casket constructed with a window for the face, so that he could see him any time he wanted. For a month he succeeded in postponing burial and having the casket held in a mortuary room at the Barcelona cemetery.

"At one point Rossellini thought all hope was lost of being able to return Romano to Italy by legal means. So, desperate but not defeated, he wrote to his brother, in Rome, a dramatic letter telling him to be prepared, together they would smuggle out the corpse. According to the director's instructions, signor Renzo was supposed to go to a French port and rent a motorboat with which to reach a certain spot of the Costa Brava during the night. Rossellini, for his part, had now been in Spain long enough not to attract notice. He would request permission to bury his son's body in a little cemetery on the coast and, only at the last moment, would divert the truck to the agreed place. The letter left no doubt about the director's intentions, nor can it be said that he ever renounced something he wanted with all his might. No obstacle has ever managed to stop him.

"Fortunately the permission to transport Romano's body to Italy arrived before any rash decisions had been made, and Rossellini made the trip from Barcelona to Genoa squatting beside the casket. In Genoa I convinced him to go on ahead to Rome alone, while I took charge of following the coffin. Some minor railway accident made the train five hours late and we arrived in Rome in the middle of the night. But Rossellini, chilled to the bone, was there waiting, accompanied by a friend, Mario Micheli, a film worker. When he saw me he didn't say a word, and we stayed that way, beside the railway car, waiting for dawn. Then we arranged for the corpse to be transported to the church of St. [Robert] Bellarmine, at Piazza Ungheria, where the funeral took place. Rossellini walked with his head lowered, an absent expression, his face marked by tiredness and weeping. It was a Rossellini destroyed, who inspired only sympathy and tenderness, solidarity and compassion. A Rossellini that no one, I think, has ever been able to find again since then."[126]

Roberto had telegraphed Marcellina daily during the 26 days he had been away. "The same night Roberto left Spain," wrote Marcellina, "I dreamed of Romano. He appeared serene and luminous. 'Don't worry, mama,' he said, 'I'll be near you both and you shouldn't worry about my body. You remember the end of *Pinocchio*, when Pinocchio has become a real boy and sees his old body abandoned on a chair, and he says, "How funny I was when I was a puppet!"? I see myself the same way, now.'

"An hour later I got the telegram in which Roberto let me know that he had overcome all the obstacles and was bringing the child's body back."[127]

In the depths of depression Roberto deposited himself in an apartment in central Rome. Far from bringing him closer to Marcellina, Romano's death had only increased his estrangement from her, for he couldn't help holding her responsible for his son's death. Nor did it bring him closer to Renzino; quite the contrary. He found lots of time for Franco his nephew, but little for his own six-year-old, who reminded him of Romano, and unfavorably at that.[128]

Venice

Paisà was to debut in a few days at the first postwar Venice Film Festival. "*Paisà* will be epoch-making," Gianni Puccini had predicted in *Film Rivista*.[129] But in Roberto's absence the film had not been finished—the editing needed to be refined and the sound redubbed—and so at Venice, where it was scheduled for the final day, speculation was constant: it will come, it won't come.

Mario Del Papa went to Rod Geiger. "Roberto needs you," Del Papa explained.

Roberto hadn't seen Geiger since April. He had been feuding with him for nearly half a year. But Geiger came and moved in with him, and it nearly led to Geiger's own suicide, so contagious and desperate was Roberto's behavior. He would lie in bed crying or have Geiger drive him to the cemetery crypt, where he would sit, hour after hour, gazing at Romano's face through the little window in the casket. It was "a love affair," Geiger said, "Roberto Rossellini is a very emotional thing for me, even today."[130]

In Venice the speculation ended only the night before, when Roberto, Geiger, and Mida arrived by plane (without Roswitha), carrying a print assembled at the last moment by Renzo Rossellini. It was almost half an hour too long. The dozen people who had seen it privately in Rome on September 10 had not been impressed.

At the critics' screening on the morning of September 17, the MGM Lion provoked considerable fuss. Otherwise the séance transpired in an atmosphere of ice. People felt let down and unsatisfied after so much anticipation. Outside afterward, Roberto, sad and deathly thin, fielded a series of stupid questions and fled to his room at the Albergo Luna. "The critics don't understand anything," he told Mida as he closed his door, tears running down his face.[131] For the Festival awards, the critics selected Renoir's *The Southerner* as best film and cited *Paisà* near the bottom of a list of movies accorded "special mention"—after *Les Enfants du paradis* (Carné), *The Oath* (Chiaurelli, USSR), *Hangmen Also Die* (Lang, USA), *Henry V* (Olivier), and *The Undaunted* (Donskoi, USSR); but ahead of *Panique* (Duvivier) and *Il sole sorge ancora* (Vergano).[132]

The Russians liked it. They gave a party with rivers of vodka and Geiger got riotously drunk.

More importantly, the public screening that afternoon at four had been a success, a huge one. The public voted it the *best* film at the festival.[133]

Roberto ignored the good and nurtured the bad. He never forgave the critics. "I remember," he said eight years later, "the immense shock I had when *Paisà* came out. I deeply believed in the film, it's one of the three I prefer [with *Francesco giullare di Dio* and *Europe '51*]. The first Italian review I saw talked about the 'gangrenous brain of the director.'"[134]

It never occurred to Roberto to doubt himself; it never occurred to him that his critics might be right. Or if it did, he never let on: this was his Roman bravado. Passion ruled his life. He was depressed by Romano. Once back in Rome he collapsed into bed again, declaring to Geiger that life was not worth living.

This too, they say, was Roman. He had given little of himself to his son while he was alive, he would give little of himself to the five other children he sired. But now the cult of Romano became the central ritual of his life. For decades he would not leave the city without "saying a prayer on Romano's tomb" which, since he always did everything at the last minute, meant that he not infrequently missed trains and planes. No matter: he checked that the flowers were fresh, that the plants had no yellowed leaves, that the earth had not dried, or that the vases lacked for water. He gave the attendant huge tips and balled him out mercilessly at the slightest lapse. "For Romano," he told Manni, "there'll never be enough flowers."[135] He kept the boy's glove and a drawing, avoided a friend who had called him an "angel" when he was alive, and refused to eat bananas (which were rare then: a carton Roberto had ordered for Romano, who loved them, had arrived after the death). The Fiat was given to Manni; Roberto could not bare the sight of it; after it became a rusty useless wreck, he stored it in his garage for years, unwilling to allow it to fall into strange hands. There was a Mass each year on the anniversary. If the date fell while Roberto was in Paris, he would have a priest friend come there from Rome to say it.

Romano's death was the fourth shock of Roberto's life, after his lung operation, his father's death, and the Occupation. It was incomparably the greatest. All his films, from then on, would seek answers to death. All his heroes would cling to life only tenuously. He would even define the hero of neo-realism as "just a little creature beneath something that dominates him and that, all of a sudden, will strike at him terrifyingly, just at the moment he feels comfortable and isn't expecting anything. What is important for me is the waiting."[136]

Press notices from Venice were mixed. Barbaro, whose semi-pan of *Roma città aperta* had so upset Roberto the year before, thought "['Florence'] more suggested than narrated, the monastery incident more ambitious than clear." He liked "Sicily" and "Naples" for the "sad tenderness" with which Rossellini treated his characters' fates; loved "The Po Delta" where "emotional intensity is born from figurative and artistic action even more than from the epic theme"; and applauded the poetic tone, "vaguely elegiac and sorrowful," of Rossellini's "crudely realistic images," the "moving re-evocation of a history too recent to be considered with dry eyes," and the "purity of the director's intentions."[137] The review was tantamount to official blessing by the Communist Party.

But many critics were churlish. One dismissed it in less than a line as "superficial." Another took two: "Lyric and naturalist in character, with widely scattered anecdotes, very good photography, and an agreeable pursuit of human truth," but inferior to *Il sole sorge ancora*. Bologna's *Giornale dell'Emilia* was disappointed; the film was sketchy and wearisome and addressed less to Italians than foreigners, who were let off too easily. Udine's *Libertà* objected to displaying Italy's squalor. *Il Tempo* thought the stories not at all gripping, mere pretexts for a travelogue. *Cine Illustrato* called it "unbearably slow, ineffectually edited, clumsily written, uselessly detailed, and fundamentally superficial. . . . The mediocre craftsmanship . . . never seems ennobled by truly poetic motives. And in Rome's *Il Buon Senso* ("Good Sense") Francesco Callari wrote: "The Festival closed miserably today with the usual presumptuous and failed operetta. . . . *Paisà* is not a film and tries to be more than a film." There is no linkage between the stories; "Sicily" is worse than the tritest newspaper story; "Romagna's" dubbing makes it false. But in "The Po Delta" "the director's foggy brain clears and manages—it was about time—to get things moving."[138]

In *La Rivista del Cinematografo*, the film organ of Catholic Action, Marcello Vazio considered each Venice entry in turn and found them each disappointing. With *Paisà* "even the last hope disappeared. . . . *Paisà* is a disconnected film, composed of six episodes, false things full of rhetoric and bad taste that want to tell the world and us in particular about the war we knew and suffered through. . . . We, and the public with us, would not have believed yesterday, and can never believe today in the episode of the Sicilian girl who . . . grieves over a fallen American a few hours after their landing . . . , nor in the snow-white sentimentality of a [Roman] miss hardened by sad daily life, nor can we ever believe in all the other episodes that seem drawn from a certain type of literature that flourishes today in the weekly variety shows. As for the so-called 'Catholic' episode . . . our discretion and kindness prohibit our expressing an excessively bad judgment." Only "Naples" was at times interesting and free of artificial sentimentality, with the black man aptly sketched without the usual stereotypes. "The rest is total darkness. The Americans actors are very bad . . . , their participation seems inexplicable; the frequent use of documentary footage is in bad taste . . . ; it was not too smart to have the Americans speak their language and the Sicilians, Bolognesi, and Neapolitans their dialects. The audience in Venice had to consult the printed plot summary often, to figure out what was going on. A note apart about the numerous, painful lines of the PWB type placed with laudable diligence in the mouths of various Yankees (. . . *War is a curse*. . . . *We Americans love middle-class dress*. . . . *We Americans, now that we've arrived, will give you liberty and white bread*. . . . *We Americans have an old mother at home who's waiting for us*. . . . *If the Japanese hadn't attacked Pearl Harbor* . . .). Obviously Rossellini wants, very strongly wants, to get to Hollywood."[139]

Yet for better or worse, *Paisà* was the most discussed film at the Festival. Vazio tells us that one "squad" of critics was enthusiastic; judging by reviews, there were at least a dozen of them. "*Paisà* proves we can finally march—and not in last place—on the great highways of the free European cinema" (Rome's *Nuovo Messaggero*). "One of the best Italian films of the last decade ... a perfect synthesis ... a necklace of fragile little pearls held together by only a thread ... anguish, seen not from the individual's point of view but from the group's" (Venice's *Gazzettini*). "Unrhetorical but passionate ... everything breathes a sense of war's pain and fatality (Venice's *Mattino del Popolo*). "Rather than a documentary, it is a study of the [period's] ethical-historical phenomenon through a series of psychological factors artistically interpreted" (*Alto Adige*). "The final episode is a masterpiece.... The day of victory will come, [it says,] but with how much blood and how much pain! Yet still there is certitude of peace with justice. Today this certitude has given way to hope: if this too is not delusion! This is why we must not forget!" (Verona's *L'Arena*)[140]

Pietrangeli (Visconti's assistant on *Ossessione*) attempted to defend the movie by conceding that every complaint against it was valid. "There is always an inner, bitter resentment lurking behind even the most faded images, which erupts at times with impetuous violence ..., redeems the murkiest, crudest story, and bears it into our hearts and minds.... It is precisely from such incoherence and uncertainty, from such astonished, logicless contemplation of the terrifying reality surrounding us, that in fact is born that indefinable force of conviction ... which in some distant tomorrow will perhaps remind us, intensely and clearly, of this confused, sorrowful time, witnessed with bewildered desperation by Rossellini."[141]

Defending Rossellini by cheering incoherence, lack of logic, and offhanded technique would be a familiar tactic in the years to come; a similar *défense à outrance* would also be pursued on behalf of Renoir, the New Wave, and the New York underground. Perhaps our ways of seeing have changed since 1946, or perhaps some people didn't know how to see back then, but it looks obvious today that Rossellini's technical prowess could scarcely be more refined and majestic. His "carelessness" is not an affectation employed for its own sake, as with the New Wave. His genius lies not in his incoherence and "documentary" style, but in the precision and richness of his characters. Not just the English officers but all of *Paisà*'s characters "are painted by a novelist, not photographed by a reporter." One of the few critics to sense this was Remo Borsatti, who praised *Paisà*'s technique ("There's not a single false word.... I can't think of another film like it. If you want a literary comparison, think of Hemingway born under Rome's sky"); asserted its sufficiency ("a full, dense, rich world"); and pinpointed its method ("This Rossellini is a communicative man who knows what he wants and miraculously transfuses his feelings and his intentions into the actors; thus the notes he touches are always correct and clear").[142]

At a special invitational screening in Rome September 27 at the palazzo Altemps *Paisà* was greeted with applause after each episode. Again the MGM Lion caused comment.

It was true Roberto wanted to go to Hollywood. Besides Selznick, Wanger was also showing interest. It did not bother Roberto that he would not fit in in Hollywood. But it did bother Geiger, and Roberto was embittered by shoddy gossip that Geiger had sabotaged the American visa. Geiger had settled into a villa with Valentina Cortese (sharing her with conductor Vittorio Sabata), and Roberto was on the outs with him again. Momentarily emerging from his conviction that nothing was worth doing any more, on September 24 he signed a two-year pact with Lawrence alone, for ten percent of his earnings. No one bothered annulling the earlier contract with Geiger and Lawrence; like many subsequent contracts, the new one was a means by which Roberto could entice fresh bank loans. Lawrence had no intention of owning Rossellini. He was so uneasy about conflicts with his military status that he had not allowed his name on *Paisà*'s credits and, a few months later, would turn down $25,000 from Selznick for Roberto's contract, "because I wasn't into selling bodies."[144]

After the Altemps screening, Roberto re-edited and redubbed *Paisà*, and cut it down to 126 minutes—changes contemplated before Romano's death. Trabucco who saw both versions reported that "Sicily" was the most altered, "Florence" the least; that "The Po Delta" was changed "excessively"; and that "Rome" was "cut differently" and improved.[145]

Cannes

Anna Magnani had encountered Roberto at the Palazzo Altemps screening, found him emaciated and drained, and embraced him silently. He cried, closed up in defensive silence. It was natural for Anna to try to repay the comfort he had given her the year before; they both used cocaine to divert their minds. With Renzo's help, she coaxed Roberto onto a train for Cannes. *Roma città aperta* was to be shown October 5 at the Prévert Festival (as the first postwar Cannes Film Festival was called) and because *Roma* had still not been bought by a French distributor, it was important for them both to be there.

Marcellina packed Roberto's bags and accompanied him to the station. There she met Magnani for the first time, both of them as embarrassed as young girls. When Roberto learned Anna had neglected to book a cabin and none was free, he insisted she take his and sat outside in the drafty corridor. After an hour, flabbergasted, Anna summoned him inside. Perhaps there had been sex earlier, but not romance. A year before she had even slapped him hard in the face in the middle of a performance of *Aida* at Rome's outdoor Baths of Caracalla, whereupon they had both stalked out, and Roberto had had an angry fight at a picnic over Anna with Amidei, who wanted her himself. Now common tragedies drew Roberto and Anna together.[146]

"My brother and Anna took me to Cannes," Roberto recalled years later, "and I followed, I followed like a sheep, because I no longer cared about anything.[147] They were watching my every moment, afraid I'd commit suicide.[148] I had a relationship with Anna already but we weren't living together—I was trying to escape because I knew that if I agreed to share her existence, I'd suffer the worst horrors of my life. So I tried to defend myself.[149] At Venice [two weeks before] *Paisà* had been a disaster. At Cannes *Roma città aperta*, for lack of anything better, was presented by a delegation of Italians who despised the film utterly.[150] It bombed amid torpid indifference. . . . True, it was shown at the worst time, two in the afternoon, when everyone was digesting with their eyes half open. My brother and I were practically alone in the auditorium."[151]

Rossellini melodramatizes in recollection. The day he left Cannes, October 8, he wrote Roswitha that *Roma* had gone over "very well." And whatever the Italian delegation's opinion, just two months previously the picture had won the "Nastro d'Argento," Italy's Oscar, in three categories—best scenario, direction, and actress (Magnani).[152] But it did not win at Cannes. The French preferred a French film on the French resistance, Clément's *Bataille du rail*. *Roma città aperta* finished fifth, behind *Symphonie pastorale* (Delannoy), *The Lost Weekend* (Wilder), and *Brief Encounter* (Lean), and ahead of *Maria Candelaria* (Fernandez, Mexico) and *The Last Chance* (Lindtberg, Switzerland), with all of whom it shared the "Grand Prize."

This was not wonderful, but neither was it "total indifference." Indeed there was a triumph of sorts, for a galaxy of Italian movies had appeared at Cannes, including *Il sole sorge ancora*, *Shoeshine*, and Lattuada's *Il bandito*, and *Roma città aperta* was signalled out as the herald of a revolution. "In the history of cinema, a new era has begun," wrote the critic of the weekly *Gavroche*; "The Italian films illustrate it as did in other times Swedish, German, American, and Russian films. . . . It is really a miracle to see an art recreated that had already seemed to have reached perfection." "The Italian cinema," agreed Alexandre Astruc in *Combat*, "is perhaps, in its ensemble, the most interesting, original, and new of anything shown at the Cannes Festival, where diverse productions from the whole world were invited to compete." "The Italian cinema was the revelation of the Cannes Festival," reported Georges Sadoul in *L'Écran Français*. "A torrent of daily life is invading the screen. . . . If Alberto Lattuada's *Bandito*, an uneven but strong work, was talked about, the film everyone admired was Roberto Rossellini's *Roma città aperta*."[153]

Because of *Roma città aperta*, wrote François Chalais in *Carrefour*, "we suddenly have to review the whole history of a nation, forget a thousand certainties, cancel numerous dates. . . . For this reason I think Italy will owe more to Rossellini than to De Gasperi or Togliatti." "Rossellini has given us back the [true] face of the Italian people so cruelly distorted by the politicians, bad actors, and tenors," Huguette Micro wrote in *Canard Enchaîné*; "Italy for us used to be D'Annunzio's emphatic declarations, Mussolini's spectacular redundancies, Scipionesque pastiches, *Quo Vadis?*'s Roman orgy, *Rodomonte* printed in a million copies. Now all these prejudices have to be revised." "Foreign works have gone further than ours in human realism," wrote André Bazin. "No French director has dared show what nevertheless dominated the clandestine adventure [of the Resistance]: torture. . . . *Roma citta aperta*'s torture scene prolongs seamlessly and naturally the action's sober and vigorous realism. . . . It is doubtful that such description would be possible in literature without falling into turgidity or sadism. And yet how much stronger the movie image is! But cinema is the art of reality."[154]

Concluded Patrice-G. Hovald: "The French critics literally imposed *Roma città aperta*'s distribution in France."[155] And it was a lucky thing for Italy that they did. Her fate was shortly to be decided at the Paris peace conferences. According to Roberto, "Ambassador Quaroni, who represented Italy at Paris immediately after the war, tells in his memoirs how miraculously his mission became easier (he was surrounded by general distrust) with the apparition on Parisian screens of a few Italian films."[156]

Paris: A Legend Begins

From Cannes, Roberto and Renzo continued on to Paris, without Magnani. He telegraphed kisses and love to Roswitha every other day, got back to Rome November 1, took her to Capri November 4, established a home for the two of them (he said) at Matermania 26, and, leaving her there, came back to Rome the next day.

On November 9, he took the train back to Paris with Rod Geiger. *Roma città aperta* was opening there at last,[157] and Joe Burstyn was coming from New York, at Geiger's request, to meet Roberto, discuss their next projects, and clear up *Paisà*'s American distribution.

They found the hotels crowded with diplomats at the peace conference. They were both broke in any case, and felt fortunate when a friend tipped them off to a cheap little bordello on rue Leclerc that, besides four rooms reserved for trade, had four others for longer-staying guests. After *Roma* opened on November 13, Roberto was able to borrow money from its distributors, the Hakim brothers, and by signing a contract with producer André Paulvé.

Roberto gave money to Geiger and had a fling with Josette Day, wife of Marcel Pagnol and star of Cocteau's *Beauty and the Beast* (which Paulvé had produced). According to Geiger, Roberto made love to her in the rear of a screening room while showing *Paisà* to a producer and then installed her in the bordello. For his liver's sake, Roberto still wore his hot San Pellegrino bottle. The question came up whether to move to the ultra respectable Hotel Raphael. No, they concluded, the bordello was a more interesting place to hold court.

Joe Burstyn arrived, as well as a writer, Basilio Franchina, who had been at Tagliacozzo with Visconti during the Occupation, had supervised *Paisà*'s French dubbing and a few of its shots, and was adapting four subjects for Rossellini: *Christ in Concrete*; *Native Son* (Richard Wright, 1940); *Napoli* (a chorale story set in postwar Naples); and something titled *Clandestine Emigration of Italians into France*. *Christ in Concrete* had been

Roberto's idea, *Native Son* was Geiger's; but all the projects reflected Geiger's commitment to combating social exploitation. From the OSS sergeant who had played *Paisà*'s Jewish chaplain Geiger had learned the Army had been monitoring him and reading his mail because Sylvia Sidney's mother had told them Rod was a "Commie." (Sylvia Sidney had been among Joseph Geiger's acting students from early childhood. Rod Geiger had ended his brief, prewar membership in the Communist Party when he had realized it opposed too many of the things he admired in America.)

Roberto was keen to make *Christ in Concrete* in New York; he had told Sadoul it would be his next project; but he vacillated about leaving Europe during an era he found fascinating and stimulating. Thus he was instantly attracted when a new idea intruded—a picture about Nazi Germany with Burstyn and the Hakims, *Deutschland im Jahre Null (Germany Year Zero)*. Geiger opposed it; he thought Roberto had been too involved with the Fascists and was too unaware politically to be able to understand Germany. He would change his mind later, after he saw and loved the picture. Meanwhile Roberto put his projects with Geiger aside, and Geiger felt betrayed. On the return to Rome he had the upper berth and threw bugs on the sleeping Roberto.

The Parisians adored *Roma città aperta*. In *L'Écran Français* Georges Altman wrote: "I doubt any film has ever attained such grandeur in authenticity. . . . It is perhaps the first time in a movie theater that a film has impressed me not just as alive, but as palpitating, as hurling to heaven so much pain and so much rage. . . . It is a wonderful and terrible film. A film without pity. A lady beside me, her eyes full of tears, was murmuring, 'They've no right to show this.' Why do they? Because it was like that. At this degree of tragedy, one no longer wonders whether it is 'artistic' to show a man tortured by the Gestapo. . . . We have reached the era of the witness-film."[158]

"As for the actors," wrote Jean Desternes in *La Revue du Cinéma*, "there aren't any, ever. . . . A heavenly grace seems to have descended upon them: of not acting in front of the camera, of just being themselves. It's as though they surrender themselves to us. Of course they are acting! But we forget it, because of the suffering that eats away at their faces, because their situation in the universe at this given moment is anything but a conventionally theatrical one. There's a woman walking with a priest. . . . She has nothing special to say to him, she speaks simply about her worries without using 'author's words.' . . . She's that woman . . . , affirming obviously her existence: [she's] there, and that's the way it is."[159]

On Saturday night, November 16, *Paisà* was given a special screening for film club members, organized by André Bazin for the Féderation des Ciné-clubs, funded by *L'Écran Français*, and held at the Maison de la Chimie. Bazin was already emerging as a leader in promoting movies as a major art form; soon, through his editorship of *La Revue du Cinéma* and *Cahiers du Cinéma* he would become the most influential film critic in history. The audience for *Paisà* was large—workers, intellectuals, ex-partisans, and POWs, all of them intensely interested. Bazin spoke afterwards. Overcome by just having experienced what he thought to be the most important and revolutionary movie of all time, he struggled almost unintelligibly to express his emotions, and found it impossible to pronounce the word "cinema."[160]

Bazin's reaction typifies the French response to Rossellini. Whereas Italians almost invariably talked about crudeness, even lamented melodramatics (especially *Roma*'s torture scenes), but always spoke of *style*, what stunned the French was "reality." For the earthy Italians (and Rossellini among them), film always had an ideological purpose: to provide a model, an explanation, a sermon. But for the existential French, the ideal movie was first of all an "imprint of reality," a "witness," and only secondly an ideological experience. In the wake of World War II, what Italians sought was an ideology, a workable mindset toward their history, and practical solutions to material problems; Fascism had been a caesura and was now an ellipsis. Whereas what the French wanted was valid sensation, a feeling of the earth beneath their feet; their capitulation to Nazism had been shattering. And so Roberto, when interviewed in Paris, melded into his partners in conversation, agreed that his work methods were existential, and encouraged people to hear what they wanted to hear.

Distortions and exaggerations soon became canonized as historical truths of what had not yet become known as "neo-realism."

"To choose my players in *Paisà*," he told Sadoul, "I would start by setting myself up with my cameraman in the middle of the locality where I planned to realize this or that episode of my story. People idling nearby would group around and I would choose my actors from the crowd. You see, if you're dealing with good professional artists, they never correspond exactly to the idea you yourself have made of the character that you want to create. To succeed in really creating the character you've dreamed of, the director has to undertake a struggle with his player and end up bending him to his will. It's because I have no desire to waste my strength in such battles that I only use actors-by-occasion. And then it's difficult to harmonize the good professional with the 'amateurs.' So I've preferred to renounce using the good actors.

"Amidei and I never finished our scenarios before arriving on the locations where we planned to realise them. The circumstances, the players that chance brought us, usually led us to modify our initial plans. And even the dialogues, like the intonations, depend on the amateur players who are going to say them; it's enough just to give them the time to get used to the surroundings.

"*Paisà* is thus a film without actors in the proper sense of the term. The American Negro whom you found remarkable in the Neapolitan sequence, claimed to have played some small roles, but I perceived that in reality he had lied to me in order to get work. All the monks from the convent scene are real monks. The minister and the rabbi from the American army who dialogue with them are also a real American minister and a real American rabbi. It's the same for the peasants and the swamp folk who live around Ravenna [in "The Po Delta"] and speak the dialect of the region, just as the Sicilians in the first sequence speak Sicilian. The English officers [in "Florence"] are as authentic as the German soldiers whom I took from among the prisoners. And if you found talent in the young American who plays in the Roman episode, you should know that he never posed before except in front of the camera of a photographer who used his picture for razor-blade advertisements."[161]

In a second Paris interview Roberto described his methods in similar terms.[162] His specific inaccuracies—Dotts Johnson had not lied about having experience; the girl was not a Sicilian; Amidei had had little to do with either movie's dialogue—are dwarfed by the blatant false impressions. It seemed best not to mention the six months of scripting, the precomposition and dubbing of dialogue, the use of professional actors in the leading roles, the constant creation of character, the use of studio sets in "Rome," the melodramatic employment of cutting, ellipsis, and music, and the constant labor of "harmonization" of reality and drama. Roberto liked the image he saw of himself in French eyes: an "amateur" reacting spontaneously to reality. The following summer he told *The New York Times* that *Paisà* contained shots of Rome and Florence before they were liberated, which he himself had taken "with a small camera he had contrived to keep, in the hope he might some day be able to sell the film as newsreel."[163]

Some Parisian critics repeated New York's folly. "A stand-up comedian was engaged to play the ecclesiastic and Anna Magnani was a music-hall singer," asserts Desternes.[164] Meanwhile, a greater legend was being born. The "actors met at a café" became "people found on the street" who re-enacted their lives in an improvised "documentary."

Roberto returned to Rome November 22, spent a night with Roswitha, went back to Paris on the 30th, came back to Rome with Burstyn for a New Year's Eve party at the 57 Club with Roswitha, Magnani, and Geiger, and went back to Paris.

The Hotel Raphael was his home through most of 1947. Nothing was more flattering than to be lionized by the Parisians. French had been his first language; the "new ideas" in the cenacolo had come from France. "France is culture's cradle," he liked to say. "We've all wailed there, more or less, and smiled when we opened our eyes to its spirit's light."[165]

Parisians had mythical dimensions for Roberto. These were people he'd read about all his life, but never seen, until now. And they adored him!

It was embarrassing, but only at first. Everyone he met invited him to dinner parties. "Wit sparkled like wood in the fireplace. Each person sported dazzling finesse; their keenest indulgence was intellectual pleasure."[166]

By day he walked the streets of *vieux* Paris, with its cafés, art galleries, retrospectives, restaurants, antique stores, and bookshops. "I loved the chimneys, their faded shades, red, black, and gray."[167]

Forget New York! "It was in Paris, [finally], that an enthusiasm arose [for my films] that I had ceased to hope for. So great was the success that in Italy film people started reconsidering their opinions of me."[168]

Paisà and Paisani

But that reassessment was still years away. In Italy in November 1946, *Paisà* was still unreleased. Roberto and Conti were bickering over money, and the ghastly reviews from Venice made them fear a fiasco.[169] The picture would require careful handling and political support.

The Communist Party rode to the rescue in the person of Antonello Trombadori, director of its cultural section. Trombadori was a painter's son, a poet, journalist, and art critic, one of the perpetrators of the Via Rasella bombing, a future member of Parliament, and, one pacific soul observed, "the only person I could imagine following into battle, even to death."[170] "When I saw *Paisà*," Trombadori said, "it was as though I had been struck by lightning. I protected Roberto Rossellini right away. It didn't matter if he was Christian Democrat, disorganized in ideas, a voyeur. His camera never lied, his films represented a unity of ideology and truth, he was a great artist. I said we should contribute, should collaborate with him."[171]

It was decided to open *Paisà* at first only in Milan (where the Party's influence was strong), albeit rather inappropriately on December 13, 1946, during the Christmas season.

L'Unità went all out. A headline proclaimed *Paisà* "THE GOOD ROAD FOR THE ITALIAN CINEMA." *Roma città aperta* had "imposed Rossellini throughout the whole world," Fabio Carpi declared, but *Paisà* was "one of those films that remain in the history of the cinema." The American players—*pace* Vazio—were a pleasure after an overdose of Gary Cooper. "The Po Delta" was one of the "highest, most intense, most efficacious" sequences in all cinema. Even the monks episode was "rich in humor, flavor, moderation."[172]

Other critics sounded less sincere. The Socialist *Avanti!* admired facts "grasped in reality" with few adjectives; but the monks were empty, the Florentines chatty, "Rome" sentimental, and Rossellini expressed emotion like a surgeon, coldly.[173] Similarly *Oggi* rated "Florence"'s end and all "The Po Delta" among "the most beautiful things in European cinema"; but *Paisà* was terribly uneven, and non-professional actors were not to be recommended.[174] *Il Nuovo Corriere della Sera*'s review was vicious: "[Rossellini] cuts himself off from the vibrations of our days with the objectivity . . . of the foreigner, if not of posterity, and has the secret of an almost total absence of passion."[175]

Paisà opened in Rome three months later, again with Trombadori's support. Alberto Moravia, as Roberto recalled, "went to the theater in Rome every day to present it, trying to explain to the audience, which was minimal, what they would see."[176] In *L'Unità* Barbaro transmuted his Venice reservations into praise. "Even the fact that the connections of the episodes are not entwined around any external link, but that their synthetic pregnancy . . . is demanded of the spectator, is a title of the high nobility of this great film, which opens a road, in content and form, for the new Italian cinema."[177] And the Communist *Vie Nuove* took up the theme. "*Paisà* . . . is a new rebuttal to those who would yoke us to things foreign even in film and who would deny the Italian people its 'own' cinema, its 'own' culture. . . . There's a life-throb in *Paisà* . . . , the life and sufferings and aspirations of our people . . . , their hunger and ruination, materially and morally, but their great will for recovery and renewal as well. . . . [But] many paid critics will say that *Paisà* is just another mediocre movie. Every device of sabotage will surely be leveled against it."[178]

In fact many critics only feigned respect.

Avanti! gushed over Rossellini's "possibly authentic talent" and "noble" intentions, but *Paisà* was banal and trite.[179] Castello conceded "a few pages will remain in an ideal anthology of our cinema," but moaned "Romagna"'s mixture of irony and reflection, "Sicily"'s slow prolixity, "Rome"'s obvious rhetoric, and other grave defects in "narrative harmony."[180] Gian Luigi Rondi, in *Il Tempo*, after saluting Rossellini as "a tragic and bitter poet" also drew the line: "Let's be clear, the film, despite the great noise it has aroused, only at times breathes the air of real poetry."[181]

Concluded Trabucco: "Rossellini may be the filmmaker of the day in New York and Paris . . . , but is he also in Italy?" Replying to his own question, he rated *Paisà*'s episodes—"Sicily" 8; "Naples" 9; "Rome" 7; "Florence" 6.5; "Romagna" 8; "The Po Delta" 9. "In sum, a film that does honor to Rossellini, even if it is not a masterwork."[182]

The *Paisà* Debate

Almost everyone respected *Paisà*—it won the Nastro d'Argento for best subject, direction, and music (Renzo)—but hardly anyone loved it. "It's the Italian film which the French have called 'one of world's best,' which American crowds applaud enthusiastically in New York, and which in Italy people are trying to boycott every way they can," wrote Casiraghi that June.[183]

Trabucco, for example, gave "The Po Delta" a 9 but at the same time objected it was "excessively hurried, and the slaughter of the peasants . . . needs explanation." And Visconti called *Paisà* "a rather discontinuous film [which] can't stand comparison to *Roma città aperta* as a whole."[184]

Some people trumpeted *Paisà*'s newness. Its defects were irrelevant, however numerous, argued *Il Giornale d'Italia*. "What is new and authentic is . . . its total contempt for any acquired rule, cinematic convention, or superficial embellishment. *Paisà* is a film in which it is impossible to distinguish between the scenario and the shooting, because so much is taken in by Rossellini's lens, intuiting and capturing reality in the same instant it happens, before taste, feeling or reflection intervene to corrupt its purity.

One never senses posing, trickery, or professional theatricality; just the faith in the value of things in themselves which distinguishes the artist from the decorator."[185] "It comes as no surprise that [the inevitable discontinuity of Rossellini's architecture] is arousing passion, hostility, and argument," agreed *Il Messaggero*. "Rossellini has posed for the first time in Italy the problem of film as art and history."[186]

But "reality"—even "captured at the instant it happened"—was no substitute for entertainment; nor was a political vision; and audiences did not know *how* to be entertained by Rossellini, then as now. They wanted clear stories, identifiable characters, and easy sentiment—which they found only in "Rome," the episode they liked best. *Paisà*'s first-year gross of 100,300,000 lire was good enough to rank it ninth among Italian movies (behind *Il bandito* and *Vivere in pace*), but not good enough to recoup costs. It ran less than half as long as *Roma città aperta* had.

For critics as well, even for those who praised it, *Paisà* seemed inept. By traditional standards Rossellini was unable to tell a story, develop a character, direct an actor in anything but violence, create interesting photography, or edit a film.

"We were high school students when the war ended," wrote Paolo and Vittorio Taviani. "One afternoon . . . we went to a movie, just for the hell of it. They were showing *Paisà*. And even though the theater was half empty, the people were protesting against the film. What they didn't like was what represented a shock for us: the rediscovery on the screen of what we had just left behind us outside on the street. We ended up getting into a couple of fights with some of the audience. Our decision was made: we had understood what we wanted to do in our lives. The movies."[187]

"None of us immediately realized the greatness of *Shoeshine, Bicycle Thieves* . . . , *Paisà* and *Roma città aperta*," admitted Carlo Lizzani, one of the *Cinema* group and author of a standard film history. "Many of us were very reserved at first toward De Sica's films and even Rossellini's, precisely because they seemed formally impoverished to us, too concerned with recording bare, crude images. All of us, not just the ones at *Cinema*, had always been preoccupied with style. Attention to content, love for reality, desire to make Italian films about Italy, all that came later, when we matured. But at the beginning we thought of ourselves as the partisans—the priests, even—of a new language. The old revulsion for cinema as just plain recording, whether of theatrical comedy or real life, didn't let us immediately understand the quality of Rossellini, and we were perplexed at a style like his that was so simple and objective. When foreign critics and audiences of other countries gave [Rossellini's and De Sica's] films the incredible reception we know, and began to see them as the tip of a big iceberg, there was a certain surprise. We came to terms with it"—but not until the 1950s—"by telling ourselves that we had been immersed in a movement, and that the French and Americans had all of a sudden discovered that a great period in Italian cinema was going on. We who were its protagonists had not immediately recognized it, and naturally so, because we were blinded by the differences separating us."[188]

A second problem was that attitudes had changed during the eighteen months since the fall of 1945, when *Roma* had caused such a stir. People were tired of "reliving history." "Haven't we had enough war films?" complained a critic at Venice.[189]

People were tired of crude style and of crude content even more. It was no longer a priority to win sympathy from foreigners. "Why," asked the Catholic Rondi, echoing a groundswell of complaints against the new cinema, "why send abroad such depictions of Italian women [as in 'Rome']? Isn't it enough what the soldiers going home will say? And the same goes for the Neapolitan episode which . . . uselessly depicts a slice of Naples' misery, which we would have preferred had stayed here with us."[190]

Suddenly the new cinema was objectionable *because* it was successful in New York and Paris. Why "wash our dirty linen" while the world's elite stare at us? People were ashamed at so many girls forced into prostitution ("Rome"); at official abuse of orphans (*Shoeshine*); at unemployment (*Bicycle Thieves*); at mafia exploitation in the most primitive regions (*La terra trema*); at the plight of the aged poor (*Umberto D*); at drug addiction, gay sex, and collaboration with Nazis (*Roma città aperta*). De Sica was accosted by the father of a middle-class family coming out of *Shoeshine*, "You ought to be ashamed of making movies like this! What will they say about us abroad?"[191]

In Paris, in contrast, where people wanted a new cinema in order to make new myths, they were saying the new cinema was reality. "The news becomes historical document. The historical document, human document. The human document, poetry" was how Claude Mauriac explained *Paisà*, Croce-like.[192] The new cinema would explore and it was the chimera of exploration, not its analytic results, that dazzled Parisians. Jean Desternes's not quite metaphoric assertion—"We really penetrate into the swamp"[193]— was only a warm-up. When *Paisà* finally opened in Paris (a year after Venice, six months after Rome: September 26, 1947), Georges Altman declared: "The public has to be told right away: they have never seen anything like this. For the first time, images taken in the form of newsreels release an impression of eternity. . . . [*Paisà*] is life stripped nude, reportage art like Hugo's *Choses vues*. Yes, things seen by a witness who is a poet. . . . One might say there is no longer dramatic, technical, or artistic mediation between the subject and the one capturing it. It all throbs, as though within hand's reach. It's all so direct, the screen and we are henceforth one. With *Paisà* one sees, one has seen. It is to this day the masterwork of a screen style entirely submissive to the real, to the ferocious nudity of the truth."[194]

Even in Italy, critics took up the chorus—finally. When *Bianco e Nero* resumed publication in 1948, its editor, Luigi Chiarini, took the opportunity in his first editorial to salute Rossellini for using "the camera as a clear eye to look at life deeply and without rhetoric."[195]

Why should Roberto have disagreed? For the rest of his life, he would humbly explain that he simply "captured things in themselves" and it was enough. The phrase resounded of Heidegger and politely hinted that, while other moviemakers dealt with artifice, Rossellini touched the real. This was seductive, but silly. Photography "captures" no matter who presses the button, and how can one thing be less real than another? Bazin's lust to get beyond conventions and to see things unfiltered ("in themselves") led him to claim that film, as a mechanical medium, gave an "unmediated imprint" of the real. But Bazin was being theatrical; he never dreamed generations of American academics would take him seriously. He knew humans mediate the imprint by fashioning the mechanism, and again by gazing at the imprint—and who watches movies just for an imprint? Hadn't the Italians seen the war? What use could they have for *Paisà*—unless to experience *someone else* seeing the world? We want to experience mediation, not the lack of it.

It is strange to find people speaking of a "newsreel look" as though newsreels were neutral, unemotional documents. Is there anything more melodramatic than famous war photos? Why did critics deny the art to assert the real? Clearly we assert the art in order to value the real. There is more reality outside my window than on any movie screen. It is not unmediated recording that makes "The Po Delta" impressive; it is artistic cunning, like Murnau's *Tabu*. "Every movie I've seen since [*Paisà*], if it didn't seem descended from that convulsive lesson of truth, has seemed almost artificial," said Luis Berlanga.[196]

"Neo-realism is fiction that becomes more real than reality," said Rossellini.[197]

Hope and Despair

Rossellini, Lattuada said somewhere, "taught Italians not to be ashamed to look themselves in the face." Indeed, this had been Roberto's explicit goal with *Paisà* from the moment he began changing the American perspective of Klaus Mann's scripts.

In 1961 he commented majestically: "The Italian cinema rose from the war's ruins, courageously recounted our tragedy and confessed our faults, but also told of our hope, our faith in life and people. It served to orient us in the sea of destruction surrounding us, and to tell the world of our tragedy and the true face of Italy."[198]

But in 1949 he had spoken less loftily: "*Paisà* was a film produced in anger, anger at all the gross unnecessary suffering caused by the war. . . . It was conceived at a time of highly emotional heart-searching, of bitterly sought national justification, [of] despair, guilt, introspection, disappointment [and] justification."[199]

Most critics have been overwhelmed not by *Paisà*'s theme of hope, but its theme of despair. "Never has a contemporary Italian artist revealed the tragic sense of human existence so purely," exclaimed Di Giammatteo. Even when Rossellini's characters possess "indomitable moral strength," their "every tiny gesture is permeated with impotence." Rossellini "inserted Italian culture into ... existentialism, [doing] with cinema in Italy, what Sartre—with aesthetically inferior results—was doing in France with literature and theater."[200]

Others complained, eventually, that Rossellini's tragic sense mocks Resistance ideals. *Paisà*'s brusque, jumpy style "shows that for Rossellini life has no order which is knowable by the human mind, that human desires and hopes always clash against an unforeseen destiny that is imposed on us from above."[201]

But Marxist objections—like Borrelli's (*Paisà* is "anti-historical") or Buache's (*Paisà* doesn't highlight class struggle as history's primary motive force[202]) or Brunette's (Rossellini was so "unabashedly bourgeois" that he couldn't distinguish between the arbitrarily conventional and the natural[203])—do not appear to have been raised in the postwar period, when the PCI was backing the movie. And other Marxists, and Catholics too, justified *Paisà*. "Man exalts himself by making himself ever more humble before war's destruction," argues Baldelli. "The film's force, then, lies not in global exaltation of historic testimony ... , nor in the present prospect of rebirth, but in the diminishment of despair, intolerance, and bitterness, as populist characters become protagonists of their own situation."[204]

Still, it is not necessary to invoke primitivism, existentialism, populist assertiveness, transcendentalism, or even bourgeoisieism to explain Roberto's attitude. More simply he was Roman quintessentially, Neapolitan by predilection, and nothing was more natural than that pessimism and impotency should mingle with persistence. Rome, after all, was the city where Garibaldi once tried to start a revolution, only to have nobody show up because it was raining. Revolutions, like new ideas, came from the North, from "Italy" and other strange places. Rome was not "Italy," nor even less was Naples. There people were too wise, too weary, too old, too cynical; they knew they couldn't change the world. Existentialism? Fascism? Marxism? Populism? Class struggle? Nationalism? So many foreign ideas, windmills for dreamers and tyrants. For Rossellini truth is the street-boy Pasquale telling the black MP he'll steal his shoes if he falls asleep.

Moods and attitudes were Rossellini's subject, and people, but not things or events. He does not so much show reality as indicate a frame of feeling within which shame and sin attach to the great slow current of time. The world felt no need to know what the war had been about, at least the victorious nations didn't; but Italians did, and no such facile answers as victory over tyranny could correspond to the roles Italians had played. They needed to feel who they were, and Rossellini gives them themselves. What *Roma città aperta* struggled to do, *Paisà* achieved.

Slopes of Hope

Una voce umana, Deutschland im Jahre Null, Il miracolo

Paris lifted Roberto out of his depression. He lived alone in the Hotel Raphael, far from home, far from reminders of Romano. Paris filled the void. In contrast to the constant spite and intrigues of Roman life, the worship of Paris was revitalizing. He had thought of himself as a playboy and a wastrel; now intellectuals—*French* intellectuals—were calling him a seer, a metaphysician, a prophet for his age. Also in Italy, as a result, people were looking to him as the artist of the moment, a national-popular artist, a Lincoln at Gettysburg, the poet laureate of the new Italy. Emissaries from the Vatican and the Communist Party were flittering around, endeavoring to win his friendship and exercise influence. Romans for centuries have lavished distinction on anyone with the slightest celebrity, and Roberto for the rest of his life would be unable to walk the streets or enter a restaurant with anonymity. He began to surround himself with sycophants who kowtowed and called him "maestro." Old friends found him big-headed and inaccessible.

Roswitha was left behind. Roberto still loved her—more tenderly, perhaps, than he would his other lovers. She had been his companion through the crucial experiences of his life—the war, the break-up of his marriage, the fall of Fascism, the Occupation, the liberation, *Roma città aperta*, and *Paisà*. Now for these reasons he avoided her. Years later he would recall how, swimming with her at Capri at the moment of Romano's death, "I heard a voice tell me: 'Your son Romano is dead.'"[1]

He sent Roswitha money regularly, if late, at Parco Pepoli or their home on Capri, and telegrams every other day pledging love and adoration. He had brought her son Viktor from Vienna and accepted the nine-year-old as his own. But since Romano's death he had spent hardly one week per month in Italy, and not even one night per month with her.

He had made her pregnant the night his son had died. Did he know?

It is impossible to say. Roswitha Schmidt herself refuses to speak of it. It seems improbable that he would not have known. But he had scarcely looked at her since August. Friends tried to persuade Roswitha to protect her interests; Roberto would have welcomed their child and it would have bound him to her. But for these very reasons she might not have wanted Roberto to know. All her life she'd been defenseless, now she was disconsolate. Her mother, a morphine addict, had killed herself, and her officer father's new young wife had hated her. Then had come Viktor when she was eighteen. Now she was pregnant and on the verge of being abandoned. Roberto's family, she felt, had not forgiven her for breaking up his marriage with Marcella. In her fifth month—December—she took the ferry to Naples and had her baby aborted.[2] At New Year's she joined Roberto for a party in Rome.

At the end of January he returned to Italy for a month, went twice to Capri, briefly, and fell insanely in love with Magnani in Rome.

"Roberto brought Anna to my house one evening," Marcella De Marchis recalled. "He wanted me to get to know her, he wanted my opinion, in as much as, after Romano's death, Roberto was virtually a son to me. You could see how much they were in love with each other. They were two beautiful, shining lovers, and they didn't hide it. They'd stopped 'just to say hello before going out to eat,' but ended up talking till two that night. At a certain point I went to the kitchen and made some sandwiches. It was a beautiful evening. Roberto had come to me as though . . . as though he were seeking my blessing. Now there was this sort of respect between us. And I, when they were leaving, told him, 'Hold on tightly to this beautiful love.'[3]

"Voluntarily and out of love of Roberto I had assumed the difficult role of 'wife in the shadow' and would never have done anything to get in his way. I felt alone, though Roberto was always nearby like the most affectionate of brothers, and I tried to reconstruct a life for myself. But my efforts were sterile and doomed to failure. I was too tied to my past. . . . I well knew that, despite appearances, no woman would ever be able to take my place in my husband's life, and this sufficed to make my renunciation less difficult. . . .

"I caught diphtheria that year, and for fear of contagion the doctor had me send Renzino away. Roberto was off working and did not know that I had had a collapse. . . . But Anna came with her own doctor and stayed until Roberto returned. . . .

"Perhaps all this may appear somewhat inconceivable to anyone accustomed to measuring life by the usual yardsticks, but everything that happened to or around Roberto was always outside of the ordinary. He always had the extraordinary ability to conciliate even life's most disparate elements and to make the unacceptable acceptable. His capacity to give something of himself to each person and to induce them to do as much is incomprehensible to anyone who does not know him."[4]

Roberto knew, however, that Magnani was a devouring whirlpool of insecurity, lust, and fury, and that for a free spirit such as himself, to love her was to court insanity, all the more so since he himself was in despair. For as long as he could, therefore, he resisted her by periodically putting distance between them. And by clinging to Roswitha. But part of him craved insanity.

*

At the end of February he was back in Paris, where he was supposed to be working on the German film. He wrote "Rosy" he would find her father when he got to Berlin (which was off-limits to ordinary citizens without Four-Power authorization). Relieved to have escaped Magnani for the moment, he reassured Rosy sincerely, "You know you're the sweetest and most important thing in my life, along with my children."[5] Two weeks later, on March 19, he set out on a tedious 600-mile drive to Berlin, in company with Franchina and Marlene Dietrich's husband, Rudolf Sieber, who was representing Burstyn.

"Without any preconceived idea," he wrote some years later, "I went to Germany, not to shoot but to visit and bring back a story idea. I arrived in Berlin in the month of March, by car, around five o'clock in the afternoon, as the sun was going down. It was necessary to cross the whole of the capital to get to the French sector. The city was deserted. The grey of the sky ran down into the streets and by standing up one could look over the roof tops. To find the streets under the ruins they had cleared the debris into piles. In the cracks in the asphalt grass was starting to grow. Silence reigned, each sound counterpointed it and emphasized it all the more. A solid wall through which the road ran was constructed out of rotten organic matter that gave off a sickeningly sweet odor. We were floating on Berlin. I turned down a wide avenue. On the horizon was the unique sign of life: a big yellow panel board. Slowly I approached this huge sign which stood on a stone block in front of a tiny storefront, and I read: 'Israel Bazaar.' The first Jews had come back to Berlin. This indeed was the symbol of the end of Nazism. . . .

"The Germans were human beings like us. What could have led them to this disaster? False morality, the very essence of Nazism? abandonment of humility for the cult of heroism? exaltation of force rather than weakness? pride rather than simplicity? This is why I decided to tell the story of a child, of an innocent whom the distortions of a utopian education inspire to perpetrate a crime [killing his invalid father] thinking he's accomplishing an heroic act. But the little flame of morality is not extinguished in him: he kills himself to escape this uneasiness, this contradiction."[6]

Roberto wired Roswitha. Her father and half-brother were well. He had telegraphed Trombadori to help get them passports out of Germany.

A week later he was back in Paris, made a quick trip to Milan, and on April 6 returned with Anna, who was to receive an award for *Roma città aperta*. She was life itself, after Romano, and worth even madness. And madness it was. No matter the setting, no civility or restraint was possible. Their antics were on stage for the whole world. At The Raphael they were likened to electrical charges: every time they made contact a tempest was inevitable. Calm would follow just as suddenly, with cooing "Robbé" and Roberto crooning "Stellina mia!" Outside the theater the Paris police had to erect barricades to hold back the crowds.

Roberto telegraphed Roswitha. "Believe me I want your peace of mind and happiness. Have faith. You're my whole life, all my love. Have patience. Keep in touch daily. I adore you."[7]

Roberto told *L'Écran Français*, "I'm planning to take Germans from the street and put them directly in front of the camera," then added an important qualification—"but for them to come alive on the screen, they first have to have something to express"—and then doubled back again: "People say I manage to get what I want out of my players. But what I want is to help them express themselves. And thus to transmit the milieu they live in, the class they belong to, the diverse reactions of people in given circumstances." But just the same, "Photo-genius isn't in the opening of the camera but in the choice and presentation of the document. . . . This is neither reportage nor Zola-like naturalism. One must achieve a new form of artistic expression . . . whose poetry is drawn from reality."[8]

Roberto's immediate poetry was Paris. "My friends were named Jean Cocteau, Marcel Pagnol, Jacques Maritain, Edgard Faure, André Malraux. . . . I remember the intellectuals around kind Maritain. One night I encountered François Mauriac, his gaze anxious, his voice frighteningly aphonic, walking with uncomfortable slowness.[9] I also met Gaston Bouthoul, the sociologist, whose person and work represent one of the most important discoveries I've made. Bouthoul, who was the first to study the phenomenon of war ('polemology'), said that in almost every society there exist phenomena whose function seems to be to push aside or destroy an important portion of the young population."[10] And there was Jean Cocteau, "thin, inspired, a poet. We went together to see Marcel Achard, Henry Bernstein, Marcel Pagnol."[11] Cocteau became a good friend. "He was greedy and showy in his thought as in his clothing. He desired everything, went through everything, surrounded himself with everything: scarves and poems, inventions and precious textiles. Total display!"[12]

Cocteau thought *Paisà* was "wonderful." "A man expresses himself through a people and a people through a man, with perfect artlessness," he proclaimed.[13] And Roberto liked Cocteau's *Blood of a Poet*. But it was Anna who brought them together and pressed them to collaborate on a film of Cocteau's monologue, *Una voce umana* (A Human Voice). She had performed Cocteau's version ("*The* Human Voice") on stage—in Rome five years earlier, at a gala in her honor—and had scored a success despite Serato's advice that it would be too morbid. She was the sole character—a woman agonizing alone in her room, as she breaks up with her lover on the telephone. Inevitably the situation reminded Roberto of his introduction to Magnani a few years earlier, when she, in fury at the missing Serato, had reenacted one of their fights before collapsing onto her couch—with the phone beside her.

The forty-minute film was shot in two weeks in a studio at Place Clichy at the end of April and beginning of May. To finance it Roberto used advance money Burstyn had provided for the German film and tried to get his assistant, Basilio Franchina, to connive in concealing the diversion of funds, which led to fights between them. Aside from Cocteau's "dialogue," there was no script. Anna, her dog Micia, and Roberto were free to improvise and to shoot late in the evening; Franchina supplied an Italian translation and prompted Magnani on the telephone. Later she recorded a dubbing in French.

Una voce umana is the first instance in which the style and techniques of "neo-realism"—although that term had still not come into use—were applied to subject matter not connected with the war and its aftermath. Some critics therefore attacked it as a diversion from more important matters. It was an "experiment," Roberto insisted: cinema was a new art, full of all sorts of intoxicating possibilities, and now the camera was a microscope and he an entomologist.

"What I did . . . was never done before. Before all else, it's a formidable technical inquiry which in itself ought to be enough to make a film's success. But there's something better: there's an individual captured, put under the microscope, scrutinized to the core. There's the study of a human face, the penetration into the hidden wrinkles of a physiognomy. And this, if I'm not mistaken, is an inquiry into expressive means that no one ever dreamed of trying.[14]

"Cinema can take us by the hand and lead us to discover things the eye might not notice. . . . Only the novel, poetry and cinema allow us to dig into characters to discover their reactions and the motives that make them act. Pushed to an extreme in *Una voce umana* this experiment has served me since in all my films, because at one moment or another during a shooting I feel the need to put the script aside and follow the character in her most secret thoughts, thoughts she may not even be conscious of. This microscope side of cinema is part of what constitutes neo-realism: a moral approach that becomes an aesthetic fact."[15] "The American underground," he added in 1963, "has taken this to the point of insanity, filming a man sleeping for seven or eight hours."[16]

Rossellini was wrong; the indecent microscope had been an experiment before in two movies he surely had seen: *The Champ* (1931), in which King Vidor's camera pursues a little boy whose father has just died; and D. W. Griffith's 1919 *Broken Blossoms*, where the camera stares at Lillian Gish going insane locked in a closet. Vidor's movie has the same aura of newsreel reality. His boy expresses his emotions by walking around and not being able to escape, just as many Rossellini characters do.

Roberto gave *Una voce umana* to Anna as a love gift and eventually released it as part of a two-part movie, *L'amore* ("Love"), with a title card announcing, "This film is a homage to the art of Anna Magnani."

His detractors have seen it as evidence of misogyny. "A D'Annunzio-like regurgitation," wrote Ferrara.[17] And Oms explained: "Cocteau and Rossellini roll up in dirty linen a woman in love, hanging desperately on the telephone. [Rossellini thinks] human love degrades the woman."[18]

And even Rossellini supporters have seen his camera's unrelenting inquisition into so embarrassing, intimate, and humiliating a spectacle as evidence of the essential cruelty of realist art. "In 25 shots," said Cocteau, "he filmed cruelly a documentary of a woman's suffering. Anna Magnani displays her soul, a face without make-up."[19] Similar charges had been made against Griffith and Vidor.

But other viewers have been awed. For Eric Rohmer *Una voce umana* embodies Rossellini's constant theme: "solitude both physical and moral . . . , the isolation to which, in the Rossellinian universe, every creature, by dint of its terrestrial condition, sees itself always condemned in one way or another. . . . With no other director is it so difficult to distinguish content from expression: it is because he never tries to be symbolic that Rossellini's art is immediately profoundly symbolic, that this 'documentary on a woman's suffering' can be considered . . . as the archetype of all suffering, of suffering itself, the earthly image of damnation. . . . There is not one of the most realistic passages of Rossellini's films that is not like the echo, the palpable reflection, of an order which is not that of flesh and creature. Even in his most profane subjects he is the most, perhaps the sole, indisputably religious author that cinema, that the entire art of the twentieth century has known. On screen Cocteau's sketch is enriched by a new, wholly moral dimension. . . . Theatrical staging only has the possibility of upholstering the text better, whereas [Rossellini's] cinema helps us assume a distance from the text. The greater our initial pain at first at participating, the greater will be our ultimate bond. . . . By what mystery occurs this sort of reversal that every Rossellini spectator has experienced at least once? I do not yet feel close to figuring it out, but everything leads me to think that the respect [he] observes not only for things as they are but for time in its exact, undifferentiated duration has something to do with it. The search for 'continuity' which for some is only an aesthetic choice is with him put forward as an ethical choice."[20]

Adriano Aprà, taking up this theme of solitude, emphasizes the film's dialectic between the closed-in room and the rest of the world, present in sound and memory (daily life, a song on the radio, a child crying, steps, a door closing, voices on the phone), its dialectic between an absolute attitude toward life which leads to death, and an attitude of a universe which goes on living. If you live like Magnani, you die; if like the absent universe, you go on. She has determined to live her life like a "terrorist," like Irene (*Europe '51*), Karin (*Stromboli*), and Edmund (*Deutschland*), except that instead of their itineraries and encounters, here everything is concentrated in the final act, as though we assisted at just Edmund's suicide, Karin's cry "My God!", Irene's reclusion. Rossellini's cinema is one of erection and ejaculation: after the maximum of life and pleasure comes collapse and death. Rossellini's characters dare, then kill themselves, overcome.[21]

After 11 P.M., when shooting had finished, Roberto had been meeting with Jenia Reissar, Selznick's European representative. The American producer had heard rumors of M-G-M's contract offer falling through because of visa problems and, eager himself to sign Roberto to a long-term contract and fearful of the competition, had been pressing Reissar since the fall of 1946 to bring Roberto to terms. Intermediaries had proposed a seven-year, fourteen-picture contract, with fees ascending from $35,000 to $125,000 for a total of $1,070,000. But Selznick had rejected these terms as exorbitant financially for even an American director. (Magnani at the time was getting $14,500 per picture plus a profit percentage—a pittance by Hollywood standards, it made her by far the highest paid performer in Italy.) And Roberto had rejected the terms as exorbitant existentially. "I would not tie myself down for seven years in Hollywood—if they had offered me one million for one picture I would have gone. I could use the million to make pictures I like."[22]

Negotiations then continued with Reissar for one-picture deals. His desire, he told Reissar that May 1947, was for a dramatic story based on contemporary events. *Of Mice and Men* or *The Grapes of Wrath* would have been ideal subjects for him, he said. And he made three suggestions. One, of course, was *Christ in Concrete* (Roberto falsely claimed Geiger's option had expired). Another was a story to be woven around the 80,000 American soldiers waiting in Naples for demobilization. The third was *Messalina*, scripted by Fellini, with Magnani in the title role and Fabrizi as her husband, the Roman emperor Claudius. Roberto wanted to reproduce Rome not in the customary epic fashion but as it really had been, built of wood, with just an occasional marble palace. In June, however, Selznick, perhaps because Rossellini insisted on being an independent producer, announced through Reissar that he had no subject for Rossellini at the moment. Roberto, very disappointed, then proposed, without result, Faulkner's *Pylon*.

This account—digested from correspondence between Selznick and Reissar[23]—contrasts with Roberto's more poetic account.

"In 1946 . . . poor Selznick offered me a contract in America for two years, for two million dollars, which was then a lot of money. I didn't have a cent.[24] "We negotiated by telegram, he sending me thirty-page telegrams and I replying in two words.[25] When I thought it over well—I went to Frascati for a year—I realized that I'd be a slave, and so I offered to hire *him*. He was really insulted. Then when we met later [in 1949] we became very good friends, so much so that when he died, he remembered me in his will as a good person [and bequeathed a silver cigarette case]."[26]

Nonetheless, as we shall see, Roberto was happy when in March 1948 Selznick, inspired by *Paisan*'s New York success, initiated a second series of negotiations.

Roswitha's silence pained him, he wired her in late May; he was alone and sad without her, he lived only to see her happy. He was sincere but had been promising to come to Capri "in a few days" since April and since mid-February had seen her only a single day (perhaps). Nor had he paid any more attention to his new picture. All he had to show for seven months of "work" were a few pages of notes. Anna was consuming him. He was speeding toward a crisis of his own making.

He had decided to call the film *Berlin* (later *Germany*) *Year Zero.* The title was lifted, with permission, from the book, *L'Année zéro de l'Allemagne* by the philosopher and film critic Edgar Morin. But no one knew this and the title puzzled everyone, and out of spite Roberto refused to explain even to Burstyn and his partner Arthur Mayer. "Rossellini's free-wheeling methods demanded a great deal of faith from anyone associated with [him]," Mayer moaned. "Every time we made an advance we wistfully asked what the picture was going to be about.... Whatever does the name *Germany Year Zero* mean..., we wondered.... 'Until the picture is finished it is sufficient if I know what it means,' was all the satisfaction [we] got. After a suspenseful period, Burstyn and I finally gave up. The picture was eventually completed, actually financed in large measure by the more trustful French government."[27]

Burstyn's faith had not been bolstered by the *Voce umana* theft, nor by the revelation that the U.S. rights to *Paisà,* which Burstyn thought were his alone, had been sold by Roberto *also* to Burstyn's chief competitor, Ilya Lopert. Now, to find new funds, Roberto had to improvise furiously. The French government would provide permits and accommodations and, through Union Générale Cinématographique, the giant nationalized distribution and theater network, a cameraman, a producer, and part of the money. A German company, Sadfi, would provide most of the equipment and crew. For the rest of the money Roberto found two Italians: Salvo D'Angelo, the producer who had gotten the Vatican to finance De Sica's *Porta del cielo,* and Alfredo Guarini, Isa Miranda's husband, who agreed to bankroll Roberto's company, Tevere Films. Roberto would use this sort of multi-national combination frequently in the future. It made it impossible for anyone to control him, gave him a profit percentage and, more importantly (since almost none of his films made any money henceforth), a pre-profit percentage through the ability to divert innumerable "production expenses" into his own pocket. "I know," Josef von Sternberg observed in 1968, "that making a film creates hundreds of problems, each one of which has somehow to be solved. From what I read and see and hear, I doubt if today's problems are worth solving. Today's director, it seems to me, has to have the cunning of a card cheat and the sophistry of a gigolo."[28]

The trusting Roswitha had finally been obliged to recognize that Roberto was living a double life. Her "husband" had at last come home to Capri on May 24, only to rush back immediately to Rome, where Magnani was. On June 2 he'd wired from Paris he would return in a week "expressly to stay with you." On June 11 he'd wired from Rome he would arrive June 12. On June 12 he'd wired he'd arrive June 13. On June 13 he'd wired he'd arrive June 14. On June 15 he'd wired he'd been stranded all night halfway from Naples when his car broke down and now was back in Rome. "Have faith," he wrote on June 18, "I'm sad without you." On June

19, back in Paris, he'd wired that he was sending money and a ring and soon they'd be together "always."[29]

He had been with Magnani all the while.

The crazed Roberto, accustomed from birth to privilege in a country accustomed for ages to according it, now regarded even his emotions as D'Annunzian heroics for others to admire. Perhaps his cocaine encouraged him, but it did not determine his moods. "This love of mine for Anna Magnani," he asked Mario Del Papa one day, "Don't you think it's important? *Truly* important?"[30]

Renzo wrote Roswitha, June 16, that more than ever he was determined to save Roberto from "his dangerous moment of weakness." The "danger" was in Rome, he argued, and Roswitha's best interests lay in keeping Roberto away from Rome and at work on the film, whose delay was threatening Roberto's career and Roswitha's financial support.[31]

Five days later, Roberto left Paris for a week to Brussels, where *Paisà* was receiving an award at the World Film Festival. Needing story synopses in French, German, and English at the last moment, he had turned to Marlene Dietrich. Dietrich was attached to Jean Gabin at the moment, but after seeing *Roma città aperta* and *Paisà* had joined the queue adoring Roberto and had pushed Cocteau, Jean Marais, and Edith Piaf to do the same.[32] She would cook him pasta, fetch espresso, tell stories about Germany, and try to explain German psychology. On her recommendation in April he had engaged Max Colpet, a German-Polish scriptwriter who had been a leading figure in the cultural renaissance in Vienna and Berlin during the twenties.[33] "Sure," she had announced, "I can do the English translation." She had spent the next two days at Max Colpet's house typing, breaking her fingernails, and chain-smoking Camels. She was sympathetic and maternal toward Roberto, and a little afraid of him.

Roberto returned to Paris on the 26th, left the next day for Rome, and that night in Naples saw Roswitha. Thirty-three days had passed since their last meeting.

In Rome the next day, at Trombadori's suggestion, Roberto engaged Carlo Lizzani as his assistant to replace the disgusted Franchina. The future director and historian was then 25 and had been an officer in the Communist Youth Movement. The Party's interest in Roberto was complex, as Lizzani has explained: "Our apprehensions, perhaps ingenuous, concerning the risk that Rossellini might abandon his big German adventure in the middle of the road, or that he might make a film that was not on a par with *Roma città aperta* or *Paisà* were born of the feeling of those years that united a vast group of intellectuals [who saw in the . . . cinema a kind of common flag, a decisive one that could give Italy a new image]. It was quite common practice at the time to circulate amongst ourselves the scripts we wrote, keeping each other informed about the films we were preparing, exchanging advice and opinions. In particular we who had matured in the *Cinema* group, and a certain number of Marxist intellectuals, [both of us] close to cinematic neo-realism, followed with trepidation every step, every plan and project of the man we considered the principal exponent of our [movement]."[34]

Roberto, according to Lizzani, had insisted he fly to Paris immediately, July 1, had signed him to a contract there, and then vanished. "I had a wonderful time in Paris, supported by a strange French company that paid me for waiting for Rossellini and studying documents on the Germany of that time. Roberto [had] told me, 'Tomorrow we leave for Berlin.' But he was not able to leave because he was caught up in a thousand financial problems and had to see Magnani who, terrified of flying, was unable to come to Berlin."[35]

Roberto had gone to Berlin July 4, and had cabled Roswitha that her father and brother were well.

"Basilio [Franchina] has let off steam to me," Lizzani wrote to Trombadori. "He is disgusted with Roberto who doesn't give him a penny and is sending him to Italy without any money at all (he did promise him, though, that he can work on the film *Pirelli* [which never came about]). He claims to be Roberto's only friend and to have salvaged the few relationships (Dietrich and Colpet) Roberto still has in Paris. He is also disgusted with Magnani who has apparently been speaking very ill of Roberto wherever she goes. In other words he considers Roberto little less than a madman or a delinquent. He says he can't wait to get back to Italy, having slaved seven months like mad with nothing to show for it, to have allowed himself to be taken in by Roberto's fascination and to have been tricked by it. . . . Renata [Gaede] also considers [Roberto] a madman and an exploiter. She's been here a month [without getting her pay] and living in debt. . . . Colpet also seems to be obliged to live very adventurously in order to stay at his side and work with him!"[36]

They were all housed at The Raphael. Renata Gaede, a Berliner and friend of Roswitha's, had had a romance with Renzo Rossellini in Rome during the war. Roberto, with typical parsimony, had given Lizzani 10,000 francs (about $20) to pay for the hotel, his meals, and his travel to Berlin. On the other hand, 25,000 lire a week were being paid into Lizzani's account in Italy (versus the 12,000 a week Fellini and Mida had been paid during *Paisà*).

"Dietrich too is rather frightened by Roberto's follies. She understands that a man of talent cannot live the life of a middle-class man, but she finds that Roberto is exaggerating things. She is very fond of him and would really be the right woman for him, but Roberto doesn't take the slightest notice of her advice. Among other things, Roberto had promised Dietrich's husband the job of production manager, had him come rushing over from America and then dumped him. Dietrich isn't sore at him about this, but just can't realize how 'Rossellini', the man whose name would be sufficient to get anything out of his producers, is incapable of imposing upon them those elements that would be more useful (at this point Basilio explains to her that in order to get personal financial facilitations, Roberto is prepared to sacrifice anything, first and foremost his friends, his engagements, his promises). She marvels at the relationship between Roberto and Anna, at how she treats him and keeps him in her grip.[37]

"Roberto has urged me absolutely to prevent Colpet from working on the dialogue. He told me that during the Paris-Berlin journey he slept right through two nights and one day to avoid discussing the script with Colpet."[38] Colpet's family had died in the concentration camps, he had vowed never to return to Germany, and had changed his mind only at Dietrich's urging, for the sake of the film and his own career.[39]

Franchina soon quit and, after a heated discussion and somewhat against his will, agreed to his name being removed from the titles.

Lizzani arrived alone in Berlin, July 14; Roberto had gone to Rome and Paris. "My first impression . . . : Roberto was right, it was a sensation of fear. It's like approaching a giant, a giant conquered and cut up into pieces but still able to move and react. The men with their semi-military clothing seem only *temporarily* dressed as civilians. It is like entering a fortress occupied only a short while ago, with the war ended only the day before. [The war had ended more than two years before.] . . . Behind the women, the children, and the very young one can feel the burden of millions of dead and of violence. . . . I don't believe Berlin can be rebuilt. The smell of corpses is everywhere, and here and there hubs of excited movement, men, women, and children with sacks, carts, a few cars, trams, etc. The hunger is frightening. Thousands of Berliners . . . will commit suicide this coming winter, chiefly because there is absolutely no solution in sight."[40]

The film's interiors would probably be shot in Italy. "This could be good for our interests," Lizzani wrote, referring to the PCI, "in the sense that since the interior shots are those that have the most dialogue there will be several of us who can, at the right moment, exercise influence upon him. . . . But from the point of view of reality and his aesthetic position? This is already a sign of 'botching it.' I fear Roberto . . . has little interest in the film. He is very excited by the chaotic situation in which we are involved because, as he says, what he likes best about film work is being able to create complicated financial and organizational situations, and in this way play with people. The fact of being able to make a film with the French, the Russians (who are, according to the latest news, supposed to be supplying the equipment) and the Vatican (the Pontifical Commission is supposed to help us with our food), sends him into raptures."[41]

Meanwhile Roberto left his crew in Berlin and for weeks did not respond even to telegrams. Marcella wrote Roswitha ostensibly to commiserate, really out of concern for her brother. It was good he was 2,000 kilometers away from "the danger," she thought, but she'd heard his situation was sincerely critical, and since his "new preoccupation" could be disastrous for everyone, she hoped Roswitha would stay cool.[42]

Roberto finally left Paris and showed up in Berlin at the end of July. "Du bist meine Alles," he wrote Roswitha.[43]

"The first evening Roberto was already extremely fed up, and I was afraid he might take off from one moment to the next. Then we began . . . to spend a few strange and curious evenings and now he is becoming fond of Berlin. Chiefly he is very happy to have found a certain Treuberg, an old friend from his youthful days in the Roman society of fifteen years ago (now a Communist and counselor of DEFA)."[44]

Said Roberto: "On the list of available technicians [in Berlin] I found the name of an old boyhood friend, one I had not seen for twenty years— Count Bubi Treuberg. Count Treuberg, who had just been released from prison where the Nazis had kept him for many years, became my right-hand man, and has since joined my permanent filmmaking company."[45]

Franz Treuberg had emigrated to London before the war and was friends with the most famous anti-Nazi German intellectuals. He had studied at the University of Rome in the thirties. DEFA (formerly UFA), in the Russian zone, was the support point for all foreign film units shooting in Berlin, for which reason Roberto wanted to be recommended through the PCI to the German Communist Party. "Roberto was already a star," Lizzani later recalled, with the result that "for a month . . . all we did was go to receptions, cocktail parties and meals at the American, Russian, or French bases. Everyone was happy. We were lodged at the Maison de France and so in this festive climate carried on the film's preparation on the basis of a scenario that changed constantly."[46] "The Americans, British, French and Russians tried to outdo each other in their help to me," said Roberto. "This included hard-to-come-buy food rations and lodgings, camera and other technical equipment, jeeps to carry us and our equipment, and military escort to see us on our way."[47] They met the Russian Mikhail Chiaurelli, whose films were constructing Stalin's personality cult, and Colpet's friend Billy Wilder, who was shooting exteriors for *A Foreign Affair*—into which he would insert a scene satirizing Rossellini's boy Nazi plot. Lizzani met his future wife.

They showed *Paisà* and *Roma città aperta* to small invited groups. *Roma* had been voluntarily suppressed by the German film industry's Freiwillige Selbskontrolle, which had declared it showed "the historical truth, but in exaggerated form. . . . Today, in a new European situation, agitation must be feared from public screenings against certain nations and must be avoided for common interest."[48] When *Roma* was finally released, in 1961, a preface was added: "This film is not directed against the German people. It does not accuse German soldiers. It depicts the struggle of freedom-loving human beings against arbitrariness and tyranny."[49] *Paisà*'s screening, on August 10 or 11, was applauded warmly and reviewed without suggestion that it was anti-German. It had been shot, one journalist wrote, "not with actors but human beings . . . who lived through a life we can [identify] with (unfortunately). [Rossellini shows surprising objectivity] toward his own people, too."[50] "What we Germans today feel so tortured and fascinated about is the clear-sighted, realistic tone of that film," commented another.[51] *Paisà* was not released publicly until October 1949, when the one anti-German segment, "The Po Delta" episode, was deleted so that the picture ended in the monastery.

"For my cast," Roberto explained, "I roamed the streets of Berlin, looking for satisfactory physical types.... The old father I found sitting on the steps of a public home for the aged. Curiously enough he had been an actor for silent pictures in the early 1900s. The sister attracted my attention by the expression of resigned despair on her pretty face as she stood on a food line. She was a ballet dancer in a chorus who supported her mother and herself. The Nazi brother comes from an outstanding academic family. He and his father were both imprisoned by the Gestapo. Besides these leading players, in my wanderings I collected a Wehrmacht general, an ex-wrestler, a professor of literature and the history of art, a beautiful model, groups of boys and girls who were dying of boredom on the streets of Berlin. Most of my players had never acted before, but anyone can act provided he is in familiar surroundings and given lines that are natural."[52]

On August 7 Roberto had cabled kisses to Roswitha and told her Manni would be coming with a letter. He cabled again August 11, worried by her silence, and again August 12, and again August 13. Manni had been sent to retrieve the ring which Roberto had given Roswitha two months before, and which Magnani was demanding as rightfully hers.

Lizzani wrote to Trombadori: "Roberto is very enthusiastic about [Treuberg], and naturally this new friendship has brought about Colpet's definite fall from grace. On the other hand, you know how Roberto is, he hasn't yet got the courage to liquidate Colpet and so we are forced to work with strange subterfuges, hiding in Treuberg's house ... working nights on the script, etc. etc.... We stay up until four in the morning, talking every now and then about the film but for the most part about the weather and other things.

"It can happen that we find ourselves at night and without knowing how in the middle of a huge villa in which 300 Swiss living in Berlin are celebrating a national holiday and stay there until the next morning with no particular reason. Or we could sit for hours at table with Hans Albers and a short, insignificant fellow who we later discover is the owner of one of the biggest circuses in the world ... and who begins to tell you how he brushes the elephants' teeth, trains bears, and breaks down the door of his house with a thrust of thumb when he forgets his keys.[53]

"At the end we found ourselves with fifteen pages in hand that, however, were fifteen very precise pages. For example: 'A horse falls, people approach the dead horse, quarter it, each takes a piece of flesh, the child sees the scene, goes by and away.' "[54]

When shooting finally began on August 15 not only did the dialogue remain to be improvised, but the story itself was still only a rough outline. So distracted was Roberto that he had started to believe his own publicity myth: he was Rossellini, he didn't need a script. Now he threw away even the outline, scant as it was, and began gropingly to compose his film anew.

In its original form, Edmund, a ten-year-old raised in the Hitler Youth, blames his father's anti-Nazism for Germany's defeat. Motivated by the invalid father's own death wish, the family's poverty, and a teacher's opinion that useless people should be disposed of, the boy murders his father with poison. He then re-encounters a man who at the start of the film had picked him up from a ditch where he was crying and who had begun telling a "fable" about how he had gone into exile in 1933. Then Edmund had walked out on him in the middle of the fable. Now he finds the man—a German Communist Resistance leader—so simple and human, so different from anything he has ever experienced, that, understanding the fable's eternal values, he is re-educated toward becoming a true citizen of the world.[55]

Lizzani explains that this man—the "Emigrant," to be played by Treuberg—was meant to stand for "the political exile destined to represent, in a Germany destroyed by war and still poisoned by the miasmas of the recently-collapsed regime, the part of Germany that had not surrendered to Hitler's dictatorship. Thousands of German anti-fascists, Communists, Social-democrats and Catholics . . . had been interned in concentration camps, murdered or forced to flee abroad. It seemed natural to me and Trombadori [and] Rossellini that in a first portrait of Germany such as Rossellini was preparing, there should be room for the idea of hope."[56]

It was in order to preserve this political idea that Trombadori had put Lizzani at Roberto's side. And Lizzani had tried to authenticate it by getting local Communists' opinions about the left's chances in the New Germany.

But in fact, the Emigrant is an obtrusive calculation in the story. A similar character (a homosexual Communist) had been inserted into *Ossessione* with similar purpose: to point the way. Similar too, though to a lesser degree, were the Communists Amidei had contributed to *Roma città aperta* and the partisan leader he had tried to insert into *Paisà*. Now, after Romano's death, ideological figures had even less appeal to Roberto.

Once production began Roberto worked fiendishly, always out of doors, near Potsdamerstrasse. "Someone asked him why he never blew up," *The New York Times* reported. "He exhibited scarred knuckles and replied: 'That scar came from *Open City*. That one came from *Paisà*. I can afford only one explosion to a picture and I have to be sure I'm at the boiling point before I let go.' The result is a liver ailment which has reduced a gourmet to a diet of boiled spaghetti or potatoes with oil and no sauces, wines or liquor."[57]

Directing in French and shooting in German, Rossellini was dependent on Colpet to translate his instructions. "During the shooting in the streets of Berlin I was struck by the indifference of the people. In New York, in London, in Paris, or Rome, a motion picture camera and a filming crew are an irresistible magnet for the citizenry. The people of Berlin, it seemed to me, were interested in only one thing: to eat and to survive. This, I believe, is the fruit of a defeat unparalleled in history which has annihilated the conscience of an entire people."[58]

To play Edmund, Roberto had been determined to find a boy who resembled Romano, and had kept Marcellina informed of his progress with daily telegrams. Lots of boys were presented; none of them would do. It was when he had accepted an invitation to visit the Barlay circus during off hours—he was curious to see the trick-playing elephants—that he had spotted eleven-year-old Edmund Meschke, a real circus boy, born in the circus, an acrobat, the son of a clown and riding master. Roberto had brought him to his hotel, had him wash his hands and comb his hair, and had taken him to lunch. His resemblance to Romano was uncanny.

"You must be very rich," the boy said, "only very rich people can have a tablecloth in Germany."

"You'll say that in my film," said Roberto.

"All right. What is the name of my film?"

"*Berlin, Year Zero.*"

"What does it mean?"

"You'll understand it when you see it."

"Not before then?"

"No. Before then it will be enough that I know what it means."[59]

But did Roberto know? His story was still unfinished, the film two months behind schedule, and he wanted to suspend production and get back to Anna in Paris. The producer refused. Roberto came to work limping and wearing a martyr's expression. "I fell down . . . dislocated a bone . . . or maybe it's a fracture." The production insurer demanded a medical consultation. "My doctor, the only one I trust, is in Paris," announced Roberto, as he hopped a cab direct to the airport. Once in Paris, instantly healed, he toured the nightclubs with Anna, spending a fortune.[60]

A week later Anna was back in Rome and Roberto in Berlin, desperate again. With whisky he bribed an American pilot to fly him to Rome. They drank the whisky during the trip and landed in Naples by mistake. The pilot sank into deepest slumber and Roberto looked for a taxi to take him to Rome. Three hours later he was hugging Anna and asking for money for the taxi. "Sure, dear! How much is it?" she cooed. Then all hell broke loose. An hour later Roberto was at the Rome airport trying to find another pilot to corrupt to get back to Berlin.[61] At Berlin airport, where Colpet picked him up, Roberto took one look at Colpet's girlfriend-of-the-moment and promised to cast her as "The Emigrant" (now female).

Roberto's drugged lunacy with Magnani alarmed his family. He was falling back into the prodigal ways of his youth and destroying his professional reputation. Now Roswitha, whom they'd counted on to keep him on a steady keel, was up in arms, having heard of his escapades at last. How could Roberto have been so imbecilic, Renzo bitterly complained, to think he could keep such noisy, ridiculous conduct a secret from her forever? Ever practical, Renzo tried to convince Roswitha she was being rash to throw away her financial claims after five years with Roberto; she had rights, she should fight for them, not run away; and besides, Roberto's attachment to her was profound, whereas Magnani was inevitably a transitory adventure, probably ending already.[62]

Meanwhile gossip had it that Magnani was trying to get Roswitha deported.

Roswitha had written Roberto. Instead of responding, he wired her August 19, 23, and 30, and September 8, 9, 13, and 16 to "stay calm." He'd be there soon.[63]

During his absences Roberto assigned Lizzani to direct certain shots, including important parts of Edmund's final walk through the ruins (passing the fountain and church; playing with his feet). "He was of the opinion," said Lizzani, "that the framing could be done this way or that, but if one shot enough [footage] and if the idea were clear, the material would be good in any case."[64] Roberto's bizarre notion of his own expendability would frequently trouble his fans and producers in years ahead. He had absorbed the Crocean attitude that art is in the conception, not in the manufacture—Shakespeare is distinguished from the rest of us by his imagination, not his craft—and would put it into Alberti's mouth in *The Iron Age* and *The Age of the Medici*. In *Acts of the Apostles* Christianity will oppose afflatus to law, as in *Deutschland* Edmund will oppose his leap to Hitler's words.

By mid-September, after forty days in the wilderness, Roberto was free to quit Berlin. The production would move to Rome. Theoretically this was justified by the need to use Italian money in Italy; actually Roberto just wanted to get out. He did so immediately, to Paris for two weeks, then Rome around the 26th, leaving Lizzani to pick up the pieces.

"Don't torment yourself," he cabled Roswitha on September 19. "Have faith in me. You know I've always acted for the best."[65] On September 29 Anna forced him to write. She stood over him the entire time.[66] "She goes or I go," the gossips quoted her as saying; but it was compassion, not jealousy, that motivated Anna this time.

"Roswitha my dear—after so much silence I am speaking up to tell you something painful, I know, but it's stronger than I am."

He had been living for months with Magnani, struggling all the while against his own "madness."

"I've waited so long to tell you that I love Anna, because I was struggling and hating myself that I was unable to give up everything for you, today the thing is too mad, it's deranging me, and I tell you this only now, it can be a slim consolation for you, but so you can be certain that this is happening for something very serious, for something that is fatal."

Roswitha had always understood him and he wanted her to understand him now. He would send her money. He would bring her father to Italy. He did not want to see her until they would have "absolute control of ourselves."

"Have faith in your future, don't beat your head, even suffering is good because it matures us. Forgive me, my Rosy—I kiss you tenderly."

The envelope was addressed to "Roswitha Rossellini."[67]

In Berlin, Lizzani had packed up and secured exit permits for the Germans from the military authorities of all four occupying powers. In Rome more weeks passed while sets were constructed and Roberto attended to Anna and went to Paris where *Paisà* was opening. It was November when production resumed and a surprise was waiting when the first rushes were viewed. Actors who had gone through a door in Germany looking thin and emaciated came out of the door in Italy looking plump and healthy—thanks to a month's worth of Vatican-supplied pasta and olive oil. Production was suspended for fifteen days while the Germans dieted.[68] Colpet's girlfriend showed up, as instructed, and discovered Roberto no longer knew who she was.

Now money problems brought back memories of *Roma città aperta*. Pay was far from certain. Roberto showed up late one evening with a bag full of the day's receipts from theaters all over Rome, having worked out a deal with Gemmi, a theater owner. But he was seldom around. Anna was filming *Assunta spina* on the same lot and he seemed to find that production more congenial than his own. Half-day holidays got stretched into two- or three-day holidays while Roberto in his brand new bright red Cisitalia sports racer drove down the coast with Anna to Amalfi. There he was a king. She admired a sea view, and he rented a whole cluster of houses overlooking the spot. (They weren't for sale; he tried.) At Christmas time, he dragged Anna out of bed to a toy store. He'd remembered some ragged kids they'd seen playing in a gutter. They loaded up the car, drove out to where the kids were, and played with them on the street. Then they realized they'd been imbeciles: they hadn't thought to bring food.

Back at the Titanus Studios Marcello Bolero had a problem. Roberto had planned the camera movements and rehearsed the boy for a complicated scene in which he would go through a series of rooms to fetch the poison. But once Roberto had gone, leaving it for Bolero to shoot, the scene would not work. The boy would get lost or make a wrong turn, or the camera would miss the action. "It was horrible, exhausting, and took the entire day, uselessly." Roberto showed up late that evening. "But that's the way it's supposed to be," he explained. "The camera follows its own course. Sometimes it sees the boy, sometimes it doesn't."[69]

Increasingly, Rossellini's camera, rather than being a simple tool for stream-of-consciousness as in *Una voce umana*, was becoming a tool for exploration, independent at times from the spectacle and drama it was photographing.

Once the picture was done, at a cost of $115,000[70], "most of the German players were unwilling to go back to their desolate homeland," Roberto recounted. "With only temporary visas they could not openly stay in Italy so they scattered through the countryside hoping to elude the police. A few escaped, but most were caught and sent home."[71]

Roswitha Schmidt's father and brother, who had been brought into Italy as part of the troupe, also had to go back when they failed to find work.

"Most Germans who have seen my film reacted as I thought they would, negatively. They found the story too pessimistic. A few, however, were willing to accept the grim realism of the story. Many members of the cast were appalled when they saw the finished film, at what they had unconsciously perpetrated. Edmund, after the long strain of the difficult role, became ill and had to go to the hospital for a couple of weeks.... My goal was the same as in any work I have done. I wanted to reproduce the truth exactly as the camera saw it for that audience throughout the world which has a heart capable of love and a brain capable of thought."[72]

But except for a Munich film club screening in 1952, Germans were not to see *Deutschland* in Germany until it was televised in 1978. Hans Habe, who rebuilt the German press, was irate when he saw it, abroad, in 1949: "A terrifying film..., not artistically, but because it would be terrifying if the world saw the new Germany as Rossellini does." The title says all Germans are like the sister who prostitutes herself, the father who eats half the family bread, the pederast teacher who tries to seduce Edmund. "But Germany in year zero was not like that, and I can prove it, for I lived through it while signor Rossellini in year zero was having trouble explaining his recently lost enthusiasm for Fascism to the occupation forces and Italy's brave underground fighters. An anti-German picture? No, a picture with no tendency at all... but full of frivolity, which is worse than anything intentional. Rossellini picks flowers from the grave of a nation... and vomits into the coffin.... It's more diabolical a swindle than Hollywood could have ever thought up."[73]

Roberto at the time defended his sociological intentions. "I made a child the protagonist in *Germany Year Zero* to accentuate the contrast between the mentality of a generation born and brought up in a certain political climate and that of the older generation as represented by Edmund's father. Twelve-year-old Edmund is the prototype of the German child who has survived the catastrophe of his native land. Whether he excites pity or horror I do not know, nor did I wish to know. I wanted to reproduce the truth, under the impulse of a strong artistic emotion."[74]

In fact Roberto had been loathe to confront Germany, had turned away from it as much as he could. "I couldn't make you cry," he explained later, "because after what Italy had been through I detested the Germans.... I show what I saw. I didn't like what I saw."[75]

Everything conspired to produce not the judiciously weighed *documentary* everyone had expected, but a subjective, almost instinctual outpouring. Perhaps a truly *instinctual* film was impossible; so much time—hours, often—had to go into setting up each individual shot. But Roberto—with his grief over Romano; his arduous romance with Magnani; his termination of the longest romantic attachment of his life; his complicated financial maneuvers; his hubris in embarking on a production without clear ideas, script, or story outline; his running away and avoidance of his film as one avoids homework in school; his not knowing himself how the story would work out, so that even after shooting had ended, he still had to devise an ending[76]—Roberto created conditions of such chaos and confusion that instinct was the only order left.

As he shot, whether from inattention or purposefulness, his focus shifted from the social group to the individual. All the secondary characters—the boy's sister, brother, and girlfriend—receded into the background. Every emotion crystallized onto Edmund, the incarnation of dead Romano. Now Rossellini doesn't just illustrate behavior as before; he follows obsessively henceforth, "spying on every minute reaction of consciousness, into the most secret self."[77] Little things Romano once did, like the way Edmund plays with a piece of pipe as though it were a gun, became integrated into the film. In *Paisà* there had been optimism despite destitution; there was never doubt Pasquale would survive; and originally *Deutschland* was to have ended with Dietrich saying, "The little boy can finally rest" over his living body. But now nothing has turned out as Trombadori and Lizzani had hoped. Germany's fate has melded into Romano's, Roberto's personal agony has melded with Germany's in a struggle of light and darkness. There's no wise and kindly German Communist resistance leader now, so Edmund isn't redeemed. He kills himself instead. He wanders through ruins, alienated from children and adults alike, plays in an abandoned building, sees his father's body trucked away on the street below, and calmly leaps to his death. Year zero. "Everything that goes before held no interest for me," Roberto admitted. The whole film "was conceived specifically for the scene with the child wandering on his own through the ruins.... I only [felt] sure of myself at this decisive moment."[78] The titles read, "This film is dedicated to the memory of my son Romano. *Roberto Rossellini.*"

But it was supposed to have been a German *Roma città aperta* or *Paisà.* It was supposed to have given a message of hope. Of course people felt cheated. What social worth could it have? Where could it lead? Lizzani, trying to make the best of it afterward, tried to explain: "At contact with the German reality, the most tragic in Europe, [Roberto's] strongly impressioned personality led him to a story of a despair without issue; of a boy, wounded by a destiny stronger than he, by a malefic heredity which continues to poison and destroy even after disappearance of the criminal Nazis.... Rossellini sensed that ... he had touched bottom and sought thereafter to regain the difficult slopes that would lead to hope."[79]

But the Communist is describing only the material, political side of Rossellini's film. A woman comes to kneel beside Edmund, reminding us of a *pietà*—the generic composition of Christ's mother holding her son's dead body. We realize that Edmund has sensed the horror of himself and his world—has, like the Italians in *Paisà*, confronted shame and leapt from an impulsive longing for liberty. Thus paradoxically Edmund's death is an affirmation of the spirit, no more nihilistic than the deaths that end *Roma città aperta* and *Paisà*. Edmund becomes a kind of Christ figure. Rossellini is turning to God for answers.

After Romano's death, all Rossellini's films, to some extent, will attempt to confront death.

"When I lost my nine-year-old son . . . ," he reflected decades later, "I naturally asked myself all sorts of questions. Strangely, my father's death had not made me pose these sorts of problems. But the death of my son was a terrifying thing, because I think that to confront death . . . there's a need for a dose of gigantic heroism. So I searched, desperately, for consolations. Where do you find them? You find them either in reality reality reality, that is, in imagining life as a biological phenomenon with a scientific precision, etc., etc., etc., with all its coordinates. And then there's another aspect, isn't there, that's completely metaphysical? So I was in a tempest—an enormous one, I'd say, in this period—yet it seems clear to me that I accepted the biological rather than the other aspect. And yet . . . perhaps because of the education, so Catholic, so Christian, that I had, this idea of the hero was born in me . . . , [this idea] of risking everything."[80]

By this time—1971—tension between science and faith had become a key to Rossellini's work. But years of searching—and filming—had passed before he had "accepted the biological side"—if he ever really did. "I never believed, I never had faith," he often claimed, after 1968.[81] But he did believe, always, in his fashion.[82] He was no more capable of separating matter from spirit than he was of separating himself from Romano, the living from the dead. Solutions excluding the dead will not be acceptable in *Europe '51, Voyage in Italy,* and particularly *Deutschland,* when, groping through the dark pains of "metaphysics," he craved faith desperately. Over scenes of devastated Berlin, these words prefaced the film: "When ideologies stray far from the eternal laws of morality and Christian compassion that are at the base of human life, they finish in criminal madness. Even the natural wisdom of childhood becomes contaminated thereby, and gets dragged from one horrible crime to another not less grave, in which, with the ingenuousness of innocence, it believes to find a liberation from guilt."[83]

Edmund's "other" crime, then—his suicide—is an impulse for freedom.

Adriano Aprà shows how Rossellini's dual concern—his search for solutions to Germany and death—finds expression in the point-of-view crosscuts (the "eyecuts," Aprà calls them) that now suddenly abound in *Deutschland* in contrast to the camera's more objective perspective in *Roma città aperta* and *Paisà*. Edmund looks at /the ruins; then /jumps to his death. Hitherto new Italian cinema had emphasized objective reality (Aprà says) and Rossellini had been assimilable into materialist projects for creating a new world. But now such approaches seem dead ends to Rossellini; objectivity holds no solutions. The trouble lies within us, in what we believe; and so he turns to subjectivity, and accents "eyecuts." The problem—

for Roberto after Romano, for Europe after the war—is to construct a *way of looking*, "to deal with things that cut across the 'eye of reason.'" Thus in the movies to come, those with Ingrid Bergman particularly, Rossellini will examine everything that "cuts eyes": his movies will have lots and lots of subjective point-of-view shots. Perhaps an investigation of the irrational will suggest solutions. In any case, so-called "objectivity" will henceforth be colored by the subjectivity of definite cultural perspectives.[84]

King Vidor once said, "Something about the lens is very akin to the human consciousness which looks out at the universe. I am a camera—we are all cameras. We are recording eyes, you know, we look out and record and we use our consciousness to do this. The motion-picture camera is the [tool closest] to the human sense of observation and sense of the universe. When the men land on the moon, I land on the moon—because I am conscious of it, and I take it into myself, and I am landing on the moon. This is what happens with a motion-picture camera. It approximates the consciousness that everyone has."[85]

Edmund inhabits a "Martian" landscape, says Rosati. The Third Reich's last soldier, the sole not to submit, he expresses himself only in walking, yet he moves in a strange way, not because he is already old, but because he is the boy of the future, whom the world is not ready for, an ambiguous symbol of something horrible and dying, of something sublime and blooming. Year zero is at an end when Edmund lies dead on the ground.[86]

Edmund is completely "other," agrees Aprà. He has nothing to do with the so-called realist attitude. He's an absolutely insane character, whose eyes, like the baby's in *2001: A Space Odyssey*, are already open in his mother's womb; he has understood everything; he's 2,001 years old. Nor does the film have anything to do with realist attitudes. It's an expressionist film: reality is deranged at a luministic level: light without sfumato, irreal, lunar, Martian. Light expresses Edmund's rapport with reality. Sharp, sourceless splotches of light when he crosses the street; light from an oven suggesting hell; crepuscular, asphyxiating light after murdering the father. "Edmund reaches the door; it's dark, night. He comes in, turns on the light, comes up the stairs, sits at the top, puts his hand on his face, the light goes off, he startles: if you like, the decision of suicide comes from that light that goes off . . . : a decision of life and death due to a luministic fact, as in Sternberg. He goes out into the night, and at the door there's an incredible light, a 5,000-kilowatt beam put there purposely. This is a fantasy film that breaks completely with reality, so there's no need for verisimilitude, no obligation to follow some hypothetical consequentialness [logic], either narratival, psychological, or luminist. [Critics had savaged Rossellini for insufficient narrative logic.] The organ sonata, for example: during a walk where the camera follows only Edmund without any external reference, at a certain moment the roofless church is framed, just it alone, like a wedge placed there purposely, and the effect is absolutely irrealistic, because the continuity is contradicted and complicated by this unique extraneous element. The same thing occurs at first sight of the church on the mountain at the beginning of *Il miracolo*, an abusive forcing of the spatial continuity. It's like the sight of the slums in Naples in *Paisà*: not subjective from the Negro who looks and sees, but two distinct universes which encounter and confront each other. . . . Rossellini, forcing realistic space/time continuity trusts not the image but the idea behind the image: he wants us to believe in the idea, not in the image; and the idea follows other than realistic courses. And this implies, for example, that the church in *Il miracolo* could be a desire, a dream, an aspiration that is realized, comes true, becomes actual, at the film's end."[87]

Edmund enacts the Rossellinian masterplot we noted in *Paisà*. He wanders a maze, half-consciously seeking a solution to the catastrophe of his life. The insert of the church and organ and, climactically, the sight of his father's funeral from high-up in the cave-like abandoned building trigger Edmund's sense of guilt, a desire to join his father, a wish to be pure: thus his impulse: he leaps. It's the only way to be pure. In so doing he destroys his Nazi heritage and, escaping history, creates the year zero from which a new beginning may be made.

Edmund's story combines three familiar myths: the hero who assumes the burden of a nation's faults; the redemption of destroyed virtue by one person's suffering; the notion that true insight into reality is accorded to simple souls (children, saints, fools, the insane). Present also are the "three great recurring metaphors" that, according to the Jesuit Fantuzzi, run through the whole of aesthetic-mystic Christian literature—and most of Rossellini: the labyrinth in which the soul gets lost and seeks itself; the chasm into which the soul falls; the mountain up which the soul climbs wearily.[88] Religion, previously, had been peripheral to Rossellini's concerns; the religious elements in *Roma città aperta* and *Paisà* had been more humanist than transcendent. But upon Romano's death, a transcendent God became a vital necessity, and for the next ten years Rossellini's movies try to bridge the gap between this world and the next, between the living and the dead. In *Paisà* he had looked to the human heart as source for impulse; in *Deutschland* he begins to look to God and religious symbolism as its sources: the church, the organ, the funeral, the *pietà*. By *Il miracolo* and *Stromboli* Rossellini will have become an Augustinian, convinced of the corruptness of our nature and our lack of freedom, of our inability to unite mind and heart, scientific knowledge and feeling—and thus achieve freedom—without a process of healing that is impossible without God's help. At the time of *Deutschland*, however, Rossellini is still groping, still too close to Romano for commitment. Velati observes that faith and surety in religious myths seem on the verge of crumbling in *Deutschland*: "The camera is always in movement, as though the author does not succeed in finding parameters he can trust enough to make judgments."[89] But faith, like death, requires no judgment. Over Edmund's *pietà*, the camera is still. It's a sort of salvation.

The Catholic Brunello Rondi, contrary to our interpretation, views Rossellini as "despairing of history." He says people complain that no reason is given for Edmund's solitude, but the reason for his solitude—for others' rejecting attitudes toward him in this infernal, biblical, destroyed city—is less important than the fact of solitude, its negativity, its eternal note of despair. In Rossellini suffering, the call for total love, attains absolute desperation, and is glacial, without redemption, without exit. After this film we neither know nor even hope that a better world will come or that humanity can find a path. Rossellini is no historian or dramatist; he does not know how to investigate the profound crises of history and milk all possibilities of tragedy. His is the world of the victim who, when he falls, falls never to get up again, as under the burden of forces more than human, in a desperate religious vision of evil suffered by innocents.[90]

But the soul has to reach bottom in order to locate itself and rise again, retorts Fantuzzi. Rossellini's originality consists not in his metaphors but in his using them for "spiritually realistic descriptions" of the impulses that shake a soul, "for it's he who leaps with Edmund and it's he who climbs with Karin (in *Stromboli*); it's again he who gets lost in the labyrinth, who seeks and finds himself; and all this is seen as a miracle (or a succession of miracles) that happen in daily life . . . the intervention of divine grace into everyday life."[91]

In *Roma città aperta* and *Paisà*, points out Aprà, many paths existed offering varied realities: Magnani's, the priest's, the worker's, the intellectual Communist's. But now Rossellini has lost humanistic faith; in *Una voce umana* and *Deutschland* the many streets cease to exist; he creates a tabula rasa, eliminating all possibilities. But possibilities are therefore infinite: Edmund opens the world for us.[92] Rossellini should have condemned Edmund, but he makes him a saint instead.[93] "It's a film so atrociously pessimistic," wrote Truffaut, "that the leisure is left to the spectator to think that young Edmund kills himself to save humanity whereas it's more likely that he can't bear living lies.[94] The moral . . . was . . . : this land has been destroyed physically and morally. Little Edmund kills himself to escape contradictions and lies, but his suicide will perhaps be a sacrifice: reconstruction is needed."[95] "Ultimately his choice between playing and death matters little to us; what mattered was to show its freedom," concludes Philippe Niel.[96]

It is these last interpretations that Rossellini intended. "There is a real light of hope," he said in 1967. "The child's gesture of committing suicide is a gesture of abandon, of weariness, by which he leaves behind him all the horror he has seen and believed in, for he has acted exactly according to a precise ethic [in killing his father]. He senses the vanity of this and the light lights up in him and he has this moment of abandon . . . , as when one becomes aware . . . ; he abandons himself to this great sleep which is death, and from there is born the new way of life, the new way of seeing, the accent of hope and faith in the future, in the future and in people."[97]

Thus "year zero" means the point before history begins. It is when we can begin again from nothing.

It was "the most beautiful Italian film" he had ever seen, said Charlie Chaplin.[98]

Anna

Typically, after sending a message to Serato begging him to drop dead, Roberto had assumed a paternal role toward Magnani's son Luca. Anna, still nominally married to Alessandrini, maintained a certain independence: her own apartment on Via Amba Aradam and her own room at the Excelsior, across the hall from Roberto's small, inside, sixth-floor cubicle. "At a certain point," De Marchis writes, "there was no one at the Excelsior Hotel where Anna and Roberto lived who was not current with their skirmishes and their inevitable grand reconciliations. Their life was very brilliant. They went to all the parties together and dined gaily in all the capital's most famous nightclubs."[99]

"Anna would sleep all day long," said Roberto. "She'd get up at eight at night, whereas I'd start swobbing away at 7:30 in the morning. I'd get back late and wake her up. 'Ohhhh! What time is it?' 'Eight o'clock.' 'Ohhh, can't you wait five minutes?' 'No. I can't. Look, let's go eat, okay?' She'd get up slowly, she'd get dressed, and we'd go out to a restaurant. We'd sit down at a table and order something to eat. She'd stare at me like this: 'My God, what an ignoble spectacle . . . ! You eat so greedily!' 'Well, I'm hungry, after all!' 'Okay. I'm not eating.' 'Ah! You want to play the victim?' 'I'm not playing the victim. If you don't mind, I'm not eating!' 'But, eat something! You immediately look for the chance to play the victim.' And I'd go back to eating. 'Hey, mister!'—to someone we didn't know at a nearby table—'Look at him! Is he a greedy eater or not?' The gentleman, very embarrassed: 'Ah, he has a good appetite!' 'Oh you're a hypocrite.' She did things like that, every day, until two or three at night, and then, at that moment, all of a sudden there'd be a surge of joy, ecstasy, reconciliation. And at 7:30 I'd get up to go."[100]

Roberto, on his side, ill supported Anna's absences back to Via Amba Aradam and threatened to throw himself off the balcony. The first time she broke her nails holding him back. The second time she went to the balcony and called serenely: "Come have a little jump."

Their squabbles were inevitable, thought Marcella De Marchis, given the double jealousies, human and artistic, that rose out of their interdependence. Passionate and egocentric both of them, their affinities drew them apart; instinctively, each sought to prevail over the other.[101] "They saw themselves in each other," said Father Antonio Lisandrini, Roberto's Franciscan friend, "and also their contradiction. It was a phenomenon of identification and contradiction. 'I've put my mark on him!' she'd boast. They spent an entire week in the bedroom without coming out. Finally Roberto slipped away while she was in the bathroom. She came after him

in her bathrobe, through the corridors and lobby of the Excelsior, screaming at him."[102]

Roberto, while slowly completing *Deutschland*, had been worrying
about *Una voce umana*. It was impossible to release a 35-minute movie by
itself. It looked almost impossible to find a suitable companion subject.
"He read mountains of books," said Fellini. "He asked friends and writers,
artists and tramps. Often he'd get as pale as possible and declare dramatically: 'I have to start shooting in five days!' and he'd stare at us—Tullio
Pinelli and me—almost with hate. I could only smile back, sweetly.[103]

Once, when Magnani saw Fellini in a restaurant, she said to him, "Instead of sitting here eating and getting fat and losing your romantic air of
dying from hunger, why aren't you writing me a wonderful story for your
crazy friend Roberto?"[104]

At the Excelsior a few days later, Fellini told her a story about a whore
who is kept imprisoned all night in a star's bathroom. It was an idea he
would use a few years later for *Le notti di Cabiria*. Magnani listened with obvious impatience. "Federì," she said, "do you really think that someone like
me lets herself be locked up in a toilet by some shit of an actor?"[105]

"One day at Amidei's," said Fellini, "when we'd gone over all the ideas
suggested till then, the situation looked positively distressing to us. Sergio
Amidei was pacing the room gravely, murmuring softly: 'We need . . . we
need . . .' Pinelli was nervously and noisily paging through the thick volumes
of Pirandello's novels. Rossellini was shaking his head silently and with an unbelievable severity was rejecting to himself numerous proposals that we didn't
even hear. It was 3:30 in the afternoon. All of a sudden, I saw, very exactly, the
story's two principal characters, and I felt, vaguely, its mechanics. But I'm timid.
I didn't have courage to propose a story that had taken form that very second. I started yawning to gain time and think. Finally, with a stupid, embarrassed little laugh, I said I remembered reading, long ago, a story I'd really
liked. Amid a skeptical silence, I babbled confusedly that it was about a mystic
fool, who one day meets a tramp, and takes him for Saint Joseph, etc., etc.

"The story had made Rossellini stand up, Amidei stop walking, and
Pinelli close his books. All three came near me: 'Where'd you read it?
When'd you read it? In a book of short stories? In a magazine?' Amidei
was like a prosecuting attorney. Cursing the timidity that now prevented
me from being the true master of the situation, I went on lying, entangling
myself in any names and titles I could think of: 'A French magazine, no,
Russian. I don't remember. Maybe it was a book, maybe . . .' Finally, making a worthy effort, I revealed the truth. It was my own idea. Entirely
mine. 'Word of honor. I swear it!'

"The enthusiasm died down. Amidei was watching me suspiciously.
Pinelli was grinning, a bit surprised. Rossellini was phoning Magnani, already giving orders for getting started."[106]

*

She loved the story—*Il miracolo (The Miracle)*, it was called. Together with Pinelli and Fellini, Roberto and Anna left immediately for Amalfi where at the Hotel Luna, a converted convent, they worked on a treatment. The opening scene was intensely difficult: Nannina, a demented vagabond played by Magnani, encounters a tramp whom she takes for Saint Joseph and, amid a carnal ecstasy that for her is religious, unwittingly conceives a child by him. Pinelli and Fellini spent two weeks on just this one scene, trying to establish the proper tone, the perfect mixture of enchantment and realism, carnality and piety, that would propel the entire story. Nannina would be mocked by her townsfolk; but firm in her belief that she was carrying the Christ child, she would climb to a mountain church and give birth amid a joyous clamor of bells. Edmund's death has been answered.

A sense of life's sacredness pervades all Rossellini's cinema, but rarely so emphatically as in *Il miracolo* (and *Voyage in Italy*), where biblical symbolism mingles with pagan and animist motifs, where the sacred is never distinguished from the sexual. Nannina's presence is physical, almost animal-like. She chews on grass while murmuring "Che paradiso"; a goat wakes her after intercourse; her pregnancy is identified with a waterfall (water, the source of life in primitive mythology); her wanderings through the maze of the town and its people suggests a way of the cross, even to a crown of thorns and an assent to Calvary; and there in the cave-like church she moans "Mio santo figlio" caressing her belly. Impulse is physical in this film but unlike *Deutschland* truth bursts forth not to end an old world but to found a new one, "perhaps to make the revolution."[107]

"Everything is carnal almost to the point of obscenity," Guarner remarks.[108] "An adventure and a cosmogony all at the same time," Godard describes it.[109] They both paraphrase Saint Paul: "All nature groans the pains of childbirth until is revealed in man and the whole cosmos the glory of the children of God." But the only miracle foreseen in Fellini's script had been a fantasy one, in which we would share while bells from all over Amalfi join the bell rung by Nannina. But Rossellini, after shooting this ending, amputated it. "For Rossellini the miracle is a real fact," Rohmer observes; "he didn't want to depict the poetry of craziness but the grandeur of faith triumphing over craziness, as in *Stromboli* and *Europe '51*, over all systems, all explanations. 'This film,' [said] Rossellini, 'isn't a symbol: these people are like that, I've shown them the way they are.' "[110]

Roberto participated in the writing from time to time. He was supposed to be quitting smoking but would cheat when Anna wasn't around, and then hide the butts in his sleeve. "La Magnani was a sort of divinity or mystery queen," recalled Fellini. "She appeared only toward one, always preceded by a menagerie of dogs: bassets, Alsatians, dark, snapping beasts that announced her like a menacing little court. She was always tired, excited, or in a bad humor. She seemed offended, threatening, and resentful, but actually her manner hid timidity and unhappiness."[111]

She quarreled endlessly with Roberto. What did they quarrel about? According to De Sica, "she maintained that in a previous fight, Roberto had come at her with a bottle, not with the blunt end, as he claimed, but with the sharp end, as she said. And so it was true that he, Roberto, wanted to kill her, it was true he was a criminal. This was the tenor of their fights, repeated two or three times daily."[112] "In two hours of Anna there's everything," Roberto declared; "summer, winter, tenderness, fury, jealousy, fighting, break-up, goodbye, tears, repentance, pardon, ecstasy, and then, once again, suspicion, anger, blows."[113]

No sooner did Fellini get back to Rome than Roberto phoned insisting he return. Magnani wanted something rewritten, he claimed. The real reason, Fellini divined, was something else. Roberto was afraid to stay alone with Anna in the hotel at springtime. He was scared, too, that she might walk out on the film. Federico's presence would have a calming effect. The next morning, out of the blue he suggested Federico play the part of Saint Joseph. It was obvious he wanted him around for protection. "He went on insisting, like a child. So I accepted."[114] Besides, why not? Acting might be fun.

"What would have been the point of trying to find someone else?" argued Roberto, later. "When Federico talked about a character, he became the character. Besides, he loves acting."

Federico smiled. "Acting, I think, is the easiest job in the world. It's weird how the brain ceases to function as soon as you find yourself in front of a camera. You forget all your worries. Others think for you. Your responsibilities are reduced to a simple, modest effort of memory. And then everyone's watching you, everyone's taking care of you. During the few days I was a 'star,' all I had to do was raise my hand slightly, and right away twenty people would start crying, 'Cigarettes! Cigarettes! A cigarette for Saint Joseph! Quick!' Yes, it's a nice life, really."[115]

Saint Joseph had to be blond, however, and Fellini's hair was dark. Roberto insisted he have it dyed. Fellini gave in; he wondered what he'd look like. What he did not know, when they entered a Naples barbershop, was that Roberto and Aldo Tonti, the cameraman, had already talked to the barber. They were on a delicate mission, they had explained. They had this friend, a very nice guy, really, but he had changed sexually and become a bit of a pederast, and he wanted his hair dyed, but he was very sensitive. "I understand," said the barber, who promised to make light of the affair. But there was an air of repressed laughter just the same, when Fellini walked into the shop. And he walked out a blazing yellow. "Fellini's return to Rome with that impossible hair," laughed Pinelli, "was quite an event"[116]

Roberto had handed Fellini a million-lire check to convince him to do the picture, then had asked for it back an hour later. Now he gave him a dark red topolino worth 650,000 lire; it was Fellini's first car.

Rossellini, said Tonti, "put all his talent into this new work. And he wanted everyone to know it was a homage to his companion. . . . He was up at the first light of dawn. La Magnani, however, rose around two in the afternoon, and this rather limited our work hours when scenes involved her."[117] It also made it difficult to photograph her in the morning sun, which they needed to get an air of enchantment in the light. "I can't do art at nine in the morning," she groaned. But work would have been slow and meticulously difficult in any case, because even more than in *Deutschland* Roberto wanted his heroine to be tracked continuously and closely by the camera, and other angles were melodramatically high. Yet many days went by with no work at all, dedicated instead to "tower hunts": Anna just had to have a Saracen tower like Leonor Fini's, her painter friend—at least until a freak little avalanche on the Amalfi-Positano road terrified her into renouncing her expeditions. She paid twenty dollars for a fisherman's cottage instead.

The sparrows didn't cooperate either. They refused to stay put while Magnani crossed a meadow. After a bit of lead was tied to fifty of them and guards were posted to keep cars away, it finally appeared they would get the scene. Then came a big American car. Marcellino Caracciolo signaled politely, but it kept on coming. Magnani screamed scatalogically, and the rest of the troupe joined in. "You bastard! Cunt! I piss in your nostrils!" shouted Roberto. The car went away but five minutes later came back, and stopped. Out stepped a big Texan, who took a rifle from his luggage compartment and, aiming at Roberto, started toward him. A hundred fifty yards separated them. But Roberto, instead of running away, started toward him. "Come on," he jeered. "Fire. Bastard. Pppppprrrr! Come on, fire. I'll kill you! Brrrrrrrrrr!" Unprepared for lunatics, the Texan fired twice in the air, got back in his car, and left. The scene was ruined, however. The cowardly crew had trampled the sparrows in their haste to flee.[118]

Amalfi was Roberto's favorite place. It fit *Il miracolo* perfectly. "There are many beggars," he said. "Some poor devils are convinced they've seen Satan. One of them told me one day, 'I've met the werewolf, I ran over him on my bicycle last night.' They are mad, crazed by the sun. But they have a power few of us possess—the power of the imagination.[119] I once asked Fra Raffaele if he had ever had visions. 'Yes, all the time.' 'What do you see?' 'The saint.' 'Which saints?' 'All of them.' 'And the Virgin Mary?' 'Yes, signore, from head to foot.' From head to foot, not just in close-up! That's how I conceived Anna Magnani's part."[120]

The Amalfitani were born actors. One old beggar took to his role tormenting Magnani as though born to commedia dell'arte and improvised a skit with clattering milk cans. Another was given Fra Raffaele's lines about visions; this was Peparuolo, who would play an important role in *Francesco* a few years later.

On March 29, 1948 *Paisan* finally opened commercially in New York. "It is rare, indeed, that the public is presented with a film in which a whole new way of expressing staggering ideas is daringly displayed," wrote Bosley Crowther in *The New York Times*, in praise of "the cryptic and crude visualizations of Rossellini's 'documentary' style."[121] Conti, inspired by Roberto's desire to exact money from his American partners, had refused to deliver prints to Foreign Film Productions, which had led to a suit, which had at last been resolved when Landau, sick of his alliance with always feuding lunatics, sold his interest to Conti on February 17, 1948. Meanwhile Burstyn and Lopert made peace, agreeing to share the profits. For the English edition, Roberto had put stretches of Italian dialogue into English. On his own initiative Burstyn changed the title, adding the "n"; inserted maps and narration between the sequences, sometimes slightly changing the newsreel footage; added a map notably between the monks and "The Po Delta" sequences, where Rossellini, in order to link the fraternity theme, had had no intercalary material at all; and put into slow motion the moment when Jim is shot in "Sicily" and, duplicating the scene of the German soldier shooting, placed this prior to Jim's death as well as after it, to clarify what happened. The Legion of Decency condemned again: *Paisan* tended "to condone illicit killing" and contained "suggestive sequences." Burstyn's publicity agreed, showing, Arthur Mayer wrote, "a young lady disrobing herself with an attentive male visitor reclining by her side on what was obviously not a nuptial couch."[122] But it was more because of the American soldiers speaking English, according to Fae Miske, Burstyn's secretary, that *Paisan* substantially outgrossed *Open City*. The earlier picture had played exclusively at the World Theater, but *Paisan's* GIs attracted interest from theater owners all over the country.[123] No foreign film had ever done so well. According to Arthur Mayer, the gross was close to $1 million.[124]

David Selznick decided to reopen negotiations. "We have been indecisive," he declared, "I blame myself." He wanted to have "the whip hand" and "tie up" Roberto exclusively. But Roberto was being cagey. RKO had offered him $125,000 for sixteen weeks, he let it be rumored, while suggesting various profit-sharing and distribution deals with Selznick and insisting on an "association" rather than an "employment" agreement. Both men were anxious to do *Mary Magdalene* in Technicolor and English with Alida Valli, Greta Garbo, or Jennifer Jones. (It looked as though a flurry of big Biblical pictures was about to begin.) A circus story; a toreador tale; a drama set in contemporary Palestine with Jennifer Jones as a middle-class refugee; and a version of *Camille* in two episodes (renunciation and death) with Magnani and Louis Jourdan were also discussed. Roberto was "enormously enthusiastic" about Jennifer Jones, Selznick bragged, a bit gullibly: Roberto was well aware that Selznick was about to marry her.[125]

To negotiate directly, Jenia Reissar, Selznick's London representative, had gone to Rome in mid-April. ("*The Miracle* has been passed for screening by the Vatican—so Rossellini tells me!" she reported.[126]) Rossellini was coming to London in May to present *Deutschland im Jahre Null*, and Selznick sensed a deal was about to finalize. "There have been many rumors that Ingrid Bergman is dealing with Rossellini," he noted on April 28, and sent Reissar three separate cables that day urging speed.

"On the evening of [May] 7th," wrote Roberto, "I got a call from Mr. Potsius of Minerva Films ... who told me he wanted to see me to give me a beautiful present. I thought he was referring to my birthday [May 8], as I'd sold him *Roma città aperta* for a mouthful of bread when it was a 'bomb' and he had profitably 'exploited' it when it was a 'masterpiece.' The next day he brought me [a] letter, which he had already read. Sometime before Minerva had been burning its accumulated correspondence and Mr. Potsius had opened all the letters without checking if they were actually for him."[127]

Later he said he had been feuding with Minerva, and had repeatedly hung up on them when they had phoned. But when the letter arrived he made a concession. Normally, like many Romans, Roberto had little respect for mail. He not only didn't answer letters, often he didn't bother to open them. If it was important, they'd telephone, he said. But on this occasion the strange handwritten letter on blue stationery, plus the foreign stamps, plus Potsius's obvious excitement perked Roberto's curiosity. He asked Liana Ferri to translate it for him.

"Dear Mr. Rossellini," the letter said, "I saw your films *Open City* and *Paisan,* and enjoyed them very much. If you need a Swedish actress who speaks English very well, who has not forgotten her German, who is not very understandable in French, and who, in Italian knows only 'ti amo,' I am ready to come and make a film with you. Best regards, Ingrid Bergman."[128]

Such a communication should have galvanized Roberto. The writer was the top female star in Hollywood. Her last three pictures had grossed over $17.5 million in the U.S. alone. If she agreed to film with him—and she was begging to—Roberto could virtually write his own contract with the Americans and his personal credit in Italy would be almost unlimited.

Instead, to Ferri's surprise, he just sat there looking blank. "Well, who is this Ingrid Bergman?" he finally asked. Not surprisingly, since Bergman's films were only now beginning to play in Italy and since Roberto couldn't care less about most movies, especially Hollywood commercial ones, he had never heard of her. Marcella, though, remembered seeing her in *The Bells of St. Mary's.*[129]

It did not take Roberto long to realize he had hit the jackpot. Typically, he started phoning everyone he knew, confiding the news to each in greatest secrecy. "I've got Bergman!" he told Amidei. "Yes, her, Ingrid Bergman. What, you don't believe it? Look, I've no time to joke. I need a subject, right away, something Italian, but suitable for an actress like her. Right away, okay? See you tomorrow!"[130]

To Bergman he sent an immediate cable:

I JUST RECEIVED WITH GREAT EMOTION YOUR LETTER WHICH HAPPENS TO ARRIVE ON THE ANNIVERSERY OF MY BIRTHDAY AS THE MOST PRECIOUS GIFT STOP IT IS ABSOLUTELY TRUE THAT I DREAMED TO MAKE A FILM WITH YOU AND FROM THIS VERY MOMENT I WILL DO EVERYTHING THAT SUCH DREAM BECOMES REALITY AS SOON AS POSSIBLE STOP I WILL WRITE YOU A LONG LETTER TO SUBMIT TO YOU MY IDEAS STOP WITH MY ADMIRATION PLEASE ACCEPT THE EXPRESSION OF MY GRATITUDE TOGETHER WITH MY BEST REGARDS.[131]

Open City had mightily impressed Ingrid back in 1946. "The realism and simplicity ... was heart-shocking," she recalled. "No one looked like an actor and no one talked like an actor. There was darkness and shadows, and sometimes you couldn't hear, and sometimes you couldn't even see it, but that's the way it is in life. . . . It was as if you were *there*, involved in what was going on, and you wept and bled for them."[132] But it wasn't until the spring of 1948 when, wandering around New York, spotting Rossellini's name by chance outside a theater, and going in alone to see *Paisan*, that Ingrid had decided to write Roberto. Then, she claims, no one had any idea who he was or how to get hold of him. So her letter, written but unmailed, had lain around for weeks, until Ingrid, stopped on a Hollywood street by an autograph hunter who turned out to be Italian, was given an address: Minerva Films, Rome, Italy.

Ingrid's inability to obtain Roberto's address was typical of her. The reason Selznick knew of her "dealing" with Rossellini even before Rossellini did was that it was his wife Irene (daughter of M-G-M mogul Louis B. Mayer) who had put into Ingrid's head the quaint idea of writing Roberto personally, rather than going through the customary chain of agents and representatives. And it was David Selznick who had brought Ingrid from Sweden to Hollywood in 1939 and had managed her career with absolutism for seven years. True, he had built her into the nation's biggest female star. But he had pocketed most of her earnings and featured her in a series of memorable roles—*Casablanca, For Whom the Bell Tolls, Gaslight, Saratoga Trunk, The Bells of St. Mary's, Spellbound,* and *Notorious*—that had left her feeling unfulfilled and frustrated with Hollywood in general. As soon as her contract had expired, Ingrid had left Selznick's aegis and embarked on a series of independent, unmemorable productions—*Arch of Triumph, Joan of Arc, Under Capricorn*—at salaries of up to a quarter of a million dollars a piece—enormous sums by the day's standards, plus profit percentages as high as forty percent. Ingrid's romantic streak equaled her money hunger. She was eager to work with directors she admired—William Wyler, Billy Wilder, George Stevens, and Rossellini, among them—and Irene Selznick had suggested she write short notes to each of them.

In a four-page letter Roberto outlined to Ingrid his idea for a movie: "Some time ago ... I think it was at the end of February last, I was traveling by car along the Sabine (a region north of Rome). Near the source of the Farfa an unusual scene called my attention." It was a detention camp for displaced women from all over Europe, surrounded by barbed wire and police. "A guard ordered me to go away. One must not speak to these undesirable women." But one of them, a Latvian, attracted him. "In her clear eyes, one could read a mute intense despair. I put my hand through the barbed wires and she seized my arm, just like a shipwrecked person would clutch at a floating board. The guard drew near, quite menacing. I got back to my car."

The memory haunted him. He obtained authorization and returned to the camp. The woman was gone. She had married a soldier to escape the camp. "Shall we go together and look for her?" Her husband had taken her to Stromboli, a tiny island north of Sicily with a small population of primitive impoverished fishermen—and a continuously active volcano. "She followed this man, being certain that she had found an uncommon creature, a savior, a refuge and a protection after so many years of anguish and beastly life. . . . But instead she is stranded in this savage island, all shaken up by the vomiting volcano, and where the earth is so dark and the sea looks like mud saturated with sulphur. And the man lives beside her and loves her with a kind of savage fury, is just like an animal not knowing how to struggle for life and accepting placidly to live in deepest misery. . . .

"I am certain, I feel, that with you near me, I could give life to a human creature who, following hard and bitter experiences, finds peace at last and complete freedom from all selfishness. That being the only true happiness which has ever been conceded to mankind, making life more simple and nearer to creation."[133]

How typical of Roberto was this letter! The invitation to adventure together, the evocative storytelling, the mystic morality, the sense of suffering and truth! How typical too was the calculation: as though from Ingrid's short note he had instantly divined just the right tones to captivate her. How typical, finally, were the lies: Roberto had not even seen the detention camps. It was the producer Carlo Ponti who, after reading about them in the papers, had gone visiting along with Fellini, Pinelli, Flaiano, and Amidei. A tall blonde girl had come after them as they were leaving, running parallel to their car from inside the fence—an image that had so moved Amidei that he thought of it immediately when Roberto demanded a subject for Ingrid.[134] Nor had the tall blonde girl gone to Stromboli, so there was no point "looking for her" (and they never did). And Stromboli itself was not Roberto's idea but Renzo Avanzo's, who two years earlier had been cruising around the Lipari Islands shooting underwater documentaries with Uberta Visconti in a motorized fishing boat, and had been so awestruck by the sight of Stromboli that he had written a story around it for Magnani, and had proposed it to Roberto.[135]

In the meantime, *Deutschland im Jahre Null* was shown in London with success. No one seemed to feel it was up to *Open City* or *Paisan*, Reissar reported, "but our English critics raved about it!!"[136] No, it wasn't as good as the others, concurred the distinguished documentarist Basil Wright, but "it has more real movie in it than anything else one is likely to see in a long time. Rossellini has got right inside the physical and psychological Berlin of today; that is, he has completely understood the feeling of living in a slow, dark, and hopeless nightmare of mental and bodily misery. . . . What one misses is the different sympathy of observation which could have come had the director seen Berlin *as an Italian*; it is no doubt one of Rossellini's greatest assets that he is able to enter so deeply into the feelings and outlook of those around him, but here he has identified so completely that it might be a film made by a German."[137]

Selznick, meanwhile, was convinced Rossellini was verbally committed to him and that only a few details remained to be worked out. Reporters were phoning, the press was rife with rumors, and he was eager to broadcast the good news. But Reissar advised otherwise. "It is not safe to make any announcement," she wrote, "as Rossellini changes his mind too often. I am afraid you will be as amazed as Mr. Lewis and I were, when Rossellini arrived here [London] last Friday, ostensibly to discuss with me a story he had in mind for Miss Jones, but actually to change the terms of his contract!.... Rossellini tried to pretend that I had misunderstood his original suggestion, but Mr. Lewis [who had been present earlier] soon put him straight about that! Rossellini got out of it by saying that he must have expressed himself badly." Roberto maintained he had not changed his terms, and that Reissar's letters had been mistranslated. She did not believe him. "Rossellini's behaviour is typically Italian, and personally I do not trust him. This is the second time he has changed his mind about terms and conditions.... [Furthermore], at the outset of our negotiations, [he] assured me he could not only provide all the finance for our picture, but also find the dollars. It is now clear that he has no financial backing at all, and that in order to make a picture he either has to get the finance from a producing company, or a distributor. The more I deal with Italians, the more I realize how untrustworthy they are and how little importance they attach to their words and obligations."

In this context Roberto did little to offset Reissar's suspicions by proposing he produce a picture for an agreed sum and pocket the balance if he brought it in for less. He explained, she wrote, that "that was the way pictures are made in Italy—which is true! and that if he is willing to take the risk of guaranteeing completion at an agreed figure, he should also be in a position to offset that risk by making a little on another picture."[138]

A few days later, Selznick received a letter.

"Dear Mr. Selznick," wrote Roberto, "I am very happy to know that we are on the verge of an agreement, and it thrills me particularly the idea of making a picture with Miss Jones. It's all right with 'Maria Maddalena,' but I have been trying to find an idea for the first picture to make with her.

"After leaving Miss Reissar in Milan, I have crossed one of North Italy's finest regions, very well-known, I think, in the States also: the one around Lombardy's lakes (Como, Bellagio, Stresa, Villa d'Este, Isole Borromeo). They are very impressive and colourful places, sometimes sunny, sometimes grey and melancholy (that's where the downfall of Fascism took place, and where Mussolini was shot). I was thinking about Miss Jones, and I immediately felt it to be the ideal setting for her character and qualities. I came back to Rome, and I thought of a very modern story, dealing with an emotional impact, that I cannot help associating with certain Greek classics, for instance, Eurypides' 'ALCEST'.

"The story evolves around three characters. The first, a young American woman, who will have to pass through a very varied sequence of emotions. A wealthy American businessman, who has come to Italy to rest, where he discovers he is ill in a way that makes it necessary for him to spare all his energy, giving up his work and any kind of emotion. In his selfishness, he also wishes to give up his wife, who is very much in love with him. The American has brought with him, as a companion and guide, a very cultivated young man, an ironic restless person, who takes advantage of the other man's illness to dominate him spiritually and estrange him from his wife. I shall make of this playboy a typical example of a certain type of present-day youth, indifferent and empty. But the most important character remains the woman. At first, a young wife in love, then almost a nurse, then a woman overcome by her husband's selfishness, and by the disquieting emotion the young man inspires in her. But the young man, an intellectualist, spiritually perverse, could not satisfy her. Therefore, before the three, against a background of the lake, with an implicit feeling of uncouth restlessness, grows an angry circle of impossible loves, that are typical of contemporary society, as I see it, eager to find what it cannot, because it pursues it through the wrong ways. It will be a picture that will condemn the egotisms, the perversions and the hatreds of our epoch. In a dramatic ending, I'll make the woman a symbol of redeeming love as it should be felt, she being the only one among them all, who has understood it. I feel this will be the message that all are waiting for, and I think Miss Jones is particularly suited to this character.

"I should be very grateful if you would inform Miss Jones of this plan, and I am sure she will be attracted by such an engaging role, of which I am convinced she is able.

"I hope you will let me know soon your ideas on this matter, so that I may start preliminary work. Personally, I am very set on this idea, and I'd like to work at it before any other one. . . ."[139]

Indeed it was a "modern" story, twenty years ahead of it time for a film. But Selznick, although regretting postponement of the Palestinian and biblical films, characteristically applauded it. "I like very much [its] background and approach," he wrote Reissar, "and I think it could have tremendous showmanship—if he has not changed his mind between the time he sent the letter and the time I received it."[140]

Selznick's irony was all the more delicate in light of revelations that had arrived along with Roberto's letter. Reissar had met Roberto for dinner in Paris in mid-June and he had pulled out Ingrid's letter and asked her to translate it into French for him. (It was Reissar, incidentally, who had discovered Ingrid for Selznick.) "From the time I read the letter," she recalled, "the whole dinner was spent talking and asking about Ingrid Bergman. He knew about her. He was like a child with it. He kept asking questions about it. He kept taking the letter out."[141]

Apparently it never occurred to Reissar that Roberto knew the letter and was using it as a negotiating ploy.[142] A few days later she got a call from Seymour M. Peyser, a well-known attorney with the firm of Phillips, Nizer, Benjamin & Krim and a vice-president of Lopert Films, who announced he was Rossellini's American lawyer, and that Roberto had asked him to look over his contract with Selznick. "Rossellini never told me he had an American lawyer," Reissar wrote Selznick, with evident frustration, "or that he had seen him in Paris the day before I arrived." A friend in London then informed her, confidentially, that Rossellini was "spending most of his time" with Laudy Lawrence and Ilya Lopert, discussing a deal with them, and "*presumably* assuring them he was free to do so." But when Reissar saw Roberto, he "couldn't have been more charming, or *seem* more enthusiastic. . . . He told me that his collaborator, Amidei, was busy working on a 30-page treatment of the story for Miss Jones for [a production to begin in] November." Together they ironed out the contract terms, but, she wrote, "I am, as I have always said, absolutely uncertain of Rossellini, and of any other Italian with whom we are dealing. As you have already discovered in the case of [N] and [N], they have very little sense of obligation."[143]

"I must say that Rossellini has succeeded in confusing me," Selznick conceded in a five-page memo to Reissar. "Before we get through with these Italians, I suppose we will all be white-haired from their vacillations and changes of minds and curious attitudes toward contracts; but I feel we should be patient with the extraordinarily gifted group with whom we are working." But haste was necessary. "The tremendous and growing interest in Rossellini on the one hand, and his unprecedented vacillations on the other" meant they might lose him, a danger "aggravated by the fact that Ingrid Bergman and others who are after Rossellini may talk him into changing his mind." Selznick hoped Reissar would "assiduously" encourage Rossellini "to sign up Bergman for one of our pictures." (Ingrid had already refused lucrative offers from Selznick to lure her back, even for a single picture.) "Bergman knows that Rossellini is tied exclusively to us. Dietrich also knows it but insists that he has not signed a contract with us; and between Dietrich and her pals among directors, such as Billy Wilder, Bergman and others, we are likely to have many people urging Rossellini not to sign with us." Joseph Cotten had also received a story from Rossellini. "When I told him that Rossellini was to be with us," Selznick continued, "he said this probably accounted for what I gather was a rather assiduous pursuit of Cotten by Rossellini's representatives in America whomever they may be. . . . I am curious as to how many stories Rossellini has floating around and as to how many people. I urge that you [tell him] he is only harming his position in Hollywood, hurting [his] prestige . . . , and damaging rather than enhancing his chances of getting stars . . . by having a lot of people drift around with a lot of stories for which Rossellini allegedly wants them but which don't materialize. . . .

"I assume that we will not deal with Mr. Peyser as Rossellini's representative without instruction from Rossellini. I believe Mr. Peyser to be a responsible lawyer of some standing and I know that he represents Ernest Hemingway. But Rossellini is so curious and so vacillating that perhaps he changed his mind about his attorneys between the time that he told Peyser to contact us, assuming that he did, and the time that Peyser actually did contact us.

"I think you had better keep after [Rossellini], and in close touch with him; that you had better have Arabella [Lemaître, Selznick's new Rome representative] keep in daily contact with him; and that you had better both continue to advise him of the enthusiasm of myself, our organization, yourself, Miss Jones, etc."[144]

Arabella went often to see Roberto at the Excelsior. She was young, beautiful, and stylish. It was the beginning of a life-long friendship. Magnani, she recalled, regarded any female as a potential rival (Roberto even had to keep it a secret when he screened *L'amore* for Marcellina), and would come down to the lobby to inspect her. "Try not to use foul language in front of Arabella," Roberto had asked. "Why not?!" Anna had shrugged. "If she understands, there's nothing wrong with it, and if she doesn't, there's nothing wrong either."[145]

"There is no telling what he intends to do!" Reissar wrote to Selznick. "Undoubtedly I'll have to go to Rome to get the contracts signed. . . . [Perhaps] I can get action from him, when I am on his doorstep! [He] accepted all the points you mentioned over the phone—i.e., accepted them verbally. What he will do when he gets the drafts is a different matter." Meanwhile, he had a story in mind for Dorothy McGuire about a girl in southern Italy chosen to play the Madonna, but blackmailed by a suitor threatening to reveal her father is a former American gangster; she stands up to him, however, and he tells what he knows. The crowd approaches the grotto menacingly on the feast day, but her radiant faith so stuns them that they proclaim her a saint instead. "As you see," commented Reissar, "Rossellini is not lacking in ideas—the difficulty is to get him to concentrate on one or two, not to be continually changing from subject to subject.

"I am writing to you separately about Magnani—from whom I haven't had a word since I wrote, making her an offer. She is as near a lunatic as I've ever come across, and if you hear that I have been put into a mental institution, you'll know that the Italians have driven me there!!"[146]

Anna's lunacy was fatiguing, but it turned Roberto on. "Years after his rupture with Magnani," recalls Jean Gruault, "he still took obvious pleasure recounting how, during a violent argument while they were driving through the Villa Borghese, she suddenly chased him out of the car and, grabbing the wheel, made to run him down. He scampered like a rabbit down the park paths, pursued by the big Buick, its driver evidently determined to destroy him. Exhausted, he finally reached a crossroad where there's a small circular antique temple. He hurried up the steps, four at a time. Magnani screeched to a halt and, seeing him cornered up there, looking so ridiculous, so pitiable, couldn't help laughing. (Remember how she laughed?) She leaned over to open the door and cried to him, almost tenderly, 'Come on! Get in!' It was his favorite love memory."[147]

According to Magnani: "Our fantastic rapport was limited to our work. In our life together it all fell apart, disintegrated, dissolved. I spoke *Ro-*

magno, he Chinese. I was straightforward, he devious. I loyal, he a snake. When I finish my three hours of theater, my day filming, I go back to being a woman, I want to go back to being a woman; but not Rossellini, no: he had to go on acting all the time."[148]

"Roberto ate you up," was the way Rod Geiger put it.[149] And with Anna it was a case of mutual devouring. Her affection for Roberto was enormous, yet she was always afraid of being overwhelmed by him, of being diminished in her personality, and it made her jealous and possessive. "She was terrified, terrified of everything," said Roberto. "She wanted to do *Mother Courage* and I spent hours on the phone with Brecht, discussing interpretation of the text."[150]

Her jealousy, as Roberto continued to philander, was well founded. "Once we bought some oranges on the way back to Rome," Gigetto Pietravalle recalled, "and when we got to Via Amba Aradam Anna, who'd been happy and peaceful all day, began to get suspicious about Roberto's intentions the rest of the evening. She asked the usual questions: 'But you, where are you going now? What are you doing? What are your plans?' At a certain point Roberto got sick of it and turned his back on her, leaving her on the doorstep holding the oranges. Anna froze for a moment then attacked Roberto furiously, throwing an orange at his head. Roberto took flight, pursued by Anna, who managed to burst dozens of oranges all over him. I tried to stop her, as usual, but it was hopeless, and I got a dose of oranges on my head too. Roberto and I were dripping orange juice from head to toe by the time it was over."[151]

In late June, Peyser told *Variety* that Rossellini had contracted for Ilya Lopert to be his American agent and advisor and to distribute *La macchina ammazzacattivi* ("The machine that kills bad people"), which he had just started filming. Lopert, a Russo-Lithuanian with a Grenoble degree, had gone to Rome in April with Peyser, bringing De Sica his Oscar for *Shoeshine*[152] and looking for more such goodies. (De Sica, still in debt from *Shoeshine*, had sold it to Lopert, who bragged it had made him a million dollars.) In Paris Roberto showed them *L'amore*. There was no question of buying it, however. He lacked rights to *Una voce umana*. (Cocteau, as Reissar explained to Selznick, "forgot" he had sold the rights to Abramovitch, and the latter, after the film was made, refused either to sell the rights or allow it to be shown![153]) Roberto also showed them Bergman's letter and the outline for *Stromboli*. Lopert had offered to conduct negotiations with the actress. But Peyser, according to a Selznick agent, felt Roberto was in no position to make pictures in the U.S., or to make a deal with Bergman— because of Magnani. He had sent Rossellini a letter, for example, but because the letter mentioned Bergman, Roberto had been afraid to retain it and had left it instead with Lopert's man in Rome. At one point Magnani had insisted that Roberto cable Lopert calling off all negotiations with Bergman, and Roberto had dutifully complied, first sending the cable, then retracting it by telephone.[154] He had written Bergman in London on July 10 suggesting they meet the first or second weekend in August. Meanwhile, Peyser was trying to clear up his visa problems—a move the Selznick forces saw as an attempt to take Roberto out of their hands—and, to make matters worse, Darryl F. Zanuck, 20th Century-Fox's production chief, was on his way to Rome. "It is almost certain he will go to work on him," cabled Selznick.[155]

Neo-realism = mc²

(Some Theory)

I don't think it's possible to say more bad things about a film than were said about *Germania anno zero*," Rossellini remarked of the Italian-dubbed release of Deutschland im Jahre Null.[1]

"The night of *Germania anno zero*'s premiere was bitter indeed," agreed the Communist partisan hero Gian Carlo Pajetta. "The sight of Berlin in ruins hadn't 'grabbed' the audience. Friends had waved hastily at the director. Negarville and I, maybe because we'd learned that life has its bitter days and that even ruins can have a dark beauty, stayed with Rossellini, there, at a table on the sidewalk outside the Cinema Barberini, as though for a farewell. . . . Perhaps we sensed the era was over when Rome had been so small. Cars were going by, not trucks any more. The year zero of the new Italy was behind us. And not all the hopes had become reality."[2]

Germania anno zero's commercial release would be held off until December. But its invitational screening that May 30, 1948, as part of a series of premieres for the "Circolo del cinema," marks a turning point not only in Rossellini's career, but in Italian culture as well. *Ladri di biciclette* and *La terra trema* had not yet been released, the word "neo-realism" had barely entered Italian consciousness, and already the new Italian cinema was over, a thing of the past, dead. The postwar was over; the Cold War had begun.

A Moral Position

No one agrees about "neo-realism." There is controversy over what it was, dispute over when it died, argument about how it began. It has been contradictorily defined by filmmakers themselves as a matter of content, politics, technique, approach, style, or attitude.[3]

Textbooks parrot that neo-realism was dedicated to exposing Fascism's distortions; to furthering political change; to doing away with plot and script, actors and dramatization, sets and lighting and montage; and to following real people in real time through an actual slice of daily life—and in each case opposite statements would be more accurate. Fascism was avoided in Italian film until the 1960s. Neither political nor social change was specifically promoted; movies had always been vaguely socially conscious. "Neo-realist" movies generally had plot, script, professional actors, dramatization, studio sets and lighting, and elaborate montage. Rossellini was famous for his ellipses, not his respect for real time. Rather than slices of daily life, neo-realist movies emphasized privileged, melodramatic moments.[4]

Neo-realism was a commitment to construct a new culture—a new reality. Transcending any party or faith, inspired by both Christ and Gramsci, its priorities were fraternity and open-mindedness. Neo-realism was not a style, nor a content. It was a "soul," in Chiarini's words, that had been forged during the Resistance and that *tried to look* at Italian realities "with, above all, an insistence on sincerity toward oneself and others."[5]

"There doesn't exist a *technique* for capturing truth," Rossellini agreed.[6] "Only a moral position can do it"[7]—a *desire* "to understand, to understand fully,[8] . . . a greater curiosity about individuals," not merely their "surface" but "the most subtle aspects of their soul."[9]

For moviemakers, in practical terms, capturing truth meant getting free of convention. "Artists during the Fascist era," declared Gianni Puccini, who had been *Cinema*'s guiding luminary during the Fascist era, "were so ignorant of poverty and real-life drama that they had had to imagine it; exploration was tentative then, our eyes were unable to open. But unlike the closed time of *Ossessione*, today is an epoch of discoveries. Emphasis on current events forces artists to study nature, whereas formerly they studied Pudovkin or Lubitsch. . . . The great films were inspired by daily life before they reconstructed it—Chaplin's bitter, ragamuffin America, Rossellini's real Rome and Berlin, Stroheim's fictional Vienna, Vidor's slavery-drenched cotton fields. Recourse to actuality produces an immediate shower of truth and life. We are just learning to explore this uproarious human forest that is Our Country."[10]

"Learning to explore . . ."

Just at this time, spring 1948, Croce proposed that the postwar Liberal Party adopt, as its sole purpose, the insurance of creative interaction among all the other parties—the continuance of exploration. No other purpose but that. Capitalists and Communists would coexist in "harmonious discord," insured by the Liberals, who would be above ideology.

Croce's proposal was rejected, because the Cold War had begun—a cold civil war in Italy—and a curtain was falling across the fraternity and open-mindedness of the Resistance. The soul of neo-realism splintered; eyes closed again; nature was no longer the prime source of truth; fraternity was no longer a priority.

Thus the term "neo-realism" has come to designate a loosely defined postwar period. In this sense, although neo-realist priorities continued to define many moviemakers in many different ways, neo-realism died in 1948.

"Neo-realism" Claimed by the Left

After 1948, a mini Cold War began over the corpse. Both left and right tried to claim parentage, and thus the right to define neo-realism's agenda.

The word itself was new. It does not appear to have been used by anyone during the period most properly defined as neo-realist—the 1944–48 period of postwar solidarity. It is known to have been used very rarely in the early thirties as a literary term,[11] and twice during the war in reference to thirties French films (Renoir, Carné, Duvivier); but never to designate Italian films.[12]

By the time "neo-realism" was first used to designate the new Italian cinema, in the April and June 1948 issues of *Bianco e Nero* and the May 1948 issue of *La Revue du Cinéma* (Paris), all the monuments of neo-realism had already been made or started, and the postwar fraternity in the soul of neo-realism had already come to an end with the Cold War rupture marked by the April 18 elections.

Staking out the right's claim, Chiarini declared the word had been coined afresh "beyond the Alps," and had no connection to earlier usage.[13] "We Catholic critics have invented the term 'neo-realist school of cinema,'" echoed a French Dominican living in Italy, Felix A. Morlion, in the June 1948 *Bianco e Nero*, and no one is known to have contradicted him. Morlion's article, like Puccini's, was a key neo-realist manifesto. Fraternity was its theme.

"As a foreigner who discovered Italy after working in thirty countries of Europe, America and Africa," wrote Morlion, "it is only here that I have regained my optimism about Western culture. In Italy, intelligence, imagination, and sensitivity are immensely creative because they are linked to a simple and rich human tradition, the fruit of twenty centuries of heroism and sacrifice: the Christian tradition"—which for Morlion's purpose meant that "in Italian art, as in the Italian mind, there is not yet a division between the left and the right, or to put it better, between materialism and the spiritual. Human reality is a spiritual reality, even for the man who is not a disciplined church-goer." Neo-realism proclaims the subsistence of human reality's spiritual riches even during war, misery, and the alienations of modern life. And, added Morlion, specifically denying the relation between neo-realism and the *pessimism* of the French films celebrated by the *Cinema* tradition, "that is why the Italian cinema will not have its *La Bête humaine*, *Quai des brumes*, or *Le Jour se lève* [Renoir 1938, Carné 1938, Carné 1939]."[14]

Morlion's neo-realism proclaims "the deep, dynamic and truly human reality" that transcends differences between left and right—between Marx and Christ—with a Christian accent.

In contrast, a Gramscian accent is apparent in Puccini's manifesto, quoted above, in the preceding issue of *Bianco e Nero*, April 1948. For Puccini, the moral position for continued "exploration" is that cinema remain "popular and national."

This was the dream Roberto had heard evoked so often during the long evenings of the Occupation—the notion that after the war a new culture, a new reality, would be constructed, with its authenticity guaranteed by a base in popular culture.

Previously, Puccini wrote, Italy's mandarin culture had made eyes unable to open, which had led to Fascism and disaster. Now eyes are able to open "precisely because Italy's recent history has brought to light classes and social strata that intellectuals knew nothing about before." Today, even in depicting a middle-class person, artists can profit from a critical perspective previously unknown.

For Puccini, a moral position was a working-class position. For many on the left, neo-realism became identified with a political agenda. Eventually the left would claim proprietorship. Neo-realist antecedents were identified as Barbaro, Visconti, and certain collaborators of the prewar *Cinema*, all of them Communists.[15] During the 1950s, Zavattini's columns would repeatedly insist on a linkage of neo-realism, literature, and left-wing humanism.

It then gradually became apparent that Rossellini felt that society could not be transformed from without by a political agenda, but only from within by individual self-education; that his characters were seldom informed by a proletarian perspective, and he himself even less so; and that his dilemmas were spiritual rather than material, and led to individual illuminations rather than choral ones. The left increasingly found Rossellini "involuted" and irrelevant; intimate rather than public. By 1978, Lino Miccichè, a Socialist, following the Marxist Pio Baldelli's landmark study of Rossellini,[16] was able to write: "It turns out that the author of the first neo-realist film (*Roma città aperta*) and of one of the masterworks of neo-realism (*Paisà*), far from being at the center of that neo-realist 'ideology' of which he was for three years considered the symbol par excellence, had actually—despite appearances—been moving collaterally to it or, better, in a coincidence that did not go beyond the humanism of the initial postwar period. . . . [Neo-realism] was not an aesthetics [but] an 'ethics of an aesthetics.' It was the answer of a new generation of filmmakers to Vittorini's question: 'Shall we ever have a culture capable of protecting people against suffering instead of just comforting them?' "[17]

What lies "beyond humanism"? God or a political agenda? What is art's social function? Is a movie failing its function if it does not go "beyond humanism"?

What lies beyond for Rossellini, it is true, is sometimes divine grace and always an intuition. Although Rossellini, like Croce, assigned a much greater role to judgment in later years, even his treatments of Socrates, Pascal, and Descartes regard it dubiously. No one ever has a diabolic intuition in a Rossellini film: all evil results from corrupt judgment. Ideology, then, must always compromise a moral position. As a result, after 1948 Rossellini to some people seemed as irrelevant as Croce.

The French Winds

Strange French winds confused the definitions of "neo-realism" even more than did disputes between Catholics and Marxists. French critics, whether or not they had invented the word "neo-realism," had taken the lead in promoting it. And their notion of neo-realism was light-years away from the straightforward social agenda of the Italian Left.

Italy had scarcely been touched by existentialism and phenomenology during the Fascist years. Roberto's boyhood exposure to a cosmopolitan thinker like Bontempelli was extraordinary and nourished his alienation from Roman provincialism. French existentialism had arisen out of exasperation with "positivists": with Marxists, on the one hand, who thought consciousness and culture were determined by economics and whose triumph was the Soviet Union; and with Freud, Jung, Durkheim, Lévi-Strauss, and Saussure, on the other hand, who thought that by grasping "structures" or patterns we can reduce history to a backdrop of deeper psychic reality and whose triumph was making sameness more real than human individuality. In France, Bergson, Merleau-Ponty, Maritain, Bernanos, Simone Weil, and almost everyone found positivism spiritually empty. Life is not facts but vast vivid experience, they exclaimed, in an animated cosmos where matter is bound up with spirit, mystery, and mind. For valid knowledge, we need intuition, faith, love, and sexuality. The true revolution must begin inside individuals, by increased awareness and "risk taking." In art "style" is not technique but an earned self-awareness, an inner orientation enabling an outward search.[18]

Such ideas infected Rossellini in Paris and animated the rest of his life—because he had heard them long before, in his father's *cenacolo*. It was by means of "unschematized intuitions" and by searching out "precognitive moments of exaltation," said *Esprit*'s Charles Du Bos, that the new criticism was to be achieved[19]—a prescription corresponding not only to Bazin's critical method, but even more to the "Bergsonian" working conditions that Rossellini created during *Deutschland im Jahre Null* and "The Po Delta." "This kind of 'realism'," declared Maritain, "is in no way realism of material appearances; it is realism of the spiritual significance of what exists . . . , permeated with the signs and dreams that are commingled with the beings of things. . . . There is no abstraction in it save the abstraction that brings out from things the meanings with which they are pregnant and recreates on the canvas the essentials, and just the essentials, of their significant elements."[20]

The best film style, according to Roger Leenhardt, *Esprit*'s film critic, seems style-less. Our duty is not to interpret but to render, not to teach people but to study the universe. Eisensteinian cinema goes in the wrong direction. Cinema should not manipulate through rhetoric but transcribe reality and engage worthy subjects.

Thus for Felix Morlion, neo-realism was "a magic window that opens out onto the 'real.'"

The Italian Soil

In Italy, however, movies, far from being magic windows, were extensions of popular theater. Unlike the abstract French, Italians were concrete.

Things held no "mystery" for them but *ideas* were suspect and "truth" was problematic. In America, history is what happened; we would be puzzled if each television station had its own truth and dispensed substantially differing accounts of major happenings. "Accurate, unbiased reporting," we are told, is why such confusion does not occur. The actual explanation lies in agreement about how to interpret events: a hegemonic ideology that excludes unconsensual attitudes.

Comparable agreement did not exist in Italy in the 1950s. There the sort of paralysis that stymies us over "non-consensuable" issues like abortion (where opposing premises—or ideologies—refuse any common ground for dialogue) affected almost every aspect of everyday life. A news story would be told a dozen different ways in a dozen different newspapers. Each paper spoke from a defined ideology; Communist *L'Unità* saw things differently than Catholic *Il Tempo.*

The Italian habit of experiencing almost everything, including art and culture, in ideological terms has weakened only in the last few years. For millennia, contesting parties pronounced dogma and exterminated dissent. "Rhetoric" spoke in absolutes, always hypocritically. Centuries taught Italians to be conformist outwardly, but tolerant, cynical, and practical inwardly. With each person convinced of *his* "reality," consensus required ideology—a theory, philosophy, mindset, political program, or faith. For Plato, ideas alone mattered, things not at all. For the Church, faith alone mattered; things led to temptation. For the Greeks, Lombards, Arabs, Franks, Normans, Germans, French, and Spaniards who invaded Italy, and for the contesting city states, their interests alone mattered. In contrast to northern Europe, where philosophic thought struggled mightily to keep abreast of empirical science, in Italy the Copernican revolution never occurred; after the suppression of Galileo in the seventeenth century, innovative thought, whether scientific, philosophic, or historical, was squashed. The intellectual ferments incited by Pascal or Locke never occurred. No attempt was made to reconcile religion and science. Italian genius turned to music. When a philosopher did appear, Vico, he concluded that human reason was incapable of understanding the natural world, that science could not yield truth, that the only things that can be known are those humans themselves create. "Reality," then, did not exist as an external anchor for ideas, not as for Americans. Only views and interpretations existed. The cart became the horse. In America it was thought that reality determined ideas; in Italy it was obvious that ideas determined reality. Rhetoric and willpower can transform reality, said the Fascists and Gramsci too. Since the world exists only in our imagination, we can make of it anything we choose.

Fusion

French and Italian thought intersect from opposite directions. A French-man's abstractions concretize theory; an Italian's theorize the concrete (compare Maritain and Puccini). Thus in reacting to the war and reassert-ing spirituality, French thought was phenomenological and existential, whereas Italian thought was pragmatic and historicist.

The first reviews of *Roma città aperta* and *Paisà* demonstrate these dif-ferences. The Italians talked about traditional literary values: crudeness, melodrama, and *style*; film had an ideological, social purpose: to provide a model, an explanation, a sermon. Movies are theater. The French talked about *reality*: film is an imprint, a witness; only secondarily ideological. Movies are experiences. As we saw apropos of *Paisà*, Italians sought an ideology, a mindset toward history, solutions to practical problems: Fascism had been a "parenthesis," as Croce put it. Whereas what the French sought was sensation, a feeling of the earth beneath their feet: so many national myths lay shattered.[21]

We have seen how a fusion occurred; how Rossellini's films, nursed back and forth between Italy and France, were increasingly discussed in Italy with the new French buzzwords, which Rossellini himself picked up: letting "things speak for themselves"; "showing" rather than "demonstrat-ing"; and leaving the spectator "free" to draw his own conclusions.

And we have seen that, contemporaneously, another rhetorical fusion was occurring. Neo-realism, which had begun as a quest, became a demon-stration of the competing new realities that left and right sought to construct.

These various fusions, however, muddied the purity of the afflatus that had inspired neo-realist films: to allow our eyes to open. Phenomenologists (climaxing in Ayfre and Bazin) were reintroducing the mystery, metaphys-ics, and existentialism Croce had thrown off. Marxists and Christians were reintroducing dogmas and politics. No wonder "neo-realism" ended up a muddle. Each person saw it as supporting his own position. Crocean roots were ignored, because nobody wanted to be caught mentioning him. Within months they were all hurling anathemas at each other and the film-makers. Contradictions between theory and fact, between what "neo-real-ism" decreed the movies were supposed to be and what the movies actu-ally were, was solved by the left by expelling Rossellini from the neo-realist canon, and by the phenomenologists by increasingly intellectualized rheto-ric. Yet none of them had had any right to define "neo-realism"; they had all come along after the movies had been made. In this ridiculous debacle festers the promiscuity of truth. Theory, when it becomes convention, arro-gates our life's experience and closes our eyes.

Rossellini insisted that his own "ideology" included, and was superior to, all other ideologies.[22] But Church and Party marked the Great Divide under the 1960s, and people who dreamed of a transcendent humanism sometimes found themselves labeled seditious by the Americans, diabolic by the Vatican, and mystical by the Party. But the dream survived and led to Vatican II. Particularly it subsisted in Rossellini, who befriended Morlion during *Stromboli terra di Dio* (1949) and *Francesco giullare di Dio* (1950) and mourned the dream in *Europe '51*. At the end of his life Rossellini was planning a film on Marx's Christian qualities after making another showing Christ's Marxist qualities.

Church, Party, and Cinema

In fact, Church and Party in Italy shared the same basic cultural values; their leaders had gone to the same schools; their legions of restoration and revolution had united in the Resistance.[23] Now Church and Party competed in trade unions and culture. Both involved themselves deeply with cinema. In contrast to the negative role of the Church in America, the Church in Italy, despite its censorship activity, treated movies as a vital cultural expression rather than an insidious consumer product. In America Catholics were forbidden to see most neo-realist pictures; in Italy they were encouraged to by Catholic publications and priest-critics. Clerics served as historians, archivists, and researchers, and administered many film series. Parishes ran most of the second-run theaters, and still today most commercial 16mm distribution is conducted by a firm of nuns. The Church's direct participation in film production has been slight, but its *indirect* influence—through Church-owned banks and corporations and the Christian Democrat party—was immense. Unlike the American Church, it tried to identify with the avant-garde.

The Party rivaled the Church, paralleling its efforts in finance, publishing, film clubs, festivals, and serious criticism. Like the Church, it had a vested interest in being in the forefront of progressive culture; like the Church, it actively competed for allegiance. Like Fathers Morlion and Lisandrini, Communists Trombadori and Lizzani hung out with Roberto and worked on influencing him.

Both Church and Party had altered dramatically since the twenties. Then the Vatican, mistrusting Catholic involvement in mass politics, had connived in suppression of the huge (Catholic) Popolari Party while striking bargains of its own with Mussolini, who had then ended a half-century stand-off by paying an indemnity for the seizures of 1870, acknowledging the Vatican State's independence, undertaking to persecute Communists and Masons, and restoring crucifixes to courts and classrooms. Six decades of Catholic isolation had come to an end, but the Pope had been bitterly criticized. It was said he had traded manna for moolah, legitimated the dictator, and sold out civil liberties. Yet that same year Pius XI's encyclical had protested "the concept which makes of the State the end and of the citizen, of man, the means, monopolizing and absorbing everything in the State." By virtue of its concordat with Mussolini, the Church had remained almost a state within the state. Its networks of parishes, schools, and Catholic action groups meant it was training the leaders of the future. It meant the average Italian, unlike the average German, had principles higher than the State.[24] It meant that when the regime had crumbled and foreign armies wreaked fear and desolation, there was a vast and (sometimes) kindly organization ready to protect and shelter, reaffirm life's direction, and assume control. Now there was alliance with America. Father Felix Morlion, for example, had been established in the Vatican by the chief of the American OSS, "Wild Bill" Donovan. Morlion himself, before the war, had started an intelligence service called Pro Deo, which was Catholic, anti-Communist, and anti-Nazi intelligence. His reports to the OSS—known within the OSS as the Black Reports—had been mostly sermons. But Donovan had gone to considerable trouble to evacuate Merlion from Lisbon to New York during the war, and then in 1944 to get him into the Vatican.[25]

Compared to the Vatican, the Italian Communist Party was ambivalent. As Barzini has remarked, it often appeared "a pitiless, centralized, and well-knit organization, which will destroy all class enemies, conquer the world, and run it autocratically, according to inflexible scientific rules, in the interest of the proletariat." But in reality it was two quite different parties in juxtaposition: "millions of fanatic, uncultivated, and easily influenced people . . . efficiently controlled by a relatively small number of mild scholars, most of whom abhor violent words, wear glasses, and speak with soft voices."[26] In *Ossessione* and *Roma città aperta*, Communists are accurately depicted as variations on Christian sainthood, for in their real-life daily contacts they embodied Franciscan virtues of generosity and kindness, fraternity, and yea-saying.

The Party's history had thus been less an outward struggle against capitalism than an inward contest between its two aspects. Its founder Amadeo Bordiga was so intransigent a revolutionary that he divided the left, frightened the middle classes out of their wits, and rallied the timid to the side of the Fascists, with the result that his now-tiny Party was driven underground and nearly destroyed.[27] It employed that underground status to cultivate the impression that Communists were the regime's only opponents. In actuality they were a minority and a help to the regime more than a hindrance. Stalin, too, divided the left. To gain advantage against Trotsky, he forced all Communist groups in Western Europe to sever their ties with socialists and thus fatally weakened the left's ability to oppose Hitler's rise and the Second World War.

The Party's role in the Resistance had been heroic but ambivalent; Communists had accounted for more than half of the 72,500 partisans killed during the Resistance, but some partisans, trained in Russia, had put the Party's advantage ahead of the struggle against Nazi-Fascism. Togliatti's April 1944 announcement, four days after his return from twenty years in Russia, that the Party would cooperate with the democrats was also ambivalent. Was the radical shift in policy (ordered by Stalin) dictated solely by recognition that, as Togliatti later explained, "the British and the Americans had no intention of allowing the Italians to decide their own future"? Or was Togliatti's temperament equally decisive, his hatred of violence, his preference for achieving "positions of power within the bourgeois State . . . [whereby] to provoke progressive transformations of the institutions from the inside"?[28]

Togliatti, in any case, eliminated fanatics and terrorists, disbanded all clandestine armed organizations, endorsed the Lateran accords with the Vatican, and built up "an élite of intellectuals in his own image, pale, Left Hegelians, Marxist-Leninist theologians, who wore glasses, thought intricately, studied history and sociology, and delivered speeches lasting half a day." By and large these were former followers of Croce who wanted to participate in the process of change, who like Giorgio Amendola had been convinced by Croce's disciple Piero Goberti that only the working class could embody liberty for the future. Croce himself opposed Communism for the same reason he had opposed Fascism: their faith in violence and negation of liberty impeded slow and normal evolution of political life. But to his disciples his notion that we ought simply to agree to disagree and let the process decide seemed insipid.

Nonetheless the Italian Communist Party retained a Crocean stamp. Goberti had "historicized" Marxism, rejecting Marx's utopian and definitive break with history and instead insisting on "permanent revolution," on movement toward the next phase of a perpetual struggle that can never be concluded.[29] Thus it was natural for Togliatti to consider "bourgeois liberties" as a conquest for all people for all times that should be respected and preserved by the Party.[30] As the most authoritative non-Russian theoretician and as a survivor of the 1920s Comintern, Togliatti carried immense authority. His opinions, particularly after Stalin's death, determined the policies guiding all parties in the West. But he was also a loyalist, a faithful executor of Moscow's, and Stalin's, directives. One might admire him and other Party leaders and trust their sincerity, but who could be sure the Party would respect liberty if it gained power?

Certainly the Church was not sure, given Stalin's Draconian purges of religion. In its determination to thwart Communism and correct past mistakes, it was purging pro-Fascist clergy, funneling millions of dollars into the Christian Democrats, at whose head it had placed Alcide De Gasperi, a Popolari parliamentarian it had sheltered from Mussolini in the Vatican Library. De Gasperi had been heading the coalition government since the end of 1945. But the left-leaning results of the 1946 election had been disappointing and much more would have to be done.

Early in 1947 De Gasperi, under pressure from the U.S. and the Vatican, expelled the Communists from his ruling coalition. Nonetheless, Togliatti continued to cooperate, convinced that De Gasperi would be unable to govern without the PCI and that fraternity was the means to acceptance. The Church, in contrast, condemned all attempts at fraternity. It excommunicated Catholics who voted for the PCI, forbade Communist literature, and outlawed Communists as godparents or wedding witnesses. The U.S. National Security Council debated an invasion to prevent the elections, then decided to subvert them instead and, in the event of a Communist victory, to topple the Italian government by paramilitary intervention. In the next elections, April 18, 1948, the CD won an absolute majority. Dawning prosperity contributed to this victory, through Einaudi's economic policies, as did the Marshall Plan, American funding of the CD, threats to withhold food, and the CD's absorption of moderate ex-Fascists; whereas the left was hurt by Russia's takeover of Czechoslovakia and its own quarreling. Above all, the CD owed its triumph to parish priests, Catholic organizations, and the hierarchy.

The bishops had overseen the Christian Democrats' choice of deputies. They saw to it now that Italy became a stalwart of the Atlantic Alliance and that persecution of Communism began. There was no McCarthyite blacklisting, as in the U.S., for sympathy for communist ideas was widespread. But local prefects dissuaded café owners from permitting Communist meetings, Communist recreation camps were closed down, and Communist organizations were expelled from public buildings.

Such measures seemed increasingly justified, as Communism took over China and began spreading into Korea and an ungodly Stalinist terror descended upon Eastern Europe.

But Italian Communists believed they were fighting the good fight for liberty. Many of them perceived Marxism as a program for effecting Christian principles on earth. Khrushchev's denunciations of Stalin and the invasion of Hungary would come as shattering revelations. But that wouldn't happen until 1956. In the postwar period, the horrifying tales against Stalin—widespread torture, concentration camps, exterminations of twenty million Soviet citizens—seemed a discountable continuation of Mussolini's anti-Communist propaganda specifically because America and the Vatican were so unswervingly hostile. And the CD encouraged this interpretation by illegal seizures of PCI property, use of state funds to finance CD party machinery, and a policy of staffing ministries, municipalities, and state-owned corporations with incompetent sycophants. In the industrialized North, where the Resistance had put factories under popular workers' and community control, the old owners were put back in control. Were not such practices a continuation of Fascism? Could it be denied that those who had profited from Fascism were now back in power, that the hopes of the Resistance were betrayed, that the poor were still poor? Even people who detested Stalin now felt they had no choice but to suffer solidarity with international Communism. Yet for them communism did not mean persecution of religion, abolition of personal property, or an end to democracy. It meant abolition of intolerable pockets of misery in Sardinia and the South, a government dedicated to fairness rather than privilege, a free, creative society in which each individual could develop his own sensibility; it meant, as Francesco said in *Roma città aperta,* the coming of spring.

But instead of spring there had come more of the same old thing, with money-grubbing politicians in collusion with a Church so reactionary that it opposed even socialized health care for children. What had happened? What had gone wrong?

Gramsci

It was in answering these questions that Gramsci proved useful: his substitution of cultural Marxism for materialism, his insistence that a just society required a wedding of workers and intellectuals. With Croce, whom he considered "the greatest thinker in Europe today,"[31] Gramsci had argued that objective reality cannot be "mechanically" accepted, that nature cannot be understood apart from human history, that history will not automatically generate progress, that the future has to be shaped by our will and ideas, that the shining goal of our endeavor is liberty ("the creation of a society in which there could be the greatest amount of freedom with the minimum of coercion"[32]), and that the process of revolution is intellectual rather than materialist. Knowledge, he said, is not something we *learn*, something we *receive* by studying things; it's something we *produce*.

In 1930, when Gramsci had spoken out from prison against Stalin's order to sever ties with the Socialists, his comrades had severed their ties with him. But after Stalin's death, Gramsci's anti-totalitarian vision was resurrected and Gramsci, rather than Bordiga, came to be regarded as the Party's true founder, saint, and martyr.

Quest for Reality

Neo-realism was more than exploration. It was *making*. It no sooner "discovered" or "captured" reality than it reconstructed it, and created a new reality, which bore the maker's mark. Croce wanted that mark to express the originality of an individual rather than the conventions of an ideology. For Rossellini, the former was a moral position, the latter an immoral one. Between making a movie and making a culture, there are only practical differences. A movie becomes a convention when copied; a culture needs constant renewal by each individual.

Yet after two world wars, ideology was in even greater demand. Church and Party supplied answers. Croce and Rossellini, in contrast, gave no answers. Even God's grace only helps open our eyes. Each person has virtually to recreate the world from zero. Rossellini was proof of his own gospel: he ended up trying to recreate the intellectual and technological history of the world—merely as a prelude for a next step.

Church and Party made life much less onerous, even comfortable. Perhaps it is for this reason that neither Christianity nor Marxism was ever tried. Instead, whole dimensions of meaning were assigned a priori, became slogans, then proved untrustworthy, leaving a void and strangulation. In Pirandello's comedic vision, we each possess our own internal logic, conflicting notions of reality never meet, we argue eternally in limbo.[33] Ah, but maybe cinema, with its "magic window onto the real," can solve our reality crisis, help us "rediscover" the "real"? Art has always had this possibility, and movies, unlike literature, spoke to the masses and, Church and

Party understood, could midwife a national-popular culture (at the time, the Italian equivalent of American multiculturalism today).

The artists and critics were products of the same middle-class, literary culture that they faulted. Rather than taking a proletarian perspective, they instructed the folk. Films like *Shoeshine, Il sole sorge ancora,* and *Caccia tragica* (De Santis), as Ferrara argues, typify the "interclass Resistance culture that ingenuously envisioned the intellectual as going toward the people and mythifying them." Rather than portraying common lives in simple unaffected language, the intellectuals transformed the people "into an inside-out image of themselves, while depriving the intellectual of any deep rapport with real society." Poverty, for example, was denounced indignantly amid lachrymose elegies, magnanimous embraces of simple souls, and an almost constant sense of fatalism, with the result that De Sica, Visconti, and their followers, ended up as self-indulgent distortions. Rossellini's perspective, in contrast, although it is Catholic and middle-class, is capable of viewing the poverty in "Naples"'s Mergellina caves as simply there, without that distorting fatalism.[34] Perhaps Gramsci's idea of an alliance between the working class and the bourgeois intellectual as a guarantee of liberty derived less from faith in the masses than from Croce's notion that true freedom encourages the creation of more aristocrats not more workers. But as the Cold War froze, exploration became defined as revealing the "structures"—of class repression or personal redemption—that Marxists and Christians discern.

In 1949, Zhdanovism, the cultural form of Stalinism, became the Party position, and Stalin was not led by Christian principles. Culture, declared the PCI in a missive "Against Imperialist and Clerical Obscurantism," had only one role: to serve political goals. Art was propaganda in service of the Party. Neo-realism erred by not being "positive" about the working classes. Filmmakers were urged, via Pudovkin and Barbaro at Perugia in 1949, to combat capitalism by attending to content rather than form and by developing positive role models to embody the "people's" struggle. The protagonist of De Santis's *Bitter Rice*—Silvana Mangano—was not such a hero, charged Trombadori in a polemic in *L'Unità*, for she was not "typical" of the Italian working woman: "It is in the healthy men and women—mothers, wives, husbands, sons—who fight for their daily bread that truth appears the richest." (In response, De Santis, in his next film, *Non c'è pace tra gli ulivi,* simplified all the characters to reflect black-and-white class struggle.) "Formalism, pessimism, subjectivism, insufficient social commitment" were all condemned, along with anything "bourgeois and cosmopolitan." Visconti was singled out by Barbaro (now teaching at the Polish Film Academy in Lodz, after being expelled from the Centro Sperimentale by the Christian Democrats) for aping Renoir's "erotic ambience" in *Ossessione* and for "lacking any lucid ideas" in *La terra trema.* (For the rest of his life Visconti submitted his scripts to Trombadori before shooting.) Only films that "analyzed" (i.e., evoked) economic and class structures to reveal oppression were henceforth acceptable. Human nature would be what Stalin decreed it to be.

Christian Democracy, for its part, reimposed precensorship in 1949, decried sex, mobilized newspapers, denied export permits, and manipulated production subsidies to eliminate the "dirty linen" so intrinsic to neo-realism. De Santis charged the State with assassinating neo-realism.[35] In fact, many movies were censored and their exhibition discouraged. "Each and every work," said Rossellini, "even every attitude or line was watched for its possible and probable political significance. A large number of taboos emerged and discussion was minimized, restricted, and dried up. A tendency was born to make 'escapist' films. In this state of affairs neo-realism was dead."[36] Lizzani's 1954 *Chronicle of Poor Lovers* was banned even though Pratolini's novel had been in bookstores all over Italy since 1947 and had been translated into 25 languages. Minister Andreotti singled out De Sica in specific attacks in the press; *Shoeshine, Bicycle Thieves,* and *Umberto D* were slandering Italy to the whole world as a place of misery, meanness, social conflict, and unemployment; shouldn't such films be denied export permits and prevented in the future? Criticism of the government was regarded as Communist subversion—even criticism of the Fascist government. A 1950 reissue of the 1930 *All Quiet on the Western Front* was censored for anti-militarism. When Aristarco and Renzo Renzi published a screenplay, *L'Armata Sagapò,* critical of the Italian Army's behavior in Greece during World War II, they were arrested and hauled before a court martial (offenses against the military being outside civil jurisdiction) and the subject still has not been filmed today, although virtually every scenarist in Italy has attempted to treat it.

An Answer?

The reality that Rossellini's movies increasingly sought to explore was not things but ideas, human reality. Ideology becomes the subject matter, not the method of his movies. Sometimes it seems there is no "reality" in Rossellini, nor any "sanity"; only a theater of ideas. His characters suffer from ideology in *Paisà, Europe '51, Deutschland, Vanina Vanini, Voyage in Italy,* and all the history films. Characters forever seek to remake the world according to their own ideas—Louis XIV, Saint Paul, Christ, Nazis and Communists, Pascal, Descartes, Cosimo de' Medici, Alberti, Augustine, Socrates, and Garibaldi. "From a very humble position you can face everything and you can revise the whole conception of the universe," Rossellini said.[37] "I'm always for the 'crazy' people."[38]

Thus, rather than being a mere reaction to Fascism, Rossellini's neo-realism is a reassertion of Italian liberalism—of our ability to create a "new reality." Rossellini may emphasize the melodrama (and tragedy) of risk-taking that, in the absence of a heavenly spotlight, every decision entails along the way to a new reality, and his characters may cry out to God more than Croce would have liked. But no matter how alone and bereft, they never descend into the morbid self-preoccupation of Camus and Sartre, they never conclude life is absurd or irrational. Just as Croce, in opposition to the egocentricity of existentialism, moved away from the mortal person and toward enduring actions, so too Rossellini's characters, however eccentric, always implement their private revelations into the public sphere of history. Such commitment to community seems typically Italian. It is exemplified not only by Rossellini's historical personages but by the "suicides" of the Allied soldiers in "The Po Delta" and Carmela in "Sicily," Irene's seclusion with the insane in *Europe '51*, and Nannina's giving birth in *The Miracle*. Karin's destitute cry to God on Stromboli is a prelude to action, and Edmund's suicide in *Deutschland*, clearly inserted within history, is neither the effete curse it would have been in Sartre's hands nor the Sisyphean involution Camus would have made of it. By focusing on our individual interaction with history, Croce's historicism, like Rossellini's cinema, is an alternative to the relative helplessness of structuralism—to our primitive tendencies, when threatened by chaos, to grasp for sameness, pattern, and stability; to pigeonhole; to reduce myths to a limited number of archetypes that govern our inner life; to uncover the "scientific" laws of Marxist determinism. Instead we can create new realities. Croce desired—and Rossellini tried to implement—a cultural understanding, a grasp of the world humans have made, in order that we might experience how our individual agency meshes with history, in order that history and culture will spark our creativity and responsibility. We are more ourselves probing the history *we* are creating than probing laws and archetypes that supposedly produce change without changing themselves.[39] In face of the horrors of the world wars and the confusion of modern life, Croce and Rossellini, rather than bewailing "fate" (under whatever name), hailed the eternal freshness of life and welcomed the winds of freedom, risk, and rapture.

Debacles

La macchina ammazzacattivi

Roberto began his next film in Amalfi in June 1948. *La macchina ammazza-cattivi* ("The machine that kills bad people") is a morality fable about a photographer, who is given a camera that kills people by petrifying them as their image is snapped. He sets about liquidating Amalfi of bad people, but discovers that good and evil are intertwined and that the saint who gave him the camera is really a little demon trying to earn points. When the photographer forces the demon to make the sign of the cross, an explosion puts everything back as it was.

Rossellini presents the story as a *commedia dell'arte*. It opens and closes on a puppet stage with its characters as figurines. It inserts topical political allusions, lampoons each character's moral defects as a lesson in tolerance, and proclaims its moral at the end: "Cultivate the good without going too far, reject evil if you want to be saved, do not rush to judge, and think twice before punishing."

La macchina is also a satire on the specific notion—associated with "neo-realism" and Zavattini in particular—that verisimilitude is a conduit to reality, moral understanding, and political action. Rossellini's photographer assumes photography empowers him to remake the world as though he were God (or a movie director).[1] Instead he discovers the camera is an invention of a demon and surface evidence is illusory. Art and life demand imagination, not just facts.

Celestino, the photographer, represents the left, assuming moral certitude that "we have to kill all the bad people to enter the kingdom of heaven." The town leaders represent the Fascists and Christian Democrats. "*Vinceremo*," they cry, echoing Mussolini's war slogan; and one official, frozen dead in the act of saluting, has to be buried in a coffin with a periscope extension for his arm, an allusion to Mussolini's arm which, also frozen in rigor mortis, had to be broken for his coffin to be closed. Like the Christian Democrats, the leaders are eager to twist the laws, and even to sell off Italy to the Americans to line their own pockets. Some American visitors are likened to the Germans (a radio is "German or American," someone says) and are totally "out of it": humorously when they search for bathrooms, crudely when they try to buy a memorial cemetery for a hotel site ("The bodies can be taken somewhere else").[2] The sexy niece represents The American Girl: half naked, sweet and dumb; in contrast to The Italian: covered-up, acerbic, and street-smart. A chubby lover vaguely recalls Roberto himself, as does everyone's chronic indebtedness. "You should honor the signora's wishes," Celestino is told, "you haven't paid her rent for years." "But I pay her 600 percent interest!" he cries—echoing Roberto's perpetual fate.

The American subplot continues a series of Rossellini movies, after *Paisà*, about Nordic types encountering Italy (*Stromboli, Europe '51, Voyage in Italy, Viva l'Italia, Era notte a Roma, The Age of the Medici*). But it was added as a lark. Through Seymour Peyser (Lopert's attorney), Roberto had met Marilyn Buferd—Miss America of 1946—in Paris and had brought her to Italy where, it was explained, she was translating his letters to Ingrid. "Put her in the film," he told Renzo Avanzo. "But there's no spot for her!" "So change the story." Then Bill Tubbs, the chaplain in *Paisà*, wrote from New York that he needed work, so Roberto created the subplot for Tubbs and his wife Helen, and cast Marilyn as their niece.

Magnani hated her. "Why don't you cut the act?" she admonished as Buferd leered at Roberto across a frosted drink; "I was a whore before you were born!"

Marilyn went home. "It's hard to put into words exactly what he has," she told a reporter, "but I can tell you this: Rossellini is more than a man; he is an act of God. . . . Why, when I was leaving for America, he gave me a pair of clips and a bracelet of old design which had been in [the] family for years and which easily cost ten thousand dollars."

U.S. Customs appraised them at sixty dollars.[3]

Roberto was in his element in Amalfi. He loved the land and the people; he was surrounded with friends and family. Anna and Marilyn were in Amalfi, Marcellina in Rome, Roswitha in Capri, and Ingrid in the bush. Renzino and Franco came to visit; Renzo was writing the music; Amidei, Eduardo De Felippo, Sarazani, Liana Ferri, and Giancarlo Vigorelli, an erudite Neapolitan friend, were writing the script; Avanzo, Alberto Manni, Mida, and Cesano were assisting; Gaio Visconti, Luchino's cousin, was taking stills. One day, after setting up his camera near the sea, Roberto was overcome by it all. "We should all kneel down," he declared, stepping back, "and thank God for such beauty!"[4]

To play the devil he found a man of 82 who lived in the hills, had never seen a movie, and only wanted a thousand lire a day ($1.65). Unfortunately, the devil would drink his thousand lire, then disappear to sleep, leaving no devil for Roberto to shoot. The photographer was another amateur, Gennaro Pisano, a local carpenter whom Roberto economically employed to build the sets as well. Too late he noticed the reluctance of the local townsfolks to play opposite the carpenter—who in fact was a coffin-maker, which was too much for the Amalfitani.

The big problem was Roberto himself. More distracted than ever, he shot slowly, took long vacations, worked intensely in spurts. Perhaps it was the cocaine. When inspired, he composed wonderfully complex shots rhyming the movements of the camera with those of the actors. Other times he would leave for Rome in the morning and not return till after midnight. The troupe had worked for him before; they would wait sometimes out of terror, more often seduced by his charm, always grateful for the overtime. Then, trying to catch up, Roberto would do in hours what another would need days for. If practical difficulties intruded, if the amateurs made mistakes, he'd explode, calm down, and shower his unnerved troupe with excessive generosity. The ingenuous and experienced Pisano most often found himself Roberto's target and reacted eventually with a nervous breakdown, forcing Roberto to cut scenes and simplify.[5]

Among many reasons to postpone work, Roberto's favorite was deep sea diving. "He's in training for Bergman," Buferd observed.[6]

He shed fifteen pounds but in three months worked only three weeks. Creditors would come, he would turn on his charm, take them for a big meal, get them drunk, and bring in Marilyn.

Anna battled him constantly, the same old battles of one-upmanship. Even after Buferd left, she could not relax; Bergman loomed on the horizon.

Roberto was waiting for a telegram from Lopert that would confirm a meeting with Bergman in Paris. He took care to forewarn the hotel concierge, in order to pledge him to secrecy. Obediently, when the telegram arrived and Roberto was in the dining room eating with Anna, the concierge completed its delivery with a stage whisper, and Roberto slipped it into his pocket nonchalantly. Anna picked up her plate of soup—*stelline in brodo*—and threw it in his face.[7]

Rod Geiger stopped by a day or two later. He found Roberto "all excited" about Bergman and already laying plans to seduce her.

Roberto's interest in *La macchina* evaporated. In mid-August he left for the Venice Festival.

In Sicily, Visconti had been trying to use Rossellini's methods. The Party, via Trombadori, had provided six million lire for him to film Verga's *I malavoglia*. The project evolved into *La terra trema* instead, and the Catholic Salvo D'Angelo found the rest of the money through the Bank of Sicily. Visconti, a self-indulgent millionaire duke who, until the April 1948 elections, firmly believed the left would triumph, was the Party's own answer to Rossellini. "From the very beginning," recalls Franco Zeffirelli, "I found [Visconti's] upper-class Communism faintly ridiculous. Later I was to see how the 'Party' used celebrities and intellectuals like Luchino to burnish its image, and I came to despise his blindness. In our circle of friends we called Luchino 'Philippe Égalité' and would joke with him that he should pray to God that the Communists never [come] to power lest he end on the scaffold like his namesake."[8]

Visconti's idea was to use actual Sicilian fishermen speaking their own dialect, as Roberto had done with people of the Po Delta. It was Zeffirelli's job to choose the performers, tell them the story, and help them invent their own dialogue. It soon became clear that there was no such thing as 'real' when the camera was present. The policeman was supposed to 'play' a policeman; the lawyer, a lawyer; the priest, a priest; the peasant, a peasant; but they were utterly lost. They had never had to think through what being themselves meant in the way that an actor does constantly, always imagining himself inside other people. So they fell back on acting conventions familiar from popular films and touring theatricals. "The results would have been funny if it hadn't been for the glowering presence of Luchino. Our non-actors fell back on melodramatic gestures, pompous set speeches, anything but the 'reality' he sought. . . . Whenever possible I would collect the next group together as far from Luchino as possible and try to coax them through their scene."[9]

Commented Roberto: "People too often think that neo-realism means having someone unemployed play someone unemployed. I choose actors solely for their physique. You can choose anyone, off the street, . . . [but] when he finds himself in front of the camera, he's completely lost and will try to 'play'; it's this that must absolutely be avoided. This man has gestures, always the same. But with the same muscles at work in front of the camera, he gets paralyzed, forgets himself—so much that he doesn't even recognize himself—he thinks he's become an exceptional being because he's going to be filmed. My work is to put him back into his real nature, to reconstruct him, to reteach him his habitual gestures."[10]

La terra trema was the only major neo-realist film of the period that truly tried to explore the "structures" of social abuse. It looked like filmed theater, even more than Flaherty (whom Visconti was perhaps thinking of); its images were magnificent; and its dialect was unintelligible to Italians. The Venice screening, September 1, was a disaster complete with hecklers and fistfights. Roberto came with ill will; Visconti in his eyes was a brazen plagiarist. But his prejudices gave way to admiration as he watched, then to enthusiasm. Visconti, he ruminated, was a true artist.

Venice gave him few other pleasures. *L'amore* was a dull dud compared to *La terra trema*, lacking the "success" of a scandal. The most Roberto had managed was to embarrass the Biennale president when he and Anna, sitting on either side of him, spent the screening holding hands across his lap. Cocteau had jumped up after *Una voce umana* and embraced Magnani, and jumped again after *Il miracolo* to embrace Roberto. But it was obvious to everyone that the applause had been for her, that the audience had found both parts of *L'amore* tedious.[11] (*Germania anno zero*, its failure all but certain, was not presented at Venice, though still unreleased. Did Roberto fear a harsher repeat of the Festival's hostile reception of *Paisà*, two years before?)

David Selznick was still negotiating, still confident that Roberto had committed himself. Indeed, Roberto had wired Jenia Reissar in late July

1948 to come to Rome to complete their contract, and she had responded offering to come in two weeks, and he had not replied. Instead she read in a newspaper that he had agreed with Boris Morros and Alexander Paal to shoot an episode of *A Tale of Five Cities* (to star Isa Miranda and be scripted by Amidei) and to supervise four other directors in the other episodes: Wolfgang Staudte, Autant-Lara, Paul Rotha, and a Hungarian named Keleti.[12]

Then on August 23, out of the blue from Venice where *Duel in the Sun* had been shown, came a telegram to Jennifer Jones: "CONGRATULATIONS FOR YOUR WONDERFUL PERFORMANCE IN DUEL HOPING TO BE WORKING WITH YOU SOON REGARDS ROBERT ROSSELLINI."[13]

Selznick wired Reissar. "What do you make of . . . this? Jennifer would like to reply. . . . I was bewildered by it." He had just read in the newspaper that Bergman had "definitely made a deal with Rossellini." But, he said, "I do not want Rossellini to think Miss Jones is rude in not acknowledging his gracious congratulations."[14]

Next, on September 16, Roberto asked Arabella Lemaître to have Reissar meet him in Paris between the 23rd and the 27th at the Hotel Raphael. "He said that this time he wants to sign," Lemaître wrote Reissar, "and that he is certain you will close the deal. I presume that now he is piping down a little bit and as it looks like he is not having all the success he thought he would have, he wants to sign just to show that he too is signing a contract with Selznick. You know I am [a] good friend of Roberto and I hate to say things against him. I have talked with people who have worked with him in this last picture. Everyone of them is disgusted. Imagine that he did not even accomplish (finish) the picture himself. He left Maiori and asked Amidei to finish it! Everything was so disorganized; they hardly ever worked during the day, and only because he had to go fishing. People who know him close and even relatives say he will never change, and I am afraid that if he signs a contract with Mr. Selznick the one who will be in trouble all the time will be Selznick."[15]

Reissar forwarded Lemaître's letter to Selznick, adding that she had talked with a lawyer for De Sica, Rossellini, and the American Embassy. "[Ercole] Graziadei told me . . . Rossellini is a 'prima donna' and one never knows what he is going to do or how he is going to behave, and he did not consider him a serious business man."[16]

Nonetheless Selznick, while admitting Lemaître's report was "frightening," asked Reissar to have a "candid conversation" with Rossellini. She replied she would call him when he got to Paris.

Roberto decided to drive to Paris in his bright red Cisitalia. He had been invited by André Bazin to present a film (*Germania? L'amore?*) at the Studio de l'Étoile for Objectif 48, an elegant, intellectual film club. Typically, he tarried in Rome and set out for Paris only that same morning, carrying the film with him. It would be close, he knew, but it wouldn't be boring. He enjoyed pushing his bright red Cisitalia to supersonic speeds, and when she developed motor problems, that only made things more interesting.

Eager to share his fun, he took to phoning Bazin or Doniol-Valcroze each time he stopped for gas, food, or water.

At 7:45 the theater was filled. "I'm fifty kilometers from Paris!" he announced. At 8:05 he rang again: "I'm in Paris! Give me precise directions!"

Like a bullet he streaked through Saturday night traffic and, dashing into the theater, deposited the film into Bazin's waiting hands. "I've set a Paris-Rome record," he proclaimed, breathless and happy.[17]

Loyally, Jenia Reissar phoned the Hotel Raphael on Thursday the 23rd. Rossellini had gone out, she was told; no one knew where he had gone. She left a message and called again Friday. Same result. Roberto never returned her call.

"That is typical of Rossellini!" she told Selznick. "He is temperamental and irresponsible." He hadn't answered Peyser's letters about the contract. He still hadn't sent the story for Jennifer Jones he had promised months ago. "[*L'amore*] met with no success at all in Venice, which must have maddened him as all his friends were praising it. I wouldn't be surprised if that weren't the reason for the 'walk-out' on his last picture!"[18]

"You win," Selznick at last conceded. "I think we would be leading with our chins to deal with this man."[19]

The reason Roberto was in Paris, unbeknownst to Reissar, was to meet Ingrid Bergman, which he did on Sunday, September 26, at the Hotel Georges V. She had come with her husband, Petter Lindstrom, from London, where she was filming *Under Capricorn* with Alfred Hitchcock. With Roberto, besides Ilya Lopert, who as producer of their prospective film had arranged the rendezvous, was Rudolph Solmsen, an American producer whom Roberto had enticed into participation in *La macchina*. The meeting lasted about two hours and was held in great secrecy. Ingrid, by her own account at the time, was nervous and awed and quivering with excitement: "I was looking at those dark eyes of Roberto's." He seemed so shy, so subjugated by the other men, she thought; she feared the businessmen would scuttle their artistic project and longed to throw her arms around him and assure him she was on his side.[20] Roberto, by his account, as reported by Marcella De Marchis, "came back from Paris more surprised than moved. Until then he had known Ingrid only through her films and wasn't expecting to find so much timidity in so famous an actress. Ingrid blushed every dozen words, spoke in a mixture of English and French and, as usual, was dressed with great simplicity. When Roberto told me the story of their secret meeting, I had the feeling that he had not been upset by the woman but only by the actress and, given our friendly relationship, there was nothing in the event to cause me to worry."[21]

Roberto didn't require potent motives to seduce a woman. Mere whim or a comrade's dare was sufficient. Still Ingrid loomed as a particular challenge. She was tall, blonde, and Nordic; also she was a Hollywood superstar and (symbolically) American. Sexually, racially, professionally, geo-politically, she embodied Roberto's insecurities, and thus everything he had to conquer. His ambition was not to go to Hollywood and become a great Hollywood director, as so many Europeans (though no Italians) had done; his ambition was to *beat* Hollywood, to vindicate Italian cinema over American movies, to avenge Italy for the humiliations of America's occupation. Bergman was a means to this end. To friends in Rome he outlined his tactics. "Swedish women are the easiest in the world to impress," he said, "because they have such cold husbands. The love they get is an analgesic balm instead of a tonic."[22]

Behind Roberto's bravado, these first accounts suggest, lay another reality. From the moment Roberto and Ingrid had first laid eyes on each other, their empathy was overwhelming.

Poor Solmsen! Roberto had abandoned *La macchina* completely. There were shots of the photographer snapping a picture, but none of whom he was filming; there was a shot of Marilyn waving, but none of whom she waved to; and so on. "If I had the nerve," groaned Solmsen, "I'd show *Machine* as it is. Nobody would understand it, but that wouldn't matter. The highbrow critics would go crazy over Rossellini's new trend toward surrealism."[23]

Solmsen sold his holding back to Roberto, although how he accomplished that trick is not recorded, and four years later Roberto—or his assistants—completed the film, despite the 82-year-old demon's premature demise. *La macchina* debuted in May 1952, attracted no notice, and sank into an oblivion from whence it has never emerged—a fate by no means merited. "A scherzo full of whimsy, loaded with all the southern atmosphere, both tragic and comic, of the *commedia dell'arte*," wrote Gino Visentini, justly, in *Bianco e Nero*.[24]

Poor Genesi! Roberto owed his lab, Technostampa, so much money that Genesi was amazed Roberto came to the phone and agreed to an appointment the next morning at eleven. Of course he wouldn't show up. But he did! They talked for an hour, so entertainingly that after Roberto left Genesi realized he hadn't asked for the money. "I could have killed him," he swore.[25]

Lemaître's and Reissar's assessments were correct. Critically, Roberto was on the defensive. *L'amore* opened ever so quietly in November 1948, while *Germania anno zero*, after its disastrous screening in May, was held off until December.

"Everyone thought *Germania anno zero* inadequate to its historical situation," Di Giammatteo recalled. "Perhaps reality had been illuminated in many of its secondary aspects, but the nucleus had escaped Rossellini's interpretation. There had been no amply meaningful synthesis as in *Paisà*, just a series of uncoordinated intuitions, of which nary one could really be called penetrating."[26]

Hadn't the same thing been said of *Paisà*?

People were unfair, remarked Massimo Mida. "Once again they wanted a polished and relaxed discourse from him, from him who instead preferred a language that was modern and nervous."[27]

People resented that Rossellini was not more like Visconti or De Sica.

Worse than the head-shaking in Rome, was Auriol's notice in Paris's (and Bazin's) *Revue du Cinéma*. "Roberto Rossellini," he wrote, "has been raised so high that, without being unkind, we can bring him down from his honored terrace to a less lofty level where his head, no longer lost in the clouds, will be more readily available to the beam of a flashlight." *Deutschland* left him indifferent. It was hasty and superficial, Rossellini was lazy and puerile. Incapable of getting deeply to the heart of things, because he didn't know German and had spent little time in Berlin, he had tried to be sensational instead, like a student who's clever at hiding his ignorance.[28]

Auriol was an important critic—he had founded the original *Revue du Cinéma* in 1927—and was saying aloud what most people were thinking privately. Tales of Roberto's antics, with the film club exploit as proof, had added to doubts about his seriousness. Were *Deutschland*'s "deficiencies" in content and plot really due to Rossellini's "modern, nervous language"? or were they due to his assumption that he could get along without good writers and depend on the moment's inspiration? Besides, *Deutschland* seemed so unrelievably negative! As far as the left was concerned, it offered no constructive contribution whatsoever to the building of a new society.

Yet by now Rossellini was a sort of national treasure. Instinctively some critics adopted deferential and even defensive tones. The picture received first prizes at the Locarno Festival, where it played July 11.[29] The respected Communist Aristarco praised its filmic and psychological riches.[30] And *L'Écran Français*, while conceding its superficiality, lauded the filmic language as "revolutionary.... Direct contact between the camera and reality is not a metaphor. Image-writing spurts from the brain and sensibility of the filmmaker just as does the word-writing of a novelist."[31]

Phenomenology, however, was no substitute for passion. "It doesn't touch the heart, it turns it to stone," complained one critic.[32] "[It is] coldly objective . . . like a newsreel . . . , unemotional," concurred another.[33] "Rossellini," concluded another, "put all his bets . . . on the hope of always being lucky. . . . He also wanted to make a lot of money, and so he paid more attention to production problems than artistic ones. . . . Born with the ambition of making the world tremble, born with an implacable indictment in a Dostoyevskian atmosphere, [*Germania*] got reduced to modest proportions by a production mediocrely planned and conducted."[34]

Even Bazin was lukewarm, responsive more to the idea of the thing than to the movie itself. "It's not a movie but a sketch, the rough draft of a work Rossellini hasn't given us." As a reportage it's insufficient intellectually and physically. But as a character sketch it's too long. "Having failed to make Germany's *Paisà*, Rossellini gives the impression of artificially stretching out an action that would have been perfect compressed into twenty minutes. But this said, it would be unjust to remain insensitive to the profound originality of the direction. Rossellini is the sole director in the world ... who knows how to treat his action ... without distinguishing it from the ensemble into which it is inserted. A trolley that passes, a stone that rolls, a piece of wall have exactly the same formal importance as the detail which gives the image its dramatic sense. What's wonderful about this, is that this detail gains increased force thereby, since the author has obliged us to discern its meaning. ... [Although sudden, the boy's suicide] seems natural and necessary, because Rossellini was able, from the outside, to lead us to understand the child's inner drama. It suffices to compare *Deutschland im Jahre Null* to ... *Shoeshine* to realise the radical difference in means. It is impossible to cry at Rossellini's films, because he never uses directly emotional methods and because he constantly requires the exercise of our intelligence to inform our heart. The meaning of things and events is offered to us still shut up within the amorphous gangue of reality."[35]

Objections to *L'amore* were less restrained. "A cross between the works of the Marquis de Sade and the first epistle to the Corinthians," quipped England's Dylis Powell.[36] "It tries to pass off as evangelically 'poor in spirit' a woman actually 'poor in mind,'" joked *Cinema Nuovo*.[37] "Frankly ugly ..., false ..., even the mountains seem false," *Cinema* charged.[38]

Rossellini's juxtaposition of earthly love in one episode with divine love in the second proved he couldn't make up his mind, thought Mario Gromo: "If the first episode is competent filmed theater, the second comes close to looking like an unintentional parody of the Nativity, its tone recalling the faked rusticness of certain furniture makers. With *L'amore* Rossellini's parabola reaches a crisis."[39]

"Rossellini has completely abandoned neo-realism," charged *L'Unità*; *Una voce umana* was "D'Annunzianismo" and *Il miracolo* "a negative experience."[40] *Una voce* was "theater, not cinema," objected *Avanti!* and *Il miracolo* had "more the flavor of a variety sketch than religious drama. It doesn't grab, move, enthuse, or involve spectators."[41]

Bazin, although grateful Rossellini was escaping neo-realism's prescribed subject matter, thought *Una voce* "simply scandalous in its cinematic laziness. It's obvious Rossellini doesn't even worry about where to put his camera; he depends on his actress's body language." *Il miracolo* was much better. "Magnani is prodigious, the landscapes beautiful, the story sensational, but throughout the film we admire more than we're moved. There's a taste of intelligent bravura, of someone who can calculate his effects well and knows when he has good material."[42]

Il miracolo did have its defenders—even at *L'Unità*, where Ugo Casiraghi judged it "a good film, possibly a masterwork." In London, C. A. Lejeune called it, as a piece of craft, "the most beautiful among all Rossellini's works."[43] The Jesuit Fantuzzi later remarked how its "contrast of fall and hope could not be neater. The protagonists of the two episodes ... push their inner experience (desire for consummation and death in one case, enthusiasm for love and life in the other) to the point of insanity."[44] And the Catholic Agel, in response to Gromo's parabolic groan, also argued that *L'amore*'s antithetical episodes throw its moral into relief: "to a sterile and destructive suffering can be opposed a fecund and regenerating suffering."[45]

Such Christian interpretations were what others objected to. *Il miracolo* was an "evasion," charged Di Giammatteo, using the buzzword for a cop-out. Rossellini used to manifest a "primitive sensibility in contact with adequate material"; but now primitive material had become an end in itself.[46]

Auriol shook his flashlight scoldingly at Rossellini's self-indulgence. "He limits his role to being a witness. . . . One almost gets the impression that it is the irresistible virago Magnani who has directed *L'amore*, while Rossellini has done nothing but decide what gets shown, like the worst naturalist novelists. . . . He has combined different elements that do not go together harmoniously: on one hand, an expert actress incarnating the pregnant mad woman with an exaltation that is both prodigious and irritating . . . ; on the other, the ordinary life of a town, flattened by a newsreel-like photography that strips it of its picturesqueness . . . without the everyday grayness bringing out (or hiding, or diminishing, or nuancing) the violence of the unusual. . . . On one hand [the movie looks like] a 'documentary' as banal as Pagnol's old exteriors; on the other, [it is] theater, almost a populist mystery-play. The whole thing [is] held together by the most primitive technique, with indecisive cutting and chance ideas. . . . Rather than the triumphant pioneer of some supposed 'neo-realism' . . . , Rossellini strikes me as an 'anarchist.' Dangerous because of the illusions he is capable of spreading among young inexperienced filmmakers, this artistic anarchist is even more dangerous to himself. And I adjure him to rediscover his style or *a* style . . . , to make himself a creative force again, and to impose his personality on his admirers once more. His latest films have virtually no form, and what lacks form exists only as lifeless, moldable material. It would be sad to see a man of cinema of Roberto Rossellini's quality commit 'suicide' because, reveling in his 'genius,' he just goes on making work instead of works."[47]

Evidently, Roberto had misunderstood his Paris fans' reactions to *Roma città aperta* and *Paisà*.

At any rate, by the end of 1948, when Fernaldo Di Giammatteo met him for the first time, Roberto was being bombarded from all sides with an inchoate avalanche of adverse criticism—and by Di Giammatteo too, who judged him an "evader." "Here I am," Roberto told him, "fighting a really big battle, here I am making gigantic efforts to stand up to competition, the weight of the industry, the amorality of private impositions, to break the vicious circle that is threatening to suffocate us all, and look how I'm repaid. I work and fight for everybody and everybody persists in not understanding me. Is it possible—you tell me!—is it possible to go on this way, under these conditions?"

Wrote Di Giammatteo: "He confronted me with defiance and stared hard at me with those lively and penetrating eyes of his, as though I were the guilty one, the only guilty one, in this unpleasant situation. As if the injustices of which he felt himself the victim, and which were wounding him profoundly, were my doing.... Rossellini wasn't polemicizing with the cold arguments of reason, nor did he want to defend himself against criticism. He neither begged excuses nor accepted debate. Precise and ringing, his words seemed to want to strike down ... the barrier between us, to conquer my resistance, to bend me by the force of his convictions. Anyhow, why resist? I'd heard about Rossellini's 'fascinating personal charm' and now I found myself about to succumb to it."

"They say I'm ambitious," Roberto continued. "But what does ambitious mean? Is a man ambitious who tries not to go to sleep, who doesn't give in and fossilize in the success of a formula [i.e., films like *Roma città aperta*]? Is a man like that ambitious? Tell me frankly. Is he ambitious?"[48]

Seymour Peyser thought he was. While Lopert had gone to California with Bob Benjamin to meet with Bergman, Lindstrom, and her agents, Peyser had been dispatched to Rome to finalize arrangements with Roberto. He was not treated kindly. Roberto dragged out negotiations for a week. Appointments to see him were a problem, Magnani was a problem, money was a problem. Even when Peyser gained access to the presence, Roberto, enthroned amid a miniature court of flunkies coming and going, bowing and kowtowing and calling him "maestro," kept changing the subject. The offers, obviously, were insufficient, Peyser decided, and after more days and nights on the doorstep, he offered $50,000 plus a percentage.

"You have the materialist mentality," Roberto rejoined. "You must know what's in my heart."

"Okay, Roberto. How much is in your heart?" rebutted the exasperated lawyer.

Roberto hated producers. He boasted to his friends that he wanted to make them suffer. So more days passed. But Peyser had been warned of Roberto's unscrupulous manners in negotiations and his patience gave out one night at 4 A.M. He sent word he was leaving Rome that morning at nine if Roberto had not signed. Back came the contract. Roberto had signed for a few thousand more.

They flew to Paris. Roberto, admiring the stewardess, invited her to dinner in the city, and afterward took her to bed.[49]

In Paris he had been invited to speak at IDHEC, the Institute for Higher Cinema Studies.

"There was a magnificent, moving reception, which I certainly did not merit," he told *L'Écran Français*. "They had put up garlands and written '*Vive* Rossellini!' on the walls. They led me into a large hall and had me sit in a big, lovely armchair and all of a sudden I saw a hundred deadly-serious faces staring right through me. 'May we ask Monsieur Rossellini some questions?' someone asked. I said yes, of course. So one young student, very intelligent, stood up and asked me why, in a certain sequence in *Paisà*,

I had used a pan after a close-up, and why the low-angle shot that followed ended up exactly on this point of the scenery rather than...' I confess these questions completely floored me. I had no explanations to give. But I'm afraid that if this young man ever makes films, he'll confuse cinema with algebra."[50]

To *L'Écran*, Roberto defended his work methods. "Maybe people think I'm crazy, but I refuse to know how my film will end on the day I begin to shoot it! I'm incapable of working in a corset. A detailed script to be followed step by step, a studio full of equipment, all that preplanning with scenery and lighting, it's totally odious to me. How do I work? Does anyone ever know how he works? What I can say, is that when I undertake a new film, I start with an idea without knowing where it will lead me. What interests me in the world is the human part and this adventure, unique for each one of us, of life! I'm an individualist before anything else. Every person is unique in their kind, though everyone appears to resemble everyone else. It's something biological: my heart, my lungs, my arteries wouldn't suit anyone else, even though they all have hearts and arteries that are similar. It's because I'm not afraid of the truth and because I'm curious about the human being that I look like a great realist! And I am, yes, if realism is abandoning the individual in front of the camera and letting him construct his own story by himself! From the first day of shooting, I install myself behind my characters, and then I let my camera run after them."[51]

Neo-realism = ∞

(Some More Theory)

In contrast to the universal grumbling about Rossellini, everyone agreed that De Sica's *Bicycle Thieves* (*Ladri di biciclette*) was everything they wanted a neo-realist film to be.

This most famous of all neo-realist pictures opened in Rome on December 22, 1948. Not only did it win De Sica his second Oscar, but it was voted the greatest film ever made in *Sight and Sound's* 1952 poll of international critics, and placed second and third in two other polls. In contrast, no Rossellini picture ever won an Oscar or a place on a ten-best international poll, and rarely placed even on individuals' lists. Even Bazin voted for *Bicycle Thieves* rather than a Rossellini film.[1]

Bicycle Thieves had not been an easy film to produce. De Sica was not taken seriously as a realist filmmaker; his dreary projects were anathema to producers. On the variety stage he could sing Italian songs with a foreign accent to packed, enraptured audiences in *Za bum*. But *Shoeshine* had played to empty halls, briefly. So when De Sica tried to get financing for *Bicycle Thieves* in Italy, France, England, Switzerland, and America, no one would give a lira except Selznick, perhaps, and only if Cary Grant were given the starring role. Only by accident did De Sica find sixty million lire in Italy from a private backer.[2]

It was Zavattini who had introduced De Sica to Luigi Bartolini's book *Ladri di biciclette*. But it was in Amidei's apartment, by deference and necessity since Amidei would work nowhere else, that De Sica and Zavattini went for their script sessions for the first month—at the end of which Amidei lost his temper and threw them out. "Certain things I didn't agree about irritated me, and I asked them to go away. De Sica went down and outside found Rossellini, who told him I had these explosions but that they passed. Maybe this one passed too, but not until much later."[3] By then the picture was finished.

Many things about "Za" infuriated Amidei, among them his obsession with minutiae. Days had been wasted, preparing *Shoeshine*, deliberating the color of the horse. During *Bicycle Thieves* typical were the moments when Zavattini would declare, "I think the protagonist should go out with a baguette of bread and mortadella wrapped in a newspaper on which can be read the word 'Unità.'" And Amidei, after a glacial silence, would explode, "God in heaven! What the hell's 'Unità' doing there? Why not just 'tà'?" And De Sica, after another long pause, would murmur, "Dear friends, I think what we need is an apple, a red apple, one of those varied-colored ones, half red and half shaded, which he'd leave the house biting into."[4] (In the film, an omelet is wrapped in an anonymous newspaper.) A more substantive difficulty was the worker's wife who, in the film as we now have it, disappears after the opening scenes. To Amidei, who prided himself on sound construction, this was unacceptable. And, he explained, "I had basic doubts about the whole idea. I didn't think it was 'Italian.' It didn't seem right that at that moment a comrade, a Communist, a worker who lived in a project and whose bicycle had been stolen, wouldn't go the Party office and that they wouldn't find a bicycle for him. The film was ignoring the sort of solidarity that existed then. Why? Because behind it, even though it was modified, remained Bartolini's character, who went off looking for the thief."[5]

Michele Scalera had made the same objection, except for a change of party, when De Sica had tried to sell the project to his studio.[6]

Bicycle Thieves' ante-premiere for an audience of students was held at the Barberini some weeks before the public opening.[7] Anxious and not wanting to be noticed, De Sica crept into the hall after the lights went out and sat with Maria Mercader in the back row. Roberto, not saying a word, took the seat beside them, slid a cigarette between De Sica's lips, and lit it for him. He didn't realize De Sica had gone almost a year without smoking and that his little gift would start him up again, never to stop.

The students liked the movie, the critics liked the film, Amidei admitted he'd been wrong ("I'm a shit!"[8]), but audiences stayed away. Somebody had decided to open *Bicycle Thieves* for Christmas. "Give us our money back," De Sica heard one father complain, "and tell large families what a gyp this movie is!"[9] The picture closed after a few weeks and De Sica found himself in Paris trying to sell it. At the Salle Pleyel his friends organized a soirée for 3,000 of the city's artistic and intellectual elite. That night De Sica was even more nervous than before—the print had almost not arrived; Graziadei had had to smuggle it through customs—but the result was a triumph. "The most emotional night of my life," De Sica called it.[10]

Once again an Italian film, unappreciated at home, found immortality abroad.

But for *Deutschland im Jahre Null* there was no welcome anywhere. "I had shot *Deutschland im Jahre Null* exactly as I wanted to, and when I see it again today, I come out of the projection totally wrecked," Rossellini said. "It seems to me that my judgment of Germany was just—not complete, but just. Nevertheless, and against all expectations, *Deutschland im Jahre Null* was quite badly received, and it was then that I began to ask myself questions. The film world had reorganized, had gone back to its prewar habits and style; people were judging *Deutschland im Jahre Null* by that prewar aesthetic, whereas they had loved *Roma città aperta* and *Paisà* for what had been new about them. Moreover, the political world had also reorganized and was judging the film politically. The reviews of *Deutschland im Jahre Null* taught me what the journalists thought about the German problem (or what the editor of their paper thought) but were of no use to me on the critical level. At that moment I found myself confronted with a dilemma: either prostitution or sincerity."[11]

Rossellini was under double attack. Audiences, producers, and politicians hated neo-realism of any sort; neo-realism's advocates found Rossellini an embarrassment.

Bicycle Thieves' success solidified the tendency to think of neo-realism as social realism rather than Crocean exploration. This was true particularly in England where Labor had come to power, and so it became true in America where England was in power in culture. *Paisà*, although admired, had met basic misperceptions in England, expressed in the same terms that had lambasted *Deutschland* on the continent. "These incidents have no apparent link of purpose and the continuity within them is poor," wrote one critic.[12] "[Rossellini] may one day feel ashamed at having merely done well in haste by a theme that deserved to be done better at leisure," wrote another.[13] "['The Po Delta'] just stops . . . on a note of sudden, hurried, almost insignificant despair," wrote Basil Wright, who was immune to Rossellini's style and passion, and thought that *Paisà*, like *Roma città aperta*, needed more "sense of statement. . . . The so-called 'documentary approach' . . . makes for realism . . . but to the extent that it inhibits the artist . . . from imposing his ideas on his raw material, from exercising his right to shape and to exclude, it is not conducive to the making of masterpieces."[14]

Deutschland was taken as justifying these admonitions, and *Bicycle Thieves*, a paradigm of social-realist cinema, brought them into focus. Besides, *Paisà's* anti-British sentiments still rankled.[15] "We must, I think, revise a number of opinions that we have formed rather prematurely about the Italian cinema," led off Lotte Eisner in *Sequence*. "Too much importance has been attached to Rossellini, too little acknowledgment has been given to Vergano and [D]e Sica. . . . It is not enough for those who were disappointed with *Germania Anno Zero* to say simply that its director—in fact sensationalizing a hasty sight-seeing tour and handicapped particularly by his ignorance of the language—could not grasp the German mentality nor get past its dragooned insensibility. [Auriol had said the same—also without telling *what* Rossellini had not grasped.] For the episodic *Paisà*—though this is not sufficiently realised—was only one stage towards the method of facile improvisation and sketchiness for which Rossellini is now reprimanded. . . . In relating [D]e Sica to the new Italian realism, one feels that his method is more complex than Rossellini's, more controlled, disciplined by a feeling for structure and plastic values that is still developing."[16] Rossellini has shown "an impressive talent for dramatized journalism," agreed Adam Helmer in the same issue, but De Sica seemed "a surer and more profound talent."[17] Even Rossellini's taste in boys was attacked. "An adorable street urchin plays [*Bicycle Thieves'*] son with a delightful spontaneity and simplicity," wrote Eisner. "How different from the stiff, expressionless, too beautiful and grown-up boy that Rossellini chose for *Germania Anno Zero*."[18]

In *Sight and Sound*, Simon Harcourt Smith catalogued Rossellini's deficiencies: (1) No continuity; static, formulaic characters; rough, incoherent cutting; cold intellectuality (unlike *Bicycle Thieves*); no finished films, just rough cuts. (2) Verbosity (because of the absence of a script). (3) Puritanical sex: "his evident and perhaps unconscious loathing of sex (which haunts him. . .) . . . , never recognizing that sex can occasionally leave the mud" results in a "profoundly false view of human existence." (4) No sustained inspiration. (5) In *Il miracolo* the persecution of Nannina for her pregnancy is unrealistic; pregnancy invariably draws compassion from Italians.[19]

Britain's moans differed little from the finger-wagging *Roma città aperta* had initially encountered in Rome. De Sica was preferred because he better fulfilled traditional story values.[20] He had none of Rossellini's off-putting qualities. Instead of incomprehensible tales, weakly constructed, about half-demented characters who find solutions no one else could relate to, De Sica provided straightforward people (compare his boy with Rossellini's neurotic boy), straightforward problems, straightforward suspense, and tearful situations that made everyone cry. Most importantly, *Bicycle Thieves* was about what neo-realism was supposed to be about (unemployment among the desperate proletariat) and was filmed the way neo-realism was supposed to be filmed (on actual city streets, in a working quarter, gray and gritty).

De Sica represented the tradition of quality; Rossellini looked shoddy. De Sica represented important social concerns, Rossellini eccentric ones. De Sica was universal, accessible, and warm, Rossellini individualistic, difficult, and cold. De Sica spoke publicly to the masses as an avatar of the new, socialist age; Rossellini spoke in secret to individuals as a relic of bourgeois egocentrism. *Bicycle Thieves*, Bazin would proclaim, was "the purest expression of neo-realism . . . , the zero point, the ideal center around which gravitate, each in its own orbit, the works of the other great directors."[21]

Paisà a satellite of *Bicycle Thieves*? The two seem hardly to inhabit the same galaxy.

Perfect Aesthetic Illusion of Reality

"The more I go on," confessed Adriano Aprà, "the more I am convinced that either we recognize that Rossellini was the unique neo-realist filmmaker, in which case we need to redefine the term, or else Rossellini was never neo-realist and all the others were, in which case the term has a negative, disparaging meaning.

"In other words, either De Sica, who is a gentleman content to look at reality as it is, is a neo-realist filmmaker, and so Rossellini, who has never been content to look at reality as it is, is not a neo-realist filmmaker. Or else neo-realism means going beyond the vision of things as they are and so Rossellini is neo-realist and De Sica a vulgar naturalist or something like that. It suffices to watch the films without blinders for it to be clear that what are supposed to be the constants of neo-realism (looking at reality so that between the lens and the 'naturalness' of things there be the least possible number of diaphragms) in Rossellini does not exist at all and that his 'naturalness' is something completely different. . . .

"Rossellini is someone who looks at reality with the will to change point of view every time [e.g., *Paisà*]. . . . What is Rossellini's neo-realism? Rossellini does not believe in reality, but in what lies beyond reality, in the stars, or in what lies beneath reality, in stomachs, in placentas."[22]

Reality as it is, indeed, was De Sica's neo-realism for Bazin. Of *Bicycle Thieves* he exclaimed: "No more actors, no more story, no more mise en scène, in other words, ultimately in the perfect aesthetic illusion of reality: no more cinema."[23]

But this is nonsense—as Bazin himself quickly concedes, by adding that a great deal of art is required to create a sense of artlessness.[24] Rossellini, yes, believes in what lies behind reality; but De Sica (De Sica–Zavattini, we should say) is no more committed to straightforward reproduction of reality than Walt Disney. Far from being natural, far from looking at reality as it is, *Bicycle Thieves* turns everything into theater. Unlike "The Po Delta," it was not improvised but thoroughly scripted and thoroughly directed, with De Sica acting out all the parts for his actors to mime. It is not honest in its photographing of Rome (which is made to look gray, depressed and ugly by falsification—by eliminating trees and anything un-ugly from any location shown, by concealing the beautiful piazza a few yards away, by exposing for sunlight while filming in shadow). It is not honest in its depiction of the Roman people (who despite Fascism, war, occupation, and poverty never lost their natural buoyancy and animation—until De Sica set about inducing a zombie-like comportment into his players and eliminating any emotion not sad, angry, or indifferent). It creates a Rome existent neither geographically (cuts connect widely separate locales as though they were proximate) nor socially (Amidei's bicycle objection) nor emotionally (totally flat and gray). And everything in the film is carefully (and beautifully) coordinated to a musical score and edited with the same musical mixture of master shot and details that Hollywood studios used. We may accept *Bicycle Thieves* as poetry, but not as any kind of realism—unless surrealism. De Sica said so himself: "Neo-realism is not . . . reality. It is reality filtered through poetry, reality transfigured. Most films today are made in a realistic style, but they are actually opposed to neo-realism."[25]

Yet the theorists persisted in saying what neo-realism was and getting it backwards. Even Moravia pontificated that "neo-realism's preferred reality is essentially that product of mood that excludes intrigue, psychology, and characters."[26] Perhaps Moravia was thinking of Zavattini's famous description of the ideal neo-realist film as ninety unedited minutes in an average worker's average day. He certainly wasn't thinking of any of Zavattini's actual scripts, which are so melodramatically edited and pointed that they often resemble lachrymose comic strips in slow motion. Unlike in Rossellini's movies (which even less resemble the Moravia/Zavattini ideal), mood comes first in every De Sica–Zavattini film, before people, who are the puppets of that mood (usually just one emotion, which pleases the critics, unlike Rossellini, who usually has too many) that dresses, paints, and shapes them, and follows them like a shadow. Think of any sequence of *Bicycle Thieves* or the entire film, its characters dominated by two or three sensations: the title might just as well have been *Anxiety*. In contrast, people in Rossellini films (Pina, Manfredi, Don Pietro, *Paisà*'s characters, Edmund), although not masters of their emotions, are clearly their emotions' originators, not their puppets—and they page through whole dictionaries of emotions in single short takes.

In *Bicycle Thieves*, as in much traditional theater, sustained mood symbolizes concepts, as do the characters—which is why socially-minded critics wanted everyone to see it: for its sermon. For some bizarre reason literary people love films inhabited by "symbol-people" (in contrast to the labyrinthine depths of *Voyage in Italy*'s people, whom they judge shallow). As Franco Zeffirelli said, *Roma città aperta* is exactly what a neo-realist film was not supposed to be: "[It] succeeded because immensely experienced performers like Magnani and Aldo Fabrizi . . . were suddenly allowed honest dramatic roles, an opportunity that they seized with gusto. It was only later that I realized just how much this was an actor's cinema and not, as was thought at the time, a director's."[27] "What naturally first struck the public," Bazin agrees about *Roma*, "was the excellence of the actors."[28] In comparison, *Bicycle Thieves*' father and son are so everyman-ish that they are no one in particular, everyone in general, in short, no one: simply symbols, foci for our concerned emotions, our mood.

In De Sica–Zavattini, essence precedes existence. There is not exploration, just repetition. *Shoeshine*'s boys are misery, rebellion, and hope—they are individuals only secondarily. In Rossellini, existence precedes essence. *Roma città aperta*'s boys strike us forcibly as *there*; their "meaning" will be aleatory.

Rossellini's characters, when they start as types, expand into persons who freak out questioning their role-playing ("Naples"'s black MP, "Romagna"'s chaplain, *Il miracolo*'s town fool, Karin in *Stromboli*, Irene in *Europe '51*). De Sica–Zavattini's characters remain types, plumbing, fathoming, and contemplating their simplest self-definition: it is the *idea* of the victimized worker that moves us, not his particularity. Is this the "new reality"? Is this the way to change the world?

They are poets in different directions, De Sica and Rossellini. They belong to "different aesthetic families," Bazin says.[29] Rossellini amplifies the range of his characters' sensations, whose heightened presence excites the filmic world they inhabit. Streets, landscapes, rooms, and objects, though straightforwardly photographed, shimmer on the screen not as "mere reality" but as romance. This is what is meant by "expressionism" or "melodrama." The filmic storyworld is active, projecting mood rather than receiving it. We feel the filmmaker's personality as strongly as we feel the objects he photographs. "The Po Delta"'s marshes, *Deutschland's* spot-lit rooms and streets, *La nave bianca's* looming cannon testify to Rossellini's use of angle and lighting to force environment to become an actor rather than a backdrop. De Sica does this too, but his actors only repeat their backdrops. In Rossellini, people and their surroundings rarely complement: they contend, they set each other off, their opposition enhances each of them. World and characters are alive, incredibly variegated, provocatively distant each from the other. Within the fiction, too, there is distance and opposition. *Roma città aperta's* heroes are almost always viewed by someone who is nonheroic and outside the action. Don Pietro, for instance, watches Manfredi being tortured. And the German colonel (or Marina) watches them both and becomes the chief subject of analysis rather than Don Pietro or Manfredi.[30]

Something similar occurs in *Bicycle Thieves*, where the son serves as a foil for his father's emotions. The simplicity of their relationship is the movie's subject and climaxes by overwhelming the question of the bicycle.[31] We watch De Sica's twosome with less interference from the camera, the world, or other watchers than in *Roma*; the dialectic is clear and sustained.

De Sica and Rossellini are poets in different directions, but within the same school. Dialectic between individual and environment (actor and event) is a trait of "expressionism" which Bazin claimed for "realism," which shows how evasive such labels can be. That dialectic, intensely experienced in Murnau's *Nosferatu, The Last Laugh,* and, above all, *Sunrise,* had changed movies forever in the mid-1920s. Murnau had decried shots that were "beautiful" or "interesting" for their own sake—which had formerly been the norm for a "good" film—and now had demanded shots that would "intensify"[32] the dramatic interplay between actor and set. King Vidor, whom Rossellini and De Sica took as their model, had applied Murnau's intensity to events of the day. Many great directors can be grouped into this "realist-expressionist" school with its two opposing tendencies. With the caveats that these tendencies descend from common parentage and share common aims, that they oppose each other as yin to yang rather than as black to white, and that any assertion must admit a dozen exceptions, see the following chart (Figure 1) outlining the opposing tendencies.

It was for a variety of reasons, then, that the De Sica–Zavattini brand of neo-realism seemed better suited to the needs of a cinema dedicated to social reform.

For Rossellini, social reform was a personal odyssey. In *Roma città aperta,* under Amidei's influence, he had respected certain symbolizing conventions of the Resistance (Marina's prostitution shows she is bad). But in *Paisà,* he had rejected Resistance conventions (Francesca's prostitution is

FIGURE 1

Lang • Eisenstein • Hitchcock De Sica	Murnau • Ford • Sternberg Rossellini
SOCIAL REALISM: *promote change*	AESTHETIC REALISM: *experience*
Theater	Travelogue
Symbol	Characterization
Action (character's working out of a dilemma)	Passion (character's consciousness of a dilemma)
Shape (stasis)	Gesture (motion)
Geometric picture (flat)	Angular stage (deep)
Reality stylized (anti-realist)	Style for realism (realist-illusion)
People as agents of determining milieu: mechanical	People acting freely within determining milieu: organic
Méliès	Lumière

"STERN MORALISTS"	"PHOTOGRAPHERS"
Drama in intellect: -in psychology -in subjectivity -in (Eisenstein & De Sica) doctrinaire analyses of character-less events	Drama in aesthetics: dialectic between milieu and character.
Films address mass audiences publicly	Films address individuals privately
Techniques excite emotion— "Protest"	Techniques incite dialectic— "Wonder"
Morally unambivalent: clear solutions	Moral tangles: no facile solutions

"JANSENISTS"	"FRANCISCANS"
People innocent: the system makes them evil, unhappy, and alienated.	People sinful: they create the system.
Alienation bad: divorces individual from community.	Alienation good: individual critiques convention.
Hope, happiness, security only in community	Hope (and fault) in each individual
Heroes: paragons of simplicity	Heroes: anguished complexity
Villains: complex	Villains: simplistic
Eisenstein: system encourages our worst traits, punishes best ones. **Lang/Hitchcock**: alienation leads us into lunacy and misery, away from communal security.	**Murnau**: alienation = love. In *Tabu* society destroys lovers. **Sternberg**: love brings wisdom. **Ford**: Christ-like isolation

Vidor: we search alone, but our answers
are realizable only within the family.

De Sica: alienation produces social rejects.	**Rossellini**: alienation = love.

viewed sympathetically from her side; the partisans are "chicken thieves"). And in "Naples," "Romagna," *Deutschland*, and *Il miracolo*, the characters inhabit moral universes that are so solipsistic that the characters are neither ideological nor even "typical." Rossellini's characters, even when confronted with *problems* that others share, almost never come up with *solutions* that others can share. Edmund's leap to death, like Nannina's leap from alienation to "sanctity," is far indeed from the sort of "model" social-realist critics wanted movies to provide. Hitchcock would shortly become famous for moving his camera to follow his characters and concentrate on their inner emotions; yet even he would not dolly and track after a heroine so obsessively (or with such melodramatically high angles) as Rossellini does Nannina in *Il miracolo* (after trapping the same actress in a room in *Una voce umana*). "Neo-realism," Rossellini declared, "consists in following a person . . . through all their discoveries, all their impressions."[33] Thus the disconcertion over *Una voce umana* and *Il miracolo* is quite understandable. They *are* inquiries into private worlds.[34] The characters do pursue private obsessions beyond the limits of everyday sanity—into shame. The social application of their experience is difficult to grasp. The illumination Rossellini's heroes experience is not a sense of themselves as agents of their class or community but, as Croce would prefer, a sense of their individuality as a poetic impulse opening to new, original experience. "Thoughts are the shadows of our sensations—always darker, emptier, simpler," wrote Nietzsche.[35] For Rossellini or Croce, such illumination encounters reality; but for many social realists, it is merely mysticism, an "evasion" of actual social problems. Yet surely the evasion at the end of *Bicycle Thieves* is just as flagrant as the (alleged) one at the end of *Stromboli* or *Il miracolo*.

Rossellini defended his course to Di Giammatteo: "The sort of realism I inaugurated with *Roma città aperta* and *Paisà* is no longer useful today. It was fine when it seemed criminal not to suggest to people the need to sink their hands in, to feel what things are made of. Today other things push me. Today I believe we have to find a new and solid base on which to build, on which to represent man as he is, in the union that exists in him between poetry and reality, desire and action, dream and life. For this I made *L'amore* and *La macchina ammazzacattivi*, which is perhaps my most original film. . . . My new convictions are summed up and explained [there]."[36]

"I see the Madonna every day," says Peparuolo, in *Il miracolo*.

"I'm a monk twenty years and have never seen a miracle," retorts a younger man.

"He's a materialist," explains Peparuolo.

Rossellini's critics chorused "Involution!" It was joked that he brought his confessor onto the set. De Santis and Visconti were struggling to make people aware of how fishermen, rice harvesters, and Calabrian peasants were being exploited like beasts right now in Italy today. But Rossellini was obsessed with interiority, dreams, and ideas—upper-class, cop-out problems. Even sensitive friends like Trombadori concluded, "Rossellini was outside of all that. He didn't pose questions of realism or anti-realism, or whether it was necessary to continue to probe and engage social problems. He wanted to be a great Hollywood director."[37]

Ayfre at the Front

Italian art from Giotto to futurism had sought to speak to the masses in public terms, and had almost always functioned as propaganda for the Church or other powers. Rossellini, in contrast, seemed northern European, with his Vermeer-like intimacy, his private revelations in caves, and his existentialism. For this reason he was viewed suspiciously by Italians and would find his ardent champions among Bazin's disciples at *Cahiers du Cinéma*. His way was prepared by Amédée Ayfre, a priest of the Confraternity of St. Sulpice.

Ayfre had come to Paris in 1949 to study philosophy with Gabriel Marcel and Maurice Merleau-Ponty and discovered cinema. Never has there been a more exciting time and place for doing so. Almost every day brought the discovery of some new titanic masterpiece at the Cinémathèque Française. And these discoveries were being celebrated in fashionable intellectual journals like *Esprit* and *La Revue du Cinéma*. Film clubs were springing up all over the capital.

Ayfre saw *Allemagne année zéro* at a little club near Trocadéro on October 27. The discussion afterwards was awkward and desultory. Ayfre listened in silence, went home, wrote his first essay on film, and sent it to Bazin at *Esprit*. Ayfre had been oriented by Bazin's articles, but his scholastic formation inspired him to organize Bazin's disheveled ideas,[38] and in so doing Ayfre established a "phenomenological" approach to movies that inspired the richest veins of cinema theory, analysis, and experience. *Deutschland* works, Ayfre thought, not as a documentary but as a psychological study of the boy, and not of child psychology in general or of boy-victims of the Nazis in general, but of *the* boy himself, of his "global human attitude" in this specific situation, where his abrupt passage into adulthood is required.[39]

What is special, Ayfre continues, is the *way* the film studies Edmund's passage to adulthood. An actor would have played—would have translated via gesture, body language, and words—the feelings the director wanted the character to feel. But here there is no introspection, tell-tale grimacing, or symptomatic behavior: this boy never "plays." We can't say he plays well or poorly; he's beyond that. We can't say he's sympathetic or antipathetic; he simply lived and the camera has watched. We can't specify how he feels after killing his father (regret? remorse? despair?). We can't say if he kills himself deliberately or if he had a sudden dizzy spell. "It's the child's whole being that's in play here, and it's for just that reason that he doesn't 'play.'" What Rossellini gives us is a "total human attitude." A total sense of existence is therefore derivable from the film. But such a sense is not, as in so many novels, plays, or films, a pre-existing thesis that the film will demonstrate. Essence does not precede existence in Rossellini, essence is part of the attitude the film studies. Thus meaning is always ambiguous for us outsiders. Just as we don't know if the boy's death is suicide or accident, so too Marxists, Sartrians, and Christians will dispute its cause and meaning: a crystallization of the economic disorder of a decadent society? a polarization of the world's absurdity? a testimony of a world where God's love cannot penetrate? "Rossellini himself does not decide. He poses an interrogation. With his existential attitude he confronts us with the mystery of existence." Rossellini's novelty is his having made the child into a sign, a sacrament almost, of a humanity which, despite all our progress, constantly has to go back to zero and ask again the same questions about what it all means.[40]

In later articles Ayfre would enrich our experience of Rossellini's other movies via this notion of "sacramental cinema." Now he argued that neo-realism should be rechristened "phenomenological realism."

Bazin agreed. In *Esprit*, November 1949, Bazin talked about De Sica's treating each event in *Bicycle Thieves* in "its phenomenological integrity"; he had made similar points in the past, he added, but without the term "phenomenological." In January 1948 he had written that "facts in themselves [acquire a] sort of ontological autonomy that makes them a succession of closed-off monads, strictly limited by their appearances."[41] Also, in his first review of *Deutschland* Bazin had remarked on Rossellini's giving equal attention to unimportant and important details.[42] And in a second review, had anticipated some of Ayfre's other ideas:

"Rossellini's . . . kid is eleven or twelve, it would have been easy and even normal for the script and acting to put us into the secret of his conscience. But if we know something about how this child thinks and feels, it is never by direct signs readable on his face, nor even by his behavior, for we understand it only by crosscheck and conjecture. . . . This psychological objectivity is in the logic of [Rossellini's] style. Rossellini's 'realism' has nothing in common with anything that cinema (except Renoir) has given us till now. It is not a realism of the subject but of the style. He is perhaps the sole director in the world who knows how to interest us in an action while leaving it objectively on the same level of mise en scène as its context. . . . It is not the actor who moves us, nor the event, but the meaning that we are obliged to extract from it. In this mise en scène, the moral or dramatic sense is never apparent on the surface of reality; nevertheless we cannot avoid knowing what it is if we have a conscience. Isn't that a solid definition of realism in art: to force the mind to take part without tricking with people and things?"[43]

The insights had first been Bazin's; their development and linkage with phenomenology Ayfre's. Both were following Bergson's maxim, "Art always aims at what is individual."[44] Croce too, with his insistence that art contains no signs but stands only for itself, said that what "moves us" is not mood, feeling, or image, but our pure intuition, our "contemplation of feeling."[45] But there was no critic in Italy to link Rossellini with Croce, the way Ayfre and Bazin linked him with Bergson, because there was no critic in Italy with their zest for movie *experience*, who wallowed so scandalously in the sensuality of movies and took them so seriously.

In Paris, Ayfre happily dragged in Merleau-Ponty to define "phenomenological description"—which, he has the eminent philosopher tell us, "attempts a direct description of our experience such as it is, without regard to its psychological genesis or to causal explanations which the scholar, historian, or sociologist might furnish."[46]

This is neo-realism, Ayfre says. It is neutral (but not passive, objective, cold, or impersonal); subjective (but without argument or thesis); and socially polemical (but without propaganda). It leaves in unimportant, irrelevant, and distracting details, so that, if afterward one wanted to understand an event as sociology, drama, psychology, or symbol, one would have the impression of working on raw events not yet abstracted. In this way, a human event is considered "globally" (without dissection or analysis), with everything possible done to emphasize existence over essence. Thus *our* attitude, as spectators, must alter radically. Neo-realism "is a call to liberty"—to look becomes an action: everything is open to question: we have to respond, we have to act. "When there's dialogue there's neo-realism; when there's no dialogue, there's no neo-realism."[47]

Rather than knowing how a film will work out before he begins it, a filmmaker like Rossellini interrogates. "One cannot deny that Rossellini . . . has tried, like Husserl [Merleau-Ponty's luminary], to go 'to things themselves,' to ask them what they themselves tell about themselves." Rossellini attempts a "total apprehension (successively total, in the manner of a creature in time) of concrete human events in which is co-present the entire mystery of the universe. In other words, for clarity of construction is substituted the mystery of existence."[48]

Mystery Mystique

Roberto would toss off Ayfre's buzzwords as his own inventions. For example: "Getting to the heart of things means this: let things speak for themselves. The director's duty is to make them speak, but things must speak only of what they are in reality and not of anything else."[49]

"I show the tree that is there," he would say, humbly, implying that everyone else was changing it.[50] But the truth is that Rossellini rarely pays attention to trees; he's busy invading a human face—Magnani or Bergman—*ravishing* them. Flattering as it was, to cite the "mystery of existence" to explain why his films were not "understood," metaphysics alienated Roberto, and the "mystery of existence," in the way the French meant it, was somewhat foreign to his Catholic soul and Crocean intuition. Even the intense fascination with *cinema* that was overtaking Ayfre's generation was a feeling he would eventually dismiss as "young and foolish."[51]

But the "mystery of existence" would rally Bazin's disciples at *Cahiers du Cinéma* and around the world. It quickly became a touchstone by which movies were transcendental art. Not only was Rossellini's reputation linked with it, but huge chunks of long-despised Hollywood, Renoir,

Ophuls, Dreyer, Mizoguchi, Bresson, Antonioni, the New Wave, cinéma vérité, Satyajit Ray, *Easy Rider*, and much else.

The flaw in the "mystery-of-existence" approach is that movie watching and movie making sometimes get confused. *Deutschland* showed how problematic phenomenology can be as a production method. We cannot postpone analysis when making a film, as we can while watching one; decisions have to be made constantly. De Sica's production methods, in fact, were the exact opposite of the results imputed to him—*un*global models of manipulation, analysis, and privileging. Nor was Rossellini free from desire to demonstrate a thesis (like the evilness of Nazism), or innocent of pre-mapped schemes (like the "master plot" governing *Paisà* and subsequent films). No one could have made a film as heuristically as Ayfre suggests.

But Rossellini had tried. By temperament he was off-the-cuff, "Bergsonian," with chameleon-like capacities to be absorbed in whomever and whatever was around him. During *Deutschland*, borne on the wings of cocaine and Paris's adoration of mystery, he rejected pre-production, relied almost entirely on instinct at the moment of shooting, and proved it was madness.

The result, curiously, was that the "idea" took on a life of its own; Rossellini didn't even have to be around to stage and film it. If the only thing important was things speaking for themselves, it didn't matter what they said or how, or who they were. Wouldn't Bazin declare, "No more actors, no more story, no more sets"? Wouldn't Ayfre lament with Zavattini that even the most neo-realist film is only ten percent neo-realist at best?[52]

Others went further than Rossellini. "Cinéma vérité" filmmakers would record events over which they had no control, and even give the camera to a player, so that things could really speak for themselves. Wasn't this Bazin's "perfect aesthetic illusion of reality"? What about Andy Warhol's six-hour film of someone sleeping?

Perfect Aesthetic Illusion of Paradox

Pursuit of reality became itself a convention. In fact, the "perfect illusion" Bazin had wanted was something altogether different: an accomplished work of artifice. Bazin was so much against mechanical art that he once denounced perspective as the "original sin of Western painting" because its pursuit of reality installed convention in place of the real.[53] Rossellini was outraged by cinéma vérité. "Documentary," their idol Jean Renoir argued, "is the falsest sort of cinema.[54] Reality has value only when it is transposed. In other words, an artist exists only if he manages to create his own little world. It's not in Paris, Vienna, Monte Carlo, or Atlanta that Stroheim's, Chaplin's, and Griffith's characters evolved. It's in the world of Stroheim, Chaplin, and Griffith."[55] Style, in Bazin's meaning, was not an artist's handwriting but his "attitude"—his moral position, his honesty.[56]

Conventions of realism, Bazin warned, get mistaken for reality and reality itself gets ignored; we reach the point of not even recognizing our own lies. (For Croce, this is the greatest evil that can befall a human being.)[57] We favor originality, but when we meet it we think it is impoverished, until it becomes convention. In Rossellini's case, people rejected *Roma città aperta* because it defied conventional realism, then turned around and said it *was* realism, then rejected his later movies as unrealistic because they were different from *Roma*, which had become the convention.[58] In other words, eyes never opened, intuition never was tried, judgment squashed any possibility of experience.

Herbert Read wrote, "Schools and academies teach men not to use their senses, not to cultivate their awareness of the visible world, but to accept certain canons of expression, and from these to construct rhetorical devices whose subtlety appeals to reason rather than sensibility. Art becomes a game played according to conventional rules."[59]

How to Experience Movies

In the realm of film criticism, Ayfre and Bazin staked out a battle line that has become perennial. On one side *cinema* criticism (movies as aesthetic experience); on the other side literary and political criticism (those who regard cinema as governed by alien aesthetics and political expediency). Those who experience movies as poetry; those who talk about them as prose.[60]

Contesting the battle are the differing ways literature and cinema engage us. There are good reasons why literature, for most people, is more absorbing and rewarding; why, for example, a book is usually thought preferable to its film version. Reading demands active intervention by the imagination for even elementary comprehension. Behind the simplest act of reading lie years of schooling in phonics, handwriting, spelling, grammar, and vocabulary. Behind the act of movie watching lies no schooling at all, except that of inattention; at best one may have had some lessons in art or music. Movies can be—and generally are—enjoyed passively, lazily, without the slightest cultivation. Music students recognize that hearing music requires highly stimulating activity, as much training as reading, and an effort that can leave one physically exhausted. The same is true of cinema. But the notion of making an effort is abhorrent to most movie goers, who want "to relax and *be* entertained." Children vegetate like zombies in front of their televisions, numbed into inability to entertain themselves.

Cinema will not be as rewarding as literature until our absorption in it becomes active: physically, emotionally, and intellectually. As with music, the most important of these is the physical: if we do not feel a cut or movement physically, like rhythm or tonality, we are not experiencing a movie and it is premature to try to discuss it intellectually. In fact, most great movies have been disdained by literary critics, who assume they are reading a book.

Jean Mitry wrote: "The novel is a story which is organized to form a world; film is a world which is organized to form a story."[61] It follows, then, that "narrative analysis" is studying radically different things when it switches its paraphernalia from literature to film. But the distinction is lost on literary critics. They take the most all-devouringly sensual of arts and treat it like a poor cousin of the least sensual. A movie's story—if it is cinema—can only be comprehended through immersion into the movie's world. Artistic intuition must precede conceptual knowledge. But literary critics, forgoing intuition of the movie, claim to abstract its "meaning" or "social significance" from its plot. How can they? The better the movie, the more their abstractions will be flawed by failure to intuit "presence," "vibes," and all the sensual aspects of cinema.

One professor once defended "structuralist study" of westerns (in which arbitrarily concocted plot summaries are compared for recurrent similarities) on the grounds that his students, all English majors, responded to it with great enthusiasm. What did he expect? Students sense there's something mysterious and different about movies, which makes them anxious. Then structuralism comes along and restores their security by removing all the mystery. Of course they're enthusiastic. They no longer have to deal with cinema.

Literary critics concern themselves with "narrative" because they comprehend film in terms of what happens, as *becoming*—as "action" illustrating an idea. Cinema critics experience movies as *being*—as world and soul experienced in an immediate now. A rose is a rose in cinema, or at least nearly so: it is a real image of a real rose that now has artistic emotion. But a "rose" is not a rose in literature: it is first of all a sign, rich in accretions but universally abstracted from any actual, individual rose. For these reasons, narrative is more important than character in literature, where character can be suggested only through event, whereas in cinema character is more important than narrative, because cinema gives us direct and immediate experience of another person, and an event is more the personality of the doer than the deed that is done. Our sense of emotion in film resembles music more than literature, because emotion is more sustained, constructed, directed; there is more sense of specific place and actual duration. What is nearly impossible in literature—virtually direct experience of another person—is the essence of cinema.[62]

Thus, as Ayfre suggests, it is inappropriate to talk about "good acting" or "bad acting" in the case of Edmund in *Deutschland im Jahre Null*, because there is not an actor on one hand and a character on the other, not an actual performance on one hand and some ideal realization on the other, but simply the presence of this particular boy on the screen, and how, then, can one talk about anything other than what is there?

But then, how *can* one talk about acting in good cinema? If the actor is inexpressive, doesn't that merely mean that the character is inexpressive? If we are really *experiencing* this person, at this moment, how can we say he or she ought to be different? In theater an actor plays Hamlet; in movies a character is only himself.[63] For "acting," Ayfre substitutes the mysteries of presence and person—which may be more or less clear, forceful, and interesting.

Land of God

Ilya Lopert wanted Roberto in America. Roberto wanted to go. They needed to finalize their arrangement with Ingrid Bergman for *After a Storm* (or *Against the Storm*), as *Stromboli* was then called.

But there were two obstacles. One—the repeatedly denied visa—was solved by Peyser, who sent the government letters he had assembled testifying to his client's good character. Afterward Peyser discovered he couldn't collect the fee Roberto had promised him.[1] The other—Magnani—was unaware she was an obstacle. She thought *she* would be making a film in America with Roberto, *Air of Rome*, about Italian emigrants, to be shot in New York that summer. At the same time she felt increasingly insecure. Her screams could be heard all over the floor at the Excelsior. One day it sounded like she was taking it out on her dog. "Get out of there, get out! Just let me at you! You lousy animal! You big ugly beast! Come out and I'll slug you with this bottle! Or stay there under the bed all night long!" But, no: it was Roberto, hiding under the bed. Another day he walked grinning out the Excelsior's front door—right into a huge slap from Anna.

She didn't really want to go to America that January. She hated to fly, she hated to wear evening clothes (she would need lots and lots of them, Roberto assured her), and anyway she would be going to New York that summer. But she didn't want Roberto to go, either.

He wasn't going, he told her. And she believed him.

"I'm taking the dogs for a walk," he said one day.

Still in bed, she nodded groggily.

Downstairs, he handed the leashes to a bellboy and took a cab to the airport. "I'll be bringing Ingrid Bergman back with me," he told Lina.[2] It was January 17, 1949, Marcella De Marchis's 32nd birthday. He carried no luggage.

Anna spent the night with Bill Tubbs, searching for Roberto at all his regular hang-outs.

Lopert was paying Roberto's expenses. He met him at the airport and hosted a party for him at his Manhattan apartment. Marlene Dietrich came in a gown cut so low it seemed about to fall off any second; the next day

Roberto told Peyser he had taken her to bed.[3] He accepted the New York Film Critics award as producer of the year's Best Film (having removed Geiger's name from *Paisan*'s initial release prints in order to avoid sharing the spotlight[4]). He downed a few Scotch highballs with a *New Yorker* correspondent and impressed a *New York Times* reporter as "a worldly conversationalist, with suave Continental mannerisms, and [with] a lot of things other than himself on his mind to talk about." He was going to Hollywood "just to look around," he told the *Times* man. He normally worked "using ancient camera equipment, picking up people here and there who have never acted before; shooting from a sketchy story outline that passes for a script and utilizing as sets genuine locales and buildings instead of studio constructed replicas."[5] He phoned Marcellina in Rome (he had postponed leaving until she had been operated on for acute appendicitis—"which had assumed terrible proportions in our family"[6]). And he cabled Ingrid in Hollywood ("I JUST ARRIVE FRIENDLY," to which she replied, "WAITING FOR YOU IN THE WILD WEST"); and boarded a train for California. "I will have Bergman in bed within two weeks," he told Lopert.[7]

At 1220 Benedict Canyon Drive that January 25, a red carpet had been laid down—thirty feet of it leading up to the door. It was "like the arrival of Agamemnon," remarked Peter Wegner, the Lindstroms' house guest.[8] "I was uncontrollably nervous," admitted Ingrid. "When he walked in, I couldn't talk. I tried to light a cigarette, but my hand trembled so much that the flame died out."[9] She was 33, he 42.

Ingrid held a party at her house that evening. At the plush Beverly Hills Hotel, where Roberto and Lopert had taken rooms, Rossano Brazzi organized a reception. "Since Rossellini only spoke French and Bergman English, it was my duty to interpret," Brazzi said. "I recall saying to Jean Negulesco, toward the end of the lunch, 'I bet it won't be long before these two won't have any need at all for an interpreter.' "[10]

Brazzi lent Roberto money to buy Ingrid a diamond. Max Colpet lent him money to buy her flowers and, since Anatole Litvak had left him his keys, he lent them Litvak's house to use as well.[11]

Lopert's agreements with Bergman and Rossellini called for him to produce and distribute their film. He was also to finance it and had no problems doing so. Thus Bergman is disingenuous in her autobiography when, never mentioning Lopert, his role in setting up the project, or her contract with him, she writes, "By this time I still didn't know who was to put up the money" and gives the impression that the film had never had a producer or distributor.[12] She and Roberto ditched Lopert. He had served his purpose. Now they thought they could do better.

Ingrid wanted Samuel Goldwyn. Roberto could not hope to get along with any of Hollywood's major industrial firms. But Goldwyn was a Polish Jew who had come to America and risen from poverty. Always a maverick, he had fought so much at Goldwyn Pictures that he had been kicked out of his own company before it became the "Goldwyn" in Metro-Goldwyn-

Mayer. Later when there was talk of his joining M-G-M himself, he said, "Not unless you rename it 'Metro-Goldwyn-Mayer and Goldwyn.'"

Goldwyn, in short, was the sort of American Roberto would like. And he did. He started out talking French, then switched to an English of his own invention: Latin words with their ends cut off. The accent was horrible but he made himself understood. Goldwyn was enchanted. "We had long conversations over numerous lunches, dinners, and breakfasts... always of an aesthetic order," Roberto recalled. "He explained everything his great experience had taught him and undertook to convince me of the necessity of working with a detailed shooting script.[13] He was my first English teacher, because he always said the same phrases: 'Listen, Mussolini'—he called me that because it also ended in ini—'from the bottom of my heart, I'll tell you...' And he would repeat how a script was absolutely necessary. And I always replied, 'Yes, but me no script!'[14]

"Some of his arguments were extremely judicious. But I was absolutely against [having a script].... Since I shoot in real interiors or in exteriors that haven't been touched-up beforehand, I can only improvise my stagings in function of the setting I find myself in. Thus the shooting script's left-hand column would still be blank, even if I had one. And since I choose my supporting players on the spot, at the moment of shooting, I can't write dialogue for them before seeing them that wouldn't be extremely theatrical and false. So the right-hand column would stay blank, too. Besides, I very much believe in the inspiration of the moment."[15]

Goldwyn admired talent, had ambitious tastes, and his policy was to hire directors and actors, cameramen and set designers who possessed artistic credentials. But for Goldwyn it was the *writing* that made a quality movie. His pictures were screenplays filmed, and excellent examples of their genre. Thus he was the *least* appropriate producer in Hollywood for Rossellini. Moreover, as an independent producer struggling against behemoths, a carefully pre-planned production was essential for his survival. Otherwise he had no way to watch costs. This was the same problem that caused Italian producers to throw up their hands at the prospect of working with Roberto. Worst of all, the money Goldwyn spent was his own, and one or two bad pictures could put him out of business.

"One evening Ingrid and I were summoned by phone to his office. He had called a press conference and announced the film to the journalists. We were very surprised, but went just the same, and were photographed signing a fake contract.[16] Afterward, a reporter asked, 'So, Samuel Goldwyn persuaded you to use a script, huh?!' And I said, 'No, no, no, not true.' So I ruined the press conference and embarrassed Samuel Goldwyn."[17]

Nonetheless, Goldwyn held a dinner party at his house and Roberto showed *Germany Year Zero* to a room full of Hollywood celebrities and potentates. Afterward, recalled Ingrid, "Not a word. No applause. Complete silence. Twenty people. Not a sound.... Freezing cold silence from all these people." Instinctively she walked over to Roberto, put her arm around him, and kissed him on the cheek. "I had to protect him."[18] The kiss was instantly famous.

Petter Lindstrom, who had escorted Ingrid, was left to fend for himself. As time wore on the party grew large and noisy. "Ingrid was standing with Roberto in a corner twisting a button on his brocade vest and looking into his eyes with a tiny inviting smile," wrote Hedy Lamarr. "She was beautiful and it was clear her charm was being appreciated."

"When I saw Ingrid and Roberto, hand in hand, stroll over to Petter, who was still standing alone trying to look happy, I was drawn closer, to hear what would be said. . . .

"Ingrid very coolly said to Petter (while Roberto looked on smiling), 'Mr. Rossellini is going to take me home. May I have the key, please?'

"I could see Petter was terribly embarrassed yet reluctant to make a scene. Hesitantly he brought out his key chain, opened it and slid a key off. Without one word he handed her the key, and she didn't say one word in return. Then Ingrid and Roberto walked out."[19]

The next day Goldwyn discussed the situation with his son Sam Junior. "I can't understand a guy who says, 'I want to make up the scenes when I see the actor.' I'm crazy about Ingrid. Everyone in town is offering her scripts. Why does she want to get into a story without a script? There's got to be something else going on. They're either having an affair or about to have one."[20]

According to Bergman, Goldwyn phoned her, reiterated his confusion over Roberto's methods, and announced he was withdrawing. "This kind of movie, I won't put money into it," he said.[21]

Roberto, to the contrary, claimed that he had walked out on Goldwyn at the press conference, after declaring in front of everyone that he would never make the film on Goldwyn's terms, and Bergman had followed him.[22] "From that day the discussions . . . took a decidedly more definite turn, to such a degree that I declined his offers shortly after."[23] Goldwyn wanted too great a percentage, he added. No other sources confirm Roberto's account.

"In Hollywood," he said, "the city with the highest density of intellectuals in the world, I felt very out of my element; I barely understood that atmosphere of contempt and wounded pride, that frenzied chauvinism, in short. I must admit that I made some very good friends, but the atmosphere was inimical from the first, without the reasons for it being clear to me—at least at the time.

"One day Ingrid was invited to a reception as the guest of honor. On return she told me, completely astonished, that on her right was seated a Hollywood bigshot [apparently, Darryl F. Zanuck, the production chief at 20th Century-Fox[24]] who, after having tried to dissuade her from shooting a film with me, told her that I had come to see him a year earlier, in Europe, to beg him to take me to Hollywood, and that I had behaved so insistently that he had had to insult me to get rid of me, and that he had thrown me out, telling me he had no use for a type like me!

"I of course knew this person only by name, and when he was pointed out to me in a Paris restaurant [in 1954], I remarked my surprise that a man as clever as twenty foxes managed to prove himself smaller than even one.[25]

"I had made a terrible gaffe the moment I arrived in America. All the press had come to see me and asked, 'What do you think of the cinema?' And I, I gave a reply—totally innocent, I swear it was innocent—I said, 'Look, do you want to talk about canned sausages or cinema? Because there are two cinemas; there's not a single cinema. You either do a well-crafted film or you involve yourself in an industrial enterprise.' This remark was a terrible insult for all Hollywood. So I had everything against me there."[26]

Including *Time* magazine. Roberto's remark—"I don't need stars, but I have nothing against Miss Bergman because she is a star"—was innocuous, even sympathetic. But in attributing it to "Italy's swarthy, balding director" *Time* made it sound gross and flippant. (Americans were usually surprised to find that Roberto was not "swarthy" but white.) Similarly, *Time* feigned offense at judgments of Hollywood that were far milder than the Algonquin wisdom of New York critics. ("I am not one who says Hollywood is terrible. . . . Hollywood is a great place," Roberto said. "It is like a sausage factory that turns out fine sausages. I go back to Italy where I have freedom."[27])

In Italy, Roberto was always "in family." The great figures in film, literature, art, politics, and the Church were people he knew well; more importantly, they were people who knew him, understood the sort of person he was, and who, no matter the dispute, never exploited to their advantage Roberto's ingenuous habit—so disastrous in America—of saying whatever crossed his mind.

Americans saw Roberto as devious. But it is a testimony to his endemic naiveté that he thought he could make films for Hollywood on his own terms. In Italy, Roberto had controlled his films by cultivating alliances, acting as his own producer, and finagling his own financing. The rules were not much different in Hollywood, but Hollywood was another world, and Roberto wasn't willing to spend years building a political base there.

He already had a considerable fan club. Billy Wilder held a small, stylish dinner at his home. Bette Davis, Frank Capra, King Vidor, John Huston, Olivia de Havilland, Edward G. Robinson, Jean Negulesco, Joan Bennett, and Alfred Hitchcock all met him, even Bergman's ex-boyfriend Gary Cooper. *Paisan* had been screened privately in Hollywood a year before, by Rod Geiger, to Chaplin, Renoir, Brecht, Thomas Mann, Hans Eisner, Charles Laughton, and others.

So what Goldwyn feared to do, Selznick was eager for. Despite Roberto's contretemps with Jenia Reissar, the two men got along famously. Selznick showed him *Portrait of Jenny* starring his wife Jennifer Jones (and directed by William Dieterle). And Roberto invited Selznick and Jones to the Los Angeles premiere of *Paisan*. But their mutual wooing was hopeless.

Ingrid, as Lindstrom put it, had "firmly decided never to make another contract with [Selznick]."[28]

Otherwise, industrial Hollywood was unwelcoming. Martin Quigley, the influential editor of *Motion Picture Herald*, spoke for many when he denounced films "from the unhappy foreign left, dripping with the bitter juices of the complaining art of a defeated world." Dore Schary, head of production at M-G-M, hadn't liked *Paisan* at all when Geiger showed it to him, but he had wanted to sign up one of the monks. "He's under contract to God," Geiger had replied.[29]

The executives could not abide Roberto's failure to keep appointments, answer letters, or negotiate in good faith. They were suspicious of his strutting, Latin sexuality. They perceived, correctly, that he took pleasure in humiliating them. Roberto had a way of shedding his manners when it came to Americans. He pranced around declaring everything was wrong. Shown a huge construction of a battleship with a painted blue sky behind it, he shook his head in vigorous disapproval. "There lies the corpse of movie making!" He let it be known that, in his opinion, the big Hollywood studios were so concerned with camera angles, trick shots, and elaborate lighting that they destroyed the basic vitality of stories and people.[30]

To circumvent Hollywood's obstacles Roberto tried, as he had with Selznick, to "associate" himself with a producer on "equal" terms: the producer would supply the money, Roberto would make the decisions. Such deals were not infrequent in the late 1940s: Ford, Capra, Wyler, Hitchcock, Hawks, and Stevens had made them, and many actors as well. Roberto's mistake was in thinking he could make them with Selznick and Goldwyn, the most notorious busybodies in Hollywood, who routinely recut films behind their directors' backs and even hired second, third, and fourth directors to shoot additional scenes. Roberto was aware of this; the scandal of *Duel in the Sun* had been the talk of the Venice Film Festival. Roberto knew that his hero, King Vidor, had walked out on it because Selznick for months had required him to reshoot scenes dozens of times, as the producer daily changed his mind about a line or hem.

Was Roberto, then, walking into the lion's den—or trying to—with his eyes wide open? Not exactly. He had toyed with Selznick in Italy, procrastinating until Selznick gave up. He had refused Goldwyn's terms in Hollywood until Goldwyn gave up. He would go on holding out until his conditions were met.

Yet Roberto possessed a fatal flaw that neither he nor Hollywood was willing to recognize. Hollywood's great directors fulfilled their personal artistry while making movies that captivated uncultivated audiences all over the world. Rossellini was not box office—except on the art circuit.

Lopert, naturally, had stopped paying Roberto's expenses. "Rossellini is a liar and a cheater, and now he has fooled me again," he complained to Lindstrom.[31]

Since Roberto was now without funds, Ingrid invited him to stay in the little guest bungalow fifty feet behind the Lindstroms' house, where Peter Wegner, a Czech refugee and medical protégé of Lindstrom's, was also living. Roberto borrowed two thousand dollars from Lindstrom and then more money from Ingrid's agent and her insurance salesman.

He phoned Marcellina regularly—"every night," according to her. And he sent cables to Anna. But his days and hours were passed with Ingrid. They drove down along the coast and up into the mountains, dined in restaurants and night spots, and even went to drive-ins. He was particularly eager to see King Vidor's pictures (and was surprised by Vidor's timidity when they met). The film he would make with Ingrid would resemble Vidor's typical mixture of documentary, sentimental theatrics, iconic passion, and star personality. His characters would struggle like Vidor's, gripped by love and ideals but never in control of their own lives.

His characters were like Ingrid. At 33, she had been married to Lindstrom for almost twelve years, and had a ten-year-old daughter, Pia. A week after Roberto's arrival she had begun remodeling the house, adding a maid's room and nursery for a second child who, though not yet conceived, was to be a boy named Pelle. But now, she said, "every time a workman hit the roof with a hammer, it was like a nail going into my head."[32]

She was restless and bored. She seldom stayed home or spent time with Pia. Her marriage had been shaky for years. Lindstrom, she complained, governed her life coldly. But she was shy and insecure and required him to front for her in her professional negotiations, even though he was in the throes of the difficult transition from dentist to doctor. And meanwhile she did as she pleased. There had been many affairs. Victor Fleming, Gary Cooper, Gregory Peck, and photographer Robert Capa were among her rumored companions. In Hollywood society, in an age when women felt unprotected without tons of make-up, Ingrid perpetually aroused female resentment by not wearing any—and not needing to. Sex meant little to her, but the prospect of romance stirred every cell in her body. Like many actors, she found real life arid and unfulfilling. Inchoate longing, confused and directionless, numbed her.

Her dream life was shaky too, however. She had been eager to be free of Selznick's tutelage, but her independent productions were destroying her. *Arch of Triumph*'s losses—some $4 million—were said to be the largest in Hollywood's history, and *Joan of Arc*, her lifelong fantasy, had been another disaster. She reacted with depression and heavy drinking. "She was obsessed with her failures," said Lindstrom. "She kept saying, 'I have to get out of Hollywood. I hate Hollywood. . . . In Hollywood, you're never any better than your last pictures. I have to do an artistic feature in Europe.' "[33]

Enter Roberto. Nothing stirred him so powerfully as a suffering, sad-eyed woman. Like Roswitha and Magnani, Ingrid was the insecure product of a tragic youth. When she was two her mother had died; at thirteen her father; and at fourteen the maiden aunt who had taken care of her, alone in her arms. Now she was captive in the dragon's castle, and Roberto saw himself as the knight in shining armor who would right every wrong and bestow every garland of happiness. "When I saw Ingrid there, surrounded by all those people, I wanted to *destroy* Hollywood," he declared.[34]

Little wonder, then, that Roberto seemed a solution to all of Ingrid's problems, personal and professional. "Roberto was so warm and outgoing. When I was with him, I didn't feel shy or awkward or lonely perhaps for the first time in my life. He was easy to talk to and interesting to listen to. Most of all, he was alive, and he made me feel alive."[35] Their film would revive her career. Hitherto she had played nuns and saints and goddesses. Now a fisherman's slap would signal finis to that image. "Oh," she was heard to sigh at a party, "Oh, it's going to be so marvelous to get out of this predictable society!"[36]

It was Lindstrom who was charged with finding Ingrid's ticket out. But with Goldwyn gone, Petter, as Ingrid put it, "had a hard time finding someone else to back the picture. Then one day he said he was going to talk with Hughes."[37] Or, better, Ingrid herself should phone the eccentric millionaire. For Howard Hughes had a crush on her. He had recently purchased the RKO studio—"for you," he had told her, although there seem to have been other similar reasons.

Hughes arrived fifteen minutes later in tennis clothes. "How much money do you need?" he asked, totally ignoring Roberto.

"Listen. Don't you want to hear the story?"

"No. . . . I don't care what sort of story it is. Are you beautiful in it? Are you going to have wonderful clothes?"[38]

"Hughes," recalled Roberto, "had a tone of great contempt, great superiority. He was the sort who says: 'I don't give a damn about the film he wants to make! To make you see who I am, I'll make the contract and assume the distribution, and he can make any kind of film he wants.'"[39]

Roberto could not have asked for more. But there was more. He would receive twenty percent of the net profits, Ingrid forty percent. Against this, she would be advanced $17,500 per week, up to $175,000, in addition to a $50,000 subsidy provided by the Italian government. There was also a verbal understanding that the two would make a second picture for Hughes. Lopert was not included in the deal; only his expense-account charges were reimbursed by Hughes.

Roberto left Los Angeles on February 28. The day before he had presented everyone with gifts. For Pia, he had bought dolls, a doll house, and a giant ($75) Elsie cow. And he had promised Lindstrom, whom he swore he loved as his own brother, that he would protect Ingrid from gossip, introduce her to Magnani, and take separate boats to Stromboli. "He used to stand in front of the fireplace and tell us how religious he was," Pia recalled.[40] A few days later the bills arrived for Roberto's parting gifts: he had charged them all to Lindstrom.

*

It was close to midnight, March 2, when Roberto landed in Rome. Despite the hour, he picked up Marcellina and Renzino and took them to the Excelsior, where he presented his seven-year-old son with a magnificent cowboy suit and Indian headdress from America. To Marcellina, though, he was reserved, atypically. He had always told her everything, now he closed up like a clam. He told her nothing of what had happened in Hollywood and during the next few weeks avoided being alone with her. "Such unusual behavior pained me," she said. "I understood something really important must have happened."[41]

Lina couldn't resist teasing. "So, where's Ingrid Bergman?" she asked.

"She'll be here in two weeks," he replied,[42] and embarked on a course of reducing baths. He may have been flippant, but he was totally in love, almost consumed by it. He phoned Ingrid frequently. This cost fourteen dollars merely for the first three minutes—almost a week's wage for many Italians. Calls were relayed by radio, since the transatlantic cable had not yet been relaid, and reception was often horrendous. Supposedly, the phone company once broke in demanding 700,000 lire ($1,150) that Roberto already owed, before letting him continue. He sent the money right over.

In *L'Elefante* he published an account of his plans. "Hardly had the news spread of a coming Rossellini-Bergman film in Italy, than Hollywood circles became alarmed and there was a turmoil of offers and deals. But the only thing that interested me was to work with absolute liberty, to be able to make the film according to my intentions, and my point of view was shared fully by Bergman. This was the essential. As for the rest, in 45 days in Hollywood, amid meetings, receptions, and discussions, I made the necessary arrangements without having to compromise or submit my ideas to opposing judgments and sensibilities. In a word, without commercial concessions of any sort."[43]

Anna was due in London to receive an award for *Onorevole Angelina*. She had hoped Roberto would go with her, but now of course he was swamped with work. Sending Fabrizio Sarazani in his place, Roberto took them to the station, kissed Anna tenderly, whispered parting words, and stayed waving on the platform until the train disappeared. She didn't imagine how convenient her departure was.

Ingrid arrived two days later, March 20. A large crowd gathered at Ciampino. To the Italians she was a fairy-tale princess and Roberto was the boy next door they were proud of. He boarded the plane with an enormous bouquet of long-stem roses and she kissed him and said, "Je t'aime." Not until that moment, she said later, did she realize it was Roberto the man who inspired her.[44] Among her luggage were two fur coats, two fur jackets, many dresses, most of her jewelry, her clipping books, personal letters, and photo albums.

Pushing through the crowd, Roberto escorted her into his Cisitalia. Outside the Excelsior another crowd waited. In Ingrid's suite Roberto's friends had gathered for a 3 A.M. champagne party. Little gifts were strewn about the room and marvelous caricatures by Fellini depicting Ingrid and Roberto on Stromboli decorated the walls.

A press conference the next day nearly became a riot. Roberto smuggled Ingrid out a back door to the nearby hilltown of Fregene. There, in a villa provided by sister Marcella's in-laws, they holed up for most of the week discussing the picture with Amidei and partying with friends. Renzino came at Ingrid's invitation and was most impressed by her height; secretly he had fallen in love with her the year before, watching *For Whom the Bell Tolls*. At Ingrid's insistence, Roberto took her to Ladispoli. The years had turned paradise to squalor, but the magic reliquaries of Roberto's memories set Ingrid to emoting. "*La grande ignora*," De Sica dubbed her: "She's completely crazy. It's a bidonville and she was enchanted."[45]

In London Magnani was at the Dorchester. Sarazani went out to get the papers. "I bought *Le Figaro* and saw a vivid photograph of Ingrid Bergman's arrival in Rome. In the hotel, Anna was having breakfast. I didn't have the courage to give her the paper, but after a few minutes I was withered by one of peremptory demands: 'And the paper?' 'I didn't get one today,' I tried to lie. 'Give it to me,' she said, 'don't tell lies to me.' In one look she understood. The picture upset her. I had never seen her in such a condition. She wanted to cry, wanted to phone friends in Rome to see if they had seen Roberto, if they knew what he was doing. For three days she didn't eat, and I couldn't either. I didn't want to leave her alone for fear she would do something irreparable."[46]

Ingrid was presented to Fabrizi, De Sica, Cervi, Girotti, Zavattini, Carlo Levi, Amato, and De Santis at a supper in Trastevere.

Marcellina did not meet her, "but her presence wasn't necessary for me to intuit the extent of Roberto's change." When Roberto phoned she told him the time had come to settle their situation with a civil divorce. "Knowing Roberto, it was easy for me to imagine how hard it would have been for him to have initiated a request of this sort."[47]

She saw Roberto the next day at the Excelsior, and "while at least forty people from the troupe came and went bustling with preparations for going to Stromboli, we made the decision to see our lawyer the next morning, which was the same as the day of departure. Roberto was very affectionate with me. He had returned to the cordiality of one time, which was all I desired from him for me and my son. The great weight that no doubt had been oppressing him before my offer had fallen from his heart and this cleared up our relationship."[48]

Marcellina's 1942 Hungarian divorce had not been ratified in the Italian courts prior to Hungary's postwar Communist regime's canceling its wartime accords with Italy. Since civil divorce still did not exist in Italy, it was decided Marcellina would go with Renzino to Vienna and attempt to obtain a divorce there.

Franco Riganti advised her against this step. "I love Roberto more than myself," she told him. "Since his happiness is to be with her, I give him up."[49]

Many telegrams, during the next four months, passed between Stromboli and Vienna.

Roberto took Ingrid to Naples, of course. At the temple of Paestrum he picked her a rose from an ancient briar. On Capri he introduced her to Roswitha. In Amalfi they stayed at the Luna Convento. At Cantanzaro the mayor closed the schools and declared a holiday and the whole town turned out to greet them. At Salerno he left the car to chat with some fishermen, and came back fifteen minutes later to announce he had hired her leading man: "Two of them, one short, one tall. You can take your pick."

From Amalfi Ingrid had written Petter. "It is not altogether my fault, and how can you forgive that I want to stay with Roberto? It was not my intention to fall in love and go to Italy forever. . . . You saw in Hollywood how my enthusiasm for Roberto grew and how much alike we are, with the same desire for the same kind of work and the same understanding of life."[50]

Anna spent four million lire calling Rome from London—almost $7,000.[51] She had been left by Alessandrini for Regina Bianchi; by Serato for Lea Padovani; and now by Rossellini for Ingrid Bergman. In Milan, on her way home, she saw a weekly recounting Rossellini's ruses to get her (Magnani) out of the way, and his love tryst with Bergman at the Luna Convento. Perhaps she recalled the line in *Una voce umana* where she had begged her lover not to take his new woman to the same hotel.

Once back in Rome, she turned to Renzo and Amidei for support. "Anna had an enormous affection for Roberto," Amidei recalled, "and the moment of separation was very difficult for her. She suffered an awful lot. I subjected myself every evening to those Roman rides with Anna, aboard that Buick with that terrible dog, and she was really hit by it, not just as a woman but also as an actress. In reality Rossellini represented the maximum, professionally speaking. It marked her for a long time."[52]

The Buick was part of her heritage from Roberto. He had wanted one of those big American cars that Italians, after escaping to the U.S. during the war, brought back afterward, as American citizens, and sold in Italy, claiming to have given them as presents. "Nothing will happen! Nothing!" they promised at the time of sale. But in fact the cars were contraband. And Magnani, who had paid five million lire ($8,000) for a Buick Roberto had ordered, had eventually found herself in a mess with the police that had nearly cost her her passport. Roberto had broken his contract to do *Air of Rome*, too.

She was not without allies. Film circles generally felt she had been treated shabbily, and held it against Roberto. His friends too were against the whole business with Bergman. "We disapproved," said Renzo Avanzo, "but not from a moral point of view. Nobody gave a damn about that. We disapproved because we knew that, with her, he was through making the kind of pictures he should be making. She came out of a proper, serious, commercial world of filmmaking. He didn't fit in with that. They were enamored with the idea of what they could do together artistically—and it was a lousy idea."[53]

"I was worried about what Ingrid would mean to my brother's life," said Marcella. "I worried because Ingrid's coming here would bring all those awful things—not her, of course—the paparazzi, all of that, so we couldn't live anymore."[54]

And Amidei: "From the very first day I told him, 'But Roberto, what does it matter to you? What does Bergman matter to us?' But in him, in truth, there was also a bit of vanity. You need to think what Italy was in 1948 and what Bergman was, what Hollywood was, what it represented. What Bergman represented for a young Roman! Roberto was a great protagonist, would have been so even if he hadn't been a director, I always say. *Roma città aperta* and *Paisà* had had success, the whole world talked about them. Yet Roberto had the physical presence to carry success with great elegance, with great casualness. He could have been a minister, a cardinal, a banker, never anything mediocre. He was basically a realist who knew how to get by in the political realities of his time. But I must say the truth, that, thinking it over from afar, I think that, all told, Bergman in Roberto's life was more negative than positive."[55]

On April 4, Roberto and Ingrid set sail from Sicily in the *San Lorenzo*, a dilapidated forty-foot fishing schooner leased for the film. The trip took four hours. At the end, Stromboli, "The Gateway to Purgatory," loomed 3,000 feet out of the sea, smoking. The volcano occupied almost all of the five-square-mile island. Only a few rocky acres remained for the inhabitants, 500 of them. Their lives were hard and primitive. The young emigrated and returned, sometimes, to die. There was no electricity, telephone, or running water; there were tons of flies, but no animals, not even a chicken, scarcely any vegetation, and just a single tree. Ingrid stood under it one day and the islanders suggested she pay for its shade. The volcano rumbled constantly. "Avanti," Ingrid would say, when her door rattled; but it was only the volcano.

Walking on the beach one day, she revolted at the sight of a fisherman slitting open a live turtle. "We must put that in the film!" Amidei exclaimed to Roberto. Then, seeing Ingrid staring at him, he added, "To horrify your character when she arrives on the island." "Oh," she sighed, "it'd be even worse if a child did it!" Roberto exchanged a smile with Amidei. "Ingrid is ready for neo-realism," he said.

Ingrid and Roberto were installed in adjoining bedrooms in the schoolmaster's two-story pink-stucco bungalow, the best house on the island. For Ingrid a make-shift shower had been constructed; water heated on the stove would be poured into an oil drum on the roof. She had as well her secretary, Ellen Neuwald, who had accompanied her from America, and a personal maid, Elena di Montis, whom Roberto had acquired from Magnani. A chef had been brought from Bernini's in Rome. Each morning Roberto brought wildflowers.

Filming began April 10. Roberto summoned a workman and told him he would be Miss Bergman's leading man. He was Mario Vitale, one of the Salerno fishermen. "When do I kiss her?" he asked immediately. "You don't," replied Roberto. "But you get a hundred thousand a week ($67). Isn't that enough?"

The second Salerno fisherman, Mario Sponza, became the lighthouse keeper, whom Bergman's character seduces into helping her escape. To play the priest, Roberto picked one of his Nazareno schoolmates, Renzo Cesano, whom RKO had dispatched to work on the script. Cesano later played gangsters on American television; he had the face Roberto wanted.

The crew numbered 65. The islanders themselves filled most of the supporting roles. They could hardly speak Italian, only their dialect, and Ellen Neuwald had to make them memorize phrases in English. They knew nothing about the film's story. "Don't you dare tell them what the lines mean," Roberto commanded. "Just drill the lines into them. I'll supply the meaning."[56] Most of them had never seen a movie in their lives, or even a play. When Roberto brought a projector from the mainland and showed them a western, they tried to duck out of the way; the horses would run them down, they feared.

To get them to say their lines at the right moment, Roberto would yank on strings he had tied to their toes.

These were novel methods for Ingrid. In Hollywood each day's scenes and the exact words to be spoken were scheduled months in advance. Roberto invented episodes on the spot, then jotted down dialogue on the backs of envelopes. She waited contentedly, nonetheless, knitting, always knitting. Moviemaking is mostly waiting for actors; perhaps they are on camera five or ten minutes in a day. Ingrid's tranquillity never failed to astonish the Italians, for whom waiting is tantamount to hell's fire.

What alarmed Ingrid was how work cauterized Roberto. His easy-going manner sharpened to a needle of concentration. Filming was a demanding, torturous experience and usually drained him of humor. When she laughed at the toe-strings, he lost his temper. There was no collaboration on his sets, no sense of a director and a troupe working together. "He'd say, 'I want you to do this and that and this is the way I want it and I don't want any nonsense,'" said Ingrid.[57]

But he was rarely specific. Actors never quite knew what they were doing or why. "As I say, he knew what he wanted, but he didn't know exactly the words, and very often he would say, 'Well, this is a scene here. You walk down the street and you meet so and so. So you say to her anything you want. . . . 'Well, of course I was stunned and frightened.'"[58] She had no string on her toe; she had no way to know when the others had finished talking.

And he paid no attention to her. "You're not even looking at me!" she sighed.

"Yes, I am. You're moving so that I can see the things around you better."[59]

Eventually there came an explosion. "I blew up. I was absolutely shaking with rage. "You can *have* these realistic pictures . . . ! To hell with them! These people don't even know what dialogue is, they don't know where to stand; they don't even *care* what they're doing. I can't bear to work another day with you!"[60]

But he never hesitated one second in front of a setup, she noted. "He is full of new ideas, unafraid and with an authority that makes the whole crew adore him. His violence, if something goes wrong, can only be compared to the volcano in the background. His tenderness and humor come like a surprise immediately after. I understand well that people call him crazy. But so are people called, if they dare to be different."[61]

Soon it became "a communication by thought process. I could read his eyes. Even when he couldn't explain in words what he wanted, I felt *what* he wanted.[62] He was very inspiring and it was wonderful to look at him, because his eyes were burning. He gave you a tremendous concentration, just by looking at him; and I remember I always asked him to sit very close to the camera so I could look at him before I did anything. It was a command more than collaboration."[63]

"Roberto was in a strange state of tension," thought Amidei, "because, when it came down to it, what interested him was not so much to make a good film as to capture Ingrid—and not for speculative reasons but for love. He was really in love."[64]

And trouble was rumbling. On April 13, columnist Cholly Knickerbocker rumored there was romance afoot. *Life* printed a picture of Ingrid and Roberto romantically holding hands in Amalfi. Papers around the world picked up the story. Quickly and widely, Ingrid's conduct was decried as outrage and insult, as public contempt for the moral values of the family. Colorado's U.S. Senator, Edwin C. Johnson, took to the podium to urge she be forever banned for "moral turpitude."[65] Joseph Breen, whose job as head of the industry-sponsored Production Code Administration was to guard appearances, sent Ingrid a severe warning: the stories, he said, "may very well *destroy your career as a motion picture artist*." Walter Wanger, *Joan of Arc*'s producer cabled her to beware. Many of Hollywood's most important figures followed suit. MCA dispatched her agent, Kay Brown, in person; she arrived in high heels and a mink coat and had to be carried ashore on a sailor's back.

The impetus for the scandal, it was said, came from Roberto himself, who, entrusted with mailing Ingrid's letter to Lindstrom, had ingenuously shown it first to one or two of his friends. Such chattiness was reserved for male friends. It was Ingrid who eventually told his sister Marcella they were in love; Roberto never said a word. But it would not have occurred to him that there was reason for secrecy. He was proud of it. As was she. Anyone who had seen them had known what everyone was now saying.

And now as week-old newspapers and letters began to arrive on Stromboli, along with reporters, and the bizarre dimensions of the scandal started becoming clear, Roberto and his friends were baffled. Their sexual morality belonged to another world; they were incapable of recognizing what was happening. "Kay Brown is so American. It's terrible," grumbled Marcella.[66]

It was inexcusable. An invasion of privacy. It was more of Hollywood's hostility, its vendetta against Roberto for "stealing" their big-box-office star.

"Why the scandal?" Roberto asked rhetorically in 1955, and answered: "Hollywood was not friendly to me. The world of Hollywood received the news [that we would make a movie] as if it were an insult and blow to its prestige."[67] Exaggerating, he claimed Senator Johnson had called him an infamous Nazi collaborator, a blackmarketer, a well-known cocaine addict, a hypnotizer of women, and the well-known head of a ring of drug dealers.[68]

His culture was accustomed to D'Annunzio-like artists and to public outrageousness as an expression of individuality. But Ingrid too adopted his attitude. It does not seem to have occurred to her, either at the time or years later when she published her autobiography, that as an American star she was obliged to respect American morality.

Roberto suggested postponing the film for six months while they sorted out their private lives: everyone could go home and RKO could just write off everything it had spent so far. It was an absurd suggestion and even he knew it. At the same time he turned down Hughes's offer of $600,000 in exchange for all of their interest in the film (except for Italy, Albania, Yugoslavia, and Turkey). Everyone, including Roberto and Ingrid, thought the publicity was creating a gold mine.

Nonetheless Roberto regarded the reporters, specifically the American and English reporters, as a personal insult. When Michael Stern and Robert Conway of the *New York Daily News* announced they were coming to the island, he invited them to make the trip on his schooner. When they arrived in Messina, however, he sent an assistant to tell them repairs were being done and there would be a delay. The same thing happened the second day, causing them to miss the weekly mail packet, Stromboli's only regular link to the mainland. Suspicious now, they booked a private boat, whereupon the police came banging on their hotel room door at 3 A.M. Conway refused to talk to them until morning, but then they were escorted to the police station and held until noon, when the commissioner appeared. They weren't under arrest, they were informed, but Stern had recently embarrassed the government by interviewing the outlaw hero Salvatore Giuliano while 15,000 soldiers were hunting the hills for the same Salvatore Giuliano. Was Stern in Sicily to see Giuliano again? Roberto Rossellini, it appeared, had suggested this was the case.

Finally the reporters set off in their boat, ran into a storm, and spent the night on Lipari. On the sixth day Stromboli was gained. Roberto greeted them cheerfully. "Make yourselves comfortable," he said. "I'll join you soon." And he went off on a boat and didn't return until they were gone.[69]

Lindstrom had been cabling Ingrid to phone, unaware that Stromboli had no phone. If she wanted a divorce, he wrote, she should return and get one, and explain matters to Pia. When all hell broke loose in the press, he flew to Rome, refusing to speak to reporters, and compelled a meeting, May 3, in Messina. Roberto arrived with Ingrid and an entourage: Kay Brown, a lawyer, Martha and Art Cohn (who was translating the dialogue), and others.

By now Roberto was paranoid from anxiety over the press and Lindstrom's intentions, and insisted on complicated, cabalistic devices: entering the Hotel Reale via torturous back passageways, and posting guards of his own at the exits, lest Lindstrom attempt to spirit Ingrid away. When Petter attempted to speak to Ingrid alone and locked the door, Roberto went insane and called the police. They came, but after questioning Lindstrom saw no means of stopping a husband from talking to his wife. Roberto stormed downstairs, got into his Cisitalia and for the next hour or two drove in circles around the hotel, racing the motor, "Vroom, vroom, vroom."

According to Ingrid, Lindstrom hurled insults at her for half the night. "It was absolute hell. I cried so much I thought there couldn't be any tears left. . . . When I talked to Roberto he argued one thing, and when I talked to Petter he argued another."[70] According to Lindstrom, nothing of the sort occurred. He agreed to a divorce on condition she see Pia first, which she agreed to do, in London, if he would wait there a couple of weeks until, as she expected, the filming on Stromboli would be finished. These decisions were announced to the entourage to be conveyed to the press, along with a promise to maintain separate houses on Stromboli and to be more discreet. Then, ignoring Roberto's subterfuges, Lindstrom walked out the hotel's front door.

Outside there was only a teenager with a camera. Ingrid and Roberto drove off in the Cisitalia, but ran out of gas after a few minutes and had to hitch a ride with the lawyer and Kay Brown in their Fiat.

On Stromboli, a photographer watched them land. "She looked tired and haggard. Roberto practically danced off the boat, hugging everyone who was close to him. She stood there white-faced for a moment, and then she said sharply, 'Roberto, come on!' He followed immediately. You could tell he had won and she was still in a great quandary."[71]

The equivocations issued to the press only added fuel to the scandal. Boatloads of tourists now began to arrive and gawk. Roberto was accused of procrastination. His crew didn't mind. "It was like a vacation," one of them recalled, "because the director and actress were thinking about making love, and the work went on, and on."[72]

RKO objected strenuously. Their first representative, putty in Roberto's hands, was replaced by Harold Lewis, an aggressive six-foot-four troubleshooter who fared no better. With consummate politeness Roberto enlisted Lewis's aid in getting supplies of fresh water to the top of the volcano, in making the tuna run, in having the volcano erupt. "I didn't realize," said Kay Brown, "that RKO and MCA, in fact all things American, were taking over as 'the enemies' as far as Roberto and therefore Ingrid were concerned."[73]

In fact, the water, tuna, and volcano were real obstacles. Roberto had no desire to prolong his stay on the bleak, uncomfortable island; his problems were legitimate, particularly the weather. Always before and always after *Stromboli* he was a director infamous for uncommon speed and economy, even if some days he did not work at all. But his methods were too bizarre for RKO: to RKO everything Rossellini did was wrong, and RKO's hostility was harassing the crew too. "Now RKO tries in every possible way to kill him," Ingrid wrote to Joe Steele. "All these stories and the outrageous way the Rome office of RKO behaves have broken Roberto's spirit.... [He is] too sensitive to take all the abuse and also work like a machine."[74] RKO encouraged the press scandal for all it was worth while loathing Roberto, his wiles and ways. On one occasion, Marcella, urgently needing to warn Roberto of Lewis's approach, whistled a tune from the *Vespri siciliani* overture—a Verdi opera recounting Sicily's revolt from foreign oppression and slaughter of its overlords. Roberto instantly recognized the tune and its meaning.

In June, ignoring the Americans' protests, Roberto took Ingrid to Rome for a week. This seemed to justify RKO's complaints. In reality, they wanted to know if Ingrid was pregnant. And she was, for two months, with Roberto's baby.

This was a crisis indeed, and a secret shared with no one but Father Lisandrini. Ingrid's first impulse was an abortion. To Roberto, the thought of his child dying sent shivers of horror through him. Romano's death had precipitated Roswitha's abortion; now here was a third child. Roberto blamed himself for Romano's death, irrationally. He could blame himself for Roswitha's abortion as well. What would he do this time? Father Lisandrini was there counseling responsibility: wasn't this the theme of the film? "When I learned that she was going to have a baby, I had to make a decision. It would have been very easy to do something about it. Remember, abortion doctors exist in our country, too. But if we did that, I would have felt as though Romano were dying a second time."[75] This was a potent argument and he used it. He even changed the sense of the whole film in order to emphasize it. Now his heroine's realization of moral responsibility would reflect Roberto's in real life, and thus Ingrid's as well. As he directed the actress and created Karin, Roberto would direct Ingrid as well; he would even hand her over to a Dominican for lessons on how to call out to God for what she/Karin was going to do. He would even marry her, although fully aware they were incompatible. As Ingrid remarked, "[Romano's death] almost killed Roberto. He felt guilty because he was on Capri with [Roswitha] when he got the news. He speaks of Romano all the time. He'll never get over it."[76] Later, she confessed to Joe Steele: "In the beginning, I did not have the courage to go through with [having the baby] but slowly, through Roberto, I gained the strength and the courage, and now I am not afraid any longer. . . . It would have been possible, when I had regained my health after *Stromboli,* to do something about it. But, after all, what a poor, miserable way out."[77]

(In 1960, when Dominique Aubier was living in Roberto's house and working on a script for *Pulcinella,* her dog, an exotic female she was planning to breed, got loose and became pregnant. Aubrier announced she would have the dog aborted and Roberto refused to allow her to remain in his house.)

They returned to the island with a puppy, a black bull-terrier, a gift from Marcella, whom they named Strombolicchio. The Strombolians thought he must be a mule; they had never seen a dog before. An old woman, reading Roberto and Ingrid's fortunes, prophesied they would separate the day Strombolicchio died.

To film the tuna run they had to go to Sicily, to Olivieri near Castroreale, and then wait with the fishermen, cameras ready, for eight days. It became one of the high points of the picture, although some critics complained it was like a documentary. Roberto disagreed: "The episode is not at all documentary-like. . . . I tried to reproduce that eternal wait under the sun; and then that terrifyingly tragic moment when they kill: this death that breaks out after an extraordinary, patient, lethargic, even benevolent wait in the sun. That was the important thing, from the point of view of [Bergman's] character."[78]

Another company was filming the tuna run at the same time, for a movie called *Volcano* starring Anna Magnani.

Anna had accepted $100,000 from Renzo Avanzo, Roberto's cousin, to make her own volcano film on Panarea, an island next to Stromboli. The story was the one Avanzo had written for her and proposed to Roberto back in 1946, when he had "discovered" Stromboli. Now that story was being directed by William Dieterle, from Hollywood, with dialogue by Erskine Caldwell. Dieterle had made *Portrait of Jenny,* which Selznick had screened for Roberto.

"I never interfered with [Rossellini's] love life," Anna told the press. "My relationship with him was always a veritable nightmare. . . . When he was living in Ingrid Bergman's household, he sent me secret cables. . . . He phoned me every day until that Ingrid Bergman announced she wanted a divorce. . . . I only regret Rossellini . . . left me without a director for my next picture."[79]

Of course the truth was not so placid. "When you are with him," she had said at the crest of her adventure with Roberto, "you feel that you're at the edge of a spiritual whirlwind. He isn't just a man. He is a hurricane."[80]

Now her life was in a vacuum. "She made no secret of her anger to anyone," said Rossano Brazzi, her co-star. "Every evening, when shooting was through, she'd go to the end of the island, from where the other Eolians could be glimpsed, and shout colorful curses in the direction of Stromboli."[81]

People speculated on Roberto's power over women. "Is he very well endowed?" Zeffirelli asked Magnani two years later. "No, he's a son of a bitch. That's why we all fall for him. He's a cunt."[82]

"He made you feel you were the only thing in his life," said Maria Mercader, De Sica's wife—Roberto phoned her almost every morning for twenty years.[83]

"He ate you up," said Rod Geiger.

"He whispered in their ear," said Vittorio Mussolini.

"I still remember the kisses, the embraces, his completely physical, equally physical, way of saying 'I want you to be happy and I know you want me to be happy,'" said Paolo Valmarana.[84]

"He creates a dream atmosphere around him," said Amidei. "The women around him live in a dream world. He is very tender but at the same time can be brutal and vulgar. He is the true man of today. The rest of us are silly romantics with foolish notions about how gently women should be treated."[85]

"Girls were a sport," said Enrico Fulchignoni, one of Roberto's best friends. "He liked to take different women to the same restaurant and have the same food." He had a childish mentality, a need to please, and to be loved. He used his charm for that. His insecurity took the form of not attaching himself to anything or anyone. Security would have entailed discipline. He wasn't afraid of betrayal in a relationship but of discipline, of obligations. "The substance of affection did not exist in him." The pain he caused others meant little to him.[86]

Ingrid was easier to understand. As a girl she had been clumsy, the brunt of teasing and of the deaths of her parents and aunt. She had always wanted to be an actress "because then I'm not myself," and stardom had not changed her. "Even today," she said around 1957, "when I go into a restaurant, my greatest torture is walking through the room until I reach my table in the farthest corner."[87] The fantasy she found as an actress she sought in real life as well. "She always imagined herself in love with the leading man or director in every picture she did. Each job was an expedition on Cloud Seven," said Walter Wanger.[88]

Roberto's life was acting, too, a sort of bravado to nullify his insecurity, a fabulously successful performance. Women admired his assurance, his defiance. "What is there to be frightened about?" he would say.[89] Ingrid was introverted, Roberto splendidly extroverted. "He made everything larger than life," she marveled; "life took on new dimensions, new excitement, new horizons."[90] Even Joe Steele, Ingrid's former press agent, who was in love with her and came to Sicily at her request to try to salvage her publicity, could not deny a measure of admiration for the man he regarded with jealousy and contempt.

"I felt an instant impact: this was no ordinary man," Steele wrote of their first encounter (also noting "the ubiquitous spaghetti"). "His wide brown eyes were inquisitive yet uninformative. His smallish mouth curls enigmatically like mouths I had seen in Florentine paintings. His chin was pointed and slightly receding. His hair thinned backward over a well-formed head. His skin was white, not swarthy. He was no taller than Ingrid, and his midriff showed signs of middle-age softness and expansion. No maiden's dream of Don Juan, this 'other man,' but he exuded charm from every flaw."[91]

After days "lost" (!?) waiting for them, the tuna came. "The blue Mediterranean turned a bloody red, and Rossellini, the realist, got his scene; a scene of savage violence, which in the finished picture, ran for half a minute, and signified nothing.

"The technical staff was ordered back to Stromboli," wrote Steele, "and Rossellini announced that the rest of us—Donati, Marcella, the Cohns, Mrs. Neuwald, myself and, of course, Ingrid—would be off to Taormina, the justly famed resort. . . .

"'But why do we go there?' I asked.

"'Ah, it is beautiful!' said Rossellini. 'You will like. We rest a few days, yes?' He gently curled the little lock of hair behind his left ear.

"Rest from what?" wondered Steele. "Sitting around for a week, waiting for the tuna . . . ?"[92]

In Taormina, Roberto donned skin-diving gear and went spearfishing. The others sat on the beach and hours passed with the sun. Chilly and hungry, they tried without success to wave him in. Roberto's "rude preoccupation with himself" was neither conscious nor intentional, thought Steele; "this pronounced absorption in the mood of the moment was but one facet of a many-sided personality." An annoying one. "If only he had caught one little fish, he would have come," explained Ingrid. "He hates to give in."[93]

Steele had heard tales of Roberto's mercurial temperament, how once in a restaurant he had beaten a photographer in a blind rage and held him for the police, then paid his fine, embraced him, and taken him back to join the table.

Ingrid had been "restless and unhappy," she said. "I was always holding it inside of me, until sometimes I felt I would burst.[94] With Roberto I don't feel shy or afraid or lonely for the first time in my life." She threw back her head and gazed at the sky. "I feel free for the first time. . . . I love Roberto. One day, when I am free, we shall be married. He is a great artist, and it is exciting and full of wonder to watch him work. I shall be content to be near him and, in a way, make his career my career. If he will let me I shall be happy to work as one of the crew—help cut his pictures—anything."[95]

But if Roberto, for Ingrid, was a hero and father figure, what was she for him? Being a hero becomes boring and taxing, especially for someone who hates responsibility and just wants to be "one of the boys." In

Roberto's life no subservient woman could hope to be more than a servant. Ingrid's stardom gave Roberto stardom. But he did not approve of stars; he did not admire Ingrid or any actor artistically. He had not even bothered to see her movies.

Already he sensed she was not the woman he needed. Among other things she was notoriously slow-witted. "I knew after the second day it wouldn't work out," he told Maria Mercader a year later.[96] Yet he loved her. At the moment, mutual affinities—their uncertain personalities, perpetually searching and unfulfilled—united them more fundamentally than mutual profit. At the moment, his *obligations* to Ingrid—his knight errantry to the dragon's prisoner—took the form of love. Had Ingrid not fled Lindstrom, had a world scandal not thrust her upon Roberto, had she not become pregnant, the whole thing might well have been just another passing affair.

Instead, every pressure mounted, forcing them closer together. RKO, unappreciative of the tuna, was issuing ultimatums: finish the film or we'll shut you down. The press scandal, excited continually by new equivocations from Ingrid and Roberto, grew and grew. And the baby inside Ingrid grew too.

They both needed divorces urgently, if an illegitimate birth—and a far worse scandal—were not to ensue. And it was now two months that Lindstrom had been waiting in London, expecting Ingrid at any moment, as she had promised. For him, a debilitating ordeal.

Steele never suspected Ingrid was pregnant. He insisted she should see Petter; Petter had a right to that, it was the only way to stop the scandal. Roberto wouldn't hear of it. He ranted and raved and grabbed a gun. "If Ingrid she go back to that man, I kill myself. . . . Ingrid is lost if she stay alone with him. That cold man—he is *dominante* Ingrid. She have no will when he look at her!"[97] Steele didn't understand anything; he thought Roberto was crazy.

In the end, Ingrid did not go, neither to Petter nor to Pia. Instead she sent Martha Cohn to meet Lindstrom in Paris and ask for a divorce. He refused, insisted she see Pia first, and went back to California.

Ingrid in her autobiography blames Roberto for this fiasco and for her cruelty to Petter and Pia: he wouldn't let her go see Petter, she says, and no one could stand up to him. She depicts herself as a weeping mother and Roberto as a maniac; to prove her helplessness she cites episodes of madcap temper years apart.

But was Roberto's behavior unreasonable? He had seen almost nothing of Petter in California. He knew of him only what Ingrid had told him—and was constantly repeating. It was she who painted him as a "cold, dominating tyrant." It was she who maintained she had no will of her own in his presence. And she was carrying Roberto's child now. If Lindstrom were anything like what she described, would he not try to seduce her? Would he not lure her back to America with promises and then ensnare her there in a thousand entanglements? Wouldn't any man desperately in love try to do that? Wouldn't Lindstrom, a doctor and a Swede, sway Ingrid to that easy solution which she, all through August, continued to vacillate toward—despite the efforts of Lisandrini, Roberto, and the heroic example of the character she was playing? Could Roberto permit this "cold, dominating tyrant" to abort his unborn son?

Ingrid, in her book, never suggests these explanations for Roberto's attitude; she never mentions her temptation to end her pregnancy. Instead she says he was a maniac and "Italian." Previously she had blamed Lindstrom for her decisions. He had been her "patsy" in Hollywood, said Walter Wanger. "She was always going off half-cocked, making crazy financial commitments, and he was the one who had to extricate her. . . . For instance, when she went to New York to play [Maxwell Anderson's] *Joan of Lorraine*, she announced she was tired of Hollywood and through with the movies. She wrote me that she was the happiest woman in the world and that, from now on, the theater was for her. But three months later, she was bored. She couldn't wait to rush back to Hollywood. She got Lindstrom to take the rap for her by getting her out of the play."[98]

"The volcano," said Roberto, "was very good to me. The finale was supposed to be like that, though it was difficult to see how it could be made. But it started erupting quite happily. I always have confidence that these things will work out."[99]

Actually it wasn't so remarkable. A volcano expert had tracked Stromboli's previous eruptions and determined its likely performance during Rossellini's sojourn.

More remarkable is how the star's own life came to parallel the film's lofty allegoric ideas—ideas that now, in Rossellini's mind, were entitled *Land of God*.

But this too was predictable. Rossellini wanted to film only what was real. When a real situation didn't exist, it had to be created.

The lofty idea in *Land of God* came partly from Father Felix Morlion. In the passage of its central character, Karin, from opportunism to responsibility, Morlion saw an allegory—the need to implement Resistance ideals into daily life. As Roberto, under Morlion's influence, put it at the time: "The only thing certain in Europe today is that nobody believes in anything. . . . What is needed is a film that can transcend both politics and economics and give man back faith in himself as well as a new apprehension of God."[100]

Land of God, he explained, is "a portrait of a human being who has come out of the war a moral wreck—who has had to abandon everything, even morality, in order to survive.[101] She had been through the war, through both collaborationism and the concentration camps, and has been clever enough to find *all* the right answers, [but] she comes to a point where she finds herself lost in a maze. The very structure of the world she lives in turns into a maze.[102]

"What interested me was to treat the theme of cynicism, a sentiment that represented the greatest danger of the postwar. Karin, speculating on the ingenuous love of a soldier, a poor primitive creature, marries him for the sole purpose of getting out of the internment camp. She trades barbed wire for the island. But there she finds herself even more penned in; she had dreamed of something else. . . . She is a victim of stupid little things: a husband who is a brute, a little island without vegetation, and doubly prisoner by being pregnant. Being pregnant is for her stupid, humiliating, ignoble, and bestial. So she decides to leave. But on the summit of the volcano—which she has to climb over to reach a small port on the other side of the island—in the middle of hostile nature, broken by fatigue, bent by primitive terror, in animal-like despair, she unconsciously calls out to God. 'My God' is the simplest, most primitive and common invocation that can come out of the mouth of a creature overcome by suffering. It can be a mechanical invocation or the expression of a very high truth. In either case it is still the expression of a profound mortification that may also be the first glimmer of a conversion."[103]

Karin, then, represents "shipwrecked" Europe; she is a prostitute like Paola (*Desiderio*), Marina (*Roma città aperta*), and Francesca (*Paisà*). In the manner of her sexuality—her inability to relate to others *except* sexually—she vaguely resembles Bergman, who also is a "fallen woman" shipwrecked in Europe. Karin/Bergman rises again, through oppression, struggle, and agony, and in accepting responsibility for her actions discovers a sense of release, a freedom from desperation, a new resolution (all of which Renzo Rossellini's music conveys compellingly).

"This is the film's dramatic construction," Rossellini continues (referring to his analysis, not mine). "But it was not difficult to discern my intentions—I shall even say my prayer—if one took the trouble to read the Bible verse placed on the screen after *Stromboli*'s titles: 'I gave to those who were asking nothing of me. I let myself be found by those who were not looking for me.' (Isaiah 65, cited by St. Paul)."[104] (On the English language prints: "I was found of them that sought me not: I was made manifest unto them that asked not after me." [Romans 10:10.])

Karin's intentions, however, are *not* so clear. As night falls she collapses on the volcano, sobbing, "I haven't the courage. I'm afraid. I'm afraid. I'm afraid." But at dawn she awakes and exclaims, "Oh, God, what mystery, what beauty!" Resuming her climb, she collapses again: "No, I can't go back. I can't. They [the Strombolians] are horrible. They don't know what they are doing. I am even worse. I'll save him [her baby]. Oh, my innocent child. God! My God! Help me! Give me the strength, the understanding, the courage! O God! O my God! Merciful God! God! God! God!" And the camera pans to some flying birds. The End.

Does Karin go back to her husband? Or does she go on fleeing?

"I don't know," said Roberto. "That would be the beginning of another film. The only hope for Karin is to have a human attitude toward something, at least once. . . . There's a turning point in every human experience in life. . . . My endings are turning points. Then it begins again. But as for what it is that begins, I don't know."[105]

Amidei's original treatment knew. It was constructed around Karin's reconciling herself to life on the island. In the version Rossellini presented to Bergman in November 1948, sunrise on the volcano ignites a religious confession and Karin plunges childishly into the sea, overcome with joy and an urgent need to return and improve her husband; she even puts on the long black dress the island women wear. Karin is also a more diabolic character in this version; she takes pleasure in exciting the island men and feeling their lust; she wants to stir up evil to avenge the wrongs men have done to her. In a second treatment, prepared just before shooting, Karin also chooses her husband. She tries to escape with a fisherman, is driven back by a storm, then gets chased up the volcano by her husband, whom she tries to kill by starting a rock slide; exhausted, she collapses in tears, invoking God; then, "Finally at peace, she returns to the village, become[s] humble, [and] goes back to her home."[106]

One tempting explanation for the change is that Roberto, once he found himself on Stromboli with Ingrid, decided that it was implausible and repugnant that Karin could accept either the island or her husband. Yet in fact the change had not been made even six months after leaving the island. The first screening, probably in February 1950, was a private one in Rome, hosted by Roberto, of the English-language version. Vittorio Bonicelli, reported on Rossellini's authority, "She will go back."[107] And the same conclusion was made by others who attended that screening. "She resigns herself . . . to going back," Moravia wrote.[108] Evidently this was also Bergman's understanding; even 25 years later she said, "Of course [Karin] would realize that there was a duty that she had to go back and have the child and live with her husband."[109] And in the version released by RKO in February 1950, a version which was butchered but initially assembled according to Rossellini's storyline, a voice-over at the end tells us Karin goes back.

On the contrary, in the movie itself, as we can see it today (even in the RKO version until the voice-over intrudes), neither Karin's words nor the trajectory of her story support the conclusion that she goes back. Whatever she does, *that* choice appears more repugnant—and unworkable—than ever.

The matter was obfuscated, deliberately made open-ended and unresolved, by changes Rossellini made during the year that passed between the critics' screenings and *Stromboli*'s general release. Now he didn't want Karin to choose—except to choose to have her baby. He wanted her to become *able*, for the first time her life, to make a moral choice. His emphasis is on her decision for life and, in a final cut for Italian release, on the miraculous. But now, as Bergman adds, after contending that Karin does go back, ". . . at the same time you don't know it, you have to guess it . . . ;

there *was* no end, which is what the public objected to."[110] ("Everyone agreed," quipped Roberto, "that I was a cretin."[111])

The *nature* of Karin's experience has also been obfuscated due to Rossellini himself, who propagated new explanations for the movie as the years passed and his religious commitments weakened. Already, by 1954, he was distancing the movie from the religious intentions he had had while making it five years earlier, by suggesting that Karin's call to God, although perhaps a "first glimmer of conversion," may also be "mechanical... unconscious... animal-like despair."[112]

But religion was a source of truth for Roberto in 1950, perhaps the sole source of truth. He appended Bible verses to *Stromboli*. And in his final cut (the Italian release), he made explicit what had been implicit in his rough cut (his English-language release). He retitled the movie *Stromboli terra di Dio* ("Stromboli Land of God") and added six shots to chronicle the definite experience of Grace—which, contrary to his assertions a few years later, is not at all "unconscious" and couldn't be further from "animal-like despair."[113] Perhaps Roberto made the changes to court the Vatican. But he did not do so insincerely. He was listening to Simone Weil, who said that "Grace fills empty spaces, but it can only enter where there is a void to receive it."[114]

Time and again in the early fifties, Rossellini gave explicitly religious explanations of his intentions. To *Sight and Sound* he explained that "the girl who in the cruel, corrupt world of the concentration camps had lost her faith, regains it in the hour of supreme castigation—when revolting against the God in whose existence she had refused to believe."[115] To the communist Georges Sadoul he said: "If one can speak ... of my spiritual cinematic itinerary, I would say that *Deutschland im Jahre Null* is the world arrived at desperation through the loss of faith, whereas *Land of God* is the rediscovery of faith."[116] To the Catholic *Rivista del Cinematografo* he said: "*Deutschland im Jahre Null* was the film of destruction. People were beginning to see the sun again, the light; were beginning to look at life with new eyes. . . . [In *Stromboli*], after looking at life, I tried to get the protagonist to see the One Who gives life, God."[117] And shortly before *Stromboli*'s screening at the Venice Festival, he published the following declaration of his (Morlion-influenced) intentions:

"One of the toughest lessons from this last war is the danger of aggressive egotism. Adopted initially as defense, egotism soon became second nature, giving individuals invincible security, true, but also a new solitude, without hope.

"For some time I matured the idea of treating, after the war dramas, this postwar tragedy ... that transfers the whole world to inside the creature and produces the disdainful certainty that one can live without love, humility, or comprehension. Reduced to its simplest terms, it turns out to be, with a new accent but with age-old significance, the struggle between Creator and creature.

"[With Bergman and Stromboli] I found natural dramatic oppositions. If the protagonist was a limit case, so was the island.... Thus the structures of ancient tragedy were the only ones I thought adequate to give life to this struggle between Creator and creature. The woman protagonist, cynical and egoistic, who has against her that double silent chorus: the people with their narrow-minded incomprehension, and nature, hostile and inclement. Ignored, unseen but omnipresent, is her real antagonist: God.

"It is against Him that the protagonist is actually fighting when, with typical perversity, she revolts against the chorus. At every step she is torn between her own feelings of proud rebellion and rejection, and other feelings of obedient submission that are dictated to her by an unknown inner voice hidden in her soul.

"God, her antagonist, will reveal himself to her only at the end, after triumphing over both chorus and protagonist and leading her to the summit of aching despair, after forcing her to invoke the light of Grace that frees her from her inhuman solitude."[118]

Roberto identified himself with Karin, who had not been pregnant in Amidei's treatment, but who, like Ingrid, became pregnant during the production, and like Ingrid had struggled to decide to have her baby. The option of abortion could not be mentioned in the movie, given the climate of the time. Nor could Roberto explain *Stromboli's* ending by soliciting applause for Ingrid's decision not to have an abortion. Such an explanation would have been not only suicidal (which would not have stopped Roberto) but unchivalrous (which always would). But in fact Ingrid, in her 1949 letter to Steele announcing this decision, even uses the same words "strength and courage" as Karin does announcing her decision. Ingrid, like Karin, was not a protagonist by nature. If five years later we find Roberto pondering whether "strength and courage" may have been only "animal-like despair," perhaps it is because after five years of marriage he was also weighing noble intentions.

Still in Roberto's mind, Karin was paralleled not with Ingrid but with himself, with his noble intentions and the adventure he wanted for Ingrid. "There is autobiography," he said in 1952, "in the feelings of the woman brutalized by reality and turning back to fantasy [i.e., Romano's death], with a longing to expand, to embrace the whole world without letting go of reality, finding inner liberation in the call to God which is the final thrust of the film. She looks at the problem for the first time, almost unconsciously. It is only in the presence of nature, of her own self, and of God, that she has come to understand."[119]

There can be no doubt, then, that Roberto intended *Stromboli* to depict our (and his own) helplessness without God. Religious motifs abound: peaks, chasms, and labyrinths; life is pilgrimage, stations of the cross; the world (mineral and flesh) is viewed almost gnostically, charged with divine life. Karin's wandering through the labyrinth of houses with the child crying in the distance is analogous to St. John of the Cross's description of the soul that goes out from his house in the night to go searching for God.[120]

Rossellini's films are passions, fundamental oppositions of love and death (carrying life and death), night and day, hell, purgatory, paradise. Like Nannina, Karin ascends the mountain. But Karin sees the stars only after the volcano.[121] No solution, no freedom, no healing is possible until, under the cave-like dome of the stars at night, God's grace descends and sparks a miracle: the impulse that causes her to cry out to Him the next morning. And then her pose reproduces *Ecstasy*, a Bernini marble of St. Theresa in the church of Santa Maria della Vittoria near Roberto's boyhood home.[122] For Rossellini as for Augustine, our ability to determine ourselves depends on areas that we cannot ourselves determine; even our ability to turn to God depends on God. "He was always searching," said Bergman, "for some meaning or some higher person that would be up there and that we couldn't find. The search was to come at least one step closer."[123]

Nonetheless. By 1960 Rossellini's rhetoric had altered radically. "Many have wished to discover in *Stromboli* an allegory of the problem of Grace. They have exaggerated and have not understood," he declared.[124] "What is mysticism?" he asked in 1975. "It's to put yourself in the hands of God. [But] the main thing in life is to be you, to be completely active, to be completely responsible, to have the chance to be bitten, to be spat upon your face, and sometimes even to achieve something. This, I think, is more exciting. When you put yourself in the hands of God, or destiny, or anything like that, it's a sort of coward's position. And I don't like cowardice at all."[125]

Are these reasons to deny that *Stromboli* is an allegory of "the problem of Grace"? The problem of Grace—which the Church wrestled over for centuries, and the Reformation was fought over—is that we are helpless without it, but salvation depends also on our own willpower. Karin never "puts" herself in the hands of God. God finds her. All during her life she has been "afraid." It is only now that she rises out of the "coward's position," becomes herself, accepts responsibility and her own willpower. And this was Rossellini's understanding in 1949. As Morlion notes, "inner security" for Roberto meant "not mystical, abstract resignation to God's will, but totally conscious acceptance of one's concrete human condition even in sorrow, and thus a capacity to be coherent with oneself."[126]

Thus the point of the movie isn't Karin's animal-like dependence or what Karin is going to do. It's that liberty requires strength, understanding, and courage, and that Karin at last accepts responsibility. Rossellini's point is clear, when he cuts to some flying birds for his last shot. Karin has been given freedom. Karin has achieved freedom.

"I am willing to break my neck to do something new," Bergman had told reporters.[127] During Karin's final scenes she nearly did. The volcanic surface was hot as tar. Wearing sandals, she trembled and suffered spasms of pain as Roberto, forsaking his customary quickness, rehearsed her over and over, deliberately creating "a real situation"—of agony. A production executive, Lodovici Muratori, was overcome by fumes and died of a heart attack. Ingrid struggled on.

Afterward she was still dissatisfied. Karin's transition, she felt, appeared unmotivated and purely a gesture of faith, insofar as it was based on an invocation to a God who does not respond to humans. Said Morlion, "We discussed it at length with Roberto and with Ingrid, who both felt themselves in some respects mirrored autobiographically in the characters' situations. Finally, chiefly because of Bergman's extraordinary inner sensitivity (she asked me for the writings of Saint Theresa of Avila to read), we realized the scene would have to be redone. It had to be made clear that Karin, as she repeats her calls to God, changes radically in her inner attitudes. God's response to the scream of anguish had to be not in liberation from pain or promise of compensation but in Karin's coming to realize that, to be at peace with herself, she has to accept life with love, even when life is suffering. And it is precisely this that Ingrid tried to express in the definitive version of the scene that, with Roberto's agreement, I directed myself. My contribution, though, was rather modest. I limited myself to individuating with Ingrid the vocal intonations that, in the repeated screams of invocation, might suggest the gradual passage from vainly waiting for a miracle to change Karin's existential condition from outside her, to a lucid and thoroughly loving acceptance of it."[128] (Six months after this incident, shortly before Ingrid gave birth, Morlion wrote Joseph Breen, the Hollywood Production Code administrator, praising her for her acceptance of motherhood. In retaliation, New York's archbishop, Francis Cardinal Spellman, arranged the cancellation of a visit Morlion had been about to make to the United States.)

On August 2, after 102 days, Roberto and Ingrid left Stromboli, spent a week in Amalfi, and moved into a furnished apartment on Via Giovanni Antonelli in Rome. Meanwhile, in an attempt to withdraw from public attention, Ingrid had Steele announce she was divorcing Lindstrom and quitting acting. The attempt was futile. On August 6, Rome's *Corriere della Sera* rumored she was pregnant and three days later Hedda Harper, Hollywood's scandal monger, arrived to see for herself. "Why, Hedda, do I look it?" Ingrid finessed, and Harper told America it could relax.

Marcellina De Marchis returned from Vienna in time to join Roberto for the annual August 14 memorial service and a visit to Romano's tomb. The divorce ruling had not yet come through. "Neither of us spoke of the subject close to both of our hearts. Only [later] did I come to understand the real reason for Roberto's singular torment at the time."[129]

He presented Ingrid to Marcellina shortly thereafter, preparing the way by telling Ingrid that Marcellina had never recovered from Romano's death and was still a bit crazy. Ingrid, accordingly, brought a bouquet and did herself proud in niceties toward her future husband's wife. Marcellina, for her part, told Ingrid to ignore Roberto's headaches. Ingrid ignored the advice instead and spent years ministering to the headaches. But she took

Marcellina's advice about what to feed Renzino, whom she began having for lunch on Saturdays. Sometimes Marcellina would wait for her son outside on the street.

On August 29, for Ingrid's 34th birthday, Roberto hosted a party at Nino's (where he had often eaten with Magnani and Roswitha) and gave Ingrid a diamond scorpion brooch. But the flowers he sent Marcellina (also 34) on the occasion of their wedding anniversary, September 26, meant more to Marcellina than diamonds. "Dear Marcellina," said his card, "despite everything you have always my tenderness and my deep, deep, deep affection." In October, Roberto and Ingrid moved into a ten-room apartment at 49 Viale Buono Buozzi, in Parioli.

In an attempt to gain Ingrid's divorce, Monroe McDonald, an American lawyer residing in Rome, was dispatched to treat with Lindstrom. His technique was to tell columnist Cholly Knickerbocker all the mournful details of Ingrid's marriage and childhood, and then to use the press to threaten to "take off his gloves" and "blast" the case wide open if Lindstrom didn't cooperate. Petter had given her only $300 when she left for Europe, charged McDonald. (In fact, she had always had access to her bank account, had transferred thousands of dollars to Italy, and had collected $205,000 in weekly payments from RKO.)

Bergman was appalled at McDonald's tactics. Lindstrom, on the verge of settling, now retired into a shell. Renzino got into fights at school, was hit on the head with a stone, and required stitches. And Pia, taunted by her friends, had been withdrawn from school and sent to Minnesota where, even there, newsmen pursued her disguised as salesmen. When Ingrid phoned, Pia asked when the picture would be finished and her mother would be coming home. At Christmas, Ingrid told her.

Deutschland im Jahre Null opened in New York in September 1949 as *Germany, Year Zero*. There was the same "shattering sense of futility" as in *Paisan* and *Open City*, wrote Bosley Crowther in *The New York Times*, yet "a strange emptiness of genuine feeling." The characters were "barren and lethargic," Edmund was a "sallow and futile little thing."[130] But *The Times'* other critic, Howard Barnes, disagreed: "The most savage and shattering of [Rossellini's] several masterpieces . . . illuminates the destruction of Nazism as no other examination of the postwar period."[131] And *Time's* Manny Farber wrote perceptively: "Roberto Rossellini's trademarks—nervous editing, off-center compositions, the camera moving faster than the figure and often at a tangent to it—are aimed at approximating the uneasy experience of the human eye, which never quite catches or catalogues everything in its path. In his mimicry of actuality, the point of focus shifts widely and illogically, the actors are in constant motion, or their talk is whirling on at a great speed, falling or rising in intonation so that the audience is not sure whether it is meant to be heard or not. . . . [Toward the end,] the shot of a family walking to the father's burial, the girls in their short black dresses, wobbling on platform shoes, has the forlorn dignity of a Chaplin ending, plus a less calculated pathos."[132]

In *The New York Times*, Renzo Rossellini gave his thoughts on film music:

> I have written scores for eighty-two motion pictures. . . . Twenty years of composing for symphony, ballet and theatre as well as films have convinced me that the cinema is as great as any of the arts. . . . The musical score can be the indispensable complement to the full expression of a film. It can be the means of revealing innermost psychological characteristics; it can evoke the flavor of a place or time; it can be decorative as well as functional. However, it must arise out of a true and artistic necessity. . . . My own feeling is that there is the best integration between story and score when film music interprets the theme. . . . In *Germany, Year Zero*, the music was written to form a whole with the steely German language, the rubble and dust of the bombed streets. It was meant to express all of this and to underline the grim realism of the film. I composed the score of *Germany, Year Zero* after the final editing. I always choose to work on a picture after it is finished. Thus I am relatively apart from the other groups concerned in the project. . . . While film music is often of concert caliber, excellent enough to be played independently of the picture for which it was written, it is my opinion that it should not be detached from the motives which gave it life. The Rome publisher, Ricordi, has asked me to authorize a concert version of the score of *Germany, Year Zero*. Orchestra conductors have requested permission to play it. I have been tempted, but I cannot bring myself to permit the music to be used apart from the film in which it finds its ideal justification, for which it was conceived and written.[133]

Under Capricorn also opened in September—Ingrid's third box-office failure in a row.

Shooting had finally wrapped on *Stromboli* (as Howard Hughes had decided to call the film) on August 22, after nine days at the displaced persons camp in Farfa. Its eventual cost was said to be about $800,000, $200-$300,000 over budget.[134] This would have been a bargain for a made-in-Hollywood Bergman movie, less than half-price. But the figure is awfully high for an Italian movie, even after subtracting Bergman's $200,000. With much the same crew, Rossellini had made *Paisà* for $100,000, a much more difficult production. American studios commonly charged a production 25 or 30 percent in excess of its actual cost to defray studio overhead.

The fights got worse.

The stock of the Berit Company (the Bergman–Rossellini production company) was to have been held in escrow as protection for RKO; but Roberto had never turned it over. Two negatives had been shot simultaneously for English and Italian versions; now RKO seized both negatives, but was unable to export them without authorization from Berit, so Harold Lewis hid them in Rome. Meanwhile Roberto sent Hughes a bill for an additional $25,000 in salary on the grounds that he had had to work three months more than his contract had called for—and "kidnapped" the single negative of the final three days' shooting.[135] Hughes kept a private plane waiting at Ciampino for twenty days, but Roberto insisted that he and Ingrid be excused from returning to Hollywood, as they had previously contracted to do, for *Stromboli*'s post-production—its dubbing, scoring, and final editing. He claimed Hollywood was out to get him; he said cocaine would turn up in his luggage as he went through customs.

Hughes, not suspecting the real reason was Ingrid's pregnancy, had to give in. The extra money was paid, Roberto surrendered his negative and put the Berit stock in escrow, and RKO, giving back the Italian negative, agreed to allow him to edit it in Rome, as a model for the American version.

Roberto did the editing himself, sitting very quietly and pensively at a moviola. To carry his torch in Hollywood he sent Renzo, who sailed in late November from Naples. It was an unfortunate choice. Renzo was even more offended by "America's" roughhousing of Roberto than Roberto himself. Everything he encountered in America disgusted him, Hollywood most of all, where his hotel was "The Garden of Allah."

Renzo was willing to concede a technical superiority to Hollywood. "But," he said, "the culture and intelligence of their executives is inferior to that of any of our doormen. And not only that: intelligence is effectively outlawed in Hollywood, and the production of a film, at every phase, is now entrusted entirely to those functionaries who are considered business experts. . . . In producing a film one is required to remember that the median mentality of the spectator is that of a twelve-year-old child. This is a rule it is absolutely forbidden to break."[136]

Renzo had no power over Hughes. And RKO, with little appreciation for the flatter pacing of a European film, and even less for the subtlety of Rossellini's ending, did its best to turn his rough cut into a Hollywood movie. Thirty-five minutes were chopped out, material within the film was isolated into a documentary-like prologue, the wait for the tuna was abbreviated, and a voice-over narrator was employed to explain everything. At the end, instead of leaving Karin on the volcano calling to God, she is made, by dint of clumsily assembled out-takes and the narrator's explanation, to turn around and start back down to her husband.

In Italy this was interpreted as a deliberate mutilation: by Amidei, as a ploy to sabotage the picture and thus recover Bergman; by Ingrid, as love-spite by Hughes because of her failure to come back to him. "I was in Hollywood with Howard Hughes," said Gina Lollobrigida. "He was mad at Rossellini because he had succeeded in taking away Ingrid from him. He really wanted to get her back. I never saw a person so angry."[137]

Roberto sued, an action that appalled Italian producers, who wanted American business. Even his own lawyer thought he was crazy to try to fight Hughes. Elettra, still wearing black in obedience to her earlier vow, now promised to give up fruit, if her son were granted victory. She loved fruit.

*

Early in December 1949, with Ingrid bundled up beside him in her black fur, Roberto picked up *Il Tempo*'s film critic Gian Luigi Rondi and his brother Brunello and drove them in his Cadillac to Technostampa for a first, private, projection of *Land of God*. All through the screening Ingrid was tense and Roberto agitated. The sound had not yet been mixed, and he imitated the sounds of the crying child that Karin hears in her room. Except for the tuna and a few other sequences, Ingrid did not like the picture at all. Brunello Rondi observed that "her sweet stubbornness in repeating this judgment was absolute. Rossellini accepted it lovingly."[138]

God's Jester

Rossellini's next film was to start shooting January 17, 1950 (Marcellina's birthday again). Unlike *Stromboli terra di Dio* which had been put together at the last moment, *Francesco giullare di Dio* (*Francis, God's Jester*) had been years in planning. It was, Marcellina noted after Rossellini's death, "the film Roberto continued to love more than any other he made."[1] *Francesco's* spirit hovers over *Stromboli*, the movie before it, and *Europe '51*, the movie after it.

Roberto had expounded his ideas on Francis of Assisi to Jenia Reissar back in April 1948. "Rossellini explained that it is the story of a man who is a non-Catholic, who renounced riches for poverty, in order to prove to himself and to others that contentment and peace of mind are not due to riches, and are an inner quality which rich and poor alike can enjoy," Reissar reported to Selznick, apparently oblivious to Roberto's blarney. "Saint Francis was followed into this voluntary exile from the world by his ex-mistress, who renounced her great love for him and became his faithful follower."[2]

"Peace of mind" was a constant, if involuted, theme for Roberto in the years following Romano's death. Such had been Karin's quest in *Stromboli*, Edmund's in *Deutschland*. In the fall of 1948, when Roberto had first met Morlion, he had confessed his pride that he had put the monks sequence into *Paisà* "to show the ability of faith in God to generate serene acceptance of suffering." This was blarney seasoned for Morlion, but honest. Rossellini's characters were going to be the same monks he had used in *Paisà* and Rossellini's message was going to be the same as well. He intended "to make a film in which Saint Francis and Saint Clare, despite their superhuman ability to renounce everything and give themselves to others, would behave like ordinary individuals—exactly like the partisans in *Paisà* or the characters in *Roma città aperta*, normal people who had faced death with simplicity, not because they had a vocation for heroism but merely because they wanted to stay human. To stay faithful, even at the cost of life itself, to certain values they had deeply interiorized without ever explicitly wondering about them."[3]

In collaboration with Fellini, Roberto put together a "treatment" consisting of 71 lines of dialogue on 28 pages drawn from the *Fioretti* ("Little Flowers," i.e., inspirational stories) and other almost-contemporary Franciscan legends, notably the *Life of Brother Ginepro*. Fellini made the initial selections among these anecdotes,[4] and eleven or twelve stories were eventually chosen to chronicle events during the short period between Francis's return from Rome, where he had received Innocent III's blessing, and his followers' dispersion out into the world, where their numbers rapidly multiplied from a dozen to tens of thousands.

"I didn't intend for a moment to make a biographical film," Rossellini explained. "The personality of Saint Francis is so immense that it would be impossible to do him justice within the framework of a film of normal length. That is why I confined myself to a single aspect of his personality . . . : *The Jester of God*. The accent is entirely on Saint Francis's whimsical, unruffled approach to the crudities and trivialities of everyday life."[5] Like Fellini's other collaborations with Rossellini—*Paisà*'s monks sequence and *Il miracolo*—*Francesco* was a story of simple faith.

Its curt, anecdotal structure suited Rossellini after his uncomfortable struggles with long, novel-like subjects. Both *Deutschland* and *Stromboli* had suffered from off-the-cuff methods that had precluded script preparation beforehand; nor had Roberto, once those productions began, been temperamentally inclined to develop subsidiary characters and intrigues to the degree feature films demanded. Indeed, as he freely admitted, only certain situations in these pictures had attracted him; most of his time had been spent unenthusiastically filming the scenes needed to get to the parts he liked. Obviously a movie containing *just* privileged situations and nothing else would be his ideal. Accordingly, *Francesco*, like *Paisà*, would be a series of virtually self-sufficient episodes—some of them little more than vignettes—informally linked in subject and theme. Titles introducing each vignette would accentuate this episodicness (e.g., "How at night Francesco praying in the forest encountered the leper"). There would be no suspense, no plot working out a drama, not even a character undergoing change. Francis would be the central personage less often than Ginepro.

It was a scheme calculated to make the most of Rossellini's abilities—and the least of his commercial appeal. Yet the Vatican was encouraging, and somehow the publisher Angelo Rizzoli, heedless to warnings by Franco Riganti and nudged on by Pepe Amato, was induced to put up the money.

Ingrid, meanwhile, had written Joe Steele in Los Angeles revealing the big secret. Yes, she was pregnant. Steele, devastated, desperate to help, and terrified that more scandal would destroy Ingrid's chance to profit from *Stromboli*, had rushed to Hughes, pledged him to secrecy, and begged him to release the film immediately, before the secret became public. The result was an eight-column headline in *The Examiner* the next morning, December 12.

Renzo was incredulous. "Roberto is my brother and he would not have kept it secret from me," he told Steele. But Roberto had not told Marcella either. And now as months of pressure climaxed Roberto went into hysterical collapse. "His hair [was] standing on end in a thousand curls, his clothes in a kind of upside-down fashion," Ingrid wrote Steele the next day. She herself, she added, was as calm as "a kind cow grazing in the sun." But Roberto? "All day he screamed at me to take something for my nerves. Which I did just to please him. A long time after [that], he shouted at the top of his voice, 'I beg you, take something for your nerves. You are driving me crazy. I can't stand to see you hysterical. Do you hear what I'm telling you? Do something about it!' . . . All disheveled, he fell in bed and slept, woke up with a horrible headache, has been sick all day, rushing around in a robe, screaming and yelling, then falling back in bed to be served some food because he was too weak to sit up."[6]

Ten days later Roberto and Marcellina met at their lawyer's office. The Austrian court, accepting Roberto's claim (not true, he told Steele) that he had been under the influence of drugs at the time of their wedding, had granted their annulment on December 23.

"Roberto, seeing my emotion, pressed my hand in his and said, 'Marcellina, these are just pieces of paper. Remember, feelings don't change and a life isn't opened and closed like a faucet.' "[7]

Roberto sent Marcellina azaleas for her birthday, January 17, and that same day began *Francesco*. Despite the cold and pouring rain, fire hoses were used to augment the torrent descending upon Francis's little band as, returning from Rome, they find themselves expelled from their hut by a farmer who has appropriated it for himself and his donkey—whereupon Francis lies down in the rain and commands his brothers to walk on his face. Saint Paul's words preface these events: "God has chosen the foolish things of the world to humiliate the learned, the weak to humiliate the strong, the vile, the despicable, and things that are not, to annihilate all those things that are." (1 Corinthians 1:27–28)

The filming took place in the countryside between Rome and Bracciano. Fellini had no part in it. To invent incidents and write dialogue for him as he went along, Rossellini had Brunello Rondi and Father Alberto Maisano, the master of novices from the convent of Baronissi (near Nocera, fifteen miles north of Maiori) whence Roberto's Franciscan players—all of them novices—had come. Lisandrini and Morlion were also involved, but as consultants rather than writers. The sole professional actor was Aldo Fabrizi; Fellini had cast him in a Fellini-esque role as the grotesque tyrant Nicolaio.

"I was very moved by their innocence. It was magnificent," said Rossellini of the monks. Fra Raffaele, for example, was a gardener rather than a priest, but "a very wise old monk" nonetheless. "He said he was a poet. I asked what kind of poetry he was doing. He said, 'I wrote a poem about a rose.' I asked him to tell it to me. He closed his eyes and lifted his face toward the sky and said, 'Oh, Rose!' And that was the whole poem. How can you have a better poem than that? It was also a sign of tremendous humility."[8] (And also an instance of what Croce meant by genuine speech, where every word is different every time it is pronounced—of poetry in Croce's sense: poetry does not make statements of any kind, neither of principle nor fact; poetry provides a picture of something individual, which may or may not exist.[9] In later years Roberto would refer to such poetry, in cinema, as "the essential image.")

Fra Raffaele had pet phrases too. One of them—"Grazie per il soccorso spirituale e temporale" ("Thanks for the spiritual and temporal assistance")—he used even when bade good night, and Rossellini had had him say it in *Paisà* when the Americans give him chocolate. "Fra Raffaele lived in sweet and dreamy silence, from which, from time to time, he would exit with singular phrases," wrote Brunello Rondi; "sometimes one had to tempt him and provoke him as with children."[10] Does God speak to us? they asked him. "Oh . . . ? God . . . ? God speaks in silence."

Fra Raffaele died halfway through the filming of *Francesco*. Roberto saw him laid out and ready for burial. They would have to rewrite and reshoot his scenes. But a few days later Roberto returned to the chilly convent near Bracciano where the Franciscans were staying, and what did he see but Fra Raffaele walking around. He had sneezed while they were burying him.[11]

From Maiori, Roberto also brought Peparuolo, the seventy-year-old beggar from *Il miracolo*, to be Giovanni il Semplice, a simple soul who joins Francis's company. "He was so full of desire to help me and he loved me so deeply, he always cried, 'Ah, now I have finally found a father,' and that was me, because I helped him a little. He was full of good will. He was called Peparuolo, which means someone with a red nose, because he used to drink. I said to him, 'Now this is the scene. You see that is Saint Francis. You come into the scene and you say to Saint Francis, "Oh! Saint Francis, I want to be with you." Do you understand?' 'Yes, sir.' 'We can rehearse, we can try,' I said, and so we started. 'So I appear and see Saint Francis and I ask . . . ' he said. 'No, listen, that is my explanation, you don't have to repeat that. Have you understood?' 'Yes, yes, yes.' 'So try again.' 'I appear, I go to Saint Francis and I say, but that is your explanation, but I have to say . . . ' He was all the time repeating the whole idea, and it was impossible to detach him from it.

"In order to use him, because he was such a character, my assistant brought him from far away while I prepared the scene. Without saying anything, otherwise he would have repeated my words. I called him with a gesture and pushed him into the middle of the scene and he improvised.[12] It worked perfectly, and it was very funny too.

"At the end of *Francesco*, all the monks decide to spin themselves around to determine what direction they will go in, and as he was lame he turned around very slowly and it took him half an hour to fall down.

When he fell he was supposed to say, 'I'm pointing to Embolo,' but he couldn't understand it however much we tried to explain. When he fell, Saint Francis asked him where he would go and he said, 'After that bird,' because there was a bird flying by. It was a priceless phrase and I kept it in."[13]

"I couldn't tell," Victoria Schultz said to Rossellini, "if you were being ironic with the brothers' naiveté or not..."

"*They* were ironic first of all, because the great message of Saint Francis, to my view, was to turn down all solemnity. Everything was very, very simple and Saint Francis was always laughing at himself because he was a silly, poor man. . . . The piety is there too. How can you reach such a humble thing like piety if you look at yourself with pride. You must just reverse the thing for the real values to come up. The truth is something very, very small, very, very humble and that is why it is so difficult to discover it. If you have no humility, how can you approach the truth? How can you make an error? You can build an opinion, but that is pride."[14]

Fra Ginepro's disarming openness ultimately faces down a roaring conqueror enclosed in a suit of armor.

"The scene with the tyrant of Viterbo is in the *fioretti* of Fra Ginepro. . . . At that time they didn't [wear] armor, it was created later, but [we committed this] falsification to give the character power, [to contrast] a little human being [Ginepro] and a robot. . . . It is very rare to find [the *fioretti* of Fra Ginepro]. Generally, when the *fioretti* are published it is cut out because it is the silliest, yet it is the most valuable. . . . They wanted to be silly . . . , to be just very foolish, because through silliness you can find the truth."[15]

"For me it was very important at that moment to speak out as strongly as possible against duplicity [*furberia*]," Rossellini reflected in 1964. "Simplicity seemed to me then, and still does today, a truly . . . awesome weapon. Innocence will always confound evil. I'm absolutely convinced of this. We've had a clamorous example of it in our time in Gandhi. This is one of the great revolutions achieved in our century using the weapons of non-violence, innocence, and candor. . . . Historically, [the Middle Ages] were cruel and violent centuries, and yet in those centuries appeared Francis of Assisi and Catherine of Siena. The fact that Saint Catherine of Siena was able go from Siena to Avignon to bring the Pope back to Rome, to travel through a bandit-infested Italy without anyone daring to touch her, is important. [In] the *Fioretti* . . . what interests and moves me is to find a man who certainly isn't a nitwit, but who had the courage to be humbly a man, with all his weaknesses."[16]

And in 1974 he told students at Yale: "Saint Francis called himself a jester, a clown, a juggler, because he wanted to make fun of all sorts of pride, because the main point was that from a very humble position you can face everything and you can revise the whole conception of the universe."[17]

God's Jester is a political film. Rossellini wanted to make the revolution, like everyone else. But like Croce he saw the liberation of the human spirit—the courage to be one's self, particularly when we know we'll look ridiculous—as the key.

Working under Rossellini, Rondi was struck by the director's "creative felicity, conviction and ardor, his delicious abandon in composition, and his exhilarating tenderness." Rossellini seemed "intense and clear, and intuitively alive to the world and people." Of course he was impatient and quick, too. But the lazy interludes spent chatting with friars and crew when the rainy winter imposed its delays, were to his liking. "Often," said Rondi, "he repeated his idea that the true mode of good living was the time just after a meal with friends, scarcely talking, without getting up from table. He was serious." Roberto was convivially Roman, with that species' sober—rather than pagan or sensual—love for primitive simplicity. "In contrast, De Sica, after *Bicycle Thieves*, thought himself as important as Thomas Mann and showed it in his way of walking. (I once said hello to him clearly, three feet away, right in front of him, but he passed right by me dreaming in his own wave.) Rossellini never had the slightest pose [or] altered his own humanity." Nor did he have any respect for his big long Cadillac: muddy shoes and soaking wet tunics were welcomed without the slightest misgiving.[18]

To play Saint Clare, Roberto was determined to enlist Arabella Lemaître, Selznick's agent, because, he told her, she resembled Giotto's painting where Clare "has the face of a crazy woman." Lemaître refused, but Roberto waited until the night before, then phoned saying he was in a mess, couldn't she help him?[19] In Clare's encounter with Francis, the two sit in long shot with their followers in immobile stillness, and a narrator tells us that the sky became so red with their love that people thought it had caught fire. How far this is from Zeffirelli's sappy sexuality in *Brother Sun, Sister Moon* (1973).

Two decades later Roberto would cast Lemaître's daughter as the Virgin Mary in *The Messiah*.

On January 23, a Turin appeals court had accepted the Austrian annulment's validity. The Vatican had promptly denounced the action as a violation of the Lateran accords (by which Italy acknowledged the Church's sole jurisdiction over matrimony) and had declared that Rossellini was still married in *its* eyes. Nonetheless, Roberto had found an end run around the law and was free. Now, since the battle continued with Lindstrom over custody of Pia, the question was whether Ingrid would obtain her Mexican divorce before her baby arrived.

She didn't. The divorce came February 9. Renato Roberto Giusto Giuseppe came February 2, seven pounds fourteen ounces. "He certainly is Swedish," remarked Roberto, looking at his son. "They always arrive ahead of their appointment."[20] To Marcellina he said it was as though Romano had been reborn. He would be called Robertino. By a Fascist law still in force, children could bear neither foreign names nor the same first name as their father.

To insure privacy Roberto stationed Manni in the room next to Ingrid's. Manni kept the key to her room and would unlock it for nurses and doctors—after checking them. Three agents watched the hospital gate, three the garden, and two more roamed the corridors.

Three jeeps full of riot police also arrived. Reporters were climbing the walls of the Villa Margherita hospital, perching in the trees and charging into wards and operating rooms. Magnani's *Volcano*, which had premiered the night before, was ignored completely. Offered $8,000 for baby pictures, Roberto took eleven in 35mm, gave them out for free, and was accused of profiteering. "About a week after our son was born I received a phone call from a Hearst reporter. It was the fiftieth call that day and so I said, 'Will you please get off the line, you people are driving me crazy.' Would you believe it—the next day there was an eight-column headline in a Los Angeles newspaper reading: 'ROSSELLINI FEARS MENTAL HEALTH.'"[21]

The peasants appearing in *Francesco* came with a basket of ricotta. A monsignor came, offering to find the baby a suitable home. For godfather, true to form, Roberto chose his banker, Enea Bazzano, director of the Banca Romana. Robertino didn't cry when given salt during the Baptism. "See, he has his father's strength to endure bitterness!" Roberto boasted.

"How nice is this baby of sin," remarked Lisandrini.

"What do you mean?!" retorted Roberto. "This is a child of love."[22]

Two weeks later in Cortina, Marcellina, concluding the writing of her memoirs, tried to sum up her feelings of life with Roberto. "If I look deep into my soul, I find there an infinity of bitterness quite beyond anything so tawdry as rancor. To forget is very difficult, to forgive is easier. And the two seem profoundly different to me.... My life with Roberto was always full and intense, even when it seemed over. I had married an exceptional man, agreeing to call myself Rossellini when his artistic gifts were unknown to everyone. I left this name at the moment of his greatest fame. In compensation there remains to me something that no one, except God, can ever take away from me: my son."[23]

To take care of Ingrid and Robertino when they went home from the hospital were a maid, a nurse, a wet nurse, a secretary for Ingrid, Pietro the chauffeur, a second maid, and a butler and his wife, the cook. They all fought constantly with each other. Roberto fought constantly with all of them. Elena di Montis, the small stubborn Sardinian governess, would stand up to him. The others would flee in tears.

"Raging island . . . raging passions!" proclaimed RKO's posters for RKO's re-made *Stromboli*, which showed Bergman kissing Vitale passionately as they burst from the volcano's erupting mouth. The tawdrily mutilated movie was released February 15 to 300 theaters simultaneously—in an attempt to cash in on its notoriety before people discovered how "bad" it was—and RKO reported a first week's gross of $2 million, probably a hyperbole to spur business. *Variety* claimed that no movie in history had received "even 10% of the space and radio time racked up by *Stromboli*."[24]

In the second week attendance dropped to nothing. The reviews were horrendous. "Incredibly feeble, inarticulate, uninspiring, and painfully banal," judged Bosley Crowther.[25] "There is no depth to Ingrid Bergman's performance, no vitality in Roberto Rossellini's direction," wrote *The Herald Tribune*. "There is neither sense nor sensation to be found in it. *Stromboli* profits only from notoriety: as a film drama it is a waste of talent and a waste of time."[26] "A bleak, draggy little picture," said *Time*, noting "obviously artistic intentions . . . , well-shot scenery . . . , an exciting tuna sequence," but a "clumsy denouement. . . . Virtually nothing suggests the Rossellini who directed *Open City* and *Paisan*. . . . Bergman is surrounded by such mediocrity that her performance seems pathetically wasted. Would-be moralists who are trying to punish her and Director Rossellini for their private transgressions by banning *Stromboli* might serve their own ends better by having the picture shown as widely as possible."[27]

The "clumsy denouement" was RKO's tacked-on ending with voice-over commentary telling us Karin goes back to her husband. Roberto had lost his suit in the U.S. In addition he was powerless to prevent RKO's releasing his rough cut in Europe. "I'm living proof of the brutality that dominates Hollywood," he grumbled to a Communist paper.[28] Only in Italy would he control the movie.

And there, the award on March 19 of the first *Premio Roma* to the still unseen movie was controversially interpreted. According to Bonicelli, the award was intended "not only as a noble word in defense of two persons humiliated by a scandal campaign, but also as a courageous proclamation of the validity of a work of art."[29]

But Roberto, whom some wanted excommunicated, was not invited to receive the award in person. "Although lack of success in America seems due to public resonance of events of no concern to us," explained Flaiano, "the Italian award has appeared to some as a sign of gratitude by the Christian-Democrat jury on the Campidoglio toward a director sensitive to the needs of Catholic cinema. Amid such confused hypotheses and distorted judgments the innocent one, the film, would have been torn in half, had not Rossellini decided to show it [a few days later] to the press and Rome's film people in its original [English] edition [but titled *Land of God* not *Stromboli*]." The ante-premiere resolved the doubts. "*Stromboli* will remain when all the controversy it has aroused has been forgotten."[30]

Yet the lost fight with RKO had involved the entire Italian film industry. "Had *Stromboli* been a staggering success," said Amidei, "it would have been a success for Italian film authors comparable to the success for Italian architects after Rastrelli's success in Russia. [But] when the film didn't do well, the doors of the American cinema were closed a bit to the Italian cinema."[31]

Blame for this fell on Roberto, adding to the acrimony accumulated from his treatment of Magnani and scandal with Bergman. During the winter and spring following *Stromboli*'s shooting, Fellini had been one of few in the cinema crowd to see him frequently.

Stromboli's fiasco was a direct result of Roberto's betrayal of Lopert. Once before, at the time of *Paisà*, he had tried to rid himself of a specialized distributor for a Hollywood major: Burstyn for M-G-M. This time, alas, Rod Geiger wasn't around to stop him. Had Lopert rather than RKO produced *Stromboli*, Rossellini would have retained control of its final cut, and the movie, cultivated on the art circuit rather than sacrificed to the quick buck/quick death of a mass release, would have been recognized as the deeply personal statement it was. Instead, Roberto had bartered his soul.

On March 14 came more blame, arising from the floor of the United States Senate in the person of Edwin C. Johnson. "She was voted the most popular actress in 1948," the senator crooned. "She was by very long odds my own favorite actress of all time.... Millions of American movie fans adored and idolized her. Not only was her interpretation magnificent beyond description, but her home life was ideal, where she lived quietly and happily with her devoted little family. She was a sweet and understanding person with an attractive personality which captivated everyone on and off the screen. God has been very good to Ingrid Bergman.... No one can reflect upon her sudden plunge from the highest pinnacle of respect to the gutter without feeling that she is the victim of some kind of hypnotic influence... : the vile and unspeakable Rossellini.... RKO publicity brazenly termed Rossellini inspired. If this swine is inspired, he is inspired by the devil. Women have moved in and out of this treacherous viper's life in a never-ending stream.... When Rossellini, the love pirate, returned home to Rome smirking over his conquest, it was not Mrs. Lindstrom's scalp which hung from the conquering hero's belt—it was her very soul. The soul of Hollywood's greatest star.... When a money-mad homewrecker like Rossellini gets caught red-handed in a bedroom raid of this kind and gets shot like the dog he is, the unwritten law in America usually turns the slayer loose with a generous pat on the back. That is what we here think of such degenerates."[32]

Johnson's idea to prevent future such goings-on was to require actors to have licenses, which could then be revoked for misconduct. Quipped columnist Irving Hoffman: "Just because a Swedish actress went to bed with an Italian director, Ethel Barrymore would have to stand in line to get a license to act."[33]

"They said," said Roberto, "that I was 'the chief of a gang of drug smugglers from Mao Tse Tung's China whose object was the destruction of the brains of American film people.' "[34]

Meanwhile in Italy, where Pius XII had designated 1950 a "Holy Year," Roberto was being accused of an opportunistic "about-face" on religion, to render himself pleasing after the Bergman scandal.[35]

This irritated Roberto more than the ravings of a U.S. senator. He hotly denied any "about-face." *L'uomo dalla croce, Roma città aperta,* and "Romagna" had all been about priests, not to mention *Il miracolo.* "In *Open City* and *Paisan,*" he retorted in *Sight and Sound,* "all the acts of heroism, of human kindness obviously spring from faith, and the brutalities of war from cynicism and absence of moral code. In the tragic emptiness of the postwar world shown in *Germany Year Zero,* the struggle between faith and mere opportunism is still more accentuated. For the child standing unconsciously between the two extremes, it is a tightrope balancing act. In *Stromboli,* the girl, who . . . has lost her faith, regains it."[36]

Franciscanism fulfilled Christ's ideal. Thus, "to repropose today certain aspects of primitive Franciscanism seems to me the thing that best responds to the needs and deep aspirations of humanity, who, by forgetting the lesson of the *poverello* and enslaving themselves to ambition for wealth, have lost even the joy of living.[37]

"During *Paisà* I discovered the Franciscans. During *Francesco* I tasted their joy to such an extent that I urgently wanted others to taste it too. . . . In a period of my life particularly full of bitterness and disappointments, I found a clear and precise model to sustain me in making this film on Saint Francis."[38]

"His characters," Bazin would write, "behave as though obsessed by the demon of movement; the little brothers of Francis of Assisi have no other way of rendering glory to God than the foot race."[39]

But behind this model foolishness lay deep purpose, Rossellini explained. "Saint Francis was born at a moment when ideal love became absolutely detached from any sort of eroticism. Until that moment love was only erotic. A profound turning point that promoted a very vast view. . . . It was no longer a question of conquest but of identification." Thus, "from a very humble position," Francis changed "the whole conception of the universe."[40]

Bazin saw this new, vast view echoing the epistemology of the thirteenth-century Franciscan Duns Scotus. Aquinas, like a positivist, had said the individual is unknowable, only the universal can be known; whereas Scotus had insisted, like Croce, that the individual is immediately intuitable.[41] We do not replace the individual with our idea of the individual, we do not "conquer" the individual. This is Francis's concept of love.

Was this the same Rossellini Senator Johnson depicted as a conquering, treacherous viper with women's scalps hanging from his belt? The Rossellini who was so proud of his scene of Francis kissing the leper that he phoned Lisandrini the evening he shot it and described it over and over in every detail?

"It's an identification of truth," Rossellini explained, "a sort of humility, an acceptance of everything with your brain, that is the main point. Francis was afraid to kiss a leper: it's terrible, and dangerous, too. And he got over all that. The main purpose in life is to be courageous."[42]

"Rossellini, Fellini, and I all agreed," said Morlion, "that the spectator had to be made to understand that Saint Francis, precisely because he was a man like any other, would have felt the same repugnance, the same terror for the leper as people always had. It was necessary, therefore, that the sound of the bell immediately suggest the idea of the outcast, of a filthy, mortal danger to flee from. Then the saint's kiss would symbolize self-coherence, a choice of love so total and absolute that it could overcome horror of death and even be able to stare deeply into death's eyes. Without this, Franciscan serenity would not have had any sense."[43]

Brunello Rondi noted Francis's acute sense of hearing while lying on the grass, and how the "moonlight, sweet meadow, and nightingale all contrast with that horrible reality that all of a sudden appears." In this sequence we find "the characteristic 'heroic' process that animates the best Italian Cinema; the character, visibly maturing second by second, breath by breath, feels growing within him an understanding, a revelation, a need for choice and decision, and completes an act that permits him to overcome himself and join a new harmony."[44]

We can see this "heroic process" occur in all Rossellini's "heroes" in all his movies.

The twin faces of mystery combine in this scene, writes Alain Bandelier: incarnation and transcendence meet in the leper's kiss. It can't be described. We need to glimpse in shadow these two men joining, led by some force; to see with Francis a face ravaged by leprosy like the landscape by night; to hear through the thick silence the tinkling bell come nearer, as though from another world; to hear Francis's cry embracing the earth, our earth, a cry thrown up from the depths of man and the depths of God, the groan of the Spirit joining itself to our spirit, making our immense question into an infinite Word. We need, with Francis, to kiss the face of this man who no longer has a face and adore there the face of God, that face which one cannot see without dying.[45]

The essence of Rossellini's genius and the constant focus of his inquiry, says Alain Bergala, lies in his camera's exploration of the enigmatic rapport between people and the world: how people relate to landscape, to each other, to the transcendent.[46]

Driving past the estate of a Roman prince one morning, Roberto spotted an old woman, obviously poor and hungry, being manhandled by two guards for taking some mushrooms. "I never saw Rossellini so furious," said Rondi. He got out of the Cadillac and assaulted the guards verbally. "Arrest me too!" he screamed.

They let the woman go. A similar intervention a few weeks later on behalf of a prostitute on Via del Tritone didn't go so smoothly, however.

The police took Roberto at his word and put him under arrest—until they learned his name, when they got scared and let him go.

That spring Roberto purchased a seven-acre beachfront estate in Santa Marinella, fifteen miles up the coast from Ladispoli, for approximately $100,000. Besides the main building with eight rooms there was a caretaker's cottage and a third, dilapidated house. When guests came Roberto would don a face mask, wade out, and catch the seafood for their dinner. Parked in the garages were his Cadillac, a Chevrolet, an old Fiat, a Fiat stationwagon, a new red Ferrari 2000—his proudest possession—and Ingrid's $6,000 Lancia. Tied to the dock was a schooner.

How could Roberto spend so much? Besides Santa Marinella, there was the apartment in Rome, the large staff of servants, all the living expenses of Marcellina and Renzino, not to mention lavish outlays for restaurants, clothes, and trips abroad. Where did the money come from? One theory is that it came from Ingrid. Her settlement with Lindstrom that April gave her $140,000, in addition to her $200,000 from *Stromboli*. But Roberto, at least in theory and perhaps in fact, had, as he put it, a "Sicilian" attitude toward taking money from his wife. And Ingrid, perpetually insecure, was none too free in such matters. Four months after contributing $10,000 out of her property settlement toward Pia's welfare, for example, she had asked for it back.

In any case, Roberto never actually paid for either the Ferrari or for Santa Marinella. He borrowed instead. His old friend Sansoni, the wealthy, bizarre Bolognese who'd married a Wülf was his principal creditor. From time to time Roberto would pay Sansoni interest, at a high rate. But he never paid the capital. When he was constrained to part with Santa Marinella in 1964, he gave it to Bornigia, his car dealer, who then paid off Sansoni.[47]

Roberto and Ingrid were married May 24 by proxy in Juarez, Mexico, while simultaneously exchanging vows privately in Rome's Chiesa della Navicella. Amidei, Fellini, and Liana Ferri were witnesses. Roberto gave Ingrid a gold chain bracelet with a little gold police whistle. Magnani was at The Raphael, however, which put a glitch into their plans to honeymoon in Paris. Paris without The Raphael was inconceivable. So, having deposited Robertino with Elettra in Fiuggi (it took two cars, Roberto driving one, Renzo the other, to transport all the baby luggage), the couple went off to Capri. There Roberto dove too deep, hurt his ears, and was practically deaf for a few days. After stopping in Fiuggi, they drove through Florence and Pisa to Portofino and visited Alexander Korda and his yacht.

The romance had already started mellowing, however. Ingrid complained to Joe Steele that she hardly ever saw Roberto, aside from the honeymoon. If he weren't off filming *Francesco*, he was running around Rome making deals, exploring opportunities, or just dropping in on friends, as he had always done. At home, of course, he rarely emerged from bed. Even the simplest well-laid plan was more than likely to turn into disaster. A week before their wedding, for example, Ingrid had invited Artur Rubinstein and his wife to dinner but Roberto, caught up in editing *Francesco*, failed to come home. She phoned him during the third cocktail, again during the spaghetti. During the coffee, he arrived—but went straight to his room. And didn't come out. "I'll just go and see . . . ," she said. He was in bed: "I have a headache. Don't disturb me." "I'm going to die," she said, "I can't go back and tell them you've gone to bed." But she did. "Oh, that's too bad," they said. Whereupon Roberto walked in, cried "Maestro!," threw his arms around Rubinstein, and the two talked non-stop till four in the morning.[48]

This was the Roberto his friends and family knew and put up with. It was not a Roberto Ingrid could put up with. The adventures never stopped. The next day a photographer snapped Rossellini and Rubinstein eating together. Roberto grabbed him, calling for the police. A fist fight broke out and Rubinstein joined in. Then Roberto accompanied the photographer to the police station and paid his fine.

Selznick, visiting Rome that June, thought he noted in Ingrid "a very definite nostalgia for her contractual past with us. . . . [She's] completely finished with Rossellini's type of pictures." He had heard, he said, that she had been talking to Goldwyn again.[49]

"I saw her the first time in their house," said Fellini. "She was the way she always was in films, a queen, serene and pacific and saintly. . . . She had this necessity of always trying to understand. Sometimes she couldn't understand why we were laughing." Everyone would laugh except Ingrid; then the joke would be explained, and she would laugh alone. "I remember Ingrid's innocence. She was very naive. For those of us who knew Roberto well, it was amazing to see them together, always surprising."[50]

To Lisandrini, Ingrid confided that Roberto was the first man who had made her feel like a woman. "He was a good man for her," the Franciscan recalled, but "she was not a good woman for him."[51] She was "a woman without passion," as far as Roberto was concerned.[52] He went on visiting Tilde, his favorite whore, explaining to friends that Ingrid was prudish about oral sex, and joked, "If some day you want to get married, don't get married to an actress, because they're actresses also in bed." He had certainly known enough of them. Yet he loved Ingrid. Dancing at a nightclub with Ingrid, he bumped into Magnani. "So how's this one?" Anna queried. "Huh? My wife?" he responded, taken aback. "Go fuck yourself!" she retorted, and danced off.[53]

Roswitha, meanwhile, abandoned on Capri, had finally had to return to the mainland and seek bit parts to support herself. Her possessions, left at Parco Pepoli in Roberto's care, had all disappeared; she accused Manni of taking them. Roberto himself she rebuffed, along with his family.

Ingrid and Robertino spent most of August in Fiuggi. Elettra had grown deafer with the years but Ingrid found warm friendship in Fiorella Mariani, Marcella's daughter. They called each other sister. Sixteen physically but older mentally, Fiorella had suffered through her own parents' separation and empathized with Pia. Although Ingrid was eager to see Pia, she was refusing to do so unless Lindstrom brought her to Italy. "She never understood why Pia was so angry," Fiorella recalled. "I said, 'You went away. There is no excuse for a child.' "

Fiorella like everyone else found Ingrid and her uncle an odd match. "[Roberto's] intellectual life ... was a hole between them. She was not a cultivated woman. If he was reading about something that had nothing to do with Ingrid, they could not talk. She was not the kind of woman who could help him intellectually. She realized that but she didn't care."[54]

On August 26, 1950 both *Francesco giullare di Dio* and *Stromboli terra di Dio* were presented at Venice. "Roberto was so nervous, so sick to his stomach, we thought he would never make it," wrote Ingrid. On those hot summer afternoons, the theater was normally half empty, but for *Francesco* it was "packed to the ceiling. . . . I cannot describe with what warmth the picture was received. The applause *during* the running was like that in a theater when you expect the actor to take a bow."[55]

The theater was packed again that night. *Stromboli* had still not been seen in Italy and black-market tickets were fetching as much as 5,000 lire. *Stromboli* too was greeted enthusiastically, but with less applause than for *Francesco*.

Stromboli had been withdrawn from competition at the last moment, in order to focus attention on *Francesco*, to which a little documentary introduction on Giotto's Franciscan frescoes had been added for the occasion.[56] But neither picture reaped good reviews; nor, despite an extremely weak field, did *Francesco* place among the twelve prize winners.[57] "I recall the critics' bewilderment at Venice," wrote Gino Visentini, who thought *Francesco* one of the "purest and most poetic moments" in all cinema. "Rossellini had simply forgotten about the camera. He had produced images that were Franciscan rather than cinematic, that had none of the usual literary, mystical polish. . . . People said that isn't Saint Francis, those are just poor beggars."[58]

Francesco and the Critics

Francesco flummoxed just about everybody.

The left followed Aristarco. *Francesco* was overly "formalist." It presented a "false reality," one "not inserted into a critical vision . . . from which Francis's immense importance could be grasped."[59]

Moravia agreed. *Francesco* showed the "concrete humanity" of Francis that had been emaciated by D'Annunzianism, but failed to confront Franciscanism in its essentials.[60]

The picture should have emphasized Francis's opposition to the Church of his day, said Casiraghi in *L'Unità*, but Rossellini hadn't given *any* historical context. "He suffers from the same crises as some segments of

Italian society who, instead of confronting with clarity and Franciscan humility the grave and real problems of the moment, hide away in contemplation and aestheticism."[61]

Francesco not only lacked "realities," continued Tommaso Chiaretti in *L'Unità*, Morlion and Lisandrini had emasculated Francis. Simplicity is always the same, agreed Di Giammatteo: there are no specific problems, no individuated characters. *Francesco* is just a collection of holy cards deprived of emotion, moaned Sadoul.[62]

"Its most obvious fault is precisely its lack of realism," Leprohon explained. "These twentieth-century monks, fat and contented, comfortably clothed in grey homespun, the disciples of an order which is now part of the religious establishment, in no wise suggest the original Franciscans, vagabonds in every way—half-starved, ragged, and so sickly-looking that they frequently scared women and children. Nor is there anything in the chosen setting to suggest the Umbria of the Franciscans, with its forests, its ravines and fast-flowing streams, its remote caves."[63]

Non-communist reactions were even less sympathetic. Despite a series of public sermons on the movie's behalf by Lisandrini, *Francesco*'s audiences, as Chiaretti observed, became lost, and mistook for sarcasm what had been intended as poetry. The movie is ugly and presumptive, growled the Augustinian Father Piaz: how dare this Rossellini come preaching messages? The movie is irreverent and devoid of faith or inspiration, moaned Bezzola. *Francesco* was made opportunistically for the Holy Year, grumbled Flaiano, with friars more like boy scouts than penitents, and a "poverello" saint who is a pathetic lie in a county where poverty is considered the worst of faults. Even Edoardo Bruno at *Filmcritica* agreed Rossellini had become so "involuted" that he no longer knew "how to look at reality" and was oblivious to the contemporary consequences of his preaching world peace and communism.[64]

Francesco's first supporters also agreed with its detractors. "From the end of the war till today," wrote Gian Luigi Rondi, "Rossellini . . . has been searching for God. . . . Now after *Stromboli*, the drama of the soul against its creator, of the *earth's* unwillingness to be accepted, comes *Francesco giullare di Dio*, where the drama not only resolves in the *earth's* (the *terra di Dio's*) willingness, but . . . is the soul's effort against itself to give itself as fully as possible to God. . . . After the biblical tragedy (. . . on the mountain) comes the Franciscan modern drama (. . . on the plain) . . . , an almost magical 'evocative cinema': souls . . . bloom on the Umbrian meadows, meet and part, and each time collide as in a game of musical harmonies; they assume bodies just enough to be 'seen,' but obey none of the laws real human life normally obeys." Thanks to Rossellini's absolute simplicity, "everything seems born here, all of a sudden, by mysterious miracle, everything seems ready to vanish at the first breath of wind, at the first profane incredulity. . . . Rossellini's latest cinema is still *cinema of truth*, but henceforth it deals with an 'interior truth' even deeper and more mysterious than that which psychoanalysis claims to discover."[65]

A similar theme was followed in *Epoca* by the poet Aldo Palazzeschi: "The leading role is entrusted not to facts but to the characters' movements wonderfully framed in the landscape, to their courses and pauses on the meadows and the country roads. The bodies have the lightness and happiness of birds. . . . I would say the director followed not a script but a luminosity in his mind. We are at Franciscanism's fascinating moment: its youth. . . . At the end you realise you have walked along the mysterious cutting edge of poetry as along a razor. The test was not easy: it was a question of rendering a fragrance."[66] *Francesco*, concluded Bolzoni, was the moment, after the world-without-God trilogy (*Roma, Paisà, Deutschland*), "when the divine is married to the human."[67]

Rondi's line denies carnality and politics, whereas Roberto had intended a polemic. He bragged for the rest of his life that "*The Jester*" was "a film that divided the convents" and that, when he showed it in Paris to the papal nuncio Angelo Roncalli, the future John XXIII put his hand on Roberto's arm and said, "Poverino, poverino, you don't know what you've done."[68]

Thus closer to Rossellini's intentions was Chiarini, who argued that the movie is not a "homily" but a "terribly polemical . . . act of faith in people . . . and thus in life, because it presupposes and wants here on earth the triumph of the poor over the rich, the weak over the powerful, good over evil.

"Joy is already in Francis and his . . . companions because . . . they are certain of the coming of a pacified world that will have no more need for madmen [like themselves]. Sublime illusion? Poetry? Reality, replies Rossellini with his film, a reality which existed for a group of people whose actions were truly their thought, their sole mode of being ['Oh, rose!']. . . . Rossellini has nothing mystical about his mind" and his point escapes those who prefer to see opportunism.[69]

Later critics, too, either loathed or adored *Francesco*. On one side, Oms called it "incontestably one of the most faithful images" of Franciscanism, and—thus—a "monument to stupidity": it proves the derivation of "cretin" from "Christian." "If [Francis and Clare] had shut themselves up in the hut or made love in front of the brethren, then Francis would have made an elegy to the flesh, would have renounced preaching, to live. But . . . the film is far from such grandeur. It stays stupid. Brother Pig here, Sister Lettuce there, I cut off your paw, I take off my clothes, I roll in the mud, I get people to spit in my face and kick me in the ass, etc. It's not to be believed."[70]

On the other side, Pasolini ranked *Francesco* "among the most beautiful in Italian cinema," Andrew Sarris put it eighth on his all-time best list, Truffaut called it "the most beautiful film in the world," and Moravia, reversing himself twenty years after, declared it "absolutely extraordinary, if for no other reason than for the expressive problems solved one after the other almost miraculously." Even Bosley Crowther applauded: "These little incidents, filmed in the outdoors in the most simple and almost amateurish way, have an innocence and naiveté about them that establish, at least, a gentle mood of wonder at such faith and humility."[71]

Never has a film with such lousy grosses—less than $13,000 in Italy—spawned such controversy.

Pio Baldelli and Brunello Rondi carried on a debate for twenty years, and spawned heirs to continue it. Baldelli echoed that Rossellini preferred mystic cop-outs to actual problems. Francis was one of his puerile "crazies" who, "defenseless but vibrating with secret vital strength, the sole beings alive in a land of dead people and bleached tombs," descend from *Paisà* through *Il miracolo, Stromboli, Europe '51* (and Fellini's *La strada* and *Le notti di Cabiria*) to argue that true spirituality expresses itself at the level of instinct rather than rationality (Croce again). But Rossellini strips Francis's life of potency by depicting it as effortless. Moreover, he falsifies his sources, by eliminating the visions and miracles in the *Fioretti*—the poetic world in which these characters and stories make sense.[72]

Brunello Rondi replied that camera-trick miracles would have ruined the fable-like atmosphere.[73] Rossellini chose a lyric moment in Franciscan history; why does Baldelli insist such happiness is irrelevant to our times unless contextualized in struggle and tragedy—the eternal refrain of the provincial critic. To show a revolution happening, there's no need to show marching armies or pontiffs being dragged off by their hair; sometimes it only requires the light in the heart of one man. *Francesco* is not a *Life of Gorki*; it is not concerned with the soul of facts but with states of soul: the impalpable but concrete circulation of a new humanist light.[74]

This debate focused on the sparseness. Everyone agreed Rossellini had reduced ambience to the essential. Nicolaio's castle has become a camp, a town is scarcely glimpsed, decor does not exist. Rossellini himself described the costumes as "simple, timeless, and, purposely, costumes that aren't costumes."[75] Such "poverty of means partakes of eternity," argued the scenic designer, "and annuls the mise en scène."[76]

Ferarra lambasted the "impoverishment," echoing Baldelli. The friars become like trees, abstractions outside of history, in a metaphysical present. For the polemical positions Francis took in his own age, Rossellini substitutes glib D'Annunzian mysticism (as in *Il miracolo*). We are not in thirteenth-century Umbria, but a timeless world with landscapes made virginally lyric to the point of boredom.[77]

Guarner, echoing Rondi, parried that "whittling" convention down to ideas made *Francesco* "the first *true* historical film." Time is abolished so that a distant past can be examined in the present. *Roma città aperta* had turned news into history; now history (or legend) becomes news. The sparseness make "the Franciscan message entirely relevant to the present and the little brothers of Saint Francis remain alive forever. . . . This approach remains an essential of Rossellini's work and foreshadows his films for television."[78]

Serceau, in 1986, agreed. Faithfulness to details of history or legend would have blunted Rossellini's point—Franciscanism's originality as ethical behavior. Contrary to Baldelli, this point is not mystic. Not only are there no miracles, but devotional moments (like Clare's visit) are juxtaposed with comic ones, contemplation with action, beatitudes with madcap charity, aesthetics with ethics. The juxtapositions get to the heart of Franciscanism. The institutionalized Church would relegate a Ginepro—who gives away his cloak and makes soup for fifteen days—to servility within its organization, but Francis sends him forth to preach because of his fervor. The Franciscans reject institutions, sensing a contradiction between material concerns and apostolic mission; the hut they live in, for example, is no sooner sanctified by Clare's visit than it is abandoned for itinerant preaching. Contrary to Baldelli, Rossellini's slant is neither mystic nor puerile.[79]

It was to the cultured, calculating Gandhi that Roberto compared Francis. "The expression [of Francis's way] was irrational, but he in fact was deeply rational. All our saints are foolish, Italians are very foolish, but in fact they are deeply reasonable."[80]

Henri Agel, although one of *Francesco*'s greatest enthusiasts, misses this point. To attain God, he writes, Francis's companions want to free themselves from all intellectual mechanisms, common sense, and wisdom. Like real Children of God, their conduct absurdly and scandalously rejects the mental processes of civilized adults. And God makes his home with them. The world's madness is God's wisdom, the world's wisdom is God's madness, says Saint Paul.[81]

No. Rossellini's point is not liberation and revolution for their own sake, but the Crocean one of a more disciplined ethical sense, an incarnate spirituality, as in *Voyage in Italy* or *India*. Francis changes the ethical concept of the universe because he has the courage to be genuinely himself. Ultimately it is Francis's originality that *Francesco*'s detractors object to; they would not have complained about Zeffirelli's *Brother Sun, Sister Moon*, Curtiz's *Francis of Assisi*, (1961), Alessandrini's *Don Bosco* (1935), King's *The Song of Bernadette* (1943), Brahm's *The Miracle of Our Lady of Fatima* (1952), or Cloche's *Monsieur Vincent* (1947)—all of which supply answers rather than questions.

Writes Jean-Claude Biette: "No actor could communicate the spiritual glow of the anonymous [monk that Rossellini] chose to incarnate Saint Francis. . . . The gestures, expressions, words, and deeds of a saint confound any prior conceptions about sanctity: they cannot be other than indecipherable, unreceivable, and uncodifiable. In contrast, *Thérèse* [Alain Cavalier (1986)] proffers perfectly reassuring images of sanctity. The Church could not dream of a more correct incarnation of convention, a more complete sacrifice of the individual to fixed idea. . . . This Thérèse de Lisieux [is] treated like a puppet in the film. . . . Rossellini [in contrast] dispensed no agreed-on image of sanctity. He looked at the facts, going so far as to love their opacity. The most mysterious actions, he seemed to say in his films, must be enlarged by time and space and considered in context of that vaster movement that is life."[82]

Ironically, Brunello Rondi saw *Francesco*'s sparseness as initiating an anti-novel narrative in favor of interior, irrational fragments. Rondi could have traced this new style from the rough approximations of *Paisà* to the rich, Dreyer-like exactness of *Francesco*. He did see it leading to *Voyage in Italy* and *La strada*, to all of Antonioni, Pasolini's *Accatone*, Ray's *Pather Pancali*, and Godard's *Breathless*. He calls it (after Soldati) a "new atonal cinema": its narrative, like atonal music, is freer, more abstract, more given over to pure gestures; it lacks an irresistible movement toward initially posed goals. He concludes that *Francesco*, although its imitators all deal with anguish and alienation, is the first movie to explore the irrationality of the new cinema.[83] Agel also hails *Francesco*'s sparseness as a "new aesthetic of insignificance."[84]

Yet Francis, with Zen-like calm, has only to raise an arm to move the cosmos.

Stromboli and the Critics

By March 1951, when *Stromboli terra di Dio* opened in Italy, six months had passed since Venice, and two years since Ingrid's arrival. She was praised with cordiality, Rossellini with defiance—no Italian wanted to credit America's racist smears—but the movie itself was incomprehensible and greeted with hatred. Positions against the "new" Rossellini hardened.

Aristarco had launched the attack at Venice. Covering *Stromboli* and *Francesco* together, he made his celebrated denunciation of Rossellini's "involution." He meant that Rossellini, instead of digging into public and social problems, was "turning inward" to psychological portraits of individuals—and *fictional* individuals at that. In the left's view, Rossellini had abandoned "neo-realism" for a movie "made to measure" for a Hollywood actress.[85] He had sold out.

Most everyone agreed. Rossellini was "no longer looking at reality" and was unfaithful to the Liberation's moral position (Bruno). A realistic film is "choral" by definition, but in *Stromboli* everything seems seen by foreign eyes and the islanders, scarcely sketched at all, are closed-up and hostile (Mida). None of the characters (or actors) is interesting except Karin (Bergman)—who's best all alone on the volcano against "the immensity of the starry sky" (Moravia). Rossellini has shifted "the theme of his inspiration" away from the real islanders onto the "unjustifiable and gratuitous" Karin (Chiarini).[86]

Critics damned Karin, while praising Bergman. (How can this be?) Karin is "schematic." Her transformation is inadequately explained. The ending is arbitrary (Aristarco). A film *can't* end with a miracle and an unexplained character (Bruno). What's the point of a drama that has no intention of resolving? (Casiraghi).[87]

L'Unità asked how Karin's grace would help change society, and replied it wouldn't. *Stromboli* is static, involuted, decadent and D'Annunzian—aestheticized mysticism combined with erotic autobiography, like *Deutschland* and *L'amore*.[88] Rossellini tells us we can confront complex problems by enriching our personalities, but Karin undergoes no enrichment and her "resignation" makes no sense (Di Giammatteo). Her character is unclear because Rossellini's ideology is unclear; *Stromboli* starts out a social drama, ends up a spiritual one (Chiaretti). Her character is unclear because Rossellini trusted too much to improvisation (Lanocita) and is inept at psychological cinema (not being introspective like Wyler, Stevens, and Lean). Bergman has turned him away from what he does best to what he does worst (Mida). He has kowtowed to American interests (*L'Écran Français*).[89]

"On the ruins of Nazism," moaned Oms, "Rossellini says we must either construct a new world or sow seeds of eternal values, and he chooses the latter. . . . Karin decides to be a good mother: some values surpass the world."[90]

A "Catholic" defense began in France—not in *Cahiers du Cinéma* where Astruc remarked that "probably only the Italians can still think volcanoes are the voice of God"[91] but in the maverick *Gazette du Cinéma*. Eric Rohmer had sat through half the film feeling the same dissatisfaction as the Italians. By the end, he had reached a different conclusion.

"*Stromboli* is the story of a sinner touched by grace," he wrote, "but . . . not the odyssey of a conversion, with all that that entails in hesitations, regrets, hopes, and slow and continuous victories over oneself. God's majesty shines here with a brilliance so hard and so terrible that no human conscience could bear even its palest reflection. This great Catholic film unrolls its pomp solemnly, all exteriorly, and accords to interior life only what can be guessed at. . . . Rossellini's art is one of the most unfit for expression of interior life. [Karin's whines] signify nothing more than the jerks of the little rabbit strangled by the ferret or the tuna pierced by the fishermen's pikes. They *are* herself and, stripping her of all mystery, reveal only her empty interior. . . . Were cinema only the art of plumbing the interior of souls, I'd be ready to give all of *Stromboli* for that single shot [in Hitchcock's *Under Capricorn*] where Ingrid Bergman's [similarly searching character], her face pressed against her bed, her lip heavy, her eyes half-closed, reflects in an instant such a wealth of diverse feelings (fear and self-control, candor and calculation, rage and resignation). But Rossellini's design is quite different. . . . What it loses in moral depth, the universe of this film rediscovers in religious grandeur. A sort of tragic horror nails our regard and imposes on the world a view which is neither completely that of a man, by what it excludes of compassion, nor completely that of God, by what it still inspires of terror. . . . I can think of only a few works of our time that have so magnificently, so directly exalted the Christian idea of grace; few works have, without rhetoric, by the sole evidence of what they give us to see, proclaimed more loudly the misery of man without God."[92]

Years later Rohmer reflected on his review. "My aesthetic and ideological itinerary . . . started with existentialism, with Jean-Paul Sartre. His essays . . . revealing Faulkner, Dos Passos, and Husserl too, gave me a lot. . . . It was Rossellini who turned me away from existentialism. It happened in the middle of *Stromboli*. During the first minutes of the projection I felt the limits of the Sartrian sort of realism I thought was going to be the film's. I detested the way it urged me to look at the world, until I understood that it was urging me *also* to go beyond that. Then came my conversion. That's what's so terrific in *Stromboli*, it was my road to Damascus: in the middle of the film, I was converted, I changed perspective. . . . What I tried to do in my review . . . was to show how values that were completely rejected at that time—values of grandeur, of making something great out of something great, whereas the current ideology was to make something out of nothing—cinema permitted them to exist."[93]

In reviews of subsequent Rossellini pictures, Rohmer would radically correct his remaining misperception—about Rossellini's "expression of interior life." For now, Gian Luigi Rondi was almost alone in perceiving what is best in Rossellini—the richness of his characters' inner lives.

In Karin's heart, Rondi explained (echoing Rossellini's own published explanation[94]), is "all the desperation of Europe"—its egoism and arid lack of faith—and when Karin calls out to God to help her against herself, Rossellini offers a problem as ancient as man but ignored by cinema until today: the problem of grace. Instead of the truth *of* man, Rossellini's theme in now the truth *in* man: conscience, the interior. Thus Rondi concedes Rossellini's involution but defends his dramatization. Karin's psychology is constructed with exemplary rigor and meticulous order, Rondi notes, with each nuance in its precise place, yet so subtly that her feelings are often apparent only in her eyes: it's her thirst for suicide that leads her to call for God. Long shots of her recur like leitmotifs of her solitude amid surrounding incomprehension. "We watch her wandering amid the village's empty houses, anxiously seeking a voice, a face, a soul that understands." (Aristarco too admired this sequence.) Pans of the volcano and island open sinister caesuras, their mute presence substituting for the menacing voice of the chorus (*pace* Mida!). But in Karin's soul hides God . . . who reveals himself from the beginning in Karin's conflicting feelings of revolt and submission: her struggle with grace (*pace* Rohmer).[95] Thus even the long shots bring us to the richness of Karin's inner life.

As even things do. Claude Mauriac thought he heard "the plaint of tortured nature—Ingrid is quiet, but the stones are crying"—and he attributed this effect to the glaring sunlight on the white cubicle houses and the torpid stillness. "Later, the young woman is at home, alone. Bare walls, a few poor furnishings. And look how the simplest household utensils take on as much importance and beauty as Ingrid's face. So it happens that a sort of animation takes possession, from the inside, of this still life (the black of that pottery and its form belong to Braque, but the arabesque of the bed makes one think of Matisse); of this still life whose immobility, like that of Matisse and

Braque, is only apparent. The movement that we have not seen is here, and, if we cannot call it excessive, it is only for the reason that 'too much,' like 'not enough,' is foreign to accomplished works of art. In this economy of means seems to reside, ultimately, one of the secrets of cinema."[96]

Concludes Guarner, "What is clear is that Rossellini is no longer primarily interested in telling a story but in investigating feelings and analyzing personalities."[97]

Rondi concluded that "anyone with honesty and heart, sensibility, and intelligence must recognize this film's high merit in marking the hour of cinematic art's surest victory and its return to God." Was he thinking of Senator Johnson and his cohorts in America?

Regardless, he scarcely mollified *Stromboli*'s critics. Casiraghi had headlined his review: "THE INCREASINGLY CLERICAL VENICE FESTIVAL: A Sermon from Rossellini in a Sacristy Atmosphere."[98] An Agel could rhapsodize about Karin "enveloped in a cosmic symphony . . . : she opens up and dilates infinitely, participating viscerally in the grand planetary, animal-and-vegetable rhythms, feeling the child tremble in her body. She sought evasion, she has found true liberty: an exultant insertion into totality."[99] But for Bonicelli it is precisely "that damn exaltation"—Rossellini's "caveman's dream"—that ruins an otherwise "acutely intuited" story of modern solitude.[100]

In fact, Agel, like Guarner, slides into gnosticism (Karin's "insertion into totality") and nullifies the drama of grace. Karin is indeed consumed in carnality. Instinctively, like Nannina in *Il miracolo* (who also chews on grass and gives herself up to nature) or like some never-repressed, over-sexed flower child who's learned how to get her way, she is at a loss to relate to anyone or anything other than sexually: Antonio, the volcano, the lighthouse keeper, even the priest, even the child, even God. The island women call her "immodest," which is hardly untrue, and a compliment in Rossellinian terms, for whom the demonic (in the Greek sense) lurks in earth, air, fire, and water. *Stromboli* is the Rossellini movie most concerned with the universe, says Guarner, with man's dependence on nature (like *Man of Aran*), a study of a relationship between a woman and the world. Karin, isolated from everyone, realizes her true enemy is the island. Henceforth the only possible dialogue is between her and Stromboli. When she's sobbing in her home, other cries answer like magical echoes; when she lights the kitchen fire, the volcano starts to erupt as if it had always been waiting for her signal. The smallest human action seems to have strange and enormous consequences. No actress's tears and sobs are ever likely to be so carnal as Karin's.[101]

Guarner suggests that Rossellini may be more pantheistic than Catholic. But his point is moot, given the "scandal of the incarnation" that invests Catholicism on one hand, and Karin's autonomous situation on the other. This is the human side of the problem of grace: much as Karin might like to be part of the world, she cannot. Ungari likens her to an extraterrestrial trapped here and trying to return to her planet of origin. "On an island full of sun, where everyone is hot, Karin alone is cold. At the end she remains suspended between her planet, our planet, and the stars, to which she will never arrive."[102]

Such estrangement is typical of Rossellini's characters. Ayfre has analyzed how, in certain privileged sequences, they construct a void between themselves and what's around them, how they are incapable of just simply "installing" themselves in the world in the "bourgeois" manner or (as Karin tries to do) imposing on their environment the colors of their state of soul. Rossellini depicts Karin's interplay with things both objectively and subjectively: we share her impressions and attitudes, see what she sees, feel what she feels. Her estrangement brings us closer to her interior life, but we are everywhere discouraged from identifying with her. Instead there is a constant "shifting" (between landscape and Karin, things and Karin, her alienation and sense of self) that disorients and disturbs us, that makes us feel the fundamental uncertainty of the creature in the world but not altogether *of* the world. No director is so concerned with the multiplicity and "otherness" of creation. The "alienation" in certain sequences—Karin in the labyrinth, Edmund in the ruins, Nannina climbing the mountain, Irene (*Europe '51*) at the factory, or Katherine (*Voyage*) on her tours—is due to the solidity of the world which is not ourselves. Thus Rossellini, simply and subtly, achieves a sense of estrangement (which is simultaneously a sense of interiority) similar to what Resnais obtains through literary counterpoint and Bresson through a certain technique of acting.[103]

"Karin on the volcano makes love with God," asserts Aprà.[104] True, but only after her other seductions have failed. Rossellini's alienation sequences all end with a cry, which ought not to surprise us, for everything in them prepares such an explosion.[105] "With me God has never been merciful," says Karin in a line that many a character in *Desiderio, Roma, Paisà, Deutschland, Una voce,* and *Il miracolo* could echo. As in Ford, God is merciful mostly to fools. All Karin's life has passed in mindless fleeing (all over Europe and nearly to Argentina), mindless sex (even with Nazis), mindless manipulations (Antonio), mindless impatience (the tuna), mindless amorality and impropriety, and this total "innocence" has led her from one prison to another. Yet on Stromboli she has come up against another mindlessness: the islanders, as brute a reality as their volcano. They seduce her ("You'll see. I live on a very beautiful island," Antonio tells her), resent her sensitivity, reprove her individuality (e.g., her decorations), enfeoff her to the Church, and board her up in her house. It is this mindlessness that is Karin's problem, not Stromboli, not the dilemma of whether to stay or flee. Is the world of Stromboli, where rabbits, tuna, and Karin are savaged, worse than the world beyond, with its wars, despotic governments, and concentration camps? All the worlds of Rossellini are predatory, from *Fantasia sottomarina* on. One can flee to the mainland, or up a volcano, or to Argentina, but there is no escape.

It is this realization that motivates Karin's transformation. For the first time, she is truly alone, with no one to manipulate—and a child to love. The Strombolians are "horrible," but "I am even worse." She asks God not for escape, but for understanding, strength, and courage.

"That's just about everything, isn't it?" said Bianchi.[106]

But it is not "resignation." It is the opposite. *Stromboli*'s detractors, misunderstanding Karin's emotions and the movie's ending, demanded motivations for a transformation that does not occur. It was the damn miracle that bugged them.

Gramsci had hailed "the moral and intellectual reform, which in Italy stemmed from Benedetto Croce, whose first premise was that modern man can and should live without the help of religion,[107] [and which] appears to me even today to be the major contribution made to international culture by modern Italian intellectuals, and it seems to me a civil conquest that must not be lost."[108]

Wasn't Rossellini losing it? Wasn't he fleeing to mystic solutions?[109]

Even Catholic Brunello Rondi accused Rossellini of having the limitations of a purely lyric poet: of wanting a happy society but not caring how to achieve it.[110] Was this not another private revelation, one that like the chaplain's in *Paisà* eludes public consensus while purporting to represent "all the desperation of Europe"?

Indeed, despite Rossellini's later equivocations, the miracle is there, prepared by religious motifs throughout the film but beyond choice, thought, or even faith. As Bergala points out, we may miss it. Grace intervenes between shots. "I don't describe the point, but the waiting," Rossellini said.[111]

But *Stromboli*'s critics grossly simplify the problem of grace, and its richness as a human theme. Rossellini's miracles, unlike Hitchcock's or Dreyer's, never rupture normality: things continue under a new light, with changed meaning.[112] Far from being a lyric poet unconcerned with how to make dreams come true, Rossellini was saying that society's problems are rooted not in materiality (Karin on the volcano discards the bags she has clung to for security) but in our evasions. Far from being a mystic cop-out, *Stromboli* simply ends at the first moment in Karin's life that she stops running away.

Fabio Carlini calls *Stromboli* a "non-authoritarian film"—one that leaves us free to continue or not the course Karin or Nannina's son will take, the streets Edmund cannot find.[113]

In contrast, consider Hitchcock's most existential melodramas, *Rebecca* and *Suspicion* (1940–41). Like *Stromboli*, their plot twists are arbitrary, even inane, and their real interest is concentrated on the fleeting emotions of their fleshy heroine, Joan Fontaine in both cases. Like Karin, she is a young woman surrounded by an alien, hostile milieu. Like Karin, she is bewildered by constant conflicts between emotion and reason. Like Karin, she is a flower child who lives in the moment, hears emotions rather than words, and has difficulty relating to men other than sexually. And Hitchcock, even more than Rossellini, labors to create a sense of place and mood and wants to watch his heroine suffer.

But the Fontaine character never comes to grips with her insecurity, never recognizes responsibility for her life. Solutions are thrust on the flower girl as arbitrarily as her problems were. She never grows as a human being. Karin does. Rossellini, unlike Hitchcock, takes a moral position.

Stromboli's public, however, felt gypped. "The spectator has been told with great publicity that this is the love story of the half century, the most explosive film of the year, and so on," explained Doniol-Valcroze. "But in place of all that, he sees a long, austere film that drives him out into the street. His disappointment is natural. Nonetheless it's surprising that the critics remain insensible to such great art, science, and beauty." "Maybe *Stromboli* is boring to some people," sighed Claude Mauriac, "but what's more boring than an art exhibit or a concert for someone who hasn't eyes to see or ears to hear?" "[It] didn't work for my audience, who suddenly saw me as an ordinary woman," said Ingrid Bergman.[114]

All of which Ennio Flaiano had predicted just after the Rome ante-premiere in *Stromboli*'s first review: "*Stromboli* will remain when all the controversy it has raised has been forgotten. We'd like to say it's a masterpiece: certainly it's the work that makes us see Rossellini no longer as 'instinctive' or as a documentarist but as an author who knows how to carry his story to nobler and more barren conclusions. *Stromboli*'s strength . . . is in its extraordinary narrative economy, its descriptions of places and characters that don't come out smelling contaminated by literature and aestheticism. In other words, places and characters don't seem the result of a script written in a city but of an idea mulled over at length on location, and put into images and episodes that innately express their drama. There's no odor of their author's self-satisfaction or skill, or even of his desire to please his public." In contrast, Flaherty's *Man of Aran* resembles an aesthetic exercise by a director who gets to the poor through good literature. And in fact Flaherty got to Aran through Synge, who himself had gotten there through other literary sources. But Rossellini landed on Stromboli with no other baggage than his camera. He doesn't "admire" the islanders' exertions, any more than an entomologist admires ants' exertions; he studies them. His film is raw; his characters neither invite our sympathy nor manage to appear other than they are: unjust, cruel, egoistic, and jealous. "*Stromboli*, we want to say, is (like *Monsieur Verdoux*) one of the few films that makes us understand how, in contrast to it, lies are the habitual inspiration of cinema—of that cinema that has created its own ethical language and presents life, people, and things (despite their being all around us and well-known to us) in a light without hope, because false." If someday we realize how deviant and oppressed our imaginations have become, perhaps then we'll realize that we owe our condition to the movies that now we find so entertaining. But Rossellini shows life on *Stromboli* as it is: reduced to struggle, weariness, patient suffering. Honor, dignity, modesty, and faith are not virtues but elements indispensable for life, like hygienic laws. Frivolous and lost, Karin is designed for confrontation. When her husband, seeing she likes the ferret and knowing that each creature plays an assigned role in this world, obligingly gives it a live rabbit to kill and eat, he is surprised and uncomprehending when she bursts out screaming. But the only thing left for Karin is to hope to understand why life is so hostile and boring, and this is what she prays to God for on the volcano: to understand. "The film is an anti-romance that restores life to its due proportions. And so we bet it won't have much success with a public that hates truth and is used to vomiting up decently anything that's 'too strong.'" Nonetheless: all of *Stromboli* is up to the level of "The Po Delta" in *Paisà*—"although its secret aim this time is higher and farther."[115]

"Never did a director treat his actress with less love or consideration," agreed Rohmer. "One may search in vain in this film for any echo of [that] adventure that still titillates the press."[116]

Yet doesn't Rossellini's *style* relate to his romance with Ingrid? "Neo-realism consists in following someone, with love, in all their discoveries, all their impressions," he said.[117] Doesn't his camera follow Karin this way? Through every discovery and impression, yes; but its gaze, its "love," is rarely tender; more often it is unsparing, cruel, even rapacious.

There's no off-space in Rossellini's storyworld, writes Charles Tesson, except the set's "fourth wall" (the camera), toward which Ingrid Bergman exposes herself and risks herself, and from which Rossellini with his camera watches her as though watching "a mouse in a cage," from slightly above, like the volcano. For example, the scene with the priest, which begins unforgettably. Bergman confronts the camera's stare, alone in the frame. At first she is confident, even flaring with anger; then she vacillates, as if ultimately what she cannot endure is the camera's stare, which is like a black hole, a consuming (and surprising) vertigo of desire. It takes the sudden intervention of the priest, his entrance into the shot, to stop her plunge in mid-flight and to hide her with his body—which is contrary to Rossellini's desire, and Ingrid's desire, to keep her in the frame alone, for the sake of the black hole of the director's eye. Two-shots in Rossellini tend to have one body too many, so one of them blocks the view of the other, typifying the entanglements of desire. Rossellini's Christianity resembles Dreyer's and Bresson's—when the priest offers her faith, she wants only his body. The camera describes their ballet wonderfully, their feints and parries. Ingrid's desire to flee corresponds to her agitated desire's inability to stay in one place, to the actor's desire not to stay on camera. "Stromboli is not a film about redemption through love but about the Assumption of a desire . . . : that incredible shot of Ingrid Bergman, her body sensually offered to the rising sun's caress, fulfilled, sacrificed on the altar of the film. What draws her up there to the volcano's summit, after all those obstacles . . . , if not the desire finally to be alone in the shot, *once and for all*, face to face with that crater, that beloved . . . eye behind the camera that draws her to give herself to him, desperately?"[118]

Timmory had thought Bergman overly done up for her role, to please Americans. Americans, not at all pleased, had been put off by her lack of glamour. Today we might dismiss both judgments and agree instead with Flaiano that she looks "so new, so liberated from the compromises that hid her true value" as to be sexier in her naturalness than she had ever been in America. "I had only seen a couple of her films," wrote Rossellini before starting *Stromboli*, "yet I had had the distinct impression that she had managed to resist triumphantly Hollywood's diva-ism and mannerism. There is something absolutely healthy and natural in her that deserves to face the huge exteriors of a volcanic landscape."[119]

Europe '51

"Some people," said Anna Magnani, "die of indigestion, others of shrewd-ness. Rossellini thought he'd calculated everything, then, whoops! Flat on his face!"[1]

Roberto was unemployed for the first time since the war. Always he had begun his next picture before finishing the current one. Now various projects were bruited about—*Christ Stopped at Eboli, Socrates and Santippe,* a film in Spain for Korda—but sixteen months would pass before he would begin shooting again. It wasn't a congenial situation.

"Speed means a great deal to me," Roberto told a journalist while aim-ing his Ferrari down a narrow highway at 140 mph. "When I drive at this speed, or faster, I get such a feeling of living more intensely, such a feeling of power, that I feel capable of knocking any obstacle out of my path. All my personal and professional problems resolve themselves when I'm at the wheel, particularly at night."[2]

Roberto was frustrated, but he had outlets. Ingrid only had drink. On November 1, 1950, Petter Lindstrom had finally obtained an American di-vorce. Ingrid had been given joint custody of Pia and half her vacation time, but only in the United States. The twelve-year-old daughter she had left behind, clearly hostile, had told the court that her mother had not been home for more than three to six months at a time during the last seven years, and nine days later had changed her name to Jenny Ann and be-come an American citizen. Ingrid was unwilling to come to the United States and no Christmas gifts arrived from her for Pia that year.

A few weeks later *The Miracle* was denounced by the Catholic Archdio-cese of New York as "an open insult to the faith of millions of people in this city and hundreds of millions throughout the world."[3]

Burstyn had obtained the picture from Lopert and opened it December 12 at New York's Paris Theater as part of an omnibus film, *Ways of Love.* The other two ways of love, Renoir's *A Day in the Country* and Pagnol's *Jofroi,* had been greeted enthusiastically by the New York press, *The Miracle* tepidly for the most part, with the notable exception of Bosley Crowther of

The New York Times who had thought Magnani "a shattering tour de force" and the film "by far the most overpowering and provocative of the [three ways of love], probably the most intense dramatic piece that we have had from the sensational Italian director."[4]

Then on December 22, New York Commissioner of Licenses Edward T. McCaffrey, a Bronx ward heeler and former head of the Catholic War Veterans in New York, had threatened to suspend the Paris's business license. He had found *The Miracle* "officially and personally blasphemous."[5] Burstyn had beaten off McCaffrey with a court order, because the Motion Picture Division of the New York State Board of Regents had already reviewed and licensed *The Miracle* twice, once for Lopert, once for Burstyn. But on December 30, as ads for the Paris proclaimed "*The Miracle* is back!", the Archdiocese of New York had entered the fray.

In Italy, where the Vatican had the right under the Italian constitution to have the government suppress films, no protest against *The Miracle* had been made—and scarcely anyone had gone to see it. But in New York, the Legion of Decency, which had previously condemned *Open City, Paisan, Shoeshine,* and *Bicycle Thieves* and would shortly condemn *Umberto D, I vitelloni,* and *La strada,* now condemned all three *Ways of Love* and lambasted *The Miracle* as "a sacrilegious and blasphemous mockery of Christian and religious truth."[6] Francis Cardinal Spellman complained that "the perpetrators of *The Miracle* unjustly cast their blasphemous darts of ridicule at Christian faith and at Italian womanhood, thereby dividing Religion against Religion and race against race." He called for "federal and state statutes to curb those who would profit financially by blasphemy, immorality and sacrilege" and admonished *all* Catholics, not just those in his archdiocese, to stay away from the film and any theater showing it.[7] Crowds flocked to the Paris Theater.

Cardinal Spellman himself never bothered to see *The Miracle,* which may be why he saw nothing odd about climaxing his harangue against it with a call to combat "the greatest enemy of civilization, atheistic Communism."[8] Loyally, the Catholic War Veterans, soon joined by the Holy Name Society, began picketing the Paris in numbers sometimes exceeding a thousand with signs reading "This is the Kind of Pictures the Communists Want" and "Don't Be a Communist—All the Communists are Inside."[9] Prospective Catholic patrons were handed leaflets saying (untruthfully) that by seeing the film "you are . . . disqualifying yourself as a Catholic."[10]

Token non-Catholics picketed the pickets. Several times police emptied the theater in response to bomb threats. One of its phone lines was cut, another line was thought to be tapped, as well as that of Burstyn's lawyer. Fire inspectors issued summonses when standees strayed into the aisles and began an investigation of "bribe-giving" at the Paris. Pressure from the archdiocese prevented the New York Film Critics from using Radio City Music Hall for their annual awards, one of which was to *Ways of Love.* In February the Board of Regents, after hearings, revoked *The Miracle's* license on the grounds that the film was sacrilegious.

The Church's victory was momentously Pyrrhic. For decades film content had been severely curtailed by numerous local censorship boards and an industry-adopted code that had been virtually dictated by the Church, thanks to a 1915 ruling by the U.S. Supreme Court that movies were *not* covered by the free-speech clause of the First Amendment. Now Burstyn appealed the Board of Regents' revocation, and in February 1952 the Supreme Court reversed itself. Movies, it now declared, were indeed protected by the First Amendment. Within a few years, film censorship of any sort became almost impossible, thanks to Cardinal Spellman and a miracle.

Ingrid finally saw her daughter in July 1951. Lindstrom had agreed that the London home of David Lean and Ann Todd would be neutral ground, and Ingrid had arrived there by train, incognito.

She was not well received. More than two years had passed. Petter, fearing Ingrid might resort to kidnapping, spent the night on guard at the bottom of the stairs. A day or two later, to everyone's surprise, Roberto arrived. No doubt he was needed.

Ingrid had never had time for Pia. She had deserted her often for long periods, beginning with a three-month trip from Sweden to Hollywood when Pia was eight months old. Now, encouraged by Roberto, she embarked on a long and expensive custody suit.

Selznick came to Rome that fall. "I don't think either has a quarter," he wrote Reissar. He wanted to back them in a twenty-minute Technicolor remake of *Una voce umana.*[11]

What had happened to Ingrid's $340,000? Was she hoarding it for a rainy day? Had Roberto swallowed it? As usual he was spending extravagantly, living wildly, and arriving home unpredictably with bunches of strangers expecting to eat, and it was all too much for Ingrid. Worse, she wasn't a star anymore, or even an actress—for Roberto wouldn't hear of her working with anyone but him. She was a housewife, and neglected, as Roswitha had been.

She tried to convince friends she was happy. "I don't think so," Jean Renoir observed. "Rossellini—who is charming—is not a 'spouse'. Everyone here knows that things cannot last with his attitude. He had arrived after lunch under the pretext of business, not hungry because he had already eaten a sandwich. I even ask myself if he doesn't already have his eye on someone else."[12]

The love affair had ended long ago. Fights were frequent. Strombolicchio would be sent upstairs to Marcella. In September a friend told reporters the two were separating and Ingrid would do films with others.[13]

That same month Ingrid became pregnant and hid it from Roberto as long as she could. *Europe '51* was about to begin, and she was afraid he'd be angry.[14]

Renzo Avanzo explained the situation. "Roberto is an ass, impractical, a dreamer. But she is a bourgeoise; he is not. That is the difference. He is used to running around until five in the morning, getting ideas from people, and he loses his imagination if dinner is to be eaten exactly at nine o'clock. She likes the floor so polished that you skid on it and almost break your neck. . . . I was bored silly whenever I visited her. After he got married, Roberto didn't dare to bring his old friends to his bourgeois house and wife. Old friends of Roberto would stop me in the street and say, 'Roberto never sees us any more.' 'Of course he doesn't,' I'd tell them. 'How the hell could he bring *you* home?' "[15]

In eleven days in October 1951, Roberto shot a twenty-minute episode for a French–Italian omnibus film, *Seven Deadly Sins*, called "Envy" ("*L'invidia*"), adapted from Colette's *The Cat*. It is about the wife of an artist (Orfeo Tamburi, playing himself) who tries to kill a cat that gets more attention than she does. It was Roberto's own quandary: a complaining wife devoid of sympathy either for his art, his friends, his pastimes, his intellectual interests or—most of all—his economics.

Mida saw "the quarrels of a couple who definitely lack any authentic ties for living together" in "Envy." Like most of the press he regarded the short film as "nothing but a purposeless intellectualistic game," evidence of the falsity into which Rossellini was falling, once away from documentary.[16] Disagreeing violently, Hovald (following Rondi's take on *Stromboli*) judged "Envy" as "the demonstration itself of Rossellinian art," the first in a series of masterpieces that through emphasis on "intentions in glances, silences, tiny traits, tightened lips and taciturn expressions . . . were going to alter the face of the cinema."[17] In this respect, Rondolino sees "Envy" anticipating Eric Rohmer's films.[18]

"Envy" marked another change in cinema as well. It was the first European picture to adopt Hollywood's use of tiny photoflood lamps to achieve softer light with softened shadows and more finely focused eyes. Its photographer, Enzo Serafin, continued this new style in *Voyage in Italy* and Antonioni's *I vinti* and *La signora senza camelie*. A few years later it would become the characteristic look of the movies of the French New Wave, as the small lamps could easily be mounted with clips in rooms or buses where older, bulkier equipment had made shooting impossible before.

Europe '51

Plot summary: Frustrated by lack of attention, the Gerards' young son throws himself down a staircase during his parents' dinner party and dies soon after. His mother Irene (Ingrid Bergman) blames herself and is disconsolate. Urged on by her Communist cousin Andrea, she turns her grief toward helping the unfortunate. When she disappears for days at a time while taking a poor mother's place on an assembly line and tending a dying prostitute, her husband becomes suspicious. And when she is held by the police after helping a teenager escape (so he can turn himself in), her husband has her committed to an insane asylum. The lawyer and judge endorse his action, and so does Irene, for there she finds people to whom she can be useful.

"I was shooting *Francesco* and telling Fabrizi stories from the *Fioretti*," said Roberto. "He listened to me carefully and turned to his secretary and said, '[Francis] was crazy' and the secretary said, 'Absolutely crazy.' That started me thinking."[19]

"Roberto," Ingrid recalled, "was talking to me about . . . what we would do if Saint Francis came back today. What would we do? We would do the same thing. He would be laughed at. . . . He said, 'I am going to make a story about Saint Francis and [Francis is] going to be you.' It was just, how would we behave in '51 if a woman gives up a rich husband, a rich life, all her friends, everything, and goes out into the street to help the poor?"[20]

"I was also thinking of something that happened in Rome during the war," Roberto said.[21] "A friend of mine—we were friends because we went underwater-fishing together—was one of the famous neurologists in Italy . . . : Professor Bini, one of the most honest persons I have known. And he told me this story. It's one of the elements I used to construct the environment of the film. . . . During the war . . . there were ration coupons. Everything was bought with coupons. And there was a guy in Via dello Statuto [near Piazza Venezia] who had a textile store and kept strictly to the rules. He didn't sell a meter of cloth without receiving the corresponding coupon. Then, with his wife pressing him to do what everyone else was doing and sell on the black market, at a certain moment this poor man decided to black market.[22] But one day when his wife was serving a customer, he came over and said, 'Signora, take this cloth, I make you a gift of it because I don't want to be a part of this crime, I think war is horrible.' Of course, after the customer left, the man had a fight with his wife and she made his life impossible at home. But the moral problem didn't go away.[23] He had decided he'd behaved ignobly; so many tragedies had been occurring around him, and he'd been profiting from them.[24] Since things couldn't be settled and since his wife went on committing crimes against his moral law, what did he do? He . . . gave himself up to the police. 'I did this and this and this, I have to get all of it off my conscience.'[25] The police, confronted with this freak behaving so strangely, sent him to the insane asylum for observation.[26] There, [Bini] told me . . . , 'I examined him and realized the only thing the man "had" was a moral problem. I was so shaken that that night I was thinking about it and said to myself, "I have to judge him as a scientist, not as a man. As a scientist I have to see if this man behaves like the average person. He does not behave like the average person." Therefore I committed him to the insane asylum. . . . Science has its limits. Science has to calculate, see, measure, be regulated by what it has achieved, what it knows. Anything beyond its limits has to be completely forgotten.' "[27]

Europe '51's heroine is like the cloth merchant. Purifying impulse inspired from shame is a theme basic to Rossellini. A moral position is abnormal, unconventional by definition (in Croce too), which is why it can change "the whole conception of the universe." Inevitably Roberto looked toward Simone Weil (1909–43), a brilliant Jewish–French academician who actually did "go the people"—by disowning her career and affluence to share the lot of the industrial proletariat—and who then discovered Christ. "My body and soul were in shreds," she wrote of her months on an assembly line. "This contact with unhappiness had killed my youth. . . . Being in the factory, confused in everyone's eyes and in my own with the anonymous masses, the unhappiness of the others went into my flesh and into my soul. Nothing separated me from them, for I had actually forgotten my past and was looking forward to no future, finding it difficult to imagine the possibility of surviving these labors. What I had endured then marked me in a manner so enduring that today still, when a human being, whoever it is, no matter the circumstances, speaks to me without brutality, I can't prevent myself having the impression that there must be some mistake and that the mistake will of course unfortunately disappear. In that place I received forever the mark of slavery, like the mark from the red-hot iron the Romans put on the faces of their most despised slave. Since then I have always thought of myself as a slave."[28]

Rossellini duplicates precisely every emotion of Simone Weil's factory experience—visually rather than verbally, such being his art. Factory work mechanizes the individual, as in Chaplin's *Modern Times*, a process comparable to violence in war. Violence corrupts victor *and victim*, Weil contended, writing as a Jew in Vichy France. So to share the victims' plight and assert her responsibility, she died from fasting at age 33. Irene, in *Europe '51*, is similarly intense. Morbidly obsessed like Roberto himself with responsibility for a son's death, she determines to share others' torments as a means of confronting her shame, and eventually elects life as an inmate in an insane asylum. But first she is consigned there by her family and the state, as happened to the black marketer—and to Roberto in his youth. "It was in speaking of his terrible memories that Roberto became convinced he had found the solution for his film," said Morlion.[29] Perhaps he had read Simone Weil, who wrote: "In this world, only those people who have fallen to the lowest degree of humiliation, far below beggary, who are not just without any social consideration but are regarded by all as being deprived of that foremost human dignity, reason itself—only those people, in fact, are capable of telling the truth. All the others lie."[30]

"I must admit, I'm always for the 'crazy' people," Rossellini said in 1970, explaining himself on Crocean grounds; "I've noted this . . . every time I've had to realize that we live in orthodoxy because it's comfortable, a way of avoiding responsibility. I believe all ideological patrimonies should be part of our culture and formation, [but] not as doctrines to which we're tied by sentiment and habits dictated by orthodoxy.[31] The world is young . . . but it ends up being dominated only by the dead, because through orthodoxy it's the dead alone who dominate us, not the young.[32] My aspiration, my great dream, is that each person be himself, with all the risks this entails, including the risk of being crazy.... If you're authentically yourself, you have such a load of honesty that it must per force lead to something.[33]

"It's not as if every act of our lives is based on reason. I think everyone acts under the impulse of the emotions as much as under the impulse of intelligence."[34]

Simone Weil wrote similarly. "There is no difficulty whatever, once one has decided to act, in maintaining intact on the plane of action those very hopes that a critical examination has shown to be well-nigh unfounded; in that lies the very essence of courage."[35]

And, condemning "we" as an illegitimate middle term between the soul and God: "The intelligence is defeated as soon as the expression of thoughts is preceded, explicitly or implicitly, by the little word 'we.' And when the light of the intelligence grows dim, in a rather short time love of the good gets lost."[36]

But: "Never has the individual been so completely delivered up to a blind collectivity, and never have men been less capable, not only of subordinating their actions to their thoughts, but even of thinking.... We are living in a world in which nothing is made to man's measure.... Work is no longer done with the proud consciousness that one is being useful, but with the humiliating and agonizing feeling of enjoying a privilege bestowed by a temporary stroke of fortune, a privilege from which one excludes several human beings by the mere fact that one enjoys, in fact, a job."[37]

Simone Weil was Marxist, a hater of capitalism, a tireless agitator for workers' rights. She was original for her time (and unpopular among some Communists because of it) in distinguishing a spiritual element in Marx in contrast to "the vulgar materialism of Engels and Lenin."[38] Like Roberto, who has Irene demand "a paradise not only for the living" but also for a dead child,[39] Weil concluded that only religious contemplation could sustain workers amid the joyless monotony of toil. She rejected materialist solutions for the world's problems, political parties in general and revolution most of all. "It's not religion, it's revolution that is the opium of the people," she said.[40]

In contrast to the fiercely virginal Weil, another influence on *Europe '51*, Herbert Marcuse, not only believed in the revolution, he insisted Dionysian sexual liberation was its *sine qua non*. He had started Roberto thinking toward *Europe '51* even before Weil and Saint Francis. Roberto said, "I was very friendly with a French intellectual, a militant in the French Communist Party, one of the ideologues of the party. In '48 or '49 or at the end of '47 he showed me a book that according to him was scandalous, a book by Marcuse [*Reason and Revolution*, 1941]. It was from this that [*Europe '51*] was born."[41]

Mixing Marx and Freud, claiming political problems are inseparable from psychological ones, Marcuse (not unlike Weil) charged that our civilization is founded on repression of sexual gratification and other instincts; that our happiness is subordinated to discipline and work; and that the result is totalitarianism. Freedom means free individual gratification, a new harmony between emotion and reason; laws must be self-given by the individual.

"Reading Marcuse certainly didn't turn me into a Marcusian. But that book did unexpectedly let me see another way of seeing things."[42] In the sixties, Roberto the bohemian would acclaim the hippies as a step in the right direction. Rossellini the artist was more sober. Marcuse was too much like Karin in *Stromboli*, confusing sex with freedom and whining that the chips were stacked against him. *Europe '51*'s agenda is that of the Resistance and Morlion: responsibility rather than evasion. And Weil's despondent gospel of sacrifice also gets Franciscanized. "People today," Roberto said, "only know how to live in society, not in community. The soul of society is the law, the soul of the community is love."[43] Franciscanism can also cure Marcuse's repression. "In each of us there's the jester side and its opposite. . . . Today there's a tendency to suppress the first brutally. The world is more and more dividing into two groups, those who want to kill imagination and those who want to save it; those who want to die and those who want to live. This is the problem I confront in *Europe '51*. . . .

"The ability to see both sides of man, to look at people with benevolence, seems to me an attitude exquisitely Latin and Italian. . . . For me it's extraordinarily important to have been born into such a civilization. I feel we saved ourselves from the disasters of the war, and from misfortunes no less terrible, precisely because of our concept of life, which is specifically Catholic. Christianity doesn't depict everything as good and perfect. It recognizes mistakes and sin but also admits that salvation's possible. It's the opposing attitude that allows only the infallible, coherent, perfect person. . . . In our civilization, Latin and Christian, we don't enshrine truth. We're full of irony and skepticism; we keep on searching for truth.[44]

"If you want to give a subtitle to the film I'm directing, call it *Europe '51, or The Tragedy of Conformism*. We're all voluntary prisoners and thus victims, through cowardice or unconsciousness, of our desire to be in harmony with everything and everyone. Idolators of what's normal, we live in continual terror of possibly becoming exceptions.[45] People talk about liberty, but the first thing they add is, 'Liberty, yes, but within certain limits.' . . . The fact is that people today want to be free to believe in a truth that is imposed on them; no one looks for his own truth any more. . . . The world has always advanced when there was real liberty.[46] [But] in a world consumed by ideology, what liberties do we enjoy? Only one: to give our adhesion to one of the three or four dogmas being marketed. . . . If you don't use the right words, you're dead.[47] Irene [in *Europe '51*] is insane, as far as the world's concerned. She's a woman who wanted to make her life profoundly moral . . . but that's not what people do. So she ends up behind the bars of an insane asylum. . . . There's a need for heroes in the world of today, that's for sure."[48]

Europe '51, like *Francesco*, tells the Rossellini "master plot." The humility of an individual, jolted by love, threatens existing social order. Human progress is due to those who go to extremes; a pinch of Franciscanism isn't enough, humility has to be uncompromising.

The radicalness of these ideas is thrown into relief by the conventionality of the feminist protest novel that was the movie's first source—*before* Francis, Weil, the black market, and Marcuse. Alba De Céspedes's *Quaderno proibito* is a quietly moving chronicle of a woman having a mid-life crisis, while she and her family confront the changing mores of postwar Italy. It is written as the diary of a woman afraid to have a diary—hence the "Forbidden Notebook" of the title—a woman who needs to assert and find herself as a person, but who has been beaten down, not so much by social convention as by her own uncertainties about her own feelings. The novel has no big scenes, just the ordinary, "neo-realist" events of anyone's life.

In contrast, the movie adds one melodramatic situation on top of the next: suicidal children, communists, prostitutes, slum mothers, fugitive criminals, deaths, police, psychiatrists, hypocritical priests, an insane asylum. In the novel, the heroine's courage never leads her out of her class or out of her family. The movie makes her as far-voyaging and disruptive as Joan of Arc. Rossellini melodramatizes De Céspedes's novel in order to radicalize it— melodrama is a form of radicalization—and this radicalization is due less to Francis, Weil, the black market, and Marcuse than to Roberto himself, whose "solution" for De Céspedes's novel was in his memories of his own incarceration in a rest home.[49] As a result, in place of De Céspedes's wise and compassionate chronicle of daily life, Rossellini constructs a myth of heroism, a heroism that defends "insanity" against the worse insanity of convention.

Such a tack was bound to confuse critics more than audiences.

The script's endless problems had consumed Roberto's sixteen months between pictures. Its original producers had been French (Franco-London Films); it was to have been shot in Paris. Roberto had Fellini and Tullio Pinelli sketch out the plot with the Dominican priest Felix Morlion in Rome, then brought them to Paris toward the end of 1949. "He knew Fellini had never seen Paris," Pinelli recalled, "and he didn't want to miss being with him on his first encounter. He was waiting for us at the station at seven in the morning and spent the whole day and whole night with us touring the city." The tour included so many nightclubs that Roberto, who usually shunned alcohol, got thoroughly drunk. "We had a great time. But with the film we had serious difficulties. To begin with, we had to take positions on rival currents of contemporary thought and the French producers didn't want anything to do with it. In Rossellini's hotel room there were long sessions with [Jean-Paul] Le Chanois, Charles Spaak, Fulchignoni, the producers, and all sorts of comers and goers. . . . When you get near Rossellini you have the impression of entering into contact not with a man but with a world of which he is the center. Thirty people speaking different languages are forever entering and exiting whatever room he's in; phone calls arrive from three or four faraway cities; the unexpected is the order of the day. He, perfumed and elegant and fiddling with a lock of hair on his neck, slides smoothly from one person to another with the sweet smile of an eighteenth-century abbot. But suddenly the prospect of a car trip or a new film idea takes hold of him totally; he becomes emotional, buoyant, enthusiastic, excited. There are few people whose lives have been as draining as his, and his constant childish capacity for emotion and enthusiasm, for seeing things in ways that are always fresh and new, is truly admirable."[50]

Roberto was in a strange mood, beset by terrible headaches and, despite pressure from his producers, unable to get down to work. Specifically he was tormented by the suicide of the boy in his story. Fulchignoni, who now lived in Paris, found him Chazal, a prominent juvenile court judge, to consult. Then three or four psychiatrists who specialized in the passage into insanity. Then other intellectuals.

Le Chanois wrote a screenplay for the film. He was one of the most respected filmmakers in France, a Communist writer-director of more than twenty pictures. Born Jean-Paul Dreyfus (1909–85), "Le Chanois" had been his undercover name in the French Resistance and he had kept it for his professional career. *Au Coeur de l'Orage* ("At the heart of the storm," [1948]) used footage of Resistance activities that Le Chanois himself had shot during the war. Jacques Lourcelles describes *Agence matrimoniale* (1952) as "at the crossroads of a French neo-realism and the tradition of the well-written, highly detailed—but apparently nonchalant—moral tale (a genre that Becker has brought to perfection). This little human comedy, rich with a hundred characters, presents a meaningful and varied canvas of lower-middle-class French society at the end of the war."[51] Just about what Rossellini wanted for *Europe '51*, except that in Le Chanois's screenplay, everything Irene does is soundly motivated and reasonable, and religion is less important to her. She leaves her husband for love of André, but so corrupts his Communism that he is expelled from the Party and they break up; and after her husband locks her up, a happy end is arranged: Irene gives up her claims to her husband's wealth, accepts a divorce, and goes to live with the poor in their tenements.[52]

Still the project got nowhere. Fellini, not understanding French, feeling completely left out, and not getting paid, went back to Rome with Pinelli. The producers departed too. They had always been worried about getting involved with Rossellini. After the prodigious sums squandered on *Stromboli* and the failure of *Francesco*, the scenes at the Hotel Raphael had not been reassuring.

Back in Rome, Roberto found a new producer—Carlo Ponti, who thought he could use Bergman and Rossellini to compete against De Laurentiis.[53] Ponti conceded total authority to Roberto—he never came near the set—but for the first time since 1943 Roberto owned no percentage of his picture and the salary—$100,000 for both Ingrid and him—was humbling. He had always loathed Ponti as a pompous ass; in 1945 he had taken Rod Geiger to Ponti's courtyard at two in the morning and howled "Ponti! Ponti" outside his window. Now he sent Manni every morning to wait at Ponti's door for daily expense money and every day was cheered to hear how much this had infuriated Ponti today. It was another of the ways Roberto alienated anyone who ventured to produce his films. Often he insisted it was his moral duty to defy, humiliate, and ruin producers.

To replace Le Chanois, Fellini, and Pinelli he found new writers, waves of them. First, breaking with Father Morlion and avoiding his phone calls, he courted the Communists Trombadori and Mida; then Sandro De Feo, Ivo Perilli, Brunello Rondi, and Diego Fabbri; then Mario Pannunzio and Antonio Pietrangeli, the assistant director; then finally, since most of the film would be shot in English, Donald Ogden Stewart, Ingrid's friend, a famous M-G-M screenwriter who had signed a dozen of M-G-M's best known movies in the thirties and forties and was now blacklisted.[54] Surrounded by so many voices representing so many ideologies, Roberto was assured of getting his own way.

He tried to cast Luchino Visconti as the Communist intellectual, was turned down, and used another director instead, Ettore Giannini. Fellini's wife, Giulietta Masina, was enlisted for a cameo role; she had made her debut in *Paisà* and had won the Nastro d'Argento as best supporting actress in Lattuada's *Senza pietà* (1948). For the last time, Roberto made a place for his friend Bill Tubbs, who died a few months later.

Aldo Tonti was a necessary choice as photographer. *Europe '51* would contain, Roberto said, "many very difficult scenes that had to be shot with the camera on a dolly following the actors around the whole time."[55] Such scenes were Rossellini's obsession, nearly impossible to shoot, and Tonti had done the impossible for him once before in *Il miracolo*. Tonti could also give *Europe '51* the black, expressionist look it required; he had done it before for Alessandrini's *Caravaggio* (1941). In fact, no Rossellini movie would be so carefully and artistically lit, so worthy to stand beside the most beautiful achievements of Hollywood's finest lighting cameramen. Roberto, having given his basic instructions, was able, just like a Hollywood director, to leave lighting, technical problems, and the impossible in Tonti's hands, while he concentrated on actors and composition.[56]

On November 11, 1951, Roberto, Ingrid, and Tonti began a fundraising short, *Radda Barnen* ("Red cross"), documenting the efforts of the Swedish nuns at the Convent of Saint Brigid in Rome to funnel gifts from Sweden to child victims of a flood in Polesine.[57]

Then *Europe '51* began. "The work was very complicated," Tonti recalled. "We were surrounded by throngs of journalists and photographers all the time, and Roberto was constantly changing the scenario, shooting all over Rome with the troupe, going from one end of the city to the other. What I remember is that Ingrid, ever so calm and serene, would sit in crannies knitting away, always, always, during the wearisome waiting for something to be shot. Then she too would walk and walk, and the grips would say, 'Hey, when are they going to stop making her act with her feet and start having her use her head?' "[58]

When Ingrid stopped walking, the troupe moved to the Ponti–De Laurentiis studio on Via della Vasca Navale, but nothing changed except the hours. They shot from one until nine or ten, then screened rushes and ate. Sets had been constructed but no one, Roberto included, knew what would be done from one day to the next. If he did tell Pietrangeli to rehearse the extras and prepare a scene for the morrow, he was sure to change everything by the time the morrow came. Then a writer would scribble down some lines. They were shooting in English.

"Only twice did I have my dialogue the night before a scene was to be shot," said Alexander Knox. "Both times, the lines were changed when we met on the set in the morning. All the rest of the time I had no dialogue until a few minutes before the camera turned. Once I was lit for a close-up and the camera had started turning before anyone realized that I had not been given any dialogue. I just sat there, smiling fatuously at Roberto and cameraman Aldo Tonti, and smoking a cigarette. Suddenly, Rossellini spoke. 'Look at Ingrid,' he said, 'and tell her you're not going out tonight.' I laughed, turned again to Ingrid, and said obediently, 'I'm not going out tonight.' The camera was still turning. 'Basta' Rossellini said at length. The camera stopped turning, the lights faded, and I leaned back. 'Well,' I asked, 'am I going out tonight or not?' 'I don't know,' said Roberto. 'But I'll know in a week or two—and I won't have to come back into this set.' "[59]

Knox enjoyed Roberto's methods. And Ingrid, so nervous and excited about working again that she was unable to sleep and had caught a cold, seemed reconciled to them. Putting her knitting aside and taking up her new lines, she would spontaneously and effortlessly enter into her part with complete conviction. "Bergman was completely in love with Roberto. She followed him with the utmost enthusiasm," said Tonti, who adored Ingrid and was benightedly unaware that her marriage wasn't Camelot. "I never heard her make the least observation, the least criticism of his way of doing things. If Roberto said something, for her it was as though the oracle had spoke[n]."[60]

Roberto, normally authoritarian on the set, was particularly so with Ingrid. One time she had to come close to the camera and he told her, "Get rid of that dirt spot under your nose!" And for once she lost control of herself: "What? We've been going to bed together for—I can't remember—X number of years, and you've never realized I have a beauty mark under my nose?"[61]

She did make a suggestion one day, in an effort to calm a gathering storm over a staging problem. Roberto grunted, "Yes, yes," and went on doing it his way, over and over, with increasing irritation. She tried again and he exploded. Everyone froze. She tried being sweet and he got madder and screamed a vulgarity at her, three times. She just stared at him. "Everyone realized at that moment that their love was over," comments Manni, who relates this story.[62]

Bergman had no understanding of what Roberto was trying to do in film, and he opposed her working for others. Now he told the press she was retiring from the screen. He had finally realized she was pregnant. "An actress, a *real* actress, cannot consent to go in and out of a character the way a secretary goes in and out of an office, she cannot be at the disposition of every commercial deal the way an employee is at the disposition of every order for transfer. In sum, it is precisely in order to remain an actress that Ingrid Bergman has left cinema. Just as I did not make a film for two years in order to remain a director. . . . I had nothing to say and a lot to do, private things that consumed time and energy, and so I've been silent until this moment. Now I have something to say."[63]

Stromboli excepted, Rossellini's postwar pictures had been cheaply and quickly made, as was *Europe '51*.[64] But his abilities were overshadowed by continuous derision in the press, to which he made insufficient obeisance. Once, when a mogul was about to give him millions and asked to see a script, Roberto fumbled in his pocket and pulled out a tattered scrap of paper with illegible scribbling. He himself admitted, "Often I don't remember later what I have told [producers, selling them ideas], and I am very embarrassed."[65]

It thus helped his reputation that Alexander Knox, who had been nominated for an Academy Award for *Wilson* and had a reputation for seriousness, rose to his defense. "Nobody," he wrote in *The New York Times* in 1953, "could make the mistakes that [Rossellini] has made and get away with them if he were not a bit of a genius. They are not the mistakes of a stupid man. (He won't thank me for that statement. He will ask 'What mistakes?' with a pained surprise in his voice, implying that they don't exist.)" Hadn't D. W. Griffith's methods been similar? "'The best effects, the best moments and the truest drama in my films,'" Knox quoted Griffith, "'were always off the cuff, spontaneous. Making films must be, for the director, a creative process, not a process of mass production or the mere assembly of prefabricated parts. The director must remain flexible, he must be able to be inspired by the film he has already shot and remain free to accept that inspiration.' "[66]

Also helpful to Rossellini's cause was the February 1952 issue of *Bianco e Nero*, the prestigious film journal edited from the Centro Sperimentale di Cinematografia. Five articles and a filmography constituted the first serious survey of Rossellini's art. Roberto himself, in a ten-page interview with Mario Verdone,[67] finally gave public evidence of his brilliance in discussing his work. A new image began: Rossellini the thinker. Even more than the writings of Bazin and Ayfre, Roberto's own words, through a majestic series of interviews, would inspire a cult for his art that would surpass in intensity, if not in population, the public's cult of derision.

He was not in turn inspired by the movies his countrymen were making. De Sica, Castellani, and Emmer aside, he looked on most "neo-realists" as vulgarizers and popularizers of his own personal poetry. Critics generally endorsed his low estimate; one commercial, sentimental vein of neo-realism went on so long repeating itself that it earned its own name: "pink neo-realism." But even Roberto's friends suspected his judgments were colored by jealousy.

Fellini, for instance, had kept Roberto abreast of his first solo film, *Lo sceicco bianco (The White Sheik)*, through scripting, shooting, and editing, and had shown him the rough cut. "During the projection I was in the grip of a thousand feelings," Roberto said, "because I saw on the screen Fellini as I had known him intimately for many years. I felt old and disturbed because he seemed so young."[68] Fellini was eager for his "maestro"'s verdict; he knew Roberto wanted success for him as a friend and would feel threatened at the same time. Roberto unhesitatingly gushed enthusiasm. "Phone me tomorrow morning," he added. "We'll talk about it together and you'll see how with a few cuts it will look like a real little masterpiece."

Next morning Fellini phoned, Roberto was still in bed, and Manni went to tell him. "He suddenly turned into a wild animal," writes Manni. "He told me he'd never seen a worse film, had absolutely no interest in laying a hand on it, had no time to waste on beginners." Cursing Manni for not telling Fellini he wasn't home, Roberto stormed into the bathroom and slammed the door.[69]

He kept Fellini at bay for a week, then suggested he redo a boat scene that too obviously had been shot on a beach rather than in the water. Pooh-poohing Fellini's objection that there was no money left, he insisted impatiently, "If on a painting by Raphael there's a bit of dust, it should be blown off!"[70]

A good deal of Roberto's pique was because *Lo sceicco bianco* had been made from *Paisà*'s profits, which Mario Conti, *Roberto's* man, had chosen to invest in Fellini rather than in Rossellini.

Fellini understood. "Robertino was very encouraging. It meant a great deal to me. I respected him as a director, and his praise at this crucial, early moment in my career was important to me. Shortly afterwards, I told him that someday I hoped I would be able to repay him for his generosity. He said that I could repay him by encouraging someone else. Someday when I was in the position of being one of the most important Italian directors, which I surely would be, he said that I should remember him and help someone younger than myself."

Thirty-six years later Giuseppe Tornatore showed Fellini a work print of his *Cinema paradiso*. "I remembered Rossellini. [He] had been there for *me*. I thought of his words."[71]

Two years later, to convince Anthony Quinn to appear in Fellini's *La strada*, Ingrid and Roberto invited the actor "to a wonderful dinner and afterwards they screened *I vitelloni*, so he could see my work. . . . Robertino was very persuasive and he always got what he wanted, but he told me the dinner and showing my film was Ingrid's idea."[72]

In contrast to Roberto's cat-and-mouse friendship–rivalry with Fellini was his relationship with Jean Renoir, "the dearest of all . . . , more than a friendship, an extraordinary love. . . . But strange as it may seem, we never talked about film when we were together. We had so many other things to say to each other."[73]

Their backgrounds were similar. Renoir was apolitical, anti-bourgeois, anti-conventional. Like Roberto, he had grown up in a well-off family, had had a spotty education, and had passed his time partying, spending feck-lessly, racing cars (also a Bugatti), and chasing girls. Like Roberto, he had flirted with the Communists when they were useful to him, but kept aloof from parties and groups. Like Roberto, his movie had suffered amid post-war politics. *La Règle du jeu* had been banned again in 1945 (before finally being released a year later) and scenes in *La Grand illusion* were censored. Like Roberto, Renoir had spectacular marriage problems.

Renoir had been afraid to go back to France after the war lest he be arrested for bigamy. His California divorce from his philandering first wife, Catherine Hessling,[74] from whom he'd parted twenty years ago, was not recognized in France; she was suing him, and he was paying her lawyer as well as his own. To clear up the affair, Renoir had planned to divorce his second wife, Dido Freire, in order to divorce his first wife, in order to re-marry his second wife. But he had been unable to find cause under Califor-nia law.

Renoir had known Ingrid before meeting Roberto. Soon after his arrival in Hollywood in 1941, Selznick had asked him to do a Joan of Arc film with her, she had cooked him crawfish, and he had proposed Mary Webb's *Sarn* instead. Ingrid had said yes, but no producer had been willing to see her disfigured with a harelip, as the role required. In November 1949, after an anxious 48-hour visit to Paris, Renoir had gone to India to make *The River*. In the spring of 1951, still avoiding France, he had come to Rome. Renzo Avanzo had hired him to make *The Golden Coach* in English with Anna Magnani.

Renoir bought a Jaguar and stayed a year and a half. Magnani learned English for the movie but, as usual, would show up two hours late looking as though she hadn't slept and by the fifth rehearsal would be blooming like a young girl. "I love to tell that story," Renoir said, "because it's typical of *the* great actor. Their art is stronger than their physique, the spiritual takes precedence over the material."[75] When Magnani became over-wrought, Renoir, like Roberto before him, would take her by the arm for a ten-minute walk and they'd come back laughing.

Unlike Roberto, however, Renoir was genuinely fond of America; ulti-mately he chose to live there rather than in France. He had been bitter at Frenchmen in France collaborating with the occupation and Frenchmen in exile complaining about America. Determined to shun them both, he had begun the process of becoming an American citizen in 1942. "It's simply because I feel more at ease in this wide country than in narrow Europe. [My son] Alain's like me, he doesn't think of himself as a refugee but as an American."[76] When Alain enlisted, Jean explained, "It's the least of politenesses. The Americans offer us hospitality, it's normal for us to fight for them."[77] Renoir had liked making movies in Hollywood, too. In Rome he regretted that he hadn't insisted on "a good American editor" for *The Golden Coach*. He ended up cutting and assembling most of the picture himself. Meanwhile his stories inspired Roberto.

Renoir passed weekends at Santa Marinella watching Roberto and Ingrid with their children. He described the scene like one of his father's paintings. "There was nothing intellectual about it. They were like animals with their young, so tactile and sensual. The joy of touching the baby's skin! They were always rolling around on the floor with the twins [who were born in June] and the little boy. Once, I remember watching Ingrid doing that and I thought to myself, 'This is just like a mother dog with her puppies.'"[78]

Often Renoir talked of his adventures in India. Ingrid wrote Joe Steele, "Now Roberto says he wants to go to India and to Japan to make pictures . . . Oh, brother! With a caravan of women and children!"[79]

In March 1952, with *Europe '51*'s editing unfinished, Roberto embarked on a second project for Ponti–De Laurentiis, *Dov'è la libertà . . . ?* ("Where is liberty?"). He was enthusiastic about working with the famed comedy star Totò, for, as *Roma città aperta*, *L'amore*, and *Stromboli* demonstrate, Rossellini had not understood that neo-realist filmmakers dislike having stars in their movies. He was also enthusiastic about his idea for the movie (lifted from Chaplin's *Modern Times*): a mild-mannered convict is released from prison, but finds the world so inhospitable that he puts himself back in jail. "In Rossellini's universe, the only serious problem is solitude," Claude Beylie wrote.[80] Rossellini declared, "*Dov'è la libertà . . . ?* is . . . a side-product of *Europe '51 . . .* , an attempt to investigate the same situation. Then there's the extraordinary character of Totò."[81]

But, as so often with Roberto, creative enthusiasm evaporated when it came to working out an idea, and boredom (his and ours) was the result. Soon he was seeking excuses to avoid the set. He showed up one day at 6 P.M. with helmet, big red Ferrari, and effusive apologies to the entire crew, who had been waiting some hours. "I had to run an errand for Ponti," he explained. "No problem," Totò replied politely; "Now *you* can wait." And he left.[82]

Producers may have hated Roberto. But his crew loved him. They were the highest paid laborers in Italy and with Rossellini there was lots of overtime. He used the same people for each picture, was jovial with them, and would play cards with them during breaks. But he came less and less to the studio and after three months, with only about 15,000 feet of negative shot, and a fight over money with Ponti, it was evident that he had abandoned the picture. Worse, he had filmed only bits and pieces of each sequence. It looked like a complete loss.

An earlier disaster, *La macchina ammazzacattivi*, was released in May 1952, four years late. There was no publicity and the few reviews were only a few words long. Visentini (*Bianco e Nero*) said it was one of Rossellini's best. Lanocita (*Corriere della Sera*) said it was his worst, and not funny, either.[83]

Dov'è la libertà . . . ? would be salvaged after only two years, and fare somewhat better in March 1954. Roberto had handed his footage to Mario Monicelli along with the suggestion that the gaps in the story could be dealt with by adding a voice-over and framing the whole thing as a flashback between scenes of Totò on trial.[84] De Laurentiis had called on Fellini to shoot, according to Fellini, "a minuscule sequence, only a pair of shots: Totò leaping on the lawyer Talarico's head and biting his ear. Just that. But I felt intimidated and ill at ease."[85] According to Roberto, "As it stands [*Dov'è la libertà . . . ?*] was very much hacked about, it was much more cruel. The producers softened it to make it more lightweight."[86]

The picture had its defenders. Visentini liked its nimbleness. Sala thought it was touching and created a lively new character perfect for Totò. Pierre Kast (*Cahiers du Cinéma*) said he was stupefied by its cruelty and Swiftian bitterness, and called it Rossellini's most beautiful film. Others, Mida, Kezich, and Chiaretti in *L'Unità*, thought it raggedly made and moralistic.[87]

Later critics find the movie interesting as a comedy version of *Europe '51* and thus a key to Rossellini. Claude Beylie writes that all Rossellini heroes obstinately oppose hypocritical appearances with ferocious solitude. "A human being, from the instant he feels truly human and not just a puppet, is isolated in the midst of everyone else, who claim to be like him though they are only caricatures of humanity. Life now is no longer possible with them, at their level." Whereupon the heroes go back to prison, into insane asylums, exile, monasteries, or the underground. "Where then is liberty? In oneself, in conscience and lucidity refound."[88]

But Beylie is wrong. Rossellini heroes may find illumination in solitude but, like Francis of Assisi and King Vidor's characters, they immediately pursue a *social* application. Irene doesn't choose "solitude"; she chooses a community in which she can function usefully. Karin chooses to raise her baby. A glaring exception to this rule, *Vanina Vanini*, is stupid and self-centered (like Marina in "Rome"); Salvatore in *Dov'è la liberta . . . ?* is just like her—and a parody of Irene in *Europe '51*. He acts from selfishness, Guarner points out, appoints himself arbiter of order and morality, and sulks because he is unwilling to recognize that his petit-bourgeois notions of happiness are based on illusion.[89]

On June 18, Ingrid gave birth to twin girls: Isabella Fiorella Giovanna Frida, seven pounds three ounces; and Isotta Ingrid Giuliana Elettra, eight pounds five ounces. When Roberto got news of the first twin, he turned white as a sheet, looked as though he were going to faint, then wept like a baby. Ingrid had been so enormous that she had entered the hospital three weeks before.

Ingrid's attention was riveted on a Los Angeles courtroom where Judge Mildred D. Lillie was hearing her suit that Pia come to Italy that summer without her father. Her attorney, Gregory Bautzer, labored to make a case for a mother who would not come in person while Lindstrom's attorney, Isaac Pacht, presented evidence of her and Roberto's bad character, including Senator Johnson's allegations of narcotics, immorality, and Nazi collaboration. Roberto, amid more than $3,000 worth of phone calls and telegrams, wanted to come defend himself. But Judge Lillie declined to adjourn the trial or admit a $1,000 telegram from him or affidavits from other absent witnesses. "I don't love my mother. I like her," thirteen-year-old Pia admitted, under questioning by Bautzer on June 13. "And you don't miss her?" "No." "And you don't have any desire to see her?" "No. I would rather live with my father." "Do you feel that your mother doesn't care about you now?" Judge Lillie asked. "Well, I don't think she cares about me too much." "Why do you say that?" "Well, she didn't seem very interested in me when she left. It was only after she left and got married and had children that she suddenly decided she wanted me." "Do you love your mother?" Bautzer pressed. "No, not very much. I mean I have seen her enough, and I know I have met her, but I haven't seen her enough to really love her. My father has mostly been taking care of me. I lived with my father mostly."[90]

Judge Lillie, maintaining that Pia was not chattel to be "passed back and forth between parents to satisfy their pride, convenience and desires" and, noting that no obstacle prevented her mother from visiting her in America, ruled against Ingrid on June 24.

The next day, summoning reporters to her hospital room, Ingrid raged against Lindstrom and the verdict and vowed to "fight like a tigress" for custody of Pia. "I gave up most of my financial substance . . . just to have Pia with me during the summer," she claimed. "You can say that I am practically broke and my husband is providing for me."[91]

Among Ingrid and Roberto's guests during this period were Joseph Cotten, William Wyler, Tennessee Williams, Alexander Korda, Marcel Pagnol, Richard Wright, John Steinbeck, Ernest Hemingway, Swedish sculptor Carl Milles, Eddie Albert, photographer David Seymour (a colleague of Bob Capa), Jean Renoir, Artur Rubinstein, and Moravia. Most of these men came to see Ingrid. But she, said a friend, "kept talking about those parties with the beggars and monks, [and] one day she said, 'They only come to see Roberto, not me!' Then I realized that she had become unhappy. At [his] parties, Ingrid would always be off to one side." "I'm only a spectator!" she moaned.[92] And Roberto at Ingrid's parties was equally discontent. "I was filming *Roman Holiday* and I was invited out to Santa Marinella with Billy Wilder," said Gregory Peck. "Ingrid had gone to some pain to prepare a

Hollywood lunch. She kept apologizing for Roberto not being there. She was very hurt at his nonappearance. He finally showed up. He didn't sit down. He leaned on a chaise, yawning and stretching. He was rather indifferent to the Hollywood crowd. I thought he was acting like a spoiled kid."[93]

Some theorized Roberto felt threatened, fearing the Hollywood crowd would tempt Ingrid to go back. More likely he was, as usual, intolerant of American rigidity in conversation. He could charm people when he felt like it, just as Ingrid could: a single friendly smile from her could create a lifelong acolyte. But just as frequently her stiffness, distraction, and tipsiness were as offensive to Italians as Roberto's irreverence was to Americans. "We went together to see an Edoardo comedy," relates Valmarana, "and afterward went backstage. Roberto loved it, but Ingrid just wouldn't emote enthusiasm. 'Yes, it's pretty,' was all she would concede by way of praise."[94] More and more Roberto came to attribute his every complaint against Ingrid to her "Nordicness." She summed up her dissatisfactions with Roberto in his "Italianness."

In preparation for Venice, Roberto edited and dubbed *Europe '51*, working by night and sleeping by day in summer heat. He desperately needed a success, and *Bianco e Nero*'s prediction—"the most mature, important, and authoritative film from Rossellini to date [and] probably the major work of the cinema since the war"—only raised the stakes.[95]

Years later, *Europe '51* would be looked on as one of the rarest moments in film history. "An attempt is made," Guarner would write, "to express a far-reaching moral conflict, which is incarnated in a woman's face, merely by means of a series of actions, sketched out in a few strokes with a simplification that touches on abstraction. Ultimately, it is this face that gives coherence to an otherwise notably discontinuous film, in the same way as the image of Falconetti or Anna Karina fills the gaps in [Dreyer's] *La Passion de Jeanne d'Arc* and [Godard's] *Vivre sa vie*. . . . One had to look for significance in [the] images rather than in [the] ideas. The film is an ascent from the darkness of the beginning towards a dazzling light of the end, when Irene . . . regain[s] her inner freedom. . . . It is quite astonishing how a film like this, passionate to the point of indecency, manages to advance steadfastly towards the extreme bareness of the conclusion, which is bathed in an unearthly, Nordic light and has an austerity worthy of Dreyer [and] the spiritual quality of [Dreyer's] *Ordet*."[96]

No critic saw *Europe '51* in such dimensions in 1952, basically because, following Rossellini's lead, they assessed the picture as social commentary rather than spiritual odyssey. In fact it was as odyssey that *Europe '51* was a box-office success in Italy—the only Rossellini movie to earn money in Italy in the fourteen years between *Roma città aperta* and *Il generale Della Rovere*. But as a "woman's picture" and as a "melodrama," its popularity could be dismissed by critics. Everywhere else the film was a dud.

At Venice, where it closed the Festival September 12, it was applauded clamorously and shared the International Prize with Ford's *The Quiet Man* and Mizoguchi's *Life of Oharu*. But the jury awarded its Gold Lion for best film to *Jeux interdits* (Clément, whose *Bataille du rail* had bested *Roma città aperta* at Cannes), and the critics awarded their prize to *The Quiet Man*.

And when the reviews appeared—both for Venice and the commercial opening in January—the verdict was unanimous. The ambitions were laudable; the first fifteen minutes, till the boy's death, were wonderful; Bergman was wonderful; the rest was travesty.

There was scarcely a single dissenting contemporary opinion. Reviewers differed only in the degree they respected Rossellini's intentions.

"Ten years ago Rossellini understood that cinema, and modern art generally, needed dedicated and conscientious research into reality above all else," wrote Trombadori, the Communist cultural leader who had championed the maker of *Paisà*. "In [*Roma città aperta* and *Paisà*] he began to discover the importance of having political and social perspectives broad enough to treat life's decisive problems with the force of art and imagination. . . . [But] in *Deutschland im Jahre Null* and *Europe '51* [Rossellini] almost seems be to repudiating [the need for research] and to be turning instead to feckless, arrogant cinema, without study and without understanding of the problems, the facts, and the human soul." Granted, the artistic problems of putting ideological conflicts into a film are formidable. But Rossellini wants to make a film about conflicts without having studied their nature and background, and thus ends up making everything seem gratuitous. "He wants to make a film of visual counterblows and sudden narrative swerves and instead maintains always the same [abstract] level: the characters, ideas, and feelings have no chiaroscuro and scarcely ever have life." Aside from theosophic sophisms sugared with Franciscanism ("It's hate toward oneself that must generate love for others"; "In love toward sinners resides perfect happiness"; "Man is walled up in his anguish"; "Work is condemnation"), there's no big idea to give perspective, substance and drama to everything else; there's just "a series of notes for a drama awaiting development." Ideas and characters are representative not of reality but of the most superficial middle-class expectations, for example the Communist, who tells a mother guilty of her son's suicide that it wasn't her fault but capitalism's!

Nonetheless, Trombadori concluded, "I'm still not yet ready, personally, to believe in the twilight of Rossellini, man and director."[97]

Others were less benevolent. Castello *(Cinema)* thought Rossellini's good intentions unfulfilled by puppets prating formulas in contrived drama. Chiaretti *(L'Unità)* thought Rossellini ever more involuted: "his immoderate ambition . . . calmly announces: 'I'll make a film on the crisis of the European conscience in mid-century, I've understood this crisis and shall indicate the ways to solve it and the public should listen to the new Gospel of Rossellini.' [But Rossellini] doesn't concern himself with vulgar problems like Umberto D's pension [in De Sica's movie]. . . . He puts everything on an ideological plane. The poor neighborhoods aren't actually real for him . . . , they're an aspect of the world soul, outside of time, an abstract category. . . . To those who ask for bread and work Rossellini answers that work is condemnation and offers a saint. As if we don't have enough saints already." Mida decided that "Rossellini has repeated the errors of *Stromboli*, failing to invent, around the figure of Irene, a functional and human chorus"; some episodes were convincing then, nothing is now. Aristarco (*Cinema Nuovo*) noted Irene's resemblance to Karin—complex, egotistic, egocentric, foreign, a representative of sorrowing humanity, living in a world without faith, atheistic, seeking not good but good living, full of conformists like the Communist and priest. But Aristarco still condemned the movie as so superficial that "one suspects Rossellini's accusation of moral deafness and conformism was almost a desire to hold out his own hands, as people do who know themselves guilty and accuse others of the same fault." Mario Gallo, at Venice, sarcastically declared that Rossellini's problem did not exist ("If priests, magistrates, and doctors actually behaved like this, we would have real reason to despair not only of Europe '51, but of Europe '61, '81, '91"), then, after the Rome opening, Gromo rejected Rossellini's solution as well. The Socialist *Avanti!* charged that *Francesco* had been "insincere," *La macchina* "decidedly badly-made," *Stromboli* "exasperating," and now *Europe '51*, whose Irene lacked "true and proper social solidarity," resembled "the questioning of a medieval man who, waking up today in Europe '51 or '52, after long lethargy, suddenly notices that the world is divided into rich and poor and a social problem exists."[98]

These critics—all from the left—had a point. The Christian Democrats had gained political control through an alliance with big industry while abandoning Catholic social doctrine. The result was Italy's "economic miracle." But the miracle was based on low wages, union repression, high unemployment, and the denial of any share in the miracle for the working classes. Rossellini was glossing over the actuality of class warfare by suggesting that charity and tolerance were sufficient solutions.

But Catholics too lined up against the film. *Rivista del Cinematografo* liked the anti-Communism, but disliked Irene leaving her husband ("Saints don't do that"), and judged the movie a botched compromise between thesis and art. Ghelli (*Bianco e Nero*) pointed out that it was probably the first film to deal religiously with "the essential problems of the philosophy of existence," but he lamented that Rossellini declaims the spiritual more than he describes it, and entrusts his message more to intensity of emotion than to poetry. Rossellini showed emotion only toward Irene, said Rondi. How, wondered Lo Duca (*Cahiers du Cinéma*), could Rossellini not have seen that his film was turning into bad propaganda? How could he have used actors who overwhelm his ideas with their nullity? Didn't he notice how every time Ingrid isn't in close up, soap-opera caricatures take over and even the montage comes loose?[99]

Moravia recalled that Irene is modeled on Simone Weil, "perfectly personifying that third force" between capitalism and communism; Weil, like Irene, thought modern labor a curse no revolution could alleviate. "But

Simone Weil, apparently so solitary and desperate and rebellious to every order or constituted society, was supported by culture astounding for its encyclopedic vastness and intellectual sharpness. Rossellini, discounting Weil's communion with great European cultural traditions, has stripped from the third force its most valid justification. Weil can easily be defended intellectually, but reduced to emotions, as here, [she] becomes eccentric, self-destructive, and above all isolated in a way Weil never knew, because Weil was the expression of a whole society, that of Europe's highest culture. . . . This is the film's conceptual weakness: Irene's purely sentimental position, her real isolation, which cannot exist in reality; even Indian santons and hermits are part of human society." Characters, moreover, are carelessly improvised; the narrative is demonstration, not drama. Still, it took courage to bring to the screen questions usually forbidden there.[100]

"To fall for having dared too much is not to fall badly, not at all," Lanocita admitted *(Corriere della Sera).*[101]

What *was* "enormously interesting," Di Giammatteo thought, is how Rossellini runs in terror from reality, hides in insanity, and claims that only conformists regard Irene as crazy—when in fact Irene *is* crazy: unable to break out of the solitude caused by her son's suicide, she makes solitude her *raison d'être.*[102]

In contrast, the critics couldn't find words superlative enough for Bergman. "Perhaps never before has she shown the measure of her talent in so clear, vibrant and communicative a manner as in this impossibly difficult and thankless role," Moravia admired. "The only way to endure *Europe '51,*" Lo Duca instructed, "is to let yourself be hypnotized by the 'presence' of Ingrid Bergman, which is far from impossible. . . . If the film had been nothing but a monologue for her, only *for her,* we would have believed in it. It may even be that the actors we found so bad actually aren't, but only seem like mere larva next to Ingrid."[103] Though disqualified for a Venice award since her voice had been dubbed by an Italian, Bergman won the Nastro d'Argento as the year's best actress.

And Roberto? What was his reaction to the unanimous verdict that he had betrayed himself, neo-realism, and history?

"He didn't give a damn," said Morlion. "The more they went on, the more he was convinced he was correct and had every right to continue straight ahead in the direction he had been going." Truly he was impervious. Roberto never gave his critics' doubts the slightest credit: they were all part of the problem. "All the political forces hated [*Europe '51* because] they felt exposed," he claimed years later.[104]

In 1954 Roberto, in an interview in a Catholic magazine, explained that, along with *Paisà* and *Francesco, Europe '51* was his favorite of his movies, because "I felt I expressed myself with the most sincerity. . . . I want my cinema to be a message of faith, of hope, of love . . . , an appeal to humanity. . . . In all my films there's an anxiety for faith, hope, and love . . . , there's always the problem of the spiritual, of the decline of human values." *Deutschland* showed people looking at life again with new eyes after the war; *Stromboli* tried to get Karin to look at the giver of life. "*Europe '51* depicts man's retreat into himself. It came out seeming more anguished, less constructive, due mainly to the fact that my earlier point, *Stromboli*, wasn't understood. In contrast to Karin, who solves everything for herself, Irene is in my opinion a martyr through the lack of understanding of those around her. Everyone is worried, but no one is capable of understanding and helping this woman. . . . Irene lives in a community of moles, and so she feels pity. This feeling of pity seems to me the most human gesture in the whole film, thus becoming a gigantic rock on which to build. It's basically man's participation in the divine spark. . . . Many people have accused me of ambition, of presuming to present the whole European world; they've generalized negatively, without understanding that I was trying to establish a dialogue between a suffering humanity worrying over ideals and hopes, and Him who gives that humanity its justification and meaning. . . . A dialogue of simplicity and humility in search of faith. If humanity were to rediscover faith I am convinced it would have the solution to its every anguish and every torment. Faith like love of one's neighbor, humbly, simply, joyfully. I've been comforted and sustained by many letters from people of every sort and station declaring they understood what I was trying to say, which is that people need to be helped, because they feel lost and abandoned. It's the start on the way to God. For this reason I believe *Europe '51* is a step forward in respect to *Stromboli*."[105]

Roberto had a few defenders. In *Bianco e Nero* Visentini called *Europe '51* "probably the greatest work cinema has produced since the war." In *Filmcritica* Edoardo Bruno called it "one of the most important, the most up-to-date, the most perceptive. . . . [Rossellini] shows an inner itinerary with the piercing light of an S-ray machine." In *Il Piccolo* Cosulich said Rossellini "is probably the only director who openly invites our cinema not to limit itself to the simple recording of phenomena and conflicts, but to give the most unprejudiced interpretation of them." Contini (*Il Messaggero*) praised *Europe '51*'s "genuine originality in language, fluid cutting and elaborate camera movements, all regulated by the rhythms of the drama." And in Paris Claude Mauriac, fascinated with Irene's complex ambivalence, said that *Europe '51* attains "true grandeur and true beauty," and hailed Rossellini's courage at "deliberately ignoring one of the fundamental rules of the movie game—that the audience's own moral comfort is not to be threatened."[106]

And there was Fellini. Told *Europe '51* had been unconvincing, he retorted that critics were usually too abstract, blind to physical beauty, and wrong to be suspicious of Rossellini's new directions. "I always like him. I like everything he does."[107]

Basically the problem with the critics was their intellectual resistance to melodrama. Naturally Chaplin liked *Europe '51*. He'd come to Europe in September 1952 in the midst of a rabid press campaign accusing him of anti-Americanism, Communist sympathies, and sexual turpitude, in response to which the U.S. government had revoked his reentry permit. Like Roberto, Chaplin resolved not to return. The two America victims had met in Los Angeles. Chaplin had admired *Open City*, and Roberto had recently spent a day "venerating" *Monsieur Verdoux* again and again.[108] In Rome in late December, Chaplin phoned to say he couldn't come over; he was besieged by reporters and couldn't escape the Grand Hotel. No problem, replied "Napoleon," as Chaplin called Roberto, who appeared in person soon after to lead the comedian to freedom via the hotel's kitchens. They were still rapt in conversation at six the following morning.

Later that day Marcella took Chaplin to see *Europe '51*. It was in Italian, and she had to explain details, but Chaplin appeared to understand without her help. He cried from one end of the movie to the other, like a fool, completely without restraint. Marcella was embarrassed. "It was the story of my mother," Chaplin explained. "She was unusual, she had ideas for humanity; she died in a clinic too."[109]

In both men's films the magic moment is always an ingenuous impulse of love, "a spark of the divine"—as in *City Lights* when the tramp looks at the blind girl. Or as in "Shadow and Substance," a story Chaplin gave as a gift to Roberto, about a Nannina-like creature in a monastery, where all the monks, seemingly good, are really bad, and she good. Chaplin proposed that Orson Welles play the abbot.

Italia mia

Meanwhile, Roberto's friends on the left had been making valiant efforts to save him from himself. On May 20, 1952, Antonello Trombadori addressed an open letter to him in *Vie Nuove*: "Why have you turned your back on your characters? These characters are the godparents of the revived Italian cinema and will go around the world as qualified ambassadors of our pains and our hopes. Don't you see that they're not dead? . . . And aren't you afraid that, in losing sight of them, you may lose the very reasons, most intimate and true, of your art and of your humanity?"

Trombadori's phrases rang of *commedia dell'arte*, the better to conjure the fidelity of art and politics. Some months later the summons was renewed and clarified by Massimo Mida. Rossellini's problem, he wrote, was his "retreat" from "choral" films, from documentary, in favor of *Europe '51*'s abstract characters and the "smell of falsity." But there was "a reason for hoping Rossellini will rediscover his fullest form. . . . With *Italia mia*, a 'reportage' on the Italy of today, Zavattini can indeed lead Rossellini back to the characters that have made him famous all over the world . . . and to his most authentic inspiration."[110]

According to Zavattini, Zavattini had originally contracted for *Italia mia* ["My Italy"] with Vittorio De Sica, to whom he had sent a four-page synopsis for three stories in September 1951. Then he and De Sica had accepted an offer from Selznick to make a film in America, but Zavattini, a Communist fellow-traveler, had been denied a U.S. visa. Whereupon in

1. Brother Renzo, Roberto, sister Marcella, cousin Eugenio, grand uncle Zeffiro.

2. Father Angiolo Giuseppe Rossellini.

3. Mother Elettra, Marcella, Renzo, Roberto (1910), from the magazine *L'Illustrazione Italiana*.

4. *La nave bianca.*

5. *Un pilota ritorna.* Massimo Girotti,
home at last (end of film).

6. *L'uomo dalla croce.*

7. *L'uomo dalla croce.* Alberto Tavazzi,
Roswitha Schmidt, Attilio Dottesio.

8. *Desiderio*. Roswitha Schmidt in center.

9. *Roma città aperta*. Rossellini on location. This DeVry camera was also used for *Paisà*.

10. Anna Magnani, Vito Annicchiarico.

11. *Roma città aperta.* Rossellini, Sergio Amidei.

12. At the first screening of *Roma città aperta* at U.S. Information Agency (August 28, 1945). Klaus Mann, Rod Geiger, Maria Michi, Andy Anderson, Stan Miller, Rossellini.

Caricatures drawn by Federico Fellini

14. Rod Geiger, Fellini.

Caricatures drawn by Federico Fellini

15. Rod Geiger.

16. Photo of Fellini pasted onto his cartoon of "the saints": Geiger, Fellini, Rossellini.

17. Aldo Fabrizi, Bill Tubbs, Rod Geiger (Rome, 1946).

18. *Paisà*: "Florence." Renzo Avanzo, Fellini, Harriet White.

19. *Paisà*: "Florence." Renzo, Roberto, Romano, on the set.

20. *Paisà*: "The Po Delta." (Starting third from left): Achille Siviero (Cigolani), Fellini, Dale Edmonds, Rossellini.

21. *Paisà*: "The Po Delta." The infamous German generator.

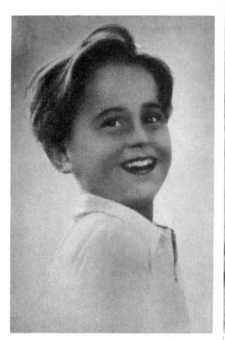

22. Son Romano.

23. Romano, first wife Marcella De Marchis.

24. Roswitha Schmidt, Roberto, Romano (Venice, 1946).

25. New Year's Eve, 1946–47. Anna Magnani and Rossellini join the party at Rome's 57 Club.

26. *Deutschland im Jahre Null.*
Edmund dead.

27. *Deutschland im Jahre Null.* Frame enlargement.

28. *Deutschland im Jahre Null.* Edmund Meschke, Rossellini.

30. *L'amore*: "Il miracolo." Anna Magnani, Federico Fellini.

29. *L'amore*: "Una voce umana."
Anna Magnani.

31. *La macchina ammazzacattivi*. Frame enlargement.

32. *La macchina ammazzacattivi.*
The *commedia* begins.

33. *Stromboli.* Ingrid Bergman.

34. *Stromboli.*

35. *Stromboli.*

36a, 36b. *Stromboli*: the miracle. Frame enlargements.

37. *Francesco giullare di Dio.*
Spinning at the end. Frame
enlargement.

38. Rossellini visits his
monks years later.

39. *Francesco giullare di Dio.*
Aldo Fabrizi in armor.

40. *Francesco giullare di Dio.*

41. *I sette peccati capitali:*
"L'invidia."

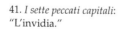

42. *Europe '51.*

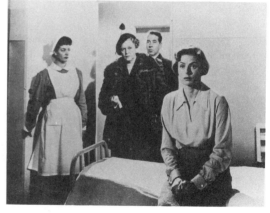

43. *Europe '51*. Frame enlargement.

44. *Europe '51*. Frame enlargement.

45. *Europe '51*. Frame enlargement.

46. *Europe '51*. Frame enlargement.

47. *Dov'è la libertà . . . ?*

48. "The Chicken."

49. *Voyage in Italy.* Ingrid Bergman, George Sanders.

50. *Voyage in Italy.* Frame enlargement.

51. *Voyage in Italy.* Frame enlargement. "Life is so short."

52. *Voyage in Italy.* Frame enlargement.

53. *Voyage in Italy.* Frame enlargement.

54. *Voyage in Italy.* Frame enlargement. Final shot.

55. *Fear.*

56. *Fear.* Frame enlargement.

57. Son Robertino, twin daughters Isabella and Isotta, with mother Ingrid Bergman.

58. *Napoli '43.*

59. *Giovanna d'Arco al rogo* (theater version).

60. Filming *Giovanna d'Arco al rogo.*

61. *Giovanna d'Arco al rogo.*

62. *India Matri Bhumi.*

63. *India Matri Bhumi.*

64. *India Matri Bhumi.*

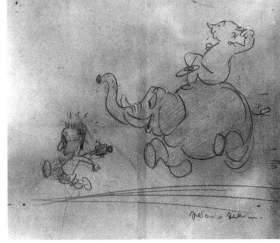

65. Drawing by Federico Fellini of Rossellini and Tonti in India.

67. *Era notte a Roma.*

66. *Il generale Della Rovere.* Rossellini,
Hannes Messemer, Vittorio De Sica.

68. *Viva l'Italia.*

69. Rossellini directs *Viva l'Italia.*

71. Renzo and Roberto Rossellini at the time of Renzo's opera, *A View from the Bridge.*

70. *Vanina Vanini.* Sandra Milo, Laurent Terzieff.

72. *Anima nera.* On the set.

73. *RoGoPaG:* "Illibatezza."

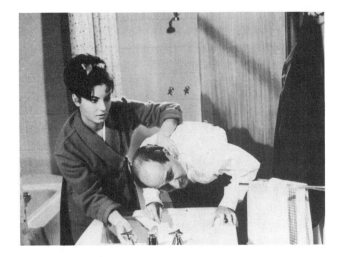

74. *RoGoPaG*: "Illibatezza."

75. *The Iron Age.* Young urine to make iron.

76. Rossellini and Sonali Sen Roy at press dinner, Savoy Hotel, Malmo (Sweden, 1965).

77. *La Prise de pouvoir par Louis XIV.*

78. *La Prise de pouvoir par Louis XIV.*

79. *La Prise de pouvoir par Louis XIV.*

80. *La lotta dell'uomo per la sua sopravvivenza.*

81. *La lotta dell'uomo per la sua sopravvivenza*

82. *La lotta dell'uomo per la sua sopravvivenza.* Christopher Columbus and son.

83. *Acts of the Apostles.*
Schüfftan mirror in place.

84. *Acts of the Apostles.*
Stephen.

85. *Acts of the Apostles.*
Edoardo Torricella
(Paul) in center.

86. *Socrates.*

87. *Socrates.* Juan Atienza (with cigarette in mouth), assistant director; Ricardo Problete (cigarette in hand), cameraman; Jorge Herrero (on Rossellini's right), director of photography.

88. Roberto, all the children, at Amalfi.

89. Roberto holds grandson Alessandro.

90. Boating off Amalfi.

91. *The Age of the Medici.*

92. *Augustine.* Rossellini, Jean Dominique de La Rochefoucauld, Dary Berkani.

93. *Blaise Pascal.*

94. *Blaise Pascal.*

95. *Cartesius.*

96. *Cartesius.*

97. *Cartesius.*

98. *Anno uno.*

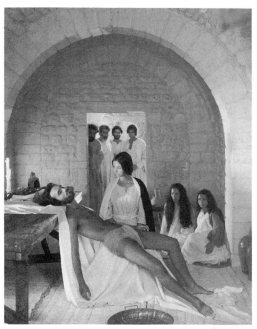

100. *The Messiah.* Mita Ungaro (Mary).

99. *The Messiah.*

101. *The Messiah.* Frame enlargement.

102. *The Messiah.* Frame enlargement.

103. *The Messiah.*

104. *The Messiah.* Rossellini on the set with Silvia D'Amico.

105. Roberto at Cannes with daughter Isabella and Alberto Sordi (1977).

April 1952 Rossellini had (according to Zavattini) invited himself into *Italia mia* (forcing the retirement of Alfredo Guarini as producer and the entry of Ponti, to whom Roberto was under contract) with the idea that they would plan the picture in June and shoot it at the end of July, and Zavattini would participate in the final montage ("the completion of the script"). And a month later Trombadori's open letter appeared—in effect urging Roberto to do *Italia mia*.

But Rossellini had then proceeded to be busy, a "phantom," until November 4, 1952, when they made an exploratory trip to Luzzara and the Po delta (and encountered Cigolani, one of the partisans "killed" in "The Po Delta"). Zavattini says Ponti then annulled their contract "for extra-cinematic reasons" (!) and Rossellini, giving Zavattini some earnest money, announced he would produce the film himself. He would shoot one episode immediately, then do *Voyage in Italy*, then complete *Italia mia*. He wanted to travel all over southern Italy, in addition to Rome and Naples "where pigs fall from the third floor." He wanted to tackle politically controversial subjects—chemical poisoning in the Cerveteri swamps, Fanfani's housing projects. Zavattini favored a populist, apolitical approach and insisted on a firm script-structure to begin with, after which Rossellini could do as he liked. But once back in Rome, Rossellini vanished into silence. "I had to go through a veritable way of the cross to get to him." Thereupon (two months later) Rossellini told him that 1953 was completely filled with other projects.[111]

According to Roberto, in contrast, Zavattini was part of an influential, politically engaged group (Roberto's friends Mida and Trombadori . . . ?) that "with the help of a certain terminology" (the press?) had cornered the market with ready-made values; made it possible for columnists "deprived of taste, intuition, and feeling" to substitute this terminology for their own judgment; created "enormous confusion"; and divided filmmakers—with the result that producers went on making "so-called commercial" movies.[112]

Nonetheless, "people wanted a try made at this artistic marriage. So a long trip was made to the Po delta and Scardovari looking for impressions and locations for the common project. At Scardovari we split up to scour the zone for inspiration. After much vagabonding we met again. Zavattini screamed at me exultantly: 'I've found it. There's a bunker with a whole family living in it.' He wondered why his enthusiasm found no echo in me, and asked, 'Don't you think that's extraordinary? A family in a bunker at the mouth of the Po?' 'No,' I replied, 'the fact doesn't seem at all extraordinary to me. With all the houses made out of cane and straw in this region, to live in a bunker is like living in a palace.' A long pause followed. Then Zavattini asked, 'Didn't you find anything?' 'Yes, I found an old friend from Scardovari who was cursing because the land was flooded on only the other side of the Po. On that side it carried the houses away but brought a wave of supplies and the affluence of government aid. 'The next time,' he mumbled between clenched teeth, 'I'll blast an opening right onto Scardovari with dynamite, because it's not fair.' "[113]

"In effect . . . , those people, after living through that tragedy, had benefited from all sorts of aid that had practically changed their [lives], while these people on the bank where we were, not having enjoyed any aid, had to go on living in the same conditions as always.

"When I told this story to my filmmaker friend and would-be collaborator, he visibly darkened and accused me of wanting to make a pro-government film.[114] So I got so mad and for a hundred-forty-four kilometers I insulted him. I dropped him at his place and left and we did not collaborate any more."[115]

Renzo Renzi was also on the Po trip. The day after encountering Cigolani, he writes, "Rossellini began to disappear. He said he had gone to visit a cemetery where his relatives were buried. That evening, after another absence, he came back insisting he had seen flying saucers. . . . Meanwhile Zavattini fretted over these absences. He had gotten enthusiastic about the delta, his curiosity drew him everywhere. In sum, he was continually at work, while his director was continually on vacation. . . . When he was there, Rossellini didn't stand out, his presence was hardly noticeable. He phoned home twice a day to Rome and followed Zavattini, who was always busier than ever. He played cards and billiards in the Porto Tolle *osteria*. Once we went to a variety show in a wooden hall. Afterward we waited together for the poor singers and dancers. Rossellini took the dancers' bags and carried them, simply. One of them, an ex-rice-weeder, told him her whole life story, then went away saying, familiarly, 'Give my best to the Mrs.!' . . . By the last day, the most intense, Zavattini had already thought up ten, twenty subjects, all told in minutiae: a shoe on the river; a little boy who goes fishing for crabs on the beach but only knows what they taste like; etc. Rossellini, on the other hand, continued his profound, stubborn laziness. In the afternoon, perhaps to spite Zavattini's busyness, he loaded him onto a little bark and had him taken out among the river canes in the valley. The rest of us, whom the bark couldn't carry, stayed on land with Rossellini shooting clay pigeons, since in the meantime Rossellini had also gotten hold of two hunting rifles.

"On the way back toward Bologna, Zavattini had lots and lots of ideas and didn't talk any more. Then Rossellini told us a wonderful story about the beach chairs, which the poor people of the delta use when they make love on the deserted beaches. How had he learned it? . . .

"Zavattini had talked about a film to be shot all in the streets, all improvised, without a real script. . . . But impressionism and improvisation weren't enough to get them together. Zavattini is curiosity, activity, duty; he writes stories to combat injustice, to get practical results, the sooner the better. Rossellini is all these things too, but he mixes in an element that can upset the whole game: contemplation. Just look at his films. He's an activist . . . but he unites activism with mystic evasion. . . . This attitude is reflected even in his character. His uncertainties, his failures, and on the practical level, films half finished, half abandoned. He gets involved and gets tired, but the tiredness comes from a sense of the vanity of action, which he then gets involved in again because, along his imagination is the other motive, moral duty. Action and contemplation playing at opposite extremes."[116]

"*Italia mia* wasn't cinema," Roberto told Trombadori, "just a series of photograms." (Photograms are Italian comic books that use photographs instead of cartoons.)

"The Chicken"

The small world of Santa Marinella should have comforted someone as insecure as Ingrid. Besides Roberto, three children plus Renzo occasionally, two governesses, five or six servants, her own secretary, her caretaker's family of five, her three dogs (one cocker spaniel, one Labrador named Loiacomo after Totò in *Dov'è*, one bull-terrier Strombolicchio), a cage full of doves, and a couple dozen chickens roaming around, there were all the guests.

But the intimate movie Roberto made with Ingrid that fall of 1952 shows a fretful soul, one perpetually redeemed by her sense of humor, but concerned about clean floors and tidy dinner parties and threatened by Santa Marinella's convivial confusion. "Ingrid Bergman" or "The Chicken" is an episode in an anthology film, *Siamo donne* (*We the Women*), in which actresses re-enact scenes from their private lives, "neo-realistically," as it were. Anna Magnani, for example, recreates one of her early vaudeville acts in an episode directed by Visconti. The omnibus film was a typical Zavattini idea; he produced and scripted as well. An Alida Valli episode is directed by Gianni Franciolini, an Isa Miranda by Luigi Zampa, and one with two aspirants, who won a *Film d'Oggi* contest for the chance and were never heard of again, is directed by Alfredo Guarini.

Ingrid recounts a comic quarrel over an obnoxious neighbor's chicken that so pesters her that she steals it and hides it in a cupboard, only to have her perfidy unmasked in front of guests and the neighbor. "Ingrid represented the opposite of Anna," Roberto said. "She was innocent, tender. She forced herself to act rationally, whereas Anna was suspicious and violent. Ingrid was absolutely timid, feared everything, even being in public. She dressed badly. She was maladroit."[117]

"The Chicken" is a story of embarrassment, humiliation, confession, and of being stripped naked, as *Fear* would be. But it is played as comedy, the most genial movie Rossellini made, an honest portrait by a man about a woman he loved—but, as neo-realism, honest more in faithfulness to Rossellini's feelings than to Bergman's actuality. Ingrid's three children and Loiacomo are also in it. "It was just a piece of fun," said Roberto. "It was almost all improvised. It's not something that really happened, but it's true to life."[118]

A few critics saw the movie for what it is.[119] Di Giammatteo even declared it the best Rossellini film since the war trilogy.[120] But most critics, although conceding it had a certain grace, were overwhelmed by its "inconsequentiality" and disturbed by its fun.[121] "Sometimes graceful, but too preoccupied with the vapidity of its subject" read one notice. "Least successful because least meaningful," read another. "It may be that Ingrid Bergman actually did fight with a neighbor over a chicken, but that's not enough," read a third. And Penelope Houston in the prestigious *Monthly Film Bulletin* waxed censorious: "The episode with Ingrid Bergman, gazed at with family eye, simply embarrasses. The actress and the director have confusedly recounted an inconsistent, semiserious episode that needed a particularly light touch. They weren't able to give it."[122]

To such criticism Rossellini would likely reply: "That means I'm a cretin." Why are almost all his detractors blind to the obvious? Embarrassment, confusion, and inconsistency are Rossellini's choices, not his mistakes.

Otello

One of the things Roberto had been doing that December while Zavattini had been hunting for him was staging a production of Verdi's *Otello* with Ramon Vinay and Renata Tebaldi, Gabriele Santini conducting, that opened the season at Naples's San Carlo Opera House. "The lyric theater has to be renovated," its superintendent, Pasquale Di Costanzo, declared, on inviting Rossellini. Said Roberto, "I'd never set foot on a stage, the experiment attracted me." He reread Shakespeare and Boito's libretto, listened to records, and tried not for a "neo-realist interpretation" but an orthodox one without the crust of "tradition" unforeseen by Verdi and Boito.

He was not charmed by opera singers. "It's all this talking about the voice and the notes and the tones—oh God, they're so boring. And they have no idea what's going on in the world. They have no idea if a war is going on, or if we're being attacked by Martians. They just don't care. It's all this tra-la-la-là! The only thing in their lives is the sound of their voices and the next aria."

But he bowed before the exigencies of operatic casting. "Iago is sly, perfidious, ironic. He should have a wretched physique equal to his character. But Iago is a baritone and the role falls to Gino Bechi, who's as tall and athletic as Otello. Then we have the opposite phenomenon: Cassio, who in the tragedy is a kind of Ridgeway succeeding MacArthur. He must be played by the second tenor Piero De Palma, who's the smallest of three central characters." So Roberto gave him elevated shoes.[123]

Before and during the performance Roberto was uncontrollably nervous. As was Ingrid. "It was all so thrilling," she exclaimed. "Roberto has done very well and I am so proud of him. I never saw the opera before, but those who have say there is no comparison. Roberto has caught the stage bug and talks of nothing else but what to do next in the theater or the opera. . . . Everybody loves him at the opera. He is so *calm*, they say. I almost died! That he could make all those singers move around and act like normal people is a miracle."[124]

Rossellini's *Otello* was greeted as an exceptionally fine production.[125]

David Selznick had come to Rome that fall. Jennifer Jones was shooting *Indiscretion of an American Wife* with De Sica and, as King Vidor said, when it came to Jones "[Selznick] definitely had an obsession. He would breathe hard when he watched her scenes on the screen, and even as they were being shot."[126]

"Every day," De Sica said, "he sent me forty- or fifty-page letters, detailing everything. They were in English; when I translated them, I arrived at work no earlier than noon. So I stopped reading them and began throwing them away as soon as they arrived. I would agree with everything he said and do things my own way. . . . The film was made for Jones. . . . She was hypersensitive in real life. . . . I had terrible problems with that production. I produced the film myself and spent my own money to rent Terminal Station at night and to fill it with trains and people. At least twice, she arrived distraught, having quarreled with her husband, Selznick, and she threw her hat in the toilet, so that we had to fish it out because we had only one which she used in every scene in the film. Then she took her shoes off and ran back barefoot to the hotel, leaving me and all the other people in the railroad station. Twice she pulled that trick on me, and it cost me four million lire each time."[127]

Jennifer Jones began her next picture immediately, John Huston's *Beat the Devil*, with Ingrid's old partner from *Casablanca*. They would go on location a few miles from where Ingrid was to film her third collaboration with Roberto. In a mid-December letter to Joe Steele she was philosophical. "[George] Sanders saw [*Europe '51*], and didn't like it—so what can you do? Chaplin and Selznick love it—so what can you do? Humphrey Bogart says he dislikes everything Roberto does—even without looking at it—so what can you do? . . . [Sanders] will be here [in Naples] on the 4th [of January], but so far we have no script, not even an outline, just an idea with no ending."[128]

Voyage in Italy[1]

To write the lives of the great in separating them from their works necessarily ends by above all stressing their pettiness, because it is in their work that they have put the best of themselves.   —Simone Weil

"George Sanders looked at me," wrote Ingrid, "and said, 'What is this? I'm coming here to do *Duo* and now it's going to be something else? He's changed his mind?'"[2]

"My agent," Sanders recalled, "had told me there was no script, but this had caused me no particular concern because even in Hollywood I had often started on films without a script.... When I arrived in Rome, however, I was informed that there would never be a script.... In this somewhat pathologically jocular mood ... I decided to persevere in the strange adventure, although my misgivings increased with every passing day."[3]

Sanders was receiving $60,000 for his perseverance, and had come to Italy to escape Hollywood and a collapsing marriage with Zsa Zsa Gabor. He enjoyed playing the snob. He would have been bemused had he known his director was being paid with an apartment instead of a salary, and this because Roberto's financier, a Roman contractor named Adolfo Fossataro, had built an apartment house at 62 Viale Bruno Buozzi so modern-looking that he hadn't been able to get anyone to live in it—until he gave away the ten-room top floor to Roberto and a lower floor to Totò.

To get actual money, Roberto came up with—in his opinion—a brilliant idea. The production budget would be paid out to him in weekly allotments, and what he did not spend each week he could pocket. "People talk about neo-realism and a heap of other things in regard to Rossellini," scoffed Sanders; "it's a fantasy. In reality, if Rossellini shoots on the streets, it's because sets cost money. I've seen stingy people, but I've never met anyone who could equal him."[4] Even so, Roberto's deal backfired: by never working more than four hours a day and not at all on many days, he went over budget nearly every week and had to pay the difference out of his own pocket.

Duo had been abandoned because the rights to Colette's novel had already been sold, leaving Roberto, at the last moment, with cast and crew already in Naples and rearing to go, freer than even he wished to be, to do as he liked. Colette's 1934 book had dealt with a fashionable marriage ending in suicide when a tradition-bound husband is unable to respond to his wife's needs and the wife refuses to feel apologetic for an old love affair. The story had appealed to Roberto's lifelong fascination at the non-correspondence between people's dress and appearance and their emotions, and he retained Colette's conflict for his non-Colette film, adding a third character absent in Colette to draw out those subterranean emotions: the raw world of nature—Naples—in which the fashionable, hothouse couple would find themselves immersed like the GIs in Italy in *Paisà*.

Roberto liked to contend that clothes long ago divided civilization into two categories. Sanders and Bergman would represent "sewn" civilization, whose dependence on animal skins had produced efficiency. But the movie would introduce them to "draped" (toga-like) civilization, with its sweeter, more relaxed, less alienated, less artificial concept of life.[5] "A great many couples are real companies . . . , partnership ventures. They marry because one of them can do a certain type of work, while the other has a certain number of acquaintances. So the wife does the public relations, the husband is the economic operator. . . . That's all their life is. The couple in *Voyage in Italy* is well matched this way. They're people who—outside of work, their job, their daily duties—don't know what to say. It's vacation that depresses them, especially vacation. The fact of becoming owner of a beautiful villa in one of the most beautiful areas of the world counts for nothing, because they don't know what to say any more. . . . What the film shows is sudden, total isolation. . . . It struck me that the only way a rapprochement could come about was through the couple finding themselves complete strangers to everyone else."[6]

Thus the third character, Naples. "It was very important for me to show Italy, Naples, that strange atmosphere in which a very real, very immediate, very deep feeling is mixed, the feeling of life eternal. It's something that's completely disappeared from the world."[7]

Voyage in Italy, like *Il miracolo*, would be another "message of faith, hope, and love." Once again "the problem of the spiritual, of the decay of human values" would be the movie's "connecting thread." "The protagonist is led to visit a cemetery: to contemplate death. For us Italians, in fact, death is only a phase in passage toward real life . . . , only a bridge. . . . Naples is the site of the film because it's the city of the oldest things, projected into the real future, with an innate, quasi unconscious comprehension of eternal values and truth."[8]

Roberto also drew heavily on a script, *New Vine*, by Antonio Pietrangeli about a quarreling English couple touring Naples in a Jaguar, an Uncle Homer, and the unearthing at Pompeii of a couple making love; but the Pompeii sequence is not a climax and the script's drama is quite different.[9] Roberto had the novelist Vitaliano Brancati on the set during part of the shooting, and the two had put together a thirteen-page synopsis (which we have not found), in which the romanticism of a poem instigates the couple's crisis; but neither this poem nor much else from this synopsis, whose ending was different, got into the finished movie, and in any case Roberto kept its existence a secret.[10] As far as anyone connected with the production knew, not even an outline existed. This meant no one knew which actors would be needed when or where, what costumes they would need or what props, how a set would be decorated, or even if there were to be a set. Just before shooting was to begin Marcello D'Amico, the production manager whose duty it was to know all these things, cornered Roberto at the Continentale, where he and Ingrid and the three children were taking up most of a floor, and insisted he reveal what would be done the next day. Roberto, tearing two leaves from the account books, icily wrote 340 words (in Italian) covering five pages of the double-folded leaves (see Figure 2). It was more than D'Amico had asked for, and all he would ever get.[11] Roberto chased him away the next time, so viciously he was afraid to come near him again and had to depend on what he could learn from Enzo Serafin, the director of photography.

"We have finally started," Ingrid wrote after Rossellini began on February 2, 1953. "It started with a lot of titles, but Roberto came out with *Viaggio in Italia*. Although I don't think it's too good, there's always a certain

FIGURE 2. Rossellini's outline for *Voyage in Italy* (translated from Italian).

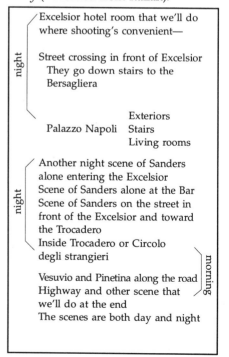

Car trip
Bentley

day
A straight stretch on road to Terra-cina near km 94 and we stop just before first curve before Terracina alongside fields on left where the buffalo are

Stop at Terracina precisely at the bar on the road out of Terracina, at the corner before the turn off for the sea.
(try to do it with hidden camera as much as possible)
Stretch of road to Formia where are walls on either side—

night
Poggioreale scene. Some streets in Naples now from inside the car
Arrival at the Excelsior

night
Excelsior Lobby arrival scene
" " when they go to bar
Excelsior Bar

night
Excelsior hotel room that we'll do where shooting's convenient—

Street crossing in front of Excelsior
They go down stairs to the Bersagliera

Exteriors
Palazzo Napoli   Stairs
Living rooms

night
Another night scene of Sanders alone entering the Excelsior
Scene of Sanders alone at the Bar
Scene of Sanders on the street in front of the Excelsior and toward the Trocadero
Inside Trocadero or Circolo degli strangieri

morning
Vesuvio and Pinetina along the road
Highway and other scene that we'll do at the end
The scenes are both day and night

FIGURE 2 (Continued)

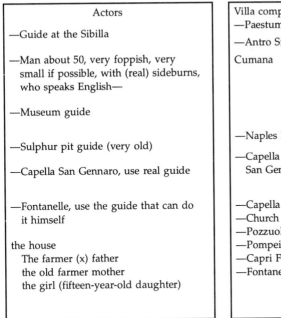

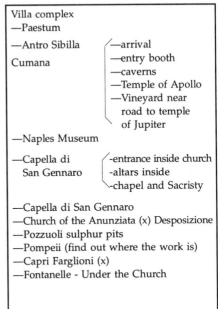

(x) indicates an indecipherable word.

```
Sibilla

Antro

                first group to
Villa           be prepared

Museum
where the biggest material is needed
_____

—Bentley
Topolino giardinetto with NA license
  plate
1100 Cabriolet Musetta or Augusta
```

style to all of Roberto's titles.... Sanders has had several nervous breakdowns due to not even seeing *one* word on paper. He has been quite a problem, even though he hasn't yet begun to work in the picture."[12]

Said Sanders, "I was in a state of such bewilderment that I asked Rossellini to release me from the picture."[13]

Ingrid too began to doubt. Roberto went on filming her staring at ancient Roman statues in Naples's National Museum, day after day, for two entire weeks, in freezing cold. But not all day. "Before noon, I'm a cripple, I can't work," her director admitted.[14]

Sanders didn't like getting up early either. So when Roberto needed a shot of him getting off the Capri ferry, which docked at 10 A.M., and wasn't prepared to go there himself at that hour and thus couldn't ask Sanders to either, he instructed the cameraman to photograph any tall man he could find.

"My interest," said Sanders, "was reduced to a state bordering on stupefaction. Nevertheless, it was impossible to say what contribution these scenes made to the picture as a whole, as the story of the film was never understood at any time, by anyone, least of all by the audience when the picture was released."[15]

Distraught, Sanders took to calling Zsa Zsa and his psychiatrist nightly, trans-Atlantic. Roberto was incredulous. "Fifty dollars an hour just to talk to a psychiatrist! In Italy you go to confession and the priest says, 'You will repeat 25 Hail Marys and go in peace, my son.'"[16] Zsa Zsa stopped by for two days in mid-February, on her way to a rendezvous with her lover, and, according to her, cheered George up by reenacting a supposed love session with a priest whom they had met on a train and whom kinky George had urged her to have sex with.[17]

Sanders finally had his turn before the camera after production moved to a villa belonging to the Conte Caetani on strada Vesuviana in Torre del Greco, about 25 miles from Naples—a perfectly lovely villa without heat or bathrooms. But Sanders would often arrive in the wrong clothes (since no one knew what the right ones were), whereupon he would be driven back to his hotel to change while Roberto and the crew happily played cards. Or Sanders, waiting as instructed in his hotel lobby, would be simply forgotten. One day he was waiting at two in the afternoon. "When the car finally came at 4:30 A.M. the following morning I was unready, unwilling, unable, unshaven, and having lost all sense of proportion calling long distance to Zsa Zsa, who could not come to the phone anyway because she was under the hair dryer. I was led like a man in Sing Sing's Death House to the waiting car which whisked me away to some Neapolitan back street where Rossellini had set up the camera to shoot the momentous scene for which we had all been waiting so patiently. He had his scarlet racing Ferrari with him [a new one!] and he kept eyeing it and stroking it while the cameraman was fiddling with the lights, getting the scene ready. Finally when all was ready Rossellini changed his mind about shooting the scene and dismissed the thunderstruck company. While we watched him in stupefied silence he put on his crash helmet, climbed into the Ferrari, gunned his motor, and disappeared with a roar and screeching tires round the bend of the street and out of our lives for two whole days. . . . [W]hen he returned . . . he retired to bed [with a migraine headache] while the company sat around for another whole day."[18]

When Roberto did get to work, the crew could always escape by exploiting his love for skin diving. "One of the men," Sanders reported, "would come running up to the great Maestro and, looking back over his shoulder with breathless excitement, point out to sea. 'There!!! *Out there, out there!!!!*' he would cry. 'A huge fish as big as this.' And with arms outstretched and awestruck face he would stare at the spot on the water he had indicated earlier. The effect on Rossellini of this little charade could not have been more electrifying than if he had received a full-scale jolt of insulin shock treatment. 'Wrap it up,' he would shout through teeth chattering with excitement, while with trembling hands he changed into his skin-diving outfit."[19]

On the set, Roberto's "method" was to chat for hours with Brancati. Ingrid sat knitting ("Penelope's weave," the crew called it). Sanders sat with his eyes closed. Once Roberto decided what to do, dialogue would be scribbled on shirt cuffs and they would begin, whereupon Roberto would change everything. The key—and beautiful—poem scene on the terrace was directed with Roberto stretched out half asleep. Then he moved the entire company to Capri, did nothing for several weeks, shot a single short scene at night that could have been done anywhere else, and brought everyone back to Naples. "His way of working is a poem," Sanders declared, "and since I don't appreciate at all this type of work, Rossellini said I was impossible."[20]

Ingrid was equally distraught. She couldn't improvise, she hated to improvise, which Roberto well knew. Yet whenever she'd ask what she was supposed to say, he'd snap, "Say whatever's on your mind!"[21]

"Ingrid was extraordinarily intelligent—instinctively," Roberto recalled. "But she has really such fantastic mastery of her craft that she refuses to do anything by instinct. There were constant quarrels between us, because I was improvising and she wanted to rationalize. 'But make me understand!' 'But you don't have to understand, just do it! Why do you care?' "[22]

And her marriage was floundering. "It would be hard to guess whether there was any real happiness in the relationship," wrote Sanders; "she was in tears a good many times."[23] If Roberto left she would come alive and start downing martinis. He reappeared one night unexpectedly and indignant. "I leave my poor children with you and look! I've come back to take their temperatures and you're in an alcoholic stupor!" As soon as he left she went back to her martinis.[24] The film moved to Amalfi in April, near Ravello where Bogart, Jones, Huston, Peter Lorre, and Robert Morley were shooting *Beat the Devil* and happy to see Ingrid. "I went up every night for dinner and laughs, as we don't have many laughs on our set."[25]

And her husband's antics were embarrassing her terribly; she felt responsible to her Hollywood colleague—who couldn't stand her. "I hate working with her; she's a conceited bitch," Sanders told Zsa Zsa.[26] Roberto would put his arm around him, "My friend, it isn't the first bad movie you've been in. Nor will it be the last. So cheer up."[27]

"It simply defeated him," Ingrid said. "I remember . . . in the hotel room we used as a dressing room, the tears were just pouring down his cheeks. . . .' I am so unhappy in this movie,' [he said]."[28]

"Poor George Sanders," Roberto chuckled years later. "He was so unhappy. He called me one night at four o'clock in the morning. 'What happened?' I said.

" 'I have decided to commit suicide.'

" 'I think it's a good idea.' What do you say? Just because he was unhappy in the film, it's too much to commit suicide. So I say, 'Well, what is wrong if we do another bad film? There can be another bad film. It's no damage for you, for me, for anybody in the world. So why do you want to commit suicide? I think it's too dramatic.' So he got really hurt against me and hated me deeply and made a lot of interviews saying a lot of bad things."[29]

It was all a plot. Roberto broke appointments deliberately, left the set deliberately, kept changing his mind and writing dialogue on shirt cuffs deliberately. He did more. He gave Sanders no direction, no hint about his role, ever. To the contrary, he did everything he could to intensify the actor's sense of lonely isolation. Everyone was in the same hotel, except Sanders. Everyone partied and ate together evenings, except Sanders. Even to visit him was forbidden. "It's his role, he's supposed to be like that, tense and anguished," Roberto explained.[30] Of course, he wanted Ingrid that way, too. It was his principle: if there's no "real" situation to film, create one. "You have to make [actors] work for you. You can use anything, even an actor's temper. . . . Don't you think [Sanders] was obvious for the part? It was his bad moods rather than his own personality that suited the character in the film."[31]

He worked to inspire maximum embarrassment between Sanders and Bergman. Wasn't this their situation in the film? Similarly, he worked to inspire love between Sanders and Mauban—their situation in the film. After keeping her isolated and forlorn in Naples, he threw her together with Sanders in Capri, one of his own favorite sites for romance. He even put her leg in a caste to keep her submissive. But nothing happened. So he shot the two short scenes he could have shot anywhere else, in which nothing happened: just as Alex is about to make his move, she tells him how happy she is that her husband's returning tomorrow.[32]

At Naples' Accademia delle Belle Arti on February 16, Roberto defended his methods. "The director is the one who realizes a scenario. The author is the one who from time to time creates scenes, lines, dialogues."[33] He was an author. "If we're thinking of a film spectacular, it can be correct to have an ironclad scenario. If we're thinking of a realist film such as has flourished in Italy, one which poses problems and searches for truth, one cannot proceed with the same criteria. Here inspiration plays the preponderant part. So it's no longer a question of an ironclad scenario but of film itself. A writer puts down a sentence, a page, then crosses it out. A painter uses carmine, then makes a green brush stroke on top of it. Why can't I also cross out, redo, and change? This is why a script can't be ironclad for me. If I thought so, I'd consider myself a writer, not a director. I study and think about the subjects of each of my films at length. The script is laid out, since it would be absurd to want to invent everything at the last moment. But the episodes, the dialogues, the scenery, are adapted day by day."[34]

And, years later: "You remember Ingrid, in *Voyage in Italy*, was unhappy because I made her walk all the time? But by having her walk I showed everything around her, furnished the spectator with all the elements he needed to select by himself, to see, to judge. The character, yes, but also a series of contextualized messages with which to explain her, to explain the situation in which she was, the environment in which she saw and the things she touched, and the reactions which that environment, those things couldn't help but excite in her."[35]

Skin diving, too, was part of the method. "When I chase fishes under water I resolve all the directing problems waiting to be solved; after underwater fishing, I reach the camera with clear, precise ideas in my head."[36] Serafin confirms that Roberto was unusually serene during *Voyage in Italy*. He rarely repeated scenes and listened attentively when Serafin suggested uses for the reflected-light techniques he had pioneered, and Roberto had so admired, in Menotti's *The Medium* and the famous bridge scene in Antonioni's *Cronaca di un amore*.[37] Ingrid agreed: "There was never any hesitation. He knew that he would take his camera and move it. Of course there were days when he doesn't work—when he just can't work, because he's stuck on something, he can't find it. He'll just go away on a pretense or something, or he's going to have a terrible headache, or he's going swimming, or SOMETHING, which upsets the film company. But it was just because he was searching for what the next move was going to be. Then he might shoot something that is of less value, to get to what he really wanted to do and then there would come a marvelous scene again. He doesn't work regularly. He works on his own inspiration, whenever the mood comes over him, which naturally can very often be difficult for companies to accept."[38]

Especially when they don't like the results. Nearly a year and a half would pass before *Voyage in Italy* would manage to find a distributor, and then it would be foredoomed to obscurity by a mid-summer release, July 1954. And it's hard to fault this decision, commercially. *Voyage in Italy* was not sellable even as an art film; it flies in the face of both convention and the conventions of unconventionality. Too many, of the few who saw it, saw (and see) nothing but pointless plotless meandering. "Tedious hokum," Leonard Maltin's 1991 *TV Movies* calls it.[39]

Nonetheless, Alain Bergala, who concedes the movie starts as though it's not ready to start, demonstrates that Rossellini's apparent non-events are anything but.[40] Alex and Katherine Joyce (Bergman and Sanders) drive a while; then stop and change positions; then slow down for a buffalo herd; then take a left fork while the camera gazes lingeringly toward the right, as though wanting to go *that* way instead. Is it that Rossellini can't decide? Why can't he, his couple, and his story get going, like the car that whizzes by them?

Bergala thinks Rossellini is warning us that he'll not pilot this film, nor will some know-it-all scenario take charge. "Rossellini is dreaming of an ever-alive film that at every second would give the impression that the script is not impairing the characters' liberty, that they can go as fancy pleases, right or left. . . .[41] [Thus he] begins by absenting himself as much as possible . . . , free[ing] himself from the burden of executing his own program [and] becom[ing] the curious observer of his own film-being-made."[42]

Yet Rossellini could scarcely be more present. Nor events be more predestined. Alex and Katherine will try to take charge, each in turn, all through the movie. That's why they change positions now. But they'll always fail. It hasn't occurred to them that control is mostly illusion.

ALEX: Where are we?
KATHERINE: Oh, I don't know exactly.

These are the first lines. Obviously the movies can't go straight toward a goal; the heroes are only beginning to realize they don't have one.

ALEX: I'm just bored because I've got nothing to do.
KATHERINE: This is the first time that we've been really alone ever since we married.
ALEX: Yes, I suppose it is.

Their marriage roles have become undefined and aimless. *They* have become undefined and useless. They shelter in their Bentley threatened by Italy, horrified at reckless drivers, the blood of squashed bugs, possible malaria. They're annoyed not to be in control anymore.

ALEX: What noisy people! I've never seen noise and boredom go so well together?
KATHERINE: Oh, I don't know. Uncle Homer lived here for forty years without getting bored.
ALEX: Uncle Homer was not a normal person.
KATHERINE: I must write to my mother.

They want "normalcy." They try to block out Italy, they think of writing home to mother. But old solutions are no longer relevant.

ALEX: You know, I was just thinking what a fool I was three months ago in London. It would have been so easy for me to solve the Lewis deal. There were at least three solutions that were better than the one I chose, and I just couldn't think of them.
KATHERINE: And you think of them now.
ALEX: Now they seem very clear to me.

Now there are always options. Freedom frightens, "bores." It's too arbitrary. To stop or go, right fork or left fork, may make all the difference in the world, or none at all. No scenario pilots us. This isn't London. Everything's up for grabs.

But Pirandello isn't Rossellini's point. What's real and wonderful in *Voyage in Italy* are the characters. If Rossellini can make a *ménage à trois* of two people and Naples, it's because both people and places, in his movies, are loci of feeling. Like Stendhal he romanticizes emotions and concentrates them in oppositions. A few seconds pinpoint a passion, an insight, a psychology, whose contemplation the next few seconds short-circuit with a new passion, a new perspective. Katherine makes no pause between a bitterness ("At home everything seemed so perfect") and a flirtation ("but now that we're away and alone" . . .), which Alex at first neutralizes with a gesture, then returns sardonically ("Now that we're strangers we can start all over again at the beginning. Might be rather amusing, don't you think?"), only to have Katherine reject him in turn ("Let's go down to the bar"). As they descend the stairs, a salon tune, yearning and lost, graces their bewildered voyage.[43]

We don't feel *actors* here, even if we never entirely forget we're watching Ingrid Bergman and George Sanders, because we sense we're piercing through the actor, the shell, the hyperpersonality—the "Ingrid Bergman"—that stars hide inside of. No wonder these characters always seem embarrassed!

This "pinpointing" is totally unlike Visconti or Huston. This is the antithesis of everything popular cant (and most critics) believe films are supposed to be. Rossellini never inflates an idea with rhetoric, never belabors a personality tic, never gives his perpetually off-balance actors a chance to construct a character or build a performance. Yet as with Matisse (the comparison is Mauriac's and Rivette's) there is a sureness with which each simple trait expresses the uniqueness of a character, a situation, or a feeling.[44]

"Direction of the actors is exact, imperious, and yet," Rohmer observes, "the film is not at all 'acted'.

"There are innumerable conventions of *naturalness* that have been created in movies . . . and that, over fifty years, have refined a cinematic language which, prior to Rossellini . . . , even the most original filmmakers felt they should take advantage of. They knew a certain way of winking an eye, holding the head, or moving the body would, by a sort of conditioned reflex, excite a particular emotional reaction in the spectator. . . . They made art, personal films in fact, using a common fund of conventional material. But for Rossellini this material does not exist. His actors . . . have gestures and attitudes like every other human's, but they incite us to look for *something else*, behind that behavior, than what our natural inclination as spectators would lead us to discover. The old relationship between sign and idea is shattered: in its place emerges a new and disconcerting relationship. This is the high and new conception of realism we discover here. . . . Rossellini and Murnau . . . , because they reject the easy facility of psychological style and despise innuendo and allusion, have had the extraordinary privilege of leading us into the most secret regions of the soul . . . , not the troubled zones of the libido, but the broad daylight of consciousness. Because [*Voyage in Italy* and *Sunrise*] refuse to illuminate the mechanics of choice, both films safeguard its freedom all the better."[45]

This "new disconcerting relationship" between gesture and character is often explained as a precursor of Antonioni's intense contemplations of modern alienation and neurotic identity. But it was in reaction to such themes that Rossellini campaigned for years against Antonioni's movies as utter abomination. Antonioni's existentialism is psychological and postmodern; Rossellini's is Catholic and Romantic. Antonioni is subjective: the world outside his characters radiates their subjectivity impressionistically; Rossellini's equally subjective characters always find themselves colliding with an objective reality that is stubbornly *other* than themselves and anything they can imagine. We have traced his "disconcerting relationship's" evolution from the first glimmerings of existential isolation in *La nave bianca*, *Un pilota ritorna*, and *Desiderio* through *Una voce umana*'s "individual captured, put under the microscope, [and] scrutinized to the core"[46] and *Il miracolo*'s and *Stromboli*'s relentless tracks. Always a "disconcerting something else" haunts our heroes. Rossellini's minimal direction of actors—his tendency to structure their environment rather than their characterization—had resulted in the "global" non-interpretations that so pleased Ayfre. Nonetheless his art lay in our sense that characters were not mannequins but true individuals. Their "signs" always indicated desperation, yearning, inner voids that, frighteningly, could evidence that *our own selfhood* is nothing but self-delusion socially conditioned. And wasn't this at least partially true of Roberto's self? Self and society, mutually dependent in their dialectic, one guaranteeing the other, seem sometimes merely idea and ideology: no amount of verbiage from philosophers, priests, and politicians can anchor them. For that anchor, Rossellini's heroes require *experience* so intense as to seem personal revelation. His new society requires the new man, who can be produced only when so reduced to desperation, so stripped of sustaining social and ideological props, that Reality—the "disconcerting something else"—at last overwhelms all defenses. It is tempting to see *Voyage in Italy* as an experiential paraphrase of Gerard Manley Hopkins's phrase, "The world is charged with the grandeur of God." Roberto's oft-professed claim, in his late years, that he had never believed in God, is perhaps less a brag of atheism than a confession of anguish by a man who, like Irene, wants to believe, questions his sincerity, and concludes that he does not have the faith that moves mountains, and who yet is overwhelmed amid his efforts to be rational.

In *Voyage in Italy* almost everything Katherine and Alex do in the opening scenes traces increasing dissolution of selfhood. Their switching seats should mark mutual support. But supports are in jeopardy, falling away. Her horror at insect blood marks her vulnerability to life; his horror at the speeder marks his. Countless imponderables—awkward intonations, blurted phrases, hesitations, uncertainties in carriage and gesture—lead us everywhere to sense their growing awareness that they don't know what to do next—with each other, with themselves, in all the tiny small things of life that ground their existence. They begin to doubt they know who they are. As the film begins, they have already begun their voyage through the most elaborate of Rossellini's mazes. Rossellini described the movie as "the variations in the relationships of a couple who are undergoing the influence of a third personage: the outside world around them."[47] Truffaut describes the movie as a series of variations about a "feeling," a way of being.[48]

Rossellini's direction of his actors may seem quite different from his "global" non-interpretation of Edmund in *Deutschland im Jahre Null*. Yet the difference is more quantitative than qualitative. If Edmund gave us one hint every five seconds of what may have been going on inside of him, Alex and Katherine give us twenty. Otherwise Rossellini has not changed. There is still no "acting." The person inside the actor is still revealing himself by accident and inadvertence. He succeeds in becoming a character in a fictional story only by dint of Rossellini's putting him in successive situations. Ingrid Bergman is made to walk around all the time. George Sanders finds himself hauled off in the middle of the night to mouth incomprehensible lines of disconnected dialogue in a situation he doesn't understand in a scene he doesn't understand in a story he doesn't understand about characters he doesn't understand. He hasn't the slightest notion of what's going on, and he's probably been told that he's wearing the "wrong" clothes. But Rossellini links this situation with another. And a character is born.

The process might be called "character by accretion." Or "de-cretion": Rossellini knocks stubbornly against his actors' habits as Naples presses continually against the Joyces' resistance. The outcome is thus inevitable and, regardless whether it matters who drives the car or which fork they take, everything the Joyces do comes to possess a ritualistic aura. Events press for contact with epiphany—the outpitched-startlement on the young-discus-thrower statue; the gaze out to sea when Katherine ascends to the Temple of Apollo; the Zen-like pans toward open space concluding the Pompeii sequence—and thus at every other moment the movie threatens to explode. But no, Alex and Katherine go calmly on with the process of living. Yet each near-epiphany has left its measure of irreparable disconcertion. Whether Alex or Katherine go right or left, the only real choice either will ever have is that of accepting grace.

> COUNTESS: They say that all Neapolitans are loafers. Now, I'd like to ask you: Would you say that a shipwrecked man is a loafer? In a certain sense, we are all "shipwrecked." You have to fight so hard, just to keep afloat.
> KATHERINE: Well, it looks like a very pleasant shipwreck to me!
> DUCA [an old man]: Especially when I look into your eyes. They're like stars in the night.
> KATHERINE: [laughs: becoming slightly hysterical]

Grace comes, as in *Stromboli*, without forewarning, loosening the control we thought we had. "In this film in which everything seems nonessential," writes Rohmer, "everything, even our own craziest mental digressions, is part of what's essential. You can take this claim for whatever it's worth. In face of a work on this level, one doesn't plead extenuating circumstances."[49] Alex, shipwrecked by his non-start courtship of Marie, encounters a prostitute (Anna Proclemer, Brancati's wife) in a scene so protracted, so like Murnau, so expressionistically lit that it seems to pass in a ritualized trance much like some emotional climax in Mizoguchi. *Slowly*, as she watches, he stops, looks, walks, looks again, gets in his car, drives off, stops, turns, drives back, stops, looks, turns around again, stops. Dialogue underlines what is felt even more powerfully visually: the improbability of these two encountering each other in life, their inability to communicate (like *Paisà*'s boy and black person). Alex himself finds the scene corny (as Katherine did the duke's compliment); but he cannot shelter himself from his own deep emotions (as neither could Katherine). Rossellini never tires of telling us, claims Rivette, that "human beings are alone, and their solitude irreducible. . . . Human destinies trace separate curves, which intersect only by accident; face to face, men and women remain wrapped in themselves, pursuing their obsessive monologues; delineation of the 'concentration camp world' of people without God."[50] But we're in Naples. So Alex and the prostitute, Katherine and the old duke, their mutual isolation unmarred, nonetheless give each other what each needs that moment; their lives change; it is a kind of love scene. It is improbable that such scenes would occur, but this time they do, like moments in our own lives that didn't have to happen, but do, and sometimes alter our tack.

> PROSTITUTE: Two nights ago a friend died. A woman friend. Thirty-two years old. In a nightclub. She put her head on the table. And she died.
> ALEX: But how? What of?
> PROSTITUTE: It was her heart. She had a baby seven months ago.
> ALEX: I'm sorry.
> PROSTITUTE: If you didn't call me just now, I think I would have thrown myself into the sea.
> ALEX: Well! Isn't that a little extreme?
> PROSTITUTE: Maybe. But it is what I would have done.
> ALEX: Now look here, after all, there are lots of
> PROSTITUTE: Listen, where do you want to go? To your home? Are you in a hotel? Where do we go?
> ALEX: Nowhere. Just forget it. I'll take you for a drive and then I'll drop you off wherever you want to go.

Voyage in Italy is about two people who fear to relate to anything sensual (to romantic dukes, desperate prostitutes, sexy statues, tour guides, pregnant women, flesh, sex, spaghetti, garlic, wine, scenery, their villa, bugs, buffalo, life, death, each other, themselves), who nonetheless spend the whole movie going without pause from one overwhelmingly intense spell of relating to another, until at last they consent to join in, to sing their solos confidently in a cosmic madrigal. The band plays, crowds of people parade by, a bandleader smiles knowingly at Alex and Katherine kissing. Miracles happen every day here.

Miracles are necessary when everyone is shipwrecked. Katherine, shipwrecked by flesh, is assaulted by flesh. She can handle ideas, emotions abstracted from flesh. But not flesh. She had a poet friend, now dead—

> ALEX: Were you in love with him?
> KATHERINE: No. But we got on terribly well together. I saw a great deal of him at Copling Farm. Then he got desperately ill. I couldn't even visit him. For almost a year I didn't see him. Then on the eve of our wedding, the night before I left for London, I was packing my bags, when I heard a sound of pebbles on my window. [*whistling in background*] Then, eh, the rain was so heavy that I couldn't see anyone outside. So I ran out, into the garden, just as I was. And there he stood. He was shivering with cold. He was so strange and romantic. Maybe he wanted to prove to me that in spite of the high fever he had braved the rain to see me. Or maybe he wanted to die.
> ALEX: How very poetic! Much more poetic than his verses![51]

Katherine expects the statues to be like his verses—

> *. . . temple of the spirit.*
> *No longer bodies, but pure ascetic images,*
> *compared to which mere thought*
> *seems flesh,*
> *heavy,*
> *dim*

—but gets a shock.

> KATHERINE: To think that those men lived thousands of years ago, and you feel they are just like the men of today. It's amazing! It is as if Nero or Caracalla, Caesar or Tiberius would suddenly tell you what they felt, and you could understand exactly what they were like.
> ALEX: Then they're not ascetic figures?
> KATHERINE: No, not at all. Poor Charles! He had a way all his own of seeing things. What struck me was the complete lack of modesty with which everything is expressed. There was absolutely no attempt to . . .

Rossellini had filmed her gaze at the statues as he would film her gaze at everything else, as he filmed Edmund's gaze in *Deutschland*—in "eyecuts," as Aprà calls them. In both movies, cuts from eye to object mark Katherine's or Edmund's inability either to admit or deny the world they see outside them.[52] One time Edmund admitted it and killed himself. Katherine acknowledges abstractions but fears emotional realities. Charles's verses blind her to Alex's suppressed love.

And Charles's same verses blind Alex to her suppressed physical yearning. Alex, Katherine's complement, has fewer eyecuts than she, because he is assaulted less by flesh than by emotion. Flesh he can handle. Emotions terrify him, specifically his own. Husbands are often this way in Rossellini, intellectuals, whether in the stentorian style of *Roma città aperta*'s males who console their women with high ideals, or in the banal, self-pitying, female-phobic style of Ingrid Bergman's husbands in *Stromboli*, *Europe '51*, and *Fear*. They are treated vilely by their women and can themselves be brutes, Alex too. Rossellini heroes typically react like Aeneas with Dido and cast their women from out their paths (Manfredi in *Roma*, Girard in *Europe '51*, Missirilli in *Vanina Vanina*). But in contrast, Alex not only has redeeming politeness; he is a true romantic, maybe the only one in all Rossellini. Katherine keeps him defensive.

KATHERINE: Jealous?
ALEX: Is that what you think?

***

ALEX: . . . It's your fault. The whole thing is your fault.
KATHERINE: I think you ought to know that it didn't take me long after we were married to realise what was wrong. There was always criticism in your eyes, criticism until it crushed me.
ALEX: Nonsense! But it is rather surprising to hear you say that what I felt was important to you.
KATHERINE: What do you mean?

***

ALEX: Now look, I don't want to talk about this any more. You know, I'm getting absolutely sick of this crazy country. It poisons you with laziness. I want to get back home, back to work.
KATHERINE: Oh, at last that big word! I haven't heard you mention it for some time: "work." I expect that you'll be talking about "duty" next.
ALEX: Do the words "work" and "duty" mean nothing to you since you've been here?
KATHERINE: Don't be a hypocrite!
ALEX: Now, that's enough. I think the best thing for us is to stay away from one another. I'm going to Capri.

***

KATHERINE: Tell me that you love me.
ALEX: Well if I do, will you promise not to take advantage of me?

Voyage concludes with "Tell me that you love me"; Antonioni's *La notte* with "You don't love me anymore, say it." Rossellini heroes finally manage to be ingenuous, Antonioni non-heroes perpetually wish they could.

In Crocean terms, one achieves poetry (ingenuous, idiosyncratic speech) or remains prose (collective speech). Rossellini's people suffer from a surfeit of originality, Antonioni's from an insufficiency. Rossellini's wander till grace shows them their unique role in society, Antonioni's till opiated by futility.

Similarly, Rossellini's social context is not Vidor's. In *The Crowd*, reality wears down the would-be-hero's offensives until, accepting relative insignificance, he sheds alienation by joining a movie audience as a spectator of life's cruel comedy. But in Rossellini individuals don't dissolve into crowds; there's no sort of cosmic soul. It's the Joyces' *defenses* that reality wears down until they discover not the crowd, but each other; previously spectators, they become actors—heroes. All the difference between Catholicism and Protestantism, between draped and sewn civilization, is here. Rossellini, Catholic, draped, and sensual, is the least Manichaean of major filmmakers. "Not merely Christian, but Catholic; in other words, carnal to the point of scandal," as Rivette proclaimed.[53] Thus spirit does not, as in Vidor (or Antonioni or Tolstoy[54]), strive to free itself from the world; spirit *is* the world, its other-face, as energy is to matter. In Rossellini's Naples, miracles are endemic. That the earth is alive, that even metal and stone have biological life, that this world is "not only for the living but for the departed: something eternal" (as Irene wants in *Europe '51*), is reiterated in every scene: Vesuvius's linked smoking craters; sexually-alive statues; flirtatious old-men tourguides, restaurant diners, party hosts; pregnant women; quarreling lovers; siesta lovers; Pompeii's petrified lovers; crypts of cared-for bones; pagan caves and temples; racing cars, songs, sea, sunlight.

What's special here is that the aesthetics of the miraculous are produced by direct evidence of things themselves—by the way Rossellini experiences them. The realism of neo-realism, as we know, is in the subject, not the object. In any other movie, a shot from a car speeding down a highway is smooth. In *Voyage in Italy* it bounces and wobbles—and it's the first shot in the film—with the result that, even while we protest such technical "amateurishness," we sense a specific road, in a specific countryside: a road not merely *seen*, passively, but actively and physically imposing itself upon us—disconcertingly, like the statues later.[55] ("*Voyage* manages solely by its own magic," says Rohmer, "to endow the screen with that third dimensionality that, for three years now, the best technicians of two worlds have been trying to achieve."[56] "A wonderful mise en scène that 'shows' instead of demonstrating, that 'points' instead of suggesting," says Truffaut.[57])

Specific, disconcerting, physical, alive, an imposition: such will be every person and thing in Naples. Even the spaghetti is pesky. The air, the dead, the statues *impose* on us their aliveness, their feelings—one might say, their religion. The word is flesh, the flesh is the word; that is the miracle. We don't suspect this theme when the road is obstructed by buffalo, two minutes into the movie. But I think we still sense something suspiciously miraculous about these buffalo, a suspicion set off by contrast with the

Joyces but confirmed by the buffaloes' gait, body motions, and symbiotic linkage with landscape and herdsman. When the same point is made in *India* —elephants filing toward a river—the miracle is clearer immediately, the elephants lumber awesomely. In *Italy* the miracle is partly juxtaposition: the buffalo come just after another annoyance: squashed-bug blood on the windshield. Life and death: word and flesh. Antiquities live on, dead bones are cared for, people petrified when Vesuvius erupted and buried Pompeii are still making love, fires smolder underground, waiting their chance to boil up into the world—as they smolder in the Joyces and in all Rossellini's heroes.

"This is the great heroic side of people," said Roberto, referring to the "feeling of eternal life, the presence of the miraculous" he had discovered in Naples in his youth.[58]

"Such a philosophy is foreign to the art of our time," argued Rohmer in 1955, thinking of Nietzsche, Nazism, Stalinism, and secularism in general. "The greatest works—even those most tinged with mysticism—seem to find their inspiration in a quite opposite idea. They present a conception of man as a deity—if not entirely God—which is an enormous temptation to our pride and has almost deadened us."[59]

Marcello D'Amico saved the tiny five-page "scenario" Roberto had so disagreeably given him. Twenty-one years later he gave it back to the director framed in glass. Then they broke the glass and Roberto wrote on the bottom of the last page: "Tutto qui, Roberto" ("It's all here, Roberto").

Which is not true, even though the point of this story, as it is usually told, is that it is true. What Rossellini began with was not even an outline, it was a bunch of "notes," as for *Deutschland im Jahre Null*. He then composed his movie from day to day, editing as he went. Some scenes, once he saw them in sequence, would be thrown out and new ones invented. Transitional scenes had to be invented, too, since he never worried about linking high points until later. How the various locations would function, or what would be filmed there, was also up in the air.[60] The Pompeii sequence, for example, was entirely improvised; it wasn't even planned as the climax of the movie until after it happened. Early on, Roberto had gone to meet the curator of the Pompeii excavations, and on the way had gotten Vittoria Fulchignoni to tell him about the man's book. He had then presented himself as one of the archaeologist's most ardent readers,[61] with the result that later, when something—they didn't know what—was about to be unearthed, the curator phoned Roberto at the last minute. Only while the actual excavation was being filmed did anyone know the discovery would be a couple, let alone a couple together. "We went there and it happened in front of us, there's no fakery, it's documentary!" said Serafin. "They more or less knew there would probably be somebody there, but that it would be a couple, face-to-face with the couple that is separating, that was really something! I assure you that there was no preparation."[62] Similarly, the "miracle" in *Voyage*'s final sequence was not rehearsed or even anticipated.[63] As Rossellini was filming Maiori's annual procession, a cripple dropped his crutches and walked. Almost equally fortuitously, Rossellini was using a crane, which he virtually never used, but without which he would not have been able to record the miracle when it occurred.

These events stand with Stromboli's obliging eruption as evidence of Roberto's good luck. But both events show how Roberto doggedly put himself in good luck's path. *Something* was bound to happen. And those somethings became the plot's actual author. Had a couple not been excavated at Pompeii, the sequence could not have been so spectacularly extended into the Joyces' separated-but-together flight through Pompeii's dead streets, with the awesome pan and music that reply to the banal words, "Life is so short." The entire movie would be different. Thus, as in *Roma città aperta*, Rossellini ends up filming something like a news story. *Voyage in Italy* often evokes the style of a home movie of the Joyces' remarkable vacation, because it *is* a home movie: a recording of what happened to Ingrid Bergman while her husband filmed her attempts to make love with—of all unlikely people—George Sanders (a situation her husband, not at all ingenuously, had set up), and how they went here and there, looking for something to see. But, as Croce demands, Rossellini does not simply film "history"; he re-experiences the past from a contemporary and subjective viewpoint. Thus he is quadrupally present in his movie: as organizer of the historical documents; creator of those documents; perpetrator of the events documented; and off-screen participant in the same events. But he has often not created the events themselves. If something happened at Pompeii or Maiori or another place, he had arranged to profit. He arranged to profit if something happened between Sanders and Bergman or Sanders and Mauban. He nudged possibilities along (as he had the off-screen love affair behind *Paisà*'s "Sicily"). But he didn't know *what* would happen, *how* it would happen, or even *if* something would happen. And he put his "actors" in a similar position, interdicting their ability to "perform." It isn't so much that he "concealed" from them any knowledge of the film's story or who and what their characters were—so that they *could not* possibly play a "role"—it's that he himself didn't know what the story or characters would be until they "happened."

Voyage in Italy is the closest Rossellini ever came to a subject identical with his work methods. In an oeuvre notorious even by Rossellini's own admission for unequal inspiration it stands as the sole feature tightly constructed, shot, and edited.

Ultimately even Sanders conceded. "For all his eccentricities Rossellini was a very charming man, and he treated me with every consideration. When the picture finally came to an end I found myself strangely reluctant to part company with the flamboyant Roberto, the bravely smiling though tear-stained Ingrid."[64]

In the mid-1950s Rossellini and his advocates were unambivalently lucid regarding *Voyage in Italy*'s ending. "It's better than a reconciliation," wrote Truffaut; "It's a veritable consecration taking place. The union of [Alex and Katherine] will be henceforth without defect.[65] *Voyage in Italy* is a film about a state of soul, about a difficulty in being (together) that finally becomes, by force of things, *the dignity of being* purely and simply."[66] Katherine and Alex are no longer undefined and useless.

By the mid-1960s, however, European thought had done an about face. To admit that love triumphs *because* of Catholicism now flew against the accepted wisdom that liberation was required from precisely the Neapolitan-Catholic ideology that Rossellini shows; and since that ideology *must* be false, so too the Joyces' love must be false. *Voyage*'s melodramatic excess was proof of false ideology and false romanticism, not an indication of reality. A new generation of ardent Rossellinians suddenly declared it more profound to see the ending not as Neapolitan Catholicism's inevitable overwhelming of two ideologically impoverished English Protestant liberals, but as cynical moralizing—"Oh, they're hallucinating! The marriage won't last!"

And in a much reprinted interview in *Filmcritica*, Rossellini, as he had with *Stromboli*, went along with the effort to cynicize his romanticism and to deny his characters' conversions and his own religious intentions. In contrast to his former glowing rhapsodies on the fertility of Naples's religious culture, he now lamented its futility. "What the film shows is sudden, total isolation. . . . It struck me that the only way a rapprochement could come about was through the couple finding themselves complete strangers to everyone else. You feel a terrible stranger in every way when you find yourself alone in a sea of people of a different height. It's as if you were naked. It's logical that someone who finds himself naked should try to cover himself up."

So is it a *false* happy ending?

"It is a very bitter film basically. The couple take refuge in each other in the same way as people cover themselves when they're seen naked, grabbing a towel, drawing closer to the person with them, and covering themselves any old how. This is the meaning the finale was meant to have."[67]

It's like Beethoven claiming that the *Ninth Symphony* and *Fidelio* are bestial.

And it's equally fallacious. *All* Rossellini movies tell us to grasp the moment, those after 1965 as fiercely as those before. People who object that *Voyage in Italy*'s ending is unconvincing, because it is too sudden or because this love will not last, fail to perceive that the Joyces have never actually ceased to love each other down deep, that it is fear and worry over tomorrow that has kept them apart. As in *Francesco* and *Europe '51*, to be radically "oneself" means unbridled surrender to pure impulse, and thus to proclaim a "self" that is necessarily moral and good, because fully in sync with everything—God, reality, the cosmos, soul, biological instinct, "that strange atmosphere in which a very real, very immediate, very deep feeling is mixed, the feeling of life eternal."[68]

Bazin called this "atmosphere," this Naples, a Naples filtered by the players' consciousness—sometimes enriched thereby, sometimes "poor and limited, because the heroine's mediocre, middle-class consciousness is itself of a rare spiritual poverty. The film's Naples is not false, however (whereas a three-hour documentary's might be), but a mental landscape simultaneously objective like pure photography and subjective like pure consciousness."[69]

This subjective realism, Rossellini had then argued, is true "neo-realism," purer and deeper than his earlier films.[70] Like Murnau's "realism," which Rossellini adored, it is expressionistically based in mental landscapes; like *Sunrise* and *Tabu*, Rohmer argued, it makes "nature the active element, the principal element in the story." (*See Figure 1 in Chapter 12.*) But *Voyage in Italy* goes beyond *Sunrise*, proclaiming not only order but disorder as well: the miracle. "We accompany the heroine along the spiritual path that leads from the platitudes of the ancients on the fragility of man to the Christian idea of immortality. And if the film succeeds—logically, you could say—through a miracle, it is because that miracle was in the order of things whose order, in the end, depends on a miracle."[71]

At first glance, then, Rossellini would appear to be marshaling heavy infantry against human self-determination. Nature is the only active element; environment determines us; order is proclaimed; and in this order it is business-as-usual that miracles perpetually disrupt things. "Very bitter" indeed.

Yet Rohmer insists that Rossellini shows "the broad daylight of consciousness" and refuses "to illuminate the mechanics of choice in order all the better to safeguard its freedom."[72] And Rivette insists on the same paradox: "One simply has to compare the miracle in [Hitchcock's] *The Wrong Man* with the one in *Voyage in Italy* to see the clash between two diametrically antithetical ideas, not only of grace (in the first film, a reward for zeal in prayer; in the second, pure deliverance lighting, within the very moment of despair, upon raw faith that is totally unaware of itself), but also of freedom, and to see that this preoccupation with necessity—or with logic, to use one of Rossellini's favorite terms—is carried to such lengths by these film-makers only the better to affirm the characters' freedom and, quite simply, to make it possible: a freedom quite impossible, on the other hand, in the arbitrary worlds of Cayatte [*Oeil pour oeil*, '57] or Clouzot [*Espions*, '57], in which only puppets can exist. What I say of recent film-makers is also true, it seems to me, for the whole of cinema, starting with the work of F. W. Murnau; and *Sunrise* remains a perfect example of rigorous dialectical construction."[73]

The dialectical attitude of Catholicism, like the attitude of most faiths, is that creation is sustained at every moment by miracle and thus we are contingent creatures, yet nonetheless that self-determination is part of the miracle. One could argue that in *Sunrise* finding Janet Gaynor alive is unlikely and presented as a miracle, whereas in *Voyage in Italy* finding Katherine and Alex in each other's arms is merely inevitable, due not only to the steady pressure of grace (Naples), but to a condition obvious from the first scene: that they *choose* to love each other. As in a South Sea Island picture, the lovers gracefully succumb as much to the beauty in themselves as to the sea, flowers, and surrounding sky. This "miracle" is constant, continuous, in every moment of life; it is life. Yet nonetheless Katherine and Alex choose it; it is freedom. "The Incarnation mixes the supernatural into daily life," wrote Amédée Ayfre. "With the couples in *Stromboli, Voyage,* and *Fear,* only by the manner of presentation do their vicissitudes of tenderness, jealousy, and indifference become more than psychological flux and become charged with a weight of eternity. Grace or miracles intervene never as a rupture or as extraordinary (as in Hitchcock and Dreyer) but through the continuity of phenomena under a new light, a changed sense. This is why events like Karin's cry on the volcano, the 'miracle' in *Voyage,* or Nannina's 'my holy child' are always ambiguous without ever being vague."[74]

Yet they may be sudden. In *Stromboli*, Karin's conversion is less the result of continuous pressure all through the movie (although there *is* that) than of God's sudden intervention, which may indeed be likened, as in Saul of Tarsus's case, to a "rupture" in the normal course of events. But even in *Stromboli,* as in *Voyage in Italy,* "Romagna" and "The Po Delta," *Francesco giullare di Dio, Europe '51,* and *Fear,* the rupture that is the dramatic subject is not the rupture in the normal course of events that a miracle causes but rather the rupture of individuals from other people and even from themselves, a rupture in which they have consented. And the difference between Rossellini and Murnau is that Rossellini believes in grace and Murnau only in miraculous chance. Indeed, because chance spectacularly thwarts the inevitable in *The Last Laugh* and *Sunrise,* we are all the more moved when chance fails in *Tabu.*[75] Rossellini, in contrast, shows how difficult it is to be Catholic and not have a happy ending, thanks be!

At the Stake

Giovanna d'Arco al rogo, Fear

R od Geiger was back in Rome, and in jail.
In 1947, after the $25,000 advance for *Boris Godunov* had vanished into Sam Spiegel's pockets, Geiger had sold all his percentages in *Open City* and *Paisan* to Landau, who had then sold his interests to Conti. Conti, according to Geiger, had given Geiger five percent of *Paisà* worldwide, but then had subsequently declined to pay out any money without written evidence of their agreement, which Geiger had given to Rossellini, who refused to get involved.[1] (Of the original investors, only Lawrence retained his share in *Open City*.)

That summer Geiger had gone to Hollywood with his second wife Katja. There he had put together a production of *Christ in Concrete* with Luise Rainer, J. Edgar Bomberg, and Karen Morley and had fascinated Bertolt Brecht. Brecht rolled laughing on the grass with him, moved into his home, and laid plans for Rod to direct Brecht's *Galileo* with Charles Laughton in Italy the following summer.[2]

In October 1947, however, the House Un-American Activities Committee began its hearings on Communist infiltration of the motion picture industry and summoned Brecht to testify. Geiger, Chaplin, and Thomas Mann coached him for the event, Brecht gave the Committee Geiger's Manhattan address as his own, and left for East Germany after receiving the Committee's thanks. But a number of writers and directors—subsequently famous as "The Hollywood Ten"—refused to cooperate and were blacklisted by the studios.

In protest, Geiger hired one of them to direct *Christ in Concrete*—Edward Dmytryk. Dmytryk had attacked racism in his 1947 *Crossfire* and had just been sentenced to a year in jail for refusing to say if he had ever been a Communist.

To persuade Geiger to drop Dmytryk, Dore Schary offered financing for *Christ* and a lucrative five-year contract at M-G-M. But Geiger, even though he was beginning to realize Dmytryk was wrong artistically for *Christ*, felt he should try to change the world. He turned Schary down and hired another of The Ten, writer Adrian Scott. And thereupon all hope vanished for American financing. Chaplin offered to help but his brother vetoed the deal.

But Geiger had found money in England and had made *Christ in Concrete* there in 1948 as *Give Us This Day* with Sam Wanamaker and Lea Padovani (who had just split from Orson Welles's *Othello* and bed). *Give Us This Day* had won the First Grand Masterpiece Award at Venice and would make good money in Italy. But when Geiger had brought his film back to the United States in December 1949, he had discovered that it was almost impossible to exhibit it with Dmytryk's name on it. Dmytryk himself, meanwhile, had been naming names to the Committee, Geiger's among them, whereupon Dmytryk had been released from prison and removed from the blacklist, and the State Department had refused to renew Geiger's passport. Geiger had had pictures lined up in England, including *Robin Hood.* But it had taken him three years to get his passport back, and then only with intervention from Congressman Adam Clayton Powell, by which time his English deals were dead.

So Rod Geiger had found money in Italy, had gone there at the end of 1952 to make *The Giant* with Primo Carnero, and had discovered his backers were broke. He had gone to Germany for new money, but back in Rome had learned his assistant had been arrested for handing out bad checks. Worried, he had driven with Katja and their three children to Naples, where Roberto was making *Voyage in Italy.* Who better to seek advice from?

Roberto was still miffed about *Christ in Concrete*, but he was reassuring. "Everything will be alright."

Back in Rome, the police were waiting at Geiger's door. They took him to the Regina Coeli prison and locked him up.

Italy had no bail system. Joe Burstyn came flying from New York to help, but had a heart attack and died on the plane. Chaplin sent letters of comfort. Conti refused assistance, rudely. Roberto got lawyers and gave money to Katja. After two months, Geiger got a hearing, Primo Carnera flew to Rome at his own expense, and the charges were dropped.

Free but broke, he asked Fellini for a loan. Fellini had nothing himself; his wife held their funds. The two drove around Rome looking for money. A few hours later, none the richer, they shrugged and laughed: not a lira between them.

A few days later Roberto lent him about five thousand dollars.[3]

At the end of April 1953, with *Voyage*'s shooting finally completed, the Rossellinis moved up the street from 49 Viale Bruno Buozzi to the new ten-room apartment at 62, along with a housekeeper, a cook, a governess for Robertino, a wet nurse for the twins, and Helen the maid.

"Each day is an adventure," Roberto told a journalist, and bemoaned the fate of the individual in modern society. "The man or woman who today has the courage of his or her private convictions fills us with a nameless terror. The individual is dangerous and, therefore, society feels that it must eliminate this danger by somehow eliminating the individual. . . . Italians today are sick of realism. They want Technicolor."

The Technicolor Ferrari, "a wingless rocket ship," the brightest red Ferrari could find, roared through Rome with "total disdain for the vulgarities of traffic regulations," added the journalist.[4]

That spring Roberto raced the Ferrari in Italy's dangerous 2,000-kilometer "Mille Miglia." He announced a film project to chronicle the glorious deeds of racing champions like Fangio, Farina, Ascari, and Villoresi, and to immortalize himself, enlisted Aldo Tonti to ride beside him with a 16mm camera. They started at 5 A.M. from Bergamo. Tonti had fallen in the bathroom that morning and was in constant pain, but because he *was* terrified and didn't want Roberto to think he was trying to chicken out, he dared not mention it. The speedometer said they were going 180 mph, he noted, but everyone kept passing them. After a hundred miles, in Padua, Roberto was ready to give up. After four hundred miles, in Rome, at Ponte Milvio, they met photographers and Ingrid, who handed Roberto a three-day supply of sandwiches. "Home! Let's go eat at home!" he said.

They had done less than half the course. Tonti had three broken ribs and could not move. Roberto thought he was chicken.

Ingrid had champagne waiting, and four-year-old Robertino slapped Roberto across the face: "That's for making my mother cry!"

Said Roberto, "I pretended to be hurt and ashamed. So then he turned me around and said, 'My poor father! You're so old and so crazy.' "[5]

In June, Ingrid and Roberto took off in the Ferrari for a party in Stockholm. He drove more moderately, around 140 mph, for 31 hours without sleep to Hamburg and missed the ferry to Denmark. "I burst out crying," Ingrid wrote. "Roberto just laughed and said, 'This is part of the fun of travelling.'" He drove another eighteen hours, and when they got to Stockholm at three in the morning, the party was still in progress.[6] "It was worth it, seeing all those people I hadn't seen in years."[7]

In July, between business trips to Milan, Belgium, and Germany, Roberto directed a production of *La gioconda* at Naples's outdoor Arena Flegrea with a prestigious cast—Cavalieri, Barbieri, and Di Stefano; Serafin conducting. Ponchielli's opera offered Roberto fewer opportunities for invention than had *Otello*. But he did manage to have a corpse carried on stage, despite Boito's instructions to the contrary.[8]

At home, guests were constant—Lillian Hellman, Jed Harris, Gabriel Pascal, Irene Selznick, Dorothy Thompson, Sidney Bernstein, Robert Sherwood, John Steinbeck, Larry Adler, Sam Spiegel, Leonard Lyons, Gary Cooper, and Rockie his wife, "and a lot of the old dear friends," added Ingrid.[9]

But not Pia. She made Ingrid promise on the phone not to go to court about her, and said no one was preventing her coming to see her mother. "Only *she doesn't want to!*" Ingrid exclaimed.[10]

In October 1953, Selznick held a four-day test run in Middletown, Connecticut for *Europe '51* (retitled, by Rossellini, *The Greatest Love*). Selznick's agent (Arabella Lemaître?) wrote Roberto the results:

I must say in all candor that I was unprepared for the reaction I found. There was a great deal of expectation in the audience when the picture title flashed on the screen. I could also say that there was great admiration for Ingrid's performance throughout most of the picture, but it was generally speaking a noisy audience which giggled and laughed at the wrong places and when the picture was approximately half over, there were a great number of walkouts before the picture concluded. The audience was primarily comprised of women, although there were some family groups. I would say . . . the patrons found the film too long, which feeling was intensified by several scenes which they felt were overdrawn and by the ending, which left many in the audience confused. There was also a surprising amount of comment concerning the lack of lip synchronization. . . . Innumerable people came up to me to find out whether there was something wrong with the sound track because of [this]. We received 153 questionnaires [out of 2200 distributed: a low return]. 80 of these questionnaires comment unfavorably upon the lip synchronization.

Based on the test run, she added, various changes were desirable: (1) Edit the cocktail party to minimize synch problems ("repeated titters in the audience"). (2) Eliminate Giggetto's singing (in English), which "was greeted by uproarious howls." (3) Eliminate Andrea's mention of the class struggle: "[T]his raises an unnecessary problem at the present time here . . . ; the conflict of ideology . . . is adequately developed in a more subtle manner without these words." (4) Trim Bergman's anguish at prostitute's death: it was "too much" for American audiences and caused "groans." (5) Trim scene between Ingrid and priest, which caused "an unfavorable audience reaction that was vocal." (6) Transpose two scenes for clarity.[11]

Selznick ultimately did not release the movie, and if this was a matter of decision (another distributor had already paid for the rights), it's hard to fault him, no matter how much one esteems *Europe '51* and deplores most of the proposed changes. None of Rossellini's pictures is executed with more care visually and less care aurally. The film had been shot in English but with only a scratch track, so the actors had had to come back weeks later to record their dialogue. Their dubbed voices are disembodied both from the moving mouths on screen and (worse) from ambient sound. Some have Italian accents, others sound like they're from England, Texas, or the Bronx. "That means I'm a cretin," Roberto retorted, when questioned about a similar debacle in 1972 with *Age of the Medici*, which American public television rejected as unusable.[12] Obviously he was oblivious. Indeed, what Connecticut was laughing at was actually a *re-dubbed* version Roberto had made in December 1952 after a single, disastrous semi-public screening that October. "I remember that New York premiere," said Aldo Tonti. "The people laughed and I couldn't understand why a tragic story inspired such hilarity. They said it was because of the dubbing done by Italians who spoke English in funny ways."[13]

Apparently neither Roberto nor Ingrid understood what was wrong. Nor were they willing to trust a competent collaborator, or spend money for better dubbing. Italians never object to poor dubbing. *All* movies are dubbed in Italy, even Italian ones. Even sophisticated Italian film critics, fluent in English, will seldom concede they are missing anything as a result of dubbing, nor do they understand the intense antipathy to dubbing in America. Certainly Roberto had not wanted to make a fool of himself in front of Ingrid's English-language audiences, especially after *Stromboli*'s fiasco, but he had. Worse, he had done it with a good part of the Italian film industry looking on.

That disastrous October 1952 screening had been part of an industry-sponsored "Salute to Italian Film Week." The festive evenings at the Little Carnegie were not advertised and only a few tickets were put on sale for the public. A hundred thousand dollars had been spent to bring 29 bureaucrats and personalities from Italy, to fly in eleven critics from out of town, and to host innumerable parties and receptions. The purpose of the shebang was to launch Italian Films Export (I.F.E.), which was the government film directorate's effort to set up an American distribution network for Italian films—fourteen offices nationwide, plus a dubbing studio in New York. Dubbing was the key to the American market, I.F.E. insisted. People like Burstyn and Lopert disagreed, but *they* had not been invited to the festivities: they were what I.F.E. was displacing. Roberto (not Ponti, *Europe '51*'s owner in Italy) had accepted $150,000 from I.F.E. for *Europe '51*'s U.S. rights; but he still had not given I.F.E. said rights, and he had been flirting with Selznick. Prior to *Europe '51*'s I.F.E. screening, *Variety* remarked that all Italian films in America had earned only twice this amount in 1951–52, and that even within the bureaucracy there was sentiment that I.F.E. ought to put itself under Burstyn's management.[14] What the sentiments were after *Europe '51*'s reception is not recorded. But the movie was re-dubbed and given a new title.

Europe '51 had been partly re-edited after Venice for its Italian release, and re-edited again for the English-language edition, and now yet again for two slightly different English-language editions of the re-dubbing. Elena Dagrada made a comparison of these editions (see the filmography for details) and argued that certain changes may have been motivated to placate Catholic audiences. For example, the scene in which Irene is confronted by a priest who behaves like a pompous idiot is progressively trimmed in each version, first, Dagrada suggests, to avoid a harsher rating than "Adults" in Italy, then to avoid similar criticism in the U.S. and France. Other changes tone down references to Fascists and Communists, delete lines that hammer on the deficiencies of all institutions (the justice system, healthcare, the Church, society), and add lines to deflect Irene's bitter denunciation of work as damnation. The Catholic *Rivista del Cinematografo* had objected that work can be redemptive, that it is not true that the world's structures are fundamentally determined to negate Christianity, and that a Christian must have more Hope.[15]

The priest is still a pompous idiot in the English editions, however, and the bitter denunciations are still bitter. Changes were not made that would placate otherwise (theoretically) offended Catholics. Indeed, what has been removed or altered can in every case be seen as a sharpening of the movie's focus. For example, it is satisfying in the Italian version to watch Irene repeatedly challenge the slimy priest, taunting "Why are you afraid?!" and to watch him cringe in confusion, but none of this remains in the English version; now Irene no longer indulges in a bullying that is inconsistent with her intense compassion. Similarly her fourth repetition that work is damnation is re-edited so that Irene now quotes Christ, "Thou shalt love thy neighbor!"—because it is empathy and love that are to be her life's theme, not hatred and cursing.

But none of these themes seem to have mattered to American audiences when Roberto's "message of faith, of hope, of love," unaltered three months after Selznick's test, was given its release by I.F.E. (after all!) simultaneously in 67 New York metropolitan theaters. It was seldom seen again. Gina Lollobrigida reported: "The question arose: Was *Europe '51* to be considered a pro-Communist film? The 'Communist' thing seemed at that time to interest, I'd say torment, the Americans more than anything else. To establish whether a production was or wasn't Communist was the essential point in the U.S. They made me judge of the debate. I said candidly that, for me, to find a clear political thesis in the film was very difficult."[16]

Fortunately at the very moment Americans were snickering at *Europe '51*, French critics, experiencing English-language from a foreign-language perspective, were urging a reassessment of the picture.

"Reservations have no importance," said André Bazin, "compared to the totality of a film which has to be understood and judged through its mise en scène. What would Dostoyevsky's *The Idiot* amount to, reduced to a logical summary? . . . What counts is that each sequence is a sort of meditation, a cinematic song. . . . It's not a question of demonstrating but of showing. . . . Rarely has the presence of the spiritual in people and the world been expressed with such dazzling there-ness. . . . Whereas De Sica pages through reality with ever more tender curiosity, Rossellini keeps unwrapping continuously and stylizing, sorrowfully but pitilessly. [Yet] Rossellini does not let his actors act, he does not have them express this or that feeling, he just forces them [to] be in front of the camera in a certain way. In such a mise en scène, the respective placement of the characters, their ways of walking, their movements on the set, and their gestures have much more importance than feelings elaborated on their faces, or than what they say. Besides, what 'feelings' could Ingrid Bergman 'express'? Her drama is way beyond any psychological nomenclature. Her face is only the trace of a certain quality of suffering."[17]

Rohmer concurred: "It proposes solely per force of what it offers our eyes—the gaze, the attitude, the physical existence of this woman and those around her—to prove the existence of the soul itself." And Rossellini eschews the conventional ways of doing this by suggestion. He adopts an atheistic perspective, offers "the spectacle of a world without God where there is no other law than the pure mechanism of cause and effect, a universe of cruelty, horror, banality, and derision. . . . [Yet] this film has for subject the solitude of a soul at grips with narrow-minded incomprehension and condescending solicitude. . . . Rossellini's genius is to know how to discover so narrow a union and at the same time so infinite a distance between the kingdom of bodies (his material) and the kingdom of the spirit (his object)."[18]

The adoration of a few Parisian critics contrasted with the cackles of everyone else. One disaster after the next had struck Roberto since *Paisà*—a death, two divorces, an abortion, scandals, drugs, chronic financial distress, constant mockery in the press, moral denunciation, ideological denunciation, and seven failed films. What did it matter that *Siamo donne* opened in October and his episode with Ingrid got only cool reviews? *Voyage in Italy* couldn't even find a distributor—and wouldn't for a whole other year. Yet Roberto kept going, ever enthusiastic, always with dozens of balls in the air. "You know how hard he always works," Ingrid wrote Joe Steele, "but the way he has been going these last few weeks is incredible. Sometimes it is hard for him to make ends meet. And the somersaults he has to go through!"[19]

She, in contrast, was accustomed neither to enthusiasm, lack of success, nor somersaults. Yet she who was hesitating by nature found herself married to someone for whom recklessness was a religion. Particularly galling was Roberto's enthusiasm over *lack* of money. Ingrid was always anxious about it, Roberto insouciant. They couldn't buy rugs, she complained. Tirelessly, she confronted him with: "But why do you want to reform the world?"[20]

Yet in her fashion Ingrid was just as impulsive as Roberto. Friends wanting to be sympathetic would make the evident observation that life with someone as willful and improvident as he must inevitably clash with motherhood, children, and solid Swedish order. But the only actual difference was that Roberto was simply determined to charge ahead, whereas Ingrid craved the knowledge of money in the bank. Far from being a staid Swede, she had run off young to the theater; thrown herself into one love affair after another; deserted a child; thumbed her nose at propriety; and dived into a culture so diverse from her own that her eccentricity became the theme of her life and pictures. The scandals had helped her by singling her out from the crowd. Naturally she now jumped at a third chance to play Joan of Arc.

Joan

Said Roberto: "I was in Naples to stage *Otello* and had an extraordinary good time doing it. . . . And they asked me if I wanted to do something for Ingrid, which was *Joan [of Arc] at the Stake* [*Jeanne d'Arc au bûcher*, an oratorio with music by Arthur Honegger and text by Paul Claudel]. And I said, 'Let me read the libretto, let me see.' The libretto couldn't be found; they sent me the records. And one evening at home I listened to the discs. And while listening images came into my mind of *Joan at the Stake*. The entire staging was in my imagination, because *Joan at the Stake* had words, and it had music, but it had not been conceived for the stage."[21]

Honegger and Claudel were gods of French music and literature. Ida Rubinstein had commissioned *Jeanne d'Arc au bûcher* from them in 1933. Already for her, Debussy and D'Annunzio had written *Le Martyre de Saint Sébastien*, Stravinsky and Gide *Perséphone*, and Ravel *Bolero*. Ida was a mime, Claudel was in love with her, and to test her his text instructed that she stand still in front of the orchestra with her hands tied to a stake. Except for the stake, there was to be no other scenery, staging, or costume, and this is the way the oratorio had always been presented. Roberto's vision was of Joan untied and given the movement of her thoughts. And everything would be shown. "Everything is staged, everything is *seen*. It starts with her burning at the stake, she ascends to paradise, meets Saint Dominic, etc., etc."[22]

Roberto scribbled his plan on the back of an envelope and held rehearsals for a month. His production would resemble medieval paintings or passion plays (as Renoir's *Golden Coach* had resembled a *commedia dell'arte*). To change scene from landscape to church, he would use rear-projectors and lantern slides, fake flames and colored spots, stars, mist, and passing clouds. His curtain would open with a small girl tied to the stake stage-rear, flames would rise up, and Ingrid would ascend out of the darkness on an elevator, in black, with only her face showing, which would represent her mind looking at her past. The moral would be that freedom means commitment, accepting chains, and going to the stake, like in *Paisà*.

The premiere of *Giovanna al rogo*, in Italian, December 5, 1953, was broadcast to great success and eventually issued on discs. Reviews of Ingrid were ecstatic. Rossellini was said to be revitalizing opera.[23] Six more performances followed in Naples. Plans were made to repeat it in the spring at La Scala, Milan, then in Paris, London, Barcelona, Palermo, Stockholm, and South America.

It was a triumph, provocative, and much discussed. But the triumph was Bergman's and the provocation Rossellini's—as with all their efforts together. *Cinema* went after him with a big broom: the scenic effects were indebted to Disney's *Fantasia* and the worst kinds of holy cards; the lighting was worse than Cecil B. DeMille's; Ingrid's misfortune was to have met Rossellini rather than Dreyer. "In his famous *Fioretti* [Rossellini] demonstrated his inability to understand the simple, sincere faith of Francis's companions, whose legend he touched with truly profaning hands; as a director his temperament is fundamentally irreconcilable with Ingrid's. Hers is an art of inner expression as much as Rossellini's is one of external, ephemeral moments of occasionally genial inspiration."[24]

Unheeding, Roberto charmed a producer, Giorgio Criscuolo, into financing a film version, quickly. Scarcely a month after the premiere, the music was recorded (twice, in Italian and French); then, while sets were constructed, Roberto raced around in his Ferrari. "If I don't get back, come pick me out of some ditch," he'd say each morning.[25] Shooting started February 1 and lasted eighteen days, at a cost of about $100,000. "For the first time, I think," said Ingrid, "he carefully planned every step of every shot in great detail. The story and dialogue were there and could not be tampered with. The result was that all his creative energy and talent were concentrated in invention and direction."[26] Roberto did walk out in the middle of one rehearsal, on the pretext that he had to take Caraceni, his electrician, to his tailor for a new suit; actually, it was because he needed to think.

The movie *Giovanna d'Arco al rogo* was visually recomposed. "I did use the same cast and costumes, [but] it would have been too easy and no fun at all just to photograph *Joan* the way we did it at San Carlo."[27] In place of projections, which wouldn't have photographed well, he used mirrors.

The mirrors—the "Schüfftan process"—would serve Roberto frequently in his later historical recreations. A painting, for example, of the Acropolis is placed some meters behind the camera; some meters in front of the camera is a large glass; the upper portion of the glass is sprayed with reflective material to turn it into a mirror (reflecting the painting behind the camera); what the camera photographs is the reflected image plus the "reality" it sees through the portion of the glass that is still clear. Eugen Schüfftan was a German cinematographer; his process had been used for years, notably in Lang's *Die Nibelungen* (1924) and *Metropolis* (1927); but Schüfftan had painted directly onto the glass. Rossellini's modification, developed with Mario Fioretti, was to reflect the painting onto the part of the glass that had been turned into a mirror. This permitted camera movements.

"*Joan* was an attempt to rediscover the style, the mode of expression, of the cinema's beginnings," said Roberto, citing Méliès.[28] "It's a very strange film. I know they'll say my involution has gone as far as it can go, that I've gone back under ground. It's not at all filmed theater, it's cinema and I'd even say neo-realism, in the sense that I've always intended."[29]

Aside from the thirteen-minute "Napoli '43" shot in Ferraniacolor for the episode-film *Amori di mezzo secolo* in November, while *Giovanna* was in rehearsal, this was Rossellini's first picture in color. He had wanted CinemaScope too, but had failed to get it. His photographer Gabor Pogany recalls, "We decided to shoot in Gevacolor because it was more 'Nordic,' it didn't have the brilliant colors of Technicolor. In fact we wanted a pallet of thin tints. I worked a lot with gelatins and filters to get a 'Flemish' look, made up of half tones.

"Roberto always shot without the script. He had it all in his head, because he would think about the film the whole day long, continuously. He was a great smoker and wrote his direction notes on cigarette packs, so it was one of the crew's duties for someone to follow him around collecting the empty packs, lest 'ideas get lost.' But on the set Rossellini 'saw' the film, he became von Karajan directing his orchestra. For a director of photography it's exciting to work this way. I really felt like a first violin playing with everyone else following me. In *Giovanna d'Arco al rogo* I had a fairly difficult job, because in fact the rehearsal hall we were shooting in wasn't designed for film but for theater staging. And I was used to lighting, not to painting with light. There are lots of directors who go into torment worrying over every single frame. Rossellini knew exactly where he wanted to go, without having to think about it. What's more, Ingrid Bergman was an extraordinary actress. I was able to shoot an entire thousand-foot load of film without a break, without a mistake. It was really a sin to stop. Today people tend to work more quickly and the photography ends up being excessively uniform, flattening the film. With *Giovanna d'Arco al rogo*'s lighting we were greatly inspired by silent cinema: when there's no talk, you have to make the images talk and to give the impression, with light, that words would be superfluous. Actually we had enormous fun doing the photographic tricks, especially the mirror ones. There was a great deal of trick work done in the laboratory, for example the first scenes, when Rossellini shows paradise, or when Joan of Arc ascends."[30]

Joan is "a point of view on a point of view," say Guarner and Beylie. Rossellini keeps Joan separate as she watches the events of her life, and Joan herself we see always enclosed by circles, "from the point of view of God or, if you prefer, from the point of view of the eternity of the myth (Claudel: 'The Joan we contemplate is the eternal Joan.')." Says Beylie, "Endowed with utterly staggering beauty, [she is] the most stupefying image of sanctity I know of, hovering in 'infinite spaces,' way above terrestrial life." Joan is a displaced person witnessing her own life, yearning for freedom, like most Rossellini heroines.[31]

Ingrid loved her role. This was not the staunch maven of her Maxwell Anderson Joan, too man-ish, nor the clever Joan of George Bernard Shaw, whom Ingrid naturally considered too boy-ish. This was a gently feminine Joan.

On January 13, 1954, *Europe '51* (now *The Greatest Love*) had opened in the United States. "Dismal and dolorous" was Bosley Crowther's verdict in *The New York Times*: "a bleakly superficial and unconvincing piece of old-fashioned fol-de-rol, notably lacking explanations or understanding of its central character. [The other] characters are incredibly obtuse and wooden. ... It's hard to believe the same man who directed *Open City* put these buffoons on the screen."[32]

In February, *Amori di mezzo secolo* opened in Rome, containing Rossellini's little sketch of lovers who meet and die under the bombs of a World War II air raid. *Cinema* called it conventional and grotesque. *L'Unità* said it was the "umpteenth disappointment" from Rossellini.[33] More was on the way.

In March, *Dov'è la libertà . . . ?* opened. Paladini said Rossellini had betrayed his old friends' commitment to search for truth.[34] *Cinema Nuovo* said it was one of the Rossellini films that couldn't be understood or shown, like *La macchina*. "The breakdown of the artist is complete . . . and there are rumors that the recent *Voyage in Italy* is causing similar problems."[35]

In April, *Giovanna d'Arco al rogo* opened at La Scala to another enthusiastic reception.[36] Roberto and Ingrid each received one million lire per night. Ernest Hemingway and A. E. Hotchner came visiting at the Hotel Principe & Savoia. Hemingway, who adored Ingrid, had not forgiven Roberto for reading to the press Hemingway's private letters to her at the time of the scandals. Hotchner describes Ingrid cringing over how rich the Milanese were ("Why, in comparison the houses in Beverly Hills are shacks!") and saying she hadn't gone skiing because of how much it "would cost to outfit the children and the nurse." Hotchner pictures Roberto as "a short man, going to paunch and baldness; he had a small, reluctant smile on his face," and didn't even laugh at jokes. And he had only a partial pint of Black and White Scotch to offer them—which Hotchner declined, "not wanting to put him out of business." And he made Ingrid cancel a dinner date with them, so that instead she could attend a speech he was giving to some civic group, "and we all understood what that meant."[37]

In June 1954, the Rossellinis—Ingrid, Roberto, three children, two maids—took *Joan* to the Paris Opéra. Jean Renoir published a salutation in *Arts:*

> It's impossible for me to describe the place where I first saw Roberto Rossellini. It must have been a hotel room. It could also have been the Capitoline Hill, the port of Naples or the Place de la Concorde. I was only seeing *him* and I was trying to grasp the subtle connections between those arms, that nose, that face, that voice and *Open City, Paisà* and all the films of his that I love so much. Suddenly I understood. This man exists first by his eyes. It's the sense of vision that establishes his bridge to the rest of the world. It's by his eyes that he absorbs, that he records, that he penetrates: two good drills capable of piercing the toughest surface. After that, his heart follows, and then his brain starts to dissect. What does Rossellini see at this moment in Paris? I'm waiting impatiently for him to tell me about our city the way he told me about Naples—Italy's holy city, according to Rossellinian theory. I wish him welcome.[38]

Renoir had only recently arrived himself from his home in Rome, to an apartment on Rue Frochot, near Place Pigalle. His self-imposed exile from France had lasted fourteen years. He was starting his first French movie since *La Règle du jeu* in 1939, *French Cancan.*

Roberto and Ingrid had come at the invitation of Maurice Lehman, the director of France's national lyric theaters, who had seen *Joan* in Naples. "But," said Roberto, "once in Paris, it was a whole different song." Everyone was terrified of Claudel, including Lehman, who insisted that *Joan* be presented as Claudel had instructed, as an oratorio in concert setting.

"Why did you ask me to come?" Roberto said. "Look, I can go see Claudel and tell him my reasons."[39]

Claudel was in Savoy, 300 miles away.

"Saturday 12 [June]," reads Claudel's diary; "Visit of Rossellini for an hour, in his big twelve-cylinder Ferrari. He explained to me, rather anxiously, his mise en scène of *Jeanne*."[40]

Claudel served tea and very sternly lectured on the *purpose* of the oratorio. "I was on the train, coming back from Brussels, when I had the vision of Joan's chains breaking. It's on this vision that I've constructed the whole thing as an oratorio."[41]

It was vital, Claudel concluded, for Joan to be tied to the stake, dying before our eyes, the whole time.

Whereupon Ingrid confessed she ran around a lot.

Claudel was aghast. He threatened to block the performance. Roberto asked him to come to the dress rehearsal, offering to withdraw the production—which was completely sold out for six performances—if Claudel didn't like it.

The poet came, bearing his cane. "At the announcement of his arrival," said Roberto, "all the people who usually came to the rehearsals fled like a flock of pigeons. We were alone in the auditorium."[42] Claudel sat in the front row. "I was in the back row, because I was afraid of getting hit with the cane."[43]

Claudel watched without a word, without a cough. At the last words, "God is the strongest," he stood up and shouted: "Ingrid is the strongest!" Turning around, he shook the cane at Roberto: "You. Come here!"

Claudel bestowed his blessing. As did Honegger, who came to rehearsals, coached Bergman at his home, and wined and dined with the company at the Tour D'Argent on opening night. Both men liked the fact that Ingrid played Joan as an ordinary girl and used her natural voice, rather than the heroic declamation, customary in oratorio, that every other Joan had employed. Claudel published a piece in *Le Figaro* endorsing Rossellini's approach; ideas count more than the letter, he argued.[44] And in his diary added, "R's conception is much more dramatic than mine. The ending with the apparition of the cathedral is decidedly superior."[45]

Jeanne d'Arc au bûcher had only recently been presented at the Opéra in an oratorio staging by Jean Doat. *Les Lettres Françaises* noted that the Rossellini's "conception of the work is in movement and variety whereas Doat sought grandeur in the static. . . . The public reacted quite contrarily: some for, some against, both sides fiercely so. . . . Visually, Rossellini's conception is extremely attractive . . . , [but] the concert format, more than the theater, accords to thought its escape: how vagabond is the imagination when scenic realization does not impoverish its dream!"[46]—an iconoclastic pensée applicable to all visual art.

In fact, it was the scenic richness that *Le Monde*'s critic, René Dumesnil, praised. "Such is the nature of Rossellini's art that, far from failing to recognize the power of dreams, he knows how to make them his allies and to capitalize on their best and surest effects. He suggests as much as he shows. He persuades without insisting. He knows the value of a suggestion that is checked as soon as it is sketched. He is a master in the play of nuances and tonal contrasts, and it is a suite of unforgettable tableaux that he puts before our eyes. His discernment is prodigious and economic simultaneously, economic when an allusion suffices, when he stresses a single trait at the expense of meaning: hence the landscape so purely French, the cluster of trees beside a river, the Gothic cathedral emerging from the mist at the moment of torture, what powers of suggestion do they lack? And everything is like this, calculated to the smallest detail in a long preparation to appear more natural, more spontaneous, at the brief instant of execution."[47]

Whereas reviewers in other cities scarcely acknowledged Rossellini as a contributor, in Paris some critics gave more attention to him than to Bergman.

Most were thrilled. The production was covered as the great event of the season. The President of France came, along with most of the governments of France and Paris, with the Garde Républicaine lining the Opéra staircase with drawn sabers; the opening was a benefit for ex Resistance fighters. Ingrid's deficient pronunciation was remarked on, in contrast to that of Claude Nollier, who had been the glory of Jean Doat's staging (and who ended up dubbing Bergman in Rossellini's film). Among other things Ingrid couldn't pronounce "France" or "Rouen." But some found her accent "charming," or even "Gothic." She took ten curtain calls.

Truffaut

That same month François Truffaut published a trio of articles canonizing Rossellini. Truffaut was 22, a protégé of Bazin's. He'd been converted at seventeen, instantly, the moment he saw *Deutschland im Jahre Null*. When Roberto had come to Paris in March 1954 for the opening of *Siamo donne*, Truffaut had jumped at the chance to interview him in partnership with Eric Rohmer.

Truffaut found, in the words of his biographer, a Rossellini who "seemed very vulnerable. [Rossellini] was not sure about anything. If he was not always understood, he thought it was his fault. He was disoriented most of all by the shifts of the critics, who had nearly always been murderous when the films come out, then increasingly dithyrambic as time passed. . . . François was touched by the fragility of the man. . . . The doubts of maturity, the disarray of this famous man troubled him deeply."[48]

Truffaut began one of his pieces: "You sense it watching his films. It's confirmed as soon as you exchange a few words with him. Roberto Rossellini is a man alone, abandoned." Old comrades had not been able to follow his evolution; what he meant by "neo-realism" was not understood. "Like Renoir, Rossellini is more instinctive than intellectual. He feels things more than he understands them, and thus can express them without trying to demonstrate anything." Films like *Europe '51* were totally misperceived by the critics: "Such art, such refinement, such mastery are naturally at the opposite pole from melodrama and one would have to be a real idiot to confuse Rossellini's extraordinary sensibility with [the melodramatic]."[49]

This article, in *Radio-Cinéma-Télévision*, was signed with a pseudonym, François de Montferrand. Truffaut had doubled himself, on his way to becoming an army. Interviews under his own name appeared simultaneously in *Cahiers* and *Arts*, and over the next twelve years Truffaut and *Cahiers* would promote Rossellini more ardently than any other filmmaker: five interviews; a three-part essay from tapes recorded by Roberto; a goodly percentage of the finest reviews written by the era's most sensitive film critics; constant cameo pieces; and one-liners in almost every issue. "It was when he evoked Faith that Rossellini best expressed what *Cahiers'* young Turks saw him as a model of," writes Truffaut's biographer.[50] Or, as Truffaut himself put it, Rossellini epitomized an attitude toward art, toward cinema as art's greatest exemplar—that aesthetic experience of life is more profound and intimate than mere "understanding." This was Croce and Bergson, converted to radical Catholicism.

Thus *Cahiers'* first interview with Rossellini begins by conceding nothing. For Truffaut and Rohmer, the ramparts were already occupied, the banners batting in the wind:

> CAHIERS: One of *Cahiers'* collaborators, Jacques Rivette, wrote recently: "On one side is the Italian cinema, on the other the work of Roberto Rossellini." He meant that you hold apart from the neo-realist movement, under whose banner almost all Italian directors line up.
>
> ROSSELLINI: Yes, from a certain type of neo-realism. But what does the word mean? You know there was a congress in Parma. They talked a very long time and the term's meaning is still confused. Most of the time it's just a badge. For me, it's mostly a moral position from which one looks at the world. It then becomes an aesthetic position, but the point of departure is moral.
>
> CAHIERS: Loving your films as we do, and thinking we understand them, it's almost as difficult for us as for you to comprehend the reasons of those who don't like them. The newness of your style confused many of our colleagues: the fact is that some of them have reconsidered their initial impressions; for example, many of those who didn't like *Europe '51* at Venice changed their opinion when the film came out in Paris.[51]

The three-way conversation was concentrated into an apparent monologue in Truffaut's *Arts* piece. Rossellini is made to say: "Look, they insult me on every side. It's not a comfortable position, but I say it as frankly as I think it: the praises often offend and wound me more than the insults, because in most cases they're back-handed compliments. Those who make them understand nothing. When I say *Stromboli* is my favorite film, it's not to amuse the balcony. It's not because it was greeted with a chorus of contempt. *Stromboli* is a very important film for me. I'm convinced that if you don't like it, there's no reason to like the others. I'm a simple man, and I swim in a tide of myths that people build up around me without the least justification."

He cited the transcendental Catholic Bernanos as his favorite writer, added he was having trouble obtaining rights to *Dialogue of the Carmelites*, and retorted to the false myths, like the supposed caesura in his work after *Deutschland.* "And another myth: my perpetual improvisation! The classic conventional image of a buffoon who thinks he's a creative genius! The truth is so much simpler . . . : It happens that I often have the development of my scenes in my head, so I have no need to write it down. . . . The only improvisation I do is to obtain a better rhythm, to maintain a state of tension that has to break in a finale that I want to be unexpected and brutal. The latest myth is in describing my films as 'symbolic.' I know very well that the tortured Communist in *Roma città aperta* can evoke the face of Christ on the cross, that the child in *Deutschland im Jahre Null* dies to save the world, that Irene's itinerary in *Europe '51* is a way of the cross. But I've always worked so that this comes 'after' the film, 'in addition to it,' as a second and richer meaning."[52]

Truffaut's intentions were serious and analytical. And earnest. In compressing and rephrasing Roberto's lines, he turned what had been a tentative conversation into a French manifesto, a defiant posture of revolution against the status quo, a theoretical discourse calculated to appeal to the French, and thus an excellent angle, indeed the only possible one, for marketing Rossellini's "new" cinema within French culture. Roberto himself would learn quite well how to play this role in order to get French financing for his projects in the decades ahead. But Roberto's actual manner was more casual and self-deprecating than Truffaut depicts, and much warmer. And in America Truffaut's tactics backfired. His version was picked up by *Newsweek* as grist for satire. The American press had already created a derisive image of Rossellini during the Bergman scandal. Now *Newsweek* evoked an egomaniac, titling its short piece "Good Old Roberto":

> The goal of every movie director, often well suppressed, is to be considered an artist. Some of them are. Interviewed by the Paris weekly *Les Arts* [sic] last week, Roberto Rossellini, one of the best-known in the art brackets, critically discussed the problems of a successful movie man with art, the critics, and even financing:
>
> "A critic wrote the other day that there is Rossellini on one side, and the Italian cinema on the other. He is terribly right. I am trying to react against the weakness which makes men voluntary prisoners—not to say victims—of cowardice or thoughtlessness, of their wish to be in harmony with everyone and everything . . .
>
> "I shall tell you something which I have told no one: The tragedy of my life is that all the happy occurrences—let us say, the successes—come to me three or four years late. In other words, I work in the most absolute moral solitude . . .
>
> "People insult me on all sides . . . people say also that I have become a producer because I have such a thirst for power.
>
> "Would you like to know the truth? I finance my pictures because no one will finance them for me. Everybody refuses them with enthusiasm.
>
> "Cocteau, whom I saw a few days ago, remarked about this with striking clarity: 'At other times, art was an abstract thing and money a material thing. Today art has become a material thing as much as money has become an abstraction.' "[53]

Truffaut's praise had become poison. *Newsweek* was instructing "normal" people to view Rossellini as an odorous example of the pretenses of the contemporary art scene. By disguising its scorn as factual reporting, *Newsweek* discouraged readers from wondering if Roberto were truly like this.

Realism for Rossellini was exactly the opposite: a constant acknowledgment that we are seeing *only* an individual's personal view, plus a constant urging that we question these views. What was revolutionary was his humility. *Newsweek* saw it as pretension.

Alas, Ingrid found herself agreeing with what "normal" people thought of Rossellini's movies, even though "normal" people were condemning *her* more than him (and were attacking him often because of her). "The world hated the Rossellini version of me," she wrote.[54] She agreed with the Italian refrain that he had swerved from neo-realism's true mission. "I never stopped thinking that if he had not done those movies with me, for me, his success would have continued gloriously. Our love, my love, broke that success."[55]

Ingrid herself did not understand her movies with Rossellini. More to the point, she didn't *like* them. "He didn't know what to write for me."[56]

"Roberto tried to bring her into his world," said Fellini. "The world of Roberto is sensual and contradictory. Ingrid's world is a nice, clean, comfortable one, without drama, not filled with anguish and desperation."[57]

She detested Roberto's habit of casual lying. She disliked his friends. She would shut herself in her apartment and communicate with him by phone. "Ingrid's a cold, Nordic bourgeoise," said Renzo Avanzo; "Roberto's a creative artist, a Bohemian."[58]

"Did Ingrid love Rome?" Bonicelli asked Roberto.

"It was a city too small for her. She needed to walk a lot, to go hundreds of kilometers on foot."

"You're joking!?"

"No, it's a fundamental difference. For Ingrid activity is motion. For me it's contemplation, thought, dreaming. If she had been bored in the Roman way she would have gotten 25 pounds fatter and our marriage would have been saved."[59]

She drank copiously. He refused even wine. Marcella would keep her company, trying and failing to keep pace, while Roberto stared at them with utter contempt. Ingrid would get drunk, he would get mad, she would sleep on the terrace. Sex had virtually disappeared from their marriage after the twins. Roberto was unwilling to take the responsibility of fatherhood, she complained; he would disappear for days, the children would need him, and no one would know where he was. Or he would take the twins with him—and leave them in the car for three or four hours while he visited someone.

Some thought it was chiefly money that drove them apart. At one point the few furnishings they had, but had not paid for, were carted away.

Ingrid hid her Italian Oscar, the gold "Donatello," under the mattress that was left them.

It was a problem that could easily have been solved. Even in 1954 the name Rossellini was still thought to have enough box-office value that, at Roberto's suggestion, Salvatore Persichetti, the producer of *Orient Express*, paid him thirty million lire ($50,000) merely to cite him as "supervisor."[60] In September, Ingrid and Roberto went to São Paolo, Brazil, to discuss a film to be co-produced with Fernando de Barros of Unifilmes and written by Amidei, *Os Mucker do Rio Grande do Sul*.[61] (On the way back, they were unable to avoid a change of plane in the United States, where customs offered them a temporary visa, and Roberto replied, "I do not recognize your country. For me you do not exist."[62])

But nothing came of the Brazilian film. Repeatedly, Roberto and Ingrid engaged others in elaborate projects, then vanished without a word. They approached Carlo Ludovico Bragaglia at the end of 1953 to start a company in which Bragaglia and Roberto would alternate directing a series of films. At his own expense, Bragaglia rented and furnished offices on Via Paisiello, engaged a cabinet minister (Angelini) as president to help raise funds, and took numerous trips with him. It was decided that Roberto would direct Ingrid in *Dialogue of the Carmelites* and Bragaglia flew to Paris to negotiate the rights. "I discovered they were divided among three authors. One had written a little novel, another had worked out the main plot, and a third had done the dialogue. I talked with this last one and, in a rush to get back to Rome, asked him to start negotiations with the other two. When I got to Rome, I left immediately with Angelini for Naples, where Rossellini was engaged in shooting [*Giovanna d'Arco al rogo*]. But to our great astonishment we discovered that Roberto and Ingrid Bergman had vanished. Later we learned they had gone to Paris, where after a short time they separated. Angelini and I decided to consider the venture of the production company closed."[63]

It was a familiar story.

Ingrid flirted with proposals—from Zeffirelli, Fellini, Visconti, De Sica, and many another—and Roberto was blamed for not "allowing" her to work for anyone but him. She wanted to, according to her, and she resented Roberto's refusal. "It was a period when he was very jealous; she would have accepted" agreed Visconti.[64] "In Roberto's terms, I was his property," she wrote. To discuss it was to wound him and create a scene. "He liked to fight."[65] "Somewhat the same tensions recurred that had ruined the love with Anna," Marcella De Marchis observed. "Roberto was possessive as usual, extremely jealous, and would not allow Ingrid to work anymore."[66]

"Ingrid is a woman of very strong character, very decided, seven times stronger than I am," countered Roberto. "If she wanted to do something it certainly wouldn't be I who'd talk her out of it. But what did they propose for her when she was in Italy? Look at the titles: *Cavalleria rusticana*, *La figlia di Jorio*, *La contessa Mara*, even *Helen of Troy*. She only had two serious offers: a film with Blasetti, *La fiammata*—but she was expecting the twins and the whole thing fell through—and *Senso* by Visconti, but Ingrid did not feel herself in it: our Risorgimento said nothing to her, she didn't understand it, her culture is too different. It was she, in any case, who refused the part; I didn't say a word."[67]

In the fall of 1954, Ingrid rejected a number of proposals from Kay Brown in London. Hitchcock too was rebuffed repeatedly. To Hemingway she was adamant: "No, no more Hollywood.... Life is short and the years run away and you must do everything you really want to.... I get movies to read all the time, same old plots bent a little this way or that." And she wrote to Joe Steele, "I probably would do a picture without Roberto, but it would have to be so wonderful that he would understand my wish to do it." And a year later wrote to Rod and Katja Geiger: "When Roberto says: we can't work here anymore, it meant because the pictures they make here are too bad, not that we can't find any work here!!!"[68]

After Ingrid left Roberto, she went straight to "more Hollywood." Except for *Autumn Sonata* with Ingmar Bergman (with Roberto's approval the year of his death), she continued to shun Visconti, De Sica, and Hitchcock in favor of commercially oriented directors.

Fear

In September, Ingrid began making a movie in Munich with Roberto, three children, and two maids. He was just back from driving the big red Ferrari in the Stockholm Grand Prix. She was thankful that Lindstrom had remarried, because "maybe he won't have so much time to hate me anymore." She was worried about the children needing new shoes that she couldn't afford and about the five servants left at Santa Marinella with nothing to do.[69] She was making *Fear* but she thought of it as *Angst* (the inferior German edition shot contemporaneously with the English one), perhaps because that was the mood she was in. She didn't hide her resentments on the set. Her co-star Mathias Wieman counseled her, "You are being torn in pieces. You'll go insane if you continue this. Why don't you leave Roberto?"[70]

"One doesn't pass through such storms with indifference," Roberto confirmed. "There was absolutely no autobiographical intention . . . [but *Fear*] does reflect things a bit."[71]

"*Fear* is a terribly ugly film, one of the famous lost opportunities," said Sergio Amidei, who wrote the script and supervised dubbing the English edition into Italian. "Roberto and I had 'divorced' after the Bergman and Magnani story. To tell the truth, I had taken Magnani's side, but there were lots of other things as well." Roberto was repeatedly throwing away opportunities to do great things with Bergman, he thought. They hadn't spoken for two years.

"I'd gone to South America and talked to Perón about film, because I'd seen a film about the inhabitants of the Plata delta, one of the biggest deltas in the world, formed by the confluence of the Uruguay and Paraguay rivers. And I said to Perón, 'You see, this gentleman made a film on the world's biggest delta and it looks like the Po delta, Rossellini made a film on the Po delta and it looks like the Plata. To make great films we need great directors.' So he said, 'Bring me Rossellini and he can do what he wants.' And in fact I already had the idea of doing the story of a girl in the Andes who sees the passage of San Martín's army when the liberator of Argentina crossed the Andes, fell upon Chile and beat the Spanish, putting an end to Spanish dominion in South America. I got back to Rome May 1 and went to Rossellini's, we made up, etc., etc. He was so, so, so enthusiastic about the South America idea.

"And instead came this deal to make *Fear* from a mediocre story by Stefan Zweig. With a fairly mediocre actor. But now Rossellini was a bit tied to his complex of things, wives, and children. . . . Not that he had changed, he still had that extraordinary ability to seduce you, but undeniably he had things weighing on his shoulders that he had to solve. . . . He had problems making ends meet. But more and more unconsciously inside him there was being created a state of mind that he really didn't like this kind of cinema. It didn't interest him anymore, he was doing it against his will, to tell the truth. Deep inside him he was beginning to see the idea of the sort of cinema he [would make in the 1970s], a more didactic cinema, more tied to a need to make things known to people at the same time he learned them himself."[72]

Zweig's *Angst* is about a husband who discovers his wife has a lover and hires a blackmailer to terrify her into a confession he thinks will be reconciling. Instead he has to intervene to stop her from taking poison.

Said Roberto, "I was interested because it was Germany ten years after [*Deutschland*]—obviously a change I made in Zweig's story [written in 1910]; and because it's about the reconstruction, material reconstruction, yet still a search for a moral solution for problems; and because it's about the importance of knowing how to confess, because it's in knowing how to confess that we achieve a certain humility and, above all, a grand spirit of tolerance.[73]

"What's important is the woman's lie and her confession. The German actor I chose [to play her husband] has really the face of an honest man."[74] "I wanted to show the importance of confession. The woman is guilty and can free herself only by confessing."[75]

Accordingly, the movie ends with confession, reconciliation, and suitably beatific music.

Was Roberto on the husband's side (and hostile to Ingrid)?

In fact his movie goes in the opposite direction. Zweig's point had not been the efficacy of confession, but the evil of arrogance, which Rossellini amplifies. He added a residue of the Nazi past into the setting and cast as the husband an actor with Nazi associations, Mathias Wieman.[76] He transforms Zweig's husband into a research science who tests animals past their limits of endurance, and then unfeelingly tests his wife the same way. He has him pursue and spy on the wife with a face of manic hatred rather than honesty. And he has the wife resort to suicide not from fear of exposure, but from horror and despair—because he has her *learn* that her husband is behind the blackmail. The woman's lie and guilt now seem irrelevant; it is the diabolic husband who needs the humility of confessing. He arrives just in time to stop her killing herself.

The film ends forty seconds later. He says forgive me, she collapses in his arms, the music plays a lullaby, and the movie ends. It is the most elaborate example of Rossellini's "improvisation to obtain a better rhythm, to maintain a state of tension that has to break in a finale that I want to be unexpected and brutal."[77]

But Rossellini's dramatic resolution contradicts his proclaimed intentions without making any sense on it own terms. We hate the husband, whose self-righteousness appears too little shaken, and do not comprehend the wife forgiving him so easily. Nor has she confronted her lie and guilt. The conflict of their immediate emotional separation has been resolved, but the moral conflicts of the film's plot are more glaringly at odds than ever.

It is the same situation as in *Stromboli*, where we were concerned with the questionable sincerity and undefined consequences of Karin's sudden outcry to God. In *Fear* it is true to life that the wife might confront her own fear and ignore her husband's cruelty *initially*, even if such myopia outrages the conventions of fiction, and it is true that a man of blunt righteousness might not initially confront his own evilness. What will happen during the next year is not Rossellini's concern, any more than it was his concern what Karin would do next on the volcano. His concern is the growing "tension" that leads up to the purifying moment of impulse, and that moment itself. The rest would be mere sequel.

Fear's subject, Truffaut perceived, is "only a feeling. The script is a suite of variations on this feeling.[78] Each incident leads us back to the themes of death, shame, and confession. The mise en scène consists, as always with Rossellini, in continually following the heroine along her via crucis by rich, complex camera movements that do not leave her for a second. We see what she sees, then we see her seeing and reacting. She goes down the stairs, walks to her car, drives, stops, starts again, and lives, amid cornered and frightened glances, an adventure truly Hitchcockian—although Rossellini's means and end are obviously more noble than those in a film by the master of suspense."[79]

Rossellini's obsessive pursuit recalls *Una voce umana*, "an individual captured, put under the microscope, scrutinized to the core," as he admitted.[80] Especially in the seven-minute take leading up to her suicide-by-injection attempt, the way Rossellini watches Irene Wagner's disintegration associates him with her husband, who stood watching the agony of a lab rabbit. This is a Hitchcockian aspect: the storyteller's sadistic voyeurism and our participation in it. Amidei and other friends thought Ingrid's success in *Joan* made Roberto want to punish and dominate her.[81] Yet although his camera follows her, she frequently has her head turned away, with the result that *Fear* lacks the intimacy and immodesty of *Europe '51*, *Stromboli*, or *Voyage*, and relies more on bodies moving into shadows and pools of light, on harsh surfaces and monstrous, dehumanized faces. There is not punishment or dominance, but neither is there the great empathy of earlier movies.

This impersonalization is even truer in Rossellini's treatment of the husband. There are *two* wrongs in *Fear*, but we discount Irene's because Albert Wagner's "honest" face displays constant blind aggression, and rarely the weakness and sorrow that would render him empathetic. *Fear* is a mad scientist story: he represses his anger into "science," subordinates women and children to "theory," and becomes himself a purely theoretical entity.

"Germany" also is theoretical. Neither interiors nor urban exteriors feel German, or give a sensation of being anywhere particular. In *Deutschland*, which also has abundant light and shadow, there is also an actual cityscape to define the boy, whereas in *Fear* there is only a milieu of the imagination. Irene is not merely untrue to her husband; she has lost almost all contact with any reality that is not shadowy. Yet she always insists on driving. And she feels alive in the country, where there are no pools of light and shadow, but where she puts on folk clothing, neglects her children, and drenches herself in dreamy, mystic union with nature. Much of the French New Wave, Truffaut particularly, is anticipated in the drive through the woods to the Wagners' house. *Cahiers'* Jacques Sicilier, who saw *Fear* in Germany, nonetheless contends that it "is really the sole film that takes account of German realities"—the mixture of technology and weekends in the country—and calls it "an essay on cruelty. The couple from *Voyage* is destroyed, implacably. From the depths of heart and soul of his characters Rossellini makes monsters surge. *Fear* is a film that gives pain, a bit like the razor in *Un Chien andalou*."[82]

Zweig, depressed over the Nazis, had committed suicide in Brazil in 1942. But *Fear*, contrary to what Sicilier argues, brings a new beginning: this couple's worlds will be different from now on, as a result of this moment of impulse. The "moral search" has found something.

Fear was shot in thirty days. Roberto began each of them with a twenty-mile drive across Munich to Franz Treuberg's house, where he would fill a liter bottle with espresso. He drank coffee and smoked constantly. Ingrid rather liked her part because it gave her a chance to act. But as usual Roberto spent days filming her walking around, and as usual she wanted to understand the scene and he would refuse to explain. They would do a scene in one language, then again in the other, never exactly the same way. Sometimes there were ten takes.[83] Roberto had to depend on a translator, Beate von Molo, who appears in the credits as "Dialogue Director." Klaus Klinski has a walk-on. Ever practical, Ingrid posed in costume for some magazine ads for Carpano aperitifs.[84]

Rossellini appears not to have attended to the post-production. He left for London where *Joan of Arc at the Stake* was opening on stage October 20. As a result, *Fear* and *Angst* were edited quite differently. The final take, for example, has a cutaway of the husband arriving in *Angst* but is seamless in *Fear*. The drive through the trees, possibly the most physically beautiful shot in the film, is missing in *Angst*, as are the Ophuls-like tracks in the corridors of the opera house. These last precede a kind of Hitchcockian "set piece," when the blackmailer trades glances across the auditorium with Irene sitting with her husband. It is an odd sequence, because it is over-elaborated for Rossellini and wants to suggest Hitchcock. But Roberto loathed Hitchcock's cinema, and as rivals for Ingrid both men were publicly contemptuous of each other. In *Angst* a performance of *La Bohème* is going on; in *Fear* a solo pianist plays Chopin's G-minor Ballade. Perhaps Rossellini left it for his editors to decide. But if the *terms* of a Hitchcockian montage do not matter, Rossellini suggests, neither do the angles: Rossellini's do not rhyme! When Schultze stares at Irene, she places Irene as sitting stage right. But when Irene stares at Schultze, she places herself as sitting stage left. Rather than being disorienting, this non-rhyming accentuates the autarchy of the two characters. In contrast, in Hitchcock a character like Schultze gets caught up in the cogs of the editing, and does not emerge as having any life outside those montage moments.

Joan of Arc at the Stake, in English in London six nights a week for a month, was a triumph for Bergman, and as in Paris was covered as the event of the season. The *Times* evoked Ingrid as "differentiating the human and the divine, vivid in action, sustained in repose." *The Sketch* said, "She evokes the sadness of things supremely well.... The quality she possesses is more than beauty: it is strangeness in beauty."[85] Again, as in Paris (but never in Italy), many noted Ingrid's Swedish-American accent ("Eet iss I, Joan of Arc!").

The production itself did not please; applause was tepid. London's Stoll Theatre had so small a stage that the orchestra and singers had had to be dispersed among 22 boxes all over the auditorium—quite beyond the conductor's ability to control their balance. The chaos encouraged drama critics' frustration over a spectacle that was neither realism or fantasy, opera nor oratorio, theater nor cinema, spoken nor sung, and yet was all of them muddled together. "An unutterably vulgarized spectacle ... butchered to make a film producer's holiday," quipped one wag. "Superbly staged," another allowed. "Pretentious, pseudo religious and boring," psalmed a third.[86]

"I am not bitterly disappointed because I understand," replied Rossellini, who had not taken a curtain call. "When *I* first saw the oratorio there were things about it I did not like. But now I know I was wrong. The critics are wrong too because *they* do not understand."[87]

Even Claudel at the Paris Opéra, however, had complained that from his seat he could not see the Cathedral, which suggests that Rossellini was not reconciled to the medium of live theater.

The production would lose £10,000, even if sold out, the producer said.

Three weeks before, *Viaggio in Italia* and Fellini's *La strada* had opened in Rome on the same day, October 1, 1954: *La strada* in three theaters, with huge ads, after its triumph at Venice; *Viaggio* at the Fiamma with, in a few papers, a tiny ad. *Viaggio*'s gross for all Italy would amount to less than $100,000. Eight years later *Cahiers du Cinéma* would vote it the finest movie ever made in Italy, but in 1954 Italian critics, like a herd of lemmings, saw it differently:

"The sole possibility left to Rossellini, to have himself considered a great director, is for him to retire definitively from the screen, and to have his last four or five films withdrawn from circulation. In certain circumstances, changing profession is without doubt the wisest thing one can do." (Marino Onorati, *Film d'Oggi*)

"*Viaggio in Italia* is nothing but a confirmation of Rossellini's absolute, terminal, irremediable decadence. . . . There is no plot, no dialogue, no scenario, no direction. It's a mess of images that creeps along, tediously. . . . Any journalist could have given us more, just by photographing the famous monuments. . . . An ugly film, a true and actual insult to the intelligence of the spectators." (Ezio Colombo, *Festival*)

"[It's true what the critics say, that with each new film Rosssellini shows] how incapable he is of saying anything at all anymore, how incapable of anything he is, except failure. . . . But this can't be said of *Viaggio in Italia*, where his intentions are so modest to begin with, and the results even more so." (Mario Gallo, *Avanti!*)

"Inadequate and dilettante-ish in the worst sense, even more than usual. . . . The actors, lacking guidance from the script, are insecure, boring and vague. Rossellini should read Flaubert's letters to Louise Colet, in which he says that a novel (or film) represents serious commitment and demands dedication and sacrifice." (Tullio Kezich, *Sipario*)

"Exasperating in its slowness . . . , without any trace of the human empathy that made earlier characters so throbbing." (*L'Unità*)

"The touring scenes are superfluous and the soundtrack is too full of Neapolitan voices." (*Corriere della Sera*)

"Sanders was right to complain. . . . The basic defect . . . is the absence of any 'psychological' causes that would justify the characters and story. . . . When the director forces Katherine to mumble, in close-up, monologues expressing her anguish and resentment toward her husband, the borders of the ridiculous are exceeded." (C. G. Castello, *Cinema*)

"Extreme superficiality . . . unfocused, pretentious, even dilettante-ish . . . decadence . . . involution . . . a vulgar tourist expedition." (Fernando Di Giammatteo, *Rassegna del Film*)

Even faithful Gian Luigi Rondi jumped ship, declaring that characters and themes were only sketchy, the drama deficient in logic, the whole never coalescing into a finished aesthetic unity.

All were agreed, a French colleague noted, that "Rossellini owes all his reputation to an extraordinary moment in our country's history [the postwar]. It was enough then just to use news footage. The difficulties began when Rossellini found himself face to face with himself. He has never resolved them."

Even Bergman, for once, fared badly. "Rossellini has not only managed to destroy himself but [Bergman] too," decried Castello, adding that his destruction of an international star cast worldwide shame on the entire Italian film industry. Ingrid's sole defender, Mario Gromo (*La Nuova Stampa*), was fascinated by her character's marvelous moments of fatigue, resignation, and endurance; her watchful waiting, her wanting to know, her refusal either to rebel openly or to submit. But Gromo gave *all* credit for this to Bergman, and none to Rossellini, and why? Because none of these "precise touches" were in the dialogue.[88]

Has any other film been attacked so savagely by so many critics—ever? Rossellini had not merely made a bad movie. He had forsaken social commitment for Hollywood escapism, had been buying respectability by peddling religious dribble, had made all Italy look incompetent and, after all this, didn't even have a proper sense of shame.

Maybe such a view of Rossellini was inevitable at this stage of the Cold War. Rossellini's historicism, his assumption that knowledge is chimeric, offended Christians and Marxists alike, and required that progressive forces stake him out. Rossellini's heroes were climbing the volcano and finding reality, but they weren't coming down to tell us what to do about war and poverty; they were just running around acting stoned, like Francesco. This was the "insult" that had to be condemned. God, capitalism, and communism were locked in a titanic struggle, and Roberto was deflecting the issues.

Rondi's panegyric reviews of Rossellini's films, year after year, had been religious tracts as much as film criticism. One suspects he was defending Catholicism rather than Rossellini, when, apropos of *Viaggio in Italia*, a film in which he could find nothing to praise *except* the Catholicism, he would write: "Despite the contrary opinion of idealists and Marxists, only Christianity has a complete understanding of reality, and only Christianity, thus, is completely realistic."[89]

Edoardo Bruno was virtually the only critic eager to defend *Viaggio*, the only one to find it intensely moving.[90]

And Fellini was one of the few industry figures to give Roberto unqualified support. He was being attacked for many of the same reasons himself.

Obvious differences mask the similarity of Rossellini and Fellini. Rossellini is modern, Fellini baroque; Rossellini regards, Fellini surrealizes;[91] Rossellini is historical, Fellini metaphysical.[92] Fellini is an "exasperation" of Rossellini, as Orson Welles is an exasperation of John Ford.

But at Venice in 1954 *La strada* was greeted in the same terms as *Stromboli* four years earlier. For some, it was a parable of Christian love, grace, and salvation. For others, it was a deplorable abandonment of orthodox neo-realism.[93] The awards committee embittered the controversy by giving a Silver Lion to *La strada* and ignoring (because of anti-Communist pressure from above, it was rumored) Visconti's *Senso*.[94] Shouts and whistles greeted Fellini when he went to the podium, and a scuffle broke out between Fellini's assistant Moraldo Rossi and Visconti's assistant Franco Zeffirelli.

Aristarco declared Fellini guilty of bourgeois individualism. *La strada* wasn't a bad film, but its "poetry of the solitary man" was *wrong*, a wrong perspective. Aristarco cited Pavese —"We started out with the intention of coming to know and understand reality more profoundly, and the result is that we are closing ourselves up within a fictitious world inimical to reality"—and insisted that Fellini is "an eternal adolescent... jealously preserv[ing] the subtlest poisons of prewar literature. ... He seeks out his own emotions along the treacherous paths of suggestivism and autobiographism, and mistakes agitation for an intense need for poetic expression."[95]

Fellini replied in *Il Contemporaneo*, a cultural journal financed by the Communist Party. "*La strada*," he wrote (but he might equally have written *Paisà* or *Europe '51*), "seeks to realize the experience which is the most basic for opening up any social prospect: the joint experience between man and man. ... Our trouble, as modern men, is loneliness, and this begins in the very depth of our being. Only between man and man, I think, can this solitude be broken, only through individual people can a kind of message be passed, making them understand—almost discover—the profound link between one person and the next. *La strada* expresses something like this with the means available to the cinema. Because it tries to show the supernatural and personal communication between a man and a woman who would seem by nature to be the least likely people to understand each other, it has, I believe, been attacked by those who believe only in natural and political communication. ... I do not believe in 'objectivity,' at least in the way you people believe in it, and cannot accept your ideas of neo-realism which I feel do not fully capture, or really even impinge upon, the essence of the movement to which I have had the honor, since *Roma città aperta*, to belong."[96]

For Aristarco, the ideal neo-realist film would expose the socioeconomic "structures" underlying reality. But such a film would seem anti-realist to Rossellini and Fellini (and Bazin[97]), because it would materialize the spiritual; and it would seem anti-art because it would subjugate appearances to structures, existence to essence. Complained Fellini, "Realism is neither an enclosure nor a pan of a single surface. A landscape ... has several thicknesses and the deepest, which a poetic language can alone reveal, is not the least real. What I want to show behind the epidermis of things and people, I'm being told is irreal.[98]

"Rossellini didn't know he was doing 'neo-realism' when he shot *Roma città aperta.* Since then people have tried to build a wall around neo-realism and hoist a flag over it. And now they're criticizing Rossellini and me for jumping over that wall."[99]

All such debates occurred in a rarefied world. The real Italy had about 12,000 movie theaters in 1954, of which 3,500 were church halls, 8,500 were in small towns, ninety percent grossed less than $150 a day, and half grossed between $15 and $80. The average Italian paid 21¢ for a ticket sixteen times a year, 1.1 percent of his income. The average theater attracted 80,000 people a year. But sixty percent of Italian films lost money. They had to compete with 300 imports a year and almost 6,000 reissues, most of them with Hollywood budgets greater than an Italian filmmaker could dream of. One hundred fifty-seven features were made in 1954, but (*if* figures are to be believed) only two-thirds of the median cost of $275,000 was recouped in the home market, even after $80,000 in government subsidy.

Roberto swore he was through with Italy. Amidei wrote to Fulchignoni in Paris, November 9:

> Dear Enrico, if you happen to see Roberto, tell him I was very sorry I couldn't see him before his departure, which, in his words, is final. Maybe he'll come back, but when? Each year there're fewer of us left. And Roberto's leaving makes me feel all the weight of the years. With him goes the last friend of my youth. (My second youth, to tell the truth, since my first one had already ended when I came to Rome 21 years ago.) I met him the day I arrived, with Vergano and Poggioli at the Restaurant on Via Zucchelli, and for all these years I've felt deep affection for him, and precisely because I cared about him I haven't always managed to forgive his "betrayals."
>
> Now that he's gone I really want him to learn that I always think of him with so much affection.
>
> I'm not surprised he's leaving! Who wouldn't like to get away from here?
>
> But some of the fault for finding himself so low, without hope of solution, is also his, but will he recognize it? I hope so!
>
> Tell him I wish him all the best, and any time I can be of service to him, and I can, he should make use of me.
>
> I embrace him and I embrace you,
>
> Sergio[100]

Roberto's reaction was to laugh. The substance of affection did not exist for him, according to Fulchignoni; he was too insecure to have attachments. Betrayal did not shame him, it was obligations he feared. Amidei accepted this; he considered Roberto a genius.[101]

Amidei's valedictory to an era and a generation was written just weeks after another letter, one that heralded the next era and generation.

"I was in Germany and one day I received a letter from a signor Truffaut, whom I absolutely did not know," Roberto said in 1963, forgetting that Truffaut had interviewed him in Paris in March. "I had made *Voyage in Italy* and the French distributor, who was also the co-producer, had completely changed the film, and had changed its title to *La Divorcée de Naples*, and had even changed the story. In the letter young Truffaut told me how he had promoted action by the French critics to block the film and to have it distributed in a undubbed print with subtitles. And he succeeded. From this event was born my friendship with these boys, who have always been close to me since then and probably love me much too much."[102]

Roberto went to Paris in November 1954 and invited Truffaut to dinner and a small screening of a workprint of *Jeanne au bûcher*. Robertino sat playing with a small lead figure of Joan, Truffaut noted.

"When I met Rossellini . . . , his discouragement was total. He had just finished *Fear* and was thinking seriously of giving up film.[103] He proposed my working with him, as assistant, as friend.[104] I was his assistant for three years, during which time he did not expose a single foot of film!"[105]

Roberto would phone frequently. He had just been talking to someone and had a new idea. They'd start filming in a month. Truffaut was to find every book on the subject and set up meetings with innumerable people. They had to "move."

Roberto amused the Parisians. He was "brilliant, seductive, droll, brimming with anecdotes"—especially at dinner.[106] His laziness was no less impressive. In bed, or stretched out in a chair, he would recite elegies on laziness, slowly. He would contend that the Roman Empire had been built on laziness: witness how Roman statues always show people leaning on something, whereas Greek statues are free standing.[107]

Wandering around a large Paris department store one day, he came upon a kangaroo looking so sad locked up in its cage that his heart went out to it. He bought it and took it to The Raphael, shocking the hotel staff. The children would feed it bananas but the free kangaroo would box anyone who came near it. Finally the manager insisted it be taken away. "After that we used to go visit it at the Rome Zoo," daughter Ingrid recalls.

In December, Roberto opened the season at Naples's San Carlo for the third time. But Pizzetti's 1936 setting of D'Annunzio's *La Figlia di Jorio* did not offer opportunities comparable to *Otello* or *Giovanna d'Arco* and Rossellini's contributions were hardly noticed.[108]

On December 22, 1954, *Jeanne d'Arc au bûcher* opened in Barcelona, in French. "It is dreary to rehearse Joan again," Ingrid complained to Joe Steele. "I have already given at least sixty performances, and now I have to begin from the beginning. I was so bored with the rehearsals here, how bored am I not going to be in Palermo and then Stockholm!"[109] She found the city dirty and smelly, objected to Roberto taking Robertino to a bullfight, and was amazed during the opening performance to find her husband on stage dressed as a monk telling the unrehearsed players where to go. One performance was broadcasted.

Roberto phoned Truffaut a few days later from Chaplin's house in Vivey, Switzerland. Truffaut should meet him in Lyon at once, they were driving to Lisbon, to discuss filming Henry de Montherlant's play, *La Reine morte*, the story about Inez de Castro, the murdered mistress of a fourteenth-century Portuguese prince who, after he became king, exhumed her body, had it crowned queen, and compelled his court to pay it homage. There was also talk of filming *Juana en la hoguera* with Akbero Ruschfell and Amalia Rodriquez.[110] Truffaut took the first train. At station Bellecourt the big red Ferrari was waiting and roared off immediately. "He drove night and day. I had to tell him stories to keep him awake and he handed me a mysterious bottle to inhale any time I felt close to falling asleep."[111]

Lisbon didn't work out. Driving back through Castile, the Ferrari's steering broke at full speed. In a small village Roberto found a mechanic to fabricate a part for him and was so grateful he decided he'd do *Carmen*. In Paris he found a fifteen-year-old dancer who was ideal, but producers, knowing Roberto, demanded a detailed treatment, so he had Truffaut put one together with scissors and glue and three paperback copies of Prosper Mérimée's *Carmen*.

"The film," said Roberto, "will be about death, in black and white, and shot in actual locations, in the streets and piazzas, with beginning actors, all very young. [Spain] is a fantastic country, an extraordinary people who look death in the face. To the point of descending into the arenas to look at it closer. The Spaniard is alone, always. The Spanish singer sings for himself and replies to himself, the dancer dances with himself, the toreador combats with himself, since the bull does not even look at him. A bull that looks at the matador is excluded, slaughtered, as unworthy of what is expected of it."[112]

Nothing came of *Carmen*. The distributors wanted stars—Marina Vlady was mentioned—and Roberto was obsessed with a new idea. He was having secret meetings with a Soviet diplomat, on the street, always somewhere different. He was going to do a Soviet *Paisà*. He found someone to translate *Pravda* for him every day, read whatever he could find on Russia, and started finding stories. One was about a man who thinks he spots his wife having a rendezvous, follows her, and, from afar, keeps seeing her in the arms of different men—until he discovers that the state-run department store has just received a hundred new dresses, all the same. Roberto's humor didn't appeal to the Soviet diplomat.

Other projects included D. H. Lawrence's *The Plumed Serpent*, to be filmed during a five-month tour of Mexico and South America with *Joan of Arc at the Stake*; a *Faust* after Murnau with Gerard Philipe and Frederic March; a film on the Renaissance drawn from Stendhal's *Italian Chronicles*.[113]

"When Rossellini wrote a scenario," said Truffaut, "he never had problems. The point of departure was enough. Given such and such a character, his religion, food, nationality, and pastimes, he could only have certain needs and certain desires. A discord between needs and desire sufficed to create the conflict which would evolve naturally by itself, if one took account of the historical, ethnic, social, and geographic realities of the character's origin. Nor was there any problem how to end the film. The finish would be dictated by the sum, optimistic or pessimistic, of all the conflict's elements. . . . Rossellini detested . . . anything decorative, anything that did not serve the idea of the film or the personality of the characters. If in my own films, I've tried to follow simply and honestly a single character in an almost documentary manner, it's to him that I owe it."[114]

Joan opened in Stockholm (as *Jeanne d'Arc på bålet*) February 17, 1955. A huge crowd had gathered at the train station to greet Ingrid, Roberto, and their children. At a palace ball Ingrid was presented to King Gustav, who almost immediately asked for her husband. "Well, he's hiding behind a pillar over there, Your Majesty, because he hasn't got tails."[115] Roberto emerged on summons: the king wanted to talk Ferraris.

The opening attracted the prime minister and most of Sweden's leading social and theatrical figures. One of Sweden's most famous writers had translated Claudel's verse, Nils-Olof Franzén. Public success was so great that the run was extended from ten performances to 22. The Swedish press, however, was cool and at times resentful. One satirist in particular, Stig Ahlgren, who had already poked fun at the king, spied an easy target: "The criticism both here and abroad has been acid against Ingrid Bergman. Her register is too narrow. Her tone of voice is too trivial. She doesn't know what passion is, etc. What she earned when she acted as Joan of Arc was not small change. . . . [But] to compare her with professional actresses is both mean and unjust. She travels around and is shown for money. The promoter is Roberto Rossellini, with whom she has three children and one Rolls-Royce. With art this traveling company has nothing to do. . . . But why criticize? . . . Ingrid is not an actress but a clever businesswoman. . . . Ingrid Bergman is a commodity, so far a desirable commodity which is offered in the free market. She is paid according to the same pricing mechanism that is valid for herring and pig iron."[116]

Roberto had gone back to Paris after the initial performances. Ingrid was left to face the hostility alone. When she found herself being attacked by an editorial "which took all honor and everything away from me" on the very day she was appearing, at the request of the same newspaper, at a charity performance, she turned on her critics and passionately appealed to the audience about "the lies . . . lies which I cannot answer!" The papers reversed themselves.[117] "It was great fun when war was declared and I answered back," she wrote Joe Steele.[118]

Ingrid's countryman, Ingmar Bergman, confessed years later that Ingrid had always exercised "an enormous erotic attraction" over him. "I thought that when she appeared in Sweden in *Joan of Arc at the Stake*, the reception was very unfair. I didn't think the director [Rossellini] helped her much; it seemed to me she created herself. I thought it was a great scandal when all the critics together tried to kill her . . . some sort of revenge. . . .

Secondly, of course, the truth is the oratorio was not perfect. Sometimes it was—I had the feeling as I sat there, that it was close to catastrophe, but in *my* truth—fifty percent of Ingrid's performance was absolutely stunning, absolutely marvelous; twenty percent was acceptable, and thirty percent was absolutely catastrophic."[119]

The oratorio's final run was in Palermo's Teatro Massimo at Easter, April 27, 1955. The Rossellinis spent three weeks in Sicily. Honegger and Cocteau had both died that winter. Meanwhile reviews of the film *Giovanna d'Arco al rogo*, and also of *Fear*, had begun to appear. The violence of the Italian press was so unspated that it became cliché.

"Roberto and Ingrid," wrote the respected Angelo Solmi in *Oggi*, "will either have to change their style of work radically—or retire into dignified silence. The abyss into which Bergman and Rossellini have plunged can be measured by *Fear*. This is not because this picture is any worse than their other recent films together, but because after half-a-dozen tries with negative results it confirms the inability of the couple to create anything acceptable to the public or the critics. Once the world's indisputable No. 1 star and successor to Greta Garbo, Miss Bergman in recent pictures has been only a shadow of herself."[120]

Even *Joan*'s admirers admitted it was not a film easy to like. Jacques Doniol-Valcroze, seeing it a second time with Pagnol, Straub, the Bazins, and Truffaut, remarked that "the enterprise remains astonishing, incredibly 'perverse' . . . and if there are dull or boring parts here and there, this is due to Claudel, not Rossellini."[121] Truffaut, insisting that only five out of an audience of 300 had walked out of a test screening, proclaimed, "Rossellini, who contrasts the 'too human' face of a celestial Joan with the stereotyped masks of people 'dead to life,' has made an appeal to all preceding cinema (Murnau, Méliès chiefly) and has found a naive work style totally related to the oratorio's.[122] Just as it is necessary, in order to appreciate Claudel, to take his words literally 'à la lettre,' exactly for what they are worth, so too in order to love Rossellini's film it is necessary to rediscover the innocence of a spectator seeing a film for the first time. Twenty years of allusive and elliptic cinema, and thousands and thousands of films that exist only in terms of each other, have created a situation where a film as elementary as *Jeanne* takes on the allure of something dangerously avant-garde and abstract."[123]

"Bergman dubbed herself in French with a Swedish-Italian-English accent that ends up exactly like a Lorrain accent," wrote Doniol-Valcroze in January. But by the May test screening Truffaut was moaning that the "merchants," who "never go in the intelligent direction," had replaced Bergman's "beautiful Bourguigon-Lorrain accent" with the "banal, very 'Comédie Française' voice" of Claude Nollier.[124]

Hovald thought the Ministry of Education had a duty to sponsor the film all over France. In fact it never got beyond a single screening at the Cinémathèque in July, where Agel reported most of the audience was bored and silent, even when Roberto appeared in person to answer questions. "He explains himself with a humility equaled only by Renoir. He even greets some people's aggressive incomprehension with a smile. I asked him if his work as a whole corresponds to a spiritual itinerary. He answered with moving sincerity that Christianity for him was neither something he thinks much about nor an ideological position, but rather a question of temperament, a way of being that his films express precisely. But the spectators, in the presence of this man who speaks about his art with the simplicity of an artisan and the inner fervor of a believer, did not manage to slough off their inertia, their tepid film-clubbish apathy. Were they impervious to greatness of this most astonishing of Italian filmmakers, or is it that film clubs corrupt people?"[125]

Critics were evidently corrupt as well. Almost all of them, in Italy and France, thought the movie a "lyrical bore."[126] *Cinema Nuovo* called it "extreme creative poverty and infinite boredom." In *Figaro Littérature* Claude Mauriac asked, "How can one be at the same time one of the inspired inventors of neo-realism, and responsible for this naive resurrection of theatrical pseudo-realism of the most dated kind?" "It is to be marveled that a production house and distributor accepted a film of this kind," agreed an Italian critic.[127]

La paura (Fear) was a worse debacle. It played in Rome only three days, but still generated odium and diatribe. "For some time the name of Rossellini has meant artistic and commercial bankruptcy. Critics each time feel compelled to repeat the story of his unheard-of decadence, while the publicists now feel it is indispensable to keep his name off the advertisements. This is what happens after one has over-abused the public's patience," wrote Casiraghi in *L'Unità* when *La paura* played Milan in January. By the time it opened in Rome, "on a Sunday toward the end of July, a certain guarantee of commercial failure," *Il Borghese* could chortle about "the *Fear* of being a director. The director of neo-realism has not realized that no film can be valid if [it] is without internal structure, if it is made without purpose and, as the posters would have us understand, without a director." *Cinema Nuovo* called it "catastrophic," the direction "dilettantish," the photography "pretentious," the scenario like a comic strip (*fumetto*): "Is this really the same director who did *Paisà*? . . . Is it possible that in 'Germany Year Ten' Rossellini could not find anything more inspiring than this mini-drama of bad, family jokes between a jealous husband and an unfaithful wife?" *Epoca* said, "The whole drama is indigestible, irritating, and anti-commercial. [Was it] Rossellini's intention to make his offering to the family altar by showing the horror of adultery and that (like Mussolini) the husband's always right[?]" *Variety* judged, "*Fear* gives evidence of [Rossellini's] artistic decline. . . . Had it not been Miss Bergman in the femme lead, pic might have been a total flop."[128]

By now, as Ojetti wrote in *Cinema*, "the violent campaign" against Rossellini was looking like "an actual real work of demolition . . . , a lynching."[129]

A rearguard defense began.

Bianco e Nero editorialized that Solmi in *Oggi* failed to take into account the specifically Italian "misunderstandings, jealousies, and calumnies" that were sabotaging Rossellini's efforts and inducing even his most committed colleagues to abandon him. *Cinema* agreed that Rossellini's "error" was his refusal to choose one ideological camp over another, thus leaving himself naked to attacks from all sides.[130]

But *Bianco e Nero*, although defending Rossellini, was conceding the inferiority of the films, as Ingrid Bergman did as well: "Roberto was always under pressure because we needed money. He could never concentrate on just being a director."[131]

She blamed herself; the critics agreed. *L'Unità*, in praising *La paura*, found "all the more reason to regret [Rossellini's] abandonment of his own country and his neo-realist way of looking at familiar things." *Cinema* advised him to remake *Roma città aperta* if he wanted "to reconquer the sympathies of the critics."[132]

Rossellini retorted—"If they want another *Roma città aperta* or *Paisà* or *Germania anno zero*, let them make another war, but let THEM do it; then I'll make the films"—but was ignored by friends who thought they knew better.[133]

Zavattini in his "Diary" in *Cinema Nuovo* wrote, "I had a great desire to write Rossellini and tell him to come to Italy and go back to work here with calm, with humility, because he would make more masterworks. He is unpopular in Italy, despite being one of the men to whom in these years Italy has owed the most!"[134]

A few months later, *La paura*'s distributor withdrew it, re-edited it, and re-released it as *Non credo più all'amore* ("I don't believe in love anymore"), without success, and then as *Incubo* ("Nightmare"), also without success. *Non credo più* ends not with Irene's suicide attempt, but with scenes of her country house and a voice-over telling us she has left her husband and gone back to caring for her children. Rossellini had not authorized this change, but it was the ending most reviewers had urged. No one mentioned the resemblance to Howard Hughes's fabrication of a "satisfying" dénouement for *Stromboli*. But, then, no one saw it.

Enrico Fulchignoni, who headed UNESCO's Film Section, had an office across from The Raphael and was constantly introducing Roberto to interesting people. Spotting him from his window one day, he called him inside, presented him to Jean Rouch, and talked him into sitting through a three-hour silent work print of Rouch's *Jaguar*, with Rouch narrating, and most of the *Cahiers* group also present.

"Never," Rouch recalled, "had a man done so much and been so humiliated for what he had done. I think that when we saw Roberto Rossellini arrive in Paris, after *Voyage in Italy* (which for me . . . is a film as important for the history of cinema as Chaplin's *Woman of Paris*), and when we knew that this film had been received by Italian critics as . . . nothing . . .

(whereas in it there is everything we are still trying to do today), we had in front of us a man humiliated. And it was strange to see this sort of gladiator coming from defeat, coming to France in search of something.[135] A beaten man, a wounded gladiator, but still a volcano, with never a single moment of dejection. Alone, a foreigner, without followers anymore in his native country, he was capable of carrying the revolution into our Parisian film circles, where we thought we had everything, and he, instead, with one stroke, showed us that we had nothing. He—who after the disaster of *Voyage in Italy* seemed to have lost everything—stimulated us, talked to us, saw and judged our films, pushed us to make others more courageous, more 'different,' and then went away."[136]

Jaguar intrigued Roberto, both because Rouch was one of the first to shoot a feature in 16mm, and because he had shot in Africa—in the "Third World"—a "typical" story with non-professional native players. Both were ideas Roberto would imitate. Now, when Rouch told him he was planning to dub in dialogue for *Jaguar*, Roberto suggested instead that he have his actors *tell* the story—as Roberto had done in the short "The Chicken." Equally intriguing, Rouch was using the first Nagra ever made—the lightweight battery-powered tape recorder that would soon revolutionize location filming. In combination, 16mm and the Nagra offered a filmmaker, particularly ethnographic, adventurous, "neo-realist" filmmakers, unprecedented opportunities. A single person could carry everything he or she needed in a small car. Production costs, compared to 35mm, could be reduced to almost nothing. It was the liberation from industrial control that Roberto had been fighting for. He urged Rouch, in his next film, to use the same approach, but this time with a *real* man. And he asked everyone present to find him stories for a film of his own—in India.[137]

Voyage in France

It was in this atmosphere that *Voyage in Italy* opened in Paris that April. *Cahiers du Cinéma* published two of the most ardent essays of film criticism, defining themselves, their era, Rossellini, and modern cinema.

For Rohmer, as we saw, it was an event as shattering as the first performance of Stravinsky's *Rite of Spring* or the first *fauve* painting by Matisse.[138]

For Rivette, taking off from Rohmer, what was like Matisse's crayon was Rossellini's "unwearying stare": "Think of any Rossellini film: each scene, each episode will recur in your memory not as a succession of shots and compositions, a more or less harmonious succession of more or less brilliant images, but as a vast melodic phrase, a continuous arabesque, a single implacable line which leads the characters ineluctably toward the as yet unknown, embracing in its trajectory a palpitant and *definitive* universe." Wasn't this like Matisse, the way, "on the canvas, a spontaneous curve circumscribes, without ever pinning down, the most brilliant of colors; a broken line, nevertheless unique, encompasses matter that is miraculously alive, as though seized intact at its source[?] On the screen, a long parabola, supple and precise, guides and controls each sequence, then perpetually closes again."[139] Doesn't *Voyage in Italy* have something like the "despoiled" quality of Matisse's pictures, where anything not essential is brutally omitted?

"If there is a modern cinema, this is it. . . . It seems to me impossible to see *Voyage in Italy* without experiencing direct evidence that this film opens a breach, and that the whole entire cinema must pass through it under pain of death. . . . Here, undoubtedly, is the culmination of art. . . . With the appearance of *Voyage in Italy*, all films have suddenly aged ten years. Nothing is more unpitying than youth, than this unequivocal intrusion by the modern cinema, in which we can at last recognize what we have been waiting for confusedly. . . . Here is our cinema, for us who in our turn are preparing ourselves to make films (Did I tell you? It may be soon)."[140]

"What first strikes you," wrote Truffaut, "is the novelty, the audacity. . . . This movie resembles those that will be made ten years from now, when filmmakers the world over will give up imitating the novel in favor of the filmed confession and the essay. . . . At times, points of emotion come to liberate the heart oppressed by a continuous dramatic tension that acts 'physically' on the spectator.[141] *Voyage in Italy* is not like anything ever done in cinema."[142]

What so impressed Rivette, Rohmer, and Truffaut?

Rivette likens it to "a television aesthetic . . . , a *direct* aesthetic," and concludes his article by declaring that the first thing to be done is "to come to an understanding on the meaning of the word *realism*, which is neither a scriptwriting technique nor a style of *mise en scène*, but a state of mind: *that a straight line is the shortest distance between two points*; (judge your De Sicas, Lattuadas, and Viscontis by this yardstick)." Television is a straight line; De Sica and Visconti twist the straight line. "Rossellini is not subtle, he is prodigiously simple."[143]

It was something deeper than the "phenomenological realism" of Bazin and Ayfre. It was a "realism of the soul,"[144] a Catholic realism.

"[Rossellini's] filmmaker's eye cannot be stressed too highly (and who can doubt that this is where his genius primarily lies?)." His eye sees, through phenomena, to the realism of the soul. It leads us, "ensconced in the darkness, holding our breath, eyes riveted to the screen," to "violate with impunity the *physical* intimacy of people who are quite unaware of being exposed to our fascinated gaze; and in consequence to the imminent rape of their *souls*."[145]

We are obsessed not just by each moment, but by their succession, which seems in hindsight to have been inevitable and leads us to give a more or less greater "weight of time" to each gesture. Thus, "within the illusion" that phenomena are simply succeeding one another," the mind is forced "to conceive another law than chance for their judicious advent." Rossellini is a "seer," which Rivette defines as "the faculty of seeing through beings and things to the soul . . . they carry within them." And what is that other law than chance? "Order itself, the heart of creation, the creator's design," says Rivette (evoking Goethe).[146]

But Rossellini doesn't argue or demonstrate, he shows. "And we have *seen*: that everything in Italy is a lesson and participates in a profound *dogmatism*, and that in Italy one suddenly finds oneself in the domain of the spirit and the soul." And these, if not "pure truths," are certainly "perceptible truths, which are even more true. There is no longer any question of symbols here"—just direct evidence [Croce]. Yet "everything now encountered by the gaze of this distraught woman, lost in the kingdom of grace, these statues, these lovers, these pregnant women who form for her an omnipresent haunting cortège, and then those huddled corpses, those skulls, and finally those banners, that procession of some almost barbaric cult, everything now radiates a different light, everything reveals itself as something else; here, visible to our eyes, are beauty, love, maternity, death, God.[147]

"All rather outmoded notions; yet there they are, visible; all you can do is cover your eyes, or kneel. There is a moment in Mozart when the music seems to draw nourishment only from itself, from an obsession with a pure chord; everything else is just approaches, successive explorations, and withdrawals from this supreme place where time is abolished.... [Likewise] cinema is never greater than in certain moments that transcend and abruptly suspend the drama.... Nothing in Rossellini better betokens the great filmmaker than those vast chords formed within his films by all the shots of eyes *looking* [Edmund in Berlin; Magnani on *Il miracolo*'s mountain; Bergman on Stromboli, in Rome's suburbs or Naples]; or [those moments when] vertiginous awareness of self grips [a character]. Whence comes the greatness of *Roma città aperta* or *Paisà*, if not from this sudden relaxation in human beings ... confronting the impossible fraternity ... ? Bergman's solitude is at the heart of both *Stromboli* and *Europe '51*.[148]

"But Rossellini is not merely Christian, he is Catholic; in other words, carnal to the point of scandal." So soul is always tied to flesh (phenomena). Rossellini depicts love as carnal, whereas the fashion is for angels or eroticism. "And it must be admitted that ... Rossellini often goes to the limits ... of what is decently admissible.... But Catholicism is by vocation a scandalous religion; the fact that *our body* also participates in the divine mystery, in the image of Christ's body, is something hardly to everyone's taste.[149]

"There is no doubt that these hurried films, improvised [like Matisse] out of very slender means and filmed in a turmoil that is often apparent from the images, contain the only real portrait of our times; and these times are a draft too. How could one fail suddenly to recognize, quintessentially sketched, ill-composed, unfinished, the semblance of our daily existence? These arbitrary groupings and abstract assemblages [in compositions of Matisse and Rossellini] of characters eaten away by boredom and lassitude, how well we recognize them! how perfectly they are the irrefutable, accusing image of our heteroclite, dissident, discordant societies. *Europe '51, Ger-*

many Year Zero, and this film which might be called *Italy '53*, just as *Paisà* was *Italy '44*, these are our mirror, scarcely flattering us. Let us still hope that this year will be faithful to the image of past years in these kindred films, and will secretly orient itself toward an inner order, toward a truth which will give it meaning and *in the end* justify so much disorder and confused haste."[150]

Rossellini's films, then, were documentaries showing the world being saved, perhaps they were even guidebooks for salvation. To be both (and many things besides) has, historically from the earliest myths and rituals, usually been art's prime function. "Rossellini deals with the very meaning of life and happiness," writes Leprohon.[151]

Cahiers promoted *Voyage in Italy* in almost every issue for the next few years. In August they began publishing an autobiographical essay tape-recorded by Roberto, "Ten Years in the Movies."[152] And André Bazin, carrying the torch to the enemy's citadel, published in *Cinema Nuovo* an open letter to Guido Aristarco, "In Defense of Rossellini." To Aristarco's shock at Rossellini's success in France, and to his objections that since *Deutschland* Rossellini had abandoned social realism and daily life for increasingly obvious moral messages, Bazin replied that neo-realism ought not to be predefined and that Rossellini, rather than piling up appearances, was trying to get at the essence of reality.[153]

In response, Aristarco's colleague Aldo Paladini repeated the argument discussed in Chapter 12, that Rossellini's films are "flawed by an erroneous sense of current reality," that he focuses on the *exceptional* people, who end up "acquiring value in themselves, independent of any tie with a vaster resonance, and for different reasons than those by which they might have universal value."[154]

Bazin replied in September, agreeing that Rossellini, in comparison to the emphasis on social reality in Zavattini–De Sica, was more concerned with moral issues. But, maintained Bazin, the exceptional solutions Rossellini's heroines find for themselves send shock waves through society; the dramatic event resides not in their individual action, but in the tissue of life.[155]

That same month *Voyage in Italy*, titled *Strangers*, opened in the U.S. *Variety* had counseled a year before that "some re-editing would help the pace considerably, with a hasty ending a sure trouble spot, since lacking proper motivation in its present form. . . . Tale is unevenly told with some unhappy bits of dialog and sometimes shows the roughcut form, which for this director is the final version." Now a second *Variety* reviewer pronounced it "dull and plodding fare . . . with hackneyed dialog badly dubbed. Miss Bergman, although poorly photographed, nevertheless lends charm to an indefinite role."[156] Lawrence J. Quirk in *Current Screen* said, "It all seems pointless and dull." And *Films in Review* announced it was "poorly written, incompetently directed, atrociously edited."[157]

"Recall," wrote Alain Bergala in 1984, "that with his Bergman films Rossellini was in the process of inventing nothing less that the modern cinema and that most of the French filmmakers that matter to us today, some thirty years later—Godard, Rivette, Rohmer, Truffaut, Straub—learned in these films, and in others by Jean Renoir, that the cinema is above all a moral affair, that the best way of filming is always the simplest, that real art avoids artistic effects like the plague, that true freedom is logical and does not care about rules and habits, and that filming should only be done in a state of urgency and necessity."[158]

After *Fear*, Rossellini would be able to make only a single film during the next five years, and even for that one he would have to rely on sponsorship by the government of India. No doubt he found solace in late spring watching another exile, Chaplin, make *King of New York* in Paris.

Ingrid Rescued. India Beckons.

"It was really my old friend Jean Renoir who rescued me," Ingrid exclaimed.

Renoir had proposed doing a film with her. She had objected, saying Roberto would not let her. Renoir had spoken to Roberto. And "to my intense surprise Roberto said, 'What a great idea. Certainly you must work with Jean.'"[159]

Roberto accompanied her to where Renoir was working and they sat on a curb waiting for him to come out. "I give you Ingrid. She is very unhappy," Roberto announced to his friend.[160]

In June 1955, Ingrid announced from Santa Marinella that she and Roberto were "splitting artistically." The choice of words was her own.[161]

Then she sent the Rolls-Royce to bring Hedda Hopper to Santa Marinella for lobster, squash, figs, loquats, cheese, and an interview. "If Ingrid was going to renew her film career, she needed Hedda on her side," notes Leamer.[162] She chatted charmingly about Selznick, America, and Hollywood and everything except Roberto, looking radiant, as Roberto sat beside her silent. After the powerful columnist left, Ingrid berated Roberto for his silence and he defended himself: "She was such a bitch!"[163] "Ingrid's love idyll is over," wrote Hopper.[164]

To his own journalist, in *Epoca*, Roberto argued that Americans felt threatened by Ingrid and wanted to destroy her myth. They'd destroyed even her recordings for the blind. An American monsignor had tried to take away Robertino for adoption. In Italy, attempts to destroy her alliance with Rossellini were part of a policy aimed at destroying independent film. The government hated the independent filmmakers; its new rules for obtaining subsidies excluded the independents, such as himself, even though it was little independents who produced almost all the movies Italy exported, and even though the year before six of the twenty independent films had been successful but only *one* of the 160 commercial films. (In theory, the government subsidy usually provided a third of a picture's budget; in actuality, accounts were rigged and the government often provided the whole of it.) Thus Ingrid would be going to Paris, Roberto concluded, and he to India. "THERE IS NOTHING FOR US IN ITALY ANYMORE" read the headline.[165]

Renoir had rescued Roberto too—with the dream of India. In London in June, Roberto had met Nehru, India's prime minister, at a reception. Nehru had introduced him to his foreign minister, Sir Raghavan Pillai. Roberto had talked up his project and the minister had replied they would do the film together.

"Roberto is leaving for India the end of this month," Ingrid wrote Rod and Katja Geiger that September 1955.[166]

"The producers don't want to let me work anymore," Roberto explained. "What I have to say no longer interests them. This is why I've accepted the offer the Indian cinema has made me. I've been given carte blanche. In India I'll be able to study the atmosphere, analyze the major problems, find someone who will permit me to evaluate the occult, fakir, and philosophic traditions in relation to current thinking, new ideas, and accepted values. It will, in sum, be the whole Indian civilization with its grandeur, its past and its future, that will take my hand and write the story, which I'll shoot in total freedom."[167]

Departure was postponed. He consumed tons of journals, papers, books, anything he could find on India. He would travel overland, following Marco Polo's route, filming all the way; France's biggest daily, *France Soir*, would publish his weekly impressions. Departure was announced for January 5, 1956.[168] Descriptions of elephants and mysteries held him spellbound. He would listen eagerly to Renoir or anyone who could talk about India.

"I was eating a delicious plate of spaghetti *al dente*," said Aldo Tonti, "when Rossellini outlined his project to me. 'We're going to a wonderland. . . .' he began. 'We won't be going like other people. We'll go by car. . . .' And, with his well-known powers of persuasion, he illustrated how it would be possible to make the most unforgettable film in the whole history of cinema. I accepted."[169]

Tonti was one of the world's top cameramen. To his credit, besides *Il miracolo* and *Europe '51*, were a goodly percentage of neo-realist film and much else: *Ossessione, La porta del cielo, Il bandito, Il sole sorge ancora, Roma città libera, Senza pietà, Il mulino del Po, Le notti di Cabiria*, and Vidor's *War and Peace*.

Ingrid, meanwhile, continued to fret over Pia. Lindstrom had been in Stockholm during *Joan* but had not contacted her. So Renzo's son Franco went off to America on his own initiative, with a round-trip ticket and fifty dollars for a slow freighter and a bus to Colorado, in order to meet Pia and plead Ingrid's cause.[170]

The Renoir picture, *Elena et ses hommes* ("Elena and her men"), was a disaster. Ingrid's French was incompetent in the French shooting; she blamed Roberto for speaking only Italian to her. Most of the rest of the cast was lousy at English in the English shooting, and poor Renoir, who had had to shoot versions in two languages, both of them lousy, had had to simplify continually. It was "one long nightmare," he groaned. The English version, *Paris Does Strange Things*, "was a massacre. They re-edited it. They even shot a beginning and end.... It upset me so much that it was six months before I could enter a movie theater and look at a screen again."[171]

He also had to contend with the tumult in Ingrid and Roberto's marriage. Renoir had not "rescued" her. He had helped start a divorce gracefully, only to see it explode violently while he was trying to make his film, from late November 1955 to late February 1956. Kay Brown, who had tried to intervene at the start on Stromboli and had failed, now showed up at the end in Paris and dangled *Anastasia* and $200,000.

Roberto exploded; he would drive his Ferrari into a tree.

"But I did it anyway, I was tired of being broke,"[172] Ingrid said. She signed the contract, January 19, 1956.

"Dear Roberto," she wrote, putting "dear" in English, "since we have decided to separate . . ."[173]

She signed a letter of separation promising that their children would be shared and live only in Italy or France. Roberto declared he was going to India and taking the children's passports to Italy and never coming back. Then he went and lay on his bed; she came, put her head on his chest and cried, and after crying a long time began to laugh. They went down to his new red Ferrari. He had gotten it just that day and it would go faster than the old one. She sat in it and with her fingers made a sign of the cross on the wheel, the way they did on their children's foreheads putting them to bed at night.

Roberto had also bought a Land Rover, a van, and an electric generator. Ingrid, Tonti said, had been unable to "believe her eyes. She had always looked on everything concerning Roberto's fantasizing about what she called his 'Dreams of India' as just a pleasant way of passing time. Now she was stupefied seeing things materialize. She gave me a pair of rugged boots of smooth leather with rubber soles, and with her usual friendly smile told me, 'These are the only thing[s] to wear when one meets elephants.'"[174]

But by mid-February Roberto was back at The Raphael. Visas, permits, and finances had forced one delay after another. The rainy season had started. He would have to wait until fall.

Fifteen years later, speaking English with effort, he described how he had felt: "I risked too much and we were hated, I don't know why. . . . We had big problems as we had three children . . . and she thought it would be wise to return to the industry just in order to save the material means of our life. I appreciated that thought very much. I believed it was wise. Unfortunately, I was as unwise myself and I did not want to be the husband of a great star. So very peacefully, very quietly and with a full understand and tremendous human compassion we decided to break. It was very hard, because we loved each other we had three children. It was very, very painful. I thought the best thing to do was to go very far, and I decided to go to India."[175]

"If I'd been concerned with exploiting Ingrid's economic value," Roberto told Bonicelli in 1959, "I'd have made, and would have had to have made, much different films than I did. [But] I've always aimed at experiment."

"Were you concerned about what you took away from her: celebrity, career, money, etc.?" Bonicelli asked.

"Why should I have? I didn't take anything away from her. We had simply decided to do a certain thing together."

"Before the film with Renoir, had she ever asked to work with others?"

"No. The first conflict was over *Anastasia*. . . ."

"What arguments did she use to convince you?"

"She didn't convince me, even if her argument, from a practical point of view, was incontestable. . . . There were two irreconcilable points of view. She wanted to save everything by renouncing our dreams. I wanted to save everything by exasperating our dreams."

"Why did you go to India?"

"Our *Voyage in Italy* was over."

"Do you recognize faults in yourself?"

"Yes. Pride, intransigence, debts."[176]

In 1976 he added, "After struggling eight years . . . , Ingrid put an end to the dream we'd nourished together. Can one blame her? She had risked her whole career for me—and what a career! She had put on the table, for her part, the most formidable stakes a woman ever gave a man she loved. As for me, I had held firm until the end. Until the end I had stayed faithful to the image that Ingrid had in running to me from her Hollywood castles. . . . Perhaps it [is] my *gallismo* [a word invented by Brancati to describe the cocky state of Italians in love] that stopped me from ever retreating from the idea Ingrid had had of the director I was, since that was the director she had come for: the idea of a free man. But, in so doing, I broke definitively with a whole world. And this rupture led me to organize my self-defense. For either I was crazy, sick and dangerous; or else I had fought for something worth the pain and had a thought worth pursuing. It was from this frontier that I left the instinctual to go to the rational"—India.[177]

Meanwhile, he lived off his friends, borrowing here and there, coming around to eat, and so on. Never did he show any sign of depression. He stopped at UNESCO one day and chattered two hours with Fereydoun Hoveyda, Iran's representative and a critic at *Cahiers*. Eventually Hoveyda noted it was time for lunch and asked if Roberto would prefer to walk or take his car. "Oh, I have a car," said Roberto. He had a taxi outside, whose meter had been running the entire time.[178]

He would invite people to The Raphael, where they would fall under his spell and he would absorb them along with their information. "'Tell me about Persia,' he'd say, and suddenly it would be 5 A.M.," recalls Hoveyda.[179]

Roberto contended that in order to know a country, like Iran or India, it was necessary to collect stories and anecdotes. With equal interest he would engage people on drugs in lengthy conversations, and was perpetually fascinated by porn shops, amateur strip tease shows, and transvestite cabarets. Ingrid never understood any of this.

There was comfort in the young French critics who admired the movies everyone else was execrating—*Voyage in Italy, Francesco,* and *Stromboli.* "That a group of young journalists aiming to become filmmakers had chosen him as their master broke his solitude and reawoke his immense enthusiasm," said Truffaut.[180]

They would spend whole nights together, for the joy of solidarity. More than a maestro or spiritual father, Roberto was an older brother.[181] He enthusiastically added his name to an open letter defending Max Ophuls's *Lola Montès* against its savaging by the French press.[182] And the fights were terrific. He argued the merits of Pagnol and they the wonders of Nicholas Ray and Joseph Mankiewicz. With *Rebel without a Cause* and *Barefoot Contessa* they were successful and, said Truffaut, he even got "really excited over *Bus Stop* [and] explained 300 prodigious details to me that I had not understood. For him [Joshua] Logan is an American Rossellini and better than Ray."[183] But also for him, Truffaut's beloved Hitchcock remained a "mystifier" who treated viewers like children[184] and, accordingly, when Chabrol and Rohmer did a book on Hitchcock, Roberto declared it was nothing but "masturbation."[185] In contrast, he admired Buñuel's extremely theatrical *Charme discret de la Bourgeoisie* as "absolutely real."

Roberto faulted French cinema for ignoring the realities of contemporary France and to correct this situation he conceived a series of 16mm films to be supervised by himself, directed by his "disciples" at *Cahiers,* and produced and financed by Henry Deutschmeister (Franco-London Films). Deutschmeister had brought Renoir back to France for *French Cancan,* had produced Renoir's staging of *Julius Caesar* at Arles, and had tried to launch the film version of *Jeanne au bûcher.* Roberto said Deutschmeister was the only Jew Hitler had had to pay to leave Germany—because of the real estate deals he had brokered for Nazi officials before they had come to power.[186]

Roberto had Truffaut convoke a meeting in *Cahiers'* office, and asked for scripts. Chabrol offered a first draft called *Le Beau Serge* (which he eventually shot when he inherited some money) and Roberto balled him out and said it was puerile.[187] Rohmer, whose earlier project with Truffaut on the modern church Roberto had liked,[188] presented a quite different, four-page story, *Le Signe du Lion* (which he eventually shot with the help of Chabrol) and, Rohmer said, Roberto "criticized it violently, telling me it had no 'generosity' and an uninteresting protagonist. During a discussion, quite protracted, I came to the realization that this man whom I admired had concepts very different from mine and that the films I wanted to do were totally different from his."[189]

Godard, Straub, Reichenbach, Aurel, Rouch, Hoveyda, and others were interested. Rivette was the most committed. He went to The Raphael with his friend Jean Gruault. They were greeted by the twins, who ran to their father's chair for safety, Gruault recalls, while Roberto, "with one [of] those noble gestures he had the secret of, invited us to sit in front of him. After a moment spent staring at us through his half-closed eyes with a sharp, piercing expression that was simultaneously malicious, attentive, and tender, and after questioning us a bit about our tastes and activities, as though he were giving us an exam, he launched into an exposition of his project."

At the same time Roberto was struggling to repair a wind-up toy one of the twins had broken. He suggested they start not with a story idea but with a place, the Cité Universitaire, where, he maintained, there was a conflux of mores, mentalities, races, levels of life, religions, and ideologies that, in concentration, mirrored the problems of the whole contemporary world. Rivette proposed a plot idea about a pure girl coming from the provinces and who could play the girl. "No actor is irreplaceable," Roberto interrupted, gesturing toward Ingrid's door. He advised them before writing a single line or concocting a single idea to go there and research it thoroughly. "Years later Roberto liked to say, half seriously, half in jest, 'I taught you everything.' Which is an exaggeration," Gruault wrote, "but certainly he did teach (and it is not nothing) the necessity, before writing any part of a script, of preliminary investigations on the location or of the documents, and of contact with the people."

At the University they found, with an African student as guide, that each foreign house enjoyed extraterritoriality and that "a place designed for fraternity and understanding had become a laboratory where were being prepared, under the cover of serene study, all the conflicts, revolutions, genocides, and convulsions that would shake the planet in the decades that followed. Roberto, by launching us onto this minefield, had again given proof of his extraordinary flare."

They submitted a complete shooting script called *La Cité* and were paid 100,000 old francs (about $200), which they split, except that Rivette gave 30,000 of his half to the African.[190]

Truffaut also received 100,000 francs and a contract to direct *La Peur de Paris*, an early version of the adventures of Antoine Doinel, on November 21, 1956.

"I went to French producers with a project including *400 Blows*, Chabrol's first film, many ideas of Godard's . . . , but I didn't succeed," said Roberto.[191] Deutschmeister, who had pledged twenty million francs, lost interest. And Roberto himself left for India.

"He disappeared," said Chabrol, "the cameraman he promised never arrived."[192] The disciples thought they had been taken for a ride.[193] He had signed contracts with Rouch, Hoveyda, and others, and they could have sued him.[194] "We felt seduced and abandoned," said Rouch.[195] "He was always saying 'I'm a *moral* man and I want to show people *moral* portraits' . . . and I want to recall this position of moral cinema because rarely have I encountered a man so marvelously immoral, like Roberto. This immoral man, completely immoral, was in his films of a morality absolutely exemplary and this transformation is one of the things which has most struck me. He came to stimulate us in Paris in the fifties—conventional, middle-class, intellectual, self-satisfied; but also people who *ate* cinema, and into this world arrived this wizard, a pied piper who made us dream for a year, obliging us to cultivate our garden, and disappeared. Well, this completely immoral act was the most moral act and gave life to Truffaut, to Godard, to Rohmer, to Rivette, and to myself. I never would have shot *Moi un noir* if Roberto hadn't incited me to do it and that was more important than the millions of lire he promised us and didn't have and more important [than] that marvelous cameraman [Aldo Tonti] he promised and who in the end went to make *India*."[196]

The would-be moviemakers, having been led by Roberto almost to the promised land, refused to turn back. Chabrol's *Le Beau Serge* came out in 1958. *La Cité*, much changed, materialized as *Paris nous appartient* in 1960. Truffaut's *400 Blows* appeared in 1959. It "owed a lot to *Deutschland im Jahre Null*," Truffaut said.[197] And even though Rohmer's *Le Signe du Lion*, when it appeared that same year, was "totally different" from Rossellini's pictures, more like De Sica than Rossellini, all of Rohmer's subsequent films are more like Rossellini than De Sica: they continue Rossellini's search for the spiritual within phenomena.[198] "Truffaut," wrote Gruault, "would never have had the idea for a film like *L'Enfant sauvage* [*The Wild Child*, 1970] and I would have been incapable of writing its script, without Rossellini's example which, for us, was capital."[199]

The *Cahiers* people had wanted to make films like those by the directors they most admired. They wanted to make "Hollywood" movies. Naturally Roberto discouraged this, given his own struggles. He argued that Hollywood movies—including all movies not independently produced—were deliberately made expensive in order to discourage people outside the system, and in fact it was insane to try to imitate them. Besides, their high costs made it impossible to work in freedom.

"At first," said Jean-Luc Godard, "I thought the only way was to make *Citizen Kane*, like Welles." Then he saw *Voyage in Italy* and, being a dialectical sort, combined it in his mind with the movies he liked that were diametrically opposed to it: Hollywood gangster films. "And then I said to myself, 'Look, all you need to make a movie is a man, a woman, and a car.'"[200] In 1959, *Breathless* appeared.

"Basically," said Roberto in 1965, "if I made any contribution to [the New Wave], it was by preaching to them to the point of satiation that, first of all, they must not regard cinema as something mystical. Film is a means of expression like any other. Films have to be made as simply as writing with a pen. What's important is to know what to write, and what's important is that each person writes what it pleases him to write—not what it might please someone else for him to write: the result would be nothing but insincerity. Absolute liberty with the camera comes from this demythification of the cinematic rite."[201]

"Rossellini's great lesson is that anybody can make movies," said Rouch.[202]

"Look around you, I told them. Express yourselves in complete freedom. Give up worrying about making films that might not be formally acceptable. Give up complicated techniques, forget about direct sound, the big screen, color. Use a hand-held camera, use 16mm."[203] (Today he would say: use video.)

"I tried to promote what was verified in that explosion that was the New Wave. I preached what has always been my concern, what I've always tried to do: liberate yourselves from the big industrial structures, make films very cheaply by using cheaper techniques. . . . We never talked about aesthetic questions. I think what they really saw in my films was a disrespect for traditional forms of cinema. There was a period when there wasn't a single critic who didn't accuse my films of being badly shot or me of being casual or careless. Well, the attacks from those tradition-bound critics excited these guys."[204]

Concluded Fereydoun Hoveyda, "First of all [the New Wave directors] learned from him to work on limited budgets and to state their views as simply and directly as possible. They also learned to present human beings as they really are and always in their natural environment."[205]

Such is the "school" of Rossellini, the only point of coherence of an otherwise incoherent school encompassing Rouch, Fellini, Godard, Rohmer, Olmi, Jansco, Rivette, Antonioni, Truffaut, Baldi, the Tavianis, and numerous others.[206] "I was always trying to create a movement and I never succeeded," said Roberto, "because I understood very well that to create a movement you must crystallize yourself into a position. Well, the moment you crystallize yourself, you've fucked yourself, you've castrated yourself, haven't you?"[207]

In this sense, as Truffaut declared, Roberto was "the father of the New Wave."[208]

The father was now fifty years old and trying to hold onto Ingrid. He had kept up negotiations for the South American tour of *Joan* until the last moment, hoping she would change her mind, long after he knew it was hopeless.[209]

She was determined to do *Anastasia*. To get out of the South American contract, she paid $37,000. To focus her attention, she sent her children to Santa Marinella with Elettra, Marcella, and Fiorella, and did not see them again for nearly six months.

The shock of going back to Hollywood, even in London where *Anastasia* was shooting, was greater than going to Stromboli had been. Helen Hayes, who played the grand duchess who has to decide if Anastasia is an imposter, recalled, "We played that confrontation scene for nearly two weeks with all the different cuts and takes. She had been working with

Rossellini and she said, 'I don't understand these takes.' He didn't do any of that, and she couldn't get herself back. It was a nightmare ... slow death."[210]

Spyros Skouras had signed Ingrid over the opposition of Fox executives Darryl Zanuck and Buddy Adler, and despite the mixed results that a poll to ascertain her box-office acceptability had produced. Skouras cheerfully reimbursed Ingrid her $37,000 when he found out about it and, as a further favor, arranged in April for Roberto to direct *Sea Wife* in Jamaica with Richard Burton.

J. M. Scott's *Seawyf and Biscuit* is about a nun shipwrecked with three men on a raft. Roberto, with producer André Hakim's agreement, caused something of a shock by casting sexy Joan Collins as the nun (Collins was thrilled), and rewrote the script with Bruce Marshall, changing the nun to a novice who, after resisting temptation, would take her vows with a maturer sense of vocation.

On June 10, 1956, he flew to Jamaica, arriving a day after the rest of the crew, due to migraine headaches brought on, according to Bergman, by fear of flying and superstitions that harm would befall Robertino, or, according to Franco Rossellini, by aversion to the whole arrangement.[211] The last time Roberto had been obliged to work as a hired director (*Europe '51*) he had had total control, and even so he had childishly taken out his indignation on Carlo Ponti every day. Now he had contracted for a commercial adventure film with 20th Century-Fox. A "sell out" of such magnitude can only be accounted for by Ingrid's ingenuous remark that if he had made a success of *Sea Wife*, "things between Roberto and I might have been very different."[212] One wonders whether Roberto, even with all the will in the world, would have been able—physically, temperamentally—to do it. He quotes Ingrid beseeching him: "I beg you in the name of our children, don't read the contract. If you read it, you won't sign it. And we need so much that you do this film. For once, do what I tell you!" And he adds, "I signed the contract, moved by the sentiment of my duties toward my family: in fact, an act of pure despair."[213]

In this frame of mind, when Ingrid left for London, Roberto had announced to *The Daily Mail* that she and he would "be free from our present commitments by the end of the year and we then hope to begin our next picture. It is too early to decide what it will be. ... Is it a good thing artistically for a couple like ourselves to work occasionally apart? Not necessarily but at any rate it does no harm. ... Whatever rumors you may have heard to the contrary, I can tell you that professionally, as well as personally, we remain happy together."[214]

When Roberto arrived in Ocho Rias, he learned that the second-unit had begun shooting without him, that Burton wanted his part enlarged, that the producers wanted more of an adventure film and less of a "moral" film, and that the man from the Breen Office was insisting that Roberto's changes would offend Catholics and that the old script would have to be used. Roberto was furious that they had started without him. He argued from 10 P.M. to 3 A.M. against the script changes. He pointed out that the Catholic film office in Italy had approved his script. To no avail. The film went on shooting with associate producer Bob McNaught directing.

Roberto spent a week in his hotel room refusing to comment as the argument continued. He hadn't a cent, but nonetheless gave a generous check to a Jesuit church. Finally he flew back to London.

Ingrid met him at the airport, red with vexation, "What have you done? What have you done?"[215]

Through his agent, MCA, Roberto announced he was suing Fox for his salary, £30,000, contending that Hakim, after accepting his changes, had begun filming the old script before the problems with the Breen Office could be resolved. "I'm not accustomed to descending to compromises. . . . The producer grossly violated the contract," he said.

"My *Sea Wife* will have more adventure and less psychology," countered McNaught.

"I couldn't do otherwise," Hakim pleaded.

"Too bad!" said Joan Collins.[216]

According to Rossellini, Skouras now told him that in signing the unread contract he had promised not to change a word of the script, that Hakim had been wrong to encourage him to rewrite it, that Fox was obliged to pay him his entire salary, except that Hakim's wife (Darryl Zanuck's daughter) had put her own money into the film, and did he want that on his conscience? Roberto replied by signing a blank sheet of paper. "Write what you want. I can't stand all these tears," he told Skouras. And left.

Whereupon Skouras called him back from the street and presented him to his staff as "the only gentleman I've ever encountered in the movies."

Skouras wrote £10,000 on the paper.[217]

Earlier that year, 1956, the Théâtre de Paris had asked Roberto to direct a play about Judas (by Carlo Suares?). As usual he plunged heart and soul into studying the period and the man. But he hated the lead actor, there were huge fights, and Roberto was the one who got fired. "Roberto was absolutely destroyed by this experience," Ingrid wrote. "I had to take him in my arms and say, 'Something else is round the corner, I'm sure there'll be something else.'"[218]

There was. The theatre owner, Rumanian producer Elvire Popesco, regretted the firing and proposed that Roberto direct Robert Anderson's play *Tea and Sympathy*. Popesco then asked Ingrid to play in it. Ingrid had refused an earlier Popesco offer for Tennessee Williams's *Cat on a Hot Tin Roof*. Now she and Roberto signed contracts for *Tea*.

A few months later, he got around to reading the play, threw it against the wall, said it was the most awful thing he had ever read, declared he would not direct it, and absolutely forbade Ingrid to appear in it. According to Ingrid, his reaction was based solely on his chronic discomfort with anything dealing with homosexuality (*Tea* is about a woman who makes love to one of her husband's students who is afraid he is gay). Ingrid says that later when she wanted to send Robertino to a Swiss boarding school, Roberto blew up: "What! That's where it all starts, in those boarding schools!"[219]

Members of Roberto's family were gay, and he was anxious about his sons. On the other hand, he had always had many gay friends and enjoyed visiting gay hang-outs. Homosexuality occurs seldom in Rossellini's films; it denotes depravity in *Roma città aperta, Deutschland im Jahre Null*, and *Agostino d'Ippona* (1972), but it is not viewed unfavorably in *The Age of the Medici* or, significantly, in "Isa's Decision," a story Roberto would write for Ingrid a few weeks after reading *Tea*, and which is *also* about a woman wanting to redeem a man from depression and homosexuality.[220]

Moreover, homosexuality is explicit in Rossellini's story, whereas in Anderson's play it is only suggested, teasingly. Anderson's man is barely seventeen, and his middle-aged heroine acts partly out of nurse-like pity for him, but more out of revulsion at her gay-bashing, jock-asshole husband; there is no actual homosexuality in his play, only various forms of fear of it. In contrast, Rossellini's man is also middle-aged, the heroine's former husband, and has an actual homosexual roommate; the heroine acts out of overwhelming passion and is in no way influenced by her present marriage, which on either side has never been more than a business partnership.

Roberto's opposition to Ingrid appearing in *Tea and Sympathy* was due to its conventional, teasing maudlinity, not to its gay theme. Once again, she lacked the intelligence to understand him.

And she insisted. It was the third and final step in what Ingrid called her "rescue," following *Elena* and *Anastasia*. *Tea* was commercial and popular hit on Broadway; the heroine is a kind of Joan of Arc; Ingrid's fans would adore her in it; Minnelli's film of it starring Deborah Kerr, had been released in the U.S. in September and makes a wonderful case for it. On the other hand, Roberto was right to want Ingrid in his own movies. Nothing in her subsequent career of mostly tawdry, commercially-motivated pictures comes remotely close to the quality of her Rossellini movies. Posterity is immeasurably poorer. But to Ingrid, popularity and money were more fulfilling than making pictures that no one liked, that no one saw, that made no money—and that, one after another, were inciting torrents of public abuse against the man she loved. Besides there were the children. "I understood him, but I was powerless to alter the way things were," she said.[221]

And he understood her. But each felt that it was the other who was causing the "artistic divorce" that was becoming a marital divorce. She scolded him over *Sea Wife*. He slapped her in the face on a Paris sidewalk and jeered that, compared to Marilyn Monroe, who was marrying Arthur Miller and taking Actors Studio classes, Ingrid Bergman was going in the opposite direction. He was deserting her for six months, going to India; on the other hand, she refused to come with him. The most humiliating thing had happened.

Ed Sullivan had told his television audience, one of the largest in America, that, even though Ingrid had done "seven and a half years of time for penance," he was reluctant to show them a clip from *Anastasia* without first soliciting his audience's permission. More respondents had said no than yes—6,433 versus 5,826.[222]

Sullivan had shown the clip anyway. Ingrid was determined to rescue herself.

Roberto kept trying. In early September, summoning Truffaut to Santa Marinella, he worked two weeks on "Isa's Decision." But at the beginning of October Ingrid began rehearsals for *Tea* with Jean Mercure, who had replaced Rossellini, and Roberto was preparing again to leave for India.

At this moment, Russia sent troops into Hungary. For a few days there was real fear that war would break out. Kindling the fear was the traumatic shock inflected on the European left, who until now had clung to Russia as the best hope for a free society. Amidei, hysterical, phoned Marcella at 1 A.M. and went on for two hours—while begging her not to reveal his distress to Roberto, who had always mocked Amidei's naiveté about Communism. Roberto was going to take the children to Rome, where he thought they would be safer if hostilities began. Then at this moment, Ingrid suddenly had to have an appendix operation, reviving the still-raw shock of Romano's death.

Tea and Sympathy opened December 1. Half the audience would walk out before the intermission, Roberto predicted. He sat in the dressing room, refusing to look toward the stage. "The play was the experience of another world, not his Latin world," said Renoir. "He wanted so much to bring her into his world."[223] At the final curtain, said Simone Paris, "I never heard anything like the applause. His face was red with fury. He stood there a moment and then stalked off."[224]

"As I bent over [to bow] I turned my head and looked at Roberto. Our eyes met. We looked straight at each other. I knew then my marriage was over even though we might stay together. I had to go out to a party with Roberto and all his Italian friends that night. We laughed a lot. Nobody talked about the play. Nobody said anything about its being a success. The following day Roberto packed his suitcases in The Raphael Hotel and I went to the railway station to see him off. I don't know why he took a train. I remember his suitcases were full of spaghetti. As we stood there in the noise and the smoke amid all the people, I had this very strange feeling that this was the end of an episode and that things would never be the same again."[225]

The Great Mother

I remember the night before I left for India I could not sleep. Anxiety, excitement, and also a bit the anguish of the adventure that I was about to attempt, provoked my insomnia. Dark ideas were racing through my mind. Would I come back? Would I see my old places again? It was the beginning of December. Bed was a torture that night. I got dressed and went out into a cold and starry night. I went like a pilgrim to take another look at Rome, my city. I stopped my car in Piazza Michelangelo on the Capitoline. I went to contemplate my Rome from the side of that hill that looks over the Forum and the Palatine. Farther off, I could see the somber mass of the Colosseum contrasting with the whiteness of the marble columns of the Temple of Venus. In the street below, the street that passes between the Forum and the Tarpeian Rock, footsteps were sounding in unison. Two men were walking in the night on that street that is still paved with the stone blocks of the ancient Roman street. They were talking. Their deep voices, guttural and heavy, reached me, but I could not make out their words. They came near and passed beneath where I was (I saw them for only a moment in the light from a street lamp). I could barely make out the beginning of a sentence from one of them, the one with the deeper voice. I heard him distinctly begin by saying: "Mi'mma!" After that I could not make out the other words, which were muffled in the noisy echo of their footsteps. But I heard again at a moment when they started speaking louder, "Mi'mma!"
[In dialect:] "My mother"!
How important the mother is in the life of Romans!
—From an unsent letter written by Roberto Rossellini in India.[1]

From Rome, Roberto and Tonti flew to Athens, then Cairo, Khartoum, Saudi Arabia, and Karachi, where they spent the night. Roberto was carrying a hundred kilos of spaghetti. "Rossellini seemed little by little to wind down from his usual talky self," Tonti said. "The closer he got to his goal, the more he was silent [and] absent, like the fakirs we were going to meet."[2]

They were flying because the Suez crisis had closed borders and made the Marco Polo overland route impossible. And because in the meantime a

Paris–Bombay airline had become interested. But Roberto intended to return overland, via Kabul, Teheran, Baghdad, Amman, Jerusalem, Damascus, Beirut, Istanbul, and Athens.

The original invitation to do a film had come from Indian producers, the Borkei Brothers, after they had seen *Paisà*. Roberto would supply the negative stock, much of the expense, and have worldwide rights, except for India. The Indian Ministry of Information and Broadcasting would supply $25,000, a camera, a pair of utility men, an assistant, and modest means of transport. Eventually a French theater chain, Union Général Cinématographique, came up with a distribution contract and a minimum guarantee, enabling Roberto to borrow a hundred million lire (about $160,000) from the Banca Romana for his ad-hoc company Aniene Film. And Fulchignoni arranged for UNESCO to commission a series of documentaries. *India* was to be one of a series of films highlighting problems of the contemporary world.

The trip's many delays had made the Borkei Brothers anxious. Now, on December 9, 1956, as they flew into Bombay where the Indian film industry was centered, the captain received a radio message asking if Rossellini were accompanied by Ingrid Bergman and Marilyn Monroe. The moment they landed dozens of photographers and reporters swarmed around, ignoring Roberto and searching despairingly for Bergman and Monroe. At customs Borkei was waiting with the Italian consul and two local actresses. At his signal they draped garlands of flowers around Roberto's neck.

He moved into a large air-conditioned suite in the splendiferous Taj Mahal Hotel. At noon a sumptuous reception and luncheon were given in his honor by the Indian film industry. Almost everyone in film was there. That evening he was taken to an amateur theater, where he posed for photos with the actors.

"I was stupefied, knowing what I knew [about how England had 'vampirized' India in 'the most formidable economic and social pillaging that one nation has ever known'], I was stupefied to find in the middle of every square that bronze grandmother with her widow's bonnet, her jowls, her imperial nose, Queen Victoria reigning on her enormous throne! In Italy I'd seen, when Fascism fell, how the statues they'd put up were knocked over. . . . 'But what do you want?' my Indian friends replied to me. 'That's part of our history. And besides, she gives shade.' "[3]

Borkei provided Roberto with a car and a guide. The guide told him lies all the time, Roberto said. Roberto wanted the "real" India, whatever that was. "I didn't visit any Indian monuments. When I happened to pass by the Taj Mahal I turned my head. And I refused to go see the frescos of Ajanta; I sat in the car while my traveling companions went to make their devotions to art. That door opens only on dead, embalmed truths, which doubtless have their hour, but which don't have anything to do with the real country anymore."[4]

Roberto already had two local assistants. Krishnashwamy, or "Kitù," he had met in Rome, as a student at the Centro Sperimentale on an Indian government scholarship. Jean Herman was French, Truffaut's friend, and a former film student at IDHEC; he had been teaching art history at the University of Bombay for a year and was married to an Indian, Lila, whom he had met in Paris.

But to get to know India through its people and its stories Roberto still needed the right kind of guide. Renoir had encouraged him to meet Harisadhan ("Hari") Das Gupta, a 33-year-old documentary filmmaker whom Renoir had met at the University of Southern California in 1946 and who had been Renoir's assistant during *The River*—which had been at the origin of Roberto's dream of coming to India. Das Gupta's circle, said Renoir, "was the very model of the enlightened middle-class Indian. It included professors, lawyers, doctors, civil servants, people of liberal outlook. Many of their daughters had gone to the Santiniketan University. This school, founded by Tagore, managed to perpetuate Indian customs while teaching the essentials of Western culture."[5]

Das Gupta stopped briefly at the Taj December 10, with his wife Sonali, a very traditional Indian lady and a Santiniketan graduate. Roberto asked Das Gupta to come back in a week and, although Sonali had scarcely spoken, handed her his notes for the film and asked for her thoughts.[6]

Das Gupta was due to start a film of his own in Jamshedpur. He was distressed not to be able to work with Rossellini. He had been part of the Calcutta Film Society and admired Rossellini's pictures. And Roberto could open doors for him. It was an opportunity lost artistically and professionally. So in his place he suggested his wife Sonali, and showed Roberto a treatment she had written. Perhaps he had noted the empathy between his wife and Roberto, but he had not discussed his scheme with her.

Sonali reacted with shock and resistance.[7]

Roberto, in his hotel room, had surrounded himself with pictures of his children and Ingrid. He missed her intensely. The wounds of their parting were vivid. He phoned and wrote her frequently.

Anastasia previewed December 14. It was a huge and swift victory. A few days later she had won the New York Film Critics award for best actress.

But Ingrid was devastated by the separation too. Robert Anderson, who had written *Tea and Sympathy*, came to Paris; his wife had just died after five years of cancer; and with a mixture of romance and nurture, like her stage persona in *Tea*, Ingrid threw herself into helping him through the first days following the death. "She had such energy. She never wanted to go to bed," said Anderson. "She would polish off a big bottle of champagne or Scotch, and it would mean nothing to her. . . . She was very caring. She nurtured me for weeks and this was a very selfless act. Of course, she needed me too. She didn't have patience for people who were sad too long. She said, 'If you had children you'd have to shape up sooner than this.' She took me everyplace. . . . She was the toast of Paris."[8]

*

Roberto said, "One person helped me more than any other to see and understand. This was India, who would become my wife."[9]

Sonali Sen Roy (Das Gupta) was 27, from a well-to-do Brahman family in Bengal, a thousand miles away. She had studied figurative arts at Santiniketan, a university designed by its founder, the Nobel laureate composer, poet, and novelist Rabindranath Tagore (1861–1941), to be an "abode of peace" (*santiniketan*), "where the world becomes one nest." Tagore had replaced traditional instruction by rote with emphasis on development from within, so that spirit might find expression in poetry, story, drama, essay, music, dance, and painting.[10] (India's most famous filmmaker, Satyajit Ray, had been a Tagore student—as well as Renoir's other assistant during *The River*.) Sonali wore the traditional sari and caste mark; modesty, duty, and inner harmony had been her life. She had two sons: Raja, four, and Arjun, four months. The notion of working independently of her husband bordered on the scandalous.

"Jean Renoir . . . had given me a list of contacts he had made in India," Roberto said. "On this list was the address of India. India was Indian to her finger tips. India rid me of all the preconceived ideas that, despite myself, I still had about her country. She gave me the keys. Women in India are the austere guardians of tradition. Whereas the men have been obliged to mix with the West and often look at Oxford or Cambridge for ways to be more English than the English, the women have maintained their cultural identity intact. This is their strength."[11]

> *How important the mother is in the life of Romans! How many mothers I had known! How many gluttonous mothers overnourished by their children's love! Apoplectic women, with very high blood pressure and lucid red skin, 'blown up' by the rich food they gluttonously engorge in exorbitant quantities, covered with gold. They are the true deities in every Roman family.*
>
> *In front of me was the minuscule mass of the Palatine Hill on which Rome had been founded. This Rome that had filled fifteen centuries of history, that was born as a small village, and whose traces are still so profound! What mysterious strength had allowed it to conquer the world? Maybe a hint about that mysterious strength lay in those words that had risen up to me from the street below: "Mi'mma!"*
>
> *Seven-hundred-fifty years before Jesus Christ, what was the geographic position of this portion of the world? Marshes all around. Amid the marshes rose the seven hills . . . fifty yards high. And swamps everywhere all around up to the Alban Hills and, on the other side of the Tiber, the Gianicolo which formed the farthest outpost of Etruria. . . . The only place where the Tiber provided an outpost was just to my right, the Isola Tiberina [a tiny island in the river]. Facing me, fifty yards from the Tiber and very near the Isola Tiberina, was the Palatine. A little hill of tufa. Like the*

Etruscan cities that rose up on other tufa islands ... [its] steep walls of tufa provided a natural defense. So ... the Isola Tiberina was perforce the traffic lane between the Etruscan world and the primitive Italians entrenched on the arc of hills in the marshy plain. At that point of obligatory passage surely outlaws would have gathered ... and also prostitutes. People say the female wolf [Rome's icon] symbolizes the prostitute. These outlaws made a little revolution. They built on this rock, on these natural defenses, their village. It was from this day that rather than continue as humble beggars, they imposed their strength and required a toll be paid.

Like all primitive civilizations, the surrounding cities were patriarchal. Rome perhaps represented the first revolution against the patriarch.

"Mi'mma!" The thought of mother brings tears to every Roman's eyes. It is a fact that the father, even today in Rome, is still "a harlot's son"! There is still a struggle against the authority of the father, who is considered authoritative, egotistic, and unjust, and in Roman families there is a perpetual complicity between mother and children.

Look again at the legends of Rome's foundation. They are always legends about a woman who was treated unjustly, and it is this woman who gave life to Romulus and Remus [Rome's mythic founders]. What is the first legend about Rome's foundation? In Plutarch's Lives there is a story of a monster, sent from the gods, who presented himself at the court of the King of Alba one day. A gigantic phallus. It is certain that a guest like that was a bit embarrassing, and the King of Alba, frightened by this guest, begged his daughter to sleep with him to sweeten him. The daughter, frightened both by the authority of her father and by the monster, begged her faithful slave to take her place for the night. This is what was done, the slave slept beside the monster and became pregnant with the two twins, Romulus and Remus.

If this is what actually happened, and if it is true [as Croce says] that history is a series of struggles between people to attain freedom, then this Rome would represent freedom [because it was matriarchal].

It is difficult to pull oneself away from ideas so fascinating. It is a fact that, if one part of humanity has always sought to attain freedom, for centuries other peoples have struggled to create slaves. It is a struggle that still continues. In small communities, what is the first form of slavery? The submission of the woman to the man.

In the history of slavery, the first slave was certainly the woman. Maybe this is why they are called the weaker sex, even though, historically, women have certainly endured pains that are greater and worse than those endured by men. So if my fantasy is correct, it is understandable why the Sabine women who had been kidnapped by the Romans were so quick to implore their fathers and brothers—and maybe their deceived husbands, too—to put down arms and renounce any spirit of vengeance against these Romans, even though they had kidnapped them. And if Rome has represented freedom for at least half of humanity, it can easily

> *be explained why victory ceaselessly smiled upon it [during the Roman Empire]—because it found natural allies everywhere it presented itself.*[12]

Years afterward, Sonali reflected: "His encounter with India was special, the 'Matri Bhumi,' the Great Mother Enchantress who charms, softens and cultivates . . . not everyone, but those she chooses. Roberto abandoned himself to her naturally, willingly, without any resistance."[13]

Sonali is referring to Rossellini's film, *India Matri Bhumi* ("India mother land") and to his encounter with India. But Sonali was "India" and "Matri Bhumi." Who of us, deeply under another's spell, will not identify places with them? And what if the spell is everything, spiritual and sexual, philosophical and emotional, a whole new culture, a person and place we discover ourselves suddenly part of?

Roman mothers, in Roberto's vision, were overnourished and nourishing, victim and empress, whore and deity. Roman men have often regarded Roman wives and mothers in this way, and Roberto never entirely left his Roman wife. But from his first venture outside of his Italian peninsula, his adventures had been focused on foreign women: Titi Michelle, Assia Noris, Roswitha Schmidt, Ingrid Bergman. Sonali would personify not only an entire sub-continent but a victim to be rescued as well.

As Roberto saw more of Hari Das Gupta, the attraction of Sonali increased. Tonti said that the moment Sonali walked into the hotel room, "I knew that to Rossellini this meeting was dangerous. . . . I have never seen him come to life more. He was the essence of charm, but he was full of energy. He bounded and bounced. He walked up and down the room waving his arms. He talked about India as though he had lived there all his life. His conversation sparkled and flashed. We all sat fascinated."[14]

For the next three days Roberto talked constantly of Ingrid and his children. He fought his desire to see Sonali. A fortune teller, however, read his palm and told him, "You are a passionate man. You have known many loves. But . . . you have come to India to meet the greatest love of your life. And you cannot avoid it."

He went white.[15]

For an artist like Rossellini it was never an option to withhold himself from attraction. Sonali was the key to his movie.

The question came up of employing her as an actress. She did not like the idea, for reasons that were partly cultural, and Das Gupta had to explain to Roberto that (in Sonali's words) "outside of a certain cultural elite, film work had a very bad reputation in India." Even on the one occasion that Sonali had worked on a film with her own husband, "the outside world, *his* world, had reprimanded him."[16]

Sonali's exclusion from the film world was all the more remarkable in that the particular "film world" in question was not one of adventure and dancing girls, but of documentaries, social commitment, and her family. Her maternal uncle was Bimal Roy, an Indian version of Rossellini, an independent producer-director of neo-realist pictures like *Two Acres of Land*, which had won the International Prize at Cannes in 1954, and *Gotama the Buddha*, a government commission for Buddha's 2,500th birthday. It is difficult to imagine a *more* respectable milieu. Yet Sonali was excluded by moral decency.

The question then came up, to Sonali's surprise, of her working for Rossellini as a scenarist. He badly needed a local collaborator, she was ideal. Das Gupta was for it. She was not. She had been embarrassed by her husband's showing her story to Rossellini; he had talked with her about her working for him. "I remember in any case that I showed myself reluctant, even after he continued to insist with Rossellini that he should have my collaboration."[17] She had seen only one Rossellini film, *Roma città aperta*, at the Calcutta film club.

Lila and Jean Herman were in the room as well. Roberto, rarely looking at Sonali, but keeping her across from him and playing with his knot of hair, began one of his spell-binding monologues, talked on for hours with hardly an interruption, and invited them all to dinner.

Meanwhile he had begun to have doubts about his producer, first when Borkei lined up a series of meetings for him with Bombay industrialists; second when a distinguished gentleman approached Roberto and politely asked for the return of his car; definitively when Borkei disappeared that same day.

He wrote Fulchignoni that "Indian producers are of the same style as our own, but even more abject, because they do really good business here . . . with incredibly lousy films." About 300 movies were made each year. "Among the producers one only finds people of unheard of vulgarity. To produce a film here they take two, three, four years. The actresses and actors, who are really the equivalent of tarantella dancers at [Italian state-sponsored] after-work parties, have so many engagements that they rent themselves by the hour and each production waits for its turn with them.

"The Indian government has developed documentary films as best it can through the Film[s] Division (the equivalent of our Istituto Luce). . . .

"So it's unthinkable to be able to do anything with the local producers. I've had to wait to see if, and how, and how much, the government is interested in my project."[18]

The government officials had been in America and then at a party congress. Roberto had had to wait. He had borrowed a Plymouth station wagon from Das Gupta.[19]

Finally, on January 7 he was able to go to New Delhi where, the next day, he saw Pillai, the secretary general of the Ministry of Foreign Affairs whom he had met in Rome. Pillai put him in contact with the Minister of Information and Broadcasting, Dr. B. V. Keskar, who gave him an appointment for the twelfth. Meanwhile, he got a call to see Prime Minister Nehru on the tenth. Keskar accordingly saw him on the ninth, and they quickly reached agreement. Roberto wrote Fulchignoni: "They will cover the expenses in India and I will give them the film for this market and also the [16mm] documentaries that I will do.

"The meeting with Nehru was extremely cordial. He is an extraordinary man, meek and strong, very modest, but conscientious and, if need be, authoritarian. During the conversation he told me what he would be doing in the next days. I expressed interest and, in brief, the next morning I left with him and followed him for four days through the most diverse places and ceremonies."[20]

Years later he recollected: "In Nehru's presence, I always felt the impression of a holy man, and the real, physical desire to put my head on his shoulder and ask protection—which I never did."[21]

Roberto as always sought a father, whom, like many Westerners, he expected to find in India in the guise of Wisdom. "I was very much attracted by India because I consider that Gandhi was the only completely wise human being in our time of history. I was attracted by India for that reason. . . . In India I saw what it means for a human being to be simple and wise and not to be tied to material interests."[22]

He had met Mahatma Gandhi in 1931 in Rome. Gandhi had been on his way to the London Round Table Conference. "The Fascist government saw [Gandhi] as an absolutely wonderful weapon to use against the Britannic Empire, so much so that Gandhi was obliged to stay in Rome a bit longer than he'd planned. Chance had it that he was the guest of [Countess Carnivali Braida, to whom I had recently sold the house we had lived in until my father's death]. When I heard Gandhi would be there, I called the countess. 'Might I come?'

"'Come.'

"Gandhi, during the thirties when the world was like a pot about to boil over, carried immense symbolism. He represented the power of the spirit. He represented destitution and weakness, capable in their redoubtable meekness of making legions retreat and shaking an entire empire . . . [like *Francesco*].

"In familiar surroundings where the furniture was still arranged as I had always known it, I saw a small man with quick gestures, who looked alertly and nimbly around him at people and things. There was nothing detached or immaterial about him, rather the sensation of a presence awake to the world. This holy man was like a very clever mouse, adroit and rapid. The cat had to watch out.

"History has canonized Gandhi. In contrast, it tends to depict Nehru as a politician, a Third-World Machiavelli. But it's Nehru [who was much different] who gave me the impression of sanctity. . . . His whole person breathed spirituality, harmony, an intelligence at peace with the world.

"Nehru was in touch with things, too. He was the 'prince of the concrete,' in fact. He was a convinced socialist who had taken upon himself the task of making India into a modern democracy. He knew how long and difficult the road would be. The mills of democracy turn slowly, for they have to wait for the grain to ripen. And men grow less quickly than wheat.

"In this bogged-down country, engaged with such gigantic problems, with everything needing to be done at once, the temptation to resort to the radical methods of dictatorship was constant. Many thought so. Some didn't hesitate to say it. Every nation has a pot of dictator sauce simmering on the back burner. How much greater is the desire to make use of it, when poverty is sitting at people's bedsides?[23]

"Yet Nehru, trying to build democracy in a situation demanding dictatorship, would write newspaper editorials under a pseudonym attacking himself. . . .

"India . . . is *par excellence* the land of realism."[24]

Roberto phoned Tonti in Bombay to rush immediately to Delhi. "Now the adventure begins," he said. At noon, November 11, they boarded a special train heading east to the University of Nalanda, a sort of Buddhist Mecca founded in the fifth century. The train was filled with Buddhist priests who had come from Tibet for the occasion. An old priest sat across from Roberto, full of gray wrinkles, looking about a hundred years old. Roberto would try to talk—"*Italiano, italiano*"—and the old priest would widen his mouth from ear to ear, display black butts of teeth, and moan. One priest turned out be a Genovese; he confessed he was unable to explain what he was doing there.

Twenty hours later, the train stopped and they boarded cars for the last seventy miles. Nehru and the Dalai Lama arrived by plane. The seventh-century relics of Hymen Tsang had been found. There were many speeches.

On the thirteenth, Roberto and Tonti flew on Nehru's plane to Hirakud, in Orissa, where a 25-mile-long dike, a 248-square-mile man-made lake, and a hydro-electric dam were to be inaugurated, ending millennia of devastation from the yearly floods of the Mahanadi River—a million people had died from them in 1866. The prime minister came out of his private cabin as they neared the dike.

"He told the pilot to survey this immense thing. We had come for the migration. There were still 35,000 men working, sometimes in 113-degree heat, so it was like the building of the pyramids. Of course the pilot immediately turned the plane so it was on Nehru's side and I, on the other side, couldn't see anything at all. And Nehru gestured to me to sit beside him, on the same seat. . . .

"So I was seeing Nehru's profile as he gazed at this immense work, and through him I was seeing it. I was suddenly very moved at seeing Nehru's immense sadness. He wasn't at all gazing with joy or exaltation, but with a deep sadness. He had this lip, heavy like this, and I was so moved that I made a ridiculous gesture, I caressed him on his arm and I said, 'God bless you.' And he turned toward me threateningly, with a sudden hate, and then he caught his hate and put his head down and his arms between his legs, and did not raise his head again, because he had caught himself giving me a gesture that was almost insulting.

"I didn't say anything, I stayed seated, and when we were landing I went to my seat, then we landed, they opened the plane, outside were soldiers with the military band, etc., then he got out, he played his role as

Prime Minister, and I got out with him as the guest of the prime minister and I stayed behind him through all this high ceremony.

"I never spoke to him about this. I did ask [his daughter] Indira [Gandhi], 'What was it?' She couldn't give me an explanation. Probably it was because I had surprised him in a moment of profound emotion, and of sadness. Sadness because he knew what it had cost.

"I had even been a little bit scared, thinking maybe it was because I had said 'God' and he's not religious. But he says almost what Feuerbach says: 'God is a need of man,' he says in a way that's very clear."[25]

Tonti took still photographs and shot 16mm Kodachrome all the while. The next day they flew with Nehru to Calcutta and boarded a special train to Santiniketan, to a graduation ceremony at Tagore University where Nehru had been chancellor. That night Roberto and Tonti slept in Nehru's private railway car.

The next day, January 15, during the three-hour trip back to Calcutta, Roberto talked to Nehru about his project. Originally, as described in a letter of introduction to Indira Gandhi from the Indian ambassador in Rome, his intention had been a film on Shri Vinobha Bhave and the land reform movement.[26] Now, besides the documentaries Tonti had been shooting—a series evoking India's progress—Roberto would make a 35mm feature, also in color, which would resemble *Paisà*, with an episode for each of India's nine regions. Nehru responded: "I'm prepared to give my full support. Go back to Bombay and get to work."[27]

They reached Calcutta at 6 P.M. At ten they were on a plane to Bombay and being buffeted by a storm. The six-hour flight took fifteen hours.

In Rossellini's absence, Das Gupta had continued to pressure Sonali. "I don't know [why]," she said. "But I asked him often and in vain. I can only guess. . . . Maybe he thought that collaboration with so famous a foreign director would justify my working with him later."[28] By the time Roberto returned, she was still afraid she could not do an adequate scenario, but she was willing to try. Das Gupta and Rossellini began talking about a contract and salary for her, and she left the room. As an Indian woman, she would have preferred to work without payment, in order not to assume obligations which in the long run she might be unable to keep. Already there was the conflict, potentially scandalous, that Rossellini wanted her to come on location.

Nonetheless she consented, and in February, for about ten days, came to the Taj after lunch. Herman and Kitù, her co-scenarists, were usually running errands, and Tonti was out shooting, so Sonali bore most of the burden of the script. She enjoyed the work. Relations with Roberto were extremely proper; they entranced each other with words. Among the stories he had brought with him was one about monks by Fereydoun Hoveyda. (Roberto had given him a check for 100,000 francs [about $200], which he had asked him not to cash. On his return, he borrowed the money back, and never repaid it.) And there was the story, "The Land Donor," about a Gandhi disciple, which Roberto had originally submitted to Nehru. "Up to now," he wrote Fulchignoni on January 25, "I have shot four documentaries which I've shipped to Rome. . . . One on Bombay and the life of this city, one on a village of fishermen, one on an industrial village, one on the trip with Nehru. I am doing another on a village in the mountains where on Sundays there is a market to which the tribes from the interior come with their products, and since the zone is full of monkeys, I'm doing one also on these animals. The [feature] film project is still about the same, but naturally . . . I have taken out a few episodes and put in new ones."[29]

Roberto added that he was sending 350 color photos, seventy in color of the Nehru trip, a thousand in black and white, and that up to now they had shot about six hours in 16mm.

(In actuality, at least two of the documentary subjects supposedly sent to Rome had not been shot yet.)

Das Gupta invited Rossellini twice, with Tonti and other friends, to their small third-floor apartment on Warden Road, a quiet street near the elegant Malabar Hills. Sonali made roast chicken for them, although she and Hari were vegetarian. Roberto wore a white cotton suit, sandals, and a flaming red handkerchief around his neck. On his second visit, he was given an Indian costume, which he immediately put on.

Sonali introduced Roberto to an impressionist painter, a Muslim named Hussein, who had lived for a time in Paris and needed marital advice, a subject on which Roberto felt himself an expert. Hussein had an Indian wife of whom he was a little tired, and he had met a Yugoslav in Paris whom he wished to take as a second wife, but she objected to such an arrangement and there were visa problems. After a few days' thought, Roberto advised Hussein to go to Yugoslavia with a bachelor friend who would marry the Yugoslav so that she could get a passport, then to re-arrange things when she got to India. Meanwhile Roberto bought twenty of Hussein's canvases, which rarely sold, and sent one to Nehru in hopes of promoting him. Hussein took a friend to Yugoslavia, as Roberto had instructed, but for one reason or another the plan failed.

"Whenever Roberto would come into the hotel," Sonali recalled, "a group of bellboys would run toward the elevator to take him up. Often there would be a silent dispute among them, which Roberto could not notice but which was eloquent enough that the Indians remarked on it. . . . Without fail more than one bellhop would hurry up, even if he only had just one simple bag. . . . He was considered the 'Baksheesh-wala sahib,' the gentleman who gives tips. Roberto would look at his change, and the Indian rupee didn't seem to be worth much, and he would generously distribute tips every time he came in or out. The servants would often tell him tragic stories of floods, sickness, or other calamities their families were suffering in some far off villages. No matter where Roberto would go—Bombay, Delhi, or Calcutta—it was always the same. All the servants who took care of Roberto's room seemed to have the same problems, but he never worried about the authenticity of their stories, he continued to be the good 'Baksheesh-wala sahib.'"[30]

Although Hari Das Gupta had encouraged his wife to work with Rossellini, he gradually became uncomfortable with the situation. His in-laws were complaining. Occasionally he would say things to her like, "Don't think you're so intelligent because you're working for him. If I had been able to do it, I would have been better."[31]

He had begun something innocently and now found himself and his family ensnared in a growing controversy. Opposition was brewing against the foreigner. But the foreigner did not know it. "The tariff he had asked [for] was what he usually asked," explained Sonali, "but it was so moderate in relation to that of the usual directors, that he had made, without intending to, important enemies in the film industry. People who had decided to destroy his work in India."[32] The Films Division of the Ministry of Information was in fact paying Indian producers fees so much higher, that the matter was raised in parliament. Rossellini's offer to *donate* his documentaries only exacerbated the irritation he was causing local producers. Having his picture with Nehru appear in all the local papers did not help, either.

The film industry had held a luncheon and reception for Rossellini when he arrived. "I hadn't been there," said Sonali, "because I had never been part of the film world. But I was there at the good moment. I was working on the script with Roberto's collaborators when the director of the hotel presented himself very embarrassed. The film industry organizers had charged the hotel to present the bill to Roberto. Naturally Roberto paid the bill with good humor. He was very amused and consoled his Indian friends in their chagrin. They had been doing their best to convince Roberto of the proverbial hospitality of the Indians."[33]

Roberto had planned to commence shooting in 35mm February 2, to coincide with Robertino's birthday. But meanwhile Keskar—the Minister of Information with whom Rossellini had his agreement—died and now questions were asked, and delays imposed.

"A freshly named Minister of Information summoned me to ask me what I was doing.

"'A film.'

"'What film?'

"'You have the project in your files.'

"'Yes,' he said, 'it's a film that is not pro-Indian.'

"'What do you know about it? Read it.'

"'Very well, I'm going to have it examined closely.'

"He called me back two weeks later. 'You have to stop.'

"'But why?'

"'A film like this can only hurt India.'

"'Tell me how. I have no intention of hurting India. . . . Give me an example.'

" 'Here's one right off. Just the sort of thing that isn't right. You have an episode with a tiger that becomes a man-eater. The behavior of the tiger is not right.'

" 'I got really angry. I told him, 'Listen. You're Indian and I'm Italian. But you're not a tiger, and neither am I. Why are you beating me over the head with this tiger?'

"I had to go find Nehru in person, to ask him to have my authorization to film restored. Doubtless this was one of the occasions when he had to admit, not without melancholy, that democracy was not yet mature in India. 'A long, long march,' he told me. 'We have to be patient.' Then he appointed two of his collaborators, Pillai . . . and P. N. Haskar . . . to plead my case to the tiger minister."[34]

A few weeks passed. The tiger was still wrong.

Finally, Nehru took the Rossellini project away from the Ministry and created a special high commission. Indira Gandhi was one of the members. "She understood Roberto and his need for freedom of action," Sonali recalled, affectionately.[35] Indira Gandhi took Roberto aside and said, "You know, we're always so short of people that the worst always get put in the Ministry of Information."[36]

Roberto's room at the Taj now became a ministry-like office through which trekked producers, technicians, students, all anxious to meet the "Buddha of the cinema." He had prints of *Paisà* and *Francesco* flown from Italy. He announced to Tonti, "This is the land in which I'll do the miracle. From India I'll launch a new word into the world. Here will be born a new cinema."[37]

"Roberto really works like a Roman," Herman remarked. "He believes strongly in the word. Everyday he re-examines a scenario that is being constructed little by little through constant conversation. He arrived with rather 'Franciscan' ideas. . . . He immediately decided that India was a country he would understand perfectly, because, like Rome, it was a 'draped,' extroverted civilization. . . . He thus decreed that between the Indians and him complicity was possible."[38]

In a country where so much milk is produced, there is no cheese. Why? What does this imply? Why this absence of systemic search for the comforts of life?

What struck me on my arrival in India was the obvious aspect of the crowds, their active laziness. I think of laziness as one of the great signs and movers of civilization. Sweet, dreamy laziness is the expression of active, thinking brains. Sweet, dreamy laziness (which has nothing to do with sloth) is the pleasure of light, detached meditation, of the proper balance in life. And one aspect of this is being a gourmet. That is, to have the pleasure of tasting. That certainly make[s] us better, quieter. The joy of living, like life, is a gift of God, even if it is intimate, and the more it is intimate the more it sweetens our character, make[s] us patient and tolerant, gives us the proper balance of daily existence....

In Naples there is a museum that probably has the richest collection of Roman statues. I remember the extraordinary impression I got the first time I went there. What I had learned about the Romans from history books no longer seemed true. All the statues—and Roman art was profoundly realistic—showed individuals ... in positions of repose. Even Hercules (the famous Farnese Hercules) was leaning lazily on a club. I remember two marvelous bronze athletes. They are shown an instant before their exploit. You can clearly sense that they have just gotten up from a position of repose, and that they are readying themselves for effort with a vague and mysterious smile on their lips. They seem amused at themselves—an ingenuous, childish amusement. It is really the desire to taste life, to feel the joy of their muscles in movement, and then to sink back joyfully into repose. You can almost sense that their nude bodies smell of the fresh wet grass that they've just risen from, and that they will drop back onto with greater joy, out of breath, at the end of their race. On a wall there is a wonderful bas-relief. It represents Dionysius (who is wisdom) bearded and old, going to a love rendezvous. In fact, at the other end of the piece of marble one discovers a nude woman stretched out on a sumptuous bed waiting for him. He looks at her from a distance with curiosity and detachment. And two fauns are pushing him on at the height of the reins, while two others are picking up his feet one after the other to make him take steps.

This bas-relief is a lesson in wisdom. It is desire that one tastes until the end, it is the dream that leads us to its realization, and that makes us savor it fully.... I have ranked the Latinos in the group of ... toga-ed people [with the Indians. But also] because I wish, as a Latin, that we could utilize the lesson of modern India....

[Its] advantage and danger is that the Indians, from lack of any dogmatism, are always ready to accept and try anything that might be good. The teaching of Buddha ... expresses this attitude with perfect clarity. He says, 'Do not accept blindly what I tell you, but test it and if it suits you, accept it.'

Here [in India] technology is accepted, but more vivid is the feeling that only certain problems can be solved by it....

I have ... discovered with a certain stupor that Hindu thought is absolutely rational....

[Meditation and mysticism are] ... products of the Indian soul. The feudal kings got fat and rich profiting from the fact that individuals, in search of personal perfection, always strove for renunciation, as a virtue—with the result that humility degenerated into complaisance toward poverty. It was a way of making slaves....

Today the country, having won its freedom, has gotten to work to modernize ..., adopting science but preserving philosophy. And if certain forces, long accustomed to domination, seek moralistically to exalt [this de-

*generated form of] Indian humility as a virtue . . . , other forces are acting
to revitalize true humility, a humility that is tolerant but also aware. . . .*

    *And it will not be bad if they improve their cuisine as well, and re-
cover a taste for things which—though seemingly less important—nonetheless give just and virtuous joy, and which will help reform a balance momentarily lost. The art that has been expressed by the great civilizations
has alone remained master of successive civilizations, and yet has remained
as monument of an historic period. Signs of new art are beginning to be
glimpsed in this country and these are the most comforting signs.*[39]

Fox had wanted Ingrid to go in person to America to receive the New
York Film Critics award. To enable her to make the trip, they had bought
up three performances of *Tea and Sympathy*. She was apprehensive, given
American hostility. There could be public protests. Hemingway wanted to
come along and protect her. She knew Roberto was against it. His brother
Renzo had even written to say it would be a kind of breach of promise. But
she went on January 19, 1957 and her reception was a triumph.

It was only a two-day visit. She writes in her autobiography that, although she had seen Pia only once since 1949, in London in 1951, she felt
obliged to put off seeing her daughter now. But Pia herself recalls a second
London meeting in 1953, and Petter Lindstrom says there was a third in
1955, and a secret fourth one in New York, also in 1955.[40] Bergman could
have made such trips without Roberto's knowledge.

Roberto left Bombay on February 19, at last. At two that afternoon,
Tonti, Tonti's son Giorgio, Kitù, Herman, and Habib from the Films Division, along with luggage, film, two 16mm cameras, a 35mm, and sound
equipment, crowded into the station wagon, which Roberto had bought
from Das Gupta, and Roberto drove them south 700 miles almost non-stop,
arriving in Bangalore at ten the next morning.

After two months in India, he had not been able to shoot a single foot
of 35mm, and accords with the Indian government had still not been formalized. Now, because of the intolerable amount of bad talk that would
have resulted, he was not able to have Sonali on location, although the
script was far from ready and although he had never before filmed, indeed
was incapable of filming, without a scenarist at hand. Even more than
Paisà, which had been re-scripted by Fellini in response to whatever was
encountered en route, the whole concept of *India Matri Bhumi* was to respond to as-yet undiscovered situations. Already, the chance trip to Hirakud had inspired an unforeseen episode. How could Rossellini—who
needed dialogue written day by day—even vaguely pre-plan what he
would shoot a month from now in the strange, exotic places he was headed
for?

The impossibility of Sonali travelling with the troupe made it inevitable that Rossellini would have to commute back and forth to her frequently. Did he fully realize the consequences of this when he left Bombay?

Or when he chose Sonali as his principal collaborator? Time would prove he had made a fatal mistake.

After a few hours rest in Bangalore, they drove another fifty miles south to Mysore to see the film's first location, the jungle of Kalapur, teeming with bamboo, wild monkeys, and elephants. They would return here in two weeks. First they would circle down to India's southern-most tip for the documentaries.

They went back to Bangalore for the night and the next morning drove to Gandhi Gram, where they spent three days. Gandhi had founded a school here for "nurses of the spirit"—widows, cast-off women, unwed mothers, lonely hearts. It was a Spartan regime. You slept on two boards and ate rice and vegetables. Roberto began to have doubts. There was not even bread. He stayed in the guest house most of the time, while Tonti roamed around shooting. The third day he made himself an egg-and-to-mato omelet.

He was, admitted Herman, "the only director I ever heard say, 'Today I'm not inspired. Excuse me. I feel stupid. I can't work.' He would disappear into his room for two days while we waited, stretched out on his bed with an ice bag on his forehead. Kitù kept trying to write, but Rossellini would not read a line. 'You're wasting my time!' he would say."[41]

Migraine headaches would incapacitate him to the point that he was unable to speak for days. He would buy drugs in wholesale quantities. Ingrid was continually sending shipments of Synthol, a cooling ointment Roberto claimed helped his headaches. A well-outfitted hypochondriac, he carried a whole chest of medicines wherever he went. Without European nourishment, his weight had dropped seventy pounds, to 160.

They had already learned that the beautiful roads indicated on their maps were the dreams of some ministry; the actual roads were often nothing but trails. The rutted one to Quilon was particularly bad. The weather was horribly hot. Then at Quilon, on the Arabian Sea, they found all the comforts of home. Twelve Norwegians were running a United Nations fishing project, teaching the people how to use motorboats, new nets, and an ice factory. The black, thorium-rich sand on the beach, the Italians were told, had been used to manufacture the first atom bomb. They stayed here about a week shooting one of the documentaries.

"I'm an old filmmaker," Roberto said. "The fun of being behind the camera is finished for me. But, I tell you, I loved 16mm. . . . It has possibilities, and a freedom, unknown in 35mm. [And color] definition is infinitely better in 16, because the stocks are made for amateurs and thus offer a very wide latitude and let you do extraordinary things."[42]

Roberto was fascinated to find a temple elephant, huge and obviously very old. In each spot of shade, it would come to an abrupt halt and have to be cajoled to pass through the sun to the next shady spot. When Roberto attempted a photograph, the owner intervened furiously and refused to let a photo be taken until he pulled from a bag two large wooden tusks and attached them to his stubborn animal.

Roberto, as much a phone maniac in India as in Italy, had been calling Bombay constantly. After a few days in Quilon, he angrily announced that Sonali had gone to Calcutta and that he had to go to Bombay to finalize the accords and flew off, leaving the troupe to continue without him. In actuality, he was facing a disaster: his scenarist had quit.

Das Gupta had started his documentary, *Indian Iron and Steel*, for the Tata firm, which had huge factories near Jamshedpur, 200 miles west of Calcutta. Claude Renoir, Jean Renoir's nephew, was photographing the picture. Satyajit Ray had done the script but Sonali had been helping with it, and the Das Guptas were staying with Hari's parents.

"I was going on with the work for Rossellini," said Sonali, "when Hari suddenly began to say things like, 'Why do you care so much? Why are you trying to be so efficient?' I reminded him that he had wanted this work, he had wanted the contract. He replied contradictorily: he wanted me to work, but not too much. I began to understand that he was seeing in my zeal an annoyance, if not a suspicion. His remarks grew more frequent, ending with my telling him, 'If this work has to try your patience, it's better to stop it.' And I stopped."[43]

Tonti and the troupe left Quilon on March 2, drove to Cape Comorin, India's extreme tip, where there is a temple dedicated to Gandhi, then to Madurai. When Tonti phoned the Taj Mahal Hotel, he was told Roberto had flown to Calcutta. From there he had gone by charted plane to Jamshedpur. By the time Tonti finally got him on the phone, he was anxious over the delays. "We're facing disaster," Tonti told him. But Tonti never understood the disaster posed by the lack of a scenarist. They agreed to meet in Bangalore.[44]

The crew arrived on March 8 in the station wagon. Electric generators and arcs had arrived by train. Roberto came the next day by plane. By the time they reached Kalapur they were bleached white by the trail's powdery dust. There was no water, except for the Cauveri River, no electricity. Tons of ants. The nearest telephone was fifty miles away in Mysore. There was a crude cabin in the jungle for the crew, but Roberto planted himself in Mysore where, he said, he could hear the voices of Europe. Alas, it was not so easy to taste Europe's food. India's was constant frustration. He showed a cook how to make *risotto con zucca*, rice with pumpkin squash. He was losing weight more quickly than during the German occupation of Rome.

In Mysore he acquired a monkey named Raimu. Raimu, he said, was "never affectionate and gave me hell." Raimu had been terrified by a cobra conjured up by a snake charmer, and had flung himself around Roberto's neck, trembling with fear, and as always with Roberto, this had been a sure ploy, like a damsel in distress. It would be fun to bring home a monkey for Robin, Isa, and Dindi. After considerable haggling, Raimu's owner sold him for a high price. Endless troubles began. "He saw the cobra again a few days later. But this time Raimu pushed me back, jumped on the cobra, and started to bite its head off. The charmer had to jump in save the snake."[45]

In Kalapur a special *Keddah* was being organized for the film. Normally the *Keddah*, an ancient way of using elephants to hunt elephants, was held only every five years and required two thousand beaters.

Rossellini was in "top form," Tonti said, and on March 10, finally, they shot their first 35mm Gevacolor. They had been in India for three months. But the *Keddah* did not get onto film, the camera broke.

Roberto, taking Herman and Kitù, jumped into the station wagon, drove non-stop eighteen hours to Bombay, dropped off his assistants and the camera at the repair shop, and without a moment's rest phoned Sonali, went to the airport, and flew to Calcutta.

He found her with her in-laws, confused and embarrassed. She had not done any more work. She tried to hide from him. Her family did not understand; they turned on her whenever she tried to explain. Roberto came back the next day and stayed almost a week nearby. He befriended Das Gupta's brother, to put more pressure on Sonali.

Tonti spent this time alone in the jungle. The rest of the crew had retreated to Mysore. He was charged with photographing monkeys and elephants and bamboo for the documentary. He found a particularly lovely watering hole where each day more and more monkeys came, until finally there were over 200. After a week he was thoroughly filthy. Roberto drove up, impeccable in white suit, silk scarf, and hunting cap, and said, "White man, where do you come from?"[46]

Roberto had flown from Calcutta. Herman had brought the camera back in the station wagon. They started the *Keddah* again, but after two days the camera broke again. Roberto had been talking about Sonali since his return and writing to her. He would take the camera to Bombay again. Tonti irrupted.

" 'Look,' I raged, 'You stay here and do your job. I'm sick of being left alone.' We stormed at each other. Then as suddenly as the row began it finished. Roberto took my arm. He said, 'Aldo, I cannot lie to you. I am fascinated by this woman. She is the most intelligent woman I have met in all my life. If you like, I'm in love with her. But it is not an ordinary love. Our minds are attracted.'

" 'But you are married, Roberto.' I said. 'To another beautiful and intelligent woman. And you know that you love Ingrid.'

"He wept. 'I do love her. I do love her. . . . Why do you think these are here?' he shouted, waving his hand at the pictures."[47]

Tonti prevailed. Herman flew the camera to Bombay; Roberto stayed in Mysore. A few days later, March 27, news came over the radio that Ingrid had won an Academy Award for *Anastasia*. "Roberto was very proud and happy for her."[48]

Then Das Gupta phoned. He needed to borrow some inexpensive arc-lamp screens, so Roberto, insisting on taking them personally, flew to Calcutta. Tonti went back to his jungle in a foul mood, grumbling. "The fool!"

The next day, a bull elephant charged him as he was filming it. He dropped to the ground. Its feet landed inches from his head; he could stare at the footprints afterward.

Near Jamshedpur, Sonali and Roberto visited a temple of the goddess Kali. And ran into Renoir's nephew. "My God, one couldn't recognize Roberto, he was always so sweet, so nice!" Claude Renoir exclaimed.[49]

"One evening," said Roberto, "I arrived somewhere around eight. There was a private path leading to the bungalow. . . . There was a barrier across the road and I stopped and honked for someone to open it for me. No one came. There was a small house on the side, so I got out and knocked on the door. An Indian responded . . . , 'I'm coming right away. I heard your horn. I waited a moment because there was a tiger sitting there. Did you see him?' 'No.' 'Oh, it's nothing!' He opened the barrier and let me drive in. He showed me the bed, which is always in the center of the room, since snakes come in and stay near the wall, because they're timid and afraid. And then the guy said to me: 'Even if you're very hot, please don't open the mosquito netting.' There were mosquito nets on the windows and door. 'Yes, okay. Why?' 'You see, there are quite a few tigers around here and it's not prudent to open the nets!'"[50]

On April 2, Herman got back to Mysore with two cameras. Roberto returned the same day with a silver cup for Tonti. "I'm not a little boy, Aldo. I know what I'm doing. And whatever you think, I can still make movies."[51]

In the next five days they shot the entire elephant episode for *India Matri Bhumi*, which ranks, with "The Po Delta" episode in *Paisà*, among the jewels of twentieth-century art.

Jean Herman marveled at Rossellini's capacity for work. "He will bury us all. He drove eighteen hours always talking, always working. No respite: he needs to change place rapidly. This man, although rather corpulent, has enormous physical agility; his motor is a sort of permanent anguish, punctuated with brief moments when one rediscovers the true Italian who wants to make spaghetti. He managed to direct actors who did not speak at all the same language as he, by putting them on the rails of a simple story and asking them to do what they do every day. He directed them without their knowing it.

"Yes, he had enormous moments of discouragement. He is a notorious manic-depressive but he would rise from his ashes. It would happen to him to bury himself in his room, in the dark, but it was in order the better to revive. More than discouragement or fatigue, it's the incomprehension that undermines him. This man has searched all his life to understand. He needs to swallow things and spit them out again his way, amplified. It's as if he wanted to swallow the Ganges at its mouth and spit it out at its source."[52]

The episode tells the story of a typical elephant man, a *mahout* who, like all *mahouts*, has to spend his every waking minute caring for his elephant, but meanwhile he sees a girl, proposes through her father, and marries, while his elephant trods modestly into the jungle to mate.

Each episode of *India Matri Bhumi* reworks these three themes: life is hard, toil never ceases; rewards are modest or non-existent; extreme realism is required.

And there is a fourth theme: the sensibility that we exist within a symbiosis of humans, animals, and nature, of earth, air, fire, and water.

"India is the discovery of another world," said Rossellini. "There's a measure of man there which seems absolutely perfect and rational to me. We call it mystical and we say something completely mistaken; and if we say it's not mystical we make another mistake. The truth is: they try to be completely rational, to see man as he is, scientifically, biologically as he is. And one of the human components is mysticism which, from an emotional point of view, is perhaps the highest expression of man. As there's respect for all human manifestations, there's respect for that, too. Indian thought seems mystical, and it is, but it's also profoundly rational. The zero was invented in India, the thing most rational and metaphysical at the same time. This attempt to see all human tendencies is the fascinating thing. In a world like ours in which one must be either white or black, the tinted halves, the shades, don't exist. But the world, and people even more, are made of shades."[53]

One might object that *India Matri Bhumi*'s symbiosis of matter and spirit is too general, that it differs little from similar visions in most other Rossellini films, or in Tolstoy or Vidor or other gnostics. It is true that Rossellini—out of deliberate choice, he said[54]—does not give much detail about Indian food, artifacts, religion, philosophy, personality, or even social custom.

On the other hand, few moments in cinema come close to the sensibility of being *there*, of being specifically in this Kalapur–April 1957 symbiosis, than does the scene of the elephants after work, lumbering down to the river to be bathed. Godard described it infamously: "*India Matri Bhumi* is the creation of the world."[55]

Can one create a world without creating a myth? *Roma città aperta*, *Paisà*, and *Deutschland im Jahre Null* may have been undertaken as searches to rerun the past, but the rerun's purpose was to figure out what had happened, which means to find meaning, to historicize the past, to create myths (in all three instances: a coming Spring—a new reality). These films are unusual in "neo-realist" cinema in being set in the past, although after 1959 most Rossellini films would be set then. At times these films have a "newsreel" or "home movie" feel to them and *purport* to be in a fictional present. But inevitably the camera draws back or characters walk off, in order to suggest a moral and to historicize what we've just seen; and the films begin that way, too. In contemporary subjects too, *Stromboli*, *Europe '51*, or *Voyage in Italy*, the withdrawing camera, at the delirious climax of the heroine's consummation, mythifies and "historicizes" the now. Rossellini's myth is usually rebirth (renaissance, risorgimento, new reality).

Perhaps had he not been so insistent in proclaiming his "moral" task of showing things as they are, had he more frankly conceded his own Romantic engagement with "reality," his critics might have given him an easier time.

What, after all, is more quintessentially Romantic than the desire to engage reality? In Rossellini's early films his engagement is moralizing. By *Voyage in Italy* no moral needs to be drawn by a retreating camera, it is already present in the first frames—Naples. Reality is the product of the people and the things around them that they look at (and historicize). Edmund looks at Germany and kills himself; the Joyces' overt moralizing gives way before Naples. By *India Matri Bhumi* such melodramatics are tempered. Roberto said: "History, like science, does not exist in India. Science and history started to be known with the English, I think. Everything there becomes mythology, fable. Historical thinking, I believe, is not very alive in India, and moreover they are right, because history is always written to modify things and to persuade people.[56] Things are there, especially in this film. Why manipulate them?"[57]

History becomes now; the mythic age is now.

India Matri Bhumi refuses melodrama—in order to validate fable. Matri Bhumi—the Great Mother Enchantress who charms, softens, and cultivates. There is no need for Rossellini to mythify what is already mythological, to manipulate what is already myth. As Naples was Catholic, India is fable. Both cultures live in a present which is also the past. But in *India* episodes (or entire movies) do not climax with revelation, with the protagonist finally tuning in to everything that has been going on around him or her; in India the revelation, if there ever were one, occurred sometime before the episode begins, we have no need to shift time in order to find meaning, history, and myth. Characters, as in the old Rossellini "master plot," still wander in labyrinths, and still have revelations, and still have the sense of the miraculous. But there is no longer the tension between the "chorus" and the uncomprehending foreigner that traumatizes every Rossellini picture since *Un pilota ritorna*. Now the miracles of personal revelation occur not in sudden, extraordinary events, but over the measured passage of time, as time reveals its reflection of eternity, through the ordinary unwinding of life. There is not a hint of melodrama in the *mahout's* love story, remarkably. Still, he treasures his moments no less. His sense of the miraculous is no less intense for being permanent.

In place of history there is eternal cycle. All four stories in *India Matri Bhumi* relate passage from one phase of life to another: people marry, have to relocate, grow old, die, learn to stand on their own. In Europe, Rossellini had said he would show India's passage into the modern world; in India (to the fury of many Indians), he subordinated historic chronicle to the immanent eternal, to the passage of individuals into greater understanding. Deliberately, he absented history from his film, indeed, absented *any* instruction in ideology or artifacts as well, because to emphasize them would have suggested that Indians are a product of their history and culture, whereas Rossellini's intention is to show exactly the reverse, that Indian history and culture are second-order manifestations of Indian sensibility, of the way passage reveals the particular relating to the general. Croce did the same thing with the kingdom of Naples, when he rejected the thesis that climate and topography had determined its history. There is no end of differences, for example, between the *mahout's* way of falling in love and, say, Roberto Rossellini's way of falling in love, because of their different sensibilities. And different differences can be gleaned from almost every single thing we see the *mahout* do, throughout the episode, even from things apparently unrelated, like the way he washes his elephant. "The Indian always stays in touch with the great things, even in the most banal gesture, in the most typical daily acts," said Roberto.[58]

It is a bit as though we are in India as tourists, watching the people around us. We don't understand their language, we haven't studied their art or history, we haven't opened our guide book, and we've missed the Taj Mahal. We've gotten off the plane without knowing where we are. But we are quiet and attentive, and we watch for a very long time, intensely, and we commune with a world no books could let us into.

On April 8, Roberto flew to Calcutta a fourth time. Meanwhile Tonti, Herman, Kitù, and Habib began a thousand-mile trip in the station wagon to Hirakud. The roads were worse than ever. The air was fire. There were mountains, forests, and deserts, and frequent detours to get across swollen rivers that had no bridges. The thousand miles took a week. In Hirakud, temperatures were over a hundred degrees. Roberto was already ensconced in the sole air-conditioned room and did not emerge until the next day. (The color film stock also had to be rushed from one air-conditioned room to the next; otherwise heat and humidity would ruin it.)

Again they shot an episode in five days.

In "Hirakud," one family's passage in life counterpoints India's emergence into the modern world. Man and wife have worked nine years here; their four-year-old child was born here. Now the dike is finished; 35,000 workers have to go somewhere else. The wife is upset. The man revisits the hydroelectric dam; a memorial commemorates 128 workers who lost their lives. For a moment the electric gizmos frighten him; he has to force himself to reject fears of magic and remember that this is science. At sundown he takes a sacramental bath in the lake the work has created, near a small temple that will soon be submerged. At night they give a party and say goodbye to their friends. The wife collapses in hysteria; ill-temperedly, he lashes out at her. Next morning they walk sadly up the road with the children and possessions. The shot recalls the boys walking down the Gianicolo at the end of *Roma città aperta*, but then the horizon held the future, now it holds the past. Rossellini historicizes.

The next sequence was to be shot near Calcutta. But no script pages had come from Sonali. So, with the Hirakud episode all but finished,

Roberto gave Tonti two sheets of instructions for filming the remaining shots (the bath among them), and flew to Calcutta a fifth time.

He arrived tired, with a sore throat and a broken rib from a car accident; he had wrapped the rib himself with insulating tape. The tension in the house was palpable, even the alarm. Sonali was silent and humiliated. "You won't work in Calcutta," Das Gupta told him. "My mother is old and doesn't understand."

"Understand what?"

"Sonali working for a foreigner. You can construct the same ambience in Bombay."[59]

Roberto returned to Hirakud, assembled his crew, and announced he had changed his mind. Instead of continuing their peregrinations to Calcutta, Benares, Bodh Gaya, and elsewhere, as planned, they would shoot all the rest of the film around Bombay. "The last time I went there I looked around and saw that the landscape works wonderfully."[60]

Everyone was stupefied, says Tonti.[61]

Tonti assumed this total change in concept from an ethnographic adventure to a studio-like approach was made so that Roberto could be near Sonali, and because everyone was exhausted. In fact, Roberto could not continue commuting thousands of miles back and forth to his scenarist, and his plans to shoot an episode near Calcutta had been, in effect, vetoed by Sonali's in-laws. It was a solution to film in Bombay, where he could work with his scenarist. *Paisà* too had falsified locations frequently.

Roberto got back to Bombay April 24 by train. The Das Guptas had already returned. At five the next morning, Sonali phoned to say that their work should be considered ended. She refused to explain. Hari took over the phone with a mixture of pleas and insults.

The cacophony in her life, Sonali recalled, had grown in "a slow crescendo, eventually intolerable. But the crisis openly erupted when we returned to Bombay in April. . . . We had had a hellish night. I was thinking the call would put a stop to everything."[62]

Roberto drove over. He found curious servants, crying babies, and confusion, and took the Das Guptas back to the Taj.

Sonali was in love with Roberto, Hari told him, and they were separating. Roberto, caught between pity and indignation, tried to reason. Sonali sat in silence. Eventually she went home with Hari.

The next night around midnight, she appeared at Roberto's door. "Have patience. Let me stay for ten minutes, then I'll go away."

"At this hour of the night? Where will you go?"

They had taken Raja, their four-year old, to the train station, she explained, to spare him the crisis by sending him to his grandparents in Calcutta. On the way back, in a taxi, Hari had made her get out at the hotel. She wanted to be sure Hari had left, before going out again and returning home.

Roberto was furious. "For me there's only one thing to do and I shall do it, even if it costs me my life. From the moment that your husband chases you from the house, I will offer you my room."[63]

He slept next door. "There had been nothing particularly between us until then," he said.[64] "Nothing before May.[65] Everything happened afterward."[66]

Sonali said, "How is it possible that I left my home voluntarily, if it's true that I sent my older son to Calcutta? It's clear I was thinking I'd stay at home, otherwise there would have been no reason to send the child away. And the other child, so small? I would have carried him with me. . . . Yes, I know, in the eyes of the world, [my staying at the hotel that night] is what proves my guilt. Or at least my fatal error. But do you imagine what a respectable woman, a human being, feels like, treated this way? At a certain moment you give up—to pride, to fatigue, you don't have strength to struggle anymore."[67]

Tonti got back the next morning. "Rossellini called me to his room. He wanted to discuss work. It seemed my hunch about Sonali had been right [that it was over between her and her husband]. As he opened the door I felt myself go cold all over. There was Sonali Das Gupta smiling at me."[68]

According to Tonti, she became hysterical as she tried to explain that her husband had forced her to choose between them, that she felt one with Roberto artistically.[69]

Das Gupta phoned. Their second son, eight months old, was crying. Roberto sent Lila Herman in a taxi for the baby and a nurse, phoned for a third room, and went out with Tonti to work on *India Matri Bhumi*'s third episode.

Das Gupta now began phoning for Sonali to come back. She refused to reply. He tried to get Roberto to persuade her to return, then asked friends to intervene. On April 28 Sonali's father arrived: Dr. K. Sen Roy, former surgeon general of Lucknow, with the filmmaker Bimal Roy and his wife. Sonali scarcely acknowledged them.

Her father addressed Roberto. "You're married, aren't you, Mr. Rossellini . . . ? And you have children?" He looked at the photographs. "And before this wife you had another? And with all this you want to marry my daughter?"

"Yes, what's strange about that?"

"You're inhuman."

"It's inhuman to love? I've known women from all over the world, but never one like Sonali."

"Let Sonali go, Mr. Rossellini. Go back to Italy. You, Sonali, go to your husband who's waiting for you!"

"Never again," Sonali replied.

Covering his eyes with his hand, the father left the room.[70]

Roberto was indignant. Sonali was the victim of a feudal mentality, he thought.

She wanted to hide. "I thought that all I could do for my dear ones was to try to disappear." She stayed in her room the next 48 days, abandoned by family and friends. She read, painted still lifes, and dreamt. She was afraid to go out. "I'm sick and tired. They can do what they want with me." Trained to silence and non-violence, believing in the futility of repaying offense with offense, she would not fight back.[71]

Das Gupta was as much a victim as his wife. He had innocently endorsed her contract, thinking it would benefit both of them. Whereupon pressure had started from every side—parents, in-laws, colleagues, industry, government, everyone. Like the man frightened by Hirakud's electricity, he doubted his enlightenment. He drank. He became an instrument for those in the industry who resented Rossellini, who would willingly spend large sums of money to fan a scandal.[72] After two weeks, at the end of his frustration, fatally, he formally petitioned the Foreigners' Registration Authority in Bombay to cancel Rossellini's visa.

Roberto had gone on with the film, shooting every day between nine and one. Now the press started phoning. The Italian consul called to warn. Das Gupta made threats. Demonstrations began outside the hotel. Kitù quit, out of loyalty to Das Gupta. Roberto, alarmed by lurking figures, staked private security guards outside Sonali's room round-the-clock. When he went out, he had Lila or Jean Herman stay with her.

He phoned Ingrid on May 17, waking her at 3:27 A.M. His tone was nonchalant. He told her there was going to be a scandal, that it was not true, that there was a conspiracy. In her autobiography, Bergman writes that she knew then that he had another woman, that she was relieved *he* had left *her* and had someone to love and look after him, and that she felt pleased both for Roberto and for herself. Until now she had not thought of divorce, she says. She had expected the marriage to go on, one way or another. Hitchcock had come to the play and offered her three scripts; she had rejected them all.

On May 19 the story broke in India. The newspapers wanted Rossellini expelled. The next day Llovack from the *New York Daily News* arrived. Seven years earlier he had "covered" the Bergman scandal. In the *Daily Mirror*, Bill Slocum wrote, "Sonali had everything Roberto searched for in a woman: a husband, a baby and a thirst for romance." And an "old Broadway actress" opined, "Ingrid is the saddest thing one can be in the world: a woman betrayed and alone. She has two Oscars, four children and a great talent. But the man for whom she destroyed her own reputation is driving a Ferrari with an Indian woman."[73]

According to the newspapers, Rossellini said, "Absolute nonsense... humbug... It's not the first time a newspaperman has indulged in fantasy." Sonali, asked if she were expecting a child, is said to have replied, "I refuse to talk about it. It's all too absurd.[74] I'm here because my husband wanted me here. Rossellini's enemies started a campaign to destroy him, using me."[75]

In Paris, Ingrid, looking radiant, expressed total confidence. She told reporters: "I think someone is trying to hurt my husband."[76] On May 27 she wrote Joe Steele, "The Indian hoopla is made-up stuff (or at least part of it; what does a wife ever *really* know!). Roberto told me on the telephone that all this started with a journalist whom he threw out of his room."[77] According to Simone Paris, "There were nights when Ingrid would arrive at the theater barely able to hold back her tears. When she heard about Rob and that Indian girl, she sobbed hysterically backstage."[78]

She was devastated for him.

In Bombay, giant billboards were advertising *Anastasia*. The monsoon had started. Roberto and Sonali were besieged within the hotel. "It was like an hallucination, a sort of nightmare. Remember the story by Mérimée about the man who dreams he's on an African beach and the natives come with a sack they're going to throw into the sea, and inside the sack is a woman who has to die? Well, in Bombay, I felt as though I were living through that absurd and frightening dream."[79]

He was 51; Sonali, 27, had fallen in love with him completely.

A week passed and he was summoned to Delhi. Pillai informed him that publicity about Sonali would have to stop if the film was to go on.

In Bombay, Tonti, despairing of Roberto's marriage and career, profited from his absence to try to convince Sonali to go back to her husband, for Roberto's sake. He found her half-packed already. In tears, she asked him to take charge of getting her out of the hotel. Lila intervened: she should not leave before Roberto returned.

Roberto, still in Delhi and determined he was right, protested to Nehru. He had a contract with Sonali. Nehru respected Roberto as a gentleman. He stuck by him and expressed distress at his break with Bergman.

Leaving his holy man, Roberto cried. Returning to Bombay, he went not to the Hotel but to the house of Italian friends in the Malabar Hills. From there he sent for his luggage. He would not see Sonali again in India.

He tried to console Tonti. "Don't worry about all this trouble, Aldo. Everything *will* turn out all right. I shall not see Sonali again. . . . Our work is over."[80]

Four days later, on a foggy, windy night, the Hermans sneaked Sonali out through a service entrance and took her to a house on Marin Drive, in another section of Bombay than where Roberto was staying.

Roberto went on shooting. By necessity, but also by deliberation, the original scheme for the film was abandoned. ("It would have been a very long film," he joked later. "Fortunately I encountered every sort of difficulty."[81]) The nine episodes were reduced to five. Four stories were abandoned which now seemed explicative or moral-laden: "Community Projects," about government engineers who help villagers reform their agriculture; "The Widow," about a woman who keeps her husband's factory going after his death despite her brother-in-law's opposition; "The Importance of Meditation," about a mountain community which detours a road so that truck traffic will not make its three hermits leave—and learns that silence once lost is hard to regain; "The Land Donor," about a rich man who gives everything away and becomes a beggar.[82]

Also abandoned was the concept of organizing the stories around three general themes: structural transformation ("Community Projects," "The Land Donor," "Hirakud Dam"); conflict with tradition ("The Widow," "The Importance of Meditation," "The Wedding"); and humans and animals ("The Mahout and His Elephant," "Ashok and the Tiger," "Dulip the Monkey"). Rossellini now realized that explicit cultural data would detract from his essential.

"[The documentaries had been] a way for me to prepare for the feature film. . . . I tried first to observe, simply to report, without taking any position. . . . In the film, in contrast, the material is dramatically elaborated. What I tried to express is the *feeling* India gives . . . , the inner warmth of the people. . . . What struck me when I got back to Europe was the total absence of nature around us."[83]

He had been struck also by Rivette's comparing him to Matisse, to Matisse's way of "despoiling" his subjects, by stripping away anything unessential. Roberto had not been conscious of this "despoiling" in *Voyage* or *Paisà*. Now he went about it with "new effort, but when I succeed, my joy has no limits.[84]

The essential drama was between people and nature, as in *Voyage* and *Stromboli* and *Deutschland im Jahre Null*—with the difference that in all previous Rossellini films, people had sought to evade nature (at least until the last scene), whereas from now on they would confront it methodically. "I tried to express the soul, the light inside these people, their reality, which is a reality that is absolutely intimate, unique, and attached to an individual, with all the sense of his surroundings. For things around have a meaning, since here is someone looking at them, or at least this meaning become unique by the fact that someone is looking at them: the hero of each episode who is at the same time the narrator."[85]

People and nature. People looking, like Edmund's constant stares in *Deutschland* or Katherine's in *Voyage*. The meanings they give to what they see, as in Flemish paintings. "Reality."

"What's important are the ideas, not the images. It's enough to have very clear ideas and to find the most direct image to express an idea. There are a thousand other ways besides film to express ideas: writing, for example, if I were a writer. *The sole thing film possesses in addition is the possibility of putting into a single photograph ten things at once.* There is no need to be analytic in cinema—while being so."[86] Like Dos Passos.

The *"ten things"* are the people and the "things around" that "have a meaning"—the land beneath your feet, your house, the elephant you wash, the trees, the sounds you hear, your clothes you feel, the straw basket of stone you carry, the lake you have made. The *"ten things"* are the formal elements of film.

The third episode, "Ashok and the Tiger," then, was based on an actual event recounted to Roberto in Rourkela, a village in Orissa, and concerns a tigress with two cubs that becomes a man-eater, after being rendered starving and neurotic by industrial incursions into the jungle. But we scarcely glimpse the tigress. The movie is really about the life rhythms of an old man, how he relates to the dawn, his wife, prayers and washing, his cattle, the jungle, and being old, and about his conviction that the world is big enough for tigers too. Perfectly illustrative of Rossellini's twin theories of despoilment and of showing ten things at once, is the scene of the old man and his wife waking up in their hut in the morning and speechlessly going about the washing and praying and other things they have done every morning of their lives together. Like a Vermeer or a Matisse painting, it is the inconsequential that is essential.

The specific drama is that the old man both accepts passage and resists it. It is again the dilemma of the particular and the general, the temporal and the eternal. But now the old man does not resist like Edmund in *Deutschland* or Karin in *Stromboli* or Katherine in *Voyage*, by evasion, suicide, escape, or turning away. Instead, like the thousands who stone by stone constructed the resistance of Hirakud Dam, the old man resists by engaging methodically with every moment of experience—and by keeping the world big enough for tigers.

The fourth episode, "Dulip the Monkey," was originally to have developed this notion of animals' dependence on man, already illustrated in the elephant story. A trained monkey (Raimu) is left destitute when his master dies from a cobra. Not understanding death, he tries repeatedly to stir him to action. Even later, when he arrives in a village by himself and does tricks for the crowds, he still expects the master to scoop up the coins people throw. At the end, because there is no other choice, he follows the people when they leave "and continues to search in vain among thousands of walking legs for the big-boned ones of Anil, his old friend, the gentlest of his friends."[87]

Roberto explained: "His master dead, the poor monkey, who is now neither monkey nor human, feels the need to go both among the monkeys and among people, to go backward and forward. This indeed is the drama of each of us. It's the struggle we're all in."[88]

Originally, before the location moved to Bombay, the story was to have had a more religious ambience. Now death from sunstroke has replaced the somewhat biblical snake. And a fairground crowd has replaced the pilgrims at Bodh Gaya, with its fabulous eleventh-century temple and, it is said, the very tree under which Buddha found enlightenment.

Eventually, after *India Matri Bhumi*'s first non-public screening, in order to give the whole film an upbeat ending, a new conclusion was filmed. Now the monkey finds a new master and a new job in a circus. But in the Bodh Gaya version, Dulip the monkey did not find enlightenment, he never understood the master's death, he just went on searching.

Raimu is endearing in Roberto's film when he tries to protect his master's body from the vultures or gets chased away by the wild monkeys. But in Roberto's house, Raimu was the servants' nightmare. He missed his master and their outdoor life vagabonding from village to village. Imprisoned in strange surroundings with strange people, he jumped ceaselessly around the rooms and was insupportable. Roberto had Raimu flown to Delhi, where his friend Giuliana Cambi was director of the Swiss Hotel and possessed a large garden with lots of trees. But Raimu's insecurity and anger increased in confinement during the trip, and in Delhi he hated being tied to a tree with a long chain. When Aldo Cambi tried to feed him, Raimu bit his hand, got loose, and was never seen again.[89]

Meanwhile, the government's cooperation and assistance were being withdrawn. Money became scarce. The station wagon was sold. The permits were running out. The fifth story, "The Wedding," about love blooming in an arranged marriage, had not been started. Sonali's father was asking the government to cancel Rossellini's visa and to deny a passport to Sonali.[90] On Marin Drive, the harassment of Sonali was systematic. Her electricity would be cut off, her milk deliveries stolen. If she ventured out, people hired by the film industry would frighten and follow her. She wasn't permitted to see her four-year-old son. For the first time in her life, she was alone, outcast from her family.

Trips to Delhi did no good. Nehru had gone to London; the ministers he left behind were not sympathetic. At the beginning of July, Roberto phoned Ingrid and asked her to get to Nehru.

Unknown to Roberto, Ingrid at that moment had fallen in love with Lars Schmidt, a theatrical producer living at The Raphael.

The relationship had started in June when she had lied to Schmidt, claiming she had to take care of her children, when actually she was lunching at an outdoor restaurant in the Bois de Boulogne with Robert Anderson, who was passing through Paris.

As it happened, Lars Schmidt was at the same restaurant. "Ah, Miss Bergman, so this is the way you take care of your children," he said.

"And she looked up at me and she blushed," he recalled. "I'd never seen anyone blush like it. Then she looked at me with this most divine smile. And that night I called her again. And that broke the ice completely."[91]

Only dimly aware of what Roberto's problems were, Ingrid phoned Ann Todd, who was friends with the Indian ambassador, Nehru's sister. Flying to London, she spoke to Nehru at an embassy luncheon on July 5. Obviously concerned, Nehru told her he would do what he could.[92]

Three days later at Orly airport, Ingrid met Pia. Seventy-five reporters were there as well. In answer to questions about Roberto, Ingrid replied, "We will spend the summer together at our Santa Marinella villa as we always have since our marriage."[93]

Mother and daughter spent the next six weeks together in Paris, Rome, Santa Marinella, and Capri, with Pia's half-brother and sisters and the whole Rossellini tribe. Pia, almost 19, fell in love with Italy and the camaraderie of the Italians. "She is so much more than I ever hoped for," Ingrid wrote Irene Selznick.[94]

Roberto, after his experience with Nehru, was curious to see a "real" Hindu saint. Someone suggested he visit Kammo Baba. Kammo Baba lived in a perfectly ordinary suburban Bombay house, surrounded by no signs of renunciation. He was well informed, intellectual, and charismatic. People would come and sit. His wife would serve tea. "I went into the house. There was the 'saint.' He was a guy with a beard. He was smoking Indian cigarettes one after another. I approached. He asked my name. He started to caress me [near my neck]. He didn't say anything special, he didn't predict my future. He was gentle, he was tender, like a mother, if you like. Little by little I felt myself relaxing. After a quarter of an hour I started to cry. After a half hour I was sobbing. After three quarters of an hour I was wiping my tears. And after an hour I left completely comforted and perfectly happy. I had bathed my nerves, maybe. And that was the Indian 'saint.' He didn't do anything extraordinary. He did this exercise of love."[95]

Roberto phoned Sonali, insisting she had to visit Kammo Baba. She came home scoffing, unimpressed by tourist banalities. That night she woke up in the middle of the night. At the foot of her bed was a tiny man. "Why are you resisting me?" he said.

The question seemed entirely reasonable. Then the tiny man vanished. She felt ridiculous.

In the morning she went back to Kammo Baba's. She arrived early. He was still saying his prayers. He glimpsed her from the corridor and looked up. "So you got my message, did you?"[96]

Roberto was determined that Sonali come to Europe. To her it was an unthinkable idea, to leave India. Yet no sort of life could be possible for her in India now. Moreover, by late July she knew she was pregnant. Roberto was able to assure her his marriage with Ingrid could be dissolved; since Ingrid had forgotten to register her divorce from Lindstrom in Sweden, they were not legally married. This angered Sonali: why hadn't he told Ingrid? "We always keep a window open," he replied.[97]

In any case, in face of the determined opposition of Sonali's husband, father, and family, plus the newspapers, it was unlikely that the government would issue her a passport.

She therefore went to Nehru. He had known her at the University of Tagore, where five of her uncles had been professors and one uncle had been rector. He had always called her by a pet name.

"Chocolate would be easier, Monkey," Nehru said, when she asked for the passport. But she got it. Nehru was also Minister of Foreign Affairs at the time. "If he had not been, I would have had problems," said Sonali.

Nehru's friendship did not end when Sonali and Roberto left India. He kept close to them, would send mangos, and phone any time he passed through Rome. He would say: "How is Monkey doing? Tell her to write straight to me and not go to embassy!"

Indira Gandhi continued the mangos and phone calls after her father's death. When Roberto died, hers was the first telegram to arrive.[98]

"I had never walked so much in Bombay as just before leaving it," Sonali wrote. "Now that my departure was certain, I was afraid. A real panic assailed me in the morning when I would go out to walk casually around the city, like an idiot. Nothing in my education had prepared me for the idea of expatriating myself. I did not in fact belong to that category of Indian women who dream of going to Europe or marrying what we call a 'Sab.' When my father had proposed it to me, I had refused to go to Paris to study at the Sorbonne.... Until now I had innocently identified with everything that made me a non-Westernized Indian woman."[99]

Work on the film came to an end in July. The negative was sent to Italy in August.

Tonti was stranded two months in Bombay, unable to leave because of problems with income taxes and hotel bills that Roberto was unable to settle. In Rome, Tonti's wife had been hospitalized. Along with the tax authorities, the hotels, and the hapless Banca Romana (who would recoup hardly a lira of its hundred million), Tonti besieged Franco Riganti in Rome with phone calls, bills, and letters. A year earlier, Riganti had declined to go to India as Roberto's production manager. Now he learned that his own friend had put his name on all the paperwork anyhow![100]

Roberto's business manager, Giulio Mauro, took care of Tonti's wife's hospital bills and finally in September Tonti was able to leave. In ten months in India he had worked perhaps fifteen days on the film.

Roberto left Bombay in August and took up residence in Delhi at the Maiden Hotel, run by Aldo Cambi from Florence. Across the street was the Swiss Hotel, run by Cambi's wife Giuliana, where Sonali was staying. At last Roberto had found food. "The first thing he would do in the morning," relates Sonali, "was to call Aldo for what the Italians call a *chiacchierata*, a chat . . . , and ask what the day's menu was. Aldo loved making fun of Roberto and keeping him in suspense. 'Is there an Italian dish on the menu?' If yes, 'What is it?' They made a game of it. One day Aldo announced: 'For dinner we shall begin with something Italian.' 'What?' asked Roberto, very excited. '*Angeli ai capelli*,' Aldo replied nonchalantly. 'I've never heard of that. What is it? What is it," asked Roberto enviously. 'Be patient. It's a surprise.' Aldo refused to give details. Roberto waited impatiently for the evening meal, hoping the first course would be pasta. That evening he was at his table, waiting. The waiter, as instructed by Aldo, advanced solemnly holding high a silver platter. He placed it in front of Roberto with a loving look. On the platter was a plate; in the middle of the plate was a piece of bread, beautifully carved, with a piece of cheese at the center and a bit of decoration underneath. Roberto did not say a word. Aldo began to laugh quietly and after a moment of surprise Roberto burst out laughing. He began to call Aldo every sort of dirty name, shockingly, in highly colored Florentine dialect.

"People would ask Aldo, 'How's Roberto today?' " Sonali recalled. " 'Oh, he has three problems today?' 'What problems? Why three? How do you know?' 'Oh easily, because he had three knots this morning.'

"When Roberto was thinking or concentrating, he habitually played with locks of his hair behind his neck, rolling them into knots," Sonali explained. "Some mornings there were none, other mornings more than three. But Roberto never got discouraged. It was a test, for a man of such vitality and such enthusiasm for life."[101]

Roberto spent almost all the day in the air-conditioned hotel, having headaches, taking medicine, playing cards with Aldo or solitaire. He had accumulated tons of books and objects and was having problems sending everything home. He had a great deal of free time in India, he told a journalist. "Every evening I sat in my hotel room, read some Italian newspaper two months old and set myself to writing for two or three hours. What do I write? Everything that goes through my mind, sometimes arguments, sometimes anecdotes, but I write. I write to myself, with simplicity and difficulty. I've already written a dozen articles on India and am a good way through doing a book. Yes, I really think this could be my new road."[102]

He wrote in long hand, never having learned to type.

When night came he would talk on and on about Sonali. He would not leave India until she did; if he did, she might lose courage. David Lean squeezed Sonali's shoulders and shook his head: "My, my, my, such little shoulders! You don't know what big loads you're going to have to carry!"[103]

Bottom Up

Il generale Della Rovere

Sonali arrived in Paris October 6, 1957, with her one-year-old son Arjun and Lila Herman, whose relatives met them at the airport. It was cold. Sonali was afraid. She'd never been out of India. No one knew she was in Paris. Roberto wanted her to stay hidden and she intended to.

He himself did not leave India for another two weeks. In Geneva, where he had to change planes, reporters insisted on taking his picture with Jayne Mansfield. In Paris it was 5 P.M., October 22, and it had just finished raining. The press blocked Roberto's way. Ignoring their questions, he mumbled, "It's all untrue, untrue, untrue."[1]

Ingrid was at the airport waiting. She ran up, threw her arms around him, and kissed him on both cheeks, as Italians do. She did talk to the reporters. "I am very happy," she told them. And repeated the kiss a few times more, so that they could photograph it.[2]

She had to get to the theater. *Tea and Sympathy* was still playing. Two thousand sold-out seats every night. Roberto came in fifteen minutes before the end—his entrance was remarked on by the audience—and Ingrid took only two curtain calls. He knew she thought it spiteful of him to refuse to watch her play. It was another thing that she did not understand.

At The Raphael the scene was sullen. The children were in Rome. He sat in silence twisting his hair. Did he want a divorce? Ingrid asked. He sank deeper into silence. To Ingrid it seemed endless. "Yes," he said slowly, "I'm tired of being Mr. Bergman."[3]

He did not know about her involvements with Robert Anderson or Lars Schmidt. Nor had she mentioned to him that she had already met Sonali. Sonali had come ingenuously in person to deliver a letter entrusted to her by Roberto for Ingrid, without it occurring to her that Ingrid would assume that Roberto's new woman was curious to meet his old one. Sonali had had no reason to believe that she had disrupted Ingrid's relationship with Roberto.

Roberto immediately asked Ingrid to promise never to take the children to America, never to fly on TWA, never to marry again. She began to laugh.

Nothing had changed. She still wanted him to see *Tea and Sympathy*. Jean Renoir could understand his refusal, not Ingrid. "That I can't forgive," she declared. "It was so small, so petty. When he returned from India, his only comment was, 'Are you still playing in that piece of junk?' "[4]

She brought him together with Renoir, left them alone, and Roberto poured out the whole story. Renoir wrote to his wife Dido, "This man is in the ridiculous and lamentable state that romantics call *la passion*. For the authors of *fabliaux* [fables] in the Middle Ages, it was the subject of jokes. . . . He is very unhappy. Sonali is hiding in Paris and he doesn't dare see her. . . . Ingrid pretended to take all this lightly but when Roberto left to wash his hands, she had a brief collapse in my arms, which distressed me."[5]

Roberto attended a dinner for the premiere of Chaplin's *A King in New York*, and with Bazin witnessed Truffaut's marriage to Madeleine Morgenstern on October 29. On October 31, *Tea* finally closed, and he flew the next day to Rome with Ingrid, to their Viale Bruno Buozzi home. To save money, she had taken advantage of his absence to divide the apartment in two and sub-lease the other half, and had sold several cars and a horse, as well. Roberto thought her economies idiotic. On November 7 Fellini came for breakfast—he had just returned from the New York opening of *Nights of Cabiria*. After breakfast, they drove amiably with their lawyer to sign a separation agreement in front of a judge. And then came back home together. The next day they found their dog Strombolicchio dead in the bathroom.

To a friend Ingrid wrote: "Hollywood and America was the spring, the sour season. Rome and Italy the summer, the richest season, my maturity. Then comes autumn, which may very well be beginning now for me as well."[6]

Ingrid was to have custody of the three children, who were to be educated in Europe in the Italian language, and Roberto was to pay 600,000 lire a month for their support ($975). The last clause was for appearance's sake; Roberto didn't have even one lira.

The amiability of their separation was mirrored inversely by public savagery. An interview with Tonti was serialized sensationally in London's *Daily Sketch* and Italy's *Il Giorno*. Roberto never spoke to Tonti again. They found themselves in the same airport lounge a few years later, and Roberto ignored him.[7]

In Italy a wave of popular hatred roared up against Roberto. Italians had loved him for winning Ingrid for Italy; now they loathed him for losing her. Their poor Ingrid had been betrayed and abandoned for some Indian woman, an *unseen* Indian woman, with two children, whose family he had destroyed—and where was she anyway?

Most of Roberto's friends abandoned him. A famous diva bragged to the press, "If he steps foot in my house I'll have him thrown out by the butler."[8]

He was prepared for the hostility, or at any rate endured it with a measure of resignation. "It's sad to see myself turned into a scandal-sheet character," he told a friend. "But I'm sure I'd feel even worse if I let myself get involved in the game of interviews and statements. . . . Despite everything I'm still full of hope, or rather, I want to be. I need silence and meditation. I have a deep need to express myself completely, and maybe now I'll manage to do it."[9]

He might give up film, he said, and become a writer. But he hadn't gotten far with the book on India he had promised Leo Longanesi the year before.[10]

In *Epoca*, a short column by Alba De Céspedes was probably the most sensitive journalism during the entire Bergman–Rossellini story. She wrote that it was natural for everyone to take sides, "because in defending Ingrid or Roberto, everyone ultimately is defending themselves, their own character, their own aspirations. Indeed, just as years ago the Bergman and Rossellini encounter stirred up the problem of love in our modern world, today their separation puts marriage in question.

"When the two famous lovers managed to get married, I remember seeing them smiling in photographs, and feeling an indefinable sense of compassion for them. They seemed to me at that moment condemned to having to demonstrate that they were happy for all the rest of their lives. . . .

"Maybe I shall be the only one to believe that Ingrid and Roberto still love each other—as so many couples love each other after seven years of marriage: in a way that the past, the notoriety, and their personalities had impeded their accepting. Perhaps the embrace at Orly was not expressing the joy of being together again—as it might have looked—but the desperation of being forced to leave each other."

Their careers had been a study in contrast, De Céspedes wrote. Ingrid had started young, with constant, self-imposed discipline. Roberto had become famous all at once. She had always known her part. He had trusted in improvisation, used amateur actors, and had never known what he would have them say the next day. "He was always looking for himself; she had found herself.

". . . Ingrid Bergman has proven to us that today a woman can extract herself from a situation that, for serious reasons, causes her pain or humiliation, because by her own work she is able to provide for herself and her children. . . . If the greater part of the public supports her, it is because she has always paid for her actions and accepted responsibility for their consequences, because, ultimately, among her many famous parts she has played the woman of today, divided between her duties and her passions, her family and her work: and has done it with inimitable grace, with admirable dignity, and with that convincing human strength whose cost only the strong know."[11]

In November, Ingrid went to London to begin shooting *Indiscreet* with Cary Grant. She had wanted the children with her; Roberto had insisted they stay in Rome. Meanwhile his lawyer, Ercole Graziadei, filed suit in Rome for an annulment, on the grounds that Bergman, by failing to register her Mexican divorce, had still been married to Lindstrom at the time of her proxy marriage to Roberto in Mexico, which was thus invalid.

At Christmas the family was reunited on Viale Bruno Buozzi. Roberto lay with his head on Ingrid's lap, the children around them. To the puzzled reporters outside she sent a bottle of glögg, and began to pack. Lisandrini, the Franciscan priest, was there.

"Aren't you going to take the Guttuso?" Roberto asked her, indicating a canvas his famous painter friend had given her.

Ingrid looked at it doubtfully. "Is it worth anything?"

"Oh yes!"

"Hmm. I'll take it then."

She left the room and Lisandrini looked at Roberto aghast. "You're crazy! She's loaded with money and you're penniless! Why . . . !?"

Roberto stared at him, amused. "You too, huh? Brother of Saint Francis!"[12]

Melancholically, he left Rome alone, but asked Fellini to keep him company as far as Civitavecchia, because he had to drive past Santa Marinella. "I'm going to Paris and will never come back. But I need a friend beside me to say farewell to that piece of road," he said. Passing the house, he began to cry like a child.[13]

"It was always raining in Paris," Sonali reflected; "an obsessive rain, slow and continual, that gave sadness and fear."[14] She took long long walks. She refused to wear Western dress, and went unnoticed in her sari. Sometimes, afraid to speak French, she had problems getting home. One time she took a cab and felt kidnapped. She had been afraid of the sticks everyone was carrying, until she found out they were baguettes.

She was still in hiding. Her presence in France was an absolute secret. But there were rumors. To elude reporters, if he went to see her, Roberto would walk a few blocks first to the Cinémathèque Française, where Mary Meerson and Henri Langlois kept a different-looking overcoat for him, which he would change into before leaving by another entrance. Sonali was staying near Place Vendôme, Rue Danièle-Casanova 19, in Henri Cartier-Bresson's apartment. The famous photographer had been Renoir's assistant on *Day in the Country* and *La Vie est à nous*. The apartment was on the top floor, the walls were all windows, so it was always dreadfully hot or dreadfully cold. The bed rested on phone books. The phone could be answered only after a single ring, a hang up, and a ring again. Mary Meerson called one morning at six.

"Roberto, my dear! You don't know what a lucky dog you are! What fantastic good luck! I'm so happy for you!"

"What happened?"

"Just go buy *L'Aurore*. Lower than this one cannot sink! Which means that as of today you're on your way back up!"[15]

In Paris on December 29, 1957, Sonali gave birth prematurely. The baby girl spent her first weeks in an incubator. She was kept secret. French law did not require parents' names on a birth declaration. Mary Meerson was sent to file it. "Raffaella Paola," she wrote on the form, as instructed—and then, on a whim, added her own name, "Mary."[16]

Officially, Roberto was still at The Raphael, in a small room on the top floor, for which he paid a risible price. Even more than before, he was dependent on the hand-outs of friends. He would eat at restaurants until his credit was exhausted, then switch to a new one happy to have a celebrity. One on Rue Marbeuf put "Lasagna Rossellini" on the menu. "His friends are obliged to follow him to restaurants that he chooses," Sonali said, "and the condition is that they have spaghetti on the menu." And even so, "He says you eat well only from Bologna on down. Everywhere else is barbaric, France included."[17] Justly distressed at France's notion of tomato sauce, he often had pasta with just butter and cheese.

Renzino was eighteen now, working at the Cinémathèque, and sometimes living with Sonali not too happily. The twins, Isa and Dindina, never met Sonali during her eighteen months in Paris, and Robertino saw her only once. "You're an Indian?" Robertino asked skeptically. "So how many Americans have you scalped?"[18]

At New Years Ingrid told Roberto she wanted to marry Lars Schmidt.

He was furious. He was defensive. He was terrified. He was going to lose his children! He swore no "foreigner" would get them. Preventing this became his priority.

Ingrid, waiting impatiently for her divorce, scarcely saw her children during the next ten months. She stayed in London for *Indiscreet*, visited Sweden with Schmidt, then went to Wales to film *The Inn of the Sixth Happiness*. In May she asked Roberto to send the children there from Paris, and was surprised by his refusal. "He gets low and depressed, he says, and to have the children around is his only comfort. I guess it doesn't matter that I haven't seen them for five months!"[19]

She saw them for one weekend in June. Then Roberto took them to Santa Marinella for the summer.

"Everything I put up with, I put up with for them,"[20] he told Oriana Fallaci.

Once again he was returning to an Italy he had sworn he was through with forever. He had lasted six months. Italy was hostile country, even worse than after *Voyage in Italy*. It had been journalists who had chased him out then. Now he was "inundated with unpopularity" from all classes. And there were debts. He was not driving the Ferrari, but a Fiat 600, and gossip said it was rented. At Viale Bruno Buozzi the furniture had been seized. Santa Marinella was threatened. If he walked into a bar for a coffee, in his white suit and sandals, people would recognize him and jeer. "What about Sonali? Where've you put her?"[21]

"The Indian actress has been living for some months in Paris," Oriana Fallaci reported, but "her address is unknown." She is "protected like Cardinal Mindszenty is protected in the U.S. embassy in Budapest."[22]

One magazine jubilantly published a picture of her. But it wasn't Sonali.[23]

Even Fellini got nowhere. "Is it a male or a female, Robbé?" he asked. "Neither male nor female."

"What does that mean, Robbé?"

"That means it's nothing."[24]

He went to see Peppino Amato at Palatino Film. "Come up with an idea," Amato told him, "just an idea, and I'll have you carried in triumph. I'll slam shut the mouths of those fools who swear you're finished!" But the conversation ended abruptly when Roberto learned Magnani was on the lot.[25] She was the last person he wanted to see.

India had been more civilized, Roberto told Fallaci, and France was more civilized too. "I'm happy to live alone in Paris now. They're not curious there, they leave you in peace. They manage to respect people—without nosing around in other people's private problems."[26]

The marriage court had granted a provisional annulment June 30; Sonali had filed for divorce in Bombay the same day. But Catholics were askance at the blatant mockery of marriage laws, and the Italian government announced it would appeal the annulment. Ingrid and Lars, in Paris with Pia, would have to wait months longer. The newspapers chuckled gleefully. Meanwhile Isabella had got appendicitis, Roberto refused to send the children to her for two weeks more, and Robertino would phone her from Italy: "Poor papa, he has been crying all night!"

Would he ever sell his television documentaries? Ingrid wondered. She had been telling him so for years that his bad luck was his own doing. She knew he would never believe it.

In Geneva that February 1958, he was asked at a film club what his plans were.

"My great project is to get down to a really serious, organized fight against the 'official' cinema. . . . The death of cinema that preoccupies us is here, very near. The doctor hasn't tested its pulse yet, the death certificate hasn't been filled out yet, but it's possible that cinema is already dead. I am out of it. I am very happy, because I can watch from a distance."[27]

Roberto had been editing his 16mm footage in Rome—on two moviolas in Marcella De Marchis's living room. In January he had sent an old friend, Romolo Marcellini, to India with a cameraman, Renzo Filippini, to film background footage: a meeting of Brahmins in Kashmir; Delhi scenes; a tiger in a Bombay zoo. Marcellini also shot exteriors for "The Wedding," whose interiors Roberto planned to shoot in Rome, with Sonali as the bride.[28]

On August 18, 1958, throwing away an offer from Carlo Ponti for him to do Moravia's *La ciociara* with Magnani and Sophia Loren, he flew to Brazil to realize an Amidei project which he had not pursued at the time of *Fear* but which now, after India, seemed more critical. "Rossellini was perhaps late in coming to a kind of awareness of problems," Amidei said. "I recall coming back from Brazil and bringing him [Josué de Castro's] *The Geography of Hunger* on which he eventually constructed a whole theme. These problems didn't particularly interest him in their political and regional aspects, as much as they did as the great problems of humanity: hunger, water, energy, science. That really got him excited. Rossellini was different from the others, Roberto got really interested in problems. When he read the newspaper, he'd also read the business pages, and all the things an artist isn't supposed to be interested in, according to the old tradition."[29]

Roberto spent three weeks in Brazil (August 16–September 7), received streams of visitors at Rio's Copacabana Palace, travelled, gave a host of interviews, and left on September 7, promising to return in November to start shooting.

But the Brazilian press and the Ministry of Foreign affairs were afraid that Castro's book would spread a negative image of Brazil abroad—and noted that Rossellini was a filmmaker in decline. The picture was never made.[30]

As for *La ciociara (Two Women)*, De Sica and Zavattini made it, and Sophia Loren won an Oscar. Was Ingrid right?

Said Truffaut: "By 1958, Rossellini was well aware that his films were not like those of other people, but he very sensibly decided that it was the others who ought to change."[31]

In September, Ingrid and Lars purchased a gray stone farmhouse in Choisel, 25 miles outside of Paris. Now that she was settled, she expected the children, whom she had not seen since the end of July, to live with her and commute 45 minutes to an Italian school in the city. Roberto of course objected to their living with Lars, especially when he discovered that the farmhouse was solely in Lars's name. He kept them at Santa Marinella as long as he could.

Finally on October 15 they arrived with their governess, Elena di Montis. But Roberto was at the train station too, and after a long acrimonious scene with Ingrid, put Robertino in his car and drove off, telling him Ingrid was stealing his sisters. She took the twins to Choisel and rushed back to see her lawyer.

The next day Roberto surrendered Robertino, who asked his mother why she had not stolen him too. Roberto insisted on having legal custody of the children, who should live with him in Paris and not suffer the long commute. Ingrid insisted they should live with her at Choisel, conceding Roberto every weekend and two summer months in Italy. From her point of view, her offer was generous. From Roberto's point of view, she was reneging on their agreement of absolute parity, according to the needs of school or vacation, and was attempting to establish sole custody, in effect.

The quarrel embittered. Word began to leak out of Sonali's whereabouts, which threatened not only her privacy but Roberto's ability to retain his children by Ingrid. Sonali was exiled to a villa owned by the American painter William Copley, in Longpont, near Menthlery, twenty miles outside of Paris. In Rome, the moment Roberto heard from Fellini that Marcella De Marchis was to start working the next morning as a costumer for Fellini's *La dolce vita*, he insisted she come instead to Paris to work with him; and the next morning, December 22, he drove her there in her own Fiat 600. He had no car of his own, nor work even for himself, and wanted her to convince Ingrid not to marry Lars, but Marcella had jumped at his offer. She had just ended an eight-year relationship for him. She had let him edit in her apartment; she had taken it on herself to intervene with a producer who was refusing to put another lira into the scandal-ridden movie; and she had hurried to Venice to stay in a hospital there with Robertino, who was eight and had a hernia. Whereupon her boyfriend had called it a day. In Paris she found herself happily at the center of a family reconstituted for Christmas—Roberto, herself, Renzino, Franco, Robertino, Isa, and Dindina. But this old family had almost no contact with Roberto's new family, which was now the center of his life—Sonali, Raffaele, and Gil. At Easter Marcella went back to Rome.

On December 21 Ingrid had married Lars in London, even though she was still married to Roberto in Italy. Roberto heard from the children that they had been photographed with their "new papa" and immediately filed a custody suit in Paris. He produced a promise from his mother and sister Marcella to live with the children in Rome, and argued that Ingrid was a Protestant with no family and twice a bigamist, and that her name was not on Robertino's birth certificate. But Ingrid had money, a home, a husband, whereas he just had debts. A month later, the French court gave Ingrid temporary custody.

It wasn't defeat; it was only the first skirmish of a three-and-a-half-year war. Roberto had learned from the custody battle for Pia. He filed suit in Italy. He complained to a Roman judge that the long, cold, daily commute between school and Choisel was bad for the kids. Eventually Ingrid felt compelled to rent an apartment for them at The Raphael, where they lived with Elena di Montis. For visitors, they had their parents. If they had to go to Choisel, Robertino would say, "Papà, don't be so upset. We'll be back tomorrow."[32]

"Rossellini," said Alberto Manni, "always showed love for his children but always kept a certain distance, then became impatient and got angry with them. Even as a father, then, he was a tangle of contrasts, because he wanted to have the children nearby, wanted them to run wake him up in the morning, but couldn't stand being disturbed while he was asleep. He wanted them to play in the room while he worked, but couldn't stand it if they made the slightest noise. He wanted them to be at the beach with him, but would get mad if they blocked the sun or threw sand on him. A real disaster. Then he would often be consumed by sudden jealousies, excessive fears, terror over some sickness. If the children were in Paris he would jump on the first airplane to join them. If they were at home and had the slightest temperature, he would phone Doctor Matteuzzi, day or night, and ask him to cure them immediately."[33]

The long-promised monkey finally arrived from India. Roberto told them it was Raimu. (Not until 1971, when Isabella saw *India* for the first time, did she realize this had been a fib.) "Raimu" quickly got himself banned at The Raphael and was taken to Choisel. Roberto made no objections to the monkey living with Lars Schmidt.

In January 1959, the India "reportages" began appearing on television in Italy and France.

Television had come late to Europe. In 1956, America had 35 million television sets. In contrast, France had 600,000 and Italy 200,000, where two state-owned channels functioned only in black and white and only during the evening hours. No major European filmmaker had paid any attention to television. Rossellini led the way, determined to exploit its immediacy. "Television is an evolution of cinema," he declared, stating as though it were obviously a proposition everyone was pooh-poohing.

Few people cared about immediacy; that was Rossellini's definition of cinema, not the public's. Roberto understood this and, having made his point, immediately shifted ground.

"To discuss cinema today in strictly aesthetic terms is arid and useless. . . . There is only a single question: how to awaken consciences. . . . I firmly believe that we in film and . . . television can educate the public in a certain way."[34]

At a colloquium with Renoir, he was more specific. "In modern society people have an enormous need to understand people. But modern society and modern art have completely destroyed [our native tendency to wonder conscientiously about what it means to be a human being]. The human being no longer exists. . . . There are very few people researching the human being. The great mass of people have been doing everything that has to be done for humans to be forgotten. Inevitably, the public has been educated to forget the human being."

On the one hand, we have fallen victim to "vertical barbarian invasions"—increasing specialization makes us ignorant of anything outside our own field. On the other hand, the arts have become obsessed with ersatz problems and ersatz human feelings. "Love, passion, tragedy, all the feelings have been deformed. . . .

"But today the problem of the human being is posed profoundly, dramatically, in the modern world. Television, suddenly, gives an immense liberty. . . . The TV public is a public fundamentally different from film's. In a movie theater, you have a public which has a mass psychology. With television you address ten million spectators who are ten million individuals, individually. So the discourse becomes infinitely more intimate, infinitely more persuasive. . . . I did an experiment in film with *Una voce umana*. I wanted to insist on film's ability to penetrate to the bottom of characters. Today on television we're rediscovering experiments like this. . . .

"I'm trying to set up an enterprise that will permit a whole slew of products to be made, not just one film. If you start making a mass of productions, you contribute . . . to forming public taste, you help the public to understand a few things.

"[But] it's extremely difficult for me to find a subject right now. . . . I can't find a story, since there aren't heroes in life anymore, just tiny acts of heroism. I miss that extraordinary élan and enthusiasm of a man who throws himself into some sort of adventure. But maybe that does still exist in the world after all. What I am going to try to do is a research, a documentation on the state of man today, throughout the entire world, and as we find inspiring dramatic themes and heroes, we will go on to the level of making fiction films."[35]

Roberto had been speaking at a colloquium moderated by Bazin in October 1958. A few weeks later, after Rossellini and Renoir had visited him at home to admire his iguana, André Bazin died at age 40. He had championed cinema's capacity to give us an imprint of reality. One of his final acts was this colloquium discussing how cinema, via television, could educate people to human realism—and so help fulfill the dreams of the illuminists in France and Italy epitomized by *Esprit* and Croce.

Rossellini's first essays into television did nothing to inspire confidence, however. He did not show the promised documentaries, which, he said, were still to come (but never did). Instead he showed raw footage assembled by subject matter, unedited into formal patterns, let alone into story fragments. He himself appeared in each of the ten half-hour shows, chatting with a television journalist about what they were seeing, while on a movie screen in front of them Tonti's 16mm footage was projected—in black and white. Roberto's charm never came through; he was wooden and dry, the interviewers even more so, in both the Italian edition (*L'India vista da Rossellini*—"India seen by Rossellini") and, with the same India footage, the French edition (*J'ai fait un beau voyage*—"I had a good trip").

In February, Roberto and Sonali told their story publicly in a series of four articles in *Tempo* with Roberto's friend (and eventual scenarist) Vittorio Bonicelli. They talked about what had happened in India and about Raffaella, the fight with Ingrid; their goals in film.[36]

Roberto revealed that his debts had totaled 300 million lire ($500,000), "now largely paid," he said.[37]

But he did not say how. According to Mario Del Papa, Roberto's money problems had grown so serious that he could have gone to jail, but Mauro his business manager had managed to arrange a bankruptcy discharge. Since there is no personal bankruptcy in Italy, the debts had had to be ascribed to business losses by the production companies that Mauro had set up for each production.[38]

Sonali, meanwhile, during her first two years abroad, had received only three letters from her parents. In one of them her father, who had read in a newspaper that she was alone and abandoned in Paris, had sent her a ticket home. She had had no contact with Raja, who was now six. She had asked everyone not to speak of her to him, so that he would feel her absence less. They had told the boy his mother was dead, but he did not believe them.

Finally on May 9, 1959, Sonali made her first public appearance—at Cannes, where *India Matri Bhumi* was premiered, out of competition. Her voice and Roberto's had dubbed in the sobbing in the Hirakud episode. "The Wedding" had not been filmed; the woman's situation in it, Roberto had decided, was "too prostitutional."[39] In effect, only the first two episodes had been fully realized; the other two had had to be pieced together.

"The afternoon show at the Palace du Cinéma got a crowd such as we have not had this year in the big hall," reported *Corriere della Sera*. "The expectation was enormous. So much had been spoken and written about *India*."[40]

It was received with respect, not enthusiasm.

Casiraghi, in *L'Unità*, hailed Rossellini's return to a style like *Paisà's* after the "frightful decadence" of the Bergman films. But alas, Rossellini's work still seemed improvised and unfinished. It was "humble, often indistinct, and sometimes suspect of mystification." On the other hand, *India* was a laudable attempt "to penetrate poetically into an aspect, albeit secondary, of the reality of an immense continent."[41]

Lanocita, in *Corriere della Sera*, rhapsodized about color and sound, yet felt disappointed. By the time *India* opened in Italy, March 1960, he had joined *L'Avanti!*, *Il Nuovo Spettatore*, and *Cinema Nuovo* in judging it, in *L'Unità's* words, a jumble of "notes for a film still to be made" and in regretting that Rossellini had not followed the neo-realist examples of Bimal Roy and Satyajit Ray. "*India* seems different than at Cannes [due to] the lack of the big screen . . . , the reworked montage . . . , the application of [additional] spoken commentary that's not always successful."[42]

Bonicelli, wanting to defend *India*, argued that it solicits unusual participation from us, because of its unfinished, summary style and its intuition of a "new language"; its representation of pure feelings freed from chains of logical narrative made it one of the first "abstract" films. Similarly, Morandini argued the incorrectness of judging *India* as a documentary. "Rossellini's photos aim at the essence of reality rather than the particularities of existence. . . . Seldom has anyone in film managed to give us so grand, profound, and exalting an idea of work as Rossellini in the dike episode."[43]

Unfortunately the French distributor, UGC, did not like *India* at all, pronounced it unfinished, and refused to release it; it was never shown commercially in France. "They were ashamed of it. It wasn't like my prospectus.[44] One thing, I think, that shocked them, is that the film's commentary wasn't by an [anonymous] voice: each story was told in the first person. I'd found some Indians who could speak French but with an accent."[45]

At a festival in Moscow *India* was booed and people walked out. In India itself it was never shown. "India was ashamed of it," said Roberto.[46] In Italy, it grossed fifteen million lire ($24,000).

Nor have its problems ended. *India Matri Bhumi* is now represented by an extraordinarily inept 1987 "restoration" of an incomplete print of the Italian edition. Almost ten minutes are missing, including almost all of the final two-minute sequence; Rossellini's sustained meditation on a bird soaring in the sky is replaced by three short shots in Bombay and an ejaculation about "the crowd!" The color throughout is so diminished that much of the magic has disappeared. No serious search has been made for the original 16mm Kodachrome or 35mm negatives. Fortunately, the single print of the French edition was restored with much better (albeit still diminished color) by the Cinémathèque Française in 1994. Unfortunately it is the execrable Italian edition that has been subtitled and disseminated all over the world.

Cannes 1959 was the year not of Rossellini, but of the "French New Wave": of Resnais's *Hiroshima, mon amour* and Truffaut's *The 400 Blows*. The year before, Truffaut had been banned from the Festival because of his acerbic journalism. This year he won first prize for direction. The "New Wave," with its raw, personable, immediate look, was sweeping aside commercial, conventional moviemaking in France. Roberto liked both movies a lot.

It was to Rossellini that *The 400 Blows* owed the most—to that first shock of immediacy Truffaut had felt when he had seen his first Rossellini film, *Deutschland im Jahre Null*. But Truffaut's discipleship was noted by few critics other than Truffaut himself. Had it been, the fact that *The 400 Blow*'s success made Rossellini an ancestor would have confirmed the general impression that Rossellini was passé. Ironically, only in Truffaut's own circles was it acknowledged that real innovation usually looks like deficiency at first, and that far from declining since *Paisà* Rossellini had gone beyond his postwar trilogy and even *Voyage in Italy*.

Truffaut had printed Roberto's new declaration of principles in *Arts* in April: "First of all we need to know man as he is [and] to get to the point where things speak for themselves, of what they are in reality. It's instinct that interests me. If that's what critics call 'neo-realism,' I agree."[47]

But it was not what *critics* had meant by "neo-realism." Rossellini's gaze in *India Matri Bhumi* is contemplative, sometimes awesome, but always attentive and listening. What critics had responded to in "neo-realism," what they responded to now in the "French New Wave," was aggressive, violent use of the camera, like Magnani's murder in *Roma città aperta*. Explained Roberto, "With us, nearly always, the artist is delivering a message: a representation for others (often an aggression). In India, art is always a type of intimate joy. The artist creates for his own satisfaction, he has to please himself, and the objects born of his art stay there where each person can see them, as he passes by.[48]

"The slightest act of daily life contains extraordinary dramatic power.[49]

"It's in how you shoot a scene that you can really bring in your own authorship, your own observation, your own morality, your own particular vision of things.[50] Cutting is no longer essential. Things are there.... Why manipulate them . . . ? Montage is a bit like a magician's hat. You put in all the tricks and out comes a pigeon, a bouquet of flowers, and a pitcher of water."[51]

Rossellini's more contemplative style would become the norm for most of the art-film world in the seventies. But in 1959 it seemed that youth was elsewhere. Everyone was talking about Truffaut's "romance with the camera"—by which they meant his vigorous gymnastics, his energy. Whereas with Rossellini, Jacques Lourcelles thought, "the author seems to be saying: 'I didn't have anything to do. I took walks. Here's what I saw, what I understood, what people told me, what I found interesting. I haven't tried to be complete. I'm not drawing any conclusions.' Having a free spirit can also mean not making yourself do anything."[52]

Only Godard appears to have noted that a new era had begun, and that the revolution he himself would help inaugurate with *Breathless* was already passé:

> *India* runs counter to all usual cinema: here the image is only the complement of the idea that provokes it. *India* is a film of absolute logic, more Socratic than Socrates. Each image is beautiful not because it is beautiful in itself, like a shot in [Eisenstein's] *Que viva Mexico!*, but because it is *the splendor of the true* and because Rossellini starts with the truth. There where the others won't arrive except in twenty years perhaps, he has already gone on from. *India* embraces world cinema, as the theories of Riemann and Planck embrace geometry and classical physics. In a coming issue, I shall prove why *India* is the creation of the world.[53]

Godard is paraphrasing the remark by Roberto cited earlier, from the April 1959 *Cahiers* interview:

> What's important are the ideas, not the images. It's enough to have very clear ideas and to find the most direct image to express an idea. There are a thousand other ways besides film to express ideas: writing, for example, if I were a writer. The sole thing film possesses in addition is the possibility of putting into a single photograph ten things at once. There is no need to be analytic in cinema—while being so.[54]

Like Truffaut's first films, Godard's would resemble Rossellini's more in their immediacy and pyrotechnics than in their ten-fold simplicity. Godard has a million ideas, commentaries, perceptions, and feelings that he wants to put into his films; he frolics in thought, as he frolics with montage. Rossellini wasn't so gay, so baroque. He wanted to get to the essence of things; more and more, like Matisse, he wanted to despoil them of anything unessential. He was rethinking what kind of films he wanted to make, now that he couldn't make any, just as he had during an earlier period of forced unemployment, during the German Occupation.

"I'm not avant-garde. The avant-garde, what is it? It's novelty for the sake of novelty; it's always a question of form rather than substance. . . . But film's true function is as a medium that can touch the large masses.[55]

"I came back from India with a new outlook. Wouldn't it be interesting to make ethnographic films on Paris or Rome? For example, a marriage ceremony . . . ?"[56]

"Abstract art has become the official art. I can understand an abstract artist, but I cannot understand abstract art becoming the official art, since it is really the least intelligible art. Such phenomena never happen without reason. What is the reason? It's that people are trying to forget man as much as possible. Man, in modern society and in the entire world, except probably in Asia, has become the gear of an immense, gigantic machine.

"He has become a slave. And all the history of man is made of passages from slavery to liberty. There is always a certain moment when slavery has held sway, and then liberty has retaken the upper hand—but very rarely, and for very brief periods, because no sooner is liberty attained, than immediately afterward slavery is reconstituted. In the modern world a new slavery has been created. And what is this slavery? It is slavery of ideas"[57]—of ideas everywhere, in novels, radio, films, pop music, advertising, and so on.

The draped Indian "tries to open his mind to every knowledge and to achieve a poetic synthesis of the world." But among the sewn European "hyperspecialization is the deep evil."[58]

"Since I've been making films, I've heard it said that films have to be aimed at a public whose average mentality is that of a twelve-year-old child. It is a fact that cinema . . . , like radio, television and all mass spectacles, has accomplished a sort of cretinization of adults and, in return, had enormously accelerated the development of children. Hence the lack of balance in the modern world, and the impossibility of understanding one another. . . . Our whole civilization is in question today. . . .

"What function can cinema have? It can put people in front of things. . . . It can make known other people, other problems."[59]

"I have a big project for South America, particularly Brazil and Mexico. I will send crews of young people to each country . . . , a writer, a photographer, a sound engineer, a crew chief. . . . I will study with my collaborators the problems posed: food, agriculture, schools, languages, habitat, etc. . . . The work . . . will give each spectator the possibility of a discovery. The art will only be the end product of these preliminary efforts. My job will be to make films which will be a poetic synthesis of each country."[60]

Three years later, he insisted, "[*India Matri Bhumi*] is probably the best example . . . of everything I have said regarding my ambitions in cinema. It's a film that I really made experimentally. . . . I tried to put onto film what I was thinking theoretically."[61]

Meanwhile, Ingrid in April 1959 had petitioned an Italian court to make Roberto pay nine million lire in back–child support. She knew he was still broke. She was fighting Roberto in the press as she had tried to fight Petter Lindstrom in the press.

In May, Roberto had begun his response by declaring that he might become a French citizen, because only in France, he had told the Italian press, did "the words democracy and liberty have any meaning. . . . When I was young in Rome, the worst thing for a youth of my generation was fanaticism. After the war I've found this fanaticism at every step I've taken in my country. In America I think it's even worse; there they hide under false labels.[62] I want to preserve my children and my future companion from the harm that people want to do to me. As much as I can, I hide the newspapers that write about Ingrid and me. The little ones suffered a shock when their mother got married. . . . What embitters me is that the Italian press is so quick to pick up anything that throws mud on me. Maybe it's accidental, but these stories always appear either just before a court hearing or in the middle of some important professional effort. It almost seems as though there's a coordinated psychological war being directed against me. I know I'm no saint, but that's no reason to make up defamatory articles or continually provoke me. I live surrounded by provocation."[63]

By going to a Roman judge and crying on his shoulder about how much he loved his children, Roberto got custody of them for the entire summer, thwarting Ingrid's plans to take them to Sweden in July with "the foreigner." She was furious.

Roberto had won in court that May because he had finally succumbed to the lures of a producer. Now he was a father of means, no longer a has-been. By September he would rise from the status of international pariah into the ranks of Italy's most commercial filmmakers.

In his terms, of course, it would be a fall. "You once told me," he said to Renoir, "that the word *commercial* means films whose aesthetic is what the producer wants."[64]

Il generale Della Rovere

Il generale Della Rovere was a project Roberto at first refused, as he had refused anything that would distract him from the purpose he had found in his life. After all, cinema was dying. But Amidei wanted to turn Indo Martinelli's four-page article into a film, and when Amidei's producer Maurice Ergas showed Roberto the article, Roberto read it avidly.[65] It was a story that had actually happened. During the Occupation, a cashiered cavalry officer, Giovanni Bertone, had been leeching money by pretending to sell information to families of people arrested by the Germans. Then he himself had been arrested by the Germans, put into Milan's San Vittore prison as a spy, and forced to impersonate Giovanni Braccioforte Della Rovere, the general commanding the Italian partisans. But ultimately Bertone had chosen execution as General Della Rovere rather than betray his comrades.

"I accepted right away," Roberto told *Arts*. "I was immediately intrigued by the strange case of this character, who had really existed, who had been simultaneously a deplorable swindler and an authentic hero."[66]

Then came the doubts. The project was concocted melodrama. "I'm not a novelist. I'm in the present.[67] I don't make commercial movies, only experimental ones."[68]

Jean Douchet asked him if the story had been imposed on him, and he replied icily: "People never impose a film on me."[69]

In fact he felt guilty; the story exploited a sacred subject. "You think it's okay, don't you, to shoot a story about the Resistance?" he asked Massimo Mida.[70]

He had capitulated, as Ingrid wanted. He had sold himself, retreated from his dreams, "disgraced" himself.[71] "I'm afraid the film may be a great success and, despite everything, I hope it is.[72] I had to do something to save my life; it was really a nightmare."[73]

Now success with *Il generale Della Rovere* was a matter of "life and death."[74] Roberto's value had shrunk so low, there was little he could do to advance his great project. But, loathe to admit that a detour through commercial cinema might be sensible, he let himself succumb to a dare:

"Papa asked me to be his assistant," said Renzino, "not because he wanted me to make films but because the producer, Ergas, was giving him money on one condition—that the film be ready for Venice, at the end of August. And we were in May! We organized things so that we could shoot during the day and edit and dub at night. It was insane. We approached it almost like a bet we had to win. And then father hadn't worked for years, so it was a necessity."[75]

They said he couldn't do a fiction film. He would prove them wrong. Amidei was turning Montanelli's article into a 300-page script "according to very classical canons."[76] Rossellini would put it onto film with all the vulgar commercial tricks and conventions everyone thought he didn't know how to do.

Production had been budgeted for twelve weeks and 320 million lire. Shooting started July 3 at Cinecittà, with Venice seven weeks away. Roberto shot it in 27 days, in sequence, the first fifty pages the first two weeks, the final 250 the second two weeks, and completed the 137-minute picture one-third under budget. At Venice it was the first Italian movie to win the Golden Lion since 1947. The critics bowed before it. "Finally Venice had a film at the level of its ancient traditions . . . : noble, serious, elevated; a work that engages, that will long engage, critics and jury, filmmakers and public; that will be discussed, that will seen by everyone, and that will 'last,'" wrote Casiraghi in *L'Unità*.[77] And he was typical.

"The disorganized, capricious Rossellini of legend reveals himself in this film as a most scrupulous and methodical craftsman," declared *Cineforum*. Bonicelli, in *Tempo*, agreed: "It is robust, well constructed, even edifying. In sum, it has all the qualities that are almost never attributed to Rossellini."[78]

Roberto was more ashamed than ever. "There were all these people who felt very very proud, because finally I had given in, had obeyed, had respected the rules."[79] He was no longer the slippery eel of Fascist days.

Yet in truth he had not respected the rules. Commercial films were usually made with a master take followed by various closer shots of the same material, and Roberto loathed the tedium of having the actors repeat the same business over and over the same way. So he tried to do whole scenes in long single takes. He could shoot faster this way, too.

Toward the end, during a prison protest, he used his beloved Pancinor zoom for the first time, mounted on a dolly. In India his attempts had been unsuccessful. Now he could rove in and out freely, and give rhythm and dynamics to his long takes. The only remaining obstacle was that the cameraman operated the zoom rather than Roberto. So Roberto spent hours figuring out how to build a remote control. An old aviation engineer told him about interlock action, he got machinery out of an old American plane wreck at Rome, and soon a wire linked the zoom to a joystick that he could manipulate sitting on his stool beside the camera. Friends were quick to note he had found a new way to be lazy. He was in heaven.[80]

"In each of my films, I want to capture reality. But reality doesn't exist, it's always subjective. So sensations and feelings have to be stolen the instant they happen, which creates a semblance of realism. This is why I try to avoid any dramatization. . . . And it's why I refuse now to look through the camera. I have enough experience to know where the frame will be. This gives me total freedom to concentrate as completely as possible on what I'm filming, so I'm never tempted toward cheap effects."[81]

Reality in *Il generale Della Rovere* is theatrical. A few interiors are real, but exteriors had had to be recreated, and their air of emptiness infests the picture—which often seems empty anyway, given that protracted scenes replace the rich incisiveness of Rossellini at his best, and the long takes disperse everything. What's real is Vittorio De Sica as Bardone (the film's Bertone), who is so intriguing that he makes even the painted backdrop of Milan in the final scene feel convincing. At any given moment, we don't quite know Bardone's motives for behaving as he does (as with Edmund in *Deutschland*), and this is the film's chief success.[82] Whereas Montanelli's character simply delighted in playing his role well, Rossellini's has a deviant Neapolitan heart, troubled at its own mixture of love and vacuity, and yearning to display itself.[83] It's the struggle of the individual against solitude,[84] as in every Rossellini hero.

To get De Sica to underplay his scenes, Roberto had constantly to direct him without his realizing it. Sometimes he would tease him by eating coffee granita with whipped cream, while the actor was struggling for inspiration.

"I'll never forget the scene of Della Rovere's monologue when he comes out of his cell," said Vittorio Caprioli. "Bombs are falling and he tried to calm everyone down. We began shooting, in the studio. At 'Action,' De Sica launched into a long rigmarole, and what hamming! Roberto followed him without fuss, as though nothing were wrong. Then, at the end, went up to him: 'Vitto! You were so great, fantastic, it couldn't have been better. But—and then I swear we're going home, just to keep Ergas happy, who's bitching at me for just doing single takes—please do another one for me, anyway you like, it doesn't mean anything, just get him off my back!' De Sica said, 'Certainly, Roberto, sure, right away!' Except that now, certain he had given a great interpretation of the scene the first time and that that take would be used, he repeated the monologue hastily, throwing it away. He was stupendous and that was the take Roberto chose.

"During my [own] death scene, I was there trying to die and Roberto was leaning over me a foot from my face, the whole time, saying, 'Come on, Vittorio, hurry up and croak. Don't bust your balls so much. I want to leave, I've an appointment, die quickly, what are you waiting for?' And I was bursting with laughter and couldn't repress it. When it was over, 'Roberto, please, let me do another! I was laughing at you and ruined everything!' 'Don't be stupid! Without sound, what difference does it make if instead of holding in your sobs you're trying not to laugh?' . . . And he was right."[85]

It is difficult today to imagine the controversies that *Il generale Della Rovere* aroused in Italy. Pius XII's death in October 1958, followed by John XXIII's exhortation to open up the past, had inspired a tumultuous national examination of conscience. The war had not been a popular movie topic since *Paisà*, and movies had never confronted Fascism. Any suggestion of Italian collaboration, any unflattering reflection on the Army, had been taboo—even in reference to World War I.

"The Italian cinema, theater, and press were prohibited from speaking of the Great War in other than flattering terms," said Monicelli, whose exposé, *La grande guerra*, had gone into production shortly before *Della Rovere*. "After news of my film was made public, the press (*Il Giorno* and *Corriere della Sera*) published articles by well-known journalists demanding that it be stopped. Even before shooting began, there was a whole campaign against it: 'Sordi, Gassman, Monicelli, [and the writers] Age and Scarpelli can only profane the 600,000 dead of the First World War.' Once the film came out, it was a real rupture. A film could finally say that those men went off to fight without knowing why; the war didn't have anything to do with them. . . . They were poor devils, badly dressed, badly fed, ignorant and illiterate."[86]

Naturally the Army also disapproved of civilians masquerading as generals. The Ministry of Defense flatly refused to lend Rossellini a few rifles and uniforms for *Il generale Della Rovere*, and demanded that all references to a "general" be deleted. Meanwhile, the Ministry set up a special commission of generals that decided to have Bertone's body dug up. The commission argued that Bertone had spied for the Germans right up to his death, had been executed only because the Germans had wanted to get rid of him, and therefore did not deserve to lie buried with the other 63 martyrs of Fossoli.

Martinelli retorted that he himself had been in San Vittorio for eight months with Bertone, that he himself had been condemned to death and had escaped by means of a fake transfer order, that he himself had told Bertone the details of his escape the day before, and that Bertone had looked him in the eye and told him it was his duty to escape.[87]

Il generale Della Rovere and *La grande guerra* shared the Gold Lion at Venice and revitalized a genre; a small flood of war films followed in its wake. Whereas *Il generale Della Rovere* blames everything on the Germans and avoids the topic of Fascism, in 1960 Vancini's *La lunga notte del '43* was self-accusatory and for the first time showed Italian terrorism—the night of December 15, 1943, when eleven randomly picked civilians had been shot in Ferrara in reprisal for the assassination of a Fascist official. The Fascist commander, at his trial in 1946, had claimed, "I was the soldier of an idea, not the hired assassin of a system." And in the movie he is shown as a respectable citizen in 1959, welcoming Franco, the son of one of his victims, home to Ferrara, and smiling during a soccer game, "Why, you look more and more like your father."[88] Many Italians had served Fascism from principle and saw no reason to be ashamed.

Perhaps Roberto, too, is confessing in *Della Rovere* by putting himself into his movie among the Italians in the Gestapo waiting room. Perhaps he is saying that he, too, like Bertone and many of his generation, was complicit in these years. A year later, in *Era notte a Roma*, he has his hero declare, "The Italians are like banners in the wind. When everything was going well, everyone was a Fascist. Now that things are going badly, there isn't a single Fascist left."

But in fact the line in *Era notte* serves less to indict Italians than to indict the *English* hero, who like his compatriots in *Paisà* sits around cracking pompous jokes while the Italians make bombs. Indeed, virtually all the Italians in Rossellini's eight war movies are born-again resistors; the two or three exceptions are monsters damned beyond hope of redemption, like Marina in *Roma città aperta* and Tarcisio in *Era notte*.

Perhaps the difference is that Roberto was 37 in 1943, Vancini 17. Vancini's sense of history is more Catholic—he didn't need to be born-again—and the demon of fascism is sensed as more insidiously present decades after the war. "It's been very convenient for a lot of people," Vittorio Mussolini remarked in 1987 while surveying the rooftops of Rome, "to have my father to kick around all these years."[89]

Some Communists did not like Rossellini's born-again attitude. The ex-partisan Gobetti charged, "The political reflection is impoverished. The Resistance is reduced to its simple human dimensions, and the individual who sacrifices himself does so by an isolated act of awareness, deprived of any ideological meaning. The resistance to Nazi barbarity is purely emotional, simple horror in face of German atrocities, it never takes on a character of engagement according to options defining a definite future."[90]

In Montanelli's story, in fact, Bertone's decision is specifically ideological. He enjoys playing the part and, à la Pirandello, simply follows his role to its obvious dénouement. It is the uniform that changes him—an ideological overcoat. This was unacceptable to Rossellini (whose resistance was religious, not merely ideological) and also to Massimo Mida, who retorted to Gobetti that Rossellini's hero intuits "authentic human values" on one hand, monstrous Nazi criminality on the other, and thus his choice between them is not Montanelli's tragic joke but a conscious moral choice.[91]

But, Rossellini's critics respond, this is the same abandonment of historic and political problems that flawed *Roma città aperta*. Neither Christian attitudes nor "authentic human values" are sufficient. Gooey emotions will not change the world. A rational line of action will.

Irene, in *Europe '51*, aroused the same sort of problems as Rossellini's Della Rovere. Both heroes are uninterested in rational lines of action; Rossellini argues for the abnormal individual whom others judge hysterical. His heroes and heroines all struggle with solitude and self-depredation, and by taking action assert their integrity, their belief in certain values, their defiance of others. Bardone, by his death, chooses his identity.

Poet Laureate

Era notte a Roma, Viva l'Italia

Il generale Della Rovere reinforced the impression that Rossellini was a national asset—as long as his theme was wartime Italy. Provided he go on repeating himself, he was even "commercial."

This was precisely the "type-casting" Roberto had spent the last decade trying to move away from. *Della Rovere's* success left a bitter taste—but offered opportunities not to be missed.

He would do a series of movies evoking historical myths cherished by Italians. First the "safe" project, another picture about the Occupation, his fourth, *Era notte a Roma*. Then three movies on the theme of the "Risorgimento," the resurgence of the Italian people: *Pulcinella*, the pre-Risorgimento, Naples populist revolutionaries, and the *commedia dell'arte*; *Vanina Vanini*, the Risorgimento's beginnings in Papal Rome; and most spectacularly, *Viva l'Italia*, the 1860 climax of the Risorgimento: a movie planned for the 1960 centenary salute to Garibaldi and the creation of Italy. Rossellini would play his role as his nation's cinematic poet laureate.

Simultaneously he would plot the destruction of commercial cinema which, he noisily contended, had given him opportunity for the wrong reasons. At the Venice Festival, August 29 and 30, 1959, he presided over a four-session conference of 25 filmmakers from six countries on the theme of the "new cinema." When the transcript was published, the conference was aptly retitled, "Papa Rossellini and the First Consistory of the *Nouvelle Vague*."[1]

Papa repeatedly ruled out of order any discussion of aesthetics. "We need to see film's situation not as art but as industrial organization. . . . The revolutionary aspect of the New Wave consists [not in a new style, but] specifically in its revolutionary means of production: they saw they could make films cheaply."

Such films, Papa said, normally could not have hoped to get shown in theaters, and therefore could not have gotten financing in the first place, because the "official cinema's principal policy is to make expensive films." As "son" Truffaut explained, producers were earning a percentage of the *budget*—$200,000 for the average French film; it just wasn't worth their time to get involved with $30,000 films. So normally independents had to seek financing outside of cinema.

But now, Papa enthused, with the advent of television, box-office receipts had plummeted, thousands of theaters were struggling to survive, some major studios had gone bankrupt. Now theaters wanted movies they could rent cheaply. "We have to profit from this crisis in official cinema. We've been trapped by myths. We want to . . . gain entrance to a particular society . . . and then be revolutionaries within it. But you can't be revolutionaries from the inside, you have to be outside."[2]

Papa himself was on the inside now, but he wanted to be outside too. He was able to reject *trasformismo* more loudly now than during Fascism, but only because it was the fashion now to be noisy, whereas then softness had been the mode.

So a week later, continuing his polemic, Roberto published an open letter to the new Italian Minister of Tourism and Spectacle in *Paese Sera*, *Schermi*, and *Cinema Nuovo*, charging that government policies had long favored industrial magnates at the expense of the authors and workers who were expressing the nation's artistic, cultural, and labor interests. Roberto, regarded as Catholic, was declaring solidarity with "neo-realism" and the left, but also with New Age technocrats. "Daily examples convince me that cinema and television have . . . been serving up a synthetic and artificial product of culture and knowledge, with the result that these media may have promoted the mental development of babies, but they have restricted the mental horizons of adults. . . . Cinema and television should establish contact between the specialists and the complex, varied world around them. Instead cinema and television have betrayed this duty . . . [and the government] has ended up protecting bad taste, moral diseducation and banality."[3]

He had established a home for Sonali and their children in the ground floor of a house on Via Nomentana, with pine trees and a large backyard, a bit far from the center of Rome. Sonali had come out of hiding and was making batiques for Giovanna Rali and Sandra Milo. Eventually she would open a store featuring expensive Indian fabrics.

The children by Ingrid had been living separately all summer at Santa Marinella. When fall came, Roberto refused to let them return to Paris for school. Instead he filed for sole custody, arguing that Ingrid was no longer entitled to Italian law because her annulment had been upheld in Sweden but overturned in Italy. (The Italian appellate court had finally ruled that the Italian lower court had acted incorrectly in granting the annulment without documentation from Sweden.) "I don't see why I should be forced to return my children to Ingrid, who is living with a man they cannot stand," he told a reporter.[4]

Ingrid flew from New York, discovered the children were no longer at Santa Marinella, and called her lawyer. She ran into Roberto on the way into court. "Why can't we be friends the way we always were?" he asked, then told the judge she was a bigamist.[5]

To no avail. He was ordered to surrender the children by 5 P.M. the following day, October 15. At 4:55 he phoned Ingrid, then telegraphed the police that she was wrongfully in possession of Robertino's passport, because her name was not on his birth certificate. To no avail.

He was unrelenting.

He flew to Paris most weekends to see the children and harass Ingrid, but also to prospect for cash. He had three families and an undefined educational project to provide for.

He owed money to everyone. This was normal, indeed it was perpetuated deliberately. It diluted his credibility, but eventually it always worked for him. "You have to make debts! Lots of debts!!" he proclaimed, proudly. "It's easy! No one tries!"[6]

Was he insouciant or ethical? Irresponsible or principled? Was he taking the only means possible to accomplish something worthwhile, like during *Roma città aperta*, or was he simply supporting his three families and elegant habits? Was money something outside consideration, irrelevant to his relations with others, or was it the essence of his relationships—a game of bondage, a sport, complete with all the sado-masochistic qualities of Roberto's friendships and love affairs? He was a big baby, looking up at you with love and confidence. How could you refuse him? He did not talk much; he listened and gradually took possession of your soul. Resistance was impossible. He became you, shared your every feeling as though it were his own. He talked a banker into a twenty-million-lire loan once at a dinner party; afterward the banker was furious at the hostess for having seated him beside Cagliostro.

It was a game, like the pursuit of women, that Roberto played obsessively, in every waking moment.

He phoned the actor Vittorio Caprioli as soon as he heard he was in Paris making *Zazie au Métro* with Louis Malle. "Vitto! I need a million and a half urgently!"

"You're crazy! You're asking me? I haven't got a lira!"

"Look, be resourceful. Spread the word that you have a property I really like, and, you'll see, they'll pay!"

Caprioli knew this was pure Rossellini. A few days later he found himself in a restaurant with two producers, Tonino Cervi and Sandro Jacovoni, and in a moment of whimsy, decided to see what would happen.

"You know, I've an idea for a story for Roberto."

Their ears perked up. Quickly he improvised a story: an Italian comes to Paris, to "go international," but eventually returns home disillusioned.

"Great! Great! And Rossellini wants to do it, really?" both producers exclaimed.

Caprioli phoned Roberto, who swooped down seconds later. "Vitto's a genius," he told the producers. To lock the deal, he accepted an advance of a million and a half, with another million for Caprioli.

"See? Didn't I tell you? I was right, wasn't I? Film is like that. Incredible. Magic!"

So Caprioli went on talking, about another film, set in Positano, one he wanted to direct himself.

They gave him another million.

Caprioli went back to Rome and, thanks to another producer, directed his first film, *Leoni al sole*. In the meantime, Roberto had disappeared and Caprioli heard that Cervi and Jacovoni thought Caprioli had bilked them—with the result that they obliged Caprioli to direct Roberto's film himself, and it became a hit, *Parigi, o cara.*

All thanks to Roberto.[7]

Thanks to Roberto, it had become almost a rite of passage for a producer to have been one of his victims. Many never forgave him. Others were philosophic. "I lost quite a bit of money," said Carlo Ludovico Bragaglia of his 1953 project with Roberto, "but, after all, I fell victim to Rossellini's charm solely through my own ingenuity. He was a dear friend, a man capable of getting himself forgiven for anything. Roberto was a great seducer, a man of overwhelming communicativeness, an audacious histrionic, an uproarious rogue, with flashes of pure genius. But, above all, a friend! It was difficult to resist his feline charm and capacity for intimacy, and not just for women."[8]

Era notte a Roma

Era notte a Roma ("It was night in Rome") was shot in 45 days at Cinecittà, beginning in February. Everyone pitched in: Roberto's mother Elettra, brother Renzo, sister Marcella, son Renzino, nephew Franco, first wife Marcellina, Amidei, Del Papa, their friends and lovers. Amidei's script had been tinkered with continuously by Trombadori, Fabbri, Brunello Rondi, Amidei—Communists and Catholics—and Roberto himself, and was still being tinkered with as filming began. Roberto would arrive around midday, still vague about the scene to be shot, work out his ideas while dressing the set or hanging out with the crew, and at the last minute decide on the dialogue.

"I found Rossellini dictating the scene to his assistants, Franco and Renzino, who were writing down the lines by hand," said Gianni Amico. "I was astounded, because it had been a very elaborate script, for which an absolutely absurd figure for the time had been paid! Seeing my perplexity, Rossellini said to me, 'Amico, we had them write it, now do we actually want to use it, too?' It was a perfect reply, summing up a whole way of putting oneself face to face with cinema. For me it was a total and complete demythification!"[9]

Roberto would fly to Paris each Sunday and return Monday. Nonetheless he edited as he shot and by May, in time for Cannes, 1,200 hours of negative had been reduced to 157 minutes.

Era notte was another Amidei project, like *Della Rovere*, and intended for Giovanna Ralli as "Rome" had been intended for Maria Michi; Amidei had been putting the deal together even before *Della Rovere* had begun shooting. The producers were strongly Catholic: Brunello Rondi and the Jesuit Centro Columbianum in Genoa; plus there was a 25 percent participation by two Americans using blocked funds, Harry Shapiro and Louis de Rochement (of *The March of Time*). Inevitably *Era notte a Roma* was anticipated as a return to *Roma città aperta*. But fifteen years had passed; urgency had yielded to reflection. Inevitably there was disappointment.

Some would approve. "In the Rossellinian geography of nocturnal Rome, there is the carefully detailed evolution of a truly populist participation in the Resistance—unreflected, instinctive, reluctant, sentimental, and full of contradictions, but solidly concrete and very human," wrote Morandini.[10]

Some would moan. "Mere retrogression," said Visentini, who almost alone had defended Rossellini all through the fifties: "Dignified and clean, of course, but devoid of insight, atmosphere and inspiration, *Era notte a Roma* is the film of a fine craftsman, a good technician, not of an artist."[11]

Some would complain. "The populist solidarity that chorally animated *Roma città aperta* has been transformed into pop cliché," denounced the Communist *Cinema Nuovo*. "Credit and responsibility, once the common domain of democratic forces, have become perquisites of the apostolic palaces; and the reassessment . . . of the people, deeds, and heroism of the period, far from historicizing them, has gone in absolutely negative directions."[12]

All three verdicts are valid.

Strong men, heroes, stood at the center of *Roma città aperta*, waging apocalyptic battle. At the center of *Era notte* lurks a vulnerable young woman, spaced-out and stumbling through the night. Grand ideals were at issue in *Roma*. The "things around" and day-by-day survival are the problems in *Era notte*, as in *Deutschland*.

Esperia (Giovanna Ralli) has been profiting from the Occupation by trading in the black market and is drawn into the Resistance reluctantly. When the Germans torture her lover, she gives away his secrets to save him, but the Gestapo kill him anyway, and set her free just as the Allies arrive. In Amidei's story, she confesses and kills herself. In the movie she is left in agony—as in *Stromboli*, except that this time there is no illumination. No Rossellini heroine so utterly reaches bottom. Liberation comes too late. Year Zero.

Unfortunately the movie's force is deflected by indirection. The English Major Pemberton (Leo Genn) is initially set up as the principal character. We begin with his voice-over, which Amidei had planned would continue throughout, intending Pemberton to mediate our experience, just as the

American was to have done in Amidei's plan for *Paisà's* "Rome" episode. Thus, for example, Amidei has Pemberton interrogate his Italian hosts: "I've never heard one Italian say, 'I'm a Fascist.' How can you explain how Fascism lasted so long, with no Fascists?"[13]

But Rossellini is obviously bored by Amidei's preoccupations with what foreigners think. And Rossellini is even more obviously obsessed with Esperia. He stops Pemberton's voice-over after its first instance, lets inspiration sag whenever the script lingers on the Englishman, and gratefully encourages Esperia to erase Pemberton as any sort of emotional focus every time she appears. Pemberton is pensive without thoughts, a supercilious bore. He stands watching the whole movie long, shrinking from soldier to baggage, too preoccupied even to escape, impotent. Reduced to his moment of impulse, he murders savagely, but experiences little of the catharsis of the typical Rossellini hero. Yet his fate parallels Esperia's. *Roma città aperta* and *Paisà* hallowed the Occupation as Resistance, as the inevitable triumph of oppressed morality; *Era notte* concentrates on the inevitable human failure in morality, on shame. The movie shoots down the myth of the Resistance, but Italian reviewers didn't notice: it was too soon.

Physically, as well as dramatically, *Era notte* is less theoretic than *Della Rovere*. The locations are authentic, near Tor di Nona and San Salvatore in Lauro. But neither movie has the taste of Rossellini caring deeply. There is not the despoiling appetite of *Paisà, Stromboli, Voyage,* or *India,* to get at the essence of things—except sometimes when Rossellini is watching Esperia.

Renzo Rossellini had had to write his score of *Era notte* in ten days, after seeing a rough cut without sound effects or dubbing. After twenty years he still resented the working condition movies imposed on him. Some composers, "betrayers of music" he called them, wrote only for film, with the result that "98 percent" of all movie music was simply music reused from other films. Roberto would make him write a great deal of music, Renzo complained, then only use some of it: "'No, here there are effects. No, here there's an important dialogue.' And the music, work, and sweat disappears, gets soft, almost inaudible. . . . The man [Roberto] never wants anything sentimental. As soon as he senses the least hint of it, he immediately says no." At the start of *Era notte,* to explain why they hide, "it's the music that has to narrate their fear, by contrast. The landscape is so beautiful, almost happy. The music had the job of making it felt that people are hiding under this sun, amid this nature."[14]

Roberto, however, would never listen to Renzo's ideas. He left him utterly on his own.[15] "I rather he play in my films than in my house," he quipped.[16] Temperamentally, the brothers lived in different worlds. "When he takes a bath, he brings his life savings with him," sneered the prodigal.[17]

Era notte was a try-out for the Pancinor zoom. The lens at this date was neither luminous nor sharp and it broke down repeatedly. Roberto carried a set of ten screwdrivers and would spring happily to its repair, taking three hours sometimes, singing to himself all the while, enthusing over its virtues, while cast and crew sat around waiting. "The Pancinor is like a camera suspended in air. It's like having the camera in your hand. The director can put the accents where he wants, *during* the shooting of the scene. And this way we eliminate the rigidity of cutting and speed up the rhythm—which changing angle by cutting inhibits, because cuts impose a tempo of their own. Now I use the dolly to change angle, and the Pancinor to move in and out. Cuts make dialogue stiff; the actor has to stop all the time and then assume a new attitude. Now instead, the director can steal expressions on the actors, without their being aware of it, while the dialogue continues.

"We used to go toward figures. Now the effect is of figures coming toward the public, toward the pit, separating themselves from the background. There's a technical reason for this: If I start with the zoom at 35mm, the depth of field is greater, everything is in focus. Then gradually, as I proceed to 50, 75, 100, 155, the depth of field diminishes more and more, leaving in focus only the subject and putting everything else out of focus. The effect is possible because everything happens within a single take. Or, vice-versa, if I start at 155, my subject is isolated in space. Then gradually as I withdraw to 100, 75, 38, I can show him in an ever vaster field, and not only that, but in surroundings ever more in focus, ever more concrete. I can go from the most complete isolation to the most complete contextualization.

"In addition I obtain a profound unification of the scene. Using montage, I can cut only at the beginning and end of the shot: everything else is tied together, fixed and decided at the moment of the shooting. To give an example: formerly, with cuts, you might proceed like this: presentation of the ambience, then the character, action, and a bit of poetry, and then repeat it: ambience, character, action, poetry. Now instead, there's a 'stratification,' an amalgam of these elements. This is the result of the evolution of technique. Take the case of painting: the primitives didn't know half-tints or perspective. Their pictures, all on one plane with pure colors, were beautiful within these limits. Then these other things were discovered, and technique became more complicated, and permitted a more complicated representation.

"To obtain this 'stratification' while shooting, naturally you first have to establish the 'notes,' which are the fabric of the discourse. Then you add pedal, color, and rhythm, all of which are things you decide on and find during the execution. So, my operator and I first establish the notes, the base line of the discourse, and then, during the filming of the scene, we try for the other qualities, in how we move the camera and the Pancinor—the speed, sharpness, and rhythms."[18]

Within a few years Roberto improved the Pancinor. It went from 25 to 250mm, with interlock motors to produce a breaking effect to reduce oscillations, and a remote control mounted beneath. It was not possible to look through the lens during shooting.

Jean-André Fieschi, in a long article in *Cahiers du Cinéma*, hailed the Pancinor as Rossellini's "second youth" and the discovery of "a new conception of space": formerly the stage space was basically stationary, now it is basically fluid. In *Viva l'Italia*, with Garibaldi at the center, space will be treated "masculinely," aggressively moving forward and opening out, as the liberating idea of Italy spreads through conquest. The zoom's distortions of space—"figures coming toward the pit"—incarnate the melodrama's theme. So too in *Era notte*. But with Esperia at the emotive center, stage space is "feminine"—internal, retreative, passive, offering shelter from the terror outside, closing ever more tightly in upon itself, homemaking. The circle formed by the gazes of the five persons in the attic turning from one to the other, accompanied by the camera, is "the very image of communion being established." It is a feminine community, inwardly anchored, whereas Garibaldi's will be masculine, outwardly expanding.[19]

> "Art can make you understand through emotion what you
> are absolutely incapable of understanding through
> intellect."[20]

At Cannes 1959, *India* had been overshadowed by the New Wave. At Cannes 1960, *Il generale Della Rovere* and *Era notte a Roma* were overshadowed by *La dolce vita* and *L'avventura*. With these movies, one historian would trumpet, Fellini and Antonioni "restored" the strength and vitality of the Italian cinema; radically altered traditional forms of construction and expression; came to grips with dramatic and moral taboos; and thereby accomplished a revolution that was both aesthetic and thematic.[21] Rossellini seemed even more passé than before. For the second year in a row, new stars had risen, stars he had helped launch, while his own star had dimmed.

Fellini's spectacular successes, *La strada* and *Le notti di Cabiria*, had won Fellini the license to make *La dolce vita*, an indulgence in navel contemplation that came close to ending his career. So insulting was the press's initial reaction that Ricordi, his producer, refused for a month even to talk to him. The Vatican issued hints of excommunication. Whereupon the public, thus stimulated, stormed the box offices in droves and the critics, not to be outsmarted, wrote new reviews.

Fellini pooh-poohed both the moral outrage and the prurient delight. His movie was about how the frenzy of modern life removes room for faith, he insisted, and was intended to be "a cry of anguish" to shake us out of our lethargy.[22] But like Cecil B. De Mille's audiences, Fellini's paid to see sin; his sole stark film, *Il bidone*, had been his only total flop. Naturally it was the only one Roberto approved of.[23] Roberto had become pro-flop. Now he declared *La dolce vita* a "manual of criminality,"[24] the lowest point reached by Italian cinema since neo-realism. [Watching it was] the saddest and most negative moment of [my] life . . . , an expressive vice that it pained me to encounter in a friend."[25]

Roberto's jealousy amused their mutual friends. Fellini joked too: "He looked at me the way Socrates would have looked at his disciple Crito, if Crito had suddenly gone insane."[26]

But Roberto's stand on principle was sincere. He felt compromised himself, because, as he saw it, he had descended to the commerciality of *Della Rovere*. Now he felt Fellini's betrayal personally. Fellini had been with him; now he had sold out. In fact, Fellini was bored by Roberto's speeches about television as a teaching tool, had no interest in making history films, and thought Roberto's pique ridiculous. What did nettle Fellini was that he was from Ferrara and *La dolce vita* was about Romans, and Roberto, a Roman, had called it "the film of a provincial."[27]

Antonioni's movies goaded Roberto even more than Fellini's. Finally he refused to see them; when *L'eclisse* came out in 1962 he gave money for tickets to Jean Gruault, his wife, and Sonali to see it and report back, when he wanted to hear only bad things. Nonetheless at Cannes 1960, when *L'avventura* was greeted with raucous hostility, Rossellini's name had appeared first on a joint declaration defending *L'avventura*'s importance.[28]

Antonioni epitomized the banes of modern life, in Roberto's estimation: complaining and immaturity, introversion and narcissism. "We have to have the courage to admit that in the past hundred years all art has been reduced to complaining. An artist is lesser or greater depending on how much he complains. They call it 'denunciation.' The fact is that it's complaining, because if it were protest it would be carried out differently, more aggressively. Besides, once you become aware that something's wrong, you have to be prepared to break away from it and put it right. But this eternal moaning and protesting about how much is wrong is something quite different."[29]

Sadomasochistic fascination, "infantility . . . , total vanity, sickness. . . . People either [moan and groan] or devote themselves to gratuituous acts of petty cruelty."[30] Art had become escapism, an indulgence in fantasies, phony problems and phony emotions—sponsored by postwar politics, which had stifled discussion of real problems. (Wasn't that what Fascism was said to have done?)

Neo-realism, Roberto defined, had been "the representation of authentic passions"[31] and had been sponsored by the Resistance's commitment to authentic culture. Now, where cathedrals had been planned, Antonioni and Fellini were erecting a religion of confusion and involution. (Andrew Sarris commiserated, "For the time being, what we call Western Man finds the sunset more meaningful than the sunrise."[32])

Roberto denounced his own movies no less severely: they had been "full of complaining."[33] He had drooled over his characters' anguished quests and ignored their subsequent efforts "to put it right." But at least (until *Era notte*) he had usually climaxed his movies with illumination, whereas Fellini and Antonioni just dragged despair on and on. "Tell me that you love me," says Katherine at the end of *Voyage in Italy*; "You don't love me anymore, say it," says Marcello Mastroianni at the end of Antonioni's *La notte*.

Yet Rossellini's illumination had never led beyond a burst of love, and it had progressed even that far in only five instances, "Romagna," *Stromboli, Francesco, Europe '51*, and *Voyage*. Elsewhere illumination had ended with question marks ("Naples," "Rome") or death (*Roma città aperta*, "Sicily," "The Po Delta," and *Deutschland im Jahre Null*).

Only in *Francesco, Europe '51*, and *India Matri Bhumi* do characters live out their illumination in daily life; illumination is an attitude rather than a spur to concrete solutions—which is what everyone had complained about *Stromboli*'s end. Worse, concrete solutions fail in *Della Rovere* and *Era notte*; it is the moment of impulse that Rossellini mythifies as the "Resistance," rather than the calculated action that must follow (as in "The Po Delta" and *Stromboli*). He favors authentic emotion, not rational action. Illumination occurs in caves, cellars, prisons, attics, miraculously, despite the characters even though within them, not because they have sought it. *Era notte* ends with fright, with Esperia's total involution as she trembles in the night. Where is the exit?

Roberto had decided. He was changing his course. And he wanted Fellini with him. "Complaining, as a rather irrational attitude, doesn't seem to me to get you anywhere, when you have extremely concrete things to struggle for. The concrete things in life end up getting pushed aside."[34]

Now Roberto's effort was to find useful, concrete action. Fellini and Antonioni, he complained, were going in the opposite direction.

He took to citing Aristotle: "It's not true that free time is the aim of work: work is the aim of free time."[35]

He emulated Socrates, making proclamation of his own ignorance into an on-going act of public virtue, while simultaneously proclaiming his daily steps to "demolish" his ignorance "little by little."

The aim was twofold: to depict useful struggle; to do something useful oneself. History films might fulfill both aims. They would show people turning private illumination into reality. "Art can make you understand through emotion what you are absolutely incapable of understanding through intellect."[36] What better way was there to examine concrete struggles than through efforts in technology, science, and ideas? What better way to discover new subjects and "authentic passions"? "You can find extraordinary sources of emotion where you would have never suspected they could exist.... I propose to be not an artist but a pedagogue. And there will be such a quantity of things that are so extraordinary, that will give you such a quantity of emotions, that I shan't be an artist, but I shall succeed, I'm sure, in leading someone to art."[37]

A Rossellini inquest into the past would focus on things Italian. Good stretches of Italian history would be relived in *Acts of the Apostles, Augustine of Hippo, Francesco, The Age of the Medici, Vanina Vanini, Viva l'Italia, Sicily*, and *Anno Uno*. There would be an Italian emphasis in the five-part *Iron Age* and the twelve-part *Lotta dell'uomo per la sua sopravvivenza* ("Man's struggle for survival"), as there had been an Italian emphasis in seven of his eight features on World War II. Non-Italian themes would not stray far from the Mediterranean: *Socrates, Louis XIV, Descartes, Pascal, The Messiah, Joan of Arc.* Numerous unfilmed projects would affirm a Franco-Italian base: *Caligula* [an outgrowth of the *Messalina* proposed to Selznick in 1947], *Marco Polo, Pulcinella, Denis Diderot, Niepce and Daguerre* (the inventors of photography).

In contrast, other unfilmed projects suggest that Rossellini found it difficult to launch foreign themes, and perhaps was less inclined to do so: *Cyrus the Great, The Civilization of the Conquistadores, The American Revolution, The Industrial Revolution, Marx, The Life of Mao, The Geography of Hunger,* a history of science, and a history of moral evolution.

"Choice" of subjects and media would be dictated by what Roberto could get funding for. "Educational" subjects like Rossellini's were unthinkable for movie theaters in 1960. Historical subjects since 1895, with scarcely an exception, had always depended on romance and adventure, big stars and big spectacle. In even the best of them the character of the hero was the emphasis, not the "concrete" efforts of the era. But television was something else. In America, *You Are There, The Hallmark Hall of Fame,* and Dupont's *Cavalcade of America* had been treating audiences since the early fifties with weekly historical re-enactments that were creative, instructive, and entertaining. Probably Roberto had not heard of them; nor had his European critics and collaborators. Ironically the revolution that Roberto accurately saw himself leading in European cinema had long been normal life for American television. Roberto too would eventually have to turn to television, but not until the end of the sixties, when his cinematic revolution had failed, and then not just because he saw television as the medium of the future but because it offered financing. In Italy and France he would be able to exploit to his advantage the mandate that state television produce educational subjects to justify its tax-supported monopoly. Ironically too, Roberto was now acknowledging some justice in the left's long charge of involution in his work; but in order to get funding for his television projects he would be obliged to turn to multinational corporations and the Christian Democrat Party, which controlled television.

He envisaged a group effort, with himself as avatar of a new genre. Most filmmakers shared Fellini's disinterest. No matter, Roberto for the remainder of his life campaigned unceasingly for "didactic" films, for films that would resemble each other not in style, but in being informative.

Yet what did "informative" mean? *Which* information should be given? How? And what of the limitations and subjectivity of our knowledge? A "moral attitude" was required, a Crocean sense of responsibility. It was this moral attitude which the style that Rossellini was developing wanted to explore and implement. It was the same effort to relive the past that had given birth to "neo-realism."

Viva l'Italia

Meanwhile, 1960, Italy's centenary year, provided a rare opportunity for a serious movie about history. At first there had been hopes for a government-sponsored epic with episodes by everyone—Fellini, Visconti, Pietrangeli, Blasetti, De Sica, Rossellini. Then De Laurentiis had almost begun something with Camerini. Finally there was only Rossellini, whose *Viva l'Italia* premiered at the Rome Opera House before the President of Italy. Like *Francesco giullare di Dio* it would attempt to apply Rossellini's moral attitude—his "neo-realism"—to an elusive and controversial episode at the roots of Italian identity—Garibaldi's conquest of Sicily and Naples. (For the history, see endnote.[38])

Rossellini's version of Giuseppe Garibaldi is a visionary who turns his private illumination into a new reality, like Francesco and Saint Paul. With a thousand untrained volunteers, he conquers two kingdoms, gives them away, "makes Italy," and then goes home to work his farm. To an orderly mind, to the *other* makers of Italy, this kind of hero is embarrassing; it is more convenient to think of history's great ruptures as ideas whose time has come by a process of internal development, of dialectical materialism or manifest destiny. People like Paul and Francis and Garibaldi struck their contemporaries as lunatics. They outraged convention, propriety, and social order, and forced everyone to live different lives as a result, and they have never been forgiven. It is the weirdo side of Garibaldi that Rossellini emphasizes.

Roberto saw himself as Garibaldi. He had been Garibaldi as a boy. He had staged scenes from Garibaldi's life in his parents' living room. Garibaldi was the hero of his heart, his model; he knew him intimately. "I'm Garibaldi!" he said, when friends objected that his Garibaldi sat around lazy and eating, instead of being on horseback. "How do you expect me to ride a horse?!"[39]

Identification was an axiom of Croce's historical method. (As cited earlier: "Do you wish to understand the true history of a neolithic Ligurian or Sicilian? Try, if you can, to become a neolithic Ligurian or Sicilian in your mind."[40]) Everyone in Italy identified with Garibaldi or another hero; naturally everyone did so differently. The actual Risorgimento had pit every faction of its day in competition; and they had all been arguing about it ever since. There were as many histories of it as there were factions. Necessarily, *Viva l'Italia* would be a reflection on history itself. A weirdo Garibaldi was bound to irritate.

Said Roberto: "I don't think we have clear ideas about the whole story of our Risorgimento . . . or on history in general, because, as we know very well, history has always been done by an author who wrote for a prince. If he was a genius like Virgil, what he wrote became *myth and reality*. And these are the sources one draws on to do history.[41]

"So it's no accident that at the beginning of the film, standing beside Garibaldi, you see Giuseppe Bandi, who was his aide de camp and later the faithful chronicler of the Sicilian expedition, [because] it's from Bandi's diary [*I Mille da Genova a Capua*] that we took the narrative thread that was our guide in making the film. Nothing you see in *Viva l'Italia* is invented.[42] [Bandi] was no poet [like Virgil], but he did write down everything that happened. You have only to read him and you can see what Garibaldi was like. . . . Garibaldi was expecting the arrival of the Bourbon generals to negotiate the surrender of Palermo. They entered his room as he was peeling an orange, and he divided it up and gave a segment to each of them.

"*Viva l'Italia* is a documentary made after the event, trying to figure out what happened.[43] I tried to place myself in front of the events of a century ago the way a documentarist would have done who had had the good fortune to follow Garibaldi's campaign with his camera, and who, afterward, had 'mounted' the campaign's salient episodes into a feature-length film. I shot the episodes with the same scrupulousness as a documentarist, except I had to shoot them, unfortunately, a century later.[44]

"The film involved us in three months of hard work, chiefly because of the difficulties posed by the geography and climate. The Sicily campaign was shot in mid-summer on the same locations where the events shown took place." Rival clans were employed to increase the passions of the contending forces. "The crew was overcome by the heat and the organizational difficulties. . . . Just to find forty broken-in horses for the meeting [between Garibaldi and King Vittorio Emanuele II] at Teano took weeks of effort."[45]

Italians laughed at Renzo Ricci playing Garibaldi with infirmities and a fair amount of ham, and Rizzoli compelled Roberto to have his voice dubbed by Emilio Cigoli (who regularly dubbed Gregory Peck).[46] But for Roberto this was the man.

"I was born in a house where everyone talked about Garibaldi. My grandfather Zeffiro was with Garibaldi and had letters from Garibaldi. As a little boy I played with the boot from Aspromonte, which we had in our house until 1918, when my grandfather gave it to the Garibaldi Museum. So Garibaldi was part of my family, just like the boot I'd put on to play. My Garibaldi is the one my grandfather described to me, with all the admiration and adoration he had for him.[47] I remember a letter I kept until the war, until along with lots of other things it was taken from my house in Ladispoli [by the advancing Allies—but Roberto sold the letter, according to his sister, and the beard too[48]]. Garibaldi wrote to my grandfather like this: 'Dear Zeffiro, I acknowledge receipt of six pairs of wool socks, two pairs flannel undershirts, one wool undershirt. Thanks. Most affectionately, Giuseppe Garibaldi.'

"Do you think I could imagine Garibaldi any other way? Every available source suggests this picture of Garibaldi: the Garibaldi of 1848, of the [short-lived] Roman Republic, who to go up the Capidoglio had to have himself carried on someone's back, because his rheumatism was so bad that he couldn't stay on his feet. And this was twelve years before the expedition of The Thousand.[49]

"Garibaldi and his men . . . succeeded only because the populace rose up in support of him, but the populace would not have moved if Garibaldi had not been near. While [he] was advancing on Naples, the politicians were already moving to deprive him of victory and snatch success from his hands. After conquering the Bourbon forces Garibaldi had to face a battle with himself: Mazzini urged him not to consign the South to [Vittorio Emanuele II of Piedmont], and the temptation was great. But Garibaldi's greatest merit was probably his never losing sight of his original goal: the unity of Italy. His 'I obey' was a conscious renunciation at the moment when he could have demanded and claimed everything. It's an example that hasn't been imitated since.[50]

"His character fascinated me. He's someone I associate with Francesco and the protagonist of *Europe '51*. In fact he did have enormous simplicity. There's his letter to White's husband on bureaucracy that is extraordinarily ingenuous, but also profoundly, profoundly acute—a precise examination of a world under constriction, a letter that could really be used as a textbook. Garibaldi was a romantic at heart: he wore a poncho, had a beard and long hair. And somebody with a beard and long hair has to move in a certain way, otherwise you would cut off your beard and hair, because it's more comfortable. All these things, the need to put together all the elements that could help me delineate the character, pushed me to the point that there is not, in the entire film, a single line of dialogue that is not taken either from letters or proclamations. I took, in other words, the same sort of minute care that is necessary to recompose a mosaic, so as to betray absolutely nothing. Even for the meeting with Mazzini, where there were no witnesses, I consulted the letters the two exchanged and other letters from Mazzini on the subject. . . . Dialogue done this way can seem a bit boring, because of its antiquated forms and words that aren't used in our language anymore. Consequently the realistic aspect of the dialogue no longer is realistic, if compared to our times, but remains realistic because it's historically exact.[51]

"Of all my films, I'm proudest of *Viva l'Italia*.[52] I consider it important as a work of research, as the most carefully done of all my films, and then because I feel it to be intimately true. I must confess, at the risk of sounding ridiculous, that when I watch *Viva l'Italia*—and it's the only one of my films that I've seen two or three times—my hair stands on end and tears come to my eyes."[53]

He was still playing with the boot. This "work of research" was a boyhood dream; this history would be "myth and reality"; these events would be full of "authentic passions [and] such a quantity of emotions."

The soaring romanticism of the Teano scene exemplifies Rossellini's "myth and reality" approach. Garibaldi, having conquered Sicily and Naples, waits with a few followers near a farmhouse and two or three peasants on an otherwise empty country road. The day is chilly; he complains of rheumatism. Hearing bugles, he gallops off on a white horse to meet the king, who is riding at the head of his staff. Garibaldi, waving his hat, hands over his conquests, proclaims Vittorio Emanuele "King of Italy," and in return receives a gruff "Thanks" and the order to place his army in reserve. Garibaldi waits on the roadside as the king's officers parade past, staring contemptuously, refusing to salute him. Outside at the farmhouse, Garibaldi is given some bread and water by a common peasant.

Historically, the weather and rheumatism are correct. But the actual road was crowded. There were lots of peasants, lots of *garibaldini*, and a band was playing in the field. Long columns of Piedmontese soldiers passed in review before Garibaldi. Finally, to the tune of "The Royal March" and preceded by carabinieri, appeared the king, with a train of guards, chamberlains, and orderlies, all of whom resented Garibaldi. The words spoken in the film are textual; but there was considerable small talk as well. The king resented being cheered by the peasants and spurred his horse to escape them; Garibaldi galloped after him, and they resumed their conversation. The farmhouse was in a little village, not nearby; and Garibaldi went inside to eat.

Rossellini's changes compress the reality, purify it, strip away the "unessential," sharpen the drama and heighten the "myth." They amplify the emotions. It is not "documentary" that everything is green, white, and red—the Garibaldian tri-color that became the flag of "Italy"—before being absorbed by the blue of the Piedmontese uniforms; or that an invisible symphony orchestra is playing "Garibaldi's War Hymn"; or that, after the Piedmontese staff pass by, the camera jumps back hundreds of yards to frame a verdant landscape as romantic as Constable. But, then, a document is not history.

"Is it accurate?" is a question people always ask. What does it mean to be accurate? Does it make any sense to signal out the textual accuracy of the words which the movie's Garibaldi and king speak, when we know that how they were spoken is equally important, and when we know that we have no way of knowing an accurate from an inaccurate inflection? And what of the person speaking the words? How important is it that "Garibaldi's" clothes and deeds are accurate when, obviously, the human being is not accurate—because this human being is not the real Garibaldi and so, essentially, nothing, absolutely nothing, he says or does can be accurate?

Each book on Garibaldi tells a different story, portrays a different man. Each memoir by each participant recounts a unique experience. Any description of Teano will put some things in, some things out, and assign to them differing meanings and emotions.

Thus, Rossellini describes history as myth and reality.

Questions of accuracy and interpretation provoked stormy fights first among *Viva l'Italia*'s scenarists, then among its viewers in a long series of newspaper letters.

In accounting for the creation of Italy, some of Roberto's writers (Fabbri and Petrucci) wanted to emphasize the diplomatic process (Cavour and Vittorio Emanuele); others the ideological process (Mazzini); others (Amidei and Trombadori) the popular revolt, without which Garibaldi's efforts would have been futile.[54]

Roberto wanted to emphasize the hero, Garibaldi, and did. As always, he was obsessed by private illumination. He treats Garibaldi no differently than he treated Magnani's or Bergman's characters, or Edmund in *Deutschland*. He follows him obsessively, with no pretense of doing justice to the world of people around him. As in *India*, the list of things left out, or myopically depicted, is endless. Cavour, for example, figures solely as an obstacle and Vittorio Emanuele is slimy, because such was Garibaldi's assessment of them. *Viva l'Italia* is not an attempt to dramatize the "balanced" history one hopes to find in schoolbooks or encyclopedias. Critiques of *Viva l'Italia* and later history movies seldom comprehend Rossellini's "myth and reality" intentions.

Amidei did comprehend, and he disagreed. He had been pushing Roberto to make information movies but their quarrels over Roberto's approach had been constant since *Roma città aperta*. *Viva l'Italia* brought a definitive rupture. "I didn't respect the scenario at all," Roberto said, "so I got insults, threats, registered letters—'Take my name off the film!' 'Put my name back on!' What was I supposed to do? I left on the names of people who had done a script that was absolutely not used."[55]

It was Rossellini's untroubled concentration on Garibaldi that provoked disagreement—and that ultimately made *Viva l'Italia* more interesting than a more conventionally judicious approach would have been. Cavour feared the red-shirted *garibaldini* as dangerous radicals who would establish a socialist republic; he sent in the Piedmontese army to take control of the revolution, to squash the people and impose capitalist hegemony. Cavour let the radicals and people make the revolution, then claimed its birthright in the name of the middle classes. His pattern was repeated after World War II. The Resistance—the populist revolution—was dissolved by the forces of order, by those who had been wearing the guise of Fascists and who now claimed the Resistance as their own.

In the movie people do rise up everywhere to support Garibaldi; there is even a lovely interlude where a merchant's daughter (Giovanna Ralli) sacrifices herself, like Carmela in *Paisà*. But Rossellini never alludes to the decisive strategic role the populace played: the terror the peasants loosed upon the landlords, their formations of mafia bands, how they supplied Garibaldi and compelled the Bourbons to abandon the countryside and concentrate in the towns, towns which the Bourbons then preferred to surrender rather than see destroyed. Nor does the movie allude to how first Garibaldi and then, for years to come, the Piedmontese army waged civil war against these same peasants. Amidei had wanted *Paisà 1860*. He said, "In both films we confront an army of liberators who conquer lands and peoples whose real problems they know nothing about. In both films we witness meetings between individuals who have trouble understanding each other. The people put too much hope in the liberators, and the liberators have too vague, abstract, and utopian an idea of liberty to attract the South's famished masses."[56]

Amidei was furious that Rossellini glossed over the tragedy of the Risorgimento—which became a shield behind which new conquerors suppressed the aspirations of millions of people and imposed yet another century of enslavement. He objected (as did the other scenarists) to the affectionate respect with which Rossellini treated the Bourbon generals, to the sentimental emphasis he puts on Francis II (played by Croce's nephew) watching his army run away at Volturno, or on the fact that Francis, whose government had continued his family's centuries-old policy of slavery and terror, now refused to let his army operate as though on foreign territory.

Amidei's objections are valid. But Roberto had not set out to wail a dirge to a debacle, but to sing a paean to a triumph and to exhort the individuality of truth. Each of us can be Garibaldi. Each of us can "revise the whole conception of the universe." Rossellini chose to emphasize "two points: the courage to undertake the Expedition of the Thousand with 993 rifles, with seven rifles less than the Thousand . . . , with three balls apiece. And then him, what he was: a romantic, so extremely simple, which was his great strength, wasn't it? . . . And yes, a little crazy—which was what was the most wonderful thing about him."[57] Rossellini's emphasis, as Louis Norman says, "refuses the heroic view of Garibaldi as the hammer striking the enemy [and shows him instead] as the fulcrum which enables a small force to dislodge a large weight. In a sense the film is a study of charisma. . . . [Garibaldi's] modest appearance belies an inner power."[58]

Thus, *Viva l'Italia* spends its first twenty minutes in a succession of scenes at night and in small rooms ("caves"), but then Rossellini zooms from a 25mm medium shot of Garibaldi on a hill, scans across the broad fields below, scans up the steep terraces opposite, and stares across the hills to the village of Calatafimi, among whose storybook mound of roads and buildings at 250mm we can barely discern columns of Neapolitan troops. We have come to the moment where "we make Italy," to the signal victory of Garibaldi's life, to concrete action, to a new era in cinema: never before has a camera done anything like this, never before have we seen anything so vast. "Hey, Garibaldi, look what we've done!" says one of the redshirts after the battle, thoroughly amazed.

Surely Italy itself proves that "history" is inseparable from spectacle. Sagesta, the Roman forum, Saint Peter's, all historicize the past and engulf it with emotions. History that is not art is not history, one might argue. The artist-historian must show his heart, not just his hand.

Rossellini, curiously, habitually hid his heart from his scenarists, which explains why he always used so many of them. Trombadori, for example, could not understand Roberto's insistence on including a scene of Alexandre Dumas greeting Garibaldi in Palermo, even though Trombadori himself had translated Dumas's writings on Garibaldi into Italian.[59] Only much later did he perceive that it was Dumas that had been Roberto's model: Roberto had wanted a Dumas-like movie with magic, élan, and poignancy. Dumas would be Roberto's model for *La Prise de pouvoir par Louis XIV*, as well. Dumas's romantic characters, like Louis and Garibaldi and Esperia, always learn that life will defeat them. "The tragedy in Rossellini is that the present becomes history; from this fabric are born our despair, joy, hope, and disillusion," observed Edoardo Bruno.[60]

Recent critics, bizarrely, have found *Viva l'Italia* emotionally cold. Mira Liehm, an adulator of Visconti, hates it as "a series of populist picture-post-cards . . . [Rossellini's] aim was not a dramatization of the events but a historical newsreel shot partly on authentic locations. . . . His 'facts' look contrived, and his 'pure history,' deprived of any subjective insight, is bland and uninteresting."[61] Rudolf Thome, a Rossellinian, loves it as "a newsreel. The events of a past time are reconstructed in their chronology. Objectively and without emotion. Almost without taking sides."[62] Gianni Rondolino, another Rossellinian, dislikes it for the same reasons: it "lacks critical digging and enlarging of horizon . . . , a transformation of realistic elements into poetic ones."[63]

Complaints in 1961 were similar. "A series of Sunday supplement covers . . . with no real characters." "Rossellini can't construct characters . . . , his Garibaldi [is] no longer symbolic but not yet human." "Rossellini doesn't believe in it all, he has no passion."[64] According to Guido Fink (*Cinema Nuovo*), the film was a "banal . . . compromise between a national-popular western and a minute, pedantic newsreel."[65]

The same objections had greeted each Rossellini since *Paisà*: background, characters, and motivations were too sketchy; style was incoherent. In Turin, *La Stampa* came out with a special article to placate the indignant Piedmontese.

Many critics, on the other hand, frankly loved *Viva l'Italia*.[66] "*Viva l'Italia* conquered the public," wrote *Paese Sera*'s Liverani, "by its constantly interesting action, animated storytelling, and the beauty of the memories that our Risorgimento's glorious and sad drama evokes in us, memories inherent in our identity as Italians, memories that came back to us yesterday, with faces materializing out of the past and almost breathing, as the illusion of reality—Garibaldi, Bixio, Bandi, Mazzini, the King of Naples, Vittorio Emanuele II."[67]

The most acidic review prompted a response from Rossellini. Tommaso Chiaretti, in the Communist *Il Paese*, had complained, like the others, that the film did not take sides, was unmoving emotionally, had a Garibaldi just as conventional in slippers as on a charger, and lacked analysis of the political forces in Sicily or the liberal social origins of the Thousand. "Frankly," Chiaretti concluded, "the film is little more than nothing. Except for Luciano Trasatti's beautiful photography, it is on an inferior level formally and technically, in ideology, story and spectacle."[68]

How, Rossellini wondered in a letter to *Il Paese*, could the same management report in one paper (*Paese Sera*) that the movie was wonderful, and in its other (*Il Paese*) have its critic beat him up like a Fascist goon squad? Ever since *Roma città aperta* critics had first hated, then loved his films. How could he orient himself amid such confusion?[69]

In reply the editor invited debate, and over the next three weeks, 27 letters appeared from many of Italy's most distinguished men.

Nine took Chiaretti's side: film critics Mida, Baldelli, Quaglietti, Miccichè, Muzii, the historian Paolo Spriano; Andres Aretini, Francesco Aluffi, and *Il Paese*'s editor, Mario Melloni. "Garibaldi wasn't popular because the morning of Teano, coughing against the humidity, he ate some ricotta and bread with a poor peasant," Melloni wrote. "Garibaldi was popular because he had around him the men he did. . . . But Rossellini tells us nothing about them . . . , their origins, the deep reasons for their loyalty."[70]

Twenty defended Rossellini, including Ugo Pirro, Paolo Alatri, Edoardo Bruno, Sandro De Feo, and Giuseppe Patroni Griffi. Guttuso saluted *Viva l'Italia* as "a populist fresco." Mario Praz likened it to *War and Peace* and *The Charterhouse of Parma*. Mauro Bolognini called it "an authentic masterwork." "I freely gave in to a very great spiritual joy," said Tinto Brass.[71] "It's a film that is basic in the history of Italian cinema . . . , history with a modern sensibility . . . ; the most beautiful battles I've ever seen on screen . . . ; Teano was unforgettable," declared Mario Monicelli. "My impression," Francesco Rosi wrote, "is that the expedition of the Thousand must have been the way Rossellini has us see it, a crazy, marvelous adventure following a fascinating man who managed to drag everyone along in virtue of his passion, boldness and geniality. . . . It's as if Rossellini were following the Thousand with a camera."[72]

Goffredo Parise condemned *Viva l'Italia*'s detractors as "spoiled by decadence and photographic snobbism."[73]

Alberto Moravia, concurring, said it was his impression that Italians are ashamed of the Risorgimento. It gets falsified in their school books, and they unconsciously want to see it deglorified; they know that Italy is older than the Risorgimento and they don't want to acknowledge a debt to it. Thus Rossellini tried to please people by reducing the Risorgimento to something familiar; but Italians don't want that, either. Nonetheless Rossellini did well to stay "midway between an amiable chromo and the intimacy of history without tinsel." It's absurd to contend that he ought to have written a socioeconomic history of Garibaldi. It's difficult to make any hero sympathetic, but especially Garibaldi, "because Garibaldi, like all actual nineteenth-century heroes, was always just one millimeter away from something not so rhetorical at all: always a millimeter away, but never falling." The movie has some of Rossellini's best scenes: Calatafimi, Volturno, the king leaving Naples. And it is a rather successful attempt at writing contemporary history, of the moment we are living. The critics and public lack subtlety, Moravia concluded.[74]

Audiences had laughed and critics had winced at Rossellini's naked use of famous Garibaldi phrases like, at Calatafimi, "Here we make Italy, or we die!" But it was just Rossellini's nakedness, Marta Berti felt, that transformed these worn-out clichés that Italians had learned in their childhood into "part of an ingenuousness that gives the film freshness . . . [and makes it] tender and stirring, without rhetoric or false modesty."[75] Menon, ten years later, argued this "tender, absolutely anti-rhetorical" impression was the result of Rossellini's preservation of the era's archaic rhetoric, to the point of making Bandi speak the written language of his own memoirs, whereas minor characters were free to speak modern Italian. Ironically, two-thirds of the way through the movie Garibaldi, who until now "has done nothing else but spit out the handed-down sentences of history . . . , suddenly has to respond to Vittorio Emmanuele's emissary with a phrase worthy of the moment; he concentrates at length over what to say, but since the 'memorable' phrase is not there, he gives up and says, with the same tone and brilliant manner, 'I'll let you know my reply.' "[76]

Freshness, even in rhetoric: this is history that is contemporary, this is the "impulse," the inner fire that smolders in Manfredi (*Roma città aperta*) and Karin (*Stromboli*) and all Rossellini's heroes,[77] and that now in *Viva l'Italia* erupts into a crescendo of liberation across an ever-expanding space—"the enthusiastic, naive faith of a small nucleus of people in the idea of freedom for everyone, as expressed by the Redshirts . . . , by Bandi's quiet bearing, Bixio's almost boyish forcefulness, and equally by the spontaneous impulse of Rosa."[78]

Hitherto, Andrew Sarris notes, Rossellini has shown Rosa close up. "But when his heroine reaches the beach, he draws back from her to emphasize the vast lateral distance involved between a moral impulse and a moral decision. Suddenly, she makes her run with a lantern, and is killed. Garibaldi's revolution sweeps over the beaches, over the forgotten girl. The camera keeps its cosmic distance. Rossellini cannot cheapen this heroic moment with a sentimental close-up. By retaining his historical perspective, he convinces us that his heroine was indeed heroic enough to die for an idea. What is more remarkable about this image is the unity of the idea and the image. Where Buñuel's ideas sometimes transcend his images, and where Chaplin's images sometimes transcend his ideas, there is in Rossellini little or no separation between style and substance. If there be such a thing as a cinematographic language, and I firmly believe there is, Rossellini requires the least translation. . . . What we are watching is our own aesthetic and ideological distance from an event."[79]

With his relentlessly roving zoom, Rossellini continuously probes and reacts. "He is not an impassive spectator," states Robin Wood, "but a passionately involved, at times dictatorial, creator. The Pancinor [zoom] becomes the means by which Rossellini reveals and analyses the action he creates—the artist's palpable presence in his own work."[80]

Roberto had wanted to bring his children to Sicily with him. But it was June and Ingrid wanted them in Sweden. They went to court, Ingrid won, and Roberto exited looking black indeed. "All right. Take the children. Have them." So she did. But where were their passports? "Ah, the judge never said anything about passports!" The next day she took them to the airport anyway, and Roberto phoned the police, who came screaming out onto the runway, lights flashing. But there was nothing they could do. Ingrid had called her friend the Swedish ambassador and gotten Swedish passports overnight.

Weeks passed. In Sweden the children jumped every time the phone rang: was it the lawyer? In Palermo Roberto stewed. It was intolerable to think of his children in the hands of that foreigner, together on a little Swedish island, and all of them swimming nude, even the nurse Elena! And here he was shackled to Sicily. And Ingrid's annulment had finally been given. And the wooden houses in Sweden were dangerous, they would burn down. He flew to Sweden on a Saturday and got back 36 hours later, with the children, but so exhausted he had to have Renzino substitute for him on the set.

From Sicily the children went to Santa Marinella for the rest of the summer. At Christmas 1961, Ingrid practically had to kidnap them. She took their clothes one by one, left a note for Elena saying she would pick up the kids at school, and took them to Norway.

But on New Year's Eve she read how Eduardo de Filippo had been destroyed when his child got sick on vacation and died 24 hours later. Like Romano. She phoned Roberto and told him she was giving up; he could have the children.

De Sica and Gabor Pogany went to Santa Marinella that summer. "I remember," Pogany said, "Roberto was there with all his women around a table, [Marcella De Marchis], Ingrid Bergman, Sonali . . . , with the children, and himself at the head of the table."[81]

"The Cinema Is Dead" but Where Is Chastity?

Vanina Vanini, Anima nera, The Iron Age

Two years after *Viva l'Italia* Roberto stood in the Einaudi bookstore in Rome and announced to reporters that the movies were dead, "Il cinema è morto."

Alfred Hitchcock, still smarting over Ingrid, heard the news and snickered, "Rossellini is dead." Fifteen years later he hadn't stopped snickering over his witticism.[1]

It was a question of perspective. The world thought Roberto was washed up. Roberto thought the world needed fixing.

A black comedy in three acts had led to this disagreement.

At first, Rossellini's Great Plan had appeared to be striding ahead. Moris Ergas, the producer of *Della Rovere,* was in love with Sandro Milo and wanted Roberto to make a film with her that would win the Best Actress prize at Venice. What Roberto wanted, using Milo as his ticket, was another movie like *Viva l'Italia.* It looked like a golden opportunity for The Great Plan; it turned into Act One of The Great Debacle.

Ugo Pirro and Goffredo Parisi went to Sicily where *Viva l'Italia* was shooting to discuss a vehicle for Milo called *Una donna a giorno* ("A woman a day"). Pirro stayed two months and enjoyed many a friendly evening with Roberto. But neither *Una donna a giorno* nor Sandro Milo were mentioned. Roberto then made a second start by asking Franco Solinas to do an adaptation of Stendhal's *L'Abbesse de Castro,* and didn't get much further. The abbess left but Stendhal stayed.

Stendhal was a romantic storyteller with a flare for the dramatic moment. He was also a perceptive diarist of Italian life and mores who brought history alive. As a French diplomat living in Rome in the 1820s, he had formed his impressions precisely during the period that had ignited the Risorgimento. He was exactly what Roberto wanted. Rulership of the Papal States had passed in the 1820s from the moderate hands of Pius VII and Consalvi to the reactionary terrorism of Leo XII and his successors, with the unintended effect of inspiring a Resistance movement that culminated a few decades later with Garibaldi, Italy, and the end of the Papal States. Parallels with the more recent Resistance were obvious.

Roberto, with the life and mores of the Papal States in mind, wanted to call the film *Chronique italienne* ("Italian Chronicle"), after Stendhal's *Chroniques italiennes*. Ergas, with Sandra Milo in mind, insisted they call it *Vanina Vanini*, after the Stendhal story, narrated like a chronicle, which they had decided to adapt.

In *Cahiers du Cinéma* trumpets pealed Rossellini's vision. "We shall see reconstructed, around Stendhal's novel, the world of politics and social life—even of hygienic, sexual, and eating life—which conditions the behavior of its heroes. We will know how they used to wash, what medicines they took, what they used to eat, how they made love. *Vanina* will thus be the first realistic western film, the first to try to express the *totality* of a world, which will also be the totality of Stendhal's world, since it borrows traits, [Stendhal's beloved] 'small little facts,' lines of dialogue, and even entire scenes from almost all of Stendhal's other works and from authors he loved (Casanova and Montesquieu, for example). In short, a Stendhal novel as Balzac would have written it (he was dying of envy)."[2]

The trumpeter of this manifesto was Jean Gruault, who had been summoned to *Vanina Vanini* only at the last moment. It was December 1960, elaborate sets had already been constructed (including two-thirds of Piazza del Popolo as it was in 1820), cast and crew had been assembled, and there was no script. Solinas and Trombadori had put together a rough treatment that satisfied neither Rossellini nor Ergas; it was a "flat, insipid synopsis," according to Gruault, and lacked an ending. "They'd managed to empty Stendhal's story of its humor and charm, while exaggerating incidents to their taste: a terribly serious description of an admission ceremony into a Carbonari *vendita* [a cell of the revolutionists] (which Roberto retained, while emphasizing how ridiculous it was) [and] subtle allusions to contemporary politics (they were confusing Rossellini and Autant-Lara)."[3]

To flesh out this treatment, Ergas, without consulting Roberto, had hired a French novelist, Monique Lange, who had just published her first book, *The Plane Trees* (the picture was a French co-production). Lange had flown to Rome, talked to Solinas, waited a week for Roberto to see her, and flown back to Paris when he refused to give her an audience (nevertheless she receives screen credit). Thereupon Roberto and Ergas had gone to Paris too. "What Roberto was looking for, rather than a Stendhal specialist, was someone who knew his own films well and loved them without reserve. This rare bird he knew he'd find only in François Truffaut's entourage."[4]

The rare bird was Gruault. He was finishing an adaptation of *Jules et Jim* for Truffaut, who summoned him to The Raphael. Roberto remembered him from the *La Cité* script with Rivette in 1956. Gruault was an inspired choice. Like Roberto, he was fascinated with period re-creation and how environment affects individuals (notably in his *Mon Oncle d'Amérique* [Alain Resnais, 1980]). His scripts for Truffaut resulted in Truffaut's most

Rossellinian movies: *Jules et Jim* (1961), *L'Enfant Sauvage* (1969), *Two English Girls* (1971), and *The Story of Adèle H.* (1975).[5] Truffaut had been able to pay him almost nothing for *Jules et Jim*, so he got him a contract with Ergas for twice as much.

Gruault's tasks were to redo what Solinas and Trombadori had done, add love scenes, and find an ending. He got to Rome in February, in time to watch Rossellini film a Schüfftan mirror shot of crowds at the Quirinal, with children in the background for a trompe l'oeil. By then, however, despite dialogue often transcribed from Stendhal, *Vanina Vanini* had ceased to be Stendhal. Soon it wouldn't be Gruault or Rossellini, either.

Stendhal's sense of psychology had proved too paradoxical for Rossellini. Stendhal writes of Vanina, for example, that "she made long visits to Missirilli, who spoke to her as he could have done if twenty people had been present. One evening, after having spent the day detesting him and firmly promising herself to be even colder and more severe with him than ordinarily, she told him that she loved him. Soon she no longer had anything to refuse him."

Rossellini's lovers, in contrast, are boringly straightforward. His Missirilli (Laurent Terzieff), Gruault admitted, is more like "a Russian nihilist of 1890" than an 1820 Romagnolo.[6] And Vanina has become, in Roberto's description, "a heavy girl who just has to give her hand to someone in order to swoon. [She is] cynical, a noble Roman who believes in absolutely nothing, who satisfies certain specific instincts."[7]

These simplifications, according to Rossellini and Gruault, were dictated by Sandro Milo being a haunchy 25 rather than a slim eighteen. But in fact there is no woman so full of contradictions as Stendhal's in any of Rossellini's movies, nor in his private life. Roberto made Vanina correspond to the fat Roman mother he had mused about before going to India. Gone too is Stendhal's humorous and protracted (and un-Rossellinian) duel of love/hate; now the lovers plop (Roberto-like) into one another's arms almost at first sight.

Given the change in Vanina, the logic of Stendhal's ending ceded to a Rossellinian one; Stendhal's broken-hearted Vanina cynically makes a brilliant marriage, Roberto's enters a convent. Rossellini, like Stendhal, dwells on a single emotion that becomes tragic and absurd; but he has no stomach for Stendhal's humorous undercutting of his characters when their emotions are most serious. One of the film's best moments is a confrontation between Vanina and Cardinal Cantazara, in which ecclesiastical hierarchy is satirized with unctuous dialogue written by Roberto's Franciscan, Lisandrini.[8] The Church and Carbonaro movement are paralleled as rival religions with similar rituals, but with the angelic virtues belonging to the latter, the diabolic monstrosities to the former; Vanina's monstrous love mirrors her monstrous ecclesiastic world as both kill the Carbonaro. But gone from Rossellini's scene is Stendhal's lunatic context, in which his Vanina sneaks into the Cardinal's room at night disguised as a page and threatens him with a pistol; now their meeting preserves formality.

Rossellini's intentions were befuddled by Ergas even as he streamlined Stendhal. Production was interrupted constantly by fights. Ergas, according to Gruault, kept adding scenes for Milo and replacing her Stendhalian dialogue, which he thought "comic-bookish," with "solemnly insipid" rewrites by Diego Fabbri.[9] Milo had not wanted the role to begin with and was frustrated by Rossellini. She was forced to repeat long takes endlessly due to technical failings of the Pancinor zoom; she had no way of knowing whether she was in close up, long shot, or out of the frame entirely; and everyone was so obsessed with the remote-controlled Pancinor that when her wig caught fire from a candle, no one noticed.[10] Ergas, meanwhile, was pressuring Gruault to make Roberto cut out "the stuff that slowed down the action," and when Gruault refused, reneged on 300,000 lire he owed him and replaced his and Lisandrini's names on the credits with those of Solinas, Trombadori, and Lange.

What Ergas wanted cut was specifically the detailing of period life and thought that, in Roberto's mind, had justified his making *Vanina Vanini*—and which might have made Vanina herself interesting. "All human history," Gruault had quoted Rossellini saying, "is made up of passages from slavery to liberty. There have always been moments when slavery was winning." "And it is one of those moments," Gruault had continued, "that *Vanina Vanini* will describe, proposing also a way for liberty to regain the lead—martyrdom, the sacrifice of one's life, as proposed and even imposed by the oppressed to the oppressor, making the oppressor, almost despite himself, into an executioner, and handing him over to the people's hate."[11]

In March or April 1961, while shooting the ball scene in Naples's Palazzo Reale, Roberto recruited Gruault to The Great Plan and required him to renounce both pure film and political cinema. "We were going to undertake a different sort of radical revolution," Gruault recalls, "a revolution of the human mind. Man had 'opinions' but knew nothing about himself. We were going to teach him, through cinema, which would finally be useful for something, to know himself, where he came from, how, over the centuries, he had become what he is. We would succeed where Socrates had failed."[12]

In a similar vein, Roberto published open letters to the Under Secretary for Spectacle denouncing the fashionable but malicious (and Antonionian) preoccupation with "false problems: incommunicability, sexual aberrations, and solitude." In published remarks at a Round Table on Italian Cinema in Milan he again proposed that the media should "spread among the masses the real essence of the great discoveries and modern technology" in order to "permit people to become aware of the complex world we belong to."[13]

For quick bucks, Roberto put his name onto three television documentaries, none of which he had much to do with. *Torino nei cent'anni* is a 46-minute film by Federigo Valli, linked to an exposition in Turin for the Risorgimento centenary. *Torino tra due secoli*, also by Valli, shows twelve minutes of Turin today. *Benito Mussolini* (U.S. title: *Blood on the Balcony*) on the other hand, was to have been directed by Rossellini, based on Federico

Chabod's *Storia dell'Italia contemporanea*, to be developed by politically engaged scenarists, and to feature interviews with Parri, Nenni, and Rachele Mussolini, in addition to archival footage. Instead, the producers commissioned a straightforward montage from Pasquale Prunas, which Rossellini disavowed.

In addition, in March he staged, simply and efficiently, his brother Renzo's gloomy, naturalistic opera *Uno squardo dal ponte* (*A View from the Bridge* by Arthur Miller) at the Rome Opera.[14] Visconti had staged the play. Ingrid sat with Roberto at the general rehearsal, Sonali on opening night.

But most of the time, while, unbeknownst to Roberto, Ergas was destroying *Vanina Vanini*, Roberto was thinking about *Pulcinella*.

Pulcinella

Pulcinella had been a pet project since 1954. Roberto had loved Renoir's *commedia dell'arte* movie, *The Golden Coach*, and Anton Giulio Bragaglia had said, why not some *commedia dell'arte* for Ingrid?[15] In 1959, Roberto had asked novelist Dominique Aubier to do a treatment, and she had spent a few months on it while living with Roberto and Sonali, even shifting houses with them from Via Nomentana to Via Appia Antica 230. But her interests were esoteric and she had turned *commedia dell'arte* into Free Masonry.[16] In 1961, right after *Vanina*, Roberto put Jean Gruault in contact with Henry Deutschmeister, who was going to produce *Pulcinella* in Yugoslavia with Charles Aznavour and Anna Karina. Gruault came to Rome to do a treatment in July and stayed into winter.

The story, according to Gruault, was based on the life of Michelangelo Fracanzani, who lived in Naples during the 1600s and introduced the stock character of the Pulcinella into France. Rossellini's Michelangelo was a combination of four people: the actual Michelangelo; his uncle and father; and their relative, the painter Salvator Rosa, who had been mixed up in Naples's 35th revolution—which had begun in 1647 with a fight between a gardener in Portici and a vendor in Naples, over who would pay a detested tax imposed on fruits and vegetables by the Spanish viceroy—and which was nicknamed "De Masaniello," after a poor 23-year-old fisherman who was one of its leaders. It was the sort of revolution that appealed to Roberto immediately. He had learned of it from Vittoria Fulchignoni, who had been reading him Alexandre Dumas's account of it in *La Corricolo*, and simultaneously Roberto and Gruault had begun transforming it into scenes and dialogues.

The 35th revolution was crushed. Michelangelo fled with a group of comedians and wandered in quest of liberty through Rome, northern Italy, Lyon, and Paris, to the court of Louis XIV, playing the Pulcinella all the while. A voyage through the seventeenth century also appealed to Roberto; he had long wanted to film Catherine of Siena's 1376 trip from Siena to Avignon. (He had Gruault do a treatment of that, too.) Michelangelo, on his journey, encounters a castrato from the Sistine Chapel (a character from

Casanova's memoirs, one of Roberto's favorite books)—whom he discovers to be a woman while making love to her inside "The Big Mouth," a stone sculpture by Bomarzo. Caterina is violent, bizarre, and jealous, and enjoys provoking jealousy in others. For years she comes and goes, sometimes following the troupe, at other times disappearing for months and making Michelangelo's life a torture. But each time she reappears she recalls him roughly to his duty as a man of the theater, and as a man: to reject the gilded slavery offered by the great, to tear away lies, tell people the truth, and show how things really are.[17]

"*Pulcinella* was a vast parable of [Roberto's] own existence, of his own intellectual and moral journey . . . very idealized," Gruault explains. "Roberto could talk about himself . . . only *in parables*. This was how he used to talk about himself during his life; as soon as he got into general ideas or abstractions, he would wander off into commonplaces. This is why movies, no matter what he claimed, were his natural language, as vehicles for fables and stories."[18]

Gruault stayed at Santa Marinella with his wife, Marcella Mariani Rossellini, Sonali's children, two of their friends, and two guinea pigs. Roberto would come weekends, dive for sea anemone, and cook big dinners for many guests. To convince Gruault's wife to translate for him, he would gaze soulfully with big dog's eyes: to say no seemed a betrayal. Driving through the countryside, they would sing Garibaldi songs from *Viva l'Italia*. Roberto would discourse on the Etruscans, how they built stone tombs for their dead and lived in fragile wooden houses, how the women were equal with the men, but were shared in common, together with the children. He considered himself Etruscan, as a Tuscan, so Pulcinella must have been Etruscan too. He knew the names of almost all the trees, which "he envied for being able to fuck—he never said 'make love'—without having to change place." Being a filmmaker gave him slight satisfaction; he was much prouder of being a seducer. One of his favorite stories was how a Parisian whore had refused payment and wanted only an autographed picture to keep in her purse. During the week Roberto would wake up Gruault at dawn by phone, to recount his ideas of the night; he slept only by day and in pieces. He had invented a character he insisted be used, Palmariello, who would be his mouthpiece, an old man "with an ignoble mouth"—in Roberto's mouth "ignoble" became a rare and positive quality, like Peparuolo in *Francesco*; Michel Simon would play him in *Pulcinella*. Caterina would pass him off as her father, before people discovered he was her husband. "You think you're logical," Palmariello would say to Michelangelo, "and everything you do is illogical. You're chasing a dream. And you want to make reality conform to your dream. You're so consumed by your dreams that reality's not even amusing anymore—although it's a thousand times more fantastic than all your dreams. It's thanks to Caterina that I began to see things clearly. While watching her, while watching her live."[19]

*

"It was impossible," Gruault wrote of Roberto, "not to surrender, at least for a time . . . , to his generosity, his kindness, the human warmth that his entire person radiated. How could one resist the fascination of his extraordinary (I was going to write 'acrobatic') intellectual virtuosity, his understanding of people and things that he could translate into a multitude of colorful, vibrant anecdotes, of which his films are only a very pale reflection (and those who knew him will not contradict me on this point). This immense hiatus between the project and its execution, between the man and his work was certainly not insignificant in the numerous disaffections that constantly marked his career. He would lose a friend, a collaborator, he would immediately find others whom he expected to be more devoted, more faithful than their predecessors, but toward whom he did not feel obliged to be himself scrupulously loyal. He treated his friends the way he treated his women. And then there were emotional reunions and again quarrels. But his charm was always turned on. He was a sorcerer. A good sorcerer."[20]

Alas, if only the sorcerer had bothered to stop by *Vanina Vanini*'s editing room once in a while, he could have prevented its massacre. In fact, Roberto checked nothing until just before Technicolor sent the prints to Venice.

Then he publicly demanded that the picture not be shown and that the prints be sequestered. But on Sunday, August 27, 1961, *Vanina Vanini* was shown. The result, says Miccichè, was "one of the biggest fiascoes ever."[21]

"Everyone at the Festival was talking of this *Vanina Vanini* of Rossellini's as though it were expected to be his masterpiece," Sandra Milo recalls. "The film was being distributed by Paramount, which had made an enormous publicity barrage. The days before the projection I was a countess, courted, followed, invited everywhere, adored by everyone. . . . We made an entrance into the theater with flashbulbs bursting in our faces, and two hours later exited amid the insults and whistles of the half of the audience that [hadn't] walked out long before the end. . . . I'd wanted to get away [too], I couldn't stand all the guffaws, the yelling, the harsh words. But Paolo Stoppa squeezed my arm and said, 'Courage, Sandra, dignity and comportment!' "[22]

Milo was "catastrophic" said Claude Mauriac.[23] She was not an actress at all, most of the Italian press concurred, and it had been a cruel folly to use her own voice, with her execrable pronunciation. It was "a sort of Waterloo," remarked Mino Argentieri.[24] And for Rossellini too. The movie was a comic script, a bloated soap opera, it never should have been selected for Venice, it confirmed that *Della Rovere* had been only an anomaly in Rossellini's degeneration. Even *Cahiers du Cinéma* thought it "lazily" directed.[25] *Variety* called it "inept."[26] Solinas and Trombadori published a letter objecting to their being credited with a film that was not their work.[27] That noisy three-sided battle, everyone agreed, was simply a storm to avoid facing the obvious fact that they had all made a horrible movie.[28]

Vanina Vanini was an abortion. We don't find out "how they used to wash, what medicines they took, what they used to eat, how they made love." Nor is there more than a glimmer of the populist revolution that will lead us from slavery to liberty, as in *Roma città aperta*. There are wonderful action scenes, marvelous crowd scenes, snippets of real life, and Lisandrini's gripping scenes; at least half the time we are watching Rossellini at his best. But the other half of the time we endure some of the most wearisome love stuff ever filmed. Neither Vanina nor Missirilli possesses the slightest fascination; they are outlines, nothing more, that talk and talk.

For the first time, the producer had won, Rossellini had lost. How did Ergas succeed in trapping a man as "strong, supple, and ungraspable as an eel"?[29] How did Ergas succeed where Fascists, Communists, Americans, the Vatican, Christian-Democrats, and dozens of producers had failed?

Roberto had three families to care for, plus the son of his domestics Pasquale and Iva,[30] plus his adventurous bachelor-like existence. He was 55 and tiring, and no longer so nimble. His constant need for money had made him repeatedly give in to Ergas's demands during preproduction and production. Finally, his insouciance during postproduction gave Ergas the opportunity to do anything he wanted. And what Ergas did, without interference, was to destroy the *negative* of the entire first three reels of Rossellini's rough cut, half an hour: the execution of the Carbonaro whom Missirilli comes to Rome to avenge; a preliminary love story between Missirilli and Countess Viteleschi (Martine Carol: Ergas had feared she might eclipse Milo); a scene where a priest refuses to let his too-sacred cincture be used to make a bandage for a wounded person; discussions of the origin of liberal thought; allusions to the American revolution; a visit to the bookstore just outside the Piazza del Popolo police-check where forbidden books could be bought; and, from the middle of the film, a Renoir-like farce where Missirilli, trying to escape the servants at Castle San Nicolo, comes upon the chaplain whipping himself in penance for his lust for Vanina. There were also numerous changes in Vanina's dialogue, insertions of rehearsal scenes with Milo where Rossellini had experimented with subsequently discarded approaches to her interpretation,[31] and, most disastrously replacement of the dubbed voice of Andreina Pagnani with Milo's own. "Poor Sandra Milo," Rossellini explained, "didn't have good diction. She aspirated, instead of raising her voice . . . , and was difficult to understand."[32] The picture had been shot in French, in any case. But Ergas had needed Milo's own voice because without it she would have been disqualified from winning the Volpi Cup at Venice.

Vanina Vanini starts out (in the mutilated version) as though it is going to be one of Rossellini's most inspired efforts. Martine Carol was Ophuls's *Lola Montès*, a movie Roberto admired, and he conjures a similarly enchanted storybook world, in decor and atmosphere, in Ophuls-like circular and linear movements of the characters, and even in use of the zoom to mimic Ophuls's camera movements as reflective of romantic, impulsive consciousness. The world depicted, however, is the most inhumane of any Rossellini movie, and Vanina, for all her innocence, is part of its mechanisms. Like other Rossellini heroines, she will find truth in a "cave": the attic, then the castle, where she loves Missirilli; but the impulse that her revelation of love inspires (a love Rossellini depicts as joyless) will lead only to more slavery, torture, death, and her own entombment in the cave of a convent. As Aprà has pointed out, Vanina is a vampire carrying love and death. We see her first at the ball introduced in a dialogue between a pederast and a castrato, moving among ugly, horrible dead people. She is a vampirized vampire, as in the scene where she is posed all in black between two rapacious cardinals in red.[33]

Much discussion of *Vanina Vanini* has centered around the difficulties of merging history and fiction,[34] as though *Vanina Vanini* were a case to study, rather than two quite different movies that have been randomly merged. The sole copy of Rossellini's edition, his work print, was deposited with the Cinémathèque Française and destroyed in a fire; given his boredom with the love story, his earlier compromises with Ergas, and above all, his inability to make interesting characters out of Vanina and Missirilli, it probably was no more successful as a total work.

Rossellini sued to block release of the film. Gruault came to testify that Rossellini had been the unique scenarist of *Vanina Vanini*. "And then no one spoke of it again. I think he withdrew his suit after an arrangement (financial, probably) with Ergas. A year or two later I went to dinner at The Raphael and was surprised to find him among Roberto's guests."[35]

Anima nera

Rossellini was blamed for *Vanina Vanini* and Sandro Milo. For his career it was a disaster like *Stromboli*. And this time his own black soul had connived in his destruction. Now, in Act Two of The Great Debacle, his black soul tried suicide.

A play called *Anima nera* ("Black soul") had debuted in Bergamo in April 1960 and was in the midst of a successful two-year tour of principal cities. Gruault describes its author, Giuseppe Patroni Griffi, as "a sort of Italian sub–Tennessee Williams—what Roberto detested most in the world."[36] But Gianni Hecht-Lucari was thinking of filming it as an Italian–French co-production and Roberto was thinking of money. "I bitterly regret [it],"[37] he insisted a few years later; "I'm ashamed of it. [It was] a form of prostitution.[38] I think it's awful. After it, I gave up films altogether."[39] "Maybe," added Gruault, "it was to soothe his conscience and cut short my criticism that he made me one of the accomplices to his crime."[40]

To close the deal, Roberto assured Lucari that Jeanne Moreau would be in it, a total fabrication.[41] Because Lucari had tempted him and was a producer, Roberto, as a grand seigneur, was determined to loathe and punish him, and to take as much of his money as he could; it was only just.[42] When Lucari gave him the 500,000 lire Gruault was to be paid, Roberto never gave the money to Gruault, who had to get it a second time from Lucari. From all reports, Roberto rushed through the film with manifest contempt at every opportunity. He shot as off-handedly as possible, in 27 days of January 1962, leaving in shots of onlookers, not caring if actors mistook their marks and played their scenes off camera, and having Annette Stroyberg recite the "Hail Mary" in Danish when she couldn't remember her lines in French. On one occasion he told Vittorio Gassman, "Look, Vittorio, you're an intelligent actor, the director's presence is disturbing you, you know everything to do," and he left for the day, leaving Gassman to direct the scene.[43]

"When the rough cut was finished," said Matteo Spinola, "there was a very private projection for De Laurentiis [who had bought the picture for distribution], and [Silvia] Mangano said to her husband: 'Dino, even though you're going to lose a bagful, I've never seen anything so funny!' Rossellini had left already, during the film. It was then edited by Gillo Pontecorvo, who put it together as best he could."[44]

Anima nera was scarcely noticed by the Italian press at the time of its release. It was passed over in relative silence by Rossellini's usual defenders, even in Paris, as an act of solidarity with his proclaimed contempt for it. In *La Notte*, Valentino De Carlo wrote, "Rossellini's sole concern seems to have been to break up the dramatic action into a myriad of short scenes situated in the most casual places, as if this were enough to change mediocre theater into good cinema. Having resigned as an artist, Rossellini is a rather flat and careless manager of actors."[45]

Anima nera's off-handedness and modern tone has often suggested comparisons with the New Wave, as though it were a kind of *hommage*—or back-handed rebuke; but it is more likely Roberto had *La dolce vita* in mind, and the general degeneration of Western civilization that he had taken to bemoaning. Now, in a sort of satire of our fascination with degeneration, he seems determined to rub our noses in our own navels. *Anima nera* should be taken in context of Rossellini's next film, the short "Illibatezza" ("Chastity"), in which a lonely fetishist masturbates while his projector covers him with shots of the girl who rejected him.

Anima nera's soundtrack is a brutish cacophony of traffic, broadcasts, and jackhammers. The locations, far from casually chosen, are uniformly squalid and off-putting; a dockside set was constructed with mirrors to accentuate alienation. Appliances litter streets and rooms like the aftermath of a nuclear war. Everyone hustles frantically for money and power. The characters are all unlikable; both the innocent young wife (like Vanina Vanini) and the wise old whores belong to the same species. Peter Brunette complains about Vittorio Gassman's clawing, desperately physical character: "[Adriano's] treatment of all the women in the film . . . is brutish."[46] But all the women treat all the women at least as brutishly. It's the way the whole world wags. "Rossellini's camera transforms the bourgeois nature of the play into a document on four faces, four different modes of existing in relation to others," writes Jacques Joly in *Cahiers du Cinéma*. "The mobile camera, the incessant moving around of the characters, the perpetual invention in the gestures and looks, and above all the manner of pushing each of them into nervous crisis and hysteria, end up creating an impression of truth, in love as in hate."[47] Thus *Anima nera* is off-putting, but hardly uninspired; unlike much of *Vanina Vanini*, there is not a scene in which Rossellini seems bored. His contempt infects his set and his actors; each of them projects constantly—toward their world, their friends, their selves. Just as some subjects gain by being treated with lightness, majesty, or brio, *Anima nera* gains from Rossellini's contempt. Contempt makes it a *true* horror movie, more vampiric than *Vanina* or *Fear*, infused with contempt as other movies are with summer sun or winter chill. What makes it horrifying is that Rossellini's compassion for his characters is at least as intense as his contempt for them. Tenderness is always valid, he contended, "because you can look at even the most terrible crime in the world with compassion as well as hatred. I think it's right to look at people with affection and make an effort to understand what's going on inside them."[48]

Brunette misses what makes Rossellini Rossellini when he writes, a bit royally, that "*we* are unable to identify with either [Adriano or Mimosa] because we cannot decide which one is less dislikeable."[49] A moral attitude consists of more than likes and dislikes.

Similarly Brunette mistakes Roberto's homophobia for simple dislike. He quotes Adriano's speech from the play, "You know I don't like to talk about myself, or else I'd have to admit that if I'm alive I owe it to the love of a German. . . . They killed him on the Via Rasella with the others: the night before he had let me escape"; and notes that in the movie the word "love" is omitted, so that Adriano declares, "I owe it to a German." Concludes Brunette: "The motif of homosexuality is used . . . in a manner unfortunately little advanced from *Open City* and *Germany Year Zero*: it is the marker or sign of corruption, a locus of evil. Then it signified Nazi corruption, now the corruption of a materialistic society."[50]

Roberto was homophobically fascinated by homosexuality—he loved visiting sex shows, sex shops, and, when there were no women present, telling obscene stories. His liaisons with men were as emotional as with women; and he liked sex in foursome. There is a particularly rancid scene of the "sub–Tennessee Williams" sort in *Anima nera* when a butchy lesbian reveals to Adriano's wife that Adriano had a sexual affair with her brother—a revelation prolonged grotesquely, drop by drop, with everyone being too shocked to say it outright. But Rossellini is quite conscious of the absurdity; he rightly draws our attention away from the "revelation" and onto the brutish hypocrisy of conventions that pass for "normal," with the result that we instantly pity Adriano, and less for the butch's hatred of him than for the wife's contempt for him. Not just homosexual relationships are brutish here, but all sexual relationships—which is to say, in this self-revealing mirror of

Roberto's self—all relationships, because there is none of them that is without a sexual element.

There is a strip tease in a depressing nightclub that is more embarrassing than erotic. It fascinates Mimosa, rather than Adriano, because the dancer is ashamed of herself and takes no delight in exhibitionism. *Anima nera*, like *Vanina*, documents repression, and the hypocrisy, the torture, the sado-masochism that result from denial, from not-seeing and not-saying.

But this is just where, in a sense, Rossellini "fails" with a "modern" cinema about modern life, and why he felt so frustrated with commercial movies: actual nudity and actual sex are as necessary to the honesty of his subject as they were to Oshima's *In the Realm of the Senses* (1976), but he must repress them, which adds to the jackhammer cacophony, because sex and nudity take on a false value when, like the subject of homosexuality, they are brutishly avoided. In other words, Rossellini's movie indulges in the same "sickness" as its characters. Joly reported that in Rome, after a short first run, the picture could be seen only in strip-tease theaters, since most of it takes place in or on a bed.[51]

King Vidor commented, "I am not horrified at sex on the screen. I think it's probably pointing toward some sort of terrific honesty. . . . It's only an illusion, but so is life. We look out upon the world, and it's a drama, it's a story, it's a script, you know. But then, it's what you do with it. . . . You have to open up new cans of reality all the time. [You] have to delve a little deeper. . . . Movies are the instrument for enlightenment."[52]

Movies were also the instrument for enlightenment for Rossellini, enlightenment about people. Joly saw *Anima nera* as conformation of "Rossellini's determination to stick to characters more than to a subject or a milieu."[53] But if neo-realism had been a "window" onto reality in the 1940s, in the 1960s it had become a wall. In Rossellini's pursuit of truth in contemporary subjects, he had run into a dead end, an unbreachable wall, which was his inability because of censorship and his own pudency to follow the questions of contemporary life beyond the portals to a "forbidden knowledge," beyond boundaries that prevented realities from being shown, or even talked about directly, with the result that lies, not actuality, became the focus of Rossellini's movies set in the present. Here indeed is "involution."

Perhaps involution was the reality of the present; perhaps movies were enlightening us about it. But to what purpose? "Cinema," Roberto moaned, "among all the arts is probably the most responsible for the enormous process of conditioning and stupefaction that has been going on."[54]

Anima nera and *Vanina Vanini* stupefied producers. "Danger" signals flashed around Rossellini now. Roberto as usual responded by taking the high ground.

His friends joked he was trying to be Socrates. He went around asking, "Why aren't there ever any heroes in European films today?" He needed to find heroes: people who broke out of lies, or at least people who affirmed their own truth.

At *Cahiers du Cinéma* he sparked a discussion. Jean Domarchi thought Rossellini had made a penetrating criticism against the whole European cinema. Jean-Louis Comolli disagreed: Rossellini himself was an exception to the pessimism, along with Renoir, even more than Bergman and Antonioni. Rossellini went "beyond doubt." A film might end in a feeling of abyss and vertigo, explained Rivette, but in context of a "cosmic plenitude forthrightly unveiled" rather than a void; we see the possibility of hope.

"It is not heroes who make tragedy, but tragedy that makes heroes," Comolli continued. "In Renoir's films, and even in Rossellini's, the characters are heroes because the films, at their deepest secret levels, are tragedies: *La Règle du jeu, Toni*. And *Stromboli*, or *Voyage in Italy*."

Yet not even Rossellini was finding contemporary heroes today, Rivette pointed out. The fact that he had to go back to Garibaldi or Francis of Assisi demonstrated that "no form of heroism in the classical sense or in the American sense is possible in the European society of our day."[55]

In fact, Roberto was no longer so optimistic, so willing to settle for a miracle as he had been at the time of *Stromboli*. He had been 43 then, he was 55 now; "hope" had a different meaning. *Anima nera*'s final shot (*not* in Patroni Griffi's play) zooms from the girl-wife determined to play house to Adriano in despair: no solution.

Yet, as Comolli said, this lack of solution, this "tragedy," is the *creation* of the hero, not his fate. In *Anima nera* the hero does make his tragedy. And if we make our world, we can make it better. Thus when Roberto played Socrates, his method was not to dialogue toward conclusions, but to sermonize hope.

He would claim, Socratically, that education that guides us conditions us, that the word "education" comes from the Latin *educere*—to lead.

"But," he would say, "I refuse to lead. . . . We have to go in search of truth in a way that's infinitely more free."

But he was leading: "The important thing is to inform, to instruct." And he was willing to inform by stimulation rather than logic. "Art has an important role to play . . . , art can make you understand things by emotion that you're absolutely not capable of understanding by understanding."[56]

He claimed, Socratically, to be presenting facts. In actuality he was imposing conclusions—facts perceived by his moral attitude, which thus were conclusions regardless of how pure his moral attitude might be. Thus Roberto claimed that all ideologies were contained by his own ideology,[57] which was the Crocean notion that truth has to be discovered by an individual on his own. We shouldn't have someone else chew our spaghetti for us before we eat it, he said.[58] Great pasta requires a great cook, too.

"Our society wants to do something to educate people, to lead them toward an end. But on the contrary, people have to find their own way.

Either you believe in democracy or you don't, that's the main point. But how can democracy be established without knowledge. . . . ?

"I don't think there can be a greater joy than thinking, and I think this joy could spread very quickly, if it were made possible for people. . . . The last century was dominated by a dream of liberty, this one is dominated by respect. Latitude for discussion and judgment has become minimal. . . . There is no longer a critical attitude. . . . We live in a society that does everything to make people as superficial as possible." The ideas people express often sound as though purchased at the supermarket. "We've become so conditioned that we have no more capacity for joy, for the thrill of discovery." Art is part of the conditioning, movies too.[59]

The Great Plan

"It's time to act," Roberto told *Cahiers du Cinéma* in April 1962, shortly after shooting *Anima nera*. "I probably won't quit making movies, but it won't be my main activity anymore." He would concentrate on writing essays. "It's been terrible trying to write; I'm more comfortable with film. I've had to go back to zero and begin all over again, to get a technique, a language. It's no fun at all, but it was time I faced this problem, because all my talk has been totally in vain."[60]

He had still found no backing for Josué de Castro's *The Geography of Hunter* nor for Ottiero Ottieri's *Donnarumma all'assalto*, a 1959 novel about Olivetti's attempts to employ local workers in a new factory in a backward region of southern Italy. Nonetheless he had laid plans for a production house, FIDEC, which would make 25 television documentaries a year for four years. By using the Pancinor and mirror images, the budget would be only two billion lire a year ($3.25 million), which he hoped to obtain from the Ministry of Public Instruction, the Cassa del Mezzogiorno, and private industry. He outlined the subjects he would cover (see Figure 3).

I carabinieri

Beniamino Joppolo's satiric anti-war play, *I carabinieri*, had been banned in Italy after playing Paris and Vienna. Pressed by Rossellini and Guttuso, Gian Carlo Menotti agreed to defy the ban by presenting it at Spoleto's "Festival of the Two Worlds" with Rossellini directing and Guttuso painting imaginative backdrops and a curtain reminiscent of *Guernica*. But the play was greeted with whistles and hostility at its opening night, June 28, 1962; some considered it a movement by Marxist forces into the Festival. Due to complaints by the Carabinieri, it was not repeated. "In the theater there is no creation," Roberto declared a few years later, "there is the work of neatness and order: trying to make everything clear, everything that's in the text."[61] But at Spoleto Rossellini's naturalistic style was

FIGURE 3

A) Pre-history: Paleolithic, Mesolithic:
   1. Caves and lake dwellings.
   2. The arts.
   3. The origin of cultivated plants.
   4. First raw materials and techniques.
   5. Hunting and fishing.
   6. Writing.
   7. The appearance of domesticated animals
   8. The search for pasturelands, areas suited for cultivation, and those rich in game.
   9. The emigrations.
B) History:
   1. The Italic peoples.
   2. From smoothed stones to metals:
      a) The bronze age.
      b) The iron age.
   3. History of thought, political doctrines, work.
   4. Some biographies suitable for illustrating the subjects in the preceding section:
      a) Socrates.
      b) Aristotle.
      c) Alexander.
      d) Demosthenes.
      e) Virgil.
      f) Horace.
      g) Lucretius.
      h) Seneca.
      i) Augustus.
C) History of mathematics and geometry.
D) History of the the mechanical arts, anatomy, hydraulics, ballistics, astronomy, architecture, sculpture, and painting of the Renaissance. Appearance of the experimental method, the democratization of the sciences. A few biographies suitable for illustrating these subjects:
   a) Leon Battista Alberti—his scientific conception of the arts, according to which mathematics is the common ground of the work of the painter and the scientist.
   b) Gutenberg—invention of the printing press as first means of spreading knowledge.
   c) Copernicus.
   d) Leonardo.
   e) Bacon: founder of the experimental method.
   f) Galileo.
   g) Descartes.
   h) Newton.
   i) Leibniz.
   l) Réamur.
   m) Volta.
   n) Linneo.

E) History of geographical discoveries:
   1. Columbus
   2. Vespucci.
   3. Cortés.
   4. Cook.
   5. Peary.
   6. Amundsen.
F) The encyclopedists:
   1. Montesquieu.
   2. Voltaire.
   3. Rousseau.
G) History of the industrial revolution with various chapters indicated by the following biographies
   1. Watt.
   2. Fulton.
   3. Ampère.
   4. Faraday.
   5. Geoffrey Saint-Hilaire.
   6. Cuvier.
   7. Comte.
   8. Maxwell.
   9. Helmholtz.
   10. Clausius.
   11. Kelvin.
   12. Bernard.
   13. Pasteur.
   14. Lyell.
   15. Suess.
   16. Darwin.
   17. Becquerel.
   18. Curie.
   19. Rutherford.
   20. Bohr.
   21. Einstein.
   22. De Broglie.
   23. Federic and Irène Joliot-Curie.
   24. Fermi.
H) History of metallurgy.
I) History of chemistry.
L) History of agricultural and food problems.
M) History of industrial progress.
N) History of our food.
O) History of the means of transport.
P) History of economic developments.
Q) History of the search for development of transformation of energy sources: from water to petroleum to nuclear energy.
R) Geography: in this field can be realized programs useful in teaching and also marketing and psychological research.
S) History of the problems of southern Italy.[62]

thought a bit heavy-handed, and some of his characterizations too arch.[63] It was his first and last non-operatic work for theater.

Afterward he liked to tell how he had needed three minutes of music for a scene change, which no one had written. So, the day before, "I got a microphone. With a fork I went 'pan pan'; with a piano, 'ting, ting'; and then I got a guy with a violin to go 'zing, zing'. I recorded my three minutes of music, and the people took it very seriously. . . . On the program I put 'Music by Jean Pach'. It's incredible that you can fake this way. But was I faking?"[64]

Gruault described *I carabinieri* to Godard, who was intrigued. At his request Gruault recorded a tape for Godard of Roberto telling the play's story, and this became the basis for Godard's 1963 *Les Carabiniers*—and the sole reason for Rossellini's screen credit for the scenario.[65] Godard paid Gruault through Roberto, who, however, kept the money. Godard, said Roberto, "was the most honest man I've ever known."[66]

"In respect to Rossellini," Godard has often said, "I've always felt, in private life too, an adopted son. He's the only one I learned anything from. He's one of the few in film whom I admired and still admire (with Hitchcock, Eisenstein, and others)."[67]

Roberto, however, never saw *Les Carabiniers*, nor any other Godard film, with the exception of *Vivre sa vie*, and then only at Gruault's insistence. By 1960, watching movies bored him, with rare exceptions, such as *400 Blows*, *Jules et Jim*, *Fahrenheit 451*, and anything by Renoir. "He came out furious [from *Vivre sa vie*] and dragged me aside to ball me out for having made him waste his time," recounts Gruault. "Next day we saw each other again, Jean-Luc and I, at The Raphael. Jean-Luc was to drive Roberto to Orly and I was to pay his hotel bill, which was quite exorbitant (in the months ahead it took me all the pain in the world to get reimbursed). On the way to the airport, he maintained a silence heavy with menace. Suddenly he barked, in a voice prophetically low-pitched, like Cassandra announcing the fall of Troy or Isaiah threatening an impious people with the greatest evils: 'Jean-Luc, tu es au bord de l'antonionisme!' ['Jean-Luc, you're bordering on Antonioni-ism!'] The insult was such that poor Godard lost control of the car for a second and nearly made us join the scenery."[68]

(Godard remained curiously quiet on the subject of Antonioni until 1964, when he put *Red Desert* on his ten-best list. Truffaut, always loyal to Roberto, was still damning Antonioni in the 1970s, and in specifically Rossellinian terms—quite unjustly: "First, his lack of humor. He is so terribly solemn, so terribly pompous. I don't like the image he projects of himself as *the* psychologist of the female soul. When De Gaulle was trying to restore the confidence of the French in Algeria, he said, 'French men and women, I have understood you.' Antonioni stands like that and says, 'Women of the world, I have understood you.' And he follows the fashion [smuggling grass in his shoe]. That shows his childish need to keep up with youth. My hostility to Antonioni helped me make *L'Enfant Sauvage*.

One of the big themes today is the difficulty of human communication. This is very nice; it makes for good conversation among intellectuals. But when you come in contact with a family that includes a deaf-mute child, only then do you realize what lack of communication means. I wanted to show a real lack of communication in my film, not the modish variety that involves Antonioni.")[69]

"Pulcinella è morto!"

Inevitably came Act Three of The Great Debacle.

Deutschmeister had given Gruault a second contract to do the dialogues for *Pulcinella*, or *The Passions, Cockoldum and Death*, as the project was now titled, and had sent a crew to Yugoslavia to scout the first locations. "I have to shoot *Pulcinella* in May or June," Roberto had told *Cahiers* in April 1962.[70] Then Deutschmeister canceled. "It had become impossible to mount an important co-production with Italy on the name of Rossellini," explains Gruault, "and the Italians couldn't bear seeing their Pulcinella played by a French singer of Armenian origin. . . . It was a terrible blow for Roberto—and incidentally for me."[71]

The heart went out of Roberto. He would continue going through the motions, commissioning a *Caligula* from Gruault for Alberto Sordi that had too much sex for television,[72] and believing even in 1973 that he was about to start *Pulcinella*. But it was the end of Rossellini the moviemaker. In *Pulcinella*, Michelangelo Francanzati dies acting on stage, the curtain drops, and Caterina comes through it. "Pulcinella is dead," she announces.[73]

"Il cinema è morto!"

Thus the news conference in the Einaudi bookstore. The movies were dead.

"There's a crisis today not just in film but in culture as a whole," Roberto announced. "Film, which is the instrument *par excellence* for spreading ideas, has had the merit of making this crisis evident, almost palpably so. For this reason I intend to retire from film and dedicate myself to television, in order to be able to re-examine everything from the beginning in full liberty, in order to rerun mankind's path in search of the truth."[74]

Roberto was bitter. Not only *Pulcinella* but also *Socrates* and *Sagapò* had been canceled. *Socrates* was to have been produced by Truffaut's Films du Carrosse and some Greek, Italian, and Swedish financiers; but at the end of November 1962, Truffaut pulled out, partly in disagreement with Roberto's methods, mostly because he was disengaging from all co-productions to concentrate on his own projects. *Sagapò* was a town in Greece where the Germans had massacred Italian soldiers. The subject was so sensational that everyone in the Italian film industry had been trying to film it but had always been blocked by the Ministry of Defense. Renzo Renzi had tried in 1953 and had found himself on trial by military court martial. Nonetheless

Alfredo Bini, Pasolini's producer, had thought he had found a way. *Sagapò* would be a comeback for Anna Magnani; Roberto himself had rewritten Ugo Pirro's scenario for her. He had run away to avoid Anna a few years before. More recently he had been in Sonali's store when Anna had walked in and, since Sonali wasn't there, she had embraced him. *Sagapò* would have been a rousing box-office success for Rossellini. If military censorship hadn't prevailed, Roberto wouldn't have been standing in a bookstore announcing his demise.

On the other hand, maybe he would have sabotaged even *Sagapò*. There was a side of Roberto that had never believed he was capable of making normal movies. Almost every time he had tried he had failed miserably, shamefully, disgracefully with critics and the public. His few successes had been for the wrong reasons. He had had a heart for moviemaking once, or thought he had, but it had been crushed. Filming was torture now and failure, something he wanted to run away from. He couldn't hide his contempt. The short film, "Illibatezza" ("Chastity"), which he made a couple months before his bookstore news conference, hurled his "fuck you" at cinema itself.

"Chastity"

Bini, while preparing *Sagapò*, had asked Roberto to participate in a four-episode picture with Pasolini, Godard, and Ugo Gregoretti, all of with whom Bini had feature contracts. Thus the title *RoGoPaG*. As a theme Roberto proposed "the profound conditioning due to the boom and consumer society on individuals."[75] Pasolini liked Gregoretti's episode, loathed Godard's and Rossellini's, and tried to get Bini to release only *PaG*. Instead, thanks to Pasolini's "La ricotta" episode, the entire film was sequestered shortly after its release and Pasolini was given a suspended four-month jail sentence for "defamation of the state religion."

Rossellini had shot his episode in November 1962 at Cinecittà, after taking an unnecessary trip to Bangkok for location footage and stopping in Frankfurt for a production of *Uno squardo dal ponte* (where he provoked press criticism when he suddenly became "indisposed").

"Illibatezza" is prefaced by a quote from the psychologist Alfred Adler:

> The man of today is frequently oppressed by an indefinable anguish. And, amid his daily grind, the unconscious suggests a refuge to protect and nourish him: the maternal womb. For this man, deprived henceforth of selfhood, even love becomes the wimpish search for the protecting womb.

The story is trivial. Joe, an American tourist is obsessed by an airline hostess; to get rid of him she consults a psychiatrist who says Joe is Oedipal and to change the color of her hair; she does, Joe loses all interest in the real woman, and indulges his fantasies by means of 8mm film he took of her earlier.

Partly "Illibatezza" continues the self portrait of *Anima nera*; Joe often looks like a double of Roberto (but thinner!). Partly it develops *La macchina che ammazzacattivi*'s doubts about cinematic realism in context of Roberto's scourging of the involution of mass media. But Roberto himself was one of the prime movers behind obsession and involution in cinema. As in his films with Bergman and *Una voce umana* (of which "Illibatezza" is almost a remake), what strikes forcibly is the extreme cruelty and lucidity of the camera's eye which—as the roving zoom lens in *Anima nera* and "Illibatezza" emphasizes—is very much Roberto Rossellini's eye—his "attitude." Enzo Ungari explains that "the camera's cruelty is the condition for feeling and transmitting the pity. We're not spared anything. This is Rossellini's profound lesson for modern cinema: the implacable camera. As in [Godard's] *Vivre sa vie*, the camera never abandons its characters, [it stays] in direct contact with their life, even when it might be more compassionate to let them alone, with their miseries."[76]

Like *Anima nera*, "Illibatezza" bursts with contradictions. Rossellini, in denouncing a certain kind of cinema, produces films that are among the best justifications of that certain kind of cinema, assuming that we are conscious of the "eye," of the Crocean observer. "Man today is conditioned, fragmented, infantile, with a frenzied need for a pastime, for something he thinks will be his salvation, [so] he embraces not the truest but the strongest ideology. Art today is the unconscious lament of this man reduced to an infantile state, the logical finish of a civilization which . . . is a civilization of consumers and not of creators. How to change society . . . ? Believe in man. But modern culture, movies included, no longer believes in man. Man . . . is enslaved."[77]

Yet in these films Rossellini is caught up in the inevitable involution of Crocean historicism. If the only truth that matters is personal truth, then how can we escape from the vicious circles of self-contemplation (of involution), and progress beyond our selves in our search for reality? Where is "chastity"?

Nearly four years would pass before Rossellini directed another movie.

Where Is Chastity?

The question of chastity posed itself that April 1963 at a conference at UNESCO in Paris organized by Enrico Fulchignoni around the topic of cinéma vérité, specifically Jean Rouch's *La Punition* (1963) and Albert and David Maysles' *Showman* (1962). "When I walked into the theater," Roberto exclaimed, "I saw everyone bending down looking at something underneath the screen, as though it were an idol. I thought it must be a crocodile or an iguana. 'It's a hand-held camera! A hand-held camera!!' they kept repeating. That was the end. You can't get much crazier than that. I think this continual mythification of film and its equipment is ridiculous. . . . And I was opposed to [Rouch's] making a myth out of cinéma vérité."[78]

Irritated, Roberto at first refused to speak. Rouch was a filmmaker he had admired. Finally, after an introduction of feigned calm, he made his point: "In a work like [Rouch's] *La Punition* there's no taking of a position, so it's difficult for me to identity the role of the creator."[79]

Roberto, in other words, was asserting the essence of Crocean neo-realism: the reality of the observer; the notion that truth can only be known individually, and therefore you must know the observer.

"Coming from you this question is surprising," responded *Cahiers* critic Louis Marcorelles. "Think of *Paisà* or *Roma città aperta*, in which the objectivity is always personal."

Marcorelles had missed Roberto's point, which was Rouch's failure to be openly personal and to take a position.

Roberto went on, enunciating Croce's gospel: "There's no need to deform the truth when it becomes a confession. There is a need to resist any temptation to cheat. And you can cheat from love of your thesis. Ultimately, you make a judgment: you confront yourself, not some other person."

"We don't know how to write a film or choose the actors," Albert Maysles objected. "We only know how to observe and film unconsciously, according to a procedure that we ourselves don't understand. You judge moment by moment, directly on the screen; the audience can drag in their own philosophy. Then there's the cutting, very important, because that's where you commit yourself by your choices."

"Okay, but where's the creator?" Roberto asked.

Maysles answered, "We're looking for something with a personal meaning. In the world around us we put the best of ourselves."

"I still don't understand. . . ."

"Everything's born in a vacuum. We're dealing with the 'scientification' of automatism, of chance. The *raison d'être* is that there is no *raison d'être*. It's music played on a tricked-up piano. We don't know what we'll play. There's a great deal of accident, it's pop art, neo-realism."

"I don't understand. . . . It's a grave danger to move toward depersonalization, involuntary or no. If you go too far, depersonalization becomes enormous, it becomes alienation. We find ourselves in front of a wall. I'm old, but I want to understand."

"You talk about film," Marcorelles objected, "as if it were painting or literature. Only film is able to grasp the moment. [The films] we've just seen are a revolution compared to what you tried to do."

"Film is a means of expression like a thousand others. I've given up film because I don't like it anymore. There doesn't exist a technique for grasping reality. Only a moral position can do so."

The audience applauded. Marcorelles called them demagogues. Rouch spoke about his intentions "to provoke things that wouldn't be verifiable without the camera . . . , to ask influencing questions." Fereydoun Hoveyda denounced Rouch's film as a half-committed sketch: "You're refusing to become a director." Rohmer defended Rouch. Roberto, repeatedly provoked by Fulchignoni, kept saying, "I don't want to say anything." Then:

"I shall be very violent but with a great tenderness, a great esteem for Rouch. Maybe I'm an idiot, but I don't understand. There's a myth about the camera as though we were on Mars. The camera's a ball-point pen, an imbecile, it's not worth anything if you don't have anything to say. Your curiosity about the camera is the morbid curiosity of the feebleminded who are good for nothing. And so's your search for chance. Chance can do anything; sometimes it's amusing, but what irritates me most in this world is that people are doing everything to fall always lower and lower, to a level of non-culture that is terrifying, and this irritates me horribly. I'm not talking from malice, the pain is sincere, I experience tremendous chagrin seeing things like this, seeing things fallen to this level. Maybe I'm an idiot."

"We'll find someone to comfort you," said Marcorelles.

Fulchignoni asked Roberto, "You feel tricked . . . ?"

"It's a disaster, to see people fall so low."

Fulchignoni said, "It's a different scale of reality. We're interested in research. We're researchers. This new technique of observation forces the collapse of the preceding structures, in psychology as in physics."

"You're voyeurs."

"They're making scientific films," agreed Hoveyda; "that's where the moral problem is. This research depresses me; it's outside of cinema as we know it, outside of Mizoguchi, outside of Rossellini."

"All my life they've been insulting me."

"This film, *La Punition*," said Rouch, "is an experiment that will result in something. I'm convinced that this film has solved problems, its technique solved them. . . ."

"It's not the tool that can do everything. The Romans didn't have typewriters, nor did Tolstoy. . . . *La Punition* is the story of a director in search of authors. . . . Rouch, you have the talent to do something and you use it to undo. It's not anarchy, it's laziness."

"And on that word, laziness, sacred to Rossellinian mythology, we can end the debate," said Fulchignoni.[80]

But Roberto didn't end the debate. He went on, a few weeks later, with Hoveyda and Rohmer during an interview for *Cahiers*. "I'm wondering where the *vérité* ["truth" or "reality"] is in cinéma vérité, what this *vérité* means, what it's aiming for. . . . I don't see *where* an artistic discourse is here. . . . A painting is the discourse of someone who, instead of taking the path of a meticulous, photographic reproduction of what he sees, makes an *interpretation* of it. So this is a person with a precise position, an artistic dream of his own, a personal emotion, who receives the emotion from an object and tries to reproduce it no matter what the cost, who tries, even by deforming the object that first solicited him, to communicate to someone else, less sensitive, less subtle, his own emotion. You see how the author

enters into all this, how his choice is determined, how his language becomes the essential element of expression. But here, there's none of that. . . .
Rouch [and the Maysles] don't want [their] own personalities to play a
part. . . . I was trembling with rage—because I love [Rouch] so much."[81]

Eight months later, talking to Centro Sperimentale students, Roberto
had decided about the *"vérité."* It consisted of "thousands of gestures and
attitudes which are very well-known, they're catalogued in the dictionary.
You can just go to a dictionary and find them there. What need is there to
do this research? If it serves to go a bit further, toward a more intimate
discovery of a human, then at this point cinéma vérité is no longer cinéma
vérité, but psychoanalytical examination. And do you think anyone can do
a psychoanalytical exam with a camera stuck in their face?"[82]

Roberto's reaction to *La Punition* was unfair, many would argue. But
the biases *La Punition* provoked in him demonstrate that he saw himself as
a traditional artist rather than the iconoclastic, newsreel documentarist depicted in film histories of "neo-realism," and that he saw his coming films
as within traditional art. At the moment he was proclaiming *La Punition*
worthless because it was not art, he was also proclaiming his own humble
attempt not to make art in order to rediscover art, true art, uncorrupted by
our present infantile, plastic culture. "I used to say the same things [as
Rouch]," he admitted.

Roberto had justification for the confusion of his passions. He was 56,
he had lost everything, he was crippled with debts and responsibilities, he
was an international joke, he felt a certain disgust for the way he had lived
his life and for the films he had made, and his adventures had discovered
a vast world beyond Italy.

"At a certain point I felt so useless," he said.[83] How could he live up to
responsibility, he asked, as he had asked Geiger back in 1946 when the first
reviews of *Open City* arrived from America? The failure of Dovzhenko's
Poem of the Sea came home to him personally. "In spite of its simplicity,
people couldn't make head or tail out of it. This made me realize that nothing done in the movies is of any value from the point of view of general
usefulness. There are only a few people who understand. Most people get
nothing, or even feel offended."[84]

Yet here was Roberto, broke and disrespected, trying to mount a grandiose project for television that everyone thought insane and no one
wanted to support.

"A guy who starts filming the history of iron does look ridiculous," he
admitted.[85] *L'età del ferro (The Iron Age)* was to be the first step of The Great
Plan. The only other notable film on iron had been by King Vidor, naturally: *An American Romance* (1944).

Ridiculous or not, Roberto's efforts, until halted by his death, would
yield some 42 hours of "didactic" films. Audiences would judge them boring, historians deficient, and critics unappealing; their emotional and artistic riches have still only begun to be acknowledged beyond a tiny coterie of

the devout. Even Truffaut would tell Roberto he was wasting his time. And Roberto, all the while denying (with patent hypocrisy) that he was trying to "make art," would go ahead, determined to do what he could to "revise the whole conception of the universe"—and propelled as well by his constant need for money.

For some years there would be no money. His magic would stop working. He would sink to the most desperate point of his life.

"Rossellini was very disoriented," says Ermanno Olmi. "We met in Milan and I spent some of the richest weeks of my life, because we were together day and night, talking about everything. He told me about his need to get out of the narrative schemes of cinema. He was as excited as a boy about television, but mostly . . . he was fired up about putting history into images, the history of humanity, the facts, the fundamental and significant moments from which people today can find directions, can extract reflections particularly useful. And he told me about this history of iron, of how it had changed people's economy and life.[86] In film circles no one listened to him anymore.[87] I talked to the directors of Edison, and we made the initial investment with 'La 22 dicembre.'[88] A few friends regretted having done it, [but] this kind of operation can't be measured solely in terms of money."[89]

La 22 dicembre was a little Milanese production house 51 percent owned by Edisonvolta, the electric company. Olmi had been making shorts on dams and electricity for Edison, which had participated in his first two features, *Il tempo si è fermato* (1959) and *Il posto* (*The Sound of Trumpets*, 1961), and had then set up La 22 dicembre. La 22 dicembre had financed a few features, including Olmi's *I fidanzati*, but was also interested in didactic documentaries for television and hoped to attract support from RAI. RAI, the state television monopoly, had begun transmission in 1955; by 1957 it was reaching ten million viewers, and was almost ripe for a project like Rossellini's. Television's mandate in Italy was for information and culture primarily, not entertainment; its director once banned a semi-classic dancer for wearing flesh-colored stockings and then became a Trappist.

Olmi showed Roberto *I fidanzati* and Sonali was in tears. "It's stupendous," Roberto said. "Let's go to the office and call Truffaut in Paris."

"Hey, François, at Cannes there'll be this film of Olmi's. I just saw it, it's really great, tell all our friends!"

I fidanzati got a fabulous reception at Cannes.[90]

The Iron Age

L'età del ferro (*The Iron Age*), in five one-hour segments, cost the risible sum of one hundred million lire ($160,000). Some of this came from La 22 dicembre. Half was provided by Italsider, Italy's government-controlled steel company, which wanted publicity for its fifth and biggest mill, which it was inaugurating at Taranto as part of the government's eternal efforts to develop the South. Roberto had approached Italsider a year or two earlier, before drawing up his encyclopedic plans for the still-born FI-DEC. (It wasn't the first time he had appealed to private industry before. In 1946 he had talked to Pirelli about a film about a factory, but nothing had happened, because Pirelli had wanted to sing the praises of its management, whereas Trombadori had wanted a labor conflict.)

The Iron Age, Roberto emphasized, would involve spectators as though they were watching a current newsreel, or "documentaries shot before movies were invented."[91]

He had described *Viva l'Italia* in similar terms. He wanted "to study certain spontaneous attitudes in man, et cetera, [and] since I'm looking for something absolutely sincere and absolutely true, I try to do away with too much preparation." Like Rouch. But unlike Rouch, he would construct his characters. "I take an individual who seems to me to have the physical look for the role, so that I can tell my story. And since he isn't an actor, but an amateur, I study him thoroughly, I appropriate him, I remake him, and I use his muscular aptitudes, his ticks, in order to make a character out of him. As a result, the character I originally imagined may change en route, but gets to the same destination. I don't abandon my first idea and end up with something else, if so I wouldn't have accomplished anything."

"Absolute sincerity" requires a "moral position" of tolerance, understanding and love, "thus also, of involvement. You see how things . . . always get closer to what you are yourself, to what you want them to be. From the moment you distance yourself from any judgments, any involvement, any sympathies . . . and say, 'Be as you are, I don't care,' it's no longer a moral position, in fact it's an attitude that's very cynical."

The moral position is a Crocean position. Opposed to it was contemporary art, which was cruel, the way the world was cruel: vainly: abusing and humiliating people for the infantile fun of watching them squirm. "Art today is either complaining or cruelty," which was inconsistent with the sensitivity that a moral position required, Roberto maintained. If you discover people will drown if they fall into the water, it's ignoble to throw people into the water every day so that you can watch them drown. But if you react by learning to swim so you can save them, this is a moral position—which "is why I've decided not to make movies anymore. [Rather than just] painting myself . . . , I think it's my duty . . . to learn to swim and be a life guard."

Art has gotten completely corrupted, Roberto insisted; it had disintegrated into abstractions, and caused us to lose not just language, but the alphabet on which language depends. Before we could do anything useful we would have to re-establish the letters of the alphabet. "It's not a question of transforming art, but of finding it again . . . , of making the big effort to re-establish language, [so that] each word will find its meaning again, its value, and present itself as the fruit of profound thought, so that language becomes a real language, and not, as now, a bunch of labels stuck on samples of things that we hardly know exist. At that moment it will be possible to take up all the forms of art again. . . .

"A civilization always bears art as its fruit. All that remains to us from it are the monuments, or the works of poets, for example, who in their own time had a minimal role within the civilization they illustrated. But when a civilization [is declining] its art dies at the same time, or even before.

"So what is to be done? To exist, a civilization needs art. To exist, art needs very clear ideas. Today we regard the world of technology and science with contempt. . . . What effort have we made to understand [it], *from a moral point of view* . . . to find in it all the sources of emotion necessary to create an art? There is an enormous divorce between the evolution of humanity . . . , which is a technological evolution, and the artists, who used to be capable of . . . assimilating this evolution. . . . If the artist isn't the fertilizer of things—irreversible things—he is totally failing in his duty. . . . Art is life, a way of perpetuating life, of giving a reason to things, of exalting enthusiasm."

Instead of complaining about alienation, an artist should show that we *can* communicate. "This is the artist's function: to conquer things, to find the new language. . . . How was the Renaissance born? The Renaissance was born at the moment when artists became aware of the immense step that humanity had made in technology and science. And what did they do? They became savants. They studied anatomy and perspective . . . , plunged into . . . science, appropriated it, rethought it, and raised it to the ranks of high art. . . . [So] you can find extraordinary sources of emotion in places where you would never have imagined they existed. . . . I'm going to put the story of iron onto film. Isn't that ridiculous?"[92]

The Iron Age was shot in the summer and fall of 1963. Roberto, involved in his reading, consumed by his efforts to promote The Great Plan, and turned off by moviemaking, left the actual direction to his son, Renzino. Marcellina De Marchis did the costumes, as she had been doing for Roberto since *Viva l'Italia*. Marcella Mariani Rossellini was the script girl, and her son designed the sets. By employing his family Roberto was able to keep costs down while increasing his own salary, since he rarely passed on their earnings to his relatives. He also saved wear and tear on his aging nervous system, because he was no longer surrounded by people like Amidei who would argue with him at every step. In the past, in *Viva l'Italia* as in *Roma città aperta*, Roberto had deliberately pit rival screenwriters and researchers against each other, and had expected them to fight with him as well. From now on, in contrast, placidity replaced contention, and the films were the poorer for it.

The first three episodes, each introduced by Roberto surrounded by books, trace the development of iron from the Etruscans—who around 900 B.C. were "the first to create a center of industrial activity, which brought about a profound revolution in equipment, attitudes, and the world economy, 'economy' . . . as an element that determines the profile of a civilization."[93] The Greeks built roads from southern Italy north for the iron. We see iron being used for boar hunting, armor, guns, and war. Footage from

Luciano Serra pilota, Paisà, Deutschland im Jahre Null, Gallone's *Scipione l'Africano,* and Gance's *Austerlitz* is mixed with Renzino's anecdotal material of Pyrrhic burial dances, a Chinese alchemist experimenting in a Franciscan monastery, a blacksmith using a small boy's urine to temper armor, a sixteenth-century dandy being fitted out in armor, and speeches by Leon Battista Alberti on art's need for the sciences. "I was concerned not to limit the subject to an examination of the technical procedures and the production of weapons and instruments, but also to reconstruct the environment, the ways of living and thinking, and the prejudices, superstitions, and aspirations. In this way, it seems to me, the logical processes of development appear in all their evidence, humanized."[94]

The fourth episode resembles an episode from *Paisà*: a true World War II story of the adventures of a Piombino steel worker. The Germans are stealing his factory and transporting it to Germany, and he tries to follow the train by bicycle. The point, as in *India*'s Hirakud episode, is that technology becomes intimately bound up with individual lives, a point that in the fifth episode is expanded to illustrate iron's role in Italy's postwar recovery.

By December 1963, *The Iron Age* was finished but Roberto had not yet secured RAI's cooperation. Nor did he have any money. He tried to use *The Iron Age* to launch the vast program for which it was only a trailer. He showed the Etruscan sequences to people from Canadian television in Paris in December, then at a documentary festival on Capri. "My wife and I," recalled Gruault, "would vainly lug the reels from one private projection to another" without result.[95] Santa Marinella had to be sold, the big red Ferrari as well; the bailiffs carried off the furniture from Via Nomentana and from Viale Bruno Buozzi. Roberto had not paid for the furniture to begin with—and would repurchase it at auction.

Elettra, his mother, had died the year before.

By January 1964, Roberto was penniless, his credit was exhausted, Sonali was talking about jumping out the window.

At that moment Rod Geiger phoned from Sweden.

Roberto hadn't heard from Geiger since he'd helped him in 1953. Now Geiger's wife, Katja, had become a big fashion designer in Sweden. Rod was probably the only person in the world who owed Roberto money, and he wanted them to make movies together again.

Roberto flew to Copenhagen February 6 and spent a week with the Geigers in their farmhouse home in Huarod near Malmö (a short ferry ride from Copenhagen). Roberto calculated and compounded interest and accepted about $21,000. And he sold Rod on the idea of filming *The History of Human Feeding through the Ages.* "Don't tell the lawyers you paid me back!" he said.[96]

In Rome, Ingrid's children were living with a cook and a housekeeper, Argenide Pascolini, who had replaced Elena di Montis. Sonali would come most days, Ingrid every month or so. Maria Mercader and her children would come some afternoons to play. "They were very alone," she said.[97] In 1964, Pia Lindstrom, now in her twenties, moved in and got to know Roberto. He was at a low point, she recalls, and very depressed. They would always set a place for him for the mid-day meal. Two or three times a week he would show up. They scarcely saw him otherwise. When he did come, he would arrive late, after they'd waited and waited, make fourteen calls about money, gulp down his now-cold pasta, kiss everyone wildly, say "I love you," and speed out the door. Once or twice he came in the middle of the night and "borrowed" the money Ingrid had sent for house expenses—and never paid it back. To Pia the whole situation appeared absurd and terrible. The children never had anyone to tell their troubles to. Roberto would check himself into a hospital clinic for ten days of rest, then his life of confusion would start up again in the clinic.[98]

At home with Sonali he spent most of the time in bed with books and the phone. After dinner he liked to watch television with the children and make comments. He would never raise his voice to them, or stop them from doing anything. If he were coaxed out to a movie, he would often fall asleep as soon as the lights went out. Sonali never managed to get any of them to like Indian food; she, on the other hand, continued to wear Indian dress and to resist integration into Italian life. In Rome she worked for the Indian government, representing high-quality Indian artisan work. The one asset remaining to Roberto, because it was not in his name, was a small house near Amalfi where the children passed the summers, now that Santa Marinella was gone. Sonali would cover up thoroughly to shield herself from the sun. When Roberto was there, his presence dominated everyone. They waited each morning to see his mood.

On September 23, Roberto was back in Sweden with Sonali and a suitcase full of medicines and Indian perfumes. They stayed several months with the Geigers. Or rather Sonali stayed while Roberto came and went, and undid the household, particularly in regard to food. Geiger had gotten an initial $100,000 together from himself, Thor Ohssons (a department store owner), and Gunnar Brimmer (Swedish Dixie cup), and they had set up a company, Toga Films, for a co-production with Istituto Luce in Rome. Roberto signed a contract with Rod and Katja giving him a weekly stipend, and at the windmill house they worked daily on a treatment in five episodes. Roberto was very much in it for the money, Geiger thought, yet totally absorbed, and surrounded by books and notes. "He had read deeply, all the way back." Rod lent Roberto $50,000 despite Sonali's warning, "Don't! You'll never get it back!"

In December they went to Paris to solicit assistance from UNESCO, and then to Rome to talk to the U.N. Food and Agriculture Organization. The president of India was going to help, and RAI. Rod suggested looking up Fellini and quickly understood, from the way Roberto offered to give him Fellini's number, that the penalty for calling him would be a week of silence from Roberto. In Stockholm at Philips they saw a demonstration of the first video recorder and held frequent screenings in their town house of *The Iron Age*. At one point they fought and Roberto went to stay with relatives of Katja's. Most of the time, said Geiger, "he clung to me as though he came out of my stomach. I said to Katja, 'I'm not his father, I'm his mother!'"[99]

The Iron Age was finally telecast in Italy in February and March 1965. It attracted an average of 2.6 million viewers, a small number for television, but an enormous number for a didactic documentary, especially since RAI had played it on Friday nights at 9:30 in competition with more popular programs. Some commentators, like Edoardo Bruno, greeted it as "the premise of a new discourse . . . , the first historic work of our contemporary culture."[100] Others, like Pio Baldelli, scorned its "hymns, incense, and hosannas" to Italsider and its failure to acknowledge the exploitation of workers that the postwar recovery had entailed.[101]

Roberto would reply that there was already too much lamenting. "In an era of pessimism optimism may seem an infamous crime.[102] You have to go back to Jules Verne to hear the positive side! The great turning point, the industrial revolution, a transformation that involved so much social injustice and so many ideas denounced today, came when man developed science and put it into practice through technology. . . . People had been slaves, had always supplied their own motor force, helped a bit by animals, then windmills and watermills. . . . But then the motor forces was *invented* . . . . A fantastic conquest, wasn't it? A whole new dimension was introduced into our lives and our possibilities! Prometheus's discovery of fire was sung by thousands of poets, illustrated by thousands of painters, depicted by thousands of sculptors, and that was the beginning. But tell me who has told us something about these other things?"[103]

Alas, *The Iron Age* is boring, if not all of the time, certainly most of it. The feeble scenario scarcely scratches the surface of the technology of making steel, the cultural contexts, and the personal adventures. Renzino's direction looks like Rossellini, but never feels like Rossellini; there is none of the intensity, invention, or poetry that marks Roberto's hand, and none of the depth. Instead there is an appalling tendency to inflate scenes worth thirty seconds into ten minutes.

By the end of March 1965, *The History of Human Feeding through the Ages* had turned into a 95-page text, still incomplete, *The Extraordinary History of Our Food*. And Roberto was proposing two companion series, each twelve hours long, on the industrial revolution and "the scientific revolution."

A substantial treatment of *The Industrial Revolution* survives. It begins by depicting the sordid facts of eighteenth-century life: the poor food, wretched housing, and lack of drainage; Edward Gibbons relates that his father named all his sons Edward, so that one might survive and perpetuate his name. Then come minor technical discoveries: the flying shuttle

(1733), the steam engine (1795). William Lee invents a knitting loom and it is denounced as a pernicious scheme to deprive workers of bread. But mass production lowers prices and population soars. "No art has sung the great conquests achieved by man during the period of the industrial revolution," Rossellini remarked.[104] Yet Western rationalism in its most extreme form—Aristotle, the Bible, and Marx—is today replacing every other civilization, including that of China.

There are discussions of Adam Smith; Aquinas versus Luther on interest; the medieval synthesis of the two cities; medieval pride versus Renaissance cupidity; what caused our century of genocide?; the tendency of any society to stabilize its structures through violence and education; mass media's attempt to ossify our structures and enslave us by exploiting our ignorance; Erich Fromm; desire to refind the womb by enlisting in an organization; how liberal humanism has been reduced to commerce and politics; the nature of revolution; English empiricism versus dogmatism; interdependence of military and industry; how segregation of art and science leads to art today becoming politics; how Romanticism tried to bolster faith but turned negative with the French revolution and the triumph of capitalism. The nineteenth-century image of a man with beard, side-whiskers, top hat, tall collar, cape, and stick is ridiculous but dangerous in its self-assurance, vanity, and dominance; but this man is aware of being for the first time in history the master. Why has modern art ceased to sing the myth of Prometheus?[105]

Rossellini's "scripts" for didactic films were generally of this sort: a ménage of essay, anecdote, and various texts, without dialogue or dramatization or any hint of "treatment"; a font of raw materials on which to elaborate at the moment of shooting.

Canadian television seemed a likely backer for *The Industrial Revolution* through Gian Vittorio Baldi. Baldi was a Bolognese filmmaker with strong social commitments and a background in television documentaries. In addition to his realist shorts (*La casa delle vedove*), he would shortly direct two features (*Luciano*; *Fuoco!*) and produce pictures by Pasolini (*Porcile*; *Appunti per un'Orestiade africana*), Straub-Huillet (*Chronicle of Anna Magdalena Bach*), Bresson (*Quatre nuits d'un rêveur*), and, almost, Dreyer (*Jesus*). In 1962 he had organized A.I.D., the International Association of Documentary Filmmakers, with John Grierson, Joris Ivens, Paul Rotha, Lionel Rogosin, and others, had contacts in Canadian television, and was happy to get Roberto named president of the jury for Canadian competition at the Sixth Montreal Film Festival, August 1965. Also Baldi knew Canadian Prime Minister Pierre Trudeau, which was good, because Roberto liked to meet the top man wherever he went.

Before leaving they joined with Gianni Amico, Adriano Aprà, Bernardo Bertolucci, Tinto Brass, and Vittorio Cottafavi in issuing a "Manifesto" declaring the duty of modern art to lead us out of confusion.[106]

In Montreal, at the Ritz Hotel, Roberto entered the dining room to spontaneous applause from the women there. Baldi even got Roberto a job, a commission from Fernand Cadieux for suggestions on how to raise the educational level of an underdeveloped area of Canada. Roberto spent two days on a small plane, wrote three pages, and received $10,000. Together they drove down through New England. Baldi noted Roberto's addiction to bed and constant smoking—and to a self-imposed discipline of never taking more than two or three puffs from each Chesterfield and throwing away the pack long before it was empty.

Roberto's film projects encountered opposition which, as in India, only the prime minister was able to clear away. Eventually they sold *The Iron Age* and a production deal for *The Industrial Revolution* to Max Cacopardo, the director of Canadian Broadcasting, and Pierre Juneau, who headed CBC's film section; both men were partners in John Grierson's National Film Board and its documentary program. They all met to sign the contracts at Lac Queareau. On the hotel menu were "Spaghetti Rossellini" (hazel nuts, rughetta, garlic) and "Spaghetti Baldi" (roasted peppers and tuna). Then the Canadians stipulated that Roberto direct the series himself, not Renzino, and Roberto exploded, tore the contract in pieces, and stormed out of the meeting.[107]

That was the end of *The Industrial Revolution*, although Roberto went on hawking it for the rest of his life.

In September 1965, also with Baldi, he went to Brazil for a UNESCO conference on cinema and television in Latin America. "I contacted all the Brazilian directors," Baldi recalled, "because Roberto wanted to speak to them about his cinema, his way of making films. And so it was, with a large participation and a big success. Glauber Rocha helped me very much. Also present were Paulo Emilio Salles Gomes, Luiz Carlos Berreto, Nelson Pereira Dos Santos, Carlo Diegues, Paulo Cezar Saraceni, Leon Hirszman, Geraldo Sarno, Thomas Farkas, and the documentarists from São Paulo. Roberto claimed he had been the father of the French New Wave with the lessons he had given Truffaut and Godard. He wanted to do the same with South American cinema."[108]

Roberto was given some snake rattlers and carried them for good luck. "He tried to meet with the president of Brazil," said Baldi, "and I think after much patience he managed to do it, too."[109] In November, Roberto was besieging ministries in Venezuela.

"The world should expect something from intellectuals and artists, a clarifying function . . . , a compass," he insisted everywhere. "It's useless to go see an artist's work in order to say, 'Look how uprooted and alienated he feels!' You can see such phenomena well enough in a hospital. Much more interesting cases, too. The real human problems aren't simply problems of communication, or anything so subtle. . . . In 2000, 35 years from now, there will be six billion people. What value does anything else have? People have to be strong enough to face this fact, which is a result of our conquest of medicine, food, science, and technology. . . . Art's great mission should be [to liberate us from our conditioning]. But art has always had the opposite objective. Wasn't Virgil an 'agit prop' for the Roman Empire?

What has been one of man's great efforts? To subjugate others. And the methods . . . have been infinite: magic, eloquence, rhetoric, history, everything to try to subjugate people to people, and . . . with the least effort. The best way to have a slave is to keep a slave who is voluntarily a slave, convinced that he's great, free, and doing his job. . . . In the modern era [such conditioning] has become rationalized and scientific."[110]

Rod Geiger's investors were starting to realize the extent of Roberto's grand plan—a history of practically everything—which Geiger, unimpressed by *The Iron Age*, wanted carried out with ample budgets. Fortunately, his investors had deep pockets.

Katja was giving a big show in Paris, the Geigers took rooms at The Raphael, and Roberto undertook to engage their butler for them, an excellent butler, he determined during an interview, even though the man had robbed his last client. They had dinner with Marlene Dietrich who chatted of the many meals she'd cooked for Roberto, and Roberto helped Katja rehearse a speech in French. He was not speaking to Ingrid at the moment, and since she would come in the afternoons, he came in the morning, eager to hear, via the Geigers, Ingrid's news of their daughter Isabella, who was being diagnosed for spinal curvature.

Soon after, who knows why, there were fights and the partnership broke up. Eventually Geiger wrote asking for repayment of the $50,000 loan. Roberto replied nastily, reminding Rod of how much Rod had learned from him, and complaining about some religious paintings Rod had given him in Rome in 1953. The paintings had not been completely paid for, as Rod had told him at the time, and Roberto expected Rod to pay off the balance. Geiger replied with a nasty letter of his own. The only thing he had ever learned from Roberto, he said, was how to trick money out of people. Roberto did not reply.[111]

Rod Geiger, like Roswitha Schmidt, is not acknowledged by Rossellini in his writings and interviews, except once, where he tells how he once went to Naples to give "an American soldier named Rod Geiger" a copy of *Roma città aperta* "in exchange for a $28,000 note—"of which I've never seen a penny," even though Geiger sold it to "someone named Joe Burstyn" and it scored "the biggest success anyone had had for a long time in the United States."[112]

The explanation was simple. Roberto thought he had found deeper pockets. Where indeed was chastity?

La Prise de pouvoir par Louis XIV

According to Roberto, he had been in Peru "to acquaint myself with the reality of [Third-World] problems," had been given a ticket to a bullfight, and had found himself sitting beside a Standard Oil executive who advised him to seek support from "'a man who is a new genius . . . , Jean Riboud.'

"I said I knew him very well, he was married to an Indian woman, which was our connection."[1]

Riboud had recently become president and C.E.O. of Schlumberger, Ltd., one of the world's ten biggest corporations. Schlumberger operated in 92 countries; almost half of its revenues came from a technique for locating mineral deposits that had been invented by its founders, Conrad and Marcel Schlumberger. The Schlumbergers were Alsacian, Protestant, pacifist, and socialist; scientific research was their corporate priority, not profits; they contributed heavily to socialist causes, to the civil rights movements, to Black and Hispanic political candidates, to almost anything challenging the status quo, and to artists.

Jean Riboud had been in the French Resistance and had spent two years imprisoned in Buchenwald. He was a socialist and by temperament always in revolt. He served, for example, on no other corporate boards and supported French President François Mitterrand's desire to nationalize 46 private enterprises. He did serve on the board of the Cinémathèque Française, however, as a friend of Henri Langlois. His wife, who knew Sonali through Cartier-Bresson's wife, was Krishna Roy, a niece of Tagore and a graduate of Wellesley College.[2]

Roberto asked Mary Meerson to phone Riboud for him.

"Roberto came," said Riboud, "to tell me: 'There are the underdeveloped countries and there is the incredible power of television; you should see what people are doing with it, or rather what they're not doing with it. It's possible to speak to all these people by making a sort of human epic tracing all the history of man's survival.' I was exhilarated by Roberto as I've never been exhilarated by anyone. I did a very difficult thing. I went looking for people to ask them for their money."[3]

Roberto also cultivated John de Menil, who ran Schlumberger in Houston. He invited de Menil and his wife to a speech he gave to Parisian Jesuits about his Great Ethical Plan. De Menil's wife was Dominique Schlumberger, Conrad's daughter, a passionate patroness and collector of modern art (whose private museum, designed by Renzo Piano, who had also done the much different Pompidou Center in Paris, became one of Houston's architectural gems in the 1980s).

On April 22, 1966, Riboud and de Menil created Horizon Two Thousand, Inc., in Houston, with themselves as directors, along with Schlumberger's Finance Chairman Paul A. Lepercq. This Texas charitable corporation would funnel $500,000 to a second Schlumberger creation, Logos, S.A.R.L., in Paris (created July 21 and "owned" by Rossellini, Jean Thuillier, and Claude Baks), which would raise another $500,000 and produce a twelve-hour *Man and His Food: The Story of Survival* in partnership with Alfredo Bini's Arco Film in Rome. Henri Langlois and Gian Vittorio Baldi were also involved, but Baldi pulled out on his lawyer's advice that "it's not advisable to sleep in a cage with a tiger."[4] Claude Baks was Schlumberger's omsbudsman, charged with keeping alive a sort of permanent cultural revolution within the company; he shared Riboud's interest in film and worked with Langlois and Rossellini on Riboud's behalf. Roberto was advanced $5,000.

Roberto did not forget the Pope. With some maneuvering he got a twenty-minute private audience with Paul VI and told him about his Great Plan, how optimistic he felt at the extraordinary stirrings of young people despite the alienation and moral decay of modern life, how he wanted to encourage people to think, and by thinking to recapture the heroic sense of life. "Do you know," Paul interrupted, "what that heroic sense of man is called in Christian terms? It's called sanctity."[5]

Roberto's heroism was his tenacity. Almost four years had passed since he had quit commercial cinema, almost three since *The Iron Age*; and he was still scrounging money at every amoral chance, while The Great Plan scarcely advanced. The tax people were after him and his daughter Isabella was facing a difficult spinal operation. No matter. He persisted. His resources were "the six attributes of the adventurer," as enumerated in *The Bridge of San Luis Rey* by Gruault's beloved Thornton Wilder: "A memory for names and faces, with the aptitude for altering [one's] own; the gift of tongues; inexhaustible invention; secrecy; the talent for falling into conversation with strangers; and that freedom from conscience that springs from a contempt for the dozing rich he preyed upon."

Indeed it was due to Jean Gruault, more even than Schlumberger, Ltd., that Roberto's tenacity finally triumphed. Gruault, stimulated by Roberto's example, had spent his years away from Roberto devouring essays, memoirs, sociology, ethnography, economics, archeology, and anthropology, and relearning Latin and Greek. Through a production bureau headed by the historian Jean Dominique de La Rochefoucauld, he had also gotten involved in television, specifically in a new series *Les Hommes de Caractère* ("Men of Character") founded, partly to please De Gaulle, by Claude Contamine, the new head of French television. Gruault wrote a successful episode about Schliemann, the archeologist who discovered Homer's Troy. Next Gruault plunged into Louis XIV.

La Rochefoucauld was doing a film on Louis XIV at Contamine's request; the subject suited Gaullist policies. He consulted Louis's memoirs, at Contamine's suggestion, thought they read like Louis's instructions to his grandsons on how to rule, and therefore went to a well-known historian, Philippe Erlanger, who was completing a book on Louis, and asked him to write out a synopsis of the principal events during the seven months, March to September 1661, between Mazarin's death and Fouquet's arrest, precisely the period during which Louis, till then king in name only, took power and began to rule. "Historians of Louis XIV," Erlanger explained, "have generally failed to recognize that in deciding to seize the reins he was taking a resolution as serious as if he were accomplishing a *coup d'état*. The monarch had not governed in fifty years."[6] La Rochefoucauld's film would be about how to rule. He gave Erlanger's synopsis to Gruault to dramatize.

Gruault knew Louis only from pictures in history books. But during several meetings with Erlanger he acquired the minute trivia indispensable to a scenarist. What did you say if you met the king in the hallway? What would the king say? How did he talk to his mother? How did he sleep and wake up and eat and walk and hold his council?

For dialogue, Gruault went to Louis's contemporaries: Saint-Simon, Mme de Sévigné, and Voltaire's *Le Siècle de Louis XIV*, from which he lifted Colbert's monologue to the dying Mazarin on the condition of France. "Thus," says Gruault, "the film is not an adaptation of Erlanger's book, although the telefilm served to promote the book, and vice versa: the two came out at the same time."[7]

Jacques Rivette, who had just finished *La Religieuse*, Gruault's adaptation of his own play, tentatively agreed to direct, with Jean-Louis Brialy as Louis. Gruault, Rivette, La Rochefoucauld, and various others were all to meet for lunch at Chez Francis, but Rivette's phone call caught Gruault as he was leaving for the restaurant. Rivette didn't want to come to lunch, do another costume film, or work for television. At the restaurant they discussed replacements. Jean-Claude Michaud, an associate director of ORTF, turned to Gruault. "What if we asked your friend Rossellini?"

Gruault had not heard from Roberto for a year or two. For Roberto he had written treatments for *Satyricon, Viva Catilina!* (Catherine of Siena), a life of Cyrus the Great (commissioned by the Shah's sister), a history of Islam, and a history of the Lumières. Roberto was mad at him because he had given up on *Caligula*. Nonetheless Gruault phoned Roberto in Rome "with resignation and without much hope."

Roberto answered the instant it began to ring, Gruault recalls. "He must have been sitting beside his phone (and in fact he had been, he confirmed) waiting in vain for quite some time for a sign from the outer world that would lead him out of an irremediable situation. . . . I think he packed his bag immediately, borrowed money for his ticket, and ran to the airport.[8] [Years later], in his moments of abandon and tender gratitude—he did have them—Roberto confided to me two or three times: 'With *Louis XIV*, you saved my life!'"[9]

In Paris the next day, Roberto met La Rochefoucauld and Gruault for breakfast, then the television people for lunch at Chez Potel et Chabot (better than Chez Francis). Later, at The Raphael, according to Gruault, Roberto laughed that "he didn't know anything more than I did about this fucking Sun King, except that he had heard he had invented a trick to get the nobles to forget their claims and leave him in peace; he led them to the point where their sole preoccupation was to have ribbons and lace sewn on their clothes and feathers stuck on their hats—in other words, he invented *fashion*, domestication, domination through fashion. At first glance Roberto had put his finger on the essential point. Everything else (court gossip, great political decisions, everyday mores, fights between people, etc.) was organized around and out of this central idea, which Roberto, without knowing anything else, had, the moment he had gotten involved, known to put first. Once again everything was leading back to a fable, the parable of King Louis."[10]

In actuality, Roberto was repeating what La Rochefoucauld had told him that morning. La Rochefoucauld had gotten the idea of dress from a Thackery cartoon unrelated to Louis, and while walking around in the Louvre, seeing the costumes of the era, and thinking of the energy coming out through the people's heads, since, because of their costumes, it was otherwise impossible for them to move.[11]

Gruault reworked his initial continuity on the idea of taking power, using the new direction indicated by Rossellini. Otherwise Roberto did not interfere; he was in Rome during pre-production reading Erlanger's book, while Marcella De Marchis (without screen credit) attended to 400 costumes, 206 wigs and 200 pairs of shoes. La Rochefoucauld and Gruault cast the picture and found the locations; La Rochefoucauld knew the Duc de Brissac, in whose furnished chateau near Angers most of the film was shot. La Rochefoucauld also found Jean-Marie Patte, an office clerk and occasional director of amateur avant-garde plays at the Cité Universitaire, to play Louis, for 10,000 francs. It was objected that Patte was too short, at five-foot-four, even though Louis was five-foot-three, because five-foot-three was fairly average in 1661; in fact, the men surrounding Patte, if not all the women, are taller than him. Some of the other casting was more arguable, Erlanger admitted. The reason Louis's mother, Anne of Austria, speaks with a German accent is that the actress was Austrian. "Anne of Austria was fat and a Spanish princess. But Katharina Renn plays her as she was morally: dry. We flattered Marie-Thérèse [Louis's wife] who was not pretty. As for Mlle de La Vallière [his mistress], she limped and was frankly ugly."[12]

On the first day of shooting, in June 1966, Gruault went to Roberto's room and found him in bed. He had read the script for the first time during the night and said it was shit, which was what he usually said. He began to simplify, drastically cutting monologues and dialogues. Having gotten what he wanted from Gruault, he distanced himself from him and kept him off the set.

"Gruault's scenario," La Rochefoucauld observes, "was very superior to what Scaffa and [Roberto's] sister Marcella would be able to supply him with [for later films]. It was an abundant text, overflowing, generous as Gruault is and full of propositions, completely in the style of the work he had already done with Truffaut, Rivette, and others.

"RR, however . . . , took a liking for me. I was something new and he loved novelty. He had the feeling that he was starting a new career. And he certainly did not like starting it with a scenario of which he would be the 'director' and not the 'author' creating it according to his inspiration of the moment. It was out of the question to shoot a script by crossing out the numbered sequences from start to finish.

"With him it was the Reign of *Change.* This will for freedom from a text written in advance had its effect at the level of the dialogue. So, more from instinct than calculation, it was agreed that I would be present during the shooting and rewrite the dialogues according to his ideas and the exigencies of the location and situation. During the shooting, the film, which at first was more or less faithful to Gruault's . . . truly 'living' work, was modified. RR and I had found an idea—and we know how important it was for RR to have one idea, one rule, per film—and this idea of Louis XIV's was the *domestication* of the chaotic force of the *Frondeurs*, who always had their boots on ready to jump on their horses and escape the king's control, domestication by a sort of mummification under the weight and cost of court costume. Obviously this was not in the scenario and if the beginning of the scenario, notably all the very beautiful scenes around Mazarin's death, was Gruault's, its continuation was modified to express the idea that excited RR! So I lived more or less at Brissac [where we were shooting] and Roberto would indicate the sequences to me the evening before they were shot the next day, and I would write dialogue for them, knowing the actual places and decors."[13]

Before committing a scene to paper, Roberto needed to be on the set in contact with the actors and to find the rhythm. He used Gruault's dialogue until Mazarin's death, then, keeping Gruault away, more or less invented the rest of the picture, with La Rochefoucauld writing lines as needed. The scene of a mannequin being dressed in the king's new costume was Rossellini's addition, as was the scene of Fouquet's arrest, viewed from the king's second-story window. A recreation of the infamously elaborate fireworks party at Fouquet's chateau, Vaux-le-Vicomte, was, when Roberto ran out of money, replaced with an intimate card game that is one of the high points of French cinema.

Roberto's immediate problem, the first day, was the French crew. They had never imagined his bizarre shooting methods, which had gone out of style with Lumière in the 1890s; they objected to working in spaces so small that cross-cutting would be impossible, and then grumbled and argued at Roberto's long takes and remote-controlled zoom. Roberto wrote directly to Contamine. "I agreed to make a rich and very spectacular film within the budget of ninety million old francs [$180,000] that you allotted me. I want to show, contrary to cinema's bad habits, that it is possible to do so. Unfortunately I am finding the same phony complications and ridiculous defiance at any demystification of the mythology surrounding photography. In reality, making this film with so little money will require a great deal of ingenuity, ruse, and skill, but this is provoking great disorder among various collaborators, for example if I refuse to move the camera more than is needed, or something else equally grotesque, they have the impudence to say behind my back that I'm going to rush through the film with a few zoom shots."[14]

Roberto was upheld and the crew soon admired how he never hesitated on where to place the camera. For his part, Roberto, after initial objections, accepted Claude Leclerc's way of shooting color as though it were black and white, which was contrary to the Italian style at the moment but which within a few years became an industry standard in Europe. The ghostly light of Mazarin's death scene was Leclerc's idea. For almost the first, and certainly the last, time in his life Rossellini was filming with direct sound—and it is wonderful for once to hear actors throw out their lines with abandon, like the sinuous Fouquet or the courtier who yells, "Le Roi!"—a remarkable sound—whenever the king appears. The crew was one of the most efficient he had ever had. The "mirror" shot, the superimpressions of the Louvre on the Seine at the beginning (it covers up a big electric power plant), is spectacularly more successful than the cruder examples in successive films.

Roberto ate hard-boiled eggs and strong espresso during the shooting, and took delight in displaying card tricks. The Mazarin, Giulio Cesare Silvani, superstitious about playing a dying man, kept a radish in his hand underneath the sheets for good luck.

That first night at a restaurant Roberto sniffed his nose drops and ate little. For one thing he was in France, where there was nothing worth eating; more critically he was "plunged into anxiety" over Ferrari doing badly at Le Mans. At 10:30 he grabbed Gruault and some of the crew into several cars and drove sixty miles to Le Mans. The Fords were winning, the Ferrari was sick, Roberto had tears on his cheeks. "We go back!" he grumbled after fifteen minutes.[15]

He refused to discuss their characters with the actors. "No! No! Why does [the player] have to be involved, poor thing? If he gets involved he suffers all the time. He must not be involved *at all*. He has only to be capable enough to attract out attention."[16] Katharina Renn, Louis's mother, tried and tried to discuss and got nowhere and was furious; Jean-Marie Patte never even tried, he just did it, and after a while Roberto accepted his idiosyncrasies. "If you want to work with non-actors, you have to invent what a non-actor can give you. What he can give you is physical presence, and certain kinds of movement. No more than that, than he is used to doing. If you study him a little, and you give him the occasion to do those kinds of things, he becomes a very good actor. Otherwise no. Even just putting his finger in his nose. Any sort of thing, but *his own* way of doing it. . . . If you use his attitude in a contrary situation for that attitude, that attitude immediately becomes dramatic. If you use his way of being so immobile, and you make him a character who is tremendously violent, you have a character. Many qualities must be played in contrast. . . . Dramaturgy is the ways of finding conflicts. . . . To get realism you need tricks. Otherwise you will never get the reality. Feeling and acting are never *real*, if you depend on them it's impossible to get the real thing. If you have somebody facing the camera and he has to appear moved, that's difficult. But if he's turned slightly away from the camera, and lowers his eyes a little and turns, it's a great emotion. Only that great emotion is nothing at all. [Perhaps I need an emotion from a character,] but I don't need *his* emotion. I can build an emotion. If you have someone move or talk very slowly, and then suddenly accelerate, you have emotion. It's mathematical. Change of rhythm: immediately you have an emotion."[17]

Patte was painfully timid, had terrible stage fright, and could not remember a single line. "Stay the way you are. I'll use your timidity," Roberto told him.[18] Patte's fright became Louis's motivation for taking power. Patte's inability to remember became the majesty of a king who searches for words and rarely looks at people—because Patte's eyes were busy elsewhere, reading dialogue from a blackboard. "Physically he was exactly the type of man I needed," Roberto said: short and stocky. "Physical appearance is always greatly tied to psychology. No doubt. It is a rough estimation, but he is *that*. Because he was so stiff, he seemed very strong and to have a great will. . . . In front of the camera he was trembling and unable to move. So [eventually] I realized I had to play everything on the man's stiffness, no? I made him even more stiff! If you put the blackboard at the right distance, his eyes [wouldn't] move at all. . . . He was so ashamed that for him it was absolutely impossible to walk straight. He was always walking [without] putting his heels on the floor. Just for a joke I left in a few frames of that. . . . If you use that awkwardness properly, it will come out as a character. . . . Remember when he cries [during a scene with his mother]? [He was] lying all the time to his mother pretending to cry. Then he goes to the stairway and begins to go down it like a kid [skipping] just for a second."[19]

Thus in retrospect Roberto could describe his intentions in *La Prise de pouvoir par Louis XIV* ("The taking of power by Louis XIV")[20] as an effort "to show the human sides of a king, even if he's the 'Sun,' the timidity underneath the pride, the weakness under the apparent strength.[21] . . . The important thing is to discover people as they are. It's the most moving thing in the world. . . . If we look at a human being, what do we have? His intelligence, his desire to take action, and then his immense weaknesses, his poverty. Ultimately things become grandiose because of this. I was terribly impressed, very young, when I heard that Napoleon at the siege of Toulon was shaking with fear, like a leaf. An officer near him said, 'But you're shaking with fear!' And Napoleon answered, 'If you were as scared as I am, you'd have run away.' It's this double nature that touches me in people. This wide, wide gap. He's small, lost, an idiot, naive. And he does great things."[22]

Louis XIV, indeed, is closer to a horror film than a history lesson. Fear dominates everyone during the whole first half, fear of the turmoil that will follow Mazarin's death, fear the *Fronde* rebellion will rise again. Colbert is genuinely terrified; Louis paces nervously, constantly charging into the focal point of compositions. "Je crains . . . je crains . . . je crains" is his refrain—"I'm afraid." He stares downcast; we can't see his eyes. He inspires confidence in no one. Everything is dark and claustrophobic. Then the sun rises and space opens up, as in *Viva l'Italia*. "You always have to try to emphasize the emotion," said Rossellini, "because it's a question of a human enterprise."[23]

Colbert, on the morning of Mazarin's death, outlines an ambitious program of public works, financial reform, and national development. "His dull, monotonous voice, [his airing of] ideas that are [apparently] the result of long consideration, and his quiet, thoughtful delivery form an outstandingly accurate psychological portrait," observes Guarner; "[Rossellini intends] to bring out the flat tone of everyday conversations between ordinary men, not actors making music with words."[24]

But with Louis the situation is quite different. Someone shouts "Le roi!" whenever he shows his head. So in response to Colbert's weighty suggestions he replies: "I'll do that and as soon as I get back to the Louvre, I want you to be sure to summon my tailor. Don't forget this. It's of the highest importance." Unlike Colbert, Louis realizes "men are ruled by appearances, not by the true nature of things."

Horror yields to comic satire. The costumes are absurd. Louis makes everyone jealous by inviting one courtier to watch him feed his dogs. "When you're dealing with sons of bitches you want to be a little bit more of a son of a bitch than the others. It's absolutely instinctive and natural," Roberto argued.[25] "[Louis] uses the superficiality, coquetry and vanity of the people, nothing else. And vanity is something that exists and is very solid."[26]

Louis XIV initiates totalitarianism via consumerism. "I think if man has one capability, it's this: discovering morality. . . . The sole faculty belonging to man, and to him alone, is judgment. . . . Man must dominate his civilization or change it.[27] *Louis* describes the technique of taking power, which is a useful thing to know.[28] For Louis XIV [making people feel they had to dress that way] became a psychological and political action; thus we're dealing with an absolutely empirical understanding of people. . . . That he managed to enfeeble the *Fronde* by creating Versailles, wigs, and so on, is rather curious. And something else that's curious is how all this was carried out within a specific economic development, at the beginning of a specific sort of . . . mass production."[29]

*

"[Louis] lives in representation," Rossellini said. "He lives for other people, but also to climb on their heads. Until that last scene where he asks to be alone and gets rid of his costume. There he redeems himself. His conquests have made him bitter. He speaks of the sun and of death, which one cannot look at. It's doubt. Louis XIV becomes human again . . . , he stops the big masquerade the others have played following him, from stupidity. . . . What I love in this character is his absolute audacity: the scene with the tailor, for example. He's even insolent. But at the same time you feel his terrible timidity."[30]

The heroes who die at the ends of *Roma città aperta, Paisà,* and *Deutschland im Jahre Null* lose themselves as they enter history, as their films' titles imply: like the partisans' bodies sinking into the Po at dawn, they subsume themselves into the collective and its history, accept their role as sacrificial lambs, as Christs, and acquire a mythic dimension. Bergman's heroines in *Stromboli, Europe '51,* and *Voyage in Italy* mature similarly, as does the worker in *India* who admires the dike he has helped build, or Della Rovere who chooses death in order to become history.

Louis's death is his transformation of himself into the Sun King; neither death nor the sun can be stared at, he explains, and we understand that death and the sun are good places to hide, that Louis has invented the apparatus of the monarchy and the totalitarian state in order that people not see him. All alone, at the end, he reads François de La Rochefoucauld's maxim: "There is a loftiness that does not depend on fortune. It is a certain air of superiority that seems to destine one for great things. . . . This quality enables us to usurp other men's deference and places us further above them than birth, rank, and merit itself. Neither death nor the sun can be gazed at fixedly."[31]

In the scene just before this, the king walks in the garden attended by the court *en masse*—"lugubrious and deathly, like a harvest of dead spirits in the Elysian Fields"[32]—and we realize that Louis has ensnared his court in a "collective suicide,"[33] that he has "turned a meal into a baroque funeral mass,"[34] and that the Revolution will surely come, bringing more death. Closeted all alone, he contemplates his self-imposed mummification. Now the death of Mazarin, protracted over the film's first thirty minutes, is mirrored by a more general death, an involution into a void, protracted over the film's final thirty minutes. Rossellini's camera has never been so intrusive, even in *Una voce umana.* He shows the myth, as well as the reality behind the myth, like Ford in *Fort Apache* or *The Man Who Shot Liberty Valance.* "Looking critically"—one of Roberto's definitions of neo-realism[35]—posits the camera as a tool of inquiry. Rossellini never spoke of the camera as Bazin did, as a means of recording; for Rossellini it was a "microscope,"[36] "an instrument of torture,"[37] an aggressive rather than passive instrument. No filmmaker ever used it as he did. He does not "present." He does not allow events to speak for themselves. Instead he perpetually attacks them, moving in and out, trying to get closer to this or that. Ophuls is always moving, too; but Ophuls's motions "present" his events and become in turn the rhythms of the movie and its characters' lives. Rossellini's camera, in contrast, does not comment or analyze; indeed it seldom expresses, narrates, or even follows an event. Instead, it inquires; instead, it perpetually intrudes *into* an event.

A good Crocean, Rossellini's camera inquires with a purpose: "critical" does not mean "detached." History is the story of liberty emerging—or, as here, of one of those "moments when slavery is winning."[38]

Thus it is incorrect to define "historical neo-realism," as *Cahiers* did, quoting Michelet: "a search for a quite uncertain contemporaneity, for an impossible integral resurrection of the human past."[39] Rossellini's ambitions were not so presumptuous. "I have drawn up a plan that closely follows my own study program.[40] I try to reconstruct the emotion that I had while learning the thing.[41] I shoot films in order to try to understand."[42]

While shooting the royal fox hunt, Roberto had to go to Florence for Isabella's spinal operation on July 3. He left it for his son Renzino to finish the fox hunt and to direct the banquet scene in a chateau at Maisons-Lafitte. For the banquet, Renzino used a crane, a device Roberto regarded as vulgar and stupid. During the hunt, Renzino neglected to keep Louis on the same horse, so that from one shot to the next the king appears on three different horses, one of them white. "Don't worry," Roberto told him, "just turn up the sound a bit, no one will notice."[43] And no one does.

Roberto instructed Renzino, "Louis is as I want him, a bit lost. Don't tell him anything! Only tell him the big actions." (Patte didn't even know who the other characters were.[44]) But Patte's characterization of Louis does change under Renzino's direction. On the horse he is relaxed and smiling; while eating he is regal and self-assured. He's not at all a bit lost.

Louis XIV was shot in 28 days, five hours a day. The long "sequence shots" were already edited, in effect, and Roberto ate foie gras (duck) while putting them together. He had decided montage was not "moral" and rhymed it with *tripatouillage*—tinkering or faking.[45] Nonetheless, some sequences are brilliantly cut, the card game particularly. A few years later he said, "The image must mutate constantly; you can't stay with one image more than four or five seconds. This raises interest and involves you in the film. Try an exercise like that. You have to invent *something* every five seconds. That is the whole secret."[46]

"I was on the Venice committee in 1966," said Tullio Kezich, "and [Luigi] Chiarini told me, 'Rossellini keeps calling me from Paris saying he's made a film for French television. I'm afraid it's some awful thing but I can't dismiss it out of hand.'" So Kezich went to Paris, taking a colleague along so he wouldn't have to assume sole responsibility for a negative judgment. "I must admit we approached Roberto with great skepticism, because conventional wisdom had conditioned us to see him as a man who was finished. . . . He was waiting for us and we went right into the screening room and there, after ten minutes, Cavallaro and I were really open-mouthed, excited, because on the screen was *La Prise de pouvoir*. Afterward we went to a brasserie and Roberto was a stupendous spectacle because it was as if moment by moment he were resurrecting; you could see it in his eyes, his behavior, his speech. And it was equally wonderful for us to go back to Venice and tell Chiarini, who was staring at us as though we had gone insane, 'Show it closing night, in the main hall, it's something really extraordinary!' And in fact it was an enormous success."[47]

Louis XIV played at Venice, out of competition, on September 10, 1966, just after the awards ceremony. To show a *television* film on such an occasion was unprecedented. But even Casiraghi, one of Rossellini's bitterest critics, was ecstatic over *Louis*'s "elegance and original perspective" and "the recuperation *in extremis* of an artist like Rossellini, who demonstrates that cinema is not dead, despite his pessimism."[48] "*Louis XIV* has made us hear again the voice of a master," agreed *La Stampa*.[49] *Corriere della Sera* praised the film's "humour" (in English) and the density of character of Patte's Louis "in defiance of all the facile canons of expressive acting."[50]

Philippe Erlanger marveled, "Everything that's in the movie is in my book, nevertheless seeing it was fascinating. Everything was completely correct and yet there wasn't a thing that I recognized. I was discovering a whole new world."[51]

Moravia philosophized, "It is a history film because in it one can recognize a certain conception of history . . . , history as ceremony and ritual. . . . Mircea Eliade in his book *Images and Symbols* makes a distinction between so-called historical time, linked to human action, and . . . cosmic time, linked to cosmic cycles. The first is the irreality of daily life; the second the reality of eternity. To make the irreal real . . . man has only one means: to ritualize daily life. Ritual . . . suspends history; daily life, immersed in ritual, becomes symbolic and atemporal. In Rossellini's film, Louis XIV's advent to power is the advent of life as ceremony. Everything is ceremony in this film: Mazarin's death, the king's morning toilette, the council, the meals, the kitchen, games, hunting, love, even Fouquet's arrest."[52]

In France, *Louis XIV* was aired Saturday, October 8, 1966, and attracted an audience of twenty million—more than a third of the entire population; color broadcasting had just begun. "Chamber pots are in their place under the beds. No one washes. The doctors sniff the perspiration of the sick. People eat with their fingers. They don't change shirts to sleep, etc. . . . One has the impression of watching a live news report about some primitive tribe with backward mores and barbaric luxury," wrote Jean Cotte.[53] "Its purpose is to show the birth of a certain number of 'mythologies,'" said Fieschi in *Cahiers du Cinéma*.[54]

A month later *Louis* opened theatrically in a Paris art house, La Pagode, played seven weeks, then eight more weeks in two other theaters, with 35,590 admissions. This was remarkable, coming after the television broadcast. (Given the bias against television and the lack of critical discussion of its programs—still with us today—even two days' theatrical run was, and is, considered more important than twenty million television viewers.)

Roberto regaled one interviewer with anecdotes about ancient Babylon, Athens in Socrates's time, and Holland in Descartes's time—all for films he was going to make.

"It's all in books. But not in films. And it's so interesting, so passionate, that I no longer desire to shoot films that show anything else. For me, henceforth, cinema means showing this.

"I've always been a voracious reader. I don't sleep much at night. I read in bed, always a number of books at the same time, often six or seven. I find it tiring to concentrate on a single book, to wait for the end. I buy books wherever I find them. When I come to Paris . . . , The Raphael doormen always see me arriving empty handed and leaving dragging cartons of books behind me. At Rome I have thousands of them. I had to fix up a garage to store all the ones I've 'used-up'—so to speak. I buy at hazard, I go in all the bookstores. I page. I buy books in blocks.

"While reading I have the courage to note on the books' margin the ideas that come to me. Later, before shelving the books, I make up some bibliographic cards.[55] I make signs with different colors so I know what's most important, less important, what's complementary, what's basic, et cetera. And I also write down the thoughts that come to me, impressions absolutely virgin. I reread my notes on the book's pages and I write them down in notebooks under headings divided by letters A, B, C, D. Then I write 'human,' 'education,' 'thievery,' et cetera.[56] These cards, later on when I need them, will permit me to reconstruct a certain type of person. For example, one that I might pick for a sequence in *La lotta dell'uomo per la sua sopravvivenza*. In one sequence I want to show how the first king's scepter was born. It's just the stick with which prehistoric people used to search for food under rotten leaves and which, in the course of the ages, became a symbol of supremacy.

"Most often it's the books about nothing at all that are the key books for me, the ones that provoke my liveliest reactions.

"Among these recently was a book on the history of teaching written by a Jesuit, and *Introduction à l'histoire des monnaies* ("Introduction to the History of Moneys"), by René Sédillot. The effort of classification that the author of this apparently insignificant book makes fantastically excited me. The ideas he gave me have been fundamental for the direction of my research."[57]

A New Cinematic Language

Acts of the Apostles

Meanwhile, Jean Riboud and John de Menil had been soliciting money for "Rossellini's film on food." Eventually Gulf, IBM, UpJohn, and General Electric joined Schlumberger in pledging $100,000 each. In December 1966, however, GE "chickened out," in de Menil's words, and when neither Michelin, General Motors, National City Bank, nor Singer, among others, was willing to fill the gap, Schlumberger doubled its share, plus an additional 29,060 francs to have a one-hour version of *The Iron Age* dubbed into French. By the time Roberto began shooting, a few months later, Italy (RAI), France (ORTF), Egypt (Corpo Film), and Romania (Romania Film) had joined the co-production and Riboud still hoped to enlist Venezuela (the Ministry of Economic Affairs).[1] The final cost would be $1,280,000.

Schlumberger's sponsorship was opening many doors for Roberto. The success of *La Prise de pouvoir par Louis XIV* was even more helpful. RAI's director general Ettore Bernabei had already supported *L'età del ferro*. Now two program directors, Beretta and Gennarini, were inaugurating a policy of joint production with filmmakers. They solicited famous directors like Fellini, Bertolucci, and Rosi, and first of all Rossellini, because Rossellini had made *Louis XIV* for French television. RAI's Christian Democrats wanted Catholic Italy to better Gaullist France. They proposed Roberto film the *Acts of the Apostles*. They agreed to support the "film on food," which had metamorphosed into *La lotta dell'uomo per la sua sopravvivenza* ("Man's struggle for his survival.") They even, at Roberto's insistence, agreed to pay him a patent royalty when he used his zoom lens in the films he would make for them. Heroic sanctity was paying off.

Roberto and Renzino began *La lotta dell'uomo per la sua sopravvivenza* or *Battle for Survival* (as Roberto was now calling it) in 1967, paused in the summer of 1968 to make *Acts of the Apostles* and a documentary about Sicily, then returned to *Survival* (as it was ultimately titled in English). NBC Television, less wary than the Canadians, had agreed in July 1966 to finance *The Sicily of Roberto Rossellini* and to pay Roberto $25,000 to direct. "Never in the history of television has any director received more than

$15,000 for any program, not even spectaculars," his agent bragged. But although Roberto may have signed the U.S. edition, Renzino is solely credited in the Italian edition, and nothing in this thoroughly uninspired, superficial film suggests Roberto's participation. Aside from its exploitation of the zoom lens, there is little of even casual interest. Baldelli properly rejects it as a "collection of tourist images."[2]

All the while the man who a few years before had rarely bothered even to open his mail was writing letters by the hundreds; and the man who had thought himself a heroic adventurer when he left Italy for France, then again for America, then again for India, was bouncing between South America, New York, and all over Europe, tirelessly repeating the same message in interviews, meetings, assemblies, lunches, and dinners, seeking to involve himself in the affairs of people who would, in turn, assist his Great Plan. He was a missionary come back from his explorations and determined to save the world; he was a denizen of Socrates's cave who had climbed to the light and come back to tell his fellows. Thus, for example, we find him in Santiago, with his son Renzino and Vittorio di Girolamo Carlini, laying plans for a government-financed film school where Chilean filmmakers would be liberated from Hollywood methods—and would help make "The History of Human Feeding."[3] Or flying to Pittsburgh, quiet and docile, in John de Menil's corporate jet to talk to Gulf Oil directors. Or spending a Sunday afternoon with Jonas Mekas at the Film-Maker's Cinematheque in New York, looking at selected works of the American Underground, getting excited over Stan Brakhage's *Window Water Baby Moving*, and declaring that he and Brakhage were after the same thing: down-to-earth truths of life.[4]

"The cinema of the neo-realist period was a cinema that denounced," Roberto told the press. "At that time we needed to find ourselves and diagnose our social and political ills. Now that diagnosis should be followed by therapy. Otherwise it all becomes a sterile game.[5] I found a letter by Turgot that says: in order really to reconstruct the world it's necessary to revise the basis of education, which is too aimed at inculcating ready-made truths instead of giving everyone the means of discovering these truths.[6] Henceforth the sole means to put intellectual and human progress at the level of technical progress, is to know, to be aware, to understand. And the quickest method, the most immediate and accessible today, is the image. . . . I'm beginning work on a history of the struggle man made to survive, a history of his fight against death.[7] The running thread is the reconstruction of daily life.[8] We rebuilt hundreds of old machines ourselves. We looked at the original designs in the Vatican, which has records for everything, and learned how to make the machines work, and the incredible gadgets for making gunpowder—every step is exciting.[9] Progress is an exalting liberation! If an artist isn't excited by such themes, what does excite him? His own life? His moral or psychic sickness? What he or his wife dreamed last night?"[10]

Most of *Survival* would be directed by Renzino in Romania. Roberto himself directed scenes of the cavemen, a chase, and Etruscan matriarchal society; and some of the Egyptian ceremonials and interior speeches; Renzino did the harvest and some exteriors.

As in *Paisà* and *India*, Roberto wanted anecdotes that would sum up contemporary mind sets. "The pharaoh was god," he said, citing one example, "and in an old document I found the speech of the overseer of a gold mine in the desert, calling on the pharaoh to play god and do a miracle, because everybody there was dying, because they had no water. It's a long, tremendously long prayer, because he's praying to god and has to convince god to do a miracle. The pharaoh answered: 'For all natural events the merit or fault is mine. Take ten thousand people and dig a canal from the Nile to there.'"[11]

In the same vein, some troubadours encounter a group of people leading a man with his hands in chains, a bandit purchased from a neighboring village. "Why? Because in the other village they get a lot of bandits, and they put four horses to the two arms and two legs and stretch them in the public square. But these people have never had a chance to capture a bandit, so they go [to the other village] and buy a bandit, because they want to have a big show at home. I found this in the Vatican Library, an absolutely extraordinary document, because it's a theological discussion between the bandit, the people who are buying the bandit, and the troubadours. The bandit complains, 'Well, you know, I have all the disadvantages, because in the other village they're used to doing this sort of thing to bandits, and they allow them to confess and lately they even allow them to receive the sacrament. Look how unfortunate I am, they don't want to give me confession or the sacrament.' And the villagers say, 'Yes, of course. He's a bandit. If we give him the sacraments, immediately after that he's saved, but he's a bandit and must be eternally condemned.' And there's a long discussion about this kind of thing. What's more revealing? The structure of thought is revealed by dialogue.[12]

Roberto's love for sardonic cameos like these is a constant in his work. Auriol had remarked how in *Paisà*'s "Florence" sequence the two English officers "are painted as by a novelist, not photographed as by a reporter."[13] What fascinated Roberto about history was the richness of its anecdotes; anecdotes were the basis of his dramaturgy. He was like Giotto or Uccello or a *macchiaiolo*, fascinated by the image that would contain the anecdote. Like them he wove many anecdotes into series of illustrative frescoes, but in a single film. Like them, by looking at the past, he constructed a portrait of his own time.

Other episodes show fertility rites, early behavior toward sickness and death; attempts to preserve life through images and pyramids. The wonder of bread making. How candles replaced dried birds or fish for light. Lords and vassals have legalistic disputes. Wandering troubadours poeticize love and spread information. A thirteenth-century university lecturer proclaims that "mystery is failing to know." Shoeing an ox, building a chariot, waterproofing fabrics, constructing windmills, the first trains, space travel. The development of paper and of printing. Columbus's attempts to find backing; attempts to calculate the earth's circumference. Rossellini makes the distinction—very significant for him, since this is a film celebrating the *conquest* of nature—that for the pagans nature was godly and untouchable, whereas for the Jews and Christians nature was a gift of God for us to use.[14]

Survival marked a change in the music in Rossellini's films. Renzo, who had written the scores for virtually all his brother's pictures since *La nave bianca*, had wearied of the frustrating task. Due to his new duties as music director at Monte Carlo, he had less time and less financial need. Moreover, despite Roberto's efforts to impose Renzo on his television films, his French co-producers thought his music too sentimental.[15]

Renzo Junior introduced his father to Mario Nascimbene. Roberto told Nascimbene he disliked orchestral music, had decided Renzo's music was too conventional, and wanted a different sound for his television films—his new cinema.

Nascimbene's first move was to ask Renzo Senior to lunch, and ask for his permission. "I agree completely," said Renzo, "because it's Roberto's desire."[16]

Nascimbene understood Roberto's desire. He thought Renzo's music belonged to the romantic and veristic traditions of the nineteenth century, and that Renzo lacked an internal need "to inaugurate a new musical language in parallel with his brother's new film language." (As music critic for *Il Messaggero*, Renzo had "vigorously opposed innovation," according to *The New Grove Dictionary of Music and Musicians*.) In contrast, at the center of Nascimbene's craft was an electronic synthesizer, which he called Mixerama. "We would do the music while watching the scene on the screen, and Roberto loved the immediate results," Nascimbene said. Roberto would come sometimes for a day or more with his dog Baruff, who would never leave him (he would sleep on Roberto's bed and change sides whenever Roberto turned over). For the final episode of *Survival*, Nascimbene recorded a black singer, Shirley Bassey, singing "The Fight for Survival" aggressively against violent percussion. Roberto hugged him when he heard it. But almost always he left musical matters totally in Nascimbene's hands. He wasn't interested in the music, Nascimbene concluded. "You're right," Renzo said; " Roberto doesn't like to work, he'll trust you one hundred percent."[17]

Survival's Egyptian sequences were shot in Egypt, where Corpo Film was a co-producer and Roberto's contact was Nasser's cultural minister, a friend of Fulchignoni's at UNESCO. Officially Roberto was to advise the national cinema and *Survival* was to show Egypt's gradual transformation through the millennia.

One morning Renzo junior was shaving in the Seramis Hotel, fifty miles south of Cairo in the desert. Bombs started exploding. Out the window he saw Israeli planes soaring in from the west, twenty feet above the ground, launching rockets at a hill 500 yards away. From a window above, Roberto looked out in surprise. Down the street the Hilton had been bombed. Tardily the sirens sounded. Roberto had been making light of the marching soldiers and military roadblocks for days; now he dismissed the latest ruckus. "Two hours and it'll be over!" All the same he had sent Marcellina back to Rome by plane the day before.

It was June 5, 1967, the six-day war had begun. Roberto, Sonali, Renzino, and a five-man crew spent the next week in the hotel. Every day the radio told them Egypt was winning. Outside, traffic accidents to military convoys gave evidence of Egypt's lack of military capacity. Eventually the Italian embassy organized a caravan to Alexandria; Mario Fioretti wept at having to leave his camera behind. They drove past bombed villages, burnt vehicles, massacred bodies. Crowds were fighting to board the *Esperia*, a 1900 Liberty ship which the Italian government had sent, and which Fellini later used for *E la nave va* (1983). Roberto got a first-class cabin which they shared in shifts. Back in Rome, some of the crew got no pay; Roberto deducted the cost of their boat tickets and refused pay for the week they'd been stuck in Egypt.[18]

Bernardo Bertolucci said, "I remember one day Henri Langlois explained to me that the screen at his Cinémathèque was so big, from the floor to the ceiling, precisely because of the films of Rossellini and Renoir. Because, said Langlois, 'the frames of their films might all of a sudden expand, going up, down, right and left.' "[19]

But in 1968 Langlois and Mary Meerson were under attack for their haphazard ways. Prints were stored all over the country, in cellars and barns, in courtyards in the rain; accidents and fires were frequent, and no one but Langlois could find anything. On February 9, 1968, Langlois and Meerson found themselves abruptly on the sidewalk. The locks on their office doors were changed. André Malraux, De Gaulle's Minister of Culture, had put Pierre Barbin in charge of the Cinémathèque.

The newspapers, right or left, took Langlois's side. Rossellini, Gance, Truffaut, Resnais, Franju, Godard, Marker, Astruc, Chabrol, Bresson, Renoir, Rohmer, Rouch, and fifty other filmmakers forbade showings of their pictures at the Cinémathèque. In response to cables sent all over the world from the offices of *Cahiers du Cinéma*, foreign filmmakers joined the boycott. Barbin then fired forty employees and closed the Cinémathèque "for reorganization." Roberto, in Rome, phoned everyone constantly, urging them on. On February 14, 3,000 protesters were surrounded by police cars, and the police charged. In the mêlée, Truffaut and Godard were slightly injured, and Bertrand Tavernier's face was covered with blood. Godard, who'd lost his glasses, ordered a dispersal. Jean Riboud, obsessed, canceled all other business. He incited the troops to "push and push" while "at the same time . . . saying to Malraux, 'Well, we're perfectly willing to negotiate.' "[20] Riboud, like everyone else, was aware of Langlois's failings, but saw his dismissal as an attempt by the conservative government to rule France's cultural life. On March 6, Malraux conceded defeat after S. Frederick Gronich, representing the American film industry, told him that there would be no more deposits of U.S. films and that those already in the Cinémathèque might be withdrawn.[21]

The year 1968 saw protests by students in Italy, France, West Germany, the United States, Japan, Mexico, and South Korea. Roberto greeted their revolts with open arms as "a fact that responds to an absolute logic."[22] His hatred of America had turned to love and admiration during the civil rights movement; as the alternate-culture movements began, he grew awestruck. "The youth of America were born into a pragmatic world and therefore into a place where the goal of life is to take as much as possible, where there has been no class struggle, where someone from a lower class is permitted to rise into a higher one, where belonging to the upper class means having money and it is money that buys power. And yet it came about, and I saw this happen in 1967, that they took poverty as their ideal. All the hippie movements . . . have the same staggering significance of a rejection of wealth. It's a very positive sign, a return to the moral ideals which have basically always ruled the world. . . . I think that today we stand on the threshold of a marvelous epoch."[23] When students occupied the University of Rome, Roberto published a long piece in *Paese Sera* defending them.[24]

His own son Renzino was among the protestors. Thus, when the first demonstrations started in Paris, Roberto suggested he come there, and watched vicariously as Renzino joined students occupying the Sorbonne.

The police stormed the Sorbonne in June. Renzino was caught in the action. "Papa spent the whole night—a tragic night because it ended so many dreams—in his room beside a small transistor radio. Around seven in the morning the police opened the siege and allowed students to leave, and I went straight to him. He was awake, sitting on his bed, very worried, he hadn't closed his eyes. I burst out crying and he put his arms around me, overwhelmed."[25]

De Gaulle's government nearly fell. In West Germany, students forced a reform law that gave them direct participation in academic governance. In Mexico City, a student strike was suppressed and dozens killed. In Czechoslovakia, Dubček's "Prague spring" ended in August with an invasion by Russian tanks. In America, Martin Luther King, Jr. was assassinated.

Two years later, Roberto reflected, "I never felt more emotion in my life than I did during the confrontations in Paris. But then it was all over after a few days."[26]

In Rome, the Centro Sperimentale di Cinematografia had also been occupied. Whereupon a new minister, Achille Corona, had an inspiration. In January 1969 he nominated Roberto Rossellini president of the school, with Fernaldo Di Giammatteo and Floris Luigi Ammannati as vice-presidents.

*

Such was the climate when Rossellini made *Acts of the Apostles*, as his collaborator Luciano Scaffa points out. "It was a time 'of great confusion,' Rossellini believed; a time in which he thought he could read the signs of the sunset of one epoch and the announcement of a new age. It was 1968. Rossellini worked on *Acts of the Apostles* in a state of extreme curiosity. He was researching the chronicle of a passionate adventure: the announcement of the Christian alternative world."[27]

Roberto intended *Acts of the Apostles* as his contribution to the revolution. "It's not a question of fanning fire, but, if there is a fire, of merely making sure that it doesn't get smothered or extinguished by ashes of hypocrisy. . . . Global opposition to the establishment was invented 2,000 years ago, and it was spread all over the world by a handful of unarmed people, often ignorant and dressed in rags. Twelve men toppled an empire: the twelve apostles. . . . Still today the seeds sown by the apostles are bearing fruit."[28]

Luciano Scaffa was a Sicilian Catholic charged with cultural and historical projects at RAI. He would be Roberto's principal collaborator there, and co-scenarist for *Acts, Pascal, Agostino, The Age of the Medici, Cartesius,* and *Anno uno.* "It should be realised," commented Jean Dominique de La Rochefoucauld, "that Scaffa, a RAI employee representing the Christian Democrats in management circles, was among those in whom the Vatican had confidence. RR was also Christian Democratic, on the left of course and an admirer of La Pira, the [progressive] mayor of Florence, yet still Christian Democratic. Scaffa was thus [Rossellini's] 'man' at RAI, attending to his projects in the corridors of the Roman bureaucracy (!)."[29]

When the screenplay for *Acts* was presented, Gennarini called Scaffa into his office to complain. He said it was too close to 1968 in feeling. Which was not surprising. The words spoken came mostly from Luke and the Epistles; but the dramatization had been the work of La Rochefoucauld who at the time, in Gruault's affectionate phrase, was "a bit Maoist (the way his ancestor had been *Frondeur*) but without therefore denying the (blue) bloodline that connected him to the *Grand Roi* and the *Grand Siècle.*"[30]

"I don't know if it was influenced by May '68," La Rochefoucauld said. "Perhaps. In any case I worked alone, aside from some conversations with RR. It was basically an assemblage of scenes faithful to Saint Paul's voyages. . . . I don't know what happened in Rome after I sent off the treatment. But RR had me come to Tunisia, to Sousse, and there I discovered a new treatment, rather different, on which [Vittorio] Bonicelli had worked, principally—a charming and intelligent man, but also a RAI employee. My task was then to dialogue the scenes, relying on the knowledge I had of the subject. I had just been very sick—cancer—and was not in the best frame. Nonetheless the text spoken by the actors—Saint Paul and the others—is by me. RR would read the dialogue before shooting, correct this or that, just a few things, and act generally satisfied."[31]

Rossellini and La Rochefoucauld emphasize the radicalness of *Acts* by underlining its opposition to temples, whether Hebrew or Greek (or Christian—by implication), and to institutions and authority generally. We hear the familiar Rossellini refrain that "the Sabbath was made for man, not man for the Sabbath." But the most radical idea is Roberto's conviction, once again, that "from a very humble position [anyone] can . . . revise the whole conception of the universe."[32]

Were someone today to tell us that God has spoken to him, with an actual voice (the way God does on Rossellini's soundtrack), how many of us would believe him? If he said it with the *physicality* and *insistence* and *single-mindedness* of Rossellini's Paul, how many of us would think him crazy? Great conviction is dismissed in our day as delusion, or resented as intrusive, or feared as the fuel of Hitlers and rock stars. Nonetheless Paul convinced much of the world for two millennia that God spoke to him, and on his conviction Western civilization was refounded. "I try to communicate the immense greatness this man had," Roberto said. "Paul retraces backwards the roads the Roman armies trod, and a religious movement without equal rises up in this unknown traveler's footsteps."[33]

Rossellini presents Paul as Saul, a kind of Nazi leader in the Sanhedrin who is determined to stamp out any talk against the Temple (the theocratic establishment). Bragging, "Of me they can say he . . . preserved the purity of the laws," Saul throws the first stone at Stephen—which is horrifying, because there's no melodrama in Rossellini's depiction of this action, just the matter-of-fact nakedness of Saul's murder of Stephen, a nightmare that calls itself "preserving purity." By zooming from Saul's gaze to Stephen's dead body, Rossellini bonds the two men together, linking them through life and death. But it is Stephen who is alive and Saul who is dead. Stephen's still moist body hangs upside-down from a solitary tree, whose living beauty seems to extend over the arid landscape all around, as the camera-eye zooms out slowly and longly, and we find three of Stephen's friends keeping watch. In contrast, Saul cannot feel Stephen's pain, because he serves "the law." It is not he but the law, he will argue, that stoned Stephen, and moreover the law had no choice, it was "obliged" to kill a human that challenged its supremacy over humans—its right to kill humans. Stephen, indeed has been going around saying precisely the opposite: "The life of a man is worth more than the Sabbath [i.e., the law]." And Stephen had challenged the law's supremacy by carrying bread to the poor. So it is the law that kills Stephen, Saul contends.

But it is not the law; it is Saul.

This same Croce-like conflict can be found in every Rossellini film, most famously in *Roma città aperta*. Human facts versus abstract theories. Laws, texts, institutions, power, murder, death, intolerance, aridity versus love, afflatus, impulse, nature, growth.

The conflict is constant in *Acts*, which is a horror film even more than *Deutschland im Jahre Null* or *Louis XIV* were horror films, but with the difference that *Acts* is even more a textbook for a revolution. The martyr's death is linked with the growth of the tree. The law is made for man, not man for the law.

Yet people's feelings are so enslaved that such a proposition is unthinkable. "From the moment of birth," a Greek slave explains, "man is part of a grand design from which he cannot escape without running the risk of some terrible punishment." Saul and the Temple powers enforce this grand design as acolytes of horror. They convene in stony crypts surrounded by bowls of fire. Amid fantastically alien costumes, beards, chantings, processions, and grim rituals, they exact sacrifice of one victim after another in meaningless bloodletting.

The revolution is to evade such grand designs and their punishments, and to found an alternate identity and community. The difficulty the Christians have in extricating themselves from the grand design is exemplified in their endless debates over whether one can be Christian without being circumcised. They are blind to their own absurdity, like the courtiers in *Louis XIV*, which is what enables the grand design to function in the first place.

What clears vision in Rossellini is not reason but impulse, love, and miracle, the fire within us. *Acts* begins where previous Rossellini films ended. The miracle has already happened. Christianity has already become the law's rival, a revolutionizing impulse for individual autonomy.

Thus the drama in *Acts*—the constant conflict—will be between the freedom the Christians proclaim and the snares, regulations, doctrines, and potentates that assault them at every turn, from within and without, physically and psychologically. There is, for example, a famine, which causes the starving people to attack Herod's grain wagons, which causes Herod's soldiers to massacre the people, which causes James to speak out in protest, which causes Herod, who perceives that James's death will please both the Romans (as a rabble rouser) and the Sanhedrin (as a Christian), to decapitate James. Thus, the Temple's religious power is identified with political power; its interests are linked with those of Herod and the Romans; the object of all three is solely to arrogate power. Naturally Caiaphas, like Saul, feels threatened by John's question, whether John should obey him or God. Anyone who escapes the grand design threatens the law.[34] Inevitably the political problems are psychological; the powerful feel threatened, the disciples fear to renounce circumcision, Paul is dogged by the law.

His travels take him from one legalistic debate to another, with Jews, with Greeks, finally with Romans, from defeat to defeat; in between he works at treading clay, weaving, or some other physical task until, gazing at birds in flight, he understands that law ensnares his body and that his travails are stations of the cross—as so often for Rossellini's heroes. Yet he is victorious in ways no signs indicate. "Jesus spoke to me on the way to Damascus. And in a moment all the force of the law and pride . . . fell from heart." So it is possible in this horror movie for even the most horrible man to change. Once the Temple was everything to Paul; now he declares that

God "does not abide in those temples built by man nor does he need anything that we might be able to make for him. . . . We are his off-spring."

"Paradoxically," Roberto said, "there seems to have been a certain desacralization of God. The God that dominated from above and ruled everything became man, identified with man."[35]

For these Christians, their new community, unlike the Catholicism of Roberto's youth, is not a grand scheme imposed from above, but a choice, an afflatus, an *individual* impulse. Rather than fire and blood, water will unite them, in Baptism and meals. Each of them, Guarner points out, acts on his own initiative, without knowing of his brethren's actions, yet each action becomes an extension of the same idea. When a widow offers Paul money to do good works, he tells her she can do them herself, she doesn't need him. As in *Stromboli*, the stress is on individual responsibility. "Jesus will restore his Father's kingdom," Paul says, "when he has destroyed all authority, all rule, all power."

Acts' opposition to authority, law, and temple in favor of afflatus mirrors Croce's opposition to prose (where intuition is smothered by societal webs of signs) in favor of poetry (expression of an individual's genuine intuition). As Roberto reminded Rouch, the foundation of all poetry is the moral person.

Thus, in *Acts*, "the word . . . the gospel . . . the good news" is not written or even fixed in words; it is poetry. One person walks up to another, tells him Christ has risen, and is believed—without any "authority" other than genuineness. Peter in particular speaks with his entire body, like a trampoline (the actor was a French clown named "Scotch"), and so does Paul, in a different way. The revolution spreads only via one person to another; there is no mass communication, no television, radio, phone, newspaper, or printing. Just one-on-one, always. And on foot. People walk constantly in *Acts of the Apostles*, they have no other way to get from one city to another. And they listen constantly. Rossellini's heroes always listen, even Louis XIV. Listening is a great theme in *Acts*, an earnest of genuineness.

The music, very spare, simple, and elegant—sometimes only a single long-suspended tone—also makes one listen and look. It makes precious the empty time, the frequent moments in *Acts* when nothing is happening and therefore the most is happening. It has the rare musical ability of underlining the openness of space and freedom. It consists mostly of Sonali's humming and Severino Gazzelloni's flute solo, "to emphasize and differentiate the states of mind and psychology of the apostles"[36], to create a melodrama. But the effect is subtle. Occasionally there are Indian instruments: tampura (plucked strings), sitar, shofar (a Hebrew bull's horn), cicale, and the Mixerama.

The fluid pictorial style, with its continuous reframing, is the visual equivalent of the music. The pictures too make us look in. Nascimbene is right to speak of "a new film language," Guarner of a "re-invention of cinema." There is no more "allusion." In this sense *Acts of the Apostles* may

be Rossellini's masterpiece. It puts us into a storyworld like Giotto's—
"myth and reality." There is a similar sense of composition, movement and
color, and directness, but even sparer, and more spacious. Giotto's proto-
cinematic frames make sense only as captured instants of an event in motion. They are never "still photographs" like Vermeer's scenes, they never
have Vermeer's wonderfully *photographic* way of capturing a reality bursting with nuance and richness. Vermeer's scenes are timeless, whereas
Giotto's suggest motion and time, often catching an action that would be
impossible to hold for even an instant in real life. In both of Giotto's Flights
into Egypt, for example, the donkey carrying Mary and Child has both its
fore and hind legs suspended in the descending arc of a step.[37] The donkey's impossible pose solicits our attention in the same way as Nascimbene's music or Rossellini's minimalist compositions: we look in, animate
the characters, and bring them to life.

We must participate actively like this with Rossellini or we shall get
little out of his movies and judge them boring. Those who want to sit back
and *be* entertained or *be* informed invariably dislike these pictures. Those
who look in, who position themselves in a state of active *emotional* receptivity invariably love them. Connecting what's inside the image is Rossellini's
favored method (as he remarked of *India*), so we have to *feel* the things
inside the image: the colors, the donkey's motion, the pots of fire on either
side of Caiaphas, the alternation of desert and water as Philip converts the
fat eunuch.

But when we feel the things inside the image, we are feeling them not
directly but through Rossellini's camera-eye. Rossellini liked to insist that
he did not motivate characters because characters already have their motivations, and that he did not give emotions to things because things already
have their emotion. These movies make a good case for his insistence. Yet
things and characters are not the only "realities" in Rossellini's new realism; another reality is the forming and connecting and visioning of Rossellini's camera-eye. Guarner points out that its constant movement from individual to collective to individual forms a dialectic that shapes Rossellini's
notion of what Christianity is.[38] It is the same movement that Rossellini
made in *Roma città aperta* from the crowd, to Sora Pina's death, to the partisan attack. The difference is that he has found a way to concentrate this
movement into a single shot or composition, rather than having to hop-
scotch it across a succession of shots. This concentration is what Roberto
was already thinking of during the Occupation, when he told De Angelis,
"I need a depth of field that probably only the cinema can provide. I need
to see people and things from every side, and to be able to use cuts and
ellipses, dissolves and inner monologues. I don't mean like Joyce, but like
Dos Passos."[39]

Peter Lloyd describes zooms that go from detail to context. When Matthew is chosen as an apostle to succeed Judas, Rossellini zooms out, enlarging our sphere of vision as physical reality fuses with a higher, spiritual
reality: "This is the stylistic key to the film: the aesthetic is made capable of

sustaining an abstract, almost allegorical burden."[40] And the allegory changes and develops; the "aesthetic" of the zoom can do many things. Lloyd cites Peter's speech at Pentecost, and again after healing the beggar in the Temple, where both times Rossellini's zoom-out expresses the supernatural and places the merely human in perspective; whereas the zoom-in expresses the mortal and immediate. In another scene, the Greek guide is showing the Roman governor where Christ died, whereupon the camera cranes up slightly to isolate the characters in deference to their environment.[41] Like Velázquez, Rossellini is not just painting things, but the spaces between things—the connections.

Curiously, one of *Acts'* best sequences, Philip's baptism of the fat Ethiopian eunuch, justifies Rossellini's life-long contention that it did not require a Roberto Rossellini to make a Rossellini film, because it was directed by Renzino, a sequence of beautifully flowing gestures and colors, and the extremely charismatic acting of Bepy Mannaiuolo (Renzino's brother-in-law).

The point is that, as in *La Prise de pouvoir par Louis XIV*, it is our interest in the characters that makes everything else function; Rossellini's movies are about ideas only secondarily, first of all they are about individuals. The abstractions, colors, motions, and zooms take value only from the characters. (They are there for humans, not humans for them.) Buzzolan said, "If, like a great painter, Rossellini sometimes happens with a shaft of light to reproduce the melancholic splendor of a sky, or with a rapid shot to paint a soul on a face, these are things we shan't forget."[42] In Rossellini's films, said Ayfre, "one feels constantly that someone has tried truly to encounter other beings."[43] Rossellini is a novelist, not just a painter.

"Roberto Rossellini was not a director like others," said La Rochefoucauld. "He created a work (his films) baroque in its treatment of space, avid for truth in the instant, the truth of the emotion felt by him in regard to his characters, through an understanding of their interior that could resemble an identification. His scenarios . . . are not invented stories but recreations of characters with whom he could feel a commonality of desires, sorrows, joys, etc."[44]

The apostle Philip is a curious example of the sort of person one would believe in immediately, at first meeting—because he is a curious individual. The point is the Crocean one that an "idea," like poetry, cannot really exist separated from the individual who has it. Sometimes we think it can, we say an idea has propagated and spread, like "freedom" or "racism." But actually it is something else that spreads, not our original idea but a distortion of it, "prose" put together by a committee whose members are forever changing and growing in number as the idea spreads until, like Roman Catholicism in 1968, it is no longer the same idea, and instead has to be reborn by the original impulse in each individual, a permanent revolution. Thus Paul is more important than his conviction—which is why his conviction can be genuine; his word is poetry, which is why people believe him on his word. Paul is never more moving than in the private messages to friends he inserts at the end of his final dictation, because we know that this poetry has become a text, "Epistle to Timothy," and that these are Paul's last private moments before the coming fadeout seals him into history, the way the dissolves to the Lincoln Memorial seal Lincoln into history at the ends of Griffith's and Ford's films. Says Paul, "As for me . . . as for me, I am ready to give life itself as my offering. It is time now that I should go away. But I've contributed my best and I've kept the faith. I've fought a good fight. Greetings to Aquila and Priscilla, and the household of Onesiphorus. Erasmus has remained in Corinth. Trophimus-Alar was staying in his bed, ill, at Miletus: if it is convenient come here before winter. Let the Lord Jesus and his grace be with you."

Acts of the Apostles was shot in five weeks during the summer of 1968 in Tunisia, in Sousse and Keirouan, where, with some Schüfftan mirror tricks, the Grand Mosque served as the Jewish Temple. For help from on high, Roberto showed a print of *Louis XIV* to Tunisia's President Bourguiba, whose nephew had worked in Italy with Zeffirelli. To control his 34 actors in primary roles, 230 in secondary roles, and hundreds of extras, he used a system of miniature microphones and ear-pieces. There were plagues of sand storms, scorpions, and rattlesnakes, Saint Paul got dysentery, camels ran off into the desert. Roberto wanted to bring a camel home as a pet, but this, like the llama he nearly purchased in South America, was not considered a good idea by Sonali. A further ten-to-twelve days shooting followed in Ostia Antica and around Rome in September. There was no studio work at all. *Acts* was produced by Horizon 2000 for RAI, the French ORTF, the Spanish TVE, and Studio Hamburg. RAI's contribution was 85 million lire ($140,000).

Atti degli apostoli was broadcast (in black and white) in five segments on successive Sunday evenings, beginning Easter, April 6, 1969. A total of 8.6 million people watched it, on average, with an "enjoyment index" of 74 percent.[45] Surprisingly the competing program, *Settevoci*, a popular musical revue, attracted fewer spectators, 6.8 million, and an enjoyment index only slightly higher, 79 percent. In France it was broadcast (in color) and rebroadcast four times.

Yet Rossellini's "didactic" films were seldom loved. On small black-and-white television sets, they were unimpressive. (*Louis XIV* had not been released theatrically in Italy until January 1969, and then only for short runs at art houses.) A subject like *Atti degli apostoli* was unobtrusive, playing casually while the family finished Sunday supper and lolled about.

Louis XIV, a more obscure subject, had pleased only 55 percent of the 6.3 million who "watched" it in Italy in black-and-white on April 23, 1967; dissatisfaction might well have increased with more attention. The movies require a continuous *effort* which most viewers feel unmotivated to make. There seem to be no strong emotions, no enticing characters, no absorbing stories, and, worst of all, no "point." The facts are just looked at, the motivations aren't seen, Baldelli objected.[46]

He was wrong: everyone's motivations in *Louis* and *Acts* are amply present; the "facts" are gorgeously transmuted into art. But Baldelli was saying what almost everyone thought (and thinks), which is what people generally think when they fail to penetrate an artist's style. Literary critics, insensitive to Sternberg's style, complain perennially that his Marlene Dietrich characters are unmotivated. Actors would complain to King Vidor: "When I would tell a story to a star, he'd say, 'But I don't prompt any of these situations—I don't motivate them.' He'd say, 'I want to motivate them—I am the hero.'"[47]

Roberto, in congenial company, would rhapsodize happily over how he had dramatized Louis's motivations. In hostile company he acted majestic instead. "You always make the same point," he retorted to Baldelli, "[that] it's necessary to make a critique, and in making a critique, it's necessary to accept a certain point of view, and this point of view must be imposed on others. [Hadn't Rossellini himself made precisely this point to Rouch at UNESCO?] But why must I make a digest of all that? It's for the spectators to do it. It's as though we had a plate of good pasta in front of us. [You] want to eat some, but you prefer to wait until I've eaten it, and then to swallow it only after I've digested it. To avoid making an effort, you'd eat terribly disgusting pasta.[48] Since I have a lot of faith in people, I think that, if people have all the facts, they can find the answers by themselves."[49]

Spaghetti is often cooked almost that soft in France, however, and in America people were eating it mostly from cans. Jacques Lourcelles, unlike Baldelli, utterly adored *Stromboli, Europe '51, Voyage in Italy, Fear,* and *Francesco,*[50] and utterly opposed *La Prise de pouvoir par Louis XIV.* He complained what many people felt: that *Louis* seemed impersonal and lacking an authorial point of view; that the drama lacked lines of force; that the acting was uncertain, the dialogue conventional and static, the blocking academic and static; that the whole thing was too serious, too pedagogic, and ignored all the fun things—the fantasy, grandeur, open immorality, and Machiavellianism of the age.[51]

At the New York Film Festival, titled *The Rise of Louis XIV,* it was booed, with Roberto in attendance, somewhere. It was "a disappointment and, to this particular viewer, a mounting bore," said Bosley Crowther in *The New York Times.*[52] Roberto was unable to obtain even a single television or theatrical play date in America.

Paul Schrader implies that the blame for *Louis*'s debacle was that it was out of season: the Festival theme was "The Social Film in Cinema"; there was a seminar on "Reality Cinema: Whose Truth?"; and cinéma vérité was ascendant: *Titicut Follies, Don't Look Back, Warrendale, Portrait of Jason, The Battle of Algiers.*[53] No doubt Rossellini looked at least as dated opposite these pictures as he had opposite the New Wave, Fellini, and Antonioni. But surely the more serious problem was that *Louis* wasn't more like *Bonnie and Clyde, The Graduate,* or *Torn Curtain.*

Subtitles, importantly, pose an almost insuperable barrier for most Americans. Even most university students simply cannot read fast enough, and Rossellini's subtitles read like sloppy encyclopedia texts, overloaded with allusions to unknown people and events. Viewers feel deprived; they miss eye-contact, the warm intimacy so easily achieved with characters in American movies. So they don't get the points, not even the broadest of Rossellini's Chaplinesque jokes, let alone the nuanced timidity of Louis; it's as though they are being subjected to Monteverdi after a lifetime of nothing but the worst rock. Thus lines, like the bystander's remark at Louis's banquet that the king spurns forks as a novelty, are understood merely in their narrowest meaning (forks are an innovation) rather than in their dramatic context (the courtiers grasp for each gasp of gossip). In addition, the subject matter intimidates them (which it would not, were it Abraham Lincoln); many of them have little idea who Saint Paul was, let alone Mazarin. Rossellini's didactic films make them feel stupid. In *Acts of the Apostles*, the American dubbing, although preferable to subtitles, adds an element of artificiality that, as with *Europe '51*, destroys the movie for most viewers. The indirect sound depletes the characters' lines of any shred of spontaneity, ambience, or involvement with the situation at hand, especially when set beside the aplomb of *Louis XIV*. (The fault is hardly unique with Rossellini; all Hollywood films shown in Italy are dubbed with the same canned sound and disembodied voices.)

Issues of subtitling and dubbing aside, originality in art has often been perceived, initially, as deficiency. Impressionists couldn't draw; the Renaissance was pornographic; Griffith's close-ups cut off the body; Beethoven was discordant and Wagner worse.

But Roberto in America seemed determined to agree with his critics, that his deficiencies were indeed deficiencies. "I tried to avoid any dramatization," he blatantly lied at a New York press conference on *Louis*; "I wanted to remain coldly with the facts." Asked about his dispute with Rouch at UNESCO, when he had insisted that a moral position required artistic responsibility, he now *reversed* their positions: "I am not against using cinéma vérité techniques to document, to record life scientifically. I asked Jean Rouch if that's what he wanted. No, he answered, I want to do creative work. That's what I am against."[54] In other words, Roberto seemed to be telling the press that it was *wrong* to enjoy these movies (or any movies), and that the sole justifiable pleasure lay in the sensation of being exposed to facts. And people took him seriously! Even his fans. For Jacques Sicilier in *Le Monde* it was a *defense* of *Acts* to call it "anti-dramatic, anti-romanesque . . . , only the objective description of a phenomenon. . . . These characters seem as strange to us, and often as incomprehensible, as they must have to the people of their own time."[55] With advocates of this sort, Rossellini had no need of detractors.

In Italy, partly as a result of Roberto's prattle, one explanation people gave for his films was that he wanted to repeat everything the moment he learned it. Another explanation—in light of *La lotta*, where some of the twelve episodes looked like ten minutes' worth of material inflated to sixty by slow talking and dead time—was that Roberto just wanted the money (RAI had coughed up $200,000 for the series). He was ridiculed for feeding actors their lines through a radio ear-piece or having his Tunisian actors speak Arabic or just recite numbers. His use of Renzino to direct was deplored. His insouciance, particularly in post-production, was outrageous. It was well known that he suffered from a conflict of interest by being his own producer: every lira Rossellini the director did not spend on a film would go to Roberto the *bon vivant* with three families to support—a reality that could influence locations, scenery, casting, number of takes, quality of dubbing, choice of writers, and collaborators; by choice he hired his family and usually pocketed their salaries.

He showed parts of *Survival* to John Grierson, who had been a driving impetus behind documentary movements in England and Canada, and Grierson, drunk at the time, laughed like a fool throughout. Roberto ignored him and went on talking in a normal, blasé voice describing the Etruscans. Grierson pointed and howled. Roberto would comment, "You see that now . . . " Sonali suffered. Grierson declared it was for kids, he had never seen such a piece of shit in all his life.

On the other hand, the fact that Roberto was able to make these films at all was a triumph of ingenuity over minuscule budgets made possible by his Pancinor zoom, a device to synchronize strobe lights with the camera, the Schüfftan mirrors, and other inventions. "I'm always doing technical research because I'm trying to make the easiest possible instrument to use. I'm always trying to make it like a pencil. To get to that point it's necessary to get free of contraptions, production needs, capital. One of the first things is to reduce the costs of production. To reduce costs, you have to speed up the time of production, you have to spend less time on many, many things. For example, do less construction, use non-actors. People say (and I swear to you it's totally untrue) that [at the time of] *Roma città aperta* it was because nothing was available that we had to adapt to what was available and that neo-realism was born, that is, reality: real walls, real people, real dirt, etc., etc. No, on the contrary, it was a perfectly clear and deliberate choice, because what I did I had been trying to do and had done before *Roma città aperta*. The real truth is this: the rite of cinema was celebrated in the temple of the studio. And the studio was in the hands of the studio owner who, to let you in, made you pay what he wanted. And then there was a mania for absolutely perfect photography and deep focus and a million little things, etc., etc. I despised all that. The most important thing for me was to say what I wanted to say. So . . . all the little technical inventions had a fundamental importance to free myself from the system."[56]

On the other hand, the outcome of Roberto's insouciance, if not always as personal and perfected as one might wish, was not always bad.

Renzino's direction of the Columbus episode in *Survival* is lovely, lively, and engaging. Interestingly, it is not about Columbus's voyage but his (Rossellinian?) struggle to get funding for it. Rossellini's point (already made by Alberti in *The Iron Age*) is that the will to initiate a project is what is important, the actual execution is secondary; similarly Alberti would praise the architect and disparage the contractors in *The Age of the Medici* (although Roberto's own father was a contractor); and similarly Roberto would "delegate" responsibility for constructing his movies to workers whom he would try to employ in the same manner that, in commercial art, a stylist employs an artist. (He would never understand why other well-known directors did not wish to shoot his scripts.)

It was the fundamental error of Rossellini's career that he discounted the importance of his own artistic hand.

Yet again, although *Acts* is the richest of his films (with *Louis XIV*, *Viva l'Italia*, and *Voyage in Italy*), Rossellini the director had nothing to do with it aurally. Its first dubbing into Italian (which Roberto had supervised with total inattention) had been so botched in mis-synchronization, inaccuracies with New Testament texts, and lacunae from scenes not shot, that, before airing, the entire process had had to be re-done in three months by Scaffa and two Jesuit priests, Stanislao Lyonnet and Carlo M. Martini, then Rector of the Biblical Institute in Rome, subsequently Rector of the Gregorian University, presently Cardinal Archbishop of Milan and possibly the next Pope. Nor had Roberto given attention to the music. "Perhaps in my long career this was the musical accompaniment that gave me the greatest satisfaction," Nascimbene wrote. "[Rossellini] went away for three months and when he got back I had already written the music, recorded it, edited it, and mixed it myself, an operation which no composer had ever done before."[57]

Italian critics were respectful and unenthusiastic about *Acts*. It was novel for a Rossellini picture to get such banal notices.

Most critics assumed that *Acts'* 1968-ish qualities made its depiction of Christianity more humanist than messianic. Stefano Roncoroni even declared, "The merit of this broadcast is without doubt that, of Rossellini's films, it is the *least* religious, most secular, most ecumenical."[58]

To my eyes, however, *Acts* seems more religious on each viewing. For these Christians, love of one's neighbor is love of God (*not* the other way round), and Rossellini depicts them as possessed by spirit—and occasionally perplexed by it all. The Communist Baldelli perceived this possession more than the Catholic Roncoroni did, but found it objectionable rather than reflective: "The film's style is very chronicle-like; but the actors always talk as though they are divinely inspired!"[59] In fact, *Acts* is very much in the tradition of religious art: it offers a form for our contemplation of God. What would be the point of a film *about* religious experience that could not provide an artistic experience *of* religious experience? We wouldn't understand anything! Even (or especially) from a materialist standpoint, how can one depict Paul without his religious experience? As a lunatic? *L'Unità*'s objection that Rossellini demands faith rather than reflection misses this point: *Acts* is a film about faith.[60]

Paese Sera objected that by relying on a text that was, after all, a religious text, Rossellini had "implicated television in [Vatican] apologetics [and] prevented any possibility of a critical reading of that text."[61] To Baldelli, Rossellini's misplaced reliance "betrayed the socio-political roots, primarily the class struggle going on in the Roman world . . . the economic-imperialist reasons for which the oligarchy of Rome ordered Christ's death and persecuted his followers."[62]

To the contrary. *Acts* is at pains to delineate social, political, and economic motives for hostility to Christianity: these are the snares the Christians seek freedom from. Yet in face of this drama and the richness of Rossellini's "new cinema," Baldelli sees only dogma and deficiency: "Everything takes place 'as it was written' and thus has the character of a ritual, an act of faith, rather than a critical reflection."[63]

But Rossellini has not been literal with the text. He omits anything—such as Paul's teachings on guilt, sin, and sex—that might embarrass *Acts'* conflict of Christian freedom-and-love versus establishment snares-and-hate.

Socrates

(Trilogy of Desiccation I)

At RAI snares formed against Roberto during the summer of 1969 among a group hostile to Bernabei. "The bureaucracy was very slow and had little understanding of Rossellini's production difficulties," Scaffa explained. "Often he went over budget. It wasn't his fault personally, but that of his organization of old collaborators and relatives. He didn't directly take care of accounts but, not infrequently, he had to record the existence of 'leaks' which he then had to hasten to repair somehow. RAI's bureaucracy, obviously and correctly, was far from accepting the 'maestro's' invoices once they were checked, since they were quite beyond the stipulations of the contract (as everyone's always are).... Some of the program directors who succeeded Beretta and Gennarini did not like Rossellini's 'logic of simplification.' They called his films 'rough and naive.' They tried to reeducate him, uselessly, to accept norms that would guarantee an improvement of his objectionable and, obviously non-existent, interpretive roughness."[1]

On November 1, 1969, Roberto played his trump card. He submitted his resignation as president of the Centro Sperimentale to the Minister of Spectacle, blaming RAI (but not Bernabei) and announcing (once again) that he was going to France. "In Italy it's impossible to do anything serious."

To the press he detailed his troubles. "I find no possibility of work in Italy, and since to survive it's necessary to work . . . , I find myself forced to go abroad again. But my activity abroad will not permit the continuous presence necessary to fulfill my duties at the Centro. From this is born, honestly, my decision to resign. . . . It's been years since I put the idea in my head—maybe I'm crazy—to use 'images' as an instrument of education. . . . People need ample information. But here . . . it's always, 'Wait, wait, you have to be patient.' . . . I made *The Iron Age* for the TV. At first I was told, 'Let's wait for the reactions, for success.' Because what counts is not the work . . . but success. Success came, but it wasn't enough: a series of conflicting interests developed, and I was obliged to leave the country again. I made *Louis XIV* in France. It was successful. So they recalled me to

Italy. I came back and made *Acts of the Apostles*. Tell me frankly: is this a 'speculative' product that can make millions? No, it's just the documentation of what can be done with an honest effort within the very limited budgets of RAI-TV. But this type of undertaking requires at least the prospective of continuity . . . . [RAI] made promises . . . [but] after six months . . . the only concrete result is a single contract [for *Socrates*, dated July 30, 1969], which we had agreed to shoot this summer and were all prepared to start. Nothing. Autumn came and we got all prepared. Nothing. Then we prepared everything for the end of autumn. Again nothing. It's not possible to go on this way."[2]

Roberto's statements caused astonishment at RAI. Their press officer, Gian Paolo Cresci, observed that Rossellini had commitments with RAI for about three years, through 1971, was finishing *La lotta dell'uomo per la sua sopravvivenza* "in thirteen chapters [sic]," and was about to begin *La vita di Socrate*, a two-hour program for which he been given an advance of 25 million lire. Other projects were *The Thirty-Years War, Saint Catherine*, and *Pascal*, for which RAI had advanced twelve million lire.[3]

Roberto made a symbolic trip to Paris. But he had won his point. "Television in Italy is a state monopoly, so you can attack it all the time," he told some American students. "It's so good and so wonderful to attack the government. It's very exciting and amusing. The government is always very weak because they want to have the approval of everybody, so they are easily scared."[4]

But it wasn't so simple. "The Christian Democrats owned him," La Rochefoucauld pointed out, "because he owed so much taxes." They controlled RAI too. "He was constantly being ordered around. The phone would ring, he'd say he was going some place, they'd say, 'No. There's a rally in Rimini. Be there tomorrow. And he'd have to go."[5]

Houston

John and Dominique de Menil were establishing a Media Center at Rice University in Houston. Their goal was "a school that encouraged students to make films with intellectual content, films that challenged people to think about their lives," according to Rice professor Brian Huberman. "The Rice Media Center was to be a 'Trojan Horse' located in the center of 'Boom City' U.S.A. This horse was to contain media soldiers trained to see through the hype of the pro-market place, anti-intellectual ideology, and to critically evaluate the real relationships between the citizen, the government, and the private sector."[6]

With movies as an art form the de Menils were not much concerned; they supported hundreds of artists, but only two filmmakers: Andy Warhol and Rossellini. They saw few of Roberto's movies and had no illusions about him personally; it was his social agenda that they believed in. When he first came to Houston in November 1968 and showed the first episode of *La lotta*—now called simply *Survival*—the result was disastrous. *The*

Houston Post called it "tediously simplistic," objected to the all-white cast, the women's shaved legs, the urbane faces more at home sipping cappucino on Via Veneto, and "an English narration both patronizing and clumsily worded," and wondered what a New Guinea aboriginal would think of the film.[7]

De Menil also thought it terrible and kidded Roberto about it for years. But Riboud defended him, and so did de Menil's associate, Simone Swan. When Roberto proposed making a TV series about science, de Menil invited him to stay at his house, consult with Rice's science faculty, hold seminars, and assist with the Media Center. (Croce, curiously, had given an inaugural lecture at Rice before World War I.)

Between 1970 and 1974, Roberto commuted between Houston and Paris and Rome as often as thirty times a year. In Rome, Schlumberger had provided a lovely villa for him, in Sonali's name, at Vicolo delle Sette Chiese 8B, in 1968. Between Europe and Houston, thanks to an American Express card whose charges de Menil paid, Roberto flew first class, often buying the adjacent seat as well, so that he would be undisturbed. Air France gave him matches with his name on them. He read and studied incessantly.

"Enthusiasm characterized Rossellini's early days at Rice," says Huberman. Rossellini insisted that "each film should be an experiment but it must have a clear goal of putting the audience in a position of direct contact with the information they need. He called this method 'direct vision.' . . . Documentary students . . . quickly produced a series of successful films, such as *Bordersville*. . . . For years [a] black neighborhood had petitioned the government for public water services. Their appeal was ignored despite the fact that across the street a white community had excellent water and sewer services. The film presented a 'direct vision' of racism to the Houston public, and within a short period the neighborhood received water." The film was shot on super-8mm for less than $500.[8]

"I was attracted by the university and disgusted with the Media Center," said Roberto, speaking in English. "So I got around and started to know a lot of people and I immediately got the feeling how ignorant I was, and because I am a very curious person I tried very hard to reduce my ignorance, and started to grab here and there some information. And at a certain moment, I thought it would be good to try to develop some kind of way to communicate, because you know how difficult it is to communicate between one discipline and another, because there is no common language and the outsiders don't know anything about science. Theirs is a new method of thinking, of analysis, of reaching facts, very concrete, you know. So I tried. The first thing I did was in the department of biology."

Twelve scientists were working with Yellow Fever viruses, each with their own microscope. Rossellini filmed the virus. "They all came in to the projection room to see the Yellow Fever and nobody recognized the Yellow Fever. You see, each one put the light in a certain way, maneuvered the microscope in his own way, so my Yellow Fever had nothing in common with the Yellow Fever of the others. So that's terrible, you know, how can you communicate? . . . So I thought that if I were able to develop a language that could show what we see with our own eyes and what is beyond our natural possibilities, and to zoom from what we see and what it is, and go back and forth, that perhaps this would be the proper language to put the thing together and have a more precise feeling."[9]

The de Menils gave Roberto a room in their house (the first residence Philip Johnson had designed), an escort (Helen Winkler Fosdick), and a long series of lunches, where one by one each scientist was invited to meet Roberto and be seduced into cooperating. The scientists did cooperate, notably biologist Clark Read, astronomer Donald Clayton, physicist Dieter Heyman, heart expert David Hellums, agricultural historian Frank Hole, religious historian William Murdock, and thunder expert Arthur Few, with whom Roberto spent many hours sitting on mountain tops waiting for thunder. But although Roberto had done his homework in science, and had brought along *Louis XIV* to show, much of the Rice faculty regarded him and his projects with suspicion and ridicule. Even twenty years later the art faculty were joking that he always took two desserts. (But he still refused to eat bananas.)

With William Colville, a cameraman provided by de Menil, Roberto filmed hours of discussions with Rice scientists and went to Arecibo Observatory, Puerto Rico, where the world's largest radio telescope is used to study the ionosphere. The greatest thrill for Roberto was a visit to NASA. With his children around him he had watched in awe and excitement when Armstrong landed on the moon, July 20, 1969. In February 1970, thanks to Donald Clayton, he got into an astronaut's costume and was given a moon rock. He invited Clayton to Rome in 1971, along with Helen Winkler Fosdick, whom he took racing in the big red Ferrari.

Centro Sperimentale President

"School today has little use and is essentially punitive," Roberto had written in April 1969.[10] Now he would have an opportunity to try out his own ideas at the Centro Sperimentale.

"If they're crazy, give them their freedom," he declared.[11] He meant it with a vengeance. Under the old set-up, sixty professors had lectured thirty students from books, keeping them away from cameras and generally declining to talk to them individually. Roberto's first move was to fire all sixty. Henceforth it would be entirely up to the students to decide what they wanted to study, whereupon someone would be hired for a week or two to teach it.

On January 12, 1970 he met with the first class admitted under his regime, nineteen Italians and nine foreigners he had chosen himself. "I'm approaching seventy," he told them, "and I'm going to use all the years left me to throw shit on the cinema!"[12]

People are more alone than ever, he said. They have been betrayed by an education so specialized that it fails to transmit a useful image of the world, which makes us victims of progress and deprives us of our ability to choose. We become intimidated and give up our uniqueness. We abdicate responsibility and seek identity with everyone else. Modern society limits liberty, which is no longer even regarded as a good thing. "You have to learn to be free again. So you're not going to need teachers, and the curriculum will follow whatever you decide."[13]

Then, according to one of the students, Beppe Cino, he gave them his Ten Commandments:

1. The camera is a pen, a plain ordinary Bic, easy to use. It's enough to know what you want to say—if you have something to say.
2. The camera is a paper tiger. Don't mythify it.
3. Therefore the image must exist first in your head. The camera can't substitute for the absence of an image in your head. Therefore learn to think in images; it's useless to expect miracles from the camera. "You really have to reduce filming to the simplicity of a pencil, so you have no more worries about the medium and all your worries can concern your thoughts."[14]
4. Making films is easy. People say it's difficult in order to stop you.
5. When I say film I don't mean commercial cinema, which is dead, and only good for letting filmmakers tell themselves, "Ah! How wonderful I am!"
6. Make films that will be useful for others, not for yourself.
7. What's useful? Knowledge, without which we'd be beasts. The brain is used to think with, not just to wear a hat.
8. Using film to spread knowledge means doing research. Ideas and subjects aren't invented by moonlight but in the library.
9. I don't like being known as a director. I prefer to be a good pilot, a man. The principal craft is to be a man, curious, fascinated, responsible, occupied with the problems of the world.
10. My only role here is to be the guardian of your liberty.[15]

After lunch they met again and Rossellini asked them what they wanted to study. "Everyone was silent," said Mario Garriba. "So I said, 'The historical avant-garde: try to rediscover a cinema that was never developed.' He listened distractedly. So I talked about analyzing narrative structures in Buñuel's recent films. He was still silent. I described my interest in how Bresson composed his frames. Finally I said, 'I'd like to study your films.' 'Which ones?' '*Louis XIV.*' Finally he smiled. 'There are too many seductive shots in it for it to be good.' I didn't understand his reply."[16]

The course lasted two years. "An idiot can learn everything there is to know about techniques in three months. An average person—fifteen days," Roberto maintained.[17] Their first films were done with video, then 16mm, then a full-length film if individuals chose to. They gained technical knowledge, plus there were seminars on economics, psychology, sociology, or, if two or three wanted it, the history of film or advertising. No theory; no acting courses. Each student received a stipend of 75,000 lire a month and meals. They set their own rules.

"We decided to learn about instruments," Mario Garriba said. They called Mario Bernardo, took an Arriflex apart, and found nothing inside. "There had to be more to it." So they had a month-long seminar with a cameraman, Luigi Verga. Then someone stole all the cameras. "Only Rossellini could help us. 'If you don't have a camera, use your head,' he said. 'Learn that to take a shot means to take away rather than to add.'"[18] For the next few days they walked around the school with rolled-up newspapers held to their eyes, like camera viewfinders.

They decided to do a film on the struggles of nineteenth-century workers—as a collective effort. "That's a lie," Roberto said. "[A film] is never made by a group. It is formally made by a group, essentially by one person. Those are theorizations, because if you have certain kinds of political beliefs you will insist that a group makes the film. It is not true, there is always a group with a personality rising above the others and imposing itself."[19]

He left for the U.S. "We looked for other fathers: Renzo del Carria, Baldelli, Fofi, Renzo Rossellini." The student technicians arranged lectures on lighting; for a month the professor, Vasco Ronchi, talked about light using Empedocles, Democrites, Euclid, the Bible, Padre Brimaldi, and Giovan Battista Della Porta—but nothing about film, deep focus, Toland, or Welles. When Roberto got back, he told them: "The reality that has developed around us eludes us, precisely because our preparation, whether technical or cultural, is minimal. To me it seems that the world is expanding with an amazing speed. New structures and forms are appearing that we do not control anymore, precisely because we lack these technical and cultural instruments of observation and research. This is the most serious aspect of our crisis. The lack of adequate instruments forces us to limit our attention to little, minuscule, partial novelties that we keep going back to without seeing the great chain of mountains that, meanwhile, have been built under our eyes." Then, said Mario Garriba, "he put a moon rock on the table. We touch it. Nothing can be said. All our arguments disappear." Roberto said, "There are people who turn around and see the wall behind them, others see twenty centuries."

Nonetheless frustration returned. Rossellini would never talk about actual films, even his own. Instead he told them, "I was full of all the myths about movies too, when I started making films. I've tried to get away from those myths. You can only do it gradually. It's gradual because reason is slow to mature. Now something else that preoccupies me in a fundamental way is honestly, I mean, not being seductive, which means stripping the images of every element that might be seductive, in order to stay inside the things.[20] Dramatization and search for effect take you further from truth.[21] Neo-realism was a moral position, a precise effort to learn; nothing more. Then, I realized that movies contain too much seduction, and being too seductive they easily start mythifying and theorizing their subjects too."[22]

Herbert Read makes the same point about Duccio and Giotto, when they attempted around 1300 to abandon the iconic approach to painting and to give a more exact account of phenomena: "To do this the artist had gradually to discard . . . any form of idealism, which suggested the possible existence of another mode of reality, and therefore any symbolic forms which merely represented the artist's fantasy. Purity of consciousness was to be cultivated, and the artist was to give a true report of his purest state of consciousness. A tremendous effort to clear the consciousness of the conventional symbols that corrupted it was implied."[23]

What Roberto wanted, he said, was an "essential" or "simple" image, an image as simple and uncorrupted as an infant's. "If I'd been able to express myself when I was a baby, I would have been a great man. Then I became systematized, lost an immense portion of my imagination, enthusiasm, and curiosity. Everything became reduced; maybe this is why I find it easier to express myself now."[24]

In place of being a baby, Rossellini wanted to be able to "write" with *precisely* the "right word." In 1958, he had lamented that "film gets more immoral every day, because every day it gets more allusive."[25] Now allusion is eliminated. Movies like *Acts* and *Socrates* are open to many interpretations without ever being unspecific or ambiguous. Roberto self-dismissively claimed he was not trying to do art. Yet how could such precision not be poetry, in Croce's sense? "To get back to the true image, the essential image, you have to get back to before spoken language was even invented," said Roberto,[26] echoing Croce's doctrine that true poetry is an expression of such images. Thus in the movies we see a complex of things at the same time as we experience Roberto's sensibility in seeing them. Now Mario Garriba understood why Rossellini had said that *Louis XIV* had too many seductive images compared to *Acts of the Apostles*. "Ideas aren't in people's heads, they're inside the things!" Roberto said, and talked about Aristotle, Sophocles, Dante, Napoleon, Suetonius, Juvenal, Tacitus, Adam Smith, Rousseau, De Tocqueville, Nazareno Padellaro, Mao Tse Tung, Proudhon, Croce, Lao Tzu, Thucydides, Plato, Machiavelli, Richelieu, Bertrand de Juvenel, Jesus, Saint-Simon, Auguste Comte, Freud, Leon Battista Alberti, Brunelleschi, Ghiberti, Masaccio, Donatello, Michelangelo, Leonardo da Vinci, Calvin, Max Weber, Ernest Roebtsch, Copernicus, Bacon, Paracelsus, Gandhi, Huizinga, Adolf Hitler, Nehru, Thomas More, Marx, Comenius, Lenin, Nixon . . . but not one film person. Mario Garriba tried to take notes; Rossellini glared at him: "What are you writing? Don't you see I'm talking?"[27]

Roberto was making a film in Spain in which Socrates protests against writing. Socrates talks about a demon who has invented writing which he promises "will develop the understanding and reinforce the memory . . . and lead you to knowledge." But in fact, Socrates tells Phaedo, "People, trusting in writing, will no longer search their memories deep within themselves. They'll stop trusting memory and thus lose most of what they know. Instead of trying to express themselves with pain and warmth, they'll cite texts with elegance. But what can one reply to citations? . . . Once written, discourses pass indifferently from one hand to another, without being able to distinguish the most deprived person from someone intelligent."

"Writing puts dialectic in an icebox," Roberto said, meaning questioning. "Aristotle was so convinced of this that he never wrote anything, he just took notes and improvised.[28] Written culture is an authoritarian instrument: it doesn't admit contradiction, dissension, or reply. Oral culture, in contrast, is dialectical, fluid, constantly changing: an instrument of collective communication and democracy."[29] When a written accusation was posted against Socrates, Socrates felt helpless. The basis of his dialectic was in relating to other individuals, a mutual and intuitive communication. Nothing of the sort is possible with a text (although we try, in our sophistic culture: for example, this book). Eloquence, according to Roberto, replaced slaves, soldiers, and whips in Socrates's time as a means of dominating and enslaving the masses and halting the search for truth.

What Roberto was searching for was a cinema that would be "oral" rather than "written," that in Croce's terms would be poetry rather than prose, that would communicate the excitement he felt at the moment of learning things; he wanted a cinema that could be *argued* with. A contradiction in terms? Perhaps. But, paradoxically, an aesthetic language that was exact rather than impressive could be rich and multivalent, and thus as open as reality to viewers' diverse interpretations. "If I have confidence in people, I must have confidence in the viewer. If I didn't believe in people, I would no longer be a man myself, and if I set out to doubt people, I would be a monster." Thus, points were not to be underlined. "Film has the advantage that, if you know how to look at things, you can put so much into one picture that the result is quite complex, whereas writing is analytical, consisting of putting one idea down after another and organizing them." These were the same ideas Roberto had outlined to De Angelis during the Occupation. In *Acts* the camera pans around the upper table from one person to another, showing the community among the apostles. But such moments came about "in a completely instinctive way, not as a result of forethought. If they were planned they would appear cold and mechanical. They must arise from natural impulse. For example, the very long pan from the hands of these real workers and peasants to their faces, is a form of microscopic discovery, it's like watching a cell. . . . The camera works like an eye, so you can develop a system of constant direct participation."[30]

Our awareness of the eye keeps us from being a passive, easily seducible audience.

The students' first films were disasters; the shots would not go together. Would Roberto come look? "Why do I have to look at things you don't even like yourselves?" But the editing? "There are no problems. I always cut on movement. I absolutely don't give a damn whether the movement is finished or not, before connecting it to the next shot. When I've showed the essential, I cut: that's enough. It's much more important to connect what's inside the image.[31] [When I was making *Stromboli*] few of the Strombolians had ever seen a movie, and they were mystified by the cutting from one scene to another, even by the cutting within a scene. They didn't make connections. The way I shoot now . . . I establish all the connections."[32] But what, Mario Garriba wondered, about other approaches to editing, like Eisenstein, Griffith, or Hollywood? For Roberto, Eisenstein, Griffith, and Hollywood were the conventions, the idealisms, that he was trying to shake off. How could he encourage students to absorb the conventions he was struggling to discard?

The students' collective film about nineteenth-century workers fell apart in arguments over the Communist Party, semiotics, and other matters. Students changed tables in the dining room. Roberto came back from America with one of the first digital watches, advised them to read the Massachusetts Institute of Technology's and United Nations' reports from the Stockholm energy conference, talked about population explosion, exhaustion of natural resources, increasing illiteracy, unemployed university graduates, and lack of capital; and concluded that we are unequivocally at the end of a civilization. Then he introduced astronomer Donald Clayton from Houston, who spoke for an hour in English. Almost no one understood Clayton, so they started an English course. Roberto talked about Aristotle—"It's not true that free time is the goal of work, it's work that is the goal of free time"—and time was only useful when dedicated to studying science, philosophy, and literature. "One of humanity's dramas is that people are useful to society as consumers."[33]

Four students made features the first year; one, *E sul davanti fiorivano le magnolie*, was eventually shown at Venice. But the student assembly decided that two of the six directing students were not worthy to make a film. One of the rejected pursued Roberto to appeal and finally got to him at three in the morning outside his house. "You signed the agreement," Roberto told him.[34]

A year later Roberto admitted, "A school based on such freedom, I have slowly realised, is a very cruel school. People must assume their own responsibility. . . . The main goal of a school must be the human being."[35]

He had hoped to link the Centro with RAI. The students refused; they were making militant films, RAI was the establishment. They wouldn't talk to journalists either, all journalists were on the right. The next class was even worse. "I have one student," Roberto said, "whom I have to protect every day, because he's considered the most reactionary and conservative by all the rest of the students, because he's the only one who joined the Communist Party." He chose some of the most radical as his assistants for his Horizon 2000 movies.

After the first semester Roberto was rarely seen at the Centro; he justified his absence by repeating that his job was to be the guarantor of the students' liberty. "To respond to the complaint that the Centro students make against me, I would like to say that the important thing is not that I show myself and give them advice, but rather that I give them the possibility to make their own discoveries. This is why I consider that the most important result was achieved when some of these young people, who had thought they could solve all the world's problems by making a film and then saw what they had made, decided not to show their film.[36]

"One makes films in order to become a better human being,"[37] he told students at New York University in 1973. "I am very stubborn and I think that the best and the most honest thing in life is to be yourself, even if you make a mistake. So what, if you make a mistake? It is another mistake among billions of mistakes. Why should you be ashamed of your mistakes? By making mistakes perhaps you achieve something new, and at least you are yourself, which is the main thing."[38]

In fact, Roberto was helpless to increase the Centro's budget, which was less than a fifth of the minimum needed. "It was a literally disastrous two years," said Carlo Verdone, "because of the political factionalism of the students . . . and the scarcity of funds. . . . Rossellini would come back from the United States and tell us wonderful things about new machines and discoveries, but everything ended there: as a teacher he didn't begin to understand our problems. And for the final thesis there was only 600,000 lire apiece [$1,000]."[39]

Verdone made his film by using his savings plus two other students' allotments, and borrowing the rest. Meanwhile Roberto, concerned for their *bella figura*, was telling an American interviewer for Jonas Mekas's independent-film journal, *Film Culture*, that student budgets were seven million lire.[40]

The class was angry at the end of the first year. They were getting nowhere. In November 1970 they gathered at Roberto's house to lay out a program for the second year. Roberto understood the situation: their disagreements with the teaching, the bureaucracy, and each other's politics. He questioned them individually. Some wanted to do the workers film, others films about racism or sexism. Mario Garriba said he just wanted to make movies, and everyone laughed. But Roberto said, "Language isn't really a research. There are things that are done by instinct. When I talk I don't search for the words, it comes to me instinctively to say certain words that are closest to represent what I am thinking, what I'm trying to say. For example, people say film is movement, then they say it's montage, then lots of other things of this sort. Now why do we have to stay tied to this truth . . . ? It's not obligatory to respect any of it!"

At the end of the second year, Mario Garriba had managed to shoot and edit his film, somehow. But he had no money to have his negative printed. He went to Rossellini, who immediately said he couldn't help. Smiling, he added, "Wasn't it in fact you who 'just' wanted to make movies? This is what making movies means: you have to invent a way to find the money!"

Garriba's film, *In punto di morte*, won the Pardo d'Oro at the Locarno Festival in 1971. "I was bursting to tell everyone. I phoned home, my mother was busy and told me to bring her some Nescafé from Switzerland. The sole telegram came that evening: 'Bravo, bravo, bravo. In my name and the Centro Sperimentale's. Roberto Rossellini.' I hid myself in a bar and read it a hundred times."[41]

The following year Roberto was even less in evidence. He still guaranteed their liberty, but there was still less money. He'd tell them to watch Ford; they'd learn everything.

"He'd show up unexpectedly," recalled Elio Girlanda, "sometimes with his son Robertino or Sonali's son [Gil], and stay with us through lunch.... He'd talk about himself, his ever more frequent trips between Paris and New York, his discoveries and his needs, calm and serene as though he were a patriarch who had nothing to teach.... The Centro should become a place for research, he'd say, a place to exchange information to develop a new audiovisual language answering new demands and new social needs, a language with high information intensity and not simply an illustrative language, like in commercial films."[42]

Roberto actually made an announcement: "From January [1973] the Centro will be open to people from the most disparate disciplines: mathematics, biology, sociology, chemistry, psychology, who will constitute work groups to experiment toward finding a common cinematic language."[43]

But it was utopia. Nothing happened. By 1974 there was so little money there was doubt the Centro would even open its doors. "I don't know if you've seen all the attacks against me at the Centro Sperimentale recently," Roberto said to Francesco Savio, "and no one knows what a success the Centro Sperimentale is. But feelings find an outlet this way."[44]

"He knew how to handle [the students'] distrust of power by proposing revolutionary programs," said Di Giammatteo, the vice president. "But he didn't know how to annul his own power. Everyone had to accept his programs exactly. The day they began to object, he left, offended and indignant. And he didn't know how to contend with the power of the Ministry of Spectacle, who shamefully dribbled out even the few lire due us, nor with the political forces within or without. He was practiced in the subtle art of mediation, using his prestige as much as possible. When his prestige wasn't enough, he resigned. And he did it in rage."[45]

The Death of Socrates

Socrate (the title of the French and Italian editions) is a mournful film. Athens, defeated after a disastrous 27-year war, looks like Berlin after World War II; the brilliant sun does not really shine; death is all around, accompanied by a disconsolate motif in the bass. Zooms and camera movements are spare and unadventurous; tight cross-cuts bluntly underline Socrates's growing isolation; images lose force midst the philosopher's incessant rationalizations; Rossellini's camera eye seems less intense and less engaged. Paul and even Louis had charm, not Socrates. The philosopher floats through each day one-upping everyone he meets, speaking and acting with the same equanimity whether buying an octopus, defying an order to arrest Leon, conducting his trial, saying farewell to his children, or laying himself down to die. The idea is sublime, the man is off-putting.

Socrates, followed by *Blaise Pascal* and *Cartesius*, form a trilogy of "uncharm": portraits of men remarkable in the abstract but unlikable in life. Their heroes have un-charm in societies that value charm above all else, except, perhaps, for the value they place on the abstract—as long as the abstract is a variant of charm. "In this period," Roberto said, "began that whole system of seduction and eloquence . . . to [persuade] people to think as you want them to think.[46] It was the moment when democracy became perverted by succumbing to the charms of rhetoric and eloquence.[47] Before that men had been made slaves, soldiers with whips had dominated great masses of people." Now we have become enslaved by eloquence—"which etymologically means the art of persuasion. . . . To persuade [ought to be] a crime because it can harm the personality, the opinions, the thoughts of others.[48] Socrates was very aware of the danger that we are so easily persuaded of all sorts of nonsense. He was condemned to death because he wasn't seductive at all. In fact, everybody really was against him."[49]

A focus on an historical period—on *time*—is typical of Rossellini. He treats his story in each movie as though it were one of the nodal points of history, one of those intersections between one era and the next. Not just in *Germany Year Zero* or this "Athens Year Zero" but in every movie. "In this moment" one cycle of history is dying and another is being born. What moment could be more "dramatic"? We feel the moment at the end of *Roma città aperta* and *Paisà*; we feel it all through *India, Viva l'Italia, Louis XIV,* and *Acts,* and in the passion plays enacted by Ingrid Bergman's heroines. As the story progresses, everything is changing. The notion of history as a dramatic intersection of cycles dominated by specific ideas is typical also of Vico, Croce, Dumas, and *The New Testament.* Thus Rossellini cites eloquence replacing whips not as a mere technological change but as a revision of "the whole conception of the universe." Typically, he melodramatized such events. He liked to cite Huizinga's idea that "until a certain point in history, the ruling sin was pride. When greed came to rule in its place, the world was transformed" and modern economies began "on principles that religion and high ideals had condemned."[50] Is this not history as melodrama?

The melodrama in "Athens Year Zero" is the rise of eloquence from the ruins of Periclean civilization, its triumph over reason, truth, and justice, its exaction of the absurd execution of Socrates. It's again Rossellini's "myth and reality" approach.

Roberto had wanted to film Socrates's trial and death for twenty years. He had originally conceived of it as a companion piece to *Francesco giullare di Dio,* and in the same quiet, earth-shaking style. "Socrates is a man of today," he had told *Bianco e Nero* in 1951. "Socrates is bound to reach the same results as Francis, but Francis gets there through the impulse of his dreams and desires, Socrates by logic. Instinct in *Francesco;* reason in *Socrates.* In our civilization, Latin and Christian, we don't enshrine truth. We're full of irony and skepticism; we keep on searching for truth. We don't look at things materialistically just to see their surfaces, but rather to have perspective. This is how Francis looked at things, Socrates too."[51]

In 1970, reason and impulse are still allies united in common struggle against prosaic convention. But now Socrates will be linked with Pascal and Descartes in a *ménage à trois* of "desiccation" rather than with Francis in nubile camaraderie. The young Rossellini celebrated Dionysian impulse in movies that are young, despite their middle-aged characters (*Viva l'Italia, Acts of the Apostles, Voyage in Italy*). By 1970, an older Rossellini is replying with movies interposing Apollonian reason, movies that are old, that revise, as Croce did as he grew older, a now-too-sensual aesthetics, in order to argue that history is not simply an art, an intuition, but also a judgment built on reason. Age speaks to youth. And thus the great interventions of *reason* into history become the events which Rossellini's movies will purport to show: the Renaissance, the Age of Reason, Athens, the Industrial Revolution, Science, Iron—and the Hirakud dike in *India*. In contrast, technology was only seen as dehumanizing in *La nave bianca, Un pilota ritorna, Una voce umana*, and *Europe '51*. Even the automobile, despite Roberto's passion for cars, functioned in *Voyage in Italy* solely as a means of alienation.

History is melodrama. Now ideas dwarf the men who give them birth, whereas *Acts of the Apostles* and every other Rossellini movie had made the point that individuals were greater. The year 1968 appears to have affected Roberto as it did many others. "All that great explosion of extraordinary feeling was lost, became confused," he said during *Socrates*, "because it turned into passion. We have to stay within the orbit of what's rational, that's the only way to begin again.[52]

"As Bergson says, intelligence seems characterized by a natural incomprehension of life. . . . Fifty or sixty thousand years ago we *homo sapiens* appeared on Earth. Our brain with 2^{33} neurons differed profoundly from that of our progenitors, *Pithecanthropus erectus*, with 2^{32} neurons. This passage from 2^{32} to 2^{33} represented an immense change: it was then that we became dominated by the fear that derives from our new, vaster intelligence. Suddenly this new consciousness made us into beings who instead of living in and according to nature lived according to ourselves, our will, our caprice. But at the start the bewilderment must have been immense.

"The invention of language furnished us the means to live a social life, no longer a herd one, and gave us the way to confront obstacles and push fear away, [to] express our creativity and orientation. . . . [But] with large concentrations of people . . . , dialectical possibilities decreased and language gradually changed from a fervid creator to eloquence: etymologically, a means of persuasion. . . ."

This is the same Crocean point made in *Acts*, that poetry is destroyed by prose.

"Today television is used as a means to gain advantage over everyone. It is not used at all to develop a dialogue with everyone.[53] Yet progress is only one thing: the increase in knowledge."[54]

Rossellini insists on the superiority of reason over emotion, but the movies he makes throw reason away in incomprehensible monologues and concentrate instead on the human character. Moreover, Rossellini embodies the supposed superiority of reason in heroes who take Jansenistic delight in abstraction at the expense of friendship, women, sex, or love. They alienate and are alienated. They are narcissists, new forms of "involution," who yet through their ideas expand like yin into yang to revise the whole concept of the universe and change the lives of all of us who have come after them. Rossellini still has a "Great Man" sense of historical causality; *Roma città aperta*, *Paisà*, "Hirakud," and *Acts* remain his only pictures in which "the masses" initiate change. But Rossellini's Great Man invariably insists he is an ordinary person with the humility to be himself, a "crazy." Thus he can be a poet. (So it's actually a "Great Weirdo" sense of historic causality.) "The whole of human history is a debate between the small handful of revolutionaries who make the future, and the conservatives.[55] In point of fact each of us in life tries to do something and has to confront a lot of prejudice, a lot of preconceived ideas, a lot of superstition, a lot of weakness, of a lot of trickery."[56]

Roberto's plan called for a massive increase in the number of revolutionaries, of "crazies," to be achieved through an increase in individual knowledge. Thomas Jefferson's illuminist vision was similar.

Wherefore, by way of encouraging us, he holds up Socrates, Pascal, and Descartes, an un-charming trio so macabre that they don't seem so far away from the creeps who Francis Ford Coppola says structure our world in *The Godfather*.

Who was Socrates? "The main thing [for Socrates] was to be himself. His wife represents what is going on in the world. She is the expression of emotion, he the expression of rationality. This is an eternal conflict."[57]

Who was Pascal? "A very boring character who never made love in his life. When he was suffering, which was most of the time—he was always having pains of one kind or another—he used to solve geometry problems. He really wasn't much fun."[58]

Who was Descartes? "Less [sympathetic than Pascal] perhaps. He was a son of a bitch, a coward, a lazy person, but he was also intelligent. He was quite repulsive of course, not simpatico. But I don't care about that."[59]

But he does care, and so do we. What kind of progress is it whose humus is so desiccated? Heroes in commercially successful films prevail in their lonely self-conviction, their struggles are telescoped, and success is the theme. Whereas dull effort and its masochism is the theme in Rossellini after *Louis XIV*. Heroes in commercially successful films are eventually made welcome by a loving community. Rossellini's heroes shut themselves up in dark rooms and die.

There are few women in Rossellini after *Louis XIV* takes power. Was this a price of progress? Peter, Paul, and Philip are men without women; so too, at least on-camera, are most of the peacocks in *The Age of the Medici*. Alberti is a pederast; Augustine has shaken off his family; Descartes takes a servant girl just to replace his male servant; Socrates has a wife who, in Roberto's words, "represents the demon"[60]; and Pascal has only a sister determined to be a cloistered nun.

But shunting women aside does not save the heroes. Individuals still must die so that ideas may be born: Socrates, Della Rovere, Christ, the emotional soldiers at the end of *Paisà*, Edmund in *Deutschland*, and, figuratively, Irene in *Europe '51*, Louis XIV, Paul, Pascal, Descartes.

"But why does Socrates have to die?" ask Baldelli, Paolo Bertetto, and Peter Brunette, who complain that, in place of the "missing explanations," Socrates's death, like Christ's, is due solely to the fact that he "bears witness to the truth."[61]

What better reason could there be, especially in a melodrama? What Rossellini shows is that conduct that was merely offensive in happier days has become mortally offensive now that Athenian civilization is disintegrating. This change is the film's dramatic context, which Rossellini sharpens by concentrating into a few days the five years (404–399 B.C.) following Athens's defeat in the Peloponnesian War; and by concentrating into a few minutes one incident after another of Socrates's abrasive undercutting of everyone who comes within his range. The first scene shows Athens's walls being destroyed; Athenians are grasping desperately for things to believe in. And meanwhile Socrates is snatching everything away from them. By showing them their lack of substance he humiliates them and offers only elusive rationality in exchange. The world is full of opinion and completely empty of knowledge, he proclaims, and "the only thing I know is that I know nothing." His timing is lousy. He wins every engagement tactically, while losing every engagement strategically, not because he makes enemies but because he discourages rather than inspires. He is the contrary of Saint Francis, who loses tactically but wins strategically because he wins friends through emotional encouragement.

Thus, even in Athens, Rossellini's hero dies because ideas that revise the conception of the universe are never timely. By definition they threaten everybody. "In human history 99 percent of the people who have been put to death have been executed for crimes of thought and opinion. Society, any society, can forgive murderers. But anyone who thinks differently, any non-conformist, always ends up being killed."[62] New ideas isolate the thinker and destroy their own progenitor.

"I heard him speak often of Socrates," said Paolo Valmarana. "In the houses on Viale Bruno Buozzi during the golden times, with Ingrid listening half-open-mouthed in admiration and from her effort to understand Italian. In the little room on Via Ruggero Fauro during the hard times, when a cot and the moviola he was editing *India* on filled up the dark basement chamber. In the shiny Ferrari and the banged-up Fiat 500 (in the former he went slow, in the latter as fast as possible)."[63]

Roberto's friends teased him, calling him Socrates. He was always exhorting the spectator to know himself; inveighing against modern "sophistic" art that makes people slaves; using Socratic phrases like "I'm ignorant"; doggedly pursuing truth; being widely misunderstood by all but a few disciples; and, like Socrates, had come late to awareness of his doubts and the beauty of intelligence.[64]

Was the movie a self-portrait? "Chiefly for the 'he never earned a cent' part," Roberto replied. "Doing only what interests you, what you enjoy and judge useful (as Socrates did and as I try to do too) is a very expensive luxury: the practical problems of life never really get solved. Certainly Socrates is a character I feel close to."[65]

In the movie, Socrates's few human moments shine in their isolation. In fact, as Michael McKegney notes, "several of the most moving incidents (Socrates's prevision of his betrayal in the eyes of Meletus, his prayer to die among friends, and the final words he whispers of Xanthippe and the children in prison) seem to be inventions of the director."[66]

Socrates's eccentricity, Roberto said, "was his search for reality, and his desire that people learn to use their own intelligence and develop their own critical faculties in order consciously to make their own choices. His eccentricity was his refusal to be called master, his not claiming that he was imposing authoritative teachings on anyone, his belief instead in the dialectic, in the force of knowledge, in culture. . . .

"And neo-realism, what was it? A way of questioning reality, of searching for the truth."

And what does "truth" or "reality" mean?

"It doesn't mean anything: it is. Reality is. There is only one reality, not many. Maybe the totality of it cannot be completely absorbed, but one can certainly get near it."[67]

Roberto made *Socrates* at the very outset of his experiments at Houston and the Centro Sperimentale, as if he were writing already the experiments' epitaphs: *The Death of Reason.* Maybe *Stromboli* was an equally pessimistic epitaph for the experiment with Ingrid, whose new wisdom, instead of leading her to come down from the mountain and redeem him, as planned in the script, will lead her away from him instead. Ingrid's various characters are all martyrs to impulse, his to reason; but the distinction is moot: they're all from Arc. Pascal and Descartes, too, as they endure living death. Nonetheless Roberto, while making *Socrates* in fascist Spain, told two young devotees, "I spend a lot of my time with people of your age, and I know how much there is about you all that's marvelous. . . . If you have faith in people, you'll have faith in logic and rationality too. We know that however long it takes, we shall achieve it. . . . There are no limitations on man if change can be carried out not in a passion but rationally. . . . I think that today we stand on the threshold of a wonderful epoch."[68]

*

Socrates was shot in Spain between mid-April and the end of May 1970; one week at the Samuel Bronson Studios in Madrid, three weeks on location in Patones Arriba, forty miles away. Roberto was unwilling to work in Greece because of its fascist regime. Spain had a fascist regime too, and Sicily could have served as easily, but Spanish television was providing part of the minuscule 240 million lire budget ($385,000) and Roberto had known the Minister of Information, Sánchez Bella, in Rome when he had been Spain's ambassador to Italy. RAI's share was 81 million; but the network covered the shooting with a press campaign and sent journalists to Spain. The rest of the money came from the ORTF, which enabled La Rochefoucauld, who was responsible for the French edition and dreaded a repeat of Scaffa's experience with *Acts*, to impose two experienced French actors, Jean Sylvère, 60, and Anne Caprile, in the roles of Socrates and Xanthippe. The French acted in French, the one Italian, Bepe Mannaiuolo, in Italian, and the rest in Spanish.

The production was frustrating and the movie disappointing. Roberto complained that he had had to spend 98 percent of his energy just setting up the project.[69] RAI had wasted almost two years since *Acts*, and now saddled him with a punctilious consultant in an attempt to enforce standards less "rough and naive."[70]

"I had to contend with a new co-author who I think was named Rosso and [I think] a RAI employee," recalled La Rochefoucauld; "Scaffa either did not come or did not stay in Spain."[71] Roberto hated RAI's man, said Scaffa, endured him for a few days, then expelled him from the set, suspended production, and went back to Italy, "forcing the RAI director to ask his pardon for having attempted such a maneuver."[72]

Roberto, at the same time, was dividing his energies between Houston and the Centro. He was very overweight, suffered from the heat, and had to be helped up the path to the cave in which Socrates was imprisoned. He had a badly sprained toe—he had dropped a suitcase on it—which deprived him of the surest vent for his frustrations, driving. More seriously, his alter ego son Renzo had deserted the Great Plan and gone off to Chile; none of the crew had worked with him before, except for his sister Marcella and La Rochefoucauld; and because he could not speak Spanish he could not communicate directly with most of the actors, who often were hostile, or the cameraman, who did not understand the remote-control zoom. And the script had been left to the last minute, even though one treatment dated from 1957.

"RR, as often, was extremely tense and irritable during the days before the shooting," said La Rochefoucauld. "It was stormy. . . . Then came the shooting of the first scenes and, as usual, he quieted down."[73]

The movies following *Louis* would be developments within a genre and style established by *Louis*. Like *Roma città aperta*, *Louis* would inspire a host of imitators (Tavernier—*Que la fête commence*, Rivette—*Jeanne la pucelle*, Goretta—*Les Chemins de l'exil, ou les dernières années de Jean-Jacques Rousseau*,

La Rochefoucauld—*Richelieu*, Mnouchkine—*Molière*). But like after *Paisà*, Roberto himself would be unable to duplicate his initial success. For the same reason:

"The point of departure for the films following [*Louis*]," said La Rochefoucauld, "was not of the quality of Jean Gruault's work, not by a long way. . . . RR was developing his discourse on 'daily life,' but in *Louis XIV* it had existed as a reflection around a clear dramatic idea."[74]

Gruault simply had a great deal more to say about history and its characters, and a much greater ability to say it interestingly and dramatically, than did Rossellini or the treatments that Scaffa and Marcella drew up for his movies after *Louis*. Gruault did more homework; his characters and intrigues are deeper, more multi-faceted, more *crafted*. Rossellini's art was to give flesh and human personality to Gruault's bookish ideas—more flesh and personality than the bookish Truffaut or Resnais could. But without material comparable to Gruault's, Rossellini's art was less rich and robust. Because the ideas are clearer, and more developed, *Louis* does not suffer from the somnolent sequences that impair the dramatic force of the later films. Even for bored audiences, *Louis* is awesome, "too seductive," thank goodness.

But Roberto had shunted Gruault aside during *Louis*, as he had Mann and Amidei during *Paisà*, then had become irritated with him for refusing to do more TV projects, and resentful of Gruault's work with other filmmakers as invasions of his private turf. When Truffaut and Gruault made the very Rossellinian *L'Enfant sauvage* (*The Wild Child*), Roberto refused to see it. He was afraid of finding it too good, Gruault maintains. Then came *Mon Oncle d'Amérique* and it was the end. "When I told him I was going to collaborate with the decadent aesthete Alain Resnais and with Henri Laborit, a *French* biologist, a nullity in other words (for him, at that moment, the only good biologists were Americans, indeed Texans . . . ; ever since he'd started teaching at [Rice] he'd given into delirious Americanphilia), I was immediately and definitively cast into outer darkness in company with Antonioni, Visconti, Kissinger (who didn't know proper table manners), Lizzani (who had the fault of being a Communist), Cottafavi (whom I had the fault to think a good filmmaker), Godard, Rivette, Vario Merdone, Solinas, and Trombadori."[75]

(Vario Merdone was Roberto's pun on Mario Verdone. *Merdone* means "big shit.") Gruault could have added other names—Riganti, De Robertis, Scalera, Mussolini, Amidei, Fellini, Geiger, Lopert.

For *Socrates*, as usual, La Rochefoucauld would have to write the dialogue the night before. His pages would arrive on the set around 6 A.M., be translated by José-Luis Guarner and Jos Oliver from French into Spanish, and then written onto blackboards for the Spanish actors to read during the shooting, since there was no time for lines to be memorized. On one occasion Roberto arrived around ten, announced everything would be changed, disappeared for an hour with La Rochefoucauld, and came back with a new scene for the sacrifice of the cock, which they then shot.[76]

"The shooting was difficult," La Rochefoucauld agrees. "RR was not satisfied with the working conditions with the TVE. There was a continual cold wind . . . , the set decorator was arrested on the set by the political police, etc."[77] A wind storm had interrupted production for a week during the fight with RAI, which left little time or money for the actors; often Roberto would do only a single take. "The cross-cutting was due to the poor acting," says Jos Oliver. "Rossellini was always saying, 'We'll fix that in the editing.' If someone made a mistake or he didn't like something an actor did, he would continue the shot until the end, then go back and do shots to save the sequence."[78]

Most of the time was spent struggling with the wind, scraping glass, and regulating mirrors for the Schüfftan effect. Roberto had spent a good part of the budget, about a million pesetas, on a miniature model of the Acropolis (which he gave to the Cinémathèque afterward). Oliver recalls that he "had planned to introduce all the sequences dealing with the public life of Athens by a camera movement from the Acropolis to the *agora*, the market town, because the Acropolis governed all public life in Classical Greece. But there was a great deal of wind almost every day, and by the next day the whole complicated set-up [the huge painting and mirror] would have all fallen down. I don't think there's more than a single sequence left in the film where this idea can be seen. The wind thus deprived the film of one of its richest visual ideas."[79]

One cloudy day they needed light to match the previous shot. Roberto spotted a small hole in the clouds, waited, and eventually the sun shone through, whereupon he shot the sequence in a single take. "You've got to have faith," he said.[80]

Socrate received the warmest applause of RAI's three movies at Venice, September 19, 1970, although Marcorelles complained it "suffers cruelly from [an Italian] dubbing that accentuates its pedantic side."[81] Because of resistance to RAI's entry into film, neither *Socrate*, Fellini's *I clowns*, nor Bertolucci's *La strategia del ragno* (*The Spider Stratagem*) were in competition. RAI then waited a year before broadcasting *Socrate* and then, as it did with all the Horizon 2000 movies, broke it up into hour-long segments. Part One, Thursday, June 17, 1971, was seen by 4.9 million viewers; Part Two, Sunday, June 21, by 7.5 million, and the "enjoyment index" rose from 70 to 75 percent. Seventy-six percent found the story easy to follow; 75 percent thought the argument interesting; 71 percent said Socrates's mentality was modern; 80 percent said his method of dialogue was still useful; and 87 percent judged his ideas to be positive on the whole.[82]

In France, at the Cinémathèque Française, some sneered at *Socrate*, others were hostile, most were uncomprehending. What did neo-realism have to do with costumes, painted scenery, and all that talk?

*

In the U.S., RAI presented *Socrate* in Italian at the Museum of Modern Art in February 1971 and at Washington's AFI Theater in March, along with *I clowns*, *Spider Strategy*, and Olmi's *I recuperanti*. In November, *Socrate* had a brief commercial run in New York. Vincent Canby in the *New York Times* noted a lack of visual grandeur, primal emotion, or drama. "The film is a series of rather proper, spoken tableaus that seldom erupt with spontaneity. . . . Yet there is in this fidelity—in this complete refusal to let the film come between the audience and its subject—a kind of beauty and poetry that are all but unknown in the work of any other contemporary film-maker."[83]

Unfortunately, it was the inferior Italian version that Rossellini sold to New Yorker Films for subtitling in English, and the subtitles are frequently illegible and, when legible, as Canby said, "don't always make a great deal of sense." But even with proper titling, replacement of oral communication with texts would totally undermine Rossellini's (and Socrates's) intentions. And the *work* of trying to follow rapidly spoken Platonic reasoning via subtitles is downright enervating. In a real sense, therefore, neither *Socrates* nor *Blaise Pascal*, *Agostino*, *Cartesius*, or *Il Messia* is accessible without knowledge of Italian or French.

Nevertheless, attitudes towards Rossellini's "new realism" had changed in New York since *Louis XIV's* failure in 1967. *Louis XIV* had had a six-week run in 1970 and been hailed by Roger Greenspun in the *New York Times* as "surely a masterpiece,"[84] an assessment which not only re-versed Bosley Crowther's pan four years before in the same *Times*, but was seconded by *The New Yorker*, *Newsweek*, *The Village Voice*, and *The New Republic*.

In a *Times* interview with Rossellini, two weeks after *Socrates*, Canby lauded Roberto's "teaching cinema" as "the record of one's man extraordinary curiosity, of one man's exploration of the world around him, with some tentative suggestions as to how it got that way." He also, like Greenspun, tried to correct the slights of the past. Rossellini's pictures with Ingrid Bergman were now acknowledged as "documents of character-in-specific-time, cast in form of fiction. So innovative were they that only now—in this almost post-Antonioni era—are they being correctly evaluated as logical extensions of the social and political concerns of his earlier work."[85]

Bob Lawrence

Bob Lawrence resurfaced into Roberto's life by a chance meeting at Tivoli in 1960 during *Viva l'Italia*. Bob Lawrence had held onto his shares in *Open City* and *Paisan* and had become a producer, a fact which led inevi-tably to a series of misadventures with Roberto beginning in 1970. The misadventures struck Lawrence as extraordinary. In fact, they were typical of (but kinder than) the misadventures that befell everyone who worked with Roberto. Friendship was even more taxing; none of the usual rules applied, your choice was to walk away or love him with more commitment. In the lives of all his associates, Roberto was an extraordinary presence; but for Roberto himself such relationships were the norm and always had been.

In 1970, Roberto was promoting *The Industrial Revolution, Thomas More, Descartes, Diderot, Nièpce and Daguerre, Moral Evolution through the Ages, Brasilia, Stories from Merovingian Times, The History of Colonization, The History of Japan, The American Revolution, The Civilization of the Conquistadores,* and *The Whale,* and asked Bob Lawrence to help him. "Are you with me, Bob?"

Lawrence found some Texans in San Antonio, who were ready to pay a large advance for U.S. distribution rights to *Pascal* and a few other projects. Roberto refused to meet with the Texans, claiming they just wanted to see "the animal."

This was the first misadventure. Nonetheless, Roberto was desperate for money, as usual, and asked Lawrence if there were not some way to make some out of *Survival.* (The first six episodes had played disastrously on RAI during the summer of 1970, despite which Roberto had managed to get the series aired on some South American networks.) Lawrence replied that there was one sole possible market in the U.S. and Roberto, without asking to hear more, cheerfully went back to Italy and spent the money he expected Lawrence to make for him. In January 1971, Lawrence called him to a meeting in Chicago with Encyclopaedia Britannica Films. They were willing to pay $1 million for the series, they explained, which they intended to re-edit into shorter segments for classroom use, and to mine for individual frames for educational film strips (a dozen or so slides to illustrate a lecture). "Bob, we must talk," Roberto said, and led him into the men's room. He would not permit these people to touch even a single frame, he announced in tones that admitted no argument. "I don't care," he said, angry, "if only ten people see my films, as long as they see them *my* way!"[86]

This was the second misadventure. Next came *Marco Polo.* Travel to China had just become possible, Mao Tse Tung had agreed to answer twelve questions submitted in advance, and Roberto was eager to go to China and meet Mao at the end of 1971. But a fight at RAI scuttled his plan and Antonioni—of all people!—went instead to make *Chung Kuo Cina* without Mao. In the meantime, Roberto had gotten excited about *Marco Polo. Marco Polo* would have a cast of thousands, he said, and *Variety* reported his words, which alarmed a British group who happened to be developing their own *Marco Polo.* The Brits flew to New York to see Lawrence and all summer he played tough, while preparations were made and agreements hammered out. At last, fall came and everyone gathered in Roberto's back yard on Via Appia Antica. The British would finance a series of 13 to 26 fifty-minute episodes, from which a feature would also be assembled. The budgets involved were many times greater than what Roberto was used to. He would have final cut for the whole world—except for England. "Bob, we must talk," Roberto said. And that was the end of that.[87]

But new adventures lay ahead.

After the U.S., Italy, and Spain, Roberto's other field of activity at this time was Chile. One project, *The Whale*, had almost been financed by Lawrence with his Texans. *The Whale* was about wretches who live on refuse on a deserted Chilean coast. One day a colossal whale is washed up. "They had a dream. Unfortunately they had no tools, no equipment, for doing anything with the whale. Very soon, some people came from Santiago and carried the whale away. It's the story of all underdeveloped countries."[88]

A second project was a documentary on Tololo, an astronomic observatory two miles up in the Andes that Roberto liked to visit. Another project dealt with the hundreds of ghost towns in northern Chile that had been created when the invention of nitroglycerin had ended saltpeter mining. In one such town Roberto found locomotives in a huge nineteenth-century factory, with a billiard table in a corner, and billiard balls still on it—a perfect set for *The Industrial Revolution*. Still another project was about primitive Indians with skinlike bark who dove nude into the freezing Straits of Magellan and gorged on seafood.

The principal Chilean project was *The Civilization of the Conquistadores*. An earlier treatment prepared for Roberto, *The Conquest of America by Cortés* or *La via dell'argento* ("The gold route"), had treated history as legend, concentrating on Malinche, a perversely seductive Indian woman who guided Cortés through his conquests in Mexico. And there had been Amidei's story about the girl in the Andes who sees San Martin's army. The latest treatment dealt straightforwardly with the conquistadors; the exploitation of hundreds of thousands of mine laborers; the vicissitudes of the blacks; the linguistic, cultural, and spiritual conquest; the reductions; the expulsion of the Jesuits; and the colonial revolution.

All of these projects were misadventures. The only Chilean film—with, rather than by, Roberto—was an interview with Salvador Allende, who had been elected president in 1970 as a Socialist and was trying to counter U.S. hostility. In May 1971, Allende invited Roberto to dinner, dubbing him *El viejo*, "the old one," to distinguish him from Renzino, whom he had known since 1964, and who had arranged the interview. Roberto thought Allende extraordinarily tender. Allende had done autopsies as a doctor and would hold out his hands: "I've opened the bodies of at least fifteen hundred people. I know people!" When Roberto remarked that Allende lived on a street named for one of his heroes, Thomas More, Allende admitted he knew nothing about him but right away "called a secretary and asked him to get hold of everything he could find on Thomas More. He was in a hurry to know what the author of *Utopia* had really said. He was that sort of man, intellectually curious and never satisfied."[89]

In Roberto's analysis, Allende dressed fashionably and conservatively, which expressed his rationalism, but was surrounded by confusion. For example, Chile's main industry was American-controlled copper mining, which Allende wanted to nationalize. But the workers short-sightedly opposed him, because the dollars the Americans paid them were worth three times as much on the black market. "Personally I don't believe at all in the theory that he killed himself [when the military stormed his residence], because he was a man too conscious of his duties and the hopes placed in him. He knew very well . . . that to affirm his own ideas he had to force himself to every extreme of heroism, including violent death. . . .

"I asked Allende if he knew why Sisyphus was condemned, as we know, to push that enormous mass back up the mountain after it had rolled down. I maintained that the gods had condemned Sisyphus because in fact Sisyphus was a trickster. Nothing is built by trickery: temporary measures are taken, illusions are created, then everything comes rolling down. Allende smiled. His policy demonstrated that he belonged to the other party [intelligence] and wanted to act in such a way that, with his example, people would develop their own capacity to think and discern."[90]

The 45-minute interview, not directed by Rossellini and with almost no cutting, was purchased by RAI but not broadcast until after Allende's death two years later, when it was titled "Force and reason" (*La forza e la ragione*).

Blaise Pascal

(Trilogy of Desiccation II)

RAI broadcast the last six episodes of *La lotta dell'uomo per la soprav-vivenza* a year after the first six, in September and October 1971, somewhat reluctantly one supposes, and opposite Italy's most popular show, *Canzonissima*. Not surprisingly, the audience dropped to as low as 300,000. Nor did *La lotta* attract respectable critiques. The left reproached its "mystic vision of history, and thus of man"; others found it simplistic.[1] "In fact," wrote Baldelli, "it lacks even the correct information: e.g., its inexact explanation of the origin of the matriarchal system; the division of labor and systems of parentage are ignored, as are also the social origins and functions of systems of succession—through maternal or paternal line—the motives of their evolution—through the incest taboo and the successive exclusions of couplings among consanguinaries—their connections with the changes in economy: from collective to private property. Rossellini constructs the Middle Ages on the basis of selections [of which events to depict] made a posteriori by bourgeois culture, which recognizes as cultural only events that laid the ground for its own birth and throws out anything suggesting other possible dimensions of mankind."[2]

But Baldelli seems to have been the only writer who thought *La lotta* worthy of serious criticism. No one seems to have polled audience response in Italy (and we do not know where else the series was shown). The obvious question cannot be answered: did anyone learn anything, get inspired, pursue ideas, or change as a result of seeing *La lotta*?

Most of the time *La lotta* is neither engaging nor instructive. Rossellini rejects the hokum that makes commercial movies (and commercials) entertaining, yet withholds his own art as well. Nor is much information imparted; there are never any dates, technology is seldom demonstrated understandably, and abstract arguments are run through quickly, without any attempt at visualization, just talk—less "democratic" than any mere "text" could achieve.

In person, Roberto was famous for telling these same anecdotes with gee-whiz charm. And he would explain things. Why didn't he do this in *La lotta*, the way Carl Sagan and James Burke did for their educational television series a few years later?

Roberto does appear occasionally, but he is dry and wooden. He was so nervous, in fact, that he asked De Sica to come direct him; he wanted to be told what to do with his hands.[3] On camera, or in front of groups, he was ashamed to be his narcissistic self; his charm does not surface.

In any case, Roberto did not want to "teach" like Sagan or Burke. He wanted to *recreate* the event—"historical neo-realism" like *Roma città aperta*. He was not a "documentary" filmmaker despite all the cant claiming he was. He eventually gave up on his *Science* series because he could neither accept a documentary format nor find a dramatic one.

"Rossellini was a filmmaker of situations more than language," said La Rochefoucauld. "He was interested in daily life, in details permitting reconstruction of the spirit of an epoch."[4] Yet it is this Crocean *ricorso* approach to history that most requires "art" to validate "facts," and Rossellini, alas, now distrusted his art as much as his narcissism. He would denounce art as seduction, and dismiss them both as social cancers. Confusedly, he would decide that art was irrelevant to the Great Plan and would produce boring film as a result. "He didn't trust himself," La Rochefoucauld said. "He was afraid of copying himself. Thus he was afraid of scripts too; he didn't want people writing 'Rossellini stuff' for him. He didn't want to be a prisoner of what would have been written. This is the heart of the problem."[5]

How one misses the outdoors in the later didactic films! *Pascal, Descartes,* and *Agostino* are mostly closed rooms, like the beginning of *Viva l'Italia* while one waits for the vast zoom of Calatafimi, but now vastness never comes. There are hardly any street scenes, let alone sky, field, or trees. One yearns for music, dance, song, or action, for the fox hunt that bursts into *Louis XIV*.

Roberto, after *Socrates,* had intended to do *The Industrial Revolution* and then *Science*, with *Pascal* in the middle as a kind of hinge—the relationship of science and philosophy in the evolution of civilization. As things turned out, RAI decided to oppose more long films, thanks to *The Iron Age* and *La lotta*. But RAI did agree to support other elements of The Great Plan, thanks to vigorous efforts by Giovanbattista Cavallaro, a film critic and member of RAI's Administrative Council who had promoted *Louis XIV* for Venice. In less than a year Roberto would make *Pascal, Agostino,* and the four-and-a-half-hour *The Age of the Medici*.

Blaise Pascal—a Horizon 2000, RAI, ORTF co-production, in which RAI's participation was less than 100 million lire ($160,000)—was shot in seventeen days, between August 16 and September 4, 1971.

According to Roberto, Pierre Arditi was chosen to play Pascal because he resembled pictures of Pascal.[6] In actuality, if Arditi bears scant resemblance to Pascal, he bears strong resemblance to a "thinking reed"—Pascal's term for a human being. According to La Rochefoucauld, Roberto had wanted an Italian but La Rochefoucauld had insisted on Arditi, a French baker and theatrical actor, and Arditi got the part after his small son won Roberto's heart. "[Rossellini] told me, 'I can make a chair act,'" said Arditi; "and I am a chair in the film, a good chair, but a chair all the same. I never had any power over what I was doing. He controlled me like a guinea pig to whom one says go right, go left: I went right, left, I put my hand like this. At the moment of the memoir, the discovery of God, my hand had to go down like this, and then my head fall like this, and then I had to fall down because I finally had the revelation of God. It's the most successful scene in the film, but I had no voice in it. He based all his work on a style of gesture that was so precise that it ended up giving you the inner feelings."[7]

To play Descartes, Roberto at the last moment thought of Claude Baks, the Schlumberger ombudsman who was his partner in Horizon 2000, and whom he thought exactly resembled Descartes. He phoned Baks in Paris on August 30 to be in Bassano two days later, gave him his lines two minutes before the shot, and then required him to walk around on a high crooked board while reading—all of which made Baks nervous but which helped produce the character. Rossellini tried similar tricks with Arditi but never got away with them, which made him mad.[8]

On the set, once the decorator and technicians were ready, Rossellini would run through a take, simultaneously choreographing the actors and camera movements. By disconnecting the Pancinor's remote-control cable, he could look through the eyepiece; Marcella, his script girl and sister, would mark the movements on her dialogue sheet and click her fingers to remind him during the shooting, when he could not look through the eyepiece. Once she forgot and the camera ran out of film halfway through a shot.[9]

In place of a script there were 350 pages of texts and ideas. "Scaffa and Marcella, or some others, produced a very thick text," said La Rochefoucauld. "RR had made me come to Rome. On my part I had worked on a treatment with the most prestigious advisers. I lived shut inside the Hotel Forum [to complete] my first mission, to produce an outline, i.e., a continuity of scenes numbered independently of earlier treatments. This outline with a few modifications was approved by Roberto. Then it remained for me to write dialogue from day to day, with the mission *not* to communicate the texts to the actors until the night before or even the same morning! Arditi surmounted this test splendidly. Neither Scaffa nor Marcella interfered the least in the world in this work except in friendly ways. Obviously from the point of view of Scaffa, who was very orthodox and well informed on theological questions, this Pascal was a thorny subject. I must say that he was always friendly and we had no conflicts. I obtained a signed agreement with both them and RR that the French titles would cite me as co-author of the scenario but sole author of the dialogue. This was the first time it seemed important to me to be credited."[10]

On the set Roberto paid little attention to how the actors said their lines—which often frustrated them—but much attention to how the actors moved, particularly in matters pertaining to details of period behavior different from our own. As always, Rossellini stressed the *physiognomic* qualities in the actor that coincided with the interpretation of the character that Rossellini wanted to present: basically, Pascal as thinking reed. Rossellini's method with actors, far from being the global phenomenology described by Ayfre and Bazin (or the non-art vaunted by Roberto), is pure Murnau, the most stylized form of Germanic expressionism (usually considered the polar opposite of realism), in which the filmmaker's psychoanalysis of the character is expressed by body posture, gesture, music, lighting, and scenery. Nonetheless, Roberto never ran through a scene more than two or three times and often did just one take; he knew what he wanted and exactly how to get it, cheaply and quickly. Thirty of the 46 scenes were shot in an old stone house south of Rome in Magliano Sabina in the first three days; most of the rest in the Odescalchi palace in Bassano Romano. Finally, because of its multiple set-ups, the witch trial took an entire day at an abbey in Fossanova, where the Port Royal scene was also filmed. Roberto had offered Mario Garriba a job but Garriba had declined: "Everyone said that when you work for him, he eats you up."[11]

Roberto's inspiration was flowing, and everything in the film is inventive and lively, no matter how morose poor Pascal: the actors, the mise en scène, the sets, the lighting, the camera. For the first time in ten years, things were going well for Roberto. He was free at the moment from both the Centro and Rice, had found powerful corporate sponsors, and knew he would be following *Pascal* with *The Age of the Medici*.

"No one who's not a kamikaze," he said, "would make a film about Pascal,[12] a very boring character who never made love in his life. When he was suffering, which was most of the time—he was always having pains of one kind or another—he used to solve geometry problems. He really wasn't much fun.[13] Yet he was a fundamental figure in our drama: the dilemma between science and faith, science and emotions, science and hope,[14] a dilemma that still hasn't been resolved or clarified. Pascal found himself at the beginning of the development of modern scientific thought, the experimental method, and mathematics. And this development came to affect profoundly our civilization, which without doubt has a structure that is eminently religious and theological. Pascal, who wore himself out in scientific research and consumed himself in exercises in Christian perfection, expresses better than anyone two essential aspects of his century: scientific anxiety and religious piety.[15] [His] scientific interests were in perpetual conflict with his deep religious faith.[16]

"One fine day it was decided that problems would no longer be posed in a religious or metaphysical perspective, but in a scientific one. Reason became Arm Number One. People discarded dream and sensibility.

"But, to the contrary: the need was to reunite them! We're made as much out of dream as reality. To privilege one over the other is a work of castration. Empiricism, positivism, illuminism, and Marxism: they're all enterprises of castration."[17]

Blaise Pascal is so much a horror movie that it makes *Louis XIV* look like a romp. It's Dreyer's *Day of Wrath* without the entrancing woman. Everything is drenched in suffering, torture, fear, superstitious dread; everyone is writhing in desperate faith, self-mortification, and pain. As in Bresson's *Diary of a Country Priest*, we feel the intolerability of time. Rossellini's penchant for masses of black, white, and scarlet make everything seem drenched in blood and penance. Such was Jansenism from the Roman point of view.

In Dreyer we are crushed by life's hopeless agony and compensated, sometimes, by a single glance (e.g., the monk who gives Joan a cross to clasp on the stake—the sole compassionate exchange in a movie structured out of uncompassionate exchanges). Also in Bresson there are instants of grace—indeed, "everything is grace"—and Bresson's corrupt physical world is corporeal only to the extent that light's paintbrush momentarily brushes it. In Rossellini's Jansenism, there is no presence of such immediate redemption, no alternative to brute materiality. We are crushed by life's hopeless agony and appalled, always, by the heroism, the physical passion endured by the persons who make the small advances that improve human survival and lead us all toward liberty. That such advances happen seems a miracle. But they are not openings of love or grace, as in Dreyer or Bresson or earlier Rossellini. Life is no longer a voyage in Italy.

We follow Pascal from age 17, as he emerges out of his father's shadow, until his death at 39 in 1662, when we leave him. It is a story of endless misery and dogged persistence. It is a life like the Jansenist crucifix that hangs on Pascal's wall and depicts Christ with his arms stretched upward. The enunciation of Pascal's famous "wager" (that heaven may not exist but we risk nothing, and may profit much, by betting that it does) is staged during a panoply of wagers (a dice game and a love tryst) in order to *dramatize* the absurdity that is the constant context of Pascal's life and that, masquerading as order and wisdom, rules Pascal's era with terror. For example (an illustrative anecdote typical of Rossellini): a miller's son recovers from sickness after his maidservant tells him to kill a cat to get rid of the demon surely causing the illness, whereupon the miller's customers desert him convinced the maidservant is a witch, whereupon to save himself from ruin he has her arrested, whereupon the elder Pascal speeds up her trial so the miller can pay his taxes, whereupon she is tortured and burned by the justice system to save the community, the miller, the tax system, and her own soul. Thus is absurdity systematized into terror. Similarly (another anecdote): the pompous Chancellor, all but ignoring the world's first calculator that Pascal has invented, fatuously blathers about Louis XIII being the finest metal smith in France, and remarks that Pascal's family fortune is due solely to the fact that Blaise's pretty sister Jacqueline had caught Richelieu's lusty eye in a girls' play when she was thirteen. When we meet Jacqueline she is frightened all the time, eventually is allowed to flee into a monastery, and dies there. Within such contexts of absurdity and terror, Pascal's heroism is miraculous, like Dreyer's moments of grace.

Secular critics sometimes charge that Dreyer's and Rossellini's miracles are "mystic." But their movies are documents historicized, and Christian iconography does not make them religious. Both men claimed to be atheists; what they are querying is religion and two millennia of Western civilization. Just as Pascal is depicted as split (suicidally, it is implied) between faith and science, mirroring his age, so too Roberto, like many Italians of his generation, would gravitate between impulse and reason, intuition and judgment, emotion and rationality, Church and Communism (or Liberalism).

On one day, in his positivist mood, Roberto would be unequivocal: "Ultimately the problem is always the same: to free ourselves from all super-structures, from our emotions and interests, to find the detachment sufficient to observe things. This is the point: the great effort to rationalize our method of observation. Our culture's point of departure has always been emotion. Scientific thought regards things in completely different terms. . . . When I lost my nine-year-old son . . . , a terrifying thing . . . , I searched, desperately, for consolations. Where do you find them? You find them either in reality, reality, reality, that is, in imagining life as a biological phenomenon with a scientific precision, etc., etc., etc., with all its coordinates. And then there's another aspect, isn't there, that's completely metaphysical? So I was in a tempest—an enormous one, I'd say, in this period—yet it seems clear to me that I accepted the biological rather than the other aspect."[18]

On another day, more Crocean, Roberto would also be unequivocal in saying the opposite: "We're made as much of dream as reality."[19]

Scaffa, in his analysis of *Pascal*, emphasizes this second attitude, declaring that the movie's "message" is "the spiritual dimension which, according to Pascal, is capable of seeing, communicating, and intuiting with the heart, beyond cold reason."[20] Indeed, there is even a scene *invented*, a confrontation between Pascal and Descartes which never occurred in reality, in order to dramatize Pascal's upholding the primacy of intuition over Descartes's advocacy of judgment. (Rossellini's subsequent movie on Descartes will attack him as overly abstract.) "The only knowledge man needs," Pascal declares, "is the recognition that an infinity of things exist that surpass reason. Can you know and love somebody with just reason alone?"

But Scaffa's spiritual "message" is only half the movie and, like Pascal himself, has to coexist with the anti-metaphysical message of human science. To reconcile the two is perhaps not possible or desirable; both Rossellini and Pascal inspired themselves trying. "There are two types of intelligence," Rossellini's Pascal says. "One of them is geometrical; the other could be called finesse. The first has conceptions that are slow, hard, and inflexible; whereas the second has agility in thought. From the eyes it goes to the heart, and from movement on the outside one knows what is going on inside. When the two intelligences are together, how much pleasure love gives!"

And elsewhere: "The extremes of knowledge touch at their extremities. One extreme is pure natural ignorance. The other is the knowledge great souls achieve, once they have learned what is given to man to learn and have discovered that they know nothing. Those who are in the middle, who have emerged from natural ignorance but have not been able to reach the other [knowledge], have the ignorance of the wise—a flour-dusting of knowledge—and make up the learned [members of society]. These are people who create confusion and judge everything badly."

As with Socrates, knowing that he does not know is a starting point for Pascal, and also an intuition that surpasses reason—and a motive for strained patience with the sort of phony knowledge that burns women alive or insists a vacuum cannot exist because "God did not create nothing." "I believe that charity is not charity, if it not illuminated by clear knowledge."

MacBean's observation about *Louis XIV*—"Rarely, if ever, has a work of art been so solidly rooted in *things* and [their] role in the making of history"—applies even more to *Pascal*.[21] Critics inevitably draw comparisons with Brecht,[22] but Brecht employs *things* only as symbols, and lest we miss the point, there are signs (billboards) to remind us. Rossellini's *things* do not function as signs (which have no place in art, said Croce). His *things* are the realities of everyday life. They "guarantee" a certain reality to an actually non-existent world. Most historical plays and movies minimize or update the differences between now and then in dress, rooms, furniture, and implements; Rossellini stresses differences, particularly when they require more *time* to deal with than their modern equivalents (e.g., Louis undressing; Pascal's servant emptying liquid utensils). Rossellini wants to give more reality to the world of his movies, not more Brechtian symbolism. Things can tell us as much as words about our ancestors' lives. Roberto spent more time constructing Pascal's calculator than on the script; and Nascimbene "created a sonority" on the music track for the calculator, "just using clocks of the period."[23]

Yet in the movie we are never given a good look at this calculator; we don't even get to see how it works. Nor is it pointed out, when Pascal uses a syringe, that a syringe was something he had had to invent. Nor is it explained that Pascal's unusual crucifix is a Jansenist one. Nor, for that matter, is it clear what Jansenism was or what the frequently-alluded-to Jansenists are quarreling over with the Jesuits.

Such obscurities annoy the hell out of audiences, and lead to observations such as this one by Carlo Scaringi: "Television's 'didactic' abilities are appealing when it really succeeds in making historical people and moments known and understood. But this doesn't seem to be the case with

Blaise Pascal, which is slow, confused, complicated, and comprehensible only to those who already know Pascal. For the general public Rossellini's pure beautiful images will remain abstruse and obscure."[24]

It is hard to disagree. A few paragraphs in a desk encyclopedia will give anyone a much clearer and deeper understanding of Pascal's life, thought, and importance than this film does, and in far less time.

But to criticize the movie for not doing what a book does is to miss the movie, by fixating on things that do not matter to it. At heart the complaint is the same that was made against *Paisà* and *Voyage in Italy*. Rossellini has not made the film we expected him to—and which we assume he intended to make. So we ignore the movie he did make.

In *Pascal* Rossellini gives us a specific crucifix that has Christ in an unusual pose (his arms stretched upward) and hangs in the room of a man who lives life as suffering and terror and hope. Now, if we relate to everything in Rossellini's shot—if we *feel* the crucifix and *feel* Pascal's life—then we shall have no problem whatsoever with the movie Rossellini has chosen to make, and we shall achieve a kind of knowledge of Jansenism that no book can give us. It is less important that we follow the specific logic of Pascal's arguments than that we relate to his emotions in making those arguments. His sister's sensibility will tell us more about Jansenism than a theology book; Rita Forzano's performance in this role rivets our attention even when she merely stands in the background, and proves the power of Rossellini's methods when applied to a performer capable of realizing them. "Most historical movies are informative: his are kindling," Penelope Gilliatt wrote.[25]

Blaise Pascal, televised in two parts in May 1972, had by far the largest audience of any Rossellini film in Italy, 16.1 million. The "enjoyment indexes" were a bit low, 59 and 64 percent, but there was one statistic Roberto could be proud of: "RAI took a survey before showing it," he said, "which showed that only one percent of Italians had even vaguely heard of Pascal. After a single transmission . . . another survey six months later found that 45 percent of the population knew something about Pascal. And there was a big increase in sales of books about Pascal and that era in French history."[26]

In France, *Le Figaro* was ecstatic. "How can someone dare to show on television, with actors, the most mysterious genius that France probably ever produced? . . . Such an enterprise would demand as much humility as audacity. The great Italian metteur en scène Roberto Rossellini took the bet and it's a beautiful success, this Pascal. . . . It's in the daily life of the seventeenth century that you are going to live for two hours. [And] during two hours, in the harmony created by Rossellini's images, Pierre Arditi manages to make us forget that the person who lives and suffers before us is an actor."[27]

Neither *Pascal* nor any subsequent Rossellini movie received a commercial release in America. Museum showings as part of Rossellini series at Pacific Film Archives in 1973 (sponsored by Dominique de Menil) and the New York Cultural Center in 1974 received awestruck reviews in specialized journals like *Film Quarterly, Cinema,* and *Art Forum.* But not even Penelope Gilliatt's adulation in *The New Yorker* was able to secure any bookings: "The film is full of physical and metaphysical conflicts that have to be reconciled: good fortune, servants, four-poster beds shrouded in beautiful brocade, patrons ready to support the pursuit of knowledge in return for a little fawning. . . . We see clerics trying a woman for witchcraft in a context of argument that is intellectually from a world completely different from the witch-trial scene in Ken Russell's hysterical *The Devils.* It might have been written by Shaw. It perfectly supports Pascal's suspicion that a man is living in perilous times when people are full of opinions and void of knowledge. The film is like *The Age of the Medici* in its gifts. All of Rossellini's new movies are intellectually elating, benevolent in their detail, and remarkable in the time they allow for dissertations more complex and beguiling than anything else in the world's popular cinema. For these films are profoundly populist: no one could mistake as anything else their view of the possible unity of thinking, art, and horse sense."[28]

Agostino d'Ippona

Roberto argued that civilizations rise and fall, and that ours, like Augustine's, "is on the edge of the abyss. . . . Augustine lived in a period . . . rich with points analogous to our own." The war in Vietnam; the crises in ecology and energy; the poverty in emerging countries; and "above all" the confusion of the people who have power were comparable, in Roberto's film, to classical civilization dying; the empire falling before the barbarian invasions; Rome itself sacked by the Visigoths in 410; roads no longer safe; riots in the cities; factionalism among the Christians; rampant transsexuality; and "above all" the moral corruption of government officials.

Augustine's solution was to recuperate the values of his dying world through a fresh vision of history. He urged people to decide whether they were citizens of the dying terrestrial city or of the city of God. "Kingdoms . . . are only soft murmurs between two silences," Augustine says in the movie; "And while the world is shaken and falls, Christ tells us: 'Why be upset?' . . . The world is like man: it is born, grows, gets old."

"This is why I made *Agostino d'Ippona,*" Roberto said. "The idea of a dying civilization, like ours, that yet somehow preserves and projects something of itself into the future, fascinates me profoundly."[29]

Augustine of Hippo, probably more than anyone, shaped the themes and defined the problems of Western Christianity. But little of his thought is acknowledged in this film, not even his profound explorations of themes particularly dear to Roberto, like intuition and knowledge and the capacity to act with responsibility; or his sense of Christian life as a process of healing. The script is shallow even alongside *La lotta,* the production more so. One might rationalize such poverty as poetic—the characters, in bright new costumes that have obviously not been worn for any occasion outside this movie, walk in wintry light (it was always raining) around ancient ruins that have obviously not been lived in for several millennia (Pompeii, Herculaneum, and Paestrum), and in their walks encounter scarcely an implement, object, or "thing" that might mar their abstracted existence by suggesting "reality." On one of the few occasions when Roberto did require a prop, the production came to a total halt, because, to cite one example, no one could find the research about how men shaved in the fifth century. Roberto would start characters talking, stop them when he got tired, and not bother completing the scene. The few ideas Augustine gets to mention are reduced to banalities. "The world seems shaken by an invincible confusion," someone observes, and classical civilization is said to have fallen because of "moral confusion." But when has this not been so? Has civilization always been falling? Rossellini's illustrative anecdote concerns a magistrate who is loathe to decide whether as a Christian he should pardon a man or as a magistrate have the man killed; but this problem was scarcely unique to the fifth century. We are told in the film that fifth-century art (which is talked about but not shown) emphasizes the sensual at the expense of the spirit ("Literature and arts have become glorifications of man's senses and contemplation of his passions," Augustine says, ending rather than starting the topic); but when has this not been true of art? Whereupon Roberto (the grand voyeur) with shock confronts us with cross-dressing (which, it is implied, no one had done before in the Roman Empire, and now today—yuck!—they're doing it again).

The quality Rossellini admires in Augustine, as in Paul and Francis, is charity. He chose a Berber filmmaker, Dary Berkany, to play him not only because Augustine was a Berber but because Berkany had a charitable face.[30] The lines on charity come at the most moving moments, which not coincidentally are the most Rossellinian: "May discord be far from us. It is born when we love only ourselves." "You have exited from charity, thus from faith, since there is no faith without charity." "The law is made for man, not man for the law." Or, like Pascal, "Knowledge is useless if you don't respond with your heart to God's love."

On the evidence of *Agostino d'Ippona* neither Roberto nor his collaborators seem to have pondered much about Augustine's thought or the "things" of his time. The film looks hurriedly shot and *cheap*. A month before Roberto began shooting near Naples in January 1972, he told *The New York Times* the shooting would be in Algiers.[31] Scaffa and Marcella had started the treatment hardly a month before.[32] No sets this time, nor Schüfftan mirror shots either. Roberto wouldn't even spend money to show us the "too sensual" art his characters discuss, let alone take his usual pains to reconstruct lovingly a machine or two. "The film can become for future historians of cinema one of the obligatory texts to document the cinematographic use of the word," wrote Cesare Cavallieri, without irony, accurately identifying where the "film's" production values lie.

Roberto only shot about half the scenario that had been prepared, said Scaffa. "At a certain point during the shooting he found the film exhausted as a discourse. In fact, he hadn't wanted to tell Augustine's life as much as the idea that societies are born and die often unaware of their crises, and that factors of change that derive from the new cultures contribute to their decay. This is why in the film he gave preference to juxtaposing the two cities: the story of Rome's fall and the triumphal announcement of the heavenly city, utilizing testimony less of Augustine than of Marcellino, martyr and theorizer of a state that would leave to individual conscience the right of judgment on human behavior. He was not interested in shooting scenes planned on Augustine's itinerary in the desert with the monks disputing 'grace,' nor in the projected end of the film.

"Rossellini never screened his films and did little in editing them. His limitation derived chiefly from his *splendid laziness*. He did mostly what excited him. When it was a question of 'inventing' he was very active, when it was a question of 'executing' he was certainly less active. Then he often got terribly cross with his collaborators who hadn't executed well or had somehow betrayed the creative lines he'd indicated. He didn't claim these were works of art, rather that he was 'doing a work' which 'would help others' know better the people of his biographies. He often lengthened dialogues when they were scientific or moral in nature, rather than being content with the few allusions that, for sobriety and rhythm, the script gave him; when opportune, he would group dialogues and material from several scenes. All this in its didactic perspective—which occasionally strained the traditional language and rhythms of cinema.[33]

Agostino cost 250 million lire, about the same as *Socrates* or *Pascal*. Where did the money go? All of it was provided by RAI which, according to Stefano Roncoroni, had initially agreed for a film on Augustine to be shot by Roncoroni from a script by him and Virgilio Fantuzzi, S.J., whereupon Roberto claimed that if RAI were making a film on Augustine it would have to be with him, as it was among the subjects he had submitted—or meant to submit, for Augustine is absent on Roberto's Great Plan. Since RAI's first contract with Roncoroni barred giving Rossellini a contract for the same subject, it bought his entire film instead.[34]

Both Roncoroni and Fantuzzi remained ardent Rossellinians; they subsequently wrote some of the best articles on his life and work. Roberto had courted Roncoroni some years earlier, when the latter was scarcely out of his teens, phoning him just to talk at every hour of the day and night. Roncoroni's father had been the wealthy entrepreneur who had built Cinecittà. When Roberto learned the family had lost its money, he stopped phoning. When he took over RAI's Augustine project, he did not use or read Roncoroni's script, or invite his collaboration.[35]

At a special screening in RAI's auditorium in Turin in September 1972, *Agostino* was greeted in silence, followed by congratulations to Roberto and the question, "Why?" Broadcast in two weekly segments, it was seen by 4.1 million and 3.7 million viewers with enjoyment indexes of 69 and 65 percent. Two westerns, *The Rover* and *Jubal*, on the second channel, attracted four times as many viewers with enjoyment indexes of 75 and 79 percent.

Rossellini had started life as a typical product of his background—an ill-defined Crocean Catholic liberal, with a vague faith in human impulse to be sincere, and thus good, at moments of love and danger, as *Paisà* and many other movies sought to demonstrate.

On Romano's death, Roberto came to believe this impulse has its source in God. He became an Augustinian, a medievalist, convinced of the corruptness of our nature and our lack of freedom, of our inability to unite mind and heart, scientific knowledge, and feeling—and thus achieve freedom—without a process of healing that only God can give. Thus Karin in *Stromboli* and Irene in *Europe '51*, thus the succession of miracles that reawaken love in *Voyage in Italy*.

During the period following India, Rossellini's public pose became more Pelagian (i.e., anti-Augustinian), modernist, and Marxist. He began, in other words, to acknowledge the point of view of those who had most strongly attacked his earlier films.

The two hostile points of view dominated Augustine's time as well; it was in opposition to Pelagius that Augustine's theology was developed. For Pelagius, the social realist, sin is superficial and reversible; we are free, responsible, able to choose and determine our course. "It is the easiest thing in the world to change our will by an act of will," one of Pelagius's followers said. For Augustine, on the contrary, our imperfection is deep and permanent; any social good will be achieved only though extended, inner evolution and God's constant grace.

This is a kernel of Augustinian thought that has permeated Western civilization for more than 1,500 years. It is a kernel strangely ignored in *Agostino*, even though the notion of the City of God, which the film concentrates on, follows naturally from it, as does the impetus behind Rossellini's movies, from first to last.

Rossellini, whatever his public prattle, never accepted the Marx–Pelagian–Freud–Fascist notion that individual ills are basically society's ills, to be cured by proper legislation and will. His notion of "grace" became more humanist and Crocean, perhaps atheistic; but he remained Augustinian.

"I've ordered forty more books. I read ten or fifteen at once. I can't read one book at a time, I die of boredom.[36] I'm curious about everything. . . . I'm fascinated by meditation, personal slavery, reason. The study of philosophy, history, and essays isn't enough. I have 9,000 books, that is, 9,000 books that I've read, and notated."[37]

Roberto did not always get around to organizing his notes. But he was finally fulfilling the aspirations excited in him in his father's *cenacolo* 45 years earlier.

After *India*, as Fieschi wrote,[38] impulse is no longer something dormant that is suddenly awakened to life, that explodes suddenly in one, brief moment of truth (Karin shouting to God). Now it is a constant unquenchable furnace within us: pushing Garibaldi to make Italy, Paul to make the Church, Louis to make the monarchy, Pascal to make reconciliation. Roberto himself has changed from the vague decadent bourgeois encountering changes, to the old man struggling to demolish his ignorance little by little, day by day. Privately, and artistically, he remains a mixture of Croce and Augustine. *Acts of the Apostles* and *The Messiah* and *Blaise Pascal* may seem more humanist than religious in their study of Christian deeds, but they are awesomely evangelical in their depiction of the impulse that moves Christ and his followers, that transforms them, and the world too. Is God answering Karin?

The Age of the Medici

Croce went so far as to suggest that art, rather than politics or science, offered the primary means by which men could transform human life.
—Philip V. Cannistraro

In Roberto's family when he was growing up, it was his brother and sister and the house guests who were the "artists," not Roberto. Roberto was interested in girls and mechanics. In his thirties, when he started tinkering with film, his interests were still girls and mechanics, not "art." In his 39th year, when he made *Roma città aperta*, it came as a surprise to almost everyone, and not least to Roberto himself, that he was proclaimed an "artist."

But with *Paisà* he showed it was true and people began calling him "maestro" and bowing before him. And he believed them at first. He had felt himself inferior in culture and schooling before. Now he started chasing a new goddess, his movies became intensely aesthetic, the critics chuckled, and his self-doubts returned and grew through the 1950s. Was he in over his head? Wasn't it pompous to claim to be an artist? And wasn't much of the contemporary art that critics praised disgusting?

Eventually, to make the movies he wanted to make, Roberto marketed himself not as an artist, and barely as a filmmaker, but as a purveyor of educational materials. Perhaps part of him believed this was all he was. For five years he refused to direct. He insisted that Renzino take responsibility for *The Iron Age*, *La lotta*, and *The Industrial Revolution*. Yet when at last, at age sixty, he found himself once again behind the camera, making *Louis XIV* and then *Acts of the Apostles*, the muse proved difficult to resist— at least on good days.

Thus Roberto was ambivalent and defensive about art. Moreover he lacked the schooling and the command of Italian to speak the critics' language. Reluctant to say what he really felt, he took a cynical pose in public.

On the one hand, contempt: "If you start to think in terms such as 'I am an artist' you are immediately a son of a bitch.[1] Do you think it's the dream of a man who's really alive to get up in the morning and be an artist? A man's dream ought to be to be a man.[2] . . . The mythification that makes an artist into a semi-divine being is a thing that really makes me vomit."[3]

On the other hand, awe: "Art is the power to condense into one thing something that can give the viewer a wider horizon and help him understand even through emotions. Art . . . means you are fully involved . . . with brain and heart; then only are you fully involved."[4]

On the third hand, a desire to throw away his cake and eat it too: "I no longer consider myself to be an artist of the cinema, one of that god-like coterie of directors producing masterpieces to stun the world. I now see myself as scientist and craftsman. For me, Shakespeare and Rembrandt and Matisse were also scientists. The cinema must become scientific, it must learn to dispense knowledge and awareness."[5]

Accordingly, *The Age of the Medici* presents Renaissance art as an instrument of research rather than self-expression. Roberto is attacking conventional attitudes toward art. His quattrocento Florentines admire Brunelleschi's cathedral dome not for its beauty, like tourists and art books today, but as a materialization of Brunelleschi's wonderful calculations, which are wonderful because they show how intelligence can raise the level of human civilization. Art is thus politics, and the film is advocating the Liberal state as envisioned by Croce.

"Artistic activity begins when we find ourselves face to face with the visible world as though with something immensely enigmatic," wrote Conrad Fiedler.[6] In this sense, Rossellini used to refer to St. Peter's as a reply to the enigma: a summation of human knowledge during the Renaissance. "Humanism was the great attempt to make a synthesis of everything that was known," he said.[7] "The Renaissance was born at the moment that artists became aware of the giant steps humanity had made in science and technology. So, they became savants, and studied anatomy and perspective. Their preparation was strictly scientific, but was so tied to their nature, and their enthusiasm was so great, that they gave us masterpieces. . . . We need to be similar today."[8]

Instead art wallows in self-indulgence, Roberto charged, paraphrasing Croce's frustration with Proust—witness Fellini and Antonioni.[9] Apparently our civilization is not yet capable of a synthesis of the sort that produced Athens and the Renaissance.[10] "Yet why can't we, when we have such really extraordinary resources at our disposal today? . . . If we try a policy of synthesis, maybe we'll know how to put ourselves on a surer path for the future."[11]

The Age of the Medici suggests we can know. Is any movie more optimistic?

In *The Age of the Medici*, the Renaissance attitude toward "art" is described by Leon Battista Alberti (1404–72), the architect and theorist who, with Cosimo de' Medici (1389–1464), is one of the two heroes of Rossellini's movie:

Brunelleschi was supreme because he was an architect, sculptor, builder of fortresses and time pieces, skilled in hydraulic and mechanical engineering, expert in proportion and perspective. Today I still admire his most beautiful and accurate clocks. With him one can enter into the fantasy of things. The many artists who are enamored of practice without science are like boatmen who board a craft without rudder or compass and are never certain where they are going.... There is no art if it ignores the science. I would like the painter, for example, to be as learned as he may in all the seven liberal arts—grammar, dialectics, rhetoric, arithmetic and geometry, astronomy and music. But chiefly that he know geometry. Painting is science and the science of visual perspective is the exact foundation of the painting art. Painting is therefore the intersection of the visual pyramid, according to a given distance, a predetermined center, and the construction of angles on a certain surface. Here, come and look.[12]

Alberti shows a perspective. By means of perspectival drawing, drawings looked more like reality; the eye could even mistake Masaccio's flat painting of a vault for an actual vault. European painting vanquished space. It freed itself from obedience to a flat surface. The boundary of a picture became a window, a gateway to a second or substitute world—a world that, like Rossellini's attempts at a *ricorso* of the historical past, was a product of research, not of mere fantasy.

True, the results were always questionable. The substitute worlds produced by the Renaissance were always *also* fantasy. Similarly, inaccuracies in Rossellini's worlds are due not only to economy (in costumes and sets, for example) but to thematic choice. *Louis, Socrates, Pascal,* and *Agostino* were horror movies; *The Medici* is elation of a peculiar kind, and the horrors are omitted—Florence's exploited workers are unseen and unmentioned; Cosimo's malevolence is minimized; no one gets sick; nothing is dirty. Certain pleasures are omitted as well—there is no sex; there are virtually no women; the seductively charming Alberti of history is reduced to a dry, stiff pedant.

Rossellini's sexless theme, instead, is the exhilaration of a glorious, youthful adventure in which one delight after another is discovered. Music rhapsodizes this poetry—not Nascimbene's synthesizer, but a wistful, tuneful chamber-score by Vittorio De Sica's son Manuel. Under a big blue sky a storybook world beckons: witness Wadding's buoyant voyage from London to Paris, his encounter with soldiers who tell him about Joan of Arc, his chat with the rural lord who bemoans modern innovations, and, riding over a hill, his first sight of Florence: an emerald city, like Oz, a wondrous new world. Even a man who has been to China marvels at the Florentines: "You're so full of enthusiasm for the Classics. You elevate the spirit while filling the purses with gold. You have accomplished what I never thought could be done. You've made plunder into a system of ethics. You've made avarice a philosophy. And to aggrandize it all, you have maintained that gold florins are a gift of God. You've commissioned monuments and cupolas and statues and frescos to portray yourselves as humble, god-fearing men."

Rossellini's decision to stress the positive accomplishments of the era and omit its failures reinforces the film's astounding optimism. We taste the sensuous ecstasy of *intelligence*. This is no small achievement. Alberti concludes the movie:

> Have you never asked yourself why we live in so marvelous a time, so rich in hope and intelligent men? It is because we *wish* to be intelligent.... What is the action which defines the most extreme achievement of which mankind is capable? It is evidently that which man alone is able to do, not living, not feeling, for other creatures outside of the human sphere do so, but *knowing* by means of one's intellect, *knowing* with all possible intelligence.

Intelligence, however, was not enough for American television, which rejected *The Medici*. Bob Lawrence had labored hard and long to convince Roberto to shoot in English, and he was right: English soon became the norm for any Italian movie hoping for export sales. But Lawrence had not counted on Roberto's obtuseness about English soundtracks. Roberto had learned nothing from the *Europe '51* debacle; he was determined to spend as little as possible on sound. Direct sound would have required special technicians, since few Italian film crews had any experience with it, and would have appreciably raised production time, and thus costs, and there would have been new people around unused to Roberto's ways. As a compromise, an American was hired to oversee the dubbing. Roberto met him the first day, chatted amiably, agreed to everything he suggested, and told his assistant he never wanted to see the man again.[13] He would rely, if necessary, on Sonya Friedman, the American from New York whom Lawrence had brought over to translate; he liked her, he told her, because she wasn't American, she was Jewish.[14] On his set, Rossellini was not about to solicit advice or approval from anyone. Yet he let actors speak too slowly, or assigned an assistant to direct who barely understood English. In the dubbing studio (where he never ventured) two or three stupid-sounding voices compounded the slow pace of the dialogue and, last but far from least, a lack of ambient sound (which would have cost a little bit more) made the picture *sound* dubbed.[15] The result was that neither PBS nor any American television station would touch it. Roberto cursed out Lawrence saying it was Lawrence's "fault" because he hated shooting in English. He and his sister Marcella blamed Sonya Friedman, for giving him the "wrong tempo."[16]

(In actuality, Friedman speaks her own lines *express* in her brief appearance as a nun scandalized by Masaccio's crucifixion.)

No doubt sound alone was not the sole problem. Rossellini's unconventional ways of imparting information added to Lawrence's difficulty in selling the movie. Events like taxes and electoral procedures are explained to death by dreary-voiced bit players; whereas more important subjects are merely alluded to, key characters go unidentified, and there is not a single date. Francesco Sforza is introduced at a party, but with only a scattered hint of who he is and with no hint whatsoever of why he's worth noting.

(Cosimo's support of him was key to the Medici balance-of-power policy that gave Italy almost a century of peace.) Cosimo is opposed by the Albizzi, but it is not explained that the Albizzi have run Florence for the last fifty years by defending the rich against the poor, whereas the Medici have sided with the poor. Rossellini demands an unusual television viewer, one rigorously attentive and able to grasp sketchy information, names thrown in the air, and unexplained situations. Alberti talks about "perspective" with a gleam in his eye, but the film never explains what a perspective is, how it relates to drawing and mirrors, or why it was important, and we get no more chance to see the mirror boxes that everyone is oohing over than we did Pascal's calculator. Similarly, people are shocked by Masaccio's pictures, but it's unclear why. The Englishman Wadding's exclamation— "These bodies are human, but they deny that which is spiritual in man"— is not illustrated via comparisons with previous paintings, or even by much of a glimpse at Masaccio's painting. Minor characters talk like printed books,[17] which some audiences find off-putting, intimidating, and difficult to understand.

For some viewers such objections are damning. For others they are mere stumbling blocks, detours at worst, along the four-hour-six-minute path of one of the most truly beautiful movies we are likely to experience. Rossellini's decision not to explain is deliberate: "Why do I have to motivate things?"[18] Beauty in a Rossellini movie, Godard once exclaimed, lies less on the surface than in the idea inspiring the images.[19] Watching *The Age of the Medici* we experience not just an "idea," but a mindset. For example: when Cosimo comes home from exile, the camera-eye zooms out from a girl calling from a high window to encompass the entire Medici villa and its front yard. The shot has the same expression of emotion indulged to the point of rhapsody that one finds in so many quattrocento paintings, in both cases an emotion whose natural expression flows along geometric lines, an emotion whose form is always a story, a story always recounted with calculated delight, a delight achieved by obliging our eye, in order to *discover* the story, to rove from one person to the next, from one detail to the next, from one point of time in the story to another, in order to discover their relationship, their story; and Rossellini mimics this roving discovery not only in the zoom, but in the contrast between the detail shot and the landscape, and thus obliges us to find a multitude of dimensions in Cosimo's homecoming. "Action is only an extension of knowing," Alberti says; or, in other words, watching this movie is an experience of its idea. "Humanism," Roberto wrote, but he could just as well have written "*The Age of the Medici*," is "the attempt to empower the human spirit, to give it free reign, without the slightest restriction; it accents the worth and dignity of man, which we express in our ability to understand, imagine, and invent."[20]

To understand, imagine, and *invent* is what Rossellini had to do in order to create not just a substitute world, the way any fiction film tries to do, but an entire *age*, and to have it correspond, in some relevant way, to the reality which that age once actually possessed. Rossellini wanted us to experience, almost as though we were there, the commerce, banking, politics, religion, armies, literature, and art of quattrocento Florence; more, he wanted us to experience the people, how they felt, thought, lived, and behaved. Thus he had to study and understand the quattrocento, to imagine what it might have been like, and then, since neither real understanding nor accurate images are within our ability, he had ultimately to *invent* quattrocento Florence.

All history invents. History is a series of judgments, a synthesis of vaguely known events, fabricated with research but inevitably with arbitrariness into a story that purports to offer a plausible explanation of some aspect of the present in terms of the past—"myth and reality." No event has relevance in itself, without someone to interpret it; ultimately it is the story writer (the historian) who invents the relevance and makes the past into history. Yet if written history is invention, how much more is filmed history! Necessarily. It is easy to write, "Cosimo de' Medici greeted the Venetian ambassador." It is something else to provide the clothing, the room, the furnishings, the ambience, the voices, the lighting, not to mention the words, vocal tones, comportment, emotions, and actual *bodies* of Cosimo and the ambassador.

Thus more than written history, filmed history must be an interpretation. Or as Alberti says, "The human being, who is perpetually in search of himself, can find himself reflected in his own works, each one of which represents his limits and his capacity for invention."

Roberto, accordingly, was not surprised to discover at a conference in France that everyone has a completely different notion of what the word "information" means.[21] Roberto gave his own definition to an American historian: "In these films, I show the customs, prejudices, fears, aspirations, ideas, and agonies of an epoch and a place. I show a man—an innovator—confronting these. And I have a drama equal to any other drama ever conceived, or ever to be conceived. I always avoid the temptation to exalt this personality; I limit myself to observing him. Confronting a man with his time gives me enough material to construct action and incite curiosity. Shakespeare said: 'Action is eloquence. The eyes of the ignorant are more learned than their ears.'"[22]

"Is it accurate?" people are always asking. In a word, no; how could it be? We would need the real Cosimo—and even the real Cosimo would have individualistic notions of what was accurate. The question of accuracy has to be re-thought. Rossellini's Cosimo has to be experienced as we would any other movie character. Whatever Cosimo was like in reality, now he must be an interesting, empathetic individual (a locus of feeling). For it is our meditations on this person (and others) that will evoke our sensation and comprehension of the Florentine Renaissance and what it can mean to us today. "The Renaissance was not a period in time but a mode of life and thought," wrote Will Durant.[23] Accordingly Rossellini, like

Renoir in *French Cancan,* has created a city in the style of its painters: Piero della Francesca, Paolo Uccello, Fra Angelico, Masaccio, Antonello da Messina.[24] In certain wonderful moments, when the characters seem most inseparable from their milieu, like the people portrayed in quattrocento pictures, they seem to jump out of their background and to talk and act the way we might imagine people in quattrocento paintings would, if quattrocento pictures were also movies. Like it or not, what will be most "real" in Rossellini's movie-Florence will not be its authentic relics of the past—the churches, statues, and paintings—but its movie-Cosimo and its movie-Alberti.

Cosimo is a joy to hear and watch. The slightly archaic dialogue "wears" expressively on his frame, which moves sinuously and sexily, like a vampire. He dresses in black, dissimulates perpetually, slinks across rooms, speaks as from a crypt, stares piercingly even as he averts his gaze. "The Medici are bloodsuckers," a barber says, just after Cosimo, returning from exile, slides through Florence's city gate. Yet if we think of Cosimo as a sort of mafia godfather, he is more bizarre than slimy, more sublime than corrupt. His impatient, avid, and conspiratorial personality is remarkable in its control, when he must deal with political opponents who will stop at nothing to destroy him and his family; and we realize fear, or the will to survive, has made him a monster, an atavistic savage, as it did Louis XIV.

(The Medici never had a secure position in Florence during the fourteenth century. Cosimo's grandson Lorenzo left a memoir of how, when his father died, a delegation from most of Florence's leading citizens "came to our house, to condole us on our loss and to encourage me to take care of the city and the regime as my grandfather and my father had done. This I did, though, on account of my youth and the great peril and responsibility arising therefrom, with great reluctance, solely for the safety of our friends and of our possessions. For it is ill living in Florence for the rich unless they rule."[25])

Cosimo's impatient, avid, and conspiratorial personality is remarkable, also, in its comical *lack* of control, when he questions Niccolai about Greek texts for sale; and we realize from this one scene one of the key attitudes responsible for the quattrocento Renaissance: wanting to know.

"There are a couple of portraits of Cosimo de' Medici," Roberto said, "and he has a nose [that's] absolutely incredible, very difficult to find. So I searched for a nose, I didn't search for Cosimo de' Medici, and I found that nose in a nightclub. And he's very good!"[26] Marcello Di Falco was 29, worked as a cashier at Rome's "Piper Club," and had already appeared in Fellini's *Satyricon, Clowns,* and *Roma.* Roberto picked him after seeing casting photos of him.[27] On the set, he thought Di Falco had effeminate, homosexual movements, and encouraged him to accentuate them.

Alberti's mannerisms are equally interesting, also gay, but pedantic and even snotty (perhaps as a result of the English dubbing). He stares a lot too, but he does not often look at people when he's talking to them; he has a "crazy" look almost like Saint Paul's. At one point after trailing Cosimo through the streets, Alberti spots something interesting off-camera and leaves the frame by walking directly toward the camera—an extremely perverse effect for Rossellini. Apparently Alberti is pursuing a boy, who turns out to be an apprentice in Donatello's workshop, Antonio Rosselino, whom he fondles while admiring Donatello's nude statue of David as a boy. (The movie's other sex scene is a chaste kiss Cosimo gives his wife.) The real Alberti was totally unlike Rossellini's pedant. He was handsome and strong, tamed wild horses, sang and played the organ like a virtuoso, could leap feet-tied over a standing man, spoke simply, and was utterly charming. That in fact neither Roberto nor his scriptwriters were aware of these qualities of the real Alberti indicates their research did not go as deep as Will Durant or the *Encyclopaedia Britannica*, but takes nothing away from the movie Rossellini made. This Alberti is a Rossellini weirdo, like Pascal, Francesco, or Garibaldi. He puts people down with words, as the Albizi do with swords, the Church with promises, and Cosimo with money. To each their hauteur.[28]

Nonetheless, this movie is the greatest defense of capitalism ever filmed. That Cosimo returns to Florence means Donatello will return, means the Renaissance will happen. Elections are defrauded, archbishops bribed, opponents decapitated, promises broken, and out of all this money-power comes good. "States are not maintained by *Pater nosters*," Cosimo says.

Cosimo is a Jean Riboud. His dictatorship guarantees others' liberty. Florence is "very strange, unique," remarks the man who travelled to China, because Florence tolerates constant dispute, change of government, and dissension, whereas elsewhere rulers do not tolerate confusion and everyone obeys.

And so the atmosphere of Florence that Rossellini "catches," in Gilliatt's phrases, "is full of easy perambulations from one local figure to another" because Florence's "confusion" is, in Durant's phrases, "an electric atmosphere of conflict and debate that quickened the pulse, sharpened sense and mind and wit, stirred the imagination, and lifted Florence for a century to the cultural leadership of the world."[29]

Alberti says, "If the world wishes slaves, very many will become slaves. But when the world wishes intelligence, very many will become geniuses."

And Durant says, "Money is the root of all civilization."[30] Capitalism creates a world, a new age, to function in. All seem to prosper. There is trade, peace, order, a reconciliation of parts, a balance of power, and hope for the poor. Cosimo gave away in his lifetime twice as much as he left his heirs. (Cosimo's questionable tactics in acquiring wealth are passed over.)

Money is Rossellini's "miracle" in this movie—a miracle he conjured often in his private life. The movie's music chirps with delight at the apparition of a bag of gold that, appearing almost miraculously on the gonfalonier's desk, will save Cosimo from execution. The film teaches us *nothing* about economics, let alone banking and commerce. Florence's money is always depicted as strange and wondrous, incomprehensible even in its simplest aspects, a perpetual *deus ex machina*, like God's breath in *Stromboli* and *Voyage in Italy*. Florence's fortunes were founded on the cloth trade, which employed tens of thousands of workers in a process that involved thirty separate skills; Rossellini shows none of it. He chose instead to spend a major part of his budget reconstructing implements, machines, and a huge experimental clock concocted by Brunelleschi, and to give us only glimpses of these machines. In the enchanting manner of a Minnelli musical, he stages a poetry contest in which the *pezzi grossi* promenade the streets singing Latin. "Who now could imagine that Greek grammar was once an adventure and a romance?" Durant wondered.[31] Well, Rossellini for one. *The Age of the Medici* is less a documentary on Florence than a poem to kindle spirits. "The Florentine influence on the rest of Europe," Penelope Gilliatt summed up, after watching the movie, "must rank as one of the most worthy penetrations of any culture in history."[32]

Rossellini's optimism flew in the face of fashion in the gloomy 1970s. There was something suspect about these happy few in Florence, about their understanding, imagining, and inventing the world rationally and freely in order to "enter into the fantasy of things." In the "real" world of the seventies, Western civilization seemed to be falling apart; properly engaged people were confronting disasters in ecology, energy, poverty, racism, and war; and these disasters could be blamed on the sort of arrogance that Alberti was exemplifying in Rossellini's film. The 1970s argued that it was Florence that had spread planetwide the arrogant contention that money, science, and art can create utopia—and look at the results! The middle class is blinded by an unwarranted confidence. It thinks its perspective on the world is the only true one. It fails to notice that it is destroying the world and exploiting the poor. Its myopia is rooted in geometrical perspective—the perspective of the Florentine Renaissance—which assumes to regulate reality from a single point, thus from a single truth, rather than from a multiplicity of truths, and which claims, arrogantly, that its view is "real." Such middle-class reality, like middle-class morality, is crassly materialistic; its perspective obsesses with appearances and neglects the ideas and spirits that are the reality beyond the surface. Thus the gloomy 1970s.

Herbert Read, in contrast, makes the more traditional point that Masaccio's novelty was his use of perspectival technique to make a painting of a man who is no longer basically a symbol of a man, as in Byzantine painting, and no longer a typical man as in Giotto's painting, but a real presence, a substantial presence, because Masaccio's man is situated in a "real" space, a perspectival space.[33]

But Read's argument for perspective supports the arguments against it: for "real" means merely that the painting resembles what our eye sees—which is why Bazin, also arguing against perspective, denounced it as the "original sin of Western painting." Bazin argued (as many do) that perspective gradually encouraged us to shift our interest from flesh as a path to the spirit to flesh as a goal in itself. We choose to eat the apple rather than honor the word. The passage from divine Giotto to profane Renaissance was thus a movement away from paintings in which "the symbol transcended its model" and got into the "soul" of its subject, to paintings that merely xeroxed the world. The motive for this passage was to find the "real," Bazin conceded, but art's proper aspirations should go deeper than mere surface.[34]

Thus the arguments against perspective. Perspective claims to be the *only* "real" way to see the world, but actually imposes a convention which, insofar as it discredits alternatives (in art, politics, or lifestyle), may block experience of the "real."

The flaw in Bazin's and the 1970s' indictment of perspective is that there is no evidence connecting perspective with the disasters attributed to it. Art seems to cycle, over the ages, through a series of conventions moving from symbol to xerox to symbol, seeking the "real" or a glimpse of eternity or "now" alternately in spirit and matter. Every convention is a snare. An artist is perpetually in quest for a less soiled vision of reality; he necessarily violates convention and fashion; and many will judge him inept or miss his point. Giotto effected one revolution toward changing notions of what is real and how to represent it, a hundred years later Masaccio effected a second one; art does so perpetually, when it is original. When it is not original it substitutes convention for true consciousness, and profits commercially by imitating others' ideas. Thus a perspectival drawing may become a wall rather than a window. But this is no reason to condemn perspective. The important question (which is also the challenge of Rossellini's television movies) is whether we are dealing with originality or convention—with poetry or prose, in Croce's terms.

For example, the Italian middle class had similar reasons for supporting dictatorships in the Medici's and Mussolini's times. Both regimes could harmonize class struggles, bestow benefits of peace, and guarantee more liberty than the alternatives. Both regimes carried out similar policies, identified themselves with art, and floundered from aggrandizement. Cosimo was poetry, but his great grandsons and Mussolini were prose. (Pope Leo X Medici precipitated 150 years of religious wars by his methods of financing St. Peter's. Clement VII Medici was so inept in his power grabs that he lost England to Henry VIII and got Rome and Florence sacked, rather like Mussolini who made friends with his enemies and war with his friends and got Italy invaded by both.)

Why does convention take control so often?

Art, Rossellini and Alberti claim, is a "science," a way of knowing things; it constructs a substitute world in order to reach the "real" through fantasy, that is, through our imagination, which may be mathematical, artistic, or whatever.

Art, others claim, is a way of remaking the world; it constructs a substitute world so we can live there, a fantasy "real" to substitute for the really real. For Sartre, art is a way of escaping the fact that the world we live in is not our own and will eventually crush us, in death; we escape into our imagination, where we are free. Gloomy Sartre lives in the future.

Sunny Croce lives in the now. Art is a window, not a playhouse. Louis XIV may make a world to hide in, but Paul and Cosimo make a world to expand in. For Croce, and even more for Gramsci, art *is* the "real," because human reality is what humans have created, it is the "really real" and we can create it anew.

Croce, like Rossellini and his heroes, was more willing than Sartre to trust in the ability of human research and judgment to make art that is more than escapist fantasy, and a world that is better than a nightmare. Perspective's advocates sanctify perspective far less than they are accused of doing. When Alberti rhapsodizes about entering into "the fantasy of things," instead of music on the soundtrack, there are the sounds of children's voices outside on the street, and surrounding Alberti on every side are mirrors. Reality is juxtaposed with multiple real images of it. Roberto may have recalled his ambition, during the German Occupation, for a cinema of multiple perspective in order "to see people and things from every side."[35] Such a perspective is the means of civilization, not its enemy.

"The existence of an immense multitude of men is justified. Their number is necessary so that they may always and continuously realize the fullest possibilities of human will," Alberti says.

Croce's liberalism consisted of multiplicity, free debate, and constant research. Impulse alone was not enough, for art or life, as Roberto concluded. Judgment was what enabled Cosimo and Leonardo to succeed (after unwise impulses almost ended their lives); cussedness was why Mussolini and the Medici popes failed. Judgment requires original thinking, not simple adherence to convention, which has damaged societies far more than original ideas. The failures of Mussolini and the Medici, like the failings of Christianity, Marxism, perspectival painting, middle-class morality, and hubristic science have been failures not in the original "sins" but in the conventions they became.

Rossellini is so insistent on his theme of art as science that to emphasize it more, he uses Alberti to caricature philosophy, mysticism, and faith. After Cardinal Niccolò Cusano gives a Plotinian meditation on how "clarity and obscurity are opposites which coincide," Alberti pooh-poohs "the *science* of philosophy, which is all subtlety and quibbling" and accuses Cusano of evoking "the cloudy world of dreams"; and everything in Rossellini's scene conjures up a mystic aura for the Cardinal: a head-on composition; a desk crowded with all manner of tools for "science"; glowing lighting; mystic music. Rossellini is so blatant with such expressionistic devices, here as throughout his career, that one can only marvel at the notion that neo-realist style is flat and undramatized; it is clearly the opposite, a circus, like Italian music, an opera. Later in *The Medici*, by using a similarly operatic style, Rossellini links Cusano's "cloudy world of dreams" with medieval frescos fantasizing the gory myths of hell, war, and suffering; the camera-eye pans and zooms across them in company with mystic music and a priest's sermon about a saint who was actually a dog, and the point of the sermon is that *quality* of emotion is infinitely more valuable than the science behind it: a medieval point of view exactly in contradiction with Alberti's humanist point of view. Alberti scoffs at Plato's argument that philosophers should govern the republic. Philosophers can create only confusion, Alberti retorts; the world should be run by architects, in other words, by technocrats.

Yes, the Renaissance delighted in deriding old idols as much as in crowning new ones. But again Rossellini's research fails. Plato was a new idol, not an old one, and the biggest. It was Greek Platonists fleeing from Constantinople in the last days of the old Roman Empire who ignited rebirth in the West. The Rossellini who made *Socrates* should have recognized that the Renaissance sprang from a "moral position"—the triumph of Socratic morality over Aristotelian Scholasticism. "They . . . found in [Plato's] *Dialogues* a drama more vivid and contemporary than anything in Aeschylus, Sophocles, or Euripides," writes Durant; "they envied and marveled at the freedom with which the Greeks of Socrates's time discussed the most crucial problems of religion and politics; and they thought they had found in Plato—clouded with Plotinus—a mystical philosophy that would enable them to retain a Christianity that they had ceased to believe in, but never ceased to love."

Rossellini is all wrong, from Durant's position, in distinguishing the Renaissance for a supposed emphasis on science over philosophy and emotions and religion. "The same century that saw the discovery of America saw the rediscovery of Greece and Rome; and the literary and philosophical transformation had far profounder results for the human spirit than the circumnavigation and exploration [of] the globe. For it was the humanists, not the navigators, who liberated man from dogma, taught him to love life rather than brood about death, and made the European mind free."[36]

And in fact what makes *The Medici* a wonderful movie is not science but rather the emotion behind the idea of science. Multiplicity of perspective, liberal debate, constant inquiry, poetry, freedom—these are the "emotions" that Rossellini lets us experience, even if he does not always make the appropriate points in the dialogue. The movie's visual evocations of quattrocento painting add an additional level of multiple perspective, and the treasuring tones of the music add another. A substitute world in cinema can be simultaneously a storybook world, a musical world, a pictorial world, a philosophical world, and many other worlds, even a "real" world.

Filming of *The Medici* started June 12, 1971. Dominique de Menil was often present. Roberto may have suggested texts, but he did not work on the script, which was entirely the work of Scaffa and Marcella Mariani Rossellini, as translated into English by Sonya Friedman in a way that deliberately preserves the bookish qualities of the Italian. RAI financed the film alone, at an (estimated) cost of 450 million lire ($725,000). The locations were free (Gubbio, chiefly; also Florence, Todi, Fiesole, and Certaldo).

L'età dei Medici, divided into three episodes, was broadcast weekly in Italy beginning December 26, 1972, and was seen by ten million viewers. RAI did not survey their reactions. Many critics complained, even of just the first episode, that *L'età* tried to do too much too compactly, and critics took fascinated exception to one or another of *L'età*'s arguments, but almost all were enthusiastic and many were rapturous.

It is difficult to disagree (too much) with Noam Chomsky's verdict that "the real world bears little resemblance to the dreamy fantasies about History converging to an ideal of liberal democracy that is the ultimate realization of Freedom."[37]

But Rossellini is not suggesting that it does. Quite the contrary. He insists that, as in art, we must *impose* our fantasy on History. This is the "new realism."

The Medici takes an historicist perspective. Life cannot be lived, it argues, without a perspective of some sort, and so we must either accept whatever perspective fortune cares to impose on us, or else we must *choose* our own.

Such was the theme of Roberto's first book, *Utopia Autopsia 10^{10}*, which was published in Italy in 1974 and the following year in Spain. Ten-to-the-tenth-power is the number of neurons in the human brain, each of which is capable of ten thousand connections. The sole hope for our future, Roberto insists, paraphrasing Francis Bacon, is the increase and exaltation of our use of our intellect.

Cartesius

(Trilogy of Desiccation III)

Roberto wanted television to be a means to exalt the intellect. He took to citing John Comenius, "the great Moravian pedagogue," to the effect that education fails "because traditional teaching methods do not permit learning by . . . 'autopsy': seeing with our own eyes.

"Television lets us see with our own eyes. Today our irrational reasoning has precipitated us into chaos, but . . . images in their naked purity, directly illustrative, can show us the way to orient ourselves through knowledge. . . .

"I have faith in humanity, history, the future of the world, ideological coexistence. But not in the future of cinema. . . . Cinema as traditionally understood, as a system of production but even more of distribution, has been superseded by television. . . . If cinema wants to have a social function, it must be didactic, teach people something, tell people about people. . . . And isn't television fulfilling this duty?"[1]

Rossellini had discovered Comenius around 1952. He attended UNESCO conferences on him in India in 1957 and Czechoslovakia in the 1970s. Comenius (1592–1670) was a bishop of the Moravian Brethren who spent his life campaigning for free universal education in order to achieve piety in individuals and happiness in the state. His *The Visible World* is the forerunner of illustrated schoolbooks. He wrote fifty others. In 1642, he was offered the presidency of Harvard College but went to Denmark instead. Roberto liked to cite Comenius's saying that he could spend ten lessons telling his pupils about the elephant, and each pupil would imagine something different, perhaps with no connection with reality, whereas if he could show them an elephant, they would have no doubt about what it is.

Once again a discovery of Roberto's maturity was a *ricorso* of his youth. Croce's fundamental principle is that our ability to form images comes before we can think logically; we are artists as soon as we can imagine, long before we can reason. Knowledge of individuals must precede theory (contrary to academia today, which takes comfort in deriving the nature of things from principles). When reading in Comenius that "all education is exploration and discovery," Roberto must surely have been reminded of the passionate hopes placed in neo-realism during the postwar period—to explore.

When Roberto died, he left Comenius's *The Great Didactic* open on his desk, with the words underlined: "Principles are derived from the nature of things." Next to the book was (and still is, thanks to Marcella De Marchis) a picture of Comenius and a world globe. It is essentially the same composition as that of Roberto and the globe that appears in *La lotta* and in the frontispiece of this book.

Science

Between 1972 and 1974, Roberto tried to apply Comenius to a ten-hour film on Science—in, according to his prospectus, "the most spectacular manner possible.

"It will avoid the traditional forms of didactics. It will *not* consist of diagrams, drawings, animation, demonstrations, etc. . . . There will be little need for explanation because the viewer will see everything with his own eyes. Science will be offered to the spectator by direct observation of real things [just as though one were present while they are happening] and not by means of the formulas and experiments that made this knowledge possible."

The film would open with a valley full of animals, plants, and fishes, whose activities change in the course of the day. At night the stars come out. We explore the planets, sun, and galaxy, then the structures of molecules and atoms. With the aide of a special zoom camera that can perform at magnifications between 200x and 1500x or between 1500x and 4000x, and eventually to 1,000,000x, "with a coordinated variable light system which automatically adjusts as a function of magnification," we can return to the valley and focus on a plant, a frog or the valley water, and enlarge progressively to the level of a single cell.[2]

Roberto spent years and a great deal of money experimenting with the zoom and the problems of photographing cells without killing them; in some ways, it was *Fantasia sottomarina* all over again, when he had been unable to photograph fish without killing them. He took footage of an artificial heart lab, of telescopes, of NASA, and became a consultant for the National Science Foundation.

From the Menil Foundation he received approximately $300,000 toward *Science*, in addition to between fifty and a hundred thousand in personal loans, the costs of his son Gil's attending Rice University, rent on an apartment in New York and the villa in Rome, air fares, and other gifts.[3] Additional funding was received from RAI, and spent mostly on the zoom. Some of the interviews with Rice scientists, along with other footage, were assembled into a two-hour film, *Rice University*, in 1973 by Beppe Cino (a Centro student who, starting with *The Medici*, became Rossellini's right-hand man during his remaining years). But ultimately Roberto gave up on *Science* because, according to Silvia D'Amico, "he wasn't exactly sure what to do with it." To repay RAI he eventually made *Concerto per Michelangelo* without salary and gave them the *Science* footage.[4]

A second film, *A Question of People*, was commissioned in 1973 by the United Nations Fund for Population Activities, which provided $100,000—which was about what the film cost—although Simone Swan remembers the budget as $400,000 with all the money coming ultimately from the de Menils. Rossellini signed the picture but had nothing to do with it. It was assembled by Beppe Cino from a scenario written by Beppe Cino and consisted of footage from *India*, material shot by Renzino in Africa, and by others in Russia and South America. *A Question of People* was shown at a U.N. conference in Bucharest, was hated by everybody, and created a scandal because of its left-wing slant. Roberto, who had seen none of the movie until this first screening, whispered in Beppe Cino's ear that next time he shouldn't be so one-sided.[5] *A Question of People* was also the final misadventure with Bob Lawrence, who had developed and set up the idea, only to have one of Roberto's friends phone to ask him if he minded if the project were taken over by others, which left Lawrence with nothing for his labors.[6] Eventually, the footage from Beppe Cino's 125-minute film was re-assembled by Michael Heywood and V. Tarsi Vittachi into a 28-minute version with a new commentary, *People: A Matter of Balance*, for the U.N. Human Settlements Agency, with the credit, "From Filming by Roberto Rossellini."

In December 1973, Roberto took a bizarre part in a "Human Rights/Human Reality" conference sponsored by the de Menils in the chapel they had constructed at Rice. The non-denominational chapel had been designed by Philip Johnson and is dominated by fourteen paintings completed by Mark Rothko shortly before his death; Rossellini was on the chapel board, representing the "free thinkers." The conference had been intended to discuss the "failure to transform into reality" the U.N. Human Rights Declaration by focusing specifically on Dom Hélder Câmara, a Brazilian archbishop and initiator of Liberation Theology who had traded his gold cross for a wooden one and his palace for a small room, and whose defense of the downtrodden had led to the outlawing of writings by or about him, and the torture and murder of his associates. Roberto broadened the conference to include scientists such as John Calhoun (evolution), John Elkes (pharmacology), and Jonas Salk (polio vaccine), with the result that after Dom Hélder spoke from personal experience of exploitation of his own third world, of outflow of capital and torture, Salk suggested that human behavior could be modified by surgically removing pathogenic cells, thus rendering Brazilian torture unnecessary.

Cartesius

"Man is born free, and everywhere he is in chains," said Rousseau, who like Roberto could speak in sound bites.

"[Life is ours to explore but] we're afraid of being free," replied Roberto.[7] "The world is young, but dominated by the dead. We live in a cult of the dead.[8] Marx said that 'the tradition of all the dead generations weighs like a nightmare on the brain of the living.'[9] But being locked in orthodoxy means immobility. The patrimony of the past ought instead to become culture. The past ought to serve us, as experience, so that we can know what has to be done in order that we can meet the future."[10] Which is what Croce meant by saying that all history is contemporary history.

Cartesius, the third of Rossellini's films on seventeenth-century France, is constructed around this notion, as expressed by Socrates and now by Descartes, of "the search for freedom/truth" despite skepticism, superstition, and blind faith in doctrine. René Descartes (1596–1650) searches not just in books, but also by "looking with total humility *into* things themselves. . . . The new sciences are leading us to truth. . . . A good man is not obliged to read every book. . . . Knowledge does not depend just on what a man has read, but on what he has *seen*." Descartes speaks for Comenius and neo-realism.

In fact, Roberto's original idea, back in 1969, about how to do a movie on Descartes had come from "a book by Benedetto Croce on Giovanni Battista Vico, a violently anti-Cartesian Neapolitan Jesuit. Reading it, I said to myself that, to make television viewers understand Descartes, the first thing to do should be to show the incredible chaos of his times. If I manage to translate that into images . . . , I hope viewers will understand immediately why Descartes felt the need to write a *Discourse on Method*."[11]

The incredible chaos, besides superstition, included the Thirty Years War, one of the most horrific devastations in history. Rossellini's *Cartesius* scarcely alludes to that war and lets us *see* none of it, even less than does *Blaise Pascal*. We see nothing of Descartes's life in the military. Moreover, we see nothing of his scientific experiments, only a few glimpses of last night's activities scattered around the morning bedroom. Descartes also *sees* nothing. Croce thought him hopelessly abstract, which is Rossellini's criticism of him as well, and which is why showing the Thirty Years War could be considered an irrelevant distraction to the incredible chaos of the man. Except for a servant woman who bears him a daughter after one of the shortest kisses in film history, the movie lets us see Descartes's life as a series of conversations in rooms among well-dressed people, none of whom he *sees*. And this existence is too much for René. "He stayed in bed all the time, and since everyone knew him and came constantly to bother him, preventing him from work, he was forced to change house constantly. His life is a chronicle of changes of house and bed."[12]

And in *Cartesius* even this "chronicle of changes" is yet one more ellipsis of something not seen. One bedroom is like another, "France" is like "Holland": all of them characterless (all of them filmed near Rome). Action and drama in *Cartesius* are entirely inside René Descartes's head, where thought and emotion are locked in deadening struggle—and where perhaps something is amiss.

"I've closed myself up, alone, in this room for many days," Descartes says. "I've reflected on every moment of my past life that I can remember.

And I've reached this conclusion: I absolutely must liberate myself from my infancy, if I want to succeed in knowing what human reason is capable of."

This sounds like Roberto, who had grown fond of citing a famous maxim by old La Rochefoucauld: *"Plus on vieillit, plus on devient sage et plus on devient fou*—The older you get, the wiser you get and the crazier you get."[13]

"Now Roberto is all wrapped up in Descartes," Sonali noted. "Everyone in the house lives with this new person. Descartes sits in front of us, takes his seat at the table, and eats with us."[14] In *Cartesius*, Elena, like Sonali, plays the dramatic foil for the hero; with her constant proverbs she throws his dementia into both comic and tragic relief.

Descartes, Roberto said, "invented the discourse on method. By instinct we know that things are never the way they look. So we have to make an effort to figure out how they are really. The sun seems small and tepid to us, says Descartes: that it is actually huge and a furnace we have to discover ourselves."[15]

The opportunity to shoot *Cartesius* came in February 1973, in the middle of Roberto's intense involvement with *Science*. *Science* would have been the first Rossellini film *not* to take an historical—and historicist—perspective, and in that sense would have marked a break with the "metaphysical." Therefore, one would expect *Cartesius* to focus on the problems of the philosophy of science, which was Descartes's claim to fame. In Descartes's lifetime, Galileo's calculations, which showed Earth revolving around the Sun, were promoting terrible confusion, suggesting that everyone had to change radically their "whole conception of the universe," and perhaps even of God. The question was: what claim did Galileo have to veracity— or did science in general have—that could rival the claims of Holy Scripture, or otherwise justify confidence? Descartes, like most of the philosophers who followed him, tried to find mathematical certainty: a "philosophy of science." But Descartes tried to do so as a faithful son of the same Roman Catholic Church that, just at that time, had condemned Galileo's calculations as scripturally untenable.

Rossellini does expound these facts, albeit in the dib-and-dab style that some of us find so boringly difficult to follow in subtitles. His Descartes says, for example: "The *Summae* of the scholastic philosophers, founded on the doctrines of Aristotle, seem to be perfect constructions that lead to truth, when they are studied closed up inside the walls of a library or college. But they appear quite far from that when they have to confront the thousands and thousands of phenomena that are the reality of our world. . . . Who among them will ever teach us with authority anything about which there can be no possible doubt?"

These words would be difficult to follow in subtitles (if *Cartesius* is ever subtitled). But our following them is not Rossellini's priority. He is not deeply concerned with philosophy of science in the abstract. Or in the concrete: it was Descartes's momentous breakthrough—his application of algebra to geometry—that showed nature could be explored through mathematics and made modern science possible; but Rossellini never mentions this victory. Nor does he care about Descartes the devout believer, whom we never see in church, on his pilgrimage to Loreto, or praying, and whose failure to defend Galileo is ascribed more to cowardice/prudence than devotion. Descartes may protest, to the contrary, that he seeks for truth with humility and piety, by "looking into things, because . . . things are God's creatures and have the stamp of truth." Rossellini is unmoved by this "neo-realistic" mixture of Bazin and theology.

What moves Rossellini is Descartes the frightened man. "I'll close my eyes, block my ears, shut off my senses," Rossellini's René Descartes says. "I want to wipe out from my thoughts every image of physical things, and concentrate only on me, only on myself, and live closed up in my selfhood. And perhaps, scrutinizing within myself, I'll manage little by little to placate the pain and confusion of these days."

This sounds like Roberto after Romano's death, seeking "metaphysical" answers, as he called them. The crisis is existential: Descartes–Rossellini has been shattered, he loses touch with even himself. Was this a crisis answerable in philosophic terms? "I will prove to myself that a thing—a soul—that thinks, means one that doubts, that affirms, that denies, that knows a few things and ignores many, that loves, that hates, that wants, that doesn't want anymore, that remembers, imagines, and senses. . . . I have the certainty of being a reality that thinks. But from where did this certainty come to me?"

In such a context, "I think, therefore I am" becomes a mantra of consolation. As Scaffa says, Descartes is "pushed by an *anguished* need to verify his reflections."[16] His obsession, which was also neo-realism's and personalism's, was with the thinking subject rather than with the object perceived. Was he more a metaphysician than a scientist, as Croce charged? Or did he wish to make metaphysics into a science?

"I want to discover by myself, alone, how this world is made. . . . It seems incredible to me that so many people, with so much ardor, are investigating human customs, the virtues of plants, the movements of the stars, the transformation of metals, and so many other disciplines, and that almost no one bothers to investigate the human mind."

Here indeed is involution. Descartes, Pascal, and Socrates argue incessantly for the superiority of reason. But in all three cases their emotional deficiencies cast doubt on the wisdom of their obsessions. Rossellini described Descartes as less likable than Pascal even, "a son of a bitch, a coward, a lazy person. He was quite repulsive of course, not *simpatico*." And it is difficult not to wonder how sincere Rossellini was being, when he added, "But I don't care about that. He was intelligent."[17]

Shouldn't intelligence be *simpatico*, particularly in a movie made for the masses? For Rossellini it's always the hero's *deficiencies* that proclaim his or her heroism—which is a Roman Catholic perspective. Good and evil coexist in us. The heroes of science martyr themselves like Francesco and Paul to abstract causes—"Science has prevented me from living," Descartes concludes—and these abstract causes become their identities. Has the abstract replaced the individual? Has Rossellini become anti-human?

Descartes's conclusion is less regret than inspiration tinged with masochism. "I shall try amid my pain to broaden my knowledge. I shall consider, carefully, if I still can't discover inside of me something *else* that I haven't perceived yet."

Cartesius cost about eighty million lire ($130,000). RAI contributed a hundred million lire ($160,000) and the ORTF as co-producer an additional eighty million old francs ($160,000); it is not known whether Rossellini refunded the $190,000 surplus. His plan had been to shoot in France, in English, with an American actor playing Descartes, for American television. He appears to have told Jean Dominique de La Rochefoucauld, representing the ORTF, that he would shoot a second version simultaneously in French. But if this was his intention, he had not made it known to any of the actors, all of whom had learned their parts only in English, as of the first day of shooting. And in any case, the French were justifiably unwilling to have Descartes played by an American in a French film. When the smoke cleared, the production had moved to locations near Rome (including the studio at the Centro Sperimentale), an Italian was playing Descartes, and on the first morning the actors learned they would enunciate brand new dialogue in French, which would be shouted to them by Marie-Claire Sinko who, during the shooting, would be hiding behind a tree or a couch, since few of the actors knew much French. (The actual sound would be dubbed later.)

Roberto had given La Rochefoucauld's script back to him. *Cartesius* is signed by Rossellini, Scaffa, and Marcella Mariani Rossellini. La Rochefoucauld contended, however, that a good deal of his script had in fact been used, and he sued—from principle. It wasn't that Roberto stole, La Rochefoucauld maintained: an artist cannot steal, he gives life to things. It wasn't important that all the big ideas in *Louis XIV* came from others; without Rossellini they would have been worthless. But Roberto always behaved like a media star and refused to tolerate any other star. He was perpetually concocting attention, posing for photos, emitting great lines, and then turning around and moaning about having to do it. He was a *putain*, perhaps a *putain sacrée*; perhaps he ended up trapped in his profession for the sake of his profession. But after a succession of projects that always turned out less than they should have been, because of last-minute improvisation, budgetary misapplication, and the ever-present webs of Italian conspiracy, La Rochefoucauld had begun to wonder, as Gruault had, whether being part of Roberto's projects was worth the effort, given Roberto's continual game of deception. He had begun to wonder, as Gruault had, whether Roberto sought money to make films, or made films to seek money.

As a result of his suit, La Rochefoucauld was given the French rights, which proved valueless. Despite the success of Rossellini's previous history films on French television, *Cartesius* was refused by the ORTF because of its lack of authenticity.[18]

Cartesius seems not to belong to the same world as *Pascal*, although the two pictures were made only eighteen months apart. *Cartesius's* air of France is thin; its air of Holland is non-existent. Some of the locations are supposed to be the same as *Pascal's*, but they look different; some of the characters are the same, but they show up played by different actors. People themselves, so intense and operatic in *Pascal*, albeit macabre, are comparatively moribund in *Cartesius*. Descartes himself, in *Pascal*, was chubby, slow, substantial, old-middle-aged, and played by a French businessman whom, according to Scaffa, Rossellini considered to look "incredibly similar to pictures of the philosopher."[19] Yet now in *Cartesius* Descartes is bony, hyper, slight, and young-middle-aged, and played by an Italian actor, Ugo Cardea, whom Rossellini had typed in *The Medici* as the mystic Niccolò Cusano.

On the set Rossellini took command and exploded when Cardea remarked that he too had read Descartes.[20] Cardea's idea was to translate Descartes's ideas into recitation through facial mime and gesture. But Rossellini told him: "*Cogito ergo sum*—say it as though you're at a bar asking for cigarettes." Cardea protested, surprised. "Do you think," Rossellini persisted, "that Descartes was figuring out at that moment what he was saying? He had been thinking about it all his life, in fact, and this is why he would say it now without any particular expression."[21] Actors often felt humiliated by Roberto, there would be real crises. He kept stopping them if they tried to recite or invest themselves in their part; he insisted they be themselves, which is almost impossible: an actor wants to play a role. "Move around the way you do at home," he would tell them. And they wouldn't know what to do.[22]

His sister Marcella one morning forbade him to shoot. The kitchen was filthy and it was supposed to be Holland. Another explosion from Roberto: "I'm not going to waste time cleaning a château!" Marcella didn't give in. "No! Holland is clean!" "So what? I'll make Holland dirty!" The kitchen was cleaned. Roberto always ended up doing what Marcella told him.[23]

Another scene had two Dutch women sewing, but there was no sewing basket. The assistants scurried through the little town they were in; no one could come back with a sewing basket. Roberto looked around the set, spotted the pretty, modern bag that Marie-Claire Sinko had just bought on Via Fratina, took it from her, and put it in the middle of the table. "There," he said, "this is a Dutch basket!"[24]

Cartesius was broadcast a year later, February 1974, and watched by nearly five million people, with enjoyment indexes of 64 and 61 percent. "The critics," according to Trasatti, "were lavish in their appreciation compared to the earlier films, either because of the particular formal dignity of the picture or because, slowly, they were becoming convinced that Rossellini, ultimately, had not been wrong in going against the current. Television itself had matured as well."[25]

Yet the critiques are not convincing. *Paese Sera* and *Il Tempo* noted the increased denial of spectacle or intrigue or anything to involve the audience. *L'Unità* pointed out that Rossellini again favored individual genius at the expense of the times. Cipriani thought *Cartesius* "very mature, greatly interesting, and at times of the highest level of quality." Maybe somebody would still think it "boring," he added, "but who ever said that a film or television work necessarily has to be 'entertaining'?"[26]

This argument leads us to the central paradox of Rossellini's Great Plan. He wanted to communicate, Comenius-like, with the masses; but he made films which most people found insufferable. He wanted to do non-art but only succeeded at art. As Trasatti comments, "a film is boring when it is not interesting."

Trasatti goes on to complain, as he does apropos of every RAI telecast of a Rossellini film, that RAI "was afraid of Rossellini, was afraid of boring people, and as insurance offered audiences an alternative, a plate for every taste"—in this case, on its other channel, two old movies, a 1959 western (*Warlock*) and a police film with Diana Dors.[27] Brunette agrees with Trasatti: "Choosing to schedule popular fare like this against the Rossellini film virtually guaranteed that it would fail."[28]

But what was RAI supposed to do? Show a Rossellini television film on every channel? Force people to watch Rossellini?

Friends

"I am in debt to everyone," Roberto said. "[To go on] I create new debts. I am working, when I get a little money I pay a little bit. It's not amazing. No one tries. It's a very simple operation. I'm not escaping or running away. I am here, I have debts, so what? I went to the bank the other day and said, 'I need $100,000 in a few days.' They said, 'What kind of guarantee can you give?' I said, 'No guarantee. If I have a guarantee it's absolutely insane to come ask you for money. I want money because I need the money.' They know I'm always there. I pay a little bit and go on. If I pay a little bit it's a good reason to have more debts."[29]

"Money was the sole domain in which he was courageous, really courageous," said Trombadori. "He'd say: 'You have to spend as much money as possible!'"[30]

There had not been good feelings between Roberto and Fellini during the sixties. They met once by chance in Monte Carlo; Fellini greeted Sonali and ignored Roberto, which infuriated him. A few years later he spotted Fellini walking down a street, hailed him with blinking headlights, and then practically smothered him with tender embraces. But he didn't stop decrying Fellini's pictures as loudly as he could. In 1976 he told a mutual friend, "I have to see Federico, because the fact that he's made a film like *Casanova* is really pathological and he absolutely must be cured of this kind of thing, which is a serious cultural illness, because a film like this has no right to exist in the normal life of a sane artist, and it's a big perversion that needs to be repaired by helping the author himself."[31]

Roberto did like *Amarcord* in 1973. Nevertheless he phoned Fellini and told him, "If tomorrow the Fiamma [Cinema] burns down, there's hope. But if not, we're fucked!"[32]

"Rossellini's limitation," Fellini reflected after Roberto's death, "was his impossibility of abstracting himself from life. He lived life like a fantasy, superior to reality. He had the virtues and defects of all Italians, an artist without being an artisan, non-continuous, a *maestro di vita* in the most human sense of the word."[33]

"When Roberto is home, he spends entire days in bed, reading or phoning," Sonali told *Il Messaggero* in February 1973. "When I was a little girl I felt secure only with my father. Now my security is Roberto. In India we say such a person is like a big tree with a solid trunk and lots of branches. Birds make their nests there, people rest in its shade, if it rains you get under it, you feel protected. He, however, says he feels like a patient cow that everyone comes to milk. In certain things he's like a farmer. He likes the earth, he likes traditions, he likes work, family, and good food. I've never known the character of legend, the Latin seducer. . . . He never raises his voice to the children. He forgives everything: their caprices, their mistakes in love, their intolerance, their bad marks at school, their disobedience. He never punishes them. He says, 'Try to understand.'"[34]

Yet Roberto had rarely been home during the last few years. Initially, the love between Roberto and Sonali had overwhelmed monstrous obstacles, and she had inspired, guided, and supported his increasing interest in films that would be "about" something. But time took its toll. The strain of being Rossellini was harder for her than for him. He would arrive home exhausted, squeezed like a lemon peel, with nothing left for the family, with no time for significant dialogue with the children. He reigned in bed all day, complaining it was never changed, summoning servants, grumbling, spawning confusion, shouting. No one else's noise was tolerated; Raffaella's piano was at the opposite end of the house, its mute pedal always on. But around him there was never silence. The television or radio was never off; at night the moviola ground away.

Being Rossellini was a perpetual cycle of tension, exhaustion, infantile behavior, physical sickness.[35] For entire days his headaches would be so severe that he would be unable to speak. Once a year or so he would retire to a hospital for a few days and "be bled or something."[36] For Marcella De Marchis, the solution was to accept everything and rub his forehead with Synthol: she was one of the few people he totally trusted. For Bergman, the solution was to retire to her own room and get drunk. For a person of Sonali's temperament, the solution was to absorb Roberto's tensions physically, to the point of illness. "They both had to have the last word," said Lisandrini.[37]

Meanwhile, Roberto, seeking allies among his Italian families, colored the situation to his own favor, and isolated Sonali by one simple explanation for everything, "She's Indian."

She had wanted to get married, he had not, he told Jean Gruault.[38] Nonetheless, he had formally adopted Gil, which under Italian law meant that Sonali would not have been able to take her son by Das Gupta out of the country, if she left Roberto.

Women, Roberto once joked, must not have security in love. He, on the other hand, needed to trust people, but was unable to, in Sonali's opinion, and so laid traps to hold them instead, without understanding that freedom is the strongest bond. His insecurity had its comic sides. He was superstitious about hats on beds, being handed salt, cats on the road. His nonchalance about money disguised his paranoia of *appearing* to lack it. Once at The Raphael he got his socks wet and did not dare put them on the radiator to dry, for fear the maids would think he had washed them himself.[39] He would run up bills in restaurants and book stores, then claim he stopped going back because they didn't have a certain dish or type of book: "Is he mad at us?" the owners would ask. He always bought twelve of anything, for fear of being without—dozens of bottles of aspirin, hundreds of ties, twenty shirts at a time. Then he wouldn't pay. Ingrid had to face the small local merchants to whom they owed money ($1,700 to the druggist on one occasion). Sonali had to face the shirt dealer, whose shop was near her own. "They made the color wrong, I'll punish them," was Roberto's response to a dozen shirts. He was myopic, not selfish. He frequently failed to pay his servants, but had an excuse: "Why do they need money, they're eating and sleeping?" At moments he would groan at his burdens. He might appear on the balcony, glare down at the family, and scream "Eaters!" Or at dinner grumble, "I'm killing myself to provide your food," whereupon a child would run to hide.

He refused to eat onion or garlic. If they were hidden in the food, all would be fine; but if he noticed he would have headaches and cry, "Murderers!"

"I am a saint," he reflected. Months would pass without Roberto and Sonali speaking. His own things, including his moviola, were all stuffed into one room; when Sonali was not home, the other doors were locked. His children were shy and intimidated in front of him, as he had been in front of his own father. He became furious at young Ingrid once, when she bought him Chesterfield Kings cigarettes rather than Regulars. "It's terrible. You live with such remorse," he told her, lamenting his own failings toward his own father.[40] He still conducted his ritual with his father's picture. Yet, outraged by all three of his daughters' dating, he stopped talking to them, and had reconciled with only Isabella at the time of his death. His sexual prowling, according to Fulchignoni (a medical doctor), was the principal cause of his physical and mental exhaustion, and why, as his body grew older, he lacked energy and dedication when it came to shooting his films.[41] He didn't seek for women, however; they came to him. High blood pressure kept him from drinking wine, but sex relieved it, he claimed.[42]

He had chased away almost all of his old collaborators, the ones who had stood up to him. "He defends himself," Amidei sighed to Sonali, "from the good people and will never defend himself from harmful ones."[43] He was embittered toward Truffaut, who had reproached him with frittering away time on the science film and milking the de Menils, and whom he in turn accused of being stuck in the troubles of puberty. "It's true that he doesn't have any friends," Sonali said, "or at least not many in Italy. Ten years ago he had a regular group: Sandro De Feo, Vincenzino Talarico, Brancati, Batti, Fulchignoni, Venivano."[44] "I lasted," said Fulchignoni, "because I never asked him for anything."[45]

What terrified him most was the threat of boredom.

"For many many years the rapport between Anna [Magnani] and Roberto was non-existent," said Marcella De Marchis. "Anna was truly a pure soul, a woman who did not admit half tones in life, love, feelings, or friendship. Everything had to be black and white. So for a long time this absence of rapport had been punctuated by letters of insults that she wrote him, which however were masterworks of moral cleanliness. They mirrored her soul. Pacification came six or seven months before her death. Roberto went to see her, taking along the twins and Alessandro, Renzo's son."[46]

"I hadn't seen Magnani for thirteen years," Roberto said. "When I read in the paper that she was sick, I sent a note, 'If you need me, call.' That's all I wrote. An hour later she called me. 'Come here.' I went to her. She had been seeing at the same time thirty doctors in Rome, since she felt bad and feared a definite diagnosis. She greeted me with, 'Spit on my hand, buddy. Sit down. Listen. I'm really sick, seriously sick, but dying pisses me off, so you have to stay here and stop me from dying.' 'Okay. I'll stay here and I won't let you die.' I stayed there. Three days later I took her to a hospital. I stayed with her all the time, 45 days, until the end. I accompanied her to the other side without her realizing she was dying."[47]

Roberto had a new drug from Houston flown in. Magnani was operated on on September 11, 1973; her case was seen to be hopeless, Roberto did not tell her. That same day she divorced Alessandrini. Fifteen days later she died. Roberto stayed to comfort her son Luca, who had not recognized Italy's president who had come to the hospital and had tried to console him. At last Roberto succeeded in separating Luca from the corpse. "Imagine," he told Marcella De Marchis the next day, "Today I got him to smile."[48]

Artists of her stature in Europe often received state funerals. Colette, for example, had lain in the Palais Royale with a French flag a hundred yards long above her. But Magnani had not belonged to a political party. "People thought Magnani was forgotten," said Roberto. "A hundred to a hundred-fifty thousand people came, many from the South. There was huge applause" when the casket was carried out of Santa Maria della Minerva.[49]

"It was such an event," added Zeffirelli, "that the Italian President felt obliged to make a gesture, but when he tried to approach the coffin, he got more than he bargained for: Luca screamed abuse at him for not giving his mother the honor he believed she deserved, and indeed he was right. . . . Roberto himself took charge of the interment. It was an amazing scene. Ingrid Bergman laid a bouquet of vivid scarlet roses on the coffin. There was Rossellini's first wife alongside his present wife, the Indian Sonali Das Gupta, with their child; and a girl who everyone knew was Rossellini's latest mistress. He was like an oriental potentate burying one of his harem, and the odd thing was that none of the others seemed to think it was odd!"[50]

"Anna is in our family tomb now," said Marcella De Marchis, "between Roberto's father and Romano. . . . I went the morning of the funeral, to prepare everything."[51]

Sergio Amidei, when he died in 1981, was also buried in the Rossellini mausoleum, courtesy of Marcella Mariani Rossellini.

Marcel Pagnol died too in 1974. Roberto had adored him for his sense of humor and verbal wit. Shortly before his death they'd gone to a cemetery together for the funeral of a common friend, and Pagnol had remarked, "This is the last time I'll come here as an amateur."[52]

Anno uno and *The Messiah*

The "girl" Zeffirelli had noticed at Anna's burial was Silvia D'Amico. She was 34. Roberto, who was 67, had known her since her babyhood. Her father was a musicologist; her uncles Silvio D'Amico and Emilio Cecchi were well-known literary scholars; her mother Suso Cecchi D'Amico was one of the world's best-known screenwriters. Her family was part of the Visconti faction and Silvia herself had been one of Rossellini's most caustic critics at RAI. She had gone to school with Luca Magnani and had produced Anna Magnani's last three films. It was Anna's illness that brought Silvia into close contact with Roberto—at Magnani's encouragement. Like Pasquale in "Naples," Anna had warned Sonali: "Watch out! He's a big ignoble slut, an incredible son of a bitch! Kick him in the ass now and then."[1]

Sonali had been in India while Magnani had been in the hospital, and Roberto had written her not to be alarmed if she heard rumors about him and Magnani. When Sonali got home, she found people acting as though there were something she ought to know. In effect, everyone knew. Sonali's children told her that Roberto had brought Silvia home often during Sonali's absence. Ingrid's children told her that they were afraid Silvia was taking their father away. Whereupon Silvia came to lunch with her parents, and did not look at Sonali when she talked.

In December there was a retrospective in Lisbon of Rossellini's films. Portugal's fascist government had granted permission for a single screening of *Roma città aperta* without subtitles; the movie had been banned since its initial release. Fourteen hundred people jammed into the hall, applauded all through, and gave a fifteen-minute ovation. Roberto, stunned, predicted the fascist regime would fall—and six months later phoned back to say, "See, I was right."

The Portuguese had invited Sonali too; Roberto had replied he would be bringing his secretary. That same month he had moved into an apartment with Silvia at 67 East 80th Street in New York—paid for by the de Menils, who were also paying for Sonali's villa.

On Christmas night Roberto was back in Rome and dropped in on Sonali, Raffaella, and Gil. He came again on New Year's Eve.

His situation with Silvia was obvious to Sonali. He had said nothing to her, but he had been gradually moving his belongings out of the house. On December 31 she confronted him, told him he was free, and assured him he would always have a friend in her. He had no real friends, he agreed, but refused to admit there was anything between himself and Silvia. He left early the next morning in a fury, still denying everything, still refusing to take a position. Sonali never saw him again.

Roberto went to his sister Marcella's and told her that he had finally come clean with Sonali.[2] Then he went to Paris, where Silvia was waiting for him in their room at The Raphael.

On February 2 they left for New York—to the Algonquin, he told Sonali on the phone, but he would be travelling. He took Silvia to Berkeley, and to Mexico, where they were married, according to Silvia D'Amico, by a priest and before witnesses.[3]

Roberto seems not to have revealed this marriage to any of his family; both he and Silvia publicly denied it at the time, she was not named as an heir when he died, and ten years after his death his sister Marcella said the marriage was news to her.[4] But half the world heard about it on February 25, 1974.

"A reporter phoned me at night from Rome," Roberto said, "and asked, 'Is it true you were married to Silvia D'Amico in Mexico?' What insanity! I denied everything, but he wrote we were married in Mexico. It's absolutely untrue."[5]

Privately, to his sister, he blamed Sonali for leaking the story.[6] Others blamed Silvia's mother. But Roberto himself had told everyone, as he had told everyone years before about his romance with Ingrid. Love rejuvenated him and made his heart sing; it was not something he could hide, or wanted to.

He had even sent his son Renzino to Suso Cecchi D'Amico to ask formally for her daughter's hand.

Suso, twelve years Roberto's junior, had called him on the phone. "Reflect, my boy," she had counseled.

"But if I reflect, I'll be dead," Roberto had replied.[7]

Sonali learned of the marriage the day after the newspapers appeared. A friend phoned. She immediately changed the locks on the doors, sent the servants away, and refused to speak to anyone except a lawyer. Roberto had once threatened to have her deported, now she was afraid that he would, and that she would lose both her children (who belonged to Roberto under Italian law).

The children too shut off the world. They did not go to school. Raffaella was afraid to go out of the house, lest she encounter her father.[8]

In March, Roberto returned, discovered he could not open even the roadside gate, and spent the night at his sister's. Three years later Raffaella, now 20, told a journalist: "For me—I was very young then—the revelations about my father published in the papers at that time were a really ugly blow . . . and also for my brother Gil. . . . Our idol had fallen and we were distraught. Maybe my reactions were excessive then. I didn't want to see my father again, I didn't want to hear about him, and I certainly had an influence on my mother's decision to make papa go live elsewhere. Since then I've avoided my father and it's been some time since I've heard from him even by phone."[9] They never spoke again.

Roberto had lost and gained friends with each change of woman. Now his union with Silvia left him particularly isolated. It was as if he had changed political parties and gone over to the Viscontis. Some questioned Silvia's motives, as they had questioned her mother's alliance with Visconti. Silvia appeared to encourage such questions when she had Carlo Tuzii shoot a film (*Numero uno*) of her with Roberto, or when she invited journalists to photograph the two of them arriving at an airport. "He fell into a trap," said one colleague, "but maybe he wanted to. History is not made in bed." Others questioned Roberto's sanity. De Sica thought it "too absurd."[10] Roberto stopped phoning Maria Mercader, after twenty years of almost daily calls, and dropped many old friends.

"It was a passionate love that embarrassed me," his daughter Isabella recalled. "I couldn't figure out what had possessed him; I had yet to fall passionately in love myself and create the same confusion in family and friends that my father did then."[11]

That spring with Silvia he visited Renoir in Los Angeles and Jonas Salk in La Jolla, and gave a series of "Dialogues with Roberto Rossellini" at New York City's New School and a seminar at Yale to thirty students. "There was not even as much [feedback] as I got from some high school students in Oakland, California," he commented about Yale. "In Oakland I entered a huge hall with six thousand young people. It was one of the most astonishing experiences of my life, to be able to have a conversation with six thousand human beings. They didn't know my films, but they listened to me with incredible interest."[12]

Around 1970, at the suggestion of the American Film Institute, Roberto had started preparing a two-hour movie on the American Revolution.[13] A surviving treatment (by whom?) begins a year before the Declaration of Independence and ends with the Constitution. The emphasis is on issues and ideas: trade, taxes, and political theories, Thomas Paine, Turgot, and George Washington. "While orators speak and publicists argue, Washington thinks. This man, calm and slow—he was said to be awkward—is above all a gentleman farmer from Virginia." There was to be far more spectacle than in the other television films: extensive work in exteriors in many locations; shifts in locale from England to France and all over revolutionary America; battle scenes at Saratoga and Yorktown. It was to be an economic production, but often overtly poetic; for example:

4d. The village of Lexington, dawn. Major Pitcairn, commander of the redcoats, through fog, sees a band of armed peasants determined to stop him. Fighting begins (who started it?). The "Americans" disperse, leaving on the ground eight dead.

"It was a totally different revolution," Roberto said; "not a class taking power from another, but based only on ideas. A permanent revolution, still going on.[14] I think it is the only revolution that was accomplished in the world. The original idea was the creation of the Constitution, the dream rather than the reality, the conception of a power as weak as possible. It is said by Thomas Paine so beautifully, that Power is a necessary evil. That's the novelty of the American Revolution. It's not a question of anarchism, but of faith in man."[15]

Roberto tried to get funding from the Rockefeller Foundation. Historian Peter Wood was there at the time, as well as on the board of the Menil Foundation, and had edited the Menil video of the "Human Rights/Human Reality" conference. He was impressed with Roberto as being knowledgeable about the Revolution and fascinated by its ideas, but considered him too involved with great men and great ideas at the expense of social history.

To this criticism Roberto retorted: "There doesn't exist a single individual and the human species. If somebody makes a step, the others, because they are monkeys, will imitate that step."[16]

Rockefeller turned down the proposal. Roberto decided it was because he was Italian. In actuality, Rockefeller's policy was to put its money into the sciences rather than the humanities; moreover, the Foundation preferred to back safe projects rather than fund unusual people who would not have worked otherwise; finally, there was uncertainty about funding a film in the public sector.[17]

Denis Diderot was another still-born project. Rossellini's treatment (by whom?) depicts Diderot as heir to Descartes's rationalism. Inspired by Locke and Newton, Diderot adds a satiric tone—nature without God—and excludes any meaning in the cosmos that is not mechanical. He is jailed, but emerges to spend twenty years compiling the first encyclopedia, enlisting people like Voltaire and Rousseau in his cause, and suffering attacks by Jesuits and Jansenists. For Rossellini, Diderot mirrors the dissolution of his age.

In 1973, Roberto was hoping for financing from the Shah of Iran for a twelve-hour *History of Islam* and from Italnoleggio for *Pulcinella*. Italnoleggio had recently been established by the Italian government to finance and distribute films—supposedly through independent evaluation of submitted scenarios, actually through an increasingly politicized process. Roberto must have had reason for optimism, because he gave Gruault's *Pulcinella* script to his assistant, Beppe Cino, and told him to start preparing pre-production.

Nothing happened, however. Then late that fall Roberto met Father Patrick Peyton in Houston. Peyton produced a Catholic television series, *Family Theater*, was well connected, and had access to lots of money. Ac-

cording to Beppe Cino, Peyton was one of "a whole series of slightly utopian, slightly Gandhi-like characters gravitating around the Menil Foundation in those years who were in between morality and politics." According
to the de Menils, however, it was the Vatican's recommendation that got
Roberto access to Peyton.[18] And once in Peyton's presence, Roberto's
charm wrought its customary magic spell. Some time later, Peyton came to
Roberto's hotel room, where Silvia D'Amico was stretched out on the bed,
made Roberto kneel down, put a hand on his head, and announced that he
had had a dream in which the Madonna had appeared and told him, "You
must make a film on the Messiah and the director has to be Rossellini."
Peyton promised money and Roberto replied, "Well, if it's the Madonna
who says so . . . "[19]

He presented a Messiah project to Italnoleggio that December. In
March 1974, Italnoleggio replied it was interested.

Anno uno

Meanwhile, Edilio Rusconi, a right-wing industrialist, was setting up a
film about Alcide De Gasperi at the bequest of the Christian Democrats.
Rusconi's in-house producer, Gian Paolo Cresci, had been one of Roberto's
Christian Democrat supporters at RAI, and Rusconi accepted arguments
from the Christian Democrat leader Amintore Fanfani that the project
should be entrusted to Rossellini rather than to Leandro Castellani.
Roberto was awarded the richest deal of his career, 150 million lire to direct, plus an additional 75 million for the script—about $365,000 alto-
gether, out of a budget of one million dollars furnished by Italnoleggio.[20]
Silvia D'Amico was the executive producer.

The picture was originally to have been titled *Anni caldi* ("Hot Years"),
because it dealt with De Gasperi's efforts, during the contentious postwar
period, to reconstruct Italy on the basis of national unity. But the 1970s
were hot years too. De Gasperi's politics were viewed from the left as a
process of *trasformismo* through which all the hopes of the Resistance had
been betrayed, a process through which the average Italian had been
cheated and exploited—and was still being cheated and exploited. Rusconi
was denounced as a "fascist"; Roberto was denounced for selling out to the
fascists; the film was denounced as having been written and financed by
fascists.

Roberto saw the project as a continuation of the reconstruction themes
of *Roma città aperta* and *Paisà*. "I think the danger of Fascism in Italy today
is very strong [from both left and right]. So I want to remind people how
things were [after the war]. . . . I shall start again from the moment of
Paisà."[21]

Provocatively, he changed the title to *Anno uno* ("Year One").

The script's outline was written by Scaffa early one morning at the
Algonquin, just before Roberto's scandal with D'Amico broke out. Scaffa
found Roberto hard to approach for the next few months and, he said, the

film suffered accordingly. In addition, Cresci and others became involved and they had many disagreements.[22] By the time shooting began, Roberto's enthusiasm had evaporated.

"On the set," recalled Beppe Mangano, a former Centro Sperimentale student who worked as a set designer on *Anno uno* and *Cartesius*, "Rossellini sat at an angle from where he dominated the scene. Everything went on around him. He was Triton surrounded by dolphins, codfish, polyps, anchovies, and mazzancolle, bustling about in waters not often tranquil. We used to say . . . that he could direct by phone."[23]

Indeed, Roberto phoned his assistants almost daily, refusing to let them separate their private lives from his film. On the set he used radio to feed actors their lines through ear pieces. "You have to create an accident, a little surprise, an uncertainty, a sort of improvised look, a bat of an eyelid," he would say. But he was bored on the set of *Anno uno* most of the time, Mangano thought, "as if his contribution was over, once he had thought up and proposed the project."[24] He put himself, along with Brancati, in the background of a scene set in Caffè Aragno.

Silvia got sick at the end of production and Roberto took advantage of the opportunity to put her name on *Anno uno* as producer. She had a phobia of publicity and had used pseudonyms in the past. Knowing this, Roberto would tease her by having her paged on airport loudspeakers, "*Mrs. Rossellini! Mrs. Rossellini!*"

"That's why I didn't want to marry. He was younger than I was," she said. "We were always quarreling together, it was great fun.[25]

Anno uno opened with great fanfare at the Fiamma, November 15, 1974. The president of Italy was in the audience, along with Prime Minister Rumor, Fanfani, the Communist leader Enrico Berlinguer (who had to sit on the floor), and almost everybody else. It was the twentieth anniversary of De Gasperi's death. *Anno uno* had been publicized as "Rossellini's return to cinema."

"Rossellini," writes Trasatti, "said he wanted to continue his didactic work without a shadow of propaganda and preconstituted theses. But is it possible to apply the method to the history of the recent past that so heavily continues to affect our present? Many of the personages who were revived in the movie were all sitting in the hall. The material was delicate. The world evoked is not one of centuries ago. . . . And even if the man behind the camera worked without prejudices and preconceptions, prejudices and preconceptions were deeply rooted in the people who watched the film and judged it."[26]

The reception was cold. *Variety* reported Italian reviews ranged from "bad to cruel."[27] Roberto was called "a servant of the regime"—to his fury. Above all, people were bored. The movie disappeared.

Anno uno was despised more by the center than the left. Rossellini's version of De Gasperi—a bombastic, babbling know-it-all—had little to do with the dignified, reflective man they had known.[28] But it was the left that dominated the debate, as usual.

Roberto had wanted to show, said his son Renzo, "how a new way of politics was established, and how it was then turned into a creation of state power, with all the negative qualities that that implies. He . . . saw [De Gasperi] as the motor of this structuring process. . . . I think he didn't have the freedom to make the film the way he wanted to."[29]

Perhaps. But there is no evidence in *Anno uno* or among available documents to suggest that Roberto shared his son's Manichaean bitterness toward the Christian Democrats—with whom Roberto himself had been associated during the postwar period and at RAI. It seems wishful thinking for Renzino to argue that Roberto really did not, in fact, "attribute positive or negative value to De Gasperi."[30] It is the issues that are ignored in *Anno uno*, not the man—as in *Socrates, Pascal,* and *Cartesius.*

Endless monologues on politics are spat out like rapid-fire harangues and staged with staggering indifference. At one point De Gasperi strides out a door and up to the camera with two cronies who never say a word, jabbers away while minutes pass, then strides back through the door, his ever silent cronies in tow. De Gasperi complains his opponents give him no choice but to reconstruct Italy along capitalist lines, but we never learn what this means or what the alternatives were. He defends positions by asserting their rectitude. His language is that hyperglot of long-winded subtlety whose true meanings only a Roman can begin to suspect. Issues are reduced to verbiage or lacunae. No mention is made of the Mussolini-like *"truffa"* law that De Gasperi tried to pass, which would have awarded control of the legislature to the minority party with the most seats. We see De Gasperi defying the Papal party, but not De Gasperi seeking Papal help. We see him as an anti-Fascist, but not sending former partisans to prison, letting Fascists out, and keeping Fascists in government posts.[31] No wonder Philip Strick concludes that for many people *Anno uno,* "pirouetting endlessly around a succession of obscure non-events in the Italian politics of the immediate postwar period, seem[s] a non-event itself," but that no matter how incomprehensible De Gasperi's political maneuvers are, the man's failure is explained by the faces, locations, and architecture. The faces in the crowds speak of reality, the man of theory.[32]

But faces, locations, and buildings—even though they are often Rome's actual buildings—look as "theoretical" in this movie as do the conversations and the impoverished "action" scenes. They're all props for De Gasperi who himself is an actor. Zambetti accurately describes *Anno uno* as "a grotesque parade of wax museum figures, who move and talk in puerile solemn style, made of good-natured hieratic attitudes and banal sententiousness."[33]

So much for issues.

On the other hand, there is De Gasperi the man. Zambetti points out that we see a De Gasperi with rectitude and strength to act, with faith that inspires him and personal disinterest, with a spirit of sacrifice and humility. His back is constantly to the camera, weighted down. At center stage is not a statesman or a political man, but a good man, a holy man who suffers power rather than grasps for it. Ten years of history are turned into ten years of spiritual exercises.[34] De Gasperi's politics were simple, Roberto replied: "In that sense De Gasperi was really Christian . . . although [his policies] didn't succeed."[35]

Anno uno concludes with De Gasperi's bitter departure from the political scene. He makes no effort to hide his sadness at being put aside. "It would be difficult to find another Rossellini film with so melancholy a finale," remarks Trasatti.[36]

Most Rossellini movies end with greater melancholy. The difficulty is to find one in which the moviemaker is less emotionally involved. Perhaps Roberto would have backed out of the film, had he been able to. He told Luciano De Feo, Massimo Mida, and Renzino that he didn't like it and hadn't wanted to do it.[37] "The level of my father's prostitution," Renzino said, "coincided with financial need and *Anno uno* came at the lowest point."[38] Roberto did not like it, agreed Silvia D'Amico, but "he was paid very little, so he didn't do it for money."[39]

"I showed papa [Domenico] Aleotti's article in *Quotidiano dei Lavoratori*," Renzino said. "He read it silently and said, 'Have I the right to reply?' I said, 'But of course, like everyone!' And he spent three days writing a reply, very beautiful, in which he practically accepted all the criticisms but contested their tone and mode."[40]

Roberto seems to have been disturbed less by Aleotti's review of *Anno uno* than by an accompanying article, unsigned, which he suspected had been written by Renzino. Under the title, "Who is Roberto Rossellini?" it replied: "After his first experiences under Fascism . . . which it is worth recalling as 'components' of his work, it was on the wave of the Resistance that Rossellini produced his most noted and significant films. . . . [But] during the fundamental years of the class struggle in Italy, Rossellini managed to offer only banal, compromised films"—*L'amore, La macchina, Stromboli, Europe '51, Fear, Voyage in Italy, India, Della Rovere, Era notte a Roma, Viva l'Italia, Vanina Vanini.* "Let's not be surprised that now, with the latest film of the series, *Anno uno,* he passes from ambiguity and mystification to brutal defense of the Christian Democrat regime."

Roberto's reply ignored the criticisms. Instead, still in Crocean terms, he sternly takes the paper's young staff to task for being stronger in vanity than in the study of problems and how to solve them. "I think the whole human race should be liberated, not just one class, by acquiring knowledge. . . . Only knowledge can give courage. Violence . . . and Fascism are born from fear." The radicals, Roberto charges, are playing the same game as the bourgeoisie.[41]

The paper replied in the title it gave his letter: "Rossellini defends *Anno uno* but forgets that illuminism has failed and Rusconi is a fascist." The illuminists, Jefferson among them, had argued education as a guarantee of good government and progress.

Roberto would have countered that illuminism has never been tried. The question is not what we think of De Gasperi's policies, but "how can we exit from the neurotic and arrive at the reasonable.[42] ... Since De Gasperi has gone, the conflict of dialectical confusion is so intense that nobody knows what to do."[43] Education, of course, was Roberto's answer—specifically, watching his movie. "If we reread [our history], it will help us put order in our minds."[44]

A similar line of defense is sustained by Rondolino, who goes so far as to state that De Gasperi as a character virtually disappears into the background, "functioning as a coordinator of a series of social and political acts" which Rossellini is putting forth as so many theses for debate.[45]

But if the acts are obscure and if the theses can be discerned only in the lacunae, what kind of debate can there be?

The Messiah

The contract for *The Messiah* was signed July 10, 1974—at Saint Peter's in front of Michelangelo's *Pietà*, at Father Peyton's insistence. "I'll do this and more for two million dollars," Roberto wisecracked.[46]

The two million dollars came in the form of two letters of credit, however, and no one was willing to accept them. Roberto was not on good terms with the Christian Democrats after *Anno uno*. "[He] had never paid attention where he put his feet politically while walking, with often uncomfortable results," Trasatti said.[47] Moreover RAI, which was a Christian Democrat satellite, was undergoing "a profound institutional crisis," in Scaffa's phrase. "Legislative reforms interrupted many work relationships, including Rossellini's." And there was "a profound state of hostility." Rather than supporting Rossellini's film on Christ, RAI had decided to back Zeffirelli's *Gesù*—at a cost of more than eight billion lire. With that much money, Rossellini could have made thirty features.

"In order to produce *The Messiah* despite the hostility of competition," said Scaffa, "Rossellini had to make many sacrifices, and to fight. He lost the tranquil work situation that RAI had guaranteed him, and had to find a way of working in the marketplace for the first time in many years"— fourteen years.[48]

Confronted with the fact that no one would accept Peyton's letters of credit, Roberto wrote again to the Pope, on November 12, 1974. Paul VI had just gone to America, the first Pope ever to do so, and his address to the United Nations General Assembly—"No more war!"—had received huge publicity. Roberto wrote that the speech had moved him, that he was preparing a film on the Messiah, and would love to meet with him.[49] "Amid the anxiety oppressing us we look tumultuously for ideas, ideologies, beliefs, and faiths. ... In the Gospels there is everything that we humans seek now in other places."[50]

Paul VI remembered Roberto affectionately. Roberto, for his part, had put the Pope in the same category as his father, Gandhi, Nehru, and Chaplin. But on the heels of *Anno uno* he may have felt reluctant to say so publicly. Instead he announced he would do *Marx* after *The Messiah* and insisted on the similarity of Christ and Marx. "Clearly, the tendency today is to plant the label of reactionary on those who strive to encourage the diffusion of knowledge and do not flaunt propagandist arguments.... The truth is that there is no greater and more shattering and violent force than authentic knowledge."[51] He saw both Christ and Marx in Crocean terms, as he had Francis and Socrates.

Roberto told Pope Paul that he was a non-believer and wanted to make *The Messiah* for non-believers.[52] The Vatican-controlled Banco Santo Spirito accepted the letters of credit. In December, Italnoleggio requested a detailed scenario and a budget for shooting in the spring of 1975.

The contract with Father Peyton had been based on a twelve-page treatment by Scaffa which Roberto had given to Paul VI, and which someone in the Vatican had approved. The actual scenario was a pastiche of New Testament texts put together by Silvia D'Amico and, more actively than usual, Roberto himself. Silvia ("stupidly," she says) sent this scenario to Harry Jones, the producer of Father Peyton's *Family Theater*, who returned it with hundreds of little changes and a few big ones that, he announced, he would make himself if Rossellini did not.[53]

To play Mary, young at Christ's birth and old at his death, Roberto had originally hired two actresses. The older woman was so small she looked ridiculous alongside Christ. Whereupon Roberto declared he did not want to copy Pasolini, whose 1964 *Gospel according to Saint Matthew* he thought too phantasmagoric; instead he wanted a Mary "strictly tied to popular imagination."[54] His Mary is a sixteen-year-old who still looks sixteen at the end because, he explained, in popular imagination virgins do not age[55]— for example, Michelangelo's *Pietà.*

Roberto's original plan had been to begin with a two-hour film which would have traced the Messiah myths in the Old Testament, followed by a second two-hour film showing their fruition in Christ. He not only wanted traditional types playing the roles, he wanted a John Ford–like movie about the dynamics of tradition itself—"myth and reality." Accordingly he vetoed Beppe Cino's casting for Christ, assigning Cino's choice to the role of Judas Iscariot and, after toying with having the thin, long-haired Cino himself play Christ, selected Cino's twelfth candidate who, rather than the terrible, Pasolinian type Cino had wanted, was fragile and pious-looking.[56]

"*Il Messia* is counter-reformation as much on the formal level as in content," Alberto Moravia observed. "Rossellini has conducted his whole film like an operation of cinematic recuperation of the post-Tridentine figurative tradition.

"Why precisely *this* tradition? Because only a tradition like the Baroque and Mannerist one, which is only barely religious and thus easily vulgarized, is suitable for teaching—that is, is capable of being directly and triumphantly didactic, as Catholicism has been in the past and as social realism was recently." Thus the movie highlights Christ's parables and didactic character "even while working as a carpenter." The movie's form re-emphasizes stylistic traditions that have dominated religious art since Raphael—"in the choice of the actor that is Jesus, a Jesus in the seventeenth-century Italian tradition, not a bit mystic but human enough; in giving the Madonna the same juvenile face throughout the film, despite the passage of the years; in the figure of Pilate, emblematic of the impartial and impassable Roman dominion; finally in closing the film with an image that could not be more traditional, a tradition that extends to Domenico Morelli [1826–1901]: the Madonna kneeling in front of Christ's empty tomb, her arms open and her eyes raised toward the sky."[57]

Roberto's Messiah myth is Ford-like. His Christ is a revolutionary whose teaching rejects, corrects, and affirms tradition in a new conception of the universe. "It's the wonderful story of a disobedience. Is man made for the law or the law for man?"[58] Thus, Roberto fought with Harry Jones's demand that there be miracles in the film. Miracles would distort the "essential image," Roberto thought. "There's always a diaphragm between knowledge and us. Imagine! Some people, in order to believe that Jesus was a great man—or a great God, if you prefer—have to attribute miracles to him! But the guy who said 'the Sabbath is made for man, not man for the Sabbath' has made a political discourse of a fundamental importance.[59]

"The main thing is the love, and the faith in people. Maybe catechism shouldn't be taught to children, because it results in a completely different understanding. . . . They give you rules and tell you, 'If you do this you're good.' In this way they nurture cowardice, they nurture fear, the feeling of non-responsibility. Catechism reduces everything to minimal size, but in the Gospels the proportions are immense, gigantic."[60]

Here again is Rossellini's Crocean theme of prose destroying poetry and the need for individual discovery. In Jewish Messiah myths, "the power that [the Jews] wanted, in order to fight against an external enemy, became itself a sort of internal enemy. . . . Life is a continuous becoming toward an infinitely difficult, infinitely complex reality . . . and thus fatally heroic. But the structures of power express a lack of heroism."[61] To mock power Rossellini cast comedians to play the two Herods. "The guy who puts a crown on his head and stands with a scepter in his hand makes me laugh."[62] The murder of the child at the beginning of the movie stands for all the violence done by power to the poor and innocent—thus also for Christ as the sacrificial victim.[63] "Christ's message had been diverted and made into an instrument of power" by those who claim to serve the poor.[64]

When the Jews choose to have a king, they lose their identity. They surrender freedom for enslavement; they abandon virtue for obedience; they shut out experience and made a fetish of theory. "This divorce," notes Joël Magny, "occurs in each person, between the I and the Law. Law become an external constraint instead of a necessity derived from the human heart. The individual is nothing anymore, the law is everything."[65]

The same drama occurs in every Rossellini character, Magny continues: the conflict between our true self (the vital fire within us) and our false but functional social face.[66] Like De Gasperi, Manfredi, or Paul, Jesus convinces not by logic but by conviction—which *is* truth (Croce's "poetry"). Like Paul and Peter, Christ preaches as though possessed—urgently, aggressively. Compared to Christ, Roberto said, Pascal, Augustine, and all the others "are like articles in an encyclopedia. Christ *is* the encyclopedia, whole and entire."[67] Christ brings strife, disagreement, revolution. Christ is denunciatory even declaiming the Beatitudes. Christ talks while working—hammering or something—while others watch idly. The disciples who preach about Lazarus stand still, calm, exalted, and lofty. Christ walks.

"We wanted the words thrown away," said Silvia D'Amico. Christ's language is simple, without adjectives. The Pharisees use sophisticated language. "He was killed for language."[68]

He is a hero rejected, like Irene or Socrates. "Every little thing he does," said Roberto, "is an expression of unheard-of courage in context of that society, as it would be in context of any society. When he eats with the tax collectors, he had tremendous courage, and he explains it: 'There's no point going to the healthy, one has to go to the sick.' This is where Jesus makes his greatest revolution. He took on himself the evil of others."[69]

"'Law is made for man, not man for law.' Man is totally responsible, it's he who must undertake the responsibility to make the immense effort to get away from blindness, myopia, and ignorance and go look at the universe. This is man's great mission."[70]

The Messiah was shot in 42 days in June and July 1975, mostly in Tunisia. ("Israel looks like Switzerland," Roberto explained.[71]) There was still no distribution contract because there was no agreement with Harry Jones. Roberto was 69, disinterested in caution. He challenged the 105-degree temperatures like a young man, and worked fifteen hours a day. He began at the end: the tomb scene, in Gabes. None of the actors was professional; all were playing in English. Carlos de Carvalho (John the Baptist, and Silvia D'Amico's brother-in-law) had set up a sort of school to train them in English.

Mary was Mita Ungaro, the daughter of Arabella Lemaître, the Selznick agent who had played Clare in *Francesco*. Roberto wanted Mita Ungaro to run up to the tomb, find it empty, and cry. In the first take she did not cry. Roberto took her aside, spoke to her for a few minutes, and she cried when he wanted.

Roberto, afterward, struggled manfully in dozens of interviews to claim he had merely filmed "information," had made no "choices" himself, had no "opinions," and that specifically with this ending with Mary crying he had intended to be ambivalent, so that each viewer might be "free" to interpret the moment as they liked: that Jesus rose from the dead, or that his followers stole the body.[72] In an article for the Communist *Paese Sera* Roberto wrote, "I have laid out—without personal interpretation and without emotional stimulation, but as the result of careful study—the life and, above all, the thought of Jesus of Nazareth."[73]

The truth is that Roberto instructed Mary to cry from happiness, like a mother who cries when her child succeeds.[74] Nascimbene's music underlines this idea, by reversing at this moment the flute passage from the start of the movie.[75] We are free to fabricate any interpretation we wish; but Rossellini's movie proposes one explanation only.

"Roberto was crying all during the shooting," his nephew Franco said.[76]

"I got very emotional. . . . I don't need miracles to know that Jesus is God incarnated so that we can love him. Certainly he conquered me, I'm in love with him. . . . I never pray to Jesus because I don't know how to pray. But maybe I like him because he's a model, something that moves me. I had a Catholic education from which I learned the deepest respect for man, which is a teaching of Jesus's. Man is the starting point of everything. God is perfection, but man must reach it. The trouble today comes from having gone from an individual morality to a collective one, which takes away individual responsibility."[77]

After Gabes the production moved to Nefta, Sousse, and Kairouan, then back to Rome for Herod's scenes. 127 camels were used, 193 asses, 91 horses, and 490 birds. Even so, there are no sets, no professional actors, no direct sound (still!), not much montage, almost no spectacle. Roberto omitted Christ's Passion as too distracting. It is difficult to see where the $2 million went. More seriously, it is apparent that Roberto did not cry every day. Often he shot with no invention and little feeling. Silvia was astonished that he respected every comma in the script; she had expected him to change everything.[78] "I refuse to accomplish any creative act," he would declare. "The only creation possible is to build a child. That's all."[79]

Yet by searching through *The Messiah*'s two hours and 21 minutes, one can find about half an hour, particularly in the middle, of Rossellini at his most creative. When Mary tells stories of "milk and honey" with the Sea of Galilee and fishermen in the background, and the camera-eye describes a wondrous track across the scene, the result is one of the lovelier moments in the history of film. The claims that Rossellini made for his new cinema here seem justified—but because it is art and not just "information."

"I really feel we don't know how to use images. We're prisoners of verbalism, we use images as illustrations of a thought. Such images are lies. To get back to the true image, the essential image, we have to go back before even the invention of spoken language. It's an uncomfortable trip to make, because our dialectical habit is different. . . . All Jesus's parables are visual discourses. They refer to concrete things rooted in daily life. Christ's discourse is a discourse on the lowest, humblest level. The idea comes across through the image. Because he's talking to simple, uncultured people. To translate this discourse into cinema becomes something passionate. The camera has to be used as much as possible like the eye. And our eye is never completely attentive. It looks around, it takes in (often unconsciously) a multitude of things."[80]

Are Christ's tools and work an aspect of this concreteness? Do they comment on what he is saying?

"They are the *reality* you start with. . . . Only like this do things become clear. . . . Marx said something wonderful: 'The concrete is the synthesis of many determinants.' If you want to get to the concrete, you have to give a quantity of determinants which each person will then synthesize according to his or her nature.[81] What someone says isn't the only thing important: ambience is. The main thing is to put a lot of things together, a lot of data representative of daily life, how people dressed, what they did, the thought of the time.[82] The long take makes all of this contextual.[83] It's all nude and bare, but the image at every instant is showing all together so many situations, so many things . . . Look how important everything is: the land, the crickets, the wind, the water, the way people move and work. Everything is sign, everything is message. And they're signs and messages that are born from an accumulation of data. A discourse, in short, without ever underlining.[84]

"Otherwise, you have to work by analysis—montage. And as you cast your eye on one thing, then another, and another, and another, you can only make very limited choices, and the result is more confused.[85] It becomes a type of language that's more sophisticated, more eloquent. And eloquence is a way of seducing, of obliging people to think in a certain direction. Long takes prevent you from becoming seducing or leading people in the direction you want. Things are there and you can't manipulate them. In any case your manipulation is reduced to very little.[86]

"I'm obsessed with not preaching *anything*, because I believe it's wrong, a violation of the personalities of the people watching. . . . People should be given data to work with, to elaborate upon, and then—who knows?—perhaps they will be able to come up with something new. . . .

"[Civilizations] die all the time, because they're imperfect, as Toynbee pointed out. And that imperfection is always the same—they are built on the idea that power had to be delegated to a single figure to provide inspiration, energy, and work.[87]

"Christ at his baptism, is just small and frail. He takes strength, affirms himself little by little. . . . He has a precise awareness of the things that are going on, and how they're happening. He has a sharp, transcendent vision of everything around him. This is why his journey is so profound, his trajectory so magnificent. And why he's so badly understood."[88]

The Messiah was never finished. According to Silvia D'Amico, Harry Jones was disappointed by the lack of miracles and passion scenes and declared his intention to alter the movie. To prevent his obtaining the negative, she and Roberto sued themselves, demanding that they not give him the film.[89] According to Michael Morris, O.P., Jones found the movie "excrutiatingly boring. . . . An attempt was made to re-edit it and shorten the film for American audiences, but this was challenged in the Italian courts and the film was caught up in endless litigation."[90]

Meanwhile Silvia directed an Italian dubbing, using for Christ's voice the same actor as used by Pasolini. Since the actors were already speaking English quickly, and since the Italian had to be spoken even more quickly because it required more syllables to say the same thing, Rossellini's Christ emerges as nervous and angry. Rossellini had wanted just the opposite— for the dubbed voices to understate everything.

Beginning with a critics' convention in Montecatini that October, and then for nearly a year, Roberto showed *Il Messia* repeatedly. No distributor would touch it. Italnoleggio and Catholic companies rejected it—not because it was controversial, but because audiences found it boring. Once again a movie was less than it ought to have been because of Roberto's doubts about art and lack of energy. Once again his justification was his refusal to entertain.

"If I wanted success," Roberto confessed, "I wouldn't be making films like these—it would be a miracle if success resulted from them. [But] I don't believe my work is wasted, in any sense. . . . Mainly I try to live with pleasure; not to have a boring moment in my life, that's my main preoccupation. I think it would be possible for me to be part of the industry, to be a very successful director, to earn a lot of money, to be respected, important. But I rejected all that, for the sake of adventure. I'm seventy and I don't have a penny. I don't care. I go on, and I have fun."[91]

Le Messie did open in Paris in February 1976, in five theaters, courtesy of Toscan du Plantier at Gaumont. "The dubbing was a huge scandal," said Gruault. "Rossellini had chosen the cheapest possible dubber, and gone as fast as possible, without correcting anything."[92]

The picture itself got respectful reviews, however, and a dozen interviews appeared. Roberto had brought along Baruff, his big dog with hair in its eyes, and would take him even into restaurants. He had rented a separate hotel room for Baruff, and the press suggested he was behaving like a movie star. On the night of the premiere, Silvia had to apologize for his non-appearance. He was too busy preparing his next film, she announced—knowing he was in bed playing solitaire.

He played cards by himself constantly; it was a way of thinking. He adored card tricks too. When he died, Silvia and Franca Rodolfi wanted to put his cards in his tomb.

Il Messia was finally picked up for Italian distribution by ARCI, a small Marxist group that hitherto had handled only a few films from Latin America. It played briefly in Rome at the end of September 1976. "People didn't miss comparing my *Messiah* with Pasolini's *Gospel according to St. Matthew*, where you see Christ buggering pigs—and the comparison wasn't to my advantage! Pasolini's vision was judged much more intelligent than mine; I'm content just showing a man among people. . . . The highest authorities of the State didn't hide their disappointment. 'But, signor Rossellini, what do you think of Christ? That's what we wanted to know!'"[93]

The End

*Success consists of going from failure to failure without loss of enthusiasm.
. . . Never give in. Never. Never. Never. Never.*

—Winston Churchill

Roberto had his seventieth birthday in 1976. Ingrid had been in Rome and had told him she had to leave the day before. But on May 8 she hosted a surprise party for him at Nino's and gave him a wreath of flowers. Everyone was there except his Indian family and Robertino. Roberto gave his order to the waiter without realizing the waiter was Robertino. The children gave him a scroll mocking his infamous aphorisms (like "I take the bread out of my own mouth to give to the children"). He almost cried.

He felt at the peak of his powers, he told Lisandrini. But he would not make another feature film during the two years remaining in his life. *Anno uno* and *Il Messia* had been disasters, his rapport with RAI was broken, John de Menil had died, Horizon 2000 was bankrupt, the Science project had collapsed, and so had the marriage with Silvia.

"One night," according to Isabella Rossellini, "Silvia, after shedding many tears, came to the conclusion that instead of abandoning themselves to their love completely and without reservation, they should split up. A peculiarity of their love was that their great passion confused their minds and led them to make random decisions that were often just the opposite of what they really wanted. That obviously caused a lot of weeping, crises, and changes of heart. Reconciliations and breakups were a daily occurrence."[1]

During *The Messiah* Roberto had pursued a young woman playing a small role. He promised to make her a star and give her a nice apartment in Rome. He wanted her to marry him. He asked her to come along in the car one day, and Marcellina De Marchis, shouting "Wait for me," scrambled into the front seat, whereupon Roberto told her he wanted the actress beside him and Marcellina uncomplainingly got in the back. Silvia cut most of the actress's scenes out of the film. When *Il Mondo* quizzed him about Silvia, he replied: "I could be in love with another woman and not with the one the papers are talking about. I'm almost always in a state of insanity. . . . I'm not a Don Juan. . . . I don't know what it means to conquer a woman. Dedication has a certain importance, but that's all I know. [The dedication] starts immediately. [I look in a woman] for something breaking out, exploding. A state of effervescence, passion, insanity. Many women seem like atom bombs but turn out to be duds. A man falls in love with a woman because she has crooked eyebrows not because she has a good rear end. Of course, the rear end counts too. . . . It's difficult to distinguish sex from love, even if they're contiguous spheres, and it's even more difficult to distinguish sex from passion. In nature the male and female hunt together and their encounter suddenly explodes, whereas in Italy everyone has a garçonnière. . . . [A relationship ends] when there's not enough insanity. Things get practical and it's all over. I have collected a large number of mothers and sisters. There are the sad moments of breaking up, but then everything adjusts."[2]

The young actress turned him down. In September 1976 he moved into an apartment that Marcellina had found for him directly across from her own, Via Caroncini 43. Silvia D'Amico and her mother lived on the same block. Marcellina kept Baruff and fed Roberto too. He had always loved her cooking: eggs fried, then cut like noodles, with tomato, basil, and butter; or cod fried then baked with white and tomato sauces, black olives, and oregano.[3] His happiness came first for her. She had not disapproved of Silvia. "How important it was for him to have had that love at that age! How dangerous it could have been!" she said.[4] She had been having a long-time relationship herself, but cut it off the moment he told her he needed her and asked her to. In her mind his other women had always been *scappatelle* ("escapades") and her other men *flirt sportivi*; she was Roberto's wife.[5] She was never willing, however, to resume marital relations after their separation.

Sonali started talking to him on the phone again; he thanked her for her dignified behavior the year before. He bought another big hairy dog, tired of it after two days, and offered to give it to Raffaella. "Give it to me," Sonali said, "I'll sell it."[6]

Ingrid showed up at The Raphael, distressed over her divorce from Lars Schmidt. "To hell with the past," Roberto told her, "look ahead, to the future."

Driving through the Galleria Umberto one day, he nearly had an accident when a car stopped in front of him, and two youngsters on a passing motorcycle screamed insults at him. Fifty yards farther they met at a light and more insults were shouted, "Imbecile! Old asshole!" Calmly Roberto replied, "Come here and I'll break your neck." The passenger came over, Roberto slapped him so hard he unexpectedly fell down. The driver tried to intervene, got his pants tangled in the cycle, and arrived on his knees. Roberto grabbed him by the hair and slapped him twice. A crowd started to gather. People jeered at the kids: "Aren't you ashamed to treat an old man like this!?" Whereupon Roberto got mad at the crowd.[7]

His closest companion during his last two years was Daniel Toscan du Plantier, director of French Gaumont, whom he had contacted to distribute

Le Messie. Schlumberger had invested in Gaumont at Roberto's urging, in the expectation that Europe's largest commercial movie company could be an organ of education and social change. Roberto's plan was that Gaumont could create a Latin common market, evolve new relationships between cinema and television, and develop new structures for an industrial counteroffensive against the Americans.

Roberto's response to any obstacle was, of course, to pooh-pooh it. "That's easy for you to say," Toscan du Plantier objected, "you're Rossellini." Roberto screamed back: *"We're all Rossellini!"*[8]

"Once I made him watch *Europe 51*," Toscan du Plantier recounted. "He was unhappy, upset, and kept going out. Everyone felt ill at ease. I didn't try again, it would have been insupportable cruelty. He hadn't suffered for aesthetic reasons but because he was seeing again his furniture, his car, and his wife. And he said, with the Socratic irony so typical of him, 'I'm emotional because that was my dog that was on the screen.' . . . He had a horror of nostalgia."[9]

Roberto recorded hours of tapes about his life for Toscan du Plantier which, after being edited by Roberto, were published posthumously in book form in French and Italian, and then mysteriously vanished. In honor of Rossellini after his death, Toscan du Plantier, who had become friends with Isabella, asked Renzino to head Italian Gaumont, which after dominating Italian production for a few years, collapsed in bankruptcy.

Concerto

In 1977 a RAI executive in Paris proposed that Roberto make a film in the Sistine Chapel around the music of Monsignor Domenico Bartolucci and the Choir of the Pontifical Chapel of which he was the director. The film would be broadcast on Holy Saturday, April 9, a week away. "Unlike me, he knew absolutely everyone [at the Vatican]," said Father Fantuzzi. "He exchanged warm pats on the back with monsignors whom he called '*tu*' and made me blush introducing me as his friend."[10] Roberto spent three days scrambling around Saint Peter's and the Vatican, then two days editing the results. The choir was filmed on video tape, the rest in 35mm, and the whole assembled into a 42-minute video, *Concerto per Michelangelo*, with a voice-off account (not by Roberto) of Michelangelo's work in Rome. Unfortunately neither the music nor Rossellini's pictures have much to recommend them. In September, after his death, *Concerto* was entered in competition for the Premio Italia and the jury complained of the poor quality of the soundtrack.

Le Centre Georges Pompidou

The week after Roberto finished *Concerto* the French Ministry of Foreign Affairs commissioned him to make a documentary on Le Centre Georges Pompidou, or "Beaubourg," which had opened two months earlier, January 31. Dominique de Menil was one of the directors of the museum, whose phony-modernist façade is an assemblage of glass and colored pipes vaguely resembling something out of Lang's 1926 *Metropolis*. A huge area of central Paris, including the Les Halles markets, had been razed to make space for Beaubourg's aridity. The more Roberto looked, the more livid he became. "It's the tomb of a civilization. . . . Everything is useful in Saint Peter's, whereas here at Beaubourg everything is useless." Nonetheless, he pledged to make "a witnessing that will satisfy both those who love Beaubourg and those who detest it."[11]

The one-hour film took a week. But this time he had Nestor Almendros, one of the world's great cinematographers, a full crew, and all the elaborate lighting his zoom demanded. "It is as if Rossellini himself takes the spectator by the hand to show him the building," Almendros remarked. "Like all his work, it is honest, personal, and uncompromising."[12]

"Beaubourg is an important phenomenon," Roberto told *Écran*. "I looked at the 'phenomenon.' And then I made a phenomenological film. I think personally that people confuse culture and refinement a lot. Refinement for me has nothing to do with knowledge. But when people talk about 'culture' they always call it 'refined.' Before being refined, people have to think, and to know how to be human. . . . Beaubourg is a flagrant thing: it's the exposition of refinement at all costs. I don't denounce it. There's no need to, it's enough to look at it. . . . I used neither music nor a narrator in the film. I wanted to *show* Beaubourg. I hid dozens of microphones everywhere and recorded everything the public said, who are running en masse to Beaubourg. I had to cheat to put some positive opinions on Beaubourg in my film. Because there weren't any. . . . But in order to have balance and not look partisan, I had to invent some positive remarks. Imagine that!"[13]

But Rossellini was not being forthright. *Le Centre Georges Pompidou* never just "shows"; it is completely partisan, and a great movie accordingly. The museum emerges slowly out of the polluted mist above Paris with the blare of loud, bone-piercing pneumatic hammers—a combination more violent visually than Antonioni's *Red Desert* and more violent sonically than Godard's *One plus One*. In contrast, we pan gently around the rooftops of *vieille Paris* with sounds of birds, children, and piano practice. Yet Rossellini is intensely sensitive to Beaubourg's geometry—the rectangles and triangles of its façade, the walls and partitions of its galleries: none of Michelangelo's lines in *Concerto* inspired him so much. He never pauses or slows to contemplate an individual painting while floating through the galleries: he *feels* the environment, the context. It's hard not to think of Resnais's hymn to technology, *La Chant du styrène* (1958). But where Resnais dealt with flat surfaces and linear movements of the frame (like strolling through a square city), Rossellini is dealing with dimensions whose depths and angles change constantly (like strolling in Venice), not only because the spaces vary in Beaubourg but also, and chiefly, because Rossellini's slow, elaborate tracks and zooms cause their dimensions to vary constantly. The effect is architecture in motion, a progression through a Bach fugue. Beaubourg itself may be a "tomb"; Rossellini's last movie is a contemplation of the mysteries of life and death.

Roberto exhausted himself over it, according to Almendros.[14] It was completed on May 6. He phoned Ingrid and she remarked how tired he sounded.

Marx

Vittorio Bonicelli tried to tempt him. Would he make, say, a film of Stendhal's *Charterhouse of Parma*—a subject set in the same period as *Vanina Vanini*—given total liberty? "No," Roberto replied, offended.[15]

A proposal from RAI for a picture on Saint Peter, on the other hand, was tempting.[16] But chiefly he wanted to do Karl Marx or, as Silvia D'Amico's treatment was titled, *Lavorare per l'umanità* ("To work for humanity").

"The poor man! Everyone talks about him but no one understands him . . . , even though nearly everyone claims to be Marxist.[17] I've two sons who talk revolution day and night. The more conservative of the two is in the Communist Party. But the fact is they've hardly read Marx.[18] I say, know him! Then hate him with reason, or use him with reason."[19]

Roberto had decided that, as Simone Weil had declared in the thirties, "Marx's entire work is permeated with a spirit incompatible with the vulgar materialism of Engels and Lenin."[20] He was fervently hoping his movie would get him into trouble with the Communists. "After *Karl Marx* I'll be assassinated! But that's better than dying in bed, isn't it?"[21]

For Roberto, Marx was Comenius, a "defender of science," a Gramscian illuminist.[22] "Marx says again and again that in order to act it is necessary to become aware—'to know' in scientific terms. . . . At the same time he accused 'power' of keeping the downtrodden in ignorance. 'For critical thinking, the minority substitutes dogmatism.' Two thousand years ago Christ said the same thing.[23] All fashionable revolution is old-fashioned.[24] What interests me is not the antithesis between Christ and Marx but these two ideas, two ethics, around which the world turns today.[25] No one reads *Das Kapital*, no one reads the Gospels, in our Marxo-Christian world.[26]

"Marxism suggests a method whereby we can become authentically ourselves and climb out of absurdity. . . . History is the story of man, of his growth, of his development. . . . Marx [himself] was never dogmatic. [But] there exist . . . associations . . . vowed to affirm or destroy Marxism.[27] Jesus said, 'Woe to you doctors of the law who have usurped the keys of science: you have not entered yourselves, and you have impeded those who wanted to enter.'"[28]

As usual, Roberto associated himself with his latest hero. His own struggle was inspired by Marx, he felt. "One of the principal goals of my life is to demolish with a great deal of patience, day by day, my ignorance. Ignorance is a concrete bunker so solid that bombs and pneumatic drills hardly scratch it. I repeat constantly to my children: 'Be sure to take the trouble to demolish every day a bit of your ignorance.' That way, life's adventure is beautiful, because you're constantly making discoveries."[29]

The search for the basis of truth is only the apparent theme of Rossellini's philosopher movies, however. The ultimate zoom lens might peer into the atom and give us a close-up of a distant galaxy, but the search always returns us to ourselves.

In a prospectus for Gaumont, Roberto said the two-hour film would be shot in Germany, England, and, mostly, France, near the Belgian frontier, for $1 million. "I'm going to deal with the first part of Marx's life, the part people usually pay no attention to," he told *Écran*. "I'll meet Marx at the moment he leaves home in Trier for the university in Bonn, and I'll film him all during his formation, [ten years] until *The [Communist] Manifesto*.[30] [I'll follow] the itinerary of how he becomes Karl Marx—family themes: his deep love for the father, a liberal from whom he learned that 'the first duty is to work for humanity'; his friendship [with] Engels; his studies; and the great historical themes of the epoch: the industrial revolution, and the political, technical, and scientific revolutions.[31]

"The day Marx goes to Bonn, the boat that goes down the Mosel leaves at four in the morning. Marx is there with his whole family, all the family friends, and the family of the woman who will later become Marx's wife, but now there is just friendship between them. And they are there waiting for the boat and looking at the sky while talking distractedly. And do you know why they're looking at the sky? Because it's the night the comet passes. Isn't that something? And it's an absolutely historical fact. Of course I'll be accused of giving . . . some profound meaning to a detail."[32]

RAI's first channel was interested. The project was complex, costly, and of dubious exploitability, and Roberto was still on bad terms with some of RAI's bureaucracy. Nonetheless, that spring, Mimmo Scarano, who was in charge of RAI's first channel, told him, "We'll try."[33]

Cannes

"Last February," Roberto wrote in *Paese Sera*, "Favre Le Bret asked me to preside over the jury of the thirtieth Cannes Film Festival. This offer bewildered me a bit, but I didn't want to lose the opportunity. . . . My separation from 'cinema' . . . had already lasted too long and in order to recapitulate my fifteen years of reflections I thought this experience would be indispensable."[34]

He told Gian Luigi Rondi he was doing it "to distinguish the true cinema from the false cinema, the one that really serves man from the one that is just a pure stylistic exercise."[35]

Afterward, he asked rhetorically: "So, what has [auteur cinema] evolved into [after forty years]?" And replied: "Navel gazing. . . . Many so-called auteur films are a pure exercise in vain and personally schizophrenic aestheticism." Even worse was the preoccupation with "trivia" like sex and violence.[36]

Roberto had scarcely seen a movie in years. Now he sat watching dozens with a finger in his nose, so that people would think he was awake and pensive. He would fall asleep, hurt his nose, and awake with a jolt. "I have so much to do," he told Rondi. "When we're both old we'll go to Central Asia, just eat yogurt and live to be 120."[37] He wanted Truffaut to direct *Nièpce and Daguerre*. He looked forward to meeting Robert Altman, whom he wanted to direct *The American Revolution*. "I really liked *Buffalo Bill and the Indians*. I really like that way of demythifying things."[38] But after meeting Altman he told Fulchignoni, "I met a man who told me some foolish things."[39] He was perplexed by Angelopoulos's *The Hunters*, but liked Scola's *A Special Day*, because of its references to his own movies, Gubenko's *The Little Orphans* and Ridley Scott's *The Duellists*, because of their technique and economy. One movie he loved: the Taviani brothers' *Padre padrone*. He wished he had made it himself.[40]

Every day of the festival he interviewed young film people on closed-circuit television. On May 13 and 14 he presided over a colloquium, "Cinema's Social and Economic Responsibility," for which he had deliberately invited experts from *outside* the world of cinema: a biologist (Henri Laborit—Gruault's biologist), a writer (Paul Guimard), an economist (Henri Mercillon), a law professor (André-Charles Junod), and the adjunct director of UNESCO (Jacques Rigaud). Cannes had the air of a funeral for the film industry, *L'Espresso* remarked: movie attendance in the Common Market had dropped by 2.5 billion spectators during the last sixteen years; there were fewer "good" films on the market; and production was dropping.[41] But economics was the last thing Roberto wanted to discuss. "It's insane to think in economic terms. . . . The most important problem is a human problem, a problem of life, knowledge, intelligence, and orientation. . . . Where is civilization going? There are too many opinions, too little harmony. Do audio-visuals help or not to orient us? Or do they cause confusion?"[42]

Would such questions work at a market-festival as crassly commercial as Cannes? Many thought Roberto was trying to mix oil and water. He had invited 200 experts, but only five came. "The world is full of opinions and empty of knowledge," Roberto replied.

But is this why the film industry is in crisis? "Yes. Because the whole world's in crisis. They're trying to keep audiences by grabbing them by their throats with pornography and spectacle, the way they did during the fall of the Roman Empire, when they attracted crowds to the Teatro Marcello with the myth of Pasiphae recounted by an actress with a ram on top of her."[43]

Roberto's second book, *Un Esprit libre ne doit rien apprendre en esclave* ("A free spirit must learn nothing as a slave") had been published by Fayard in April. It was a discussion of the revolutions in science, technology, politics, and economics that have thrown our age into crisis—and how education, television, and Comenius offer solutions. What occasion could possibly be better for discussing such matters than Cannes? Hadn't Christ sat down with the tax collectors?

A hundred people came to the first session. "The spirit of this colloquium," Roberto announced, "is to give birth to a dialogue among film people to try to define the situation we are in. I think . . . we live in a world in total crisis . . . and that cinema mirrors it. But . . . is film simply a mirror? Or does it accelerate the process? History tells us that civilizations die by suicide. So are our current actions suicidal? How can we remedy our situation?"[44]

Roberto's panel tried to respond. The adjunct director of UNESCO contended that all films reflect fear, announcing (or denouncing) the end of something. The economist raged against the quantity and misuse of electronic messages. Hollywood was attacked, along with its influence on third-world distribution. The biologist proposed creation of an international monetary fund for cinema. One session was held in a corridor, after someone forgot to reserve the Conference Hall. Roberto smiled and smoked and said little. He bemoaned the film industry crying "crisis" because theater admissions were decreasing, whereas, if television were included, actual audiences were exponentially increasing. He scoffed at the call for "special commissions" to intervene as wet nurses, which, as we know, are "useful only to sucklings."

"But when I made these objections, many looked at me with suspicion, even with pity. And they were horrified at talk of cinema and television in the same breath."[45]

He explained again that the whole point of "neo-realism," for him, had been liberation from the "absolutely crushing structures that prevented new forces from entering into play.[46] Karl Marx said: 'Ignorance was never any use to anyone.' I add: 'Ignorance has been quite useful to those who want to put their feet on our necks.' I'm 71, I'm on my feet, and I continue to annoy everyone. I had the choice. I had had great success. I had become a star, I could have profited from that, could have lived off of it without being bored, because I get a lot of fun out of life. I preferred to go back to being annoying. I was born free, luckily. I am free, totally free."[47]

Such, perhaps, was the point of Roberto Rossellini's career in terms of the history of cinema: the example he gave of freedom.

The two-day, three-session conference continued "unofficially" for ten days. A successor was planned for the following year. Roberto, who had insisted before the festival that he had *not* made the colloquium a condition of his being president of the jury, now said that he had.[48]

Meanwhile he ignited a bomb. Determined to proclaim his thesis of collaboration between film and television, he had inspired the jury to award the Palm d'Or—the highest prize—to *Padre padrone*, which had been produced by RAI *for television*. He inspired one uncertain jury member with the gift of some expensive jewelry (which he billed to the festival). To underline the slap in the face Roberto intended, he arranged not to award that year the two awards specifically designed to honor "problematic" films without stealing limelight from the more mainstream Palm d'Or (the Special Jury prize and Best Director).

The result was just what he wanted: a hell of a scandal. "The scandal was to award first prize to a 16mm film made for television, and to do it in such a way that all would know it had been a precise and polemical choice. Everyone did realize it, and the scandal Rossellini wanted arose, but we were not always grateful to him for having lit even this slow fuse," commented Casiraghi.[49]

The administrators of the festival boycotted the stage of the awards ceremony. Roberto appeared alone. "The prize to the Tavianis is the indispensable bond between cinema and television," he declared.[50] "I have defended the true cinema without hesitation, without half measures, cleaning house of all the rest—which no longer is of service to anything or anyone, neither to man nor society, nor, consequently, to the festival."[51]

The president of the festival, Robert Favre Le Bret, who was responsible for Roberto being there in the first place, protested publicly. "I have never given my opinion in thirty years, but this year I am so upset that I cannot resist supporting the opinion of the press and the public. This award is quite incoherent to me, and even so I'm putting it gently. It is astonishing, for example, that the two films that got the best reception unanimously, I mean unanimously, in the press, received no awards. One did, yes, due to the bias of a female performance [Shelley Duvall in Altman's *Three Women*]. And I am truly sorry, because an award is important. You know that we have always tried at Cannes—and I told the jury so—to harmonize art and industry. In other words, it is necessary to reward films that can attract very large audiences. This is one way to save the cinema, if the jury had done so. I think this point was not taken into account this time. I deplore it. I have to say to Roberto Rossellini: the awards should have been totally different and should have corresponded to what we expected, as a festival where, really, some very good films were shown."[52]

The Tavianis, quite aware that their movie was out of place at Cannes, had not even wanted to have it shown there. But the more Le Bret had pressed the jury, the more the jury had united behind Roberto. "It was the first time that in a festival like Cannes a film won that had been produced outside the power groups of the commercial cinema," said Paolo Taviani.[53]

Roberto, aware that everyone was mad at him, was jubilant. "We've struck a real blow here at Cannes," he crowed at lunch the next day. From Paris, Agnès Varda had told him, "Don't forget to shit on everyone."[54] To accusations that he had wanted to please RAI for personal motives, he responded blithely. "If someone doesn't like you, drown them with love. Television doesn't like the cinema, so we'll drown it with love."[55]

Roberto drove back to Rome with Gil on Tuesday, May 31. Before dropping Gil off, he stopped to buy flowers and candy for Sonali, and at the gate on Vicolo delle Sette Chiese wondered if he should come in. He decided to leave for another time this next step toward the reconciliation he hoped eventually to achieve.

The next day, Toscan du Plantier of Gaumont and the director of RAI's second channel met and agreed to produce *Marx* in partnership.[56] The same day Favre Le Bret phoned, inviting Roberto to preside at Cannes again in 1978: the Festival had in fact been a huge success, they had decided. Roberto asked Silvia to talk to Harry Jones again about finishing *The Messiah*, and fumed about an article on Cannes in *L'Espresso* that completely missed the point he had been trying to make. Thursday was spent trying to comfort Vittorio De Sica's daughter Emy, whose mother had died Wednesday. After the funeral, he took her out to dinner.

On Friday morning he phoned Suso Cecchi D'Amico at 9:30: "I'm pretty worn out, I didn't sleep at all last night. I spent it writing an article that will re-establish the truth about Cannes and what happened. I absolutely have to publish it tomorrow in *Paese Sera*, not to fight with *L'Espresso*, but for the love of truth."[57]

"He was going away to Paris again," said Marcellina, "and at seven in the morning began phoning to give me instructions about what I had to do for him in the meantime. The bank, bills to pay, a few errands." He also phoned Silvia constantly. She was working on the script for *Marx*, they had an appointment at RAI that afternoon. He called asking her to type the article, then again to come and get it. He called Toscan du Plantier in Paris, Callisto Cosulich at *Paese Sera*, Gil at Sonali's, still asleep, and many another. "Toward midday he called again," Marcellina said, "to ask what I'd made for lunch and when he heard it was fried cod with olives in a baking dish, which he adored, he was overjoyed: 'That's great! I'll be there soon, and we can give some to Baruff too!' In other words, it was a day like any other. . . .

"Ten minutes later came another call. His voice was hardly recognizable. He panted, 'Marcella, run, come, I feel terrible!' I ran to his place, just the time to cross the street."[58]

Meanwhile he had phoned the D'Amicos. "I'm afraid I just had a heart attack. I have a sharp pain in my chest. If I can, I'll come this afternoon."[59] His voice was matter-of-fact, strong, not scared. Silvia said, "Don't tease!"[60]

Marcellina arrived. "He was standing near the door, leaning a bit against the wall, with his glasses on. 'It's a heart attack. Call the doctor quickly. Call Renzo,' he said, and he gave me the number of the clinic. I made the calls with him still standing near me. Then I convinced him to stretch out on the bed. His eyes were staring but very lucidly, his face was moist. Meanwhile Rita had come, the maid who'd been with us for years.

"There was no medicine in the house, because Roberto had never had heart trouble. My legs were trembling but I managed to take his hand calmly, 'The doctor will be here in a moment, and Renzo's coming. Wait a second and I'll get the Synthol for your forehead, it'll cool you off.' I started looking for the bottle on the table when I heard him sigh three times. Three long sighs, like when he was upset. I said, 'I'm bothering you, huh?' And looked at him through the corner of my eye. His eyes were gazing vaguely upward, with an almost ironic expression. I understood at once. With three long sighs, Roberto had gone."[61]

Silvia got there shortly after her mother. "Roberto was lying on his side, his hands protecting his heart, but he had a pulse. I thought he was playing dead."[62]

The doctor came, tried massages and injections, and pronounced Roberto Rossellini dead at 12:45 p.m., June 3, 1977. Silvia went to the living room where the others were. "Roberto is dead," she said, then believed it herself when her mother started crying.[63]

Renzino arrived, then Di Giammatteo and Leonardo Fioravanti from the Centro Sperimentale. The phone rang, Marcella recalled. "It was Paolo Grassi, the president of RAI. He wanted to talk to Roberto. 'He's indisposed,' I responded. But Renzo grabbed the receiver from my hand and screamed crying, 'No, he's dead, papa is dead.' It was ten to one, which is why the world knew immediately of his passing on the one o'clock news."[64]

Marcella put a flower in Roberto's hands. Fellini came, as did Renzino's Communist friends. Silvia typed and corrected the article for *Paese Sera*; it appeared the next day, "A Diagnosis of the Cinema after the Experience of Cannes."[65] Comenius stood open on his desk. "Principles are derived from the nature itself of things." The lousy review of *Roma città aperta* was still in Roberto's pocket.

Sonali came home and heard the news on television. She drove to Roberto's apartment on Via Caroncini and sat on the floor, which she had strewn with lilies of the valley, with her long hair streaming down.

Ingrid, in England doing a play, got the news by phone from Fiorella. Her friends forced her to go on anyhow. She cried afterward. She remembered how she had cried over the monkey episode in *India*, and how Roberto had told her that she was crying because she was the monkey always trying to protect him. "It was the best death Roberto could have hoped for," she told Marcellina on the phone. "In your arms. It was right, so right for him to die in your arms."[66]

Most of Rossellini's recent movies had ended with heroes confronting death: Louis XIV, Augustine, Pascal, Socrates. In *Roma città aperta* Don Pietro had remarked, "It is easy to die well. What is difficult is to live well."

"When everyone's standing around Socrates crying," Roberto had said, "because he's dying, Socrates says, 'Well, you don't realize that from the moment we are alive we start our voyage, our trip towards death.' This truth, very rational, is outside any sort of emotion. We always look at death in an emotional way, so we lose even the value of death."[67]

"I remained a long time alone with Roberto that night," Marcella De Marchis wrote. "It was a night of silence and quiet . . . not of crying . . . but of meditation and, above all, communion with Roberto. No ugly memory, only silent images of so many happy moments of my life beside him."[68]

"He died at a moment when he was too associated with the life of Jesus," his son Renzo said. "So it seemed to me . . . that it would be more appropriate to have a non-religious funeral . . . which would somehow relate to his next work, which he had not been able to make. . . . I asked Amendola and Pajetta to help me."[69]

Amerigo Terenzi arranged for the Communist Party to organize and pay for the ceremonies. A wake was held the next day, Sunday, at four in the afternoon, in the *Camera ardente* of the Party's Casa della Cultura. At the entrance, a large wreath of red roses displayed a red ribbon with the words "La Federazione communista di Roma." But there were dozens of wreathes and single flowers too. A large card in the room, signed by Roberto's children, said, "Thank you, papa, for giving us riches." His assets at death had been 300,000 lire ($350); his tax debts alone were estimated at between one and three million dollars. In his safe-deposit box were found a handkerchief Silvia had cried on which had "miraculously" stayed damp for days afterward, some love letters from her, and a medal. His papers were taken by Silvia from his apartment. The visitors' book at the wake, the children remarked, was signed by hundreds of women.

On Monday, June 6, a funeral procession left the Casa della Cultura and proceeded along Via delle Botteghe Oscure and Via del Teatro di Marcello to Piazza della Consolazione, where a small podium had been set up. There were a television camera, dozens of photographers, and thousands of people—including virtually the entire world of Italian cinema. Giulio Carlo Argan, the Communist mayor of Rome, referred to Roberto three times as "Riccardo" and noted his "contempt for the power of a system [i.e., the Christian Democrat establishment] that had covered him with gold for an act of submission" and underlined how the development of Roberto's art and life "made implicit his next choices: he had reached that mature threshold of modern culture where Marxism figures as the ultimate evolution of secular humanism and illuminism."[70]

The Minister of Spectacle spoke next, then Giorgio Amendola, the leader of the Communist Party, who recalled the years with Roberto at the Nazareno, the free tickets to the Cinema Corso, and their encounters during the Occupation. They had followed different paths, he a militant Communist, Rossellini "a believing Catholic, without bigotry, with a religious fervor that animated all his life, including the final choice of his matured, secular conscience. . . . In his individual life and his artistic life, he always had the courage to start again from zero. . . . We need to see *Il Messia* again to feel the generous breath of a religious sense that has not submitted to mercantilism, and his *Marx* to understand the reasons for his ultimate secular choices."[71]

His brother and sister had not agreed with this interpretation of Roberto's ultimate choices. "To my friends who have faith, I ask that at my death they gather for a prayer," Roberto had said. Brother Renzo had organized a service that morning at eleven, at San Carlo di Catinari, a hundred yards from the Casa della Cultura. Fathers Ettore Segneri, Virgilio Fantuzzi, and Claudio Sorgi said a "Mass for the Repose of a Soul." Marcella De Marchis sat in the first row; brother Renzo in the second; Sonali far in the back. The church was crowded. Political leaders came in force: Amendola, Aldo Moro, Giulio Andreotti, Amintore Fanfani, Francesco Cossiga, Giovanni Galloni. The music, violin and organ, was by Renzo, according to Roberto's wishes. "Three years ago," Sorgi said, "Roberto matured and lived, with deep artistic and spiritual tension, his encounter with Jesus while making *Il Messia*. He told me then, 'I wish people could know, understand and accept the Gospel of Jesus, his law of love. Humanity would be one big family.'"[72]

Marcella De Marchis and Sonali barely acknowledged each other on the way out, *Il Tempo* reported. Sonali embraced brother Renzo, and he cried. He had spent his life worrying about Roberto and picking up after him. His death came almost as a relief. And Roberto had gone at a moment when he was "on top."[73]

Jean Gruault wrote: "He refused to be Catholic, Communist, or anything else. But the two confessions who then claimed to share Italy argued over his remains. The first to arrive, the Communists, had the body, appropriately. The Catholics (or the Christian Democrats), far behind in second place, had to be content with the soul.... The family, lacking money, was not in a position to oppose either of these mediating operations.... [His sister] Marcella, in telling me all this, did not know whether to laugh or cry. We cried, while telling ourselves that this ambivalence, fruit of necessity, would not, in fact, have displeased Roberto. It expressed rather well what he had been. And what he had refused to be."[74]

At the end of the ceremony in Piazza della Consolazione the sun came out. Amendola gave the valedictory: "And you, Roberto, who so much worked, loved, suffered, and struggled, rest now in peace, and be at ease. Because you have given many people, with your art, a great help in how to understand, to live, and to struggle for a better world."[75]

The procession drove to the Verano cemetery and the Rossellini mausoleum. After considerable difficulties, because he had not signed the necessary papers, Roberto's body was cremated, as he had wished.

His adventures were over. Or were they?

* * *

Ironically, despite his drubbing by the left, Rossellini was virtually the only major figure in the arts who stayed loyal to the Resistance commitment to create a new culture.

—William Arrowsmith

Filmography

Running times: Reported running times of Rossellini films vary enormously between pre-release, festival screenings, commercial releases, exported versions, and extant prints.

Language: Original language is Italian, unless noted. Where two **bold-faced titles** appear for the same film, two versions were shot.

Rossellini's film titles are, for the sake of clarity, always styled in this book in the language of the original (or most original) edition (or, in default of an original edition, in English, *except* when the title refers specifically to an alternate edition. *Paisan,* for example, refers to the U.S. edition, specifically, of a film otherwise referred to as *Paisà.* Citations of titles within quotations have often been altered to conform to this usage.

• = lost film.

1937 *La fossa degli angeli* ("Grave of angels")
Director: Carlo Ludovico Bragaglia. Assistant [uncredited]: Roberto Rossellini.

Script: Curt Alexander, Carlo Ludovico Bragaglia, [uncredited: Roberto Rossellini], from story by Bragaglia.

Editor: F. M. Poggioli.

With: Amedeo Nazzari, Luisa Ferida.

•1937 *Prélude à l'après-midi d'un faune* ("Prelude to the afternoon of a faun")
Director: Roberto Rossellini.

Unreleased. Perhaps unfinished.

1938 *Luciano Serra pilota* ("Luciano Serra, pilot")
Director: Goffredo Alessandrini. Assistant: Umberto Scarpelli. Supervisor: Vittorio Mussolini.

Script: Goffredo Alessandrini, Roberto Rossellini, adapted by Ivo Perilli, Fulvio Palmieri, from story by Francesco Masoero, Goffredo Alessandrini. Dialogue: Cesare Giulio Viola.

Photography: Ubaldo Arata. Camera: Mario Craveri. 2nd unit: Renato Del Frate, Piero Pupilli. Assistant: Aldo Tonti.

Sets: Gastone Medin.

Sound: Bruno Brunacci.

Music: G. C. Sonzogno, conducted by Edoardo De Risi.

Editor: Giorgio C. Simonelli.

Producer: Aquila Film SA, Milan (Angelo Monti). Released by Generalcine. Executive producer: Franco Riganti. Managing producer: Luigi Giacosi.

Filmed at Cinecittà and in Ethiopia, June 1937–March 1938.

With: Amedeo Nazzari (Luciano Serra), Germana Paolieri (Sandra Serra, the wife), Roberto Villa (Aldo Serra), Mario Ferrari (Col. Franco Morelli), Guglielmo Sinaz (Jose Ribera), Egisto Olivieri (Nardini), Gino Mori (Aldo Serra, child).

Running time: 105'. Scenes of Mussolini were added but have subsequently been deleted.

Venice Film Festival, 1938: Coppa Mussolini (ex-aequo with Leni Refenstahl's *Olympia*).

1938 *Fantasia sottomarina* ("Undersea fantasy")
Director and Story: Roberto Rossellini. Assistant: Marcella De Marchis.

Photography: Rodolfo Lombardi.

Music: Edoardo Micucci.

Producer: Incom (Industrie Cortimetraggi Società Anonima Italiana). Released by Istituto LUCE. Production manager: Domenico Paolella.

Filmed at Rossellini's cottage in Ladispoli, summer 1938. Edited at Cinecittà.

Narrator: Guido Notari.

Released: Apr. 12, 1940 (Rome). It played at Rome's Supercinema Apr. 12–18, then at the Planetario Apr. 20–23, then at the Donizetti in Milan, June 15. It was issued in the U.S. in an Incom package that included *Criniere al vento* (Giorgio Ferroni) and *Castel S. Angelo* (Domenico Paolella). 10'27".

•1940 *Il ruscello di Ripasottile* ("The brook of Ripa Sottile")
Director: Roberto Rossellini.

Story and Text: Elisabetta Riganti.

Photography: Rodolfo Lombardi.

Music: Ugo Filippini.

Producer: Excelsior Safa (Elisabetta Riganti)–ACI (Franco Riganti). Released by Scalera.

Filmed summer 1940 near Ladispoli and at the Istituto Ittogeno, Rome.

Working titles: *Anche i pesci parlano* ("Fish speak too"); *Il pesce a congresso* ("The fish congress").

Released: May 4(?), 1941 (Rome). c. 10'.

1940 *La vispa Teresa* ("Lively Theresa")
Director: Roberto Rossellini.

Photography: Mario Bava.

Music: Simone Cuccia.

With: small girl (c. 10 years); seven types of insects.

Producer: Scalera.

Announced October 1940. Probably not released. c. 7'15" (200m).

1940 *Il tacchino prepotente* ("The bullying turkey"); working title (possibly original release title): *La perfida Albione* ("Perfidious Albion")
Director: Roberto Rossellini.

Photography: Mario Bava.

Music: Maria Strino.

With: turkey, hens, various farmyard animals.

Producer: Scalera (not credited on existing print). Distributor (c. 1947?): Fincine.

Announced October 1940. No information concerning release or distribution. Possibly limited release after the war, possibly in altered version. c. 7'15" (200m).

- *La foresta silenziosa* ("The quiet forest")
- *Primavera* ("Spring")
- *Re Travicello*
- *La merca*
- *Il brutto idraulico* ("The ugly plumber")

Various titles of shorts announced but perhaps never produced.

1941 *La nave bianca* ("The white ship")
Director: Roberto Rossellini. Supervision [and storyboard]: Francesco De Robertis.
Script: Francesco De Robertis, Roberto Rossellini, from story by De Robertis.
Photography: Giuseppe Caracciolo. Camera: Carlo Bellero, Mario Bava. Assistant: Carlo Carlini.
Sets: Amleto Bonetti.
Sound: Piero Cavazzuti.
Music: Renzo Rossellini. Editor: Eraldo Da Roma.
Producers: Scalera–Centro Cinematografico del Ministero della Marina. Released by Scalera.
Filmed February–July 1941 on warship *Littorio*, hospital ship *Arno*, and at locations at Taranto; command bridge reconstructed at Scalera Studios, Rome. Postproduction: August (and October) 1941.
With: Non-professionals (Basso, Elena), officers and men of Royal Navy, and nurses of the Corpo Volontario.
Footage of battle of Punta Stilo (July 9, 1940, when Italian Air Force mistakenly bombed Italian ships) shot by Angelo Jannarelli, Lamberto Urbani, Giovanni Esposito; used for LUCE newsreel. Footage from encounter of Capo Teulada; a shot in which grenade smashes battleship *Giulio Cesare* had already been cited for its drama in newspapers.
Shown: Sept. 14, 1941 (Venice Festival). Released: Oct. 4 (Rome); Oct. 15 (Milan). 84' (release permit). Existent print: 70'52".
Coppa del Partito Nazionale Fascista, 1941 (Venice).

1942 *I tre aquilotti* ("The three eagles")
Director: Mario Mattoli.
Script [uncredited work]: Roberto Rossellini.

1942 *Un pilota ritorna* ("A pilot returns")
Director: Roberto Rossellini. Assistant: Paolo Moffa. Supervision: Tito Silvio Mursino (aka Vittorio Mussolini).
Script: Rosario Leone [Michelangelo Antonioni, Gianni Puccini, Massimo Mida, Rossellini]; Dialogues: Antonioni, Mida, Margherita Maglione, Rossellini [Gherardo Gherardi, Ugo Betti, Luigi Chiarelli, Franco Riganti], from story by Tito Silvio Mursino.
Photography: Vincenzo Seratrice. Camera: Alberto Attili [Domenico Scala, Crescenzio Gentili].
Sets: Virgilio Marchi, Franco Bartoli.
Sound: Franco Robecchi.
Music: Renzo Rossellini, conducted by Pietro Sassoli. Musical edition: Cine Armonica.
Editor: Eraldo Da Roma.
Producer: ACI (Anonima Cinematografica Italiana). Released by ACI Europa Film. Executive producer: Franco Riganti. Production manager: Luigi Giacosi. Inspector of production: Alberto Tronchet. Flying consultant: Capt. Aldo Moggi. Military consultant: Maj. Filippo Masoero.

Filmed October 1941–Mar. 22, 1942 on locations in Viterbo and at Cinecittà or Tirrenia. Cost: L. 6,423,704 [officially; actually c. 2,500,000].
With: Massimo Girotti [dubbed by Giulio Panicali] (Lt. Gino Rossati), Michela Belmonte [dubbed by Rosetta Calavetta] (Anna, the doctor's daughter), Gaetano Masier [dubbed by Cesare Polacco] (Lt. Trisotti), Piero Lulli (De Santis), Nino Brondello (Lt. Vitali), Giovanni Valdambrini (doctor), Elvira Betrone (Rossati's mother), Jole Tinta (mother of sick child), Piero Palermini (young English officer), Officers and men of the 50th Gruppo RTV of the Italian Air Force.
Released: Apr. 8, 1942 (Cinema Supercinema, Rome). 85' (release permit). 80'23" (2320m), existent print at RAI.
Premio Nazionale della Cinematografia, best war or political film, 1942.

1943 *L'invasore* ("The invader")
Director: Nino Giannini. "Supervisor": Roberto Rossellini (purely nominal).
Released: 1949.

1943 *L'uomo dalla croce* ("The man of the cross")
Director: Roberto Rossellini. Assistants: Mariano Cafiero, Franco Pompili. Supervision: Asvero Gravelli.
Script: Asvero Gravelli, Alberto Consiglio, G. D'Alicandro, Rossellini, from story by Gravelli.
Photography: Guglielmo Lombardi, Aurelio Attili. Camera: Alberto Attili, Rodolfo Lombardi, Giuseppe Rotunno.
Sets: Gastone Medin.
Music: Renzo Rossellini, conducted by Pietro Sassoli.
Producers: Continentalcine–Cines. Released by ENIC. Production manager: Giuseppe Sylos. Military consultant: Lt. Col. D.U. Leonardi.
Filmed July–December 1942 on locations near Ladispoli.
With: Alberto Tavazzi (chaplain), Roswitha Schmidt (Irina), Attilio Dottesio (wounded tanker), Antonio Marietti (Sergei, political commissar), Doris Hild, Ruggero Isnenghi, Aldo Capacci, Franco Castellani, Piero Pastore (disfigured Russian tanker), Marcello Tanzi, Zoia Weneda.
Released: June 9, 1943 (Rome). 77'06".

1943 *Desiderio* ("Desire") (*Woman*)
Directors: Roberto Rossellini, Marcello Pagliero. Assistant director (with Rossellini in Rome): Giuseppe De Santis.
Script: Rosario Leone, Giuseppe De Santis, Roberto Rossellini, Diego Calcagno, (and for additional scenes) Marcello Pagliero, Guglielmo Santangelo, from story by Anna Benvenuiti.
Photography: Rodolfo Lombardi (with Rossellini), Ugo Lombardi (with Pagliero).
Music: Renzo Rossellini.
Producers: Produttori Associati–Imperator–Sovrania [with Rossellini]; Società Anonima Film Italiani Roma [with Pagliero]. Released by Fincine. Production managers: S. Lodi [with Rossellini], Renzo De Bonis [with Pagliero].
Filmed July 1943, ACI Farnesina studio, Rome; August–September 1943, on location near Tagliacozzo; completed October 1945 by Pagliero, Rome.
With: Elli Parvo (Paola Previtali), Massimo Girotti (Nando Mancini), Carlo Ninchi (Giovanni Mirelli), Roswitha Schmidt (Anna Previtali Mancini),

Francesco Grandjacquet (Riccardo), Jucci Keller-mann, Spartaco Conversi, Giovanna Scotto.

Working titles: *Scalo merci* ("Freight yard"), *Rinuncia* ("Renunciation").

Released: Aug. 9, 1946 (Rome); re-release after nude shots taken out, Oct. 1, (Milan); Feb. 8, 1950 (Rialto, New York, *Woman*). Feb. 28, 1951 (Paris, *La Proie du désir*). Existent print: 78'50" (2179m).

1945 *Roma città aperta* (*Open City*)

Director: Roberto Rossellini. [Assistants: Amidei, Fel-lini, Mario Chiari, Alberto Manni, Bruno Todini.]

Script: Sergio Amidei, in collaboration with Federico Fellini, from story by Amidei (and Alberto Con-siglio).

Photography: Ubaldo Arata. Camera: Vincenzo Sera-trice, [Gianni Di Venanzo, Carlo Carlini, Carlo Di Palma, Giuseppe Berta].

Sets: Rosario Megna. [Furnishings: Mario Chiari. Make-up: Alberto De Rossi. Torture scenes make-up: Nino Franchina.]

Sound: Raffaele Del Monte.

Music: Renzo Rossellini, conducted by Luigi Ricci.

Editor: Eraldo Da Roma. [Assistant: Jolanda Ben-venuti.] Scriptgirl: Jone Tuzzi.

Producer: Excelsa Film, [Chiara Politi, CIS-Nettunia; Peppino Amato; Aldo Venturini]. Released by Min-erva [in Europe]; Arthur Mayer and Joseph Burstyn in association with Rodney Geiger [in U.S.]. Pro-duction managers: [Carlo Civallero, Angelo Be-sozzi, Ermanno Donati, Luigi Carpentieri, then] Ferruccio De Martino. Assistant producers: Alberto Manni, Bruno Todini, Antonio Palumbo.

Filmed January–May 1945, at Capitani Film di Li-borio Capitani, Via Avignonesi 30, and on Rome locations (Piazza di Spagna [including interior and terrace of Amidei's apartment at no. 51], Via Rai-mondo Montecuccoli 17, 36, 15; Piazzale Prenes-tino, Chiesa di Sant'Elena on Via Casilina; interior of a church in Trastevere; an oratorio on Via Avel-lino; Circonvallazione Casilina; antique store exte-rior on Via Margutta; Ponte Tiburtino; EUR; Forte Bravetta (execution scene); Via Trionfale on Monte Mario). Lab: Tecnostampa di Vincenzo Genese (Via Albalonga 38). Sound lab: Fono Roma (Via Maria Adelaide 7).

With: Marcello Pagliero [dubbed by Lauro Gazzolo] (Giorgio Manfredi, aka Luigi Ferraris), Aldo Fabrizi (Don Pietro Pellegrini), Anna Magnani (Sora Pina), Harry Feist [dubbed by Giulio Panicali] (Major Bergmann), Francesco Grandjacquet [dubbed by Gualtiero De Angelis] (Francesco), Maria Michi (Marina Mari), Giovanna Galetti [dubbed by Roswitha Schmidt] (Ingrid), Vito Annicchiarico ["Annichiarico" on film's credits] (Marcello, Pina's son), Carla Rovere (Lauretta, Pina's sister), Nando Bruno (Agostino, aka Purgatorio, sacristan), Eduardo Passarelli ["Passanelli" on film's credits] (policeman), Carlo Sindici (police commissioner), Akos Tolnay (Austrian deserter), Joop Van Hulzen (Maj. Hartmann), Amalia Pellegrini (Manfredi's landlady), Alberto Tavazzi (priest at execution), Fer-ruccio De Martino (soldier at execution), Alberto Manni (blackmarketer).

Shown: Aug. 28, 1945, by U.S. Information Agency at Italian ministry for press and spectacle, Via Veneto 108, Rome; Sept. 24 (Primo Festival Internazionale della musica, del teatro e del cinematografo, Cin-ema Quirino, Rome), titled *Città aperta*; Sept. 27–28, Cinema Quirinetta, titled *Roma città aperta*. Re-

leased (titled *Roma città aperta*): Oct. 8 (Rome: Cinema Capranica, 28 days, and Cinema Imperiale, 22 days); Oct. 24 (Milan: Odeon, 15 days); Nov. 9 (Naples: Filangeri); Nov. 17 (Turin, 14 days). Feb. 25, 1946 (New York: World Theatre, *Open City*, 21 months; subtitled by Pietro Di Donato and Herman G. Weinberg); August 1946 (Locarno Festival). Oct. 5 (Cannes Festival); Nov. 13 (Paris: Maison de la Chimie, privately, *Rome ville ouverte*); Dec. 1 (Paris; Eldorado, Impérial, Cinécran [subtitled], Rialto [dubbed]); July 4, 1947 (London: Academy Cin-ema). Feb. 21, 1961 (Germany, *Rom offene Stadt*); Oct. 18, 1969 (Madrid, *Roma ciodad abierta*). Prints run between 97' and 108'. [Censure copy, Sept. 4, 1945: 9304 feet (103'); Cineteca Nazionale copy: 9541 feet (106'); Berlin copy: 9731 feet (108'). 1991 BBC tele-cast: 100'.]

Nastro d'Argento, 1946, best director (ex aequo with Alessandro Blasetti [*Un giorno nella vita*] and Vitto-rio De Sica [*Sciuscià*], best script, best actress. Grand Prix, Cannes, 1946 (with six other films). Academy Award nomination: best screenplay. New York Film Critics: best foreign film, 1946. National Board of Review: best actress, 1946. Italian grosses through Dec. 31, 1961: L. 124,500,000.

1946 *Paisà* (*Paisan*)

Director: Roberto Rossellini. Assistants: Federico Fel-lini, Massimo Mida, [Renzo Avanzo, Vercours, Basilio Franchina], E. Handamir, Annalena Limen-tani (translator).

Script: Sergio Amidei, with the collaboration of Klaus Mann, Federico Fellini, Alfred Hayes, Marcello Pagliero, Rossellini, Rod Geiger [and for "Florence," Vasco Pratolini; for "Romagna," Padre Vincenzo].

Photography: Otello Martelli. Camera: [Carlo Carlini, Gianni Di Venanzo, Carlo Di Palma].

Music: Renzo Rossellini. [Costumes, "Rome": Mar-cella De Marchis.]

Sound: Ovidio Del Grande.

Editor: Eraldo Da Roma.

Producers: Roberto Rossellini, Rod Geiger, for Orga-nizzazioni Film Internazionali [Mario Conti, Renato Campos, Rossellini]–Foreign Film Productions [Rod Geiger, Robert Lawrence]. Released by Metro-Goldwyn-Mayer (in Europe); Mayer-Burstyn (in U.S.). Production manager: Ugo Lombardi. Assis-tant producers: Alberto Manni, Augusto Dolfi, [Mario Micheli, Aldo Bonifazi].

Filmed January–June 1946, in: Maiori ("Sicily"); Maiori: Convento di San Francesco ("Romagna"); Naples ("Naples"); Villa Roncioni on Via Lungo-monte Lucchese, and Florence ("Florence"); Scar-dovari-Porto Tolle ("The Po Delta"); Moka Abdul, Cinema Florida on Via Francesco Crispi, Capitani film studio, Rome ("Rome"); Livorno (for tank scene in "Rome"); Via Lutezia 11, Rome (stairs in "Florence"). Lab: Tecnostampa di Vincenzo Genese.

With: "Sicily": Carmela Sazio (Carmela), Robert Van Loon (Joe), Benjamin Emanuel, Raymond Camp-bell, Mata "Sweede" Rune, Merlin Berth, Mats Carlson, Leonard Penish (U.S. soldiers [from 7th Transit Camp]), Albert Heinze, Harold Wagner (German soldiers).

"Naples": Alfonsino Bovino (Pasquale), Dotts M. John-son (Joe), Pippo Bonazzi.

"Rome": Maria Michi (Francesca), Gar Moore (Fred), Lorena Berg (Amalia, landlady).

"Florence": Harriet White (Harriet), Renzo Avanzo (Massimo), Gigi Gori (Gigi, a partisan), Renato Campos (man on rooftop), Giuletta Masina (his daughter), Gianfranco Corsini (Marco, a partisan), Ursula Werber, Rose Nadell.

"Romagna": Bill Tubbs (Fr. Bill Martin), Captain Owen Jones (Protestant chaplain), Sergeant Elmer Feldman, assistant to the rabbi of the 7th Transit Camp (Jewish chaplain), Franciscan monks from the convent of Baronissi, near Nocera, 15 miles north of Maiori: Frs. Vincenzo, Salvatore, Angelico, Claudio, Pacifico, Raffaele, Felice; Br. Vincenzo (guardian [dubbed by Carlo Ninchi]).

"The Po Delta": Dale Edmonds (Dale), Achille Siviero (Cigolani), Alan Dane, Van Loel (German officer), Hannes Messemer (German officer).

Giulio Panicali (commentator).

Working title: *Seven from the U.S.*

Shown: Sept. 18, 1946 (Venice Festival: Teatro Malibran and Cinema San Marco; c. 134′); Nov. 13 (Paris: Maison de la Chimie). Released: Dec. 10, (Turin); Dec. 13 (Milan: Cinema Diana, 7 days); Mar. 7, 1947 (Paris); Mar. 8 (Rome: Cinemas Capranica, Capranichetta, Imperialie, 7 days); June 1947 (Brussels Festival); August 1947 (Locarno Festival); September 1947 (Edinburgh Festival); Sept. 26 (Paris: Cinémas Biarritz, Français, Lynx); 1947 (Marianske Lazne/Karlova Vary festival): 126′31″ (3461m); Mar. 29, 1948 (New York: World Theatre, *Paisan*, with slight alterations by Stuart Legg and Raymond Spottiswoode, subtitled by Herman G. Weinberg; previewed Feb. 4); Feb. 21, 1949 (Los Angeles: El Rey Theatre); Oct. 13, 1948 (London: Academy Cinema): 116′; Oct. 9, 1949 (Berlin: Marmorhaus: without "Po" episode; previewed Aug. 12, 1947).

ANICA Cup, Venice (ex aequo with eight others). Nastro d'Argento, 1947, best direction, script, original music. Academy Award nomination: best screenplay. New York Film Critics: best film, 1948. National Board of Review: best film, 1948. Belgium Government Prize, excellent quality, Brussels Festival.

1947 *Deutschland im Jahre Null* (*Germania anno zero; Germany in Year Zero; Germany Year Zero*)

Director, Producer: Roberto Rossellini. Assistants: Carlo Lizzani, Max Colpet, (Franz Treuberg).

Script: Rossellini (and Carlo Lizzani) with the collaboration of Max Colpet, from story by Rossellini (on idea by Basilio Franchina). Supervision and dialogues for Italian version (*Germania anno zero*): Sergio Amidei.

Photography: Robert Juillard. Camera: Jacques Robin, Emile Puet.

Sets: Piero Filippone.

Sound: Kurt Doubrawsky.

Music: Renzo Rossellini, conducted by: Edoardo Micucci.

Editor: Anne-Marie Findeisen. [Italian version: Eraldo Da Roma]

Producer: Tevere Film [Rossellini and Alfredo Guarini], in collaboration with Salvo d'Angelo Produzione–SAFDI [Berlin])–Union Générale Cinématographique [Paris], with technical collaboration of DEFA [Berlin]. Released in Italy by Fincine; in U.S. by Ilya Lopert. Associate producer: André Halley Des Fontaines. Assistant producers: Marcello Bollero, Alberto Manni. Script girl: Renata Gaede. Production secretary: Giancarlo Campidori.

Filmed Aug. 7–September 1947, Berlin (Lützowstrasse, Nollendorfplatz, Tiergarten, U-Bhf. Nürnberger Platz, Innsbrucker Platz, Schlossplatz, Bendlerstrasse, Dancing Femina); November–January 1948, Stabilimenti Titanus alla Farnesina, Rome. Lab: Tecnostampa di Vincenzo Genesi.

With: Edmund Meschke (Edmund Koehler), Ernst Pittschau (his father), Ingetraud Hintze (his sister Eva), Franz Krüger (his brother Karl-Heinz), Erich Gühne (Henning, the teacher), Jo Herbst (Jo, the boy thief), Christl Merker (Christl, the girl thief), Alexandra Manys (Eva's friend), Babsy Schultz-Reckwell (Rademacher's daughter), Hans Sangen (Rademacher), Hedi Blankner (Frau Rademacher), Karl Krüger (doctor), Barbara Hintz (Thilde, pregnant woman), Gaby Raak (woman in general's house), Inge Rocklitz (refugee).

Dedicated to the memory of Romano Rossellini.

Running time: 72′. A version approved by the censure, Apr. 15, 1948, had a running time of 79′ (2153m). *Variety* reported 73′ for the Rome anteprima in May.

Shown: Apr. 11, 1948 (Rome: Circolo romano del Cinema); May 30 (Rome: Cinema Barberini, *Germania*); July 9 (Locarno Festival, *Deutschland*); August (Edinburh Festival). Released: Dec. 1 (Milan: Cinema Astra, 7 days); Dec. 18 (Rome: Capranica, Europa, Imperiale, 5 days); Feb. 2, 1949 (Paris, *Allemagne année zéro*); Apr. 15 (London: Curzon, *Germany in Year Zero*); Sept. 19 (New York: Ambassador); Dec. 16 (Los Angeles: Marcal); Apr. 9, 1952 (Munich: Studio für Filmkunst). 72′.

First prize (ex aequo with *La vie en rose* [Jean Faurez]) and best script, Locarno Festival, 1948.

1947–48 *L'amore: Due storie d'amore* ("Love: Two love stories")

Director, Producer: Roberto Rossellini.

"Una voce umana" ("A human voice")

Script: Rossellini, after one-act play by Jean Cocteau, *La voix humaine* (1930).

Assistant director: Basilio Franchina.

Photography: Robert Juillard.

Sets: Christian Bérard.

Sound: Kurt Doubrawsky (direct).

Music: Renzo Rossellini.

Editor: Eraldo Da Roma.

Filmed in Paris, rue Forest 15; May 1947. 35′.

With: Anna Magnani (the woman), Micia (her dog).

"Il miracolo" ("The Miracle")

Script: Federico Fellini, Tullio Pinelli, Roberto Rossellini, from story by Federico Fellini.

Assistant director: Federico Fellini.

Photography: Aldo Tonti.

Sound: Kurt Doubrawsky.

Music: Renzo Rossellini.

Editor: Eraldo Da Roma.

Producer: Tevere Film [Rossellini]. Released by CEIAD.

Filmed in Maiori, April 1948. 43′.

With: Anna Magnani (Nannina), Federico Fellini ("Saint Joseph," the shepherd), Peparuolo (monk). Magnani dubbed herself in the French version.

Shown: Aug. 21, 1948 (Venice Festival). Released: Nov. 2 (Rome). 78′. The Miracle opened Dec. 12, 1950, at New York's Paris Theater as part of an omnibus film, *Ways of Love*, which included Renoir's *A Day in the Country* and Pagnol's *Jofroi*.

Nastro d'Argento, 1949: best actress (Magnani).

1948 *La macchina ammazzacattivi* ("The machine that kills bad people")

Director: Roberto Rossellini (and for some shots: Luciano Emmer). Assistants: Massimo Mida, Renzo Avanzo.

Script: Sergio Amidei, Giancarlo Vigorelli, Franco Brusati, Liana Ferri, (Roberto Rossellini), from story by Eduardo De Filippo, Fabrizio Sarazani.

Photography: Tino Santoni. Camera: Enrico Betti. Special effects: Eugenio Bava.

Sound: Mario Amari.

Music: Renzo Rossellini, conducted by him.

Editor: Jolanda Benvenuti.

Producer: Roberto Rossellini for Tevere Film (Rossellini) [and Luigi Rovere for Universalia]; Rudolph Solmsen. Released by PDC. Assistant producer: Alberto Manni.

Filmed June–August 1948 in Maiori and Amalfi.

With: Gennaro Pisano (Celestino Esposito), Giovanni Amato (devil-saint); Marilyn Buferd (young American); Bill Tubbs and Helen Tubbs (her parents, American tourists), Joe Falletta (Joe), Giacomo Furia (Romeo Cuccurullo), Clara Bindi (Giuletta Del Bello), Camillo Buonanni, Piero Carloni (mayor), Aldo Nanni, Gajo Visconti, and inhabitants of Maiori, Atrani, and Amalfi.

Released: May 20, 1952 (Milan). 83'.

1949 *Stromboli* [English] (*Stromboli terra di Dio* ["Stromboli Land of God"])

Director: Roberto Rossellini. Assistant: Marcello Caracciolo Di Laurino.

Story: Roberto Rossellini (Sergio Amidei).

Script: Sergio Amidei, Gian Paolo Callegari, Renzo Cesana, Art Cohn, (Felix Morlion, O.P.).

Photography: Otello Martelli. Camera: Luciano Trasatti, Roberto Gerardi, Ajace Parolin.

Sound: Terry Kellum, Eraldo Giordani.

Music: Renzo Rossellini, conducted by C. Bakaleinikoff.

Editor: Jolanda Benvenuti, Roland Gross (in U.S.). [Alfred Werker, 81' RKO edition.]

Producers: Berit Film [Bergman-Rossellini]-RKO. Released by RKO. Production managers: Enrico Donati (Berit), Ed Killy, Harold Lewis (RKO).

Filmed Apr. 4–Aug. 2, 1949 on Stromboli and at Farfa.

With: Ingrid Bergman (Karin Bjorsen), Mario Vitale (Antonio Mastrostefano), Renzo Cesana (priest), Mario Sponza (lighthouse keeper), Roberto Onorati (child), and the inhabitants of Stromboli. Bergman dubbed herself in the Italian version.

Released: Feb. 15, 1950 (U.S., RKO edition); 81'. Shown: Aug. 26, 1950 (Venice Festival, Rossellini's edition, in Italian). Released: Mar. 18, 1951 (Italy, Rossellini's edition, in Italian); 105'; Oct. 20, 1950 (Paris, Rossellini's rough-cut, in English, subtitled); Kino International (U.S.); 105'.

1950 *Francesco giullare di Dio* ("Francis, God's Jester") (*Flowers of St. Francis* [U.S.]; *The Adventures of St. Francis of Assisi* [U.K.])

Director: Roberto Rossellini. Assistants: Marcello [Caracciolo di] Laurino, Brunello Gay [Rondi].

Script: Rossellini in collaboration with Federico Fellini, Felix Morlion, O.P., Antonio Lisandrini, O.F.M., [Brunello Rondi, Alberto Maisano, O.F.M.], from story by Rossellini after *I fioretti di San Francesco* and *La vita di Frate Ginepro.*

Photography: Otello Martelli. Camera: Luciano Trasatti. Assistant: Roberto Gerardi. Assistant: Enrico Betti, Carlo Carlini.

Sets: Virgilio Marchi. Furnishings: Giuseppe Rissone. Costumes: Marina Arcangeli, Ditta Peruzzi.

Music: Renzo Rossellini and (liturgical chants) Fr. Enrico Buondonno. Sound: Eraldo Giordani, Raffaele Del Monte.

Editor: Jolanda Benvenuti.

Producer: Angelo Rizzoli for Cineriz [Rizzoli]. Released by Minerva Film. [U.S.: Joseph Burstyn.] Associate producer: Giuseppe Amato. Production manager: Luigi Giacosi. Assistants: Mario Gabrelli, Mimmo Salvi, Gianfranco Parolini. Stills: Osvaldo Civirani.

Filmed Jan. 17–February, May 1950, near Oriolo Romano. Recording at Fono Roma. Lab: Technostampa.

With: Aldo Fabrizi (Nicolaio, tyrant of Viterbo), Arabella Lemaître (Clare), and non-professional actors: thirteen Franciscan monks from the convent of "Nocere Inferiore" [in the U.S. titles, actually Baronissi, near Nocera, 15 miles north of Maiori]: Brother Nazario Geraldi (Francesco), Fr. Roberto Sorrentino, Brother Nazareno; Peparuolo (Giovanni the Simple). [U.S. edition: English narrator: Lee Kresel. Subtitles: Herman G. Weinberg.]

Shown: Aug. 26, 1950 (Venice Festival): 93'. Released: Dec. 15 (Milan): 85'; Mar. 6, 1951 (Paris, *Onze Fioretti de Saint François d'Assise*). Oct. 6, 1952 (New York: 55th Street Playhouse, *Flowers of St. Francis*): 79'. The edition presented at Venice included a prologue featuring Giotto's frescoes on the life of Francesco; this prologue was omitted from release prints and from the identical British edition (*The Adventures of St. Francis of Assisi*). The U.S. edition, *Flowers of St. Francis*, omits an episode on Perfect Happiness and the intertitles between the episodes, and has English narration and 30" of exit music, and begins with the Giotto prologue, which here runs only 2'34". This leaves unaccounted for six additional minutes of footage reputedly in the Venice edition.

1951 "L'invidia" ("Envy"), episode in *I sette peccati capitali* (*Seven Deadly Sins*)

Director: Roberto Rossellini. Assistant: Antonio Pietrangeli.

Script: Roberto Rossellini, Diego Fabbri, Liana Ferri, Turi Vasile, [Antonio Pietrangeli] from short story by Colette, "La Chatte" (1933).

Photography: Enzo Serafin.

Sets: Hugo Blaetter.

Music: Yves Baudrier.

Editor: Louisette Hautecoeur.

Producers: Film Costellazione (Rome)–Franco London Film (Paris). Released by 20th Century Fox. Production manager: Paolo Moffa.

Filmed: in eleven days in October 1951 in the studio of the architect Antonio Valente, 60 Via Margutta (Rome) and in an apartment on Piazza di Spagna.

With: Orfeo Tamburi (Orfeo), Andrée Debar (Camilla), Nicola Ciarletta, Nino Franchina, Tanino Chiurazzi, Raoul Maria De Angelis, some intellectuals of the time (the guests in the first scene), and Sara (cat).

Released: May 3, 1952 (Milan); Apr. 30, 1952 (Paris, *Les Sept Péchés capitaux*); May 13, 1953 (New York). 21' (whole film: 140').

Other episodes directed by Yves Allégret, Claude Autant-Lara, Carlo Rim, Jean Dréville, Eduardo De Filippo, Georges Lacombe.

1951 *Santa Brigida*
Director: Roberto Rossellini.
Photography: Aldo Tonti.
With: Ingrid Bergman.
Approximately 10′ of 35mm footage survives at the Svenska Filminstitutet from a documentary (probably not completed or even edited) shot in the convent of the Swedish sisters of Saint Brigid, Rome, at the request of the Swedish Red Cross, for victims of the Polesine flood of November 1951.

1952 *Europe '51* (*The Greatest Love*) [English] (*Europa '51*)
Director, Producer: Roberto Rossellini. Assistants: Antonio Pietrangeli, William Demby, Marcello Caracciolo Di Laurino, Marcello Girosi.
Script: Sandro De Feo, Mario Pannunzio, Ivo Perilli, Brunello Rondi [Jean-Paul Le Chanois, Diego Fabbri, Antonio Pietrangeli], from story by Rossellini, Massimo Mida, Antonello Trombadori. [Federico Fellini, Tullio Pinelli]. English dialogue: Daniel Ogden Stewart. Photography: Aldo Tonti. Camera: Luciano Tonti.
Sets: Virgilio Marchi. Furnishings: Ferdinando Ruffo. Ingrid Bergman's costumes: Fernanda Gattinoni.
Sound: Piero Cavazzuti, Paolo Uccello.
Music: Renzo Rossellini, conducted by him.
Editor: Jolanda Benvenuti.
Producers: Carlo Ponti-Dino De Laurentiis. Released by Lux. (U.S. distribution by I.F.E. [Italian Films Export] Releasing Corp.) Production manager: Bruno Todini. Assistants: Nando Pisani, Federico Teti, Pio Angeletti, Trento Petrella. Script secretray: Sandro Corbo.
Filmed November 1951–January 1952, Ponti-De Laurentiis Studio and exteriors in Rome.
With: Ingrid Bergman (Irene Gerard; dubbed in Italian version by Rita Savagnone), Alexander Knox (George Gerard), Ettore Giannini (Andrea [André, in English] Casati, Communist intellectual), Giulietta Masina (Giulietta, "Passerotto"), Sandro Franchina (Michael "Michel" Girard, the boy), Teresa Pellati (Ines, the prostitute), Maria Zanoli (Signora Galli), Marcella Rovena (Signora Pugliesi [Strada, in English]), Giancarlo Vigorelli (judge), Bill Tubbs (Prof. Alessandrini), Alfred Browne (priest), Eleonora Baracco, Alfonso Di Stefano, Carlo Hintermann, Tina Perna (Cesira, the maid), Silvana Veronese, Alessio Ruggeri, Alberto Plebani (Signor Pugliesi [Strada, in English]), Gianna Segale (Irene's nurse), Mary Jokam, Bernardo Tafuri, Francesca Uberti, Mariemma Bardi, Alessio Ruggeri, Gerda Forrer, Charles Moses, Giuseppe Chinnici, Vera Wocht, Gianna Damiani, Rossana Rory (a guest when Irene comes back from the factory), Gipsy Kim, Marinella Marinelli, Graziella Polacco, Barbara Berg, Rodolfo Lodi, Eric Blyte, Jane Sprague, Elisabetta Cini, Dany Guy, Attilio Dottesio, Antonio Pietrangeli (psychiatrist).
Edition A) Shown: Sept. 12, 1952 (Venice Festival: Italian dubbing, *Europa '51*): 116′ (Nitrate at ASAC: 3183m, reduced from 3220m for censor seal). In a scene deleted from subsequent editions, Irene, after her vertiginous nightmare at the factory, crosses Piazza Barberini, enters the cinema [built by Rossellini's father; a Totò film is playing], and is overpowered by a documentary on how dam construction furnishes power for factories that furnish work—represented by a vertigo of water (reminiscent of the staircase vertigo where her son died).
Edition B) Released: Dec. 4, 1952 (Catania); Jan. 9, 1953 (Rome: Italian dubbing): 113′20″ (Positive prints at Cineteca Nazionale: 3134m). Cinema scene omitted. Priest scene shortened—Irene is less aggressively messianic, the priest insists on rules rather than cautioning moderation. Conference of judge, doctor, and lawyer is two minutes shorter and less uncertain.
Edition C) English language editions. All known editions: Omit opening scene of old couple on street (she complains of transit strike, he rebukes her lack of social conscience). Add extra lines to dinner scene (Irene mentions Marshall Plan); coffee scene (her mother talks of her youth); office scene (in Italian edition Andrea recalls period of postwar solidarity as best in his life; in English he tells Irene she was selfish and frivolous then but now is concerned with "the class struggle"); Giulietta scene (she asks if Irene comes from Organization of Displaced Persons). Replace Irene's Italian repetition that work is punishment humiliating everyone by her telling André, "Thou shalt love thy neighbor as thyself." Omit scenes when Irene goes out at night searching for medicine for the dying prostitute, is guided to a pharmacy, meets the doctor in the piazza. Reduces insert of George and Irene's mother during Ines's death from four to three shots. Omit a searing CU of the dead prostitute's face panning down to her neck. Omit a newspaper headline: "Mystery woman helps the escape of one of the Trastevere bank robbers. The accomplice is a foreigner—and the robber's lover?" Change the Pugliesi boy's name to Strada and delete reference to his father's Fascist past. Change judge asking if Irene is a Communist to whether she belongs to a political party. Truncate end of priest scene (Irene no longer challenges why he is afraid, and he seems less confused).
Edition C) Shown: Oct. 11, 1952 (New York: Salute to Italian Film Week, Little Carnegie Theatre, English dubbing, *Europe '51*). Rejected for poor dubbing. No other details available.
Edition D) Released: Jan. 13, 1954 (67 metropolitan theaters, New York, [new] English dubbing, *The Greatest Love*); 109′30″. Two prints are known in the U.S.
Edition D-1) Martin Scorsese's print: Michel's line to Irene, after she swats him, "You're all naked. Shame on you!" is garbled. An insert of George in scene with Irene and mother is omitted. Gigetto's song is in English. Omits a pan with Irene from Ines's window to her bed. R-edits conference of commissioner, lawyer and Gerard with CUs rather than medium two-shots.
Edition D-2) Tag Gallagher's 16mm: like D-1 except: Omits three inserts of George and Irene's mother during Ines's death. Cuts 35″ from Irene's long take with the priest (Her: "That's exactly what causes all the evil in this world, this necessity we feel to change people. . . . We should improve their nature. Who are we to dare to change them? God made them as they are. How sad it is suddenly to discover that we've been dictators in our lives to ourselves and others." Him: "Isn't it selfish of you to give way to these impulses of yours, to allow yourself to be swept perhaps to perdition?").

Edition E) Prints deposited at Cineteca Nazionale, Rome, *Europe '51*: 109'30" (2992m). Like D-1 except: retains insert of George; retains pan with Irene.

Edition F) Shown: Apr. 15, 1953 (Cannes Festival: English dubbing, French subtitles, *Europe '51*); May 5 (Paris: English dubbing; also French dubbing), Cinémathèque Française print: (2896m). Like D-1 except: has clear redub of Michel's "naked"; omits first shot on bus going to Primavalle; Gigetto sings in Italian; reduces inserts of George and mother during Ines's death to one shot; keeps conference of commisioner, lawyer, and Gerard in medium shots (as in B) rather than in CUs; two small cuts in priest scene.

Edition G) U.S. telecasts on Bravo from Janus Films, (*Europe '51*). 109'. Like D-1 except: has clear redub of Michel's "naked"; Gigetto sings in Italian; keeps conference in medium shots.

International Prize, Venice Festival, 1952 (ex-aequo with John Ford's *The Quiet Man* and Kenji Mizoguchi's *Life of O'Haru*). Nastro d'Argento, 1953: best actress (Bergman).

1952 *Rivalità (Medico Condotto)* ("Rivalry [Community doctor]")

Director: Giuliano Biagetti. Assistant: Vittorio Taviani. "Supervision": Roberto Rossellini (purely nominal).

Script, Story: Roberto Rossellini, Antonio Pietrangeli.

Photography: Giuseppe Caracciolo.

Music: Renzo Rossellini.

Producer: Liburnia Film.

With: Marco Vicario, Franca Marzi, Pietro Tordi, Carlo Marazzini, Giovanna Ralli.

1952 *Dov'è la libertà . . . ?* ("Where is liberty?")

Director: Roberto Rossellini. Assistants: Marcello Caracciolo, Luigi Giacosi. Trail scenes directed by Mario Monicelli.

Script: Vitaliano Brancati, Ennio Flaiano, Antonio Pietrangeli, Vincenzo Talarico, from story by Rossellini.

Photography: Aldo Tonti, Tonino Delli Colli. Camera: Luciano Tonti.

Sets: Flavio Mogherini. Furnishings: Armando Suscipi. Costumes: Antonelli et Ferroni.

Sound: Paolo Uccello.

Music: Renzo Rossellini. Conducted by Giuseppe Morelli. Song: Totò, sung by Giacomo Rondinella.

Editor: Jolanda Benvenuti.

Producers: Ponti–DeLaurentiis–Golden Films [Giovanni Amati]. Released by Lux. Production manager: Nando Pisani. Assistants: Mimmo Salvi, Trento Petrella. Script editor: Sandro Corbo.

Filmed at Ponti–DeLaurentiis studio and Amalfi coast (the prison), March–May 1952. Trial scenes shot summer 1953, by Mario Monicelli.

With: Totò (Salvatore Lojacono), Nita Dover (marathon girl), Vera Molnar (Agnesina), Leopoldo Trieste (Abramo Piperno), Giacomo Rondinella (prisoner who sings), Franca Faldini (Maria), Vincenzo Talarico (defense attorney), Ugo D'Alessio (judge), Mario Castellani (public minister), Fernando Milani (Otello Torquati), Augusta Mancini (Signora Teresa), Maria Bon Roseto, Giacomo Gabrielli (Torquato Torquati), Andrea Compagnoni (Nandino, the brother-in-law), Thea Zubin (Thea, the maid), Ines Fiorentini (Signora Amalia Torquati), Ines Targas, Fred and Aronne (dance champions), Eugenio Orlandi (Romolo Torquati), Fortunato, Pasquale et Nino Misiano (three retired men), Andrea De Pino, Eugenia Orlante.

Released: Mar. 26, 1954 (Rome); Mar. 29, 1961 (Paris, *Où est la liberté?*). 91'.

1952 **"The Chicken"** [English], **"Ingrid Bergman"** [Italian], episode in *Siamo donne*

Director: Roberto Rossellini. Assistant: Niccolo Ferrari.

Script: Cesare Zavattini, Luigi Chiarini, from a story by Zavattini.

Photography: Otello Martelli.

Sound: Giorgio Pallotta.

Music: Alessandro Cicognini.

Editor: Jolanda Benvenuti.

Producer: Costellazione [Alfredo Guarini]-Titanus. Released by Titanus. Production manager: Marcello D'Amico. Assistant: Giancarlo Campidori.

Filmed at Rossellini's home in Santa Marinella, in two versions.

With: Ingrid Bergman (herself), Albamaria Setaccioli (Signora Annovazzi), and Renzo, Franco, Robertino, Isabella, Isotta Rossellini.

Released: Oct. 27, 1953 (Milan); Mar. 26, 1954 (Paris). 17' (whole film: 90').

Other episodes directed by Alfredo Guarini (Anna Amendola, Emma Danieli), Gianni Franciolini (Alida Valli), Luigi Zampa (Isa Miranda), and Luchino Visconti (Anna Magnani).

1953 [*Voyage in Italy*], **Strangers** (U.S.), **Journey to Italy** (U.K., France subtitled) [English] (*Viaggio in Italia*; *L'Amour est le plus fort*; *The Lonely Woman* [short U.S. release]; *Voyage in Italy*; *Voyage to Italy*; *Voyage en Italie* [titles attributed by critics])

Director: Roberto Rossellini. Assistants: Marcello Caracciolo Di Laurino, Vladimiro Cecchi.

Script, Story: Roberto Rossellini, Vitaliano Brancati, [Antonio Pietrangeli].

Photography: Enzo Serafin. [Aldo Tonti, transparencies; Luciano Trasatti, a few shots.] Camera: Aldo Scavarda. Assistant: Alessandro Serafin. Assistants: Aldo Casalegno, Ottavio Belli, Amadeo Muscitelli, Corrado Ricci, Ennio Mancini, Orlando Pellegrini, Mario Micheli, Fernando Bonifazi, Giovanni Di Felice, Rodolfo Filodotto, Ettore Zampagni.

Sets: Piero Filippone. Make-up: Manrico Spagnoli. Gowns: Ines Fiorentini. Ingrid Bergman's costumes: Maison Fernanda Gattinoni.

Sound: Eraldo Giordani. Assistants: Venanzio Lisca, Aldo Zanni, Sergio Zega.

Music: Renzo Rossellini, conducted by him. Theme song and popular Neapolitan songs sung by Giacomo Rondinella. Theme song: "O paese d'o sole," by Vincente d'Annibale and Libero Bovio. At Bersagliera restaurant, "'E spingole frangese!" by Enrico De Leva and Salvatore Di Giacomo (1888). At hotel: "O Marenariello," by Gennaro Ottaviano and Salvatore Gambardella (1893). Visiting the villa: "Comme facette Màmmeta?" by Gambardella and Capaldo. On the terrace: "A Vuchella," by Paolo Tosti and Gabriele D'Annunzio (1892). Katherine's car trip: "O Surdarto 'nnammurato," by Aniello Califano and Enrico Cannio (1915). Katherine on terrace after visit to Cuma: "Luna Caprese," by Augusto Cesareo and Luigi Riccardi (1954). Alex returns to villa: "Autunno," by De Curtis and Bovio. Band at end: "Hymn to the Virgin of Pompeii."

Editor: Jolanda Benvenuti.

Producer: Roberto Rossellini, for Sveva Film (Rossellini)–Junior Film (Adolfo Fossataro)–Italia Film (Alfredo Guarini) S.G.C.–Les Films Ariane–Francinex (Paris). Released by Titanus. Production managers: Mario Del Papa, Marcello D'Amico. Assistants: Mimmo Salvi, Pietro Notarianni, Alberto Travaglini. Script: Mary Alcaide. Still photos: Lorenzo Papi. Drivers: Pietro Mannetti, Mario Cartocci, Ernesto Cartocci.

Filmed Feb. 2–Apr. 30, 1953, on locations in Naples, on the via Domiziana, in a villa near Torre del Greco, at Cuma, Herculanum, Capri, Pozzuoli, Campi Flegrei, Pompeii and Maiori. And in Titanus studios, Rome. Lab: Technostampa.

With: Ingrid Bergman (Katherine Joyce), George Sanders (Alex Joyce), Marie Mauban (Marie Rastelli: girl with leg in cast), Anna Proclemer (prostitute), Tony La Penna (Tony Burton), Natalia Ray–La Penna (Natalia Burton), Jackie Frost (Judy), Leslie Daniels (Leslie Harris, Judy's housemate), Lyla Rocco (Miss Sinibaldi), Paul Muller (Paul Dupont), Bianca Maria Cerasoli (Miss Notari), guests at Duca di Lipoli's: Lucio Caracciolo, Marcello Caracciolo, Paola Carola.

Released: Sept. 7, 1954 (Milan, *Viaggio in Italia*); Oct. 1 (Rome); Apr. 15, 1955 (Paris, *L'Amour est le plus fort*); 82′ [some sources say 76′]. Sept. 1 (Hollywood: Egyptian Theatre, *Strangers*, distributed by Fine Arts Films, Inc.); 85′ [*Variety* reported, probably erroneously, a running time of 80′, Sept. 28. An earlier *Variety* report of "*Journey to Italy (Viaggio in Italia)*"in Rome, Oct. 19, 1954, reported 100′, probably erroneously.]

The Italian- and French-dubbed editions lack a scene in which Alex tries to get more wine. A butchered French dubbing was titled *La Divorcée de Naples*. The British edition titled *A Lonely Woman* was reported as running only 70′ in the BFI's *Monthly Film Bulletin*, March 1958. A more recent British edition titled *Viaggio in Italia* appears to have appended the Italian titles to an English-language edition otherwise identical to *Strangers*.

1953 ["Napoli '43"], episode in *Amori di mezzo secolo*
Director: Roberto Rossellini. Assistant: Marcello Caracciolo Di Laurino.
Script: Oreste Biancoli, Carlo Infascelli, Giuseppe Mangione, Vinicio Marinucci, Alessandro Continenza, Giuseppe Mangione, Antonio Pietrageli, Vincenzo Talarico, Rodolfo Sonego, Ettore Scola; but in reality, for his episode, Rossellini, from story by Carlo Infascelli (but in reality Rossellini).
Photography (Ferraniacolor): Tonino Delli Colli. Camera: Sergio Bergamini.
Sets: Mario Chiari. Costumes: Maria De Matteis.
Sound: Ovidio Del Grande.
Music: Carlo Rustichelli, conducted by Alberto Paoletti.
Editor: Rolando Benedetti, Dolores Tamburini.
Producer: Carlo Infascelli, for Excelsa–Roma Film. Released by Minerva. Production manager: Silvio Clementelli.
Filmed November (?) 1953 at Cinecittà and on location in Naples.
With: Antonella Lualdi (Carla), Franco Pastorino (Renato), Ugo D'Alessio, Ascoli, Costa.
Released: Feb. 18, 1954 (Milan). 14′ (whole film: 100′).
Other episodes are directed by Glauco Pellegrini, Pietro Germi, Mario Chiari, Antonio Pietrangeli.

The title "Naples '43" was given by contemporary critics but does not appear in the film itself.

1954 *Jeanne au bûcher; Giovanna d'Arco al rogo* ("Joan of Arc at the Stake")
Director: Roberto Rossellini. Assistant: Marcello Caracciolo Di Laurino. Choreography: Bianca Gallizia.
Adaptation by Roberto Rossellini from the oratorio *Jeanne d'Arc au bûcher* (1939), music by Arthur Honegger and poem by Paul Claudel.
Photography (Gevacolor): Gabor Pogany. Camera: Guglielmo Garroni.
Sets: Carlo Maria Cristini. Furnishings: Marcello Caracciolo. Costumes: Adriana Muojo. Sound (direct): Paolo Uccello [Italian]; W. Robert Sivel [French]. Recording: Amelio Verona, Raffaele del Monte.
Music: Arthur Honegger. Orchestra, chorus and ballet of Teatro San Carlo, Naples, conducted by Angelo Spagnolo [I]; Chorus of Théâtre National de l'Opéra de Paris, conducted by René Duclos [F]. Music editor: M.O. De Filippi.
Editor: Jolanda Benvenuti [I]; Robert Audenet [F].
Producers: Giorgio Criscuolo, Franco Francese for Produzioni Cinematografiche Associate–Franco–London Film. Released by ENIC. Production manager: Raffaello Teti. Assistant: Federico Delfauro. Script: Mary Alcaide.
Filmed end of January through Mar. 8, 1954 at the Teatro Mediterraneo, Naples.
With: Ingrid Bergman (Joan of Arc), Tullio Carminati (Brother Domenico), Giacinto Prandelli (Porcus), Marcella Pobbe (the Virgin), Augusto Romani (the giant Heurtebise), Agnese Dubbini (Madame Botti), Gerardo Gaudisio (Justice representative), Aldo Terrosi (priest), Saturno Meletti, Plinio Clabassi, Nino Tarallo, Luigi Paolillo, and the voices of Miriam Pirazzini (Saint Catherine), Giovanni Avolanti (the ass), Florence Quartararo (Saint Marguerite), Pina Esca.
Released: Jan. 29, 1955 (Rome). 80′.
The version sung in French (*Jeanne au bûcher*) existed originally in a work print with Bergman's own voice (screened privately in Paris, November 1954 and Jan. 21, 1955), then in an (unreleased) version in which she is dubbed by Claude Nollier (previewed Paris, May 26, 1955; shown Paris Cinémathèque, July 7). The credits to this version read "Franco London Film présente / Une oratorio cinématographique / Composé par Arthur Honegger . . . / Jeanne au Bûcher / Poème de Paul Claudel."

1954 *Orient Express*
Director: Carlo Ludovico Bragaglia. Supervision: Roberto Rossellini (purely nominal).

1954 *Fear* [English]; *Angst* [German]
Director, Producer: Roberto Rossellini. Assistants: Franz Graf Treuberg, Pietro Servedio. Dialogue director (*Angst*): Beate von Molo.
Script: Sergio Amidei, Franz Graf Treuberg, Roberto Rossellini, from short story, "Die Angst," by Stefan Zweig.
Photography: Carlo Carlini, Heinz Schnackertz. Camera: Luigi Filippo Carta, Peter Haller, Johann Lym.
Costumes: Jacques Griffe (Paris) for Ingrid Bergman.
Music: Renzo Rossellini; Franco Ferrara conducting the Orchestra of the Accademia di Santa Cecilia.

Sound: Carl Becker (mostly in direct sound).
Editor: Walter Boos, Jolanda Benvenuti.
Producer: Roberto Rossellini, for Ariston Film, Munich–Aniene Film, Rome. Released by Gloria (Germany) and Minerva, then I.N.D.I.E.F. (Italy). Production managers: Jochen Genzow, Mario Del Papa. Assistants: Wolfgang Kühnlenz, Heinz Mikosch, Hans Seitz, Horst Wigankow.
Filmed September–October 1954 in Munich (Villa in der Clementinenstr.; Englischer Garten; Kabarett "Die kleinen Fische," Leopoldstr.; Fabrikgelände Siemens; Finsterwald bei Gmünd; in the Gegend von Kreuth) and in the München-Geiselgasteig studio.
With: Ingrid Bergman (Irene Wagner), Mathias Wieman (Prof. Albert Wagner), Renate Mannhardt (Johanna Schultze, alias Luisa Vidor), Kurt Kreuger (Heinrich Stoltz), Elise Aulinger (Martha, the governess), Edith Schultze-Westrum, Steffie Struck, Annelore Wied, Klara Kraft, Elisabeth Wischert, Gabriele Seitz, Jürgen Micksch, Dr. Rolf Deininger, Albert Herz, (Klaus Kinski, transvestite in nightclub).
Released: Nov. 5, 1954 (Germany): 78' [but *Variety* reports 91' for a Berlin release, Mar. 8, 1955); Jan. 21, 1955 (Milan, *La paura*): 82'; Dec. 14 (Marseilles, *La peur*); U.S.: *Fear*: 82'.
Shot simultaneously in English and German, with many differences. The English version was the basis for the Italian dubbing, *La paura* and French release. A third version (not authorized by Rossellini), *Non credo più all'amore*, 75', adds a voice-over to some scenes, eliminates scenes of the family fishing and Irene's attempted suicide, and alters the ending, so that Irene, having left her husband, has retired to the country with her children. The film was also announced in Italy under the title *Incubo* ("Nightmare"). Zweig's story had been filmed before, in 1928 by Orphid Films, Berlin; and in 1936 by Tourjansky in France (*Vertige d'un soir*). A second French production had been prepared that same year (*La Peur*, starring Gaby Morlay) but was not made.

1956 *Le Psychodrame*
ORTF, Service de la Recherche.
Director: Roberto Rossellini. Psychodramatic direction of actors: Jacob Levi Moreno, Anne Ancelin-Schützenberger.
Rossellini shot about 30' in 16mm for French TV during a congress on psychodrama in Paris. The footage was never edited.

1957–58 *L'India vista da Rossellini*
For RAI TV series *I viaggi del telegiornale*.
Producer, Director: Roberto Rossellini. Television coordinator: Giuseppe Sala. Post-production: Adriana Alberti, Jenner Menghi.
Photography (16mm Kodachrome, printed in black and white): Aldo Tonti. Television: Franco Morabito.
Original Indian music.
With: Roberto Rossellini and Marco Cesarini Sforza, who converse while watching footage shot in India.
Ten episodes, telecast:
1. India senza miti (India without myths) (27'10", Jan. 7, 1959).
2. Bombay, la porta dell'India (Bombay, the gate to India) (27'10", Jan. 14, 1959).
3. Architettura e costume di Bombay (Architectures and costumes in Bombay) (21'16", Jan. 21, 1959).

4. Varsova (19'44", Jan. 28, 1959).
5. Verso il sud (Toward the South) (29'20", Feb. 4, 1959).
6. Le lagune di Malabar (The lagune of Malabar) (24'23", Feb. 11, 1959).
7. Kerala (23'08", Feb. 18, 1959).
8. Hirakud, la diga sul fiume Mahadi (Hirakud, the dike on the river Mahadi) (25' 24", Feb. 24, 1959).
9. Il Pandit Nehru (25'51", Mar. 4, 1959).
10. Gli animali in India (Animals in India) (28'12", Mar. 11, 1959).
Total length: 251'.

1957–58 *J'ai fait un beau voyage par Roberto Rossellini* [French]
For ORFT TV.
Producer, Director: Roberto Rossellini. Presented by: Etienne Lalou; assistant: Pierre Robin. Technical collaboration: Jean L'Hôte.
Photography (16mm Kodachrome, printed in black and white): Aldo Tonti.
Sound illustration: Pierre Poulteau.
With: Roberto Rossellini and Etienne Lalou, who converse while watching footage shot in India.
Ten episodes (untitled), telecast:
1. [Bombay] (26', Jan. 11, 1959).
2. [Bombay] (24'30", Feb. 1, 1959).
3. [Bombay] (22', Feb. 8, 1959).
4. [Varsova] (26', Feb. 22, 1959).
5. [Voyage au sud (Trip to the South)] (24', Mar. 8, 1959).
6. [Malabar] (18', Mar. 23, 1959).
7. [Quillon] (22', Apr. 12, 1959).
8. [Barrage (Dike)] (24', May 10, 1959).
9. [Nehru] (24', June 14, 1959).
10. [Animaux (Animals)] (29', Aug. 6, 1959).
Total length: 239'30".
The footage shown appears to be the same as in the Italian series.

1957–59 *India Matri Bhumi* ("India mother land") [French]
Director: Roberto Rossellini. Assistants: Jean Herman, M. V. Krishnaswamy, Habib (India), Giovanni (Tinto) Brass (Rome, post-production). Additional footage: Romolo Marcellini (India).
Script: Roberto Rossellini, Sonali Sen Roy Das Gupta, Fereydoun Hoveyda. French commentary: Jean L'Hôte. Italian commentary [for the most part, a translation]: Vincenzo Talarico.
Photography: (Gevacolor, Ferraniacolor, Kodachrome): Aldo Tonti. Camera: Giorgio Tonti, Prem, Renzo Filippini.
Music: Philippe Arthuys: traditional Indian music elaborated by Alain Danielou (Ed. Ducretet-Thomson). Assistant: Christian Hackspill.
"Sound illustration": Tadié-Cinema.
Editor: Cesare Cavagna.
Producer: Roberto Rossellini, for Aniene Film, Rome–Union Générale Cinématographique, Paris. Released in Italy by Cineriz. Technical assistance: Indian Films Development (Jean Bhownhagari).
Filmed February–July 1957.
With: non-professionals.
Shown: May 9, 1959 (Cannes Festival): 95'. Released: Mar. 12, 1960 (Milan); May 26 (Rome): 91'30" (?). The recent color restoration of the French edition by the Cinémathèque Française runs 95' (2605m, including a 13" note explaining the restoration); the

restoration of the Italian edition by the Cinecittà International runs 85'.

The original French-language version was not distributed commercially after being shown at Cannes. The French restoration is vastly superior, although its color is partly faded. The inept Italian restoration has color so poor that much of the poetry is lost; also, the print chosen for "preservation" was missing most of its ending—all but three short crowd shots of the final 2' montage sequence (which ended with a bird soaring in the sky). Also missing are 23 shots plus portions of two long takes present in nine places in the French edition, but some of this latter footage may have been missing in the Italian edition itself, whose original running time is uncertain.

Working title: *India 58.*

1959 *Il generale Della Rovere* (*General Della Rovere*)
Director: Roberto Rossellini. Assistants: Renzo Rossellini Jr., Philippe Arthuys, Giovanni (Tinto) Brass.
Script: Sergio Amidei, Diego Fabbri, Indro Montanelli, (Piero Zuffi, Roberto Rossellini), from story of the same name by Indro Montanelli, based on an actual incident.
Photography: Carlo Carlini. Camera: Luigi Filippo Carta, Ruggero Radicchi.
Sets, Costumes: Piero Zuffi. Assistant: Francesco Ciarletta, Elio Costanzi. Make-up: Goffredo Rocchetti. Women's wardrobe: Vera Marzot. Hair: Maria Rocchetti.
Music: Renzo Rossellini.
Sound: Ovidio Del Grande.
Editor: Cesare Cavagna.
Producer: Moris Ergas, for Zebra Film, Rome–Société Nouvelle des Etablissements Gaumont, Paris. Released by Cineriz. Production manager: Paolo Frascà. Assistants: Carlo Giovagnorio, Manolo Bolognini, Gianni Cecchin, Zeev Havazelet. Script: Anna-Maria Montanari.
Filmed July 3–August 1959, at Cinecittà.
With: Vittorio De Sica (Emanuele Bardone, aka Col. Grimaldi, Gen. Giovanni Braccioforte Della Rovere), Hannes Messemer (Col. Müller), Sandra Milo (Olga), Giovanna Ralli (Valeria), Anne Vernon (the widow Carla Fassio), Vittorio Caprioli (Aristide Banchelli), Lucia Modugno (a partisan), Giuseppe Rossetti ("Fabrizio"), Luciano Picozzi (sweeping prisoner), Nando Angelini (a partisan), Herbert Fischer (Walter Hageman), Kurt Polter (German aide de camp), Kurt Selge (Schrantz, German officer at San Vittore), Franco Interlenghi (Antonio Pasquali), Linda Veras (a German), Bernardino Menicacci (watchman), Mary Greco (Madame Vera, bordello madam), Esther Carloni (bordello maid), Baronessa Barzani (Contessa Bianca Maria Della Rovere), Leopoldo Valentini (Giuseppe Di Castro), Gianni Baghino (Scalise), Roberto Rossellini (bystander in German commander's waiting room, in a scene between De Sica et Messemer).
Shown: Aug. 31, 1959 (Venice Festival): 139'. Released: Oct. 7 (Rome); Nov. 11 (Paris): 132'. October 1960 (New York): 139'. December 1961 (London): 131'.
Venice Film Festival 1959: Lion d'Or, (ex-aequo with Mario Monicelli's *La grande guerra*). San Francisco International Festival: best film, best direction, best script, best actors (De Sica and Messemer). Nastro d'Argento, 1960: best direction. David di Donatello

1959–60: best production. Prize, International Catholic Film Office (OCIC).

1960 *Era notte a Roma* ("It was night in Rome") (*Blackout in Rome*)
Director: Roberto Rossellini. Assistants: Renzo Rossellini Jr., Franco Rossellini.
Script: Sergio Amidei, Roberto Rossellini, Diego Fabbri, Brunello Rondi, with English dialogue by Mario Del Papa, from story by Amidei.
Photography: Carlo Carlini. Camera: Pippo Carta, Ruggero Radicchi, Sante Achilli.
Sets: Flavio Mogherini. Furnishings: Mario Rappini. Costumes: Elio Costanzi. Assistant: Marcella De Marchis. Make-up: Eligio Trani, Emilio Trani. Hair: Gustavo Sisi.
Music: Renzo Rossellini, orchestrated by Edoardo Micucci. Sound effects: Philippe Arthuys.
Sound: Enzo Magli. Special sound effects: Philippe Arthuys. Recording: Enzo Magli, Oscar Di Santo.
Editor: Roberto Cinquini.
Producer: Giovan Battista Romanengo, for International Golden Star, Genoa–Film Dismage, Paris. Released by Cineriz. Executive producer: Franco Magli. Production manager: Oscar Brazzi. Assistants: Alfred Veloccia, Ferdinando Alivernini. Script: Anna-Maria Montanari. Chief press officer: Nella Garozzo.
Filmed in Rome, the Roman countryside and at Cinecittà, February–March 1960.
With: Leo Genn (Maj. Michael Pemberton), Giovanna Ralli (Esperia Belli), Sergei Bondartchouk (Sgt. Fiodor Nazukov), Peter Baldwin (Lt. Peter Bradley), Renato Salvatori (Renato Balducci), Enrico Maria Salerno (Dr. Costanzi), Sergio Fantoni (Don Valerio) Paolo Stoppa (Prince Alessandro Antoniani), Hannes Messemer (Col. Baron von Kleist), George Petrarca (Tarcisio, the hunchback), Laura Betti (a fake nun, Esperia's friend), Giulio Calì (peasant), Rosalba Neri (professor's daughter), Carlo Reali (professor), Leopoldo Valentini (doorkeeper), Franco Rossellini (young prince Augusto Antoniani), Roberto Palombi.
Shown: May 13, 1960 (Cannes Festival): 157'. Released: Oct. 7 (Milan); Oct. 21 (San Francisco Film Festival): 142'; July 6, 1961 (Paris). Some release prints were cut to 114'.
Karlovy Vary Festival: Special Jury Prize, director and actress, Special Defenders of the Peace Prize, 1960.

1960 *Viva l'Italia*
Director: Roberto Rossellini. Assistants: Renzo Rossellini Jr., Ruggero Deodato, Franco Rossellini.
Script: Sergio Amidei, Antonio Petrucci, Diego Fabbri, Antonello Trombadori, Roberto Rossellini, from story by Amidei, Antonio Petrucci, Carlo Alianello, Luigi Chiarini.
Photography (Eastmancolor): Luciano Trasatti. Camera: Luigi Filippo Carta, Ruggero Radicchi. Special effects: Franco Cuppini.
Sets: Gepy Mariani. Costumes: Marcella De Marchis. Make-up: Eligio Trani. Hairdresser: Gustavo Sisi.
Sound: Enzo Magli, Oscar Di Santo. Sound effects: Philippe Arthuys.
Music: Renzo Rossellini: popular Italian songs, orchestrated by Eduardo Micucci, conducted by Pier Luigi Urbini.
Editor: Roberto Cinquini.

Producers: Tempo Film (Arturo Tofanelli)–Galatea (Lionello Santi)–Francinex. Released by Cineriz. Managing producer: Oscar Brazzi. Assistants: Renato De Pasqualis, Sergio Merolle, Alfredo Veloccia. Military consultant: Remo de Angelis.
Filmed on actual locations in Sicily, Naples, and Teano, summer 1960.
With: Renzo Ricci (dubbed by Emilio Cigoli) (Giuseppe Garibaldi), Paolo Stoppa (Nino Bixio), Franco Interlenghi (Giuseppe Bandi), Giovanna Ralli (Rosa), Raimondo Croce (Francesco II), Leonardo Botta (Menotti Garibaldi), Giovanni Petrucci (Fabrizio Plutino), Attilio Dottesio (Francesco Crispi), Amedeo Buzzanca (Rosa's father), Vittorio Bottone (Vittorio Emanuele II), Tina Louise (French journalist), Philippe Arthuys (Alexandre Dumas), Amedeo Gerard (Gen. Landi), Piero Braccialini (Giuseppe Mazzini), Sveva Caracciolo D'Acquara (Queen Maria Sofia), Ugo D'Alessio (secretary), Remo De Angelis (Giuseppe Missori), Armando Guarnieri (capitain at arms), Gerard Herter (journalist), Giuseppe Lo Presti (Litta-Modignani), Evar Maran (Francesco Montanari), Vando Tress (Luigi Gusmardi), Carlo Gazzabini (Giuseppe Sirtori), Franco Lantieri (Giuseppe La Farina), Marco Mariani (Major Sforza), Luigi Borghese (Lt. De Laurentiis), Ignazio Balsamo (Col. Ballavicino), Nando Angelini (Cap. Pietro G.B. Spangaro), Bruno Scipioni (Lt. Facanti), Renato Montalbano (Cap. Laprini), Sergio Fantoni, Armando Guarbieri.
Shown: Jan. 27, 1961 (Rome Opera, before President of Italy). Released: Feb. 2 (Rome): 129'.
A 90' English dubbing was released as *Garibaldi*.

1961 *Vanina Vanini* [French]
Director: Roberto Rossellini. Assistants: Franco Rossellini, Renzo Rossellini Jr., Philippe Arthuys.
Script: [Jean Gruault], Monique Lange, Diego Fabbri, Roberto Rossellini, from adaptation by Antonello Trombadori and Franco Solinas, of short story by Stendhal, "Vanina Vanini, or Particularities on the Last *Vendita* of Carbonari Discovered in the States of the Pope," (1829) in *Chroniques Italiennes*. Historic consultant: Amerigo Terenzi.
Photography (Technicolor): Luciano Trasatti. Camera: Claudio Ragona. Assistants: Franco Di Giacomo, Vittor Ugo Contino.
Sets: Luigi Scaccianoce. Furnishings: Riccardo Domenici. Make-up: Goffredo Rocchetti. Hair: Maria-Teresa Corridoni. Costumes: Danilo Donati, executed by Ditta Safas.
Music: Renzo Rossellini, conducted by Pier-Luigi Urbini.
Sound: Oscar De Arcangeli, Renato Cadueri.
Editor: Daniele Alabiso, supervised by Mario Serandrei.
Producer: Moris Ergas, for Zebra Film, Rome–Orsay Films, Paris. Released by Columbia-CEIAD. Executive producer: Manolo Bolognini. Assistants: Antonio Negri, Roberto Cocco, Carlo Giovanorio, Franco Casati. Script: Anna-Maria Montanari, Marcella Mariani.
Filmed at Cinecittà, December 1960 and winter 1961.
With: Sandra Milo (Princess Vanina Vanini), Laurent Terzieff (Pietro Missirilli), Paolo Stoppa (Prince Asdrubale Vanini), Martine Carol (Countess Vitelleschi), Isabelle Corey (Clelio, the maid), Nerio Bernardi (Cardinal Savelli), Fernando Cicero (Saverio Pontini), Leonardo Botta (Vanina's confessor), Antonio Pierfederici (Prince Livio Savelli, the

spy), Carlo Tamberlani (Monseigneur Benini), Olimpia Cavalli (chambermaid at inn), Mimmo Poli (executioner), Jean Gruault (castrato at ball), Evaristo Maran (Cardinal Rivarola), Carlo Gazzabini, Claudia Biava, Enrico Glori (a cardinal), Leonardo Severini.
Shown: Aug. 27, 1961 (Venice Festival: Italian dubbing). Released: Oct. 12 (Milan); June 29, 1962 (Paris): 118'. (Censor permit: 125').

1961 *Torino nei cent'anni*
Director: "A film by Federigo Valli directed by Roberto Rossellini." Collaborator: Enzo Leonardo. Assistant: Gilberto Casini.
Script, Story: Valentino Orsini. Historic consultants: Carlo Casalegno, Enrico Gianeri. Commentary written by Vittorio Gorresio.
Photography (16mm): Leopoldo Piccinelli, Mario Vulpiani, Mario Volpi.
Editor: Vasco Micucci.
Production: PROA (Produttori Associati) for RAI TV. Managing producer: Ugo De Lucia.
Telecast: RAI, Sept. 10, 1961 (10:25 P.M.). 46'35".
A montage documentary on Turin within Italy's history between 1860 and 1960.

1961 *Torino tra due secoli*
Director: Roberto Rossellini [=Federigo Valli?]. Assistant: Enzo Leonardo.
Script: Valentino Orsini. Text: Vittorio Gorresio.
Photography (color): Leopoldo Piccinelli.
Producer: P.R.O.A. Produttori Associati. Executive producer: Federigo Valli.
Filmed in Turin, Porta Nuova train station, *La Stampa* newspaper, Einaudi head offices, the Politecnico, and Fiat.
Released: 1961, on occasion of the exhibition, "Italia '61," Turin. 11'42".

1961 *Benito Mussolini*
Director: Pasquale Prunas. Supervision: Roberto Rossellini (purely nominal).
Script: Giovan Battista Cavallaro, Ernesto G. Laura. Commentary: Enzo Biagi, Sergio Zavoli.
Narrator: Romolo Valli.
Music: Roberto Nicolosi; conducted by Pier Luigi Urbini.
Editor: Romeo Ciatti. Supervision: Mario Serandrei.
Producers: Etrusca Cinématografica–Galatea Roma. Released by Unidis. 95'.

1962 *Anima nera* ("Black soul")
Director: Roberto Rossellini. Assistants: Franco Rossellini, Ruggero Deodato, Geraldo Giuliani.
Script: Roberto Rossellini, Alfio Valdarnini, from the 1960 play of the same name by Giuseppe Patroni Griffi.
Photography: Luciano Trasatti. Camera: Claudio Ragona. Assistant: Giacomo Maichiodi.
Sets: Elio Costanzi, Alfredo Freda.
Music: Piero Piccioni.
Costumes: Marcella De Marchis. Make up: Giuliano Lauren. Hair: Lina Cassir Tailor: Carmen Paricoli.
Editor: Daniele Alabiso.
Producer: Gianni Hecht Lucari, for Documento Film, Rome–Le Louvre Film, Paris. Released by De Laurentiis. Managing producer: Piero Lazzari. Assistants: Paolo Gargano, Nereo Salustri, Angelo Jacono. Script: Marcella Mariani.

Filmed in Rome and in an apartment on Monte Mario, January 1962.

With: Vittorio Gassman (Adriano Zucchelli), Annette Stroyberg (Marcella), Nadja Tiller (Mimosa), Eleonora Rossi Drago (Alessandra), Yvonne Sanson (Olga Manfredi), Giuliano Cocuzzoli (Sergio, Adriano colleague), Tony Brown (Guidino, Marcella's brother), Rina Braido (Lucia), Daniela Igliozzi (Giovanna), Chery Milion (dancer at night club), Armando Suspici (knight).

Released: Sept. 5, 1962 (Milan). 96'47".

1962 **"Illibatezza"** ("Chastity"), episode in *Ro-GoPaG*

Director: Roberto Rossellini. Assistant: Renzo Rossellini Jr.

Script, Story: Roberto Rossellini.

Photography (1.85): Luciano Trasatti.

Sets: Flavio Mogherini. Costumes: Danilo Donati.

Music: Carlo Rustichelli.

Sound: Bruno Brunacci, Luigi Puri.

Editor: Daniele Alabiso.

Filmed at Cinecittà.

Producer: Alfredo Bini, for Arco Film, Rome–Société Lyre Cinématographique, Paris. Executive producer: Manolo Bolognini. Managing producer: Eliseo Boschi. Released by Cineriz.

With: Rosanna Schiaffino (Anna Maria), Bruce Balaban (Joe), Gianrico Tedeschi (psychiatrist), Maria Pia Schiaffino (hostess), Carlo Zappavigna (Carlo, Anna Maria's fiancé).

Released: Feb. 21, 1963 (Milan): 33' (whole film: 111').

The title *RoGoPaG* derives from the names of the four directors: Godard (*Il nuovo mondo*), Pasolini (*La ricotta*), Gregoretti (*Il pollo ruspante*). After censorship difficulties with Pasolini's episode, the film was reissued under the title *Laviamoci il cervello* ("Let's wash our brains").

1963 *Les Carabiniers*

Director: Jean-Luc Godard.

Script: Jean Gruault, Jean-Luc Godard, from play by same name by Beniamino Joppolo, as synopsized by Roberto Rossellini.

Photography: Raoul Coutard.

Music: Philippe Arthuys.

With: Marino Masè, Albert Juross, Geneviève Galea, Catherine Ribeiro, Jean Brasset, Gérard Poirot, Alvaro Gheri, Barbet Schroeder, Jean Gruault, Jean-Louis Comolli, Odile Geoffroy, Catherine Durand, Jean Monsigny, Gilbert Servion, Wladimir Faters, Roger Coggio, Pascale Audret.

Producers: Georges de Beauregard, for Cocinor Marceau, Paris–Laetitia, Rome. Released by Euro.

1963 *L'età del ferro* (*The Iron Age*) (*L'Âge du fer*)

Director: Renzo Rossellini Jr. Assistant: Ruggero Deodato. Choreography: Franca Bartolomei.

Script, Supervision: Roberto Rossellini. Additional dialogue: Marcella Mariani.

Photography: Carlo Carlini. Camera: Luigi Filippo Carta. Assistant: Ruggero Radicchi.

Sets: Gepy Mariani, Ennio Michettoni. Costumes: Marcella De Marchis.

Music: Carmine Rizzo.

Sound: Renato Cadueri, Pietro Spadoni.

Editor: Daniele Alabiso.

Producer: 22 Dicembre–Instituto Luce, in collaboration with Italsider, for RAI TV. Executive producer:

Alberto Soffientini. Managing producer: Alfonso Donati.

Filmed summer and fall 1963.

With: *First episode:* Evar Maran, the Rome Ballet, Franca Bartolomei, Walter Zappolini (first dancers). *Second episode:* Alberto Barberito, Pasquale Campagnola, Walter Maestosi, Osvaldo Ruggeri. *Fourth and fifth episodes:* Arnolfo Dominici, Giulio Biagini, Giovanni Giannotti, Alessandro Lombardi, Evaldo Mancusi. Presenter: Roberto Rossellini. Narrators: Giancarlo Sbragia, Roberto Rossellini.

Telecast: RAI 2, in five episodes, 1965: Feb. 19 (52'33"), Feb. 26 (58'59"), Mar. 5 (49'17"), Mar. 12 (58"05"), Mar. 19 (47'50") at 9:15 P.M. Total running time: 266'44".

Telecast: France's ORTF2, in four episodes, Wednesdays 8:30–9:30 P.M., Dec. 7, Dec. 21, 1966, Jan. 11, 1967; 9:00–10:30, Jan. 25. Spain's TVE, in eight parts, Apr. 19–June 7, 1971.

A one-hour version was dubbed into French in 1966, and subsequently into English, essentially for private exhibition. Extracts from *Paisà*; *Deutschland im Jahre Null*; *Luciano Serra pilota*; *Austerlitz* (Gance), *Scipione l'africano* (Gallone).

1966 *La Prise de pouvoir par Louis XIV* [French] ("The taking of power by Louis XIV") (*The Rise of Louis XIV*)

Director: Roberto Rossellini. Assistant directors: Yves Kovacs, Egérie Mavraki. [Banquet and portions of hunt directed by Renzo Rossellini Jr.]

Script: Philippe Erlanger, [Jean Gruault, Roberto Rossellini]. Dialogue: Jean Gruault, [Jean Dominique de La Rochefoucauld]. Artistic consultant: La Rochefoucauld.

Photography (Eastmancolor): Georges Leclerc (and, for a few shots, Jean-Louis Picavet). Camera: Claude Butteau. Assistant: Bernard Zanni. Special effects: Marc Schmidt, Jean Faivre, Bernard Cinquin. Electrician: Henri Banoz. Machinist: Jean Coilbault.

Sets: Maurice Valay, Pierre Gerber. Assistant: François Comtet, Constantin Hagondokoff. Costumes: [Marcella De Marchis,] Christiane Coste; assistant: Pierre Cadot; executed by Peruzzi (Rome). Dresser: Hélène Maillet. Make-up: Nadine Jouve.

Sound: Jacques Gayet. "Sound illustration": Betty Willemetz. Effects: Daniel Couteau. Recording: Jacques Gayet; assistant: Claude Fabre. Assistant-montage: Huguette Cheltiel. Mixages: J.-P. Quinquempois.

Hunt sequence: Le Rallye Boissière, Marquis de Brissac, Vicomte de Chabot. Script: Michèle Podroznik.

Editor: Armand Ridel.

Producer: ORTF. Production chief: Pierre Gout. Laboratoire: G.T.C.

Filmed in August 1966 at the Châteaux de Brissac, Maison-Laffitte (banquet), Vincennes; mirror shorts filmed at a factory in Mantes (construction of Versailles); scenes of the Vert-Galant filmed along the Seine, near Mantes, with superimpression of images of the Louvre.

With: Jean-Marie Patte (Louis XIV), Raymond Jourdan (Colbert), Giulio Cesare Silvani (Mazarin), Katharina Renn (Anne of Austria); Dominique Vincent (Madame Du Plessis), Pierre Barat (Fouquet), Fernand Fabre (Le Tellier), Françoise Ponty (Louise de la Vallière), Joëlle Langeois (Marie-Thérèse), Maurice Barrier (d'Artagnan), André Dumas (Père Joly), Françoise Mirante (Mme de Brienne), Pierre

Spadoni (Moni), Roger Guillo (pharmacist), Louis Raymond (first doctor), Maurice Bourbon (second doctor), Michel Ferre (De Gesvres), Guy Pintat (chief cook), Michèle Marquais (Mme de Motteville), Jean-Jacques Daubin (de Vardes), Georges Coubert (de Soyecourt), Pierre Pernet (Monsieur), Ginette Barbier (Pierrette Dufour), Jean Obe (Le Vau), Jacques Charby (Le Vau's assistant), Micheline Muc (Mlle de Pons), Michel Debranne (tailor), René Rabault (M. de Grammont), François Bennard (archbishop), Georges Spanelly (Séguier), Jean Soustre (de Guiche), Axel Ganz (ambassador), Jean-Jacques Leconte (first chambellain), Violette Marceau (Mlle de Chemerault), Paula Dehelly (Mme d'Elbœuf), Jacques Preboist (musketeer), Roger Cransac (musketeer), André Daguenet (chief sailor), Marc Fraiseau, Pierre Frag, Jean Coste (sailors), Rita Maiden (Louison, a peasant), Françoise Deville (a woman), Raymond Pelissier (Pamponne), Claude Rio (Vardès), Daniel Dubois (Lionne), Pierre Lepers (chaplain), Hélène Manesse (Naiade), Jean-Claude Charnay (messenger).

Shown: Sept. 10, 1966 (Venice Film Festival). Telecast: ORTF, Oct. 8 (color). Released: Nov. 9 (Paris: La Pagode). Telecast: RAI, Apr. 23, 1967 (black and white). Italian release: January 1969. Shown: Sept. 25, 1967 (New York Film Festival). 98′.

1967 *Idea di un'isola* ("Idea of an island"); *The Sicily of Roberto Rossellini*

Director: Renzo Rossellini Jr. Assistants: Roberto Capanna, Paolo Poeti.

Photography (color): Mario Fioretti. Camera: Carlo Fioretti. Technical squad: Attivo Bevilacqua.

Music: Mario Nascimbene.

Editor: Maria Rosada.

Producer: Roberto Rossellini, for Orizzonte 2000. (Reputedly financed by National Broadcasting Company.) Managing producer: Francesco Orefici.

Narrator: Corrado Gaipa.

Telecast: NBC, Dec. 29, 1968; RAI 2 (black and white), Feb. 3, 1970, 9:15 P.M. 52′.

The American edition reputedly lists Roberto Rossellini as director.

1967–69 *La lotta dell'uomo per la sua sopravvivenza* ("Man's struggle for his survival"); *Survival*

Director: Renzo Rossellini Jr. Collaborating director: Pitt Popesco. Assistants: Roberto Capanna, Paolo Poeti, Émiliano Giannino, Ilie Sterian.

Script, Story: Roberto Rossellini.

Photography (color): Mario Fioretti. Camera: Carlo Fioretti. Assistants: Gianni Bonicelli, Marcel Reinstein.

Sets: Gepy Mariani, Virgil Moise (Eugenio Saverio, Giusto Puri Purini, Jurie Vasile, Ennio Michettoni). Costumes: Marcella De Marchis.

Music: Mario Nascimbene, Mixerama. Conductor: Roberto Pregadio. Theme song, "The Fight for Survival," sung by Shirley Bassey and the Folk Studio Singers.

Editor: Daniele Alabiso, Gabriele Alessandro, Alfredo Muschietti.

Producer: Roberto Rossellini, for Orizzonte 2000, for RAI–Logos Film, Paris–Studioul Cinematografica Bucaresti, Roumania–Copro Film, Cairo. Executive producer: Michele Bini (Arco Film, Rome). Managing producers: Francesco Orefici, Adrian Caracas. RAI representative: Angelo Lodigiani.

Filmed in Egypt, Tunisia, Roumania, and Sicily between 1967 and 1969.

Presenter: Roberto Rossellini. Narrator: Pino Locchi.

With: *First six episodes:* Piero Baldini, Renato Baldini, Rodolfo Baldini, Salvatore Billa, Massimo Sarchielli, Pino Caruso, Claudio Trionfi, Bruno Scipioni, Luciano Rossi, Franco Gulà, Elio Bertolotti, Marzio Margine, Luigi Barbacane, Alberto Dell'Acqua, Vasco Santoni, Vitaliano Elia, Giglio Gigli, Ernesto Colli, Emilio Giannino, A. Bella. *Second six episodes:* Franco Aloisi, Lydia Biondi, G. Andersen, Consalvo Dell'Arti, Valentino Macchi Giulio Donnini, Bepy Mannaiuolo, Corrado Olmi, Stefano Sibaldi, Alfredo Censi, Sandro Dori, Evar Maran, P. Ababini, Vittorio Williams, Valeria Sabel, Massimo Sarchielli, Florin Scarlatesco, Hans Krauss, Dino Jancolesco, Pino Caruso.

Shown: Nov. 21, 1968 (University of Saint Thomas, Houston, *Survival*): Part: "Neolithic Period and the Beginnings of Agriculture," c. 45′, dubbed into English; in color.

Telecast: RAI (black and white), in twelve episodes, divided into two series (the first six on Fridays at 9:15 P.M.; the second six on Saturdays at 9:30 P.M.):

1. Prima della storia, l'uomo (Prehistory: man). Aug. 7, 1970. 57′22″.
2. La civiltà che nacque da un fiume (The Civilization that was born from a river). Aug. 14, 1970. 54′31″.
3. Dall'angoscia dei miti al Dio che è salvezza (From the anguish of myths to the God that is salvation). Aug. 21, 1970. 50′37″.
4. Un'arca nel diluvio: il monachesimo (An ark in the flood: monasticism). Aug. 28, 1970. 51′15″.
5. Il medioevo, età di pietra e di ferro (The middle ages, era of stone and iron). Sept. 4, 1970. 43′42″.
6. Verso la scienza, patria dell'uomo (Toward science, man's birthright). Sept. 11, 1970. 51′49″.
7. In cerca delle Indie oltre l'oceano ignoto (In search of the Indies beyond the unknown ocean). Sept. 4, 1971. 54′39″.
8. Dall'età della magia all'età della scienza (From the age of magic to the age of science). Sept. 11, 1971. 59′04″.
9. Lo spirito scientifico conquista il mondo (The scientific spirit conquers the world). Sept. 18, 1971. 56′26″.
10. Questa nostra grandiosa civiltà della fretta (Our grandiose civilization of haste). Sept. 25, 1971. 52′13″.
11. Un'arte nuova in un mondo di macchine (A new art in a world of machines). Oct. 9, 1971. 49′15″.
12. Nonostante tutto, ancora più lontano. (Despite everything, farther still). Oct. 16, 1971. 47′55″.

Telecast: Spain's TVE, in twelve episodes between Apr. 14 and June 30, 1972.

1968 *Atti degli apostoli; Les Actes des Apôtres; Acts of the Apostles*

Director: Roberto Rossellini. Assistants: Malo Maurizio Brass, Roberto Capanna, Hedi Besbes, Abeljalil El Bahi, Mohamed Naceur al Ktari. Dubbing director: Luciano Scaffa.

Script: Jean Dominique de La Rochefoucauld, Luciano Scaffa, Vittorio Bonicelli, Roberto Rossellini, from "Acts of the Apostles" and other books of the New Testament. Dialogues: Jean Dominique de La Rochefoucauld. Theological consultants: Stanlislao Lionnet, S.J., Carlo Maria Martini, S.J.

Photography (Eastmancolor): Mario Fioretti. Camera: Carlo Fioretti. Assistant: Giovanni Bonicelli. Effects: Giusto Puri Purini.

Sets: Gepy Mariani, Carmelo Patrono, Elio Costanzi, Alessandro Gioia, Dino Leonetti. Costumes: Marcella De Marchis. Make-up: Manlio Rocchetti, Carlo Sindici. Hair: Duilio Scarozza, Todero Guerrino, Franco Rufini.

Music: Mario Nascimbene. Flute: Severino Gazzelloni. Voice: Sonali Sen Roy Das Gupta. Mixing: Meridiana Recording.

Sound: Gianni Mazzarini. Recording: Eugenio Rondani, Mario Messina. Italian dubbing: CDC (CDS, via Margutta).

Editor: Jolanda Benvenuti. Assistant: Giancarlo Tiburzi. Technical squad: Attivo Bevilacqua.

Producer: Roberto Rossellini, for Orizzonte 2000—RAI–ORTF–TVE Madrid–Studio Hamburg, in collabortion with Les Films de Carthage, Tunis. Executive producer for RAI: Vittorio Bonicelli. Managing producer: Francesco Orefici. Assistants: Renzo Rossellini Jr., Sergio Galiano, Paolo Luciani. Set photos: Giovanni Assenza. Script: Marcella Mariani.

Filmed in southeastern Tunisia around Sousse and Kairouan, at Ostia Antica, Pompeii, Sperlonga, the forest of Ceri, summer 1968.

With: Edoardo Torricella (Paul), Jacques Dumur (Peter), Bepy Mannaiuolo (Philip), Renzo Rossi (Zacharias), Mohamed Kouka (John), Bradai Ridha (Matthew), Missoume Ridha (James The Greater), Zouiten (James The Less), Hedi Nouira (Andrew), Zignani Houcine (Stephen), Mohamed Ktari (Mark), Bouraoui (Bartholomew), Ben Reayeb Moncef (Thomas), Maurizio Malo Bras (Aristarchus, the Greek scribe), Enrico Ostermann (Caiaphas), Paul Muller (Greek sophist), Daniele Dublino (Syla), Olimpia Carlisi (Lydia), Lydia Biondi (snake woman), Dino Mele (Aquila), Sergio Serafini (Christian in Rome), Gian Paolo Capovilla (Greek soldier at Neapolis), Maria Cumani Quasimodo (hotel keeper in Corinthe), Alessandro Perella, Ada Pometti, Mimmo Caruso, Valentino Macchi, Mario Zampelli, Bruno Cattaneo (another Christian in Rome).

Telecast: RAI 1 (black and white), in five episodes, Sundays at 10:35 P.M., Apr. 6, 1969 (58'), Apr. 13 (58'), Apr. 20 (64'), Apr. 27 (64'), May 4 (98'). Total running time: 341'. Spain's TVE, five episodes, daily, Mar. 23–27, 1970, preceded by an introduction in Castilian by Rossellini. France's ORTF2, five episodes, weekly, Oct. 7, 14, 21, 28, Nov. 4, 1970. Running time: c. 290'.

There is no original-language edition, the scratch track having been polyglot; see text. An abridged edition by Luciano Scaffa, approximately 280' and probably identical to Spanish and French editions, was issued in Italy by San Paolo Films on 8mm and VHS video. This same edition was dubbed into English by Don Bosco Multimedia (New Rochelle, New York) and issued in 16mm and VHS.

1970 *Socrate* [French] (*Socrate* [Italian dubbing])

Director: Roberto Rossellini. Assistants: Juan Garcia Atienza, José Luis Guarner, [Jos Oliver]. "French adaptation and Artistic direction": Jean Dominique de La Rochefocauld.

Script: Roberto Rossellini, Marcella Mariani, from adaptation by Rossellini, Maria Grazia Bornigia. Dialogue: Jean Dominique de La Rochefocauld.

Text established after the works of Xenophon, Diogenes, Laerce, and Plato, and other works and documents of the era.

Photography (Eastmancolor): Jorge Herrero Martin. Camera: Ricardo Poblete. Assistant: Miguel Garrido Salvadores. Special effects: Giovanni Bonicelli.

Sets: Giusto Puri Purini, Bernardo Ballester. Costumes: Marcella De Marchis. Costume furnisher: Tigano-La Faro. Make-up: Juan Sanchez Quesada. Hair: Julia Gonzales Garcia. Wigs: Ditta Rocchetti. Shoes: Dita Pompei. Furnishings: Set-Mancini.

Music: Mario Nascimbene.

Sound: Gianni Mazzarini, Jesus Paralta Navarro.

Editor: Alfredo Muschietti. Assistant: Giancarlo Tiburzi. Dubbing: CDC (Cooperativa Doppiatori Cinematografici).

Producer: Roberto Rossellini, for Orizzonte 2000–RAI–ORTF–TVE Madrid. Managing producers: Francesco Orefici, Antonio Matilla. Assistant: Juan Mauricio Matias. Script: Marcella Mariani. Italian dubbing by Coop. Doppiatori.

Filmed at Patones Arriba and Samuel Bronston Studios, Madrid, mid-April–May 1970.

With: Jean Sylvère (Socrates, dubbed in Italian by Guy Grosso), Anne Caprile (Xanthippe), Ricardo Palacios (Criton), Bepy Mannaiuolo (Apollodorus), Manuel Angel Egea (Cebetes), Julio Morales (Antisthenes), Jesus Fernandez (Cristobolus), Eduardo Puceiro (Simmias), Jose Renovales (Phaede), Antonio Medina (Plato), Emilio Miguel Hernandez (Meletos), Emilio Hernandez Blanco (Hyperides), Gonzalo Tejel (Anytos), Antonio Requena (Hermes), Roberto Cruz (old man), Francisco Sanz (actor), Antonio Alfonso (Eutyphron), Juan Francisco Margallo (Critias), Roman Ariznavarreta (Calicles), Francisco Catala (Lysias), Adolfo Thous (Hippias), Jean Dominique de La Rochefoucauld (Phaedre), Bernardo Ballester (Theophrastus), César Bonet (priest), Jerzy Radlowsky (juggler), Pedro G. Estecha (Phocion), Rafael de la Rosa (Trasybulus), Simon Arriaga (servant), Ivàn Almagro (Hermogenes), Constant Rodriguez (Aristephus), Stefano Charelli (Ephigenes), Luis Alonso Gulias (Aechines), Jesus A. Gordon (Lamprocles), Jose Luis Ortega (Socrates's young son). Elio Seraffini, Julio Morales.

Shown: Aug. 19, 1970 (Venice Festival). Telecast: RAI 2 (black and white), in two parts, Thurs., June 17 and Sun., June 20, 1971. Telecast: ORTF1, in two parts, Wed., Oct. 28 and Thurs. Oct. 29, 1974 (rescheduled because of strike Oct. 9–12). 120', film (61' and 56' at 25 fps on European TV).

Shown at Cinémathèque Française prior to telecast on ORTF, and at Museum of Modern Art, New York February 1971, and AFI Theater, Washington, D.C., March 1971.

1971 *La forza e la ragione: Intervista a Salvatore* [sic] *Allende*

Directors: Helvio Soto, Emidio Greco.

Photography (16mm color): Roberto Girometti.

Sound: Antonio Russello.

Filmed in Salvador Allende's house, Santiago di Chile, May 1971.

Producer: Renzo Rossellini Jr., for San Diego Cinematografica.

With: Salvador Allende, Roberto Rossellini.

Telecast: RAI 1 (black and white), Sept. 15, 1973 (after Allende's death) cut from c. 45' to 36'22" with comments by Rossellini and Enzo Biagi.

1971 *Blaise Pascal* [French]
Director: Roberto Rossellini. Assistants: Gabriele Polverosi, Andrea Ferendeles. French dubbing: Jean Dominique de La Rochefoucauld.
Script: Roberto Rossellini, Marcella Mariani, Luciano Scaffa, Jean Dominique de La Rochefoucauld. Adaptation and Dialogues: La Rochefoucauld.
Photography (Eastmancolor): Mario Fioretti. Camera: Carlo Fioretti.
Sets: Franco Velchi. Costumes: Marcella De Marchis. Assistant: Isabella Rossellini. Tailor: Togano-Lo Faro. Make-up: Giulio Natalucci. Hair: Marisa Fraticelli. Wigs: Rocchetti. Shoes: Pompei.
Music: Mario Nascimbene, Mixerama.
Sound: Carlo Tarchi. Mixage: Gianni Mazzarini. Assistant: Corrado Demofonti. Dubbing: Cooperativa Doppiatori C.D. Mixage: Meridiana Recording.
Editor: Jolanda Benvenuti. Assistant: Rita Di Palo.
Producer: Roberto Rossellini, for Orizzonte 2000, for RAI–ORTF. Executive producer: Sergio Iacobis. Assistant: Nicola Venditti. Script: Marcella Mariani. Italian dubbing: Cooperativa Doppiatori C.D.
Filmed at Magliano Sabina (near Rome), the palace of the Odescalchi at Bassano Romano, the abbey of Fossanova, Aug. 16–September 1971.
With: Pierre Arditi (Blaise Pascal), Rita Forzano (Jacqueline Pascal), Giuseppe Addobbati (Etienne Pascal), Christian De Sica (criminal lieutenant), Livio Galassi (Jacques, the servant), Bruno Cattaneo (Jean Deschamps), Bepi Mannaiuolo (Florin Perier, Gilberte's husband), Marco Bonetti (Artus Gouffier, Duc de Roannes), Teresa Ricci (Gilberte Pascal), Christian Aleny (Adrien Deschamps), Bernard Rigal (Chancellor Seguier), Melù Valente (Charlotte de Roannes), Lucio Rama (M. Moulinet), Mario Bardella (the mathematician Pierre Petit), Claude Baks (Descartes), Anne Caprile (Michèle Martin, the servant of Moulinet, accused of witchcraft), Tullio Valli (Father Marin Mersenne), Edda Soligo (the Mother Superior Angélique), Jean Dominique de La Rochefoucauld (Father Noël).
Telecast: RAI 1 (black and white, Italian dubbing), in two parts, Tues., May 16, Wed., May 17, 1972. Telecast: ORTF1, May 29, 1974. 131', film (128' at 25 fps on European TV).

1972 *Agostino d'Ippona*
Director: Roberto Rossellini. Assistants: Andrea Ferendeles, Claudio Bondì, Claudio Amati.
Script: Marcella Mariani, Luciano Scaffa, Roberto Rossellini. Dialogues: Jean Dominique de La Rochefoucauld. Consultant: Carlo Cremona.
Sets: Franco Velchi. Costumes: Marcella De Marchis. Assistant: Isabella Rossellini. Make-up: Manlio Rocchetti, Franco Ruffini.
Photography (Eastmancolor): Mario Fioretti. Camera: Carlo Fioretti.
Music: Mario Nascimbene.
Sound: Carlo Tarchi.
Editor: Jolanda Benvenuti.
Producer: Roberto Rossellini, for Orizzonte 2000, for RAI. Executive producer: Sergio Iacobis. Managing producer: Francesco Orefici. Assistants: Salvatore Scarfone. Script: Marcella Mariani.
Filmed in Pompeii, Herculanum, Paestrum, and Rome (basilicas of St. Elia and of St. Costanza), February 1972.
With: Dary Berkany (Augustine), Virginio Gazzolo (Alipio, bishop of Tagaste), Cesare Barbetti (the rhetorician Volusiano), Bruno Cattaneo (the Christian tribune Massimo), Leonardo Fioravanti (Milesio), Bepy Mannaiuolo (Severo), Livio Galassi (Possidio, new bishop of Calama), Fabio Garriba (proconsul Marcellino), Valentino Macchi (Sisto), Giuseppe Alotta (Siriaco, a Syrian merchant), Sergio Fiorentini (a sailor), Pietro Fumelli (Megalio, bishop of Calama), Giovanni Sabbatini (Valerio), Ciro Ippolito (Terenzio), Dannuzio Papini (Roman judge), Filippo Degara (Crispino), Gian Giacomo Elia (Papirio), Leo Pantaleo (Macrobio), Guido Celano (Roman exile), Maria Teresa Piaggio (Roman exile), Ettore Bevilacqua, Marilù Vilar, Carlo Schellino, Andrea Maroni.
Shown: September 1972 (Turin). Telecast: RAI 1 (black and white), in two parts, Oct. 25 and Nov. 1, 1972, at 9:30 P.M. 117'.

1972 [*The Age of the Medici:*] *Cosimo de' Medici* (2 parts) and *The Age of Cosimo de' Medici: Leon Battista Alberti: Humanism* [English] (*L'età di Cosimo de' Medici: 1. L'esilio di Cosimo. 2. Il potere dei Cosimo. 3. Leon Battista Alberti: L'umanesimo* [Italian dubbing])
Director: Roberto Rossellini. Assistants: Claudio Bondì, Beppe Cino, Claudio Amati.
Script: Roberto Rossellini, Luciano Scaffa, Marcella Mariani.
Photography (Eastmancolor): Mario Montuori. Camera: Giovanni Maddaleni. Assistant: Sergio Melaranci.
Sets: Franco Velchi. Costumes: Marcella De Marchis. Tailor: Safas. Shoes: Pompei. Make-up: Manlio Rocchetti. Hair: Maria Costanzi. Wigs: Rocchetti.
Music: Manuel De Sica, conducted by him.
Sound: Carlo Tarchi. Mixing: Fausto Ancillai.
Editor: Jolanda Benvenuti. Assistant: Rita Di Palo.
Producer: Roberto Rossellini, for Orizzonte 2000, for RAI. Executive producer: Sergio Iacobis. Managing producer: Francesco Orefici. Assistants: Carla Raiconi: Nicola Venditti. Script: Marcella Mariani.
Filmed in Florence, Gubbio, Todi, Venice, a villa at Fiesole, Certaldo, Medici Villa at Careggi, August–September 1972.
With: Marcello Di Falco (Cosimo de' Medici), Virginio Gazzolo (Leon Battista Alberti), Tom Felleghi (Rinaldo degli Albizzi), Mario Erpichini (Totto Machiavelli), Adriano Amidei Migliano (Carlo degli Alberti, Leon Battista's brother), John Stacy (Ilarione de' Bardi), Sergio Nicolai (Francesco Soderini), Michel Bardinet (Ciriaco d'Arpaso), Piero Gerlini (Poggio Bracciolini), Mario Demo (Sigismondo Malatesta), Duccio Dugoni (Bernardo Rossellino), Janti Sommer (Comtesse de' Bardi, Cosimo's wife), Ugo Cardea (Niccolo Cusano), Marino Masè (Francesco Filelfo), Lincoln Tate (Thomas Wadding), Carlo Reali, Roberto Bisacco (Niccolò Di Cocco Donati), Giuseppe Addobbati, Livio Galassi, Giuliano Disperati (new gonfalonier), Nazzareno Natale, Roberto Bruni, Maurizio Manetti, Goffredo Matassi (Bernardo Guadagni, gonfalonier of Florence), Bruno Cattaneo (Toscanelli), Valentino Macchi, Fred Ward (Niccolo de Conti), Giuseppe Pertile, John (Janos) Bartha, Ernesto Colli, Attilio Dottavio, Sergio Serafini (Lorenzo), Enzo Spitaleri, Franco Moraldi, Sonia Fridman, Bernard Rigal, Francesco Vairano, D. Bugna, G. De Michelis, Emanuele Vacchetto, Bepy Mannaiuolo, Giacinto Ferro, Honard Nelson Rubien, Dario Micaelis (Carlo Marsuppini).

Telecast: RAI 1 (black and white), on three Tuesdays, Dec. 26, 1972, Jan. 2 and 10, 1973, at 9:15 P.M. Running time: 254' (81'20"; 81'20"; 91').

1973 *Cartesius* [French]
Director: Roberto Rossellini. Assistants: Beppe Cino, Claudio Amati.
Script: [Jean Dominique de La Rochefoucauld,] Roberto Rossellini, Luciano Scaffa, Marcella Mariani. Consultant: Ferdinand Alquié.
Photography (Eastmancolor): Mario Montuori. Camera: Maurizio Scanzani. Assistant: Giancarlo Granatelli.
Sets: Giuseppe Mangano. Costumes: Marcella De Marchis. Tailor: Safas. Shoes: Pompei. Make-up: Pino Ferrante.
Music: Mario Nascimbene, Mixerama.
Sound: Tommaso Quattrini. Mixing: Gianni Mazzarini. Editor: Jolanda Benvenuti. Assistant: Rita di Palo.
Filmed at Odescalchi castle at Bassano Romano; stake scenes in a piazza in Faleria; abbey of Fossanova. Dutch exteriors of dikes and canals on the beach of Tarquinia. Anatmony staged in the studio of the Centro Sperimentale di Cinematografia, Rome, February 1973.
Producer: Roberto Rossellini, for Orizzonte 2000, for RAI–ORTF. Executive producer: Sergio Iacobis. Managing producer: Francesco Orefici. Assistants: Nicola Venditti. Coach: Marie-Claire Sinko. Script: Marcella Mariani.
With: Ugo Cardea (René Descartes), Anne Pouchie (Elena), Claude Berthy (Guez de Balzac), Gabriele Banchero (Bretagne, the servant), John Stacy (Levasseur d'Etioles), Charles Borromel (Father Marin Mersenne), Kenneth Belton (Isaak Beeckman), Renato Montalbano (Constantin Huygens), Vernon Dobtcheff (Ciprus the astronomer), Giancarlo Sisti, Beppe Colombo, Maurizio Manetti, Bruno Corazzari (Dutch officer), Bruno Rosa, Bruno Cattaneo, Camillo Autore, Jack Gillin, Raffaele Tecce, Cesare Di Vito, Cristiano Camponelli, Antonio Guerra, Stavros Tornes, Carlo Monni, Marcello Carlini, Matilde Antonelli, Penny Ashton, Angelo Bassi, Gianni Loffredo, Franco Calogero, Dante Biagioni, Mario Danieli, Marcello Di Falco, Miguel, Sergio Doria, Maria Grazia Piani, Duccio Dugoni, Soko, Nicolaas Ladenius, Enzo Spitaleri, Dan Tesdahl, Fred Ward, Anthony Berner.
Telecast: RAI 1 (Italian dubbing), on two Wednesdays, Feb. 20 and 27, 1974, 8:45 P.M. 154'. Never telecast in France.

1973 *Rice University* [English]
Director, Editor: Beppe Cino.
Camera (16mm color): William Colville.
Producer: Roberto Rossellini.
Unreleased. c. 120'.
A series of conversations between Rossellini and Jean and Dominique De Menil, Clark Read, Dieter Heyman, Donald Clayton, and other scientists at Rice University, plus footage of the telescope at Arecibo, Puerto Rico, in prospectus of the *Science* series then in preparation. An extract, with voice-over translation into Italian by Rossellini, was telecast by RAI in 1977 as part of Angelo d'Alessandro's *Roberto Rossellini: un ricordo.*

1974 *A Question of People*
Director: Roberto Rossellini [actually: Beppe Cino]. Assistants: Giampaolo Santini, Renzo Rossellini Jr.

Editor, Commentary: Beppe Cino.
Producer: United Nations.
Shown at U.N. Conference on World Population, Bucharest, 1974. 16mm color. 125'.
A 28' edition, *People: A Matter of Balance*, was edited by Michael Heywood with a new commentary written by Heywood and V. Tarzie Vittachi, for the U.N. Human Settlements Agency, with the credit, "From Filming by Roberto Rossellini."

1974 *Anno uno*
Director: Roberto Rossellini. Assistants: Beppe Cino, Nino Bizzarri, Antonio Carlucci.
Story, Script: Roberto Rossellini, Luciano Scaffa, Marcella Mariani. Historical research: Maria Stella Sernas.
Photography (Eastmancolor): Mario Montuori. Camera: Maurizio Scanzani. Assistants: Giorgio Urbinelli, Enrico Biribicchi.
Sets: Giuseppe Mangano, Andrea Fantacci. Costumes: Marcella De Marchis. Hair: Maura Turchi. Make-up: Pino Ferranti.
Sound: Tommaso Quattrini, Franco De Arcangelis.
Music: Mario Nascimbene.
Editor: Jolanda Benvenuti. Assistant: Marcella Benvenuti.
Producer: Rusconi Film. Released by Italnoleggio Cinematografico. Executive producer: Silvia D'Amico Bendicò. Managing producer: Sergio Iacobis. Assistants: Nicola Venditti. Production delegate: Renato Pieri. Script: Marcella Mariani.
Filmed in Rome, Castelgandolfo, and Matera, Sicily, summer 1974.
With: Luigi Vannucchi (Alcide De Gasperi), Dominique Darel (Maria Romana De Gasperi), Valeria Sabel (Francesca De Gasperi, his wife), Rita Forzano (Lucia De Gasperi, nun), Ennio Balbo (Nenni), Luciano Gaudenzio (Longo), Renato Montanari (Secchia), Paolo Bonacelli (Amendola), Francesco Di Federico (Saragat), Francesco Morillo (Fenoaltea), Piero Palermini (Scoccimarro), Consalvo Dell'Arti (Bonomi), Franco Ferrari (Ruini), Renato Montalbano (Spataro), Tino Bianchi (Togliatti), Corrado Olmi (Di Vittorio), Aldo Rendine (Romita), Nicola Morelli (Badoglio), Rita Calderoni (journalist), Renato Scarpa (Jesuit), Maria-Teresa Piaggio (Catholic Action woman), Enzo Loglisci (Catholic Action member), Franco D'Adda (Tuscan DC leader), Giorgio Lovine (Sicilian DC leader), Ubaldo Granata (Ligurian DC leader), Camillo Milli (Emilian DC leader), Armando Furlai (Roman DC leader), Gianni Rizzo (Turin DC leader), Tom Felleghi (Venetian DC leader), Laura de Marchi (Laura), Vittorio Ripamonti (Don Signora), Cesare Nizzica (an old Roman) Mariella Fenoglio (girl), Gianni Di Gregorio (young man), Riccardo Bosco (young Communist), Fabrizio Iovine (Catholic Action member), Omero Antonutti (Communist), Enrico Marciani (Liberal), Sergio Nicolai (partisan disguised as priest), Adriano Micantoni (Milanese socialist), Carlo Bagno (Milanese Communist), Dante Fioretti (Liberal), Bruno Cattaneo, Adriano Amidei Migliano, Mauro Vestri, Carlos de Carvalho, Achille Brugnini, Vittorio Anselmi (journalists), Ettore Carloni (doctor), Edda Ferronao (Nilde Jotti), Ivano Lattanzi (Scelba), Gianni Rizzo (Roman DC leader), Renato Pinciroli (typographer), Stavros Tornes (Parri), Bepy Mannaiuolo, Pinuccio Ardia (old gentleman at Grand Hotel), Bill Vanders (journalist), Nais Lago, Biagio Pelligra (at café), Bruno

Rosa, Piero Vida (café customer), Giancarlo Fontini, Antonella Forsano, Sergio Gibello, Riccardo Mangano, Carlo Bagno (Milanese Communists), Roberto Rossellini (at café). Released: Nov. 15, 1974, Rome. 123'.

1975 *The Messiah* [English] (*Il Messia; Le Messie*)
Director: Roberto Rossellini. Assistants: Beppe Cino, Carlos de Carvalho, Abdellatif Ben Ammar. Choreography: Giancarlo Vantaggio.
Story, Script: Roberto Rossellini, Silvia D'Amico. (Carlo Maria Martini, S.J., Lucianno Scaffa.) Consultant: Don Ettore Segneri, S.D.B. [Dialogue for French dubbing: Jean Gruault.]
Photography (Eastmancolor): Mario Montuori. Camera: Gaetano Valle, Giuseppe Berardini. Assistants: Giuseppe Buonaurio, Liberto Pisani, Stellio Firenzini, Mark Lombardo.
Sets: Giorgio Bertolini. Assistants: Fethi Dammak, Hassan Soufi. Costumes: Marcella De Marchis. Decorations: Giovanni Del Drago, Osvaldo Desideri. Make-up: Manlio Rocchetti. Graphics: Maurizio Silvi. Hair: Galileo Mandini. Costumes executed by: Maison Raparelli. Postiches: Rocchetti-Carboni. Shoes: Pompei Luigi Soc.
Sound: Alain Contrault, Tommaso Quattrini.
Music: Mario Nascimbene. Flute: Severino Gazzelloni.
Editor: Jolanda Benvenuti, Laurent Quaglio.
Producer: Orizzonte 2000–Procinex (Paris). Released by ARCI Nuova Comunicazione. Executive producer: Silvia D'Amico Bendicò. Associate producer: Enzo Provenzale. Assistants: Roberta Revetria, Nicola Venditti. Administration: Ettore Quattrini, Sergio Bologna, Paolo Lombardo. Executive producer (Tunisia): Tarak Ben Ammar. Managing producer (Tunisia): Aloulou Cherif. Assistants: Lilia Ben Salem, Hassine Soufi, Habib Chaari. Script: Marcella Mariani. Stills: Gianni Assenza.
Filmed in Tunisia, Monte Cassino (temple interior), and around Siena (shots in an old church), June 2–July 25, 1975.
With: Pier Maria Rossi (Jesus, dubbed in Italian by Enrico Maria Salerno), Mita Ungaro (Mary), Carlos de Carvalho (John the Baptist), Fausto Di Bella (Saul), Vernon Dobtcheff (Samuel), Antonella Fasano (Mary Magdaline), Jean Martin (Pontiu Pilate), Toni Ucci (Herod Antiphas), Vittorio Caprioli (Herod the Great), Flora Carabella (Herodias), Tina Aumont (woman taken in adultery), Anita Bartolucci (Samaritan), Denise Bataille (Herod's sister), Cosetta Pichetti (Salome), the apostles: Raouf Ben Amor (Judas), Luis Suarez (John), Hedi Zouglami (Simon Peter), Renato Montalbano (Matthew), Raouf Ben Yaghlane (Andrew), Fadhel Djaziri (Nathanial), Mark Lombardo (James, son of Alphe), Moncef Ben Yahia (Thomas), Antonio Carlucci (Simon the Cananite), Ridha Missume (Philip), Slim Mzali (James, son of Zebediah), Mohamed Ali Belkadhi (Thadeus), Samir Ayadi (a pharisee), John Karlsen (Caiphas), Mustapha Ferchiou (Jesus as child), Abdellatif Hamrouni (priest), Yatsugi Khelil (Joseph), Abdelmagid Lakhal (another pharisee); Claude Betan, Francesco Costa, Rossano Jalenti, Mathia Machiavelli, Lorenzo Piani, Paolo Rovesi, Giuseppe Scarcella, Renato Scarpa, Moncef Ben Arbia, Madar Ben Jemine, Habib Bel Hareth, Mohamed Ali Ben Hassine, Mourad Ben Hmida, Abdellaziz Ben Othman, Mohamed Ben Slimane, Martine Benedetto, Sonad Charni, Hedi

Daoud, Hima Daoud, Faouzia Debbiche, Rachid Gara, Kamel Hannachi, Nourredine Kasboui, Saada Kasboui, Akrout Khaled, Amor Khalfa, Béchir Ksouri, Nourredine Assaoui, Habib Laroussi, Jiji Le Garrec, Louzir Mokhtar, Moheddine Mrad, Béchir Nafbouti, Brahim Mohamed Salah, Mannai Slaheddine Mongia Tabour, Mohamed Touhri, Ahmed Tounsi, Salah Seghir, Salma Zehar, Mokdad, L. Berta.
Shown: at Montecatini (Italian dubbing), Oct. 25, 1976. Released: Feb. 18, 1976 (Paris, French dubbing); Sept. 30 (Rome, Italian dubbing). 145'.
Although shot with a scratch track mostly in English, an English-language dubbing was never executed.

1977 *Concerto per Michelangelo*
Director: Roberto Rossellini. Assistant: Laura Basile.
Photography (video, plus 35mm Eastmancolor transferred to video): Mario Montuori (film), Giorgio Ojetti (video).
Music: Monsgr. Domenico Bartolucci.
Filmed at the Vatican week of Apr. 2, 1977.
With: Choir of the Pontifical Musical Chapel, conducted by Monsgr. Domenico Bartolucci. Narrator: Alberto Lori.
Producer: RAI 2–TG 2, coordinated by Guido Sacerdote.
Telecast: RAI 2, Apr. 9, 1977. 42'.

1977 *Le Centre Georges Pompidou* [French]
Director: Roberto Rossellini. Assistants: Christian Ledieu, Pascal Judelewicz.
Photography: Nestor Almendros (Eastmancolor 5254; Mitchell Mark 2; Angenieux 254-250 zoom; 1.33). Camera: Emmanuel Machuel, Jean Chabaut. Assistants: Anne Trigaux, Emilio Pacull Latone.
Sound: Michel Berthez, Philippe Lemenuel. Mixing: Dominique Hennequin. Gaffer: Jean-Claude Gasché. Grip: Jacques Frejabue.
Editing: Véritable Silve, Colette Le Tallec, Dominique Taysse. GTC Laboratory.
Producer: Jacques Grandclaude, Création 9 information. Released by A.D.P.F.
Filmed Apr. 30–May 6, 1977.
Telecast: ORTF, June 4, 1977; RAI 3 (*Il centro Georges Pompidou*), Oct. 1, 1983, 8:30 P.M. 56'.

THEATROGRAPHY

1952 *Otello*
Opera by Arrigo Boito, after William Shakespeare.
Music: Giuseppe Verdi.
Staged by: Roberto Rossellini.
Musical direction: Gabriele Santini. Chorus: Michele Lauro.
Sets: Carlo Maria Cristini. Costumes: Casa d'arte Peruzzi Florence.
Lighting: Giovanni Marino.
With: Ramon Vinay (Otello), Renata Tebaldi (Desdemone), Gino Bechi (Iago), Piero De Palma (Cassio), Vittoria Garofalo (Emilia) Gianni Avolanti (Roderigo), Augusto Romani (Lodovico), Antonio Picillo (Montano).
Presented: Teatro San Carlo, Naples. Dec. 13, 16, 18, 21, 1952.

1953 *La gioconda*
Opera by Arrigo Boito.
Music: Amilcare Ponchielli.

Staged by: Roberto Rossellini.
Musical direction: Tullio Serafin. Chorus: Michele Lauro.
Sets: Carlo Maria Cristini. Lighting: Giovanni Marino.
With: Anna de Cavalieri (Gioconda), Fedora Barbieri (Laura Asorno), Mario Petri (Alvise Badoero), Lucia Danieli (blind woman), Giuseppe Di Stefano (Enzo Crimaldi), Ugo Savarese (Barnaba), Silvio Santarelli (Zuane), Eraldo Gaudosio (singer), Silvio Torelli (pilot), Gianni Avolanti (Isepo Barbarigo).
Presented: Arena Flegrea, Naples, July 4, 8, 12, 19, 1953.

1953 *Giovanna al rogo*
Oratorio by Paul Claudel, *Jeanne d'Arc au bûcher*. Italian version: Emidio Mucci.
Music: Arthur Honegger.
Staged by: Roberto Rossellini.
Musical direction: Gianandréa Gavazzeni. Chorus: Michele Lauro.
Sets: Carlo Maria Cristini. Lighting: Giovanni Marino.
With: Ingrid Bergman (Joan of Arc), Tullio Carminati (Friar Domenico), Augusto Romani (the giant Heurtebise), Agnese Dubbini (Madame Botti), Gianni Avolanti (ass), Gerardo Gaudisio (court envoy), Marcella Pobbe (the Virgin), Giacinto Prandelli (Procus), Florence Quartararo (Saint Magaret), Myriam Pirazzini (Saint Catherine).
Presented: Teatro San Carlo, Naples, Dec. 5, 6, 8, 11, 13, 18, 22, 1953 (with Busoni's *Turandot*).

1954 *Giovanna d'Arco al rogo* [Italian]
Oratorio by Paul Claudel.
Music: Arthur Honegger.
Staged by: Roberto Rossellini.
Musical director: Gianandrea Gavazzeni. Chorus: Vittore Veneziani.
Sets: Mario Mantivani, Nicola Benois.
With: Ingrid Bergman (Giovanna), Memo Benassi (Domenico), Carlo Badioli (Heurtebise), Ebe Ticozzi (Botti), Giuseppe Nessi (L'asino), Enzo Sordello, Dario Caselli, Enzo Feliciati, Mario Carlin, Dino Lucchetta, Alfredo Caporilli, Walter Marconi, Rodolfo Danton, Franca Duval, Giacinto Prandelli, Emma Tegani, Cloe Elmo, Michele Cazzato, Eraldo Coda, Gino del Signore, Silvana Zanolli, Enrico Campi, Carlo Fori, Giovanni Mascolo.
Presented: La Scala, Milan, Apr. 22f, 1954 (with Ravel's *Daphne et Chloë*).

1954 *Jeanne au bûcher* [French]
Oratorio by Paul Claudel, *Jeanne d'Arc au bûcher*.
Music: Arthur Honegger.
Staged by: Roberto Rossellini. Staging assistant: Jean Doat.
Musical direction: Louis Fourestier. Choeurs de René Duclos. Orchestra of the Paris Opera.
With: Ingrid Bergman (Jeanne), Vidalin (Dominique), Romegnoni (Cauchon), Guihard (Ste. Margherithe), Chabal (Ste. Catherine), Van Herk (virgin).
Presented: Paris Opéra, June 21, 23, 25, 26, 27, 28, 1954 (with Adam's *Giselle*).

1954 *Joan of Arc at the Stake* [English]
Oratorio by Paul Claudel. English version by Dennis Arundell.
Music: Arthur Honegger.

Conductor: Leighton Lucas. Chorus: John McCarthy.
Sets and lighting: Cesare Cristini. Costumes: Adriana Muoyo (from Florence).
With: Ingrid Bergman (Joan of Arc), Valentine Dyall (Brother Dominic), Robert Algar, Anthony Newlands, Audrey Nicholls, Thelma Litster, Harry Hapgood (Porcus), Kim Grant, Alfred Hallett, Norman Lumsden, Nancy Thomas, Elizabeth Cooper, Eugenie Castle (The Virgin), Richard Carey, Gabrielle Day, Leslie Kyle, Jack Leonard, Andrew MacPherson, Robert Algar, Irving Childs (The Boy). Eleanor Beam's Children. Michael Greenwood, Barry Shawzin, Cecily Plowright, Naomi Benart, John Chesowrth, Terry Gilbert, Ann Gardner, Norman Morrice, Dorothy Buttery, Alison Norwood, Norman Dixon, Ronald Verrell. Ambrosian Singers.
Presented: Stoll Theater, London, Oct. 20–Nov. 13, 1954 (with Adam's *Giselle*).

1954 *Jeanne d'Arc au bûcher* [French]
Oratorio by Paul Claudel.
Music: Arthur Honegger.
Staged by: Roberto Rossellini.
Musical direction: Pérez Simó. Conducted by César de Mendoza Lassalle. Choeurs: Luis Moreno-Palli.
With: Ingrid Bergman (Joan), Claude Etienne (Fra Dominico), Gustav Rubbel, Louis Arquier, Pierre Foret, Jean Llort, Georges Bistagne, Joseph Cortés, Armand, Massé, Albert Duverger, François Baillés, Patrick Monerot-Dumaine, Frédéric Pujula, Rose M. Carrasco; Pilar Tello, Teresa Batlle, Pilar Torres, Bartolomé Bardají, Diego Monjo, Julio Catania, Maria Teresa Girvés.
Presented: Liceo, Barcelona, Dec. 22, 1954 (with Bartók's *Blue Beard*). Broadcast Jan. 4, 1955 (with Act II of Rimsky-Korsakov's *Invisible City of Kitzes* and Act II scene 4 of Tchaikovsky's *Eugene Onegin*).

1955 *Jeanne d'Arc på bålet* [Swedish]
Oratorio by Paul Claudel. Swedish translation: Nils-Olof Franzén.
Music: Arthur Honegger.
Director: Roberto Rossellini. Assistant director: Bengt Peterson. Choreography: Julius Mengarelli.
Conductor: Stig Westerberg. Chorus: Arne Sunnegård. The Opera Choir. The Childen's Choir from the Opera Ballet School. Royal Court Orchestra.
Sets: Cesare Christini. Costumes made after sketches by Adriana Muoyo from Casa D'Arte "Firenze" (Florence).
With: Ingrid Bergman (Jeanne d'Arc), Anders Näslund (Brother Dominicus), Folke Jonsson (herald), Arne Wirén (beadle), Berit Sköld (tiger), Berit Hermansson (fox), Olle Sivall (swine), Georg Svedenbrant, Sven Nilsson (heralds), Margit Sehlmark (St. Katarina), Eva Prytz (St. Margareta), Sven-Erik Jacobsson (Master Slaga), Kerstin Meyer (Tunnmor), Erik Sundquist (clerk), Dustin Ottosson, Arne Tyrén (peasants), Nils Johansson (Perrot), Sonja Norin (child), Erik Sædén (monk), Anna-Greta Söderholm (Virgin Mary), Sven-Erik Jacobsson (priest), Anna-Greta Söderholm, Arne Ohlson, Erik Sædén (voices), Dancers: Kaj Selling (King of France), Karin Bogren (Stupidity), Elis Gustavsson (Duke of Burgundy), Rose-Marie Mengarelli (Greed), Leonardo Mengarelli (King of England), Monika Tropp (Pride), Sven-Thorsten Thuul (Death), Kerstin Dunér (Lust), Svante Lindberg (Duke of Bedford), Gunnar Randin (Jean de Lux-

embourg), Mario Mengarelli (Guillaume de Flavy), Göte Stergel (Regnault de Chartres).

Presented: Kungliga Teatern [The Opera], Stockholm, 22 performances, Feb. 17–Mar. 22, 1955 (with Debussy's *Nocturnes*).

1955 *Giovanna d'Arco al rogo* [Italian]
Oratorio by Paul Claudel.
Music: Arthur Honegger.
Staged by: Roberto Rossellini.
Conductor: Glauco Curiel. Chorus: Giulio Bertola.
With: Ingrid Bergman, Alessandro Ziliani (tenor), Emma Tegani, Claudia Carbi, Iselle Favati, Mario Ferrara, Leonardo Morreale, Rolf Tasna (Domenico), Leo Pudis, Ebe Ticozzi, Cesari Masini Sperti, Vittorio Pandano, Alfredo Artale.
Presented: Teatro Massimo, Palermo, Apr. 27, 1955 (with Monteverdi's *Il Combattimento di Tancredi e Clorinda*).

1954 *La figlia di Jorio*
Opera by Gabriele D'Annunzio.
Music: Ildebrando Pizzetti.
Staged by: Roberto Rossellini.
Musical direction: Gianandrea Gavazzeni. Chorus: Michele Lauro.
Sets: Carlo Maria Cristini. Lighting: Giovanni Marino.
With: Clara Petrella (Mila di Codro), Mirto Picchi (Aligi), Giangiacomo Guelfi (Lazaro), Elena Nicolai (Candia), Maria Luisa Malagrida (Ornella), Maria Teresa Mandalari (Favetta), Fernanda Cadoni (Splendore), Antonia Maria Canali (Teodula), Giuseppina Sauri (little old woman).
Presented: Teatro San Carlo, Naples, Dec. 4, 8, 12, 1954.

1961 *Un squardo dal ponte* (*A View from the Bridge*)
Opera by Arthur Miller. Italian version: Gerardo Guerrieri.
Music: Renzo Rossellini.
Staged by: Roberto Rossellini.
Musical direction: Oliviero De Fabritiis. Chorus: Giuseppe Conca.
Sets: Piero Zuffi. Lighting: Alessandro Drago.
With: Nicola Rossi Lemeni (Eddie Carbone), Clara Petrella (Beatrice, his wife), Gianna Galli (Catherine, his niece), Ruggero Bondino (Rodolfo), Giovanni Ciminelli (Marco, his brother), Giuseppe Valdengo (the lawyer Alfieri), John Ciavola (Louis), Nino Mazziotti (Mike), Giulio Mastrangelo (an agent), Rolando Sessi (Tony).
Presented: Teatro del Opera, Rome, Mar. 11, 15, 19, 25, 1961.

1962 *I carabinieri*
Play by Beniamino Joppolo.
Staged by: Roberto Rossellini.
Set: Renato Guttuso.
With: Pupella Maggio (mother), Orazio Orlando (Michelangelo), Elio Zanuto (Leonardo), Turi Ferro, Gastone Moschini (Carabinieri), Marzia Unbaldi (Anna).
Presented: Spoleto's "Festival of the Two Worlds," June 28, 1962.

Notes

Abbreviations for Frequently Cited Sources

Arts, **1954**. Rossellini interview with François Truffaut. "Rossellini: Je ne suis pas le père du néoréalisme, je travaille dans une solitude morale absolute, je souffre d'être méprisé et insulté de tous côtés, je suis obligé de payer moi-même mes films." *Arts*, June 16, 1954, p. 3.

Arts, **1959**. Rossellini interview with Jean Douchet. "Roberto Rossellini: Le Général escroc et héros." *Arts* 739, September 9, 1959.

Baldelli. Pio Baldelli. *Roberto Rossellini*. Rome: Samonà e Savelli, 1972.

Bergala. Alain Bergala, ed., Roberto Rossellini. *Le Cinéma révélé*. Paris: Éditions de l'Étoile/*Cahiers du Cinéma Écrits*, 1984.

Bergala *Voyage*. Alain Bergala. *Voyage en Italie de Roberto Rossellini*. Crisnée, Belgium: Editions Yellow Now, 1990.

Bergala and Narboni. Alain Bergala and Jean Narboni. *Roberto Rossellini*. Paris: Éditions de l'Étoile, 1990.

Bianco e Nero, **1952** Mario Verdone. "Colloquio sul neorealismo." *Bianco e Nero*, February 1952; English translation. "A Discussion of Neo-Realism," *Screen* 4, Winter 1973–74, pp. 69–77.

Bianco e Nero, **1964**. Rossellini interview with Adriano Aprà and G. Berengo Gardin. "Un cinema diverso per un mondo che cambia." Transcript of a conference with Centro Sperimentale di Cinematografia students, December 14, 1963, *Bianco e Nero*, February 1964; reprinted in Rossellini, *Il mio metodo*, pp. 302-27.

Blue, 1972. Rossellini interview with James Blue (Houston, 1972). In *Rossellini*, a brochure for a series presented by Joseph Papp at the Public Theater, New York, May 1–20, 1979, p. 17.

CdC **37, 1954**. Rossellini interview with Eric Rohmer (signed Maurice Schérer) and François Truffaut. "Entretien avec Roberto Rossellini." *Cahiers du Cinéma* 37, July 1954, p. 7; reprints: *Film Culture* 2, 1955; *La Politique des auteur* (Paris: Champ Libre, 1972; Andrew Sarris, ed. *Interview with Film Director* (Indianapolis: Bobbs-Merrill, 1967; *Filmkritik* 303, March 1982; Bergala.

CdC **94, 1959**. Rossellini interview with Fereydoun Hoveyda and Jacques Rivette. "Entretien avec Roberto Rossellini." *Cahiers du Cinéma* 94, April 1959; reprint: Bergala.

CdC **133, 1962**. Rossellini interview with Jean Domarchi, Jean Douchet, Fereydoun Hoveyda. "Entretien avec Roberto Rossellini." *Cahiers du Cinéma* 133, July 1962; reprint: Bergala.

CdC **145, 1963**. Interview with Fereydoun Hoveyda and Eric Rohmer. "Nouvel entretien avec Roberto Rossellini." *Cahiers du Cinéma* 145, July 1963; reprints: *Filmkritik* 303, March 1982; *La Politique des auteurs*; Bergala.

Changes, **1974**. Tag Gallagher and John Hughes. "Roberto Rossellini: 'Where are we going?'" *Changes*, April 1974.

Dix ans. Roberto Rossellini. "Dix ans de cinéma." *Cahiers du Cinéma* 50, August 1955 (I); 52, November 1955 (II); 55, January 1956 (III).

Écran, **1977**. Claire Clouzot. "Entretien." *Écran* 60, July 15, 1977, p. 44.

Faldini and Fofi. Franca Faldini and Goffredo Fofi. *L'avventurosa storia del cinema italiano racconta dai suoi protagonisti, 1935–1939*. 3 vols. Milan: Feltrinelli, 1979.

Film Culture, **1971**. Victoria Schultz. "Interview with Roberto Rossellini, February 22–25, 1971, in Houston, Texas." *Film Culture* 52, Spring 1971, p. 2.

Filmcritica **156, 1965**. Adriano Aprà and Maurizio Ponzi. "Intervista con Roberto Rossellini." *Filmcritica* 156–57, April 1965; reprints: "Sur *L'età del ferro*," *Cahiers du Cinéma* 169, August 1965 [in part]; *Screen* 14:4, Winter 1973–74; Edoardo Bruno, ed., *R.R. Roberto Rossellini* (Rome: Bulzoni, 1979); Rossellini, *Il mio metodo* and *My Method*.

Fragments. Roberto Rossellini. *Fragments d'une autobiographie*. Paris: Éditions Ramsay, 1987.

Il mio metodo. Roberto Rossellini. *Il mio metodo*. Ed. Adriano Aprà. Venice: Marsilio, 1987. Partial translation: *My Method*. New York: Marsilio, 1992.

Il Progresso, **1948**. Rossellini interview with Fernaldo Di Giammatteo. "Rossellini si difende." *Il Progresso d'Italia* (Bologna), December 9, 1948; also in *Fotogrammi*, January 4, 1949.

My Story. Ingrid Bergman and Alan Burgess, *Ingrid Bergman: My Story*. New York: Dell, 1980.

Nuestro Cine **95, 1970**. Rossellini interview with Francisco Llinás, Miguel Marías, A. Drove, "Una panorámica de la historia. *Nuestro Cine* 95, March 1970, pp. 44–60; reprint: *Screen*, Winter 1973–74, p. 97.

Rossellini (**Texas**). *Roberto Rossellini*. A book published by the Ministero del Turismo e dello Spettacolo for the Progetto multimediale del Ente Autonomo di Gestione per il Cinema: "Rossellini in Texas," October 1987. Roma: Edizioni Ente Autonomo Gestione Cinema, 1987.

Rosselliniana. Adriano Aprà. *Rosselliniana*. Roma: Di Giacomo, 1987. Includes the best bibliography available on Rossellini.

708

"Rossellini parla," 1977. "Roberto Rossellini parla di Roberto Rossellini." *Paese Sera*, June 12, 1977.

Téléciné **168**, 1971. C. J. Philippe et al., "Je sais bien que le monde moderne est plein de gens inquiets, pourquoi irais-je grossir leurs rangs?" Transcript of a television program, *L'invité du dimanche*, January 24, 1971. In *Téléciné* 168, April 1971.

Chapter 1: Fantasy

1. "Roberto Rossellini parla di Roberto Rossellini," *Paese Sera*, June 12, 1977.
2. Rossellini interview with Dacia Maraini, *E Tu Chi Eri?* (Milan: Bompiani, 1973), p. 95.
3. Quoted in Ingrid Bergman and Alan Burgess, Ingrid Bergman: My Story (New York: Dell, 1980), p. 336. But Bergman misquotes in locating Elettra's mother in Venice; she lived in Rome.
4. Rossellini interview in Pio Baldelli, *Roberto Rossellini* (Rome: Samonà e Savelli, 1972), p. 251.
5. Renzo Rossellini, *Pagine di un musicista* (Rome: Cappelli, 1963), pp. 25–26. Details of Rossellini's childhood have been drawn from this collection of essays, as well as from Renzo Rossellini's other collection, *Addio del passato* (Rome: Rizzoli, 1968), and from the author's interviews with Marcella Mariani Rossellini and other members of the family.
6. Maraini interview, p. 96.
7. Ibid.
8. Marcella Mariani Rossellini to TG.
9. Roberto Rossellini, *Fragments d'une autobiographie* (Paris: Éditions Ramsay, 1987), p. 110.
10. Ibid.
11. Camillo di Cavour, *Carteggi di Cavour: Cavour-Nigra dal 1858 al 1861* (Bologna: Zanichelli, 1929), iv:144–45; quoted in Christopher Hibbert, *Garibaldi and His Enemies* (Boston: Little, Brown, 1966), p. 328n.
12. Denis Mack Smith, *Italy: A Modern History*, revised ed. (Ann Arbor: University of Michigan Press, 1969), p. 37.
13. Uncited quotations in Walter Karp, *Buried Alive: Essays on Our Endangered Republic* (New York: Franklin Square Press, 1992), pp. 18–20.
14. *Fragments*, p. 55.
15. Renzo Rossellini, *Addio*, p. 42.
16. Ibid., pp. 86, 87.
17. Rossellini interview in Francesco Savio, *Cinecittà anni trenta* (Rome: Bulzoni, 1979), p. 962.
18. Franco Riganti to TG.
19. Victoria Schultz, "Interview with Roberto Rossellini, February 22–25, 1971, in Houston, Texas," *Film Culture* 52, Spring 1971, p. 2.
20. Maraini interview, p. 97.
21. Renzo Rossellini, *Addio*, p. 42.

Chapter 2: Youth

1. Prime Minister Orlando's words, cited in Edward R. Tannenbaum, *The Fascist Experience: Italian Society and Culture 1922–1945* (New York: Basic Books, 1972), p. 25.
2. Quoted in John M. Cammett, *Antonio Gramsci and the Origins of Italian Communism* (Stanford University Press, 1967), p. 66.
3. "Rossellini parla," 1977.
4. Benedetto Croce, *Politics and Morals*, trans. Salvatore J. Castiglione, from *Etica e morale*, 1922 et seq. (New York: Philosophical Library, 1945), p. 112.
5. Ibid., pp. 113, 125.
6. *Fragments*, p. 102.
7. Marcella Mariani Rossellini to TG.
8. *Fragments*, p. 113. Rossellini incorrectly dates his pleurisy at sixteen.
9. Ibid., p. 99.
10. Marcella Mariani Rossellini's memories of this episode are vague, and no other testimony has been found.
11. *Fragments*, p. 40.
12. Joseph Henry Steele, *Ingrid Bergman: An Intimate Portrait* (New York: David McKay, 1959), p. 163.
13. Cited by Gian Vittorio Baldi to TG.
14. Quoted in Mira Liehm, *Passion and Defiance: Film in Italy from 1942 to the Present* (Berkeley and Los Angeles: University of California Press, 1984), p. 4.
15. Renzo De Felice, *Intervista sul fascismo* (Rome: Laterza, 1982), pp. 40–42.
16. Ibid., pp. 101–02.
17. Max Gallo, *Mussolini's Italy: Twenty Years of the Fascist Era* (New York: Macmillan, 1973), p. 219.
18. Quoted in Adrian Lyttelton, *The Seizure of Power: Fascism in Italy 1919–1929* (New York: Charles Scribner's Sons, 1973), p. 362.
19. Gallo, *Mussolini's Italy*, p. 220.
20. Alexis de Tocqueville, *Democracy in America*, vol. 1, part II, chapter 7.
21. Karp, *Buried Alive*, pp. 149–50.

22. Cf. William Manchester, *The Glory and the Dream* (Boston: Little, Brown, 1974), pp. 80–81; Michael Parenti, *Inventing Reality* (New York: St. Martin's Press, 1986), pp. 114–15; also, the film *Gabriel Over the White House* (La Cava, 1933).

23. De Felice, *Intervista*, p. 33.

24. Tannenbaum, *Fascist Experience*, p. 140.

25. Thomas M. Pryor, "The Personal History of Roberto Rossellini," *New York Times*, January 23, 1949. The full text is "traveling about Europe," but I have not found any person or writing to confirm that Rossellini, aside from two brief excursions to Savoy and Nice, travelled outside of Italy before 1946. And there are far too many instances of inaccurate—or misquoted or mistranslated—statements from Rossellini to accept this single quotation as evidence to the contrary. The same interview, for example, quotes him as saying that his father was a "leading architect." Rossellini would not have said this (in Italian interviews he always describes him as a *costruttore*—a contractor), but neither would he have bothered to correct it. Even to travel around Italy, however, was uncommon for Italians until after World War II; thus the *sense* of Rossellini's statement is accurate.

26. *Fragments*, p. 99.

27. Eugenio Silenzi to TG, April 1985.

28. Maraini interview, p. 97.

29. Franco Riganti to TG.

30. Ibid.

31. Quoted by Gian Vittorio Baldi to TG.

32. Cited by Marcella Mariani Rossellini to TG.

33. Cited by Fereydoun Hoveyda to TG.

34. Renzo Rossellini, *Pagine*, p. 104.

35. Quoted by Gian Vittorio Baldi to TG.

36. *Fragments*, p. 101.

37. "Rossellini parla," 1977.

38. Quoted in Tannenbaum, *Fascist Experience*, p. 258.

39. Notably while researching *Cartesius*. The fact that Rossellini has seldom been recorded mentioning Croce is probably due simply to the fact that no one else brought him up. Croce was already out of fashion by the late 1930s and almost taboo by 1970. At the beginning of the century, his attacks on Marxism on the one hand and the pedestrian ideas of the ruling class on the other, had marked him as the leader of the new liberalism. Such was his prestige that Mussolini tolerated the persistent opposition of his journal, *La Critica*. After the war seemed too tied to the discredited past to be accepted in the role he sought to play—as a rallying symbol for the fresh start of a brave new world.

    Croce, for his part, never mentioned film, with the sole (?) exception of a letter to *Bianco e Nero* in December 1948 correcting a claim by Emilio Cecchi that he thought of cinema as a "fusion of drama or narrative and visual images." To the contrary, he insisted, "distinctions between the arts, poetry, music, painting, and so on, are useful for classification, and for consideration of artworks from abroad, but are irrelevant to the basic reality that each work has its own physiognomy and that they all have the same nature, because they're all equally poetry, or if one prefers, they're all music, or all painting, and so on. So, a film, if felt and judged beautiful, has full rights." In theater, he added, "diction and mime and scenery are all one in a representation, both from a single act of aesthetic creation, in which they can't be distinguished separately because they are that very act. Nor is the art of the actor, as people are wont to say, 'interpretation' of the literary text (beautiful 'interpretation,' that robs us of the intimate vision and penetration and enjoyment of a poem read just between ourselves!). If anything, it's not interpretation but 'translation' of the text, and, as such, a 'variation' and, if it's good, a new work of art, just as a picture can be that is 'inspired' (as they say) by a poem, that is, a translation with canvas and brush."

40. Roger MacNiven, citing remarks to students at Yale University, c. 1974.

41. Croce, quoted in Gian N. G. Orsini, *Benedetto Croce: Philosopher of Art and Literary Critic* (Carbondale: Southern Illinois University Press, 1961), p. 77.

42. Croce, *Teoria e storia della storiografia* (Bari: Laterza, 1917), p. 119; quoted in R. G. Collingwood, *The Idea of History* (London: Oxford University Press, 1946), p. 199.

43. Very similar notions of *ricorso* are developed by Herbert Read in his *Icon and Idea* (New York: Schocken Books, 1965), in which he maintains that the image always precedes the idea in the development of human consciousness, and that art is the essential instrument in the development of human consciousness: "It is, in a positive sense, the principle underlying the thesis of these lectures: what has not first been created by the artist, is unthinkable by the philosopher" (p. 70).

44. Isabella Rossellini to TG.

45. Quoted in H. Stuart Hughes, *Consciousness and Society: The Reorientation of European Social Thought 1890–1930* (New York: Knopf, 1958), pp. 428–29.

46. In G. Menon, ed., *Dibattito su Rossellini* (Rome: Partisan Edizioni, 1972), pp. 76, 80.

47. Among other Rossellini buildings are the villa of the Prince of Lucedio in Villa Glori and the Banca Commerciale in Via del Corso.

48. Pryor, "Personal History."

49. The fact that Rome's Archivio Centrale del Stato contains no reference to Giuseppe Rossellini suggests that the police were not conducting an investigation of him.

50. Marcella Mariani Rossellini to TG.

51. Giuseppe Pagano, a modernist, was the era's architectural genius. He contributed to Rome University, Casa del Fascio, Sabaudia, and the Florence railway station. Piacentini's "imperial" style, heavy with

arches and monumental in scope, was more reactionary. His chief works were after Giuseppe Rossellini's death and included the Foro Italico, the Stadium of the Marble Statues, and other parts of EUR.
52. Marcella Mariani Rossellini to TG.
53. Ingrid Rossellini to TG.

Chapter 3: Passing Time

1. Franco Riganti to TG.
2. *Fragments*, p. 116.
3. Tag Gallagher and John Hughes, "Roberto Rossellini: 'Where are we going?'" *Changes*, April 1974.
4. Francis Koval, "Interview with Rossellini," *Sight and Sound*, February 1951, p. 393.
5. Fereydoun Hoveyda to TG. Hoveyda was a critic for *Cahiers du Cinéma*, served as Iran's representative to UNESCO and later as ambassador to the U.N.
6. F. Tranchant and J.-M. Vérité, "Rossellini 59: Le pays des hommes-drapés vu par un homme cousu," *Cinéma 59*, no. 36, May 1959, p. 50.
7. Koval, "Interview," 1951.
8. Baldelli, p. 253.
9. Gilbert Seldes, "A Fine American Movie," *The New Republic*, March 7, 1928, pp. 98–99; reprinted in George C. Pratt, *Spellbound in Darkness* (Greenwich, CT: New York Graphic Society Ltd., 1973), pp. 469–71.
10. François Truffaut, *The Films in My Life* (New York: Simon & Schuster, 1978), p. 277. Jean-Pierre Aumont, *Sun and Shadow* (New York: Norton, 1977), p. 32.
11. Noris's second release was La signorina dell'autobus ("The girl on the bus," directed by Nunzio Malasomma), shot at Caesar Film in 1932 or 1933 in both an Italian and a French version, *Eve cherche un père* ("Eve looks for a father," Mario Bonnard). Noris was in both versions; Aumont in only the latter.
12. Quoted in Franca Faldini and Goffredo Fofi, *L'avventurosa storia del cinema italiano raccontata dai suoi protagonisti, 1935–1939*, 3 vols. (Milan: Feltrinelli, 1979), I:13, I:12; from an interview with Ornella Ripa, *L'Europeo*, 1969.
13. Marcella De Marchis Rossellini, *Un matrimonio riuscito. Autobiografia* (Milan: Castoro, 1996), p. 86.
14. Ibid.
15. Lina Rossellini, who was there, to TG.
16. Ibid.
17. Savio, *Cinecittà*, p. 964.
18. Baldelli, p. 253.
19. Savio, *Cinecittà*, p. 964.
20. Ibid.
21. Eugenio Silenzi to TG.
22. Quoted by Ettore G. Mattia, "Rossellini «Anno Zero»" in Edoardo Bruno, ed., *Roberto Rossellini: il cinema, la televisione, la storia, la critica, dagli atti del Convegno* (Città del Sanremo, 1980), p. 189.
23. Enrico Fulchignoni to TG, May 1984; an opinion seconded by many others.
24. Franco Riganti to TG.
25. Enrico Fulchignoni, "Préface," in Michel Serceau, *Roberto Rossellini* (Paris: Editions du Cerf, 1986), pp. 7–9.
    Enrico Fulchignoni (1913–1988) was a Sicilian, with degrees in medicine and psychology. He had introduced new works by Wilder and Saroyan while directing theater; taught mass communication at the University of Rome and direction at the Centro Sperimentale (where his students included Antonioni, De Santis, and Alida Valli); and filmed *I due Foscari* (1942). After the war he headed the Film Section at UNESCO in Paris, where he promoted Third World cinema.
26. Lina Rossellini to TG.
27. Renzo Rossellini, *Addio*, p. 34.
28. Marcella De Marchis, "La mia vita con Roberto," *L'Europeo*, November 24, 1957, p. 12. In *Un matrimonio*, forty years later, De Marchis gives Rossellini's weight as about 175.
29. De Marchis, "La mia vita," p. 12.
30. Ibid. In *Un matrimonio*, De Marchis writes that Vevi's husband was her witness.
31. Ibid.
32. Ibid., p. 13.

Chapter 4: Finally Working

1. De Marchis, "La mia vita," p. 13.
2. Franco Riganti to TG.
3. Savio, *Cinecittà*, p. 815.
4. Prior to 1934, when a combination of social and industrial forces effectively banned contemporary and controversial material, American films were frequently forthright and critical. Hollywood adopted stringent codes to avoid having to deal separately with myriad local censorship policies, thus accepting the guidelines of the more rigid communities. Even so, many southern exhibitors routinely spliced out *any* shots of black people. Five major and three minor American companies virtually monopolized

distribution of film; their distribution circuits and theater chains had fallen under the control of Morgan and Rockefeller interests.

5. Cesare Pavese, *The Burning Brand: Diaries, 1935–1950* (New York: Walker, 1961), p. 320.

6. Vittorio Mussolini, *Vita con mio padre* (Milan: Mondadori, 1957), pp. 91–92, 41, 37.

7. Franco Riganti to TG.

8. Dario Zanelli, "Quando Vittorio Mussolini dirigeva 'Cinema,'" in Mariella Furno and Renzo Renzi, *Il neorealismo nel fascismo: Giuseppe De Santis e la critica cinematografica 1941–1943* (Bologna: Edizioni della Tipografia Compositori, 1984), p. 105.

9. Ibid., p. 107.

10. Mino Argentieri, in Giorgio Tinazzi, ed., *Il cinema italiano dal fascismo all'antifascismo* (Padua: Marsilio, 1966), p. 70; Tannenbaum, *Fascist Experience*, p. 236.

11. "The point about *Lancer*," its American director declared, "was that in India 400 million people were controlled by 40,000. They were kept in line by discipline. The discipline wasn't in beating down the natives, but in being very disciplined among themselves so that the natives watching it thought: 'Holy Jesus! If they punish themselves so harshly, what will they do to us!'" (Henry Hathaway, interviewed in John Kobal, *People Will Talk* [New York: Knopf, 1985], p. 619.)

12. Cf. Noam Chomsky, *Turning the Tide* (Boston: South End, 1985), p. 88.

13. "Abyssinia," *Encyclopædia Britannica*, 1957, vol. I, p. 78.

14. Quoted by Tannenbaum, *Fascist Experience*, p. 173, from a citation in Marcello Luchetti, *Educazione civica internazionale* (Rome: Unione Scolastica Internazionale, 1965), p. 99. Actually, the trade sanctions were a farce: oil and coal, without which the war could not have been waged, could still be sold, while some countries, including the United States, Germany, and Russia, refused to adopt any sanctions and continued to supply Italy with whatever she needed.

15. Patrizia Carrano, *La Magnani* (Milan: Rizzoli, 1982), p. 47. Magnani was spiteful at the time she recounted this anecdote. It's hard to imagine Roberto being doggy, no matter how hard he was trying to make a favorable impression.

16. "Anti-semitism, a movement begun at first quietly and unenthusiastically, became more active and open due to the usual zealots. As in many other things, Italians have an elevated sense of proportion and the anti-semitic campaign fortunately led to no tragedy and almost always remained simply an official point of view. I myself, out of non-conformism, took part with my Jewish friend, Orlando Piperno Alcorso, in Italy's most important automobile race, the 'Mille Miglia', with a Fiat 1100, coming in tenth at an average speed of over 103 kph [64 mph]. One evening, though, I asked my father, who told me: 'The Jewish problem has not been invented by us, and when it comes to racism the Jews can give us points. It's much easier for an Aryan man to marry a Jewish woman than vice-versa. I've received the head of the Zionist movement, Chaim Weizmann, three times, and told him I've nothing against creation of a Jewish state in Palestine, as long as it wasn't tied to England. Other times I accepted his request to allow Jews expelled from Germany to stay in Italy. In exchange, linked as he was with the Anglo-American trust, he made secret information available to the Italian Government that was useful for our war industry and agriculture. I'm presently examining a project to create large colonies in Ethiopia, where the Jews would find much greater resources than in Palestine. But I don't hide from you that the collusion of the Jewish world with the plutocracy and the international left, and our politico-military position, do not permit us to keep within our breast eventual saboteurs of the effort the Italian people are engaged in. On the other hand, it's not a serious problem: there are no more than 50,000 Jews in Italy and not a hair will be touched on any of them.' Just the same, toward the end of the year, I advised my friend to take a trip abroad. He followed my advice and he is in Australia today, quite well situated." (V. Mussolini, *Vita*, pp. 92–93.)

   Many Italian Jews did suffer, however. A Colonel Segre was conducting training exercises in Vercelli when an envelope came dismissing him from the army. He called his troops together and, astride his horse before them, shot himself. Mussolini's persecution did not take the form of concentration camps and extermination, but of excluding Jews from national life and encouraging their emigration—with many exceptions for distinguished individuals. His notion, alluded to above, that Jewish Italians constituted a potential fifth column was based on their disproportionate participation in anti-Fascist groups. His precautions against them, however, were infinitely more lenient than those taken against 300,000 Japanese Americans in the United States. Despite German pressure, Mussolini stubbornly protected any Jew, Italian or not, on Italian territory and kept Italy's borders open to Jews fleeing the Nazis. The Duce's fall, in July 1943, was a disaster for Jews in Italy. A list of Jewish Italians had been compiled, and during the Occupation, the Germans used Fascist records to locate and execute about 7,500 Jews. From September 1943 until the end of the war, the Fascists in Mussolini's puppet Italian Socialist Republic enthusiastically persecuted Jews.

17. Quoted in Denis Mack Smith, *Mussolini's Roman Empire* (New York: Viking, 1976), p. 75; from Vittorio Mussolini, *Voli sulle ambe* (Florence, 1937), p. 150.

18. Faldini and Fofi, I:45.

19. Ibid., I:45; from *Filmcritica*, no. 5, May 1951.

20. Faldini and Fofi, I:59.

21. Franco Riganti to TG.

22. Ibid. This entire account derives from Riganti.

23. Massimo Mida, *Roberto Rossellini*, 1st ed. (Rome: Guanda, 1953), p. 40; probably on Rossellini's authority. The claim is absent from the book's second edition. The Fascist censors virtually never suppressed an entire film; at worst they would demand changes. Riganti is certain the picture was never completed, although Marcella Mariani Rossellini remembers seeing it with a music track, and Roberto had managed to get a publicity photo published for it in 1935 or '36.

24. Quoted in Liehm, *Passion*, p. 4; from *Corriere padano*, October 26, 1938.
25. De Marchis, "La mia vita," p. 13.
26. Franco Riganti to TG, adding that the figure may not be correctly remembered. In comparison, the following year Vittorio De Sica was paid 20,680 lire for both directing and starring in *Teresa Venerdi*.
27. Franco Riganti to TG.
28. Baldelli, p. 251. Cf. *Film Culture*, 1971: "I was considered a young boy of ideas, but dangerous."
29. Vittorio Mussolini to TG, June 28, 1987.
30. See the very detailed treatment of this film in Stefano Roncoroni, "Il 'primo Rossellini,'" in Bruno, ed., *Rossellini* (Sanremo), pp. 54–56.
31. Mario Verdone, "Colloquio sul neorealismo," *Bianco e Nero*, February 1952; English translation, "A Discussion of Neo-Realism," *Screen* 4, Winter 1973–74, pp. 69–77.
32. Unpublished Ferrara interview with Adriano Aprà, May 5, 1987; TG's collection. In a telephone interview with TG, October 25, 1992, Massimo Ferrara referred to this film as *Il pesce a congresso*. No other record of either title exists. Undoubtedly the film was *Il ruscello*.
33. Marcella De Marchis to TG, for the figure of 5,000 lire a month. Ferrara to Adriano Aprà that his salary was 2,000 lire a month. Rossellini, in "Voglono tentare il colpo del '40," *L'Espresso*, February 1956, p. 9, says his contract was for 50,000 per month.
34. The first four titles are cited in Salvatore Ambrosino and Paolo Lugli, "Relazione a Pesaro, 1988," an unpublished research into *La nave bianca*'s production. Franco Riganti mentioned *Il brutto idraulico* to TG as a film he dimly recalled Rossellini having made.
35. Quoted by Gianni Rondolino, "Fattori degli animali," *La Stampa*, November 17, 1996.
36. Ferrara interview with Aprà.
37. Ibid. Ferrara stated that Scalera distributed *La perfida Albione* in 1940 or 1941 (Carlo Carlini also recalled seeing it at Scalera) but the print of *Il tacchino prepotente* discovered in 1996 by the Archivo Nazionale Cinematografico della resistenza in Turin lacks a Scalera logo. *La vispa Teresa* has a Scalera logo but Ferrara stated it was not distributed by Scalera. For a detailed découpage of both discovered prints: Marta Teodoro, ed., "Perduti e ritrovati. Due cortometraggi di Rossellini, *La vispa Teresa* e *Il tacchino prepotente*," *La Nuovo Spettatore 1* (Franco Angeli: Archivio Nazionale Cinematografico delle resistenze: Turin, 1997), pp. 116–44.
38. Franco Riganti to TG.
39. Rossellini to Gian Vittorio Baldi to TG.
40. June 20, 1941.

Chapter 5: The War Trilogy

1. V. Mussolini, *Vita*, p. 64.
2. Benedetto Croce, *Ultimi saggi* (Bari: Laterza, 1937), p. 37; quoted in Orsini, *Benedetto Croce*, p. 279.
3. Gian Vittorio Baldi to TG.
4. Augusto Turati, Fascist party secretary, 1927, in Gallo, *Mussolini's Italy*, p. 218.
5. Ibid.
6. "Cinque lettere a uno studente," *Nuovi Argomenti* 20 (1953), quoted in Simone Pétrement, *Simone Weil: A Life* (New York: Schocken, 1976), p. 306.
7. Gallo, *Mussolini's Italy*, p. 219.
8. *New Yorker*, February 19, 1949, p. 25.
9. Rossellini interview with Francisco Llinás, Miguel Marías, A. Drove, "Un panorámica de la historia," *Nuestro Cine*, 95, March 1970, pp. 44–60; reprint: *Screen*, Winter 1973–74, p. 97.
10. Simone Weil, "Lettre à Georges Bernanos" (1938), *Ecrits historiques et politiques* (Paris: Gallimard, 1960), pp. 220–24. Cf. "Letter to Georges Bernanos" (1938) in George A. Panichas, ed., *The Simone Weil Reader* (New York: McKay, 1977), pp. 74–77.
11. Anthony Sampson, *The Seven Sisters* (New York: Bantam, 1976), pp. 94–99. Sampson writes that it was to overcome adverse publicity from its assistance to the Nazi war effort even after the fall of France that Texaco began sponsoring the Metropolitan Opera Broadcasts.
12. *The Ciano Diaries 1939–1943*, ed. Hugh Gibson (New York: Doubleday, 1946), August 11, 13, 18, 26, 1939, pp. 119, 120, 123, 129.
13. Rachele Mussolini, *Mussolini* (New York: Morrow, 1974), p. 183.
14. Vittorio Mussolini to TG.
15. *Ciano Diaries*, March 5, 1940, p. 216.
16. Ibid., July 27, 1940, p. 279.
17. Hitler told Leni Riefenstahl on March 30, 1944: "Italy's entry into the war has been nothing but a disaster for us. If the Italians hadn't attacked Greece and needed our help, the war would have taken a different course. We could have anticipated the Russian cold by weeks and conquered Leningrad and Moscow. There would then have been no Stalingrad." Leni Riefenstahl, *A Memoir* (New York: St. Martin's Press, 1993), p. 295.
18. *Ciano Diaries*, November 10, 1941, p. 404.
19. Ibid., January 23, 1941, p. 340.
20. Ibid., November 12, 1942, p. 490.
21. Croce, *Teoria e storia*, p. 119; quoted in Collingwood, *Idea of History*, p. 199.
22. Cited by Adriano Aprà to TG.

23. *Fragments*, p. 104.
24. Rossellini to Fereydoun Hoveyda to TG. Hoveyda says Rossellini told him he cheered the proclamation of Empire. Marcella Mariani Rossellini denies he would have done so.
25. Faldini and Fofi, I:59.
26. Quoted in Jean George Auriol, "Entretiens romains sur la situation et la disposition du cinéma italien," *La Revue du Cinéma*, no. 13, May 1948, p. 60.
27. Ambrosino and Lugli, op. cit.
28. In *Cinema* (Milan), no. 7, January 30, 1949.
29. Massimo Ferrara to TG, October 25, 1992.
30. Ferrara interview with Aprà.
31. Massimo Ferrara to TG.
32. Faldini and Fofi, I:59.
33. Ferrara interview with Aprà.
34. Ambrosino and Lugli, op. cit.
35. Assessorato alla cultura del comune di Roma, *La città del cinema*. (Napeoleone: Roma, 1979), p. 84.
36. Franceso De Robertis, "Libertas, Unitas, Caritas," *Cinema*, January 30, 1949, p. 212.
37. *Nuestro Cine* 95, 1970.
38. Savio, *Cinecittà*, p. 962.
39. Franco Magli, one of Rossellini's crew, at the time of *Era notte a Roma* (1961), said: "This film is important from an artistic point of view, it's a revolution. Rossellini made one before when he shot *La nave bianca* with De Robertis. I worked on it too. Then he had shot so many short shots, all chopped up. Tack, tack, tack. We'd say, 'But won't it be annoying?' Yet it wasn't. The public liked it. Why? Because of what we used to call rhythm. Rhythm! In sum, you know, the beginnings of neo-realism. Today, though, it's just the opposite. Rossellini shoots very long shots, goes forward and back, delicately, following the action." (Quoted in Renzo Renzi, ed., *Era notte a Roma* [Bologna: Capelli, 1960], p. 36.) Rossellini would use a slower tack-tack montage in his next picture, *Un pilota ritorna*.
40. "I was struck by . . . the dogs on the deck in *La nave bianca*, or the flower hooked by the sailor." ("Rossellini parla," 1977.)
41. "People didn't like it. Some officials didn't either and my name was taken off of it. It was released anonymously," Rossellini told Pryor, "Personal History." Cf., also, *Fragments*, p. 117.
42. Marcella De Marchis to TG.
43. Quoted, without citation, in Mattia, "Rossellini anno zero," p. 190.
44. Mida, *Rossellini*, 1st ed., p. 13.
45. G. Isani, *Cinema*, no. 127, October 10, 1941. Emphasis added.
46. ". . . which is the opposite of the neo-realist method," he added. *Cinema* (Milan), no. 7, January 30, 1949.
47. Faldini and Fofi, I:58.
48. Mida, *Rossellini*, 1st ed., p. 13. The analysis that follows is TG's, not Mida's.
49. Enrico Fulchignoni, in *Bianco e Nero*, October 1941, p. 4.
50. This argument, almost identically, is put forward by Baldelli and Guarner. Less specifically, *La nave bianca*, *L'uomo dalla croce*, and *Un pilota ritorna* are classed as propaganda by Freddi, Luchino Visconti, and *Positif* magazine. In opposition to that classification, more or less strongly, are not only phenomenological Catholics like Brunello Rondi and Amédée Ayfre but also, in an odd alliance, the Communists from *Cinema* (Mida and De Santis) and the Communist daily, *L'Unità*—although on more general grounds than the interpretation offered here. Jacques Demeure ("Un débutant méconnu," *Positif* 198, October 1977, p. 36) endorses an analysis by Maria-Antonietta Macciocchi (*Eléments pour une analyze du fascisme*, Paris: Collection 10/18, 1976) characterizing, as do several other critics, the heroine as an ideal Fascist woman—sister, nurse, mother, teacher, asexual—a description, however, that would fit innumerable women in American and British films of the war period. Besides, she's not asexual.
51. Rossellini interview with Eric Rohmer (signed Maurice Schérer) and François Truffaut, "Entretien avec Roberto Rossellini," *Cahiers du Cinéma* 37, July 1954, p. 3.
52. Savio, *Cinecittà*, p. 963.
53. *Bianco e Nero*, 1952.
54. "Sens et non-sens de la Passion dans l'universe de Rossellini," in Michel Estève, ed., *La Passion du Christ comme thème cinématographique* (Paris: *Études Cinématographiques* 10–11, Autumn 1961), p. 171; reprint: Ayfre, *Conversion aux images?* (Paris: Éditions du Cerf, 1964). The references are to Sartre's *No Exit* and Rossellini's 1946 *Una voce umana*.
55. Brunello Rondi, "Realtà della persona nell'opera di Rossellini," *Cronache del cinema e della televisione*, 8–9, January–February, 1956, pp. 12–14; reprinted in Rondi, *Cinema e realtà* (Rome: Editori Cinque Lune, 1957), pp. 139–49.
56. Mida, *Rossellini*, 1st ed., p. 15.
57. "Rossellini parla," 1977.
58. *Fragments*, pp. 116–17.
59. V. Mussolini, *Vita*, pp. 141–42.
60. Although Rossellini's assignment was announced in *Cinema* 122, July 25, 1941, it seems improbable that he was assured of the job at this time, for the problems of beginning production in October would not have arisen. Riganti states that the assignment was won as a result of *La nave bianca*, which was still being edited in August, and that Rossellini's professional competence and political suitability had been questioned. On the other hand, delay was mandated by a nationwide talent contest, which did not end until September 1, that ACI had announced that summer to cast the aviator roles.
61. Franco Riganti to TG.

62. Ibid. Riganti estimates the film's final cost as between two-and-a-half and three million lire. The production's official accounts survive (in Riganti's possession), but are completely fictitious; there the cost is stated as L. 6,423,704 and Rossellini's remuneration as L. 60,000 for directing, L. 21,000 for editing, plus a portion of the script money. What Rossellini actually received can be guessed from the fact that Vittorio De Sica, a big popular star at the box office, received L. 20,680 for both directing and starring in ACI's *Teresa Venerdì* the same year. Vittorio Mussolini, by comparison, is listed as receiving L. 50,000 for the subject and L. 100,000 for his supervision. In reality he took only L. 5,000 a month from ACI as expenses. He never received money from his father.

63. Savio, *Cinecittà*, p. 605.

64. Franco Riganti to TG.

65. Faldini and Fofi, I:59.

66. Colloquium with Centro Sperimentale students, in *Bianco e Nero*, July 1958; quoted in Pierre Leprohon, *Michelangelo Antonioni* (Paris: Seghers, 1961; English ed., New York: Simon & Schuster, 1963), p. 17.

67. Massimo Mida, "Un film tra Rossellini e il figlio del duce," *Cinema Sessanta*, March 1988, p. 10.

68. Faldini and Fofi, I:59.

69. In Zanelli, "Quando Vittorio Mussolini dirigeva," p. 105.

70. Mida, "Un film tra Rossellini," p. 10.

71. Aldo Scagnetti, "Testimonianza," in Giorgio Tinazzi, ed., *Il cinema italiano dal fascismo all'antifascismo* (Padua: Marsilio, 1966), pp. 115–18.

72. Vittorio Mussolini to TG.

73. Ibid.

74. According to *Cinema*, June 10, 1940, Renoir shot six weeks, all exteriors, of *Tosca*. In fact he shot interiors as well.

75. V. Mussolini, *Vita*, pp. 91–92.

76. Cf. Célia Bertin, *Jean Renoir* (Paris: Librairie Académique Perrin, 1986).

77. "Rossellini parla," 1977.

78. Bertin, *Renoir*, p. 260, writes that Rossellini was "among the group around Visconti" and thus met Renoir at this time. But she is not to be trusted, for besides making Rossellini an acolyte of the cousin-in-law he disliked, she makes no mention of Vittorio Mussolini and claims it was Benito who invited Renoir to direct *Tosca*. Renoir himself wrote in *Arts*, June 16, 1954, that when he first saw Rossellini he tried to connect his physical appearance with *Roma città aperta* and *Paisà*, which would place their first encounter after the war.

79. Massimo Mida to TG, 1982.

80. Savio, *Cinecittà*, p. 605.

81. Faldini and Fofi, I:59.

82. Savio, *Cinecittà*, p. 962.

83. Franco Riganti to TG.

84. Marcella Mariani Rossellini to TG.

85. My willingness to accept Riganti's story as at least possible has led to suspicions in the Rossellini family that I am trying to prove that Roberto was a Fascist. Patently this is not the case, unless one equates having a card with being a Fascist, which is a notion that few in Italy entertained at the time and which, from today's perspective, is a slap in the faces of the millions who for reasons of family, profession, survival, or (as among the would-be partisans) political commitment took cards—but no more considered themselves Fascists than did Americans who paid taxes during the Vietnam War. Riganti's seriousness and veracity have been testified to by all who knew him whom I could locate, including several Communists and Roberto's son Renzo ("If Uncle Franco said it, it must be true"—although Renzo subsequently aligned himself with his aunt and mother). An inquiry to Renzo De Felice, probably the most respected expert on Fascist life, yielded the opinion that it is extremely unlikely that Rossellini could have managed not to have a card. De Marchis and Marcella Mariani Rossellini, on Roberto's authority, contend that he was protected, and excused from the necessity of having a card, by Vittorio Mussolini; in their opinion, accepting such recognition of the dignity of one's beliefs from the Duce's son was less compromising than enrolling, even *pro forma* as everyone else did, in the Party. Vittorio Mussolini, however, denies that he took any such interest in Roberto's affairs, gave him any protection, or was any more able to exempt someone from having a Party card than Amy Carter was able to exempt someone from paying taxes.

   In her 1996 autobiography, Marcella De Marchis wrote: "Roberto was never considered one of their own by the Fascists. The fact of never having taken the card of the sole party always created a lot of problems and prejudice for him. Roberto was never stipended by the regime, as were, in practice, other film people. So he always had to be clever and he always had to struggle for each new job. Vittorio Mussolini had the possibility of getting work for people independently of their belonging or not to the Fascist Party. . . . When Fascism fell many ex-members of the party began, partly to prove their innocence, to name people who had been with them. One of these was the producer Franco Riganti who had worked with Roberto. Franco was certainly Fascist and linked to the regime. After Roberto's death, in a pair of interviews, he declared that he had gotten him a Fascist Party card so that he could find work. This is how the business of connections between Roberto and the regime was born." (*Un matrimonio*, p. 29.)

86. Quoted in Luigi Barzini, *The Italians* (New York: Atheneum, 1965), p. 112.

87. Luigi Barzini, *Memories of Mistresses* (New York: Macmillan, 1986), p. 19.

88. Pryor, "Personal History."

89. Savio, *Cinecittà*, p. 963.

90. "Jean Rouch su Rossellini," in Gian Luigi Rondi, *Il cinema dei Maestri* (Milan: Rusconi, 1980), p. 31.

91. The English treat Girotti as a professional colleague and accept his initial attempt to escape as good sportsmanship. Later, during the retreat, the British commander's reply to the Italian doctor that he can't concern himself with alleviating the sufferings of the sick and wounded because he is busy trying to "create a desert" in front of the enemy, seems factual rather than brutal or callous (in contrast to the way the English are depicted in the "Florence" episode of *Paisà*). Toward the end, however, a newspaper headline mentions the British are retreating along with their "civilian hostages"; this seems the only anti-British thing in the movie.

92. Letter from Franco Riganti to TG, July 20, 1986.

93. A twenty-page treatment in 87 sequences, probably written by Rosario Leone, a Fascist, was published pro-forma on June 30, 1941 (*Un pilota ritorna* [*Ritorno alla base*], Rome: A.C.I.-Europa Film) in order to deposit it at the Ufficio della Proprietà Intellettuale (the copyright office) and obtain a nulla osta before work began.

94. Vittorio Mussolini to TG.

95. Franco Riganti to TG; confirmed, certainly, by the fact that the existent dialogue goes against the currents of Fascist rhetoric. The dialogues were dubbed but, even in the cases of Girotti and Belmonte, not by the actors one sees—a fairly common practice in Italian films.

96. Ibid.

97. Vittorio Mussolini to TG.

98. Guido Piovene, April 18, 1942; quoted in Savio, *Ma l'amore no* (Milan: Sonzogno, 1975), p. 270.

99. *Cinema 140*, April 25, 1942; reprint: Massimo Mida and Lorenzo Quaglietti, eds., *Dai telefoni bianchi al neorealismo* (Rome: Laterza, 1980), pp. 257–60.

100. Franco Riganti to TG. Also, in the film's accounts, Rossellini is the only one paid for editing.

101. Faldini and Fofi, I:59.

102. De Marchis, "La mia vita," p. 14.

103. Faldini and Fofi, I:59.

104. Giuseppe De Santis, "L'uomo dalla croce," *Cinema 168*, June 25, 1943; reprint: Mida and Quaglietti, *Dai telefoni bianchi,* p. 266.

105. Ursula Werber to TG.

106. Adriano Baracco, "Cinque minuti con . . . Roberto Rossellini," *Film Quotidiano,* September 7, 1942.

107. Savio, *Cinecittà,* pp. 964–65.

108. Opinion attributed in program notes for a Rossellini retrospective organized by the Cineteca Nazionale and Istituto Luce at the Sala del Planetario, Rome, December 12, 1970–January 16, 1971.

109. *Ciano Diaries,* May 27, 1942, p. 420.

110. Marcella De Marchis to TG.

111. This movie began shooting (but not with Roberto) as *Gli ultimi Taureg* or *I cavalieri del deserto* in the Libyan desert twenty kilometers outside Tripoli and encountered bombardments from the U.S. forces that landed in November 1942. Fellini had been sent to Libya by Riganti, and in January 1943 was forced to make a long perilous flight back to Rome through Sicily.

112. Franco Riganti to TG.

113. These two ideas derive from Roncoroni, "Primo Rossellini," p. 60.

114. Mira Liehm (*Passion,* p. 49) sees the priest's death as a repudiation of Fascism: the most heroic deed he can accomplish is to die for others; God is the only hope in a lost war and the moment of death. This is an ingenuous reading, based on an ogre-ish notion that Fascists were unreligious and unappreciative of sacrifice. Besides, the priest does not choose to die nor does he know the war is lost. He dies during victory, as Italian cavalry charge stirringly in the midst of streaming light and epiphanic music.

115. *CdC* 37, 1954.

116. De Santis, "L'uomo," pp. 263–65.

117. *Ciano Diaries,* December 13, 1941, p. 418.

118. "Schermi sonori: al fratello," *Cinema 158*, January 25, 1943, p. 62.

119. Pryor, "Personal History."

120. Vernon Jarrat, *The Italian Cinema* (London: Falcon Press, 1951), p. 59.

121. Rossellini, "Tentano il colpo del '40," open letter to Giuseppe Brusasca, Undersecretary of Spectacle, *L'Espresso,* February 3, 1956.

122. Savio, *Cinecittà,* p. 965.

123. *Fragments,* p. 118.

124. Franco Riganti to TG.

Chapter 6: World War II Comes Home

1. Faldini and Fofi, I:69.

2. Ibid., I:48.

3. Quoted in Mattia, "Rossellini Anno Zero," p. 190.

4. "For Whom Do We Write?" *La nuova Europa,* December 10, 1944; translated in David Overbey, ed., *Springtime in Italy: A Reader on Neo-Realism* (London: Talisman Books, 1978), p. 35.

5. Antonioni, for one, saw through this charade, and said aloud what others really thought—that the "people" preferred what was mediocre, tasteless, and pleasant and were oblivious to film language and

art. He proposed replacing "Andare verso il popolo" with "Portare il popolo verso di noi" ("Bring the people to us"). (Antonioni, "Dell'educazione artistica," *Corriere Padano*, March 2, 1937.)

6. Enzo Ungari, "Conversazione con Carlo Lizzani: Quando il 'découpage' sembrava una prigione," *Cult Movie*, April 1981, pp. 15–16.
7. Faldini and Fofi, I:49.
8. Ungari, "Conversazione con Lizzani," p. 15.
9. Savio, *Ma l'amore*, p. 248.
10. Franco Riganti to TG.
11. Vittorio Mussolini, "Emancipazione del cinema italiano," *Cinema* 6, September 25, 1936, pp. 213–15.
12. Faldini and Fofi, I:23.
13. Marcia Landy, *Fascism in Film: The Italian Commercial Cinema, 1931–1943* (Princeton: Princeton University Press, 1986), pp. 302–08.
14. The State, in any case, after the fivefold increase in production and proliferation of small producers resulting from the 1938 ban on American imports, was less interested in fostering the conventional than in promoting commercialism, experimentation, and variety.
15. From "L'Occhio di vetro," reprinted in Luigi Chiarini and Umberto Barbaro, eds., *Problemi dei film*; cited and quoted in Mario Verdone, *Roberto Rossellini* (Paris: Éditions Seghers, 1963), p. 16.
16. Quoted in Howard Sharpe, "The Star Creators of Hollywood," *Photoplay*, October 1936, p. 100.
17. Fabrizio Sarazani, *Il Tempo*, April 11, 1945; quoted in Savio, *Ma l'amore*, p. 249.
18. Henri Langlois, *Trois cents ans de cinéma: écrits* (Paris: Cahiers du Cinéma, Cinefranc, Fondation Européenne des Métiers de l'Image et du Son, 1986), pp. 306–07. Langlois was director of the Cinémathèque Française. In the same passage he compares Visconti to the "Milanese" Stendhal and *The Red and the Black* and Rossellini (and De Sica) to Balzac and *Splendors and Miseries of Courtesans*. "Like Stendhal, Visconti was isolated and unclassifiable; though linked to young Italians, he was separated totally from them." (Other points of truth in Langlois's comparison of Visconti with Stendhal, however, elude me.)
19. Mario Alicata, "Testimonianze," in Giorgio Tinazzi, ed., *Il cinema italiano*, p. 182.
20. Ugo Casiraghi and Glauco Viazzi, "Presentazione postuma d'un classico," *Bianco e nero*, April 1942; cited in Venturini, "Origini del neorealismo," *Bianco e nero*, February 1950; reprinted in Overbey, *Springtime*, p. 181.
21. Cited by Gian Vittorio Baldi to TG.
22. *Il neorealismo nel fascismo*, p. 127.
23. Faldini and Fofi, I:49.
24. Savio, *Cinecittà*, p. 965.
25. Faldini and Fofi, I:69–70.
26. Giuseppe De Santis to TG, April 1985.
27. Cited by Gian Vittorio Baldi to TG.
28. Franco Riganti to TG.
29. Existent copies, however, do not have these cuts. For a detailed study of *Desiderio*'s vicissitudes, see Roncoroni, "Primo Rossellini," pp. 57–59.
30. A.W., *New York Times*, February 9, 1950.
31. Brunello Rondi's phrase, "Realtà della persona," p. 13.
32. Ungari, "Conversazione con Lizzani."
33. Giuseppe Ferrara (paraphrasing Massimo Mida), "L'opera di Roberto Rossellini," in Piero Mechini and Roberto Salvadori, ed., *Rossellini, Antonioni, Buñuel* (Padua: Marsilio Editori, 1973), p. 24. Ferrara and Mida were trying to perpetuate the myth of a Rossellini whose instinctive grasp of reality transcended his political naiveté. This is balderdash.
34. Cited by Enrico Fulchignoni to TG.
35. Renzo Rossellini, *Addio*, pp. 34–35.
36. R. M. De Angelis, "Rossellini romanziere," *Cinema* (Milan) no. 29, December 30, 1949, p. 356.
37. Roswitha Schmidt to TG.
38. De Marchis Rossellini, *Un matrimonio*, p. 43.
39. Roswitha Schmidt to TG.
40. Faldini and Fofi, I:74–75.
41. *Nuestro Cine* 95, 1970.
42. Roswitha Schmidt to TG.
43. "An interview with Rossellini," by James Blue (Houston, 1972), in *Rossellini*, a brochure for a series presented by Joseph Papp at the Public Theater, New York, May 1–20, 1979, p. 17.
44. Roger MacNiven to TG, c. 1974.
45. Massimo Mida to TG. Some say it was partly because Roberto feared his wife and children would be seized and held captive to root him out, as was happening with other fugitives, that he had placed them in a convent. Marcella, however, reports that she circulated freely during the daytime, visiting friends and the Villa Borghese, and makes no mention of Roberto's fears—which may have been real even though groundless.
46. Roswitha Schmidt to TG.
47. Blue, 1972. Roswitha Schmidt to TG.
48. Cited by Adriano Aprà to TG.
49. Nino's, founded in 1932 by a Tuscan, Nino Guarnacci, moved after the war to Via Borgognona, a few blocks away in the direction of Piazza di Spagna. A few decades later, Sonali Sen Roy would open her Indian boutique a few doors from Nino's. Adjoining Via Rasella were Via Zuchelli, with another restaurant Rossellini frequented, and Via Avignonesi, where *Roma città aperta* would be shot.

50. Tullio Kezich, *Fellini* (Milan: Rizzoli, 1987), p. 114.
51. De Angelis, "Rossellini romanziere," p. 356. De Angelis was writing from memory; Rossellini could not have used the term "neo-realism" in early 1944 in reference to newsreel-like film. The term was then used on only a handful of occasions to denote early-thirties literature, and on even fewer occasions in regard to certain French films. But Carné is not newsreel-like. Cf. Chapter 10.
52. *Ragazzo,* a story of the reformation of a delinquent youth set against the unusual backgrounds of Tiber barges, pool halls, and workers' quarters on Rome's periphery, was about to open at the Corso Cinema in 1933 when it was withdrawn on Mussolini's personal order—not for reasons of censorship, but "perhaps to 'punish' the federale of the city, Nino D'Aroma, who had written the story with Sandro De Feo and who was, at that time, being covertly accused of boulangism [plotting against the regime], to the extent of losing his post." *Ragazzo* was never released, but a copy was deposited at the Cineteca and regularly shown to students until it, along with much of the collection, was destroyed by the Nazis during the Occupation. No copy of the film exists today. (Savio, *Ma l'amore no,* p. 409.) Pirro incorrectly states that *Ragazzo* was immediately destroyed by the censor. (Ugo Pirro, *Celluloide* [Milan: Rizzoli, 1983].)
53. "Espresse in un film le speranze di un popolo," *L'Unità,* June 6, 1977, p. 3.
54. Enrico Fulchignoni to TG; Rod Geiger to TG.
55. Rossellini interview, July 15, 1978, in G. L. Rondi, *Cinema dei Maestri,* p. 213.
56. Alicata, "Testimonianze," p. 182.
57. Recent thinking—which credits Fascism's rise primarily to support by the lower–middle classes rather than by industry—does not entirely refute this earlier analysis. The middle classes initially desired labor's repression, and Mussolini's corporatism, though classless in theory, but later subverted labor to capital while reaping large profits for the latter.
58. For many of the ideas in this critique of Croce, I am indebted to Leonardo Olschki, *The Genius of Italy* (New York: Oxford University Press, 1949), pp. 384–95, 450–61.
59. Quoted in Luigi Barzini, *From Caesar to the Mafia* (New York: Bantam, 1972), p. 137.
60. Wrote Gramsci: "In Italy there has always lacked and there continues to lack a national-popular literature, either in narrative or any other genre." "In Italy, the term 'national' has a meaning that is very restricted ideologically and that in any case does not coincide with 'popular [of the people],' for in Italy the intellectuals are far from the people, that is, from the nation, and are instead linked to a tradition of class that has never been broken by a strong political movement based either in the people or in the nation: the tradition is bookish and abstract, and the typical modern intellectual feels more linked to Annibal Caro or Ippolito Pindemonte than to a Pugliesian or Sicilian farmer." (*Letteratura e vita nazionale* [Turin: Einaudi, 1950], pp. 105–06).
61. Michael Stern, *No Innocence Abroad* (New York: Random House, 1952), p. 286.
62. Gaia Servadio, *Luchino Visconti: A Biography* (New York: Franklin Watts, 1983).
63. Pirro, *Celluloide,* p. 32.
64. Ibid., p. 24.
65. Unpublished Rossellini interview, c. 1976, with Paolo Valmarana, in RAI archives.
66. Pirro, *Celluloide,* pp. 53–54.

Chapter 7: *Open City*

1. This is Servadio's account of Denis's role in Visconti's liberation. Among those who dispute her credit for it are Uberta Visconti and Marcella Mariani Rossellini, who claim that anyone of any importance was being set free at this point. (Servadio, *Luchino Visconti.* Marcella Mariani Rossellini to TG.)
2. Cf. Nino Lo Bello, "De Sica's Favorite Film Never Released," *Boston Sunday Globe,* March 1, 1981, p. A4. His claim that the film was not seen until the 1980s is false; it opened and was reviewed in April 1945.
3. Lorenzo Quaglietti, *Storia economico-politica del cinema italiano 1945–1980* (Editori Riuniti: Rome, 1980), p. 37.
4. Stefano Roncoroni reports (to TG) seeing a contemporary news item in which Rossellini is said to have been summoned to testify. Marcella Mariani Rossellini claims (to TG) that Roberto did not appear.
5. Quoted by Gian Vittorio Baldi to TG.
6. Faldini and Fofi, I:19–21.
7. In Pirro, *Celluloide,* but with numerous revisions. The dialogue assigned characters has usually been invented by Pirro.
8. Alberto Consiglio, *I maccheroni, con cento ricette* (Rome: Hobby Books, Newton Compton Italiana, 1973).
9. Pirro, *Celluloide,* pp. 114–15.
10. Roncoroni, "Primo Rossellini," p. 61. Roncoroni has read Consiglio's original.
   Pirro says the title was "La vendetta di Satana" (Pirro, *Celluloide,* p. 88) and that neither Manfredi nor a cocaine-loving informer were part of it. Instead Pirro contends that Consiglio's priest story and Amidei's Manfredi story (including sora Pina) were kept separate until late in the scripting process, when Perilli suggested combining them. Whether Pirro was able to confirm Perilli's version of these events with Amidei or Consiglio is not known. Nearly everyone associated with *Roma città aperta* subsequently made vast claims, and Rossellini's tendency to divide and manipulate all of his collaborators naturally encouraged each of them to see only their own contributions, with the ultimate result that Rossellini himself was, over the decades, frequently thought to have had negligible effect on the film!
11. Pirro, *Celluloide,* pp. 88–89, for the account of Rossellini's machinations with Consiglio and Amidei.

12. Roncoroni, "Primo Rossellini," pp. 53, 61; wherein it is stated that Consiglio claimed it was he who first interested the Countess in the priest story; also, Roncoroni to TG. Pirro's account generally reflects an intention to inflate Amidei's role in the film, but is often rendered suspect by its limitation to Amidei's unwittingly myopic viewpoint and by a tendency to gets facts and names wrong (e.g., "Polito" for Politi).

13. *Fragments*, p. 129.

14. Mario Del Papa to TG, 1985.

15. Turi Vasile, *Un vellano a Cinecittà* (Palermo: Sellerio, 1993), p. 75.

16. Ibid., p. 78.

17. Pirro, *Celluloide*, pp. 98–100, for the account of Perilli and of the restaurant the next day.

18. So writes Pirro. Actually the homosexual hero in Visconti's *Ossessione* is a Communist, although never so labeled.

19. Pirro, *Celluloide*, pp. 100–06, for the account of the restaurant conversation and getting money from the countess. For the account of Maria Michi, cf. these pages as well as her own account in Faldini and Fofi, I:72, 94.

20. Vasile, *Un vellano*, p. 78.

21. Ibid., p. 79.

22. Pirro, *Celluloide*, p. 116; also, cf. Faldini and Fofi, I:90, quoting De Sica from his accounts in *Tempo illustrato*, December 16, 1954 and succeeding issues (unidentified).

23. Pirro, *Celluloide*, pp. 117–20, for the account of the meeting of Fabrizi, Rossellini, and Amidei.

24. Ibid., pp. 120–25, for the Funny Face Shop episode. Cf. also Fellini's account in Faldini and Fofi, I:91, quoting from an interview in *Il segnacolo* (Bologna), August 1961.

25. Vasile, *Unvellano*, pp. 80–81.

26. Faldini and Fofi, I:92.

27. Fellini claimed that it was at this point that *he* suggested to Amidei that the short stories be combined into a feature, that this work was carried out in his kitchen in the period of a week, that neither of them had much faith in the project, and that only when Fabrizi saw the completed script did he finally reach agreement on salary (Faldini and Fofi, I:92; reprinted from an uncredited interview in *Il segnacolo*, Bologna, August 1961). Unfortunately, Fellini's penchant for fantasy and for making good stories even better makes him an unreliable source for detailing events. It is likely, moreover, that Fellini would have shared Rossellini's preference for free, episodic constructions (as in *Paisà*), rather than Amidei's preference for the well-written drama.

28. All the film's contracts, handwritten and generally made with Amidei (acting as producer on behalf of Politi's Nettunia Productions), are in Roncoroni's possession.

29. Pirro, *Celluloide*, pp. 128–30, for the account of Diena and the political squabble.

30. Marcella Mariani Rossellini to TG.

31. Massimo Mida, Giuseppe De Santis, Mario Del Papa, Franco Riganti, to TG.

32. Grandjacquet's contract, as well as those of most others, is dated in January and made with Amidei, as Politi's representative.

33. Pirro, *Celluloide*, pp. 133–36, for Michi's choice of Pagliero and the finding of Feist.

34. Jone Tuzzi, in Faldini and Fofi, I:92.

35. Rossellini interview, in G. L. Rondi, *Cinema dei maestri*, pp. 213–14.

36. MacNiven, Yale 1974.

37. Rossellini interview, in G. L. Rondi, *Cinema dei maestri*, p. 24.

38. Rossellini, "L'intelligenza del presente," in *La triologia della guerra* (Bologna: Cappelli editore, 1972), p. 13.

39. Rossellini interview, in G. L. Rondi, *Cinema dei maestri*, p. 24.

40. Renoir, writing in *Pour vous*, no. 456, August 12, 1937, declared: "What I want to show . . . is the grandeur of the individual in the middle of a collective action. . . . I would be lying if I would say that, in this struggle of ideas, I remain impartial. I am shooting *La Marseillaise* with a very firm conviction: I want to make a partisan film but in good faith." Upon the film's release the Communist Aragon wrote: "The great miracle of Jean Renoir, and which alongside Hollywood's 'reconstructions' amounts to the condemnation of a false and academic genre, is to have made *La Marseillaise*, despite the costumes, despite the scenery, despite the theme, a film so actual, so scorching, so human, that one is caught up, transported, swept away during more than two hours as if it were our own life being debated under our eyes. And in fact it is our own life." (*Ce soir*, February 10, 1938.) On the contrary, *La Marseillaise* was booed by the right (including Henri Jeanson, Marcel Achard, and Roger Leenhardt in *Esprit*) as too left-partisan.

41. According to Marcella Mariani Rossellini (to TG), who was present.

42. Thomas Meder to TG.

43. Pirro, *Celluloide*, pp. 157–58, for the account of the dispute over the torture scenes and the Russian generals.

44. In *Star*, Silvano Castellani listed Magnani for the part on January 20, 1945; but on February 3, Adriano Baracco listed Calamai.

45. Mira Liehm calls Pina "the first independent modern woman to be portrayed in an Italian film" (*Passion*, p. 146). The claim seems dubious. Even by the standards of 1945, Pina, with her nagging guilt over her pregnancy, is neither particularly independent nor modern.

46. Faldini and Fofi, I:93.

47. Rossellini interview with Georges Sadoul, "Rossellini qui vendia ses meubles pour tourner *Rome ville ouverte*, a recruté les acteurs de *Paisà* parmi les badauds," *L'Ecran Français* 72, November 12, 1946, p. 17.

48. Faldini and Fofi, I:91.

49. Quoted in Franco Zeffirelli, *Zeffirelli: The Autobiography of Franco Zeffirelli* (New York: Weidenfeld & Nicolson, 1986), p. 77.

50. Roberto's penchant for abandoning the set became chronic in later years, but Marcella Mariani Rossellini insists, contrary to what Amidei and others have stated, that he did not do so during *Roma città aperta*.
51. Pirro, *Celluloide*, pp. 166–68, for the account of Amato and the dailies.
52. Marcella Mariani Rossellini to TG.
53. Amidei, in *Città del cinema*, p. 77; *Fragments*, p. 132; and Pirro, *Celluloide*, p. 178. All tell the story differently.
54. Mario Del Papa to TG.
55. Ibid. In Pirro, *Celluloide*, the impression is given that it lasted only two or three weeks.
56. Blue, 1972.
57. Quoted in Lorenzo Bocchi, "Parigi onora Rossellini," a report of a UNESCO conference, in *Corriere della sera*, January 4, 1978, n.p.
58. Cf. Adriano Aprà, *The Fabulous Thirties: Italian Cinema* (Edizione Incontri Internazionale d'arte Roma: Milan, 1975), p. 109.
59. Pirro, *Celluloide*, pp. 165–66, for story of Tuzzi and missing scenes.
60. Franco Riganti to TG.
61. Faldini and Fofi, I:48.
62. Marcella Mariani Rossellini to TG. Vito Annicchiarico interviewed by Adriano Aprà, March 18, 1995, in Aprà, *Il dopoguerra di Rossellini* (Rome: Cinecittà International, 1995), pp. 38–39.
63. *Fragments*, pp. 116–17.
64. *Città del cinema*, p. 77.
65. Some of Venturini's documents are reproduced in Stefano Roncoroni, "Giro di carte," in Adriano Aprà, ed., *Roma città aperta di Rossellini* (Rome: Comune di Roma, Assessorato alla cultura, 1994), pp. 152–62.
66. The moment can be seen and reseen in some footage of Magnani performing in the 1982 documentary *Io sono Anna Magnani*.
67. Pirro, *Celluloide*, pp. 181–99, for the account of what happened and what was said from Saturday through Monday.
68. There are many different versions of this story, although presumably all derive from Amidei. Cf.: Amidei, in Faldini and Fofi, I:92; Amidei, in *Città del cinema*, p. 78; Pirro, *Celluloide*, pp. 203–04; Carrano, *Magnani*, pp. 101–02. According to Amidei, the incident occurred behind some police barracks in Trastevere where a slightly corruptible priest ("un parroco un po' imbroglione") had permitted them to shoot the scene of Don Pietro, Pina, and the Austrian deserter. The reason the priest had to have been "corruptible" is that, as Pirro explains, an edict had gone out barring the use of any church by a film crew after the desecrations of *La porta del cielo*. According to Pirro, even the original Don Pappagallo, despite Roberto's attempts to charm him, was reluctant to defy his bishop until he saw the cherubic Fabrizi in a cassock portraying himself. But I have not been able to ascertain what church was used in *Roma città aperta*, or whether the corruptible priest and Pappagallo were one and the same. The problem with Amidei's account, however, and even more with Pirro's (who describes in detail a fight *inside* the church), is that Magnani, whatever her temper, would not have behaved scandalously in a church. Thus the fight with Serato would have had to have occurred elsewhere.
69. Blue, 1972.
70. Pirro, *Celluloide*, pp. 205–06, for the story of the arrested actor.
71. Similar incidents occurred not infrequently during other films, e.g., Pagliero's *Roma città libera*, begun late in 1945. Maria Michi, after *Roma città aperta*'s release, was cursed and denounced by people on the street. And one of the German guards (who in real life had fled the Nazis and deserted to Italy) made the mistake of showing a still of himself in an SS helmet in a bar and was thrown in jail for six months, until Rossellini heard of his fate.
72. Pirro, *Celluloide*, p. 210, Amidei quote.
73. Faldini and Fofi, I:95, quoting from an interview in *Arianna* (Milan), August 1970.
74. Faldini and Fofi, I:95, quoting from an interview by Nantes Salvalaggio in *Il Giorno* (Milan), no date.
75. Carrano, *Magnani*, p. 98.
76. Faldini and Fofi, I:95.
77. Baldelli, p. 290. Fabrizi's sister had a restaurant on the Tiber island where Rossellini supposedly liked to dine in the sixties. I went there one day in 1984, but after I revealed I was researching a book about Rossellini, I was refused service.
78. Richard Collier, *Duce! A Biography of Benito Mussolini* (New York: Viking, 1971), pp. 362–63.
79. Faldini and Fofi, I:95.
80. D. M., "*Roma città aperta* in America è il successo del giorno," *Cinelandia*, May 5, 1946.
81. Fellini told TG in 1985 that the story is untrue. Cf. Federico Fellini, *Fare un film* (Turin: Einaudi, 1980), pp. 73–74; also *Il Segnacolo* (Bologna), August 1961.
82. Stefano Masi, "L'hardware del neorealismo," in Alberto Farassino, *Neorealismo. Cinema italiano 1945–49* (Turin: Edizioni di Torino, 1989), p. 49.
83. Quoted in Sadoul, "Rossellini," 1946.
84. Gian Vittorio Baldi to TG. Fellini, for one, has often imitated Rossellini's technique (without, however, acknowledging the debt). See Bertrand Philbert, "Fellini V.F.," *Cinématographe*, January 1984, p. 30.
85. *Film Culture*, 1971, p. 19 (slightly re-edited).
86. Ibid.
87. Alfred Hayes, "Author's Note on Birth of *Paisan*," *New York Times*, March 7, 1948.
88. Klaus Mann, *Tagebücher 1944–1949* (Munich: Spangenberg, 1991), pp. 91–92.
89. Klaus Mann, *La svolta. Storia di una vita* (Milan: Il Saggiatore, 1962), pp. 441–43.
90. Rod Geiger to TG. Geiger, who was present, says Artisti Associati was Scalera. The original Artisti Associati, 1935–43, had belonged to Giorgio Genesi who owned Technostampa, the lab Rossellini was

using. The new firm did not release a picture until 1948. Scalera, however, had continued to release films from Venice during the German Occupation and survived until Welles's *Otello* [sic] in 1951.

91. Lawrence and Geiger split up in 1946 and I have been unable to reconcile their accounts. Lawrence denies he ever gave Geiger reason to hope for money from his family. Geiger retorts he had no other reason for taking Lawrence on as an equal partner. A letter from Geiger in rebuttal of Lawrence's claims appeared in Archer Winsten's column in *The New York Post*, November 16, 1964.

92. Renzo Rossellini, *Addio*, p. 99.

93. Ferruccio de Martino interview with Adriano Aprà, May 1987, in Aprà, *Roma*, p. 79. De Martino was Venturini's production manager for the film.

94. Stefano Roncoroni to TG. Roncoroni spent time with Venturini shortly before the latter's death, around 1971. But as late as February 10, 1948, Venturini accepted Rossellini's IOU for one million lire.

95. Rod Geiger to TG.

96. *Fragments*, p. 135.

97. On these same September accounts: Nettunia Production's investment is given as 2,811,893.80 lire (apparently the sum of amounts listed in April as Politi's and Rossellini's separate investments); Amidei's salary as 149,000; Magnani's as 440,000. The accounts are in the possession of Stefano Roncoroni, Rome.

98. Accounts of *Città aperta*'s cost differ. De Martino, who as Venturini's production manager ought to have known, stated it was seven million (De Martino: Aprà, *Roma*, p. 79). Amidei, possibly confusing what Venturini had paid with what he originally received from Minerva, maintained that Venturini had paid out eleven million lire (Amidei: Faldini and Fofi, I:95). Roberto, whose head for numbers was notoriously chaotic, told Sadoul in 1946 that he had needed "seven or eight million" to make the film (Sadoul, "Rossellini"); told Jenia Reissar in 1947 that it had cost twelve million (memo to David Selznick, May 4, 1948 [Selznick Archives]); and stated in 1958 that it had cost nine-and-a-half ("Roberto Rossellini vous avez la parole!" Interview in *Filmklub-Cinéclub* [Geneva], October 1958). Geiger told a reporter in 1945 that it had cost $110,000 (*New York Telegram*, December 11, 1945). In 1953 the figure, probably on Rossellini's authority, was given as $18,000 (William Murray, "The Man Who Knows No Rules," *United Nations World*, May, 1953, p. 45).

Dollar figures may vary due to the artificiality of the exchange rates. At *Città aperta*'s release the Am-lira was still officially where it had been in 1943: 100 to the dollar. But one could get much more on the black market (in 1946 the official rate climbed to 225) and everyone involved in Rossellini's deal was calculating 200.

99. *Il Segnacolo* (Bologna), August 1961.

100. One-page folded program. Although Mann refers to the movie as *Rome Open City*, the program bills it as *Open City* on its title fold and the print still bore the original title.

101. Visconti added, begrudgingly: "At that moment even some other, though similar, picture would have made us jump out of seats. *Roma città aperta*, which I saw again later, is a modest film." (Faldini and Fofi, I:137, quoting from Giuseppe Ferrara, *Luchino Visconti* [Paris: Seghers, 1964], n.p.).

102. Alessandro Blasetti, *Cinema italiano oggi* (Rome: Carlo Bestetti, 1950), p. 48.

103. Cf. Mino Argentieri, "Storia e spiritualismo nel Rossellini degli anni quaranta," *Cinema 70*, no. 95, 1974.

104. "Open City," *Film d'Oggi 20*, November 3, 1945 (reprint in a dossier of eighteen contemporary reviews in Nedo Ivaldi, ed., *Quello che scrissero . . . allora*, published for the Convegno di studi dell'aprile 1970 a Venezia, su *La resistenza nel cinema italiano del dopoguerra*, pp. 20–22).

105. Massimo Mida, *Roberto Rossellini*, 2nd ed. (Guanda: Parma, 1961), pp. 21, 29–32.

106. *Pagine*, pp. 224–25 (slightly abridged).

107. Amerigo Terenzi to TG, November 1983.

108. January 25, 1947; April 13, 1946.

109. Rossellini, "Dix ans de cinéma," *Cahiers du Cinéma 50*, August 1955 (I); 52, November 1955 (II); 55, January 1956 (III). "Dix ans," I.

110. Rossellini interview with Adriano Aprà and G. Berengo Gardin, "Un cinema diverso per un mondo che cambia," transcript of a conference with Centro Sperimentale di Cinematografia students, December 14, 1963, *Bianco e Nero*, February 1964; reprint: *Il mio metodo*, pp. 302–27.

111. "Dix ans," I.

112. Pirro, *Celluloide* (following the Rossellini legend), pp. 216–18.

113. "Dix ans," I.

114. Interview with Massimo Mauri, *Epoca 231*, March 6, 1955.

115. Umberto Barbaro, *L'Unità*, September 26, 1945. Anon., *La Voce Repubblicana*, undated (c. September 25, 1945). Vittorio Ragusa, *La Ricostruzione*, undated (c. September 25, 1945). Anon., *Il Giornale del Mattino* (i.e., *Il Messaggero*), September 25, 1945; reprint: Aprà, *Roma*, p. 96.

116. Mino Caudana, *Quarta Parete*, October 25, 1945; reprint: Ivaldi, *Quello*, p. 15.

117. Anon., *La Capitale*, September 25, 1945, quoted in Renzo Rossellini, *Pagine*, pp. 221–22; reprint: Aprà, *Roma*, p. 98.

118. Mario Meneghini, September 26, 1945; B. Ban, *L'Italia Libera*, September 25, 1945; reprints: Aprà, *Roma*, pp. 97, 102.

119. Indro Montanelli, Milan, October 24, 1945; reprint: Ivaldi, *Quello*, p. 18.

120. *Domenica*, September 30, 1945; reprint: Ennio Flaiano, *Lettere d'amore al cinema* (Milan: Rizzoli 1978), pp. 81–82.

121. *Film d'Oggi* (Milan), October 13, 1945.

122. *Cinetempo* (Milan), October 18, 1945.

123. Anon., *Il Giornale del Mattino* (i.e., *Il Messaggero*), September 25, 1945.

124. *La Nuova Europa*, September 30, 1945; reprint: Ivaldi, *Quello*, p. 12. An earlier Moravia review in *Libera Stampa*, September 25, 1945 (reprint: Aprà, *Roma*, p. 96), evinces less enthusiasm.
125. September 28, 1945; reprint: Ivaldi, *Quello*, p. 11.
126. Fabio Carpi, *L'Unità*, December 15, 1946, within a review of *Paisà*.
127. *La Ricostruzione*, undated clipping; TG archive.
128. Anon., unidentified contemporary clipping.
129. Guido Guerrasio, *Cinetempo*, November 1, 1945; reprint: Ivaldi, *Quello*, p. 20.
130. Alberto Farassino, "I rapporti con la critica," in Bruno, *Roberto Rossellini*, p. 157. Also: Umberto Lisi, "La critica, allora," *Cinema nuovo*, April 25, 1955.
131. *L'Unità*, September 26, 1945; reprint: Ivaldi, *Quello*, p. 13. According to Antonioni, the audiences received the Russian films "with reserve." *Film d'Oggi*, October 13, 1945.
132. Farassino, "I rapporti con la critica."
133. Adriano Baracco, *Cinema*, October 25, 1948.
134. Mina Caudana, in *Avanti!* November 1, 1945. His mixed review in *Quarta Potere*, October 4 (reprint: Ivaldi, *Quello*, p. 13) was also retracted in that paper on October 25 (reprint: Ivaldi, *Quello*, p. 15.
135. For this argument: Argentieri, "Storia e spiritualismo." Cf. also, Giuseppe Ferrara, "L'opera di Roberto Rossellini," pp. 19–46. Cf. also, Geoffrey Nowell-Smith, *Framework 10* (date?), quoted in Don Ranvaud, ed., *Roberto Rossellini: British Film Institute Dossier no. 8* (London: BFI, 1981), p. 10. Cf. also, Baldelli, pp. 51–53. Cf. also, Franco Antonicelli, *Cinema Nuovo 57*, April 1955: "The film has a limitation: one finds indeed the heroic myths of solidarity, of courage, of the martyr, but no critique of the past, and nothing on the new historic course opened by the Resistance."
136. See, for example, Fernaldo Di Giammatteo, "Un ritratto di Rossellini," *Rivista del Cinema Italiano*, November 1952.
137. José-Luis Guarner, *Roberto Rossellini* (London: Studio Vista, 1970), p. 18.
138. For this definition of art: Camille Paglia, *Sexual Personae* (New Haven: Yale University Press, 1990), p. 25.
139. Rossellini interview with François Truffaut, "Rossellini: Je ne suis pas le père du néoréalisme, je travaille dans une solitude morale absolute, je souffre d'être méprisé et insulté de tous côtés, je suis obligé de payer moi-même mes films," *Arts*, June 16, 1954, p. 3.
140. For world without love: Gian Luigi Rondi, paraphrased in F. Bolzoni, "Il tema religioso nel film," *Bianco e Nero*, May 1955, p. 27.
141. Henri Agel, *Le cinéma et le sacré*, 2nd ed. (Paris: Éditions du Cerf, 1961), p. 85.
142. Serceau, *Rossellini*, pp. 23–24.
143. In 1946 Rossellini cited Don Pietro's aphorism as expressive of the common feeling of all people after the war. Rossellini interview with J. P. Berryer, "Metteur en scène n. 1 du cinéma italien, Rossellini nous parle du son film, *Rome, ville ouverte*," *Alger Républicain*, January 28, 1947.
144. Rossellini, in Fernaldo Di Giammatteo, "Rossellini si difende," (Rome, November 1948), *Il Progresso d'Italia* (Bologna), December 9, 1948; also in *Fotogrammi*, January 4, 1949.
145. Regrettably, American release prints substitute a blank background during the opening titles for this dome vista. St. Paul's Cathedral is used similarly, to evoke values that cannot fail to triumph, in Humphrey Jennings' poetic documentary of London during the blitz, *Listen to Britain* (1941).
146. Centro Cattolico Cinematografico, vol. xix, 1944–45; reprint: Aprà, *Roma*, p. 120. Legion description quoted by Richard Corliss, "The Legion of Decency," *Film Comment*, Summer 1968, p. 41.
147. Arthur Mayer, *Merely Colossal* (New York: Simon & Schuster, 1953), pp. 221–23.
148. Interview, in G. L. Rondi, *Cinema dei maestri*, p. 24.
149. Genêt (Janet Flanner), "Letter from Rome," *New Yorker*, December 1, 1945.
150. February 26, 1946.
151. March 2, 1946.
152. March 4, 1946.
153. Eileen Creelman. February 26, 1946.
154. *Telegram*, Alton Cook, February 26, 1946; *Life*, March 4, 1946.
155. *New York Times*, March 3, 1946. At the end of the year, December 29, 1946, Crowther put *Open City* first on his list of the year's ten best pictures.
156. April 13, 1946.
157. March 4, 1946.
158. John T. McManus, "*Open City* Is Film Classic of Italy's Partisan Fighters," *P.M.*, February 26, 1946 (My re-translation from the Italian reprint: Aprà, *Roma*, p. 129).
159. Joseph Foster. March 19, 1946.
160. "'Man Is Greater Than You Esteem Him!': A Drama Addressed to the Peace-Makers." March 18, 1946, p. 10.
161. Rod Geiger to TG. In the *New York Times*, A. H. Weiler reported on June 9, 1946, that *Open City* had taken in $100,000 in fifteen weeks at the World, $500,000 at eight other locations. On December 22, Weiler reported $300,000 after forty weeks at the World, with a $1,600,000 gross from 275 situations nationwide. But on February 4, 1947, Weiler reported a $500,000 gross in 250 engagements—without alluding to his higher figure five weeks earlier.
162. Quoted by Douglas Gilbert, *New York World Telegram*, December 11, 1945.
163. Sgt. Sherman Davis, in a contemporary review of *Open City*, in *Stage, Radio, Screen* (a U.S. army-in-Italy publication?), undated clipping.
164. For the analysis of light: Giuseppe Ferrara, *Il nuovo cinema italiano* (Florence: Le Monnier, 1957), p. 111.
165. ". . . l'excellence des interprètes." André Bazin, "Le Réalisme cinématographique et l'école italienne de la libération," *Esprit*, January 1948; reprint: *Qu'est-ce que le cinéma?* (Paris: Editions du Cerf, 1962), IV:17; cf.

Hugh Gray's sometimes inaccurate translations, *What Is Cinema?" II* (Berkeley: University of California, 1971), pp. 16–40.

166. Guido Fink, "'Etre' ou 'avoir été': le film italien, le temps et l'histoire," *Cultures,* vol. 2, no. 1, 1974, pp. 128–33.

167. Lamberto Sechi, in a clipping of a contemporary review in an unidentified paper.

Chapter 8: *Paisà*

1. Quoted (in Italian) in Rose Nadell, "Paisà," *Cine Illustrato,* April 1, 1946.
2. Mann, quoted (in Italian) in Adriano Aprà, ed., *Rosselliniana* (Rome: Di Giacomo, 1987), p. 93. According to Baldelli, p. 56, this treatment was submitted to Allied censors. Rod Geiger tells me, however, that there was never any Allied censorship of the film and that no copies were submitted for censorship, but that copies were given to Captain Andy Anderson and others at the U.S. embassy who were assisting in the film's production. Nor is it true, as Baldelli alleges, that U.S. police followed the production, censoring continuously. Mann, in a letter to his mother, November 23, 1945, notes, "the censor doesn't exist anymore." (Klaus Mann Archives, Munich, quoted in Thomas Meder, *Vom Sichtbarmachen der Geschichte: Der italienische "Neorealismus,' Rossellinis* Paisà *und Klaus Mann* [Munich: Trickster, 1993], p. 176.)

   Roncoroni (*Primo Rossellini,* p. 65) quotes (in Italian) another version of this preface specifying "the special . . . relations between liberated and liberators during the Italian campaign."
3. Mann, quoted in Aprà, *Rosselliniana,* p. 93.
4. "THE INVASION . . . A vast armada of American boats and planes moving from North Africa to Sicily in eerie silence and darkness. Atmosphere of secrecy and suspense. / Individual close-ups—taken at random, as it were, of some characters in the convoy: / An ITALO-AMERICAN SOLDIER (Seventh Episode) with a group of friends. They ask questions about Italy. He is irritated, evasive. 'I don't know much about Italy', he says, 'and what I know isn't very pleasant. I have never been there, and wished I wouldn't have to go there now . . .' / A CHAPLAIN (Sixth Episode), on deck, with troops, praying for the success of the great venture. / A TANK DRIVER (Fifth Episode) with a bunch of buddies. They tease him because of his shyness toward women. Maybe he'll find a beautiful signorina in Rome . . . He grins, rather embarrassed and uncomfortable. / A NEGRO MP (Fourth Episode), with his colored outfit. They are afraid of what may be in store for them, but at the same time are looking forward to seeing Europe. For they have been told that the Europeans don't despise colored men. 'You can even talk with a white woman there . . .' / A FLIER (Third Episode), in his heavy bomber—grimly prepared to 'bomb the hell out of them.' / A NURSE (Second Episode), in a Red Cross ship, with other nurses and an American doctor, remembering her delightful pre-war trips to Italy. Rome was 'gorgeous', Capri was 'divine'—and what fun she had! It's such a thrill to see good old Italy again . . . / While these people are wondering about Italy, the ITALIANS are anxiously waiting for the arrival of the Americans. We see groups of Italian soldiers and civilians, women and children, in various Italian cities and villages—breathless with expectation, hopeful and apprehensive, whispering to each other: 'The Americans are coming . . . What are they going to bring?' / Then the camera returns to the CONVOY. A YOUNG GI (First Episode) cleans his rifle. He doesn't give a damn about the Italians. All he wants is to get it over with, and to go home . . . / Transition to the opening scene of the First Episode." (Quoted from manuscript in Klaus Mann Archives, Munich, in Meder, *Vom Sichtbarmachen,* p. 189n.)
5. Quoted (in Italian) in D.M., "Roma."
6. M. T. McGregor, *Time and Tide;* undated partial reprint: Roger Manvell, "Paisà, How it struck our Contemporaries," *Penguin Film Review* (London: Penguin, 1949), p. 57.
7. Campbell Dixon, *Daily Telegraph;* undated partial reprint: Manvell, "Paisà," p. 57.
8. Faldini and Fofi, I:97.
9. Rod Geiger to TG.
10. *Cahiers du Cinéma* 73, July 1957.
11. "Memorandum for Lt. Lawrence and Roland Geiger," November 15, 1945. Robert Lawrence Archives. I have rearranged the order of sentences and corrected Mann's misspelt "Rosselini."
12. November 23, 1945. Klaus Mann Archives. Quoted in Meder, *Vom Sichtbarmachen,* p. 176; Meder's translation from Mann's German.
13. Photocopy in author's archive.
14. Rod Geiger to TG.
15. Blue, 1972.
16. Hayes's idea for "Rome" preceded the *Seven from the U.S.* concept. A dramatically less focused version of it runs intermittently through his vignette novel of the American occupation, *All Thy Conquests,* published in 1946, in which "Harry" searches for Francesca, never finds her, but mistakes a prostitute for her. Hayes expanded the "Rome" idea into his 1949 novel, *The Girl on the Via Flaminia,* which became a 1954 feature film, *Act of Love,* directed by Anatole Litvak. Hayes also contributed to "Naples" and to some of the Carmela-Joe dialogue in "Sicily," but not to any of *Paisà's* other episodes. Hayes was paid $1,000.

   Mann did a British story, a story about a nurse, and a story about a chaplain and a Fascist youth ("Apennines," see below) that were also not used. He was the most important writer for the film. Mann had been paid about $2,500 for collaborating on the script. But contrary to his December 14, 1945 contract with Rossellini, he was initially given no screen credit, and in November 1948 brought suit against Rossellini and Conti. In 1949 he died and his estate was awarded only $1,750.

Amidei was chiefly responsible only for "Rome." Probably he worked on "Sicily" and quite different versions of "Naples." His "The Pastor of Predappio" (see below) and "The Partisans of the North" were not used. Neither was "The Prisoner," co-authored with Pagliero and at one point intended for Fabrizi, about a mute near Anzio who rescues an American parachutist, is abused by other Americans, and dies machine-gunning Germans. Another version of the story replaces the mute with an old man. ("Il prigioniero" appeared in *Cinema Nuovo* 57, April 25, 1955; reprints: Verdone, *Rossellini* [French trans.], pp. 124–35; Aprà, *Rosselliniana*, pp. 127–29.) Another "Anzio," (by Pagliero, in Pagliero's bad English in the Klaus Mann Archive, Munich) concerns an American priest who kills some Germans to save Italians.

17. Interview with Adriano Aprà, April 23, 1987, in Aprà, *Rosselliniana*, p. 136.
18. Massimo Mida, "Luchino Visconti e il gruppo «Cinema»," in Mariella Furno and Renzo Renzi, *Il neorealismo nel fascismo: Giuseppe De Santis e la critica cinematografica 1941–1943* (Bologna: Edizioni della Tipografia Compositori, 1984).
19. Rod Geiger to TG.
20. "Their day came in 1943, when . . . the newly landed Americans named most of the Mafia leaders mayors of their towns and villages: they were all officially classified as political victims of the Fascist tyranny." (Barzini, *From Caesar*, p. 366.)
21. Helen Tubbs to TG.
22. *Il Segnacolo* (Bologna), August 1961.
23. Baldelli, p. 56.
24. Brunello Rondi, *Il neorealismo italiano* (Parma: Guanda, 1956), pp. 143–44.
25. Di Giammatteo, "Un ritratto," p. 36, for the antinomy of impotence and indomitable moral force.
26. MacNiven, Yale 1974.
27. The "searching" theme was even stronger in Hayes's first version of "Rome" in *All Thy Conquests*, where the GI meets "Maria" and spends the rest of the book loudly hoping to see her again. Edmund, Nannina, Karin, and Irene wander street mazes in *Deutschland, Miracolo, Stromboli, Europe '51*, as do the couples in *Voyage* and *Fear* and the Amalfitani in *La macchina*. In Rossellini's later films characters are perpetually wandering from place to place (e.g., Augustine, the apostles, Socrates, Christ) or room to room (*Della Rovere, Era notte, Vanina*).
28. Blue, 1972.
29. Massimo Mida, "Dal diario de lavorazione di 'Paisà': Carmela e Robert," *Film rivista*, August 15, 1946, p. 11.
30. Mida, "Dal diario," p. 11.
31. Gian Vittorio Baldi, for this notion of Rossellini's desire to create real situations.
32. Massimo Mida, "Dal diario," p. 11.
33. Massimo Mida, *Compagni di viaggio: Colloqui con i maestri del cinema italiano* (Turin: Nuova ERI, 1988), p. 46.
34. Blue, 1972.
35. *Nuestro Cine* 95, 1970; *Screen*, pp. 97–98.
36. Federico Fellini to TG. Fellini does not recall Geiger being with him; but neither does he recall that he was not.
37. Federico Fellini, "Mon Métier," *Cahiers du Cinéma* 84, June 1958, p. 15 (translated from "Fellini parla del suo mestiere di regista," *Bianco e Nero*, May 1958).
38. Rod Geiger to TG.
39. Fellini, "Mon Métier," p. 16.
40. Rod Geiger to TG.
41. *First story:* "Apennines." Christmas in the Futa pass during the war's long stalemate. Captain Frank Martin's sermon stressing fallibility and warning against hatred incurs the distaste of other officers. Meanwhile the local mayor's wife is concerned about her husband's disappearance—she doesn't know whether he was Fascist or not—and about her son Ernesto, a hunchbacked cripple. Ernesto tells Martin the "revolutionary side" will yet triumph, democracy and Christianity are obsolete, the bourgeoisie cannot survive as it is and should accept totalitarian leadership against bolshevism. Ernesto speaks of honor, historic mission, heroism, discipline, of suicide if they lose. Despite this, the chaplain almost reaches the boy, but an intelligence officer intrudes to arrest him, he escapes, and is shot in the heart while trying to kill the chaplain, whom he believes betrayed him. Martin puts a scarf over Ernesto's tortured face. (Unpublished 23-page typescript, *Seven from the U.S.*, Synopsis of a Film, by Klaus Mann, based on stories by Sergio Amidei, Marcello Pagliero, Alfred Hayes, and Klaus Mann. Undated. Author's collection.)

Second (?) story: "The Pastor of Predappio," by Sergio Amidei. The monks sing a Te Deum to celebrate the German retreat, and free turkeys, ducks, rabbits, geese, and a fat pig that the local pastor has entrusted to them to hide from the Germans. Outside, some boys take down a road sign that the Germans had put up, "Verona Km. 150." But some Allied troops arrive, break in, steal chickens, and restore the sign. So the monks, remarking on the similarity of the two armies, put the animals back in hiding. On Christmas a crowd of chaplains come visit, with an Italian chaplain to translate. The monks offer to cook the mid-day meal, but the Americans have brought all sorts of canned foods which the monks have to accept—with resulting indigestion. So in revenge they work all afternoon and that night serve the Americans a feast exhibiting the culture, wisdom, and richness of Italian cuisine, instead of canned things. After antipasto and stuffed turkeys, the pastor of Predappio (the town in which Mussolini was born) presents the roasted pig with the words, "It's not just *that one* that comes from Predappio, this one does too." (Roncoroni, "Primo Rossellini." p. 63. A dialogued treatment by Amidei,

"Parco di Predappio," appears in Stefano Roncoroni, "Presentazione di due soggetti inediti di Sergio Amidei per 'Paisà' di Roberto Rossellini," *Filmcritica* 410, December 1990, pp. 570–75.)

Third story: "Anzio Bridge." At evening an American chaplain in civilian clothes knocks at the Trappist monastery of San Callisto, fleeing after killing two Germans at the bridge who had participated in a massacre of Italians guilty of sheltering Allied soldiers. But the chaplain, after a crisis of conscience, gives up sanctuary and goes back to the front, toward those who are dying and need him.

42. Fellini, "Mon Métier," p. 16.
43. Arnheim, a letter published in *Bianco e Nero* #4, 1948, quoted (in Italian) in Baldelli, p. 76.
44. Baldelli, p. 76.
45. B. Rondi, *Il neorealismo*, p. 155.
46. Renzo Rossellini, *Addio*, pp. 142–43.
47. Ibid.
48. Claudio Sorgi, "Il cristianesimo di Rossellini," *Rivista del Cinematografo*, July–August 1977, pp. 326–27.
49. Quoted in Menon, *Dibattito*, p. 80.
50. *Nuestro Cine* 95, 1970, pp. 97–98
51. Federico Fellini, *Intervista sul cinema*, ed. Giovanni Grazzini (Bari: Laterza, 1983), translated into French by Nino Frank as *Fellini* (Paris: Calmann-Lévy, 1984), excerpted in *Cinématographe* 96, January 1984, p. 16.
52. Fellini, "Mon Métier," p. 15. Occasional gossips have claimed that substantial portions of "Romagna" were actually shot by Fellini; Rod Geiger feels that Fellini shot most of the beginning, Rossellini the end. But Geiger was not always present and Massimo Mida, who was, insists he is "sure, sure, sure" that every bit of "Romagna" was shot by Rossellini and none of it by Fellini. Fellini himself, according to Jose-Luis Guarner who spent a week with him, has only vague memories and makes no claims either way. Kezich, Fellini's biographer, claims Fellini directed his first shot later, in "Florence." (Mida to TG; Geiger to TG; Guarner to TG. Tullio Kezich, *Fellini*, [Milan: Rizzoli, 1987], p. 127.)
53. Gian Vittorio Baldi quoting Rossellini to TG.
54. Faldini and Fofi, I:108.
55. Federico Fellini to TG. Also, Mida, *Compagni di viaggio*, p. 42.
56. Federico Fellini to TG.
57. Rod Geiger to TG.
58. "Fellini par Fellini," p. 16.
59. Fellini, "Mon Métier," pp. 14–15.
60. *La Table Ronde* 149, May 1960, p. 48.
61. "Fellini par Fellini," p. 16.
62. Quoted in Suzanne Budgen, *Fellini* (London: British Film Institute, 1966), p. 88.
63. "Fellini par Fellini," p. 16.
64. Jean Gili, "Federico Fellini," an interview, *Le Cinéma italien 2* (Paris: U.G.E 10/18, 1982), pp. 39–40.
65. This incident is recounted in Roberto Rossellini, "Neapolitan Note in a Director's Diary," *New York Times*, May 30, 1948, claiming to be extracted from a "voluminous . . . third-person" diary kept by Rossellini. That Rossellini kept such a diary is dubious. That he would have given away 100,000 lire—three or four months' wages—is scarcely likely.
66. Meder, *Vom Sichtbarmachen*, p. 242, and Meder to TG.
67. Madeleine Thornton-Sherwood (Mrs. Johnson) to TG. Dotts (Hylan) Johnson is credited on the film as Dots [sic] M. Johnson, but correctly as Dotts Johnson on U.S. publicity stills for *Paisà*. Some of the film's credits are inexactly transcribed in the Italian edition of the published screenplay (Roberto Rossellini, *La trilogia della guerra*, ed., Stefano Roncoroni [Bologna: Capelli, 1972]), and the errors are compounded in the American translation (Roberto Rossellini, *The War Trilogy* [New York: Grossman, 1973]). Poor Alfred Hayes is "V. Hayes" in the Italian edition and "V. Hales" in the American, and somehow becomes "Victor Haines" in Adriano Aprà's filmography in Alain Bergala, ed., Roberto Rossellini, *Le Cinéma révélé* (Paris: Editions de l'Étoile/Cahiers du Cinéma Écrits, 1984).
68. Serceau, *Rossellini*, pp. 71–73.
69. *CdC* 37, 1954, p. 7.
70. Rod Geiger to TG.
71. A search via the Freedom of Information Act through relevant government files revealed no records pertaining to Rossellini prior to his actual visa in January 1949, which was obtained from the intercession of Seymour M. Peyser, a Manhattan attorney for Ilya Lopert. "I do not think that I ever knew precisely the reason for the hesitancy of the United States consul in Rome to issue the visa," Peyser states. "My recollection now is that it had something to do with his affiliation in the 20's or 30's with the Fascist party. I do not think I ever had in my possession any specific information." (Letter to TG, June 22, 1989.)

   U.S. policy, however, saw ex-Fascists not as opponents but as allies against Communism. Geiger has precise memories of his embassy friends citing cocaine and the police record. He recalls telegraphing Burstyn that "February 31" would be an acceptable date for a U.S. visit and Burstyn replying that there was no such date.
72. B. Rondi, *Il neorealismo*, p. 150.
73. *La Revue du Cinéma* 4, January 1947, p. 14.
74. Serceau, *Rossellini*, p. 28. The categorization of Rossellini as a pamphleteer is mine, not Serceau's.
75. Blue, 1972.
76. Renzo Avanzo to TG, 1984.
77. Renzo Rossellini, *Addio*, p. 100.
78. Kezich, *Fellini*, p. 127.

79. Massimo Mida to TG. Toward the end of production in July Mida was sent to Livorno—the closest city where tanks could be found—and filmed for "Roma" the scenes of the tanks arriving and Michi watching. (Fellini and Mida can also be glimpsed among the crowd.) According to Mida, these (with the list above) were the only shots in *Paisà* not directed by Rossellini. But Basilio Franchina has recently said that in the same period he and Martelli filmed one shot for "Florence" at Scalera Studios (the Fascists being executed, #132 in Roncoroni's edition of the screenplay); and two shots for "The Po Delta" near Fiumicino on the Tiber River (#29? of the Germans in medium shot; and #180, *Paisà*'s final shot of the bodies falling into the river). (Franchina to Thomas Meder; unpublished.) Gina Franchina (whose husband Nino created Manfredi's after-torture make-up in *Roma città aperta*, with chewing gum; and whose son Sandro plays the boy in *Europe '51* and in 1966 made a film *Morire gratis* inspired, like *Voyage in Italy*, by a man, a woman and a car) says she helped Roberto film the flare signals for "The Po Delta" on the coast near Orbetello north of Rome. (In Alain Bergala and Jean Narboni, *Roberto Rossellini* [Paris: Éditions de l'Étoile, 1990], p. 42.) Basilio Franchina himself, at Rossellini's direction, filmed three insert shots at Scalera after regular production: in #132 in "Florence" (close shot of Fascist being killed); #29 in "Po" (Germans on the tower) and #180 in "Po" (the close shot of the partisans being dumped into the water: actually, the Tiber). (Basilio Franchina to Thomas Meder in Meder, *Vom Sichtbarmachen*, p. 313.)
80. Paolo Benvenuti to TG, based on statements by Rossellini and Count Roncioni.
81. Renzi, ed., *Era notte*, p. 60.
82. D.M., "*Roma.*"
83. Rod Geiger to TG.
84. Robert Lawrence to TG.
85. Mario Del Papa to TG.
86. Robert Lawrence to TG.
87. Rod Geiger to TG (dollar figure); Massimo Mida to TG (lire figure). In May 1947, Rossellini cited a figure of around fifty million; at that time, according to the stock exchange rate, as distinct from the official bank rate, this was equivalent to $72,000; but the lira had declined somewhat.
88. A. H. Weiler, April 28, 1946.
89. Carlo Carlini to TG.
90. Renzo Avanzo to TG.
91. "Rossellini parla," 1977.
92. "Fellini par Fellini," p. 16.
93. Ibid.
94. This version, titled "Northern Italy; Spring 1945," appears in Mann, *Seven from the U.S.* A somewhat different version by Amidei, "I partigiani del Nord," appears in Roncoroni, "Presentazione," pp. 576–84, in which there is no reference to "Byrnes's" Italian ancestry; the name "Guernica" does not appear; "Cristina" is shot; and Byrnes, taking her red handkerchief, joins her brother's band of partisans. "Guernica" is a reference to a Basque city in Spain that was annihilated by German bombers in 1937, an atrocity that became the subject of a contemporary mural by Picasso.
95. Quoted in Baldelli, p. 60.
96. Robert Warshow, "*Paisan*," *Partisan Review*, July 1948; reprinted in Warshow, *The Immediate Experience* (Garden City: Doubleday, 1962), p. 256. His remark refers equally to *Open City*.
97. Paolo Valmarana, "Cinema adulto," in Bruno, ed., *Rossellini* (Sanremo), p. 36.
98. Robin Wood, "Ingrid Bergman on Rossellini," *Film Comment*, July 1974, p. 8.
99. Valmarana, "Cinema adulto," pp. 36–38. Valmarana quotes in Italian, "Questo accadeva nell'inverno del 1944. All'inizio della primavera la guerra era già finita." In the film's American edition, the subtitles read: "This happened in the winter of 1944. A few weeks later spring came to Italy and the war in Europe was declared over." (This second sentence is incorrectly rendered in the English language edition of the script as "At the beginning, the war was over." [Rossellini, *The War Trilogy*, p. 348.])
100. B. Rondi, "Realtà della persona," p. 13.
101. Henri Agel, *Poétique du cinéma* (Paris: Ed. du Signe, 1973), p. 81.
102. Rossellini interview with Fereydoun Hoveyda and Jacques Rivette, "Entretien avec Roberto Rossellini," *Cahiers du Cinéma* 94, April 1959.
103. Emilio Lonero, "Un messaggio di fede, di speranza, di amore," *Rivista del Cinematografo*, June 1954, pp. 16; reprint: Roberto Rossellini, *Il mio metodo*, ed., Adriano Aprà (Venice: Marsilio, 1987), p. 104.
104. Valmarana, "Cinema adulto," p. 36.
105. Freddy Buache, *Le Cinéma italien d'Antonioni à Rosi* (Yverdon, Switzerland: Le Thiele, 1969), pp. 24–25; summarized in Peter Brunette, "Unity and Difference in *Paisan*," *Studies in the Literary Imagination*, Spring 1983, p. 100.
106. Paolo Gobetti, "La Résistance dans les films italiens (1945–1955)," in *Fascisme et résistance dans le cinéma italien* (Paris: Études Cinématographiques 82–83, 1970), p. 54.
107. Baldelli, pp. 66–67.
108. Bazin, "Le Réalisme," p. 31.
109. Ibid., p. 32.
110. Ayfre, "Sens et non-sens." Ayfre refers to Jacques Rivette, "De l'abjection (*Kapo*)," *Cahiers du Cinéma* 120, June 1961, pp. 54–55.
111. Bazin, "Le Réalisme," p. 28.
112. Serceau, *Rossellini*, pp. 39, 59.
113. B. Rondi, *Il neorealismo*, p. 147.
114. B. Rondi, *Il cinema di Fellini* (Roma: Bianco e Nero, 1965), p. 28.
115. Faldini and Fofi, I:108.

116. Rod Geiger to TG; Massimo Mida to TG.
117. De Marchis, "La mia vita," p. 16.
118. Alberto Manni, "Rossellini, l'araba fenice," *Epoca 1959*, No. 433 (month unknown, 1959), p. 54.
119. Franco Riganti to TG.
120. Lina Rossellini to TG.
121. De Marchis, "La mia vita," p. 16.
122. Ibid.
123. Manni, "Rossellini, l'araba fenice," pp. 53–54.
124. Lina Rossellini to TG.
125. De Marchis, "La mia vita," p. 16.
126. Manni, "Rossellini, l'araba fenice," pp. 54–55.
127. De Marchis, "La mia vita," p. 17. Vittorio Mussolini, in exile in Argentina, telegrammed his regrets.
128. Franco Rossellini to TG; De Marchis, "La mia vita."
129. *Film Rivista*, July 31, 1946.
130. Rod Geiger to TG.
131. Massimo Mida to TG.
132. Among other entries: *Lassie Come Home, Sister Kenny, Love Letters, The Bells of St. Mary's, Blood and Sand*.
133. In a poll, *Paisà* won the Premio del Pubblico di Film Rivista with 297 points, followed by *Blood and Sand* (Mamoulian, USA) with 263 and *The Southerner* with 219 points.
134. *CdC* 37, 1954, p. 2.
135. Manni, "Rossellini, l'araba fenice," p. 55.
136. "Dix ans," I.
137. *L'Unità* (Rome), September 19, 1946; reprints: Ivaldi, p. 48; Aprà, *Rosselliniana*, p. 150.
138. Anon., *Cinema* (Milan), September 28, 1946. Glauco Viazzi, "Cinema a Venezia," *Sipario*, no. 6, October 1946; reprint: Ivaldi, p. 49. Marta Schiavi, *Il Giornale dell'Emilia*, September 19, 1946; reprint: Aprà, *Rosselliniana*, p. 155. Nicolo Nemo(?), *Libertà*, September 21, 1946; reprint: Aprà, *Rosselliniana*, p. 158. Gino Damerini, *Il Tempo* (Rome), September 19, 1948; reprint: Aprà, *Rosselliniana*, p. 149. Nino Ghelli, *Cine Illustrato* (quoted without date in Stefano Masi and Enrico Lancia, *I film di Roberto Rossellini* [Rome: Gremese, 1987], p. 29). "Qui l'ottenebrata mente del regista s'illumina e riesce—era tempo—a sferrare l'azione." Francesco Callari, *Il Buon Senso*, September 19, 1946; reprint: Aprà, *Rosselliniana*, p. 152.
139. "I film presentati alla Mostra," *Rivista del Cinematografo* 7–8, October 1946; reprint: Aprà, *Rosselliniana*, p. 149.
140. Alredo Orecchio, *Il Nuovo Messaggero*, September 19, 1946; reprint: Aprà, *Rosselliniana*, p. 150. Augusto Torresin, *Il Gazzettini*, September 19, 1946; reprint: Aprà, *Rosselliniana*, p. 151. F. T. Roffaré, *Il Mattino del Popolo*, September 19, 1946; reprint: Aprà, *Rosselliniana*, p. 153. Enrico Graziola, *Alto Adige* (Bolzano), September 19, 1946; reprint: Aprà, *Rosselliniana*, p. 156. M. D., *L'Arena*, September 19, 1946; reprint: Aprà, *Rosselliniana*, p. 156.
141. *Fotogrammi*, September 25, 1946; reprint: Ivaldi, *Quello*, p. 49.
142. Remo Borsatti, *Fronte Democratico* (Cremona), September 19, 1946; reprint: Aprà, *Rosselliniana*, p. 157.
143. Rod Geiger to TG.
144. Robert Lawrence to TG.
145. Carlo Trabucco, *Il Popolo* (Rome), March 9, 1947; i.e., six months after Trabucco had attended the September 24 invitational Altemps screening in Rome. According to Rod Geiger, the print shown in Paris in November 1946 ran two hours.
146. Roberto Lawrence to TG about the slap and picnic. Otherwise: Pirro, pp. 198–99, expanding on De Marchis, "La mia vita," p. 17. But both sources incorrectly state that Rossellini and Magnani were taking a train to Paris in November to accept awards for best director and actress—evidently confusing the Italian awards with non-existent French ones, and a trip to Cannes in late September with a trip without Magnani to Paris in November. But it is possible that the Magnani–Rossellini romance began not on this trip to Cannes but on a third train trip, to Paris the following spring.
147. Rossellini to Adriano Aprà to TG.
148. *Fragments*, p. 136.
149. Rossellini to Adriano Aprà to TG.
150. "Dix ans," I:3.
151. *Fragments*, p. 135.
152. Director, ex-aequo with Alessandro Blasetti (*Un giorno nella vita*) and Vittorio De Sica (*Shoeshine*).
153. Quoted in Anon., "L'ora del cinema italiano," *Fotogrammi*, January 25, 1947; reprint: Ivaldi, *Quello*, p. 97. Ibid. Sadoul, "Rossellini," 1946.
154. Anon., "L'ora," in Ivaldi, *Quello*, p. 97. Ibid. *Le Courrier de l'Etudiant*, October 30, 1946; reprint: André Bazin, *Le Cinéma de l'occupation et de la résistance* (Paris: Union Géneral, 1975), p. 168. Cf. *French Cinema of the Occupation and Resistance* (New York: Ungar, 1981), p. 137.
155. Patrice-G. Hovald, *Le Néo-réalisme italien et ses créateurs* (Paris: du Cerf, 1959), p. 11.
156. Rossellini, "Un nuovo corso per il cinema italiano," *Cinema Nuovo* 152, July 1961, p. 305.
157. In three theaters in a dubbed edition, and in one theater with subtitles. The run closed on December 17.
158. *L'Écran Français* 73, November 19, 1946; reprint: F. Debreczeni and H. Steinberg, eds., *Le Néo-réalisme italien* (Paris: Études Cinématographiques 32–35, 1964), p. 133.
159. *La Revue du Cinéma* 3, December 1946, p. 66.
160. An ad for the screening appears in *L'Écran Français* 72, November 12, 1946, p. 8. For Bazin's emotions, cf. Dudley Andrew, *André Bazin* (New York: Oxford University Press, 1978), p. 119.
161. Sadoul, "Rossellini," 1946.

162. B. Jeener, "Roberto Rossellini, réalisateur de *Rome ville ouverte*, nous expose ses conceptions," *Le Figaro*, November 20, 1946; partial reprint: Debreczeni and Steinberg, eds., *Le Néo-réalisme*, pp. 119–20.
163. Delbert Clark, "Berlin, Year Zero," *The New York Times*, September 21, 1947.
164. *La Revue du Cinéma* 3, December 1946, p. 66.
165. Cited by Gian Vittorio Baldi to TG.
166. Ibid.
167. Ibid.
168. "Dix ans," I:4.
169. Mario Del Papa to TG, for the first explanation for the delay; Massimo Mida to TG for the second. Neither source felt secure in his opinion.
170. Reginald Torrington to TG.
171. Antonello Trombadori to TG. "J'étais fulgoré par *Paisà*."
172. *L'Unità* (Milan), December 15, 1946; reprint: Aprà, *Rosselliniana*, p. 160.
173. Alfredo Panicucci, December 14, 1946; reprint: Aprà, *Rosselliniana*, p. 160.
174. Pietro Bianchi, December 24, 1946.
175. Arturo Lanocita (Milan), December 14, 1946; reprint: Ivaldi, *Quello*, p. 50.
176. Rossellini comments recorded for the ORTF, 1962, in *Il mio metodo*, p. 202.
177. Umberto Barbaro, *L'Unità* (Rome), March 8, 1947; reprint: Ivaldi, *Quello*, pp. 50–51.
178. Franco Funghi, March 16, 1947; reprint: Aprà, *Rosselliniana*, p. 162.
179. Alberto Vecchietti, March 11, 1947; reprint: Ivaldi, *Quello*, p. 53.
180. Giulio Cesare Castello, *Il Secolo XIX* (Genoa), no date, 1947; reprint: Ivaldi, *Quello*, pp. 54–55.
181. *Il Tempo*, March 9, 1947; reprint: Ivaldi, *Quello*, p. 52.
182. Carlo Trabucco, *Il Popolo*, March 9, 1947; reprint: Ivaldi, *Quello*, p. 51.
183. Casiraghi, *Pattuglia* (Milan), June 30, 1947; reprint: Ivaldi, *Quello*, pp. 55–56.
184. Quoted in Faldini and Fofi, I:137.
185. Giorgio Prosperi, *Il Giornale d'Italia*, March 11, 1947; reprint: Ivaldi, *Quello*, pp. 53–54.
186. Alfredo Orecchio, *Il Messaggero*, March 9, 1947; reprint: Ivaldi, *Quello*, p. 53.
187. Faldini and Fofi, I:110.
188. Ungari, "Conversazione con Lizzani." Order of sentences rearranged.
189. Carlo Veneziani, *Il Mattino d'Italia* (Rome), September 18, 1946; reprint: Aprà, *Rosselliniana*, p. 149.
190. *Il Tempo*, March 9, 1947; reprint: Ivaldi, *Quello*, p. 52.
191. Pirro, *Celluloide*, p. 97.
192. Claude Mauriac, *L'Amour du cinéma* (Paris: Albin Michel, 1954), p. 107.
193. *La Revue du Cinéma* 3, December 1946, p. 66.
194. *L'Écran Français*, September 30, 1947; reprint: Debreczeni and Steinberg, eds., *Le Néo-réalisme*, p. 137.
195. Chiarini, "Avviso," *Bianco e Nero*, March 1948, p. 3.
196. Luis Berlanga, "L'emozione più grande," *Il Tempo*, June 3, 1978.
197. Quoted by Jean Rouch, "Memorie e testimonianze," in Farassino, *Neorealismo*, p. 9. By 1962 this was abundantly clear to Jacques Joly in *Cahiers du Cinéma*: "In Rossellini's case, misunderstandings were long numerous. Doubtless the gravest was seeing *Roma città aperta*, *Paisà* and *Deutschland im Jahre Null* as realistic and objective portraits of two nations. What was only an astonishing intuition by the man was taken for a lucid analysis of the disarray of the two countries, as though Rossellini had been doing the work of an historian instead of presenting a series of emotionally-charged flashes on the reality of certain individuals. One can consider these films as political works, as works of a moralist and poet, but they are certainly neither works of an historian nor patient studies of the economic and social reality of a country. Nor are they oriented toward the spectator: they aim neither to educate him nor to open his eyes to reality, but demand on the contrary that he come to the characters, that he participate with the director in seeking out an inner reality, a concealed moral. To accomplish a realist task, Visconti resorted to a mode of irrealist vision [in *La terra trema*], whereas Rossellini used pieces of reality to discover a hidden meaning beyond that same reality." ("Un nouveau réalisme," *Cahiers du Cinéma* 131, May 1962, pp. 4–5.)
198. Rossellini, "Un nuovo corso," p. 305.
199. Quoted in Derek Monsey, "Letter from Rome: A Meeting with Rossellini," *World Review*, January 1949, p. 59–60.
200. Di Giammatteo, "Un ritratto," pp. 31–32.
201. Armando Borrelli, *Neorealismo e marxismo* (Avellino: Cinemasud, 1966), pp. 81, 85; quoted in Brunette, "Unity and Difference," p. 101.
202. Buache, *Cinéma italien*, pp. 24–25.
203. Brunette, "Unity and Difference," pp. 100–01.
204. Baldelli, pp. 67, 59. (Free translation.) Similarly, the Catholic Brunello Rondi argued that Rossellini transcends the negativity of European philosophic thought by placing individual tragedies within an "integral vision of history . . . seen and narrated as participation and discovery." (B. Rondi, *Il neorealismo*, pp. 19, 24.)

Chapter 9: Slopes of Hope

1. Cited by Roswitha Schmidt to TG.
2. Rod Geiger to TG on Rossellini's still intense affection for her. Roswitha Schmidt to TG on her memory and Romano. Thomas Meder to TG for details of the abortion, based on testimony of Renata Gaede to Meder.

3. Faldini and Fofi, I:198.
4. De Marchis, "La mia vita," p. 17.
5. Roswitha Schmidt to Thomas Meder to TG.
6. "Dix ans," II.
7. Roswitha Schmidt to Thomas Meder to TG.
8. Léo Sauvage, "Rencontre nocturne avec le cinéma italien," *L'Écran Français*, April 29, 1947, p. 4.
9. "Rossellini parla," 1977.
10. Rossellini, "Il regista Rossellini giudica (e assolve) la rivolta giovanile," *Paese Sera*, May 8, 1969.
11. "Rossellini parla," 1977.
12. Cited by Gian Vittorio Baldi to TG.
13. Cocteau, "A propos de la Bienne de Venise," *Carrefour*, September 8, 1947; reprint: *Du Cinématograph* (Paris: Belfond, 1973), p. 36.
14. *Il Progresso*, 1948.
15. "Dix ans," II.
16. *Nuestro Cine* 95, 1970, p. 100. The reference is to Andy Warhol's six-hour *Sleep* (1963).
17. G. Ferrara, "L'opera di Rossellini," p. 39.
18. Marcel Oms, "Rossellini: du fascisme à la démocratie chrétienne," *Positif* 28, April 1958, p. 14. The article is an infamous anti-Rossellini diatribe.
19. *La Revue du Cinéma* 7, summer 1947; reprint: Cocteau, *Du Cinématographe*, p. 155.
20. Eric Rohmer, "L'Amore," *Cahiers du Cinéma* 59, May 1956, pp. 38–39.
21. Menon, *Dibattito*, pp. 108–09.
22. Quoted in Clark, "Berlin."
23. Selznick Archives, at the Harry Ransom Humanities Research Center, The University of Texas at Austin.
24. Baldelli, p. 205; Rossellini speaking before an audience at the Centro Sperimentale in 1971. There is no evidence in the Selznick Archives of a $2 million offer. The $1,070,000, seven-year, fourteen-picture proposal appears to have been a trial balloon thrown in the air by intermediaries. "[Walter Wolff] King is making a chump out of you on this," Selznick told Henry Willson on December 3, 1946. Nonetheless Rossellini appears to have misunderstood. In the summer of 1947 he told *The New York Times* that Selznick had offered him $2 million for seven pictures. (Clark, "Berlin.")

Except for a single exchange during a later period (a two-page letter from Rossellini answered by a half-page telegram from Selznick in June 1948), there is no evidence of any direct communication between Selznick and Rossellini in the Selznick Archives before 1949. Instead, all negotiations took place in person between Rossellini and Reissar or other Selznick agents. The Selznick Archives contain no record of Rossellini's offer to employ Selznick.
25. Claude Beylie, "L'Homme qui cherchait la vérité," *Écran* 60, July 15, 1977, p. 45.
26. Baldelli, p. 205; Rossellini speaking before an audience at the Centro Sperimentale in 1971.
27. Mayer, *Merely Colossal*, p. 219.
28. Unpublished interview, May 1968, with Philip Jenkinson.
29. Roswitha Schmidt to TG.
30. Mario Del Papa to TG.
31. Roswitha Schmidt to TG.
32. Steven Bach, *Marlene Dietrich* (New York: Morrow, 1992), p. 328.
33. Max Colpet has described his affair with Rossellini in *Sag mir, wo die Jahre sind. Erinnerungen eines unverbesserlichen Optimisten* (München-Wien: Albert Langen-Georg Müller, 1976; end ed., Frankfurt: Ullstein, 1988).
34. Lizzani, letter to Trombadori, September 15, 1947 (uncredited translation into English); in *Roberto Rossellini*, a book published by the Ministero del Turismo e dello Spettacolo for the Progetto multimediale del Ente Autonomo di Gestione per il Cinema: "Rossellini in Texas," October 1987 (Roma: Edizioni Ente Autonomo Gestione Cinema, 1987), p. 89.
35. Lizzani, quoted in Faldini and Fofi, I:111.
36. Lizzani to Trombadori, July 3, 1947, *Rossellini* (Texas), pp. 73–74.
37. Lizzani to Trombadori, July 4, 1947, Ibid., pp. 74–76.
38. Lizzani to Trombadori, July 15, 1947, Ibid., pp. 77–78.
39. Bach, *Dietrich*, p. 328.
40. Lizzani to Trombadori, July 15, 1947, *Rossellini* (Texas), pp. 79, 78.
41. Lizzani to Trombadori, July 15, 1947, Ibid., pp. 77–78.
42. Roswitha Schmidt to TG.
43. Ibid.
44. Lizzani to Trombadori, August 3, 1947, *Rossellini* (Texas), p. 82.
45. Rossellini, "Germany Year Zero," Pressbook for New York 1949 release by Superfilm Distributing Corp (Author's Collection); reprint (in Italian): *Il mio metodo*, pp. 60–62. Partially published, in English, in *New York Herald Tribune*, September 18, 1949.
46. Faldini and Fofi, I:111.
47. Rossellini, "Germany Year Zero" Pressbook.
48. Quoted in P. W. Jansen and Wolfram Schütte, eds., *Roberto Rossellini* (München: Hanser, 1987), p. 278.
49. Ibid.
50. M. K., "Ein Film ohne Drehbuch," *Der Morgen*, Berlin, August 12, 1947.
51. Walter Lennig, "Neue Augen sehen die Welt," *Berliner Zeitung*, August 12, 1947.
52. Rossellini, "Germany Year Zero" Pressbook.
53. Lizzani to Trombadori, August 3, 1947, *Rossellini* (Texas), p. 82.

54. Faldini and Fofi, I:111. Before going to Berlin in March, Rossellini had outlined the plot, writing it himself on four small sheets: "Gang of boys, they rob. / Police. / Violent defense by the little boy / who escapes, reaction: cries. / Home. / The people in the house. / In presenting the / house and its characters scene in which / it's made evident / in the boy's mind the / necessity of kill / the father. / The school. / The gang—the pleasure of / sleeping outside, of a life / of adventure, the boys profit / from the disorder of the life / of society to live / as they like. The mailman character. / Various characters." Allusions follow to the SS brother, the sister, the crime and the boy's psychology, concluding: "Solitude. / Squalid little / funeral. / Little boy finally / can rest. / Finale." Quoted from material in Basilio Franchina's possession in Gianni Rondolino, "Come nacque *Germania anno zero*," *Bianco e Nero*, July–August 1987, p. 34.

55. Renata Gaede, *Fotogrammi*, September 20, 1947; Rondolino, "Come nacque *Germania anno zero*." Lizzani gives a similar synopsis (*Rossellini* [Texas], pp. 79–80). Franchina's attempts to develop this outline are examined in Rondolino, op. cit.

56. Lizzani, in *Rossellini* (Texas), pp. 79–80.

57. Clark, "Berlin."

58. Rossellini, "Germany Year Zero" Pressbook.

59. Quoted in Lauro Venturi, "Roberto Rossellini," *Hollywood Quarterly*, Fall 1949, p. 7, with an acknowledgment to "Luigi Morandi, 'Letter from Berlin', in a Roman newspaper."

60. Carrano, *Magnani*, p. 111.

61. Giancarlo Governi, *Nannarella* (Milan: Bompiani, 1984), p. 120.

62. Roswitha Schmidt to TG.

63. Roswitha Schmidt to Thomas Meder to TG.

64. Faldini and Fofi, I:111; supplemented by TG's interview with Carlo Lizzani. Lizzani did not shoot Edmund's encounter with the boys, the scenes inside the building, or his suicide; these were done by Rossellini.

65. Roswitha Schmidt to TG.

66. Ibid.

67. Ibid. Thomas Meder, *Nosferatu*, June 1995.

68. Carlo Lizzani to TG.

69. Marcello Bolero to TG.

70. *Time*, September 26, 1949.

71. Rossellini, "Germany Year Zero" Pressbook.

72. Ibid.

73. Hans Habe, in *Süddeutsche Zeitung*, September 28, 1949. Translated with assistance from Thomas Meder. Habe's own book about postwar Germany is titled *Im Jahre Null*.

74. Rossellini, "Germany Year Zero" Pressbook.

75. To Ingrid Bergman; quoted in *My Story*, p. 242.

76. Fereydoun Hoveyda to TG, on Rossellini's authority.

77. Virgilio Fantuzzi, S. J., *Cinema sacro e profano* (Rome: Edizioni La Civiltà Cattolica, 1983), p. 19.

78. *Bianco e Nero*, 1952.

79. Carlo Lizzani, *Le Cinéma italien* (Paris: Les Editeurs Français réunis, 1955).

80. Baldelli, p. 254; Rossellini speaking before an audience at the Centro Sperimentale with Florentine students, April 17, 1971.

81. Ibid.

82. Marcella De Marchis to TG.

83. Roncoroni's edition of the screenplay (Rossellini, *La trilogia della guerra*, and its American translation) identify these words as present in Italian release prints. And they exist in the original U.S. release, which was in German. They are missing, however, from the second U.S. release, in the 1970s, of an otherwise identical edition (albeit dubbed into Italian)—in which, perhaps, Rossellini sought to cover his tracks.

84. Adriano Aprà, "Rossellini oltre il neorealismo," in Lino Micciché, *Il neorealismo cinematografico italiano* (Venice: Marsilio, pp. 294–95).

85. Schickel, *Men Who Made*, p. 159.

86. Faliero Rosati, in Menon, *Dibattito*, p. 35.

87. Aprà, in Menon, *Dibattito*, pp. 38–40.

88. Fantuzzi, *Cinema sacro*, pp. 93–94.

89. Enzo Velati, in Menon, *Dibattito*, p. 24.

90. B. Rondi, "Realtà della persona," p. 13.

91. Virgilio Fantuzzi, "Rossellini e la religione," in Bruno, ed., *Rossellini* (Sanremo), p. 180.

92. In Menon, *Dibattito*, p. 40.

93. Aprà, "Rossellini oltre," p. 294.

94. François Truffaut (signed, François de Montferrand), "Dans le cinéma italien un homme seul: Roberto Rossellini," *Radio-Cinéma-Télévision* 233, July 4, 1954, pp. 4, 39; reprinted as "Un homme seul," *Cahiers du Cinéma* 410, July 1988, p. 14.

95. Truffaut, *Arts* 576, July 11, 1956; reprint: *Cahiers du Cinéma* 410, July 1988.

96. Philippe Niel, "Voyage au centre d'*Allemagne année zéro*," *Positif* 331, September 1988.

97. In Glauco Pellegrini, "Colonna sonora," *Bianco e Nero*, March 1967, p. 29.

98. Quoted in Brunello Rondi, "Lavoro con Rossellini," *Cronache del Cinema e della Televisione* 25, Summer 1958, p. 143.

99. De Marchis, "La mia vita," p. 17.

100. Cited by Valmarana to TG.

101. De Marchis, "La mia vita," p. 17.

102. Antonio Lisandrini to TG.
103. "Le Miracle," *La Revue du Cinéma* 14, June 1948, p. 16.
104. Quoted in Carrano, *Magnani*, p. 116; from Fellini, *Fare un film*.
105. Carrano, *Magnani*, p. 116.
106. "Le Miracle," p. 16. Fellini was later widely accused of deriving his story from *Adega*, a 1901 novella by the Spaniard Ramón Valle-Inclán which in its time almost became a *cause célèbre* (Guarner, *Rossellini*, p. 27). "I did not plagiarize Valle-Inclán!" Fellini declared in newspapers at the time. But the stories are virtually identical. Cf. Verdone, *Rossellini*, pp. 34–35, for a detailed comparison between Valle-Inclán and Fellini.
107. Fabio Carlini, in Menon, *Dibattito*, p. 30.
108. Guarner, *Rossellini*, p. 26.
109. *Arts* 656, February 5, 1958.
110. Rohmer, "L'amore," p. 40; quoting Rossellini in *CdC* 37, 1954. Rohmer cites Fellini's script in *Revue du Cinema* 14, June 1948. Guarner, *Rossellini*, p. 28, states Rossellini changed the ending for the 1956 Paris presentation, but there is no evidence to suggest that the Fellini ending was ever exhibited. The 1950 American edition had the Paris ending.

    "A number of my colleagues," Rohmer continues, "have compared *Il miracolo's* theme with *La strada's* . . . to inflate the importance of Fellini's collaboration. . . . On paper, *Il miracolo's* crazy woman and Gelsomina are indeed not very different, and the two films contain the same meaning, the same moral, which is also *Stromboli's*: that the creature closest to God is also the humblest and most disreputable; but whereas Fellini, with his love for the shocking, the baroque, the monstrous, only knows how to convey this idea by intellectual tricks, it is principally the visible unity of nature that Rossellini is trying to make shine. And besides, if Rossellini shows himself here, even more than in *Paisà* or *Deutschland im Jahre Null*, in full possession of his art, [in Fellini] the constant search for effect, the musty stereotypes from Vigo or Stroheim sprinkled through *I vitelloni*, *La strada* and *Il bidone* signal a style still in search of itself."
111. Carrano, *Magnani*, p. 117.
112. Quoted in M. Fini, "Prima di lei conobbi la sua risata," *L'Europeo*, October 11, 1973.
113. Quoted by Indo Montanelli, in Carrano, *Magnani*, p. 106.
114. Federico Fellini to TG.
115. "Le Miracle," pp. 16–17.
116. Federico Fellini to TG; Tullio Pinelli to TG. For the quote: Faldini and Fofi, I:199.
117. Aldo Tonti, *Odore di cinema* (Firenze: Vallecchi, 1964), p. 131.
118. Ibid., pp. 132–33.
119. *Bianco e Nero*, 1952.
120. *Nuestro Cine* 95, 1970, p. 98.
121. April 11, 1948.
122. Mayer, *Merely Colossal*, p. 233.
123. Fae Miske to TG.
124. Mayer, *Merely Colossal*, p. 218.
125. Selznick Archives: Inter-office memo from Selznick to Scanlon and O'Shea, April 6, 1948. Telegram from Jenia Reissar to Selznick, April 7. Cable from Selznick to Reissar, April 8. Letter, Reissar to Selznick, April 14. Cable, Reissar to Selznick, April 19. Letter, Reissar to Selznick, April 21.
126. Selznick Archives: Reissar to Selznick, April 21, 1948.
127. "Dix ans," I.
128. Steele, *Ingrid Bergman*, p. 162.
129. Laurence Leamer, *As Time Goes By: The Life of Ingrid Bergman* (New York: Harper & Row, 1986), p. 153. Rossellini's claim (Bergman, p. 19) that he eventually recalled seeing her in Selznick's *Intermezzo* during a bombing raid so long that he had had to sit through it three times is an obvious canard. Bombing raids were short and Rossellini would not have endured a film like *Intermezzo* even once.
130. Governi, *Nannarella*, p. 135.
131. Steele, *Ingrid Bergman*, p. 166.
132. *My Story*, pp. 13–14. Bergman incorrectly writes that she saw *Open City* in Hollywood in 1948 with her husband, Petter Lindstrom; in fact she saw it in New York with Joe Steele, her publicist.
133. *My Story*, p. 23.
134. Faldini and Fofi, I:201.
135. Carrano, *Magnani*, p. 129. Avanzo named his company Panarea Film, after the Eolian island next to Stromboli. His partners were Francesco Alliata, Pietro Moncada, and Fosco Maraini, who operated the camera. Among the documentaries were *Cacciatori sottomarini* and *Bianche Eolie*. In 1949 Panarea Film produced *Vulcano* (William Dieterle) with Magnani, and in 1952 *The Golden Coach* (Renoir) and *A fil di spada* and *Il segreto delle tre punte* (both C. L. Bragaglia).
136. Selznick Archives: Reissar to Selznick, June 29, 1948.
137. *Documentary Film News*, May 1948, p. 53.
138. Selznick Archives: Reissar to Selznick, June 1, 1948.
139. Selznick Archives: undated, typed letter (in English), on Rossellini's stationery.
140. Selznick Archives: Selznick to Reissar, June 19, 1948.
141. Leamer, *As Time Goes By*, p. 154.
142. Ibid.
143. Selznick Archives: Reissar to Selznick, June 10, 1948.
144. Selznick Archives: Selznick to Reissar, June 19, 1948; five single-spaced pages.

145. Arabella Lemaître Unghero to TG.
146. Selznick Archives: Reissar to Selznick, June 29, 1948.
147. Jean Gruault, *Ce que dit l'autre* (Paris: Julliard, 1992), p. 222.
148. Faldini and Fofi, I:65.
149. Rod Geiger to TG.
150. "Rossellini parla," 1977.
151. Governi, *Nannarella*, p. 118.
152. *Shoeshine* was awarded an honorary Oscar in 1947. "The high quality of this motion picture, brought to eloquent life in a country scarred by war, is proof to the world that the creative spirit can triumph over adversity."
153. Selznick Archives: Reissar to Selznick, June 29, 1948 (the quotation marks are hers). Selznick had wanted to stage the piece with Magnani in a New York theater, in Italian.
154. O'Shea to Selznick, reporting on a phone conversation with Peyser, July 13, 1948.
155. Selznick Archives: Selznick to Reissar, July 20, 1948.

Chapter 10: Neo-realism = mc^2

1. *CdC* 37, 1954.
2. Gian Carlo Pajetta, "Espresse in un film le speranze di un popolo," *L'Unità*, June 4, 1977. Pajetta was a prominent Communist who had been imprisoned under Fascism. Barzini described him as "an energetic, young chief [who at the end of war] stormed the prefecture of Milan at the head of a tumultuous crowd, and called Togliatti in Rome from the Prefect's own phone. [T]he leader did not hide his displeasure: 'Get out of there immediately,' he said. 'What do you think you're doing? Lenin said that either one carries out a revolution to the end or one does not start one.'" (Barzini, *From Caesar*, p. 128.) Celeste Negarville was the partisan model for Pagliero's character in *Roma città aperta*.

   One well-respected art critic, Toti Scialoja, did express open esteem for *Germania* at this time, calling it "Piuttosto bello." (Quoted in B. Rondi, "Lavoro," p. 138.)
3. Among diverse after-the-fact definitions of neo-realism:

   ZAVATTINI (1952): "The old realism wasn't expressing the real. What I want to know is the essence, the really real, inner as well as external reality.... There's a thin line between reality and the imagination, and it's that thin line that we followed at first. Our movement, which we call neo-realism, is simply an attempt to stay always at the level of the Italian people." (In Harvey Breit, "Focus on Italy's Top Scenarists," *New York Times*, November 9, 1952; reprinted [in French and retranslated here] in Debreczeni and Steinberg, eds., *Le Néo-réalisme*, p. 78.)

   MORAVIA (1954): "Neo-realism's preferred reality is essentially that product of atmosphere that excludes intrigue, psychology and characters." (*Cinema Nuovo* 33, April 15, 1954.)

   DE SICA (1956): "Neo-realism is the poetry of life itself." (In R. Gabert in *Il tetto* [Unitalia Film, 1956]; in Debreczeni and Steinberg, eds., *Le Néo-réalisme*, p. 78.)

   VISCONTI (1959): "Neo-realism is more than anything else a question of content." (*Cahiers du Cinéma* 93, March 1959.)

   FELLINI (1959): "Neo-realism is a way of looking at reality without any prejudice, without intervening conventions ..., not just social reality but spiritual reality as well, metaphysical reality, everything that's within man." (Gideon Bachmann, "Federico Fellini: An Interview," in Robert Hughes, ed., *Film: Book I* [New York: Grove, 1959], pp. 99–100; reprinted [in French and retranslated here] in Debreczeni and Steinberg, eds., *Le Néo-réalisme*, p. 78.)

   "Rossellini is the sole neo-realist director. The quality of [his] regard posed on reality has perhaps given birth to a certain current, which has since undergone diverse influences and gone off into different directions." (Fellini, "Mon Métier," p. 16.)

   ROSSELLINI (1954): "People have said, written and repeated in every key that I discovered a new form of expression: neo-realism. This is doubtless true, since, on this point, all the critics agree, and one is never right to contradict general opinion. But I have trouble convincing myself. The term neo-realism was born with *Roma città aperta*'s success ... and I'm still not sure people understood my intentions very well. But people baptized me the inventor of neo-realism. What does that mean? I don't feel at all in solidarity with the films made in my country. It seems obvious to me that each person possesses his own realism and that each thinks his is the best. Myself included. My personal 'neo-realism' is nothing else but a moral position summed up in four words: love of one's neighbor. 'On one side there's Rossellini, on the other, the Italian cinema.' That's what a critic wrote about me once, and it's terribly exact." (*Arts*, 1954.)

   "Neo-realism consists in following a person, with love, through all their discoveries, all their impressions." ("Dix ans," I.)
4. But assumptions to the contrary may be found, to one degree or another, in almost every history or textbook published in English, perpetuated even by scholars who know better. For example, David Overbey writes: "The ethical and moral position of neo-realism was, in part, born in the 'War of Liberation' and was dedicated to exploring and exposing the rhetorical lies of the Fascist period and to confronting the social reality of the present. Lies and equivocations had caused Italy's calamities and it was thought that the 'truth' would save her ..., [that] artistic expression might continue the battle to success where politics had failed.... Neo-realist theory [i.e., Zavattini, who started theorizing in the 1950s and had

nothing to do with Rossellini's films] holds that plot should disappear, for plot suggests a too-obvious manipulation of characters which blocks 'reality' from being truly represented.... Roberto Rossellini carried this tenet [which didn't yet exist] to the core of his work by minimizing narrative events [*Roma città aperta? Paisà?*] in order to observe more clearly the 'movements of the soul', and the 'movements of ideas as they are born and acted upon'." (Overbey, *Springtime*, pp. 10, 24.)

5. *Filmcritica* 5, May 1951.
6. Luigi Chiarini, "Discorso sul neorealismo," a lecture delivered April 11, 1950, published in *Bianco e Nero*, July 7, 1951; reprint: Overbey, *Springtime*, p. 141.
7. "Una posizione morale" from a debate at UNESCO, March 1963, excerpted in *Artsept*, April 1963, pp. 101–04 and in *Objectif 63* (Canada), August 1963, pp. 35–38. The two versions are integrated in *Il mio metodo*, pp. 280–87.
8. Blue, 1972.
9. *Bianco e Nero*, 1952. Continuing: "A need, appropriate to modern man, to say things as they are, to be aware of reality in an absolutely concrete manner, in conformity with that typically contemporary interest in statistical and scientific results. A sincere need, as well, to see men with humility, as they are, without resorting to stratagems in order to invent the extraordinary. A conscientiousness to obtain the extraordinary through research. A desire, finally, to enlighten oneself and not ignore reality, whatever it be.... To give anything its true value means to have understood its authentic and universal meaning.... There are those who still think of realism as something external, as going out into the open air, as a contemplation of misery and suffering. Realism, for me, is nothing but the artistic form of truth."
10. Gianni Puccini, "Per una discussione sul film italiano," *Bianco e Nero*, April 1948, pp. 12–17.
11. Don Ranvaud notes at least three earlier occurrences of the term: Ettore Margadonna, "Il realismo nel cinema europeo," *Comoedia*, May 15, 1932 (regarding *Nanook, Grass, The General Line, Tabu*, et al.); Arnaldo Bocelli in *Nuova Antologia*, 1931, quoted by G. P. Brunetta, *Storia del Cinema Italiano*, Riuniti, 1979, p. 446 (regarding recent writers); Umberto Barbaro, in preface to Italian edition of Pudovkin's *The Cinematic Subject*, 1932. ("A Critical Trajectory I," in Ranvaud, ed., *Roberto Rossellini*, BFI - Dossier number 8, 1981, p. 39.)

   Bocelli, referring to thirties literature, says neo-realist works analyze human condition vis-à-vis social environment and psychology and avoid stylistic and formal "hedonism" (e.g., *Gli indifferenti*). In contrast, later theorists of cinematic neo-realism have emphasized (perhaps not correctly) its lack of "psychology." Italo Calvino, again speaking of literature rather than film, claims neo-realists were more concerned with expression, the form of the stories to be told, than with the stories themselves; he calls them compulsive formalists who thought "the musical score is more important than the libretto" (p. 28); and holds that the importance of neo-realism is not in its subject matter or ideology (which both change) but in rejection of elegant writing, in giving written form to spoken language. (*I sentieri dei nidi di ragno* [Torino: Einaudi, 1947], preface to 1967 edition.)
12. Serandrei, when he saw *Ossessione*'s rushes in 1943, wrote to Visconti, "I don't know how one could define this sort of cinema if not with the name 'neo-realistic'" (Faldini and Fofi, I:67)—by which he meant that *Ossessione* resembled French films of the thirties.

   Barbaro's essay, "Neo-realismo," in *Film* (Rome), June 5, 1943, was a discussion of Renoir, Carné, and Duvivier.

   Cinema never used the term neo-realism before it ceased publication in 1943.

   Guido Aristarco did use the term in *Cronache* (Bologna), December 29, 1945—four months after *Roma città aperta*'s release—but, still, not for Italian cinema: "In France, neo-realism (Renoir, Carné, Duvivier) arose not from the conscious will of the critics but because there were poets with precise aspirations."

   A newer usage—but still not for Italian cinema—occurs by Georges Sadoul, *Les Lettres françaises* 148, March 21, 1947. Sadoul notes a "common tendency" among Rouquier's *Farrebique*, Lindtberg's *La Dernière chance*, Clément's *La Bataille du rail* and *Paisà*. "What characterizes this new European school, which could be called the realist school, is its reaction against the excesses that have brought about Hollywood's current decadence and that today threaten a whole sector of the French cinema. In contrast to the minute mechanics by which each piece is manufactured and polished by a hyperqualified specialist, the 'neo-realists' oppose films shot without money or equipment but which always have a feeling of life and truth. In contrast to studied fabrication they prefer the sure choice of reality which is one of the most refined forms of art."
13. Chiarini, "Discorso sul neorealismo."
14. Morlion, "Le basi filosofiche del neorealismo cinematografico italiano," *Bianco e Nero*, June 1948. Translated in Overbey, *Springtime*, pp. 115–22. The Italian films Morlion refers to as neo-realist are *Roma città aperta, Paisà, Un giorno nella vita* (Blasetti, 1946), *4 passi fra le nuvole* (Blasetti, 1942), *Sciuscià, La porta del cielo* (De Sica, 1943–46), *Vivere in pace, L'onorevole Angelina* (Zampa, 1947), and the final sequences of *Il sole sorge ancora. Ladri di biciclette* and *La terra trema* had not yet appeared to complicate Morlion's terrain.

   Morlion distinguished the "human reality" of Italian realism from similar realism in other countries. "With its tough frankness this Italian school is different from the somewhat 'sophisticated' American school, the main goal of which is to please all audiences and every censor. In its artistic and intellectual severity, the Italian cinema is distinguished from the French school, which is always dressed up with plastic and literary embellishments. Again the new Italian school differs in its freshness and spontaneity from the new English 'documentary school', which, in the hands of Carol Reed, David Lean, and Harry Watt, remains rather cold."
15. The Barbaro articles cited above, dating back to 1932; the Serandrei letter to Visconti cited above; the discussions of the *Cinema* group, although the magazine did not print the word itself.

16. Baldelli.
17. Lino Miccichè, "Per una verifica del neorealismo," in Miccichè, ed., *Il neorealismo cinematografico italiano*, 2nd ed. (Venice: Marsilio Editori, 1978), pp. 15, 25. Elio Vittorini, "Una nuova cultura," *Politecnico*, September 29, 1945. De Santis and Alicata, essaying on the realism of Verga and French cinema, called in 1941 for a "revolutionary art inspired by the sufferings and hopes of humanity." But both men were posing as Fascists and such language was typical of the rhetoric of the regime, which routinely presented itself as "revolutionary." Would their call have been understood as un-Fascist, let alone as anti-Fascist? (De Santis and Alicata quoted in Pietro Ingrao, "Luchino Visconti: L'antifascismo e il cinema," *Rinascità* 13, 1976; quoted in Liehm, *Passion*, p. 327n. 32.)
18. Andrew, *Bazin*, pp. 25–27. My summaries of French thought are greatly indebted to Andrew's book.
19. Ibid., p. 22.
20. Jacques Maritain, *Georges Rouault* (New York: Abrams, 1954), quoted in Andrew, *Bazin*, p. 22.
21. Count Carlo Sforza, Italian foreign minister, put this somewhat differently. "The Italians must forget a defeat," he said. "The French must invent a victory." (Cited in Luigi Barzini, *The Europeans* [New York: Atheneum, 1965; reprint: Simon & Schuster, 1983], p. 136.)
22. Antonello Trombadori to TG.
23. H. Stuart Hughes, *The United States and Italy*, revised ed. (New York: Norton, 1965), pp. 236–37.
24. "Mussolini," Ciano wrote in his diary, "is irritated for the nth time at Catholicism, which is to blame for 'having made Italy universal, hence preventing it from becoming national. When a country is universal it belongs to everybody but itself.'" *Ciano's Diaries*, March 30, 1940, p. 229.
25. Anthony Cave Brown, *The Last Hero* (New York: Times Books, 1982), p. 684.
26. Barzini, *From Caesar*, pp. 126, 129.
27. Ibid., p. 129.
28. Quoted in Barzini, *From Caesar*, p. 307.
29. For many of these ideas about Croce and postwar Italy I am indebted to David D. Roberts's magnificent *Benedetto Croce and the Uses of Historicism* (Berkeley: University of California Press, 1987).
30. Barzini, *From Caesar*, p. 310.
31. In 1917; quoted in Barzini, *From Caesar*, p. 137. Cf. Cammett, *Antonio Gramsci*; Walter L. Adamson, *Hegemony and Revolution: A Study of Antonio Gramsci's Political and Cultural Theory* (Berkeley and Los Angeles: University of California Press, 1980).
32. Quoted in Barzini, *From Caesar*, p. 137.
33. H. Stuart Hughes, *Consciousness and Society* for this summary of Pirandello.
34. G. Ferrara, "L'opera di Rossellini," pp. 29, 36–37, 30.
35. Faldini and Fofi, I:218; cf. also, I:222–23.
36. Rossellini, "Il neorealismo è morto ucciso dalla politica, dai tabù e dalle mode," *Il Messaggero*, July 29, 1960, p. 8; reprint: *Il mio metodo*, pp. 229–30.
37. MacNiven, Yale 1974.
38. In Menon, *Dibattito*, pp. 76, 80.
39. For these ideas on Croce's relation to existentialism, Freud, and Marxism I am again indebted to Roberts, *Benedetto Croce.*

Chapter 11: Debacles

1. Cf. Peter Bondanella, "Neorealist Aesthetics and the Fantastic: *The Machine to Kill Bad People* and *Miracle in Milan*," *Film Criticism*, Winter 1979, pp. 24–29.
2. Guarner, *Rossellini*, p. 34, for "vinceremo," radio, cemetery.
3. Stern, *No Innocence*, pp. 161, 164. Leamer, *As Time Goes By*, p. 157, cites Helen Tubbs that Magnani's remark was directed at an Italian sunbather. Stern claims Buferd was the target (p. 165).
4. Helen Tubbs to TG.
5. Mida, *Rossellini*, 1st ed., pp. 54–59.
6. Stern, *No Innocence*, p. 165.
7. Spaghetti is usually the designated ammunition in this famous story. Unfortunately, honesty obliges us to follow the account of an eyewitness, Gigetto Pietravalle. Cf. Governi, *Nannarella*, p. 140.
8. Zeffirelli, *Zeffirelli*, p. 72.
9. Ibid., pp. 84–85.
10. "Dix ans," I.
11. Achille Valdata, "Il cinema al Lido di Venezia," *Gazzetto del Popolo*, August 22, 1948, p. 3.
12. Other reports around this time had Rossellini about to do *La contessa di Montecristo* with Magnani and a script by Fellini and Pinelli, and possibly *La strada* with Isa Miranda and, again, Fellini.
13. Selznick Archives: Rossellini to Jones, August 23, 1948.
14. Selznick Archives: Selznick to Reissar, August 31, 1948.
15. Selznick Archives: Lemaître to Reissar, September 16, 1948.
16. Selznick Archives: Reissar to Selznick, September 21, 1948.
17. Andrew, *Bazin*, p. 149.
18. Selznick Archives: Reissar to Selznick, September 28, 1948.
19. Selznick Archives: Selznick to Reissar, October 4, 1948.

20. Except for the quote (from Bergman, *My Story*, p. 237), I have followed Bergman's contemporary account to Steele (*Ingrid Bergman*, pp. 167–68). Bergman's later account (*My Story*, pp. 237–39) deletes the intensity of her emotions (except for the aforementioned quote) in favor of a detached amusement at Rossellini's quixoticness. Stern's account—that the meeting took place on September 22, that Rossellini had arrived two days late, and that Bergman had almost not waited for him—would explain his failure to return Reissar's calls; but Alan Burgess (Bergman's coauthor) implicitly contradicts this chronology by citing a letter of September 23 in which Bergman wrote Ruth Roberts she would meet Rossellini over the coming weekend (Stern, *No Innocence*, p. 169; *My Story*, p. 235).
21. De Marchis, "La mia vita," p. 46.
22. Steele, *Ingrid Bergman*, p. 68; citing Omar Garrison, *Los Angeles Evening Mirror* (no date).
23. Stern, *No Innocence*, p. 166.
24. Quoted in Mida, *Rossellini*, 1st ed., p. 54 (no citation).
25. Lina Rossellini to TG.
26. Fernaldo Di Giammatteo, "Un ritratto."
27. Mida, *Rossellini*, 2nd ed., pp. 44–45.
28. Jean George Auriol, *La Revue du Cinéma* 17, September 1948, pp. 64–69.
29. The claim on *Deutschland im Jahre Null*'s titles that it was awarded "Primo premio assoluto" is untrue. It won first prizes for picture and best scenario.
30. Aristarco, *Cinema*, December 1948; quoted in F. Rinaudo, "Foyer Rossellini," *Cronache del cinema e della televisione*, May-June 1956, p. 44.
31. Raymond Barkan, *L'Écran Français* 188, February 1, 1949.
32. Enzo Colombo, *Bis*, December 16, 1948.
33. Antonio Lanocita, *Cinema*, December 15, 1948.
34. Adriano Baracco, *Cinema*, October 25, 1948, p. 10.
35. Bazin, *L'Écran Français* 189, February 8, 1949. Bazin reiterated these points in *Esprit*, May 1949, p. 689, but deleted his negative judgments when this second review was reprinted in *Qu'est-ce que le cinéma?*, III:29–32. Had Bazin, like so many others, changed his mind?
36. Quoted in Rinaudo, "Foyer Rossellini," p. 45.
37. Carlo, Falconi, *Cinema Nuovo*, no. 50; cited in Rinaudo, "Foyer Rossellini," p. 45.
38. Baracco, *Cinema*, October 25, 1948, p. 10.
39. Mario Gromo, *Cinema Italiano*, p. 107; cited in Rinaudo, "Foyer Rossellini," p. 44.
40. *L'Unità*, November 3, 1948.
41. Alfredo Panicucci, *Avanti!*, August 22, 1948.
42. *Esprit*, December 1948, pp. 904–05.
43. Quoted in Rinaudo, "Foyer Rossellini," p. 45.
44. Fantuzzi, *Cinema sacro*, p. 19.
45. Henri Agel, *Cinéma et nouvel naissance* (Paris: Michel, 1981), p. 220.
46. Di Giammatteo, "Un ritratto," p. 34.
47. Auriol, *La Revue du Cinéma* 17, pp. 68–69.
48. *Il Progresso d'Italia*, 1948.
49. Seymour Peyser to TG.
50. Roger Régent, "Rossellini: Quand je commence à devenir intelligent je suis foutu" *L'Écran Français*, November 2, 1948.
51. Régent, "Rossellini."

Chapter 12. Neo-realism = ∞

1. *Open City* was nominated for an Oscar for its screenplay (Amidei and Fellini), *Paisan* for story and screenplay (Hayes, Fellini, Amidei, Pagliero, and Rossellini), but neither won. Both *Shoeshine* and *Bicycle Thieves* were nominated for their screenplays but won, respectively, an honorary Oscar and best foreign language film. In the *Sight and Sound* polls, conducted every ten years, *Bicycle Thieves* placed first in 1952; sixth in 1962, with De Sica himself voted the sixth best director in history (*La terra trema* was ninth, *L'avventura* second, *Umberto D* a runner-up; Antonioni the fifth best director, Visconti the eleventh); in 1972 *Bicycle Thieves* didn't place; *8 1/2* was fourth, *L'avventura* fifth; Fellini ninth best director, Antonioni tenth. In the 1952 Belgium Cinémathèque poll, *Bicycle Thieves* placed third. In the 1958 Brussels World Fair poll of 117 historians it was second, and De Sica fourth. Orson Welles put *Shoeshine* fifth in 1952 and King Vidor gave a rare vote for Rossellini, voting *Open City* seventh.

  Rossellini fared somewhat better in later years, but aside from such vagaries as Andrew Sarris's putting *Francesco giullare di Dio* eighth on his 1952 *Sight and Sound* list, what Rossellini support there was came from the *Cahiers du Cinéma* group. In the 1962 *Sight and Sound* poll, Rivette put *Deutschland im Jahre Null* second, and Rohmer *Voyage in Italy* sixth. *Cahiers* responded to Brussels in December 1958 with its own twelve-best list, first choosing directors and then selecting a specific film by each; *Voyage in Italy* placed third (behind *Sunrise* and *La Règle du jeu*). In *Cahiers'* survey of Italian directors in May 1962, De Sica and Fellini were put among 36 second-tier artists, while Antonioni, Rossellini, and Visconti were the "three greats."
2. Cf. Maria Mercader, *Un Amour obstiné: Ma vie avec Vittorio De Sica* (trans. from Italian, Paris: Lhermier, 1981), pp. 91–92. Curiously, *Bicycle Thieves* was distributed in the U.S. not by Lopert (who was now

involved with Rossellini) but by Mayer-Burstyn, under the mistranslated title *The Bicycle Thief* (like the French release: *Voleur de bicyclette*). The British title was *Bicycle Thieves*.

3. Amidei, quoted in Faldini and Fofi, I:135.
4. Cited by Sergio Leone in Faldini and Fofi, I:135. Leone, 16, was De Sica's errand boy during this period; he also plays one of the talky German seminarians.
5. Amidei, quoted in Faldini and Fofi, I:135.
6. Massimo Ferrara to TG, October 1992.
7. "At the end of November or in the first days of December," according to Mercader (op. cit., p. 94). *Variety*'s critic saw it December 6.
8. Pirro, *Celluloide*, p. 127. "Sono uno stronzo!"
9. Mercader, *Un Amour*, p. 96.
10. Ibid.
11. "Dix ans," II.
12. Jympson Harmon, *Evening News*; quoted in Manvell, "Paisa," p. 54.
13. A special correspondent in the *Observer*; quoted in Manvell, "Paisa," p. 54.
14. Basil Wright, "Paisa," *Sequence*, no. 2, 1947, p. 31.
15. Commented Rossellini: "In Italy I have been called unpatriotic because the picture showed the degradation of Italian girls. Then I have been accused by the Catholics of ridiculing religion in the monastery episode. So I'm not really surprised that people in London lack the sense of humour to see the slight burlesque of the two officer types [in "Florence"] in the right perspective. As for the scathing reference to British military policy by one of the Po partisans [in response to Alexander's order, a GI, not a partisan, says the partisans "aren't fighting for the British Empire, they're fighting for their lives"], I can imagine that—separated from the political context of the time—it might sound offensive to the British. It must be remembered, though, that at the time Field-Marshall Alexander had issued a message to Italian partisans telling them to return to their homes and wait until the spring for Allied orders. He might not have realised that to any of these men, whose absence from home had been persistently investigated by the Germans, a return home would have meant death or at least deportation to Germany. Hence a widespread resentment, which that characteristic remark of the partisan reflects." (Koval, "Interview," 1951, p. 393.)
    The English—in the form of Alexander Korda—had been invited to participate financially in *Paisà*'s production, and an episode featuring them had at one time been planned, but the deal had not come off.
16. Lotte H. Eisner, "Notes on Some Recent Italian Films," *Sequence* 8, Summer 1949, pp. 52, 58.
17. Adam Helmer, "Germania Anno Zero," *Sequence* 8, Summer 1949, p. 85.
18. Eisner, "Notes," p. 57.
19. April 1950, pp. 86–88. The English were also disillusioned when they learned Rossellini had used back-projections and studio interiors in *Deutschland* and Méliès-like trick shots (the devil's popping off the screen, the frozen characters) in *La macchina*.
20. For an analysis of its traditional construction, see Frank Tomasulo, "Bicycle Thieves: A Re-Reading," *Cinema Journal*, Spring 1982, pp. 2–13.
21. André Bazin, *Vittorio De Sica* (Parma: Guanda, 1952); reprinted in French as "De Sica metteur en scène," in *Qu'est-ce que le cinéma?*
22. Menon, *Dibattito*, pp. 36–37, 38, 39. Aprà is alluding to a famous line in Jean-Luc Godard's "Beyond the Stars," a review of Nicholas Ray's *Bitter Victory*: "It's no longer a matter of reality nor of fiction. . . . It's about something else entirely. About what? About the stars maybe, and people who love to look at the stars and dream." (*Cahiers du Cinéma* 79, January 1958.)
23. André Bazin, "Voleur de bicyclette," *Esprit*, November 1949; reprinted in *Qu'est-ce que le cinéma?*, IV:59; beware trans. Gray, *What Is Cinema?*, II: 60.
24. Bazin's enthusiasm repeatedly inspired him to poetic exaggerations that, unfortunately, American academics have accepted as well-considered statements of film "theory": the notion, for example, that neo-realism is styleless; or the notion that cinema is an imprint of reality, which academics have glossed with reams of analytic disputation, as though it were intended as the foundation of cinematic ontology rather than one among many poetic insights into cinema's experiential problems (e.g., Noël Carroll, *Philosophical Problems of Classical Film Theory*, [Princeton: Princeton University Press, 1988]).
    Note, for example, this passage from one of Bazin's most ambitious essays, "L'Évolution du langage cinématographique" (*Qu'est-ce que le cinéma?*, I:145): "In Rossellini's *Paisà* and *Deutschland im Jahre Null* and De Sica's *Bicycle Thieves*, Italian neo-realism opposes earlier forms of cinematic realism by stripping away all expressionism and, in particular, by the total absence of effects due to montage."
    The points Bazin goes on to make ("As with Welles and despite antithetic styles, neo-realism tends to give film a sense of the ambiguity of the real. Rossellini's concern with the boy's face in *Deutschland im Jahre Null* is just the opposite of Kuleshov's with Mozhukhin's close-up. It is a matter of preserving its mystery . . . of reducing montage to nothing and getting reality's true continuity to pass on the screen.") are good and valid as attempts to explain Bazin's *emotions* while watching these films. But taken literally, Bazin's opening sentence: (1) contradicts his earlier assertion (in "Le Réalisme") of how much "The Po Delta" owes to the "enormous ellipses" that Rossellini's montage creates between "autonomous facts" which we then have to connect together ourselves; (2) ignores Rossellini's expressionistic affinities with Murnau in his use of atmospheric lighting in *Paisà* and downright melodramatic lighting and camera angle in *Deutschland* and *Il miracolo*—not to mention Renzo Rossellini's expressionist music; (3) ignores Rossellini's careful fiddling with his films' editing, in order to create "rhythm" and, by removing frames from the *middle* of shots, to prevent "reality's true continuity" from passing on the screen.

Bazin's attitude was common in Paris. Cocteau lauded *Paisà* for its "perfect artlessness" and Claude Mauriac announced that "never have art's lies become truth with less artifice." (Cocteau, *Du Cinématographe*, p. 36. Mauriac, *L'Amour du cinéma*, p. 107.)

25. In Charles Thomas Samuels, *Encountering Directors* (New York: G. P. Putnam's, 1972), p. 144. Sentence order inverted.

26. Moravia, *Cinema Nuovo* 33, April 15, 1954; quoted in Debreczeni and Steinberg, eds., *Le Néo-réalisme*, p. 89.

27. Zeffirelli, *Zeffirelli*, p. 76.

28. "Le Réalisme," p. 17.

29. Bazin, "De Sica," p. 74.

30. For this interaction among *Roma città aperta*'s characters, cf. Serceau, *Rossellini*, p. 34.

31. Wrote Bazin: "It is supremely clever to have virtually eliminated the role of the wife in order to embody the private character of the tragedy in the child. . . . It is the child who gives to the workman's adventure its ethical dimension. . . . He is the intimate witness, the private chorus attached to the tragedy. . . . It is the admiration the child, as a child, feels for his father and the father's awareness of it that gives the ending its tragic grandeur." ("*Voleur de bicyclette,*" *Esprit*, November 1949, in *Qu'est-ce que le cinéma?*, IV:52.)

32. Murnau, at a press conference shortly after completing *Sunrise*, was at pains to dissociate his work from criticism as indulgence in style for style's sake: "Interesting camera angle: it seems to be the most used—I think also the most abused term in pictures—talking, reading, and producing. Such a thing as an interesting camera angle should not exist. By itself an interesting camera angle does not mean a thing. If it does not help to intensify the dramatic action of the scene it is not only useless, it is dangerous, because instead of helping the dramatic action, it detracts from it. But what should the camera angle be if not interesting? It should be dramatic. That is to say, a camera angle that helps to intensify the dramatic action of the scene." ("Drama," of course, implies conflict, not mere reduplication.) (*Moving Picture World*, April 2, 1927, p. 490.)

Cf. Rossellini: "Beautiful shots! That's one thing that makes me sick! A film should be well staged—that's the least one can expect from a film person—but a shot all by itself doesn't have to be beautiful." "Dix ans," I.

33. "Dix ans," I.

34. "*L'amore,*" wrote Vittorio Taviani early in 1950, when this crisis was still very much alive, "has induced some to speak of [the] death of neo-realism, whereas Rossellini's film is a direct and necessary consequence of neo-realism. The new Italian directors, in fact, pushed by a tragic experience to turn to everyday life as [the] sole font of inspiration, soon realized that it is more fantastic than any fantasy. The screen has become for them a window wide open onto the real, from which the artist must gather the internal and invisible movement. 'Reality,' Ugo Spirito said recently, 'has been made like a window.' This explains how a Rossellini or a De Sica have managed to go from their first documentary-esque works to the modern fables of *La macchina ammazzacattivi* and *Totò il buono*." (*Hollywood*, February 18, 1950.) But Taviani's view, as his reference to Morlion's "window onto the real" suggests, was a minority one at the time.

35. *The Gay Science*, aph. 179 (revised ed., 1887).

36. *Il Progresso*, 1948.

37. Antonello Trombadori to TG (1985).

38. Ayfre defined neo-realism by contrast with two main realist orientations (*my summary*):

1. THE EMPIRICAL ORIENTATION:

1a: Documentary Technique tries for the least possible deformation of the real via a mechanical camera and elimination of filmmaker consciousness. But such objectivity is unachievable. And consciousness is less an opponent of reality than a means to reach it.

1b: Naturalism describes material entities. But in failing to distinguish human consciousness from the rest of the world, and thus in mistaking a whole aspect of reality, this approach is not truly realist.

2. THE RATIONAL ORIENTATION:

2a: Verism, conceding empirical difficulties but thinking reason can compensate, tries to reconstruct a true world in the studio. It believes a social or historical event can be exhaustively analyzed and then made perfectly clear through characters and situations. And it exaggerates or distorts to achieve a "real" effect. Truer than true, such films are "from God's point of view": the author knows his characters because he has made them himself. Thus he risks leaving out the mystery proper to authentic reality. And he puts reality at the service of a given thesis. Whereas empirical realism fell short of man, verism is beyond him.

2b: Social Realism belongs with verism, not materialism, because of its rationalist belief that reality is transparent under human effort. It believes there is some special point of view, some analytical method (such as the dialectic) which will furnish the key to reality. But again we end up with thesis films, for, like verism, social realism must accentuate in order to promote what ought to be. And we end up making reality and transforming it aesthetically, not just looking at the world as it is.

3. NEO-REALISM: PHENOMENOLOGICAL REALISM:

3a: as opposed to the rational orientation: neo-realism does not make the real, it describes it. Classic realism achieves ordered construction, unlike neo-realism, because while dealing with one angle, such as the psychological, it neglects all the others; or, concentrating on milieu, it turns characters into stereotypes; or, concentrating on meaning, it turns reality into symbol. The neo-realist aims for global description, and even includes aspects which ancients would have found unimportant or disruptive.

3b: as opposed to the empirical orientation: neo-realism does not claim to be objective. It is a consciousness that confronts the real, interrogating it, describing it, and finally revealing it. Not the cine-eye but the human eye (two of them); not physical relief but human depth.

In summary, "Neo-realism is an aesthetic orientation of cinema in which the directors . . . use all the resources of their consciousness (feelings, ideas, values, engagements) to describe concretely the real in its globality, in order to reveal its diverse levels of meaning." (Ayfre, "Un réalisme humain," *Conversion aux images?* [Paris: Éditions du Cerf, 1964], pp. 223–30.)

39. Serceau agrees: The picture is about Edmund, not Germany, Edmund's consciousness (his "attitude" [Ayfre]), which colors (and is colored by) everything that happens to him. He is surrounded by a physical, ideological, and moral catastrophe that no one has come to clean up; no reconstruction is afoot, no solidarity exists. He is sensitive to the duty and sacrifice his father demands; but he is constantly exploited by adults (who steal the scale; have him sell Hitler records); is excluded from the adult world (denied the cemetery job, a share of coal or horse meat); is triply rejected by adults (his teacher), peers (Christine), and children; and is then afflicted with moralistic reprobation (they're eager for the potatoes he brings home, but punish him for staying out all night to get them). Unlike De Sica, who in *Shoeshine* merely describes social circumstances, Rossellini uses circumstances to confront contradicting mentalities [Ayfre's "attitudes"]. (Serceau, *Rossellini*, pp. 74–89.)

40. Ayfre's "Allemagne année zéro" appears in his posthumous collection, *Le Cinéma et sa vérité* (Paris: Éditions du Cerf, 1969), pp. 139–43. The same volume contains a preface by Jules Gritti recollecting Ayfre's first movie experiences in Paris (pp. 7–12); and a "Panorama critique" by René-Claude Baud of Ayfre's film criticism (pp. 181–230). Although Ayfre's original essay was unpublished in his lifetime, he incorporated much of it word for word into his "Néo-réalisme et phénoménologie," *Cahiers du Cinéma* 17, November 1952; reprint: Ayfre, *Conversion aux images?* pp. 209–22. I have interpolated a passage from this latter version ("Rossellini himself does not decide . . . ") into my summary of the original.

41. Bazin, "*Voleur de bicyclette*," p. 49; "Le Réalisme," p. 29.

42. Bazin, *L'Écran Français* 189, February 8, 1949.

43. *Esprit*, May 1949, p. 688; *Qu'est-ce que le cinéma?*, III:30, 32.

44. Quoted from Bergson's *Comedy* (without citation), in Orsini, *Benedetto Croce*, p. 115.

45. Quoted in Tannenbaum, *Fascist Experience*, p. 251 (no citation).

46. Quoted by Ayfre, citing Merleau-Ponty, *Phénoménologie de la perception*, p. xvi(?), in Ayfre, "Néo-réalisme et phénoménologie," p. 213.

47. Ayfre, during an F.L.E.C.C. (?) conference, September 1956, *Télécine* 62 (no date), cited by Baud, "Panorama critique," in Ayfre, *Le Cinéma et sa vérité*, p. 194.

48. Cf. Ayfre, "Néo-réalisme et phénoménologie," p. 213.

49. Quoted in Valmarana, "Cinema adulto," p. 41.

50. *Changes*, 1974.

51. Ibid.

52. Ayfre, "Un réalisme humain," p. 227.

53. André Bazin, "The Ontology of the Photographic Image" (1945), "The Myth of Total Cinema" (1946), *What Is Cinema?* (Berkeley: University of California, 1971), I:9–16, I:17–22. A fine exposition of Bazin's argument can be found in Andrew, *Bazin*, pp. 70–81.

54. Quoted in Bertin, *Renoir*, p. 182.

55. Cited only by date (1958) in Jean Renoir, *Écrits 1926–1971* (Paris: Belfond, 1974), pp. 189–90.

56. Bazin, "Le Réalisme," pp. 34–35. Cf. *What Is Cinema?*, II:38–39, where Gray's translation obfuscates Bazin's point.

57. R. G. Collingwood, *The Principles of Art* (London and New York: Oxford University Press, 1938); 1958 paperback ed., pp. 282–85.

58. Apropos of *Voyage in Italy*. Eric Rohmer (signed Maurice Schérer), "La Terre du Miracle," *Cahiers du Cinéma* 47, May 1955, pp. 39–40.

59. Read, *Icon and Idea*, p. 87.

60. Intense communion with screen, physically and emotionally, inspired mystical odes to the union of mise en scène and attitude (style), as in this passage by Bazin:
   "Rossellini's mise en scène invests its object from the outside . . . with an exteriority that conveys an ethical and metaphysical aspect essential to our relation with the world. . . . Compare [for example] his treatment of the boy in *Deutschland im Jahre Null* with [De Sica's treatment of] the boys in *Shoeshine* and *Bicycle Thieves*. Rossellini's love for his characters envelops them with a desperate awareness of people's inability to communicate. De Sica's love, in contrast, radiates from the characters themselves. They are what they are, but lit from within by the tenderness he feels for them. It follows that Rossellini's mise en scène interposes itself between his material and us, not certainly as an artificial obstacle but as an unbridgeable ontological distance, a congenital weakness of the human being that translates aesthetically into terms of space, forms and structures of mise en scène. Because it is felt as a lack, a refusal, a concealment of things, and thus as definite pain, it follows that it's easier to be aware of it."

61. "Le roman est un récit qui s'organise en monde, le film un monde qui s'organise en récit." Jean Mitry, *Esthétique et psychologie du cinéma* (Paris: Éditions Universitaire, 1965), II:354.

62. Phenomenologists would agree with Vladimir Propp's assertion that in fairy tales characters are important essentially for their actions (*Morphology of the Folktale*, [Austin: University of Texas Press, 1968]). Actions and morals are the essence of folktales; personalities count for little. But phenomenologists can hardly agree with the application of Propp to cinema that literary critics make, treating cinema characters as though identical to folktale ones. A more accurate translation of Propp into cinematic criticism would treat characters as loci of emotions—which, in cinema, are actions.

63. The literary tradition "cuts" reality in order to submit it toward manifesting one meaning, which pre-exists in some fashion; subjects it to montage, which articulates scenes, organizing strong and weak times, of which the succession constitutes a story; privileges the protagonists, on whom narration centers and images are constructed, to the detriment of other sides of reality. Everything culminates in a concerted

dramatism: interpretation comes first. In contrast, neo-realism substitutes ontological affirmation (the real seized in its globality). Cf. Louis Audibert, "Roberto Rossellini," *Cinématographe* 29, July 1977, p. 20.

Chapter 13: Land of God

1. Seymour Peyser to TG.
2. Lina Rossellini to TG.
3. Seymour Peyser to TG.
4. Rod Geiger to TG.
5. *New Yorker*, February 19, 1949, p. 25. Pryor, "Personal History." The last quotation is Pryor's summary rather than a direct quotation from Rossellini.
6. Referring to Romano. De Marchis, "La mia vita."
7. Leamer, *As Time Goes By*, p. 168, quoting Petter Lindstrom's account of what Lopert told him in March 1949.
8. Ibid., p. 162, from his interview with "Petter Veger."
9. Quoted in William Davidson, *The Real and the Unreal* (New York: Harpers, 1961), p. 162.
10. Faldini and Fofi, I:204; from *Gente* (Milan), June 24, 1972.
11. Colpet, *Sag mir*, p. 262.
12. *My Story*, p. 240.
13. "Dix ans," II.
14. Roberto Rossellini to TG.
15. "Dix ans," II.
16. Ibid.
17. Roberto Rossellini to TG.
18. *My Story*, p. 242. Steele, *Ingrid Bergman*, p. 169, states *The Miracle* was also shown.
19. Hedy Lamarr, *Ecstasy and Me* (New York: Bartholomew House, 1966), p. 84.
20. Interview with Samuel Goldwyn, Jr., in Leamer, *As Time Goes By*, p. 163.
21. *My Story*, p. 242.
22. Mida, *Rossellini*, 1st ed., p. 61.
23. "Dix ans," II. Steele, *Ingrid Bergman*, p. 169, states it was Goldwyn who withdrew.
24. A few lines later Rossellini refers to him as "un homme rusé comme vingt renards" ("Dix ans," II).
25. "Dix ans," II.
26. Roberto Rossellini to TG.
27. *Time*, February 7, 1949.
28. Leamer, *As Time Goes By*, p. 125.
29. *Motion Picture Herald*, December 24, 1949. Rod Geiger to TG.
30. Mayer, *Merely Colossal*, p. 218.
31. Quoted in Leamer, *As Times Goes By*, p. 168.
32. *My Story*, pp. 200, 201.
33. Leamer, *As Time Goes By*, p. 160.
34. Quoted by Fereydoun Hoveyda to TG.
35. Quoted in Davidson, *Real and*, p. 162.
36. Quoted by Celeste Holm, in Leamer, *As Time Goes By*, p. 164.
37. Steele, *Ingrid Bergman*, p. 214. Bergman omits this detail in *My Story*.
38. *My Story*, p. 247.
39. Quoted by Renzo Avanzo to TG.
40. Quoted in *My Story*, p. 357.
41. De Marchis, "La mia vita," p. 40.
42. Lina Rossellini to TG.
43. Rossellini, "Perchè ho scelto Ingrid Bergman," *L'Elefante*, March 24/31, 1949.
44. Bergman to Monroe McDonald to Cholly Knickerbocker, *Time*, October 3, 1949, p. 28.
45. Anecdote recounted by Suso Cecchi D'Amico; Leamer, *As Time Goes By*, p. 170.
46. Quoted in P. Palumbo, "Amava suo figlio come una tigre," *Gente*, October 12, 1973; cited in Governi, *Nannarella*, p. 143.
47. De Marchis, "La mia vita."
48. Ibid.
49. Franco Riganti to TG.
50. Quoted in full, from the 1952 custody trial, in Leamer, *As Time Goes By*, p. 171. In *My Story*, p. 164, a reference to "Pelle" (the child the Lindstroms were planning) has been changed to "Pia," so that it appears that Bergman mentioned her daughter.
51. Sarazani to Marcella Mariani Rossellini to TG.
52. Amidei, in Faldini and Fofi, I:202.
53. Quoted in Davidson, *Real and*, p. 163.
54. Marcella Mariani Rossellini to Leamer, *As Time Goes By*, p. 172.
55. Amidei, in Faldini and Fofi, I:202.
56. Quoted by Neuwald, in Leamer, *As Time Goes By*, p. 175.
57. Robin Wood, "Ingrid Bergman on Rossellini," *Film Comment*, July 1974, p. 14.

58. Wood, "Ingrid on," p. 12.
59. Michel Delain, "Rossellini après Rossellini," *L'Express*, June 13, 1977, p. 17.
60. *My Story*, p. 280.
61. Steele, *Ingrid Bergman*, p. 172.
62. *My Story*, p. 280.
63. Wood, "Ingrid on," p. 14.
64. Faldini and Fofi, I:202.
65. Steele, *Ingrid Bergman*, p. 193.
66. Leamer, *As Time Goes By*, p. 178.
67. "Dix ans," III.
68. Quoted, presumably on Rossellini's authority, in Vittorio Bonicelli, "Ecco Paola Raffaella, il grande segreto di Sonali e Rossellini," *Tempo*, March 17, 1959. No confirming citation has been found in American sources. In Johnson's infamous denunciation a year later on the Senate floor, he made no mention of Nazis, drugs, or blackmarketing.
69. Stern, *No Innocence*, pp. 173–74.
70. *My Story*, pp. 294, 295.
71. Quoted in Davidson, *Real and*, p. 163.
72. Renato Terra, in Faldini and Fofi, I:202.
73. *My Story*, p. 296.
74. Steele, *Ingrid Bergman*, p. 175.
75. Stern, *No Innocence*, p. 178.
76. Steele, *Ingrid Bergman*, p. 188. Bergman is quoted as placing Magnani rather than Roswitha on Capri.
77. Ibid., p. 255.
78. *CdC* 37, 1954.
79. Cited from *France-Soir*, in *My Story*, p. 275.
80. Quoted in Steele, *Ingrid Bergman*, p. 180.
81. Faldini and Fofi, I:204.
82. Zeffirelli, *Zeffirelli*, p. 107.
83. Maria Mercader to TG.
84. "Ti voglio bene e so che mi vuoi bene." *Rivista del Cinematografo*, July 1977, p. 314.
85. Quoted in Stern, *No Innocence*, p. 171.
86. Enrico Fulchignoni to TG. In illustration, Fulchignoni cited a plaintive letter from Amidei, citing their long friendship and bemoaning Roberto's callous treatment of him. Roberto's reaction to the letter was only to laugh. The letter is reproduced on p. 442.
87. Davidson, *Real and*, p. 164.
88. Ibid., p. 145.
89. *My Story*, p. 282.
90. Ibid., p. 282.
91. Steele, *Ingrid Bergman*, p. 180.
92. Ibid., p. 186.
93. Ibid., p. 187.
94. Ibid., p. 181.
95. Ibid., p. 214.
96. Maria Mercader to TG.
97. Steele, *Ingrid Bergman*, pp. 182–83.
98. Davidson, *Real and*, p. 158.
99. *Nuestro Cine* 95, 1970, p. 99.
100. William Davidson, "Anatomy of a Scandal," *Colliers*, November 12, 1949, p. 14.
101. *La Table Ronde* 149, May 1960, p. 75.
102. Adriano Aprà and Maurizio Ponzi, "Intervista con Roberto Rossellini," *Filmcritica* 156–57, April 1965; reprints: "Sur *L'età del ferro*," *Cahiers du Cinéma* 169, August 1965 (in part) *Screen* 14:4, winter 1973–74; Edoardo Bruno, ed., *R.R. Roberto Rossellini* (Rome: Bulzoni, 1979); *Il mio metodo*; and Rossellini, *My Method* (New York: Marsilio, 1992; the *Screen* translation).
103. "Dix ans," III.
104. Ibid.
105. *Filmcritica* 156, 1965.
106. D. Meccoli, "Ingrid come Karin," *Cinema*, March 31, 1949, p. 335.
107. *Cinema*, March 1950.
108. *L'Europeo*, March 26, 1950.
109. Wood, "Ingrid on," p. 13.
110. Ibid.
111. "Dix ans," III.
112. Ibid.
113. Ibid. The English-language edition that Rossellini himself prepared (as distinct from the butchered version released by RKO) differs from the third version—Rossellini's final Italian cut—in only two respects: the English edition is titled *Stromboli* and lacks six shots toward the end. But this is sufficient to render the rough cut less explicitly religious than the final cut. After Karin collapses on the volcano, the continuity is as follows in this Italian version:
1. *CU*: "Non ne posso più. È meglio morire. Ma non ho il coraggio di [incomprehensible]. Ho paura." ("I can't go on. It's better to die. But I don't have the courage. . . . I'm afraid.")

2. Volcanic craters, less smoke than previously.
3. (=1) Karin, also more relaxed, turns, looks up.
4. Night sky, filled with stars.
5. (=3) Karin.
6. (=4) Stars.
7. *High angle*: Karin: "Dio, se esisti, dammi . . . dammi un po' di pace, dammi . . . dammi un po' di pace." ("God, if you exist, give me a bit of peace.")
8. (=6) Stars. *Dissolve:*
9. Dawn. Karin wakes up.
In the English version, shots 2, 3, 5, 6, 7, and 8 are missing; the dialogue in shot 1 is also missing. Thus there is no explicit thought of suicide; no calming dialogue between Karin and the stars; and no prayer for peace addressed to a personal God. In the butchered RKO version, a single invocation—"God!"—is added to shot 1; shots 2 through 9 are replaced by a different montage of different takes, without religious implications.

114. *Gravity and Grace*, trans. Emma Craufurd (New York: Putnam, 1952).
115. Koval, "Interview," 1951.
116. Cited (with no reference) in Stefano Roncoroni, "Gli anni 'di mezzo,'" *Rivista del Cinematografo*, July 1977, p. 269, as spoken to Sadoul. Also cited (with even less reference) in Pio Baldelli, "Dibattito per 'Francesco' di Rossellini," *Rivista del Cinema Italiano*, November 1954, p. 57.
117. Lonero, "Un messaggio," 1954.
118. Roberto Rossellini, "Perchè ho diretto proprio questo film," *Film* 31–32, August 16, 1950; reprinted in *My Method*, pp. 29–30 (my translation: miscredited in the book).
119. *Bianco e Nero*, 1952 (*Screen*, p. 76)
120. Fantuzzi, *Cinema sacro*, pp. 94–96.
121. Aprà, in Menon, *Dibattito*, p. 108.
122. Fantuzzi, *Cinema sacro*, pp. 94–96.
123. Wood, "Ingrid on," p. 14.
124. ORTF interview published in *La Table Ronde*, May 1960, p. 76.
125. Unidentified typed transcription of a Rossellini interview, in English, c. 1975.
126. Morlion, interviewed by Mario Arosio, "Il figliol prodigo," *La Rivista del Cinematografo*, July 1977, p. 306.
127. *Time*, May 16, 1949.
128. Arosio, "Il figliol," pp. 306–07.
129. De Marchis, "La mia vita."
130. *New York Times*, September 20, 1949.
131. *New York Times*, September 23, 1949.
132. *Time*, September 26, 1949.
133. "Composer's Film Credo," *New York Times*, September 11, 1949, sec. 2, p. 5.
134. Stern reports it was $300,000 over budget. Davidson ("Anatomy of a Scandal," p. 14) says it was budgeted at $600,000 and cost a million. Bonicelli (*Cinema*, March 1950) says $800,000.
135. Stern, *No Innocence*, p. 177; *New York Times*, September 11, 1948, sec. 2, p. 5.
136. Quoted in Edgard Macarini, "Sono la prova vivente della brutalità di Hollywood," *Vie Nuove*, February 26, 1950.
137. Interviewed by Leamer, *As Time Goes By*, p. 229.
138. B. Rondi, "Lavoro."

Chapter 14: God's Jester

1. Faldini and Fofi, I:205.
2. Selznick Archives: Reissar to Selznick, April 21, 1948.
3. Arosio, "Il figliol," p. 306.
4. Federico Fellini to TG. The *Fioretti* are an anonymous collection put together in the fourteenth century. Only three of the film's sketches derive from the original collection of 53 *fioretti* (nos. 8, 11, and 15 therein), in which there are few facts but many visions and miracles. The other sketches derive from five supplemental collections of *fioretti*, principally *The Life of Brother Ginepro*, wherein there is abundant humor entirely lacking in the *Fioretti*.
   Fathers Morlion and Lisandrini are credited in the picture's titles as having "participated in the elaboration." But, writes Brunello Rondi, "the 'treatment' . . . was elaborated by Fellini and by Rossellini and by no one else. The scenario and the other dialogues were written, during the shooting, by Rossellini, by me, and by Padre Alberto Maisano. . . . No one else laid a hand on the film creatively. We did have religious and historical consultants." (Rondi, "Per un riesame del 'Francesco' di Rossellini," *Rivista del Cinema Italiano*, January 1955, p. 89.)
5. Koval, "Interview," 1951, p. 394.
6. Steele, *Ingrid Bergman*, p. 268.
7. De Marchis, "La mia vita."
8. *Film Culture*, 1971, p. 13 (in English).
9. Orsini, *Benedetto Croce*, p. 67.
10. B. Rondi, "Lavoro."

11. Jean Herman to TG.
12. *Film Culture*, 1971, pp. 13–14 (in English).
13. *Nuestro Cine* 95, 1970, p. 98.
14. *Film Culture*, 1971, pp. 13–14 (in English).
15. Ibid.
16. *Bianco e Nero*, 1964, p. 14.
17. MacNiven, Yale 1974.
18. B. Rondi, "Lavoro."
19. Arabella Lemaître to TG.
20. Steele, *Ingrid Bergman*, p. 276.
21. Stern, *No Innocence*, p. 169.
22. Leamer, *As Time Goes By*, p. 206.
23. Marcella De Marchis, "La mia storia" (dated February 19, 1950).
24. *Variety*, February 22, 1950.
25. *New York Times*, February 16, 1950.
26. Quoted in *My Story*, p. 343.
27. *Time*, February 27, 1950.
28. Macarini, "Sono la prova."
29. *Cinema*, March 1950.
30. Ennio Flaiano, "L'isola di Rossellini," *Il Mondo*, March 25, 1950; reprint: Flaiano, *Lettere d'amore*, p. 159.
31. Faldini and Fofi, I::201.
32. *Congressional Record—Senate*, March 14, 1950, pp. 3281–88.
33. Stern, *No Innocence*, p. 168.
34. "Dix ans," III.
35. Luigi Chiarini, "Francesco," *Filmcritica*, January 1951, alludes to published accusations of this sort without citing where they occurred. B. Rondi, "Lavoro," makes similar allusions. Ennio Flaiano did make such accusations in *Il Mondo*, December 30, 1950.
36. Koval, "Interview," 1951.
37. Baldelli, "Dibattito per 'Francesco,'" p. 57.
38. Lonero, "Un messaggio," 1954.
39. André Bazin, "Difesa di Rossellini," *Cinema Nuovo* 65, August 25, 1955, p. 149; trans., Hugh Gray, *What Is Cinema?*, II:97.
40. MacNiven, Yale 1974.
41. Cf. Robert Bridges, "Introduction" to *Poems and Prose of Gerard Manley Hopkins* (London: Penguin, 1953), pp. xxiii–xxiv, as cited by Gray in his "Notes" in Bazin, *What Is Cinema?*, II: 184.
42. MacNiven, Yale 1974.
43. Arosio, "Il figliol," p. 306.
44. B. Rondi, *Cinema e realtà*, p. 239.
45. Alain Bandelier, "Cinéma et mystère," in Amédée Ayfre, *Cinéma et mystère* (Paris: Cerf, 1969), p. 100.
46. Alain Bergala, "Le Foyer de la cruauté," *Cahiers du Cinéma* 410, July 1988, p. 20.
47. Renzo Rossellini, Jr., to TG.
48. *My Story*, pp. 338–40.
49. Selznick Archives: Selznick to Reissar, June 13, 1950.
50. Leamer, *As Time Goes By*, p. 210.
51. Antonio Lisandrini to TG.
52. Rossellini to Franca Rodolfi, 1974; quoted in Leamer, *As Time Goes by*, p. 212.
53. Antonio Lisandrini to TG.
54. Leamer, *As Time Goes By*, p. 211.
55. Steele, *Ingrid Bergman*, p. 294.
56. The Giotto prelude (and choral music over the intertitles) were deleted from the Italian release, but showed up again in the American edition, *Flowers of St. Francis*, which, however, was shorn of the "Perfect Happiness" episode. Did Rossellini himself put together the prologue? Was it present in the initial Italian release? Did he authorize the American edition?
      He refers to the prologue in his article, "Il messaggio di *Francesco*," *Epoca*, November 18, 1950, p. 54.
57. Cayette's *Justice Is Done* was best film, followed by Kazan's *Panic in the Streets*, Delannoy's *Dieu a besoin des hommes*, and Blasetti's *Prima communione*. Moguy's *Domani è troppo tardi* was best Italian film, and awards went also to Walt Disney, Sam Jaffe (*Asphalt Jungle*), and Eleanor Parker (*Caged*). Ophuls's *La Ronde* received two prizes for scripting.
58. *Bianco e Nero*, 1952.
59. *Cinema*, September 15, 1950.
60. Alberto Moravia, *L'Europeo*, Janurary 1, 1951.
61. *L'Unità*, August 27, 1949.
62. *L'Unità*, December 17, 1950. Di Giammatteo, *Cinema*, April 1, 1951. Sadoul: quoted without citation in Rinaudo, "Foyer Rossellini," p. 45.
63. Pierre Leprohon, *The Italian Cinema*, revised English ed. (New York: Praeger, 1972), p. 136.
64. Piaz, Bezzola: *Cinema*, no date; both quoted in Rinaudo, "Foyer Rossellini," p. 45. Flaiano, *Il Mondo*, December 30, 1950. Bruno, *Filmcritica*, March 1951.
65. *La Fiera Letteraria*, December 24, 1950.
66. Quoted, without further citation, in B. Rondi, "Per un riesame," p. 95.

67. Bolzoni, "Il tema religioso."
68. Story recounted by Rossellini, in Fantuzzi, *Cinema sacro*, p. 90.
69. "Rossellini," in Chiarini, *Cinema e film: Storia e problemi* (Rome: Bolzoni, 1972), pp. 282–83, quoting from his review in *Filmcritica*, January 1951, p. 53.
70. Oms, "Rossellini du," p. 15.
71. Pasolini, in Faldini and Fofi, I:205. Moravia, "Bambini nel deposito degli scheletri," a review of *Germania anno zero*, *L'Espresso*, August 5, 1971. Crowther, *New York Times*, October 6, 1952.
72. Baldelli amplified the criticisms from his original review ("Falsificazione umana di un giullare di Dio," *Cinema* 55, February 1, 1951) in "Dibattito per 'Francesco' di Rossellini," *Rivista del Cinema Italiano*, November 1954, pp. 55–69 (wherein he painstakingly compares the film's manipulation of its sources in the *Fioretti* and *Vita di Ginepro*). Rondi's rebuttal, "Per un riesame del 'Francesco' di Rossellini," appeared in *Rivista*, January 1955, pp. 88–95. Baldelli then repeated his argument in his *Sociologia del cinema* (Rome: Riuniti, 1963), and Rondi replied again, in "La continua proposta del *Francesco* di Rossellini," *Filmcritica* 147, July 1964, pp. 369–72. Baldelli, *Rossellini* (1972), pp. 94–115, abridges his earlier argument.
73. B. Rondi, "Per un riesame."
74. B. Rondi, "La continua proposta."
75. *Bianco e Nero*, 1952.
76. Virgilio Marchi. *Francesco*'s use of Savona, "a city whose ruins lie on the border of medieval imagination" suggests the same purpose. Marchi (1895–1960) also did the sets for *Un pilota ritorna*, *Francesco*, *Europe '51* and *Un'avventura di Salvator Rosa*, *La corona di ferro*, *Umberto D*, *Don Camillo*, and *Stazione Termini*. Cited in Verdone, *Rossellini*, p. 42.
77. Giuseppe Ferrara, *Francesco Rosi* (1965), excerpted without citation in Overbey, *Springtime*, pp. 201, 224.
78. Guarner, *Rossellini*, p. 49. Guarner's Spanish word *crónica* (news story) is mistranslated in his book's English edition as "chronicle." J. L. Guarner, *Roberto Rossellini*, 2nd ed. (Madrid: Editorial Fundamentos, 1985), p. 75.
79. Serceau, *Rossellini*, pp. 179–86.
80. MacNiven, Yale 1974.
81. Agel, *Cinéma et le sacré*, pp. 75–78. Most people who see the film once, or who are distracted by other spectators, Agel concedes, come out complaining of the poverty of its style, its lack of rigor or unity, its occasional infantilism, and see nothing but buffoonery devoid of grandeur. But many who agree to see it a second time change their minds. The author intentionally leaves us free to discern or not the light of grace.
82. Jean-Claude Biette, "Cinéma chronique: On a cours d'histoire chez Rossellini," *Cahiers du Cinéma* 389, November 1986, p. viii.
83. B. Rondi, "La continua proposta."
84. Agel, *Cinéma et le sacré*, p. 75.
85. *Cinema*, September 15, 1950.
86. But Rossellini's chorus is often hostile: *Desiderio*, *Deutschland*, *Il miracolo*, *La macchina*. It is supportive only (and only occasionally) in *La nave bianca*, *Roma città aperta*, *Paisà*, and *Viva l'Italia*: films deliberately celebrating populist unity.
    Edoardo Bruno, *Filmcritica*, March 1951. Mida, *Rossellini*, 1st ed., p. 30. Alberto Moravia, *L'Europeo*, March 26, 1950. Chiarini, "Discorso sul neorealismo."
87. Aristarco, *Cinema*, September 15, 1950. Edoardo Bruno, *Filmcritica*, March 1951. Ugo Casiraghi, "Sempre più clericale il festival di Venezia: Predica di Rossellini in un'aria di sacrestia," *L'Unità*, August 27, 1950.
88. Casiraghi, "Sempre più clericale."
89. Di Giammatteo, "Un ritratto." Tommasso Chiaretti, *L'Unità*, March 16, 1951. A. Lanocita, *Corriere della Sera*, August 27, 1950. Mida, *Rossellini*, 2nd ed., p. 53. François Timmory, *L'Écran Français* 277, October 30, 1950.
90. Oms, "Rossellini du."
91. Alexandre Astruc, *Cahiers du Cinéma* 1, April 1951, p. 32.
92. Eric Rohmer (signed Maurice Schérer), *Gazette du Cinéma* 5, November 1950, p. 4. (I have rearranged sentences and added parentheses.); reprint: Rohmer, *Le Goût de la beauté* (Paris: Cahiers du Cinéma, 1984), pp. 135–38.
93. Eric Rohmer to Jean Rohmer, in Rohmer, *Le Goût de la beauté*, p. 15.
94. Rossellini, "Perchè ho diretto," 1950.
95. Gian Luigi Rondi, *La Fiera Letteraria*, March 18, 1951.
96. Mauriac, *L'Amour du cinéma*, p. 112.
97. Guarner, *Rossellini*, p. 44 (my rephrased translation).
98. Casiraghi, "Sempre più clericale il festival di Venezia: Predica di Rossellini in un'aria di sacrestia."
99. Agel, *Cinéma et nouvel naissance*, p. 224.
100. Vittorio Bonicelli, "Rossellini o dell'improbabile," in M.Valsecchi and U.Apollonio, eds., *Panorama dell'arte italiana 1951* (Turin: Lattes, 1952).
101. Guarner, *Rossellini*, pp. 40–44.
102. Menon, *Dibattito*, p. 72.
103. Ayfre, "Sens et non-sens." Cf., also, Wood, "Rossellini," p. 9.
104. Menon, *Dibattito*, p. 108.
105. Ayfre, "Sens et non-sens."
106. Menon, *Dibattito*, p. 63.

107. Antonio Gramsci to Tatiana Schucht, in Giuseppe Fiori, *Antonio Gramsci: Life of a Revolutionary*, trans. Tom Nairn (London, 1970), p. 74; quoted in Edward W. Said, "Opponent, Audience, Constituencies, and Community," *Critical Inquiry*, September 1982, vol. 9, no. 1, p. 17.

108. Gramsci to Schucht, August 17, 1931. *Lettere del carcere* (Turin, 1975), p. 466; trans. and quoted by Said, "Opponent."

109. For an interesting analysis of this question, cf., P. Ojetti, "Un discorso su Rossellini e due parole su *La paura*," *Cinema* 149, August 25, 1955, pp. 802–03.

110. B. Rondi, "Realtà della persona."

111. Bergala, p. 13. Rossellini, *CdC* 37, 1954.

112. Ayfre, "Sens et non-sens."

113. Menon, *Dibattito*, p. 68.

114. Jacques Doniol-Valcroze, *L'Observateur*; quoted in Rinaudo, "Foyer Rossellini," p. 44. Mauriac, *L'Amour du cinéma*, p. 113. Wood, "Ingrid on," p. 14.

115. Flaiano, "L'isola di Rossellini."

116. Rohmer (signed Schérer), *Gazette du Cinéma* 5, p. 4.

117. "Dix ans," I.

118. Charles Tesson, "La Méprise, le mépris: *Stromboli terra di Dio*," *Cahiers du Cinéma* 329, November 1981, p. 62.

119. Timmory, *L'Écran Français* 277. Flaiano, "L'isola di Rossellini." "Perchè ho diretto," 1950.

Chapter 15: *Europe '51*

1. Faldini and Fofi, I:204; from *Arianna* (Milan), August 1970.

2. Quoted by Georges Beaume, *Cinémonde* 884, October 9, 1950; cited in Leprohon, *Italian Cinema*, p. 140.

3. Monsignor Walter P. Kellenger, Archdiocesan Chancellor, quoted in Corliss, "Legion," p. 43.

4. December 13, 1950. According to Corliss, *The Herald Tribune*, *Journal-American*, and *World Telegram and Sun* disliked *The Miracle*; Crowther in *The Times* liked it, as did the *New Yorker* and *Newsweek*; *Time* was mixed, *The New Republic* thought it impressive but embarrassing, *Cue* called it memorable, and *Commonweal* called it tortuous and an unfit subject for movies (Corliss, "Legion," p. 42).

5. Quoted in Richard S. Randall, *Censorship of the Movies* (Madison: University of Wisconsin Press, 1968), p. 28. Randall's account is drawn from Alan F. Westin, *The Miracle Case: The Supreme Court and the Movies* (Inter-University Case Program Series, No. 64, Tuscaloosa, Alabama, 1961); Bosley Crowther, "The Strange Case of 'The Miracle,'" *Atlantic Monthly*, April 1951, p. 35; and court records.

6. Quoted in Corliss, "Legion," p. 43.

7. Ibid.

8. Ibid.

9. Ibid., p. 44.

10. Ibid.

11. Selznick Archives: Selznick to Reissar, October 25, 1951. Bergman eventually appeared in *The Human Voice*, a fifty-minute film directed by Ted Kotcheff, in October 1966 in London, and telecast in the U.S. on ABC, May 4, 1967.

12. Letter to Dido Renoir, June 7, 1951, in Jean Renoir, *Letters* (London: Faber and Faber, 1994), p. 276.

13. Mario Parpegnoli to UP in Buenos Aires, *Bis*, September 29, 1951.

14. Sandro Franchina to TG, January 1991.

15. Quoted in Davidson, *Real and*, p. 147.

16. Mida, *Rossellini*, 1st ed., p. 37; 2nd ed., p. 77. Cf., also, *La Rassegna del Film*'s judgment ("a gratuitous succession of asides"), quoted without further citation in Rinaudo, "Foyer Rossellini," p. 45.

17. Hovald, *Le Néo-réalisme*, pp. 113–14.

18. Gianni Rondolino, *Roberto Rossellini* (Turin: Utet, 1989), p. 216.

19. *CdC* 37, 1954.

20. Wood, "Ingrid on," p. 12.

21. *CdC* 37, 1954.

22. Baldelli, p. 260.

23. *CdC* 37, 1954.

24. Rossellini's comments for television, transcribed in *Il mio metodo*, p. 200.

25. *CdC* 37, 1954.

26. Baldelli, p. 260.

27. *CdC* 37, 1954.

28. Simone Weil, *Attente de Dieu* [*Waiting for God*] (Paris: Fayard, 1966), pp. 41–42.

29. Arosio, "Il figliol," p. 306.

30. Letter, August 4, 1943, to her parents, in *Seventy Letters* (New York: Oxford University Press, 1965).

31. In Menon, *Dibattito*, pp. 76, 80.

32. In Baldelli, p. 261.

33. In Menon, *Dibattito*, pp. 76, 80.

34. *Filmcritica* 156, 1965; *Screen* translation.

35. Simone Weil, uncited article in *Révolution prolétarienne*, August 25, 1933; reprint: Weil, *Oppression et liberté* (Paris: Gallimard, 1952).

36. Simone Weil, *L'Enracinement* (Paris: Gallimard, 1949), p. 30.
37. Simone Weil, "Reflections concerning the Cause of Liberty and Social Oppression," in *Oppression et liberté*.
38. "le matérialisme grossier d'Engels et de Lénine." Weil (Compte rendu), "Lénine: *Matérialisme et empiriocriticisme*," *La Critique Sociale* 10, November 1933; reprint: *Oppression et liberté* and *Oeuvres complètes*, II: 1, *Écrits historiques et politique* (Paris: Gallimard, 1988), p. 304.
    "Marx seems to think that there exists in matter a tendency to automatically produce good, a kind of principle of progress toward the good. This is neither science nor true religion; it is an inferior form of religion." Simone Pétrement, *Simone Weil: A Life* (New York: Pantheon, 1976), p. 502, summarizing argument in Weil, "Is There a Marxist Doctrine?" reprinted in *Oppression et liberté* and *Oeuvres complètes*, III:3.
39. Irene's retort to the Communist Andrea—"I'm searching for a different path, the spiritual path. In your paradise here on earth there is no place for Michelle, because he's no longer alive. The paradise that I dream of is not only for the living but for the departed"—recalls the admonition in Georges Bernanos's 1935 *Diary of a Country Priest*, "What I can nonetheless affirm to you is that there isn't a realm of the living and a realm of the dead, there's only the realm of God, the living or the dead, and we are in it."
40. Weil, *La pesanteur et la grâce* (Paris: Plon, 1948), p. 206.
41. In Baldelli, p. 259.
42. Ibid.
43. In Matteo Ajassa, "Una nuova frontiera per Rossellini," *Rivista del Cinematografo* 11, November 1963.
44. *Bianco e Nero*, 1952.
45. Gigi Cane, "*Europa '51* o la tragedia del conformismo," *Rassegna del Film*, February 1952, p. 16.
46. *CdC* 37, 1954.
47. Rossellini's comments for radio, transcribed in *Il mio metodo*, p. 192.
48. *Filmcritica* 156, 1965; *Screen* translation.
49. As related, above. Arosio, "Il figliol," p. 306.
50. Tullio Pinelli, *Cinema*, 165 (Milan), May 1956. Supplemented by TG's interview with Pinelli.
51. Lourcelles, *Dictionnaire du cinéma: Les Films* (Paris: Laffont, 1992), pp. 446–48, 18–19.
52. Laurent Billia, "Le Murmure des fonds d'auteurs: La donation Jean-Paul Le Chanois," *Revue Cinémathèque* 1, 1992, pp. 69–77. Le Chanois's script, 103 typed pages, is deposited at the Cinémathèque française, Paris.
53. This is Aldo Tonti's contention, Faldini and Fofi, I:251.
54. Stewart's credits included *Dinner at Eight, The Barretts of Wimpole Street* (1934), *The Prisoner of Zenda* (1937), *Holiday, Marie Antoinette* (1938), *Love Affair* (1939), *Kitty Foyle, The Philadelphia Story* (1940), *That Uncertain Feeling, A Woman's Face, Smilin' Through* (1941), *Tales of Manhattan, Keeper of the Flame* (1942), *Without Love* (1945), *Life with Father* (1947), *Edward My Son* (1949).
55. *Nuestro Cine* 95, 1970, p. 120.
56. Aldo Tonti to TG.
57. It is unknown whether this film was completed or shown. Rushes in the archives of the Venice Biennale include scenes of Bergman in piazza Farnese and Swedish nuns packing clothes in St. Brigid's church.
58. Faldini and Fofi, I:251.
59. Alexander Knox, "Actor's Accolade," *New York Times*, November 1, 1953.
60. Faldini and Fofi, I:251.
61. Quoted by Gina Franchina, in Bergala and Narboni, p. 42.
62. Manni, "Rossellini, l'araba fenice," p. 56.
63. Cane, "*Europa '51* o la tragedia."
64. According to Rossellini, *Europe '51* was shot in 46 days, using about 50,000 feet of negative (versus c.10,000 in the finished film), which would have been remarkable: an average Hollywood director shot 250,000. According to Tonti it was shot in three weeks on 130,000 feet, still not much. But neither man's figures merit much trust. (Rossellini, in *CdC* 37, 1954. Aldo Tonti to TG.)
65. Murray, "The Man Who," 1953.
66. Knox, "Actor's Accolade."
67. *Bianco e Nero*, 1952.
68. Quoted in Hollis Alpert, *Fellini: A Life* (New York: Atheneum, 1986), p. 77.
69. Manni, "Rossellini, l'araba fenice." Manni's memoirs are hostile.
70. Kezich, *Fellini*, p. 135.
71. Fellini, cited in Charlotte Chandler, *I, Fellini* (New York: Random House, 1995), pp. 79, 286.
72. Ibid., p. 104.
73. "Rossellini parla," 1977; *Fragments*, p. 88.
74. Ronald Bergan, *Jean Renoir: Projections of Paradise* (Woodstock: Overlook, 1994).
75. Jean Renoir, *Entretiens et propos* (Paris: Éditions de l'Étoile & Cahiers du Cinéma, 1979), p. 150.
76. Jean Renoir, *Lettres d'Amérique* (Paris: Presses de la Renaissance, c.1984), p. 102.
77. Bertin, *Renoir*, p. 258.
78. Quoted in Davidson, *Real and*, p. 147.
79. June 1952. Steele, *Ingrid Bergman*, p. 303.
80. *Cahiers du Cinéma* 122, August 1961, p. 53.
81. *Nuestro Cine* 95, 1970.
82. Mario Del Papa to TG.
83. Quoted in Masi and Lancia, p. 42.
84. Franco Riganti told me Rossellini discussed these solutions with him and Antonio Pietrangelo in the summer of 1953.
85. Fellini, *Fare un film*, p. 129. Kezich (*Fellini*, p. 135) claims Fellini directed the trial scenes.

86. *Nuestro Cine* 95, 1970, p. 54; *Screen* translation, p. 102.
87. Gino Visentini, *Il Giornale d'Italia*; and Vittorio Sala, *Il Popolo*; quoted in Masi and Lancia, p. 62. Pierre Kast, *Cahiers du Cinéma* 56, February 1956, p. 33, in the "Petit Journal" rather than a full review. Mida, *Rossellini*, 2nd ed., p. 84. Tullio Kezich, *Sipario* 197, May 1954, p. 28; quoted in Masi and Lancia, p. 63. Tommaso Chiaretti, *L'Unità* (Roma), March 3, 1954.
88. Claude Beylie, *Cahiers du Cinéma* 494, November 1989.
89. Guarner, *Rossellini*, p. 56.
90. Quoted in Leamer, *As Time Goes By*, p. 225. *Los Angeles Times*, June 27, 1952.
91. Quoted in Davidson, *Real and*, p. 164.
92. Vittorio Bonicelli, "Il nostro romanzo a Bombay fu allucinante," *Tempo*, March 10, 1959, p. 11.
93. Quoted in Leamer, *As Time Goes By*, p. 228.
94. Paolo Valmarana to TG.
95. Gino Visentini, "Rossellini o della trascendenza,"*Bianco e Nero*, February 1952.
96. Guarner, *Rossellini*, pp. 51–52.
97. Antonello Trombadori, *Vie Nuove*, January 18, 1953.
98. G. C. Castello, *Cinema* 99, December 15, 1952. Tommaso Chiaretti, *L'Unità* (Rome), September 14, 1952. Chiaretti was equally severe at the film's commercial opening, *L'Unità*, January 9, 1953. Mida, *Rossellini*, 1st ed., pp. 32–33; unpalliated in 2nd ed., pp. 66–67. Aristarco, *Cinema Nuovo*, December 15, 1952. Mario Gromo, *La Nuova Stampa*, September 13, 1952, p. 3; reprint: Mario Gromo, *Film visti* (Rome: Edizione Bianco e Nero, 1957), pp. 414–18. Mario Gallo, *Avanti!*, January 9, 1953. Luigi Fossati, *Avanti!* September 14, 1952.
99. Renato Buzzonetti, *Rivista del Cinematografo*, January 1953. *Bianco e Nero*, September 1952. *Il Tempo*, September 13, 1952. *Cahiers du Cinéma* 16, October 1952, p. 14.
100. Alberto Moravia, *L'Europeo*, January 22, 1953.
101. A. Lanocita, *Corriere della Sera*, January 22, 1953. Lanocita's initial, more enthusiastic reaction, at Venice, was to call it Rossellini's "best film in recent years. Each sequence is the fruit of thoughtful research." (*Corriere della Sera*, September 14, 1952)
102. Fernaldo Di Giammatteo, "Europa '51," *La Rassegna del Film*, January 1953.
103. *L'Europeo*, January 22, 1953. *Cahiers du Cinéma* 16, October 1952, p. 14.
104. Arosio, "Il figliol," p. 307. *Nuestro Cine* 95, 1970, p. 98.
105. Lonero, "Un messaggio," 1954.
106. Visentini, "Rossellini o della trascendenza," p. 19. *Filmcritica* 17, October 1952, p. 110. Callisto Cosulich, cited in Masi and Lancia, p. 58. Ermanno Contini, cited in Masi and Lancia, p. 59. *L'Amour du cinéma*, p. 114.
107. Kezich, *Fellini*, pp. 8, 135. In 1952 Kezich wrote: "If Rossellini really wants to do a film on contemporary conformism he should shoot it at the Lido [site of the Venice Festival] . . . And choose his protagonist from the mass of pageboys who run to and fro during the Mostra, carrying passwords, distributing handshakes and jotting down confidential information." (Quoted in Rinaudo, "Foyer Rossellini," p. 46.)
108. B. Rondi, "Lavoro."
109. Marcella Mariani Rossellini to TG.
110. Mida, "L'ultimo Rossellini," *Ferrania*, April 4, 1953.
111. Zavattini, "Come non ho fatta *Italia mia*," *Rassegna del Film* 12 (March 1953) and 13 (April 1953); translated in R. Hughes, *Film Book* (New York: Grove Press, 1959), pp. 122–43; and in *Cahiers du Cinéma* 98, August 1959.
112. "Dix ans," III.
113. Ajassa, "Nuova frontiera," p. 435.
114. Ibid.
115. Blue, 1972.
116. Renzi, ed., *Era notte*, pp. 34–35.
117. Cited by Adriano Aprà to TG.
118. *Nuestro Cine* 95, 1970, p. 99.
119. Morando Morandini (*La Notte*, October 12, 1953): "Maybe we're the only ones, but for us the story went marvelously [and was] told with an incisiveness with a certain sense of humor that we hadn't known in the director of *Paisà*."
120. *Rassegna del Film* 19, November 1953.
121. For example, Tullio Kezich (*Il Sipario*), said Rossellini's episode was the least engaged and concerned only with being anecdotal and amusing, "but one can't deny it's done with a certain charm." (Quoted in Masi and Lancia, p. 67.)
122. A. Lanocita, *Corriere della Sera*, October 28, 1953. F. Sacchi, *Epoca* 162, November 8, 1953, p. 8. Vice, *Il Resto del Carlino* (in Masi and Lancia, p. 67). *Monthly Film Bulletin* 251, December 1954, p. 176.
123. Renzo Trionfera, "Regola la gelosia di Otello," *L'Europeo*, December 25, 1952.
124. Steele, *Ingrid Bergman*, p. 310.
125. Cf., for example, Alfredo Parente, "Un'eccezzionale edizione dell' 'Otello' ha inaugurato la stagione Sancarliana: Vivo successo della interpretazione dell'opera verdiana con la regia di Roberto Rossellini," *Il Mattino*, December 14, 1952, which contains a detailed account of Rossellini's restorations and innovations, and the performance's reception.
126. *King Vidor, A Directors Guild of American Oral History*, interviewed by Nancy Dowd and David Shepard (Directors Guild of America and Metuchen: Scarecrow, 1988), p. 212.
127. (1971), in Samuels, *Encountering Directors*, p. 155.

128. Ingrid Bergman to Joe Steele, December 14, 1952, in Steele, *Ingrid Bergman*, p. 311. She refers to *Europe '51* as *The Great Love*, a mistake for the U.S. title, *The Greatest Love*.

Chapter 16: *Voyage in Italy*

1. No film bearing this title actually exists. Two separate British releases were titled *The Lonely Woman* and *Journey to Italy*. The U.S. release was titled *Strangers*. The French release was *L'Amour est le plus fort*. Nonetheless we have come to think of it as *Voyage in Italy* through numerous published references, and we prefer this title. The Italian title, *Viaggio in Italia*, designates an Italian-dubbed edition (from which the three-minute scene of language confusion between Alex and the cook has been cut) and is not acceptable in referring to the (English-language) original.
2. Bergman, *My Story*, p. 370.
3. George Sanders, *Memoirs of a Professional Cad* (New York: Putnam, 1960), p. 121.
4. R. Redi, "Buono o cattivo il vino nuovo?" *Cinema* 124, December 1953.
5. Rossellini's comments for radio (1960), transcribed in *Il mio metodo*, p. 193. Cf., at much greater length, Rossellini, "Mi'mma'. Lettera dall'India," *Linea d'Ombra* April 1992, pp. 60–64. In French translation, "Une Lettre," *Trafic*, Winter 1991, pp. 53–60.
6. *Filmcritica* 156, 1965; *Screen* translation.
7. *CdC* 37, 1954.
8. Lonero, "Un messaggio," 1954.
9. Copies of Pietrangeli's script—only the title is in English and is possibly a mistake for "New Wine"—exist in the Pietrangeli Archives, Viterbo, and with Adriano Aprà, Rome. An article in *Cinema*, evidently written a year earlier during the shooting, summarizes it (without mentioning Pietrangeli) as though it were what Rossellini were actually filming, and quotes George Sanders, "I heard the film will be called *New Wine*." (Redi, "Buono o cattivo?")
10. Katherine was to recite these verses on the terrace: "Vita è la nostra unica parola. /Ma l'eco di questi luoghi /risponde sommessamente: morte. /Gli uomini nascono /già contagiati di vecchiezza /e la vita /è priva di fanciulezza. /Il silenzio si adagia /su tutte le cose /come la polvere . . ." ("Life is our only word. /But the echo of these places responds meekly: dead. /People hide /already infected with old age /and life /is deprived of childhood. /Silence descends /on everything / like dust . . ."). The verses actually in the movie are: "Temple of the spirit. No longer bodies, but pure ascetic images, compared to which mere thought seems flesh, heavy, dim."

    The synopsis foresaw a gradual melting of tension between the couple; in the movie tension mounts. In the synopsis Katherine ("Caterina") demands a divorce after Alex slaps a man leering at her during a visit to Paestum, after which they are reconciled by smiles from people passing in a procession. In the movie they ponder divorce before and after Katherine runs from the buried lovers at Pompeii, and reconciliation requires an impulse generated by a miracle.

    Brancati (1907–54) wrote satirical novels. *Don Juan in Sicily* (1941) critiqued Sicilian obsessions with eroticism and machismo, a theme that reappears in *Antonio the Great Lover* (1949) and in *Voyage in Italy*.

    Cf. Renzo Trionfera, "Roberto e Ingrid nell'antro della Sibilla," *L'Europeo*, March 12, 1953. Louis Kibler, "Brancati," *Software Toolbooks Multimedia Encyclopedia* (New York: Grolier, 1992).
11. The original is in the possession of Silvia D'Amico. An Italian transcription is in Stefano Roncoroni, "Pour Rossellini," *Voyage en Italie* (*L'Avant-Scène Cinéma* 361, June 1987), pp. 14–15. A French translation appears in Alain Bergala, *Voyage en Italie de Roberto Rossellini* (Crisnée, Belgium: Editions Yellow Now, 1990), pp. 7–9.
12. Steele, *Ingrid Bergman*, p. 311.
13. Sanders, *Memoirs*, p. 121.
14. Trionfera, "Roberto e Ingrid."
15. Sanders, *Memoirs*, p. 122.
16. Quoted in *My Story*, p. 370.
17. Zsa Zsa Gabor, *One Lifetime Is Not Enough* (New York: Delacorte, 1991), pp. 109–12.
18. Sanders, *Memoirs*, pp. 123–24.
19. Ibid., pp. 127–28.
20. Redi, "Buono o cattivo?"
21. Quoted by Enzo Serafin, in Bergala, *Voyage*, p. 132.
22. Baldelli, p. 246.
23. Sanders, *Memoirs*, pp. 124, 125.
24. Quoted by Helen Tubbs, in Leamer, *As Time Goes By*, p. 232.
25. Letter, in Steele, *Ingrid Bergman*, p. 311.
26. Gabor, *One Lifetime*, p. 106.
27. Quoted in *My Story*, p. 372.
28. Ibid., p. 371.
29. Blue, 1972. For Sanders, cf., Redi, "Buono o cattivo?"
30. Quoted by Enzo Serafin, in Bergala, *Voyage*, p. 132.
31. *Filmcritica* 156, 1965; *Screen* translation.
32. Rossellini bragged about his effort to Gian Vittorio Baldi. Enzo Serafin, the film's photographer, confirmed this and added further details. Gian Vittorio Baldi to TG. Enzo Serafin to TG.

33. Trionfera, "Roberto e Ingrid."
34. Quoted in Redi, "Buono o cattivo?"
35. (1976) In G. L. Rondi, *Cinema dei maestri*, pp. 21–22.
36. Quoted in Venturi, "Roberto Rossellini," p. 10; from Lamberti Sorrentino, "Un film e un idillio," *Tempo*, April 16, 1949. Serafin to TG.
37. Enzo Serafin to TG.
38. Wood, "Ingrid."
39. Leonard Maltin, ed., *Leonard Maltin's TV Movies and Video Guide* (New York: Signet 1991), p. 1111, under *Strangers*.
40. Bergala, *Voyage*, pp. 16–26. These two paragraphs paraphrase Bergala's argument; the subsequent continuation and alteration of that argument are my own responsibility.
41. Ibid., p. 19.
42. Ibid., p. 25.
43. Peter Brunette writes, "Words are used a weapons to *prevent* communication," and quotes Leo Braudy: "[There] is an abrasion of boredoms [between Katherine and Alex], spawned by . . . inconsequential, space-filling dialogue." Yet clearly Katherine and Alex are communicating love, pain, bewilderment, and much else at the deepest levels. After years together their language is honed to rich subtlety. They use words, not to prevent communication (a contradiction in terms), but to hurt, solicit, and cry out to each other. How can Braudy say they are "bored" with each other? Their sparring is so intense and obsessive that everything they do is an attempt, unqualifiedly futile, to think of anything else *but* each other. How can he call it "inconsequential"? Rossellini has so stripped his script of redundancy that every feint, every parry is a necessary stop on their voyage into love. What could be more consequential? (Brunette, *Rossellini*, pp. 158–60. Leo Braudy, "Rossellini," in Braudy and M. Dickstein, eds., *Great Film Directors: A Critical Anthology* [New York: Oxford University Press, 1978], p. 668.)
44. Jacques Rivette, "Lettre sur Rossellini," *Cahiers du Cinéma* 46, April 1955, p. 14. Generally my translation, but occasionally that by Tom Milne, in Jonathan Rosenbaum, ed., *Rivette: Texts and Interviews* (London: British Film Institute, 1977), pp. 54–64. Cf., also, Gruault, *Ce que*, p. 192.
45. Rohmer (signed Maurice Schérer), "La Terre." Sentence order transposed.
46. *Il Progresso d'Italia*, 1948.
47. Jean Douchet, "Roberto Rossellini: Le Général escroc et héros," *Arts* 739, September 9, 1959.
48. *Radio-Cinéma-Télévision*, May 1955; reprint: *Cahiers du Cinéma* 410, July 1988, p. 15.
49. Rohmer, "La Terre," p. 40.
50. Rivette, "Lettre," § 14, p. 22.
51. The dialogue undoubtedly derives from James Joyce's "The Dead," except that Joyce's woman is neither uncarnal nor self-consumed. By naming his characters Joyce and having them claim a heritage from Uncle "Homer," Rossellini is perhaps obliquely suggesting a need for Nordic races to connect themselves to Mediterranean culture.
52. Aprà, "Rossellini oltre," pp. 294–95.
53. Rivette, "Lettre," §14, p. 22.
54. An example in Antonioni is the end of *The Passenger*.
   I mention Tolstoy to clarify the point about Vidor. The two are profoundly alike, even aside from their collaboration on War and Peace. Unfortunately, English-language studies of Vidor ignore the Christian Science outlook his films propagate. See Vidor's detailed exegesis with Louis Marcorelles, *Cahiers du Cinéma* 104, February 1960. Cf., Tag Gallagher, "King Vidor," "Hollywood Directors, 1932–55," *Trafic* (France), Spring 1995.
55. The effect is perhaps borrowed from similar shots in Renoir, particularly in *Le Crime de M. Lange* (1936).
56. Rohmer, "La Terre," p. 40.
57. *Arts*, April 20, 1955.
58. *CdC* 37, 1954.
59. Rohmer, "La Terre," p. 41 (sentence order transposed). Rohmer refers to an interview with Rossellini in *CdC* 37, 1954.
60. Interview with Jolanda Benvenuti (Rossellini's long-time editor), in Bergala, *Voyage*, pp. 143–46.
61. Vittoria Fulchignoni to TG.
62. Interview with Enzo Serafin, in Bergala, *Voyage*, p. 131.
63. Ibid.
64. Sanders, *Memoirs*, p. 128.
65. *Arts*, April 20, 1955.
66. *Radio-Cinéma-Télévision*, May 1955.
67. *Filmcritica* 156, 1965; *Screen* translation.
68. *CdC* 37, 1954.
69. Bazin, "Difesa di Rossellini," p. 149; *Qu'est-ce que le cinéma?* IV:156; beware Gray's translation, *What Is Cinema?*, II:98.
70. Quoted in Rohmer, "La Terre," p. 40.
71. Ibid.
72. Ibid., pp. 39–40 (sentence order transposed).
73. Jacques Rivette, "La Main," *Cahiers du Cinéma* 76, November 1957. (A translation appears in Rosenbaum, *Rivette*, p. 67.)
74. Ayfre, "Sens et non-sens," *Conversion*, p. 71.
75. In *Sunrise*, Gaynor is thought to have died in the storm but is improbably found, in the middle of the lake in the middle of the night, holding onto some reeds. In *The Last Laugh*, old Emil Jannings is demoted from

doorman to lavatory attendant, but a whimsical millionaire leaves him his fortune. In *Tabu*, the boy drowns when the priest cuts the rope.

Chapter 17: At the Stake

1. Rod Geiger to TG.
2. James K. Lyon, *Bertolt Brecht in America* (Princeton: Princeton University Press, 1980), p. 82. Geiger to TG. Joseph Losey had staged the play in Beverly Hills in July 1947, but Brecht intended for Geiger to direct the film. Cf., Bertolt Brecht, *Letters* (New York: Routledge, 1990), pp. 426–27.
3. Rod Geiger to TG. Some forty years later, Dmytryk apologized to Geiger—who held no grudges and blamed himself for what had happened: he felt his reponsibility should have been to speak through his movie rather than putting his belief in someone over whom he had no control. Dmytryk thought *Give Us This Day* was his best movie.
4. Murray, "The Man Who," 1953.
5. Tonti, *Odore di cinema*, p. 171.
6. Davidson, "Anatomy of a Scandal," p. 14
7. Steele, *Ingrid Bergman*, p. 312.
8. Alfredo Parente, *Il Mattino* (Naples), July 5, 1963.
9. Steele, *Ingrid Bergman*, p. 313.
10. Ibid.
11. Selznick Archives: Unsigned memo to Rossellini, October 7, 1953.
12. *Changes*, 1974.
13. Faldini and Fofi, I:251.
14. Cf. *Variety*, October 7 and 14, 1952.
15. Elena Dagrada, " Le philologue, l'Histoire et la censure: a propos d' *Europa '51* de Roberto Rossellini," in Jean Pierre Bertin-Maghit and Béatrice Fleury-Vilatte, eds., *Cinéma, Histoire* (Paris: Ecole des Hautes Etudes, 1998). Renato Buzzonetti, *Rivista del Cinematografo*, January 1953.
16. Faldini and Fofi, I:252.
17. "Europe '51," in *Qu'est-ce que le cinéma?*, IV:97.
18. Rohmer (signed Maurice Schérer), *Cahiers du Cinéma 25, July 1953. Sentence order rearranged.*
19. Steele, *Ingrid Bergman*, p. 313.
20. Quoted by Rossellini, in Vittorio Bonicelli, "Che cosa disse Ingrid quando Rossellini le parlò di Sonali," *Tempo*, March 24, 1959.
21. Baldelli, p. 242. Steele, *Ingrid Bergman*, p. 313, quotes a letter from Ingrid acknowledging the records were a gift to her from Steele and Ruth Roman. Perhaps Rossellini did not wish to acknowledge Steele.
22. Baldelli, p. 244. In fact, everything is *not* seen. A review of Rossellini's production in Paris noted: "One good reform is the suppression of the apparition of the saints and the Virgin." (Hélène Jourdan-Morhange, "Jeanne au bûcher de Paul Claudel et Arthur Honegger," *Les Lettres Françaises* 523, July 8, 1954.)
23. Guido Pannala, *Epoca* 167, December 6, 1953, p. 96.
24. Roberto Paolella, "Il teatro licio e lo schermo," *Cinema* 126, January 30, 1954.
25. Sergio Toffetti, "Roberto stava lì, seduto a capotavola . . . : Intervista a Gabor Pogany," in *Giovanna d'Arco al rogo di Rossellini*, Turin: Museo Nazionale del Cinema, 1987.
26. *Theater Arts*, May 1955.
27. Ibid. Sentence order inverted.
28. Claude Beylie, "Défense de *Jeanne au bûcher* ou la sérénité des abîmes," *Études Cinématographique* 18-19, July 1962, p. 78.
29. *CdC* 37, 1954.
30. Toffetti, "Roberto stava lì."
31. Guarner, *Rossellini*, pp. 68–70. Beylie, "Défense de *Jeanne*," pp. 72–78.
32. *New York Times*, January 12, 1954.
33. G. C. Castello, *Cinema* 128, February 28, 1954. Casiraghi, *L'Unità*, quoted in Rinaudo, "Foyer Rossellini," p. 44.
34. A. Paladini, "Dov'è Rossellini?" *Rivista del Cinema Italiano* 7, July 1954, pp. 42–45.
35. Anon., "*Dov'è la libertà . . . ?*" *Cinema Nuovo* 35, May 15, 1954, p. 284.
36. F. A., "Giovanna d'Arco al rogo"; O. V., "Le scene e la regìa," *Corriere della Sera*, April 23, 1954, p. 4.
37. A. E. Hotchner, *Papa Hemingway* (New York: Random House, 1966), pp. 99–102.
38. *Arts* 468, June 16, 1954; reprinted in Jean Renoir, *Écrits 1926–1971* (Paris: Belfond, 1974), p. 198.
39. Roberto Rossellini to TG, 1974.
40. Claudel, *Journal*, II (1933–55) (Paris: Gallimard, 1969), p. 867.
41. Quoted by Roberto Rossellini to TG, 1974.
42. Roberto Rossellini to TG, 1974.
43. Baldelli, p. 242.
44. "L'Idée mère de *Jeanne au bûcher*," *Le Figaro*, June 21, 1954.
45. Claudel, p. 867. Claudel continued: "The chorus encircling the audience [are] magnificent. Ingrid Bergmann [sic], magnificent. A temperament overflowing with energy, a surplus of gifts which she doesn't know how to use. There is *progression*—but: the angels at the beginning: cheap. The first scenes are confused, rather inferior to the earlier version. Ingrid, too agitated, gesticulates too much. The little

landscape of pseudo-France in the corner is execrable. At the end, Jeanne in the sky should dissolve, leaving the entire place to the music."

46. Jourdan-Morhange, "Jeanne."
47. *Le Monde*, June 25, 1954.
48. Gilles Cahoreau, *François Truffaut* (Paris: Julliard, 1989), pp. 110–11.
49. Truffaut, "Un homme seul."
50. Cahoreau, p. 111.
51. *CdC* 37, 1954. I have been unable to locate any publication of the sentence attributed to Rivette.
52. *Arts*, 1954. Contemporaneously, Rossellini told *Rivista del Cinematografo* (June 1954, p. 16) that *Francesco, Europe '51*, and *Paisà* were his favorites. He frequently said he never watched his films after making them.
53. *Newsweek*, June 28, 1954.
54. *My Story*, p. 392.
55. To Oriana Fallaci, *Look*, March 5, 1968.
56. *My Story*, p. 392.
57. Quoted in Davidson, *Real and*, p. 50.
58. Quoted in Davidson, "Anatomy of a Scandal," p. 15.
59. Bonicelli, "Che cosa."
60. Carlo Ludovico Bragaglia, in Lamberto Antonelli and Ernesto G. Laura, *Nato col cinema: Carlo Ludovico Bragaglia: Cent'anni tra arti e cinema* (Rome: Associazione Nazionale Circoli Cinemtografici Italiani, 1992), pp. 93–94. The contract stipulated that Rossellini would not interfere in the montage.
61. *Diario de São Paolo*, September 1, 1954.
62. Rossellini to Gian Vittorio Baldi to TG. The incident may have occurred in September 1954, when Rossellini was returning from Brazil alone.
63. Bragaglia, in Antonelli and Laura, *Nato col cinema*, p. 94.
64. *Cahiers du Cinéma* 93, March 1959, p. 9.
65. *My Story*, p. 392.
66. De Marchis, *Un matrimonio*, p. 79.
67. Interview with Massimo Mauri, *Epoca* 231, March 6, 1955. Rossellini repeated in 1959 to Bonicelli that "Ingrid herself refused [*Senso*] because the part was too far away from her, she didn't understand it." (Bonicelli, "Che cosa," p. 16.)
68. Davidson, *Real and*, p. 158. Hotchner, *Papa Hemingway*, p. 90 (1954). Steele, *Ingrid Bergman*, p. 316 (September 1954). Rod Geiger to TG, September 1955.
69. Steele, *Ingrid Bergman*, p. 316.
70. *My Story*, p. 392.
71. Baldelli, p. 135.
72. Faldini and Fofi, I:338.
73. Unpublished remarks for ORTF, 1962. In *Il mio metodo*, p. 202.
74. Cited in François Truffaut, "Rossellini '55," *Arts* 499, January 19, 1955, p. 5.
75. *CdC* 37, 1954.
76. Mathias Wieman was a *Staatsschauspieler*. He wrote articles on the moral duty of the actor during wartime and, during the last months of the war, toured to entertain the troops.
77. *Arts*, 1954.
78. "Petit Journal," *Cahiers du Cinéma* 45, March 1955, p. 39.
79. Truffaut, "La Peur," *Arts*, July 11, 1956.
80. *Il Progresso d'Italia*, 1948.
81. Rondolino, *Rossellini* (1989), p. 225.
82. Sicilier, letter to Hovald, cited in Hovald, *Le Néo-realisme*, p. 124. Sicilier, "Letter from Berlin," *Cahiers du Cinéma* 52, November 1955, p. 56.
83. Carlo Carlini to TG.
84. One appeared in *La Settimana Incom*, February 12, 1955.
85. *London Times*, October 21, 1954. Louis T. Stanley, quoted in Bergman, *My Story*, p. 383.
86. Harold Conway, *Daily Sketch*, October 21, 1954. John Barber, *Daily Express*, October 21, 1954. Anon., *Stage*, October 28, 1954.
87. *Daily Express*, October 23, 1954.
88. *Film d'Oggi*, October 1954, quoted in Masi and Lancia, p. 63. *Festival*, quoted in Masi and Lancia, p. 64. *Avanti!*, October 2, 1954, p. 33. *Sipario*, October 1954, p. 33. *L'Unità*, December 2, 1954. *Corriere della Sera*, Anon., October 3, 1954. *Cinema*, December 1954, p. 739. *Rassegna del Film*, October 1954, p. 47. Rondi, *La Fiera Letteraria*, October 24, 1954. François Vinneuil, quoting his Italian colleagues, in an uncited review at the time of *Voyage in Italy*'s Paris opening (April 15, 1955), quoted by Claude Beylie, "Les bons et les mauvais guides," *Voyage en Italie* (*L'Avant-Scène Cinéma* 361, June 1987), p. 136. Castello, *Cinema*, December 1954, p. 739. *La Nuova Stampa* (Turin), September 23, 1954.
89. *La Fiera Letteraria*, October 24, 1954.
90. *Filmcritica*, November 1954, p. 225.
91. Hovald, *Le Néo-réalisme*, p. 177.
92. Renzi, "Introduction," in Renzi, ed., *Era notte*, p. 66.
93. Alpert, *Fellini*, p. 77.
94. The Golden Lion went to Castellani's *Romeo and Juliet*, Silver Lions to *La strada*, Mizoguchi's *Sansho the Bailiff*, Kurosawa's *Seven Samurai*, and Kazan's *On the Waterfront*.
95. Guido Aristarco, *Film Culture* 1:2 (1955), pp. 30–31; reprinted in Peter Bondanella, ed., *Federico Fellini: Essays in Criticism* (Oxford: Oxford University Press, 1978), pp. 60–61.

96. "Letter to a Marxist Critic," *Il Contemporaneo* 143, October 25, 1954. Quoted in Alpert, *Fellini*, pp. 98–99.
97. Bazin, "Difesa," p. 149.
98. Quoted in Hovald, *Le Néo-réalisme*, p. 176.
99. Ibid., p. 188.
100. Enrico Fulchignoni to TG.
101. Ibid.
102. *Bianco e Nero*, 1964.
103. François Truffaut, "Il préfère la vie," in Verdone, *Rossellini*, p. 199; reprint: Truffaut, *The Films in My Life* (New York: Simon & Schuster, 1978).
104. Cahoreau, *Truffaut*, p. 112.
105. Truffaut, "Il préfère la vie," p. 199.
106. Jacques Doniol-Valcroze, *Cahiers du Cinéma* 44, February 1955, p. 41.
107. Fereydoun Hoveyda to TG. Cf., in Verdone, *Rossellini*, p. 7.
108. Cf., long reviews by Mario Baccavo, *Roma* (Naples), December 5, 1954, and Alfredo Parente, *Il Mattino*, December 5, 1954.
109. Steele, *Ingrid Bergman*, p. 317.
110. *Triumfo* (Madrid), January 5, 1955.
111. Truffaut, "Il préfère la vie," p. 200.
112. Quoted in Truffaut, *Arts*, January 19, 1955, p. 5.
113. Cf. Jean-Marie Straub, "L'oeuvre de Rossellini, a-t-elle une signification chrétienne?" *Radio-Cinéma-Télévision* 265, February 13, 1955.
114. Truffaut, "Il préfère la vie," p. 201.
115. *My Story*, p. 384.
116. *Vecko-Journalen*, February 26, 1955; quoted in Leamer, p. 234. Bergman (*My Story* p. 385) appears to be quoting a somewhat different text: "It is both malicious and unfair to compare her to professional actresses, as has been done. It just happened that, after making one film failure after another, nothing else remained for Rossellini and Ingrid Bergman but to travel from one city to another, from one country to another, showing Ingrid Bergman for money."
117. Steele, *Ingrid Bergman*, p. 318.
118. Ibid., p. 319.
119. Quoted in *My Story*, p. 558.
120. *Oggi*, February 3, 1955; quoted in Lawrence J. Quirk, ed., *The Films of Ingrid Bergman* (Secaucus, N.J.: Citadel, 1970), pp. 143–44.
121. *Cahiers du Cinéma* 44, February 1955, p. 41. A private screening January 21, 1955, of the work print, which Truffaut had seen with Rossellini in November 1954. The test screening, with Bergman dubbed by Nollier, was May 26, 1955, as part of the "Journées du Cinéma" at the Maison de la Chimie, Chalon-sur-Saône.
122. Truffaut (signed François de Montferrand), *Radio-Cinéma-Télévision* 28, June 1955; quoted in Hovald, *Neo-realisme*, p. 122.
123. Truffaut, *Arts*, June 1, 1955.
124. *Cahiers du Cinéma* 44, February 1955, p. 41. *Cahiers du Cinéma* 48, June 1955, p. 38, (signed Robert Lachenay.)
125. Hovald, *Neo-realisme*, p. 122. "Petit Journal: 7 juillet," *Cahiers du Cinéma* 50, August 1955.
126. Anon., *Festival* 112, February 19, 1955. Gian Luigi Rondi thought it uninteresting as cinema (*Il Tempo*, January 30, 1955). Gino Visentini, *Giornale d'Italia*, January 30, 1955, was, as so often before, almost alone among Italian critics in finding words of praise.
127. *Cinema Nuovo*, March 10, 1955, p. 191. Claude Mauriac, *Figaro Litteraire*, July 31, 1955. Alessandro Ferraù, *Bolletino dello Spettacolo*, February 17, 1955.
128. *L'Unità* (Milan), January 23, 1955. Ojetti, "Un discorso." *Il Borghese*, quoted in *Cahiers du Cinéma* 62, August 56, p. 36. Anon., *Cinema Nuovo*, March 10, 1955, p. 191. Filippo Sachi, *Epoca*, January 30, 1955. Hans, *Variety*, March 16, 1955; from Berlin. A notice from Rome by Hawk, *Variety*, March 3, 1955, was far more positive, but thought the "theme" would keep earnings moderate. Visentini, as with *Joan*, gave *Fear* virtually its only enthusiastic notice in Italy. "His film is clean, hard, lucid and simple: like reality exactly seized with the precise intuition and grace of the artist." (*Giornale d'Italia*, quoted in Masi and Lancia, p. 72.)
129. Ojetti, "Un discorso," *Cinema*.
130. Giuseppe Sala, "Variazioni e commenti su Rossellini," *Bianco e Nero*, January 1955, pp. 99–100. Ojetti, "Un discorso," *Cinema*.
131. Davidson, *Real and*, p. 177.
132. Anon., *L'Unità* (Rome), July 26, 1955. Ojetti, "Un discorso," *Cinema*.
133. Rossellini quote dated as August 1954, cited in Ojetti, "Un discorso," Cinema.
134. *Cinema Nuovo*, April 14, 1955.
135. Rouch, "La ricerca della 'verità', in Bruno, ed., *Rossellini* (Sanremo, 1980), p. 47.
136. "Jean Rouch su Rossellini," in G. L. Rondi, *Cinema dei maestri*, p. 31.
137. Jean Rouch to TG, February 1991.
138. Rohmer, "La Terre," p. 40.
139. Rivette, "Lettre," §3, pp. 15–16.
140. Ibid., §0–1, pp. 14-15; §16, pp. 23–24.
141. Truffaut, *Arts*, April 20, 1955.
142. Truffaut, *Radio-Cinéma-Télévision*, May 1955.
143. Rivette, "Lettre," §9, p. 19; §16, p. 24; §12, p. 20.
144. For these terms, cf., Pierre Macabru, "Un Cinéma contemplatif," *Arts*, June 21, 1961; reprinted in Verdone, *Rossellini*, pp. 177–78.

145. Rivette, "Lettre," §8, p. 18; §9, p. 19. Milne translation. My emphases.

146. Ibid., §10, p. 20.

147. Ibid., §12–13, pp. 20–21.

148. Ibid., §13, pp. 21–22.

149. Ibid., §14, p. 22.

150. Ibid., §5, p. 17.

151. Leprohon, *Italian Cinema*, p. 137.

152. "Dix ans de cinéma," *Cahiers du Cinéma* 50, August 1955 (I); 52, November 1955 (II); 55, January 1956 (III). Rossellini interrupted the work and never returned to it, although Truffaut made some attempts with him in September 1956.

153. *Cinema Nuovo* 65, August 25, 1955, pp. 147–49. Original French text in Bazin, *Qu'est-ce que le cinéma?*, IV:150–60; trans. Gray, *What Is Cinema?*, II:93–100.

154. "Il caso Rossellini," *Cinema Nuovo* 69, October 25, 1955, pp. 306–08.

155. Bazin, "De Sica et Rossellini," *Radio-Cinéma-Télévision*, September 1955; *Qu'est-ce que le cinéma?*, IV:112–16. Bazin goes on to reiterate points he had made in his 1952 book *Vittorio De Sica*.

   Bazin was never as ardent in casting votes for Rossellini's movies as he was in defending them theoretically. *Cahiers* had not yet instituted its monthly "Council of Ten," but in their January 1956 year's-ten-best lists *Voyage* was ranked *first* by Agel, Astruc, Chabrol, Demonsablon, Rivette, Rohmer, and Truffaut; *second* by Bitsch and Doniol-Valcroze; *third* by Bazin; *sixth* by Richer; *out-of-the-running* by Audiberti, Braunberger, Kast, Kyrou, and Resnais. Those who did not give first place to *Voyage*, including Bazin, generally favored Dreyer's *Ordet*. Bazin put *La strada* second, while *French Cancan*, another movie he would champion in theoretical terms, was ranked fifth, behind Aldrich-Odet's *Big Knife*.

   Similarly, in Council of Ten voting for *Fear* in August 1956, the highest rating (three stars: "a must see") was accorded by Agel, Doniol-Valcroze, Goute, Lachenay, Rivette, Rohmer, and Truffaut. But Bazin gave only two stars ("see").

156. Hawk, October 19, 1954. Whit, September 28, 1955.

157. Cited in Quirk, *The Films of Ingrid Bergman*, p. 140.

158. Alain Bergala, "Celle par qui le scandale arrive," *Cahiers du Cinéma* 356, February 1984, p. 12.

159. *My Story*, p. 394.

160. Leamer, *As Time Goes By*, p. 237.

161. Ibid., quoting an A.P. dispatch, *Citizen News*, June 7, 1955.

162. Leamer, *As Time Goes By*, p. 237.

163. *My Story*, p. 238.

164. *Los Angeles Times*, June 29, 1955.

165. M. Mauri, "Per noi in Italia non c'è più nulla da fare," *Epoca*, August 8, 1955, pp. 34–39.

166. Rod Geiger to TG.

167. *Cinema Nuovo*, November 10, 1955, p. 346

168. Ibid., December 10, 1955.

169. Tonti, *Odore di cinema*, p. 182.

170. Franco Rossellini to TG, 1987.

171. *Cahiers du Cinéma* 78, December 1957, p. 22.

172. Davidson, "Anatomy of a Scandal," p. 15.

173. *Tempo*, March 17, 1959, p. 13.

174. Tonti, *Odore di cinema*, p. 182.

175. *Film Culture*, 1971, p. 14.

176. *Tempo*, March 24, 1959, p. 33.

177. *Fragments*, pp. 154–55.

178. Fereydoun Hoveyda to TG.

179. Ibid.

180. Truffaut, "Il préfère la vie," p. 199.

181. Marie-Claire Solleville, in Rondolino, *Rossellini* (1989), p. 233.

182. Jean Cocteau, Roberto Rossellini, Jacques Becker, Christian Jaque, Jacques Tati, Pierre Kast, Alexandre Astruc, "Lettre ouverte," *Le Figaro*, January 5, 1956; reprinted in *L'Avant-Scène Cinéma* 88 (*Lola Montès*), January 1969, pp. 108–09. The initiative for the letter was Becker's and Astruc's, under the influence of arguments put forward by Truffaut. "This film is not a divertissement," the letter argued; "It makes you think. But we believe the public *also* likes to think. Why should someone appreciate a book of a certain quality and reject a film of equal quality?"

   The argument has a Rossellini ring to it. Truffaut, in *Arts*, December 28, 1955, had written: "If the public is annoyed by *Lola Montès*, it's because they've scarcely ever been encouraged to see films that are really *original* and *poetic*."

183. Truffaut, *Correspondance* (Renens, Switzerland: 5 Continents-Hatier, 1987), p. 123.

184. Jean Gruault, in C. J. Philippe et al., "Je sais bien que le monde moderne est plein de gens inquiets, pourquoi irais-je grossir leurs rangs?," transcript of a television program, *L'invité du dimanche*, January 24, 1971, in *Téléciné* 168, April 1971.

185. Fereydoun Hoveyda to TG. Cf. Eric Rohmer and Claude Chabrol, *Hitchcock* (Paris: Editions Universitaires, 1957). In English as, *Hitchcock: The First Forty-four Films* (New York: Ungar, 1979).

186. Gruault, *Ce que*, p. 178.

187. Fereydoun Hoveyda to TG. Wrote Chabrol, "Rossellini made an apparition in our offices above the Cinéma Georges V. . . . He asked us for some scenarios. I wrote the first version of *Le Beau Serge*. Rossellini

judged it to be without interest." (Claude Chabrol, *Et pourtant je tourne . . .* [Paris: Laffont, 1976], pp. 136–37).

188. Truffaut, *Correspondance*, p. 104.
189. Aldo Tassone, "Entretien avec Eric Rohmer," in Sergio Toffetti and Daniela Giuffrida, eds., *Eric Rohmer: Un Hommage du Centre Culturel Français de Turin* (Milan: Fabbri Editori, 1988), p. 18.
190. Gruault, *Ce que*, pp. 178–79.
191. *Bianco e Nero*, 1964.
192. Chabrol, *Et pourtant*, p. 137.
193. Renzo Rossellini, Jr., to TG.
194. Fereydoun Hoveyda to TG.
195. In Rondi, *Cinema dei maestri*, p. 31.
196. In Bruno, ed., *Rossellini* (Sanremo), p. 47
197. Truffaut, "Il padre della Nouvelle Vague," *Il Tempo*, June 3, 1978.
198. Cf., for example, C. G. Crisp, *Eric Rohmer: realist and moralist* (Bloomington: Indiana University Press, 1988).
199. *Téléciné*, April 1971.
200. In Rondi, *Cinema dei maestri*, p. 54. Taking Godard literally, Sandro Franchina, the boy in *Europe '51*, made *Morire gratis* in 1966 with nothing more than that. Godard's *Le Mépris* (1963), which is also about a man, a woman, and a car and was shot in Italy, is loaded with continuous references to *Voyage in Italy*, not least in the way Georges Delerue's score constantly evokes Renzo Rossellini's. In Godard's 1959 *Breathless*, Jean Seberg's character was originally to have interviewed Rossellini, rather than, as filmed, Jean-Pierre Melville.
201. *Filmcritica* 156, 1965; *Screen* translation.
202. In Bruno, ed., *Rossellini* (Sanremo), p. 46.
203. "Rossellini parla," 1977.
204. *Bianco e Nero*, 1964.
205. From a speech given at Bard College, Annandale-on-Hudson, New York, June 1988.
206. Tommaso Chiaretti, in the collection *Venti anni di cinema italiano* (Rome: Sindicato Nazionale Giornalisti Cinematografici Italiani, 1965), p. 231.
207. Cited by Gian Vittorio Baldi to TG.
208. *Il Tempo*, June 3, 1978.
209. Enrico Fulchignoni to TG.
210. Leamer, *As Time Goes By*, p. 242.
211. *My Story*, p. 448. Franco Rossellini and Fereydoun Hoveyda to TG.
212. *My Story*, p. 448.
213. *Fragments*, p. 150.
214. *Daily Mail*, May 21, 1956.
215. *Fragments*, pp. 151–52.
216. Demenico Meccoli, *Epoca*, July 1, 1956. See also, *Daily Mail* June 16, 26, and 27, 1956. Franco Rossellini (to TG) said Rossellini was angry that the second unit had started without him. Bergman (*My Story*, p. 448) gets the story wrong by saying Rossellini arrived to find they had started without him and walked around absolutely useless until he phoned her and she told him to come back to London, which he did "very dispirited." According to Fereydoun Hoveyda (to TG), Rossellini told him that he had had no intention of doing the film and went to Jamaica merely in order to collect his retainer, which he would otherwise have forfeited. This explanation may be true, or just face-saving or, more likely, indicative of Rossellini's intense ambivalence about doing the picture; at any rate it does not agree with Rossellini's memoir in *Fragments*, pp. 149–54. Truffaut, presumably on Rossellini's authority, reported in *Arts*, July 11, 1956, that Rossellini left because of the script changes.
217. *Fragments*, pp. 152–54.
218. *My Story*, p. 398.
219. Ibid., p. 402.
220. "La Décision d'Isa: Scenario," in Bergala, pp. 151–60. An endnote states "Scenario dictated by Roberto Rossellini to François Truffaut in 1956."
221. In 1958. Steele, *Ingrid Bergman*, p. 323.
222. *New York Times*, August 5, 1956; *Newsweek*, August 13, 1956; cited in Leamer, *As Time Goes By*, p. 246.
223. Davidson, *Real and*, p. 175.
224. Ibid., p. 173.
225. *My Story*, p. 403.

Chapter 18: The Great Mother

1. Rossellini, " 'Mi'mma.' Lettera dall'India," *Linea d'Ombra* April 1992, pp. 60–64. Also in Andrea Martini, ed., *Utopia e Cinema* (Venice: Marsilio: 1994), pp. 205–14. In French translation, "Une Lettre," *Trafic*, Winter 1991, pp. 53–60.
2. Tonti, *Odore di cinema*, p. 183.
3. *Fragments*, p. 169.
4. Ibid., p. 159.

5. Renoir, *Ma vie et mes films* (Paris: Flammarion, 1974), p. 236.
6. Renato Barneschi, quoting Sonali Das Gupta, in "Sola mia madre mi comprese,"*Gente*, September 23, 1959.
7. Ibid.
8. Leamer, *As Time Goes By*, p. 244.
9. *Fragments*, p. 181.
10. Erik Barnouw and M. V. Krishnaswamy, *Indian Film*, 2nd ed., (New York: Oxford University Press, 1980), pp. 24, 94.
11. *Fragments*, p. 181.
12. Rossellini, "Mi'mma."
13. Sonali Sen Roy, "Notes," in Adriano Aprà, ed., *Rossellini: India 1957* (Rome: Cinecittà International, 1991). Without page numbers.
14. Aldo Tonti, *Daily Sketch*, November 27, 1957. Doubtless re-written for publication.
15. Ibid.
16. Quoted in Vittorio Bonicelli, "Il nostro romanzo."
17. Barneschi, "Sola mia madre."
18. Rossellini, letter to Enrico Fulchignoni, dated January 25, 1957, *Filmcritica* 390, December 1988, p. 571.
19. Tonti says it was a Ford (*Odore*, p.188); Max Gordon a Dodge ("Le avventure indiane di Roberto Rossellini," *Tempo*, November 28, 1957); Jean Herman a Plymouth (*Cinéma 57*, September 1957). Both Tonti and Herman lived in it for thousands of miles and several months. Tonti's photos show a Plymouth.
20. Letter, January 25, 1957.
21. Cited by Adriano Aprà to TG.
22. *Film Culture*, 1971.
23. *Fragments*, pp. 162–63.
24. Cited by Adriano Aprà to TG.
25. Ibid.
26. Letter, November 28, 1956, reproduced in Fernaldo Di Giammetteo, *Roberto Rossellini* (Florence: La Nuova Italia, 1990), p. 119.
27. Gordon, "Le avventure."
28. Bonicelli, "Il nostro romanzo."
29. Letter, January 25, 1957.
30. Sen Roy, "Notes."
31. Sen Roy quoting Das Gupta, in Bonicelli, "Il nostro romanzo."
32. Sen Roy, "Notes."
33. Ibid.
34. Cited by Adriano Aprà to TG.
35. Sen Roy, "Notes."
36. Bonicelli, "Che cosa."
37. Gordon, "Le avventure."
38. *Télécité* 168, April 1971.
39. Rossellini, "Mi'mma."
40. Leamer, *As Time Goes By*, p. 246.
41. Jean Herman to TG, 1986.
42. Rossellini interview with André Bazin and Jacques Rivette, "Comment sauver le cinéma," *France-Observateur* 410, April 10, 1958; reprint: Bergala, pp. 95–101.
43. Bonicelli, "Il nostro romanzo."
44. Tonti, *Daily Sketch*, November 29, 1957.
45. Cited by Adriano Aprà to TG.
46. *Odore di cinema*, p. 180.
47. Tonti, *Daily Sketch*, November 28, 1957.
48. Ibid.
49. Gordon, "Le avventure."
50. Rossellini spoken commentary, *J'ai fait un beau voyage*, episode ten.
51. Tonti, *Daily Sketch*, November 29, 1957.
52. *Télécité* 168, April 1971.
53. *Filmcritica* 156, 1965; *Screen* translation.
54. *CdC* 94, 1959.
55. *Cahiers du Cinéma* 96, June 1959.
56. Rossellini's spoken commentary, *J'ai fait un beau voyage*, episode one.
57. *CdC* 94, 1959.
58. Tranchant and Vérité, "Rossellini 59."
59. Quoted in Gordon, "Le avventure."
60. Ibid.
61. Ibid.
62. Bonicelli, "Il nostro romanzo."
63. Gordon, "Le avventure."
64. Domenico Meccoli, *Epoca*, May 17, 1959.
65. Bonicelli, "Il nostro romanzo."
66. Meccoli, *Epoca*.
67. Bonicelli, "Il nostro romanzo."
68. Tonti, *Daily Sketch*, November 29, 1957.

69. Ibid.
70. Bonicelli, "Il nostro romanzo."
71. Ibid. Gordon, "Le avventure."
72. Sonali Sen Roy to TG.
73. Quoted in Nantas Salvalaggio, *Epoca*, November 17, 1957.
74. Quoted in Steele, *Ingrid Bergman*, p. 332.
75. Gordon, "Le avventure."
76. Quoted in Steele, *Ingrid Bergman*, p. 332.
77. Ibid.
78. Davidson, *Real and*, p. 173.
79. Bonicelli, "Il nostro romanzo.
80. Tonti, *Daily Sketch*, November 30, 1957.
81. CdC 94, 1959.
82. There also appear to have been some links between the stories. The family leaving Hirakud are going to Rourkela, which is where the old man has to deal with the factory's effect on the tigress; and perhaps the same trucks are disturbing the hermits in the mountain village.

    According to Jean Herman: "At the outset, [the picture] had a very social focus. But it must not be forgotten that Hari Das Gupta was high caste and the scandal was terrible. A part of high society recoiled; they had received Rossellini as one of their own and suddenly he took one of their own. It was a huge impropriety. Thus there was an enormous shutting of doors against him in India, while in Italy the same thing was happening because of Ingrid. He was surrounded." (Jean Herman, interviewed by Alain Bergala, in Nathalie Bourgeois and Bernard Benoliel, eds., *India: Rossellini et les animau* [Paris: Cinémathèque Française, 1997], p. 38.)

    Cf., Roberto Rossellini, "L'India tra il vecchio e il nuovo," six of the stories, prefaced by Antonello Trombadori, *Il Contemporaneo*, January 11, 1958, pp. 10–11. Also, Interview, CdC 94, 1959.
83. CdC 94, 1959. My emphasis.
84. Ibid.
85. Ibid.
86. Ibid. My emphasis.
87. Rossellini, "L'India."
88. CdC 94, 1959.
89. Sen Roy, "Notes."
90. *Blitz* (Bombay), July 7, 1957.
91. Leamer, *As Time Goes By*, p. 251.
92. Steele, *Ingrid Bergman*, p. 332, confuses events by putting Bergman's meeting with Nehru in November. Bergman was his source and, like her (*My Story*, p. 424), he states that the reason for her appeal was that the Indian government was blocking export of Rossellini's negatives to Italy. Both books claim the negatives were subsequently released, and cast Bergman in a heroic role as their liberator. Sonali Sen Roy, in contrast, states (to TG, 1986) that there was never any problem with getting the film out.
93. Leamer, *As Time Goes By*, p. 254.
94. Ibid., p. 255.
95. Rossellini spoken commentary, *J'ai fait un beau voyage*, episode one.
96. Sonali Sen Roy to TG.
97. Ibid.
98. Ibid.
99. Sonali Das Gupta, *Altro mondo* (Milan: Longanesi, 1961), p. 33.
100. Franco Riganti to TG. When Rizzoli elected to distribute *India* in Italy, he repaid Banca Romana "a tiny amount" on its loan.
101. Sonali Sen Roy, "Notes."
102. *Epoca*, November 10, 1957.
103. Gordon, "Le avventure."

Chapter 19: Bottom Up

1. *Epoca*, November 3, 1957.
2. Leamer, *As Time Goes By*, p. 256.
3. *My Story*, p. 426.
4. Davidson, *Real and*, p. 175.
5. Letter to Dido Renoir, October 27, 1957, in Renoir, *Letters*, p. 367.
6. *Epoca*, November 17, 1957.
7. *Daily Sketch*, November 26, 27, 28, 29, and 30, 1957; *Il Giorno*, November 30, 1957 and successive days. Aldo Tonti to TG.

    Tonti, according to Rossellini and Sen Roy, had never understood the events in India. Subsequently, according to Tonti, he never understood why Rossellini was mad at him, or connected Rossellini's ire with words to reporters; Tonti was not a worldly person and probably neither suspected—nor was even aware—of the sensationalized way his account would be presented by the press. (He was, for example, unaware of the existence of Bergman's best-selling autobiography—also in Italy—in which she speaks of him affectionately.) Tonti, said Renzo Rossellini, Jr. (to TG), was only defending his own professional reputation, which could have been damaged by the fiasco in India.

8. Bonicelli, "Che cosa."
9. Rossellini to Marie-Claire Solleville, in Rondolino, *Rossellini* (1989), p. 256.
10. This is conjecture, based on silence and the absence of any published writings on India during these years. But perhaps a book will be found among the Rossellini papers, if anyone is ever permitted to see them.
11. *Epoca*, November 17, 1957, p. 46.
12. Antonio Lisandrini to TG.
13. Oriana Fallaci, *L'Europeo*, August 17, 1958.
14. Barneschi, "Sola mia madre."
15. Gian Vittorio Baldi to TG.
16. Mary Meerson to TG.
17. E. Granzotto, "Il mio Roberto. A colloquio con Sonali Sen Roy," *Il Messaggero*, February 22, 1973.
18. Bonicelli, "Ecco Paola."
19. Steele, *Ingrid Bergman*, p. 340.
20. Fallaci, *L'Europeo*.
21. Ibid.
22. Ibid.
23. Ibid.
24. Ibid.
25. Ibid.
26. Ibid.
27. "Roberto Rossellini vous avez la parole!" Interview with François Bardet, Alain Buholzer, Arnold Kohler, Jacques Rial, *Filmklub-Cinéclub* (Geneva), October 1958; reprinted (in Italian) in *Il mio metodo*, p. 148.
28. Romolo Marcellini to TG.
29. Faldini and Fofi, I: 338. Josué de Castro, *The Geography of Hunger* (*Geopolitica da fame*); English translation (Boston: Little, Brown, 1952).
30. *Jornal do Brasil*, August 16, 1958, p. 3; August 19, pp. 3, 7; August 20, p. 7 (Interview); August 23, pp. 6, 9; Sepember 7, p. 6. *O Estado de São Paulo* [? or *A Gazeta*], August 19, 1958 (Interview); *A Notícia* (Rio), August 23, 1958. *A União* (João Pessoa), August 24, 1958 (Interview). Alex Aviany[?], "Rossellini, Josué e Geografia da fome," *Revista da Semana*, no date [evidently August–September 1958] (Interview).
31. Truffaut, "Il préfère la vie," p. 202.
32. Bonicelli, "Ecco Paola."
33. Manni, "Rossellini, l'araba fenice."
34. *France-Observateur*, April 10, 1958.
35. André Bazin, Jean Herman, Claude Choublier, "Cinéma et télévision: Entretien d'André Bazin avec Jean Renoir et Roberto Rossellini," *France-Observateur*, October 23, 1958; reprint: Bergala, pp. 106, 107, 109, 111.
36. Bonicelli, *Tempo*, March 3, 10, 17, 24, 1959.
37. Bonicelli, "Ecco Paola."
38. Mario Del Papa to TG.
39. Romolo Marcellini to TG.
40. Arturo Lanocita, *Corriere della Sera*, May 10, 1959.
41. *L'Unità*, May 10, 1959.
42. *Corriere della Sera*, May 10, 1959. Corrado Terzi, *Avanti!* March 13, 1960. *Il Nuovo Spettatore Cinematografico* 10–11, April 1960, pp. 273–74. Alberto Ferrero, *Cinema Nuovo*, September 1960. Enzo Muzii, *L'Unità*, December 29, 1959. Arturo Lanocita, *Corriere della Sera*, March 13, 1960.
43. Vittorio Bonicelli, *Tempo*, March 29, 1960. Morando Morandini, *La Notte*, March 13, 1960.
44. *Fragments*, p. 187.
45. *Téléciné* 168, April 1971.
46. Cited by Gian Vittorio Baldi to TG.
47. *Arts*, April 1, 1959.
48. Tranchant and Vérité, "Rossellini 59."
49. *Arts*, 1959.
50. *France-Observateur*, October 23, 1958.
51. *CdC* 94, 1959.
52. Jacques Lourcelles, "Journal de 1966," *Présence du Cinéma* 24–25, Fall 1967, p. 98.
53. *Cahiers du Cinéma* 96, June 1959.
54. *CdC* 94, 1959.
55. *France-Observateur*, April 10, 1958.
56. Tranchant and Vérité, "Rossellini 59."
57. *CdC* 94, 1959.
58. Tranchant and Vérité, "Rossellini 59."
59. *CdC* 94, 1959.
60. Tranchant and Vérité, "Rossellini 59."
61. From a series of introductions to his films filmed by the ORTF in 1962, in *Il mio metodo*, p. 202.
62. *Corriere della Sera*, May 10, 1955.
63. Domenico Meccoli, *Epoca*, May 17, 1959. Rossellini said the report that he would become a French citizen was a misinterpretation. He had meant during the worst periods that it was something he considered.
64. *France-Observateur*, October 23, 1958.

65. The article appeared in a number of Italian periodicals, then in *Reader's Digest* and in many translations, and is included in Indo Montanelli, *Pantheon minore* (Milan: Longanesi, 1950).

66. *Arts*, 1959.

67. Renzo Rossellini, Jr. to TG.

68. *Nuestro Cine* 95, 1970.

69. *Arts*, 1959.

70. Mida, *Rossellini*, 2nd ed., p. 90.

71. Baldelli, p. 232.

72. *Arts*, 1959.

73. Cited by Marcella Mariani Rossellini to TG.

74. Luc Moullet, *Cahiers du Cinéma* 102, December 1959.

75. Faldini and Fofi, II:100.

76. Faldini and Fofi, I:95. Montanelli was one of Italy's best known journalists, but he was not a novelist. His relations with Amidei, and Rossellini as well, came to a halt when, according to Amidei, he published a novelized version of Amidei's script, virtually a paraphrase, acknowledging only in a preface to the first edition—a preface that was not reprinted in subsequent editions or in any of the many translations—that he had taken the novel from the script. Said Amidei, "A Spanish producer told me, 'When I read the book in Spanish, I asked myself: "But what did Amidei do? Nothing! It was already all written!" ' " (Faldini and Fofi, I:398.)

77. *L'Unità*, August 31, 1959.

78. Nevio Corich, *Cineforum*, May 1961. Bonicelli, *Tempo*, September 15, 1959. Bonicelli added, "And for this very reason its fundamental defect is that it is the least Rossellinian of all Rossellini's films."

79. Baldelli, p. 232.

80. Renzo Rossellini, Jr. to TG.

81. *Arts*, 1959.

82. Guarner, *Rossellini*, p. 79.

83. Corich, *Cineforum*, May 1961.

84. Luc Moullet, *Cahiers* 102, December 1959.

85. Faldini and Fofi, I:399.

86. Monicelli interview, in Jean Gili, *Le Cinéma italien* (Paris: Union Générale, 1978), pp. 182–83; cited in Liehm, *Passion*, p. 163.

87. Stelio Martini, "Montanelli polemizza, Rossellini gira," *Tempo*, July 28, 1959.

88. Liehm, *Passion*, p. 164.

89. Vittorio Mussolini to TG.

90. Alicata, "Testimonianze," p. 182. Paolo Gobetti, "La Résistance dans les films italiens," p. 55. Baldelli, p. 151. Serceau, *Rossellini*, p. 118.

91. Mida, *Rossellini*, 2nd ed., p. 90. Corich, *Cineforum*, May 1961. Guarner, *Rossellini*, p. 78.

Chapter 20: Poet Laureate

1. *Schermi*, December 1959. Portions reprinted in *Il mio metodo*, pp. 207–20.

2. *Schermi*, December 1959.

3. "Lettera aperta," *Paese Sera*, September 8, 1959; reprinted in *Schermi*, October 1959; *Cinema Nuovo* 141, September 1959; and *Il mio metodo*, pp. 221–25.

4. *New York News Syndicate*, October 14, 1959.

5. Leamer, *As Time Goes By*, p. 269.

6. *Changes*, 1974.

7. Vittorio Caprioli in Faldini and Fofi, II:71.

8. Bragaglia, in Antonelli and Laura, p. 94.

9. Faldini and Fofi, II:100.

10. Morando Morandini, *Schermi*, June 1960; quoted in Masi and Lancia, p. 85.

11. Gino Visentini, *Giornale d'Italia*, October 18, 1960; quoted in Masi and Lancia, p. 86.

12. Lorenzo Pellizzari, *Cinema Nuovo* 149, January 1961, pp. 56–57.

13. Amidei said: "The idea for the film was born from my instinctively nationalistic reaction to Marshall Montgomery's famous declarations. Rossellini's new film wants to show anyone who thinks like the English general that tens of thousands of Allied prisoners crossed Italy from north to south, always finding asylum even when on the door they knocked on was the German announcement threatening death [to anyone giving them shelter]. *Era notte a Roma* in fact tells the story of three Allied prisoners who find asylum in the home of a working-class Roman woman and their pilgrimage makes them pass from initial distrust to progressive understanding of the Italians as they are—generous even to risking their lives." (Quoted in Baldelli, p. 154.)

14. In Renzi, ed., *Era notte*, p. 63.

15. Marcella Mariani Rossellini to TG.

16. Jean-Luc Godard, *Introduction à une véritable histoire du cinéma* (Paris: Albatros, 1980), p. 253. Godard describes Renzo's music as "monstrous."

17. Amerigo Terenzi to TG.

18. In Renzi, ed., *Era notte*, pp. 40–41. The quotation reads like summary notes by Renzi, rather than Rossellini's actual words.

19. Jean-André Fieschi, "Dov'è Rossellini?" *Cahiers du Cinéma* 131, May 1962, pp. 15–25. The circle shot is missing from the U.S. edition, which at 144 minutes is 13 minutes shorter than the original. *Era notte* was edited to 116 minutes for commercial distribution in Italy, but was restored to 157 minutes for video release. Also missing from the U.S. edition is the only passionate kiss in all Rossellini.

20. Rossellini interview with Jean Domarchi, Jean Douchet, Fereydoun Hoveyda, "Entretien avec Roberto Rossellini," *Cahiers du Cinéma* 133, July 1962; reprint: Bergala.

21. Leprohon, *Italian Cinema*, p. 167.

22. Ibid., p. 169.

23. Brunello Rondi, in Faldini and Fofi, II:16. Rondi says Pasolini also thought *Il bidone* was Fellini's best film.

24. Renzo Rossellini, Jr. to TG.

25. Brunello Rondi, in Faldini and Fofi, II:16.

26. Kezich, *Fellini*, p. 136.

27. Alpert, *Fellini*, p. 14.

28. *Bulletins du Festival de Cannes*, May 16, 1960.

29. *Filmcritica* 156, 1965.

30. Rossellini interview with Fereydoun Hoveyda and Eric Rohmer, "Nouvel entretien avec Roberto Rossellini," *Cahiers du Cinéma* 145, July 1963.

31. Rossellini, "Il neorealismo è morto," 1960.

32. "Rossellini Rediscovered," *Film Culture* 32, Spring 1964.

33. *Changes*, 1974.

34. *Filmcritica* 156, 1965.

35. *CdC* 133, 1962.

36. Ibid.

37. *CdC* 145, 1963.

38. In 1859 Italy was divided into four parts: the Kingdom of Sardinia (Turin, Piedmont, Savoy, and Sardinia); the Papal States; the Kingdom of the Two Sicilies (Naples, Southern Italy, and Sicily); the Austrian duchies of Lombardy, Venice, Parma, Modena, and Tuscany.

But that year Vittorio Emanuele II and his prime minister Cavour annexed Lombardy after a bloody war with Austria fought on Piedmont's behalf largely by France, under Napoleon III. In recompense, Piedmont ceded Savoy and Nice to France.

But, unexpectedly, Tuscany, Modena, Parma, and Romagna revolted and joined Piedmont. And now Cavour feared to alienate France. Napoleon had wanted a strong Piedmont as an ally against Austria, not a strong "Italy" as a European rival. Moreover, to appease French Catholics, Napoleon had stationed a French garrison in Rome since 1849, when the French, after defeating Garibaldi's forces, had suppressed the Roman Republic and violently reimposed Pope Pius IX.

Cavour therefore opposed, hindered, and refused to arm Garibaldi's expedition to Sicily in May 1860. And after Garibaldi's stunning victories, Cavour feared that Garibaldi would continue on to occupy Rome and incite French intervention. Worse, Cavour, a rabid monarchist, feared Garibaldi would establish a republic, because Garibaldi had been a follower of Mazzini, who had led the republican revolution in Rome in 1849, who had been the firebrand behind the idea of "Italy" since 1831, and who, Cavour falsely believed, was a socialist. ("Socialism" in 1860 was as terrifying as "Communism" in 1950.)

But Garibaldi's priority was a united Italy. So despite Cavour's enmity and his own loyalty to Mazzini, Garibaldi bestowed his conquests on Vittorio Emmanuele and proclaimed him King of Italy. The king resented such a gift from a radical outsider, marched south with his army, and absorbed Garibaldi's forces and conquests.

Garibaldi, refusing all rewards and hugely resented by the Piedmontese, went back to farming on Caprera. He was no less obsessed with uniting Rome to Italy, however, and subsequent Garibaldi expeditions were defeated in 1862 by the Italian government at Aspromonte, and in 1867 by the French at Mentana.

Finally, in 1870 the Franco-Prussian War compelled Napoleon to withdraw his troops from Rome, which capitulated shortly after to the Piedmontese army. Garibaldi was purposely excluded from this final victory by the Piedmontese, who did not wish to share their glory with a socialist and a weirdo.

39. Marcella Mariani Rossellini to TG.

40. Croce, *Teoria e storia*, p. 119; quoted in Collingwood, *Idea of History*, p. 199.

41. *Bianco e Nero*, 1964. My emphasis.

42. Rossellini, "Non ho fatto un Garibaldi eroe del west," *Tempo*, October 29, 1960; *Il mio metodo*, pp. 231–33.

43. *Filmcritica* 156, 1965.

44. Rossellini, "Non ho fatto."

45. Ibid.

46. Said Ricci: "In my whole film career . . . the only thing I'm satisfied with is Rossellini's Garibaldi in *Viva l'Italia*." (Savio, *Cinecittà*, III: 954.)

47. During the shooting, a nephew of Garibaldi's showed up, proclaiming, "The name Rossellini was a myth in my family!" (Zeffiro had been a friend and benefactor of Garibaldi's son, Menotti.) Marcella Mariani Rossellini to TG.

48. Marcella Mariani Rossellini to TG.

49. *Bianco e Nero*, 1964, p. 319.

50. Rossellini, "Non ho fatto."

51. *Bianco e Nero*, 1964.

52. Ibid.
53. Ibid.
54. Enrico Fulchignoni to TG.
55. Baldelli, p. 235, modified by repetition on p. 236.
56. Quoted in Mino Argentieri, "Lo stivale di Garibaldi," *La Fiera del Cinema*, October 1960, p. 39.
57. Baldelli, p. 250.
58. Louis Norman, "Rossellini's Case Histories for Moral Education," *Film Quarterly*, Summer 1974.
59. Antonello Trombadori to TG.
60. Edoardo Bruno, letter on *Viva l'Italia, Il Paese*, February 21, 1961.
61. Liehm, *Passion*, p. 293.
62. Bergala and Narboni, p. 128
63. Rondolino, *Rossellini* (1989), p. 269.
64. Gregorio Bapoli, *Il Domani*, February 10, 1961. Enrico Rossetti, *L'Espresso*, February 12, 1961. *Il Nuovo Spettatore Cinematografico* 20, March 1961, pp. 208–10 (a critical anthology).
65. March 1961, p. 156.
66. E.g., Morando Morandini, *La Notte*, February 11, 1961; Ercole Patti, *Tempo*, February 4, 1961; Filippo Sacchi, *Epoca*, February 26, 1961.
67. Maurizio Liverani, *Paese Sera*, January 28, 1961.
68. *Il Paese*, January 28, 1961.
69. Ibid., February 1, 1961.
70. Ibid., February 18, 1961.
71. Ibid., February 21, 19, 7, and 5, 1961.
72. Ibid., February 19 and 17, 1961.
73. Ibid., February 19, 1961.
74. Ibid., February 17, 1961.
75. Ibid., February 15, 1961.
76. Menon, *Dibattito*, p. 103.
77. The theme of inner fire in Rossellini's work was explored by Jean Douchet, "Roberto Rossellini," in "Cinquante-quatre cinéastes italiens," *Cahiers du Cinéma* 131, May 1962, p. 53; and subsequently developed apropos of *Il generale Della Rovere, Era notte a Roma*, and *Viva l'Italia* by Fieschi, "Dov'è Rossellini?"
78. Guarner, *Rossellini*, p. 92.
79. Sarris, "Rossellini Rediscovered," p. 60.
80. Wood, "Rossellini," *Film Comment*, September 1974.
81. *Giovanna d'Arco al rogo di Rossellini* (Turin: Museo Nazionale del Cinema, 1987).

Chapter 21: "The Cinema Is Dead" but Where Is Chastity?

1. Hitchcock quoting himself to TG, 1976.
2. Jean Gruault, "La Photo du mois," *Cahiers du Cinéma* 120, June 1961, p. 43.
3. Gruault, *Ce que*, p. 196.
4. Ibid., p. 197.
5. Curiously, Truffaut inadvertently hurt Rossellini's feelings by telling him that *Viva l'Italia* reminded him of Renoir's *La Marseillaise*. (Ibid., p. 239.)
6. Ibid., p. 213.
7. *Filmcritica* 156, 1965.
8. Serceau, *Rossellini*, pp. 159–69, gives an extended contrast of Stendhal's and Rossellini/Gruault's handling of similar themes.
9. Gruault, *Ce que*, p. 213.
10. Sandra Milo, in Faldini and Fofi, II: 223.
11. Gruault, "La photo."
12. Gruault, *Ce que*, p. 218.
13. Open letters to Renzo Helfer. "Soltanto la Magistratura ha il dritto di giudicare," *Paese Sera*, May 2, 1961 [quoted above]; "Rossellini risponde all'on. Helfer sul problema della censura nel cinema," *Paese Sera*, August 3, 1961, reprinted in *Il mio metodo*, pp. 236–51. Helfer's response to the first letter appeared as "L'on. Helfner risponde a Rossellini," *Telesera*, June 19, 1961. Address, at "Tavola rotonda sul cinema italiano," organized by Titanus, Milan, July 1, 1961; distributed in typescript; published with slight abridgment as "Un nuovo corso per il cinema italiano," *Cinema Nuovo* 152, July 1961, reprinted in *Il mio metodo*, pp. 252–64.
14. A recording of one of the performances was released on two semi-pirated LPs on the "Legendary Records" label.
15. *Cinema* VII:128, 1954, p. 100.
16. Gruault, *Ce que*, p. 220.
17. Ibid., pp. 221–22.
18. Ibid., pp. 222–23.
19. Ibid., pp. 223–24; except for the comparison with Peparuolo.
20. Ibid., p. 206.
21. *Avanti!* August 29, 1961.

22. Faldini and Fofi, II:326.
23. *Les Lettres Françaises*, July 5, 1962.
24. *Vie Nuove*, September 9, 1961.
25. Jean Douchet, *Cahiers du Cinéma* 124, October 1961.
26. September 6, 1961.
27. They detail at great length the extensive changes made in their treatment. *Paese Sera*, September 26, 1961; reprinted in Verdone, pp. 74–77.
28. Gian Maria Guglielmino, *Gazzetta del Popolo*, August 28, 1961; reprinted, as a summary of press response, in *Il Nuovo Spettatore Cinematografico* 24, August 1961. Cf. Rondolino, *Rossellini* (1989), p. 274, that most of the Italian press took this attitude.
29. *Fragments*, pp. 116–17.
30. Gruault, *Ce que*, p. 215.
31. Cf. Jacques Joly, "Les Infortunes de *Vanina Vanini*," *Les Lettres Françaises*, July 5, 1962.
32. Baldelli, p. 238.
33. In Menon, *Dibattito*, pp. 110–11.
34. Cf., in particular, Rondolino, *Rossellini* (1989), pp. 274–76.
35. Gruault, *Ce que*, p. 217.
36. Ibid., p. 226.
37. 1966, introducing *La Prise de pouvoir par Louis XIV* at Venice; quoted in Guarner, *Rossellini*, p. 78.
38. Baldelli, pp. 231–32.
39. *Nuestro Cine* 95, 1970.
40. Gruault, *Ce que*, p. 226.
41. Ibid.
42. Gian Vittorio Baldi to TG.
43. Faldini and Fofi, II:227.
44. Faldini and Fofi, II: 227.
45. September 6, 1992.
46. Brunette, *Rossellini*, p. 245.
47. "Petit Journal," *Cahiers du Cinéma* 140, February 1963, p. 39.
48. *Nuestro Cine* 95, 1970.
49. Brunette, loc. cit. Italics added.
50. Ibid.
51. *Cahiers du Cinéma* 140.
52. Schickel, *Men Who Made*, p. 159.
53. *Cahiers du Cinéma* 140.
54. *CdC* 133, April 1962.
55. Group discussion, "Les Malheurs de *Muriel*," *Cahiers du Cinéma* 149, November 1963, pp. 20–37. Rivette referred specifically to Antonioni's *L'eclisse*, an allusion which would have annoyed Rossellini.
56. *CdC* 133, 1962.
57. Antonello Trombadori to TG.
58. Baldelli, p. 250.
59. *CdC* 133, 1962.
60. Ibid.
61. *Filmcritica* 156, 1965.
62. Quoted in Rondolino, *Rossellini* (1989), pp. 288–90, from a 27-page typescript in the Rossellini papers in the possession of Silvia D'Amico Bendico.
63. Alberto Perrini, *L'Espresso*, June 1962; Roberto De Monticelli, *Epoca*, July 8, 1962.
64. *CdC* 145, 1963.
65. In Godard's *Introduction à une véritable histoire du cinéma*, p. 307, Godard states that Rossellini "had made a great many changes" to the play and that the scenario for Godard's film "is by Roberto Rossellini, and I changed absolutely nothing in the scenario; I shot it, I did my own dialogues, but the actual organization of the scenario, the idea of the two peasants," etc., all comes from Rossellini. In fact, Rossellini's "scenario" consists of only about fifteen minutes of his taped voice recounting Joppolo's story. (The tape is still in the possession of Jean Gruault, who very kindly made a copy of it for me.)
66. Quoted by Jos Oliver to TG.
67. Godard interview in G. L. Rondi, *Cinema dei maestri*, p. 54.
68. Gruault, *Ce que*, p. 226.
69. (1970), Samuels, *Encountering Directors*, p. 53.
70. *CdC* 133, 1962.
71. Gruault, *Ce que*, p. 228.
72. The *Caligula* treatment is printed in Baldelli, pp. 341–84 (without credit to Gruault or anyone). La Rochefoucauld (Serceau, *Rossellini*, p. 167) asserts Rossellini preferred not to make the film rather than yield to an American demand that he have Dustin Hoffman play Caligula (but this may have been on principle rather than any objection to Hoffman). After many years, according to Franco Rossellini, Roberto gave the idea to him, and in 1980, in parnership with *Penthouse* magazine, Franco produced a *Caligula* as a $15 million porno film directed by Tinto Brass.
73. The *Pulcinella* script is printed in Italian in *Filmcritica* 374–75, May 1987. Typescript versions in French and English versions exist also. A theatrical adaptation directed by Manlio Santanelli was performed at Rome's Teatro Argentino, February 16, 1987.
74. Quoted in *La Stampa*, June 4, 1977, p. 7.

75. Ugo Gregoretti, in Faldini and Fofi, II:239.
76. In Menon, *Dibattito*, p. 31.
77. Ajassa, "Nuova frontiera."
78. *Nuestro Cine* 95, 1970; *Bianco e Nero*, 1964.
79. "Table-ronde: cinéma vérité," *Objective* 63 (Canada), August 1963, pp. 35–38. A second transcription exists in "Débat à propos de *La Punition* et *Showman*," *Artsept* 2, April 1963, pp. 101–04. The two have been collated in *Il mio metodo*, pp. 280–87.
80. Ibid.
81. *CdC* 145, 1963.
82. *Bianco e Nero*, 1964.
83. *Filmcritica* 156, 1965.
84. Ibid.
85. *CdC* 145, 1963.
86. In Faldini and Fofi, II:81.
87. Faldini and Fofi, III:111.
88. Faldini and Fofi, II:82.
89. Faldini and Fofi, III:111.
90. Tullio Kezich, in Faldini and Fofi, II:81.
91. Sketch for a letter, January 6, 1963, in Rossellini papers, quoted in Rondolino, *Rossellini* (1989), p. 290.
92. *CdC* 145, 1963.
93. *Bianco e Nero*, 1964.
94. Rossellini, undated document in Menil Collection, Houston.
95. Gruault, *Ce que*, p. 228.
96. Rod Geiger to TG. Cf., Mauritz Edström, "Än Mullarar Vulkanien Rossellini," *Dagens Nyheter*, February 9, 1964.
97. Maria Mercader to TG.
98. Pia Lindstrom to TG, September 21, 1984.
99. Rod Geiger to TG.
100. *Filmcritica* 154, February 1965.
101. Baldelli, p. 178.
102. "Lettera alla seconda Mostra Internazionale del Nuovo Cinema" (Pesaro), typescript circulated May 30, 1965; *Il mio metodo*, pp. 355–61.
103. *Filmcritica* 154, February 1965.
104. Rod Geiger to TG.
105. *The Industrial Revolution*, typed manuscript; author's papers and elsewhere.
106. "Manifesto," presented July 7, 1965, at Rome's Foreign Press Club; reprinted in *Cahiers du Cinéma* 171, October 1965; *Il mio metodo*, pp. 353–54.
107. Gian Vittorio Baldi to TG.
108. Ibid.
109. Ibid.
110. *Filmcritica* 156, 1965. According to Fereydoun Hoveyda, Rossellini put forward similar arguments during a private dinner with Truffaut and other *Cahiers* writers. (Hoveyda to TG.)
111. Rod Geiger to TG.
112. *Fragments*, p. 135.

Chapter 22: *La Prise de pouvoir par Louis XIV*

1. *Téléciné* 168, April 1971.
2. Cf. Ken Auletta, *The Art of Corporate Success: The Story of Schlumberger* (New York: G. P. Putnam's Sons, 1984).
3. *Téléciné* 168.
4. Gian Vittorio Baldi to TG, quoting Giuliano Sparti.
5. *Rivista del Cinematografo*, July 1977.
6. Interview cited by Claude Mauriac, *Figaro Littéraire*, September 17, 1966.
7. Jean Gruault, letter to TG, July 26, 1988. Cf., also, Gruault, *Ce que*, pp. 231–35. Also Jean Dominique de La Rochefoucauld to TG, and letter to TG, August 24, 1988. Erlanger's notes consisted of "one or two pages," according to La Rochefoucauld, "quelques dizaines de pages" according to Gruault (twenty or thirty?).

Gruault's letter compares his technique of creating "pastiches of 'classical' language" to Thornton Wilder's dialogue in *The Bridge of San Luis Rey*. Curiously, there is a passage in Wilder's 1948 *The Ides of March* (New York: Harper, 1948) that not only outlines *Louis*'s thesis, but in its first sentence paraphrases the film's famous last lines:

"Neither the sun nor the situation of man permit themselves to be gazed at fixedly; the first we must view through gems, the second through poetry. . . . It is by poets that all men are told that we press forward to a Golden Age and they endure the ills they know in the hope that a happier world will arrive to rejoice their descendants. Nor it is very certain that there will be no Golden Age and that no government can ever be created which will give to every man that which makes him happy, for discord is at the heart of the world and is present in each of its parts. It is very certain that every man hates those who have been placed over him; that men will as easily relinquish the property they have as lions will permit their food to be torn away from between their teeth; that all that a man wishes to accomplish he must complete in this life, for there is no other; and that this love—of which poets make so fine a show—is nothing but the desire to be loved and the necessity in the wastes of life to be the fixed center of another's attention; and that justice is the restraint of conflicting greeds. But these are things which no man says. Our very state is governed in the language of poetry. . . .

"The world of poets is the creation not of deeper insights but of more urgent longings. Poetry is a separate language within the language contrived for describing an existence that never has been and never will be, and so seductive are their images that all men are led to share them and to see themselves other than they are." (pp. 78–80.)

Louis's last words, "Neither the sun nor death can be gazed at fixedly," come from *Reflexions ou sentences et maximes morales*, published in 1665 by Jean-Dominique's ancestor, François, Duc de La Rochefoucauld (Éditions Garnier, 1965, p. 11). But Gruault says he was unfamiliar with this novel of Wilder's and La Rochefoucauld says the lines were selected by Jean-Marie Patte, the actor who played Louis.

8. Gruault, *Ce que*, p. 233.
9. Ibid., p. 229.
10. Ibid., p. 234.
11. Jean Dominique de La Rochefoucauld to TG.
12. Quoted by Thérèse Fournier, unidentified Paris newspaper, October 11, 1966.
13. Jean Dominique de La Rochefoucauld to TG.
14. *Télécine* 168.
15. Gruault, *Ce que*, p. 238.
16. Blue, 1972.
17. Ibid.
18. *Le Mercredi*, September 13, 1966.
19. Blue, 1972.
20. The title is frequently misquoted as "La prise DU pouvoir DE Louis XIV." But as François Albera notes, the French construction "de" rather than "du" implies that Louis is legitimately entitled to this power; whereas "par" rather than "de" implies that he nonetheless *takes* it. The bizarre English translation that one commonly sees—"The Rise of Louis XIV"—completely misses the point of the film. (François Albera, "Le Prise de pouvoir par Louis XIV de Rossellini," *Procès* 11, 1983.)
21. Patrick Sery, "J'ai choisi d'être utile," *Le Nouvel Observateur*, February 10, 1975.
22. Jean Collet and Claude-Jean Philippe, "La Prise de pouvoir par Louis XIV," *Cahiers du Cinéma* 183, October 1966; reprint: Bergala.
23. Ibid.
24. Guarner, *Rossellini*, p. 112.
25. *Changes*, 1974.
26. Blue, 1972. I have cleaned up Rossellini's English.
27. Ibid.
28. *Nuestro Cine* 95, 1970.
29. *Filmcritica* 190, August 1968.
30. *CdC* 183, 1966.
31. See note 7, above.
32. Menon, *Dibattito*, p. 101.
33. Ungari, in Menon, *Dibattito*, p. 106.
34. Aprà, in Menon, *Dibattito*, p. 107.
35. "The language, the style of neo-realism . . . is the result of a moral position, of looking critically at the obvious." (Rondi, *Cinema dei maestri*, 1980.)
36. "Dix ans," I.
37. *Changes*, 1974.
38. Gruault, "La photo."
39. *Cahiers du Cinéma* 181, August 1966.
40. *Filmcritica* 156, 1965.
41. Enrico Fulchignoni to TG.
42. *Paris Match*, October 8, 1966.
43. Renzo Rossellini, Jr. to TG.
44. Ibid.
45. Gruault, *Ce que*, p. 236.
46. Blue, 1972.
47. Faldini and Fofi, II:230.
48. *L'Unità* (Milan), September 11, 1966.
49. Leo Pestelli, *La Stampa*, September 11, 1966.
50. Giovanni Grazzini, *Corriere della sera*, September 11, 1966.
51. *Paris Match*, October 8, 1966.
52. (1969); reprinted in Moravia, *Al cinema* (Milan: Bompiani, 1975), p. 54.
53. Unidentified Paris newspaper, October 11, 1966.
54. *CdC* 183, 1966.
55. *Paris Match*, October 8, 1966.
56. "Rossellini parla," 1997.

57. *Paris Match*, October 8, 1966.

Chapter 23: A New Cinematic Language

1. Letter from John de Menil to Thomas Watson, December 17, 1966; Rossellini files, Schlumberger, Ltd., New York. Jean Riboud to TG.
2. Gino di Grandi to Rossellini, July 18, 1966; Schlumberger Archives. Baldelli, p. 303. I have not seen the U.S. edition.
3. Vittorio di Girolamo Carlini to TG.
4. Jonas Mekas, *The Village Voice*, October 5, 1967; reprinted in *Movie Journal* (New York: Macmillan, 1972).
5. Lietta Tornabuoni, "Le Cinéma c'est fini!," *L'Europeo*, September 15, 1966 (also: *Le Figaro Litteraire*, October 6, 1966).
6. *Téléciné* 168, April 1971.
7. *L'Europeo*, September 15, 1966.
8. *Nuestro Cine* 95, 1970.
9. In Philip Strick, "Rossellini in '76," *Sight and Sound*, Spring 1976.
10. *L'Europeo*, September 15, 1966.
11. Blue, 1972.
12. Ibid.
13. *La Revue du Cinéma* 4, January 1947, p. 14.
14. Curiously, Rossellini insisted that this theme is a key to *Acts of the Apostles*, although it is never alluded to in any way therein. Cf., *Nuestro Cine* 95, 1970; Letter to Peter Wood, 1972; and, in its most complete form, the following from an undated document circulated by the Menil Foundation, Houston: "*Acts of the Apostles* underlines that the advent of Christianity in the pagan world was the seed that determined a deep change in man's behavior in the face of Nature. In the pagan world the gods were the personification of Nature itself and therefore untouchable and inviolable. In Judaic religious thought Nature was considered a gift that God had bestowed on man who was to penetrate it, understand it, and use it, if he wished to distinguish himself from animals. The change in ethics that rose from this was produced by Christianity which spread the ideas of Judaism in the pagan world. This new ethics represented the first step toward the advent of the increasingly scientific world of today: and this is another of the meanings of progress."

    In actuality, neither system of "ethics" is enunciated in Rossellini's *Acts of the Apostles*. The suggestion that the ethics of pagan Greece or Rome impaired technology or a scientific attitude, or that those of Christianity favored them, is not supported by history.
15. Enrico Fulchignoni to TG.
16. Mario Nascimbene, "Il mio lavoro con Roberto Rossellini," *Cinema Nuovo* 332, July 1991. Quotes of Renzo: Nascimbene to TG, July 1988.
17. Ibid.
18. Sergio Emidi, in Faldini and Fofi, II: 230; Renzo Rossellini to TG.
19. Enzo Ungari, "Conversazione con Bernardo Bertolucci," *Cult Movie*, April 1981, p. 22.
20. Auletta, *Art of Corporate Success*, p. 112.
21. Richard Roud, *A Passion for Films: Henri Langlois and the Cinémathèque Française* (New York: Viking, 1982).
22. Menon, *Dibattito*, p. 77.
23. *Nuestro Cine* 95, 1970.
24. Rossellini, "Il regista Rossellini giudica," 1969.
25. Renzo Rossellini, in Faldini and Fofi, II:437.
26. *Nuestro Cine* 95, 1970.
27. Luciano Scaffa and Marcella Mariani Rossellini, eds., *Roberto Rossellini: Atti degli Apostole, Socrates, Blaise Pascal, Agostino d'Ippona, L'età dei Medici, Cartesius* (Turin: ERI/Edizione RAI, 1980), p. 19.
28. Quoted, without clear citation, in Sergio Trasatti, *Rossellini e la televisione* (Rome: La Rassegna, 1978), p. 51.
29. Letter to TG, April 19, 1994.
30. Gruault, *Ce que*, p. 231.
31. Letter to TG, April 19, 1994.
32. MacNiven, Yale 1974.
33. Quoted, without clear citation, in Trasatti, *Rossellini*, p. 51.
34. Guarner, *Rossellini*, p. 129.
35. Quoted in Scaffa and Rossellini, *Roberto Rossellini*, p. 12.
36. Nascimbene, *Il mio lavoro*.
37. A Flight into Egypt by Carpaccio also has a lifted donkey leg. Perhaps it's a cliché. But Giotto uses various motion devices in the Scrovegni chapel scenes: series of successive poses by angels, beating sticks, etc.
38. Guarner, *Rossellini*, p. 122.
39. De Angelis, "Rossellini romanziere," p. 356.
40. Peter Lloyd, "Acts of the Apostles," *Monogram* 2, Summer 1971.
41. Ibid.
42. Ugo Buzzolan, *La Stampa*, May 5, 1969.
43. Amédée Ayfre, "Cinéma et présence du prochain," *Esprit*, April 1957; reprint: Ayfre, *Conversion*, p. 174.
44. Letter to TG, April 19, 1994.

45. The duration totalled 341 minutes (four episodes approximately an hour long; the final 97 minutes long). After Rossellini's death, Scaffa prepared a ten-chapter edition approximately 290 minutes in length for 16mm, Super 8mm, then video release, for the Salesian Catechetical Center at Leumann, Italy. In 1982 this edition was dubbed in American by Don Bosco Films, New Rochelle, NY, and released on 16mm and video. Since there was no original soundtrack and Rossellini had nothing to do with the Italian dubbing, and not much to do with the edition originally telecast, there seems no strong reason to regard the American edition as less authentic than the Italian. Don Bosco Films issued a *Teacher's Guide for Catechesis and Prayer* to accompany the film, and a comparison between the scripts printed here and in Scaffa's ERI book shows that Scaffa's abridgement consisted in removing entire scenes, or occasionally half a scene, rather than in tiny cuts—none of them among the film's inspired sections.
46. Baldelli, p. 235.
47. Interview with King Vidor, in Richard Schickel, *The Men Who Made the Movies* (New York: Atheneum, 1975), pp. 131–60.
48. Ibid., p. 250.
49. Baldelli, p. 176.
50. Cf. Lourcelles's articles on these pictures in his massive *Dictionnaire du cinéma*. He does not mention *Louis*.
51. *Présence du Cinéma* 24, Autumn 1966.
52. September 26, 1967; cited in Paul Schrader, "The Rise of Louis XIV," *Cinema* (Beverly Hills), Spring 1971.
53. Op. cit.
54. Quoted by Mekas, *The Village Voice*.
55. November 6, 1970.
56. Baldelli, pp. 229–30.
57. Nascimbene, *Il mio lavoro*.
58. *Bianco e Nero*, July 1969, p. 142
59. Baldelli, p. 188.
60. Giovanni Cesareo. *L'Unità*, May 5, 1969.
61. Ivano Cipriani, *Paese Sera*, April 8, 1969.
62. Baldelli, p. 189.
63. Ibid.

Chapter 24: *Socrates*

1. Luciano Scaffa to TG, 1986.
2. Ivani Cipriani, "Roberto Rossellini dice addio al Centro e all TV italiano," *Paese Sera*, November 15, 1969; reprinted in Trasatti, pp. 141–47.
3. *La Stampa*, November 16, 1969, quoted in *Cinema Nuovo* 202, November 1969, p. 144.
4. c. 1973, Roger MacNiven to TG.
5. Jean Dominique de La Rochefoucauld to TG, July 5, 1986.
6. Brian Huberman and Edward Hugetz, "The Memory of Roberto Rossellini in Texas," in *Rossellini* (Texas), p. 109.
7. Nathan Fain, *The Houston Post*, November 22, 1968.
8. Ibid.
9. MacNiven, Yale 1974.
10. "La Contestation," April 25, 1969.
11. Cited by Beppe Cino to TG, 1986.
12. Cited by Beppe Cino, in Bergala and Narboni, p. 46.
13. Quoted in Mario Garriba, "Cinema anno zero" in *Filmcritica* 374, May 1987.
14. This quote: February 1971. *Film Culture*, Spring 1971.
15. Paraphrase of material freely quoted by Beppe Cino, *Filmcritica* 374, May 1987.
16. Garriba, "Cinema anno zero."
17. Interview with Vincent Canby, *New York Times*, December 12, 1971.
18. Ibid.
19. Schultz, *Film Culture*.
20. Ibid. I have changed the incorrect rendering of the Italian word "*suggestione*" by its false cognate "suggestion" in this text.
21. *Nuestro Cine* 95, 1970.
22. 1971, Baldelli, p. 255.
23. Read, *Icon and Idea*, p. 96.
24. 1971, Baldelli, p. 264.
25. *France-Observateur*, April 10, 1958.
26. Claude Beylie, "Entretien avec Roberto Rossellini," *Écran* 45, March 15, 1976, p. 59.
27. Garriba, "Cinema anno zero." The comparison with *Acts* is added.
28. Blue, 1972.
29. Lietta Tornabuoni, "Ventotto domande a Rossellini," *Rossellini Socrate per la TV: Appunti del Servizio Stampa della RAI*, 28; reprinted in Trasatti, *Rossellini*, pp. 149–60.
30. *Nuestro Cine* 95, 1970.
31. Garriba, "Cinema anno zero."

32. *New York Times*, December 12, 1971.
33. Garriba, "Cinema anno zero."
34. Beppe Cino to TG, 1986.
35. *Film Culture*, 1971.
36. *Téléciné* 168, April 1971.
37. Quoted in *The Village Voice*, May 10, 1973.
38. Victoria Schultz, *Film Culture*, Spring 1971.
39. Carlo Verdone, in Franca Faldini and Goffredo Fofi, *Il cinema italiana d'oggi: 1970–1984, raccontato dai sui protagonisti* (Milan: Mondadori, 1984), p. 595.
40. *Film Culture*, 1971.
41. Garriba, "Cinema anno zero."
42. *Rivista del Cinematografo*, July 1977, p. 303.
43. Elisabetta Rasy, "La logica di Rossellini," *Paese sera*, October 7, 1972.
44. Savio, *Cinecittà*, p. 966.
45. *Rivista del Cinematografo*, July 1977, p. 300.
46. MacNiven, Yale 1974.
47. *Nouvel Observateur*, 1975.
48. *Film Culture*, 1971.
49. MacNiven, Yale 1974.
50. *Nuestro Cine* 95, 1970.
51. *Bianco e Nero*, 1952.
52. Llinás and Marías, 1970.
53. Rossellini, "Verso il futuro come ciechi." *La Stampa*, August 8, 1971; reprinted in Trasatti, pp. 189–96.
54. 1971; Baldelli, p. 213.
55. Llinás and Marías, 1970.
56. *Changes*, 1974.
57. MacNiven, Yale 1974.
58. Strick, "Rossellini in '76." I have cleaned up Rossellini's English.
59. *Changes*, 1974.
60. *Bianco e Nero*, 1952.
61. Brunette, *Rossellini*, p. 301. Baldelli, p. 195. Paolo Bertetto, *Sipario* 294, October 1970. "Bears witness": Rossellini, cited in Trasatti, *Rossellini*, p. 78, but followed by the correcting qualification, which Brunette omits, cited below, that society can forgive murderers but not non-conformists.
62. Cited in Trasatti, *Rossellini*, p. 78.
63. Paolo Valmarana, "Ho seguito Socrate come un discepolo," *Radiocorriere TV*, June 13, 1971, p. 40; cited in Trasatti, p. 74.
64. Trasatti, *Rossellini*, p. 75.
65. Tornabuoni, "Ventotto domande."
66. Michael McKegney, "Rossellini, Socrates, and History," *Village Voice*, April 22, 1971.
67. Tornabuoni, "Ventotto domande."
68. Llinás and Marías, 1970.
69. Tornabuoni, "Ventotto domande."
70. Luciano Scaffa to TG.
71. Letter to TG, April 19, 1994.
72. Luciano Scaffa to TG.
73. Letter to TG, April 19, 1994.
74. Ibid.
75. Gruault, *Ce que*, p. 240.
76. Jos Oliver to TG.
77. Letter to TG, April 19, 1994.
78. Jos Oliver to TG.
79. Ibid.
80. Ibid.
81. *Le Monde*, August 21, 1970.
82. Trasatti, *Rossellini*, p. 151.
83. November 24, 1971.
84. August 19, 1970.
85. December 12, 1971.
86. Robert Lawrence to TG.
87. Ibid.
88. *New York Times*, December 12, 1971.
89. Roberto Rossellini, "Un vero uomo," *Paese Sera*, August 26, 1973; reprinted in *Il mio metodo*, pp. 440–42.
90. Ibid.

Chapter 25: *Blaise Pascal*

1. Cf. Trasatti, *Rossellini*, pp. 68–69. *L'Unità*, September 12, 1970.

2. Baldelli, pp. 302–03.
3. Maria Mercader to TG.
4. Jean Dominique de La Rochefoucauld to TG, 1986.
5. Ibid.
6. Interview with Giuseppe Nava, "Perché Pascal. Quattro domande a Rossellini sull'importazione e le scelte del telefilm," in *Pascal per la televisione*, Appunti del servizio stampa 44 (Roma: RAI) May 1972, p. 19; reprinted in *Il mio metodo*, p. 419.
7. In Bergala and Narboni, p. 45.
8. Jean Dominique de La Rochefoucauld to TG.
9. Marcella Mariani Rossellini to TG.
10. Letter to TG, April 19, 1994. In the Italian edition, La Rochefoucauld is cited only for the dialogues.
11. Garriba, "Cinema anno zero."
12. Rasy, "La logica di Rossellini."
13. Strick, "Rossellini in '76."
14. Rasy, "La logica di Rossellini."
15. Nava, "Perché Pascal."
16. Letter to Peter Wood, July 20, 1972, distributed in mimeograph by Pacific Film Archives, Berkeley, during a Rossellini retrospective, October–December 1973; partially reprinted in *The New Republic*, July 2, 1977, pp. 27–30; reprinted integrally in *Il mio metodo*, pp. 425–32.
17. Claude Beylie, "Brève rencontre," *Écran* 34, March 1975, p. 17.
18. 1971, Baldelli, p. 254.
19. Beylie, "Brève rencontre."
20. Scaffa and Rossellini, *Roberto Rossellini*, p. 175.
21. J. R. MacBean, *Film Quarterly*, Winter 1971–72.
22. Cf., for example, Brunette's excellent discussion of claimed comparisons with Brecht, *Rossellini*, pp. 286 and 394, n. 10. Nonetheless, 1950s television series like *Cavalcade of America* and *You Are There* were surely more Brechtian than Brecht or Rossellini.
23. Nascimbene, "Il mio lavoro."
24. "Rossellini e Pascal," *Avvenire*, May 17, 1972; quoted in Trasatti, *Rossellini*, p. 91.
25. *The New Yorker*, May 13, 1974.
26. Strick, "Rossellini in '76."
27. Georges Walter, "La télévision: Le Pascal de Rossellini," *Le Figaro*. Undated photocopy in papers of Jean Dominique de La Rochefoucauld.
28. *The New Yorker*, May 13, 1974.
29. Quoted in Scaffa and Marinai, p. 235. Cf., also, Rossellini, *Utopia Autopsia 10^{10}* (Rome: Armando, 1974), p. 20. Sentence order transposed.
30. Trasatti, *Rossellini*, p. 99.
31. December 12, 1971.
32. Scaffa wrote Rossellini on October 21, 1971, "We are working with alacrity with Marcella on the Saint Augustine, especially looking for concrete situations. We think the doctrinal aspects should just be adumbrated, whereas what should chiefly live is the character, his interiority, his critique of Roman society, and his vision of the role of Christianity in the history of the world." (Cited in Rondolino, *Rossellini* [1989], p. 313.)
33. Luciano Scaffa to TG.
34. Stefano Roncoroni to TG.
35. Ibid.
36. Interview with Costanzo Costantini, "Rossellini: Per me la vita è solo follia," Il Mondo, October 2, 1975, p. 60.
37. "Rossellini parla," 1977.
38. "Dov'è Rossellini?" *Cahiers du Cinéma* 131.

Chapter 26: *The Age of the Medici*

1. *Changes*, 1974.
2. G. L. Rondi, *Cinema dei maestri*, 1980.
3. Trasatti, *Rossellini*, p. 86.
4. *Film Culture*, Spring 1971.
5. Cited in John Hughes, "In Search of the 'Essential Image,'" *The Village Voice*, May 10, 1973. The actual quote has "consciousness" for "awareness." Rossellini was probably translating *coscienza* by the cognate, "consciousness."
6. Conrad Fiedler, *On Judging Works of Visual Art*, my paraphrase of the translation by Henry Schaefer-Simmern and Fulmer Mood (Berkeley: University of California Press, 1949), p. 48; cited in Read, *Icon and Idea*, p. 17.
7. Interview with J. Grant, "Je profite des choses," *Cinéma* 206, February 1976.
8. *CdC* 145, 1963.
9. Benedetto Croce, "Proust: An Example of Decadent Historical Method," *My Philosophy* (New York: Collier paperback, 1962), pp. 220–27.
10. "Colloque Rossellini" (Cannes Festival, May 14, 1977), *Cinéma Québec* 52, 1978, p. 39.

11. Claire Clouzot, "Entretien," *Écran* 60, July 15, 1977, p. 44.
12. Partly my translation of Italian version.
13. Beppe Cino to TG.
14. Sonya Friedman to TG. Friedman's name subsequently became familiar as subtitler of Lincoln Center broadcasts on PBS.
15. Penelope Gilliatt who otherwise adored it noted, "The dubbing of the Medici film is bad, but *Pascal* is subtitled." She was apparently unaware that *Pascal* had been dubbed in Italian whereas *The Age of the Medici* had been shot in English. (*New Yorker*, May 13, 1974.)
16. Robert Lawrence to TG. Sonya Friedman to TG. Marcella Mariani Rossellini to TG.
17. *La Voce Repubblicana*, January 10, 1973.
18. Baldelli, p. 248.
19. *Cahiers du Cinéma* 96, June 1959.
20. Rossellini, *Utopia*, p. 86.
21. MacNiven, Yale 1974
22. Letter to Peter Wood, 1972.
23. Will Durant, *The Renaissance* (New York: Simon & Schuster, 1953), p. 69.
24. This list is Sergio Maldini's, in *Il Resto del Carlino*, January 16, 1973.
25. Quoted in Judith Hook, *Lorenzo de' Medici* (London: Hamish Hamilton, 1984), p. 53.
26. Blue, 1972.
27. *Il Mattino*, December 28, 1972.
28. The boy in Donatello's shop announces he is the brother of the architect Bernardo Rosselino, from whom Rossellini liked to claim descent.
    Marcella Mariani Rossellini, one of the two scenarists, told me their Alberti would have had these qualities, had she been aware of them. Cf., Durant, *The Renaissance*, pp. 107–08.
29. *The New Yorker*, May 13, 1974. Durant, p. 73.
30. Durant, *The Renaissance*, p. 68.
31. Ibid., p. 79.
32. *The New Yorker*, May 13, 1974.
33. Read, *Icon and Idea*, p. 96.
34. Bazin goes off on a long, regressive tangent here. As art struggled to capture material reality, it lost sight of spiritual reality, its proper domain, and risked becoming a xerox machine. Photography and film rescued art from such a disaster by relieving it of the necessity of trying to be photographically realistic. But then people said, to Bazin's disgust, that film images have no artistic value, because they are in fact xeroxes, and that film becomes art only in the editing, a position Bazin spent his career combating in favor of the long take. (He did not live to see Rossellini's long takes.) To refute the objection that photography does not put a human spirit *into* its material, as other arts do, Bazin argues the cinema is different in that it's the trace of the humanity that is no longer there that achieves the same effect from a different direction. Bazin's argument is expressionist, strangely enough; he is assigning the art in photography to the subject and allowing the photographic medium only a single trick. He would do better in underlining the many ways in which a photograph can be the result of expressive choices by the artist.
    In any case, Bazin's attacks on phenomenological realism are difficult to reconcile with the lauds he would sing to it a few years later.
    André Bazin, "The Ontology of the Photographic Image" (1945), "The Myth of Total Cinema" (1946), *What Is Cinema?* (Berkeley: University of California, 1971), pp. 9–16, 17–22. A fine exposition of Bazin's argument can be found in Andrew, *Bazin*, pp. 70–81.
35. De Angelis, "Rossellini romanziere," p. 356.
36. Durant, *The Renaissance*, pp. 80, 86.
37. Noam Chomsky, *Year 501: The Conquest Continues* (Boston: South End Press, 1993), p. 226.

Chapter 27: *Cartesius*

1. Rossellini, "Vedere con i nostri occhi," *Film della TV. Rassegna di programmi della radio-televisione italiana al Museo d'Arte Moderna di New York* (Rome: Servizio Stampa, RAI, November 1972), cited in Trasatti, *Rossellini*, pp. 201–03.
2. *Rossellini* (Texas), p. 171. The volume contains a series of descriptions of the *Science* series, written by or prepared for Rossellini around 1970. The figure 1,000,000x appears only at a later date, in MacNiven, Yale 1974.
3. Elsian Cozens to TG, November 15, 1985. On the yearly reports the Menil Foundation was required to file with the Federal government $0 are listed for 1971; $50,000 for 1972; $107,071 for 1973; $50,000 for 1974. Also, $100,110 in 1973 for the U.N. Film; and $1,400 in 1974 to Pacific Films Archives for a Rossellini retrospective there. Whether these moneys are the same as the $300,000 is not clear. Nor is it clear whether any of these figures include the $100,000 that, it is said, came from the de Menils via the U.N. for *A Question of People*. Quite justifiably, the de Menil family has preferred to be silent about its generosity.
4. Silvia D'Amico to TG.
5. Beppe Cino to TG.
6. Robert Lawrence to TG.
7. *L'Osservatore Romano*, June 22, 1972.

8. Baldelli, p. 285.
9. Karl Marx, Frederick Engels, *Complete Works* (London: Lawrence & Wishart, 1976) vol. 11, p. 103.
10. *Radiocorriere TV* 14, April 6, 1969; cited in Trasatti, p. 50.
11. Quoted in Michel Gall, "Louis XIV," *Paris Match*, October 8, 1966, pp. 97–98; cited in David Degener, ed., *Sighting Rossellini* (Berkeley: Pacific Film Archives, 1973), no page numbers.
12. Rasy, "La logica di Rossellini."
13. *Téléciné* 168, April 1971.
14. Granzotto, "Il mio Roberto."
15. Rasy, "La logica di Rossellini."
16. Scaffa and Rossellini, *Roberto Rossellini*, p. 391.
17. *Changes*, 1974.
18. Jean Dominique de La Rochefoucauld to TG.
19. Scaffa and Rossellini, *Roberto Rossellini*, p. 177.
20. Ibid., p. 14.
21. Fantuzzi, *Cinema sacro*, p. 38.
22. Ibid. Beppe Cino to TG.
23. Marie-Claire Sinko, in Bergala and Narboni, p. 43.
24. Ibid.
25. Trasatti, *Rossellini*, p. 117.
26. Ivano Cipriani, *Paese Sera*, February 28, 1974; cited in Trasatti, p. 117.
27. Trasatti, *Rossellini*, p. 117.
28. Brunette, p. 332.
29. *Changes*, 1974.
30. Antonello Trombadori to TG.
31. Cited by Brunello Rondi, in Faldini and Fofi: III:16.
32. Jean Gruault to TG.
33. Federico Fellini to TG.
34. Granzotto, "Il mio Roberto."
35. Enrico Fulchignoni to TG.
36. Franco Rossellini to TG.
37. Antonio Lisandrini to TG.
38. Jean Gruault to TG.
39. Gruault, *Ce que*, p. 215.
40. Ingrid Rossellini to TG.
41. Enrico Fulchignoni to TG.
42. Gian Vittorio Baldi to TG.
43. Sonali Sen Roy to TG.
44. Ibid.
45. Enrico Fulchignoni to TG.
46. Faldini and Fofi, III:110.
47. Cited by Paolo Valmarana to TG.
48. Carrano, *Magnani*, p. 250.
49. Cited by Paolo Valmarana to TG.
50. Zeffirelli, *Zeffirelli*, p. 271.
51. Faldini and Fofi, III:110.
52. Cited by to Gian Vittorio Baldi to TG.

Chapter 28: *Anno uno* and *The Messiah*

1. Sonali Sen Roy to TG.
2. Marcella Mariani Rossellini to TG.
3. Silvia D'Amico to TG.
4. Marcella Mariani Rossellini to TG.
5. Quoted in Costantini, "Rossellini: Per me," 1975.
6. Marcella Mariani Rossellini to TG.
7. Cited by Sergio Leone to TG.
8. Renato Barneschi, "Non voglio vederlo più," *Oggi*, March 13, 1976.
9. Quoted in Arturo Lusini, "Ciak: I Rossellini scappano," *Gente*, April 9, 1977.
10. Maria Mercader to TG.
11. Isabella Rossellini, *Some of Me* (New York: Random House, 1997), p. 49.
12. Roberto Rossellini to John Hughes to TG; *Écran*, 1977, p. 44.
13. A treatment and two letters to Tony Vellani, printed in *Rossellini* (Texas) book, are identified by Adriano Aprà as originating in 1970. An almost identical unpublished treatment, together with an essay (derived from the letters to Vellani), bears the date March 1, 1972.
14. Schultz, *Film Culture*, 1971.
15. *Changes*, 1974.
16. Ibid.

17. Peter Wood to TG, November 28, 1987.
18. Dominique de Menil to TG.
19. Cino, Bergala, and Narboni, p. 46. Dominique de Menil to TG.
20. Strick, "Rossellini in '76." L. Pellizzari, *Cinema e Cinema*, April 1975.
21. MacNiven, Yale 1974.
22. Luciano Scaffa to TG.
23. Beppe Mangano, "Gli specchi di Roberto Rossellini," *Filmcritica* 374, May 1987.
24. Ibid.
25. Silvia D'Amico to TG.
26. Trasatti, title p. 119.
27. December 4, 1974.
28. Cf., for example, Vittorio Gorresio, "De Gasperi tradito dal film," *La Stampa*, November 16, 1976.
29. Faldini and Fofi, III:72.
30. Ibid.
31. S. Zambetti, "Operazione De Gasperi: sullo schermo l'immagine istituzionale dell'azienda DC," *Cineforum* 140, January 1975.
32. Strick, "Rossellini in '76."
33. Zambetti, "Operazione De Gasperi."
34. Ibid.
35. Strick, "Rossellini in '76."
36. Trasatti, *Rossellini*, p. 121.
37. Luciano De Feo to TG. Massimo Mida to TG.
38. Renzo Rossellini to Peter Brunette, in Brunette, *Rossellini*, p. 333.
39. Silvia D'Amico to TG.
40. Faldini and Fofi, III:72.
41. Aleotti's review and the accompanying article appeared December 10, 1974, Rossellini's reply January 5, 1975.
42. Letter to *Paese Sera*, November 27, 1974 (reprinted in *Il mio metodo*, p. 462), in response to a review by Callisto Cosulich, November 16, 1974.
43. Strick, "Rossellini in '76."
44. Ibid.
45. Rondolino, *Rossellini* (1989), p. 331.
46. Virgilio Fantuzzi to TG.
47. Trasatti, p. 121.
48. Luciano Scaffa to TG.
49. Beppe Cino to TG.
50. A large extract from Rossellini's letter is quoted in Virgilio Fantuzzi, "Rossellini e la religione," p. 176.
51. *Framework*, Autumn 1979, p. 31.
52. Virgilio Fantuzzi to TG.
53. Silvia D'Amico to TG. Beppe Cino to TG.
54. Beppe Cino to TG.
55. Fantuzzi, *Cinema Sacro*, p. 39.
56. Beppe Cino to TG.
57. *L'Espresso*, October 26, 1975.
58. *Nouvel Observateur*, 1975.
59. *Écran*, 1977.
60. Fantuzzi, "Il Gesù di Rossellini," *Rivista del Cinematografo*, March 1975; reprinted in Trasatti, p. 170.
61. Ibid.
62. Edoardo Bruno, A. Cappabianca, E. Magrelli, M. Manicini, "Conversation with Roberto Rossellini," *Filmcritica* 264, May 1976; reprinted in E. Bruno, *R.R. Rossellini; Filmkritik* 303, March 1982.
63. Bernard Lauret, "Rendre Jesus au peuple," *Téléciné* 206, March 1976, p. 28.
64. Rossellini in *La Vie Catholique* 1590, p. 14; cited in Lauret, "Rendre Jesus," p. 29.
65. "Le Messie," *Téléciné* 206, March 1976, p. 23.
66. Ibid.
67. Fantuzzi, "Il Gesù," p. 172.
68. Silvia D'Amico to TG.
69. Fantuzzi, "Il Gesù," p. 172.
70. Television interview, transmitted June 22, 1975, cited in Sorgi, "Il cristianesimo di Rossellini," p. 326.
71. Jacques Fieschi, "Entretien avec Daniel Toscan du Plantier," *Cinématographe* 43, January 1979, p. 31.
72. Cf., in particular, a long argument in *Fragments*, pp. 45–46, made in speaking with Toscan du Plantier.
73. Rossellini, "E' reazionario parlare di Gesù?" *Paese Sera*, May 6, 1976; reprinted in *Il mio metodo*, p. 468.
74. Franca Rodolfi (unit press agent) to TG.
75. Nascimbene, "Il mio lavoro."
76. Franco Rossellini to TG.
77. *Avvenire*, October 26, 1975; cited in Sorgi, "Il cristianesimo."
78. Silvia D'Amico to TG.
79. *Changes*, 1974.
80. Beylie, "Entretien avec Rossellini."
81. Bruno, et al., *Filmcritica* 264, 1976.
82. MacNiven, Yale 1974.

83. Grant, "Je profite des choses," 1976.
84. G. L. Rondi, *Cinema dei maestri*, p. 23.
85. Grant, "Je profite des choses," 1976.
86. *Télécine* 206. Sentence order rearranged.
87. Strick, "Rossellini in '76."
88. Beylie, "Entretien avec Rossellini."
89. Silvia D'Amico to TG.
90. "How Jesus Fares on the Silver Screen," *National Catholic Reporter*, July 27, 1997.
91. Strick, *Sight and Sound*.
92. Jean Gruault to TG.
93. *Fragments*, p. 45.

Chapter 29: The End

1. Isabella Rossellini, *Some of Me*, p. 50.
2. Costantini, "Rossellini: Per me," 1975.
3. Marcella De Marchis to TG.
4. Ibid.
5. Isabella Rossellini to TG. De Marchis, *Un matrimonio*, p. 77.
6. Sonali Sen Roy to TG.
7. Simone Swan to TG.
8. Daniel Toscan du Plantier, *Les Enfants d'Al Capone et de Rossellini* (Paris: Mazarine, 1981), p. 100.
9. Fieschi, *Cinématographe*.
10. Fantuzzi, "Rossellini e la religione," p. 177.
11. Delain, "Rossellini après Rossellini," 1977.
12. Nestor Almendros, *A Man with a Camera* (London: Faber and Faber, 1985), p. 200.
13. *Écran*, 1977.
14. Almendros, *A Man with*, p. 201.
15. Bonicelli, "Una proposta per 'tornare indietro'," *La Rivista del Cinematografo*, July 1977, p. 297.
16. *L'Espress*, June 13, 1977.
17. *Écran*, 1977.
18. *Nouvel Observateur*, 1975.
19. *Écran*, 1977
20. Weil, "Lénine: *Matérialisme et empiriocriticsm*."
21. *L'Espress*, June 13, 1977.
22. Enrico Fulchignoni to TG.
23. Rossellini, "E' reazionario parlare di Gesù?"
24. *Nouvel Observateur*, 1975.
25. G. L. Rondi, *Cinema dei maestri*, p. 45.
26. *Nouvel Observateur*, 1975.
27. Rossellini, Introduction to the treatment for *Lavorare per l'umanità* (i.e., "Karl Marx"), *Paese Sera*, June 5, 1977; reprinted in *Il mio metodo*, pp. 473–74.
28. Rossellini, "E' reazionario parlare di Gesù?"
29. *Écran*, 1977.
30. Ibid.
31. G. L. Rondi, *Cinema dei maestri*, p. 45.
32. *Écran*, 1977
33. Bonicelli, "Una proposta."
34. Rossellini, "Una diagnosi del cinema dopo l'esperienza di Cannes," *Paese Sera*, June 4, 1977; reprinted in Trasatti, p. 219.
35. Cited by Rondi, in Maurizo Porro, *La Repubblica*, June 7, 1978.
36. Rossellini, "Una diagnosi."
37. Gian Luigi Rondi, "Presentazione," in Bruno, ed. *Rossellini* (San Remo), p. 20.
38. *Écran*, 1977.
39. Enrico Fulchignoni to TG.
40. Paolo Taviani, in Faldini and Fofi, III:540.
41. *L'Espresso*, June 5, 1977, p. 145.
42. *Écran*, 1977.
43. *L'Espresso*, June 5, 1977, p. 145.
44. A transcript of the colloquium appeared in "Colloque Rossellini," *Cinéma Québec*, no. 51, 1977, pp. 27–33; no. 52, 1978, pp. 35–39; and no. 55, 1978, pp. 24–30.
45. Rossellini, "Una diagnosi."
46. *Cinéma Québec*, 52:36.
47. Ibid., 55:30.
48. That he had not: *Écran*, 1977, p. 42. That he had: Rossellini, "Una diagnosi."
49. *L'Unità*, June 4, 1977.
50. Paolo d'Agostini, "Storia di un pioniere modesto e antiretorico," *La Repubblica*, May 30, 1978.

51. Gian Luigi Rondi, "Prima di lui a finzione dopo di lui la realtà," *Il Tempo*, June 4, 1977.
52. *Écran 60*, July 15, 1977, p. 33. Duvall was awarded the Prix d'Interprétation Feminine ex aequo with Monique Mercure in Jean Beaudin's *J. A. Martin Photographe*. Other awards: Prix d'Interprétation Masculine: Fernando Rey (*Elisa, Vida mia*, Carlos Saura, Spain). Jury Prize for First Work: *The Duellists* (Ridley Scott). Best musical score: Norman Whitfield (*Car Wash*, Michael Scholtz). Palm d'Or for best short: *Lutte* (Marcell Jankovicz, Hungary). Special jury prize (short): *Di Cavalcanti* (Glauber Rocha, Brazil). Homage for ensemble of his work: Peter Foldes.
    The jury consisted of N'sougan Agblemagnon, Anatole Dauman, Jacques Demy, Carlos Fuentes, Benoîte Groult, Pauline Kael, Marthe Keller, and Youri Ozerov.
53. Paolo Taviani, in Faldini and Fofi, III:540.
54. Gil Rossellini to TG.
55. Trasatti, *Rossellini*, p. 127.
56. After Rossellini's death it was initially suggested that *Marx* would be shot by the Taviani brothers, who eventually declined—"because we would have had to approach the film without being motivated by the two things Rossellini, in his last talk with us, had claimed were essential for a new film: wonder and audacity." (Faldini and Fofi, III:117.)
57. Cited by Suso Cecchi D'Amico in *Il Giorno*, June 4, 1977.
58. Faldini and Fofi, III:115.
59. *Il Giorno*, June 4, 1977.
60. Silvia D'Amico to TG.
61. Faldini and Fofi, III:115.
62. Silvia D'Amico to TG.
63. Ibid. She noted the time of Rossellini's death as 12:20. (Di Giammatteo, *Rossellini* [1990], p. 181.)
64. Faldini and Fofi, III:116.
65. Rossellini, "Una diagnosi."
66. De Marchis, *Un matrimonio*, p. 73.
67. MacNiven, Yale 1974.
68. De Marchis, *Un matrimonio*, p. 124.
69. Renzo Rossellini, Jr., in Faldini and Fofi: III:117.
70. The account of the funeral is drawn substantially from L.C., "I funerali di Rossellini," *Il Tempo*, June 7, 1977, p. 10; and from Berenice, "Rossellini, l'ultima lezione," *Paese Sera*, June 7, 1977.
71. *Paese Sera*, June 7, 1977.
72. Ibid.
73. Franco Rossellini to TG.
74. Gruault, *Ce que*, p. 240.
75. *Paese Sera*, June 7, 1977.

Select Bibliography

A huge bibliography may be found in Adriano Aprà, ed., Rosselliniana *(Roma: Di Giacomo, 1987), pp. 11–89.*

Agel, Henri. *Le cinéma et le sacré*, 2nd ed. Paris: Éditions du Cerf, 1961.

Alicata, Mario. "Testimonianze," in Tenazzi, ed., *Il cinema italiano*.

Andrew, Dudley. *André Bazin*. New York: Oxford University Press, 1978.

_____. "Rossellini oltre il neorealismo," in Lino Miccichè, *Il neorealismo cinematografico italiano* (Venice: Marsilio), pp. 294–95.

Aprà, Adriano, ed. *Rossellini: India 1957*. Rome: Cinecittà International, 1991.

_____. *Roma città aperta di Rossellini*. Rome: Comune di Roma, Assessorato alla cultura, 1994.

_____. *Il dopoguerra di Rossellini*. Rome: Cinecittà International, 1995.

_____, and Berengo Gardin. Interview with Rossellini. "Un cinema diverso per un mondo che cambia." Transcript of a conference with Centro Sperimentale di Cinematografia students, December 14, 1963, *Bianco e Nero*, February 1964; reprinted in Rossellini, *Il mio metodo*, pp. 302–27.

_____, ed. *Rosselliniana*. Roma: Di Giacomo, 1987.

_____, and Maurizio Ponzi. "Intervista con Roberto Rossellini" *Filmcritica* 156–57, April 1965; reprints: "Sur *L'età del ferro*," *Cahiers du Cinéma* 169, August 1965 [in part]; *Screen* 14:4, Winter 1973–74; Bruno, ed., *R.R. Roberto Rossellini*; Rossellini, *Il mio metodo* and *My Method*. Assessorato alla cultura del comune di Roma, *La città del cinema*. Napeoleone: Roma, 1979, p. 84.

Auriol, Jean George. Interview with Rossellini. "Entretiens romains sur la situation et la disposition du cinéma italien." *La Revue du Cinéma*, no. 13, May 1948.

Ayfre, Amédée. "Sens et non-sens de la Passion dans l'universe de Rossellini." In Michel Estève, ed. *La Passion du Christ comme thème cinématographique* (Paris: *Études Cinématographiques* 10–11, Autumn 1961), p. 171; reprint: Ayfre, *Conversion aux images?* Paris: Éditions du Cerf, 1964.

_____. *Le Cinéma et sa vérité*. Paris: Éditions du Cerf, 1969.

_____. "Néo-réalisme et phénoménologie." *Cahiers du Cinéma* 17, November 1952; reprint: Ayfre, *Conversion aux images?* Paris: Éditions du Cerf, 1964.

Baldelli, Pio. *Roberto Rossellini*. Rome: Samonà e Savelli, 1972.

Barzini, Luigi. *From Caesar to the Mafia*. New York: Bantam, 1972.

_____. *The Italians*. New York: Atheneum, 1965.

Bazin, André. "Le Réalisme cinématographique et l'école italienne de la libération." *Esprit*, January 1948; reprint: *Qu'est-ce que le cinéma*, IV. Paris: Éditions du Cerf, 1962, p. 17; trans., Hugh Gray, *What Is Cinema?*" II. Berkeley: University of California Press, 1971, pp. 16–40.

_____, and Jacques Rivette. Interview with Rossellini. "Comment sauver le cinéma." *France-Observateur* 410, April 10, 1958; reprint: Bergala, pp. 95–101.

_____, and Jean Herman, Claude Choublier. "Cinéma et télévision: Entretien d'André Bazin avec Jean Renoir et Roberto Rossellini." *France-Observateur*, October 23, 1958; reprint: Bergala, pp. 106, 107, 109, 111.

Bergala, Alain, ed., Roberto Rossellini. *Le Cinéma révélé*. Paris: Éditions de l'Étoile/*Cahiers du Cinéma Écrits*, 1984.

_____. *Voyage en Italie de Roberto Rossellini*. Crisnée, Belgium: Editions Yellow Now, 1990.

_____, and Jean Narboni. *Roberto Rossellini*. Paris: Éditions de l'Étoile, 1990.

Bergman, Ingrid, and Alan Burgess. *Ingrid Bergman: My Story*. New York: Dell, 1980.

Berryer, J. P. Interview with Rossellini. "Metteur en scène n. 1 du cinéma italien, Rossellini nous parle du son film, *Rome, ville ouverte*." *Alger Républicain*, January 28, 1947.

Bertin, Célia. *Jean Renoir*. Paris: Librairie Académique Perrin, 1986.

Beylie, Claude. Interview with Rossellini. "L'Homme qui cherchait la vérité." *Écran* 60, July 15, 1977, p. 45.

Blue, James. "An Interview with Rossellini" (Houston, 1972). In *Rossellini*, a brochure for a series presented by Joseph Papp at the Public Theater, New York, May 1–20, 1979, p. 17.

Bondanella, Peter. "Neorealist Aesthetics and the Fantastic: *The Machine to Kill Bad People* and *Miracle in Milan*." *Film Criticism*, Winter 1979, pp. 24–29.

Bonicelli, Vittorio. Interview with Rossellini. "Che cosa disse Ingrid quando Rossellini le parlò di Sonali." *Tempo*, March 24, 1959.

_____. "Ecco Paola Raffaella, il grande segreto di Sonali e Rossellini." *Tempo*, March 17, 1959.

Bourgeois, Nathalie, and Bernard Bénoliel. *India: Rossellini et les animaux*. Paris: Cinémathèque Française, 1997.

Brunette, Peter. "Unity and Difference in *Paisan*." *Studies in the Literary Imagination*, Spring 1983.

_____. *Roberto Rossellini*. New York: Oxford University Press, 1987.

Bruno, Edoardo, ed. *R. R. Roberto Rossellini*. Rome: Bulzoni, 1979.

Carrano, Patrizia. *La Magnani*. Milan: Rizzoli, 1982.

Cannistraro, Philip V., and Brian R. Sullivan. *Il Duce's Other Woman*. New York: William Morrow, 1993.

Cino, Beppe. "Il cinema? Un mestiere da imbecilli." *Filmcritica* 374, May 1987.

Clark, Delbert. "Berlin, Year Zero." *New York Times*, September 21, 1947.

Clouzot, Claire. "Entretien." *Écran* 60, July 15, 1977, p. 44.

Collet, Jean, and Claude-Jean Philippe. Interview with Rossellini. "*La Prise de pouvoir par Louis XIV*." *Cahiers du Cinéma* 183, October 1966; reprint: Bergala.

Collingwood, R. G. *The Idea of History*. London: Oxford University Press, 1946.

Corliss, Richard. "The Legion of Decency." *Film Comment*, Summer 1968, p. 41.

Davidson, William. *The Real and the Unreal*. New York: Harpers, 1961.

De Angelis, R. M. Interview with Rossellini. "Rossellini romanziere." *Cinema* (Milan) no. 29, December 30, 1949, p. 356.

Debreczeni, F., and H. Steinberg, eds. *Le Néo-réalisme italien*. Paris: Études Cinématographiques 32–35, 1964, p. 13.

Degener, David, ed. *Sighting Rossellini*. Berkeley: Pacific Film Archives, 1973.

De Marchis Rossellini, Marcella. *Un matrimonio riuscito. Autobiografia*. Milan: Castoro, 1996.

De Marchis, Marcella. "La mia vita con Roberto." *L'Europeo*, November 24, 1957.

____. "Roberto venne da me e mi portò da Ingrid." *L'Europeo*, December 1, 1957.

De Robertis, Franceso. "Libertas, Unitas, Caritas." *Cinema*, January 30, 1949, p. 212.

Di Giammatteo, Fernaldo. Interview with Rossellini. "Rossellini si difende." *Il Progresso d'Italia* (Bologna), December 9, 1948; also in *Fotogrammi*, January 4, 1949.

Domarchi, Jean, and Jean Douchet, Fereydoun Hoveyda. "Entretien avec Roberto Rossellini." *Cahiers du Cinéma* 133, July 1962; reprint: Bergala.

Douchet, Jean. Interview with Rossellini. "Roberto Rossellini: Le Général escroc et héros." *Arts* 739, September 9, 1959.

____. "Un ritratto di Rossellini." *Rivista del Cinema Italiano*, November 1952.

Faldini, Franca, and Goffredo Fofi. *L'avventurosa storia del cinema italiano raccontata dai suoi protagonisti, 1935–1939*. 3 vols. Milan: Feltrinelli, 1979.

Fantuzzi, Virgilio, S. J. *Cinema sacro e profano*. Rome: Edizioni La Civiltà Cattolica, 1983.

Fellini, Federico. *Intervista sul cinema*." Ed. Giovanni Grazzini. Bari: Laterza, 1983. Translated into French by Nino Frank as *Fellini*. Paris: Calmann-Lévy, 1984; excerpted in *Cinématographe* 96, January 1984, p. 16.

____. "Mon Métier" *Cahiers du Cinéma* 84, June 1958, p. 15. Translated from "Fellini parla del suo mestiere di regista." *Bianco e Nero*, May 1958.

____. *Fare un film*. Turin: Einaudi, 1980.

Ferrara, Giuseppe. "L'opera di Roberto Rossellini." In Piero Mechini and Roberto Salvadori, ed. *Rossellini, Antonioni, Buñuel*. Padua: Marsilio Editori, 1973.

Fieschi, Jean-André. "Dov'è Rossellini?" *Cahiers du Cinéma* 131, May 1962, pp. 15–25.

Fink, Guido. " 'Etre' ou 'avoir été': le film italien, le temps et l'histoire." *Cultures*, vol. 2, no. 1, 1974, pp. 128–33.

Fulchignoni, Enrico. "Préface." In Serceau, *Roberto Rossellini*, pp. 7–9.

Gallagher, Tag, and John Hughes. "Roberto Rossellini: 'Where are we going?'" *Changes*, April 1974.

Garriba, Mario. "Cinema anno zero," *Filmcritica* 374, May 1987.

Gruault, Jean. *Ce que dit l'autre*. Paris: Julliard, 1992.

Guarner, José Luis. *Roberto Rossellini*. London: Studio Vista, 1970.

____. *Roberto Rossellini*. 2nd ed. Madrid: Editorial Fundamentos, 1985.

Gobetti, Paolo. "La Résistance dans les films italiens (1945–1955)." In *Fascisme et résistance dans le cinéma italien*. Paris: Études Cinématographiques 82–83, 1970, pp. 54–55.

Hayes, Alfred. "Author's Note on Birth of Paisan." *New York Times*, March 7, 1948.

Hovald, Patrice-G. *Le Néo-réalisme italien et ses créateurs*. Paris: Éditions du Cerf, 1959.

Hoveyda, Fereydoun, and Jacques Rivette. "Entretien avec Roberto Rossellini." *Cahiers du Cinéma* 94, April, 1959.

____, and Eric Rohmer. "Nouvel entretien avec Roberto Rossellini." *Cahiers du Cinéma* 145, July 1963; reprints: *Filmkritik* 303, March 1982; *La Politique des auteurs*, Bergala.

Ivaldi, Nedo, ed. *Quello che scrissero . . . allora*. Published for the Convegno di studi dell'aprile 1970 a Venezia, su *La resistenza nel cinema italiano del dopoguerra*, pp. 20–22.

Jeener, B. "Roberto Rossellini, réalisateur de *Rome ville ouverte*, nous expose ses conception." *Le Figaro*, November 20, 1946; partially reprinted in Debreczeni and Steinberg, eds. *Le Néo-réalisme*, pp. 119–20.

Kezich, Tullio. *Fellini*. Milan: Rizzoli, 1987.

Knox, Alexander. "Actor's Accolade." *New York Times*, November 1, 1953, II:6.

Koval, Francis. "Interview with Rossellini." *Sight and Sound*, February, 1951, p. 393.

Landy, Marcia. *Fascism in Film: The Italian Commercial Cinema, 1931–1943*. Princeton: Princeton University Press, 1986.

Langlois, Henri. *Trois cents ans de cinéma: écrits*. Paris: Cahiers du Cinéma, Cinefranc, Fondation Européenne des Métiers de l'Image et du Son, 1986.

Leamer, Laurence. *As Time Goes By: The Life of Ingrid Bergman*. New York: Harper & Row, 1986.

Liehm, Mira. *Passion and Defiance: Film in Italy from 1942 to the Present*. Berkeley and Los Angeles: University of California Press, 1984.

Llinás, Francisco, and Miguel Marías, A. Drove. Interview with Rossellini. "Un panorámica de la historia. *Nuestro Cine* 95, March 1970, pp. 44–60; reprint: *Screen*, Winter 1973–74, p. 97.

Lonero, Emilio. Interview with Rossellini. "Un messaggio di fede, di speranza, di amore." *Rivista del Cinematografo*, June 1954, p. 16; reprint: Rossellini, *Il mio metodo*, p. 104.

Manni, Alberto. "Rossellini, l'araba fenice." *Epoca 1959*, nos. 433, pp. 53–57; 434, pp. 52–55.

Manvell, Roger. "*Paisa*, How it struck our Contemporaries." *Penguin Film Review*. London: Penguin, 1949, p. 57.

Maraini, Dacia. Interview with Rossellini. *E Tu Chi Eri?* Milan: Bompiani, 1973.

Mattia, Ettore G. "Rossellini «Anno Zero»" in Edoardo Bruno, ed., *Roberto Rossellini: il cinema, la televisione, la storia, la critica, dagli atti del Convegno*. Città del Sanremo, 1980, p. 189.

Meder, Thomas. *Vom Sichtbarmachen der Geschichte: Der italienische "Neorealismus", Rossellini's Paisà und Klaus Mann*. Munich: Trickster, 1993.

Menon, Gianni, ed. *Dibattito su Rossellini*. Rome: Partisan Edizioni, 1972.

Miccichè, Lino. "Per una verifica del neorealismo." In Miccichè, ed. *Il neorealismo cinematografico italiano*. Venice: Marsilio Editori, 1978, pp. 15, 25.

Mida, Massimo. "Dal diario de lavorazione di 'Paisà': Carmela e Robert." *Film rivista*, August 15, 1946, p. 11.

——. *Roberto Rossellini*. 1st ed. Rome: Guanda, 1953.

——. *Roberto Rossellini*. 2nd ed. Parma: Guanda, 1961.

——. "Luchino Visconti e il gruppo «Cinema»." In Mariella Furno and Renzo Renzi, *Il neorealismo nel fascismo: Giuseppe De Santis e la critica cinematografica 1941–1943*. Bologna: Edizioni della Tipografia Compositori, 1984.

——. "Un film tra Rossellini e il figlio del duce." *Cinema Sessanta*, March 1988, p. 10.

——. *Compagni di viaggio: Colloqui con i maestri del cinema italiano*. Turin: Nuova ERI, 1988.

——, and Lorenzo Quaglietti, eds. *Dai telefoni bianchi al neorealismo*. Rome: Laterza, 1980.

Monsey, Derek. "Letter from Rome: A Meeting with Rossellini." *World Review*, January 1949, p. 59–60.

Morlion, Felix. "Le basi filosofiche del neorealismo cinematografico italiano." *Bianco e Nero*, June 1948. Translated in Overbey, *Springtime in Italy*, pp. 115–22.

——. Interviewed by Mario Arosio. "Il figliol prodigo," *La Rivista del Cinematografo*, July 1977, p. 306.

Olschki, Leonardo. *The Genius of Italy*. New York: Oxford University Press, 1949.

Oms, Marcel. "Rossellini: du fascisme à la démocratie chrétienne." *Positif* 28, April 1958.

Orsini, Gian N. G. *Benedetto Croce: Philosopher of Art and Literary Critic*. Carbondale: Southern Illinois University Press, 1961.

Overbey, David, ed. *Springtime in Italy: A Reader on Neo-Realism*. London: Talisman Books, 1978.

Pajetta, Gian Carlo. "Esprese in un film le speranze di un popolo." *L'Unità*, June 4, 1977.

Pétrement, Simone. *Simone Weil: A Life*. New York: Schocken, 1976.

Philippe, C. J., et al. "Je sais bien que le monde moderne est plein de gens inquiets, pourquoi irais-je grossir leurs rangs?" Transcript of a television program, *L'invité du dimanche*, January 24, 1971. In *Téléciné* 168, April 1971.

Pirro, Ugo. *Celluloide*. Milan: Rizzoli, 1983.

Pryor, Thomas M. "The Personal History of Roberto Rossellini." *New York Times*, January 23, 1949.

Puccini, Gianni. "Per una discussione sul film italiano." *Bianco e Nero* April 1948, pp. 12–17.

Ranvaud, Don, ed. *Roberto Rossellini: British Film Institute Dossier no. 8*. London: British Film Institute, 1981.

Régent, Roger. Interview with Rossellini. "Rossellini: Quand je commence à devenir intelligent je suis foutu . . ." *L'Écran Français*, November 2, 1948.

Renzi, Renzo, ed. *Era notte a Roma*. Bologna: Capelli, 1960.

Rivette, Jacques. "Lettre sur Rossellini." *Cahiers du Cinéma* 46, April 1955, p. 14. Generally my translation, but occasionally that by Tom Milne, in Jonathan Rosenbaum, ed. *Rivette: Texts and Interviews*. London: British Film Institute, 1977, pp. 54–64.

Rivista del Cinematografo, March 1975.

Roberto Rossellini. A book published by the Ministero del Turismo e dello Spettacolo for the Progetto multimediale del Ente Autonomo di Gestione per il Cinema: "Rossellini in Texas," October 1987. Rome: Edizioni Ente Autonomo Gestione Cinema, 1987.

Roberts, David D. *Benedetto Croce and the Uses of Historicism*. Berkeley: University of California Press.

Rohmer, Eric (signed Maurice Schérer). "La Terre du Miracle." *Cahiers du Cinéma* 47, May 1955.

——. *Le Goût de la beauté*. Paris: Cahiers du Cinéma, 1984.

—— (signed Maurice Schérer). "Stromboli," *Gazette du Cinéma* 5, November 1950, p. 4; reprint: Rohmer, *Le Goût de la beauté*, pp. 135–38.

—— (signed Maurice Schérer), and François Truffaut. "Entretien avec Roberto Rossellini." *Cahiers du Cinéma* 37, July 1954, p. 7; reprints: *Film Culture* 2, 1955; *La Politique des auteurs*. Paris: Champ Libre, 1972; Andrew Sarris, ed., *Interview with Film Directors*. Indianapolis: Bobbs-Merrill, 1967; *Filmkritik* 303, March 1982; Bergala.

Roncoroni, Stefano. "Il 'primo Rossellini'." In Bruno, ed., *Rossellini* (Sanremo).

——. "Pour Rossellini," *Voyage en Italie*. *L'Avant-Scène Cinéma* 361, June 1987, pp. 14–15. A French translation appears in Bergala, *Voyage en Italie de Roberto Rossellini*, pp. 7–9.

Rondi, Brunello. "Lavoro con Rossellini." *Cronache del Cinema e della Televisione* 25, Summer 1958, p. 143.

——. "Realtà della persona nell'opera di Rossellini." *Cronache del cinema e della televisione*, 8–9, January–February, 1956, pp. 12–14; reprinted in B. Rondi, *Cinema e realtà*. Rome: Editori Cinque Lune, 1957, pp. 139–149.

——. *Il neorealismo italiano*. Parma: Guanda, 1956.

Rondi, Gian Luigi. Interview with Rossellini. *Il cinema dei Maestri*. Milan: Rusconi, 1980.

Rondolino, Gianni. *Roberto Rossellini*. Turin: Utet, 1989.

Rossellini, Renzo. *Addio del passato*. Rome: Rizzoli, 1968.

——. *Pagine di un musicista*. Rome: Cappelli, 1963.

Rossellini, Roberto. "Dix ans de cinéma," *Cahiers du Cinéma* 50, August 1955 (I); 52, November 1955 (II); 55, January 1956 (III).

_____. *Fragments d'une autobiographie.* Paris: Éditions Ramsay, 1987.

_____. "Germany Year Zero," Pressbook for New York 1949 release by Superfilm Distributing Corp. Author's Collection. Reprint, in Italian, in Rossellini, *Il mio metodo*, pp. 60–62. Partially published, in English, in *New York Herald Tribune*, September 18, 1949.

_____. "L'intelligenza del presente." In *La triologia della guerra.* Bologna: Cappelli editore, 1972.

_____. *Il mio metodo.* Ed. Adriano Aprà. Venice: Marsilio, 1987. Partial translation: *My Method.* New York: Marsilio, 1992.

_____. "Neapolitan Note in a Director's Diary." *New York Times*, May 30, 1948.

_____. "Il regista Rossellini giudica (e assolve) la rivolta giovanile." *Paese Sera*, May 8, 1969.

_____. "Roberto Rossellini parla di Roberto Rossellini." *Paese Sera*, June 12, 1977.

_____. *Un Esprit libre ne doit rien apprendre en esclave.* Translated from Italian into French by Paul Alexandre. Paris: Fayard, 1977.

_____. *Utopia Autopsia 10¹⁰.* Rome: Armando, 1974.

Sadoul, Georges. Interview with Rossellini. "Rossellini qui vendia ses meubles pour tourner *Rome ville ouverte*, a recruté les acteurs de *Paisà* parmi les badauds." *L'Écran Français 72*, November 12, 1946, p. 17.

Sanders, Georges. *Memoirs of a Professional Cad.* New York, 1960.

Sauvage, Léo. Interview with Rossellini. "Rencontre nocturne avec le cinéma italien." *L'Écran Français*, April 29, 1947, p. 4.

Savio, Francesco. Interview with Rossellini. *Cinecittà anni trenta.* Rome: Bulzoni, 1979, p. 962.

_____. *Ma l'amore no.* Milan: Sonzogno, 1975.

Scaffa, Luciano, and Marcella Mariani Rossellini, eds. *Roberto Rossellini: Atti degli Apostole, Socrate, Blaise Pascal, Agostino d'Ippona, L'età dei Medici, Cartesius.* Turin: ERI/Edizione RAI, 1980.

Schultz, Victoria. "Interview with Roberto Rossellini, February 22–25, 1971, in Houston, Texas." *Film Culture 52*, Spring 1971, p. 2.

Serceau, Michel. *Roberto Rossellini.* Paris: Éditions du Cerf, 1986.

Servadio, Gaia. *Luchino Visconti: A Biography.* New York: Franklin Watts, 1983.

Sery, Patrick. Interview with Rossellini. "J'ai choisi d'être utile." *Le Nouvel Observateur*, February 10, 1975.

Sorgi, Claudio. "Il cristianesimo di Rossellini." *Rivista del Cinematografo*, July–August 1977, pp. 326–27.

Steele, Joseph Henry. *Ingrid Bergman: An Intimate Portrait.* New York: David McKay, 1959.

Stern, Michael. *No Innocence Abroad.* New York: Random House, 1952.

Tenazzi, Giorgio, ed. *Il cinema italiano dal fascismo all'antifascismo.* Padua: Marsilio, 1966.

Toffetti, Sergio. "Roberto stava lì, seduto a capotavola . . . : Intervista a Gabor Pogany." In *Giovanna d'Arco al rogo di Rossellini.* Turin: Museo Nazionale del Cinema, 1987.

Tonti, Aldo. *Odore di cinema.* Firenze: Vallecchi, 1964.

_____, et al. "Rossellini meets his new passion." *Daily Sketch*, November 26, 27, 28, 29, and 30, 1957.

Tranchant, F., and J.-M. Vérité. Interview with Rossellini. "Rossellini 59: Le pays des hommes-drapés vu par un homme cousue." *Cinéma 59*, no. 36, May 1959, p. 50.

Trasatti, Sergio. *Rossellini e la televisione.* Rome: La Rassegna, 1978.

Truffaut, François (signed, François de Montferrand). Interview with Rossellini. "Dans le cinéma italien un homme seul: Roberto Rossellini," *Radio-Cinéma-Télévision 233*, July 4, 1954, pp. 4, 39; reprinted as "Un homme seul." *Cahiers du Cinéma 410*, July 1988, p. 14.

_____. "Il préfère la vie." In Verdone, *Rossellini*, p. 199; English translation: Truffaut, *The Films in My Life.* New York: Simon & Schuster, 1978.

_____. Interview with Rossellini. "Rossellini: Je ne suis pas le père du néoréalisme, je travaille dans une solitude morale absolue, je souffre d'être méprisé et insulté de tous côtés, je suis obligé de payer moi-même mes films." *Arts*, June 16, 1954, p. 3.

Ungari, Enzo. "Conversazione con Carlo Lizzani: Quando il 'découpage' sembrava una prigione." *Cult Movie*, April 1981, p. 15–16.

Valmarana, Paolo. "Cinema adulto." In Bruno, ed., *Rossellini* (Sanremo), p. 36.

Vasile, Turi. *Un vellano a Cinecittà.* Palermo: Sellerio, 1993.

Verdone, Mario. "Colloquio sul neorealismo," *Bianco e Nero*, February 1952; English translation: "A Discussion of Neo-Realism," *Screen 4*, Winter 1973–74, pp. 69–77.

_____. *Roberto Rossellini.* Paris: Éditions Seghers, 1963.

Wood, Robin. "Ingrid Bergman on Rossellini." *Film Comment*, July 1974.

Zanelli, Dario. "Quando Vittorio Mussolini dirigeva 'Cinema'." In Mariella Furno and Renzo Renzi, *Il neorealismo nel fascismo: Giuseppe De Santis e la critica cinematografica 1941–1943.* Bologna: Edizioni della Tipografia Compositori, 1984, p. 105.

Acknowledgments

During the fifteen years that this book was in preparation, the quantity of help I received from so many persons, and the quality of the relationships I formed with many of them, make it impossible for me to acknowledge them properly. Every effort has been made to locate and acknowledge all rights holders of material under copyright.

For interviews, information, and help († = deceased): Doris Ashbrook, †Renzo Avanzo, Gian Vittorio Baldi, Janine Basinger, Paolo Benvenuti, Marcello Bolero, Vittorio Bonicelli, Edoardo Bruno, Carlo Carlini, Beppe Cino, Elsian Cozens, Silvia D'Amico, †Renzo De Felice, Luciano De Feo, Gerald De Luca, Marcella De Marchis, Giuseppe De Santis, Manuel De Sica, Mario Del Papa, Virgilio Fantuzzi, S.J., †Federico Fellini, Massimo Ferrara, Helen Winkler Fosdick, Sonya Friedman, †Enrico Fulchignoni, Vittoria Fulchignoni, Mario Garriba, Katja Geiger, Rod Geiger, Vittorio di Girolamo Carlini, David Grossman, Jean Gruault, †Jose-Luis Guarner, Jean Herman, Fereydoun Hoveyda, John Hughes, Jean Dominique de La Rochefoucauld, Robert Lawrence, †Sergio Leone, Pia Lindstrom, †Antonio Lisandrini, OFM, Carlo Lizzani, Serge Losique, †Roger MacNiven, Romolo Marcellini, Fiorella Mariani, Michael McKegney, Thomas Meder, †Mary Meerson, Dominique De Menil, Maria Mercader, †Massimo Mida, Fae Miske, Vittorio Mussolini, Mario Nascimbene, Gerald O'Grady, Jos Oliver, Paola Olivetti (Archivio Nazionale Cinematografico della Resistenza), Ted Perry, Seymour Peyser, Tullio Pinelli, John Prizer, †Jean Riboud, †Franco Riganti, Franca Rodolfi, Eric Rohmer, Stefano Roncoroni, †Franco Rossellini, Gil Rossellini, Ingrid Rossellini, Isabella Rossellini, Lina Rossellini, †Marcella Mariani Rossellini, Raffaella Rossellini, Renzo Rossellini, Jr., Jean Rouch, Dominique Saintville (Institut National de l'Audiovisuel), Luciano Scaffa, Roswitha Schmidt, Martin Scorsese, Daniel Selznick, Sonali Sen Roy, Enzo Serafin, Eugenio Silenzi, Ursula Starrabba-Rochlitz, Simone Swan, †Amerigo Terenzi, Madeleine Thornton-Sherwood, †Aldo Tonti, †Antonello Trombadori, Helen Tubbs, Arabella Lemaître Unghero, †Paolo Valmarana, Uberta Visconti, Peter Wood.

Photo credits: Frontispiece photo by Giovanni Assenza, courtesy of Beppe Cino. Photos 9–18, 20, 21, 25, 76 courtesy of Rod Geiger. Photos 26, 30, 32–34, 39, 42, 49, 55, 59, 60, 66, 68, 69, 72, 73, 75, 100 courtesy of *Cahiers du Cinéma*. Photos 6, 7, 40, 41, 47, 48, 61, 74, 79, 85, 103 courtesy of the British Film Institute. Photos 27, 31, 36a, 36b, 37, 38, 43–46, 50–54, 56, 88–90, 101, 102 courtesy of Rainer Gansera. Photos 4, 35, 62, 67, 71, 80, 87 courtesy of Jos Oliver. Photos 5, 70 courtesy of Munich Film Museum. Photos 1–3, 8, 19, 22–24, 28, 29, 57, 58, 63–65, 77, 78, 81–84, 86, 91–99, 104, 105 from the author's collection.

For additional photo help: Pellegrino d'Acierno, Ernet Callenbach, Massimo Forleo, Catherine Fröchen, Michael McKegney, Ted Perry, John Prizer, Martin Scorsese, Andreas Ungerböck.

For editorial help: Soo Mee Kwon and Yuval Taylor at Da Capo Press.

For text permissions and additional help:
Centro Sperimentale Cinematografia.
National Endowment for the Humanities, for a research grant.
Edoardo Bruno and *Filmcritica* for permission to cite and paraphrase from Mario Garria, "Cinema anno zero," *Filmcritica* 374–75, May–June 1987.
Bantam Doubleday Dell for permission to quote from *Ingrid Bergman: My Story*, by Ingrid Bergman and Alan Burgess. Copyright © 1980 by Ingrid Bergman and Alan Burgess. Used by permission of Delacorte Press, a division of Bantam Doubleday Dell Publishing Group, Inc.
Jean Gruault for permission to quote from his *Ce que dit l'autre*. Paris: Julliard 1992.

R.C.S. Periodici for permission to reprint passages from Marcella De Marchis, "La mia vita on Roberto," *L'Europeo*, November 24 and December 1, 1957.

Ugo Pirro for permission to quote and paraphrase passages from his *Celluloide*. Milan: Rizzoli, 1983.

Daniel Selznick, President, Selznick Properties, Ltd., for permission to reproduce materials from the Selznick Archives at the Harry Ransom Center, University of Texas at Austin.

Cahiers du Cinéma for permission to reproduce materials from Jacques Rivette, "Lettre sur Rossellini," *Cahiers du Cinéma* 46, April 1955; Maurice Schérer and François Truffaut, "Entretien avec Roberto Rossellini," *Cahiers du Cinéma* 37, July 1954; Fereydoun Hoveyda and Jacques Rivette, "Entretien avec Roberto Rossellini," *Cahiers du Cinéma* 94, April 1959; Roberto Rossellini, "Dix ans de cinéma," par Rossellini, *Cahiers du Cinéma* 50, August 1955 (I); 52, November 1955 (II); 55, January 1956 (III)—all © *Cahiers du Cinéma*.

Index

Other titles of interest

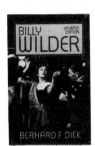